PORCH OF GRAMMAR SCHOOL.

A HISTORY

OF THE

TOWN AND PARISH

OF

NANTWICH,

OR

𝕎𝕚𝕔𝕙-𝕄𝕒𝕝𝕓𝕒𝕟𝕜,

IN THE

COUNTY PALATINE OF CHESTER.

BY

JAMES HALL, WILLASTON, NANTWICH.

"Thus times do shift ; each thing his turne does hold ;
New things succeed as former things grow old."—*(Robert Herrick.)*

NANTWICH.

PRINTED FOR THE AUTHOR.

MDCCCLXXXIII.

To

George Fortescue Wilbraham, Esquire,

of Delamere House, Cheshire,

and to the

Memory of his Ancestors,

who were long resident in the Town of

Nantwich,

and were the never-failing Guardians of its

rights in by-gone days,

This Volume

is respectfully inscribed

LIST OF SUBSCRIBERS.

A

ACTON Samuel, Esq , Hatherton House, Nantwich

AINSWORTH, Alderman John, J P , Ex-Mayor of Crewe, Heathfield, Crewe

ANDREWS, William, Esq , F R H S , Literary Club, Hull

ANKERS, Charles, Watchmaker Pillory Street, Nantwich

ANTIQUARIES, The Society of, Burlington House, Piccadilly London

ASHTON, J Thornhill, Esq , Wellington Road South, Stockport

ASTON the Rev Peter, Havelock Place, Hanley, Staffs

ATKINSON, the Rev Canon, M A , R D , The Vicarage, Audlem, Cheshire

B

BAGNALL, S, F Esq M R C S , L R C P , 1 Clarence Terrace, Runcorn

BAILEY, J Eglinton, Esq , F S A , Stretford, Manchester

BANKS, John, Esq , Farnworth, near Bolton, Lancashire

BARKER, Philip, Esq , The Grove, Nantwich

BARKER the Rev Rowland V , B A , St Paul s Vicarage, Preston

BARNETT, J N , Commercial Traveller, 11 The Barony, Nantwich   *Two copies*

BATEMAN, Thomas Esq , Chorley, Nantwich

BAVLEY, James, Esq , J P , Willaston Hall, Nantwich

BELLYSE, Mrs , Oakfield near Nantwich   *Two copies*

BENNETT, Thos R , Esq , Shrewbridge Hall, Nantwich

BENTLEY, James, Music Depot, Pillory Street, Nantwich

BIRCHALL, Edward, Esq , Willaston, Nantwich

BLACKBURNE, the Rev Foster G M A , The Rectory Nantwich   *Two copies*

BLACKBURNE, the Rev Canon H Ireland, M A The Rectory, Warmingham

BLAND, George, Esq,, M D , Park Green, Macclesfield

BLEASDELL, the Rev John, B A , Enville Place, Ashton-under-Lyme

BOLTON, Mrs Thomas, Hanley, Staffordshire

BOOLS, William Edward Esq , 7 Cornhill, London,

BOSTOCK, R C , Esq Little Langtons, Lower Camden, Chiselhurst, Kent

BOSTON, John, Esq , Wybunbury, Nantwich

BOTT, Thomas, Esq 7 Onega Villas, Green Lane, Birmingham

BOWER, Thomas, Esq , Architect, Cleerbrook, Stapeley, Nantwich

BOWERS, Edward, Coal Merchant, Woodside, Nantwich

BOWERS, William, Coal Merchant, Woodside, Nantwich

BOWKER Henry, Photographer , Churchyard-side, Nantwich

BOWKER, Thomas, Broker, High Street, Nantwich

BOWMAN, Sir William, Bart , LL D , F R S , Joldwynds, Dorking, Surrey   *Two copies*

BOYER, Matthew, Baker, Welsh Row, Nantwich

BRIDGEMAN the Hon and Rev Canon, Wigan Hall, Wigan

BROCK John, Esq , J P , Wellfield, Farnworth, Widnes, Lancashire

BROOKE, Charles Stuart, Esq , Solicitor Nantwich

BROOKS, J Marshall, Esq Portal, Tarporley, Cheshire

BROUGHTON, Delves Louis Delves, Esq , Doddington Hall, Nantwich

BROUGHTON Edward Delves, Esq Wistaston Hall, Cheshire

BROUGHTON, E W Delves, Esq , St Asaph, North Wales

BRUNT, E , Esq , F G S , F R H S , Havelock Place, Hanley, Staffordshire

BRUSHFIELD, T N Esq M D , Budleigh, Salterton, Devon

BURTON, Alfred, Esq , 37 Cross Street Manchester

C

CARRINGTON Anthony News Agent, High St Nantwich

CARRINGTON Charles, Grocer 33 Heaton Lane, Stockport

CAWLEY, Thomas, Esq , Welsh Row, Nantwich

CAWTHORN George Page, Esq , 5 Great Winchester St , London E C

CHARLESWORTH, Edward, Farmer, Stoke Hall Nantwich

CHATER, the Rev Daniel Sutcliffe, The Vicarage, Blackawton R S O Devon   *Two copies*

CHESTER, the late Colonel J L , D C L , LL D , Southwark Park Road, London

CHESTERS, Philip Hale, Grocer, Wallfield House, Nantwich

CHESWORTH, Henry, Esq Burland Cottage nr Nantwich

CHESWORTH, William Coal Merchant, Pillory Street, Nantwich

CHRISTY Stephen, Esq , J P Highfield, Bramhall Cheshire

CLARKE, John, Confectioner, Pillory Street, Nantwich   *Two copies*

CLEGG, Joshua, Grocer, Hospital Street, Nantwich

COCKAYNE, Andreas Edward, Esq , Great Lever, Farnworth, Lancashire

COCKAYNE, G E , Esq , M A , F S A , College of Arms, London

COLLINS, Mrs, St Denis Hotel, Madison St, Chicago, Illinois

COLLINSON, W S, Esq, Hawthorne Grove, Heaton Moore, Stockport

COLLISON, the Rev Henry, M A, East Bilney, Norfolk

COMBERMERE, the Right Hon the Lord Viscount, Combermere Abbey

COOK, the Rev R P, 32 Grove Road, St John's Wood, London, N W

COOPER, Thomas, Esq Solicitor, Mossley House, Congleton

COOPER, William Esq, White Hall Nantwich *Four copies*

COOPER, William, Hair-dresser, Welsh Row Nantwich

CORNES, Wm Mile-House Farm, Worleston, Nantwich

CORNES, Mrs Marianne, Baddington, Nantwich

CORNISH, J E, Esq 33 Piccadilly, Manchester

COTTINGHAM Alderman Wm, Esq, High St, Lincoln

COTTON Captain E T D, R A, Rease Heath Hall, Nantwich

CRAWSHAW, the Rev Charles, Newark, Nottinghamshire

CREWE, the Rt Hon Hungerford Lord, Crewe Hall, Chesh

CROMPTON, J H S, Esq, Vernon House, The Beeches, Didsbury

CROSTHWAITE, John Fisher, Esq, F S A, The Bank, Keswick

CRUM, William G, Esq, J P, Mere Old Hall, Knutsford

CUMMING W A Esq 348 Dickenson Road Longsight Manchester

CUMMING, A G, Esq, The Crofts, Nantwich

D

DALTRY, the Rev Thomas W, M A, F L S, Madeley Vicarage, Newcastle, Staffs

DANA, B, Esq, Berkeley Street, near Beacon Street, Boston U S America

DAVIES, John, Gas Manager, Hospital Street, Nantwich

DAVIES-COLLEY, Thomas, Esq, M D Newton Cottage, Chester

DELAMERE, The Right Hon the Lord, Vale Royal, Northwich

DERBY, The Right Hon the Earl of, D C L, F R S, Knowsley Hall

DEVONSHIRE His Grace the Duke of K G, D C L, F R S F S A, London

DIOCESAN REGISTRY OFFICE, Chester

DIXON, George, Esq, Astle Hall, Chelford

DOOLEY Henry, Esq, 22 Lower Hillgate Stockport

DOWNES, John, Esq, Welsh Row, Nantwich

DOWNING, Wm, Esq, Olton, near Birmingham

DUNNING, Thomas Stationer Welsh Row Nantwich

DUNNING, William, Esq, Professor of Music Crewe

E

EARWAKER, J Parsons, Esq, M A, F S A Pensarn, Abergele, North Wales

EATON, George, Esq, 196 Edleston Road, Crewe

EATON, James, Esq, May Cottage, Haslington, nr Crewe

EATON, John, Esq, Meadow Cottage, Church Coppenhall

EGERTON The Rt Hon the Lord, Tatton Park, Knutsford

EGERTON, Major Sir P le B Grey, Bart, Oulton Park, Cheshire

ELSMORE, Thomas Esq, J P The Woodlands, Stapeley, Nantwich   *Two copies*

F

FFOULKES, W Wynne, Esq, M A, Judge of County Courts, Chester

FITTON, Miss A, High Street Nantwich

FITTON, Samuel, Cheerbrook Farm, Willaston, Nantwich *Two copies*

FODEN, George, Corn-dealer, Welsh Row, Nantwich

FOREY, Richard, Clerk Willaston Nantwich

FOSTER, William Orme, Esq, Apley Park, Bridgenorth

FRANCE HAYHURST, Charles H, Esq J P, Bostock Hall, Middlewich

FURNIVAL, A, Grocer, High Street, Nantwich

G

GARNETT-BOTFIELD, the Rev W B Decker Hill Shifnal, Salop

GARNETT, the Rev R C, Delamere Rectory, Northwich

GARNETT, Richard Massie, Esq, Park House, Willaston, Nantwich

GELDER, Mrs R, Worleston, Nantwich

GEORGE, Ambrose B Esq, M D, Dodington Whitchurch

GILBERT, Mr Egerton C, Welsh Row, Nantwich

GILBERT, James, Shoe-manufacturer, London Road, Nantwich

GLEADOWE, T S, Esq, H M I of Schools, Alderley Edge, Manchester

GOY, James Dixon, Esq L D S St Mark's Terrace, Lincoln

GOY, Mrs M, Grantham Street, Lincoln

GOY, Matthew, Esq, Foster, South Gipps Land, Victoria, Australia

GRAFTON, F W, Esq, J P, Hope Hall, Manchester

GRASON, James, Esq, Fore Street, Tiverton, Devon

GRATRIX Samuel, Esq, West Point Whalley Range, Manchester

GRAY, Henry, Esq, 25 Cathedral Yard, Manchester

GRAZEBROOK, George, Esq, F S A, Oak Hill Park, Liverpool

GREAVES, Hilton, Esq, Hankelow, Nantwich

GREAVES, Joseph J, Esq, Bank House, Ecclesfield, Sheffield   *Two copies*

GREEN, James Clerk, London Road Nantwich

GREENALL, Sir Gilbert, Bart, M P, Walton Hall, Daresbury, Warrington

GREGSON, Samuel Leigh, Esq, Overton Hall, Malpas,

GRESTY, John Thomas, Builder, The Laurels, Willaston, Nantwich

GRIFFITHS, Edward Hounson, Esq , Henhull Cottage, Acton, Nantwich *Two copies*

GRIFFITHS John Lloyd, Esq The Spitals Stoke-on Trent

GROCOTT, F T , Clerk, Sandbach, Cheshire

GROCOTT, William, Grocer, High Street, Nantwich

GROSART, the Rev A B , LL D , F S A , Brooklyn House, Blackburn, Lancashire

GROUCOTT, Thos , Cabinet Maker Pillory St , Nantwich

GRUNDY, Alfred, Esq , Whitefield, near Manchester

H

HALE, Thomas E , Esq , Faddiley Lodge Nantwich

HALL, James, Esq , Grantham Street, Lincoln

HALL, John, Esq , The Grange, Hale, Cheshire

HALL, Thomas, Esq , Rasen Lane, Lincoln

HALL, Walter Edward, Esq , F C O , Cathedral, Denver, Colardo, U S A

HALL, William Charles, Esq , The Green Southall, London, W

HARLOCK, Samuel, Draper, Brookfield House, Nantwich

HAWORTH, J E , Esq , Spring Side House, Rossendale, Lancashire

HEAD, Robert, Esq , Congleton, Cheshire

HENSLEY, Thomas W , Esq , Solicitor, Nantwich

HEWITT, John, Esq , 17 Steam-Mill Street, Chester

HEYWOOD, John, Esq , Ridgefield, John Dalton Street, Manchester

HILL, Mrs , The Manor House, Wistaston, Nantwich *Two copies*

HILL, Thomas, Shoe-manufacturer, Pillory St , Nantwich

HILLYARD, Mrs , Dysart House, Nantwich

HINCHSLIFF, John, Printer, Victoria Street, Crewe

HOBSON, Samuel H , Shoe manufacturer The Elms, Nantwich *Four copies*

HOCKENHULL, James, Plumber, Beam Street, Nantwich

HODSON, George, Farmer, The Marsh, Nantwich

HOLME, J Wilson, Esq , 34 Old Jewry, London, E C

HORSPOOL, A , Esq , Albert St , Camden Town, London

HORTON, Mrs R G , High Street, Whitchurch

HOLLDING, J W , Draper, High Street, Nantwich

HOVENDEN, Robert Esq , Heathcote Park Hill Road Croydon, Surrey

HOWARD, J J , Esq , LL D , F S A , Dartmouth Row, Blackheath, Kent

HOWARD, Thomas, Esq , Acton, Nantwich

HOWELL, T , Esq , Clydesdale, Wistaston Road, Crewe

HOWLE, H , Esq , 13 Clifden Terrace, Higher Broughton, Manchester

HUGHES Thomas, Esq , F S A , The Groves, Chester

J

JACKSON, Joseph, Draper, Queen Anne Buildings, Nantwich *Three copies*

JERVIS, Levi, Printer 4 Churchyard side, Nantwich

JOHNSON, John, Esq , Welsh Row, Nantwich

JOHNSON, John Moore, Brick & Pipe Works, The Barony, Nantwich

JOHNSON Thomas Esq Grove Cottage Acton Nantwich

JOHNSON, Thomas, Junr , Printer, Oat Market, Nantwich

JOHNSON, William Tailor, High Street, Nantwich

JOHNSON W B , Esq , Woodlands Bank, nr Altrincham

JONES, Ambrose, Printer London Road, Nantwich

JONES, Thomas, Joiner, The Barony, Nantwich

JONES, T Rought, Esq , The Bank, Market Drayton

JONES William, Esq , J P The Grange Knutsford *Two copies*

JUBB, Francis, Publican, Pillory Street, Nantwich

K

KENT, Alfred, Esq , Montpellier Crescent, New Brighton

KENT Mrs Joseph H , Hawthorn House, Welsh Row, Nantwich.

KENT, Mrs , Heatherlea, Grassendale, Liverpool

KETTLE, Joseph Wheelwright Acton Nantwich

KNIGHT, Daniel, Stationer, High Street, Nantwich

KNOWLES the late Thomas, Esq , M P , Darnhall Hall, Cheshire

L

LAFAGE, Charles Clement, Esq , M D , Hospital Street, Nantwich

LATHAM, Baldwin Esq 7 Westminster Chambers London, S W

LATHAM, the late Joseph, Builder, Beam St , Nantwich

LAWTON, Mrs Elijah, Market Street, Tunstall, Staffs

LAXTON, the late Charles, Esq , Dysart View, Nantwich

LEA, William, Currier, Hospital Street, Nantwich

LEATHER, Miss M E , 173 Dalton Road, Barrow-in-Furness

LEE, the Rev M H , Hanmer, Whitchurch, Salop

LEWIS, Joseph, H Esq , 33 Heaton Lane, Stockport

LEYLAND, John, Esq , The Grange, Hindley, nr Wigan

LIBRARY, Bolton-le-Moors, Lancashire

————— Boston Public, United States of America

————— Crewe Mechanics' Institution Cheshire

————— Leeds Public, Yorkshire

————— Liverpool Corporation, Lancashire

————— Liverpool Free Public, Lancashire

————— London, The Guildhall

————— Manchester, Free Public, King St , Manchester

————— Manchester, The Portico

LINGARD-MONK, R B M , Esq , Fulshaw Hall, Wilmslow

LISLE, Henry Claud Esq , Solicitor, The Chestnuts, Nantwich

LOCKETT, John, Esq Market Drayton, Salop

LUNT, Owen Esq , Ashfield House, Willaston, Nantwich.

LUNT, Richard, Esq , Norfolk House, Bristol Road, Birmingnam

M

MAINWARING, Sir Philip, Bart , Peover Hall, Knutsford

MANLEY, Henry, Esq , Aston, Nantwich

MARSHALL, George W , Esq , LL D , 60 Onslow Gardens, London, S W

MARTIN, Edward Harrison, Esq , Bar Hill House, Madeley, Staffordshire

MARTIN, Henry, Esq , Solicitor, Dorfold Cottage, Acton, Nantwich

MATHEWS, William, Esq , Surgeon, The Manor House, Nantwich

McNAIR, John, Junr , Watchmaker, Pillory St , Nantwich

MILNES Ernest, Esq , Walton Cottage, Chesterfield, Derbyshire

MINSHULL, John Bellamy, Esq , 3 Rodney Terrace, West Bow Road, London

MINTON, E E , Esq , Rudyard, near Leek, Staffordshire

MONTFORT, Ralph, Esq , 3 Westwood Terrace, Leek

MUNRO, Seymour H , Esq , M D Nantwich *Two copies*

N

NAPIER, G W , Esq , Mercaistoun, Alderley Edge, Cheshire

NEWALL, W , Esq , Woodlands Villa, Hartford, Northwich

NIELD, James R , Clerk, Hawthorn Buildings, Nantwich

NIXON, Mr Henry, Acton Nantwich

NIXON Thomas Esq , Welsh Row Head, Nantwich

NORWOOD, the Rev T W , F G S , The Parsonage Wrenbury

O

ORMEROD, Henry M , Esq , 5 Clarence St , Manchester

P

PANKHURST, Miss, Willaston, Nantwich

PARKES, Alfred, Esq , Bridge Street Row, Chester

PARRATT, Thomas, Blacksmith, Hospital St , Nantwich

PARSONAGE, Thomas, Ironmonger, High St , Nantwich

PEDLEY, Mrs , The Barony, Nantwich

PERRIN Robert D , Ironmonger, High Street, Nantwich

PIERCE, Thomas, Esq , Claremont Villa, The Crofts, Nantwich

PLATT, Mr , Post Office, Shavington, Nantwich

PLATT, Mrs Joseph, Thornlea, Willaston, Nantwich

POTTS, Arthur Esq , J P , Hoole Hall Chester

POOLE Henry, Watchmaker, High Street, Nantwich

PRINCE, Mr, John, Barker Street, Nantwich

PRINCE, Thomas, Brush Manufacturer, 2 Bridge Street, Warrington

R

RADFORD-NORCUP, Alexander W , Esq , Betton Hall, Market Drayton, Salop *Two copies*

REDFERN, the Rev R Scarr, M A , Acton Vicarage, Nantwich

RICKARDS, C H Esq , Old Trafford, Manchester

RIDGWAY Colonel Alexander, Sheplegh Court, Blackawton, Devon

RIGBY, Samuel Esq , J P , Bruche Hall, Warrington

RIGBY, William, Tailor, High Street, Wolstanton, Stoke-on-Trent

ROBINSON, George, Accountant, Market St , Nantwich

ROBINSON, William, Esq , 56 Thompson Street, Higher Tranmere Birkenhead

ROUNDELL, Charles S Esq , M P , 16 Curzon Street, Mayfair, London

ROYLE, John Esq , 78 Tarvin Road, Chester

RYLANDS, J Paul, Esq F S A , 24 Stanley Gardens, Belsize Park, Hampstead, London, N W

RYLANDS, T Glazebrook, Esq , F S A , High Fields, Thelwall, Cheshire

S

SALISBURY, F G R , Esq , J P Glan Aber Chester

SALISBURY, Lazarus, Esq , Cheerbrook House, Willaston, Nantwich

SALMON, Robert H , Esq , 39 Ackers Street, Manchester

SAMUELL, Edward J , Esq , Sunny Side, Slade Lane, Longsight Manchester

SANDYS, Albert, Schoolmaster, The Crofts, Nantwich

SANDFORD, Thomas H , Esq , J P , Sandford, Whitchurch, Salop

SHARMAN R Bell Esq , Aboretum Avenue, Lincoln

SHARPE, Miss Thomasin E , Brewood House, Gunterstone Road, West Kensington *Three copies*

SKENTON, William, Clerk, Welsh Row, Nantwich

SKIDMORE, James S , Chemist, Fairfield House, Nantwich

SLEIGH, William, Grocer, Welsh Row, Nantwich

SPEAKMAN Charles E , Esq , Solicitor, Crewe

STEVENTON Edwin Senr Seedsman, High St , Nantwich

STEVENTON, Edwin, Junr , Commercial Traveller, Acton View, Nantwich

STEVENTON, Miss, Milliner, High Street, Nantwich

SYKES, Thomas Hardcastle, Esq , J P , Cringle House, Cheadle, Cheshire

T

TABLEY, The Rt Hon Lord de, Tabley House, Knutsford

TAYLOR George, Clerk, Dysart Buildings, Nantwich

TAYLOR, John, Esq Woodland Terrace London Road, Nantwich

TAYLOR, Mr Harthill, Cheshire

TOMKINSON, Henry R , Esq , 24 Lower Seymour Street, Portman Square, London

TOMKINSON, James Esq , Willington Hall, Tarporley

THISTLETHWAITE, William, Esq , The Bank House, Nantwich

THOMPSON, Alderman Joseph J P , Riversdale, Wilmslow

TOLLEMACHE OF HELMINGHAM, The Right Hon Lord, Peckforton Castle

TOLLEMACHE, Wilbraham Spencer, Esq , J P , Dorfold Hall Nantwich *Two copies*

TRUBNER & CO , Esqrs , 57 & 59 Ludgate Hill, London

TUBBS, BROOK, & CHRYSTAL, Market Street, Manchester

TUCKER, Stephen, Esq , *Rouge Croix*, Heralds' College, London

TUNNICLIFFE Aaron, Auctioneer, Beam St , Nantwich

TURNER, Duncan, Esq , M D , Ardchonnell, Moonee Ponds, near Melbourne Australia

TURNER, Samuel Shoe-manufacturer, Hospital Street, Nantwich

TWEMLOW Thomas Fletcher Esq , J P , Betley Court, Crewe

V

VAWDREY, B Llewellyn, Esq , Tushingham Hall Whitchurch, Salop

VAUGHAN, W E W , Esq , Crewe Cottage, Crewe

VICKERS, Robert, Esq . Wilton Polygon, Cheetham Hill, Manchester

W

WALKDEN, Mrs Lees, The Broomlands, Hatherton, Nantwich

WALLER, Mrs , The Barony, Nantwich

WALLEY, William, Wine-merchant, Pepper St , Nantwich

WARD, Thomas, Esq , Brookfield House, Northwich

WELCH, Percy B , Esq , 7 Clifton Rd , Eccles, Manchester

WESTON, John, Esq , The Heysomes, Hartford, Northwich

WESTMINSTER, His Grace the Duke of, K G , Eaton Chester

WICKSTEED, Gustavus Wilham, Esq Q C Law Clerk, House of Commons, Ottawa, Canada

WICKSTEED, Major Horatio Asprey, 6 Duke, St , Adelphi, London

WICKSTEED, R A , Esq , Major Governor General s Foot Guards, Ottawa, Canada

WILBRAHAM George Fortescue, Esq J P , Delamere, Northwich

WILBRAHAM, Randle, Esq , Rode Hall, Scholar Green, Stoke-on-Trent

WILD, William J , Esq , Romiley Terrace, Wellington Road S , Stockport

WILD, John H , Esq Southwood, Paignton, S Devon

WILSON, H C Esq Langley House Prestwich, Manchester

WILLIAMS, C Henry, Esq , Whixall, near Whitchurch Salop

WILLIAMS, John, Madams Farm, Acton, Nantwich

WILLIAMSON, Walter Stringer, Esq , Stapeley Hall, Nantwich

WITHINSHAW, Alfred Currier, Mill Fields Nantwich

WITHINSHAW John Senr , Esq , Elm House Nantwich

WOOD, James, Builder, Coppice Rd , Willaston, Nantwich

WOOD, Mrs Joseph, London Road, Nantwich

WOOD, Thomas, Currier, Beam Street, Nantwich

WORSEY, Sampson, Confectioner, Hawthorn Buildings, Nantwich

WRIGHT, William, Esq District Traffic Superintendent of Great Indian Peninsula Railway, Bombay

WILDE, Joseph, Grocer, High Street Nantwich

Y

YATES, Joseph St John, Esq , Wellbark House, Elworth, Sandbach

YOUNG, Henry, Esq , Wavertree, near Liverpool

YOUNG, Henry Selden, Esq , 6 Arundell Avenue, Sefton Park Liverpool

YOUNG John Esq Brook Bank, Timperley, Cheshire

TABLE OF CONTENTS.

	Page
TITLE	1.
DEDICATION	III
LIST OF SUBSCRIBERS	IV.–VIII.
TABLE OF CONTENTS	IX.–XI.
LIST OF ILLUSTRATIONS	XI.–XII
PREFACE	XIII.–XVI.

Introduction 1–9
General description Population, Field-names, Street-names, Derivation

Saxon and Norman Periods . 10–16
Domesday Survey, William Malbank, first Baron, his lands, the Castle

Norman Barons of Wich Malbank 17–24
Foundation Charter of Combermere Abbey, Abbot's Fee, Welsh Invasion, Division of the Barony, Malbank family Pedigree.

Manorial History 25–79

FIRST DIVISION OF THE BARONY 25–54
I —COUNTESS OF WARWICK'S FEE 25–39
The Praers', the Fouleshursts, Town Orders of 1538, Sir Christopher Hatton, the Crewes, Bellmen, Parish Clerks
II —LOVELL LANDS 40–54
Bishop Burnell, Great Fair, Rent Roll; Lands forfeitted, Sir William Stanley, &c

St. Nicholas Hospital 49–53

St. Lawrence Hospital . 53–54
SECOND DIVISION OF THE BARONY 55–58
AUDLEY FEE 55–58
THIRD DIVISION OF THE BARONY 59–79
The Savages, Leftwiches, Wettenhalls, Davenports, Mainwarings, Bailiffs' Accounts, Proportional shares of Barony, and Corn-mill
THE BARON'S FEE .. 63–77
The Cholmondeleys, Quo Warranto in 1500
MANORIAL COURTS .. 67–77
Town Offices; Gaol, Stocks, Court Rolls.
Night Watchmen 78
Town Charter 79

                                                                    Page
𝕳istorical Annals   .   80–251

Annals from Norman times to the Year 1580   80–103   .
THE GREAT FIRE OF 1583 .   104–110
Annals from 1580 to 1640   . .   111–136
THE GREAT CIVIL WAR AND COMMONWEALTH PERIOD   137–194
Annals from 1660 to 1883   .   .   195–251
"THE TOWNE CONCERNES," A Memorial   203–211
THE CHOLERA OF 1849   .   245–247

𝕿rades of the 𝕿own   .   .   252–271
Salt Manufacture   .   252–267
Corn Mill and Cotton Factory   267–269
Weaving and Stocking Trades   .   269
Shoemaking   270–271
Gloving, Clothing Factories   .   271

𝕿he 𝕻arish 𝕮hurch   .   272–334
THE CHURCH BEFORE THE REFORMATION   272–280
Chantries and Altars   .   281–283
Heraldic Glass and Ancient Monuments .   .   284–287
THE CHURCH SINCE THE REFORMATION   288–334
Clergy List   .   .   293–309
Monumental Inscriptions now destroyed   .   310–319
Monumental Inscriptions now in the Church   319–327
Description of the Church   ..   328–334

𝕿he 𝕻arish 𝕽egisters   .   .   335–353

𝕮harities   ,   .   354–382
The Grammar School   .   373–378
The Blue-cap School   378–382
The New Grammar School   382

𝕹onconformity   .   383–403
Presbyterian Chapel   384–392
Baptist Chapel   393–397
Friends' Meeting House   397–398
Congregational Chapel   398–400
Wesleyan Chapel   .   400–403
Primitive Methodist Chapel .   .   403

𝕬lbaston 𝕿ownship   .   .   404–412

𝕎oolstanwood 𝕿ownship   .   .   412

𝕎illaston 𝕿ownship   413–415

𝔉amily 𝔥istory
                                                                    Page
                                                                  416–499
The Maistersons   416–423
The Wilbrahams   424–439
The Church family   440–448
The Mainwarings   449–459
The Wettenhalls and Tomkinsons   460–466
The Minshulls of Nantwich and Stoke   467–471
Mrs. Elizabeth Milton   472–476
The Minshulls of Wistaston and Nantwich   477–478
The Goldsmith family   479–480
John Gerard   481–483
The Malbon family   483–486
The Wright family   486–494
The Comberbach family   495
The Wicksted family   496–498
Conclusion   498–499
ADDITIONS AND CORRECTIONS   Including the Eddowes and Bow-
    man families   500 *et seq*

General Index.

LIST OF
PLATES & ILLUSTRATIONS.

1   Arms of the Town   (Cover)
            (Quarterly, Or and Gules, a bendlet Sable)
2   Porch of Grammar School (*Plate*)   .   (Frontispiece)
            (Re-produced from a plate by C J Richardson)
                                                               Page
3   Hospital Street (*Plate*)   opposite   53
4. The Church, S W view (*Plate*)   opposite   91
5. Old Houses, High Street and Castle Lane   110
6   The Church, N W view (*Plate*)   .   opposite 167
            (Fac-simile of engraving in Lysons *Cheshire*)
7   The Crown Inn, High Street   ..   194
8   The Old Lamb Hotel, Hospital Street   265
9. The Church, N.E. view (*Plate*)   .. opposite 275

								Page
10.	Stone Pulpit in the Church	...	...	...	...	...	...	280
11.	Shields of Arms (*Plate*) ...	...	...	...	...	opposite		284
	(Fac-simile of original drawing *temp.* Eliz. *penes* J. P. Earwaker, Esq.)							
12.	The Church Interior (*Plate*)	...	...	...	...	opposite		308
13.	Plan of the Church (*Plate*) ...	...	...	...	...	opposite		330
14.	Bosses in Chancel groining (*Plate*)	...	...	...	...	opposite		332
15.	Sweet-briar Hall, Hospital Street	...	...	...	...	...	...	353
16.	Gateway to Wright's Almshouses (*Plate*)	...	...	...	opposite		370
	(Re-produced from a plate by C. J. Richardson).							
17.	Old Grammar School	...	...	...	...	...	...	...	377
18.	Grotesque Carving ...	...	...	...	...	...	...	...	395
19.	Miserere Carving ...	...	...	...	...	...	...	...	403
20.	Old Houses in High Street	...	...	...	...	...	...	415
21.	Arms and Crest of Maisterson	...	...	...	...	...	...	420
22.	Wilbraham's Widows' Almshouse	...	...	...	...	...	...	430
23.	Arms and Crest of Wilbraham	...	...	...	...	...	...	436
24.	Church's Mansion ...	...	...	...	...	...	...	...	441
25.	Arms and Crest of Mainwaring	...	...	...	...	...	...	457
26.	Arms and Crest of Wettenhall	...	...	...	...	...	...	463
27.	Arms and Crest of Minshull	...	...	...	...	...	...	470
28.	Portrait of John Gerard	...	...	...	...	...	...	...	481
	(Fac-simile slightly reduced from the engraving in Gerard's Herbal 1597-8).							
29.	Arms and Crest of Wicksted	...	...	...	...	...	...	496

PREFACE.

NE has well observed that "the past is in itself a treasure; and the same feeling which leads us back to the recollection of infancy carries us still further along the mighty waste of time." In these pages an attempt is made to trace the history of Nantwich, an ancient market town in Cheshire, from the time of the taking of the Domesday Survey to the present year; bridging over that interval of more than eight centuries with a series of local events in chronological sequence, and linking the present with the past by re-peopling the town with inhabitants of by-gone days. This self-imposed task has entailed no small labour; for, as Sterne has said, "when a man sits down to write a history, though it be but the history of Jack Hickathrift or Tom Thumb, he knows no more than his heels what lets and hindrances he is to meet with in his way, or what a dance he may be led by one excursion or another, before all is over . . . . . He will, moreover, have various accounts to reconcile; anecdotes to pick up; inscriptions to make out; stories to weave in; traditions to sift; personages to call upon; panegyrics to paste up at this door; pasquinades at that . . . . . To sum up all; there are archives at every stage to be looked into, and rolls, records, documents, and endless genealogies, which justice ever and anon calls him back to stay the reading of—in short, there is no end of it."

Of former histories, the first, published anonymously in 1774 (see page 381), was written by a native townsman, the Rev. Joseph Partridge. It was re-printed, with some omissions, in 1778 in Poole's so-called History of Cheshire, vol. ii. pp. 573–629. A second history of the town, which was little more than an enlarged and better arranged edition of the former work, was undertaken by Mr. John Weld Platt in 1818, who, however, omits to mention the existence of the earlier history from which he borrowed very freely without acknowledgment. The brothers Lysons, in 1810, and Dr. George Ormerod, in 1819, in their valuable County Histories, added very considerably to what had previously been written relating to Nantwich; and in the new edition of the latter work, much has again been added from the Cheshire Records. Of later writers, who have contributed in a less degree to the knowledge of the history of this locality, may be mentioned Miss Julia Tomkinson (afterwards Lady Rich), the authoress, in 1851, of "*Historical Facts of Nantwich and its neighbourhood;*" and Miss Elizabeth Johnson, of Nantwich, who wrote a short sketch entitled "*History of Nantwich and its neighbourhood,*" which appeared in "Johnsons' Nantwich and Crewe Monthly Illustrated Journal" from June to Dec. 1868.

obtained his information of the Civil War, which was afterwards printed under the title of *"Providence Improved"*

To the REV FOSTER GREY BLACKBURNE, M A , Rector of Nantwich, for his courtesy in allowing me to examine the Parish Registers   and for placing other documents in his possession under my notice

To the REV ROBERT SCARR REDFERN, Vicar of Acton, the REV. HENRY COLLISON, late Rector of Wistaston, and the REV. RICHARD DANDY, Vicar of Wybunbury, for their kindness in allowing me to search the Registers and other records of those Parishes

To JOHN PARSONS EARWAKER, ESQ, M A   F S A , author of *"East Cheshire,"* &c , for the interest he has always manifested in the progress and success of this work, for the loan of several rare books, pamphlets, original MSS , transcripts of documents, register extracts, &c , without whose aid much valuable information contained in these pages could not have appeared

To WILLIAM BEAMONT, ESQ , of Orford Hall, the well known antiquary and author, for his assistance in the translation of several ancient Latin deeds

To JOHN EGLINTON BAILEY, ESQ , F S A , editor of the *"Palatine Note Book,"* &c , who has furnished me with useful information at various times.

To JOHN BELLAMY MINSHULL ESQ , of London, for many particulars relating to the Minshulls of this town and its neighbourhood, and for the translation (by an unknown scholar) of the curious Latin inscription on pages 322–3

To MISS THOMASIN E SHARPE, of Kensington, for the benefit of her researches respecting the genealogy of the Goldsmith and Minshull families.

To DR T. N. BRUSHFIELD, of Salterleigh, Devonshire, for several communications.

To the REV T W NORWOOD, F G S , Vicar of Wrenbury, whose knowledge of Architecture has been helpful to me in describing the Church

To JOHN DOWNES ESQ , of Nantwich, for the loan of many useful and some rare books, to THOMAS W HENSLEY, ESQ , H CLAUD LISLE, ESQ , PHILIP BARKER, ESQ , and other residents in Nantwich, to whom I have in various ways been obligated during the time I have been engaged on this history.

To SIR WILLIAM BOWMAN BART , of Dorking, Surrey, for particulars relating to his family

To the representatives of the late HENRY BOWMAN ESQ , his brother, and to J S CROWTHER, ESQ , for their kind permission to re-produce the N E and S W views of the Church and the Plate of the Bosses in the Chancel groining, from their handsome work, *"The Churches of the Middle Ages "*

To THOMAS BOWER, ESQ , Architect, for the excellent Plan of the Church, which has been drawn specially for this work

To a friend, MR. E. E. MINTON, for the drawings of the illustrations on pages 110, 194, and 265

And, lastly, I would thank my Subscribers, without whose generous support this history could not have appeared, to whom also an apology is due for the unavoidable delay that has occurred since the first announcement of the work more than two years ago, and for the omission of the promised map of the Parish indicating the fields and field-names.   It was afterwards found that such a map would of necessity be so small as to be practically useless   The sheet maps of the Government Survey, however, are easily obtainable, and will supply the deficiency

The first illustrated book printed at Nantwich, issued from the press of Mr Edmund Snelson in the year 1787   It was entitled " *A Topographical Survey of the Counties of Stafford, Chester and Lancaster, containing A new engraved Map of each County   *   *   *   * together with elegant Engravings of the Arms of the Nobility and Gentry*," &c , by William Tunnicliffe   Those of my readers who happen to possess a copy of that work, will be able to judge of the improvement in local typography that has taken place since that date   A meed of praise is therefore due to the printer, Mr. Thomas Johnson, and to his foreman, Mr Jervis, who has spared no pains to make the volume as attractive as possible

In conclusion, I would adopt the words of old Geffrey Whitney, (the celebrated Emblem writer in the time of Queen Elizabeth,) who was a native of the adjoining parish of Acton, and say to the general reader—

> " *Peruse with heede, then frendlie iudge, and blaming rashe refraine,*
> *So maist thou reade vnto thy good, and shalt requite my paine* "

JAMES HALL

WILLASTON, NEAR NANTWICH,
            December 10th, 1883

HISTORY

OF THE

TOWN AND PARISH OF NANTWICH.

Introduction.

ANTWICH is the name of an ancient Market-town, a Parish, a Poor Law Union, a Rural Deanery, and a Hundred in the south of Cheshire. The Parish includes the Townships of Nantwich, Alvaston, Woolstanwood, and part of Willaston. Leighton, formerly included in Nantwich Parish, became in 1840 a new ecclesiastical district, under the name of Leighton-cum-Minshull-Vernon, in the parish of Middlewich.

Nantwich is bounded by the parishes of Acton, Church Minshull, Church Coppenhall, Wistaston and Wybunbury. The adjacent townships are Baddington, Edleston, Acton, Henhull, Worleston, Leighton, Coppenhall, Wistaston, Willaston, Stapeley, Austerson and Bartherton.

Situated about the centre of the Hundred, old writers locate Nantwich on the "Great and Direct Road from London to Holyhead," one hundred and sixty-nine miles from "Hick's Hall,"* and twenty miles from Chester. Since the introduction of iron roads, the situation of Nantwich must be referred to the modern and rival town of Crewe; from which railway centre it is about four miles distant on the Crewe and Shrewsbury branch of the London and North Western Railway System.

---

* "*Hick's Hall*," or the Sessions' House, was situated in St. John Street, Clerkenwell, London.

As its name implies, Nantwich is situated in a valley, through which the Weaver, here an inconsiderable stream, flows, dividing the town into two parts   Drayton, in his "Polyolbion," c 1612, calls the Weaver the "*wizard river*," and, as the valley has always been famous for its numerous salt-springs, it is still commonly believed that a subterranean brine-stream follows the course of the river

In 1819 the town was described as follows :—[*]

"A very large proportion of the buildings in the town of Nantwich are timber and plaister with large bay windows and projecting stories   This kind of architecture gives an air of gloom when introduced in masses in the narrow streets of a crowded town, and when in the lapse of time such buildings fall into the hands of the lower orders, their exterior becomes necessarily ragged and unsightly   There are, however, many respectable modern mansions of the more opulent inhabitants, in various streets of Nantwich, and in its outskirts, and more open parts, where the ancient timber buildings have trees and gardens around them, they assume an air which is pleasing and picturesque, as well as venerable "

So wrote Dr Ormerod, and in some respects the same description still applies   The greatest town improvement of this century, effectually dispersing the "gloom" of High Town, was the removal of the ' Old Market Hall" in 1868, and the block of houses and shops, in 1872, that stood on what is now called "The Square "   Still, however, a few quaint timbered houses,[†] with low, thatched roofs and small lead-latticed windows having hanging shutters, stand in an in-and-out fashion, as if with studied irregularity along the boulder-paved, narrow, and tortuous thoroughfares   At intervals are structures of Elizabethan age, timbered mansions with high peaked gables and overhanging roofs, beside substantial red brick houses with red tiled roofs, and high walled gardens, while the Cathedral-like Church, with its tree adorned graveyard, forms the centre round which the town is gathered.   It is only within the last thirty years that the existing modern fronts have put a new face on the ancient gables of High Town, (and it is to be regretted that so few attempts have been made to reproduce the Elizabethan style so characteristic of Nantwich), but there, behind, are the old oak beams of houses jammed together, as if land had always been scarce and dear, with curious shaped rooms over low, narrow passages that lead to courtyards, where the eye beholds chimneys and roofs oddshaped and crowded. Perhaps some of the oldest houses are to be found in Welsh Row and Wood Street, since the fire of 1583 did not extend its ravages to that part of the town, and it is noticeable that many of the old beams exhibit notches, mortices, &c , as if they had served some anterior purpose   Old barns, peasants' cottages and farm houses in the neighbourhood furnish the same evidence.   A few "ragged and unsightly " buildings linger to tell of "forgotten years,"

> "Whose walls with wrinkles frown,
> And people say, who pass that way,
> 'Twere well the house were down "

While in the outskirts of the town long rows of regularly built houses, with garden plots attached, have become the homes of an increased population.

The population of Nantwich Parish, according to the Government returns, is here appended

POPULATION TABLE

Date of Census	Township of Leighton		Township of Woolstanwood		Township of Alvaston		Township of Nantwich-Willaston		Township of Nantwich		Total Population of Nantwich Parish
	Houses	Popul'n	Houses	Popul'n	Houses	Popul'n	Houses	Popul'n	Honses	Popul'n	
1801	39	200	7	40	3	11		*	824	3463	3714
1811	29	156	7	48	4	33		†	873	3999	4236
1821	31	270	9	65	6	37		‡	985	4661	5033
1831	48	261	9	70	6	41	29	122	952	4886	5380
1841		§	9	64	4	40	22	91	1045	5489	5684
1851			9	65	7	37	33	147	1120	5579	5828
1861			11	65	7	28	51	228	1189	6225	6546
1871			15	75	6	23	53	222	1328	6673	6993
1881			20	117	11	57	66	333	1629	7496	8003

The numbers given above from the Census of 1881, are divided into males and females as follows.—

Parish of Nantwich	Males	Females	Total
Nantwich Town	3508	3766	7274
Nantwich Workhouse	142	80	222
Woolstanwood	59	58	117
Alvaston	23	34	57
Nantwich-Willaston	173	160	333
	3905	4098	8003

In the absence of records of the numbering of the people prior to this century, it is difficult to ascertain, even approximately, the population of towns in remote times. King William III adopted a curious mode of reckoning the population, and one that was practised for many years, viz by a diocesan inquiry into the comparative strength of religious sects Thus Bishop Gastrell, in his "*Notitia Cestriensis*," in 1722, gives the following statistics relating to Nantwich —

Total number of Families 770

Papists	5	
	9	
Presbyterians	157	} 293—Number of Nonconformist families
Anabaptists	109	
Quakers	13	

Probably, at that time, the population of Nantwich did not exceed 3,000

* No return of Willaston in 1801

† In 1811 the whole of Willaston had 35 houses and 214 inhabitants, but the return is included in Wybunbury Parish

‡ In 1821 Willaston had 41 Houses and 209 inhabitants, included in Wybunbury

§ Leighton, which has been separated from Nantwich Parish since 1840, had in 1841, 237 inhabitants, in 1851, 190 in 1861, 217, in 1871, 241, and in 1881, 172

(8) "I John Wilbor have given to Richard Wilbor one place of land in Wich Malbank in breadth between the land of Roger Cradock and the land of Tho Praers [?] and in length between the *high street* and the *Castle Hall*   Witnesses, Richard de ffouleshurst then sheriff of Chester, &c   Dated 1321"   (*Harl MSS* 1967, f 114)

(9) 'Pardon to William de Brescy for acquiring to himself and his heirs one messuage called *Chastelyord* in Wich Malbank from John Lovel   Dated 19 Sept 1341"   (Chesh Recog Rolls)

(10) "We Richard le Cooke of Beeston and Rose my Wife grant to John de Cholmundelegh and Ann his wife two places of land in Wich Malbank in ' *le Tenchersfeild*" which are called *flowerscroft* &c   Witnesses, Richard de ffouleshurst then sheriff of Chester, &c   Dated 1325" (*Harl MSS* 1967, f 115)

In the same MSS, and on the same page, are deeds in which the following local names occur —"land called *Tinkersfeild*" in 1361, "houses in *le Beme Streate*" in 1336, and "*Meelstreete* dated 29 Edw 3 1355" Beam Street is the street leading to Beam Heath, which in Norman times bore the name of *Creche*   Mention is made of Nantwich mill in an original Charter at Keele, Staffordshire, about the year 1228, in which

(11) "Philippa Mauban grants to Letisce [Letitia] wife of Peter de Stapeley land against the *mill of Wichomauben* Witnesses Hugh Decino de Wichomauben, Richard de Sandeford, Hugh de Beveresford" &c   (Ormerod's *Cheshire*, New Edit, Vol III p 495)

(12) "John de Wettenhall demised to Thomas de Edgley *the Inn of ye Swanne* and three shopes in *Churchloue* for 10 years yeilding four marks [£2 13s 4d] and 8s 4d yearly &c Dated 1424" (*Harl MSS* 1969, f 115)

Of the following names, which often occur in the fifteenth century, only one—*Monks' Lane*—survives to the present time, viz   *Flesshemonger Lane*, occurring in the Inquisition *post mortem* of John Lovell, Kt , dated 1414, "*Lothburne*" (once an open channel in Beam Street) in 1452; "a meadow formerly called the *Monkes orchard*" in 1453, "*Ratonrowe*" in 1483, and as late as 17 Hen VIII [1525-6] "*Bayartesholt*" or "*Baywards hold*" in 1468, "*Monkslone*" in 1470, and "*Peters Lane*" in 1482   (*Harl MSS* 1967, f 136-9).

Great and *Little Wood Street* and *Snow Hill* were common names for the localities of the salt-houses in the same century   *Wyche-house Bank* is a modern name

Waterlode, that is, the road *leading* to the fordable part of the river, was the lane where the great fire of 1583 began, which destroyed, amongst other streets, *Swine Market*, the *Beast Market* (the west end of Beam Street) and *Love Lane*, afterwards named *Corn Market*, and now *Oat Market*   These, from their central positions, must have been very old streets, but the earliest mention of the Corn Market with its necessary ' Inn,' still bearing the same sign, occurs in an Inquisition *post mortem*, dated 4 Sep 2 Jac I. [1605] as follows — *(translated)*

"Geffrey Mynshull gent died 26 Dec last past [1603] leaving Edward Mynshull his son and heir aged 40 years, and upwards   He died seised of a messuage and shop in Nantwich in the *Hightown* 1 cottage & stable, 1 garden and part of a garden in N by *Mounkes Lane* there , 2 other messuages & 2 gardens there in a street called the *Welch Row*, a salt-house of 12 leads in *Little Wood Street*, 6 acres of land, 6 of meadow, called the *Pear-tree field* and *Pear-tree Meadow* in Nantwich , an annual rent of 12 sh issuing of a messuage of Nicholas Goldsmith in the *Hospell St* there , another annual rent of 6 sh issuing out of another messuage or burgage being called the *Sign of the Cock* lying near the *Corn Market*, then the inheritance of Thos Bromley gent " &c   [Lands in Wistaston, &c]

Between Snow Hill and *Wall-lane*, i e the lane leading to *Wall-field*, is *Cart-lake*, which formerly contained a cesspool known as the *cuckstool-pit*, for the discipline of the "thewe" [cuckingstool] and "tumbrel" [cart], which in former days, must frequently have been in requisition so as to have given rise to the local proverb—"Scold like a wych waller " With the improvement of the manners of the inhabitants, that engine of punishment disappeared, and the proverb became obsolete, but the name of the lane still survives

Pillory Street* is suggestive of another kind of punishment in days long ago   According to the tradition of the town, James Kirkham, for a rape, was the last person to be pilloried, not, however, in this street, but in the High Town, early in the present century. *Barker Street*, from an old Latin word, *Barcaria* a tan-house, was most likely so called from the tannery that belonged to the Comberbach family during the sixteenth and seventeenth centuries   *Pepper Street*, a name of doubtful etymology, is also found at Chester, Middlewich, and in other places in the County †   These three street names are mentioned in the Inquisitions *post mortem* of Thomas Minshull, and Sir Hugh Cholmondeley, Knight, dated 1604 and 1605

Some of the field names, too, are of a most interesting character   On the eastern side of the township is the *Barony*, formerly the waste of the lord of the town. In this waste, now largely built over, are two enclosures called *Clonners fields*, a name indicating the features of the place, namely—land surrounded by bog or water, which was the actual fact not many years ago   To the south, at Shrewbridge, are *Salt Lake* and *Salt Meadow*, suggesting the presence of brine-springs   The *Mill-field* is mentioned by John Gerard in 1597 as the Milne-*eye*, that is, *island*, a tacit allusion to the antiquity of the existing mill-weir   *St Ann's Croft*, behind the tannery at Welsh Row Head, was no doubt land belonging to the ancient Oratory that stood on the *Wich* [now *Welsh*] Bridge in pre-Reformation times   But the names that carry with them the greatest antiquity are to be found on the north side of the town, viz   *Wall-field*, *Dunmllow-field*, and *Windy Harbour*   *Windy* or *Cold-Harbour* is a common name found on all the main lines of Roman Roads, signifying resting or sheltering places   *Dunmllow* is a Saxon word meaning "hill-fort-mound," and *Wall-field*, from the Latin "*vallum*, a stockade," is clearly indicative of Roman occupation   These are situated exactly in the line of the Roman way (the 2nd Iter of Antoninus) running north and south from CONDATE (now supposed by some to have been near Warrington) to URICONIUM (Wroxeter,) traces of which occur on the Government Survey Map under the names of Holford Street and King Street to Middlewich, and thence in direction of Nantwich to within two miles of the town   *Causeway Meadow*, an oblong field on the boundary of the township on the west side of the river, and *Cawsey Croft* in the adjacent township of Henhull, together with the aforesaid *Wall-field*, are all in the same straight line with the *Watfield Pavement* in Wardle, which is known to have been part of the great Roman Way (VIA DEVANA) that connected Chester (DEVA) with Leicester (RATÆ)

Both Partridge and Pennant suppose Nantwich existed as a salt-town in Roman times,‡ and the conjecture is not undeserving of credit, from the fact of the intersection of these

---

* "*Pyllery-strete*" occurs in the Exchequer Records, Ministers' Accounts 3 & 4 Edw VI [1550]   Record Soc Publ Vol vii p 111
† In one instance it occurs in this County, near Stockport, as the name of part of a Roman Road   *Pepper Street*, and "*Pepper Street Moss*," in Hunsterson, are names frequently mentioned in Wybunbury Parish Registers
‡ Partridge's Hist Nantwich, p 4 , and Pennant's "Tour from Chester to London," 1782 p 27-8

roads at *Wall-field*, in close proximity to the ancient Brine-pit, and the discovery of a
few interesting remains   In 1667 Lord Brereton related to the Royal Society, "that upon
digging a salt-pit near the Weaver, (between Nantwich and Northwich, the exact place
not being given) at two yards deep he found a pavement and some Roman coins "[*]
Mr James Pick, of Nantwich, has twelve Roman copper coins that were found many years
ago in Marsh Lane   Fifteen other coins found in a hard lump of earth when alterations
were being made in the *Wall-Lane* tanyard in or about 1849, which are helmet headed,
and have been identified as belonging to various Roman Emperors, were in the possession
of the late Mr Charles Laxton, of Nantwich

Mr Webb, in his description of the town, written in 1621, (see King's "*Vale Royal
of England*") speaks of it as existing anterior to Roman times, stating that "the *Britons*
called the town HELLATH-WEN,[†] the white pit " Little or nothing, however is known of
Cheshire in the Keltic period of history, but the etymology of the name Nantwich proves
that the Weaver[‡] valley was once inhabited by the ancient race of people now dwelling
in the secluded valleys of North Wales.

NANT-WICH is a Kelto-Teutonic word, the former syllable alluding to its situation in
a *river valley*, and the latter having reference to *salt*, for the manufacture of which the
town was in ancient times famous   "*Nant*" is common as a prefix in place-names in
Wales, Cornwall, and Brittany, but philologists are not agreed as to the derivation of
"*Wich*" as applied to the inland salt-towns, collectively called the *Wiches*   "*Wich*," a
word found in all the Teutonic dialects,[§] is said to mean, primarily "a village" or
"dwelling place,' being synonymous with the Latin *vicus*, the Greek *oikos*, the Sanskrit
vesa, from *vas* to inhabit   The Rev Isaac Taylor (*Words and Places*, p 169) suggests
that the Wiches derive their name from the Norse "*wic*, a bay," and not from the Anglo-
Saxon "*wic*, a village," and argues that the Northmen or Vikings *(creekers)* visited
certain bays or creeks *(vigs)* and there obtained salt from sea-water   Whilst that might
account for the names of places on the coast-line, where it is presumed salt was obtained
in shallow *wiches* or bays by solar and artificial evaporation, it entirely fails to prove that
the Northmen gave the name of *Wich* to inland salt-towns, inasmuch as it is recorded as
early as 716, or seventy years before they first commenced their ravages on our coasts,
that ' Æthelbald of Mercia granted certain salt-works near the river Salwarpe at *Lootwic* in
Worcestershire in exchange howevei, foi others to the north of the river, and "in the
same year he granted a hide of land in *Saltwych vico emptorio salis*, to Evesham '[||]
Although no mention of the Cheshire *Wiches* has occurred in any record prior to 1086, it
may be inferred that the name *Wich* applied to the salt-towns in this county, as elsewhere,

---

[*] Earwaker s "Local Gleanings, 4to Series, vol 1 p 40
[†] The Welsh name for salt is *hel*, and for a salt-pit, *helead*   *Wen* or *Gwyn* signifies white
[‡] *Weaver* is a Keltic river-name, found elsewhere, in *Wear* and *Ure*
[§] The various forms and meanings of this word are thus given in Charnock's Local "Etymology," p 296

Saxon { Anglo-Saxon, *wic, wyc,* / a village, dwelling-place habitation, street, monastery, convent, castle,
      { Frieslandic, *wic,*   camp, station
      { Old German, *wick, wiek, weich* }

Norse { Danish *wyk, wig,* a ford
     { Swedish, *vik,* a cove, or creek
     { Icelandic, *vik,* a little bay

[||] Kemble's "*Saxons in England*," Vol ii , p 70, quoting *Cod Dipl* Nos 67 and 68   The name *Saltwych* is a
curious combination

was of Saxon and not Danish origin, especially when it is remembered that the names of surrounding townships invariably indicate Saxon and not Danish occupation.

In "*Notes and Queries*" (1874, vol. ii.) will be found a series of articles on the derivation of this word. Among the many etymologies there adduced is the Low German word "wijck or wicca," from a Teutonic root "wih or wyc" found in every dialect, meaning *sacred*, *devoted*. Pennant speaks of the superstitious reverence for salt-springs amongst the Saxons; and thinks the old custom of *Blessing the Brine* as practised at Nantwich in the eighteenth century, may have originated in their sacred rites. Kemble, too, remarks (Saxons in England, vol. ii. p. 72) that "the pagan Germans considered the salt-springs holy; and waged wars of extermination for their possession; and it is not improbable that they may generally have belonged to the exclusive property of the priesthood; and upon the introduction of Christianity these rights would naturally pass into the hands of the King."

The rights of royalty and the severe laws against crime, as recorded in Domesday Book, (see next chapter) seem to favor the theory here advanced accounting for the origin of the name *Wich* as applied to all salt-towns. Though commonly called Nant´-wich, local pronunciation places the accent on the *second* syllable, which is also pronounced in two ways; Nant-wich´, and Nant-wīch´. Without deciding which of these is the correct pronunciation, it may here be observed that the Domesday Book gives to all the salt-towns, both in Cheshire and Worcestershire, the longer name of *wich* or *wiche*; and not the shorter form of *vic* or *wik* as in other place-names in the same record. Thus it would appear that it is not a modern affectation of speech to say Nant-wiché.

The name of the town is found spelled in various ways. Nantwich, in Cheshire, and Droitwich, in Worcestershire, are alike simply called *Wiche*, in the Domesday Survey; no doubt, by way of pre-eminence in their several districts, each county having its Middlewich and Northwich, &c. From the time of the Norman Conquest through the period embraced by the "Cheshire Records," the town is very frequently called in legal record *Wicus-Malbanus*, *Wich-Malbank*, or *Malbanewic*, a name given in honor of the Baronial family of Malbank. But it must not be supposed that the *people* called the town by those names; or that the present name, which is as old as the English language, was, after having been lost for several centuries, revived again in recent times. For occasionally even amongst documentary rolls, the ancient name occurs, e.g. in the Calendar of Fines No. 3. 13 Edw. I. [1284] &c., which is quoted on a subsequent page.

The final "*e*," which is often added, denotes the long vowel sound of "*i*," for which sometimes a "*y*" is substituted, thus :—*Nant-wyche*. The alteration of the first syllable to "*Nampt*," which appears to have taken place in the sixteenth century and to have become common in the two following centuries, can only be considered as a gross mis-spelling of the word.

The Saxon and Norman Periods.

HE earliest account of Nantwich, relating to the laws, customs, and values of the salt-works in late Saxon times and after the Conquest, is contained in the Domesday Survey of 1086. That account, which is very full and interesting, is as follows: (translated)—*

In King *Edward's* time there was a WICH in WARMUNDESTROU [Nantwich] hundred, in which there was a well for making salt, and between the King and *Earl Edwin* there were 8 salt-houses, so divided that of all their issues and rents the King had 2 parts and the Earl the third. But besides these, the Earl had one salt-house adjoining his manor of ACTON, which was his own. From this salt-house the Earl had sufficient salt for his house throughout the year. But if he sold any from thence, the King had twopence, and the Earl a third penny, for the toll.

In the same WICH many men from the country had salt-houses, of which this was the custom:— From our *Lord's Ascension* [Holy Thursday] to *Martinmas*, [Nov. 11th] any one having a salt-house might carry home salt for his own house. But if he sold any of it either there, or elsewhere in the county of CHESTER, he paid toll to the King and the Earl.

Whoever after *Martinmas* carried away salt from any salt-house except the Earl's, under his custom aforesaid, paid toll, whether the salt was his own or purchased. These aforesaid 8 salt-houses of the King and the Earl, in every week that salt was boiled or they were used on a Friday, rendered 16 boilings of salt, of which 15 made a horse-load. From our *Lord's Ascension* to *Martinmas*, the salt-houses of the other men did not give these Friday's boilings. But from *Martinmas* to our *Lord's Ascension*, these boilings were given according to custom,

---

* Taken from the "Domesday Book of Cheshire and Lancashire," extended and translated by William Beamont, Esq., of Orford Hall; pub. Chester, 1863, pp. 64-7.

as from the salt-houses of the King and the Earl

All these salt-houses, both of the lord and other people, were surrounded on one part by a certain river, and on the other by a ditch

Whosoever committed a forfeiture within these bounds might make amends, either by the payment of 2 shillings, or by 30 boilings of salt, except in the case of homicide, or of a theft, for which the thief was adjudged to die   These last, if done here, were dealt with as in the rest of the shire

If out of the prescribed circuit of the salt-houses, any person within the county withheld the toll, and was convicted thereof he brought it back and was fined 40 shillings, if a free man, or, if not free, 4 shillings

But if he carried the toll into another shire, where it was demanded the fine was the same

In King *Edward's* time, this WICH with all pleas in the same hundred rendered 21 £ in farm   When *Earl Hugh* received it, except only one salt-house it was waste

WILLIAM MALBEDENG now holds of the Earl the same WICH, with all the customs thereto belonging, and all the same hundred, which is rated at 40 shillings, of which 30 shillings are put on the land of the same WILLIAM and 10 shillings on the land of the Bishop, and the lands of RICHARD and GILBERT which they have in the same hundred, and the WICH is let to farm at 10 £

From these two WICHES [Nantwich and Middlewich], whoever carried away bought salt in a wain, drawn by four oxen or more, paid 4^d for the toll, but if by two oxen, 2^d if the salt were 2 horse-loads

A man from another hundred gave 2^d for a horse-load

But a man of the same hundred gave only a half-penny for a horse-load

Whoever loaded his wain so that the axle broke within a league of either WICH, gave 2 shillings to the King's or the Earl's officer, if he were overtaken within the league

In like manner, he who loaded his horse, so as to break its back, gave 2 shillings if overtaken within the league, but nothing if overtaken beyond it

Whoever made two horse-loads of salt out of one was fined 40 shillings if the officer overtook him   If he was not found, nothing was to be exacted from any other [*than the actual offender*]   Men on foot from another hundred buying salt, paid 2^d for 8 men's loads

Men of the same hundred paid 1^d for the same number of such loads"

From the above it appears that when Edward the Confessor ruled this land, Wich, or Nantwich, was the chief salt-town in Cheshire, and was farmed out at £21 per annum, the rent of Middlewich and Northwich being each £8 per annum.

The salt-houses, of which the total number is not given, were supplied with brine from "*a well*," and were enclosed in an area that was defended on one side by a moat, and on the other by the Weaver *   They were divided between the King, Earl Edwin,

---

* "It was the only wich so defended and the only one which Hugh Lupus did not retain as parcel of the demesne of the Earldom —(Dr Ormerod's Cheshire, vol iii 422 New Edit)   Also compare p 4 *note*

and certain thanes or freemen resident in the neighbourhood   There was a court where
justice was administered , and the internal peace and prosperity of the town was regulated
by special criminal laws and trade customs   Civil injuries and criminal offences were
atoned for by the payment of pecuniary fines   A fixed sum of two shillings (an amount
incidentally mentioned in the same record as the value of an ox) or thirty boilings of salt
was demanded in restitution to the guild-brethren, for all crimes committed within the
town, except those of *homicide* and *theft*, for the former of which the murderer forfeited
all his goods, and, being expelled from the town, became a lawless outcast   while for the
latter, which was regarded the more heinous sin, the thief, who, in Chester and South
Lancashire, might atone for his offence by a fine of forty shillings, was here to die.
Elsewhere, e g in the Rhuddlan boroughs,* offenders were fined twelve pence for all crimes,
except homicide, theft, and heinfare (*i e* enticing away another s slave ,) and, perhaps, the
severer penalties in Nantwich may be accounted for by the superstitious idea alluded to
by Pennant,† Kemble, and other writers, viz   " *the peculiar sanctity of salt-springs* '

The very heavy fines attached to the neglect of paying toll-dues, and especially that
bye-law which states that the fine could *only* be recovered from the actual offender, who
must first of all be caught, prove how very jealously the trade of the town must have
been guarded by active and vigilant officers   It is noticeable in all ancient Town Charters
granting privileges to burgesses in other parts of the county, such as exemption from tolls
at markets and fairs, that exception is always made in the case of *toll of salt in the Wiches.*
Such a privilege, indeed, could not be claimed by the freemen proprietors of salt-houses,
nor even by the Earl himself, except for salt made only for their own consumption.   Toll
of salt belonged to the King and Earl, who had " *twopence* ' and every " *third penny* '
respectively , *i e* the salt-maker received two-fifths of the profits, the King two-fifths, and
the Earl the remaining one-fifth   A privilege belonged to the inhabitants of *Warmundestrou,*
viz. the purchasing of salt at one fourth the price paid by people beyond the bounds of the
hundred , and I am inclined to believe that the local customs of the salt-trade in Saxon
times above-mentioned account for the ancient name of the Hundred—Warmundestrou—
which according to Sir Peter Leycester was lost about the time of Edward III   The
name is certainly of Saxon origin   " *War*" is the word " *ware*, ' meaning ' fixed price,'
or ' equivalent value ,' a word still used in the northen dialects in the sense of *spending*,
and also found in the common word *ware-house*   " *Mund*" literally meant ' the hand,' or
' holding out the hand to ' and then, secondarily, a token of protection ‡   " *Strou* " or
" *strow* " signifies ' a district '   Thus, according to this derivation, Warmundestrou would
be *the district of protected prices* in the salt-trade

Mr Beamont thinks the custom of rendering Fridays boilings to have been of the
nature of a tithe to the Church , but if so, it does not appear clear why the freemen
should have been exempted from payment for six months of the year, while the tenants
of the King and Earl were required to give sixteen boilings of salt every week.   Remembering that Domesday makes no mention of a church in Nantwich, this ' custom ' seems

* Domesday Book, page 73

† " *Tour from Chester to London*,' page 30, Edit 1782

‡ The same root occurs in four other Cheshire names in Domesday Book , viz   *Chelmundestune* (Cholmondeston,)
Cepmundwich (near Peover,) *Calmundelei* (Cholmondeley,) and *Wimundisham* (Wincham)

rather to have been gathered as a rent or perquisite by the officer of the King and Earl, than as tithes by the parish priest.

The two Earls were *Edwin*, the third and last of the Saxon Earls of Chester, and *Hugh Lupus*, the first Norman Earl of the Palatinate and as Nantwich suffered in the struggles that brought about that change, it will be necessary to say something about that crisis of English history.

On the death of Edward the Confessor, the strength of Saxon England was sapped by the feuds and plots of two rival families—the sons of Godwin and the house of Alfgar—given in the following pedigree —

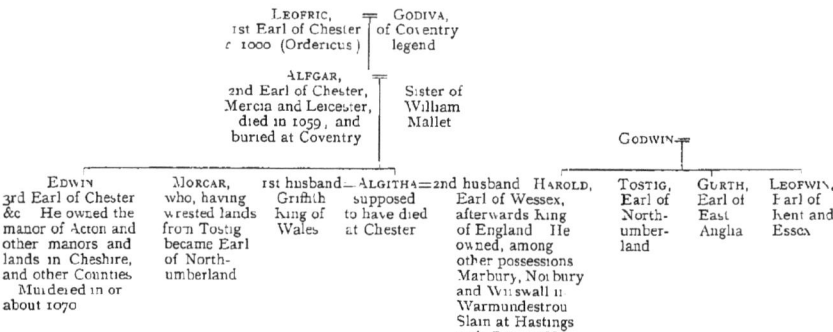

While these claimants for the crown were contending for the supremacy, William, Count of Normandy, invaded England, and, after the battle of Hastings, was first elected King by the populace of London, and then crowned by Stigand, the Archbishop, at Westminster, Christmas 1066 After this, Edwin and Morcar supported the claims of Edgar Atheling, but the King's march through central England reduced both Earls to submission, and peace was made with the Conqueror at Berkhampstead Sir Peter Leycester records, on the authority of Ordericus, that Earl Edwin, "fearing to be imprisoned, conveyed himself secretly from the court of William the Conqueror, and rebelled against him and unable to withstand, he intended to have gone to Malcolm then King of Scotland, but being betrayed by his own men, was slain by the way"* Another account given by Webb, who cites Hoveden, says, "In 1067 the Conqueror sailing into Normandy, carried this Earl and other nobles with him over the sea, not daring to trust such dangerous friends in a late acquired dominion In 1071 the King desirous to put them in closer custody, which being perceived, they secretly stole from court, and among the rest Earl Edwin made his way to Scotland, but was slain by his own companions in his journey thitherwards "+

The people of the north, however, only sullenly acquiesced in the change of dynasty, waiting a convenient time for revolt An opportunity was afforded in 1069, when Sweyn, King of Denmark, with mercenaries from northern Europe, came to contest the crown.

---

* Ormerod's Cheshire (New Edit) Vol I p 9
† Ormerod's Cheshire (New Edit) Vol I p 166

His fleet arrived in the Humber, York was besieged, and the Norman garrison there, to the number of 3000, massacred   The same year "Anno Christi 1069 the Cheshire men and the Welsh besieged Shrewsbury."* King William received the news of invasion, massacre, and rebellion, while hunting in Dean Forest, and in an outburst of wrath, swore he would be avenged   The Danish fleet was bribed to withdraw   The King, "stark as death to those who crossed him,' wasted the north country as he went with fire and sword, as far as the Tees, till his hand was "as winter on the field" An old writer says —†

> "William turned ageyn and held that he had suorn
> Alle mad he wasteyn, pastur, medow, and korn,
> And slough bothe fader and sonne, women lete thei gon,
> Hors and hondes thei ete; oneth is skaped non."

From the frequent mention of the term *"waste"* in the Domesday account of Cheshire, it would appear that the devastation in this county was scarcely less cruel and complete than in Yorkshire   In this terrible march, an opposing force made ineffectual resistance at Nantwich, for according to a deposition taken at Wych-Malbank, 1st October, 1386, at an inquiry in the Scrope and Grosvenor Suit of Arms   it was stated that "a Saxon thane, named Hame was killed at the battle of Nampwich"‡ The town suffered almost total destruction, or, to repeat the forcible words of Domesday, *When Earl Hugh received it* [Wich,] *except one salt-house, it was* WASTE "

The King's victorious march through Cheshire resulted in the abolition of the Mercian Earldom, and the establishment of a new Earldom of Chester   Raised to a Palatine county, Cheshire became *de facto* a Kingdom in itself, having its own court and parliament of temporal and spiritual barons, courts of justice, legal and military officers, &c   The whole county and part of North Wales was granted by the King § to Hugh Lupus, who held his earldom by the possession of the sword of St Edward, called *Curtein*, just as the King held the country by his Crown   Hugh Lupus in like manner granted the lands of the Saxon thanes who had either been slain or ejected, to certain Norman soldiers, whom he created Barons, the Bishop's lands only being excepted in the general confiscation.   In this distribution of lands William Malbedeng or Malbank, under the title of Baron of Wich-Malbank, received *"Wich* [Nantwich] *with all the customs thereto belonging,"*— its salt-works, court, &c,—*"and all the hundred '* of Warmundestrou, except *Wimebeire* [Wybunbury] which belonged to the Bishop *"Aldelime"* [Audlem] and *"Creu'* [Crewe,] which were granted to Richard de Vernon Baron of Shipbrook, *"Blackenhale '* [Blakenhall,] granted to Gilbert Venator, Baron of Kinderton, and *"Eleacier"* [Alsager] which Hugh Lupus retained as parcel of the demesne of the Earldom   Warmundestrou was *taxed*

---

* Ordericus

† Peter Langtoft, by Robert of Brunne, Hearne's Edit

‡ Ormerod's Cheshire (New Edit) Vol III p 144

§ Cheshire was granted in the first instance to Gherbod, a noble Fleming, the son of Matilda dau of Count of Flanders who on the death of her husband married William the Conqueror   Gherbod, however, was obliged to return to his native land to defend his possessions there   and being imprisoned, had to surrender his newly acquired honors in England ' (probably for the payment of the *mise* on the accession of every new Earl,) in the following fixed sums —

The lands of William Malbedeng,	30 shillings
The lands of the Bishop, Richard, and Gilbert	10 do
Total	40 shillings

In 1086 the rental of Nantwich amounted to £10 so that the town was again rising in importance and wealth.

There is no mention in Domesday of a church in Warmundestrou, but it is believed that one existed at *Acton*, where two priests occur as farmers of land, another at *Wybunbury* and another at *Barthomley*, each having one priest If these were all the churches in the hundred, the religious advantages in this district must have been similar to what now prevails in the 'far west' of America, or thinly peopled parts of Australia Nantwich was included in Acton parish, and Dr Ormerod supposes one of the Acton priests officiated here and in the more distant parts of the cure After the year 1000 there was great lethargy through all Christendom arising from the belief that the Millenium had passed, and the world was soon to come to an end, but towards the end of the eleventh century, a religious revival broke out, chiefly through the zealous preaching of Cistercian monks, who were welcomed to England by high and low Hence the Norman Barons of Wich-Malbank, impressed with the new ideas of these reformers, made grants of land, salt-houses, &c, for the erection and maintenance of Abbeys and Convents for this order, thus providing better religious teaching in one of the "dark places of the earth," and very probably William Malbedeng built the first *Chapel* of Nantwich, which is mentioned in his son's Charter, dated *c* 1130

The following townships in the immediate neighbourhood,—Austerson, Baddington, Coole-pilate, Henhull, Alvaston, Leighton and Woolstanwood,—do not occur in Domesday, being perhaps included in the vill of Acton, which was by far the greatest and most important manor in the hundred, containing as it did, the *"lord's hall"* with its court, (possibly on or near the site of Dorfold Hall,) a *"corn-mill,"* *"thirty-three carucates of land"* out of a total of 110 for the whole hundred, or *three-tenths* of all the arable land in Warmundestrou, a *"wood,* nine miles long and a mile and a half broad, in which there was an *"aery of hawks,"* preserved, no doubt for falconry

William Malbedeng was grantee of other lands in the Palatinate, and a complete list of the dependencies of his Barony, with their values in 1086, as given in Domesday Book, is here appended

	s	d		s	d
In DUDESIAN [BROXTON] HUNDRED			Landechene [Landican]	40	0
Tatenale [Tattenhall]	26	0	Optone [Upton (Overchurch)]	20	0
Colborne [Golborne Belleau]	6	0	Tuigvelle [Thingwall]	5	0
In RISEION [EDDISBURY] HUNDRED			Chenoterie [Knoctorum]	10	0
Ulvre [Over (Borough)]	10	0	In MILDESIVIC [NORTHWICH] HUNDRED		
In WILAVLSION [WIRRALL] HUNDRED			Eteshale [Hassall]	10	0
Wivrevene [Wervin]	4	0	Mainessele [Minshull Vernon]	4	0
Pol [Poole (Over)]	4	0	Maneshale [Church Minshull]	8	0
Salhale [Saughall (little)] with a fishery	45	0	Sprostune [Sproston]	4	0

In WARMUNDESTROU [NANTWICH] HUNDRED	s	d		s	d
Actune [Acton]	6	0	Titesle [Titley]	5	0
Estune [Hurleston ?]	5	0	Steple [Stapeley]	6	0
Wilavestone [Willaston]	2	0	Wistetestune [Wistaston]	10	0
Warenebene [Wrenbury]	5	0	Brunhala [Broomhall]	2	0
Ceiletune [Chorlton]	2	0	Pol [Poole by Nantwich]	8	0
Merebene [Marbury] }			Tereth [Frith in Wrenbury ?]	5	0
Norberie [Norbury]	10	0	Ceilere [Chorley by Nantwich]	3	0
Wireswelle [Wirswall] }			Bedelei [Baddiley]	5	0
Walcretune [Walgherton]	5	0	Stanleu [Stanley in Weston]	2	0
Santune [Shavington]	3	0	Copehale [Church Coppenhall]	12	0
Buitune [Buerton] }			Pol [Poole by Nantwich]	3	0
Haretone [Hatherton] }	10	0	Estone [Aston in Mondrem]	3	0
Wistanestune [Wistanston]	10	0	Chelmundestone [Cholmondeston]	6	0
Berchesford [Basford]	5	0	Wich [Nantwich]	£10 0	0
Berdeltune [Bartherton]	3	0	In ANTICROS HUNDRED [FLINTSHIRE]		
Werelestune [Worleston]	8	0	Claitone* [Clayton]	10	0
Bertemeleu [Barthomley]	20	0	Wepre* [Wepre]	10	0
Essetune [Edleston ?]	10	0			
Wiveledse [Dodcot-cum-Wilkesley]	5	0	Total value	£29 15	0

It cannot be positively stated whether the Malbank family resided in the town or at the "lord's hall" in Acton   Mr Platt† speaks of the "ancient grandeur of the castle erected at Nantwich by William Malbank, the first Baron,' and says it was "square, surmounted at each angle with turrets   The outer walls were defended by a moat of considerable breadth, passable only by a draw-bridge'   This account, however, is purely fictitious, and therefore of no historical importance   The earliest mention of Nantwich Castle occurs in an *Inquisition*, dated 1288 (see next chapter,) or more than two hundred years after William Malbank became first Baron of Wich-Malbank   Occasionally in the Cheshire records during the fourteenth and fifteenth centuries, the Castle is mentioned, (see page 6,) but nothing further is known of it, beyond the fact that its site is preserved in the name of Castle Street

* Probably the reward for his services in the Welsh campaign that resulted in the addition of Flintshire and part of Denbigh to the Earldom of Chester

† History of Nantwich 1818, p 73

The Norman Barons.

S has been stated, Nantwich was created the head of a Barony about the year 1070. Three Barons in succession, members of the Norman family of Malbank, were the sole proprietors of lands, woods, salt-houses, &c., here, and held their possessions *in capite* (i.e. directly) from the Earl of Chester.

WILLIAM MALBEDENG OR MALBANK,

FIRST BARON OF WICH-MALBANK.

All that is now known of this Baron is that he was a benefactor to certain Religious houses. In Nantwich he appears to have founded the Hospital of St. Nicholas "*in the eighteenth year of William the Conqueror*"* [1083-4]; and it is highly probable that he built the Chapel (or Church) of Nantwich, which his son afterwards gave to Combermere Abbey. He is said to have contributed to the building of the Nave of Westminster Abbey, and to have had his arms emblazoned there.† In or about 1093, and most likely towards the close of his life, he granted the following possessions to the Abbey of St. Werburgh, Chester.

> "Witeby, (" *Witebiam*") the third of Wepre, the Church and tithes of Tattenhall, *one salt work in Wich and two bovates of land*, and the tithes of Salghall ("*Salchole*") and Claitone ("*Claitona*") and Yroduc (" *Yroduc.*")

> These being witnesses, the Countess of Chester, Richard Banaster, Hugh son of Osborn, Bigod le Loges, Richard Pincerna"‡ [the butler] &c.

Neither the date of his death nor the place of burial, is recorded; but he left a widow, Adelia, who was surviving about 1130, and a son, Hugh, who succeeded him.

---

* Cheshire Recognizance Rolls, 8 & 9 Hen. IV.

† Dr. Ormerod's "*Cheshire*," old Edition, vol. III, p. 441. The arms assigned to this Baron were, "Quarterly, Or and Gules, a bendlet Sable;" and were afterwards used as the Arms of the town.

‡ From a Confirmation Charter of Chester Abbey cited by Sir Peter Leycester, in Latin, in Dr. Ormerod's "*Cheshire*," new Edit. vol. I. p. 13.

HUGH MALBANK,
Second Baron of Wich-Malbank

Hugh Malbank, son of William and Adelia, occurs as a witness to Earl Richard's Confirmation Charter to Chester Abbey in 1109 at which time his father was most likely dead, and, again as witness to Earl Randle's Charter to the same Abbey before the year 1128 He is, however, chiefly remarkable as the founder of Combermere Abbey, at a time when monachism was fairly established in England, and his Charter is not only a curious instance of such a deed, commencing, as it does, with an avowal of the donor's religious faith, and concluding with the Bishop's anathema, supposed to render the deed sacred and inviolate but is particularly interesting from being the earliest deed relating to the town The original Charter, undated, as was usual in deeds prior to 1300, does not exist but a printed copy, in Latin, taken from the Cotton MSS Faustina B viii 124, will be found in Dugdale's "Monasticon" (vol v p 323, folio Edit 1830) The following translation is given in Webb's "*Itinerary of Nantwich Hundred*," (c 1621)

FOUNDATION CHARTER OF COMBERMERE ABBEY

"In the name of the holy and inseparable Trinity, the Father, the Son, and the holy Ghost, I Hugh Malbank, of one part, applauding the promise of the Lord, by which he saith to his elect, "what you have done to these little ones you have done to me, enter ye into the kingdom of heaven prepared for you from the beginning of the world," on the other side fearing the threatening whereby he says to the wicked, "what ye have not done to one of my little ones ye have not done to me, go ye into everlasting fire,"—Therefore, I, oftentimes revolving in my mind this godly precept, in which he saith, "Make unto you friends of the Mammon of iniquity that they may inherit the holy tabernacle," I oftentimes revolving with myself these other precepts of our Saviour, and considering the change of all temporal things, the misery, and the shortness of human life, I am wholly resolved to change all worldly things, and the vanities of this age, for the love of God, and to exchange shadows for realities, and to those who have given themselves wholly to the divine service, to them I have bestowed this donation

In the beginning, I give and grant to my Maker, with a sincere heart, by the counsel and consent of my lord *Ranulph*, Earl of Chester, and lord *Roger* [de Clinton] Bishop of Chester, holiest of men, and *William* my son and heir, for the health of me and my wife *Petronilla* and my *children* and all my friends, for the redemption of our souls, I say I give humbly and devoutly to the Lord God, omnipotent, the place and site which is called *Combermere*, to the founding and erecting of a certain abbey of the monks of Saint Benedict, in honour of the most blessed and most glorious Virgin Mary, and the mother of God and our Lord Jesus Christ, and St Michael the Archangel, the wood, the plain, the waters, the water-courses, the fishings, the meadows, the pastures, the feedings, with all other their appurtenances, and with all other their commodities, and all things which are there, or may be made there, as well under the earth as above, for ever, to wit, between these bounds —*

     *   *   *   *   *   *   *   *   +   *

"All these metes and bounds, as well on the said place of Combermere, as of the said manor of Wilksley ["Winclestle,"] I, *Hugh Malbank*, with my wife *Petronilla*, and *William* my son, and many others, have perambulated and compassed, and have freely given to the said abbey of Combermere,

---

* The bounds, which are specified, need not be given here, as they refer to lands in Wilkesley and the immediate neighbourhood, but it is worthy of remark that some of the names may still be identified

and to the monks there serving God, and to their successors, all things being within the said metes and bounds, with all their appurtenances, without reserving anything temporal to me, my heirs or assigns, for ever , and let them make of the wood and plain whatsoever they please , and inclose, assart,* and assess whensoever they p'ease

Also I give to the same monks common of pasture for all their cattle in all my woods and pastures of Cheshire, and besides that they may take wood to burn, and timber to build, as well without as within that abbey, at their pleasure, in all my woods as freely as I to my own use, except my forest of Couhull [Coole]

And I also grant unto the same monks, the *fourth part of the town of Wich, and the tithe of my salt, and of the salt-pits that are mine, and* (of those) *that belong to others, and of my money, and the salt of the Blessed Virgin, and salt on Friday, and salt for the abbot's table* as freely as I have at my board. And let them have their *Court distinct from their townsmen, or from their tenants, and assize of bread and ale, and of all kinds of measures, and toll, and blodwit, and amerciaments, and all manner of fines of all sorts of trespasses of all their tenants and men*, as freely as I have to my own proper use

Likewise I grant unto the same monks, and to all *burgesses* or *tenants* of the same town, *common of pasture* in all *woods* and *pastures, meadows, moors* ["mors,"] *marshes, heaths* [' brueris,"] and *fields* belonging to the *said town*, and through all *"Ranesmore"* [Ravensmoor] and the *wood* of *Creche* [in Alvaston,] without molestation of any   And if it happen that any of their burgesses, tenants or men, be impleaded in my Court for any trespass, I will and grant for me and my heirs or my assigns that my aforesaid monks have the amerciaments and fines without molestation or contradiction of me or of my heirs or assigns whatsoever

I give also to the same monks a *plough land* ["unam carucam"] in the town of Acton with the *church of the same town*, and the *chapel* ["capellam"] *of Wich Malb   "* [Wich Malbank] *with all their appurtenances*

I grant likewise to the same monks and their successors free passage through all my lands every-where, with free ingress and egress, to take whatever they want, as often and whenever they please And let them have all and singular the premises, in free, pure, and perpetual alms, as freely and absolutely from all secular exaction and worldly service, with as ample freedom and peace as any alms may be enjoyed, and we may never challenge or exact anything but only spiritual benefit and prayer

Therefore, of my good will, I grant that my lord Ranulph, Earl of Chester, be principal founder and defender of the said Abbey and of the monks there serving God, and that his heirs after him share in all good things, which may be there, for ever

The witnesses of this establishment and grant are these —*My lord Ranulph, Earl of Chester*,† *Roger, Bishop of Chester*,† *Aldelia, my mother, Petronilla my wife, William my son, William Abbot of Chester, Robert a chaplain, William son of Ralph, Archibald*, and many others who both saw and heard

And I, Roger Bishop of Chester, at the pious request of lord [domini] Hugh Malbank, and other nobles, in perpetual memory hereof, and that his present gift and grant may for ever stand in force, in presence of Ranulph, Earl of Chester, and other nobles at Chester, have affixed thereto the seal of my bishopric

And therefore, if any shall any ways violate, diminish, or wilfully hinder this alms, gift, and grant, let him have the curse of God, and the blessed Virgin and saint Michael the archangel, to whom in special manner all these things are granted, together with my own [curse,] unless he be repentant of his missdeed   Be it so ' Be it so ' Amen "

* *"Assart* " i e to bring forest land into cultivation by grubbing up the roots, &c

† Either Ranulph I, Earl of Chester from 1120 to 1128, or Ranulph II, Earl of Chester from 1128 to 1153   Roger de Clinton was Bishop of Chester from 1119 to 1149
These dates approximately fix the date of Hugh Malbank's Charter , which is generally said to be c 1130

The witnesses to this charter prove it to have been a very important deed   Concerning the order of these witnesses, Dr Ormerod remarks, "the Earl, as sovereign Prince, signs before the Diocesan, and the family of the donor have precedence of the other clergy." The gorgeous pageantry, consisting of the Baron, his lady, his heir, his retainers, and many local gentry, perambulating the bounds of the future lands of the Monastery, would be a memorable event and an imposing spectacle to the Wich men of that age.   The ' *forest of Couhull,* '* excepted in this grant of lands and privileges, was reserved, according to Norman fashion, for the chase   It would be at that time, a district not necessarily planted all over with trees, but ' afforested, ' i e subject to forest law.   In later times it became an extensive wood, furnishing the "wich-wood" for the salt-works   The mention of the "*Chapel of Wich-Malbank,* ' and the tithes belonging thereto particularly defined as "*salt of the Blessed Virgin,*" &c point to the dedication of the first church in the town, and the express terms of the charter prove it to have become, henceforth, a dependency of the Abbey   Fosbroke, speaking of such churches and chapels, says, " If the benefice was given *to the table of the monks,* and not so appropriated in the common form   but granted by way of union in full right, it was served by a *temporary curate* belonging to their *own house,* and sent out as occasion required "†   This liberty of not appointing a perpetual vicar accounts for the absence in the Lichfield Registers of recorded institutions of clergymen to Nantwich Church in pre-Reformation times

The Abbot's Fee.

By the above Charter, the lands therein mentioned, including "*the fourth part of the town of Wich,*" became for ever severed from the Barony of Wich-Malbank, and were afterwards known as the ABBOT'S FEE, within the limits of which, the Abbot claimed all rents and services, the tenants being obliged to plead in his courts, whilst with him alone rested the power of amerciament or punishment   In the two great Ecclesiastical Valuations, the former taken 160 years after the founding of Combermere Abbey, and the latter above 400 years after, the revenues of the Abbot's Fee in Nantwich are given as follows —

    I *ECCLESIASTICAL TAXATION OF POPE NICHOLAS IV* (c 1291)‡

    (*Translation*)—"Item Combermere Abbey has rents in Wych Mauban, per ann £5 0ˢ 0ᵈ "

    II *VALOR ECCLESIASTICUS 26 HEN VIII* [1535]

" Rents and Profits in Wich Malbank, per ann £14 14ˢ 5ᵈ "

This fee, with its court attached, passed after the suppression of Combermere Abbey, to the Wilbrahams of Woodhey, but the exact date of the transfer has not occurred   The following record of this court-leet is from an original paper *penes me* —

    [Translated] ' *Abbot's Fee*   On the petition of the Bailiff of the same, concerning the goods and chattels of *Christopher Smith* to be made to forfeit 39ˢ 11½ᵈ which *John Bromley* in this Court recovers against him in a plea of transgression &c.   By this court he is fined 1ˢ 6ᵈ &c at Wich Malbank, the 25th day of October, Ano Dni 1649   By *Joseph Harefinch* seneschal of the same."

---

* Probably "*Coole Pilate,*" a township on the south of Nantwich
† " British Monachism ' p 269   T D Fosbroke, London, 1843
‡ Pope Nicholas IV granted the tenths of all ecclesiastical benefices to the King for six years towards defraying the expenses of an expedition to the Holy Land , and that the full value might be collected, a new taxation by the king's precept was begun in 1288 and finished in 1291 by the Bishop of Lincoln (Oliver Sutton) and the Bishop of Winchester (John de Pontifera)

In 1666, according to *Harl MSS* 2010. f. 21. the Abbot's Fee in Nantwich belonged to Sir Thos. Wilbraham, Bart , of Woodhey, and on another page of the same vol. occurs the following—

"LIST OF FREEHOLDERS IN THE ABBOTS FEE IN NAMPTWCH
BELONGING TO SIR THO WILBRAM 1674'

PHILIP CHETWOOD of O[a]kley.	JO TENCH, mercer
ROGR WILBRAM of Townsend	RICH GILL
THOMAS MAISTERSON	WILL CAPPER, vint[ne]r
THO WINSTED	JO PRATCHETT JUNR
THO SEGRAVE	ROGR VAUGHAN
JO BREREION, pson [parson]	GABRILL HODGSON
RICH WRIGHT of the Stone in namptwch	ROB TYMMIS.
ROBT WRIGHT	

After the death of Sir Thomas Wilbraham, in 1692, these lands with other Cheshire estates passed in marriage with Grace Wilbraham, his daughter to Lionel Talmash [Tollemache] second Earl of Dysart , and so descended to John Tollemache, Esq. in 1837, who was created Lord Tollemache of Helmingham, co Suffolk, in 1876, and who is now proprietor of what remains of these Abbey lands in the town, which appear to have been situated on the north and east sides of the church The court, which was held in 1819, as stated by Dr. Ormerod on the information of Henry Tomkinson, Esq , as agent of Lord Dysart, has long since been discontinued, but the name *Monk's Lane* has survived through the vicissitudes of centuries

WILLIAM MALBANK,
THIRD BARON OF WICH-MALBANK

William Malbank, son and heir of Hugh Malbank and Petronilla, succeeded his father, and was the last of the Norman Barons of Wich-Malbank in the male line In the additional MSS Brit. Mus No 6032 p 94, is a charter of this Baron, granting a salt-pit [i e a wich-house] in Wich-Malbank to the Monastery of Wenlock, co Salop, witnessed by Robert, Abbot of Chester, &c , who was probably *Robert Fitz-Nigel,* fourth Abbot of St. Werburgh, Chester, from 1157 to 1174 According to the *Quo Warranto* 15 Hen VII [1500,] contained in *Harl MSS* 2115 f 168, Wenlock Abbey still claimed " a salt-work of 8 leads, in Nantwich, free from all tolls and customs," but no mention of it is made in the Valor Ecclesiasticus of 1535

William Malbank confirmed his father's charter to Combermere Abbey, adding other donations and privileges thereto This confirmation charter is printed in Dr Ormerod's "Cheshire," (iii p. 418 New Edit) from *Harl MSS* 3868 12 of which the following is a translation —

"In the name of the Holy Trinity, I, William Maubanc, being not unmindful of the mercies of God, concede and confirm to my maker, the Lord God Almighty, to Saint Mary, and Saint Michael the Archangel, to all saints and to the monks of Combermere, in smaller alms and whatever my father gave and conceded to them I grant and confirm freely, peaceably, and honorably, and from all secular exaction, the site of the Abbey and Church of Combermere , also four carucates of land in *Wilkesle* [Wilkesley] and whatever belongs to that manor , and all fields, pastures, water-courses, roads and foot-paths ["semitis"] in the plain and wood of the said Combermere , and what they shall make in wood and plain, and whatever they shall demand, enclose, or assess, let them have all which may be there, or shall be made there, for ever, besides all deer and boars   I also give and grant fully to them and their successors common of pasture in all my woods and pastures at Stone with their appurtenances, except in my forest of "*Chouhyl*" [Coole]   Also, (I give) tithe of my salt and of my manor of Wych, and a tenth of the corrody " of my house   Moreover, I give and grant to the foresaid monks the patronage of the Churches of *Acton, Sandon, Alstonfeld* with a *chapel* also, a land in the manor of *Dycheley,* and the mill of *Checkyley,* with all the fishings, and all their appurtenances in free pure, and perpetual alms

     The witnesses to these donations and grants are these — *Arch[ibald] son of William, William, the chaplain, son of   Robert le Praers, Reginald son of Arch[ibald] of Malbank, Adam de Audeleye, William de Arca, Adam Wachet, Robert son of William, Hugh de Draycote, Roger de Henhull, William son of Hunfredi, Richard de Aresca, Clemens, clerk, and many others*"

No other mention of William Malbank has occurred †   He appears to have lived in the reigns of Stephen and Henry II, and no doubt served in the civil war on the side of the Empress Maud, whose cause Earl Randle II had espoused   The Earl proved a formidable enemy to the King at Lincoln on Candlemas day [Feb 2nd] 1141, but subsequently suffered imprisonment, and during his long absence from the Earldom, the "whole county was laid waste" by the Welsh   Successful resistance to this invasion was made at Nantwich, according to a line in *Harl MSS* 2155 p 59, inserted by Dugdale from a MS Chronicle in Bibl Bodl K 84, as follows—"*sed apud Wycum Malbanum intercepti sunt* '   In Lysons' "Cheshire, ' two dates are given for this battle, viz   1146, and about 1150, and the same authors state on the authority of Dugdale's "*Monasticon*," that "in 1133 the town [of Nantwich] was laid waste by the Welsh"‡   Perhaps these dates all refer to the same event, which may have happened about the same time that the city of Chester was burnt, namely, 11th Kal Junii [21 June] 1140   (Chronicle of St Werburgh)§

     William Malbank married Andilicia, and died probably in the early part of the reign of Henry II, leaving three daughters and coheiresses, *Philippa, Eleanor,* and *Auda,* between whom the Barony of Wich-Malbank was divided, as proved by an *Inquisition,* taken at Chester on Tuesday next after the feast of the Ascension [May 15,] in the 16 Edw I. [1288] before Reginald Gray, then Justice of Chester,‖ in time of the war in Wales, in order to show what services were due to the King at that time   A copy of this Inquisition in Latin is preserved in *Harl MSS* 2115 f 135, of which the following is a translation, reciting that —

         "Dns [Lord] William Malbank formerly held the whole Barony of Wich-Malbank, and because he died without male heirs, the Barony was divided amongst [three] daughters in the following manner

         The first daughter [Philippa] had a *third part of Wich-Malbank with the Castle of the same,* excepting those lands which the same William gave before to the Abbey of Combermere, a *third part* of the

---

     * A sum of money or amount of provisions granted for the maintenance of one of the Abbot's servants or dependants, perhaps for the officiating priest for the time being at the chapel of Nantwich

     † In Doddsworth MSS vol xxxi f 148 (Bodl Lib) is an abstract of an undated Charter, in which, *William Malbank* gives a salt-house in Wich-Malbank to *Robert le Praers*   These being witnesses "Nicholas son of William, Reginald son of Herchenbald his steward ["dapifero,"] Henry de Crewe, Roger son of Odenot [Woodnoth] Adam son of Liulph of Aldithley, Alured of Cambray, Roger his son, Adam Wachet, Peter Morbur [y], Richard le Praers "   The impression upon the seal is a Knight on horseback

     ‡ Lysons' "Cheshire," pp 304 and 699

     § Ormerod s "Cheshire," vol I pp 147 and 230   New Edit

     ‖ Reginald de Grey was Justice of Chester from 1282 to 1300

manors of *Newhill, Aston-juxta-Hurleston, Acton* and *Haslington* in demesne, a third part of *Cowell* [Coole] and *Woolstanwood* She had also the homage and services of the following lordships and vills, namely, *Bartumleghe, Crue, Leghton, Aston in Mondrem, Cholmeston, Stoke, Lan[dr]ean* two parts of *Tranmoll, Buyrton, Aluaston, Church Mynshull, Wistaston Rope, Willaston, Wytpull,* [White Poole,] *Norbury, Wirswall, Row Shotwick and Thingwall*

⚹   ⚹   ⚹   ⚹   ⚹   ⚹   ⚹

"The second daughter [Eleanor] had a *third part of Wich-Malbank,* excepting the lands conceded to the Abbey of Combermere, a third part of *Cowell* [Coole] *and Woolstanwode,* and two parts of the manors of *Newhall, Aston-juxta-Mondrem,* and *Hurleston* and *Acton* in demesne Also, she had the homage and services of the lordships and vills undermentioned, namely, of *Becheton, Hassal, Wolaston, Wrenbury, Chorle, Backford, Monks-Coppenhall, Over-Bebbington,* two parts of *Barneston, Badington, Broomhall, Sonde, Alstanton, Bartherton, Chorlton, Tiverton,* and a moiety of *Wordhull,* the same, with all services are now [1288] in the hands of James Audlegh And it is known that Hatherton is in the hundred of Wich-Malbank, but in which division of the Barony it has passed is not known Also, *Blakenhall, Chatkeley, Dudington, Briddesmere, Hunsterton* and *Lee,* are not in this Barony, but of the Barony of Shipbrook and Kinderton "

"The third daughter [Auda] had a *third part of Wich-Malbank,* excepting the lands conceded to the Abbey of Combermere, a third part of *Cowell* [Coole] and *Woolstanwood,* one part of the manors of *Hurleston* and *Acton* and two parts of *Haslington* in demesne she had also the homage and services of the lordships and vills of *Audlim, Hanrelow, Titenlegh, Marbury, Stapelegh, Badelegh, Fadelegn, Burlond, Edlaston, Barrettsponle, Weston, Wydinbury, Hough, Saunton* [Shavington,] *Walkerton, Church-Copenhall, Hennull, Alsager,* a third part of *Cherlton* and *Wightreson* [Wistason] and *Penesby* "

⚹   L   ⚹   ⚹   ⚹   ⚹   ⚹   ⚹

"Memd That the aforesaid Barony is held of our lord the King [Edw I] as Earl of Chester, in capite "

Whilst the Earldom of Chester has descended in regular succession for more than eight centuries, first through a period of about 180 years by seven successive local Earls, and since the year 1254 without interruption by Royal Earls down to the present time, H.R H Albert Edward Prince of Wales now holding the dignity which is still inalienable and indivisible, the descent of the Cheshire Baronies, on the contrary, have had a more chequered and intricate history and none of them more so than the Barony of Wich-Malbank After the death of the second William Malbank, the Barony fell into abeyance between three coparceners already mentioned, and throughout the later history, instead of a quiet succession from father to son, it exhibits a constant dependence on the rights of female inheritance, and in this manner the town of Wich-Malbank and the lands of the Hundred became vested in various families In tracing the descent of the Manor, and the divided interests, rights, customs, &c claimed, we shall find parts of the Manor were sometimes transferred in an arbitrary manner, and other parts were at times confiscated to the Crown and let to farm The chief divisions were —

1 The Abbot's Fee (already noticed)
2 The Countess of Warwick's Fee
3 The Lovell Lands   } First Division of the Barony
4 The Audley Fee   Second Division of the Barony.
5 Two Moieties, which in course of time became } Third Division of the Barony
     much subdivided

In modern times these lands and manorial rights have been held as follows:—The *Abbot's Fee*, by the *Wilbrahams* of Woodhey; the *Countess of Warwick's Fee* by the *Crewes* of Crewe Hall; and the greater part of the remaining lands by the *Cholmondeleys* of Cholmondeley, some of whom have been styled BARONS OF NANTWICH.

The subjoined pedigree exhibits at one view the early descent of the Barony of Wich-Malbank, which will be more fully detailed in the following chapter.

The Malbank Family.

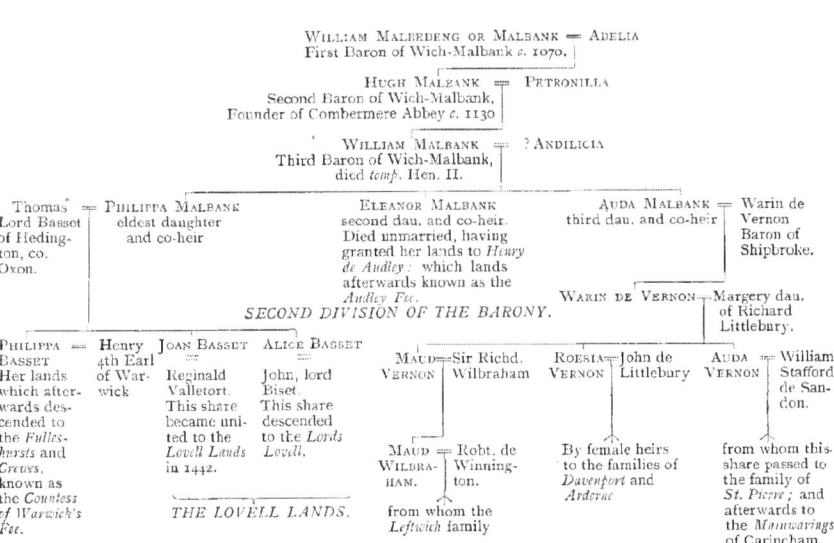

FIRST DIVISION OF THE BARONY.

I. The Countess of Warwick's Fee.

HILIPPA, eldest daughter and co-heir of William the last Norman Baron of Wich Malbank, married THOMAS, LORD BASSET, of Hedington, co. Oxon, who obtained the wardship* and marriage † of Henry de Newburgh, son and heir of Walleran, fourth Earl of Warwick who had died in 1205. When the young Earl came of age in 1212, he was certified to hold no less than 107 Knights' fees of the King *in capite*. To this princely Earl, Lord Basset gave his daughter *Philippa Basset* in marriage; and by this alliance the Castle‡ of Wich-Malbank and certain lands in Nantwich Hundred, being one third of her mother's share of the Barony already mentioned, became added to the Earl's already extensive possessions. Henry, Earl of Warwick, died 13 Hen. III. [1229], and on the death of his widow (the Countess Philippa) without issue, her share of the Barony, known afterwards as the *Countess of Warwick's Fee*, reverted to the Earl of Chester [Ranulph III], and appears to have remained merged in the Earldom until the 22 June 6 Edw. I [1278], when it passed by royal grant to RANDLE DE MERTON, who re-granted the same to SIR RANDLE PRAERS on the 25th August in the same year.§

The date of Sir Randle Praers' death is not known, but he was succeeded by his son *Richard Praers*.

---

* "*Wardship*," i.e. the custody of the body and lands of an heir during his minority,

† "*Marriage*," i.e. the guardian had the power of finding a suitable match to his "ward," which, if refused, the "ward" was subject to certain penalties. Lord Basset, no doubt, paid a large sum for the wardship of so rich an heir as the Earl of Warwick.

‡ Inquisition 16 Edw. I, in *Harl. MSS.* 2115, f. 135.

§ *Harl. MSS.* 2115, f. 186.

RICHARD PRAERS obtained the farm of the sheriffdom of Flint, the pleas and perquisites of the Courts and fairs of the towns of Flint and Ewlowe, the forest of Ewlowe, the pasturage of Bokelegh and the sea coal there for £29 per ann.* He appears to have died before 2nd Oct, 1335, when it was found he was £23 17s 5½d in arrears, and on 24th Dec 1335 his son and heir, *Thomas*, paid his relief, having succeeded to his father's estates †

THOMAS PRAERS appears to have lived at Barthomley, and, by licence from Edward the Black Prince, as Earl of Chester, dated 12th Nov. 1338, to have alienated, for the term of his life, the greater part of his lands, including the Countess of Warwick's Fee, to a neighbour, John Gryffyn of Bartherton, under the nominal tenure of one rose yearly, with remainder to the heirs of the said Thomas Praers ‡ No doubt he would be regarded as a very eccentric gentleman for by this strange transaction Thomas Praers forfeited his property to the injury of his family and his own loss while he lived. On examination, however, he was found to be of sane mind, and capable of managing his own affairs, as proved by the following Certificate from the Black Prince *(translated)*—§

"Edward eldest son of the noble King of England and of France, Prince of Wales Duke of Cornwall and Earl of Chester to all those who shall see or hear these letters greeting Forasmuch as we have been given to understand that *Thomas de Prayers* of Bertonlegh [Barthomley] in our County of Chester was a natural born fool and in his foolishness hath aliened and granted a part of his lands to the great damage of himself and ourselves wherefore we caused him to come before us to be examined and we caused him to be examined by the members of our council and others learned in the law, and upon such examination it was found that he is a man of sound memory and as such is sufficiently able to govern himself and his lands in a proper manner of which we are informed by those who have examined into it

In witness whereof we have caused these our letters to be made patent Given under our privy Seal ‖ at our manor of Kensyngton the xvj day of May in the 17th year of our most dear father King over England and the 5th of his reign over France " [1344]

By his wife Margaret, Thomas Praers had an only daughter and heiress *Elizabeth*, whose wardship and marriage he granted to Alan Cheyne [? of Willaston, nr Nantwich] on 26 Sept 1349 Probably on that day he died, as his *Inquisition post mortem* ¶ was taken only four days after, of which the following is an abstract *(translated)*—

' *Inquisition p m* taken before Sir Hugh de Hopewas Escheator of Chester at Wich-Malbank on Wednesday in the morrow of St Michael [30 Sept] 23 Edw III [1349] The Jurors say on their oaths that *Thomas de Praers* of Bertumleigh died seised as of right and in his demesne as of fee of two parts of the manor of Bertumleigh with appurtenances and of the advowson of the Church of Bertumleigh, which same two parts are held of the Earl in capite ; also one carucate of land which was worth 40 sh , and now is worth 13/4 , also, two acres of meadow worth 2/- per ann also, from rents of tenants who used to pay £16 per ann , but now only 100/- per ann , also two parts of a water-mill formerly rented at 53/4, and now only at 13/4 which tenants are dead , also the manor of Crewe , they say the site of the manor is worth nothing beyond reprisal and support of the house ; also in the same two carucates

* Chesh Recog Rolls   † Ibid   ‡ Ibid
§ The original Certificate in Norman French is printed (with the contractions extended) in *Arch Journal* 1857, vol xiv p 349-350   I am indebted to Wm Beamont, Esq , for the above translation
‖ A woodcut of the seal appended to the original document is given in the same vol on p 351
¶ Pub. Record Office.

of land formerly worth £4 per ann, now only 26/8, also three acres of meadow valued at 3/-per ann, a water-mill formerly worth 40/- per ann, now only 10/-, pastures in three places formerly worth 40/- now worth 13/4

Also, the vill of Landecan with the advowson of the Church at Wodechurch which vill was worth £8 per ann, and is now worth only 60/- in which the tenants are dead   Also, he died seised of two parts of the *Serjeancy of the fee of the Countess of Warwick* for which he paid into the Exchequer at Chester 8s 11d per ann, and they used to be worth besides the said payment 11/4, and are now worth only 6 8   The said *Thomas* held all the said manors with appurtenances and advowsons aforesaid of the Earl of Chester in capite by the service of 2½ Knights fees, &c   Also they say he has from perquisites of the Court and pleas 3/4 per ann   Also, they say that *Elizabeth* daughter of the said Thomas is his next heir and of the age of 11 years and more " &c

These estates, which had so depreciated in value in the lifetime of Thomas Praers, eventually came to the heiress *Elizabeth*, who brought the same in marriage to *Sir Robert Fouleshurst Kt*

SIR ROBERT FOULESHURST KT the next successor to the Countess of Warwick's Fee, is said to have been and most likely was, one of Lord Audley's esquires of Poictiers fame   He survived his wife, but died Nov 16th or 17th, 1389, and was buried in Barthomley Church, where a monumental tomb, having a recumbent figure of the Knight in armour, with mail gorget, conical helmet and collar of SS, although much mutilated, is still to be seen   His Inquisition post mortem is as follows * *(translated)*—

Inq p m taken before Adam de Kyngeslegh Eschaetor at Wich Malbank on the Sabbath next after the feast of St Katherine the virgin [25 Nov] 13 Ric II [1389] &c   The Jurors say that *Robert de ffouleshurst* of Crue died seized for the term of his life by the law of England of the manors of Crue Bertumlegh and Landecan in Wyrhale &c together with the advowsons of the Churches of Bertumlegh and Woodchurch after the death of *Elizabeth* daughter and heir of Thomas de Praers of Bertumlegh formerly wife of the said Robert who died seized in his demesne as of fee of the Manors and Advowsons aforesaid held of the Earl of Chester *in capite* by Knight service and by the service of 13/4 by a certain rent called Chamber rent paid per ann into the treasury at Chester at the feast of the Nativity and St John the Baptist [June 24]   Also, they say that the Manor of Crue is worth £10, and Bertumlegh 20 marcs [£13 6s 8d], and Landecan 100 sh   Also, the tithes of corn &c of the said churches are worth £20 per ann   Also, messuages in Badynton and Wich Malbank worth 40 sh per ann   Also, they say that *Thomas* son of the said Robert and Elizabeth is son and heir, and of the age of 23 years and more on Tuesday in the feast of St Edmund the Bishop [Nov 16 or 17] last past on which day the said Robert died " &c

SIR THOMAS FOULESHURST KT. who thus succeeded, occurs as a Commissioner of Array for Nantwich Hundred, having been appointed on the 11th Oct 4 Hen IV [1402] prior to the rebellion of the Percies   He probably served on the side of the King at the battle of Shrewsbury on 21st July, 1403, and dying in the same year left a son and heir, *Thomas*, then under age, and a widow, *Joan*, who obtained the wardship and marriage of her son for the sum of 400 marks [£266 13s. 4d] †

THOMAS FOULESHURST obtained possession of his father's estates on the 9th Feb 5 Hen V [1418], his proof of age having been taken at Wich-Malbank on Wednesday on

---

* Public Record Office   Although the Countess of Warwick's Fee is not mentioned by name in this Inquisition, it is clear that it descended together with the other property, rights, &c to Sir Robert Fouleshurst *jure uxoris*, the heiress of Thomas de Praers

† Chesh Recog Rolls

the morrow of the feast of the Conversion of St. Paul [25 Jan] previous[*] He married
Cicely, daughter of Ranulph Maynwaring of Peover, and "died on the Vigil of the Nativity
of John the Baptist [June 24] 1439, leaving Robert his son his next heir and of the age
of 20 on the feast of SS Lucian Maxian and Julian [Oct 17] in the same year," having
died seized *inter alia "of the serjeanty of the fee of the Countess of Warwick* for which he
rendered 13s 4d. yearly" &c. *(Inq p m)*

SIR ROBERT FOULESHURST, Knight, as he afterwards became, succeeded to the estates
of his father after his proof of age had been taken at Wich-Malbank on Wednesday next
before the Purification of the Blessed Virgin [Feb. 2] 18 Hen VI [1439-40]. He obtained
another share (a 36th part) of the barony of Wich-Malbank by his marriage with Joan
Whelok, daughter of Eleanor, the wife of Richard Whelok and heiress of Sir Richard
Vernon of Shipbrook, Kt, after the death of her mother in 1474[†] He held several
important appointments, viz the office of Bailiff and Beadle of Nantwich Hundred, which
was leased to him on 22 Jan 1444-5, for seven years at £7 3s 4d per ann, and afterwards for a further term of ten years He was Eschaetor of the county during pleasure
in 1460, was Knighted in 1461, was one of the Collectors of Subsidies in 1463 and 1474,
and one of the Commissioners of Array in the years 1480 1481 and 1484.[†] According
to his *Inquisition post mortem* he

' died on Monday next before the feast of St Nicholas the Bishop [Dec 6] last past [1498] leaving
Thomas Fouleshurst his son and heir aged 52 years on the day of St Cedde the Bishop [Jan 7 or
March 2] also last past [1497-8] He died seised [*inter alia*] of the office of the *Serjeant of the fee of
the Countess of Warwick,* a 36th part of the Barony of Wich Malbank 20 messuages burgages and
cottes with gardens adjoining in Nantwich and 24 acres of land 2 salt houses and £20 annual rent
issuing out of lands &c there " &c

THOMAS FOULESHURST, ESQ, who was in London at the time of his father's death,
succeeded but died the same year He had been appointed Constable of Chester Castle
on 4 June, 1483. His *Inquisition p. m*, which is much torn and obliterated, states that
he died seised of the same property as his father held, and that his son *Robert* was his
heir. His widow *Anna* survived until 1524, her *Inq p m* being taken on 18 June 16
Hen VIII [1524].[‡]

ROBERT FOULESHURST, ESQ, the next inheritor of these estates pleaded in 15 Hen.
VII [1500] to a writ of *quo warranto,* at Chester, before Thomas Keble and John Mordant
serjeants at law, Itinerant Justices, relative to his *Serjeancy of the Countess of Warwick's
Fee within and without the town of Wich Malbank,* on payment of 13/4 per ann claiming
also the "liberty of buying and selling all kinds of merchandise in Nantwich, and the tolls
of stallage of all merchandise, assize of bread and ale" &c § He was appointed collector
of a Subsidy in Nantwich Hundred 17 Hen VII [1502], and made esquire of the body
to King Henry VIII, as Earl of Chester He held the office of seneschal [steward] of
the town and lordship of Wich-Malbank from 14 Jan 4 Hen. VIII ‖ [1512-13] and a few

---

[*] Record Office

[†] Chesh Recog Rolls

[‡] Both of these Inquisitions are still preserved at the Record Office.

§ *Harl MSS* 2022 f 16/22 and 2115 p 186, also Doddsworth MSS xxxi f 144

‖ Chesh Recog Rolls.

months after, on 9 Sept 1513, was slain at Flodden-field, leaving two sons, *Edward* and *Thomas*, both minors, the former being "aged 18 years in the feast of the Ascension of our Lord last past" [1519-]   *(Inq p m)*

EDWARD FOULESHURST, ESQ , who succeeded, was grantee for life of his father's office of seneschal of Nantwich   His wardship, marriage, and custody of inheritance were granted to Sir William Brereton   His proof of age was taken at Wich-Malbank on Thursday next after the feast of the Annunciation of the blessed Virgin Mary [25 March] 1521, before Ralph Egerton Kt Eschaetor , livery of his lands being obtained on the 25th Oct in the same year.   He married Catherine the daughter of Sir Will Brereton , but being an idiot, an *Inquisition on a Commission of Lunacy* was taken, 13 Hen VIII [1521-2] by which his lands descended to the next heir at law, viz. his brother, *Thomas Fouleshurst* *

SIR THOMAS FOULESHURST, KT , by special writ, had livery of his brothers lands, without proof of age, on 18 April, 1525   In the previous year (25 Sept 1524) being then *"groom of the chamber,'* he obtained the stewardship of the lordship of the town of Wich-Malbank for life †   He became Sheriff of the county in 1528 , and ten years later framed a Code of Regulations for the government of the town of Nantwich, which have been preserved among the Wilbraham MSS , and are here printed for the first time

INJUNCTIONS & ORDINANCES, ordained, provided, and determined for the Common-wealth of Wich-Malbank by Sr THOMAS FOULESHURST Knight Stewarde of the same Towne by the assent & consent of the Burgesses & Freehoulders of ye said Towne at the great Court there holden the Munday next after the feast of St John of Beverley [7 May] in the thirtieth yeare of the raigne of our Soueraigne Lorde Kinge Henrie the eight [1538]

1   First it is ordered by the stewarde by the assent & consent of the great enquest that noe Baker shall make any sale bread but such as shall beare weight assysed and ordayned for the same, and that it be made lawfull and wholesome for mans body under the payne of forfeitting of the same bread soe oft as they shalbe taken with the same, and allso that noe Baker shall putt any butter in any sale cakes under ye paine of forfeitting for every time soe doing—12d

2   Alsoe it is ordered that noe bruer shall putt anie esties hopps lee or salt in their Ale from henceforth and that they shall sell yeir [their] Ale but after ijd [2d] a gallone of the best under ye shot flagon ‡ and after a halfpennie a quart shall of the best , and of the second Ale, called pennie Ale after a halfpennie a pottle§ under the paine of forfeitting—ixs [9s] soe often and for everie tyme as they be taken doing the contrary as well within the Libertye as without.

3   Alsoe it is ordered that all ffishers and other manner of vituelers that bring any vittaile to the town to sell, shall bring all their vittaile into the open markett, and that they sell no such vittaile in noe place but in the open markett under the payne of forfeitting the same vittailes

4   Alsoe it is ordered that no manner of person nor p'sons shall forstall|| nor buy anie manner of vittailes comeing to this Towne before it come to the open markett under the payne for every time soe doing to forfett—iijs iiijd [3/4]

---

* Record Office

| Chesh Recog Rolls

‡ *"Shot-flagon,"* i e The flagon which the Host gave to his guests if they drank above a shilling

§ *Pottle* is an old word for two quarts

|| *"Forestall,"* i e monopolize   The necessaries of life were first to be brought into the public market, so that anyone, who bought or bargained for corn &c before it was brought into the market came under the lash of the law

5 Alsoe it is ordered that all and every p'son or p'sons being inhabitted within this pishe [parish] shall
   yearly be cessed by the Steward or his deputyes and the freeholders being sworne on the great enquest
   [court] what every of them shall pay towardes the supportation and maintenance of the Church within
   the Towne

6 Alsoe it is ordered that the said ffreehoulders wᵗʰ yᵉ wardens of the Church shall see that all the gilte
   prests [guild priests] shall observe and keepe all such ordinances as be expressed in a certaine booke
   here afore made and sealed with the Common Seale bearing date the xᵗʰ of August in the xij [12] yeare
   of the Raigne of our soueraigne lord King Henrie the eight [1520]

7 Alsoe it is ordered that the said ffreeholders and yᵉ wardens shall cause the Clerke and other Ministers
   of the Church to do their offices according to their dutyes, and allso that they shall see a redresse and
   reformation for the misordered people as well within the Chancell as within the Church

The "*Injunctions*" relating to Ecclesiastical affairs are particularly interesting   Allusion
is here made both to habitual neglect of religious observances and want of decorum in
the priests who officiated at Nantwich Church, proving that corrupt practices prevailed
here and at Combermere as in Abbey Churches and Monasteries generally throughout the
Kingdom   In 1524 the Pope had issued a bull empowering Wolsey to visit religious
houses and punish all violations of discipline, and ultimately these disorders were made
the pretext for the suppression of the Monasteries, by which King Henry VIII replenished
his exhausted coffers   In anticipation of the dissolution of Combermere Abbey, which
took place shortly after the date of these "*Injunctions*," (viz   on 27 July, 1538), provision
is made in No. 5 for the future maintenance of the Clergy at Nantwich, by an annual
assessment of the whole town, and thus it was that in later times the parishioners claimed
the right to elect and appoint their own minister.

Reference is made in No 8 to the severe penal laws against wandering beggars, who,
being thrown upon their own resources after the suppression of religious houses, took to
plunder and became a terror to the country

The existence of *Gilds* or religious fraternities somewhat resembling modern friendly
societies, is adverted to in Nos 6 and 20   No records, however, exist to throw light on
the local customs of these ancient orders   On another page will be found a deed dated
1461 relating to the Gild.   In Webb's "*Itinerary*" it is distinctly stated that the Grammar
School in the Churchyard was formerly the Gild Hall   (See also *Harl. MSS* 2074 f 166 a
According to a Statute in the reign of Hen VIII the rents, profits, &c. of all Gilds,
together with all Monasteries, &c, became confiscated to the Crown, the same Act of
Parliament authorising the commissioners to assign the lands and property towards endowing
"Grammar Schools or such other godly intents and purposes as the same Commissioners
or two of them should appoint "   In the Chantry Roll for Nantwich, the establishment of
a Grammar School is recommended, and Messrs. John and Thomas Thrush, woolpackers,
of London, the founders of the School, probably purchased the Gild-hall from the Crown.

The remaining Orders of Sir Thomas Fulleshurst are as follows —

8 Alsoe it is ordered that the Steward the Bayliffe yᵉ Constables and the ffreehoulders of the great enquest
   shall examine all vagabonds * and suspitious psons comeing or resorting to this Towne and all other
   now here abideing and them to correct and punnishe according to the Kings statutes provided for the
   same vppon payne of euery of the sayd Steward the Bayliffe the Constables and the ffreeholders for to

* "*Vagabonds*," i e   wandering beggars, vagrants, or tramps as they are now called

forfeitt for euery tyme denyinge to doe the same haueing sufficient monition—vjˢ viijᵈ [6 8] and also to punishe all manner of psons comitting briberie and petty larceny within this towne according to the Kings Statutes ordained for the same

9   Alsoe it is ordered that noe manner of pson within this towne shall resett nor suffer mens children, servants, or light p'sons to be within their houses at drinkeing or gameinge at ten of the clocke in the night nor after supper uppon payne for euery tyme for doing to forfeit—iijˢ iiijᵈ [3/4]

10   Alsoe it is ordered that all mannei of Artificers and craftsmen resorting or comeing to this towne shall be appoynted where they shall stand to sell their wares by the officers of the Towne, that is to witt, all drapers that be forreiners except them that sell whole sale to sell noe cloath within the Towne but in the *Booth hall* * uppon the markett daie , and all shoomakers turners   potters and Ironmongers to stand in the *Pillorie Streete*, and all they that sell parsnips turneps onyons and garlicke to stand aboue the *Beete bridge*,† or else at home at their owne houses under the payne of forfeiting for for euery tyme—xijᵈ [12d]

11   Alsoe it is ordered that noe waynes [wagons] nor carte shall come through the markett places with anie manner of wood after nine of the clocke in the aforenoone upon the markett daye under yᵉ paine to forfeit for euery tyme—xijᵈ [12d]

12   Alsoe it is ordered that there shall noe waller buy anie sale loades of wood betwixt the ffeast of Easter and the ffeast of St Michael under the payne of forfeitting for euery tyme soe doing—xijᵈ [12d]

13   Alsoe it is ordered that noe manner of psons shall buy nor sell any manner of graine with other *hoop* nor *strike* but such as shall be sealed with the seale , the wᶜʰ seale shall be showed by the Bayliffe and knowne in the Maikett, under the payne of euery tyme soe offending to forfeitt—xijᵈ [12d]

14   Alsoe it is ordered that noe manner of p'son shall lay any manner of mucke at the *Water load, the Milne load*, nor between the Whitch [sic] house of John Crockett and Richard Ince his garden , nor in any manner of place neere nor within the *Kings streets* in yᵉ Towne, noi allsoe that noe manner of pson nor psons shall caste any mucke, straw nor rushes in the *channell* within the *welch owe* undᵉʳ the payne for euery tyme soe doing—xijᵈ [12d], and allso that fathers and Mrs [mothers] of euery pson soe doing shall pay the mercemᵗ [fine] for the same   And allso that noe pson nor psons shall cast any witch-house muck or clodds upon noe witch-house ground, nor in noe other place but in *weaver* undei yᵉ payne for euery tyme soe doinge to forfeitt—xijᵈ [12d]

15   Also it is ordered that there shall be a *swineheard* in this towne and that noe manner of pson nor psons of this inhabitance shall haue any swine going abroad within this Towne, but such as shall be putt into the custody of the syᵈ [said] swineheard under yᵉ payne to forfeitt for euery swine soe going abroad— ijˢ [2/-], and that the sayd swineheard shall haue for euery swine that he shall be charged with, that is twelue monethes and aboue, euene yeare 2ᵈ foi a swine , and for eu'y [every] pigg that is weaned 1ᵈ , and that noe man shall putt anie swine before the said swineheaid but such as shall be made lawfull for rooting, under the payne of eu'y [every] swine vjᵈ [6d], and that the sayd swineheard shall haue a horne and that euery daie betwixt Easter and Michaelmas betwcene the hours of seaven of the clock & eight before noone, hee to goe into the *Beame Streete*, and soe throughe streetes unto yᵉ *well*‡ in the *welch rowe* neere the tenement now in the holding of Raphe Bebington, and from thence through

* Although Leland's "*Itinerary* " states, "*It* [i e Nantwich] *is no market*," there is clear evidence that Nantwich was, and had long been a market town, before the 16th century   Leland, as a topographer rather than historian, described the town as he *then* found it   and possibly the market may have sustained a temporary check in 1535, from the serious and frequent visitations of the plague, called "*Sweating Sickness* "

† *Beete Bridge* was in Pillory Street, (see Account of the fire, in 1583)

‡ "*Ye well in welch rowe* " It stood opposite *Whtts Hall* From the way in which this is mentioned, it may be implied that this well was at the extremity, or near the end, of the town

the *high towne*, and soe through *hospitall streete*, and as he goeth through euery streete continuallie to blow his horne, for the intent that euery pson haueing any swine may put them before the sayd swine-heard, and from Michaelmas to Easter betweene the howers of eight of the clocke and nine before noone, for to use in like manner, and that the said swineheard shall euerie daye betwixt Easter and Michellmas driue and keepe all such swine as hee shall be charged with betweene the toppe of *creache* [Beam Heath] and the *crooked Brooke*, and after Michellmas until Easter to keepe the sayd swine uppon the heath in such place as the sayd swineheard shall think convenient

16 Alsoe it is ordered that there shall be a Comon Pinfolde made neere to the *Court hall* there as it hath bin in tymes past, & allso a greate payre of *Stockes*, for to be made and sett in the *high towne*, and that eurie pson of this inhabitance shall be cessed by ye Officers & the ffreeholders of the great enquest what euery of ym [them] shall pay for any thing that shall chance or fall necessary as well to serue our soueraigne Lorde the Kinge as for all other thinges concerneing the Comonwealth of this Towne

17 Alsoe it is ordered that the Steward or his deputy and the Bayliffe, and the ffreeholders of the great enquest shall assemble themselves, and meete together within the *Court-hall &* there to commune of all thinges that shall be necessarie for ye comonwealth of this Towne at all tymes hereafter, haueing sufficient monition from or by the Steward or his deputy of the daye and hower of their assembly and meeting together to them giuen by the Bayliffe vnder the payne of euery p'son failing soe to doe for euery time—iijs iiijd [3/4]

18 Alsoe it is ordered that noe man from henceforth shall weare any vnlawful weapon swithin this Towne, as Billes,* glaiues, polaxes, morrispicks, and such other, vnder the payne of forfeiting the sayd weapons and to be punished accordinge to ye Kinges Statutes made for the same

19 Alsoe it is ordered that all manner of p'sons haueing ye occupation of three dozen leads [lead pans] shall haue but a monethes wood wthin the Towne ouer the old yeare, and all other haueing lesse occu-pation than three dozen leads, to haue after the rate of three leads, vnder the paine of euery weekes wood ouer and aboue to forfeitt—vjs viijd [6/8] and yearely the Rulers for their tyme being to make search for the same, and they uppon their oathes to present all such offenders, and this act to take effect from the feast of Penticost wch shall be in the veare of oure Lord god 1539 [viz. on 25 May]

20 Alsoe it is ordered that all such p'son or p'sons as be in noe gilde within this Church that they nor none of their children shall haue at their decease and their bringing home† none of ye ornaments of the Church nor no more of the bells to be rungen for them but the third Bell that there be from hence-forth noe passing peale here rungen vnder the payne the Clarke to forfeit iijs iiijd [3/4]

21 Alsoe it is ordered that noe manner of p'son or p'sons shall for henceforth lay any flax nor hempe in *Weauer* betweene ye *Wiche-bridge* and the further side of *Ridley feild* vnder the payne to forfeitt for euery tyme—xijd [12d]

22 Alsoe it is ordered that if it shall chance hereafter variance or strife to be betweene any pson of this inhabitance for ye occupation of walling of anie witch-house or leads wthin this Towne and that both p'ties [parties] doe pretend title or interest to the same occupation soe that the Rulers of the Walling for that tyme being may nor cannot determine nor discusse whether partie ought of right to haue the sayd occupation according to the customes of this towne that the sayd Rulers shall permitt and suffer the pty [party] ye wch hath peaceably had the occupation of the said witch-house or leads by the space of three yeares for to occupie for the same, and the other partie thereof to be discharged vntil such tyme that the matter be determined according to the Kinges lawes, or vnto such tyme that the pties [parties]

* Bill i e an edged tool for lopping trees or dubbing hedges Glaiue i e a long sword or bill Pole-axe i e an axe, having a long stale or handle

† "*Bringing home*," an old-fashioned but very beautiful expression, meaning *burial*

shall be agreed for the same, and that noe p'son or p'sons being soe discharged shall from henceforth vexe nor trouble the sayd Rulers nor none of them by noe maner processe procured or obtained from anie other Court for the same under the payne to forfeitt for euery tyme soe doing xl^s [40/-]

23 Alsoe it is ordered by the great enquest and by the advice and consent of the Steward and the Kinges Lyeutent [Lieutenant] Justice agreed that if any statue or ordinance heretofore or now at this tyme made or hereafter to be made, shall at any time hereafter be found hurtfull or preiudiciall to the comonwealth of any occupation the wch shall thinke therein to be oppressed or grieved by any of the sayd statutes or ordinances, shall by the advice and consent of the others of the sayd sort or occupation make a bill of their griefes, and at ye next greate Courte after here holden the same bill present to ye Steward, whereupon the Stewarde shall cause the sayd two psons to be sworne that the said bill and all such evidence as they shall giue uppon the same shall be good and true and the meaning thereof for the comonwealth and not for the proper wealth of themselves, and then the same bill to be delivered to ye ffreeholders of the great enquest the wch bill shall be examined and by good deliberacon by the great enquest pondered and then the same to be redressed and ordered as the sayd enquest shall upon their oathes thinke most necessarie and convenyent according to their charges

24 Alsoe it is ordered that all such statutes and ordinances as haue bin made before this time for the Comonwealth of this Towne the wch be not mentioned in this booke and not revoked nor repelled shall be observed and kepte according to the true intent and meaning of ye same, and that noe p'son or p'sons of this inhabitance doe breake nor offend the same statutes and ordinances, under the payne to forfeit euerie tyme soe doing—iij^s iiij^d [3/4] ouer and beside such paynes and punishment as been cessed for the same

25 Alsoe it is ordered that in case any of the ffreeholders which now be or hereafter shall be sworne on the great enquest doe at any tyme hereafter breake anie of these statues or ordinances before or now at this time made, or any other hereafter that shall be made for the good order and wealth of this sayd towne, haueing lawfull monition for the same, that euerie of the sayd ffreeholders shall forfeitt for euery time soe doing double the paynes and mercements cessed or ordained for ye same, and that none of the sayd paynes being presented and found be forfetted shall from henceforth be minished nor made lesse by anie fearers of these Courtes nor otherwise, but that all the whole thereof shall be levyed by the Bayliffe, or his deputy, to the use and behalfe of the Kinge, and the Barons of this Towne Provided alwaies that ye ffreeholders wch shall be at any Courte or Courts hereafter sworne uppon ye great enquest shall haue full power and authoritie for to change alter or breake any statute or ordinance here before or now at this time made, or any other hereafter to be made the wch shall happen hereafter to be preiudiciall or hurtfull to the good order or Comonwealth of the Towne, or to the Inhabitants of the same soe that the sayd thinge be done by the consent and agreement of the Steward, and ye whole enquest upon their oathes at a greate *Courte* here holden with good intention for ye redressing or reformacon of the same

26 Alsoe it is ordered that there shall noe carryers of salt that buy their salt in other places, shall not sell their malt* here under the payne of eurie time soe offending to forfeitt—xx^s [20/-]

27 Alsoe it is ordered that noe man swap quarter-wood under ye paine for euery time soe offending xij^d [12d], and that there shall be noe swapping of salte for noe manner of Chaffei [i e wares] under the payne for euere time xij^d [12d]

28 Alsoe it is ordered that all Butchers shall deny noe man a pennie worth of flesh nor a ob [halfpenny worth] of flesh, and that the sayd Butchers shall from henceforth blow noe flesh under the payne of

* Webb, in his "*Itinerary*" one hundred years after, says—the salt-trade was "*chiefly done in exchange of the best malt that the shires towards the Champion* [plain] *do send in barter for it*'

xijd [12d], and that no man shall wall [i e make salt] for mending the pauement betwixte *Bartons crosse* and the *wiche Bridge*, without he putt in surtye by obligacon betwixte this and the taile of the Courte, and that noe man leaue emptie waynes in the high streetes except a lawfull cause, under the payne for euery tyme soe offending xijd [12d]"

[END OF SIR THOMAS FOULESHURST'S TOWN ORDERS]

Sii Thomas Fouleshurst lived to the last year of Queen Mary, his death and burial being recorded by Richard Wilbraham, of Nantwich, in his MS Journal thus —

" Thomas fulleshurst Knight dyed on Sonday beinge xxvi day
of September Ao 1558 And was buryed in Bartomley Churche "

His Inquisition *post mortem* is not to be found at the Record Office, but he was succeeded by his son Robert, with whom began the decay of this ancient family

ROBERT FOULESHURST, of Ciue, Esq, who married Bridget, daughter of Sir Thomas Smith of Hough, Kt ,† succeeded to his father's estates, which he was compelled to alienate, as tradition says, through extravagance. Little more than foui years after his fathei's death, he sold to Sir Hugh Cholmondeley of Cholmondeley, Kt, property in Nantwich for the sum of £107 14s 10d, thus described in the "Indenture made 20th Jan 4 Queen Elizabeth [1561-2],

" One messuage or Cottage & garden now in occupacon of *John Walthall* of the yrely rent of 4/10 one annuall rent of 14/- goinge out of the lands late of *Wm Churche* deceased one annuall rent of 2/- goinge out of the lands and tents [tenements] of *John Hill and Joan Hill widdow* one annuall rent of 6/8 out of the lands and tents of *John Bromley gent*, now in the Occupacon of *Oliver Manwaringe*, one annual rent of 10/- out of ye lands & tents of *Roger Crokett* and *Alice Crokett* widdow one annuall rent of 10/- out of the lands & tents of the *earle of Derby* one annuall rent of 10/- out of lands and tents of *Wm Bromley gent* one other annuall rent of 10/- out of the lands and tents of *Henry Mainwaringe Esqr*, now in the Occupacon of *Humphrey Mainewaringe* one annuall rent of 14/- out of one mess. now or late of *Tho Gibbons* lyinge in the highe towne one annuall rent of 10/8 out of the lands tents & hereditamts of *Roger Maisterson* gent one other annuall rent of ijs [2/-] out of the lands and tents of the sd *Rogr Mrson* [Maisterson] one other annuall rent of 12d out of lands &c of the same *Rogr* one other annuall rent of 6/8 out of the lands, tents & hereditamts of *Rogr Wright* And alsoe one other annuall rent of 9/- out of one mess and one garden in the *wiche-forest* now in the occupacon of *Randle Sontley* and late in the tenure or occupacon of Raph Sturrop deced ' [deceased]

The Indenture, which is given in full in *Harl. MSS* 2099. f 486/118, is signed and sealed by "Robert ffuleshurst," and witnessed by "Gregorye ffuleshurst" and others.

Robert Fouleshurst, who still held his 36th shaie of the Barony of Wich-Malbank consisting of "one messuage, 200 acres of land and 3/4 rent in Wich-Malbank, Crue, Hashngton, Stoke, Cholmeston, Whitpoole, Barretspoole, Aston, Leighton and Landecan, and the *Serjeancy of the Countess of Warwick's Fee, and of the Audley Fee* " was afterwards under the necessity of raising money on these possessions and rights, resulting in dishonorable transactions on the part of Sir Hugh Cholmondeley, who, it appears, designedly intended to take an unfaii advantage of Mr Fouleshurst's pressing need ‡ On the 20th May, 17 Eliz [1575] Robert Fouleshurst sold and conveyed his share of the Baiony to

---

* "*Bartons Crosse*," now simply called "*the Cross* " is in Stapeley township

† Cheshire Wills, part 3, vol liv p 46 Chet Soc Pub

‡ Information by Mr E W Jones, from his father's (the late T W Jones, Esq, Solicitor, Nantwich) papers

Sir Hugh Cholmondeley in consideration of the sum of £56 10s 0d, and on 20th Aug in the same year, Mr Fouleshurst mortgaged his Fees with other freeholds to Sir Hugh Cholmondeley for securing £420 and interest, a very unusual proviso having been introduced in the mortgage, (which ended in its destruction as will hereafter be seen) restraining Mr. Fouleshurst from redeeming the premises he had mortgaged to Sir Hugh, who, to make his security as he supposed doubly safe, required Mr Fouleshurst to levy a fine to him of the mortgaged Estates, which he accordingly did on the 20th February 18 Eliz. [1575-6], and so soon as Sir Hugh's security was, as he thought completed, he entered into the possession of the property comprised therein, and held the usual Court for the fee as Lord thereof, as Mr Fouleshurst and his ancestors had before done   Sir Christopher Hatton, Chancellor to Queen Elizabeth, having in 1581, purchased from Mr. Fouleshurst large estates, including these supposed to be irredeemably mortgaged to Sir Hugh Cholmondeley, and being advised that Sir Hugh's mortgage could not stand, he impeached it by a suit instituted for that purpose in the Court of Exchequer at Chester in the year 1582, and the cause coming on to be heard before the Chamberlain, assisted by Sir George Bromley and Sir Henry Townshend, Justices of Cheshire, on the 10th April 25 Eliz [1583] those learned Judges held Sir Hugh Cholmondeley's mortgage void, and by their decree ordered him to deliver up the same and likewise possession of the premises comprised therein, and execute a re-conveyance of the latter to Sir Christopher Hatton, which order Sir Hugh rather reluctantly complied with in the same year. An exemplification of this decree that the *Serjeantships of the Countess of Warwick's Fee and of the Audley Fee* had been assured to Sir Christopher Hatton Kt was taken on 8th April, 1593 —*(Chesh Recog Rolls)* William Smith, a contemporary writer, also says* "Mr Fouleshurst, of Crew, had rule of the town, and after him, sir Hugh Cholmley, and now, [c 1600] lastly, sir Christopher Hatton "

Robert Fouleshurst of Crewe, Esq, died on the 3rd Jan 1599, [*Wilb MS Journal*] leaving a son *Thomas Fouleshurst,*† of Coppenhall, who occurs in the Recognizance Rolls in an indenture of sale of a messuage in Church Coppenhall to Sir Richard Wilbraham, of Woodhey, dated 6th June, 1617, this property possibly being the last possession of the last heir of the ancient family of Fouleshurst.

SIR CHRISTOPHER HATTON, KNIGHT, Lord Chancellor of England, who thus became manorial lord of the Countess of Warwick's Fee, dying a bachelor in 1591, left his estates to his nephew, SIR WILLIAM HATTON (*alias* NEWPORT) who died without male issue in the 39 Eliz [1596-7], his possessions being divided between joint-heirs, namely —SIR EDWARD COKE,‡ Knight, Lord Chief Justice, who inherited a portion in right of his second wife, the Lady Elizabeth Hatton, widow of Sir William Hatton, and also SIR CHRISTOPHER HATTON, K B, half-cousin to Sir William Hatton. From these joint-heirs, the Countess of Warwick's Fee and other estates in Cheshire, (Crewe, Barthomley, Haslington, &c) were purchased by Ranulphe Crewe, Esq,§ in the year 1608.

* King's ' *Vale Royal*," printed in Ormerod s *Cheshire*, vol 1 p 137, new Edit
† Thomas Fouleshurst appears to have been living at the Hall of Shaw, in Coppenhall, about the year 1621, when Mr Webb wrote his Itinerary of Nantwich Hundred   (See King's " *Vale Royal* ")
‡ Sir Edward Coke was lord of this Fee in 1606-7, when the dispute was pending relating to the election of parish clerk in this town (See *Annals* under that date)   Sir Ranulphe Crewe was one of the Executors of Sir Edward s Will (*Cal State Papers*)
§ "I gave Sir Christopher Hatton £500 and his brother Sir Robert £100   The whole in gould being after my purchase passed   This I did out of respect to him altogether for that he was unwilling to sell but to me " (Mem in the handwriting of Sir Ran Crewe)

SIR RANULPHE CREWE, of Crewe, Knight, the purchaser of the Countess of Warwick's Fee, was the second son of John Crewe, gent, of Hospital Street, Nantwich, by his wife Alice, the daughter of Humphrey Mainwaring, of Nantwich. The well-known couplet says:-

"Sir Randle Crewe, the Lord of this [Crewe] Manor
Was born at Nantwich, the son of a Tanner"

Statements at variance with each other have been made respecting his father. The Rev Edward Hinchliffe* doubts whether he was a tanner or not, another biographer† states that he was "under the pressure of reduced means at the time of his son's birth," whilst a third writer says that the *father* of John Crewe was a tanner, and that John Crewe himself was locally known by the cognomen of "Golden Roger."‡ Nothing has occurred to prove the truthfulness of the rhyme, or to show which of the foregoing statements is the correct one, but it seems very improbable that a needy tradesman could have brought up his two sons, Ranulph and Thomas, to the highest department of the profession of the law. John Crewe's residence still exists as one of the principal houses in the town, and has old heraldic glass *in situ* which is described in the next chapter. (See St Nicholas' Hospital)

Ranulphe Crewe was baptized on 10th Jan, 1558.* Of his early life nothing is now known, but on the 24th Oct, 1597, he was elected M P for Brackley, co Northampton In the following year his father died and was buried at Nantwich.   •

"1598 Dec 20 John Crewe of the Aspell Street, Gent" [*Bur Reg*]

Having been a student at Lincoln's Inn, he was called to the bar in 1603 In 1608, as previously stated, he purchased the estates, fees, manorial rights, &c, which had passed away from his ancestors about three hundred years before, and which have been traced during that interim through the families of Praers and Fouleshursts. Together with Sir William Brereton, Kt, he is said to have been returned as M.P for his native county in 1614 § On the opening of Parliament he was elected Speaker of the House of Commons, and on the 8th June in the same year he was Knighted Mr Barlow, speaking of the advancement of Sir Ranulphe to dignity and honor, and relying on the supposed accuracy of Lord Campbell's "*Lives of the Chief Justices*," is guilty of several anachronisms, thus making him young for one purpose and old for another. He says "Ranulphe Crewe was elected one of the representatives of his native county when a *young* man in 1614," although he must have been 56 years of age at that time, that he purchased the manor of Crewe "in his *declining years,*" although the purchase was made six years before he became a county member, and pictures "the quiet old gentleman," his father, dreaming away his existence at Nantwich in pleasant fancies of the progressive advancement of his two talented sons, many years after John Crewe, Gent, was entombed in the Church, and probably after his monument was set up.

Sir Ranulphe Crewe next took the degree of Serjeant-at-law in 1614, and soon afterwards became the King's Serjeant ‖ He was Attorney-General in 1623, and, on the

* History of Barthomley, 1856, p 221
† Mr T W Barlow in his "Cheshire, its Historical and Literary Associations" 1852 p 43
‡ Pennant's "Tour from Chester to London," 2nd Edit 1811 p 43-4
§ Though it is commonly stated that he was elected M P for *Cheshire*, it is not absolutely certain that he represented his *native county*, as the Parl returns for 1614 are now lost
‖ In 1616 Justice Winch and *Serjeant Crew* were in disgrace for hanging supposed witches at Leicester, when the King, whilst there, found out the imposture of the boy said to be bewitched *(Cal Stat Pap* Dom Series, Jas I vol 88, dated Oct 12, 1616)

resignation of Sir James Ley, succeeded as Lord Chief Justice of the Court of King's Bench on the 26th Jan. 1625, but he was displaced in the following year, the judicial office being then tenable at the King's pleasure Fuller, in his "*Worthies*" says:—

"King Charles' occasions calling for speedy supplies of money, some great ones adjudged it unsafe to venture on a Parliament, for fear in those distempered times, the physic would side with the disease, and put the King to furnish his necessities by way of loan Sir Randal, being demanded his judgment of the design, and the consequences thereof (the imprisoning of recusants to pay it) openly manifested his dislike of such preter-legal courses, and thereupon 9 Nov 1626, was commanded to forbear his sitting in the Court, and the next day, by writ, discharged from his office"

Thus deprived, Sir Ranulphe afterwards lived in retirement at his town-house, near Westminster Abbey; but often visited his noble mansion of Crewe Hall, the first stone of which was laid on the 3rd April, 1615,* the mansion not being finally completed until 1636. On the 3rd March, 1631, Sir Ranulph obtained a perpetual lease of the Easter Roll of Nantwich, and in 1633 his right to the Countess of Warwick's Fee was disputed by Robert, viscount Cholmondeley, in the Court of Exchequer at Chester, but without success, Sir Ranulphe's right to the serjeancy of these fees in the Manor of Nantwich being upheld by a decree dated 30th April in that year, and subsequently confirmed by Royal letters patent by King Charles I.—*(Chesh Recog Rolls.)*

The following account of the manner of life and hospitality of Sir Ranulphe Crewe in his last days well describes the manners of country squires rather more than two hundred years ago, and is too interesting to be omitted †

"Sir Ranulphe, when far advanced in years, was accustomed to take much equestrian exercise over his Crewe and Barthomley demesnes, on his piebald gelding, accompanied by his two sons, Sir Clippesby and John, on their gray and bay nags He frequently paid visits to the neighbouring gentry, amongst whom were, Sir Thomas Smith, Sir Richard Lea, Sir Richard Wilbraham, and Sir Randle Mainwaring. at those once fine, but long since decayed seats, called Hough and Lea, in Wybunbury, and Woodhey and Baddiley in Acton, where he was welcomed by his hosts, and according to the fashion of the age, attended by retinues of chamberlains, grooms in waiting, ushers of the hall, and their several deputies Although Sir Ranulphe kept sumptuous tables, he was himself contented with very plain fare. His generosity to the poor was most extensive, and the higher classes, when in adversity, likewise shared his bounty, often receiving from him very liberal pecuniary presents He regularly gave alms to the poor of his native Street ‡ He was eminent as a lawyer, skilled in architecture, and devoted to archæological pursuits He was the preserver at Crewe of a transcript of Smith's valuable Cheshire Collections, which formed the basis of King's "*Vale Royal*," and to his grandson Ranulphe the credit is due of having promoted the publication of that work" (*Hist Barthomley*, pp. 364, 368).

---

* Wilb MS Journal It is worthy of note that Dorfold Hall was built about the same time These noble manor houses indicate the great change that had taken place in the reigns of Jas I and Elizabeth, when the family assembled in "*withdrawing rooms*" and "*parlours*," leaving the servants to the "*halls*," where in mediæval times the lord used to meet his retainers and hold his feasts

† This account is from the pen of the late T W Jones, Esq, of Nantwich, who contributed much valuable information relating to the Crewe family that has already appeared in the History of Barthomley

‡ Sir Thos Crewe (younger brother of Sir Ranulphe) of Steane, Kt, co Northampton, also distinguished himself as a lawyer and politician, sat in several parliaments became Speaker in the House of Commons, and died on the 1st Feb 1633, leaving by his will "the rents and profit of land in Buglawton to be for ever employed either to erect and maintain an hospital of some poor in the *Hospital Street*, or to be put in stock in all or part to keep the poor of *that street* in work, or to be distributed yearly among the poor of *that street*, with some allowance to the preacher" (See *Charitus*)

Crewe Hall sustained two sieges during the Civil War, on 27th Dec 1643, and 4th Feb 1643-4 (see *posted*). and before the war was over in this county Sir Ranulphe Crewe died. Concerning his death and burial Thomas Malbon, of Nantwich, writes as follows —*

"Sʳ Randull Crewe, Knighte, A greate Councellor, wᶜʰ had byn Lorde Cheefe Justice of the Kinges Benche, a Religious good man and ferme for the p[ar]liamᵗ and a man of fayre possessions bothe in Cheshire & many other places And whereof his owne Charges found & maynteyned in Cheshire (for Servys of the p[ar]liamᵗ) duringe all the tyme of the late warres vntill his Death, Tenne Soldyers & Twoe Horse & men bravely furnished, Dep[ar]ted this lyfe att his howse in westm[inste]ʳ the xiijᵗʰ daye of January 1645[-6] Beinge then of the Age of ffourescore and eighte yeres, or thereabouts And afterwards his bodie was broughte downe into Cheshire & entombed att Barthomley (whereof hee was Patron) in a fayre vaulte (wᶜʰ hee had made) the fyfte of June 1646 about Seyven a Clocke in thafter noone (beinge ffrydaye) wᵗʰout either Sermon or any Solemnitie "†

Sir Ranulphe Crewe was twice married, first to Juliana, daughter and co-heiress of John Clippesby, of Clippesby, co Norfolk, Esq, by whom he had three children, (1) Sir Clippesby Crewe, of Crewe, Kt, who succeeded to the Countess of Warwick's Fee, and other estates in Cheshire, &c (2) John Crewe, of Utkinton, Esq and (3) Juliana He married secondly Juliana, daughter of Edward Fusey, of London, and widow of Sir Thos. Hesketh, Kt, by whom he had no children

The descent of the Countess of Warwick's Fee from the middle of the seventeenth century is, briefly as follows —‡

Sir Clippesby Crewe, of Crewe, Kt succeeded his father Sir Ranulphe Crewe, and, dying at London, was buried in Westminster Abbey on the 3rd Feb. 1648-9, leaving as his son and heir

John Crewe, of Crewe, Esq, who was also buried in Westminster Abbey on 22nd Feb 1683-4, and who left as his heir a grandson, *John Offley*, then about three years of age, who assumed the name and arms of Crewe

John Crewe (*alias* Offley) of Crewe, Esq, who thus succeeded his grandfather, died on the 25th Aug 1749 His son and heir was

John Crewe, of Crewe, Esq, who enjoyed the estates scarcely four years, and died on the 18th Sept 1752, leaving a son and heir, *John*, then only ten years of age

John Crewe, of Crewe, Esq, the next successor, was created Baron Crewe, on the 25th Feb 1806, and died on the 28th April, 1829. aged 86, and was interred at Barthomley.

The Right Hon John, second Lord Crewe, of Crewe, succeeded his father, and died on the 4th Dec. 1835, aged 65. He was buried at Barthomley, and was succeeded by his son,

The Right Hon Hungerford, Lord Crewe, in whose lifetime the manorial rights attached to the Countess of Warwick's Fee have fallen into extreme decay.

* The Malbon MS, preserved at Condover Hall, Salop

† The entry in Barthomley Register is as follows —
"A D 1646 Sir Ranulphe Crewe of Crewe, Knight, buryed the fifth day of June Mortuus est 13 Jan 1645[-6 "

‡ For Biographical particulars relating to the later *Crewes* the reader is referred to the History of Barthomley

From this descent it is clear that the Countess of Warwick's Fee, which has passed through successive generations of Praers, Fouleshursts or Fulleshursts, and Crewes, has remained severed from the Barony of Wich-Malbank for more than six hundred years; and was not re-united thereto by Sir Hugh Cholmondeley in the sixteenth century as stated in the new edition of Ormerod's History of Cheshire The manorial rights attached to this fee are now no longer claimed by Lord Crewe The Court was abolished about 1840, the toll of corn was relinquished in favour of the Local Board about 1866, and toll of brine was paid by Mr Townley, the last salt manufacturer, until 1856 The right of appointing the bellman was passed to the Local Board in February, 1872 The last bellman appointed by Lord Crewe was Mr. Robert Harding, who, strange to say, was incapacitated from *"crying"* through impediment of speech, and who, rather than resign an office that had been held by his forefathers for more than a century,* was obliged to employ a deputy, whilst he himself discharged the duties of Bill-sticker, an office associated with that of Town-crier.

A very curious custom, commonly observed in the north of England and in Scotland in the eighteenth century, and known by the name of *lating* (i e. inviting), was practised by the town-crier of Nantwich in the previous century as noticed by John Ray in his *"Itineraries,"* under date Wednesday, 24th May, 1662, as follows —†

> "At Nantwich they have a Custom like that in Scotland, when anyone is dead, a Bellman goeth about the streets the Morning that the dead Person is to be buried tinkling a Bell he has in his Hand, and now and then makes a Stand and invites the People to come to the Funeral at such an Hour."

The lord of this fee also claimed the right of nominating the parish clerk, an office that has recently fallen into disuse, the last lay clerk being Mr. John Cooper The Rector now appoints a clerk in holy orders. In former times parish clerks were required to be able to sing the Psalms of David and to write, the latter qualification being necessary as they were for many years the recorders of Baptisms, Marriages and Burials of past generations, and the custodians of the Parish books A list of their names as mentioned in the Registers may not be uninteresting

LIST OF PARISH CLERKS

THOMAS BULLEYNE, signs the Register in 34 Hen VIII 1542
BROOKE, nominated by Mr Fulleshurst
THOMAS BULLEN, 1586—1606   Buried at N 7 Oct 1606
JOHN PEARSON nominated by Sir Edwd Coke, Kt , and displaced shortly afterwards by the Parishioners
THOMAS CLOWES, 1607—1639   Chosen by the Parishioners He gave the present Communion Table   Buried 3 April 1639

JOHN HUSSIE	1639—1660, nominated by Sr Ranulphe Crewe Kt Buried 2 Nov 1660
SAMUEL HUSSIE	1660—1685 Buried 22 Oct 1685
SAMUEL HUSSIE	1685—1729 Buried 10 Sept 1729
THOMAS SHENTON	1729—1736 Buried at Acton 19 Dec 1736
RICHARD YOXALL	1736—1762 Buried 29 May 1763
THOMAS OULTON	1762—1767 Buried at Acton 23rd May, 1767
THOMAS CHILD	1767—1782 Buried 21 Dec 1782
THOMAS CARTWRIGHT	1782—1806 Buried 17 Feb 1806 Aged 69

---

* The *Harding* family held the bellmanship of the town from 1736 to 1872 that is, for 136 years Another family appears to have held the office from 1586 to 1689, that is, 103 years, according to the following extracts from the Burial Register

"Homfrey Wilbram, bellman, buried 29 June 1586 '
"Nicholas Clowes, Bellman, a verie ould man, buried 7 May, 1617
"William Clowes, the bellman, 9 Oct 1638 "
Alexander Clowes, bellman, 28 Nov 1666 '

"Nicholas Clowes Bellman, 10 Jan 1672-3 "
"William Clowes, Belman, 19 March 1689 90 "
"John Hussey, the bellman 21 April 1736"
"John Harding, Bellman, 1 April 1767 "
"John Harding, Bellman, 9 Dec 1791 ' &c , &c

† "*Life of John Ray*" by Dr Derham, Edited by Lankester for the Ray Society, 1846 Appendix p 165
Brand speaks of the same custom at Hexham, co Northumberland, in 1777, and at Linlithgow as late as 1796 (See "*Popular Antiq of Gr' Britain,*' by W C Hazlitt, vol ii pp 163 and 174)

II. The Lovell Lands.

HESE lands, together with the advowson of the Chapel of St. Nicholas, in Nantwich, and the right of holding annually a three days' fair at Bartholtide, came into the possession of the Lovell family about the year 1350, and remained in that family for nearly a century and a half. Originally this part of the Barony of Wich-Malbank was divided between the two sisters of Philippa Basset, the Countess of Warwick, viz.:— *Joan Basset* and *Alice Basset* both of whom did homage for their fathers' lands in 4 Hen. III. [1219-20].*

I.—JOAN BASSET married Reginald Valletort, and the descent of her lands, which cannot be very clearly traced, is remarkable for the numerous instances of failures in male issue ; these lands having, in the course of 170 years, passed by successive heiresses into the families of SANDFORD, MAUTRAVERS, WARRENE, CHEYNE or CHANU, and BROWNING.†

JOHN BROWNING obtained livery of the same on 25th Dec. 1392; and his grandson, WILLIAM BROWNING of Melbury, co. Dorset, Esq., gave his share (a sixth part) of the Barony of Wich-Malbank in exchange for lands in Wiltshire to Sir William Lovell, Kt.‡ A copy of King Hen. VI. charter granting William Browning, on payment of five marks, [£3 6s. 8d.], licence to convey these lands to Sir William Lovell, is dated 13th Feb. 21 Hen. VI. [1442-3];§ and thus his share became united with the one next treated of.

II.—ALICE BASSET is said to have had three daughters; *Ela*, who married John Wotton, and had her portion in Worcestershire, but no share of the Cheshire estates; *Margaret*, who married John de Ripariis [Rivers]; and *Isabel* married to Hugh de Plessetis, who is said to have been the son of John de Plessetis Earl of Warwick.—(*Harl. MSS.* 2038.) These statements are given on the authority of an old local antiquary, John Woodnoth, of Shavington, in the neighbouring parish of Wybunbury, who died in 1637, leaving behind him many Cheshire pedigrees drawn up from ancient documents, and other collections, which are now preserved in the British Museum and the Bodleian Libraries. Philip de Plessetis, in 14 Edward I. [1285-6];‖ and John de Ripariis, about the same time, by an undated charter here given, conveyed their estates, parcel of the Barony of Wich-Malbank, to Robert Burnell, Bishop of Bath and Wells. An abstract of the Rivers' Charter, in Latin, is preserved at the Bodleian Library, of which the following is a translation :—¶

---

* Dr. Ormerod states this on the authority of a *Fine Roll* of that date discovered by Vincent. This *Fine* is not now to be found at the Record office.

† *Harl. MS.* 2038. f. 137.

‡ Chesh. Recog. Rolls.

§ Add. MSS. Brit. Mus. 6032. f. 43. b.

‖ *Harl. MSS.* 1967. f. 120. a.c.

¶ Dodsworth MSS. vol. xxxix. f. 151. b.

' To all present and to come, Know that I, *John de Rivers* [Riparus,] lord of Aungre have given, conceded, and by this my charter have confirmed to the Venerable father in Christ Lord R[obert], by the grace of God Bishop of Bath and Wells my manor of Wychemalbanc with the advowson of the church [*ecclesiæ*] of the same being one Knight's fee and all their appurtenances without retention whatever To have and to hold *in capite* from the lord of that fee freely and quietly in fee, and to his heirs for ever, by doing all customary services to the lord of the fee *in capite* and rendering to me and my heirs annually at Easter one penny for all services to me and my heirs or assigns belonging And I the aforesaid John &c will warrant for ever against all men and women "

These being witnesses " &c   [Names not given]

Some explanation is here necessary, for on the authority of this deed attempts are now being made to prove that Bishop Burnell was Lord of the town of Nantwich and founder of the present parish Church, implying thereby that the Church is dedicated to St Nicholas, and that it was an ancient Rectory in the gift of that eminent prelate, and afterwards of the Lovell family All this is a fictitious theory that receives no confirmation in any record The term "*manor*" here used, cannot possibly refer to the whole lordship of the town, for the *Abbot's Fee*, which included the Church or Chapel of the town, is mentioned about the same time in the Inquisition 16 Edw I * [1288] as *separate* and *distinct* from the Barony of Wich-Malbank It has been suggested that the Abbey may have alienated the Church lands in Nantwich, but the clear evidence of the Inquisition proves the falsity of the supposition The Bishop's "manor ' or share of the Barony was situated *chiefly* in Newhall and Coppenhall as will be seen in the rentals on a subsequent page. Adam, the Abbot of Combermere in and before 1296, by deed, quitclaimed all lands, tenements, woods, &c, belonging to the convent in Copenhale, to Robert Burnell, Bishop of Bath and Wells, for exchange of Greenfordhey and payment of £213 6s. 8d. to relieve the necessities of the house at Combermere,† but no such deed has occurred of the Abbey relinquishing Church lands in Nantwich until compelled to do so at the final dissolution of that Monastery, hence it is most likely that the word "*ecclesiæ*" is a clerical error for "*capellæ*," the reference being, not to the Church or Chapel of Nantwich, but, as will presently be seen, to the Chapel of St. Nicholas Hospital, in Nantwich, which was situated outside the pale of the Abbey lands in this town

BISHOP BURNELL, the grantee of manorial lands in Wich-Malbank and the neighbourhood, was Lord Chancellor to King Edward I, and a Bishop of high standing among the clergy of his day, for, on the promotion of Robert, Archbishop of Canterbury, to the Cardinal's chair, "the monks of Canterbury demanded Lord Robert Burnell, Bishop of Bath and Wells, the King's Chancellor, as their Archbishop, which demand, however, was quashed by the supreme pontiff, and brother John of Peckham, one of the order of Minor Brothers, a man of the most perfect learning, was appointed by the Roman Court to be the shepherd of the Church of Christ at Canterbury 1278 '‡ The year before, on 2nd Aug 1277, Bishop Burnell was present at the laying of the foundation stones of Vale Royal Abbey, Cheshire, and celebrated high mass on that occasion § No doubt he attended the King

* See pp 22-3, and *cf* Foundation Charter of Combermere Abbey, p 19
† *Williamson s Fines*, quoted in Ormerod s Cheshire, New Edit III 403
‡ Matthew of Westminster s Chron Vol II p 472   (Bohn's Edit)
§ "Ormerod,' New Edit Vol II p 147

on his Welsh campaign, for at Aberconwey [Conway] on the 19th May, 1283, he obtained the privilege of a chartered fair at Nantwich

' The King concedes to the Venerable father *Robert Bishop of Bath and Wells* that he and his heirs for ever shall have a fair at his manor of Wich Malbank in the county of Chester every year for three days duration namely, on the vigil, on the day, and on the morrow of St Bartholomew the Apostle, [23, 24 and 25 Aug] &c Dated 19 May 11th Edw I [1283]

These being witnesses Edward [Burnell] his brother, Henry de Lacy Earl of Lincoln,* Roger le Bygod, Earl of Norfolk and Marshall of England, Robert de Brus Earl of Warwick,† Richard de Brus, Robert son of John and others "

The above is translated from a copy of the charter in *Harl MSS* 2074 p 202, and on the same page is an extract from a Patent Roll as follows *(translated)*—

"In the year 15 Edw I [1286-7] the King concedes to *Robert Bishop of Bath and Wells* that he and his heirs for ever shall have free warren in all his demesne lands in Wich Malbanc and Copenhall in the county of Chester, so that no one &c These being witnesses Henry de Lacy Earl of Lincoln, Ottone de Grandison, John son of St John and others "

Bishop Burnell was presented by Simon, Abbot of St Werburgh, Chester, to the Rectory of Astbury in this county, before the year 1289 ‡ Being on a journey to Scotland, whither he was sent to demand the surrender of that country to King Edward I, he died at Berwick on 25th Oct. 1292, and was buried in Wells Cathedral, his possessions here descending to his brother *Edward*, son of Sir Philip Burnell, Baron of Malpas, who had died 15 Edw I [1286-7] —(*Harl. MSS* 2038 f. 136 g)

EDWARD, LORD BURNELL, who succeeded through survivorship, held his share of the Barony until 9 Edw. II.§ [1315-16], when he died without issue, his lands descending to his sister Matilda, then wife of John de Hanlow, Kt., and afterwards of John Lovell, Kt. (*Harl MSS* 2038 f. 136 g)

JOHN DE HANLOW, KT., paid his *relief*‖ of £10 for his lands described as "two knights' fees" formerly held by Edward Burnell, in 1316,¶ and was still living on 2nd Dec 1330, when he presented to the Hospital of St Nicholas, in Nantwich His death took place not long after, for in 1341

SIR JOHN LOVELL, KT , the second husband of the said Matilda, had alienated without licence a messuage and garden in Wich-Malbank, called "*Chastelyord*," to William de Brescy, who on the 19th September in that year had obtained pardon for the same ¶ Sir John Lovell died before 1350, leaving two sons of the *same name*, John, both under age The elder died about the age of twenty, in the year 1362, the younger being of the age of sixteen when his brother's Inquisition *post mortem* was taken

---

* Henry de Lacy, who held the high title of Earl of Lincoln, was of Cheshire origin, and was the 10th Baron of Halton in this county from 1258 until his death on 5th Feb 1310 (See Beamont's "*History of Halton*," p 33)

† ? Robert, son of William de Beauchamp, Earl of Warwick.

‡ Ormerod's "Cheshire,' New Edit Vol iii p 26

§ Alina, widow of Edw Burnell, in 1315 and 1316 entered actions against John and Roger Brescy, Thos Cradok, William de Pull, Roger de Bulkylegh, &c , claiming dower for lands in Wich-Malbank, in all for 2 parts of 64 acres of lands, besides 81½ acres, 10 acres of wood, 2 acres of meadow, the Serjearcy and Bedelary of Wich-Malbank, &c *(Plea Rolls)*

‖ "*Relief*," i e a fine "due for taking up the estate, which had lapsed or fallen in by the death of the last tenant

¶ Recognizance Rolls—Cheshire Records In Acton Burnell Church, Salop, is a brass and effigy to Sir John de Hanlow, who married the heiress of the Burnells

A copy of an Indenture of this Inquisition is given in *Harl MSS* 2038 f 137, of which the following is a translation

"To Edward,[*] son of the illustrious King of England, Prince of Wales, duke of Cornwall, and Earl of Chester Adam de Kingesley Escheator of Chester sends greeting Forasmuch as *John son of John Lovell Kt* who held of us *in capite* on the day of his death &c as witnessed by Bartholomew de Burghesse our Justiciary of Chester on the first day of April in the 36th year of the King our father [1363] by virtue of our letters an Inquisition was taken at Wich Malbank on the Sabbath day next after the feast of Easter [April 2] in the year aforesaid, by the oathes of Richard de ffuleshurst, Robert de Maisterson Richard de Parker, Roger de Cholmundelegh, William de Wettenhall of Cholmundeston, Roger de Brescy of Morefield [Willaston] John de Rope, Robert de Wyllaston, Ralph de Shagh, John Brescy, William de Bromlegh and Hugh of Blakenhall, Jurors, who say on their oaths that the aforesaid John, son of John, on the day of his death died seised in his demesne as of fee of a sixth part of the Barony of Wich Malbank held of our Lord the Earl of Chester *in capite*, and that quantity of the fee of the barony is of the total value of £20 per annum, and that on the day aforesaid John, brother of the said John son of John, is his heir of the age of 16 years on the day in which the same John his brother died, namely about the feast of St Michael, in the year aforesaid of the King" [i e about 29 Sept 1362]

Consistent with this Inquisition, the Bishop of Lichfield presented a priest to St Nicholas' Hospital in 1364, "*through lapse,*" and in the following year, before the heir had attained his majority, the next presentation to the vacant Hospital was made by Sir Edmund Everard Knight, the legal representative, and probably guardian of the heir

SIR JOHN LOVELL, of Tichmersh, co Northampton, Kt, afterwards Knight of the Garter, would obtain possession of his lands about 1367 He took the title of Lord Lovell and Holland about 1373 on his marriage with Maude de Holland, sole heiress of Robert de Holland; and by his marriage added the manors of Mottram, Tintwistle and Longdendale in Cheshire, to his extensive possessions in the counties of Dorset, Somerset, Oxford, and Northampton He did service in the French wars in 1368, 1374 and 1375, and on the 8th Aug 1394, was appointed by the King to take for the King's voyage, (probably to Ireland,) such ships and seamen as he should find fit in the ports of Chester, Lancaster and North Wales [†] In his will dated at Wardour Castle, co Wilts, 25th July 1408, and proved 12th Sept in the same year, he bequeaths "his body to be buried in the Church of the Hospital of St John at Brackley, co Northampton," and leaves "a vestment of black adorned with stars of gold, and certain copes to the said hospital"[‡]

His *Inquisition post mortem* as far as relates to Nantwich, taken at Wich-Malbank in Sept, 1408, before Richard de Manley Escheator, finds that "he died seized in his demesne, as of fee, of a sixth part of the barony of Wich Malbanc, with the advowson of the Chapel of St. Nicholas, with appurtenances, to wit [the following] free rents from lands and tenements, viz. —

In Nantwich	£	s	d
The heirs of William de Praers .	0	12	0
Robert Brett .	0	0	6
William de Fouleshurst, for two places of land .	0	1	6

* Edward the Black Prince, who had the wardship of John Lovell, the elder heir

† Recognizance Rolls—Cheshire Records

‡ Earwaker's *Last Cheshire*, Vol II p 113, where will be found an account of this family and their lands in the parish of Mottram

	£	s	d
Nicholas Colfox, Kt	0	2	0
Thomas de Fouleshurst	0	4	0
John de Brescy	1℔ cinnamon		
Richard de Rooper & John Muryell	0	10	0
Thomas le Maisterson, Henry Bryan, William le Fyssher Elisot ⎰ de Wetenhale Richard de Cholmondeley ⎱	8	19	0
In Newhall [from 38 tenants all named]	13	8	0
In Wolstanwood from Thomas de Bulkylegh for 150 acres of land	5	0	0
In [? *Monks'*] *Copenhall* [from 8 tenants]	7	10	3
In [? *Church*] *Copenhall* [from 10 tenants] . .	8	8	6

Total annual Rental £44 15 9

The Inquisition further states that he died on 10th Sept. last past, [1408] and that *John Lovell*, Chevalier, was his son and next heir, then of the age of 30 years and more.

SIR JOHN LOVELL, KT , who thus succeeded, died on or about the 19th Oct , 1414, his *Inquisition post mortem*, which is now defaced and almost obliterated, being taken on the following 6th Nov. finds his son and heir, *William Lovell* to be under age in the feast of Epiphany last past

" He died seised of two parts of ⅙th part of the Barony of Nantwich with the advowson of the Chapel of St Nicholas a clear rent of   shillings out of a tenement of the late William de Praers in Nantwich   &c   " 4s issuing out of a piece of land held by Thomas de Fouleshurst of *Flesshemonger lane* in Nantwich " &c   His widow, Eleanor, the daughter of William Lord Zouch of St. Maur, held part of these lands in dower, viz — " 30 acres of land and 10 acres of meadow and 38/3 rent in Wich Malbank and Copenhall, value £4 1s 0d , 40 acres of land and 12 acres of meadow and 33 4 rent in Newhall and Wolstanwood, value £6 5s 6d ,

until the day of her death, which was " Monday next after the feast of St Gregory the Pope [13 Jan] last past " [1434] when they reverted to her son Sir William Lovell Kt

SIR WILLIAM LOVELL KT had livery of the lands of his father and grandmother Maud by writ dated 12th June, 1434, being then about twenty-three years of age   From that time to the year 1444 he was summoned to Parliament , after which, special exemption from serving in Parliament for the rest of his life was granted in consideration of his eminent services in foreign parts during the reigns of Henry V and Henry VI   On the 13th Feb 1442-3, he obtained by an exchange of lands from *William Browning* of Melbury, co Dorset, an additional sixth part of the Barony of Wich-Malbank,[*] which had descended from Joan, wife of Reginald Valletort, the sister of the Countess of Warwick and Alice Basset as already mentioned   Sir William Lovell married Alice, one of the co-heiresses of Sir John Deincourt Kt , with whom he had large estates in Oxfordshire, Lincolnshire, &c He died on 13th June, 1455, desiring by his will dated 18th March, 1454-5, to be buried " at the Grey Friars Oxenford " &c.

His Inquisition post mortem is as follows *(translated)*—

"*Inq p m* taken at Acton on the 4th Aug 33 Henry VI [1455] before Ralph de Legh Escheator, by the oaths of Richard Spurstowe, Hugh Wettenhall, William Ree (?) Randle Wetenhale, Hugh

* Recognizance Rolls—Cheshire Records   Also, *cf* p 40

Multon, John Cheswys, Richard Hankylowe, David Swanwyk, William Dod, John Fyton, William Whytney and Thomas Olton, Jurors, who say that Sir William Lovell Kt, died seized in his demesne as of fee, of a sixth part of the barony of Wich-Malbank with the advowson of the Church of St Nicholas of Wich-Malbank, held of the Earl of Chester, *in capite*, by Knight's service, and of the yearly value of £24 6s 8d , also of one other sixth part of the aforesaid barony, formerly of William Brounyng, held of the Earl of Chester, as above, and of the yearly value of £6 13s 4d , &c , and that the said William Lovell, by the name of William, Lord of Lovell, Burnell, and Holland, granted [30th Sept 1441] to Bartholomew Ardern an annual rent of £13 6s 8d , to be received of the issues and profits of the said William's lands in Wich-Malbank, Munkescopenhall, Wildeheth [Willaston] and Newhall , that the said William Lovell died on the 13 June last past [1455] and that John Lovell, Kt , was his son and heir, and of the age of 22 years on the morrow of Easter last past "

SIR JOHN LOVELL, KT., who thus inherited a third part of the Barony of Wich-Malbank, died on the 14th Jan , 1464-5, leaving as his heir *Francis*, then only seven years of age , his Inquisition being taken on Wednesday next before the Feast of St John before the Latin gate [May 6] in the year 1465 In the same year, his widow Joan, who had granted these lands, with the advowson of St Nicholas Hospital, without licence, to Thomas Acton, Thomas Maisterson, and Thomas Lewes, obtained pardon for her illegal act, which made it necessary to obtain a writ of *"ouster le main,"* [*] dated 31st July, 1465, or delivery of these lands[†] to the heir, or rather his guardian, the Hon Sir Richard, Earl of Warwick and Sarum, lord of Bergevenny, who presented to the Hospital at Nantwich in 1468 [‡]

FRANCIS LORD LOVELL obtained livery of his lands on the 28th Feb 1477-8, being probably about twenty-three years old He espoused the cause of the House of York, and suffered for his loyalty. He went to Scotland in the retinue of the Duke of Gloucester, afterwards King Richard III, who, on 4th Jan 1483, created him Viscount and soon afterwards Knight of the Garter, Chamberlain of the Household, and Chief Butler of England. He fought on the side of the King at Bosworth Field, on 22nd Aug 1485 , but escaped and fled for sanctuary to St. John's at Colchester, and thence to Sir Thomas Broughton's in Lancashire. After hiding there for some months he escaped to Flanders, where he joined Margaret, Duchess of Burgundy (sister to Edward IV), by whom he was sent, with John de la Pole, Earl of Lincoln, and a body of two thousand veteran Germans, to join Lambert Simnell, the pretended Duke of York. The invasion of England being resolved on they landed in Lancashire, and advanced as far as Stoke, near Newark, where they were defeated 16th June, 1487

Lord Bacon says,[§] "there went a report, that Lord Lovell fled and swam over Trent on horseback, but could not recover the farther side by reason of the steepness of the bank, and so was drowned in the river But another report leaves him not there, but that he lived long after in a cave or vault " Hume and Lingard both state that Lord Lovell escaped from the field, and the latter historian says—" towards the close of the seventeenth

---

[*] "*Ouster le main,*' i e literally " to take off the hand "

[†] In 1475-6, March 12, Thomas Fulleshurst was appointed steward and receiver of these manors and lordships {Cheshire Recognizance Rolls)

[‡] *Johanna or Joan* the widow of Sir John Lovell Kt "died on Thursday next after the feast of St Bartholomew the Apostle [Aug 24] 8 Edw IV [1469] leaving Francis Lovell her son and heir aged 15 years on the day of the taking of this Inquisition She died seised (in dower) of a sixth part of the Borony of Wich-Malbank with the advowson of St Nicholas Chapel in Nantwich, and another sixth part of the same Barony " *Inquisition p m*

§ Bacon s *History of Henry VII* p 333 Bohn s Edit

century, at his seat at Minster Lovell, in Oxfordshire, was accidentally discovered a chamber under the ground, in which was the skeleton of a man seated in a chair, with his head reclining on a table   Hence it is supposed that the fugitive had found an asylum in this subterraneous chamber, where he was perhaps starved to death through neglect ' This discovery is mentioned in Gough's additions to Camden's "*Britannia*, thus " In pulling down the house of Minster Lovell in Oxfordshire, there was found in a vault the body of a man, in rich clothes, seated in a chair, with a table and mass book before him. The body was entire when found, but upon admission of the air, it soon fell to dust ' *

In consequence of his high treason, Francis Lord Lovell's lands became forfeited to the Crown, according to the following Inquisition *(translated)*—

"*Inquisition* taken at Chester in the Hall of Pleas there, before Thomas Wolton Kt Escheator, on Thursday next after the feast of St Hillary [13 Jan] in the 3 Henry VII [1488], by the oaths of John Hockenhull, John Mynshull, Thomas   , John Myles (?), Richard Legh of Adlington, Robert Corbet, John Brooke of Leighton, Thomas Peche [? or Touchet] Thomas Hull of Eyton, John Legh of Hawardyn Thomas Wetenhall of Cholmondeston, Geffrey   and Thomas Lee, Jurors, who say on their oaths that Francis Lovell formerly Lord Lovell, was seized in his demesne as of fee, on the 7th November 1487 the day on which he was attainted of High Treason in Parliament held at Westminster, the manor and lordship of Longdendale &c   Also of a sixth part of the Barony of Wich-Malbank with the advowson of the Chapel of St Nicholas in the same Wich and also the advowson of a third part of another Chapel of St Lawrence there, the which sixth part and advowsons aforesaid were held of the King, as Earl of Chester, and all pleas and plaints, the same being worth £24 6s 8d   Also, the aforesaid Jurors say that the said Francis died seized in his demesne as of fee, on the 7th November of another sixth part of the said Barony, which was formerly William Browning's, and held the same of the King, as Earl of Chester, worth £6 13s. 4d

Also, a third part of the manor of Monkescopenhall which he held of the King, as Earl of Chester, worth 47 shillings   And they say that Sir William Stanley Kt , Chamberlain of Chester has seized the same into his hands, but by what title the Jury are ignorant "

These lands &c were granted by King Henry VII, in 1489,† to SIR WILLIAM STANLEY, of Holt, Knight, Chamberlain of Chester, and Judge of North Wales, who had received high favours from the Crown after the Battle of Bosworth Field, where he treacherously deserted King Richard at the most critical time of the fight, and set the crown on Henry's head after rescuing him from imminent peril   Lord Bacon says,—"he was the richest subject for value in the kingdom, there being found in his castle of Holt 40,000 marks in ready money and plate, besides jewels, household stuffs, stock upon his ground and other personal estate, exceeding great   And for revenue in land and fee it was £3000 a year of old rent, a great matter in those times.   Yet, nevertheless, blown up with the conceit of his merit, he did not think he had received good measure from the King, as he expected; and his ambition was so exorbitant and unbounded, as he became suitor to the King for the Earldom of Chester."‡

His fall soon came.   On the surrender of Sir Robert Clifford in 1494, Sir William

---

* An elegant romance entitled "*The Old English Baron*," written by Miss Clara Reeve, of Ipswich, in 1777, is based on the mysterious disappearance of Lord Lovell of Minster Lovell , but the details of the story do not coincide with the true history of the family
  The Arms of the Lovells were—Barry nebule of six Or and Gules   (Dorfold MS Pedigree Bk fol 117)

† *Harl MSS* 1967 f 1186

‡ Bacon's Henry VII p 400 and 402   (Bohn's Edit)

Stanley, then Chief Chamberlain, Privy Councillor, and Knight of the Garter, was accused of favouring the designs of Perkin Warbeck, and imprisoned in the Tower, and eventually, on 16th Feb 1495, he was executed on Tower Hill, all his estates having been confiscated *

From the list of Masters of St Nicholas Hospital it is clear that the advowson of the Hospital belonged henceforth to the Crown, until its final dissolution in 1 Edw. VI [1547]. The Lovell lands were not granted away until 1530, and during that interim of thirty-five years, stewards were appointed by the Crown, who received the rents, and nominated the Bailiffs of Nantwich. Thus Ralph Egerton, of Ridley Hall, afterwards Standard bearer to King Henry VIII, and Treasurer of the Household of the lady Princess his daughter, was appointed Steward and receiver of all lands lately belonging to Sir William Stanley, in Chester and Flint, by deed dated at Greenwich 21st May 1 Hen. VIII [1509], and James Button, yeoman of the Crown, was appointed Bailiff of Nantwich, by deed dated at Greenwich 29th May 2 Hen. VIII [1510] † In *Harl MSS* 2039 f. 44 b , Richard Maisterson occurs as Steward and receiver of these Crown lands in 1525-6, of which the following is the Rental

Namptwich	£	s	d
The heirs of William Praers	0	12	0
The heirs of Nich Colfox	0	2	0
The heirs of Will ffouleshurst	0	1	6
William Brescy	0	0	6
Jo Meverell & Jo Rope	0	0	9
The heirs of Thos ffuleshurst, 1℔ cummin	0	4	0
Jo Kingsley	0	2	0
Jo son of John de Wetnall	0	6	8
Will Leeke	0	4	0
Rich Spencer	0	6	8
Hug' Madye	0	1	0
Tho Brunley	0	1	0
Rich Maisterson [Steward]	2	0	0
Tho Brayn	1	1	0
Ric Moreton	0	16	0
Jo Kinggesley	1	0	0
Nich Hengster	0	16	8
Rich Fletcher	0	13	4
Tho Taylor	0	10	0
Ric de Vernon	0	10	0
Jo son of Tho Wettnall	0	10	0
Rog preers	0	5	0
Jo Kingsley for part of the mill	0	13	4

Total—£10 18 5

* Sir William Stanley Kt built Ridley Hall, "the fairest gentleman's howse of al Chestreshyre," the gateway of which still exists

† *Calendar of State Papers, Domestic Series*, Hen VIII Vol 1 Nos 131 and 1086

James Button, who succeeded his father Richard Button in the office of Bailiff for the Lovell Lands in Nantwich, was in 7 Hen VIII [1515-16], sued by Alicia Maisterson, for the recovery of 3 messuages in Wich-Malbank *(Plea Rolls)*

		£	s	d
In *Baretspull*—Thos Moulton	.	0	9	0
In *Wolstanwood*—The heirs of Thos Bulkeley, and 6 other tenants		7	18	6
In *Acton*—7 tenants	.	2	2	6
In *Newhall*—17 tenants		3	5	0
In [*Church*] *Copenhall*—13 tenants		13	3	3½
In *Monks Copenhall*—13 tenants		11	16	1

On 23rd June 22 Hen VIII [1530] the King granted by Letters Patent to SIR JOHN GAGE, vice-Chamberlain of the King's Chamber, the lordship and town of Nantwich, and the manors and lordship of Cow-lane, Weston Wood, *alias* Ulston Wood and Acton, lately belonging to Sir William Stanley, attainted *temp* Hen. VII,[*] which grant was surrendered through invalidity in favour of SIR ANTHONY BROWNE, Knight of the Body, and Alice, his wife, by another deed of the same date, to be held *in capite* by the service of one Knight's fee [†]

In 37 Hen VIII [1545-6] the King grants to SIR WILLIAM PAGET, Knight, "all that our manor of Nantwich &c with all its privileges largely enumerated, and on 22 Octb. 1550 LORD PAGET of Beaudesart, sells the said barony, described as the manor of Nantwyche, with 40 messuages, 3 mills, 2740 acres, and £23 rent there and in Acton, Copenhall, Newhall, Aston, Cowlane, and Owstenwood, to ROLAND HILL, first protestant Lord Mayor of London, and to Thomas Legh of the same, merchant "[‡] This sale appears to have been afterwards rendered void, for on 11th March 1 Mary [1553] William Lord Paget, K G, of Beaudesart, in consideration of his faithful services, grants to his servant ROBERT FLETCHER, all his rights in the Barony of Wich-Malbank, viz —one third which was the property of the lords Lovell, and other two parts of a third, which belonged to Lord Audley (*Harl MSS* 1967 f 119 b)

On 26th April 3 and 4 Phil and Mary [1556] Robert Fletcher, in consideration of £100 sells the same to SIR HUGH CHOLMONDELEY (*Harl MSS* 1967 f 119 c)

Before treating of the second Division of the Barony of Wich-Malbank, it may be well to speak of the two pre-Reformation Religious Houses and Chapels mentioned in the foregoing Inquisitions

St. Nicholas Hospital.[§]

ST NICHOLAS HOSPITAL, where *hospitality* was dispensed to travellers, and alms distributed to the needy poor, was situated in the street still called *Hospital* Street. Founded by the first Norman Baron of Wich-Malbank this religious house continued for nearly 500 years During the last 200 years of its existence, institutions of Chaplains or Masters to the Hospital are recorded in the Bishops' Registers at Lichfield To the list of Chaplains

---

[*] Calendar of State Papers, Hen. VIII Vol 4 part III p 2920   [†] Recognizance Rolls—Cheshire Records

[‡] *Harl MSS* 1967 f 118 119, and Recognizance Rolls

[§] It is singular that neither Partridge nor Platt mention this Hospital   A salt-house belonging to the Hospital is mentioned in a deed in *Harl MSS* 2077 f 39 h as follows —"Thomas son of Richard Taylor deceased of Wich-Malbank gave to Roger Mainwaring a salt-house of 6 leads in Nantwich, lying in length between the road called le Wood Street on the south part, and the land of Roger Praers on the west part, and in breadth between the *salt-house belonging to St Nicholas Hospital*, on the east side, and the salt-house of the Blessed Virgin on the north side &c   These being witnesses John Leech &c   Dated 11th Hen VII " [1495-6] which first appeared in Dr Ormerod's *"Cheshire,"* (vol iii p 238, old Edit 1819), and which has recently been corrected in the new edition of that History, the names of two Chaplains of earlier date, and other interesting particulars relating to the Hospital, are here printed for the first time.

The CHAPLAINS or MASTERS of the HOSPITAL and FRFE CHAPEL of the BLESSED NICHOLAS of WICH-MALBANK

DNO. [Sir] JOHN, chaplain of St Nicholas Hospital, 44 Hen III [1259].

His name occurs as witness to a deed of that date among the Wettenhall Charters in *Harl MSS* 1967 f 113

WILLIAM DE LA BACH Keeper, 3 Edw. II [1309-10].

He is mentioned in the following extract of an *Inquisition* from the Woodnoth Collections in Dodsworth MSS xxvi f 144 (Bodleian Lib) *(Translation)*—

> *Inquisition* taken anno 10 Edw II [1316-7]   The Jurors say that a certain Ralph Sarazin gave to God, and St Nicholas, to the Prior and brethren of the Hospital aforesaid a certain salt house in Wich Malbank in pure and perpetual alms, which same salt-house belonged to *William de la Bach* formerly keeper of the said Hospital who in the 3 Edw II conceded the same to Hugh ffouleshurst, by the payment to him and his successors Keepers of the Hospital of 13s 4d per annum "

DNI [Sir] ROBERT DE MARCHOMLEGH, admitted, in o1 before 1330

ALEXANDER LE BLOUNT, clerk, admitted, *"iiij non' Decembr"* [2 Dec] 1330   Presented by Sir John de Hanlowe, Knight, on the death of Robert de Marchomlegh, the last rector

THOMAS CORBET, master, admitted before or in the year 1350

ROGER DL ALLERTON, clerk, admitted *"v Idus May"* [11th May] 1350   Presented by Edward (the Black Prince) eldest son of the King, as Earl of Chester, by reason of the custody of the son and heir of Sir John Lovell, Kt deceased, vacated by the death of Master Thomas Corbet the last Chaplain of the chantry or chapel of St Nicholas of Wychmalbank

JOHN DE NEWENHAM, chaplain, admitted *"xij Kln Aug"* [12 Aug] 1354   Presented by Edward, son of the King, &c , by reason of the minority of John Lovell, after the resignation of Roger de Allerton, the last Chaplain

NICHOLAS RIVELL, priest, admitted, *"xij Kln. March '* [21 March] 1364   Presented by the Bishop (of Lichfield) through lapse, (i e by the change of ownership in the advowson, through the death of the elder John Lovell on or about 29th Sept 1362) by the vacation in the Hospital or Chapel of St Nicholas of Nantwych

ROGER, son of WILLIAM OF BLACKHURST,* admitted *"ij Kln. Oct "* [30th Oct] 1365. Presented by Edmund Everard, Knight, attorney-general of John Lovell of Tichemersh; on the vacancy of the free chapell of the blessed Nicholas of Wych Malbank

JOHN OF ORMESHENED, priest, admitted 20 April, 1374   Presented by Sir John Lovell, Knight, lord of Tichemersh, on the resignation of *"dni '* [sir] Roger of Blackhurst, 19 April.

* *Blackhurst* is the name of a hamlet in Baddiley parish, which was the seat of the ancient family of *Praers*

"Dns" [Sir] John of Wodehouse, clerk, admitted 8 Decr 1376. Presented by Sir John Lovell, Knight, through the resignation of John of Ormeshened, the last Keeper, on the 27th day of November last.

Thomas Hine,* priest, admitted 31 Octi. 1395   Presented by the noble Lord John, Lord Lovell, and of Holland, after the death of Sir John Wodehouse, dean of S. Johns Chester, last rector, in the month of August last past

Master Alan of Newark, clerk, admitted 27 March, 1396.   Presented by the noble Lord John, Lord of Lovell and Holland, through the resignation of Sir Thomas Hyne, the last Keeper or Master

Randle of Bruyn, clerk, admitted . . .   1425   Presented by the rev father Lord William, by the grace of God Bishop of Coventry and Lichfield, through lapse, (during the minority of Sir William Lovell Knt.)

The cause of the vacancy is not recorded.

Master Thomas Heywode, admitted in or before 1460.

There is no mention of the name of the patron, nor the cause of the vacancy in the Bishop's Register

"Dno" [Sir] Thomas Friston, chaplain, admitted 15 Nov 1460.   He succeeded after the death of Master Thomas Heywode, the last Master or Keeper.

Randle Egerton clerk, admitted 21 Octobr. 1468.   Presented by the Honble Sir Richard Earl of Warwick and Sarum, lord of Bergavenny, in place of Lord Lovell by reason of his minority of age, the vacancy occurring through the resignation of Thomas ffryston last Master or Keeper of the Hospital or Chapel.

Richard Egerton, clerk, admitted 28 May 1477.   Presented by the most excellent Prince Edward [afterwards Edward V.] eldest son of the King, as Earl of Chester, (Francis Lord Lovell, not having obtained full possession of his lands until nine months after that date, viz   on 28 Feb. 1477-8,) after the resignation of Randle Egerton the last Master &c.

Thomas Blythe, clerk, admitted 4 Feb. 1506   This presentation is entered in the Bishop's Register at Chester as well as at Lichfield, the entry in the Chester Presentation Book being as follows   (translated)—

"To the Hospital or free Chapel of St Nicholas in Wich-Malbank, vacant by the resignation of Sir Richard Egerton, Thomas Blythe, clerk, was presented by the most excellent Lord Prince [Henry, son of] Henry [VII] by the grace of God King of England and ffrance true patron of the said Hospital, and was admitted and instituted to the same by the Revd Father in Christ and God, Geoffrey, Lord Bishop of Coventry and Lichfield, and was inducted by Robert Cliffe, the Bishop's official, and John Veysy L L D, Archdeacon of Chester on the 6th March 1506

Master William Gwyn, clerk, admitted 11 Deci. 1531.   Presented by the most excellent Prince in Christ and God now Lord King Henry eighth, on the death of Thomas Blythe last incumbent.

* *Thomas Hyne* was presented by the same patron to the living of Leigh, in Lancashire   (Ormerod's "Cheshire," New Edit vol iii p 449)

During his incumbency the Ecclesiastical Valuation 26 Hen VIII [1535] was taken, and the following return made

"FREE CHAPEL OF ST NICHOLAS"

"——— Gwynne, master of the same   Value of lands and tenements belonging to the said Hospital per annum £6 11s 4d   Tithes 13s 1¾d "

MASTER WILLIAM HILL LL B, admitted "nono die Aprilis" [9 April] 1541   Presented by the most Excellent and Puissant Prince in Christ, Lord Henry the eighth, on the death of Master William Gwyn last Master or Keeper

In the first year of the following reign [Edw VI] the Hospital was dissolved, and like others, no doubt demolished   William Hill the last Master, retired on a pension of C ᶳʰ [£5] per ann , which continued to be paid to him until 12th Oct. 4 Eliz [1561] *

The *Chantry Roll,* dated 1548, gives the following particulars at the dissolution of the Hospital

'THE FFREE CHANTRY OF SAINT NICHOLAS WITHIN THE SAYD TOWN [Nantwich]

Incumbent   Wyilm Hyll of the age of l [50] yeres   *The yerrly valewe*   viijʰ xˢ [£7 10s od]
Plate and Jewells   None   *Goods and Ornaments*   None   *Lead & Bells*   None

Shortly before the dissolution of the Hospital, and probably in anticipation of the threatened change, William Hill, "clerk," by an Indenture dated 3rd Nov. 1542, leased to *Raphe Wilbraham* of Nantwich for the term of twenty-one years at an annual rent of £6 11s 4d ,—

"all that hys *ffree Chappell or Hospitall* with all houses, messuages, tenements, lands, tythes, leadds salt wallings emoluments &c thereto belonging" &c †

This lease was however annulled when the dissolution came in 1548, and in the following year King Edward VI granted to *Thomas Bromley* of Nantwich, and his heirs for ever, in consideration of the sum of £435 16s 8d paid by him into the Crown Treasury, the following Chantry lands —‡

[1] " The Chantry House in Bunbury formerly the residence of two Chantry priests of Sir Raphe Egerton's Chantry Chapel in the parish Church of Bunbury, co Chester, together with the following lands in Wistaston &c parcel of the possessions of the said Chantry a messuage or tenement with mill, orchard, gardens, meadows, and common of pasture in the occupation of Richard Orton , a house with garden orchard &c in the occupation of Henry Nayler , a house &c in the occupation of John Bykerton a Cottage in the occupation of Thomas Lucas (all in Wistaston co Chester) , and also lands in Tiverton, Whicksall, co Salop, and Threpewood in co Flint , of the total value of £12 15s 4d ,

[2] Also a House and manse ["*mansionem*"] formerly called the *Chapel of St Nicholas* in the parish of Nantwyche, with its orchard one close adjoining containing by estimation about 2 acres, and a croft containing   acres, and one wiche house of 12 leads , also the site or vacant land of a wiche house of 6 leads , of the total annual value of £6 11s 4d

- Dated at Westminster 11th Nov 2 Edw VI " [1549]

* Mr Earwaker's transcripts of West Hall (Chesh) Papers, relating to Chantry Priests and their Pensions, between the years 1560—1568
† From an authorized copy of the Lease now preserved at Nantwich Rectory
‡ The original parchment deed in Latin, which is very lengthy, and still has the King s seal attached, is now in the possession of G F Wilbraham, Esq , of Delamere

Through the lapse of the Parish Register before 1572, it is not known when Thomas Bromley died, but he left a daughter and heiress, Emlyn, who was married to Alexander Newton of Newton, in Mottram, co. Chester whose will (proved 26th July, 1557) and that of his son George Newton (proved 19th April, 1580,) have been printed by the Chetham Society. (Vols xxxiii and liv)

These lands are also traceable in an Indenture dated 13th Sept. 1637, which states they were sold by Sir Richard Newport, Knight, to Thomas Wilbraham, Esq, of Nantwich, for £380, viz..—*

"One Messuage Tenement, or Hospitall in Wiche aforesaid known by the name of *the Hospitall* One cottage in Wiche wherein John Maddocks then dwelled one other cottage in Wiche, (then divided into two) wherein Marion Critchley did theretofore inhabit

One pasture or Croft in Wiche, called *the Hospital Croft*

One Croft in Wiche called St Anne Croft, alias Frogge Greave (except nine butts in the West end of the same Croft, being the Inheritance of Roger Wilbraham of Dorfold Esq)

One *wiche house of 12 leads* with its Appurts. in Great Wood Street

The *scite or ground of one other Wiche house of 6 leads* lying in pepper Street [near the Bridge (see Partridge's Hist p 8)] All manner of hereditaments &c Wood-rooms, Bryne Wallings, making of salt, Tythes profits &c then in the tenure of John Thrush

All that *parcel of the yard belonging to the said Hospital whereupon new Almshouses were then lately built*"

The Almshouses here referred to are Sir Edmund Wright's, who conveyed the same by deed of gift to Trustees on 30th Aug. 1638 *Hospital Croft* † is probably the same as *Almshouse Meadow* (see map), and though the Hospital is not here mentioned by name, there is no doubt that St Nicholas Hospital is intended, as proved by the Rent Roll of Roger, the son of Thomas Wilbraham, Esq of Nantwich, dated 1659, which gives *inter alia* —

	Annual Rent		
	£	s	d
"Roger Bickerton for 2 cottages & an orchard *part of St Nicholas Hospital in Namptwich*	2	13	4
William Pratchett for 2 cottages built upon a *six leads ground heretofore belonging to*			
St Nich Hosp	2	0	0
18 leads Wallinge & *tythes p'taining to St Nicholas hospitall after my father in law's*			
death, Val p ann	15	0	0
Jo Bromhall for ye 2 *Froggreaves* .	10	0	0
Tho Richardson for *St Annes Croft* ‡ .	3	0	0
The *Hospitall Croft* usually set for	12	0	0
William Jackson, Tanner, for ye *Hospitall howse*	, 4	0	0

It may be presumed that "*ye Hospitall howse*" occupied by a tanner in 1659, was in the previous century the identical residence of John Crewe, of Hospital Street, Gent, who is said also to have been a *tanner*, and who was the father of Sir Ranulph Crewe, Kt. The house of John Crewe is unmistakeably identified by old heraldic glass still existing in the three lead latticed windows of the upper over-hanging story, namely —

---

* An authorized copy of the original Indenture in the "Office of Land Revenue Records" is now preserved at Nantwich Rectory

† This meadow has no connection whatever with Sir Edmund Wright's Almshouses and never has been connected with that foundation

‡ Roger Wilbraham of Nantwich paid an annual rent of 10s to his father-in-law, Roger Wilbraham, of Dorfold, Esq for "9 *butts in St Annes Croft*" (Rent Roll)

HOSPITAL STREET, NANTWICH.

Window over the Entrance —

A shield Azure, a lion rampant Argent   *(Crewe)*

In the Window on either side —

A shield Quarterly. *First and fourth,* Argent, two barrs Or   *(Mainwaring) Second* (the glass of which is wanting in the west window) *and third,* Azure, three garbs Or. *(? Blundeville)* [*] surmounted by a crest, An Ass's head proper, issuing from a ducal coronet *(Mainwaring.)*

John Crewe, Gent, married Alice daughter of Humphrey Mainwaring of Nantwich, and died in 1598 (see Monuments)   This house belonged to the Goldsmith family in the early part of the eighteenth century   and in the latter part of the same century to the Caldwell family, whose representatives now reside at Lindley Hall near Talk-o'th-Hill co. Staff   After the death of James Caldwell, Esq, who was buried on 15th July, 1791 it was for many years the residence of his son-in-law Joseph Skerrett, Esq, who died there on the 18th Jan. 1832 [†]   The present proprietor and occupier is Thomas Bower, Esq, Architect who has recently taken down the old chimney stack, and gate-posts with balls on, at the east end of the house, and erected thereon new offices   When making these alterations some remarkable stone remains were discovered in digging the foundations. They are now to be seen in the garden behind, and Mr Bower is of opinion that they have been the capital and base of a Norman doorway   Here then is evidence, which, taken in connection with the foregoing statements, and the fact that Hospitals were usually situated at the entrance to towns, goes a long way to prove, if it does not absolutely determine, that this house, at Hospital Street end, is the exact site of the ancient Hospital and Chapel of St Nicholas

St. Lawrence Hospital.

Of this Hospital very little is known   In *Harl MSS* 2074 f. 166 *a*, it is styled a hospital *"for leazours,"* that is, a Lazar-house, or hospital for lepers   Mr Partridge says, *(Hist of Nantwich,* p 13) it is termed in several deeds *"Domus Leprosorum,'* and that, according to the tradition of the town, it stood on or near the site of a *"*Malt-house*"* then (1774) occupied by Mr James Bayley, (still standing, but now disused) very near the Almshouses at Welsh Row Head   The same writer contends for the existence of a *Priory* in close proximity to the Hospital, but no mention of any such foundation is to be found in any authentic record.   St Lawrence Hospital, as will presently be seen, was connected with the Abbey of Combermere, and the superior of the Hospital may have been the prior of the Abbey, i e the monastic officer next below the Abbot   The earliest mention of the Hospital occurs in an *Inquisition* taken at Minshull before Thomas le Yong, Eschaetor in 28 Edw. III [1354-5], as follows · [‡] *(translated)—*

---

[*] Why the arms of Randle III (Blundeville) Earl of Chester, are here introduced, I do not know

[†] "1775   June 14   Joseph Skerratt Upholsterer & Margaret Caldwell" (Nant Marriage Registers)   A large tombstone enclosed with iron railings in the Churchyard is thus inscribed   "To the memory of *James Caldwell* a native of Scotland but long resident in this Town who died in July 1791   and of Hannah his wife who died in July 1794   Also of their daughters *Margaret Skerrett* who died 12 March 1805 Aged 54   Ann Caldwell who died 6 February 1826 Aged 68   Elizabeth Caldwell, who died 10 January 1842 Aged 76,   Also *Joseph Skerrett* the husband of Margaret Skerrett who died 18 January 1832 Aged 87

[‡] Erdswick Collections in *Harl MSS* 506 p 13, and also in No 2077 f 98 n.

" The aforesaid Jurors say that (the Abbey of Combermere) is possessed of the Hospital of St. Lawrence at Wich Malbank   in which there ought to be one chaplain to sing divine service every day, and in which there ought to be three beds for the reception of poor sick people where they shall remain until they shall have recovered health, and that a certain service has been withheld for four years now elapsed, and it is now valued at 20 shillings per annum "

Combermere still maintained its claim on the Hospital in the 14 Henry VII [1498-9], when, according to the Rentals of Abbey Lands in Nantwich, (*Harl. MSS* 1967 f 19) the name of " *John ffowler* " occurs as " *chaplain of the ffree chapel of St Lawrence in Nantwich* " Francis Lord Lovell, on his attainder in 1488, was found possessed of one third of the advowson of the Hospital

The *Valor Ecclesiasticus* of 1525, returns as follows —

FREE CHAPEL OF ST LAWRENCE

" Doctor Incent' master of the same   The said Chapel is worth £4 per ann from lands and tenements belonging to the same   And there is paid to the Barons of Wich Malbank for toll of salt 4 shillings So that there remains clear, 76 shillings   Also the tithes amount to 7s 7¼d "

From the Survey of the Deanery of Wich-Malbank in 1541-2, (*Harl MSS* 2071) the amount of first-fruits claimed by Henry VIII was 6s. 10½d

The *Chantry Roll* dated 1548, at the dissolution of the Hospital and its Chapel, returns as follows —

" *THE FFREE CHANTRY OF ST LAWRENCE AND ST JAMES WITHIN THE SAYD TOWNE OF NANTWICH*

Incumbent   Rychard Wryght of the age of viij yeres [so in the original, but most likely an error]
Yerely valewe   lxxvjˢ [76 shillings]
Plate & Jewells   none
Goods & Ornaments   none
Leade   none
Bells   valewed ijˢ ? [2 shillings]

Richard Wright, the last incumbent, received an annual pension of £3 8s. 4d as late as 1562, and appears to have purchased the lands and to have lived until 1585. According to his *Inquisition post mortem* he died seised of, (*inter alia*,) " *the tythes of the formerly dissolved free Chapel of St Lawrence*,"* " a pasture called *Chapel croft*, and half of another pasture called the *Chapel-field* adjacent, lying in Acton "

Thus in pre-Reformation times St Lawrence Hospital, or Leper House, stood on the road-side at the western entrance to Nantwich, a refuge for poor emaciated creatures suffering from cutaneous diseases so common in past ages, when the poor lived in squalor and filth, were badly clothed and worse fed, while St. Nicholas Hospital or Bede House, for the reception of indigent persons and poor wayfarers, stood at the opposite end of the town   It is worthy of remark that history has here repeated itself in modern times   for Sir Roger Wilbraham, in 1613, and Sir Edmund Wright, in 1638, each founded Alms-houses, on or near the respective sites of those ancient Religious Houses.

---

* These small tythes were eventually conveyed by an Indenture dated 1st May, 1639, to the Minister of Nantwich Church and his successors   by *Margaret Woodnoth* and *Elizabeth Davenport*, the daughters and co-heiresses of Richard Wright, the son of Richard Wright, who was probably the last incumbent of the Hospital   (See *Wright Pedigree*)

SECOND DIVISION OF THE BARONY.

The Audley Fee.

 LEANOR MALBANK, second daughter and co-heiress of William the third Norman Baron of Wich-Malbank, died unmarried, having in her life-time granted her share of the Barony to HENRY DE ALDITHLEY or AUDLEY, for the sum of 100 marks of silver and the gift of a palfrey, subject to the annual payment of 40 shillings. The charter granting these lands is among the Erdswick Collections in the *Harl. MSS.* 506; of which the following is a translation:—

"To all present and to come, know, that I, Eleanor Malbank of my own lawful right have given, and by this my present charter have confirmed to *Henry de Aldithley* and his heirs, for his homage and service all that land which I have had within the borders of Cheshire, with all their appurtenances and liberties and all fee service &c. * * * * to have and to hold of me and my heirs, them and their heirs, freely and quietly for ever &c. rendering for the same to me and my heirs, them and their heirs, for all secular service and exaction 40 shillings sterling annually, at the two terms, viz.: 20/- at the feast of St. Michael and 20/- at the feast of St. Mary, annually, for safe foreign service [*salvo forinseco servicio*]. For this donation and concession Henry before gave me 100 marks of silver, and one palfrey. And I, Eleanor Malbank &c. [give general warranty].

"These being Witnesses: Philipp de Orreby Justice: of Chester, Hugh Despencer, Thomas Despencer, Roger de Montalt, Warin de Vernon, & others."

Of these witnesses, the first, Philip de Orreby, was Justiciary of Chester from 1209 to 1228; so that the Charter must date back to the early part of the reign of Henry III; whilst the others were among the greatest landowners of the Palatinate. The Despencers were feudal lords of Stockport, Roger de Montalt was Baron of Montalt and High Steward of the County, Warin de Vernon was Baron of Shipbroke, and had married Auda, the sister of the grantress Eleanor. Although the Earl's name does not occur in connection with this large grant of lands, it appears to have been necessary that this deed should be ratified, and accordingly, shortly afterwards, Ranulph, Earl of Chester, confirmed it by a Charter, which was also witnessed by Philip de Orreby, the Justiciary   This Charter affords an instance of the simple process of transfer of land in those times   A few inches of parchment, worded in the above general terms, attested in the presence of numerous local gentry, and having the seal of the grantress attached, gave to *Henry de Aldithley* sufficient title to thousands of acres!

Henry Audley married Bertred daughter of Ralph de Mainwaring by his wife Amicia,[*] and, probably, he resided at his castle of Newhall, a few miles from Nantwich, which is traditionally said to have stood in a field called "the three butts" near Sheppenhall [†] His successors, however, who are well known in history for their military exploits during the Edwardian wars, and for their pilgrimages to the Holy Land, had their chief seat at Helegh, in Staffordshire

According to the Inquisition 16 Edw I [1288] already given on p 23, the Audley Fee was at that time found to be held by JAMES AUDLEGH, who may possibly have been the son, or grandson, of Henry de Aldithley   The next in descent appears to have been SIR NICHOLAS DE AUDLEY, who married Joan de Lacy, Countess of Lincoln, and widow of Henry de Lacy, Earl of Lincoln and Baron of Halton, co Chester [‡] This fee was afterwards held in succession by his son, *Sir James Audley*, and his grandson, *Sir Nicholas Audley* [§]

SIR JAME AUDLEY, of Helegh, Knight, the famous hero of Poictiers, whose exploits are so romantically described in the pages of Froissart's Chronicles, alienated part of his Cheshire lands, in 1336-7, including "*one third part of the manor of Wich-Malbank,*' to Walter, parson of the Church of Newport, probably for the purpose of joining the expedition to the French wars, he however, obtained re-enfeoffment and pardon for this alienation on 15th Dec. 1353 [||]   His Inquisition *post mortem* taken on the 18th May, 9 Rich II [1386] finds "that he died siezed of *(inter alia)* "*a third part of the Barony of Nantwich,*' held *in capite* of the Earl of Chester, yearly value £50, &c, and that Nicholas de Audlegh Kt, was his son and heir, and 50 years of age on the 1st April last, on which day the said *James* died'

SIR NICHOLAS AUDLEY, OF HELEGH, KT, the next in succession, is stated to have "died on Saturday, the feast of St Mary Magdalen [22 July][¶] in the year 1391, siezed of, inter alia, *one third part of the lordship of the town of Nantwich,* held in capite of the King as Earl of Chester, *by service of a third part of the Barony* "[*][†] Though married, he died childless, in consequence of which his lands in Nantwich and elsewhere were divided as follows —one third part to each of his two sisters, *Margaret* wife of Roger Hillary, Kt, and *Joan,* wife of John Tochet, which two parts became re-united in the Tochet family after the death of *Margaret* in 1411   The remaining third part passed to the *Fitzwarines,*

* Ormerod s Cheshire, vol iii p 390   New Edit

† *Ibid,* p 905   Leland says, (c 1535) "There was a place of the lord Audleys in Cestreshyre, betwixt Cumbremere and Nantwiche, cauld Newhaull Tower   It is now doune There be motes and fair water   (*Itineraries,* vol vii p 31)

‡ Chesh Recog Rolls   Henry de Lacy, who was Constable of Chester, and custos of England, died at London, and was buried at St Paul s in 1310

§ It is so stated in an *Inq per B de certior* 16 Ric II [1392-3]

|| Cheshire Recognizance Rolls

¶ Another record gives 9th Nov as the day of his death   (Chesh Recog Rolls)

[*] *Inquisition post mortem* 16 Ric II [1392]

as descendants of a younger branch of the Audley family, and continued severed from the rest of the Audley Fee until it was sold, "*with all rights in Wich-Malbank*" &c to SIR ROBERT CHOLMONDELEY, BART, for £100, on the 24th Nov 22 Jac I [1624], by William, Earl of Bath as representative of the Bourchiers Lords Fitzwarine (*Harl MSS.* 1967 f 119 d)

SIR JOHN TOCHET, KT, LORD OF AUDLEY, succeeded his great uncle Sir Nicholas Audley. Mention is made of his departure to Aquitaine in the train of John, Duke of Aquitaine and Lancaster, in 1394 By his Inquisition *post mortem* he is found to have "died seized in his demesne as of fee *of a third part of a third part of the Barony of Wich Malbank*, held *in capite* of the Earl of Chester, yearly value £20 &c, on the Friday next before the feast of the Nativity" [25 Dec] in the year 1408, and ' James, son of the said John was his heir, and of the age of 12 years on the said Friday "

JAMES TOCHET, LORD AUDLEY, during his minority was committed to the custody of Henry Barton, citizen of London His proof of age being taken on the 4th Jan 1420-1, livery of his lands, including the part of the Barony held by Margaret, wife of Roger Hillary, Kt, was obtained on the 21st of the same month Like several of his ancestors, this Lord Audley was a warrior. He fell in battle at Bloreheath, in Staffordshire, on St. Tecla's Day, Sunday, 23rd Sept 1459, having been appointed to the command of the Lancastrian army, which was defeated with dreadful slaughter by Richard Neville, Earl of Salisbury

His Inquisition *post mortem* is not to be found at the Record Office, but he was succeeded by his son and heir, John Tochet, Kt

SIR JOHN TOCHET, KT, LORD OF AUDLEY, who thus succeeded, "died on Sunday next before the feast of St Michael the Archangel [29 Sept] last past [1490] leaving Sir James Tochet Kt., his son and heir, of the age of 26 years and upwards '

"He died seised of two parts of the Barony, Manor, and Lordship of Nantwich, two parts of the manor of Newhall parcel of the same Barony, with all the homage, suit, rents and services of all the freehold and customary tenants to the said two parts of a third part of the said Barony, Manor Lordship, belonging, allotted, and assigned, in Nantwich aforesaid, and in Fouleshurst,* Badynton [Baddington] Bromehall, Bertherton, Weston, Choileton, Saltersiche,† [in Nantwich-Willaston] Stapeley, Blakenhall, Wrenbury, Smallwode, Becheton, Hassall, Monks Copenhall, Worleston, Wodecote, Chorley, Aston, Newhall, Chester, Tiverton, and Acton, together with the mills, suits, Courts, and Tolls, to the said two parts of the said Barony, Manor, and Lordship belonging 6 Messuages, 70 acres of land, 5 acres of meadow, 6 acres of pasturage, 2 acres of moor, 2 acres of marsh and services and rent of 2 barbed arrows in Wirswall, the manor of Buglawton,‡ the manor of Tattenhall, and the advowson of the Church of Middlewich " (*Inquisition post mortem*)

SIR JAMES TOCHET, KT, LORD OF AUDLEY, who obtained livery of his father's lands on 3rd Nov. 1490, was the last of the family that had manorial property and rights in Nantwich. Within seven years after, these were forfeited to the Crown, by the attainder of Sir James, who had joined the Cornish Rising in 1497, and had thereby been guilty of the worst of all crimes—high treason Lord Bacon says, concerning this insurrection,

---

* There is no township now known as Fouleshurst, but a farm house, still called Fulleshurst Hall, is in Edlaston township, near Nantwich

† A field lying between Millstone Lane and Crewe Road, is named *Saltersiche*, in the Nantwich Survey of 1794

‡ Buglawton is now part of Congleton

"They [the Cornish] marched to Wells where the Lord Audley, with whom their leaders had before some secret intelligence, a nobleman of an ancient family, but unquiet and popular, and aspiring to ruin, came in to them, and was by them, with great gladness and cries of joy, accepted as their general, they being now proud that they were led by a nobleman The Lord Audley led them on from Wells to Salisbury and from Salisbury to Winchester. Thence the foolish people, who in effect, led their leaders, had a mind to be led into Kent, ... and encamped upon Blackheath, threatening either to bid battle to the King, ... or to take London within his view." The battle was fought on Saturday, 22nd June, 1497, but the rebels "being ill armed, and ill led, and without horse or artillery, they were with no great difficulty cut in pieces and put to flight " Lord Audley was taken prisoner, and led from Newgate to Tower-Hill, " in a paper coat painted with his own arms, the arms reversed, the coat torn, and he at Tower-Hill beheaded," on 28th June, 1497, being the third contemporary manorial lord of Nantwich that had been traitorous to King Henry VII

It is not known when nor in what manner these lands were regranted by the Crown, one portion appears to have become united with the Lovell lands, and was finally sold by Robert Fletcher to Sir Hugh Cholmondeley in 1556 (see posteá), while another part was obtained by the Fouleshurst family,* which in 1666, according to *Harl MSS.* 2010, f 21, was "held by *Mr Crewe, of Crewe,* and so must have become united with the Countess of Warwick's Fee in the Crewe family

* Edward Fulleshurst, in 1521, held lands in Sonde [Sound] and Coule of the Lord of Audley, in socage, yearly value £4 9s , and lands in Wich Malbank, of the Lord of Audley and the Lord Fitzwarin, in socage, yearly value £16 17s od " (Cheshire Recog Rolls)

THIRD DIVISION OF THE BARONY.

T remains to speak of the share of the Barony that fell to the third co-heiress of William, the last Norman Baron of Wich-Malbank, namely, to AUDA, who married Warin de Vernon, Baron of Shipbroke. The descent of this share is, however, confusing and unsatisfactory; and to trace in detail, and clear up the difficulties of the ramifications of these lands through many families of County gentry, is a task sufficient to discourage the most assiduous antiquary, even "Old Mortality" himself. The following brief summary will supply all necessary information on the subject.

After the death of WARIN, son of Warin de Vernon above-mentioned, this third part of the Barony was divided into two moieties.

I. One *Moiety* is traceable in the Cheshire Records through the second line of the VERNONS, Barons of Shipbroke, to the great family of SAVAGE of Clifton, near Frodsham. By a fine levied at Chester on Tuesday next after the feast of St. James the Apostle [July 25] 19 Edw. II, 1325, RICHARD VERNON granted to his near relative RALPH VERNON, *inter alia,* "a sixth part of the manor of Nantwich;" which descended by direct line to SIR RICHARD VERNON, KT., who died on 3rd Sept. 1419, leaving JAMES VERNON his kinsman heir to part of his estates, who married *Alice Savage;*[*] and who, on the 8th July, 1425, granted to trustees *"two parts of a sixth of the Manor of Nantwich,"* for JOHN SAVAGE, KT., who had livery of the same on 21st April, 1474, after the death of Eleanor, the wife of Richard Wheelock and heiress of Sir Richard Vernon;[†] at which time Sir Robert Fulleshurst, Kt., obtained the other part of the sixth of the manor of Nantwich, which thus became incorporated with the Countess of Warwick's Fee, as stated on page 28.

SIR JOHN SAVAGE, KT., of Clifton, near Frodsham, who married Catherine, daughter of Thomas Stanley, afterwards Lord Stanley, "died in the feast of St. Cecilia the Virgin

---

[*] This marriage explains how the Arms of *Vernon* and *Malbanc* came to be used in the 13 quarterings of the Arms of Sir Thomas Savage, Kt., once painted on the walls of Macclesfield Church, as given by Mr. Earwaker in his *"East Cheshire,"* Vol. II p. 492.

[†] Cheshire Recognizance Rolls.

[22 Nov] last past [1495], seised of,' *inter alia*, "a sixth part of the manor of Nantwich and of the perquisites of the Court, stalls, markets and fairs within the township of Nantwich, leaving *John Savage Esq* his grandson his heir.' (*Inquis p m* 11th Hen. VII)

To the memory of Sir John Savage and his lady Catherine, was erected a fine alabaster monument with their effigies, now standing on the south side of the chancel of Maccles-field Church *

SIR JOHN SAVAGE, KT , the next successor died on the 2nd March, 1527, and to his memory an effigy still remains in the Savage Chapel of Macclesfield Church † His Inquisition *post mortem*, states that he died seised of (as far as relates to Nantwich)—

"A sixth part of the manor of Wich Malbank, a sixth part of the issues and profits of the water-mills there,‡ and a sixth part of the pleas and perquisites of the courts &c of the town of Wich Malbank, held of the Earl of Chester, *in capite*, by the 30th part of a Knight's fee , yearly value 20 shillings , and that John his son and heir was of the age of 34 years and more

SIR JOHN SAVAGE, KT , who thus succeeded, died on 26th July, 1528, and was buried in the Savage Chapel, Macclesfield, where a handsome tomb, with effigies of Sir John and his lady, still exists to their memory § His son and heir, SIR JOHN SAVAGE, KT , sold his share of the manor of Nantwich to *Sir Hugh Cholmondeley, Kt* , on 3rd Jan 17 Eliz. [1574-5]. (*Harl MSS*. 2038 f 119 b)

II The other *Moiety* became subdivided among the three co-heiresses of the second Warin Vernon, named *Maud, Roesia,* and *Auda*

[A] MAUD, wife of Sir Richard Wilbraham, had issue Maude wife of *Robert de Winnington,* who was the ancestor of the LEFTWICH family In 1407 ROBERT DE LEFTWICH died seized of a thirty-sixth part of the Barony of Wich-Malbank, held of the Earl of Chester by barony,‖ consisting of " 2 messuages and 1 salt-pit, in Wich-Malbank, yearly value 14s 8d , a parcel of land in Acton, and one messuage in Hurdelestone, yearly value 6s. 4d " This thirty-sixth part was sold by RALPH LEFTWICH to *Sir Hugh Cholmondeley,* in the 17 Eliz [1574-5], and confirmed to him by a fine in the following year ¶

[B] ROESIA, the second co-heiress, married *John de Littlebury,* who sold this part of the Barony to JOHN DE WETTENHALL After the death of SIR JOHN DE WETENHALE, KT , (before 1400) it was divided between his two daughters, *Margery* and *Ellen*

1 MARGERY brought her share in marriage to *Geoffrey de Bromhale,* whose daughter, *Alice,* married *John de Davenport,* the ancestor of the DAVENPORTS of Bramhall Hall, near Stockport. The Inquisition *p m.* of the said Margery, taken in 1433, sets forth that she was

"seized in her demesne, as of fee, of an 18th part of the barony of Wich Malbank, and of 14 burgages, 2 tofts, 30 acres of land, 1½ acres of meadow, and 1 salt-pit of 12 leads, in the town of Wich Malbank, of the yearly value of 40 shillings , of 43s 8d rent in the same town issuing out of tenements held by *John Wright, John Walker, Thomas Daukynsone, John Hildiche, Hugh Hunt, John Brothersone,*

---

* An engraving of this monument is given in Mr Earwaker s "*East Cheshire,*" vol 11, opposite page 493 Interesting accounts of the Savage family will be found in that History , and also in Mr Beamont s History of Frodsham

† An engraving of the monument is given in "*East Cheshire,*" vol 11 p 491

‡ This *Inq* was traversed as far as regards the possession "*of a sixth part of a water-mill at Wich Malbon on the water of Weaver,*" which it appears Sir John gave to his cousin *John Davenport* (See Cheshire Plea Rolls, 23 Hen VIII)

§ An engraving of th s monument is given in '*East Cheshire,*' vol 11, p 495

‖ *Inquisitio de melius inqu rendo,* dated 26th Oct 1409 Pub Record Office

¶ *Harl MSS* 1967 f 119 h 1.

Henry de Wetenhale, Robert Alva, Roger Oteworth, John Wildbore and *William de Fouleshurst,* of 5 shillings rent issuing out of the manor of *Derfold,* [Dorfold], &c , of an 18th part of the court baron in the said town of Wich Malbank, together with an 18th part of the tolls of the same town, yearly value 20 shillings, 18th part of the tolls of salt and of 2 mills in the same town, yearly value 10 shillings, with an 18th part of 300 acres of pasture and waste, in the town of Wich Malbank, yearly value 12d all which said lands and rents formed the said 18th part of the barony aforesaid, held of the Earl of Chester, *in capite*, and of the yearly value of £6 3s 2d " &c

This share of the barony remained in the Davenport family until WILLIAM DAVENPORT,* of Bramhall, Kt , and WILLIAM his son and heir apparent, sold their interest in Wich-Malbank on 20th Jan in 22 Jac I [1625-6] to *Sir Robert Cholmondeley* for £100 (*Harl. MSS.* 1967 f. 119 d)

2 ELLEN, the other co-heiress, married *Henry de Arderne* This share, called a thirty-sixth part of the barony, and valued in 9 Hen IV [1407-8] at £20, consisted of the manor of Acton and demesne of Dorfold, but did not embrace any manorial rights in Nantwich.

[C] AUDA, the third co-heiress, married *William Stafford,* "from whom, or whose descendant of the same name," says Dr Ormerod, "this last share passed by purchase to JOHN ST PIERRE † This portion, described as an eighteenth part, was certainly held by the Pierre family as late as 36 and 37 Hen VI [1458-9] and after many vicissitudes became vested before the 3 Hen VII [1487-8] in the MAINWARINGS of Carincham, until the 13th Jan 17 Eliz [1574-5] when it was sold by RANDLE MAINWARING to *Sir Hugh Cholmondeley* (*Harl MSS.* 2038 f. 144)

The proportional shares of the privileges claimed by the various lords of Wich-Malbank in the town during the reigns of Henry VI and Henry VII, are clearly shown in the following tables —

BAILIFF'S ACCOUNTS OF WICH-MALBANK 36 & 37 Hen VI ‡

"Upon the view of the Accounts at Wich Malbanke for one whole year, beginning at the feast of St Michael, a° 36 Hen VI [1457]

	s	d	
The Ld Audeley .	53	4	} . £4
The Ld Fitzwarin .	26	8	}
The Lds Lovell & Browning .			. . £4
Vernon wth ye Dower .	£2 0	0	}
St Pere	13	4	} £4
Fulleshurst & Leftwich	13	4	}
Wetenhall & Davenport .	. 13	4	}
"The whole sum of the estreits & p'quisets of ye court for ye said whole year was			} . . £12

---

* According to the *Inquisition p m* of Sir William Davenport, of Bramhall, Kt , the grandfather of this Sir William, taken 11th Oct 19 Eliz [1577], the said Sir William died seised " of the 20th part of the manor of Wich Malban, and messuages, lands, and rents in Wich Malban, held of the Queen as Countess of Chester, and are worth £23 13s 10d per annum " (Farwaker s "*East Cheshire*" vol I p 428)

† By Inquisition p m 28 Edw I [1300], URIAN DE ST PIERRE died seised, *inter alia,* of an 18th part of the barony of Wich Malbank, and 2 salt pits there Ormerod's Cheshire, vol II p 603, New Edit

‡ Add MSS Brit Mus 6032, f 61-2, p 124-5

" *Wich Malbank*   The Accompts there of Nicolas Hewster & John Leech Baylifes there from the feast of St Michael in ye 37 of Hen VI for one whole year after all charges and decayed rent discharged   £14 10   6

[of which] The Ld Audley [claimed]	.	£3 4 6 ob ⎫	£4 16 9 ob
The Ld Fitzwaren		£1 12 3 qr ⎭	

		s d	
The part for ye Lord Lovel for himself & Browning's [part]		⎱	£4 16 10
The parte of Vernon with ye Dower		48 6 ⎫	
The pte of St Pere	.	16 1 ob ⎮	£4 16 10 ob
Davenport & Wetenhall	.	16 1 ob ⎰	
Fulleshurst & Leftwich		16 1 ob ⎭	

The following table, given in *Harl MSS* 2038 f. 134, shows the proportional shares of the Barony of Wich-Malbank before the attainder of Lord Lovell 3 Hen. VII. [1487-8].

The whole Barony of Wich Malbank is divided in 36 parts

Lord Lovell has	12 parts, namely one third of the Barony
Lord Audley has 8 parts ⎱ Lord Fitzwarine has 4 parts ⎰	12 parts, which make one third of the Barony
John Savage Kt has 6 parts ⎫ Will Davenport Kt has 2 parts ⎮ Hen Mainwaring Esq has 2 parts ⎬ . Robt Fouleshurst Esq has 1 part ⎮ Raphe Leftwich Esq has 1 part ⎭	12 parts, which make one third of the Barony

"For prouve [proof] of this deuision Rafe Egerton Esq, doth pay a fee farm rent forth of his mills in Namptwich to euery of the p'tners p'portionable to his p't [part], and the balyes [bailiffs] of namptwiche did in tymes past account for fines amersments & tolles and other casualtyes p'portionable to his divysion as by the same accompt may appeere "

A COPIE of ye RENTALL, without date [but c 1525] *of RENT paid out of ye MILNES of NAMPTWICH to ye KING & LORDES* [of Wich-Malbank] [*]

		s d		s d	
To ye King	.	.	.	13 4	Wm Church p[er] p'chase
The Ld Audeley	.	3 4 ⎫		5 0	Egerton Ld Chamb'ln p[er] p'chase
The Ld Fitzwarin	. .	1 8 ⎭			
Thomas Fulshurst 5d ⎫ Rich Leftwich 5d ⎭	10d ⎫				
Davenport with Wetenhall 10d ⎬ Randle Mainwaring . 10d ⎭	2 6 ⎬	.	5 0		
Sr John Savage Kt	.	2 6 ⎭			

"It is said that Sr Will Hanley, Kt, did erect a milne by graunt from ye King & the Barons, the King then having Lovels 3rd part by Attaynder, which Hanley had an attachment & watercourse from Sr John Bromley, Kt and it seemeth that by the attaynder of Stanley ye King had 8s 4d yearly over & above 5 shillings which came to him by the attaynder of Lovell "

* Add MSS Brit Mus 6032, f 61-2 p 124-5

The Baron's Fee.*

A S has been shown in the foregoing pages, the Barony of Wich-Malbank, with the exception of the *Abbot's Fee*, and *Countess of Warwick's Fee*, became united in the Cholmondeley family by various purchases in the years 1556, 1575 and 1625.

SIR HUGH CHOLMONDELEY, KT., died, at the age of 83, on 16th Jan. 39 Eliz. [1596-7]; and his Inquisition *post mortem* taken in the same year,

"finds that he died seised," *inter alia*, "of 19/20ths of the manor or barony of Wich Malbank, alias Namptwiche, with all its rights, which are largely enumerated, and various lands and messuages therein, including '*Le Booth Hall*,' or '*Le Court Howse*,' and another tenement called '*Escheator's Halle*;' those parts of the barony formerly the Lovell lands, and Audley Fee, being held *in capite* from the Queen as of her crown of England, by the service of a 20th part of one Knight's fee; and the rest held by the service of a 10th part of a Knight's fee from the said Queen as Countess of Chester, value per annum 40 marks. [£26 13s. 4d.]; and that Sir Hugh Cholmondelegh Kt., was his son and heir, and of the age of 46 years."

SIR HUGH CHOLMONDELEY, KT., who succeeded, married the celebrated Mary Holford, whom King James called the "*Bold Ladie of Cheshire*." He died at Cholmondeley on 23rd July 43 Eliz. [1601]; leaving Robert Cholmondeley, "his son and heir, of the age of 19 years, on the 16th June last past." [1601].

Two Inquisitions *post mortem* were taken after Sir Hugh's death, by which it was found that he died seized of, *inter alia* :—

"Nineteen parts [i.e. 19/20ths] of the manor or Barony of Nantwich with all and singular rents, reversions, services, fairs, markets, stallage, tolls, fees, Knight wards, marriages, escheats, reliefs, heriots, courts leet, view of frankpledge, profits and perquisites, amerciaments, goods and chattels, waifs, estrays, liberties, franchises, privileges and other profits and hereditaments whatsoever of the said 19 parts of the said manor or Barony of Nantwich; a messuage called the *Booth Hall*† otherwise the *Court-house* in Nantwich; a capital messuage and tenement in the same place called the *Escheator's Hall*;‡ 7 other messuages; 8 cottages; 12 gardens and 9 court-yards there; a certain place of land there called the *Taintree yard*§ containing by estimation 2 roods of land therein; another place of land there in *Pillory Street* containing by estimation 2 roods of land, with 2 barns erected; another place of land called the *Donghill place*, containing by estimation 4 roods of land; another parcel of land there in *Barkers' Street* containing by estimation 2 roods of land; 13 messuages or salt-houses there, called wiche-houses, containing in all 78 leads; and £20 9s. 10d. clear rent there."

---

* So called in *Harl. MSS.* 2010 f. 21, in a list of the Lords of the several Fees of Nantwich, dated 1666.

† *Booth Hall*, or *Court House*, afterwards called the Market Hall, stood in the High Street, which continued to be the market place until 1868.

‡ *Escheator's Hall* was situated in Beam Street.

§ *Taintree Yard*. In a Rate Book, *penes* G. F. Wilbraham, Esq., dated 1691, mention is made in Beam Street of "Mr. Broomhall's, ho[use]; Mill; Meadow & *Tentry* garden."

In the second Inquisition taken 3 Jac I. [1605-6] it is stated that certain premises in *Barker Street* and *Masons Yards* which had belonged to the *Griffins* of Bartherton, were escheated to Sir Hugh when George Griffin died at Stapeley on the 9th May 43 Eliz. [1601] without heirs of his body, he being a bastard

What follows relating to the Cholmondeley descent is, in substance, the same as that given by Dr. Ormerod in 1816. Unfortunately, no opportunity has occurred for examining the deeds and documents preserved in the muniment chest at Cholmondeley, where, doubtless, much information relating to the family, as well as to Nantwich and its neighbourhood, might be obtained that would be valuable to the local historian

SIR ROBERT CHOLMONDELEY was created *Bart* on 29th June, 1611, *Viscount* Cholmondeley of Kells in Ireland, in 1628, and *Baron*, by the title of LORD CHOLMONDELEY OF WICH-MALBANK in 1645, the last honour being conferred on him by Letters patent for his services as a zealous royalist in the Civil War   He afterwards compounded for his estates, by paying the enormous sum of £7742 and retired to *Bickley Hall* where he spent the residue of his days   He died without lawful issue on 8th Oct 1659, and from some disputes relative to the defraying of the expenses of his funeral, by the heirs of his real and personal property, his body was left uninterred for the space of one year, when, on 8th Oct 1660, it was carried to the family vault in Malpas Church in great pomp. He was succeeded by his nephew of the same name

ROBERT VISCOUNT CHOLMONDELEY, of Kells, of whom little is known, died in 1681 and was succeeded by his eldest son Hugh

HUGH VISCOUNT CHOLMONDELEY, was created *Lord Cholmondeley of Nantwich* on 10th April, 1680, with limitation to his brother George, as a reward for his opposition to the unconstitutional conduct of James II   By patent 27th Dec 1706, he was created Viscount Malpas and Earl of Cholmondeley, with the same limitation as in his former title   He was displaced from several important public offices and trusts in 1713, but restored on the accession of George I   He died unmarried 18th Jan, and was buried at Malpas Feb 30th, 1724-5

GEORGE, second EARL OF CHOLMONDELEY, *Baron of Nantwich*, &c succeeded to the title and estates of his brother Earl Hugh   Educated at Christ Church, Oxford, he entered the army, and was made cornet of horse in 1685, and groom of the bed-chamber on King William's accession   At the battle of the Boyne he commanded the horse grenadier guards, and particularly distinguished himself at the battle of Steenkirk in Aug. 1692. In the first year of Queen Anne, he was raised to be Major-general of her Majesty's forces, and Governor of the forts of Tilbury and Gravesend, and held these posts after the accession of George I. On 15th Feb 1714-5, he was constituted Captain and Colonel of the 3rd troop of horse-guards, on 15th March, created an Irish Peer, the following year, 2nd July, 1716, being advanced to an English Peerage, by the title of Baron of Newburgh in Anglesea   In 1724 he was appointed Lord-lieutenant of the co and City of Chester, and *Custos rotulorum* of the said county, and also Lord-lieutenant of the six counties of North Wales   In 1725 he was made Governor of Kingston-upon-Hull, which at that time was a sinecure worth about £600 per annum   and in 1732 George I made him General of the Horse, and Governor of the island of Guernsey.   He died at Whitehall on the 7th May, and on the 17th May, 1733, was buried at Malpas; leaving his son George his successor

GEORGE THIRD EARL OF CHOLMONDELEY, *Baron of Nantwich*, &c , was born 2nd Jan. 1702-3 , and previous to his succession to his father s title, had been M P. in two parliaments, being elected for East Loe in 1724, and for Windsor in 1727   Like his father, he was high in honour at Court , and on the accession of George II, was constituted one of the Commissioners of the Admiralty, and Governor of Chester   He succeeded his father as Lord-lieutenant of the County, and *Custos rotulorum*   and Chamberlain of the County , and subsequently held, among other offices of honour and public trust, the Vice-admiralship of Cheshire , the Governorship of Chester Castle , the stewardship of the royal manor of Sheene. and was one of his Majesty's privy council

He died on 10th June, and was buried on 21st June, 1770, at Malpas.   His successor being his grandson, George James Cholmondeley

GEORGE JAMES, FIRST MARQUIS OF CHOLMONDELEY and EARL OF ROCK SAVAGE, who was elevated to that rank of the Peerage on 22nd Nov 1815 , Baron of Nantwich, &c , succeeded his grandfather , his father, George, lord viscount Malpas, having died in 1764   He was born 30th April, 1749, and succeeded as Lord-lieutenant and *Custos rotulorum* of co of Chester, and Governor of Chester Castle   He was appointed his Majesty's envoy extraordinary and plenipotentiary to the court of Berlin 14th June, 1782 and in the following year was sworn a privy-counsellor   On the death of Horace, Earl of Orford, he succeeded to the ancient Walpole Estates in Norfolk and elsewhere was Chamberlain and Vice-Admiral of Cheshire, and Lord steward of the royal household, &c. He died on 10th April, 1827, and was succeeded by his two sons in succession , first by *George James Horatio*, and then by *William Henry*, the present Marquis.

GEORGE JAMES HORATIO, EARL OF ROCK SAVAGE, and after his father s death, *Second Marquis of Cholmondeley and Baron of Nantwich*, was born on 17th Jan 1792 He was joint-hereditary great Chamberlain of England , and died, without issue, at Cholmondeley Castle on 8th May, 1870, and was buried at Malpas on the 15th day of the same month He was the last possessor of the Barony of Nantwich, with its ancient privileges, &c

By an Indenture dated 14th Feb 1862, "all MARKETS and FAIRS held within and for the town of Nantwich, and all rents, tolls, pickage, stallage and other dues, franchises, customs, privileges, profits, easements, rights and appurtenances, belonging &c to the said markets and fairs," were relinquished by the Marquis in favour of the Nantwich Local Board

In 1869 the BARONY, a waste piece of land which had until then been retained as part of the ancient feudal barony, by the possession of which the Barons Cholmondeley claimed the right of holding annually a Court Leet and Baron for the town, was enclosed by order of the Enclosure Commissioners, who allotted it in the following manner —

A	R	P	
2	0	2	to Lord Cholmondeley in satisfaction of his rights as Lord of the Manor
8	0	0	as a Public Recreation Ground , vested in the Churchwardens and Overseers.
9	0	22	as a Public Park, vested in seven trustees, viz —the Rt Hon Lord Tollemache, Wilbraham S Tollemache, Esq , of Dorfold, E D Broughton, Esq , of Wistaston; Mr. Hignett, of Cholmondeley, and Messrs. Leonard Gilbert, Samuel Harlock, and Thomas Bowker, of Nantwich.
2	1	0	as a site for a proposed Smithfield, Cattle Market, and Sheep Market, vested in the Nantwich Local Board.

The remainder being sold in building lots to pay the expenses of enclosure

The Courts Leet and Baron were abolished about thirty years ago when County Courts were established by Act of Parliament. Copies of a few of the Court Leet Rolls, affording evidence of the powers possessed by the Barons in former times, and throwing much light on the history of the town, are fortunately preserved in the Wilbraham MSS. It will be interesting to show from these and other records, what was the extent of the privileges of this local jurisdiction, what town officers were required, what their duties were, together with other customs and usuages belonging thereto, which have now for ever passed away.

In the 15 Hen. VII. [1500] the lords of Wich-Malbank were required by writ from Prince Arthur, as Earl of Chester, to show "*quo warranto*," (i e. by what title) they claimed for themselves and their heirs manorial franchises and privileges in the town; and, as Sir William Stanley and Lord Audley had recently been attainted, the following six lords only appeared to answer the summons, namely — John Bourchier Lord Fitz-Warine; John Savage, of Clifton, Knight, William Davenport, of Bramhall, Esq ; Robert Fouleshurst, of Crewe, Esq., Randle Mainwaring, of Carincham, Esq ; Richard Leftwich, of Leftwich, Esq

Copies of the pleas put forward in this inquiry will be found in *Harl. MSS.* 2115 f. 168, 172 and 186, but they are too long to be given here. The liberties claimed and allowed were—

1 View of frank-pledge with its appurtenances, with respect to all residents therein, twice in the year.

2 A Hundred Court, with its appurtenances, to be held from 15 to 15 days

3 Waif,* stray,† gallows,‡ tumbrel, and thewe, with manorial rights in the vill of Wich-Malbank

4 A yearly fair on the feast of St Bartholomew and four following days §

5 A market weekly on Saturday, with the appurtenances of fair and market, and 4d toll from every horse or beast of burthen sold therein, picage‖ and stallage¶ in the market and fair, 2d from every cart-load of leather, and 1d for every bundle of leather sold therein, or exposed to sale

6 Pelfe*⁎ in the same manor

In explanation of the "*appurtenances*" of their *view of frank-pledge* the said lords of Wich-Malbank claimed the usual privileges of a Court Leet for any manor, viz —"assize of bread and beer, cognizance of effusion of blood, punishment of butchers and fishermen selling tainted flesh or fish, punishment of bakers by the *pillory*, victuallers or inn-holders [*pandoxatores*] by the *tumbrel*, and scolds by the *thewe* [or cucking-stool], with all fines and amerciaments of the same

* ' *Waif*," i e any goods waived (or left) by a felon, within the manor, became the property of the lord of the manor

† "*Strays*," i e animals straying into the manor, might be detained, and if after proclamation they were not claimed by the owners within a year and a day, they then belonged to the lord of the manor

‡ *Gallows* i e the right of hanging a convicted felon within the manor

§ This annual fair is now held on *one day* in the year, namely, on the 4th September

‖ "*Picage*" i e the erection of a "scabellum" [low bench or form] to expose merchandise on

¶ "*Stallage*," i e the right of erecting stalls

*⁎ "*Pelfe*," i e the right of appropriating the goods of any robber taken within the manor.

The Manorial Courts.

The *Court Leet* with its *view of frank-pledge,* was superior to all other local courts, inasmuch as it could inquire into *all* offences against the King and country "It had the power to present by jury all crimes whatsoever that happened within its jurisdiction; and not only to present but also to punish all trivial misdemeanours, as all trivial debts were recovered in the *Court Baron;* justice in these minuter matters of both kinds being brought to the doors of every man by our ancient constitution. The objects of its jurisdiction were very numerous, being such as affected the public weal or good government of the town, from common nuisances and other material offences against the King's peace and public trade, down to eaves-dropping, waifs, and irregularities in public commons.*

The *view of frank-pledge* was the survival of an ancient Saxon law, by which every freeman gave a pledge for his good behaviour to his King and country. Upon an offence being committed by a person, his *sureties* were obliged either to surrender him or pay a fine for his misdeeds.

The *Court Baron* was incident to every manor, and in ancient times sat at Nantwich from fifteen to fifteen days,—that is, allowing an interim of a fortnight and a day between each sitting The business of this Court was to record transfers or surrenders of land, and receive heriots, duties and customs, (cases that were decided by the lord or his Steward as sole judge), or to take cognizance of trespasses, debts, slanders, &c , where the damage did not exceed forty shillings, (these latter cases being tried by a local jury of freeholders).

The *Court Leet* met twice in the year at Nantwich, within three weeks after Lady-day and Michaelmas, when all persons above twelve years of age and under sixty, resident within the jurisdiction for a year and a day, were obliged to render suit and service, i e. to attend in person and answer to their names. The place of meeting in the sixteenth century would be the *"Court Howse,"* (page 63). In recent times the Court met in an old building in the Lamb Inn Yard, now used as the Masonic Lodge Room, and in the Assembly Room of the Crown Inn

The Court was presided over by the Steward of the lord, who was usually a barrister, the last being the late Richard Edleston, Esq of Nantwich. The following was the "order of the Court." Six days notice having been given, on the meeting of the Court, the *Bailiff* opened with the proclamation—

'Oyez ! Oyez ! Oyez !' [i e Hear ye ! Hear ye ! Hear ye !]

'All manner of persons who owe suit and service at this Court let them draw near and answer to their names, or send their essoignes ' [excuse]

The names were then read over, and fines imposed in case of non-attendance Then the Bailiff announced—

'Oyez ! Oyez ! Oyez !

'All manner of persons who have any more to do at this court let them come forth, and they shall be heard, otherwise they and all others may depart hence, and give their attendances at the adjourned court '

* See *"Commentaries on Laws of England,'* by H J Stephen, vol iv p 340 1845 Edit

Then a Jury was empanelled, and the following oath administered to each one —

"You shall inquire and true presentment make of all such things as shall be given in charge, or come to your knowledge, touching this present service The King's Counsel, your own, and your fellows, you shall well and truly keep, you shall present no one through hatred or malice, nor conceal anything through love or affection, but in all things, you shall well and truly present as the same shall come to your knowledge. So help you God !"

The Jury first fixed the fines on all non-attenders at court, they then received the reports of the various town officers, for the past half-year, inflicting a fine on such as neglected their duty The submitted reports having been investigated and verdicts given, the concluding business was to elect the following town officers for the ensuing year viz —

1 —*Rulers of Walling,* or Inspectors of the *salt-works,* who appear to have been annually elected until the beginning of the eighteenth century.*

2 —*Heath-keepers,* who reported concerning the ancient common called *Beam Heath.*

3 —*Leave-lookers,* or Market Inspectors, who examined all weights and measures, seized unwholesome meat and fish, and looked after the customs and tolls

4 —*Ale-tasters,* officers appointed by every court-leet to see that bakers made good bread, and brewers strong drink †

5 —*Fire-lookers,* who reported defective chimnies, &c, and inspected buildings with the view of preventing, as far as possible, destruction of property by fire

6 —*Channel-lookers* or public scavengers, whose duty it was to see that the inhabitants cleaned their parts of the streets in front of their own houses, shops, buildings, &c, and that wells, drains, &c were cleansed Mr Platt, writing in 1819, makes the following remark concerning these town officers —"If I may form my opinion from the state of the streets, either the office must be abolished or the officers defunct," and those who remember Nantwich forty or fifty years ago, bear testimony to the extreme filthy state of the town, when heaps of ashes, manure, &c, and pools of stagnant filthiness, were suffered to remain undisturbed in the principal thoroughfares of the town At a depth varying from a yard to six or eight feet below the present level of the streets, is to be found a lower pavement of blackened beams of wood, which, together with the overlying strata of black mould, are popularly believed to be the *debris* of the great fire of 1583, but, it seems more reasonable to suppose, and much easier to believe, that the old pavements have been buried by accumulations of modern times, rather than by the embers and ashes of a burnt town above three hundred years ago.

7 —*Constables,* who, having been previously recommended by the Vestry, were appointed by this Court, on their taking the *oath to serve the King and the Lord of the Manor* In point of power, they were the superior officers of the town, and, like the others, were unpaid officers It was their duty to detect crime, arrest offenders, and maintain public order. The last of the Parish Constables were *Mr John Prince* and *Mr. .. Pritchard.* The latter person was the first petty Constable for the township of Nantwich, acting under the first Special High Constable for the Hundred of Nantwich, *Mr Becket,* both being appointed under Sir Robert Peel's County Constabulary Act

* See Account of the Salt-works, where their duties are more fully explained
† The Parish Register records the burial of an "Ale-taster" during his year of office —
"1758 June 13, John Savonry, ale-officer" [Buried].

8 —*The Bailiff, or "Bedell,"* as he is sometimes called in ancient records, "was the supreme officer of the town, in reputation, and had the like respect paid him that was usually given to bailiffs of legal corporations. He was annually chosen [with the other officers] at the Court-leet after *Michaelmas,* with the consent of the Lord of the Leet, and while he had the Lord's consent and countenance he was a useful officer to the town; but, upon some displeasure taken by the Lord Cholmondeley, his election was suspended and never since renewed" (Partridge's *Hist Nantwich,* p 18) The same writer also says, (p 9 *ibid*) that Earl Cholmondeley has "*the privilege of a jail, and appointing the keeper who is generally the Bailiff to the Court Baron.*"

In the Parish Registers frequent mention is made of the town Bailiffs, but the earliest "gaoler" in those records, occurs as follows —

"1739 July 30, John, son of William Hopwood, *Gaoler* " [Baptized]

The last Bailiff and Gaoler whose duty it was to serve summonses for debts, and attend the Court to swear the same had been duly served, &c., was the late *Mr James Topham,* who was appointed by the following deed —*

"Know all men by these Presents That I the Most Noble George James Marquis Cholmondeley, Viscount Malpas, and Baron of Wich-Malbank otherwise Malbanewic otherwise Nantwich in the county of Chester Have made constituted and appointed and by these presents Do make constitute and appoint James Topham of Nantwich in the said county Plumber and Glazier Serjeant at Mace of the Court of our Lord the King for the Hundred of Wich-Malbank otherwise Malbanewic otherwise Nantwich in the said county of Chester And also of the Courts Leet and Courts Baron with view of Frankpledge for the same Hundred and likewise serjeant at Mace of the Court Leet and Court Baron with view of Frankpledge for my Manor or Barony of Wich-Malbank otherwise Malbanewic &c and to do and execute all things belonging to the office of serjeant at Mace of the said Courts respectively And also *Gaoler* or Keeper of the *Gaol* or *Prison* for the same Hundred and Barony and each of them during my will and Pleasure

In witness whereof I have hereunto set and put my hand and seal this 29th day of Sept in the year of our Lord 1825 '

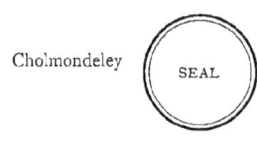

Cholmondeley

Signed sealed and delivered
(being first duly stampt) by
the abovenamed Marquis in
the presence of

William Jones

This Mr Topham † who resided at the *Gaol House* in Pillory Street, where his daughter still lives, was also the last collector of the Cholmondeley Tolls, which at that time were let for £12 per annum, he held office until the late Marquis yielded the tolls into the hands of the Local Board, in 1862, after which, by agreement dated 21st July, 1866, he received as compensation, a life annuity from the town of £40 per ann

On Fair days it was customary for Mr. Topham to announce at the Stocks in High Town, between the hours of twelve and one o'clock, the following proclamation —‡

---

* From the original deed now in the possession of Miss Topham, of the Gaol House, Nantwich

† Mr James Topham died 15th Dec 1869, aged 86

‡ From an original paper in the possession of Miss Topham

" *Oyez ! Oyez ! Oyez !*

" The Most Noble George Horatio Marquis Cholmondeley Viscount Malpas and Baron of Nantwich, in Her Majesty's name doth strictly charge and command all manner of persons who shall resort to this Fair not to hold any unlawful assembly or commit any affray or bloodshed within the limits of this town, during the continuance thereof, upon pain of imprisonment, or other punishment by fine, for disturbing the peace,

And further, that no person whatsoever presume to wear or carry any manner of Bills, Halberts, or other unlawful weapons, upon pain of fine or imprisonment, except such as attend the Steward and Bailiff of this Fair .

And all persons who shall buy any cattle, pewter, brass, iron or other ware above the price of twelve pence, are enjoined not to conceal the same, or convey them out of the Town, until they be lawfully tolled for

And notice is hereby given that the Fair for Horses is to be kept in the usual place, and if any controversy arise between Buyer and Seller, the person aggrieved may resort to the Steward, who will hear and determine the difference according to equity and justice

And further, all persons coming to this Fair may stay or depart without molestation provided they demean themselves orderly and civilly   But all Rogues, Vagabonds, and other idle or suspicious persons upon this proclamation made, are immediately ordered to leave the Town upon pain of imprisonment "

" God save the Queen, and the Most Noble George Horatio the Marquis of Cholmondeley "

The following extracts from the Court Rolls of the town, are here given from the Wilbraham MS. collection preserved at Delamere.

Court Rolls.   Barony of Wich-Malbank.

" *Paines and bylawes laid downe & imposed by the Grand Jurye at a Leet* houlden for the Barons of Namptwiche the 27° Apr   Anno R.[egno] Re[ginæ] Elizab Angliæ nunc &c. 34to [1592]*

" *Donghills.*   We doe ordaine that every perso[n] within the Fee of this Court doe remove their donghills that lye within any of the streets of this Court of Namptwiche, or within 8 yoords [yards] of any street or lane of and within the same towne on this side the feast of St John Baptist [June 24] next ensuing   and not to vse them for muckhills hereaftr to th' annoyance of the Inhabitants, or for mattr that may breed infection, vpon paine of every one that maketh defalt herein to forfait—39s. 11d

Swyne   Styes   It^m that noe inhabitant within this Fee shall set or keepe any swynestye or Privye within 8 yards of any the streetes or lanes vpo paine of 39s. 11d to be forfaitted   if aftr Midsom'. day [24 June] next any such be found to stand so erected

Water-   course   It^m we doe paine Rich Chestr yt he shall not hereaftr stop a watercourse or ditch adioyning to the Beame street vpo[n] paine of xxs [20s]

* *Leet* signifies *Law-Day*

Wm. Tench   *Itm* The Jurie doe prsent yᵗ Wᵐ Tench of the Bridgend hath not forfaited the
his Porch.   paine of 39ˢ 11ᵈ ob. [39s. 11½d] heretofore imposed vpon him for yᵗ he hath
removoued his Porch and railes adioyning to the high street, according as he
was pained heretofore   And a paine is further now layd yᵗ yᵉ sᵈ Wᵐ Tench shall remoue
the same Porche & rayles before Midsom' next upon the like paine of 39ˢ 11ᵈ ob.
[39s. 11½d.]

"Shoppes. We doe amerce [fine] John Crew of Cholmestⁿ for yᵗ he hath not removoued soe
much of his shops at the Bridgend as doth stand vpo the high street in 6ˢ 8ᵈ
& we doe paine him to remoue yᵗ incrochemᵗ before Midsom'. next vpon paine of
xxxixˢ xjᵈ ob. [39s. 11½d]

Ashes.   *Itm* we doe prsent yᵗ John Cowper & Ric· Smith haue forfaited eyther of them
the seuerall sume of 39ˢ 11ᵈ ob. for carying forth of Ashes out of this Towne
for the making of glasse contrary to the paine of the Court heretofore made 32° Elizᵗʰ
[1590], and we confirme the same ordinance of the Court therein heretofore made to be
continued and stand in effect hereaftᵣ agˢᵗ euery perso yᵗ shall offend therein *sub pœna
p'dict* [under the penalty aforesaid]

Rand[le].   Authority is given by this Inquest vnto the now Rulers of the Walling of this
Horton.   Towne of Namptwich yᵗ they forthwith stop Randle Hortoⁿ for the walling of
Pauements.   the 3 leads appointed vnto him heretofore by this court, towards the charges
of his part of repairing the Pauementˢ wᵗʰin the sᵈ Towne now by his defalt
in ruine and decay, except the sᵈ Ran Hortoⁿ doe then enter into Bond wᵗʰ some sufficient
sureties in the sume of 5 markes [£3 6s 8d] vnto the said Rulers & Steward of this
Court speedilie to repaire his pt. of the sᵈ Pauemᵗ And soe froᵐ tyme to tyme to keepe
the same repaired & amended accordinglie.

Bowles.   A paine is laid yᵗ noe persoⁿ shall hereaftᵣ cast or throwe Bowles within anie the
streetes of the Towne vpoⁿ paine to forfait for euery such offence xxˢ [20s]

Bandoggs   *Itm* yᵗ noe persoⁿ shall suffer any Bandoggs to goe at liberty within this Towne
not being strait musled vpoⁿ paine of xxˢ [20s]

Swyne   *Itm* yᵗ none of yᵉ Inhabitants of this Towne shall suffer their swyne to goe at
liberty abroad in the streets of this Towne vpoⁿ paine of 3ˢ 4ᵈ

Bellman   It is ordered & agreed by the whole homagers of this Court that euery Belman
Fishboords   of this Towne shall euery tyme hereaftᵣ when he placeth fishboords in the
sᵈ Towne, at the same tyme place and sett Rindges & Tubbs vnder the sᵈ fishboords for the receauing of the Garbage of the fish, then to be sould & shall not suffer
the Garbage thereof to be cast or throwen downe vpo the Pauemenᵗ· nor the said fishboords
to be washed or scoured vpoⁿ the Pauements vpoⁿ paine yᵗ the Belman shall forfait for
euery day wherein any defalt shalbe made iijˢ iiijᵈ [3s. 4d] And for the better putting
in executioⁿ of this Ordinance, *Tho. Church*, mercer, is auctorised to be Ouerseer herein
& to prsent every defalt.

Donghills   *Itm* yᵗ Tho Minshull mercer, Geoffrey Minshul and Hugh Mainwaring shall
before Midsumer next remoue & carry away their seuerall middinges or donghills
adioyning to the Church wall vpoⁿ paine of xiijˢ iiijᵈ [13s. 4d]

Lamporne. It^m y^t all the occupier of the lands w^thin this Fee betweene the *schoole howse*
          & the water of Weeuer shall before Whitsontyde next scoure the comon cesterne
called *Lamporne* in euery place needfull to be scoured vpon or anende [belonging to] their
seuerall lands vpo^n paine to forfaite for euery defalt xij^d [12d]

Styes   It^m y^t Wm Garnet and the wid[ow] Ince doe before Midsommer day next remooue
          their styes standing neere vnto *Misselsuch** [Middle Styche] & not to place them
again w^thin 8 yards of the Cesterne, vpo^n paine of vj^s viij^d [6s 8d]

Cucking   It^m we prsent y^t we want a Cuckingstoole & we request y^t Sr Hugh Cholmeley,
Stole   Knight, Baron of this Towne of Namptwich would in some convenient tyme cause
          a Cuckingstoole to be made & erected
              Note y^t the Cuckingstoole† & a fine new Cage‡ were both made and set vp at
          the proper costs of the s^d S^r H Cholmeley

Wich-houses It is ordered by this inquest y^t euery one of them y^t haue decayed wich
decayed   howses doe before Midsom day next sufficientlie repaire them vpo paine of
              39^s 11^d ob   Or els from henceforth not to wall in the same so decayed
It^m We lay a paine y^t Rog^r Leigh, Butcher, shall not from henceforth enclose a comon
Lane adioyning to the Boothe Hall vpon paine of 39^s 11^d
              Concordat cum papirys Cur' et exatr per T Burroughes

---

PAINES laid for the better ordering of the TOWNE of NAMPTWICH at the Great
COURT 23° *Oct.* 1592

LAW WRIGHT gen *elect Ball vill* [Bailiff elect for the Town]
WILLMS TENCH et RICH COLCLOUGHE   Const[abl]^es

RAND MAINWARING, ⎫
RICH WIXSTED   ⎪
THOS CHURCH   ⎬ *gubernates salinarm* [Rulers of Walling]
ED HEYES   ⎭

JASPER RUTTER.   ⎫
ROBTUS SPARK.   ⎪
RICUS HFUSTER   ⎬ *custod comie de Crech* [Heath-Keepers]
WMS. WINSTEED   ⎭

Orders for *Item* where[as] the Jurie is giuen to vnderstand as well by Informacon of
the Heath   others, as also by their owne knowledges, y^t diuers deceits & cuning practices
              are vsed vpo the marking day of Cattel that are to be put vpo the heath
whereby the whole layes y^t otherwise would be entered & p'fered [preferred] to be marked
vnto the Heath Keepers are so seuered & deuided, to th' intent to defraud the whole lay
for some smaller sume, then the same coming wholly together wold amount vnto, not

---

* Middle Styche occurs as the name of a lane adjacent to Welsh (or rather Frog) Row, in very ancient deeds   (See
page 4)   The "*Cesterne*" was probably the *open channel* that ran down Welsh Row to the river
† The "*Cuckingstoole*" was placed in "*Cart-lake*"
‡ The "*Cage*" stood in High Town, near the site of the old Market Hall,

onely to the great trouble of the Heath Keepers to foresee such deceitfull dealing, but also to the hindrance of this Towne, for preventing whereof, It is ordered by the Jurors of this Court for a law hereaft[r] to be continued   That it shalbe lawfull to the said Heath Keepers appointed for this year, as also for all other heath-keepers that shalbe hereaft[r] to take for euery Beast, aft[r] the proportion of the full lay the 3[i]d part of the same laye: And for euery horse the halfe laye, any former law to the contrary notwithstanding

It[m] for good considerations moouing this Jurye it is ordered & enacted for a law hereaft[r] to be continued, That the vnder Heath-keepers for y[e] yeare being, shall not haue any allowance of horse or horsegrasse vpon the heath otherwise the[n] vpon the marking day, & then paying for the same according to the p'portio' of the Layes   And y[t] for all trespasses vpon the heath they shall haue their allowance as before they haue had   And y[t] the head Heath-keepers shall not dispence with th' impounding of any Cattel by the underkeepers impounded to take away their benefitt fro[m] them, Yet notwithstanding y[t] the s[d] head heath-keepers shall haue therein an ouersight that the trespassers shall not be used wth extortion, but y[t] they shall pay for such trespasses as by law may be stood vpon & iustified, & y[t] the fees for the vnder heath-keepers shalbe vj[s] viij[d]   [6s 8d] a peece · & not more according as it was in auncient tyme

Orders for   *It[m]* it is ordered & agreed by the full consent of this Jurye that it shalbe law-
Walling   full at all tymes hereaft[r] for the Rulers of the Walling for the tyme being in euery yeare to examine by oath by them to be ministred to eu'y [every] such persons as fro[m] tyme to tyme they shall thinke convenient to be examined vpo[n] any matter y[t] shall tend vnto the breache of any custome, ordinance, paine or Bylaw heretofore made or hereafter to be made, touching the ruling of Walling   And y[t] therevpo[n] the s[d] Rulers shall at euery Leet and view of Frankpledge comonly called the great Court, w[ch] shalbe held the one after Easter, the other after Michaelmas, p[r]sent all such misdemeanors & offences w[th] the offenders as the s[d] Rulers shall find offensive ag[st] any of the Customes, ordinances and paines touching the s[d] walling, & deliuer the same in writing upon then oathes at the end of their office vnto the Jurors & homagers of euery the s[d] Courts, to the end, the Jurors may find & present the same in theire verdict accordinglie

Bryne-pit.   *It[m]* it is ordered by the said Jurye y[t] the Rulers of the Walling for this yeare
being shall haue authoritye to make a lay of ij[d] [2d] euery six leads, to be bestowed vpo[n] the repaire of such decayes as be about the *Bryne-pitt* & the water-workes thereof

Stryke.   *It[m]* it is agreed that the leaue lookers or one of them shall euery kinding [heating
of the salt-pans] goe about w[th] the stryke and measure their owne, & euery Occupiers salt to try whether the same be made sufficient or not, & to p[r]sent the offenders therein at the next gr[t] Court   And if the s[d] *Leaue-lookers* shall make defalt herein to forfaite for euery such offence the sume of iij[s] iiij[d]   [3s. 4d.]

Exchanging   *It[m]* it is ordered y[t] noe Occupier of walling w[th]in this Towne shall from
of Salt   henceforth after the publishing of this Order buy, exchange, obtaine, or ingrosse
[i e. forestall, or monopolise] into their hands any salt of any person to sell or exchange the same againe vpon paine of euery *Barrowe* of Salt so bought, exchanged, obtained, or ingrossed, to forfaitte iij[s] iiij[d] [3s. 4d]

New orders   *It^m* where[as] this Jurye haue vnderstanding y^t there are not sufficient wallers,
for Walling   laborors, & makers of salt wthin this Towne, wherevpoⁿ the owners and
occupiers of the same walling are inforced (the most of them) to retaine &
hire for the making of salt such as they can gett, although not sufficient for y^t purpose.
By reason whereof the salt is not onely made bad to the great pr̄iudice of the Masters of
the same, & of the carriers thereof, But also the s^d Masters are inforced to giue such
vnreasonable wages vnto the s^d wallers and other the labourors in y^t trade as heretofore
hath not bene accustomed   And also in consideracon of the s^d wallers & other the labourors
in y^t trade are growne so head strong and disobedient y^t neither their Masters lawfull
comandm^{ts,} nor ordinances of the Court heretofore made & p'vided for remedying of diuers
disorders & misdemeanors touching the same trade, are very little or slenderlye regarded
amongst them   For remedying of all wch inconveniences, & to th' end y^t the making of
salt may from henceforth be the better made by good and sufficient workfolkes, It is
therefore by the full consent of this Jurye, ordered, That the now Rulers of the walling
or also all others y^t shall succeed them shall haue full power to seuer [sever] and deuide
the walling within the Town to be walled in manner & forme following—

That is to say, One kinding on the one syde of the water and another kinding on the
other syde ,

And soe to keepe the course of walling according to euery mans right of occupation
as the Rulers shall appoint the same

And that the said now Rulers vpoⁿ the kinding next after the 16th Novemb^r next
coming [1593] shall cause (after lott cast wch syde shall begin) that side of the water then
first to wall as the s^d Lott shall fall out

And to th' end y^t this ordinance may be the better obayed, & put in executioⁿ by the
s^d Rulers, It is ordered likewise by the s^d Jurye,—

That if any psoⁿ shall at any tyme hereafter goe about or vndertake to kind or wall
by them selves of their owne heads, contrary to the Rulers appointm^t in this behalf, That
then it shalbe lawfull for the s^d Rulers not onely to stop & let [i.e hinder] them, But
also y^t euery such seuerall offender shall forfaite for euery such seuell [several] offence the
some of 39^s 11^d ob. [39s 11½d]

Pauements   *It^m* it is ordered that Tho Bullin, Peet^r Witherhead & Eldred Bebington
shall before the next great Court raise up their Pauements before their howses
in the Church lane equall wth the Pauement of the howses wherein Raph Buckley & the
widdowe Browne doe dwell, soe y^t the water may runne into the Lamporne, vpo paine
of x^s [10s] for each of them y^t shall make defalt

Butts   *It^m* we doe p^rsent o^r *Butts* are in decay and pray for repairing of the same &
authoritie is giuen vnto the head heath-keepers for this yeare, & for all other that
shall succeed them in that office fro^m tyme to tyme to repayre the same, & to be allowed
the charges thereof vpon their account to the Jurors of this Court

Town Officers.					
THO YARDLEY	} *Gustator kiaste.*	HENR WINSTEED	} *Supuisor ignis &c*		
ROG BICKER	[Ale-tasters].	ROBTUS WILKES	[Fire-lookers]		
ROB SAVAGE	} *Supuisor modij.*	GILB^r WOLLAM	} *Supuisor font, vill et canell*		
RIC CREWE	[Leave-lookers]	THO. SARGEANT	[channel-lookers]		

Nota q^d [quod] apud magnam cur.' tent ibm. die Lune viz vii° die May 1593, nullæ pœnæ posit. fuer'. per Jurat' 35° *Eliz*

(Translation)—*Note* That at the same great Court held on Monday the 7th day of May 35 Eliz. 1593 no paines had been imposed by the Jury

PAYNES layd downe at the great LEET in NAMPTWICH holden 22° Octr Ano° R Regnæ. Eliz 35° [1593]

A paine is laid downe that John Brett, wid[ow] Duckowes, & Tho Palins wife nor any other shall gather any colecroome [? wood ashes] to make any ashes, vpon paine of iij^s iiij^d [3s. 4d]

It^m y^t noe occupier of walling within the Towne, nor noe waller vnder them shall suffer any ashes to goe out of their wich howses, vpon paine of iij^s iiij^d [3s. 4d]

It^m where[as] Robt Spark gent was nominated & elected by the Jurors of the great inquest in this Town holden 23° Octr Anno 1592, to be one of the head heath keepers of the Heath, and Commons belonginge to the s^d Towne, and at this Court should haue made his account of such sumes of money as he hath receaued by reason of his s^d late office, & to haue made paym^t thereof vnto this Inquest, according to the usage of the s^d Court heretofore, which thing the s^d Robt Spark hath not done, although however requested by the Jurye of this Court therevnto, but doth detaine the money receaued in his hands · Therefore the Jurors doe amercye [fine] the s^d Robt Spark for his defalt to the sume of 39^s 11^d ob [39s 11½d]

And we doe further paine the s^d Robt Spark that before the 7th of Novembr next he doe pay vnto the hands of Jasper Rutter, Wm Winsteed & Ric Kinshaw or to some one of them, all such sumes of money as the s^d Robt hath receaued by reason of his s^d late office of Heath-keeper

And that he the s^d Robt Spark shall before that tyme repaire vnto the Steward of this Court for the tyme being, & take his corporall oath before him, y^t he shall fully satisffie & paye vnto the s^d Jasper Rutter, Wm Winsteed & Ric Kinshawe or to one of them, all such sumes of money as he the s^d Robt hath receaued vpon paine of 39^s 11^d ob

And authorytye is giuen by the s^d Jurye to the s^d Jasper Rutter, Wm Winsteed & Ric Kinshaw, or any 2 of them to allowe vnto the s^d Robt Spark vpon the payment of the s^d sumes, such sume of money as the s^d Robt at that tyme of his payment shall de-mand allowance of, according as the s^d Jaspr. W^m & Richard, or any 2 of them shall think meet to be allowed, and not otherwise

It^m we doe amercye the s^d Robt Spark and Robert Wilkes being Supervisors of the high waies within the boundes of this Towne for that they came not to yield their accounts of their s^d late office at the great Court holden about a yeare now last past, according as they ought to haue done, by a former usage in this Court in the sume of x$^{s.}$ [10s.] seuerally.

It^m where[as] Tho. Bagnall and others haue found themselves greived & annoyed by a Privye of John Seckersons adioyning to Tho Bagnall, who prayed the Jurye to viewe the same, The Jurors of this Court haue therevpon viewed the same and find it to be very noysome [nasty], And therefore doe appoint the sd John Seckerson to remooue the sd Privye before Christmas next, or otherwise from tyme to tyme soe to cleanse it & keep it, as it doe not henceforth annoy his neighbours about him, upon paine to forfaite 39s 11d ob.

Names of the Jury at the said Court

RICH MRSON [Maisterson] *gent*	RICUS ROBINSON
GAB[RIEL] WETTNALL, *gent*	WMUS WIXSTEED
JASPER RUTTER, *gent*	RICUS BAGNALL
JOHES MAINWARING, *gent.*	HEN MAISTERSON
GALFR MINSHUII, *gent*	ARTHUR MINSHUII
WMUS CHURCH, *mercer*	JO[HN] ALVASTON
THOS CHURCH, *mercer.*	ALANUS WRIGHT
JOHES MINSHULL, *mercer*	RIC. KINSHAWE
RICUS WIXSTEED	WM TENCH SENR

Itm a paine yt noe person hereafter from the tyme of publishing this order doe stop the passage of the Queens high way leading from the high towne to the Castle-lane, and vpon paine of iijs iiijd [3s 4d]

The aforesaid Jurors say that Ferdinand Earl of Derby is free within the Jurisdiction of this Court and ought to carve for the Court, and others say that the said Earl ought to dine with the Jurors at the next great Court

WILLIAM CHURCH, mercer, *Ballius* [Bailiff]

NICHUS GOLDSMITH	Constables	JASPER RUTTER			
ROG BICKERTON		WM WICKSTEED	Custodie co'ite		
THO WILKES	Gubernator	THO ROBINSON	[Heath-keepers]		
RIC ROBINSON	Salinarum	RIC KINSHAW			
MATT. WRIGHT	[Rulers of	WMUS TENCH SENR	Gustator Kinsie.		
HEN MRSON	Walling]	WMUS INCE	[Ale-tasters].		
JOHES ALVASTON	Supuissrs	ROBTUS SAVAGE	Supuissis ignis. &c.		
RADUS CROCKET	[Leave-lookers.]	JOHES COWPER	[Fire-lookers]		
		HEN WIXSTEED	Supuis font vill. et canell.		
		ROGER MEYRIN	[Channel-lookers]		

Concerning the following Orders of the Court Leet without date, but apparently in 1594 or thereabouts, Mr Wilbraham wrote —

"Theis last notes I had forth of some Papers vnder my Cosn [cousin] Ric. Cluttons hand."

"That the assessment made for the repayring of *Shrewbridge lane* shalbe ordered & pd [paid] vpon paine of xxs to be exacted & the Fynes by entreaty of the Jury to be imployed to the amending of that work, and the surplusage to the highwaies within the Towne

It^m y^t a six leads shalbe occupied for 3 yeares from the next making meet towards the repairing of the said lane, and that the collectors shall sett and receiue the rents thereof and acount vpo. their oathes before the Jury at the great Court   And if any surplusage be, the same to be imployed towards the repacons [repairings] of the *March lane*

It^m that John Alvaston shall haue the 9 dayes of the Pauem^t Walling wch are behind vpo Randle Hortons head   And shall from the next making meet, haue nyne leads walling dureing his life, and shall put into repaire the pauem^{ts} & wayes, & maintaine them in sufficient rep'rations   And if vpo survay of the Grand Jury in any leet of this towne there shalbe any defect of repacon. & not reformed vpo^n premonition then his estate therein to cease   And yet he to haue the Pauem^{ts} in repacon

It^m y^t euery occupier of Walling in this Towne shall bring in writing to the Rulers a note of all such walling as he will wall for, at or before the 3rd kinding in euery half y^r , & whose inheritance the s^d walling is, or at the least who is immediate Landlord to the s^d occupier of the same walling vpon paine euery one making defalt to forfait xx^s [20s]

And not to be allowed by the Rulers to wall any thing for that half yeares occupation, vntil it shalbe ordered & found due to him by the Jury at the great Court the next following   And if any perso^n making such defalt shall by strong hand attempt to wall agst the Rulers permission before it be found & permitted by the grand Jury, then euery one soe offending shall forfait for euery kinding soe walled 39^s 11^d ob

It^m that euery perso^n that shall bring in any more walling then [than] they truely hould, and are to wall for, shall forfait for euery such offence 39^s 11^d ob

It^m To confirme the orders found for o^r [our] customes recyting the names of the Jurye & to order that it may be engrossed & sealed wth the Towne seale, and deliuered to the Rulers to be deliuered ouer for euery tyme to their successors   And y^t theis paines and a paine enabling the Rulers to sweare, made 23° Oct 34° Eliz [1592] shalbe engrossed therevnto to th' end they may be better put in execution

It^m y^t noe perso^{ns} shall wall that are not buyers of wood, & payers of workfolkes wages, & wall truely to wyn or to loose without collusion [i e deceit] vpo^n payne of 39^s 11^d ob

It^m y^t no occupier of walling or other perso^n wthin this Towne shall sell any wich howse wood afte^r it shalbe brought into this Towne, vpo^n paine of 39^s 11^d ob

It^m y^t euery of the occupiers of walling shall before Midsom^r next p'vide a ladder of xvj [16] pins at the least to be at the wich-house wherein they shall wall and keep them at their wich howses in the walling weekes, vpo^n paine of 3^s 4^d And that noe perso^n shall without lycence of the owner take away any of the s^d ladders vnles it be in tyme of fier, vpon paine of iij^s iiij^d [3s. 4d]

Sweeping   *It^m* that euery perso^n y^t shall sweep any muck together in the streets shall *the Streets*   get the same away before the next Saturday morning vpon paine of iij^s iiij^d [3s 4d]

And that euery inhabitant being a householder in the high Towne shall cause the pauements agst their seuerall howses vnto the middest of the Pauement to be made clean & swept weeklye before euery Saturday morning & the muck to be carried away, vpon paine of iij^s iiij^d [3s. 4d]

Night Watchmen.

Beside the public officers already mentioned, there was formerly a band of *Night Watchmen* who were not amenable to any manorial court, but were chosen from amongst trustworthy townsmen by a "Watching Committee" of influential tradesmen, and paid ten shillings each a week, from a fund raised by subscription for that purpose They are traceable in the Registers only as far back as the early part of last century, the first mentions being as follows —

"1735 May 4 Charles Harding, *Watchman*" [Buried]

"1740 April 9 Mary, dau of William Siddals, *Watchman*" [Baptised]

"1747 May 15 Jane, wife of Thomas Taylor, *Night Bellman*" [Buried]

"1758 Sep 16 Thomas Taylor, *Night Bellman*, a pauper ' [Buried]

Until about 1832 six watchmen nightly walked their lonely rounds from 10 p m to 5 a.m , carrying with them a spring rattle, (or *bell* in former days) a bludgeon, and lantern, crying in more or less musical tones, as they tramped along the dark streets, the hour of the night and state of the weather   The last band of Watchmen, or "Charlies," were Rondull Strong* (or Strung as he was called), Robert Astles, William Green, Peter Bolis,† John Basford, and John Sutton   All these were under a Captain, or Chief, Mr John Prince, of Wall Lane, who had been a soldier in the French Wars, and was one of the last two Constables already mentioned (page 68)

In the lower room of the Old Grammar School in the Churchyard, which was then the storehouse of oil, lamps, &c Captain Prince met his men, set their rounds, giving necessary instructions to each for the night , and at the week end was their paymaster. When the police came, and gas was introduced into the town, the band of watchmen was finally dispensed with , with the exception of *John Sutton*, who continued to be sole night-watchman for High Town, until Christmas 1868, when he was incapacitated by infirmity, and after a protracted illness died Christmas 1870, having been watchman over fifty years. He was a well-known "character" in the town   It was his practice nightly to watch the shops of those tradesmen who gave him a small pittance, (10d usually) fortnightly, to try their doors , and plaintively cry "*parst ten, and a fine starry night,*" or otherwise, as the time and weather might be   After which he might have been found in some corner or passage of High Street muffled up in a top-coat, his eyes peering from under an old wide-awake hat, his hands encased in big gloves, and having fixed to his belt a bulls-eye lantern.   In these retreats he was always ready to relate how many years it was since he had been in bed at night, or tell of the robberies he had prevented, and his once clever capture of a gang of thieves in Wall Lane, to offer a pinch of snuff, or slily insinuate that he knew a place where they were brewing   For many years he had been called "Old Jack Sutton," though he was only 67 years of age at his death

---

* His proper name was *Armstrong*,—a name of frequent occurrence in the Registers, sometimes written "*Strongitharmes*,' and "*Strongarm* '

† The last survivor is Peter Bolis who now (1883) lives in one of the Almshouses in Love Lane

The Town Charter.

On the 18th March, 10 Eliz [1567-8], a Charter confirming an ancient privilege that had been claimed by the townspeople for upwards of two hundred and fifty years, was obtained from the Queen on the petition of *Roger Maisterson, Roger Walthall, John Leche, Thomas Clutton*, and others, gentlemen of Nantwich   This Confirmation Charter, which is too long and tedious in legal phraseology to be given in full, declared that—*

> "The Burgesses of Wich Malbank were entitled not to be put upon any assize, juries, recognizances, or inquests whatever with strangers concerning lands and tenements lying out of the vill of Wich Mal-bank or its liberty, or concerning any trespasses, contracts or agreements made and happening out of the same, &c   That the men of Wich Malbank were entitled to this privilege as proved by an Inquisition taken at Chester on Tuesday next after the feast of St Gregory the Pope [March 12], in the 13 Edward II [1319-20] and had then had that privilege time out of mind " &c

It was enrolled in the Court of Exchequer at Chester on the 23rd Aug 1568,† and signed by Sir John Throckmorton, Knight, then Chief Justice of Chester and Flint. This privilege of non-jurors was, nevertheless, repeatedly called in question by the legal authorities at Chester, but, was as strenuously resented and upheld by the people of the town. The Wilbraham family appear to have always exerted themselves in maintaining this town right, and thus they have left on record‡ that the Town Charter was confirmed at the Assizes held in the Common Hall at Chester on

Monday 4 July 6 Jac. I [1609]	before Rich Lewkenor Knt.	Chief Justice	
	before Henry Townshend Esqr	do	
Monday 23 Sept 20 Jac I. [1623]	before James Whitelock Knt	do	
	before Marmaduke Lloyd Knt.	do	
1654	before John Bradshaw	do.	
1664-5	before Sir Job Charlton Knt.	do	
Aug 1680	before Sir George Jeffries Knt	do.	
25 March 1718	before Spencer Cowper Esqre	do	

Dr Ormerod stated from the Copy of Enrolments and Allowances that it was confirmed ten times before 8 Will III [1695-6], and since that time by every succeeding Chief Justice   In 1762 the privilege was again challenged, rousing the watchful jealousy of "near sixty of the principal freeholders and inhabitants, who unanimously resolved to spare no expense in defending their common right § For rather more than a century after that date, the town enjoyed its privilege undisputed, until this antiquated plea was at last annulled and rendered invalid by Act of Parliament in 1873.

---

* A copy of the Charter in Latin is preserved amongst the Wilb MSS
† Chesh Recog Rolls
‡ Wilbraham MSS Collections at Delamere
§ Partridges Hist. Nantwich, p 22

Historical Annals.

ICH, or Nantwich, although not mentioned in the Saxon Chronicle, must have been an important place in Saxon times. Its importance at the close of the Saxon æra, is seen in the account given by King William's Commissioners in the great national survey, called Domesday Book, (p. 10, 11); an account that is only exceeded in length and interest in this county, by the description in the same record, of the City of Chester.

Three important events connected with Nantwich in Norman times have been noticed in the preceding pages;—the battle in 1069 resulting in the destruction of the ancient Saxon town; the grant of lands to the then newly founded Abbey of Combermere, about 1130; and another sanguinary battle in which the Welsh were defeated in or about 1140. For a period of 167 years, i.e. from 1070 to 1237, during which Cheshire had been governed by local hereditary Earls, the Welsh had been kept in check; but after the death of the last of these Earls (John Scot) in 1237, the history of this county consists of a recital of reciprocal inroads and injuries by Welsh and English, with stories of crimes, usurpations, and massacres. In 1244, says Matthew Paris,* "the Welsh being exceedingly alarmed, lest when the King had made peace with the King of Scotland, he might attack them in a hostile manner with his whole army, kept quiet, and, like hares, lay hid in peace. But when the Welsh understood that the King had returned to the peaceful delights of Westminster, forgetful of the injuries which had been inflicted on himself and his people, like bees who swarm out of their hives, they came forth from their lurking-places, devoting themselves in no slack manner to pillage, conflagration, and massacre, and shamefully routing the English, though not without considerable loss on their own part." The same old chronicler states,† that in the following year, [1245] about the time of the feast of the Nativity of St. John the Baptist [June 24], the King caused all who owed him military service to be warned to follow him on a hostile expedition against Wales; and soon after, when he was about to set out, he very courteously requested the sanction of the citizens of London, who were

* Matthew of Westminster's Chronicle, vol. ii. p. 234.
† *Ibid.* p. 243.

convened in St. Paul's, and humbly requested the prayers of the clergy " This expedition appears to have returned inglorious The King unable to cope with the brave Llewellyn, depopulated the border, causing thereby a dreadful famine, and, retreating into Cheshire, he destroyed the salt-pits of Nantwich and the other Wiches, in order further to distress his enemies During the long and feeble reign of Henry III, a murderous warfare was kept up between the Welsh and Lord James de Audley, who held a third part of the Barony of Wich-Malbank, and "who, on his return from Germany, found his lands, goods, and castles burnt or desolated A savage system of retaliation was instantly commenced, and the whole border was reduced to an uninhabitable desert, the inhabitants were cut off by the sword, the castles and houses burnt, the woods felled, and the cattle destroyed by famine "+ It was not until the year 1282 that Wales was subjugated by the terrible and victorious march of Edward I, and, in that year, the King being at Nantwich, granted protection to several persons, that their corn and other provisions should not be seized on account of the approach of the Welsh army †

On 11th May, 1283, Edward I granted to Robert Burnell, Bishop of Bath and Wells, a three days' fair at Nantwich, to be held annually at Bartholtide, on 23rd, 24th and 25th Aug (See page 42) No doubt this chartered fair would tend to raise the town again into importance, after the reverses in the previous King's reign, and possibly it may first have been held in the churchyard, until fairs were prohibited from being held in churchyards by the statute of Westminster 13 Edw I. [1284-5]

Still known as the *Old Fair*, *Great Fair*, or more commonly as *September Fair*, it has continued to be held annually for six hundred years,—at Bartholtide until the alteration of the English Calendar by stat 24 Geo II c 23 [1752], and on the 4th of September, being eleven days after, since the year 1753 ‡ No fair was held in 1631 on account of the plague, and again by prohibitory notice in 1849 owing to the visitation of Cholera, (see *postea*) The right of collecting toll on all merchandise at this fair passed with the Lovell lands to Sir Hugh Cholmondeley in 1556, and by his descendant, the late Marquis, was granted to the Nantwich Local Board in 1862 In former times vendors, in order to attract buyers, were accompanied by jugglers, minstrels and buffoons, hence this fair became the great pleasure fair of the year, and often the scene of riot and dissipation. Two instances of clowns or mountebanks, who, no doubt, had often addressed and amused the gaping crowd in their *ad captandum* way, are mentioned in the Burial Register —

"1604 Sep 22 Laurence Swettnam, capper, a merry man " [i e the funny man or clown of the fair]
"1712 Dec 29 Benjamin Gonnins, a merry-andrew "

Formerly the fun of the fair consisted in bull, bear, and badger-baitings, cock-fighting, sack-racing, bolting hot porridge or dumplings (barm-balls, or *barm-baws*, as Nantwich people called them), swarming greasy poles, grinning through horse-collars, &c , "but all these charms (!) are fled."

* Ormerod's Cheshire, vol I Introduction p xxvi (old Edit) p lvi (new Edit) Twenty years after, on the Sunday following the battle of Evesham in 1265, the Lord James de Audley, and Urian de St Pierre, seized the Castle of Beeston, and laid siege to Chester which after a defence of ten weeks surrendered to Prince (afterwards King) Edward, thus terminating the Barons' War in this county

† Lysons' *Cheshire* p 699 quoting *Rot Wall* 10 Ed I

‡ This fair which was originally granted for *three* days, was held for *four* days in the year 1500, (page 66) and has since that time been reduced to *one* day

In the years 1285 and 1307 lands in Alvaston, then known as the wood of *Creche*, which one hundred and fifty years before had been granted to the townsmen of Nantwich and monks of Combermere as common land, by Hugh, second Baron of Wich-Malbank, and which in the meantime had become the waste of the lords of Alvaston, were again secured to the town by certain deeds   From that time down to the commencement of the present century, officers were annually elected by the Court Leet to see that the common domain was equitably enjoyed.   Two Acts of Parliament have since been obtained by which the cultivation of this waste land has been extended and improved, resulting in an increased benefit to the town   (See Alvaston township)

On the 2nd July 1310, King Edward II, being on his journey to London, came from Chester to Nantwich   He was again in Chester on the 31st July, 1319, and in November of that year visited the Religious houses of Norton and Vale Royal,[*] on which occasion he may possibly have paid a visit to Combermere Abbey and Nantwich, though no chronicler has recorded the fact

During the reign of Edw III, on three different occasions, neighbouring gentlemen sought the privilege of altering certain roads in their manors near Nantwich, and at courts held before the Escheator and a local jury sworn to inquire whether if the claim were granted, it would interfere with any vested right, or be to the detriment of the crown or any subject, the following Inquisitions were taken   (Plea Rolls, Cheshire Records).

[I]   "4 Edw III [1330-1] *Inquisitio ad quod damnum* finding that it was not to the damage of the King, &c , that *Peter de Stapelegh* should close a way 220 perches long and 40 feet wide leading from Holebek towards Wich-Malbank, near Ambaldeside, on the east part of his manor of Stapelegh, so that he made another way 200 perches long and 40 feet wide on the west side of his said manor "[†]

[II]   "8 Edw III [1334-5] Inquisition finding that it was not to the damage &c that *William de Wystaston* should divert a way nine perches in length   leading under the park of the said William from Monkescopenhale towards Wych Malbank, and hold the said way to himself and his heirs, provided that he made another way in lieu of the one so diverted "

[III]   "22 Edw III [1348-9] Inquisition, finding that it was not to the damage, &c , that *Matthew de Fouleshurst* should appropriate a lane leading from the metes of Edlaston to the rivulet of the mill of Shyrardes-brugge [Shrew-bridge], to the enlargement of his manor of Newbold , that the said lane contained 46 perches in length and one perch in width , and that the way to be constructed by the said Matthew in lieu of the said lane would contain 40 perches in length and one perch in width "[‡]

In 1339-40, Nicholas the *Catchpole*, i e the collector of manorial dues in the town, occurs on the Plea Rolls in litigations respecting property in and near Nantwich

About this time commenced that period of English history known as the "days of chivalry " or the hundred years' war with France, when, if Froissart is to be believed, in Englishmen were united true nobility of character and tenderness of feeling with military valour and physical strength   A few local records during that long and fatal war, which, robbed of its romance, "drained the strength and corrupted the temper of the English people," have a curious bearing on those times, commonly known as the "Dark Ages '

[*] W Beamont's "*History of Halton*,' p 39-40

[†] ' Whether the " London Road " through Stapeley, which is still on the west side of Stapeley Hall, is the road here mentioned

[‡] In a field opposite Shrewbridge is a mound and moat   ? Whether this is the site of the manor-house of Newbold

In 1347 a pardon was granted to Thomas, son of John Noteman, of the Hospital of Stanthorn, for the death of *William de Chastel* "*prechour*" *of Wich-Malbank*, at the request of John de Beauchamp, Knight, son of the Earl of Warwick, who had the honour to carry the royal standard at the battle of Cressy, was captain of Calais, and held other high offices *

On the 3rd July, 1360, a pardon was granted to Richard Brom of Northenden, for the death of *John Blake of Nantwich*, the said Richard having served the prince in his last journey to France in the train of James de Audelegh, the hero of Poictiers *

On the 12th Dec 45 Edw III [1371] protection was granted by Edward the Black Prince, as Earl of Chester, to *William Barbour, of Wich-Malbank*, on his going to Calais on the King's service, in the retinue of Nicholas de Tamworth, captain of the said town of Calais †

On the 20th July, 46 Edw. III [1372] protection was granted by Prince Edward, Earl of Chester, to *Richard de Henehull, of Wich-Malbank*, on his going to North Wales on the Earl's service, probably for the defence of the Castle of Beaumaris †

On the 12th June 5 Rich II. [1382] protection was granted to *Sir David Cradok, Knight*, Mayor of the city of Bordeaux, on his going to Gascony on the King's service †

Gascony, as part of the Duchy of Acquitaine, had become a possession of the English crown in 1360 by the treaty of Bretigny, and in the same year, or soon after, this mayoralty had been conferred as a reward for military services. Sir David Cradock appears to have been the son of Nicholas Cradock, of Nantwich, (*Harl MSS* 506 p 124) who was living in the 3 Edw II [1309-10]. His position and wealth obtained for him, in Feb 1376-7, from Prince Richard, as Earl of Chester, the wardship, marriage and custody of the lands of John son of John de Oulton, "who was born at Erdeswick and baptized in the church of Churchmunshull," to whom, of course, Sir David ultimately gave as the most suitable match, his own daughter Pelerine. The heir came of age in 1391, at which time his guardian and father-in-law was dead, for it is stated in the "*de etate probanda*' (proof of age) of John de Oulton, that his lands were then in the custody of the executors of David Cradock, Kt, Peter and John de Legh * On the next page of *Harl MSS.* 506, is a charter, of which the following is an abstract, proving that Sir David was still living in 1384

> "I John Woodehouse Chancellor of Chester and Nicholas Wildebor chaplain have granted &c to *David Cradoc Knight*, and Ireland his wife certain lands and tenements in Wich Malbank, and lands &c within and without the county of Chester, and after their deaths, to *Richard Cradock* son of the said David and his male heirs, failing which to revert to *Roger Cradoc*, brother of the said Richard, and his male heirs &c Dated at Wich Malbank on the day of the Invention of the Holy Cross [May 3] in the 7 Ric II [1384] These being witnesses —Hugh Venables, Sheriff of Cheshire, Ralph Vernon, Robert Fouleshurst Knight, William de Praers, William de Bromlegh, Nicholas Colfox, and others"

Of the two sons mentioned in this deed, only Richard occurs in the Cheshire Records Like his father, he was a soldier and a Knight, and on his departure to Gascony in 1391 licence was obtained for *Thomas Maistresson*, of Nantwich to act as his attorney Sir Richard Cradock, Kt occurs for the last time in July and Aug 1397, in connection with

* Chesh Recog Rolls   † Cnesh Plea Rolls

Sir William Bagot, Kt, as joint grantee of the custody of the same manor of Erdeswyk, then of the yearly value of £20, and of other lands, during the minority of the three daughters of John de Oulton, who had died on the 9th Oct 1396 * To the memory of Sir David Cradock, Kt, a tomb was placed in the south transept of the present Nantwich Church †

Contemporary with Sir David Cradock lived John Wyche of Wich-Malbank, whose ancestors had long been connected with Bollington and Middlewich. This family has hitherto almost escaped the notice of Cheshire historians, although Richard de Wyche, Bishop of Chichester, who died on 3rd April, 1253, was canonized by Pope Urban IV in 1261, and was the only Romish saint of Cheshire birth, and another Richard de Wyche, brother of the above John Wyche, became a witness against Popery and suffered as a *Martyr* in the Lollard persecution. The following descent of the Wyche family of Nantwich, which is specially interesting as containing allusions to the building of Nantwich Church, is taken from a long pedigree in Hoare's Hist. of Wiltshire, vol iv & v p 35

Wyche of Wich-Malbank.

William de Wyche of Middlewich and Bolinton, temp I Edw III [1327-8]

Thomas Wyche	John Wyche of	Sir Maurice	William de Wyche	Richard de Wyche
an Esquire of England to whom the strong castle of Hennebond was committed in 1373	Wyche Malbank, 1380	Wyche Knt	of Middlewich from whom descended the Wyches of Davenham and in the 16th and 17th cent of Soss	surnamed the Lollard 1388, the contemporary and friend of *John Wicliffe* Chaplain to

Richard de Wyche	Richard Wyche of Nantwich	William Wyche	Moss Hall, Alderley	John of Ghent Duke
a Lance Bearer in the company of the Duke of Gloster Was at the siege of Rouen and Agincourt in 1415	*He contributed to the fabric of the Church there*, and his arms were in the windows of the Church His son, Hugh, left money to all the Friars in London to pray for his soul and that of his wife	Esquire to the Abbot of Saint Albans (probably John de Bostock) living 1420 ob before 1425	Cheshire (See Earwaker's "East Cheshire," vol ii p 622)	of Lancaster, Vicar of Hanworth co of Middlesex Burnt on Tower Hill as a witness against Popery 1440, aged 80 and more

Sir Hugh Wyche Knt born 1395	William	John	Thomas Wyche, citizen
admitted freeman of the Mercers' Compy 1420 Alderman and Sheriff of London in 1444 M P in 1446 Lord Mayor 1461, obiit May 1468, aged 73 buried in St Margaret's, Lothbury Left his widow £3000 gave money also *to the fabric and works of the body of the Church of Nantwich* Married Alice dau and co-heir of John Stratton Esq, and widow of W Holte of London, Citizen, buried at St Dionys Backchurch, London			and Freeman of the Fishmongers' Compy Will dated 12 Oct 1425, desires to be buried at St Magnus, London Bridge leaves 6s 8d to the *Church of Nantwich* mentions his uncle William Wyche Esq deceased Proved 20 Oct 1425

1384 On Nov 11th, William Colfox (probably of Nantwich) was appointed to the office of *Bedelary* [or *Bailiff*] of the Hundred of Nantwich, which he held by lease for three years at £12 per annum.*

* Chesh Recog Rolls
† See Ancient Monuments, and History of the Church, &c, for other notices of this family.

1385-6. On Feb 28th, Robert Daniel, of Rydelegh, Henry Brayn, [? of Aston-in-Mondrum] and Richard de Cholmundelegh, were appointed Commissioners to arrest all disturbers of the peace in the hundred of Nantwich, the King having heard of great terror and disturbance caused by bands of armed men there *

1386—1389. Between these years the celebrated Scrope and Grosvenor Suit of Arms was exciting the counties of Cheshire and Lancashire Never, on any trial were so many distinguished witnesses of every rank, from the sovereign Prince down to country gentlemen, examined the point at issue being to prove whether *Sir Richard le Scrope* or *Sir Robert le Grosvenor* had the better right to bear a blue shield having a gold band across it diagonally from left to right An examination of witnesses took place at Nantwich on 1st Oct. 1386, and again on the 6th May, 1388 It was at the first of these examinations, that John de Holford, one of the Grosvenor witnesses, deposed on oath, that at the time of the Conquest Hugh Lupus Earl of Chester, granted to Gilbert le Grosvenor a part of the manors of one of the Saxon Thanes named Hame, who had been killed at the battle of Nantwich.†

After three years' litigation, this chivalrous suit was decided in favour of Sir Richard le Scrope, but that Sir Robert le Grosvenor should bear the same Arms with a silver border Sir Robert, however, being dissatisfied, appealed to the King, who, by his commissioners, finally decided concurrent with the former judgment, but granted Sir Robert the privilege to bear a golden sheaf instead of a golden band, as being descended from the ancient Earls of Chester, which latter Arms he accordingly adopted, and the same have ever since been borne by the noble house of Eaton

In 1386, when Richard II had nearly attained the full age which entitled him to govern by his own authority, parliament sanctioned the transferrence of sovereign power to the ambitious Duke of Gloucester, who, in 1387, upon pretence of removing the King's favourites, but in reality to carry out his design of still holding the King (his nephew) in subjection, assembled an army, which met the King's forces, commanded by Thomas Molyneux, Constable of Chester Castle, at Radcot Bridge in Oxfordshire The King's army was defeated, and the gallant leader of the Cheshire men was slain Under date 20th Dec 1398 occurs a list of men in Nantwich Hundred amongst whom was distributed the sum of £183 8s 10¾d "as part of the 4000 marks [£2666 13s 4d] sent by the King out of his treasury at Westminster for the relief of those of Chester who suffered at Redcotebrugge" [Radcot Bridge] Foremost of those who thus survived the defeat and were rewarded, comes Sir Richard Vernon, Baron of Shipbroke, who afterwards died in the same King's cause, being taken prisoner at Shrewsbury and beheaded in 1403 The names are as follows —*

[SIR] "RICHARD LE VERNON,	RICHARD LE ROPE,	THOMAS LE VERNON,
DAVID LE SEINTPIERRE,	THOMAS DEL HETH,	JAMES LE VERNON
JOHN DE KELSHALL,	THOMAS LE PRAERS,	NICHOLAS WILLESONE,
ROGER ALKOC,	JOHN DEL CASTELL,	JOHN DE BUYRTON,
JOHN LE EYRE,	JOHN LE CROUTH,	THOMAS DE SONDBACH
ROGER LE WODEWER,	JOHN DE ERDELEGH,	ROGER DE STAPELEY

* Cheshire Recognizance Rolls
† Dr Ormerod quotes this deposition, in Norman French, in Hist of Cheshire, vol iii p 82 old Edit , p 144 new Edit

1388   Oct. 16th, ROBERT, the Abbot of Combermere, appointed *Justice of Eyre*, for the towns of Middlewich and Nantwich,[*] that is, he was made an *Itinerant Justice*, and went from place to place to hold Courts and try criminals   He was not, however, the first Abbot, who, in addition to his power as the greatest ecclesiastic in this part of the county, exercised high legal authority, for, in Norman times, the Abbot of Combermere, together with the Baron of Wich-Malbank, had jurisdiction in Nantwich Hundred, even in cases of capital felony [†]

1390-1   Feb 13th, Thomas le Maisterson, of Nantwich, appointed Escheator of the county, by the King, who, on 29th Oct 1391, also made him Attorney-general of the county [‡]

1392   Aug 2nd, Commissioners were appointed in the different Hundreds of Cheshire to arrest all disturbers of the peace, great complaints having reached the King of evil doings in Cheshire   The Commissioners for Nantwich Hundred were Ralph de Vernon, Kt [of Hashington] and William de Praers [of Baddiley] [‡]

1396   Oct 4th, John Bateson, late *Catchpol* of Nantwich, being in arrears to the King for 13s 10d , enters into a recognizance for payment of the same [↓]

1397—1398   On 27th Jan 1397-8, King Richard assembled his Parliament at Shrewsbury, where an act was passed raising the county of Cheshire to a Principality, the King styling himself Prince of Chester , and in the following year, when he had become unpopular elsewhere, he visited his Principality for the purpose of raising an army of two thousand archers   In Aug 1398 the King stayed at Nantwich on this journey, for on the 31st of the same month Robert Parys,[§] Chamberlain of Chester, had delivered to him, " by John Cranmere yoeman of the King's wardrobe,' &c , *inter alia*,—" two carpets of red tapestry and a green mattress, being part of the Royal bed furniture which had been left behind at Nantwich "[‡]

On Nov 18th of the same year, " the King granted to John Norley, Chamberlain, ["*garcio Camere nostre*], and Richard Letfote, the goods and chattels of Richard de Pulle [Poole] who was convicted of the death of a woman at Nantwich , the said John and Richard to answer for all the value of the same beyond £4 "[‡]

Under date 5th Jan 1398[-9] occurs the first mention of the TOWN BRIDGE, when licence was granted by the Bishop of Lichfield and Coventry, for the benefit of the inhabitants of the town of Nantwich, to have divine service celebrated in " *St Ann's Chapel upon the Bridge in the said town* "[||]   It occurs again in John de Kyngeslegh's Rental dated 17 Hen. VI [1438-9], as follows —

" Four shops which he formerly had *upon the Bridge with the Chapel* &c value 40 sh "

Partridge, in his history (page 11), says, that the street Welsh Row was anciently called " *St. Anne's and St. Anne's parish ,* " but, from what follows, it is clear that writer did not know that St Ann's Chapel stood on the bridge. No doubt in that oratory, a priest, on the payment of money, offered up prayers for the safety of wayfarers passing

---

[*] Cheshire Recognizance Rolls   [†] Ormerod's *Cheshire,*" vol 1 lv new Edit
[‡] Cheshire Recognizance Rolls
[§] The Chamberlain of Chester presided at the Court of Exchequer there
[||] Ormerod's *Cheshire,* vol 111 p 450, new Edit , quoting the Lichfield Registers

over the bridge, as in similar bridge-chapels at Congleton and Stockport in pre-Reformation times   In early times the Bridge, which was built of wood, was maintained and repaired by the town, (see Annals, 1633—1637), but in 1652 it was made a County Bridge, and in 1664 was first built of stone, that bridge being superseded by the present structure in 1803   Though formerly known as the *Wich Bridge*, it is now called, in the Government Survey Maps the *Welsh Bridge*

On 21st August, 1399, King Richard II, then the prisoner of Henry Bolinbroke, being on his journey from Flint Castle to London, came again from Chester to Nantwich, the next day he travelled to Newcastle-under-Lyme, to Lichfield on the 24th, and Northampton on the 29th, where he granted a patent of the priory of Derehurst to one *Master Richard Wyche*, (perhaps of Nantwich, but no doubt belonging to the local family of that name), arriving in London on the 2nd September, where he was deposed on the 29th of the same month

The transfer of the crown to Henry Bolinbroke as King Henry IV on 30th September, 1399, produced great fear and anxiety amongst Cheshire people on account of their former adherence to the deposed King, and from the fact that lawless bands of armed men had committed great robberies and murders in the adjacent counties of Salop, Stafford and Derby   But one of the first acts of King Henry was the granting of a general pardon to his subjects in this county   By commission dated 23rd January, 1399 1400, the following Justices of Peace for Nantwich Hundred, namely —"*John de Delves, Richard le Vernon, Thomas de Fouleshurst* of Edlaston, *Thomas le Maistresson* [of Nantwich], *Richard le Mascy del Hogh* [of Hough], *William de Beeston, William de Crue,* of Sond   *Thomas Malbon, Thomas Daukynson, Richard son of Roger de Cholmondeley, Hugh del Malpas David le Seintpere, John de Kyngeslegh, Richard de Roope and David le Crue* of Pulcroft,—were to make proclamation of pardon to all those who had through fear joined the rebels, on their returning to their homes, and, also that poor people should not be frightened '*   Amongst those who were excepted in this general act of pardon occur *William Coke*, chaplain of Wich-Malbank, *Roger de Salghall*, vicar of Acton, the latter being required in July, 1400, to find sureties in the very large sum of 200 marks [£133 6s. 8d] for his own good conduct and that of his Chaplain †

In the early years of Henry IV Cheshire was connected with the Percy rebellion, and the Welsh revolt.   Owen Glendower, who claimed to be the rightful Prince of Wales, was at war with the usurper Henry IV at that time, and though not a confederate with Hotspur, he appears to have aided the Cheshire men who still cherished the memory of the deposed King   Hence "Prince Henry" [that is, Prince of Chester, and King of England] ordered *John de Kyngeslegh* and *Richard de Bromley* to "seize all cattle within the hundred of Nantwich which had been bought of the rebels [the Welsh] contrary to proclamation against buying cattle of the Rebels " (*Chesh Recog Rolls*, dated June 1403)

On St Kenelm's day [17 July] 1403, Hotspur, who had proclaimed the late King to be still alive at Chester Castle, summoned a muster of Cheshire men at Sandiway, near Delamere Forest,† and from thence marched southwards through Nantwich, where he plundered and destroyed the house of *Thomas Maisterson Esquire*,§ (who no doubt was then

---

* Chesh Recog Rolls   † Lyson's *Chesh re*, p 834, quoting Rot Parl 1 Hen IV

‡ *Traison et mort Rich* II, p 285, also, *Harl MSS* 1989 f 381   § See *postea*

at Lichfield with King Henry's army),* and thence by Whitchurch and Prees to Shrewsbury, where, on 21st July, 1403, was fought one of the most dreadful of English battles

It was long before the Marches of Wales were at peace   On the 24th Jan 1403-4, *Richard de Bromley*, *John de Kyngesley*, *Thomas le Maistersone*, *Richard le Mascy del Hogh*, *Richard Rope*, *David de Crue* of Pulcroft, *Richard de Wybunbury* and *Hugh del Malpas* were appointed by King Henry IV to hold inquiries in Nantwich Hundred "touching those who spread false rumours to the disquiet of the people of the county of Chester, and the disturbance of the peace there, and also to array all the fencible men of the said hundred "†

Meanwhile a rebellion had broken out in the north, and in 6 Hen IV [1404-5], *John Kingsley* of Nantwich, was required to find 12 bowmen, and *Richard de Minshull* 4 bowmen   (*Harl MSS* 1988 f 135)

On the 18th June, 1406, Thomas Maisterson Esq , of Nantwich, and others "were ordered to conduct a number of men at arms and archers (viz 4 lances and 40 bowmen) of the hundred of Nantwich to the Marches of Wales in the hundred of Broxton, there to remain for the defence of the county against the [Welsh] rebels ' §

On Tuesday next after the feast of St Andrew the Apostle [Nov. 30] 10 Hen IV [1408] Nicholas Parker, of Coppenhall, who held lands in Coppenhall and Nantwich, was outlawed for the death of *Thomas Malbon* (? of Bradley), and by Inquisition taken on Thursday in the second week of Lent, his lands were forfeited to the Crown ‡

War with France having been declared by Henry V, in 1415, the Sheriff of the county was called upon to muster all knights, Esquires and yeomen, at Newcastle-under-Lyme, thence to proceed to France, *John Fox* is the only name preserved in the Cheshire records of a townsman of Nantwich that embarked in that expedition   Three years afterwards, on 30th June, 1418, *Robert Dawson* of Nantwich obtained protection on his going to France in the King's service, and in March, 1421-2, *Thomas Shermon*, of Nantwich, went thither in the retinue of Queen Catherine †

Perhaps the most remarkable man in Nantwich during these eventful war times, was THOMAS MAISTERSON, ESQUIRE, already mentioned in the preceding pages   Born as early, if not before the year of Cressy [1346], in his youth he must have heard of the Poictiers heroes, Sir James de Audlegh of Helegh, Kt , Sir Robert de Fouleshurst of Crewe, Kt , and Sir Richard de Delves of Delves Hall, Kt   He would remember Sir John de Delves Kt purchasing the Doddington estate from the Brescy family in 1351-2, and in 1364, obtaining "*license to fortify and kernellate his mansion at Doddington with stone, chalk, and wood.*"† As a young man, he was present at the battle of Navarette in 1367, with the mighty Cheshire giant Sir Hugh Calveley, who, twenty years afterwards, returned to

* Perhaps it was for this loyal service that Thomas Maisterson Esq obtained exemption from serving on juries in 5 Hen IV [1403-4]   (See *Plea Rolls* of Cheshire)

‡ Cheshire Plea Rolls

† Cheshire Recognizance Rolls

§ The military force of England was divided into (1) Feudal troops and (2) the "*posse comitatus* '   The former consisted of the tenants *in capite*, that is, those holding immediately from the King the quantity of land called a *Knight's Fee* Every such person was bound to hold himself in readiness, with horse and arms, to serve the King in war, at home or abroad, at his own expense, for a stated time (generally 40 days in a year)   This service accomplished, he was at liberty to return home , if, however, he continued in the army, he received pay from the King   These tenants granted to under-tenants lands, liable to the same conditions   The *posse comitatus* included every freeman, between the ages of 15 and 60, for the preservation of peace in England, under the command of the sheriff, and to defend the country in time of invasion They were not called out for foreign service   Thus the troops raised in the county in 1406 were the *posse comitatus*; while the muster in 1415 consisted of the feudal troops of Cheshire

England and rebuilt Bunbury Church. He was still living when John Bromley, of Baddington Hall, so heroically recovered the British Standard at Corbie in 1415, just before the battle of Agincourt, as related by Hollinshead, and perhaps witnessed the burials of the same John Bromley in 1419, and his young esquire Walter de Audlegh, in July, 1420, in Acton churchyard   The following interesting memoir written by his descendant Lawrence Maisterson in 1611, from "evidences & other writtinges of Richard Maisterson Esqr ," of Nantwich, his elder brother, is taken from *Harl MSS* 2119 f 43

"Thomas Maisterson son to Robert was a man of long life He married Katherine Dutton of Halton He served Edward III in his French Wars, went into Spain with Edwd the Black Prince in that honble Jorney wch he made for the restoringe of Peter K of Castill unto his Kingdome He fought in the vantgard with Jo of Gaunt duke of Lancaster against the French, where sir Bertram de Cleaquin constable of France, and the marshall Dandrehen were, which part of the army was in the cruelst fight, not wth standinge, that Henry the Bastard, that usurped, restored and stayed his men thrise that day when they were at poynt to fly for the great valor of the sayd Tho shewed that day, upon ther return to Burdeux, the duke of Lancaster did wyn the sayd Thomas to his service, and by Indenture interchangeably did bind him to serve him in the wairs, upon honourable termes & honourable conditions and to pay him yearly the sum of xli [£10] p ann , out of his receipts of his honor of Halton, as by sayd Indenture may appeare

"Upon their returne from Spaine he made his account wth the Constable of Bordeux & it was found that the Prince was behind wth him for his pay for himselph, his men at armes, & archers, the some of 2738 fortz of Gwyan gold wch sayd money he could neuer be payd, although the Prince appoynted his receivors in Cheshire John Sonde & Jo Allen, to make payment thereof unto him

"After [this] in the tyme of K R II [1391] he was made Eschaetor of Cheshire, and anone [again] he went into Spaine wth Jo of Gaunt, Duke of Lancaster, who went wth great forces thither to take possession of Castill & Leon, in right of his wife Constance dau & heyre to pe er King of Castill, wch jurney had no great good successe by reason of our mens sicknesse contynuinge in that hott countrey " &c

"This Tho Maisterson was written very kindly vnto by ether K R II or H IV , as I take it for cairinge of himselph so well "

"When some of the Countys [Counts or Earls] of Huntingeton, Salisbury together wth the Lord Spencer & others did stir vpp rebellion he is desyred by the Kinge to make opposition against all their p'ceedings & he will be redy to assist him wth all his power

"A letter likewise from K R II to Sr Rafe Vernon, Sr John Griffin, Sr Robt le ffouleshurst de Edleston, Wm de Praers de Baddeley, Willhm Bromley de Batington, Thomas Maisterson, and on[e] Rich de Crew Commandinge & Authorizinge them to call to gether all maner of psons in the hundred of Nantwich, wch by a day named, from the age of 16 to 60 to arme all their owne people to resist the enemy

"This man receued also frendly lres from Hen Duke of Lanc & Earle of Darby after called H IV desiringe him to be redy wth all his people by a day when he should be aduertized by his next lres [letters] etc

"He was with K H IV at Shrewsbury field against the Percys, where he fought right valiantly wch caused his house to be spoyled and all his goods carried away by the sayd percyes seruants * for wch afterward he was a petitioner to the K H IV Lastly he receued his pension of xli p ann of

---

* *Servants*, is here synonymous, perhaps, with *friends* or *favorers* of the cause of the Percies and accepting this old meaning of the word the natural inference is, that the house of Thomas Maisterson in Nantwich was plundered and destroyed by Hotspur's forces in their march towards Shrewsbury

[1 e from] K H V of whom he was greatly esteemed for the seruice done to his father & grandfather
"He lived in the last yeare of H V [1422] so as I conceaue he was hueing in the beginninge of
H VI his raigne   .

' Of all the Maistersons before, I find him to be of the greatest note and account & the best
servitor   Moreover he is called Esqr by those great princes, and one Nicolas Maisterson & Richard
his brother, & Richard his sonne were all called Esquiers in Auntient deeds, and Thomas sonne to
Richard "

On the 8th April 1427, *Richard de Werburton*, sheriff of Chester   *John Starkey*, undersheriff, *John de Wetenhale* of Nantwich, Escheator of Cheshire, *Thomas de Eggesley* and
John Hancocksone, bailiffs of Nantwich Hundred, *John de Wettenhale* of Cholmundeston and
Richard de Golburn of Henhull, coroners of Nantwich Hundred, had orders to arrest the
following persons as disturbers of the peace —Robert, son of Richard de Cholmundeley;
John le Smith, of Hurdleston, Richard de Alvaston, Thomas le Taillor, both of the same
place, and John ap Atha, of Acton, and many others in the neighbourhood *

Not only was the fifteenth century a period of civil war and rebellion, but there is
ample evidence that it was a quarrelsome age, when the lower orders, and the better sort
of people too, were often bound in heavy sums to keep the peace with their neighbours
Persons who had grievances, usually had recourse to arms first, and to law afterwards.
From their tenants, their relatives, or their neighbours, they formed armed bands, and
tried to settle disputes about lands, or vindicate personal wrongs, by a very free use of
sword, pike and bow   Like other places, Nantwich was, at times, the scene of such
riotous proceedings, and an instance has occurred as late as 1572, which will be found
fully described on a subsequent page

The following record, which is only one out of many contained in the Recognizance
Rolls, seems to relate to a serious disturbance of this kind that had taken place at
Nantwich or in its vicinity.†

Feb 26th, 1432-3, Randal le Mainwaring, John son of John de Wetenhale, Richard
de Whelok, and Randle de Wettenhall of Wich-Malbank, enter into a recog for £100 to
the king that the following persons, (most of whom appear to be of Nantwich and its
neighbourhood) keep the peace towards Thomas del Shagh, and Isabel his wife, William
Harrisone and Margaret his wife, Hugh Baker and Mary his wife, John Cutler and Agnes
his wife,—viz —‡

Nicholas de Davenport, gentleman		Thomas de Wetenhale	yoman
Ralph de Macclesfield, do		Ralph de Wettenhall	do
John de Wetenhall, of Wich-Malbank, gentleman		John de Wetenhall	do
Thomas de Wettenhale, of Alpraham	do	Henry de Wetenhall	do
John de Wetenhale, of Cholmondeston	do	John son of Tho Wetenhall	do
Hugh, son of the said John de Wetenhale		Thomas de Wetenhall of Alpraham	do
Ralph, brother of said Hugh Wetenhall		Randle de Wetenhall	do
Thomas Chanu	do	William Brett	do
Adam de Dutton	. yoman	Randal de Merton	do
Hugh de Alcok	do	Thomas de Multon	do
John de Stanyhurst	do	Hugh de Multon	do
Roger de Buren .	do	Thomas Shermon	do

* Chesh Recog Rolls
† See other instances in 37th Report of the Deputy Keeper of the Pub Records
‡ Chesh Recog Rolls

John de Pull	knave	Richard Bothe	.	.	fletcher
John Thornyclyff	do	Robert Alva	..		clerk
Thomas Whembrugge	wevere	William de Hatton		.	wright
Thomas Wevere	do	Richard Spencer			do
Nicholas Henster	waller	John Foster			milleward
Hugh de Cholmyley	do	John Organere			caryor
William Alva	do	John Hudd			mustardman
John Chobbam	. do	Thomas Baxster			baxster

"1434 Aug 2nd Warrant to the Sheriff of Chester [Hugh de Dutton of Hatton] to receive *Thomas Shaw*, of Nantwich, *mason*, (who had been confined in the inner bailiwick of Chester Castle for more than two years and a half) and to produce him on the morrow of the Purification of St Mary [2 Feb] before the King, wheresoever he might be "[k]

What the misdemeanour was that had brought about this long term of imprisonment is not recorded, but the passing notice of a *mason* whose name also occurs on the Plea Rolls ten years earlier in connection with a grant of his lands in Middlewich, points, probably, to the time of the building of the Kingsley Chantry Chapel and the completion of Nantwich Church

One of the principal residents in Nantwich at that time, was John Kingsley, Esq, who seems to have settled here from Kingsley, in Frodsham parish about the year 1400, and to have acquired considerable property here and in eight adjacent townships. His name is often mentioned in the Cheshire Records between the years 1414 and 1441, in various "suits," and on several ' commissions," as the guardian of certain heirs under age, and as the Escheator for the county After the death of his wife, Petronilla, daughter of Thomas Swettenham of Carincham, on the feast of Epiphany [Jan. 6] in 7 Hen VI [1428-9], he appears to have disposed of his Nantwich residence and other property in and near the town, according to the following copy of a deed in *Harl. MSS* 2119 f 26 d *(translated)*—

"Know &c that I John de Kingsley Esq have given &c to Randulph le Maynwaring the elder [of Peover], Ranulph le Maynwaring the younger [of Carincham, his son], John son of John de Wettenhale of Wich Malbank, John de Wetenhale of Cholmundeston, William de Wettenhale of London, grocer, Hughe de Wettenhale and John son of Thomas de Wettenhale of Wich Malbank their heirs and assigns, all my capital house in which I inhabit with all its appurtenances in Wich Malbank, and also all my burgages, messuages, lands &c in the vills of Wich Malbank, Horepulle and Whitepulle with all their appurtenances in the hundred of Wich Malbank called one 18th part of the barony of Wich Malbank, to have and to hold &c

These being witnesses Peter de Dutton, John Sneyd, Laurence Wareyn, John Maynwaringe, Laurence Fitton, John de Carrington, John Honford Kt, Thomas de Wylbram, John Maisterson, Richard Maisterson, Thomas Chana, Thomas de Multon and others

Dated on Monday next before the feast of All Saints [1 Nov] in 10 Hen VI "[1431] †

In the same year, on 10th Aug 1431, an Inquisition was taken at Chester Castle, before John de Bruyn, Escheator, and William de Bulkyley of Ayton one of the King's Commissioners, finding that *John Kyngesley*, of Wich-Malbank, Esq, had, on the 8th Feb. 1417-8, obtained and entered into the possession of Stoke manor, near Hurdelston,

---

* Chesh Recog Rolls

† This Charter is alluded to, but not quoted, in Ormerod's "Cheshire new Edit vol iii p 78 Mr Helsby states that the original "is or was, in the possession of a well known dealer in such documents,—Mr James Coleman formerly of 22 High Street, Bloomsbury *cf* page 61 The Mainwaring share of Nantwich Barony

after the death of Robert de Stoke who had died seized of the same on the feast of St Andrew the Apostle [30th Nov] 2 Hen V [1415], but by what title he held the said manor the jurors were altogether ignorant +   Record does not say whether John Kingsley, in whose life-time the above Inquisition was taken, satisfactorily proved the legality of his claim

A Rent Roll, which has recently been printed by Mr Helsby, seems to imply that John Kingsley, Esq retained a life interest issuing out of the lands &c that he had granted away by charter a few years before. It is here given *(translated)* because of the mention of local field names, most of which still retain the same names.

RENT ROLL OF JOHN KINGSLEY.   17 *Hen. VI*   [1438-9].

	s	d
, *Rents formerly of William de ffouleshurst.*		
A free rent of a place formerly in the tenure of John Wettenhall &c .	30	0
Rents called Saint Pierre land in Wich Malbank		
From John son of John de Wetenhall a free rent for Godwynsley Croft, &c .	0	9
„ Henry Wetenhall for lands in the Wyche field &c	5	0
„ John Wetenhall for croft and right of way in Edlaston &c	0	12
., Henry Wetenhall for lands in le Bromehull &c [perhaps the same as now called "The Brownhills"] · · ·	3	0
„ John Wetenhall for a garden &c ·	0	16
„ A garden near the house of John Wetenhall of Hospetylstrete .	0	12
Lands formerly of Elene mere in Wich Malbank		
From John Wetenhall and Ralph Wyldebor for a meadow called *the Barousmedewe* per ann .	6	0
„ ll Walshmon for 1 Croft formerly in the tenure of Ranulph de Wetenhall per ann	12	0
„ Thomas Wetenhale and William Da for Rydley-fylde per ann	26	8
„ John son of John Wetenhall for 2 Crofts which had been Robert Chomlegh's near *Tynker's Crofts* per ann	12	0

Beyond the fact that he did service in the wars in France and Normandy, little else is recorded of John Kingsley He is believed to have died about the year 1441, but the time and place of his death is not known, as his Inquisition *post mortem* is not to be found   There is no evidence to prove that any other person of note of the name of Kingsley was ever connected with Nantwich, and hence it may be presumed that John Kingsley Esq was the Founder of the Kingsley Chantry in Nantwich Church, which in the sixteenth century had a window decoration to the memory of "——— *Kingsley and Margaret Bromley his wife*"   Mr. Helsby, however, receives this with suspicion, doubting whether John Kingsley Esq married a second time, and suggesting, without adducing any very cogent reasons for doing so, that the heraldic glass represented an alliance between one of the Wettenhalls of Nantwich, who assumed the arms and name of Kingsley, and Margaret Bromley of Baddington +

It is very remarkable that the name *Kingsley* has been handed down to the present time, in the name *Kingsley-field*, situated immediately adjacent to property on the site of which, in former times, stood an important "mansion," called the *"Porch-House,"* adjoining

---

* *Inq per B de intrusio*   Pub Record Office
† *cf*   Ormerod s *Cheshire*, vol ii p 89, *note*, vol iii p 448, *note* New Edit

Fulshurst (now Red Lion) *Lane*, which house was sometime the inheritance of *Henry Wetenhall* of Darfold, in the time of Edward IV,"* and it is not unlikely that that house may have been the identical residence of John Kingsley, Esq

1437. Under this date occurs the will of Randle Wetenhall, (probably the same as Ranulph de Wetenhall mentioned in the Kingsley Rent Roll) which is interesting as being the earliest known will of a Nantwich townsman It was copied into *Harl MSS* 2022, f 66 61 from the original "in the possession of Mr Thomas Wetenhall of Nantwich Ano. 1691,' and is as follows *(translated)—*

"20 Oct 1437 In the name of God Amen I, Randle Wetenhall of sound mind and perfect memory do make my will &c I commend my soul to Almighty God, and the blessed Mary, and all the saints, and my body to be buried in the churchyard of the Church of Wich Malbank, on the north part near the chancel of the said Church

Item I give my best animal by way of principal +

Item In wax to be burned around my body, and on the anniversary days of my death and burial £10 in wax

Item To my servant Agnes, 1 bed, namely, 1 coverlet, one piece of fine linen and two pillows

Item To Robert Sonkey, chaplain, 2 shillings

Item To a certain chaplain in the church at Wich Malbank for celebrating [mass] 1 shilling

Item To John Barr, clerk, 1 shilling

Item To the fabric of the said Church a great *"ollam"*‡

Item I give and concede to John Wetenhall my son, after my decease all those lands and tenements my rents and services with appurtenances which Richard Eske, briner, and Bigmalens sometime held in Coole

I give and concede to the said John my son, after the decease of Ellen my wife, all my lands and tenements rents and services with appurtenances which I have in the county of Chester or elsewhere, and all the rest of my goods not before bequeathed

I give and bequeath these to Ellen my wife that she may carry out this my will, well and faithfully

I constitute and ordain William parradise, chaplain, and John Wetenhall my son, my legal and true executors

In witness whereof &c Dated at Wich Malbank on the day and in the year aforesaid "

Probate

"In the name of God &c The present will was proved before us in the deanery of Wich Malbank on Thursday in the feast of St Marcellus the martyr [Jan 16] in the Church of the said Wich Malbank, in the year 1437 8 &c "

It is difficult to say who Randle Wetenhall was Mr Helsby§ places him in the ancient Wetenhall pedigree, as the son of John de Wetenhall, who was living in the 10 Rich II [1386-7], and the younger brother of John de Wetenhall of Wich-Malbank, who was

---

* Partridge's Hist of Nantwich 1774, p 34 The *Porch-House* is mentioned as follows in the Parish Registers
  '1600 May 2 Edward Massye, Gent & Margaret Wright of *porche*' [Married]
  1607 Sep 15 Margaret, dau of Roger Wright of the *porche* '' [Baptised]
  "1609 May 29 Alice Wright widow of the *porche* '' [Buried]

† That is, the *corse present* or *mortuary*, being the best horse or cow which would be led before the corpse at the funeral, and would belong most likely to the Abbot of Combermere as a recompense for his personal tithes and offerings then, and soon after falling due

‡ *"Ollam,"*—probably some sacred vessel used in the service of the mass ? whether used at the altar in the Kingsley Chantry Chapel

§ Ormerod's *Cheshire*, vol iii p 479, New Edit

Escheator of Cheshire from 1422 to 1428, but he makes no mention of this will, nor of John Wetenhall, the son of the testator   From the Kingsley Rent Roll, it is clear there were two John Wetenhalls living in Nantwich in 1438, but as the *Inq p m* of Randle Wetenhall is not now preserved at the Record Office, it cannot be determined which of the two resided at the house in "*Hospetylstrete*"   The extraordinarily large sum left as *cerage money*, and the gift of *bed-furniture** to a faithful servant, unmistakeably prove Randle Wetenhall to have been a man of wealth

Respecting his burial place, it is stated in *Harl MSS* 2151 p 96, from Church notes taken in the latter part of the seventeenth century, that in the "Churchyard, on the outside the chancell, on the north side, is cut in stone about a yard fro the ground, this coate,"—namely, a shield bearing a cross engrailed, which was the Wetenhall coat of arms.

William Smith, in his "Description of the County Palatine of Chester" (*temp* Eliz *c* 1600), says—"The most part of this towne (Nantwich) was miserably consumed with fire in July anno 1438"   No further particulars of this conflagration are to be found   The town seems to have been speedily rebuilt, and the salt-trade resuscitated; for on 1st July, in the following year, Sir Richard Hangford, Kt, was proved to have died seized, *inter alia*, of 2 salt-pits [i e houses] in Wich-Malbank, held of the Earl of Chester, *in capite*, and valued at 10s per ann †

Between the years 1443 and 1463 the name of John Maisterson of Nantwich occurs on no less than thirty Recognizance Rolls, in which he is bound in the large sum of £100, to keep the peace with John son of John de Wetenhall, and Thomas Maisterson his kinsman   Long before the settlement of this prolonged personal quarrel, a serious riot had broken out in the neighbourhood, and on 18th Oct 1445, the following gentlemen were appointed commissioners to arrest all disturbers of the peace in the hundred of Wich-Malbank, viz —‡

JOHN MAINWARING KT	JOHN SON OF JOHN WETENHALL
RANDLE MAINWARING, SENIOR	RICHARD MAISTERSON
RALPH DE EGERTON	THOMAS MAISTERSON
ROBERT FOULESHURST	THOMAS DAWISON
JOHN BROMLEY	ROGER PRAERS
JOHN ROOPE, ARMIGER [ESQ]	RALPH DAKYN
RALPH MAINWARING, JUNIOR	RICHARD WILDBORE
THOMAS DE WILBERHAM.	JOHN WETENHALE.

The year 1459 is memorable for the renewal of the Civil War, called the Wars of the Roses, after the hollow reconciliation of the two factions in the previous year   Richard

---

* An old local antiquary says —"There are olde men yet dwelling in the village where I remayne, which have noted three things to be marvellously altered in Englande within their sound remembrance   One is, the multitude of chimnies lately erected   whereas, in their younger days there were not above two or three, if so many, in most uplandish townes of the realme   (the religious houses and mannour places of their lordes always excepted   and peradventure some great personages), but each one made his fire against a rere dosse in the hall where he dined and dressed his meate "

The second is, the great amendement of lodginge   for sayd they, our fathers, and we ourselves, have lyen full oft upon straw pallettes, covered onely with a sheete and coverlettes made of dogswain or hop-harlots   and a good round logge under their heads insteade of a boulster   If it were so that our fathers, or the good man of the house, had a mattress or flock bed, and thereto a sacke of chafe to rest hys head upon, he thought himself as well lodged as the lorde of the towne, so well were they contented   Pillowes, sayde they, were thoughte meete onely for women in childbed   As for servants if they had any sheete above them it was well   for seldom had they any under their carcase [body] to keep them from the pricking strawes that ran oft thorow the canvass, and raced their hardened hides [skins]

" The third thinge they tell of is the exchange of treene platters into pewter, and woode spoones into silver or tin ' &c —(Hollinshed's *Chronicles of England*, cap 10, describing the manners of the people in the 16th century)

† Cheshire Inquisitions.   ‡ Chesh. Recog Rolls

Neville, Earl of Salisbury, marching from Yorkshire to join the forces of the Duke of York at Ludlow, was intercepted in his progress at Bloreheath, near Market Drayton, by John Lord Audley (one of the lords of Wich-Malbank) with an army of ten thousand men raised chiefly in Cheshire and Shropshire, who bore the badge of a "white swan," said to have been given them by Queen Margaret   A savage battle ensued on Sunday, 23rd Sep 1459   The veteran Earl, though fighting against great odds, obtained the victory by first feigning a retreat and then skilfully veering round to attack the Lancastrian army that had left their vantage ground   In the fight, so disastrous to many noble families of Cheshire, Lord Audley and 2400 of his army were slain *

In 1461 Sir Hugh Wyche, Kt a mercer of London, but a native of Nantwich, (p 84) fulfilled the important office and high dignity of Lord Mayor of that City †

The few events in the County Records relating to Nantwich in the latter half of the fifteenth century, speak of the disturbed state of the country consequent upon the Wars of the Roses

On the 18th March 1476-7, a general pardon was granted to the following men of Wich-Malbank—"*Roger Darkus or Dilkes*, butcher , *James Dod , William Drake*, tailour , *Roger Fazacreley , Thomas Willey* yeoman , and *Ralph Hassall*, Gent "‡

In 1480 the *posse comitatus* was again called out, by *John Bromley, Robert Fouleshurst, Kt* , and *Laurence Roope, Esq* , who on Nov. 18th were appointed "commissioners to array the fencible men of the hundred, between the ages of 16 and 60 before Christmas following, and to command the same to be in readiness, in warlike array, to attend the Earl of Chester, upon three days notice "   That some insurrection had actually taken place, may be inferred from the fact, that the same gentlemen, together with *Hugh Eggerton,* of Wrynehill, *John Maynwaring*, and *Ralph Delves*, were commissioned on 26th Sept 1481, to arrest all outlaws in the Hundred of Nantwich   It was not until after 15th Dec 1484 that quiet was again enjoyed in the county ‡

The next time the home troops were called out was on the 10th April, 1497, when "*Sir Richard Pole, Kt* , *Ralph Delves, Esq* , *John Minshull, William Wiltraham, Thomas Starkey* of Wrenbury, *Thomas Bromley* of Wich-Malbank, *Roger Maynwaryng*, and *Ralph Birkenhead*, were commanded to array the fencible men of the hundred of Nantwich, before the 1st of May following," on account of the Cornish Rising in that year, headed by James Lord Audley, one of the lords of Wich-Malbank   The defeat of the insurgents at Blackheath, near London, on the 22nd June, and the execution of Lord Audley on the 28th of the same month, probably rendered the march of Cheshire troops to the capital unnecessary   This was the last of the three rebellions in Hen VII reign, in each of which, as has been already remarked, one of the lords of Wich-Malbank had taken a leading part, and suffered for their treason , namely, *Lord Lovell* in the Simnel insurrection of 1487 , *Sir William Stanley* in the cause of Perkin Warbeck, in 1495 , and within two years after, *Lord Audley* in the Cornish Rising

---

* On the battle-field a monument, called the *Audley Cross*, was afterwards erected, which   was repaired in 1765 at the charge of the Lord of the Manor Charles Boothby Skrymsher "—(Inscription on the Cross)

† Orridge's "Citizens of London and their Rulers "

‡ Chesh Recog Rolls

In the 15 Hen VII [1500] the Lords of Wich-Malbank were required by a writ of "*quo warranto*" to show by what title they held privileges of fair, market courts, &c in Nantwich, and, as previously stated, they had their claims allowed (see page 66) King Henry and his successor frequently adopted this course of extorting money from their subjects to replenish the royal coffers, for, on the issue of a *quo warranto* writ, if the lord and burgesses of a town failed to prove their right to hold fairs, markets, &c, those rights with their profits, as in the case of heirless property, reverted to the Crown

According to Plea Rolls dated 23 Hen VII [1507-8] *Henry Sparke* of Wich-Malbank obtained exemption from serving on Juries   This is the first mention of a family of some note that continued to reside in the town for about a century after this date   By the following deed, preserved among the Wilbraham MSS, Henry Sparke granted in perpetuity to Nantwich Church, for the benefit of the minister, a certain *walling-land* in the town. The deed is as follows *(translated)*—

"Know all present and to come, that I, Henry Sparke of Wich Malbank have given, conceded, and by this my present charter indented have confirmed to *Nicolas Harwar*, chaplain, Gilbert Walthall, Roger Brooke and Roger Sparke a wiche-house of six leads lying in Wich-Malbank aforesaid between the land of the Abbot of the Monastery of the Blessed Mary of Combermere on the west part, and the land of William Eggerton on the east part, and the land of the Priors of the Monastery of Saint Thomas the Martyr near Stafford[*] on the north part, and the King's High Street upon the south part, To have and to hold in trust &c to them their heirs and assigns for ever, ffirst I will that my said feoffees of trust shall suffer me and Elizabeth my wife to occupy the said wich-house of six leads with the appurtenances during our lives natural and to the longer liver of us to our moste advantage and after our decease I will that my said feoffees of trust and their heirs shall suffer the wardens of the Church of Wich Malbank for the time being to occupy and to take the advantage of the said wich-house &c to the use profit and behoof of the said Church to the sustentation and maintaining of God's service therein for ever

I have made and constituted my beloved in Christ, John Leche of Wich Malbank my true and legal attorney, &c   In testimony whereof &c   I have affixed my seal

These being witnesses, *Thomas Maisterson, Thomas Chetwode, Robert Harwar, Thomas Willey Richard Taylor* and others

Dated at Wich Malbank the 14 June in the 7 Hen VIII [1515]"

Two hundred years after, this property is described in the will of *Richard Horton*, Innholder of the Lamb Inn, Nantwich, (dated 1st Feb 1714, and proved at Chester 10th Oct 1715) as "one messuage or burgage with its appurtenances situate and being near the *bridge* in Nantwich, in possession or occupation of Robert Lynne belonging to the Minister of Nantwich for the time being under the payment of the yearly rent of *Ten Shillings*"   In Bishop Gastrell's valuation of the living of Nantwich in 1722[†] it occurs again —

"*House given by Mr Sparke*   .   £0 10s 0d per ann"

One branch of the Spark family left Nantwich, and settled in the parish of Plympton St. Maurice, near Plymouth, co Devon, where they continued to reside until the end of

---

[*] The property belonging to the Priory of St Thomas near Stafford is described in *Valor Ecclesiasticus* 26 Hen VIII [1535], as, Two salt-houses, valued at £2 13s 4d per annum.

[†] *Notitia Cestriensis*, p 222   Edit 1845,

the seventeenth century, according to the following inscriptions on a flat stone in the aisle of that Church —

> "John Sparke from Nantwich, Cheshire, buried here 11 July 1566
> "John his son, 14 Jan 1597
> "John his grandfather [?] 1630
> "Nicholas, his son, aged 107, at Plympton St Mary 1700
> "John, his scn, at Plympton St Mary, 1694."

Returning to the year 1515, on the 15th September, George, Earl of Shrewsbury wrote to Wolsey, then Prime Minister and Lord Chancellor of England, beseeching "that *Thomas Wilbraham* of Wich Malbank, may be called before the Council for a cruel murder done upon *Randolph More* of the same town," and further acquainting him "that the murderer is supported by the gentlemen of the county, and that More is to be indicted for his own death his widow sues for redress," and the said More "did the King good service in his last voyage beyond the sea, then being in the Earl's company"[*]

In 1525 a dispute between *Thomas Smythe* and *Robert Crocket* of Wich Malbank, concerning the claim of the former to a right of way through a field belonging to the said Robert Crocket was decided by an Inquisition, of which the following is an abstract *(translated)*—[†]

Inquisition taken at Wich Malbank on Wednesday in the feast of St Lucy the Virgin [Dec 13] in 17 Hen VIII [1525] before George Helsby Knt &c by the oathes of Richard Hassall of Honkelow, Richard Rope, senr, Hugh Wetenhall of Cholmeston, John Chenue of Wisterston [Willaston], Thomas Cranage Ralph Malbon, of Hatherton, Thomas Cheswis, Richard Kerdiff Junr, Ralph Gresti John Ithell, Hugh Aston of Aston, and John Hassall, Jurors, who say upon their oathes that to *Thomas Smythe* there ought to be a certain way diverging from Wich Malbank, as far as a certain pasture and meadow of his lying in Wistaston *alias* Willaston, namely, beginning at Wich Malbank and leading to another King's high-way that leads to Wistaston Church, and as far as a certain field of *Robert Crocket's* of Wich Malbank, and then entering into a certain broken part called a gap, continually in width three perches from the west to the south part of the same field, and leading and passing through a ditch &c &c In testimony whereof &c

On the 1st Aug 1526, *Richard Verney* obtained the grant for life, of the offices of the two bailiffs in the town of Wich-Malbank [‡] By Act of Parliament 27 Hen VIII [1535-6] Justices of the peace were appointed in Cheshire and Flint, in order that common justice might be better administered,[§] *Richard Hassall* of Hankylow, being the first J P for Nantwich He had been made serjeant-at-law for Chester on 18th May, 3 Hen VIII [1511], and on 22nd Oct 32 Hen. VIII [1540] was made vice-Justice of Chester [||]

In 1538 new orders for the better government of the town were drawn up by Sir Thomas Fouleshurst, Knight, and sanctioned by the Court Leet   (pp 29-34)

When the privileges of the Palatinate were abridged by Henry VIII, the inhabitants of Cheshire petitioned the King that they might send Knights and burgesses to Parliament, in consequence of which an Act was passed in 1542 that two Knights should be returned for the County, and two burgesses for the city of Chester, and for this new privilege a

---

* Calend State Papers, Dom Series, 1515-18, Vol 11 No 911
† Chesh Inquis Pub Record Office   ‡ Recog Rolls (Chesh Records)
§ Lysons' Cheshire, p 302 || Officers List (Chesh Records)

Subsidy appears to have been levied on the County, in 1545.

The following extract from the *Subsidy Roll* for Nantwich Hundred gives the names of the chief inhabitants of the town at that time, the value of their property, and the amount of the King's tax.

SUBSIDY ROLL.*

"*Hundred of Nantwich in the Co^y of Chester the acc^t of the Collection of the Subsidy levied in the parliam^t held at Westminster 37th year of the King's Reign, from the Residents in that Hundred for the use of the King.*" [1545].

SIR RANDLE MAYNWARYNG KNT one of the Commissioners of the Hundred of Nantwich

    for lands and tenements tax^d at an annual value of £30   .   .   £8

SIR HENRY DELVES KNT, another of the Commissioners of the Hundred of Nantwich for

    lands and tenements valued at £20   .   £3

RICHARD HASSALL, another of the Commissioners for property valued at £16   16s 0d

NANTWICH.

			s	d				s	d
Thos Maisterson for property worth £18			18	0	Robert Pyckeryng for property worth £7			4	8
John Twemloe	,,	£5	3	4	Henry Wixsted	,,	£8	5	4
Roger Bromall	,,	£5	3	4	Gylbert Wylliams	,,	£5	3	4
William ffleytcher	,,	£7	4	8	Margaret Leche, widow	,,	£5	3	4
Thomas Bickerton	,,	£5	3	4	Margaret Sparke, widow	,	£5	3	4
Richard Maisterson	,,	£5	3	4	Margaret Broke	,,	£5	3	4
Humphry Wright	,,	£8	5	4	Elizabeth Shuryngton, widow	,,	£5	3	4
Margaret Sadler, widow	,,	£5	3	4	Roger Broke	,,	£7	4	8
Richard Bebynton	,,	£5	3	4	William Bromley	,,	£11	11	0
Humphrey Maynwaring	,,	£7	4	8	Richard Robinson	,,	£10	10	0
Robert Graye	,,	£5	3	4	John Ancors	,,	£8	5	4
Ralph Mynshull	,,	£5 .	3	4	Thomas Glegge	,	£5	3	4
Joan Harwai, widow	,,	£5	3	4	Oliver Maynwaring	,,	£9	11	0
Edward Mynshull, mercer	,,	£10	10	0	John Wright	,,	£8	5	4
Roger Wright, junior	,,	£5	3	4	Nicholas Drake	,,	£8 .	5	4
Roger Wright, senior	,,	£8	5	4	Ralph Olton	,,	£8	5	4
Edmund Wright	,,	£5	3	4	Katherine Maisterson, widow	,,	£8	5	4
John Alexander	,,	£10	10	0	John True	,,	£5	3	4
Henry Wright	,,	£8	5	4	John Blackesha	,,	£12	12	0
Richard Wright	,,	£9	6	0	John Leche	,,	£12	12	0
Edward Mynshull senr	,,	£8	5	4	John Weston	,,	£5	3	4
John Seckerston senr	,,	£10	10	0	John Parker	,,	£7	4	8
William Tenche	,,	£10	10	0	Richard Wright	,,	£5	3	4
Edward Tenche	,,	£5	3	4	Roger Sparke	,,	£5	3	4
Ralph Wilbraham	,,	£8	5	4	Nicholas Goldsmyth	,,	£5	4	0
William Wettenhall	,,	£8	5	4	Robert Goodyere	,,	£5	3	4
Ralph Bebynton	,,	£6 .	4	0	Gilbert Walthall	,,	£18	. 18	0
William Kente	,,	£7	4	8	Edmund Taillor	,,	£7	4	8
Henry Bickerton	,,	£7	4	8					

* From a parchment Roll being either a contemporaneous copy or else the original roll, now in the possession of J Bellamy Minshull, Esq, of London

Then follows the list of persons taxed in the various townships of the Hundred, and at the end—

"Total of the whole Subsidy £88 5s 3d"

"Names of those elected to receive the money & to make payment into the Treasury at Westminster"

"*John Bryne, Armiger.* [Esquire]

"*John Mynshull, Armiger.* [Esquire]

"List. Extracts delivered by the Commissioners to *John Bryne & John Mynshull* collectors to the s^d Commission &c to receive payments from *Wm Bromley* of Norbury, *John Breyn* of Aston, *Thomas Titley* of Pole, & *Richard Wilbraham* of Bryndeley sub-collectors."

In 1551 England was visited for the last time with the dreadful plague known as the *Sweating Sickness,* which had appeared in the years 1485, 1506, 1517 and 1528 As the earliest recorded burial in the parish registers only dates back to 1572, it is impossible to say to what extent Nantwich suffered from the "*posting sweat,*" as it was also called, "that posted from towne to towne throughe England" The pestilence of 1551 is said to have first manifested itself at Shrewsbury on the 16th April, and in a few days 960 died there * Edmund Gee, Mayor of Chester, was a victim during his year of office—1550-1. In the month of June, 1551, at Marbury village a few miles south of Nantwich, the register records the burials of sixteen persons who "dyed of ye sweating sicknes as y^t seemeth" So serious and widespread had it become, that on the 18th July, 1551, the Bishops of the land were desired "to exhort the people to a diligent attendance at Common Prayer, and so to avert the displeasure of Almighty God having visited the realm with the extreme plague of sudden death "†

In or about the month of January, 1559-60, *Sir Laurence Smith* Kt , *Sir Ralph Eggerton* Kt , *Robert Corbet* Esquire, and *John Mynshull* Esquire, were appointed collectors of a *mize* in Nantwich Hundred,‡ which became due to Queen Elizabeth, after the death of the late Queen Mary It was an ancient custom, that lingered long after this date, for the county of Chester to raise in the course of three years the sum of 3000 marks [£2000] as a present to every rightful owner of the Earldom, levied by a rate or tax, called, in Cheshire, a *mize,* which in Nantwich town, amounted to £3 11s 6d for each year.

On the 18th March, 1567-8, at the instance of *Roger Maisterson, Roger Walthall, John Leche* and *Thomas Clutton,* burgesses of Nantwich, the Town Charter confirming the privilege of exemption to the burgesses of the town from serving on juries out of the town, was granted by Queen Elizabeth (see page 79)

Thomas Mynshull, mercer of Nantwich, in his *Book of Accounts* &c , now in the possession of George F Wilbraham, Esq , of Delamere, makes the following memorandum —

"Roger crowckett of the crowne, inhowlder was sleayne the xixth of December in the welche roe in the fiftinthe yeare of the reane of our quaine Elizabeth" [1572]

The following detailed account of the murder is here given on the authority of another MS. in the possession of G. F Wilbraham, Esq , entitled "*Examinations touchinge the death*

---

* Chambers's Encyclop vol ix p 235 and Book of Days I p 518-9

† Calendar of State Papers 1547-80   ‡ Cheshire Recog Rolls

of Roger Croket, of Namptwiche, in the countie of Chester, Gent ," consisting of sixty folios, and containing the depositions of 116 persons in answer to no less than 214 interrogatories at a Privy Sessions held at Nantwich shortly after the 22nd December, 1572, on which day the Coroner's Inquest had been held in the Parish Church

The affray, which resulted in the death of this gentleman, appears to have been the outcome of a quarrel of long standing between the families of Hassall and Croket. Richard Hassall, of Welsh Row, Gent , and his father before him, held a lease of *Ridley-field,* and before the expiration of his tenancy, Roger Croket, by purchase from the landlord, Mr. Edward Leighe, of Leicestershire, obtained the next lease, thereby giving offence to the then tenant   Much ill-feeling was manifested between the two parties, and, each having his own friends and supporters, great jealousy and excitement prevailed among the towns-people   Early on the morning of Wednesday, the 19th December, Roger Croket took possession of the field, and soon after his friend, Thomas Wetenhall, Gent , was assaulted in the fields near Townsend, by Thomas Wilson.   About 8 a m Roger Wetenhall, Gent brother of Thomas, was walking from the "*Crown*" towards his house in Welsh Row, when he was attacked by Richard Hassall, Gent , armed with a pike-staff and a dagger, in *Little Wood Street,* and pursued to the further end of *Wood Street,* where he received serious injury.   Meanwhile many people had congregated, armed with staves, &c.   One brandished a "fire-shovel," another a   dubbing-hook," and as Roger Croket was pushing his way through the crowd with a pike-staff, towards his friend Wetenhall, he received a blow on the head, which one witness (Rondell Lytler) said "would have stryken down Brayne's Bull yf he had been among them ," the force of which felled him to the ground. Immediately after, Mr Richard Wilbraham, of Welsh Row, Gent , came upon the scene at "Wood Street end near the Channel "

Several witnesses describe Mr Wilbraham hurrying to the *mêlée* "straight from his chamber, without shoes or slyppers, holding his hose with one hand, and carrying a staff in the other, his doublet being untrussed," and having "on a red petticoat with a white fur hanging out behind, and a black cap on his head "

It is clear from the depositions that Mr Wilbraham's arrival at once put an end to the affray, and so prevented further mischief   Calling to his brother-in-law, the said Richard Hassall, who was at some distance from the place where the unfortunate Croket lay, Mr Wilbraham led Mr. Hassall home, and the crowd dispersed   Roger Croket died about twelve hours after , and on the following day *Sir Laurence Smith,* of Hough, Knt , issued a warrant to the deputy Steward of the town *(Thos Clutton),* the Bailiffe *(Rondall Alvaston),* and to the Constables *(John Wixsted* and *John Brett)* to apprehend the murderer, no name, however, being given , thereupon the friends of the deceased supplied the names of Richard Wilbraham, and Richard Hassall, Gents , Thomas Wilson, Edmund Crewe, and divers others, who appear to have been arrested , and in order to make good their charge, they endeavoured, in a very strange manner, to prove that Roger Croket had died, not from *one* blow, but from many wounds   To this end, a painter *(John Hunter)* was employed to make a picture of the corpse, showing the wounds of which it was alleged R C had died.   The naked body was also publicly exposed in the street , and "during the height of the markett " on the following Saturday   At three o'clock on that day, the corpse was carried thence on a bier into the Church, to the Inquest, followed by the noisy, gazing crowd which by the Coroner's *(John Minshull Esq)* order was expelled therefrom by the Constables, who during the inquiry, guarded the Church door   The verdict of the Jury was that Roger Croket had died from *one* blow on the head , and *Randle Goldsmith* (foreman of the Jury), *Richard Edgeley* (the Coroner's clerk) and others deposed to the same in the succeeding trial at the Sessions   The decisions of both Inquest and Sessions inquiries being unsatisfactory to the friends of the deceased, an appeal was made to the Court of Assize at Chester   and Richard Wilbraham, Richard Hassall, and others were arraigned, but were finally acquitted by the Jury who were fully satisfied that the prosecution was malicious "

A list of witnesses in the trial at Nantwich is here appended, forming an interesting calendar of local names chiefly of the lower orders , many of which names continue to the present time , and when taken in connection with another list of resident Gentlemen and Freeholders, dated only seven years after, (1579) the reader will have the names of more than one hundred families, representing perhaps, not less than half the population of the town three hundred years ago

LIST OF DEPONENTS' NAMES AT NANTWICH SESSIONS TRIAL, 1572

Thomas Wetenhall of Namptwiche of the age of liij [53] years

Roger Weterhall of Namptwiche of the age of xlvij [47] years

Thomas Palyn, servant to Roger Crocket of the Crown Inn

Nicolas Maisterson, a ' corvisor," or shoemaker

Bridgett Croket, widow of Roger Croket

Hugh Lowe, a cleaver of wood at John Gibbons wyche-house

Marget Wryght

Jane Daniell, a waller under Roger Wetenhall

Richard Wryght, *alias* Kendall, a "clayman ' He was repairing a wiche-house of Thos Clutton's when the fray began

Humphrey Manwaringe, at the schoole at the schoole-house besydes the churche "

Margery Wryght

John Lovett, who dwelt by Acton Church, and came that day to N to buy a bushel of malt and had it ground at Thomas Wetenhall's " mylne. '

William Kelsall

Randall Alvaston, a ' deputie bailiffe ' He was buried 18th Nov 1593 (Par Reg)

Richard Horobyn, a servant at the Crown

Ma'get Turner

Reynold Jackson, who was "in his own wiche-house, next to Wood Streate lane end, and the contrary end to where the fray begann "

William Jackson, of Little Wood Street, son of Reynold Jackson.

Jone Jackson, wife to William Jackson

Willm Sparke a farm servant of Roger Brown of Chorley

Edmond Spariowe a weaver

Thomas Clerke, servant of Mr Edward Leighe of Leicestershire

John Wixsted, constable of Nantwich

John Brett constable of Nartwich

Ciceley Mainwaringe lived in the country and was natural sister to the mother of Roger Croket

Thomas Shenton the elder

Thomas Shenton the younger

Richard Smythe

Edward Starkey a servant of Mr R Hassall's

Cicely Huxley, a maidservant of Hassall's, she was spinning at her wheel in the hall of Mr H 's House, and "lookinge throughe the glasse wyndowe, saw the people runne in the stieete "

Margett Hare, another maidservant of Hassall s

William ffoxley, tenant of Roger Croket ⎫
John Key   ⎪ These three drove Ridley
Robte fforest   ⎬ field by order of
                                        ⎭ Roger Cioket

Johan Shyre

John Hill servant of Hassall

William Greene, of Minshull Vernon, a husbandman, of the age of 60 years

Thomas Bressy

John Houyet (? Hewitt) 'taylor of Wich-Malbank, aged 58 yeares "

Margett Blackshawe, of the Welshe Row, aged 30 years

John Gryffyn, butcher of N aged 37 years

Randull Lytler, "of Monks Copnall "

* This trial at Chester is adverted to by Roger Wilbraham, of Nantwich, Esq , in his Journal   See Annals under date 1670

John Hunter, of Namptwiche, painter
Richard Horbott of little Acton
Thomas Dodd of N shoemaker
Thomas Halmarke, of the parish of Acton
Olyu [Oliver] Brooke, of N servant at the Crown
William Jackson, "of lyttle Acton'
John Lowe, Vycar of Acton'
Agnes Clare of N servant at the Crown
Ales Gerrerd, "wydowe of Namptwiche"
Raphe Hulse, "of Wysterson"
John Sparrowe, of N brother to Edmund Sparrowe
George Harvson, of the parish of Acton
Roger Lowe, of Nantwich
Thomas Shenton, of Nantwich
Robte Goodier, described as a 'dealer for Croket
Ales Sparrowe
John Gryffyn, Gent, of Bartherton
Richard Gryffyn, Gent, of Bartherton (probably son of
    John G)
Thomas Hurleston
Henry Wryght
John Wryght
Raphe Ince, butcher
Ales Greenold
Joan Hall
Roger Parker
Margery Parker, a waller, working in Rich Robinson's
    wiche-house
Oliv' [Oliver] Parker
Ellen Ince, wife to Raphe Ince
Anne Ankers, servant at the Crown
Roger Hocknell
Margery Shenton
Margarett Smythe
Roger Brooke
Gilbert Clare
Roberte Cheney
Richard Chetwood
John Parker
Thomas Barton
Isabel Barton
John Ankers, brother to Anne Ankers
Agnes Clare
John Gibbons

Roberte Pickeringe He deposed that he came with Mr
    R Wilbraham to the fray after Roger Croket was
    wounded
Marian W xsted
John Gorste, of Wood Street, into whose house Roger
    Croket was carried
Nicholas Reade, a blacksmith in Wood St , aged 26
Richard Cally
Marget Ryder, wife to Humphrey Ryder
Jone Hulse, aunt to Croket, and sister to Hassall
Cicely Crewe
Marget Crewe, "widowe"
Mawde Leycester
Richard Aston
Ellen Turner
Ales Huxley a girl who was "sent of an arrond by her
    father"
Jane Gardener
Marget Buckley, servant to Mr R Wilbraham, she "was
    spinning in the kitchen when the fray began"
Ales Whorall, a waller, who was going to the wiche house
Marg'et Bickerton, of Wood Street
Jone Blymston, servant to Margaret Bickerton
Ales Platt
Katneryn Horobyn, sister to Margt Hall the wife of
    Thos Hall
Margery Crewe, "lived in the house next saving to Rich
    Hassall"
Richard Crewe "yeoman, of the Brydge end," who was
    called to be on the inquest, but because of his name
    was set asyde,' being probably related to Edmund
    Crewe, whom several witnesses deposed to having
    given R C "the great blow '
John Mynshull Esqre (Coroner) "came to N and vewed
    the body' of R C
John Prestland
Richard Edgeley, "clerk to the Coroner'
Richard Hulse
Thomas Cartwright
Thomas Bryndley
Richard Rodes
John Browne
Thomas Venables

"MEMORAND that *Randull Goldsmith* and xv mõe [15 more] beinge of the Coron's enqueste appeared before vs the comission^{rs} this day bringinge with them the Counter payne of theire v^{r}dicte wch they gave up to the Coron'. for the vewe of the body of Rog^r Croket, and they affirme they saw noe mõe [more] strokes uppon his body then ys mencioned in the said v^{r}dicte, whereof they have delivered us a coppy signed wth their handes."

LIST OF GENTLEMEN AND FREEHOLDERS RESIDENT IN
NANTWICH. 1579.*

ROGER MAISTERSON, GENT.	LAURENCE WRIGHT.
ROGER WALTHALL, GENT.	JASPER RUTTER, GENT.
THOMAS CLUTTON, GENT.	RICHARD GODIER.
RICHARD HASSALL, GENT.	JOHN CREW.
WILLIAM BROMLEY, GENT.	RICHARD CHURCH.
RICHARD MAISTERSON, GENT.	JEFFREY MINSHULL.
JOHN LEECH, GENT.	THOMAS MAINWARINGE.
RICHARD WILBRAHAM, GENT.	JOHN MAINEWARINGE, MAIOR.
ROGER MAINWARING, GENT.	JOHN MAINEWARINGE, MINOR.
ROBERT CROCKETT, GENT.	JOHN MAINEWARINGE, MINIMUS.
THOMAS WETENHALL, GENT.	JAMES BULLEN.
HUMPHREY MAINWARING, GENT.	JOHN SECASTON.
HENRY WRIGHT, SENIOR.	JOHN TENCH.
HENRY WRIGHT, JUNIOR.	RICHARD ROBINSON.
RICHARD WRIGHT.	RICHARD WIXTED.
THOMAS WRIGHT.	WILLIAM TENCH.
REGINOLD WRIGHT.	THOMAS CHURCH.

Richard Wilbraham, in his MS. Journal, has the following memoranda relating to a serious flood, and the building of his family mansion, called Townsend.

"*Mem.* The 26th day of November 1574 & Ao. [in the year] of the reigne Eliz. 17th. there rose a fludd upon Wever that drowned in the towne of Namptwich 40 dwellinge howses in the Welshe Rowe & 24 wiche-howses so that all of theym were aboute a yarde deepe w[i]th water in them. Weever came up to the brydge."

"*Mem.* That the byldyng of my howse dyd beygine in ffebruarie Ao. 1575."

"That my ffirst comyng to Dwelle in my howse was in the vj[th] daye of August 1580."

---

* This List, entitled "The names of all and singular Knights, Esquires, Gentlemen and Freeholders in Com. Cestriæ, for Nantwich Hundred, *temp.* Eliz. 1579," is preserved in *Harl. MSS.* 1988, f. 121-2. (Brit. Mus.)

The Great Fire.

N the night of Tuesday, the 10th December, 1583, the greater part of the town was destroyed by fire. According to the earliest printed account of the catastrophe, the outbreak originated *"through negligence of undiscreet persons brewing;"* * and this fully agrees with a Memorandum by Allen Wright, written in the earliest volume of the Parish Registers, which was afterwards copied in red ink into the first parchment Register, by Hugh Price, who subscribed his *own*, instead of the author's name. The Mem., which has been printed many times, but not always correctly, is as follows :—

"The X day of this Monnth [Dec.] chaunced a most tereble and vehement fyre begininge at the water lood† about vi of the clocke at night, in a Kitchen by Bruinge, the winde being very boysterous, increased ye sayd fyre, which very vehemently wasted and consumed (in the space of 15 houres) 600 bayes of buildinges, and could not be stayed nether by labour nor pollitye, which I thought good to comend unto the posterety as a favorable punishment of th' almightye in destroyinge the buildins and goods only, but sparing the lyves of many people (wch considering ye time space and perell) were in great jopardy yet by gods mercye, but only two persons that pereshed by fyre."

"ALEN WRIGHTE whoe ssawe the saide
ffire and wrotte this."

From this account, it may be inferred that the high wind would not only fan the flames and carry them along the thatched roofs with great rapidity; but the thousand sparks and fire-flakes shot into the air as the old oak houses one after another fell in, would be driven onward as *avant-courrieres* of destruction; while the inhabitants, terror-stricken with the suddenness and seriousness of the conflagration, must have rushed wildly in all directions to escape the roaring furnaces of the streets on that December night. On the following day, all that remained of the town on the east side of the river was the Church, the Grammar School, the Corn-mill, and a few residences in the less crowded parts of the town, at the ends of Beam Street, Hospital Street and Pillory Street, as stated in the following detailed account by Richard Wilbraham, in his MS. Journal, which though written three hundred years ago, is here printed for the first time.

"*Mem.* That the xth of December Ao. Dni. 1583 & in the xxvj yere of the reigne of or soueragne ladye Elizabeth about v of the clocke in the eveninge there began by godds sufferaunce such a ffyer in this towne of namptwiche in A howse of Jo[hn] Crewe joyning to the water loode wch howse was in the tenure of Nycolas Browne. And first beganne in his Kytchen : And by reason of an extreme greate westerlye wynde ytt speedelye burned up to the hie town : And soe burned most extremeley all that nyghte tyll ytt was upon the other Day aboute viij [8] of the clocke in the morninge most grevus & lamentable & ffearffull to beholde in wch tyme there was consumed by the same ffyeer All the buyldings in the hyghe towne upon bothe sydes from the seyd howse wherein yt began joyning to the wather

* Stowe's *Annals.* Edit. 1592. p. 1189.
† *Water-lode* is the way leading from the High Street to the Weaver, just above the Town Bridge.

lode up to the pillore strete & all the pillore strete upon boothe sydes tyll yt came to the beete brydge except one howse wherein Robt Goddier dwelled all the hospell strete vpon both sydes past the myddest thereoff & dyd staye at the howse of Thoms wryghte upon ye sowth syde of the strete And at another howse* of Mr Wylorahms of Woodehey wherein Randull Maynewaring dwelled upon ye north syde yt burned all the church lane Downe ffrom the seyd hospell streete to the churche yarde on bothe sydes and all howses rownd about the same churchyarde And from the churche yarde yt burned a stretet leding to the beast markett‡ in the beame strete on bothe sydes yt burned more the sowth syde of the same beame strete from a cesterne called lothburne draine§ to the snow hyll wth a strete leding ca!led love lane‖ on both sydes wch strete ledyth from the hie towne to the beame strete And in this crewell ffier there was left no manner of tymber bylding stick or block of Any howse in all these streetes & compasse thereof named except one peece of a wall of the howse wherein ytt began, wch peece of the same wall standing till the day ffollowing in the afoor noon As women were carrying water from weever yt fell downe & kylled a woman carrying of water whoe was wyffe of Thoms lovatt ¶ After all the tymber of these howses were cleane consumed yea the verre stonne of chymneys burnt & fell in peces & nothing left butt the brycke chymneys standing in a straung post [position] yett the ffyer burned in the heapes of fier cooles in tymber & sylle [cellars] under the yerth [earth] that the people contynewed carrying of water by the space of ii or iii dayes after for Daunger of burning the rest of the hospell strete & mylne strete the wynde contynewed soe greate And in the first nyghte the churche stode in soe greate daungr by reason of sparkes & fflames of ffyre cast upon the leade thereoff that the people dyde ffeare greatly yt wolde have been burned but god dyd prserve ytt whose name be praysed to whom I pray to Give us his Grace of repentaunce & to be warned by this his generall admonycon & soe to Amende or lyves from the hiest to the lowest for ffeare of his further punyshment Amen

The numbre of the howses wch were burned that nighte were one hundred and ffiftie wth all shoppes kytchens stables & other howses of office belonging And aboute xxxtie shoppes of several psons as dwelled in other places of the towne ij [2] horse mylles ij [2] barnes many swyne styes & swyne in them ij [2] women burned in their howses,,.* mooste lamentable to thinke of there were amongest these seyde howses vij [7] of them Innes for loging & very ffayre viz. the ship, wherein dwelled one Seckerston the cocke, Jon Walker, but Mr Willm Bromleys landes [i e landlord or owner] the bell, Richard Wryghte the Crowne Robt Crockett the harts horne Jon Maynwaring the swanne Ric Gryffyn but Joh Wydenburyes his lande [i e landlord] the beyr, Jon Seckerston, who having in his stable iijor [4] great beyres of his dyd lose theym out in the beginning to the streete whereoff the women were soe affrayed they durst nott carrye water onelesse the[y] were accompanyed wth men havyng wepons to Deffende theym ffrom the same beyres & much goodes were brought out off the howses & more stollen & moste burned in the howses

This ffire was not all quenched in the space of xxtie dayes after yt first begann but burned in the yerth & in sell[ers] of the howses wch lay in the yerth & The quenes most excellent mat'ie beinge enformed by the godly prchr [preacher] Mr Alexandt Nowell*₊* of the foreseyde burnynge of this towne And therebye moved wth greate pyttie of her highness charitable benevolence she gave towardes the re-ediffiyng off the

---

* Probably the house now known as "*Sweet-briar Hall*"   † Pepper Street
‡ Beast Market in Beam Street between Pepper Street end and Swine Market
§ Now a culvert passing under the Shakespeare Inn
‖ Now Oat Market (See Partridge's Hist of Nantwich, p 8)
¶ She was buried on the same day according to the Burial Register—
          "1583 Dec 11th Ann, wife of Thos Lovart, Kild with the fall of a wall '
*₊ They were probably the following given in the Burial Register—
          "1583 Dec 12 Margery Daughter of Rondull Duckworth .
                    Alis Blagge widow
₊ Alexander Nowell was Dean of St. Paul s, London

same towne a thousande poundes of money * And moreover Dyrected her gracious lrēs. [letters] to ye lorde Mayor & Aldermen of the Cittie of london for their charitable benevolence whereupon there was collected in all the wards of london & gyven ffrelye vijch [£700], and moreover her highress commanded her Honorable Councillors in her name to Direct & sende out lrēs to allmost all the byshopps in Englande for collec[ti]ons in their seu'all provinces & Dioces wth lyke lrēs. to moost of the best Cities & townes in Englande, and the mooste p[ar]te of the sheryffes in England for colleccons in the same Cittes townes and shires towards the re-ediffyinge the same Towne Whereupon great sumes were gathered & presᵈ [presented] but certainlie butt ffewe dyd knowe who were the Doers but the like charytable benevolence hath nott been seen & herde God saffe our gracious quene Elizabeth "

Another singular circumstance is related by Thomas Mynshull, mercer, of Nantwich, (whose shop, house, furniture, and kitchen were totally destroyed), in these words—†

"1583 I and my cowssen mathewe wright beinge the same yeare constabeles goot [got] the Day byfoore hit was browned [burned] xvij [17] cartes loeed [cart-loads] wth mvnision [ammunition] owt of our towne presed [praised] be the Lorde "

The following Letter, addressed by the Lords of the Council to William Chadderton, Lord Bishop of Chester, for a collection in his diocese, shows how these "Briefs" were issued. It has recently been printed in the "Cheshire Sheaf," No 934, and in a similar "Letter of the Justices of Peace to the High Constables of the ffranchises of Bury St. Edmunds about their collecting the charity of well disposed people towards the losses of the inhabitants of Nantwich by the Great fire," contained in Harl. MSS 368, p 126, and dated 27th March, 1584, it is also stated that 800 houses were consumed, a number, no doubt, much over-estimated.

The Letter is as follows —

" After oure verie hartie comendations

Whereas, by misadventure of fyer [which] happened within the towne of Nauntwiche in the countie of Chester upon the x day of December last, there was burnt and consumed (as we have bene verey credible enformed from our verie good lord therle of Derbie & others of good credit) to the number of DCCC [800] houses, with the most part of the goods & househoulde stuffe of the inhabitants to a verie great valew, wherebie a great number of the sayd inhabitants, beinge men of good wealth, are, with their wives, children & families, utterlie spoyled and undone, and the towne become desolate, which of late was not onlie of good wealth & trade by reason of [its] situation but alsoe of good importaunce for the service of her majestie & the realme (beinge a th'oughe-fare, lyinge convenient, for the receipt of souldiers, carrages, [i,e baggage] and munition to be sent unto the realme of Ireland).

The queens maiestie there fore, of her gracious disposition, having her self [given] towards the relief of the said inhabitants a good valew hopinge that her lovinge subiects will also have consideration of the lamentable estate of those poore afflicted inhabitants, as they would desire relief of other, upon the like visitation from Gods hands

To that ende it hathe pleased her majestie to com annd us most earnestlie, in her name, to recommende the same unto your lordship, and to require you, not onlie by your owne good example in contributinge in some reasonable manner, but by dealinge effectualye with your clergie to yeild there devotion the more largelie, to farther soe charitable and necessarie a purpose, and that vow appoint some men of good credit and reputation to collect the said contribu ion and devotion, & send the same to the citie of Chester, there to be delivered to the handes of the maior of the same citie [Robert Brerewood] and Christopher Gooodman preacher, together with your letters, mentioning the summes collected and sent, and further [to] advertise us by youre letters thereof

Wherein we praye yow to cause all convenient expedition to be used, in respect of the present necessitie of the people so as therebie they maie be speidelie relieved, and her maiestie occasioned to accept well of youre doings therein

* The statements of Partridge that " the damage was computed at 30,000 pounds," and that the Queen gave " 2,000 pounds and a grant of a considerable quantity of timber out of the royal forest of Delamere," (Hist Nantwich, p 28-9), probably rest on no better authority than the tradition of the town

† Minshull Accounts in the possession of G F Wilbrabam, Esq

And soe, trustinge that this shall surffice, we bid yow farewell   From Westminster, the xi of March 1583-4.
Your lordships verie lovinge frends

T Bromley, canc [Chancellor]   Fra Knolles
W Burghley   James Crofte
E Lincolne   Chr Hatton
R Lecester   Fra Walsingham
H Haward   Wal Mildmay
John Hunsdon

To oure verie good lord, the
lord Bishop of Chester "

Four Collectors for the diocese of Chester appear to have been appointed by the Bishop, two of whom are mentioned by name in Webb's "*Itineraiy*" (*c* 1625) viz .— *Sir Hugh Cholmondeley Kt*, (probably the son and heir of Sir Hugh who had purchased so much of the Barony of Wich-Malbank) and *Mr John Maisterson*, of Nantwich, whose burial is thus recorded in the Parish Registers—

"1586 Dec 23 Mr John Maisterson on [e] of the 4 comisshoners for coleftor "

Of the amount collected in this county, however, no particulars are known, but the following sums from various cities, towns, parishes, municipal bodies, &c. are to be found in a volume of the Calendar of State Papers

		£	s	d
"1584 May 2 The Mayor and citizens of *Chichester* to the Council " (at London)		5	0	0
" " 4 The Mayor and Jurats of *Sandwick*		13	1	6
" " 5 Wm Furnesse, Mayor, and the Aldermen of *Oxford** &c have collected and sent to Mr Tho Aldersey and Tho Brasey, merchants & citizens of London†		10	0	0
" " 12 Richard Goddarde, Mayor, and the Aldermen of *Southampton* to the Council Have sent to Thos Aldersey and Tho Brasey, of London, &c		5	18	9
" " 20 The Bailiffs and Citizens of *Lichfield*, &c .		6	0	7
" " 31 *Christchurch Oxford* Dr Tho Thornton informed the Council, that he had sent up the money collected in the *University of Oxford* for the relief of the town of Namptwich, and is sorry the state of the University did not enable them to give more &c		24	12	8
" June 28 Bishop Scorey, informs the council, he "has dealt effectually with the clergy of *Hereford* and collected and sent up £28 18s from them for the relief of Namptwich, and £5 of his own benevolence Many of the Clergy, however, "did use themselves very contemptuoushe "		33	18	0
" July 2 Anthony Collie, sheriff, Kenelme Digby, and others, Justices of the *county of Rutland*, inform the Council they have collected and sent up the sum of £8 for the relief of Namptwich and begging the acceptance of the same as from the smallest shire in England		8	0	0

---

* The following extracts from the Council books of the Corporation of Oxford show how the Orders for the Collection were carried out in that city, and how this sum was realized

"26 *Elizabeth, Apl* 13 *ffor Namptwiche* "

"Hit is agreed at this Counsell that collection shalbe made of all the comons of thys Cytie towards the reliffe of the town of Namptwiche in the countie of Chester by reason of the fire that happened theare on the xth of December 1583, in manner and forme followinge That is to saye in everie parishe collectors appoynted " &c   The amounts are as follows—

St Aldates parishe	viijs vd	St Thomas parishe	vjs
St Martins parishe	viijs id	St Mychaells parishe	iijs xjd
St Maries parishe	xjs vjd	All Saynots parishe	xs —
St Peters in the Est	vjs xd	St Peters in the Baylie	iiijs xd ob,
Magdalene parishe	vs iiijd	St Ebbes parishe	iiijs xjd
St Gyles parishe	xixd	Holliwell	ijs xd

"26 *Elizabeth*, 27 *April*   *ffor Namptwiche*
"Hit is agreed at this counsayle that the thertene shall paye towards the collecon for Namptwiche everie one ij s everie Bayliffe xvjd everie Chamberlen xijd, everie of the comon counsayle viijd and what shall want of the somme of tenne pounds in all shalbe payed and layed fortne owt of the comon treasure of this Cytie " (Local Gleanings, 1st Series, Vol II p 5)

† Thomas Aldersey and Thomas Brassey belonged to Cheshire families of those names.

	£	s	d
1584 July 17 John Wolton, Bishop of Exeter, informs Sir F Walsyngham that he has collected the sum of £20 16s 7d within the diocese of *Exeter* &c Is sorry he could not collect more as the clergy had to contribute in a similar way for relief of Sampford Peverell in Devon, lately burnt	20	16	7
,, Aug 24 The Sheriffs and Justices of Peace in *Gloucestershire* &c	56	6	0
,, Oct 10 Sir William Courtenay and others, Justices of Devonshire, &c	35	0	0
,, Oct 17 Sir Ric Grevnville informs Walsingham, that he sends a further sum of £20 for the relief of Namptwich ″ and that "the County generally complain of the great burtheus laid upon them ″	20	0	0

Some idea of the national sympathy manifested for the distressed inhabitants, and the trouble taken that charity should meet this distress, may be formed from the fact that it was nearly two years after the fire, before the collection was finally closed, as proved by the following State Paper—

"1585. Nov 13 Brief declaration of the total amount of money collected in the several counties throughout the realm, for the re-edifying of the town of Namptwich lately consumed by casualty of fire   delivered into the hands of Thomas Aldersey and Tho Brasey, merchants of London, and to the Mayor of Chester [Edmund Gamull] and Mr Goodman the preacher [Rector of St Bridget's, Chester, &c ,] including the Queen's most liberable gift of £1,000 amounting in the whole to the sum of £3224 6s 9½d."

Mr Thomas Mynshull, mercer, of Nantwich, who states in his *"Accounts"* that he commenced business in the year 1572, makes the following curious entries relative to the rebuilding of his house and shop near *"the twerling gate,"* *"*in *Pepper Street,'* and the actual sum received from Mr. John Maisterson in compensation for his loss

"pead Jhon gambole of bewrtone [Buerton] after that these towe howses weare brownte for the tember fraimes ard bringinge home & rearinge '	xxxvjli.—£36
"pead for the finishinge of botne these howses by a Just a cownt set Downe	xxxli —£30
"lead owte one howsell [houschold] fornetewre as silling [? shelves] bedstedes, stowles [stools] bowrdes [tables] and silde cheres [chairs]	ixli —£9
"pead owen a morre, carpenter, for the buldinge and for finishinge of my stabell and cloes howse	xiiijli.—£14
"pead for platte [plate] a s'ver [silver] salte, and xij [12] postell spownes, a Drinking can and foore [4] spownes	xviijli —£18
Total	£108
'that mr Jhon mestersone gave me towardes my buldinges	liijli vjs 8d —£53 6s 8d

The town was speedily rebuilt on the lines of its former streets. Camden, Smith, and Webb, topographical writers between the years 1586 and 1625, all speak in praise of the new-built town, and some of the houses with their quaintly figured gables, remain to this day, but many, during the present century, have been either defaced or demolished, and what is even worse, no artist has left to posterity any illustration of the streets of this once picturesque town   A house* in High-town, now in the occupation of Mr. Sandford, grocer, and which has been a grocer's shop at least for a century back, commemorates the rebuilding of Nantwich by the following inscription on a board in Roman capitals —

* This house narrowly escaped destruction by fire early in the morning of Thursday, 16th Nov. 1882, when the adjoining premises, occupied by Mr John Walley, draper, were burnt down

GOD GRANTE OVR RYAL QVEEN
IN ENGLAND LONGE TO RAIGN
FOR SHE HATH PVT HER HELPING
HAND TO BILD THIS TOWNE AGAIN
THOMAS CLEESE MADE THIS WORKE
THE YEARE OF OVRE LORDE
GOD 1584

When the block of houses and shops in Hightown were taken down (Christmas, 1872), another curious inscription, probably of the same date, deeply carved in oak, and which had long been hidden behind successive coats of plaster, was discovered It ran thus—

"A BEWTIFVL FACE IS A DVMBE PRAIS FAIRE WOMÊ[N]
BE DAVNGEROVS MARKES FOR YONG MENS EYES
CHOOSE NOT THY WIFE BY HIR BEWTY BVT BY HIR HONESTY " [i e chastity]

With a view to the prevention as far as possible of a conflagration so wide-spread and calamitous, water-works appear to have been at once erected on the Weaver on the north side of the Corn Mills, and wood water-mains, (simply trunks of alder trees hollowed out, and tapered at one end to fit one into the other), were laid along the principal streets, having at intervals a hole for fire-plug connections. A line in the Burial Register records the name of the person who designed and carried out this scheme

"1638 Sept 13 William Sands, *Mr* [Master] *& devisor of the water workes* " [Buried]

Occasionally portions of these mains are unearthed in almost as sound a condition as when they were first laid down, but the works on the Weaver, which, by means of a wheel, raised the water from the river and supplied the mains, were themselves destroyed by fire, together with Messrs Eddleston & Co's Cotton works, in the year 1799, and never afterwards rebuilt, the site being now occupied by gardens

News of the sad calamity described in the foregoing pages reached GEOFFREY WHYTNEY, a native of Coole Pilate, near Nantwich, who, at the time, was probably living at Leyden, in Holland The following quaint lines taken from the second part of his "*Choice of Emblemes*," published in 1586, may fitly close this account of an event that forms so important a crisis in the history of the town

"*Unica semper avis* [The bird always alone]

To my countrimen of the Namptwiche in Cheshire "

Device a Phœnix rising out of its own ashes

" THE Phœnix rare, with fethers fresh of hewe,
ARABIAS righte, and sacred to the Sonne
Whome, other birdes with wonder seeme to vewe,
Dothe liue vntill a thousande yeares bee ronne
Then makes a pile which, when with Sonne it burnes
Shee flies therein, and so to ashes turnes.

Whereof, behoulde, an other Phœnix rare,
With speede dothe rise most beautifull and faire:
And thoughe for truthe, this manie doe declare,
Yet thereunto, I meane not for to sweare,
    Althoughe I knowe that Aucthors witnes true
    What here I write, bothe of the oulde, and newe.

Which when I wayed, the newe, and eke the oulde,
I thought vppon youre towne destroyed with fire:
And did in minde, the newe NAMPWICHE behoulde,
A spectacle for anie mans desire:
    Whose buildinges braue, where cinders weare but late,
    Did represente (me thought) the Phœnix fate.

And as the oulde, was manie hundreth yeares
A towne of fame, before it felt that crosse:
Euen soe, (I hope) this WICHE, that nowe appeares,
A Phœnix age shall laste, and knowe no losse:
    Which GOD vouchsafe, who make you thankfull, all:
    That see this rise, and sawe the other fall."

OLD HOUSES.

Historical Annals.—(Continued.)

ESIDES the evils of pestilence and fire, Nantwich has had its share of suffering in times of famine. In these days of free trade and cheap food, it is difficult to realize the amount of distress amongst the inhabitants of small towns in former times, when food was at famine prices. Before the passing of the Inclosure Act in 1836, and the more recent changes effected by the Inclosure Commissioners, towns and villages had their heaths, mosses, wide, open lanes, and waste lands; and although the principal farms have existed as such for hundreds of years, yet, it was formerly thought that light land was scarcely capable of cultivation; arable land being always stiff clay land. Consequently, in wet seasons, the grain crops suffered severely, and bad harvests brought local distress; for communication was bad, and food could seldom be brought from distant places in large quantities. A few particulars are here given of times of great scarcity in 1585 and 1597.

1585. "This last yeare began a greate Derthe of corn in England wch contynewed all that yeare ffollowing beyng 1586; in wch Derthe corne was solde in this towne of Namptwiche as followeth, viz.:— Wheat, at xxxvish. the bushell or thereabouts; Rye, at xxviijsh. the bushell or thereabouts; Barlye, at xxsh. or more; Otes, at viij or ixsh. the bushell; and at harvest 1587 ytt fell in the price greatlye. Wheat came to xs.: Rye to vjsh.: and barley to vsh. or lytle more." (*Wilb. MSS. Journal*).*

1586. "This yeare passed the towne of namptwiche and dyvers other townes were vissited with a kind of frenzy or madd Ague of which Disease ther dyed the yeare aforesayd about seven score and odd persons in this towne." (*Parish Register*).

Only 138 burials are recorded; of which 98 occur from May to September; the greatest number, 30, being in the month of August. The Burial Register also mentions the following untimely deaths :—

"1587 April 12. Lawrence Woolley, slain with a goon."
"1588 Oct. 11. Wm. Gibbons kild by a fall of a rouche of wood."
"1588-9 Jan. 28. James Vernonn slain by William Louart."

With patriotic pride the parish Clerk made the following memorandum in the Register, concerning the memorable year of 1588.

"This yeare passed the Spaniards with a great navye of shipps and a great multitud of men Intended to have invaded this Realme : against whome our queene provided a great power both by land and by sea: the land souldiers camped at a place called tilbery ; but our englishe navy fought very valliantly with the Spaniards, betwixt callais and dover, wher the Spaniard had a great ouerthrow and many of them slayn and taken prisoners, and finally the rest of ther shipps by tempest were Dispersed and sunken, soe that fewe or non retorned to bring K. phillipe newes of ther Adventure."

---

* This scarcity of corn was so severely felt in Gloucestershire, that the people "were driven to the last extremity by famine, and forced to feed their children with cats, dogs, and roots of nettles." (Calend. of State Papers, Vol. 188; dated 30th April, 1586).

Other local patriots occur among "*The Names of the Nobility, Gentry and others who contributed to the Defence of this Country at the time of the Spanish Invasion in 1588*,"* as follows —

	£	s	d
"Thomas Wilbram, of Woodhey	25	0	0
Henrie Delves, of Doddington, Armiger [Esq] 24 March	25	0	0
Richard Cotton, of Combermere, Armiger 17 March	25	0	0
Thomas Vernon, of Haslington, Armiger 13 March	25	0	0
Roger Manwering, of Nantwich, 17 March	25	0	0
Richard Wilbram of Nantwich, eodem die	25	0	0
Richard Church, of Nantwich, eodem	25	0	0
Geffrie Minshall, of Nantwich, [mercer] eodem	25	0	0

In 1591 there died in the town a centenarian—

"1591 Sep 30 Richd Lewes, a 100 yeares ould "—(Burial Reg)

"1596 Aug 22 George ffallowes late come from Cales [Cadiz] in Spaine " [buried] (Par Reg)

"This yeare the Right honourable Robt Deuorax Earle of Essex accompanied with a great Army of men, & a great navy of ships put to seas in the later end of Aprill, and the xx° day of June the[y] landed at a Noble mart towne in Spayne called Cales [Cadiz] wch beinge by our navy valliantly assayled, was as coragiously defended by the Spaniards, both by lande and seas, by reason thereof the fight indured very fearce and hott the space of 4 houres, yet in the end the spaniards had the foyle, ther best ships taken, and many of the rest sonnke, and chased out of the harborow

finallie the noble Gennerall landed his men, repulst 800 horsemen upon land and tooke the towne with the spoyle thereof, and burnt it, only 2000 women he sent away very honorably wth ther goods and lyves, also at his returne he took the towne of Faro in portugall, but out of those hott countryes they brought home a kinde of fluxe which spreed ouer all England, whereof followed a great Death of people in many places, and in this towne of Namptwiche, also, the first wch dyed in this towne of the same fluxe was the befoie remembred George fallowes "—(Par Reg)

The number of registered burials in 1596 is 165 the greatest mortality being in these months—December 40, Jan 49, Feb 21, and March 18.

The year 1597 was one of great scarcity of provisions

"This yeare was a great Dearth of corne and other vittuls Gennerally throughout this Lande, for wheat was sould at foure marks [£2 13s 4d] the Bushell Rye at forty-foure shillings ye bushell barley at twenty-eight shillings ye Bushell, pease and beanes at thirty-tow shillinges, and mault at forty shillings Ale was sowlde at 4d the quart, the scaresety was soe great that many pooer people were a ffamished, and soundrey of good account were utterly impouerished "—(Par Reg)†

Richard Wilbraham mentions similar prices in his Journal, and says the famine "punyshede all degrees, especially the pore houshoulders, soe that greate syckness by ffamyne ensued & many poore dyed‡ thereoff & yff greate store of wheate & rye especially had nott been brought to london & other hauen towns from Denmarke & holland &c where there was this yeare greate plenty (by god his merceyfull prouydence) yt ys lyke wee had ffelt & hadde a greate mortalytie '

* Originally printed in 1798, and reprinted in "Local Gleanings" 1st Series, Vol II p 228-9

† This extract was printed in Gent Mag for Jan 1801 with the following note—
        "N B —*The wages of artisans at this time was 7½d per day* "

‡ The burial Reg records 92 in the year, or more than double the average mortality of other years, amongst whom is mentioned,   "George Clowes of the age of 100 yeares, 10 April, 1597"

Another native of Nantwich, the celebrated *John Gerard*, in his "Herbal" (page 63) alludes to the great importation of Rye from "Germanie and Polonia," "in the year 1596 and at other times, when there was a generall want of bread corne, by reason of the abundance of raine that fell the yeere before, whereby great penurie insued, as well of cattell, and all other victuals, as of all manner of graine"

Thomas Mynshull, mercer, of Nantwich, in his "Accounts' for the year 1597, says —

"The genes [gains] of my shop this Deare yeare did amownt vnto by my a cowntes just 10 li   £100
"The genes [gains] of my shop this yeare by resone I bowght soe lettell wares and the greatt Darthe web all was lesser by "   11yxx li   £60
"All the gene of my shop was spent but v li [£5] by resone of the Darthe and great charges I lived at and givinge a wey to the powre, for corne was at such a verie fearefull prise

Wheat the bowshell at 43sh to 45sh				Owtes the bowshell at 20sh			
Rie	,,	,,	, 42sh	benes	,,	,,	,, 24sh
Malte	,,	,,	,, 35sh	pease	,,	,,	,, 2, sh
Barley		,,	,, 30sh				

In 1603 the Parish Clerk paid the following tribute to the memory of the great Queen, whom, doubtless, all Nantwich would mourn

1603 March "The 24th daye of this Mounth Died the most noble & Renowned christianne Queene Elizabeth, our most gracyous gouernoui, when she had raigned 44 yeares and more   And the same daye was K James of Scotland with a generall good likinge of all English men proclaymed K & supreame Gouernour of England ffraunce & Ireland & he was crowned together with the Queene the 25 of July next followinge at Westminster, whose happie raignes god longe continue "

In 1604 the town was visited by that terrible epidemic—THE PLAGUE   The *Wilbraham MS Journal says —"yt vppon St Peters Day [June 29] 1604 there began a great plague in this Towne of Namptwiche, wch continued about six monthes, whereof there died in that space about 500 people, and soe by Gods mercifful providence the plague ceased "*

The Parish Register gives a more explicit account —

"1604 July This yeare together with the former yeare & the yeare followinge this Realme of England was vissited with a contagious plauge generally whereof many thousands in London, and other Townes & Cities dyed of the same   The said plauge begane in our Towne of Namptwich about the 24th of June 1604, being brough[t] out of Chester and here dispersed diversly, soe yt presently our Market was spoyled, the town abandoned of all the wealthy inhabitants who fledd for refuge into diuers places of the country adioyninge   But of those which remained at home ther Dyed from the 12th June till the 2nd of March followinge about the number of 430 persons of all deseases   Now seeing god in mercy hath withdrawn his punishinge hand, & hath quenched the spark of contagious infection among us   God graunt that we by Repentaunce may prevent further punishment & that the remembrance of this plauge past, may remain in our hearts for that purpose for ever   Amen "

No Marriage register was kept in 1604, the Baptisms are wanting from Aug 12th to the 10th March following, and only 366 burials, of which none are expressly said to have died of this horrible disease, are recorded   The clerk has notified this irregularity in keeping the Parish Books, accounting for it "*by reason of the plauge which hinder'd the good procedinge of the Regester for that yeare* "

The number of Burials entered is—

1604.	April	4	Aug.	103	Dec	11	
	May	7	Sep.	96	Jan.	3	Total 366
	June	2	Oct	45	Feb.	4	
	July	64	Nov	25	March	2	

The following extracts illustrate how whole families were cut off.

"1604 July 2 Dorothy wiffe of Richard Crocket
,, 2 The Crown mayde
,, 2 Ann Sutton
,, 5 Mris Ellen Bromley, widdow
,, 14 Henry sonne of Hugh Manwaringe gent [of the Crown Inn]
,, ,, Rodger Wright, mercer
,, ,, John Rutter, gent
,, ,, Hugh, sonne of Hugh Manwaringe, gent
,, ,, Prudence, dau of Hugh Manwaringe, gent
,, 15 Roger, son of Hugh Manwaringe, gent
,, ,, Jane, daughter of Hugh Manwaringe, gent
,, ,, William, son of Hugh Manwaringe, gent

July 18 Jasper Rutter gent
,, 18 Urselo wife of Jasper Rutter gent
Aug 5 Raphe Crockett of the Welche Rowe
,, 7 Ann Poole keper at the Crowne
,, 11 Ellen Lowe servant to Mrs Crockett
,, 12 Ann daught of Thomas Goulborne
,, 13 Thomas Goulbourne, Taylor
, ,, John son of Thomas Goulbourne
,, 14 Elizabeth Coden, Mrs Crocketts servant
Oct 30 William Houlford Minester [of Nantwich Parish] Dyed
Nov 6 Ann wife of Mr Houlford, minester "

To meet the distress a county rate, amounting to "halfe the whole pay^{mt} of the myze," appears to have been levied, and *Harl MSS* 2090 f 18-20 contain "*various sums of money collected in Macclesfield Hundred &c by order of Sessions holden at Chester 10 Oct. 1604, towards the relief of the towns of Namptwiche and Northwyche, infected with the Plague*' The Constables of the Hundreds, who collected the rate, paid the monies to appointed receivers and presented their accounts to the magistrates, who paid over the sums for the purpose intended at different times Thus about Aug 1605 the following sums were disbursed from Macclesfield Hundred, (52^{sh} 11^d then remaining to be collected)—

"*Impr* to m^r Delues his man for the Namptwich v^{li} [£6]

"*Item* delivered to Sr Urian Leigh wch was lykewise p^d vnto m^r Delues his man v^{li} [£5]

The plague appears to have been particularly fatal for five months, making its greatest ravages in Aug and Sept, as also in other years elsewhere, not only in England but throughout Europe. For months after the town was freed from the infection, all persons leaving the town were required to produce certificates of removal Thus—*

"*Richard Maisterson and 13 other residents bailiffs and constables of Nantwich to the Justices of the Peace gentry & inhabitants of Manchester.*"

"Being required to certify our knowledge touching the behaviour of John Warrant, Henry Brooke, Ellen Foulke and Cicely Smith, late of this town, and now in Manchester, while the sickness remained here, we certify that in the last visitation, they were severally visited with the sickness, and that during that time they demeaned themselves orderly, without doing anything that might breed any danger or infection to their neighbours"   [Dated] "Nantwich 31 July 1605 "

Chester suffered severely from the Plague for several years in succession, and in 1605, in consequence of this visitation, the Court of Exchequer was removed to Tarvin; and the COUNTY ASSIZES were held at Nantwich, *Sir Richard Lewkenor* and *Henry Townesend* being Chief Justices, and *Richard Broughton* vice-justice, at the time

* Calendar of State Papers, Addenda Jac 1, vol xxxviii p 478 (1580—1625)

A severe winter is noted in the Parish Register as follows —

"In this yeare 1607 was an extreame great ffrost which began about St Andrews Day [30 Nov] before Christyde, and continued till the first week of Lent following, which was about ix weekes   The extremity whereof caused great scarsety of water for Cattell soe that many dyed in sundry places of this land   Tames at London was frosen 5 foote thick   The same forced man, svche as were deseased to yeald to nature, especially ould people   The Lord in mercy soften our frosen hearts as we may better imbrace the word of god, and be freed from the lyke punishements ' —(*Par Reg*)

Amongst the old people that died was—

"*Jan 25 John Weston of Aspell Streete a man of an 103 yeares ould* "—(Bur Reg)

During the years 1607 and 1608 Nantwich, like other towns about that time, manifested opposition to the newly imposed Canon 91, [1 Jac I (1603)] which transferred the power of electing Parish Clerks from the Vestry to the Clergy, thus making the office an ecclesiastical instead of a secular one.   After the death of *John Bullen*, clerk of Nantwich in Oct 1606, in accordance with the new Canon, Sir Edward Coke, Kt as lord of the Countess of Warwick's Fee, nominated *Mr John Pearson*, master of the Grammar School, who was in holy orders, to the Clerkship, and, the consent of the Bishop having been obtained, he was duly installed by Mr John Bradwall, Minister of Nantwich Church Mr Thomas Maynwaring and other parishioners, refusing to submit to the innovation, forcibly ejected Pearson, and selected in his place *Thomas Clowes*, a native townsman, and a layman, and for that act they were cited to appear before the Ecclesiastical Court. In the end, *Clowes* was suffered to retain the Clerkship, but the following documents* afford evidence of the excited state of the town, and will be read with interest inasmuch as both Archbishops were appealed to while the dispute was pending

DOCUMENTS RELATING TO THE CLERKSHIP OF NANTWICH

[I]

"Sr Chr'er [Christopher] Hatton, Knight late Lo Chancellor of England being seised in fee (by purchase from Mr ffulleshurst] of the franchise or liberty in the Towne of Namptwch called the Countesse of Warwick's fee, wherevnto certaine Court Leets, the Bellmanship of the Towne, the Tolles of the Corne Markett and *nominacon of the Clarke of the Churche* did time out of mind belong, Did about Twenty yeares synce [i e about the year 1586] grant the sayd Clarkshipp vnder his hand and seale to one *Thomas Bulleyne*† whoe enioyed the place during his life and died in November [*sic* for October] was twelue moneth " [i e a year ago last Oct or Nov]

"After the death of Bulleyne the former grant being sent vp to my Lo Cooke‡ [Coke, Lord Chief Justice] by some of the Townesmen whoe then desired a newe grant thearof from his Lo[rdship], his Lo afterwards granted the place vnder his hand and seale to John Pearson schoolemaster there during his life in like sort as Sr Chre'r Hatton had done "

"My Lo Cooke afterwards acquaynting the Lo Bishop of Chester wth this grant the Lo Bishop gaue his assent thearvnto vpon knowledge of the p'ties [party's] sufficiency for the place   And likewise

---

* Original papers *penes me*

† The Parish Registers record,—
      "1586 Thomas Bullen & Elenor Tenche, dau of John Tenche, dyer [were married] Jan 17th
      "1587 July 25 James son of Thomas Bullen Clarke, and Ellen his wife " [Bapt]
      "1606 Oct 7 Thomas Bullen, Clearke " [Buried]

‡ Sir Edward Coke, Kt had married for his second wife Lady Elizabeth Hatton, the grand-daughter of Queen Elizabeth's High Treasurer, Lord Burleigh, and widow of Sir William Hatton, *alias* Newport, Lord Chancellor Hatton's nephew and heir

John Bradwell the Curate of the Churche there vpon Chrms day after, at the time of diuine service did assent to the grant and did then publiqly nominate the sayd Pearson to be Clarke according to the late Canons, who then tooke his place and enioyed it twoe or three moneths together "

" Afterwards some of the Townesmen incouraged the rest to displace Pearson wch they violently did, and putt one *Clowes* in his place whearvpon Pearson complayned to the Lo Bishop of Chester and other the Comission's there for causes Ecclesiasticall and by there [their] order was restored to the possession vntill he were evicted by due Corse of lawe "

" Afterwards during the Lo Archbbp [Archbishop] of Yorke visitacon some of the Townesmen were petitioners to his grace on the behalfe of *Clowes*, not acquaynting his grace wth my Lo Cooks grant to Pearson, the Lo Bishops and Curats assent thearvnto, nor the order of the highe Comission[er]s, whearvpon his grace sent some direccons [directions] to the Curate that Clowes should enioy the place But his grace being since informed of the former p'ceedings hath by his l'res [letters] reserved the cause to the highe Comissioners before whome it first depended And now some of the Townesmen goe about to intitle the Kings ma^tie [majesty] to the Clarkship in the right of the p'sonage [parsonage] Albeit his highness hath made a lease thearof to others* and that the Curate hath placed Pearson according to the Canons "

[II]

A Letter addressed to Toby Matthew, Archbishop of York, by Richard Bancroft, Archbishop of Canterbury, relating to the Clarkship of Nantwich, with particulars inclosed.

" *Saltm in Chro* My verye good Lo I haue bene moved by my loving kynd ffrend Sr Chr er Hatton to comend vnto your Grace the consyderation of the inclosed, and to intreate you that one Pearson thearin mentioned hath bene lawfullye hearetofore admitted to be Clarke of the parishe Churche of Namptwich maye still continue in that place vntill he shalbe by lawe evicted , or that your Grace wilbe pleased to remitt the cause by your letters to the Lo Bishop of Chester and the rest of the Commissioners, before whom the same is alreadye depending, their to be ordered as in theire Judgments shalbe found meet

The gentleman I doe very well affect, and wilbe redye to assist him by all good meanes in any his honest and lawfull Causes And I heartelye desyre your Grace, that for my sake the rather you will be pleased to satisfye his request in the primiss [premises] I will acknowledge your Graces kindnes thearin thankfully and requite you as your occasions shall require And so with my hartye comendacons I Comit your Grace vnto the tuition of Almighty god. At Lambeth the xth of December 1608 "

" Your Gr[ac]e verye loving ffrend

" and brother

R Cant" [erbury]

" *A Copie of the breife inclosed in r y lo of Cant h.s letter The state of the Cause Concerning the Clearkship of Namptwych* "

* 1 That Sr Xpofer [Christopher] Hatton, Knight late lo Channcelor of England, havinge the Inherytance of a certayne lybertye or frannchises in the towne of Namptwich, in the Countye of Chester, Called the Conntesse of Warwicke ffee, wherevnto the noiacion [nomination] of the Clarke of the parishe Churche and the tolle of he Corne markett there & amongst other things are incident, and did tyme out of mynd belonge vpon the death of the former Clarke who was placed by those ffrom whom he purchased the sayd ffrancheses The sayd lo Chancelor did graunt the sayd Clarkshipp by patent vnder his hand and seale to one Thomas Bullen, who quyetlye emoyed the same during his life and receaued the ffees and profitts thereof for Dyvers yeares together and vntill his death "

* The allusion here is to the lease of the Easter Roll , which was afterwards purchased by Sir Ranulphe Crewe on the 13th March, 1631

2 That aboute a yeare synce after the death of Bullen, the Inheritaunce of the sayd libertye belonging to Sr Xpofer
   Hatton Knight who is nowe livinge, And Sr Edward Cooke Knight, nowe lo Cheefe Justice of the Comon plees
   having the present interest thereof The sayd Sr Edward Cooke graunted the sayd Clarkship to one John Pearson
   who had bene schoolemaister in the sayd Towne and had lived there these 14 or 15 yeares last past with good
   comendations both for his suficiencie and honest Carriadge

3 That my lo cheefe Justice his graunt being made knowne to the Reverend ffather in God the lo Bishop of Chester
   that nowe is, And also to John Bradwall Curate of the sayd Church, the [they] did both giue their absolute assents
   and alowances, of the sayd Pearson to be Clearke, and the sayd Curate openlye published and made knowne the
   same in the said Churche at the tyme of diuine Service vppon Christmas daye last past

4 That Pearson Therevppon entered into the place and enioyed the same wᵗʰ the consents and good lykinge of the better
   sorte of the sayd parishoners But the sayd towne having no maiestrate or other ordinaire meanes of govermente,
   dyvers of the parishoners weare afterwards incited by one Thomas Maynwayringe fforcyblie to displace the sayd
   Pearson, and to place in his roome one Clowes a weauer, which the [they] did accordinglye aboute Maye last past,
   vppon prtence that he had more skill in singinge than Pearson had have[ing] first p swaded the sayd Curate by
   threatninge him to abridge his stipent [stipend], which he had of the towne to revoke his former nomination of
   Pearson to be Clearke

5 That the sayd Maynwayringe and other of his Complices being thervpon called before the Bishop of Chester and other
   his maiestyes Comissioners for causes Exclesiasticall within the said dyoces The sayd Pearson was by order of the
   Comissioners installed in possession vnty l the Cause was finally heard and ordred Whervppon the sayd Maynwayring and some others lately preferred a Petition to my lo Grace of Yorke during his visitation And hath there
   vpon obtayned his Grace his derection [i e his Grace s direction] to the Curate that Clowes shall quyetlye enioye the
   place his Grace being not enformed of the former possession of the sayd Pearson the assents of the sayde lo Bishop,
   and Curate, nor of the righte and tytle of the lord Cheefe Justice and Sr Xpofer Hatton, nor in what contemptuous
   manner the favorytts of the sayd Clowes have opposed them selves against the same, nor what vndecent and
   reprochfull speaches the [they] have used to disgrace the sayd tytle which will in particulars be proved " *

[III]

The following document, though undated, possibly relates to the year 1629, when
the next appointment of Clerk had to be made after the death of Thomas Clowes, by
Sir Ranulphe Crewe, in whose handwriting it is endorsed on the back as follows —

"*Clarkship of Namptwiche · to this Clarkshipp my title is undowbtedly good & I wyll
mantayne it*"

"A clarkshipp of a parish may belonge to a seignory ffee or mannor, & the guift thereof may be
in the Lord of that ffee or mannor for wᶜʰ I have Mr lloyd his opinion when he was Attorney
generall vnder his hand, & this is emongst other thynges in a black boxe in one of the waynscott
boxes in my evidence howse, wherein be writeinges co'cerning the Cowntes ffee There is allso their
[there], a pattent fro Syr Chr Hatton Lord of the Cowntes ffee to Bulleyn, & another to Pierson, wᶜʰ
was opposed by the towne of Nampt wyche to the Archbysshopp of York, when his grace no way
informed of the title one the other pd [possessed] besides the matter betw[i]xt Clowes & Pierson was
ended by the arbitrement of Mr Leversage, & Pierson had money to relinquish his tytle

When Brook was chosen Clarke, Mr Maysterson & Mr Walthall went to Crewe to Mr ffowleshurst
& obtayned by theyr sute the Clarkshipp for Brook, this was tould me by ould Yardley a servant. so
Mr ffowleshurst tould me thus much when he lived ould Syr Hue Chomley heavyng [having] the
Cowntes ffee morgaged vnto him, dyd afterwards reconvey the same to Syr Chi Hatton, & levyed a
ffine of the ffee & dyd graunt the Clarkshipp & belmanshipp to Syr Chi Hatton, by p'ticular names so

---

* The Parish Registers record as follows —
    " 1607 Thomas Clowes Clarke entereth "
    " 1620 May 21 John Pearson Schoolemaister " [Burjed]
    " 1639 April 3 Thomas Clowes the parrishe Clarke " [Buried]
        The present Altar Table in the Church was the gift of this clerk

as the ffine & deede make itt wthout question   Bulleyn enioyıng itt dyvers yeares after the ffine

Thus stands my title to the Clarkshipp   the ffine & deede be in the boxe where the writeinges of the Cowntes ffee be   So as I hould the disposition of the Clarkshipp to belonge clearely to me, & shalbe most unwilling to be att a controversy wth my kinsemen* & ffrend there about itt   but I shalbe excused to mantayne my right yf itt be opposed, & that I shall not fayl to do '

1607   Oct 22   On this date an Inquisition of Right of Wayt was taken at Nantwich. A full translation of the original Latin record is here given, mainly on account of the local names of places and persons mentioned therein

'*Inquisition* indented taken at Wich Malbank co Chester, on 22 Oct 1607, before Sir John Savage, Kt, Sheriff of Cheshire, by virtue of a certain writ of our lord the King, concerning a certain way, under the seal of the County Palatine of Chester, to the same Sheriff directed and to this Inquisition attached, upon the oaths of *William Dod, William Salmon, William Pratchett, John Scott, Thomas Smith, John Hollins, Hugh Brome, John Whylocke, Hugh Furnivall, William Shaw, Richard Shaw,* and *Robert Burre*, gentlemen, *Jurors*, good and lawful men of the County aforesaid, who, on their oaths, say that a certain reasonable high-way ought to be from Wich Malbank, in the aforesaid writ mentioned, as far as an Enclosure or parcell of land in *Edlaston* in the said County, called *Evetts Croft*, in the said writ mentioned, by and through a certain land of the King commonly called *Shrewbrige-lane* in Wich-Malbank aforesaid, and by and through a certain River called the *Weever*, and by and through a certain other King's highway called *Badington lane*, in Badington, in the county aforesaid, and by and through a certain "assart"‡ called the "*Intack*," lying between the same King's highway and the land of *Robert Cholmondeley Esqr*, and now in the tenure or occupation of Joan Baker, widow, in Badington aforesaid, and by and through the same lands in the tenure of the said Joan Baker, and by and through certain other lands of the said Robt Cholmondeley esq called *Walkeley*, in Badington aforesaid, in the tenure or occupation of *Anthony Wright*, of Wich-Malbank, gent or his assigns and by and through a certain rivulet, called *Newbold brook* as far as the aforesaid enclosure called *Evetts croft*, and so from thence back to the town of *Wich-Malbank*, as well for the passage of *Roger Wright* gentleman, his tenants and servants, as for his beasts, carts and carriages &c Which said reasonable way I, the Sheriff, by the verdict of the Jury &c find to be of the breadth of 12 feet, and of the length of 20 perches [?] between the places aforesaid and also I have caused to be set certain metes, bounds, and divisions faithfully marked out, and assigned to the same *Roger*, in execution of the aforesaid writ

In testimony whereof to two parts of this Inquisition the Jurors have set their seals, the day and year aforesaid

JOHN SAVAGE, Knight "

Mr. Partridge (*Hist. Nantwich, p.* 12) writing in 1774, says "A public clocke called *St. Anne's*, which continued till a few years ago, was fixed up on a dwelling in the middle of this street [Welsh Row]; which, by a recent alteration in the buildings there, hath been taken away   This clock was probably erected at the expense of the worthy family of the Wilbrahams of Towns-end, the Bell being inscribed with their name'   What became of the bell afterwards is not known, but its origin, and purpose, are fully explained in the following extract from the Wilb. MS Journal.

* Mr Thomas Maynwaring, see Maynwaring Pedigree
† The original is preserved at the Record Office
‡ "*Assart*," that is, land then or lately brought into cultivation

"*Mem* 17 May 1608 I bought of Henry Oldfield of Nottingham, Bellfounder,[*] one Bell weighing foure score & two pound, & paid him for it by *Raph Jackson & Lawrence Steeven* the sum of iij^li vj^s viij^d [£3 6s 8d], ouer and besides ij^s vj^d [2s 6d] payd for the carriage of the said Bell from Nottingham to Congleton where I receaved it, wch Bell remaineth in the howse of the said Lawrence Steeven for the use of a clock there & remayneth still properly myne owne   Also I have given lead to make two Peazes [i e clock-weights] wch weigh aboue 40 pound & my will is y^t the said Bell & peazes shall remaine to the freehould of the same howse as the inheritaunce thereof, & to be for the use of a clocke there & the benefit of neighbours   The charge for the rest of the clocke is to be performed & maintained by the well disposed neighbours of the same street

[signed] RICHARD WILBRAHAM "

Richard Wilbraham also states *(ibidem)*—

"That the Great Bell of this town of N being new Cast the 17th day of Nov in the year of our Lord 1608, and being of the weight of 2300 ℔s [i e 20 cwt. 60 ℔s], was cast at *Congleton* by *George Lee*, the Churchwardens for that yeare being *Edwd Massey & John Thrush*, whose names were set upon the Bell & this verse & these letters

Hæc campana sacra fiat trinitate beata.

	C	
R		G
	G	
T		C

In the following year the *fourth bell*[†] was re-cast. probably at the same foundry, and extensive repairs in the tower of the Church were carried out, as mentioned in the Parish Register

"In the tow former yeares, namely in anno 1608 & in anno 1609 the Great Bell was new cast and the fourth bell   Also the timber worke of the roufe of the steeple, wethercock poole, and the tow floures [two floors] in the steple were new made "

> JOHN THRUSH, gent } beinge churchwardens
> EDWARD MASSEY, gent }

In 1611 the Grammar School, in the Churchyard, was enlarged by Randle Kent, the Master, at his own cost.[‡]

Thomas Wilbraham, of Townsend, Richard Mynshull, mercer, and the Registrar of Nantwich, all mention the occurrence of an earthquake, the account in the Register, being the most characteristic, is here given —

"This same yeare on the 18 day of March 1612[-13] chaunced a terrible earthquake between 7 and 8 of the clocke in the forenoone wch came with a most fearfull noyse and horrible shakeinge, the space of 3 minutes, wch is noe doubt a sure signe that the cominge of Christ is at hand, & even at the Dores"

The first Almshouses built at Welsh Row Head, were founded, in 1613, by *Sir Roger Wilbraham, of Dorfold, Kt*, second son of Richard Wilbraham of Townsend, who has been frequently mentioned in the previous pages

---

[*] Henry Oldfield, bell-founder, is believed to have been a native of Cheshire, he married for his first wife, Mary, daughter of Richard Spencer, of Congleton, Gent   (See Earwaker's *Local Gleanings Magazine*, pp 109 and 197-8)

[†] "The lay for the reparacon of the bell frames in Namptw^ch *ano* 1607, 1608, was 16 myzes, taxed after viij^s ye pound "   (Bishop Bridgeman s Accounts in MS)

[‡] See Account of the Grammar School, *posteâ*

While these sheets were passing through the press, the long lost Parliamentary Roll for 1614, alluded to on page 36 *note*, was also being printed in the Palatine Note Book, vol iii (June, 1883), from a copy recently discovered in the Library of the Duke of Manchester at Kimbolton It now appears that Ranulphe Crewe was *not* elected M P. for his *native county* in the Parliament that met on the 5th of April, 1614, as stated by Foss, *(Lives of the Judges)*, and other biographers, but that he was returned as one of the members for *Saltash*, in Cornwall That Parliament was hastily dissolved on the 7th of June in the same year, and Ranulphe Crewe was Knighted on the following day.

A memorandum in the Parish Register states —

"This yeare last past, 1615, the church fflore and all the Iles theirof weare raised with sand a full half yarde at the least * The walles of the Church new whited and the sentences of Scripture new written theirupon "

"RICHARD GOULDSMITH
"RICHARD HARWAR } Churchwardens "

The following list of shocking deaths is taken from the Burial Register —

"1607 Nov 19 Ellen, dau of John Dutton drowned in Weever "
"1609 Dec 22 Ann Steven, widow, drowned in Weever "
"1610 Dec 26 Homfrey Sare, dyed of a fall "
"1611 Nov 13 Willm Turner, servant to Will Yorge, sadler, poysoned himself "
"1612 July 7 Robert Ince slayn by a creuell surgeon with a knife
"1612 Aug 1 George, Ostler of the Bell, drowned in the Weever "
"1613 June 9 William Dudley was slayne "
"1613 Nov 2 Jane, dau of Edward Diggens dyed by fyer
"1613-14 Jan 24 Richard Ffisher, slain with a miln hook "
"1613 Feb 5 Edmund Downes slayne with a pice at Badeley '
"1614 Aug 7 John, son of William Moore, slayne by a fall '
"1616 July 28 Ffrancis Gresty, Carpenter, was slayn by his man
"1616 May 9 William Crewe of Burland was slaine the 7th of Maye by Thomas Walthall, sadler, of this towne, and was buried at Acton the 9th "
"1618 Aug 16 Thomas Hunt by the falling of a house was slaine at a rearinge and buried '
"1618 Oct 11 Thomas Sargeant was slaine at Avdglem [Audlem] by strving, the Kings prosses †
"1618 Oct 13 Ellin daughter of William Whitworth was drowned and buried "
"1618-19 Feb 13 Thomas sone of Robert Bockeley, Taylor, was slaire by Anthony Wright the 11th of ffebruarie and was buried the 13th '
"1618 19 Feb 19 Ann, wife of John Holford, which did strangle herself '
"1619 Dec 18 Richard, son of Richard Lytler, being drowned in the garden in the well "
"1620-1 March 3 Henry Brammall was slaine with the fall of a gayt "
"1622 May 27 John sonne of James Blythe was slaine the 6th Aprill by Willm Savage & buried the 27th May "
"1622-3 March 10 Raphe sonne of Edward Breame, being drowned "
"1623 June 6 George Huxley found in Baderton wood dead & buried the 6th "
"1624 April 7 William son of Elizabeth Bookeley, stroke with an axe "
"1624 June 15 John Goldsmith bathing in the Weever the 13th day was drowned '
'1624-5 Jan 18 Henry Morrey was slaine by the falling of a tree into a saw-pit '

It is remarkable that the Parish Clerk has left no memorandum of the Royal visit in 1617 According to the Whitegate Register, "the 21st day of Auguste, being Thursdaye, King James came to Vale Royall and there kept his court untill Mondaye after." Here,

---

* See List of Charities   † This is the correct reading but the meaning is obscure

says William Webb, *(Itinerary of Eddisbury Hundred)* "he solaced himself and took pleasing contentment in his disports in the forest," and, having visited Chester on Saturday, Aug 23rd, and Knighted the forester of Delamere, Sir John Done, who lived "in a delicate house on the highest hill," on the following Monday, the King left Vale Royal for Nantwich. Thomas Wilbraham, Esq, in his MS Journal, says:—

> *"Mem* That uppon the 25th of August 1617 King James at his returne forth of Scotland came to this Towne of Namptwich, and lay one night at my howse at the same tyme there were with him the Duke of Lenox Ld Steward of the Kings Household, the Duke of Buckingham master of the horse, the Earle of Pembroke Ld Chamberlain of the K household, and diuers other Lords and Knights Upon the 26th day he went to the Church, where Doctor Dod preached before him, who shortly after was sworne his Chaplaine At his returne from Church he went to see the Bryne pitt, and aftr diner went to Bromley, to my Ld Gerards howse " [in Staffordshire]

The account of this visit, by Mr Webb,[*] (who states that the King visited the Brine-pit on the 25th instead of the 26th day) is as follows:—"His majesty was likewise pleased to appoint a sermon to be preached before him in the church, and of his princely graciousness to stay while an oration[†] was pronounced by one of the scholars of the [Grammar] school, which sermon was then performed by a divine of our own country [i e of Cheshire] both by birth and dwelling, *Mr. Thomas Dodd*,[‡] archdeacon of Richmond, and to which his majesty gave so great attention, and with the same was so affected, as it pleased his highness to grace the preacher with his princely and free election of him into the number of one of his chaplains in ordinary, which, for the honour of our country, and for an addition to the worth of this our eloquent and sweet preacher, I thought fit here to record " . "It pleased him [the King] to walk so far as to the brine-seth, and with his eye to behold the manner of the well, and to observe the labours of the briners (so they call the drawers of the brine), whose work it is to fetch it up in leather buckets fastened to ropes, and empty it into the troughs, which troughs convey it into the wich-houses at which work those briners spend the coldest day in frost and snow, without any cloathing more than a shirt, with great chearfulness And after his Majestys gracious enquiry among the poor drawers, of many things touching the nature of the same brine, and how they proceeded to convert it into salt, most princely rewarding them with his own hand, his majesty returned to the court," [at Townsend house, in Welsh Row] ' In the afternoon of the same day, after dinner, having knighted Sir Hugh Wrottesley, King James proceeded on his way to Gerards Bromley [in Staffordshire] and at his taking leave, on the confines of Cheshire, of John Davenport of Davenport, the high sheriff, who had attended his majesty through the county, the King bestowed upon him the degree of knighthood and graced him with a pleasant princely farewell,—'*You shall carry me this token*

---

[*] Webb's ' *Itinerary of Nantwich Hundred,"* in King s " *Vale Royal* "

[†] The oration has not been preserved It would probably be written for the occasion by the then aged master *Randle Kent* and no doubt would be an elaborate eulogium on the Monarch, perhaps as flattering as the one delivered by Master Thos Read, in Latin, on 3rd Sept 1617, when the King visited Warwick (See Cooke s *Guide to Warwickshire, p* 175-180, Fourth Edition)

[‡] *Thomas Dodd D D* was of the family of the Dods of Shocklach, near Malpas, being nephew of John Dod, commonly called the *Decalogist* He was baptized at Shocklach, 4th Dec 1576 At the time of the King s visit to Cheshire, he was Rector of Astbury and prebend of Chester In addition to these preferments and the royal chaplaincy, he subsequently held the Lower Mediety of the Rectory of Malpas (1623), the Archdeaconry of Richmond (c 1625), and the Deanery of Ripon (c 1634), and was buried at Malpas, 10th Feb 1647-8,

to your wife,'—graciously so meant by his Majesty, but the gentlewoman* having indeed before that attained to a better ladyship, being gone to her Lord and Saviour in Heaven "

Tradition says that the King was expected to have stayed at the then newly erected Dorfold Hall, the present drawing room, and adjoining chamber, still called King James' Room, having been specially prepared for his Majesty's visit   No doubt the Church, which had been recently "beautified," the comparatively new built town, and the Wilbraham Mansion, would present a very gay appearance before the illustrious visitors, and it is almost a wonder that Thomas Wilbraham, Esq, was not included amongst the 120 knights dubbed by the King on that very costly journey.

In the following year general excitement in the county was caused by the appearance of a comet   According to the superstition of those times—

"Comets we see by night, whose shagg'd portents

Foretell the comming of some dire events "§

such as pestilence, famine, war, or change of Kingdom, and thus, with dread forebodings, were penned the following lines in the Burial Register —

"This yeare last past, 1618, in the month of Novembre many times their appeared eastward a Blazing Starr, betokenninge godds judgements towards us for Sine   the lorde in mercye be mercifull unto us "

In the early part of 1623 there was great scarcity of corn all over England, through the bad harvests of two previous years   At such times farmers often became *ingrossers* (i e. buyers up of growing corn) and *regrators* (i e. buyers up of corn in the market) for the purpose of stowing it away   By a proclamation of the King for preventing the dearth of grain, Justices of the Peace were required to furnish certificates of the quantities of corn in their hundreds   and oblige persons to take their corn to the market town, to attend the markets themselves and see the poor supplied first, for two hours, at a lower price, to suppress all unnecessary ale-houses, and to limit the sale of barley for making malt   Thus on or about 31st March, 1623 the Justices of Nantwich Hundred reported to Sir Thos Smith, High Sheriff of the County, that they *"find very little surplus of corn, but have ordered what there is to be brought weekly to market, and attended to other points of instruction.'*†

The year 1625 must have been a plentiful year, if the following prices of provisions in the neighbourhood are correct ‡—

	s	d			s	d
A wether sheep	13	4	Malt per bushel		4	o
A flitch of bacon	8	o	Oatmeal per peck		1	o
A sucking pig	1	o	Salt per barrow	.	1	8
A calf's head	o	8	Wheat per measure		3	8
A Turkey	1	4	Rye ,,	,	2	8
A Goose	1	1	Barley ,,		2	6
A couple of Ducks	o	7	Oats ,,		2	o
Do chickens	o	6	Pease ,,		2	8
Do rabbits	o	10	A pound of butter		o	3
A Neats tongue	o	6	Ale per quart	...	o	2

* This lady was Elizabeth, dau of Thomas Wilbraham, Esq, Recorder of London, and Attorney of the Court of Wards   She had been buried at Swettenham four years before on 8th Aug 1613   Sir John Davenport Kt, the widower, died in 1625, and was buried at Swettenham, aged 76
† Calendar State Papers, Dom Series Jas I vol cxl   ‡ See Hinchliffe's "Barthomley,' p 351
§ Robt Herrick's *"Farewell to Sack "*

Towards the end of King James' reign, (i e. about 1622 or 1623), Mr William Webb thus quaintly describes the town in his "ITINERARY,"—(King's *Vale Royal*)

"Whatsoever hath been the causes or howsoever the inhabitants there have had their invancement, sure I am, there can hardly be found a town meerly uplandish, as we term it, neither traded into by waters, nor enriched by any special trades or manufactures, that hath such a knot of wealthy and landed men in so small a compass, there being within the same thirty or more, that are usually assessed in the King's majestys subsidies to pay for lands, and the greatest part of them gentlemen that pay with none of the meanest ranks "

"The buildings within the same town are very fair and neat, and every street adorned with some special mansions of gentlemen of good worth, the middle and principal parts of the town being all new buildings " &c

"It may be not amiss   to note one lustre of that town, that into the five entrances into the same, which way soever you come, your eye is entertained with a fair gentlemanly house at the end or entry of the first street every way, as, namely, that which is called the Welsh Row, with that of *Mr Wilbrahams,* that of Beam Street, where they hold yet weekly great markets of cattle, with a fine house of the *Mainwarings,* and now belonging to the right worshipful and worthy ingenious knight *Sir Dudley Norton,* secretary to his majesty's council in Ireland * that of the Hospital Street, with a fair timber-house of *Mr Randol Church,* a gentleman of singular integrity, that of the Pillory Street, with a very ancient house of the worshipful race of the *Mastersons,* and the Barkers-street or Mills-street with a very fine brick house of *Mr Wrights,* to say nothing of a great number of very fair houses and neat buildings dispersed here and there throughout the middle part of the town "

The subsequent history of these five principal houses is, briefly, as follows —

TOWNSEND HOUSE continued to be the residence of the Wilbraham family for two centuries, that is, from 1580 till 1780. In 1810 Messrs Lysons† described the house as being in a state of dilapidation, and Dr Ormerod, judging from the small portion standing in 1819, says,‡ "It appears from these remains to have been a lofty and spacious edifice of brick, with large bay windows, surrounded with numerous outbuildings of timber and plaister, and gardens with high walls of brick, ornamented with stone carvings of armorial bearings, and grotesque devices " The house and its extensive garden adjoining were sold by George Wilbraham, Esq, of Delamere In and previous to the year 1824 the house had been reduced and converted into a brewery, and in that year was occupied by Messrs George Brooke, and Quain, Brewers, and after having been so used for many years, it was at length, about the year 1855, purchased by a firm of Quakers, Messrs George Harlock & Co., who turned it into a clothing factory and built a new house, still the residence of the head of that firm.

The *Garden* belonging thereto passed through several hands,—Mr Henry Tomlinson (lawyer), Mr T W Kirkbride (brewer), and John Eyton, Esq. (banker), who in 1850 sold it to the County, and ten years after a handsome structure was raised thereon for the accommodation of the Magistrates' offices connected with the Police Establishment, and for the detention of offenders previous to committal to prison   A stone gateway, with the original ornaments (carved lionesses) which formerly stood in this garden, now adorns the

* Sir Dudley Norton was sent to Ireland as Secretary in May, 1615

† Lysons "Cheshire, p 710

‡ Dr Ormerod s Hist of Cheshire, Vol III, p 441 New Edit No drawing or engraving of this house is known to exist

grounds of Dorfold Hall, having been purchased many years ago by Wilbraham S. Tollemache, Esq , who has since added thereto busts of King James and his Consort.

The BEAM STREET-END MANSION, which Sir Dudley Norton had held *jure uxoris* since his marriage, in 1591, with Margaret, dau of Thomas Maisterson, and widow of Roger Mainwaring, passed after the death of "Lady Margaret Norton" in 1644 to the family of Dodd of Edge,* of whom it was purchased by Robert Wright, who was possessor of it in 1666 (*Harl MSS.* 2010).   It afterwards, in 1677, became the *House of Correction ,* and was ultimately purchased by John, first Lord Crewe, who, in 1767, pulled it down and built the present *Almshouses* on the site.

The HOSPITAL STREET-END MANSION was erected in 1577 by Richard Church, father of Randol Church, mentioned by Mr Webb   It is in an excellent state of preservation, and belongs to A W. Radford-Norcup, Esq , of Betton Hall, near Tunstall, Salop, who is the present representative of the Church family.   Originally it was moated   A portion of the moat is still traceable while another part has become a culvert drain forming part of the parish boundary.   It has carved work and wainscotting, and intersecting triangles form the ornament of every panel in one of the rooms.   The window over the porch seems to be the only original one , but, below two other windows, are still to be seen the following inscriptions in old English characters —

(1) " 𝔯𝔶𝔠𝔥𝔞𝔯𝔡𝔢 𝔠𝔥𝔲𝔯𝔠𝔥𝔢 𝔞𝔫𝔡 𝔪𝔞𝔯𝔤𝔢𝔯𝔶𝔢 𝔠𝔥𝔲𝔯𝔠𝔥𝔢, 𝔥𝔦𝔰 𝔴𝔶𝔣𝔢, 𝔪𝔞𝔦 𝔦𝔦𝔦."

" 𝔱𝔥𝔬𝔪𝔞𝔰 𝔠𝔩𝔢𝔞𝔰𝔢 𝔪𝔞𝔡𝔢 𝔱𝔥𝔦𝔰 𝔴𝔬𝔯𝔨𝔢 𝔞𝔫𝔫𝔬 𝔡𝔫𝔦. 𝔪𝔠𝔠𝔠𝔠𝔩𝔦𝔯𝔟𝔦𝔦.
 𝔦𝔫 𝔱𝔥𝔢 𝔯𝔳𝔦𝔦𝔦 𝔶𝔢𝔯𝔢 𝔬𝔣 𝔱𝔥𝔢 𝔯𝔢𝔞𝔫𝔢 𝔬𝔣 𝔬𝔲𝔯 𝔫𝔬𝔟𝔩𝔢 𝔮𝔲𝔢𝔢𝔫𝔢 𝔢𝔩𝔢𝔷𝔞𝔟𝔢𝔱𝔥."

(2) " 𝔱𝔥𝔢 𝔯𝔬𝔬𝔱𝔢 𝔬𝔣 𝔴𝔶𝔰𝔢𝔡𝔬𝔪 𝔦𝔰 𝔱𝔬 𝔣𝔢𝔞𝔯𝔢 𝔤𝔬𝔡, & 𝔱𝔥𝔢 𝔟𝔯𝔞𝔫𝔠𝔥 𝔱𝔥𝔢𝔯𝔢𝔬𝔣 𝔰𝔥𝔞𝔩𝔩 𝔱𝔬𝔬 𝔢𝔫𝔡𝔲𝔯𝔢."

Another inscription inside an old cupboard reads thus —

" BLESSED ART THOV THAT FEARES AND WALKEST IN HIS WAYES
FOR THOV SHALTE EATE AND HAPPIE ARTE "

The last of the Church family to reside at this *"Mansion,"* was *Mr. Sabboth Church,* who lived there in 1691, according to a Rate Book of that date   He was elected a Wright s Trustee in 1702, and was buried at Nantwich 3rd May, 1717 (Par Reg.)   In 1792, Mr. John Latham occupied this house; and for many years in the early part of this

---

* The following Pedigree from *Harl MSS* 1535, f 340 , and the Parish Registers illustrates this descent

	1st husband ROGER MAINWARINGE⊤	MARGARET dau to	⊤ 2nd husband SIR DUDLEY
	Auditor of Ireland	Sir Thomas Maisterson	NORTON, Knight
	(*Harl MSS* 2119 f 42)	Buried at Nantwich as	marr 15 Nov 1591
	Died 1 March 32 Eliz	Margaret Lady Norton	(Nant Reg)
	1589-90 Will proved 1	29 March, 1644 .	
	May 1590 Printed		
	Chet Soc Pub vol 54		Dudley Norton,
	Burial not recorded at		Bapt at Nantwich, 20 Ap 1594
	Nantwich Inq p m		Buried „ 21 June, 1658
	32 Eliz		

Richard, eldest	John		Margaret M ⫤ EDWARD DOD of Edge	
son, 13 yrs 5	2nd son		eventually heiress	Baron of Exchequer
mo at his			to her brothers	Died 25 Nov and buried
father's death			Buried at Nant	30 Nov 1648, at
			21 Sep 1648	Nantwich

century it was tenanted by Mr. John Berks, tanner; who was succeeded by Mr. James Latham From 1848 to 1858 it was the residence T W Jones, Esq, attorney-at-law; and for ten years after, it was untenanted, and a neighbouring cowkeeper was allowed to use the parlour as a granary and storehouse for hay, &c In 1869 it became a ladies' boarding school (Mrs Rhodes') and as such continues to the present time.

The PILLORY STREET-END MANSION, although "a very ancient house" in 1622, remained until the end of last century (Lysons' *Cheshire*, p 710) Thomas Maisterson, Esq, who was buried in Nantwich Chancel on the 9th March, 1768, appears to have been the last of that ancient family to reside there It was purchased by Ralph Cappur, Cheesefactor. His son George Cappur, Cheesefactor, took it down and built on the same site the present house, which descended to his son, George Cappur, also a Cheesefactor, who, about the year 1850, sold it to John Withinshaw, Esq, of this town, the present residential owner.

The "very fine brick house of Mr Wright's" in 1622, and the brick and stone house, now called "*The Elms*," in Mill Street, with its lofty and spacious wainscotted rooms, fine staircase, &c, if not identical, occupy the same site This property appears to have been renovated, and perhaps largely rebuilt in the latter part of last century Mr Samuel Acton, of whom more will be said in other parts of this work, lived here in 1691,[*] and for many years in the following century it was the residence of William Penlington, Esq, M D, who belonged to a respectable family of that name in Sandbach parish William Penlington married Joan, one of the co-heiresses of Richard Lowndes, Esq, of Hassall. Their burials are thus recorded —

"1769 Sept 8 Joan, wife of William Penlington Gent Nantwich, buried at Sandbach " (Sandbach and Nantwich Registers)

"1782 Jan 22 William Penlington Esq of Rode, Buried " (Sandbach Register)

The Penlington family appear to have been connected with this neighbourhood many years earlier, according to the following entries in the Burial Register at Acton.

"1714 June 4 George Penlington de Sandbach "

"1721-2 March 24 Janna Penlington de Sandbach, widow "

The house in Mill Street was the residence of Samuel Hodgson, Esq., wine merchant, who died 16th Sept 1807,[‡] and for many years, of the Misses Bennion, it then became the District Bank, and, after having been unoccupied for several years, was purchased for a residence by Mr. Samuel Hobson, shoe manufacturer, of this town.

Mr Webb's description of the town in 1622 concludes as follows —

"Here are also fair and profitable mills for the service and use of the town, which are the inheritance of sir Richard Egerton, Knight

"A strong timber bridge over the stream of the Weever is maintained by the town, which requires no little care and cost, by reason of the monstrous carriages of the wood in carts which is brought thither for the boiling of their salt I might speak of some charitable gifts that have been by well disposed persons given or bequeathed to charitable uses, whereof to make mention, I fear it would be rather to question their neglect, than to commend the inhabitants that perform not, for ought I know, the care that should be taken in that behalf, only the *School* which was founded there by Mr John Thrush, and Mr Thomas Thrush, of London, woo'-packers, is well and sufficiently upheld and maintained, to the

[*] Rate Book *penes* G F Wilbraham, Esq

[‡] See Monument in Lady Chapel

furtherance of teaching the children of the poor and others, and an ancient and grave school-master of of very near fifty years continuance, *Mr Randal Kent*, yet teacher there,* with a learned assistant, a master of arts of Queens college in Oxon, whose name is *Mr Shenton*, of laudable pains and industry"

To which I must not omit to add the late charitable erection of an alms-house for six poor aged men, which sir Roger Wilbraham, Knight, master of the requests to his majesty (King James) at the the town's end, there new built for the said six persons, to be chosen out of Nantwich and of Acton parish allowing them each one, an handsome lodging, a little garden, and five merks [£3 6s 8d] per annum towards their relief in the latter end of their old age "

1626   Party spirit ran high in January 1626 during the exciting election for County members to serve in the second Parliament of Charles I, which, like its predecessor, was resolved on diminishing the King's prerogative in the matter of obtaining supplies   The Wilb MS Journal records —

"*Mem* That the 30 Jan 1625[-6] there was much syding betwixt the Gentlemen of the shire about elect[ing] Knights of the Parl¹ , S¹ R₁ Gr [Sir Richard Grosvenor, of Eaton, Kt and Bart] and Mr Dan₁ [Peter Danyell, of Over Tabley, Esq] were chose "

In the same week, on the 26th Jan 1625[-6], Sir Ranulphe Crewe, Kt, became Lord Chief Justice of the Court of King's Bench, from which high office he was deprived on the 9th Nov 1626   (See page 37)

Between the years 1626 and 1630 important alterations and repairs to the Church were carried out, according to the following memoranda in the Burial Register —

"*Mem⁴* That in December last [1626] the grate orrell [gallery] over the great church doore was reared and the third day of November 1627 the same was ffynished †   *Thomas Malbon* gent & *Richard Harwar*, Apothecary, Church Wardens both those yeares"

"1629   This yeare there was a bane‡ laid throughout the whole parishe after the rate of a noble [6s 8d] the pound for the repacon [repairing] of the churche, wherewᵗʰ was very much good worke done aboute the saide churche and chauncell oles [aisles] namely   in the lead ou' [over] both church & chauncell, in cramppinge [carving] of most pte [part] of the great pynnackles of the steeple, and ou' [over] the church & chauncell   and lykewise in the cramppinge of the bosse stones in the Arches ou' [over] the North Ile   and in glassinge of the wyndowes about the churche and chauncell, and in diu'ers other necessarie workes as may att large appeare by the churchwardens accompts for this yeare ' §

"1630   *Mem⁴* That theise are to testifie unto all succeeding Churchwardens and all other persons whomsoever, That wee *Edward Church & Thomas Walthall, gents* Churchwardens of the parishe of Nantwyche for this past yeare Did allow and graunt unto *Matthew Mainwaringe* the elder, of the same Towne, gent, full libertie and lycence to erect and sett upp one Pewe or litt'e orrell on his face or front-syde of the Archpillor (upon the south syde of the churche) whereon upon the back syde the clocke now standeth, wᵗʰ a paire of stayres upon the south syde thereof to goo into the same pewe Upon condicon [condition] whereas yᵗ ys an obscure and emptie place   That the said Mathew

---

* This statement approximately fixes the date of the "*Itinerary*," for Mr Kent died in 1623-4 , his burial is recorded thus —"1623 *Jan* 20 *Mr Randle Kent, an ancient schoolemaster* " (Reg)

† On the panels of this gallery were painted fifteen shields of Arms properly blazoned, namely, those of the seven ancient Earls of Chester, and the eight Norman Barons of Hugh Lupus   The gallery was removed at the ' restoration of the Church in 1855, and "*Four panels with Coats of Arms from the front gallery of Nantwich Church,*" were sold, together with other lots of antique oak, for £18 10s , on the 27th April, 1880, at a sale of the goods of Mr John Jones, of Alkington, near Whitchurch, Salop

‡ *Bane* i e *bann*, or public proclamation, by which this parish rate was commanded

§ No Churchwardens' Accounts are now to be found

Mainwaring (wanting a convenyent place to sitt in) should at and upon his owne pp [proper] coste and charges erect and build the said pewe and stayres in such sorte and forme, as the same shall and may beautyfie and bee an ornament to the saide churche   And suitable to the other pewe or orrell sett upp on the other syde by the saide churchwardens at their owne charges   Now whereas the said Mathew Mainwaringe hath accordinglie to the greate lykinge of all the inhabitants of the said towne and the said churchwardens att his onely great and extraordinarie cost and charge erected and sett upp the said pewe or orrell with the stayres thereof, and thereby very much adorned and Beautified the said church, and fully performed and accomplished the condicon afore expressed   Wee therefore, the said Churchwardens by the full assent consent and approbacon of the gentlemen and other the inhabitants of the said Towne Have and doe give graunt assigne and confirme the said pewe or orrell with the stayres thereof unto the said Mathew Mainwaring & his heires and to then onely use for ever "
In witness whereof wee the said C W &c.*

The following names of property owners in Nantwich occur in the Subsidy Roll for Nantwich Hundred that was collected on the 6th May, 3 Chas I [1627],† namely —

NAMPTWICH

DUDLEUS NORTON miles [Knight] in terr. [in lands]	xxvs	vjs
JOHES. MAINWARINGE gen in terr.	xxvs	vjs
THOMAS WILBRAHAM ar [esq] in terr	iijli	xvjs
THOMAS MAISTERSON ar. in terr	iijli	xijs
HUGO HASSALL ar. in terr	xls	viijs
RICUS CLUTION gen in terr.	xls	viijs
JOHES MINSHALL gen in terr	xxvs	vjs
ROGERUS WRIGHTE gen in terr	xxvs	vjs
RICUS CHURCH gen in terr	xxvs	vjs
EDRUS CHURCH gen in ter	xxs	iiijs
RICUS WHICKSTEAD gen in ter	xxxs	vjs
MARIA BROWNE vid in terr	xxvs	vjs
RICUS MINSHALL gen in terr.	xxs	iiijs
THOMAS MALBON gen in terr	xxs	iiijs
THOMAS MAINWARINGE gen in terr.	xxs	iiijs
MATHEW MAINWARINGE gen. in terr	xxs	iiijs
EDRUS HEYES gen in ter	xxs	iiijs
RANUS MINSHALL gen in terr	xxs	iiijs
WILMUS WETTENHALL gen in teri	xxs	iiijs
WILMUS MAINWARINGE gen in terr.	xxs	iiijs
KATHERINE WRIGHTE vid in terr.	xxs	iiijs
THOMAS CLAYTON gen in terr	xxs	iiijs
RICUS WILKES in terr	xxs	iiijs
LEONARD SPENCER gen in terr	xxs	iiijs
RICUS GOULDSMITH in terr.	xxs	iiijs

* These two curious pews, with panelled backs, that were sometimes said to resemble four-post beds, were last tenanted by the late Michael Bott Esq (the Churchwardens Pew of 1630) and the late Dr Brady (Mr Manwaring's Pew in 1630, on the south side of the tower arch)   Some carvings from Mr Bott s Pew were bought at Mr Jones' sale, beforementioned, for £3 17s 6d

† This list of names is from a contemporary copy of the Subsidy Roll in the possession of J P Earwaker Esq F S A

Thomas Burroughes in terr.	xx^s	.. iiij^s
Wilmus. Lea in terr	x\$^s$	iiij^s
Robtus Bromhall in teri	xx^s	iiij^s
Jacobus Bullen in terr	x\$^s$	iiij^s
Johes Winsey in bonis [in goods]	iij^h	viij^s
Ricus. Arcold in bonis	iij^h	viij^s
Thomas Arcold in bonis	iij^h	viij^s
Wilmus Judson in bonis	iij^h	viij^s
Johes Stockton recusan[t] [a Roman Catholic]	o	viij^d

In Richard Mynshull's Accounts occurs the following notice of a frolicsome wind — "That the iv of Aprill 1627 beinge Tuesday there was a straunge whirlwynde that tooke up linan cloeths that lay upon the hedges one [on] the back of pepper streete, and caried up in the aire full 10 score off upon aple trees and plum trees one [on] the back of the beame streetc," and Thomas Wilbraham, Esq , in his Journal, states there was *"a violent wind upon Tuesday 4 Nov* 1628 "

The Registers contain the following memoranda —

"*Mem* That this past yeare, 1628, there were two great fasts comanded to be kept by the King Char · proclamacon solemly and generally throughout this kingdome, with fastings and prayers according to the same proclamacons The first of them was kept upon the 21st day of April last aforewritten [1627], and the later upon the 20th day of this instant March " [1627-8]

"1629 June *Mem^d* That this yeare upon Wensday att night being the 10th of this month there happened an exceeding great frost wch did great earm [harm] to frute and corne especially to rye in lowe valleys and playne grounde and distroyed fearne [?] in diurs [divers] places "

"*Mem^d* That upon Thursday be:ng the 29th of October in this yeare [1629], about 12 of the clocke in the night their happened a great and sodden fire in the house of one *Thomas Jackson** in Welche Row, beginn- inge in a chamber ou' [over] *Mr Wettenhall's* gates and lastinge for the space of almost two howers consum- inge the rooffes of three bayes of buildings and more How the fyre began it is uncertaine, but thought to be through the carelesness and neglegence of some wretchles p'sone [person] dwellinge and inhabitinge in the saide house of the said Thomas Jackson by a candle wch fyre althoughe it were very furious and raginge yett by the providence of allmightie god and very many ready and willinge people wch despathe [desperately] venturrd for the quenchinge thereof (blessed bee god) the same was staydd wthout further losse "

Mr Wettenhall's house, now called "*White Hall*," appears to have been approached from the Welsh Row by the *gateway* under one of the chambers of Thomas Jackson's house, where the fire began The front of the house, facing the south, would overlook Ridley Field, which was formerly part of the Wettenhall lands in this town

An entry in the Burial Register states —

1629 Dec 7 John Cartwright an ould man drowned in the channel [Welsh Row] between the Wich Bridge and Lawrence Wilkes house "

In the year 1630 Margaret Slade, widow of John Slade, of Poole, gent , left a charity to sixty poor householders in Nantwich, which has been annually distributed ever since.

* This *Thomas Jackson* occurs again in the Register as a "*fur-dresser*," and most likely was both tenant and work- man of Mr Gabriell Wet'enhall, who had a tannery in the town

" 1631 This yeare the 30th of July being Saturday was terrible Thunder & lightning, whereby much hurt was done in many places In Warton a windmill was torne in pieces On Houghton Mosse 23 sheep were killed with the thunderbolt, and in many other places much hurt was done With this kind of thunder, came a strange kind of Hail, & namely in Nantwich where the like hath not been seen This yeare the plague was dangerouslie dispersed in many parts of the kingdom, as in London, Yorke, Yorkshire, Lancashire, & especially in Preston, where it raged so that the own was almost depopulated, and cern rotted upon the ground, for want of reapers It was also in Shrewsbury, Wrexham & many other parts of Wales, but Cheshire was graciously preserved, where were many public fasts kept, for the turning away of Gods hand "[*]

The following Proclamation of Robt. Viscount Cholmondeley, from an original paper *(penes me)* indicates what precautions were taken to prevent, if possible, the extension of the plague again to Nantwich

"Whereas accordinge to auncyente vse and custome a faire for the towne of Wich Malbanke hathe there bin holden and kepte vpon the feaste daye of Ste Bartholomewe the Apostle yerelie, and sythence [since] yt hathe pleased God at this p'nte [present] to visite wth the fearefull & contagious disease of the plauge diu'rs p'ts & plcs in the neighboringe Shires Countyes & townes adioynjnge to this Countie of Chester out of the wch placs dyu's [divers] chapmen tradesmen artificars drou's [drovers] pedlers and others have vsuallie resorted to the said faire And for asmuch as yt is alsoe feared that some pts in this Countye of Chester is alreadye infected wth the said disease, And to th'ende that all meanes maye be vsed to p'vente the dangr of infection fiom the said towne of Wiche Malbanke and the townes & placs adiacente wch the greate concourse of people to the said faire maye be likelye to endangr, It is therefore thot [thought] fitt by the right Honble Robte Viscounte Cholmondeley, Boron of the said towne of Wiche Malbanke & Iorde of the said faire, In his Mats [Majesty's] name to Commande appoynte & give notice to all man [manner] of p'sons fforiens [foregners] strangs and others that lyve in anye remote shires Counties or townes, or in or neere to any place infected that they and eu'y [every] of them abstaine & forbeare to come vnto the said towne and faire for the space of fyve dayes, to wytt the faire daye and foure dayes nexte after And that noe clothier, drap'r, vphoulster, Brazier, pewterer, pedler, or other chapman or chapmen whatsoeu' doe either in p son resorte or to sende oi conveye any man [manner] of wares or merchandize to the said faire from any place or placs before p'hibited, But onelie suche as the Warders & Watchers for the said dayes shall accordinge to theire charge & vpon theire voluntary oathes, thinke fitt to receyve into the said towne And that this may be a sufficyente warnynge to all man [manner] of p'sons to obs've this p'hibicon vpon payne & penaltye that maye insue thereon "

"Dated at Chomeley this xiiith daye of Auguste in the seyventh yere of his Mats reigne of Englanoe Scotlande ffrunce & Irelande 1631

"God save the Kinge and the Lorde Viscounte cholmeley "

" *The man* [manner] *of the p'clamacon* Jhn Offley deputye Stewarde, Willm Iea Baylyfe to the sd Lo [lord], Randle Croxton another baylyf to the sd lo , Tho venables baylyf of the Corte [ie Court Leet] and dyu's others the 13th of August 1631, being vi dayes before the faire, came into the open m'kett [market] when yt was at the highest Venables made a soleme "*oyes, oyes,*' sure on against [it] was done, iohn offley did read the p'clamacon & venables p'nounced yt with an audyble & publique voyce, then they walked all togither to the cage t where they did the Iike, & after fixed the p'clamacon wth some neales [nails] vpon the cage poaste, where yt stoode for the space of iiij or fyve howers "

---

[*] Burghall's '*Diary*," Cole MSS Brit Mus '   † The Cage was situated in the Market-place in High Town

Accoiding to *Calend State Papers*, dated 30th June, 1631, special measures were adopted for the relief of the poor in the Hundied of Nantwich, and in the next year the principal propeity owners in the town signed an Agieement, which was entered in the Burial Register as follows —

" *Memd* It is covenanted, piomised and agreed by us the gentlemen and others the inhabitants of this Towne whose names are subscribed That by reason our Towne is greatly op[p]ressed with Inmates and Strangers continually cominge to reside amongst us, without any restraynt, in regard whereof our owne poore cannot so wel be reserued [received] as otherwise they might That from henceforward, wee will not sett or lett any of our howses or cottages to strangers dwellinge out of our Towne, excepte they shall be such as shal be able to secure the Towne, by bond to the Church wardens, [as Overseeis of the Poor] for the tyme beinge, from any charge that they or their ffamillies might diaw uppon ytt

Witness our hands the thirteenth daie of November in the seventh yeare of the raigne of our gratious souraigne Lo Kinge Charles and in the yeare of our Lo god 1632 "

THO WILBRAHAM	JOHN DELUES	JOHN BERKBET
ALEXANDER WALTHALL	RICHARD WICKSTED	MARY BROWNE
THO MAYNWARYNG	RAPHE WODNOTHE	THOMAS WRIGHT
RAN CHURCHE	JOHN JUDSON	WM MAYNWARING
MAI MASINBARING *	RANDALL HAMPTON	THO BURROUGHES
RIC MINSHULL	THOMAS MYLES	WILL GRASTON
	THOMAS SPARROWE	

In 1633 an important Episcopal Visitation, by the authority of Dr. Neile, who had become Archbishop of York in the pievious year, was held at Nantwich, presided over by William Easdaile (or Easdall) LL D , Henry Wickham, D D , (who held Yorkshire preferments and obtained notoriety as Commissioners for causes Ecclesiastical in the extiaoidinaiy litigation between Peter Smart and the Puiitans against the Chapter of Durham), and Dr Cosin, the Aichbishop's Chaplain, and Aichdeacon of the East Riding, Yorkshire, and afterwards Bishop of Durham until his death in 1672 The Parish Register records as follows —

" 1633 That Doctr Nayle, being Archbushoppe of Yorke, and houldinge his visitation this yeare, by Doctr Isdale, as principall visittoi, Docti Wycum, & Doctr Cossens, his assistante, they gave straite commandment to the Churchwardens, That the Pulpitt, the ministers seat, and clarkes seat, should be removed to the pillor, where they now stand, and alsoe that all the Pewes in the Churche should be made uniforme wch was Done accordingly, by vnitue of a Comnission from the said Archbushoppe wth confiimacon thereof And the Church new whitted & very much beautifyed with payntings and many sentences of holy scripture "

This removal of the Pulpit to the place it afterwards occupied for 222 years, was the cause of litigation between Geffrey Mynshull of Stoke, gent , (Utter Barrister of Grays Inn, and authoi of the, now, extremely scarce book " Essays and Characters of a Prison and Prisoners," 1618), and the Churchwaidens, in the Ecclesiastical Court at Chester. The Mem recoiding the settlement of the dispute, is unfortunately, the last of the series of events furnished by the Parish Registers.

---

* This is one of the many ways of spelling the name of Mairwaring. Sir William Dugdale enumerated 131 different ways in which that surname cccuis in ancient and modern deeds

1634 *Decimo die Novembr* [10th Nov] *Ma* That whereas there was a suite dependinge in the Lo Bushopps Court of Chester att Chester Betweene Jeffrey Mynshull Esqr plt and Robte Wilkes & Robte Martyn Churchwardens this prsent yeare concerninge the right & tytle of Inheritaunce wch the said Jeffrey claymeth unto a buriall place wthin the p'ish Church of Namptwich, and that his Ancestors (as hee alleadereth)* have heretofore bine buried closse upp vnto the East syde of the greate Pillor standinge on the North syde of the Church wherevnto the Pulpitt is nowe fixed, and soe vnder the ministers seate wherein hee readeth divine service, And under pte [part] of the clarks seate & the weddinge or churchinge seate therevnto anexed And from the said seate or places eastwards in length towards the seate late of Roger Crocketts deceased & nowe the seat of Edward Heyes the elder gent, by the space of three score yeares or thereabouts All wch hee affirmeth to prove by the testimony of sufficient witnesses Wherevpon att A publique assembly vpor. the tenth day of November this p'nte yeare of our lord god 1634 of the gents & others concerninge the same buriall place It there was and is fully concluded, condiscended and agreed vpon by & betweene the said Jeffrey Minshull vppon th'one pte And John Saringe preacher of gods word att Namptwich aforesaid, the said Churchwardens, gent & p[ar]ishoners of the said p'ishe on th'other pte That there shalbe noe further prceedinge in the said suite betwixt the said p ties concerninge the said burial place And that the said Jeffrey his heires executors administrators & assignes & eu'y [every] of them shall not hereafter clayme or haue any right, tytle or interest of buriall vnder the said Pulpett & ministers seate, But shall for eu' [ever] hereafter bee excluded & debarred from the same And that they and eu'ic of them for eu hereafter shall or may haue free lib tie & accesse, as in prim' [former] tymes to bury their dead wthout intervpcon wthin pte of the said clarks seat weddinge or churchinge seate, and soe in length Eastwards towards the seate of the said Edward Heyes And that upon the takinge or removinge of the said seate, the said Jeffrey Mynshull his heires & successors shall well & sufficiently att his & theire owne coste & charges erect & sett upp the said seate againe wthin the space of twoe dayes next ensuinge after any such buriall there In witness whereof to this prsent agreemt wee the said minister, Jeffrey Minshull & Churchwardens haue subscribed oure names the day and yeare abouewritten "

The following List of Pews in Nantwich Church, 1633, is from a " True copy ' [on Parchment] "from the original in the Lord Bishop of Chester's Registry faithfully made and collated by William Wilson Public Notary," now in the possession of G F Wilbraham Esq This document which furnishes another interesting list of contemporary names, is headed as follows —

"*A SCHEDULE containing the names of the severall Inhabitants and p[ar]ishoners of the parrish of Namptwich of the diocese of Chester and province of Yorke to whom Stalls or pewes are assigned and allotted in the same Church and the severall stalls or pewes soe to them allotted by vertue of a Comission and an Order or Act made on that behalfe made and graunted By the Right Word William Easdall Doctor of Lawes Vicar gen'all [general] and officiall principall to the most Reverend ffather in God Richard by the providence of God Lord Archbishopp of Yorke primate of England and Metropolitane to whom all and all manner of Jurisdic'con Spirituall and Ecclia'call within the dioces of Chester and province of York aforesaid which otherwise did belonge to the Lorde Bishopp of Chester during the continuance of his Graces Metropoliticall Visitation late dependinge was notoriously known to appertaine as followeth, viz —*

* "*Alleadereth,*" that is, alleges

Imprimis, the first Seate or pew from the Cross Ile or Alley
    is assigned and allotted unto   Maister Thomas Maisterson.

It'm the next Collaterall Stall or pew to that is assigned and
    allotted unto   m^r Thomas Wilbraham.

It'm. The first stall or pew in length on the other side of the
    Crosse Ile or Alley Collaterally is assigned and
    allotted unto   m^r Alexander Walthall.

It'm the second stall or pew which is next behind Mr. Thos
    Wilbrahams is assigned and allotted unto   Mr Hugh Hassall.

It'm the first second and third Stalles or pewes with length
opposite to the pulpitt is assigned and allotted
unto
           { Mr Thomas Maisterson,
             Mr Thomas Wilbraham,
             Mr Hugh Hassall,
             aforesaid for their wives
             respectively.

It m One Pewe seate or Stall now in the possession of M^r
    Geffrey Minshall built on high and affixed to one
    Capitall pillar wth th'appurtenances is assigned
    and allotted unto   Mr Geffery Minshall

It'm One Pewe seate or Stall now in the possession of Mr.
    Mathew Manwareing built on high and fixed to
    to the other Capitall pillar wth th'appurtences is
    assigned and allotted unto   Mr Mathew Manwareing

In the middle Range on ye South side

Imprimis the first stall or pew is allotted and assigned unto Mr [Richard] Whicksteed.

Item.	the second	do.	,,	,,	Raph Lat[ham?]
Item	the third	do	,,	,,	Robert [Parker?]
Item.	the fourth	do	,,	,,	. [Clutton?]
Item	the fifth	do.	,,	,,	[Richard Wright?]
Item	the sixth	do.	,,	,,	[Wilkes?]

The parchment is here much worr, and the names almost entirely obliterated

[In the mid]dle Range on the North side

Imprimis the fourth stall or pew is allotted and assigned unto Sabboth Church

It'm	the fifth	do	,,	,,	Mr Henery Delues
It'm.	the nynth	do	,,	,,	Edward Church
It'm.	the Eleaventh	do.	,,	,,	Mr John Delues.
It'm	the Twelfth	do.	,,	,,	Robert Wilkes.
It'm.	the Thirteenth	do.	,,	,,	John Winsye
It'm	the ffowerteenth	do.	,,	:	Thomas Sparrow
It'm	the ffifteenth	do	,,	,,	[Roger] Howrobin
It m.	the eighteenth	do.	,,	,	John Wright
It'm	the nineteenth	do.	,,	,,	Edward Massey.
It'm	the Twentyth	do	,,	,,	Margaret Comberbach & Thomas C. her son.

In the South side of the Great Ile or Alley.

Imprimis the sixth stall or pew is allotted and assigned unto Cicily Maisterson

It'm	the seaventh	do	,,	,,	Thomas Burroughes.
It'm	the eighth	do.	,,	,,	Robert Bromhall
It'm	the ninth	do.	,,	,,	John Winsted & John Browne
It'm.	the Tenth	do.	,,	,	Sabbath Church
It'm	the fowerteenth	do	,,	,,	Mr Richard Clutton, the younger
It'm	the nineteenth	do	,,	,,	Mr Roger Wright.

Which said stall is adioyreing to the pillar

| Itm. the six & twentieth do | ,, | ,, | John Sare. |

Being under the clockhouse

| It'm. the nine & twentieth do | ,, | ,, | Mr Richard Minshall |

In the South syde Ile

Imprimis the first stall or pew is allotted and assigned unto Edward ffrith

Item	the third	do.	,,	,,	Thomas Alsager
Item	the fowerth	do	,,	,,	John Jenings
Item.	the ffifth	do	,,	,,	Thomas Noden
Item.	the sixth	do	,,	,,	[Geffrey ?] Minshall.
Item	the nynth	do	,,	,,	John Maddocke.
Item	the tenth	do	,,	,,	Richard Rockett [Pratchett?]
Item	the eleaventh	do	,,	,,	Arthur Mainewareing
Item	the thirteenth	do.	,,	,,	William Barnes.
Item.	the ffifteenth	do	,,	,,	Edward Massey
Item	the eighteenth	do	,,	,,	Thomas Bickerton
Item	the twentieth	do	,	,,	Richard Venables the younger
Item.	the one & twentieth do	,,	,,	John Becket
Item.	the fower & twentieth do.	,,	,,	Edward Brayne
Item	the five & twentieth do	,,	,,	Roger Wright, glasier

In the South Side of the North Ile or Alley

Imprimis the first stall or pew is allotted and assigned unto John Tench

Item.	the second	do	,,	,,	George Mainewaring
Item	the fowerth	do	,,	,,	Mr Henery Maisterson.
Item	the eighth	do.	,,	,,	Henery Briscoe
Item	the ninth	do	,,	,,	mr Roger Wright

In the north side of the Great Ile or Alley

Imprimis the sixte stall or pew is allotted and assigned unto James Bullin.

| Item | the seaventh | do | ,, | ,, | Thomas Bickerton |

In the Old Ile

Imprimis the tenth seat or stall is allotted and assigned unto Mr Lawrence Wright

Item	the eleaventh	do	,,	,,	Mr. Thomas Church.
Item	the twelfth	do	,,	,	Mr Richard Minshall
Item	the ffowerteenth	do	,	,,	Mr Henery Delues
Item	the sixteenth	do.	,,	,,	Mr Richard Church
Item	the eighteenth	do	,,	,,	Mr Edward Heyes.
Item.	the two & twentieth do	,,	,,	Robert Bromhall.

In the North syde Ile

Imprimis the first seat or pew is allotted and assigned unto Gilbert ffourins

Item	the second	do.	,,	,	William Moore
Item	the fyfth	do	,,	,	George ffletcher
It m	the syxt	do	,,	,,	Jane Mainewareing
Item	the eighth	do	,,	,	John Watson
Item	the ninth	do	,,	,	Henery Whicksted
Item	the tenth	do	,,	,,	Raph Bostock
Item	the twelfth	do	,,	,,	Thomas Masseye
Item.	the Thirteenth	do	,,	,,	Randle Babbington
Item	yᵉ ffoureteenth	do	,,	,,	Edward Braine
Item	the sixteenth	do	,,	,,	Richard Wilkes
It'm	the eighteenth	do.	,,	,,	William Edgeley
Item	the twentieth	do	,,	,,	Mr Hugh Allen

In the North side of the South Ile or Alley

Imprimis the sixth stall or pew is allotted and assigned unto Mr Richard Clutton the elder

Item	the tenth	do	,,	,,	Mr William Wettnall.
Item	the seaventh	do	,,	,,	Roger Cumberbach
Item	the eighteenth	do	,,	,,	Eldrid Maddock.
Item	the nineteenth	do	,,	,,	Richard Venables

"Moreover by the appoyntment and direction of Authority aforesaid the pulpitt is placed and now sett adioyneing to the first pillar on the North side of the said Church and the Ministers Deske is next before the said pulpit, the Clarkes seat next before the Ministers Deske and the wedding pew immediately before the said Clarkes seat And alsoe the Stall pew or Seat where the Minister heretofore used to sitt is now allotted and assigned unto mʳ Savinge as Clarke or Curate or Minister of the said Church of Namptwich"

Thomas Wilbraham, (MS. Journal) records a shock of earthquake, a hard winter, a drought, a flood, and an epidemic, that followed in successive years, as follows —

"*Mem* An earthquake aboute 4 in the morn 1 Jan 1634-5 And in the next month fell an exceeding great snow, such as noe man then living could remember, wherein many perished The whole winter fro [m] the later end of Michaelmas term was very cold wᵗʰ frosts and snowe But untill then faire summerlike weather & the wayes very faire" . "The beginninge of this yeare fro March till July [in 1635] was noe rayne at all but very hot weather wᶜʰ burnt up the grass in most fields, & prevented many from sowing barley, & much that was sown came not up "*

"5 Nov 1636 The River Weever was so high yᵗ the water touched the planks of the wych bridge, & broke down the Jarrels, & did run with a swift current thorough my cos Hassalls gates "

The year before, at the Spring Assizes at Chester, the following order was made by the Justices, Sir John Bridgman and Sir Marmaduke Lloyd —

---

* In Sir William Brereton s "Travels, (in Scotland and Ireland, 1635) pp 76-7, allusion is made to the severe winter of 1634, and the intensely hot summer of 1635 He says, amongst other remarks "At Falkirk, in Scotland, many perished in their houses for want of relief and many houses were buried in the snow, and could not be found but by the smoke of the chimneys ' "No rain to speak of had fallen since the winter of 1634 but in the end of July was much dropping weather "

" 30th March 1635

The Inhabitants of yᵉ Towne of Namptwᶜʰ are ordered to repayre and amende their Bridge, & to make yᵉ same sufficient for Carts & Horses at all Seasons, upon paine of yᵉ forfeiture of £100 And yᵉ Justices of p[eace] for yᵗ hundred are ordered to make Report to his Maᵗⁱᵘˢ Justices of Assize

Jo Bridgman
Marmaduke Lloyd '

The above order was not immediately carried out, notwithstanding the threatened fine   But what the Judges' Order could not do, was effectually done by the flood of 5th Nov. 1636, and the Bridge was obliged to be rebuilt in the following year

'*Mem* 1637 That this summer the wych bridge was new built of tymber to yᵉ discredit of the undertakers and overseers thereof "   .

"*Mem* And this year [1638] many died in our Towne of a contagious Ague "* (Wilb. MS Journal)

Greater evils than these, however, soon befel the town and the whole kingdom,

> " When hard words, jealousies, and fears,
> Set folks together by the ears,
> And made them fight "

In 1637 the celebrated Puritan barrister, Mr Prynne, probably passed through Nantwich, on his way to Caernarvon Castle, where he was imprisoned, having been condemned by the Star-chamber Court as a libeller to be put from the bar, to stand in the pillory in two places, Westminster and Cheapside, to lose both his ears, one in each place, to pay £5000 to the King, and to be imprisoned during life   In the same year a petition had been sent from Nantwich respecting the then newly imposed *ship-money tax*, complaining that it had not been equitably assessed   Among the Calend State Papers Chas I 1637-8, vol 380, is a letter dated Jan 29, 1637-8, by Thomas Cholmondeley of Vale Royal, Sheriff of Cheshire to the Council, on the subject.

" By letters of 29 Nov last, you sent me a petition of the town of Nantwich, whereby they complained to be overcharged for their *ship-money*   Those letters came not to my hands till 28 Dec last, when I had settled a proceding in the service   Since then I have weighed the justice of their complaint, and find that that town is a great market town, and reputed the wealthiest part of the county   This, with other privileges they enjoy, moves me to conceive they are but proportionately rated with the rest of the shire, and more especially because my last predecessor, Sir Thos Delves [of Doddington], a near neighbour to their town, an ancient justice of the peace of their hundred, and better knowing their estates than myself, set the same assessment which is now upon them "

1637-8 Almshouses erected and endowed by Sir Edmund Wright, Kt, Alderman of London (See Charities).

The Wilb MS Journal furnishes the following information †—

" Thos Wilb being sworne servant to Kg Chas ‡ had sumons by the Ld Chamb of the House-hold to attend his Matᵘᵉ in his Royal Journey into Scotland comeing to York where the Court was, in such equipage as befitted his place "

---

* ·The year 1638 was one of great mortality as proved by the Registers   The number of burials in 1637, was 74, in 1638,—171, in 1639 —107

† This entry is in the handwriting of Roger Wilbraham, who handed down the records of the family for the next fifty years,—that is, from 1639—1690

‡ " I was sworne servant to Kg Charles in the place of an Esquier of his body 1 Nov 1628 " (Thos Wilb MS Journal)

The original summons, which is still preserved at Delamere, is as follows —

"After our hearty Commendacons Whereas it hath pleased the Kings most Excellent Maty to undertake a Royall Journey into the North, and therein to be attended upon by all his sworne Servants of weh number yorselfe beinge one I haue thought fitt to signify unto you his Mats Royall pleasure yt you be ready within one Moneth after ye date hereof, wheresoever His Maty shall then be with a Horse and Russett Armes for yorselfe, with guilded Nails or Studds as a Curassier, and White Armes as a Hargobusier for yor Seruant or Seruants yt you shall bringe alonge with you in befitinge equipage there to act and doe such duties & seruices as shalbe required of you Which not doubting but you will carefully performe as allsoe giue me a speedy Accompt hereof I res. "

                                    " Yor very loving ffriend

   " Yorke this 22nd   " P————(?)
   " of Aprill 1639

The Journal continues —" He was sworn a Gent of the honble privy Chamber extraordinary, dated 23 April 1639 He attended his Royal Master to Edinburg where a peace was concluded, whereupon His Majtie retired into England, and Tho. Wilb. returned by Carlisle & came to his house in Namptwich 6 July 1639 '

" The year following Thos W[ilbraham] entertained the Earl of Strafford then Ld Lieutt of Ireland & his Retinue, viz his son ye Lord Raby, Sr Toby Mathew, Sr Philip Mainwaring, then Sect. to his lordship & some others of quality in their way to London Which so great a minister of State might have had opportunity to have requited, if his Destiny, rather than Desert, had not hurried him to the block [12 May, 1641]. This entertainmt was in April 1640 "

On this occasion the Earl of Strafford, (before Sir Thomas Wentworth, Lord Deputy of Ireland), was returning from Ireland, where in fourteen days he had procured four subsidies from the Irish Commons and raise a force of eight thousand men to take part in the attack on the Scots The shortness of the visit may be accounted for by the hurry of the Earl flushed with his successful statecraft, to be in time for the opening of the " Short " Parliament on 13th April, 1640

On 18th July, 1640, "a public fast was solemnized thro' the land by the King s proclamation, for the turning away of the plague then begun in London, and the preventing the sword and other judgments hovering over our heads " (Burghall's *Diary*)

The Great Civil War and Commonwealth Period.

HEN war was inevitable, a "*Remonstrance*" or "*Declaration*" was circulated through the towns and villages of Cheshire, in order to ascertain by the signatures of the inhabitants those who would take the side of the "King and Parliament" in opposition to the Royalist cause. Several Declarations were issued by the Parliament in the months of March and May, 1642;[*] and, while public opinion was being thus tested throughout the country, the "*Gentrie and Commons of Cheshire*" sent a "*patheticall Petition*" to the King imploring his return to his Parliament.[†] The Remonstrance, which is preserved in *Harl. MSS.* 2107, is as follows :—

"*A REMONSTRANCE or DECLARACON. of vs the INHABITANTS of the COUNTIE PALLATINE of CHESTER whose names are subscribed and of manie more.*"

"Wee most humblie declare and remonstrate that we owe oʳ lawes, liberties, oʳselves and what els we can yet stile ours (next to Gods infinite mercies) to the goodnes of his Matⁱᵉ and to the great care and indefatigable paines of the Honᵇˡᵉ Parliamᵗ. To the one for discovering the varietie of oppressions that had almost overwhelmed vs and for prᵖaring and advising apt remedies. To the other for crowning these wholsome counsells with a blessed fiat: Wherein the joynt acts of a good King and a faithfull councell have so apparentlie concurred to the generall good that we cannot but looke upon all such as unworthie of future happines who doe admitt for currant that dangerous and disloyall distinction (which rings too loud in oʳ eares), videlt., *For the King* or *For the Parliament.* Our loyall affections and judgments will not permitt us to stile them true Patriotts and lovers of theire countrie that are not cordially affected to oʳ gratious Soveraigne, nor them good subjects that disaffect Parliamᵗˢ.: the King and Parliamᵗ being like Hippocrates twynnes, they must laugh and crie, live and die, together: And both of them are so rooted in oʳ loyall hearts that we cannot disjoynt them.

---

[*] See a scarce pamphlet entitled "*Jehovah-jireh,*" by John Vicars, p. 91-2 : printed 1641-2.
[†] *Ibid.*

Wherefore we declare that according to o^r allegiance and our solemne Protestation (our vowes beeing in heaven) we are resolved to spend o^r lives and fortunes in the service and defence of both, in maintenance of his Mat^{ies} most royall and sacred person, honor and prerogative, & in the preservation of the Parliam^t and just privelidge thereof and of o^r true and undoubted religion, lawes, properties and liberties which are deposited for o^r use and availe in that great and wise councell   Wee beeing confident that neither King nor subject, nor religion nor libertie can comfortablie survive the ruyne and destruction of that great body   And we further professe o^rselves enemies to all those who ever they be that shall be found Agents in making o^r wounds deeper by fostering and fomenting the unfortunat mistakes and fearefull jealousies betwixt head and body, his Mat^{ie} and the Parliam^t, and wch continuing at this distance threatens not only the dissolution of the fabrick of this blessed government, but also the losse of all his Mat^{ies} kingdomes & dominiones "

Two lists of signatures are appended to the above "Remonstrance," the *first* endorsed "*Poole, Nantwich and other p^{ts}* [parts] *their subscripcon. of ye declaracon. July* 1642," gives the following sixty-three names of persons, most of whom appear to have belonged to Nantwich

ALEXANDER EJCOCKE [of Poole]	JOHN SHENTON	WILLIAM CAPPER
ANDR BOWRY, Curat	RICHARD WRIGHT	THOMAS WHITTAKERS
W^M GEWLOR [GOORE] ministr[*]	GABRIELL WETTENHALL	ROGER WRIGHT
JOHN CARTWRIGHT	JOHN REYNOLDS	HENRIE WRIGHT
THOMAS VRSCRATE [Urscrate]	JOHN MAINWARING	ROBERT JOHNSON
RANDULL CROXTON	RICHARD CAVALES	THOMAS PENKAMANE
RANDLE GRAFTON	JOHN TOMSON	GEORGE WHITTICKERS
LAWRENCE FFLETCHER	RANDULPHE SACKLRSON	JAMES CROXTON
RAPH LEFTWICH	WILLIAM JACKSON	JOHN DOLMAN§
ARTHUR EDGLEY	MARC FOLINEUX ‡	RICHARD PATTRICKE
THO STEELE†	WILLIAM ALCOCKE	RICHARD KORKETT
THO WILSON	HENRY TRICKETT	LAWRENCE DAVIES
WILL MOULTON	WILLIAM DAWSON	JOHN DAVIES
JNO CREWE	WILLIAM TRICKETT	THOMAS TENCH
ELDRID MADDOCK	RICHARD EACHIS	GILBLRT JOHNSTON [?]
RICHARD WOODKEN	JOHN BARKER	NEHEMIAH POTTE
THOMAS PROUDMAN	WILLIAM WHEELER	ROBERT FEARINGTON
ROBERT PARKER	RICHARD WILBRAHAM	ROBERT MOTTERSHED
THOMAS WRIGHT	THOMAS MYLES	ROGER MADELEY
WILLIAM POTT	JOHN PREICE	JOHN OULTON
JOHN SLADE	JEFFREY MASSIE	THOMAS POIS

The second list, consisting of the "*Justices of Peace and Gentlemen*" in this neighbourhood who signed the "*Remonstrance,*" contains the following names —

* This clergyman's name occurs three times in Nantwich Register of Baptisms—

    "1633 Jan 9   Margaret dau of Mr Willm Goore Minister "
    "1636 June 7   Hannah dau of William Goore clerke "
    "1638 Sep 16   Sarah daughter of Mr William Govar "

† ? Whether afterwards Governor of Beeston Castle
‡ Afterwards one of the Collectors for Nantwich
§ Master of the Grammar School at Nantwich

RIC WILBRAHAM [of Woodhey]	EDWARD MYNSHULL	ROBERT WICKSTED
THOMAS DELVES*	ROGER WRIGHT	WILL'M GLEGG
JOHN MAINWARING	GEFF MYNSHULL	SAB CHURCH
JO CREWE	ROGR WILBRAHAM [of Dorfold]	JOHN DELUES
HU WILBRAHAM	RICHARD WICKSTED	THO BURROUGHES
GEO MAINWARING	WILLIAM LEVERSAGE	EDW HAYES
ROBERT HINTON	RIC LEICESTER	RIC CHETWOODE
LAWRENCE WILKES	THOMAS MALBONE 1642	GEORGE STARKEY
THO WALTHALL	WILLIAM ANDERTON, clrcus [clerk]	RANDALL HAMPTON
	THOS MAVALBARING [Mainwaring]	

The above Lists represent the local gentry and tenants who favoured the Parliament side in the great struggle   Of those on the King's side, may be mentioned THOMAS WILBRAHAM of Townsend, RANDULL CHURCH of Hospital Street, THOMAS MAISTERSON of Pillory Street, LADY MARGARET NORTON of Beam Street, ALEXANDER WALTHALL of Wistaston, WILLIAM ALLEN, Gentleman   MR SARING, the Minister at Nantwich Church, &c , and the following three persons, WILLIAM LEVERSAGE, RICHARD WICKSTEAD, and HUGH WILBRAHAM, who, occurring in the above list, seem to have changed their opinions, all of whom (except *Thomas Wilbraham* who left the town and died in 1643) occur in the list of " *Delinquents* " on a subsequent page

Of the second list of signatures, perhaps the most remarkable name (which, in the original, is underlined and dated 1642), is that of *Thomas Malbon*, of Nantwich, a gentleman in the legal profession, who left, in his own handwriting, an interesting and detailed account of the Civil War in Cheshire and the adjacent Counties, dated 1651 , and now preserved in the Library of Reginald Cholmondeley, Esq , of Condover Hall, Salop †   In an article contributed to the Palatine Note Book, I have adduced arguments in proof of the genuineness and authenticity of that MS , which need not be here repeated , and have also shown that the oft-quoted " *Diary* " of Edward Burghall, Vicar of Acton, entitled " *Providence Improved*," (dated 1663), was, as far as it relates to the Civil War, wholly obtained from the account previously written by Thomas Malbon ‡   By comparing the extracts from the Malbon MS. here printed for the first time with the Cole MS of Burghall s " *Diary* ' in the British Museum, and the abridged and altered version of the latter MS printed in 1778 ,§ it will be seen that Burghall must have had access to the Malbon MS , which he appears to have used in illustration of his peculiar views of the Divine Providence, adopting the phraseology, but frequently transposing the words, of Malbon , and, in his reproduction, omitting much of the original account, that is of importance and interest

Making allowance for the strong party colouring pervading this account, the statements here recorded, which, in many instances, can be corroborated from Parish Registers,

* Sir Thomas Delves, the son of Sir Henry Delves, of Doddington, Bart

† By the courtesy of Reginald Cholmondeley, Esq , in Feb 1882 I was allowed to make a complete transcript of the original MS , the existence of which has hitherto been unknown to local historians , I hope on a future occasion to publish it in its entirety, with explanatory notes

‡ " *Palatine Note Book*," edited by J E Bailey, F S A , Manchester, vol ii pp 133-137 (1882).

§ Poole's " *History of Cheshire*," vol ii pp 893-948   Edit 1778

contemporary pamphlets, letters, and other documents, contain a mass of information concerning local families and events, collected by an eye-witness, who, at the time, held office as one of the Committee of Sequestrators, and therefore must have been well acquainted with what was transpiring in this neighbourhood. Thomas Malbon's Account is much too long to be given in its entirety, but all that relates to Nantwich and its garrison is here given, exactly as in the original, retaining the curious spelling as affording an indication of the local pronunciation of persons of respectability at that time.

The opening paragraphs of the MS clearly show what were the first beginnings of the "*troubles*" in this part of the Country. Chester at once declared for the King, but Nantwich, the next important place in the County held with the Parliament. Some of the most influential gentlemen in the neighbourhood, viz Sir Richard Wilbraham, of Woodhey, Bart, Sir Thomas Delves, of Doddington, Bart., and Roger Wilbraham, of Dorfold, Esq, together with "Mr. Mainwaring of Peover," were taken prisoners, perhaps to overawe others who were not loyal All attempts, however, to secure Nantwich for the King, proved unsuccessful, and throughout the struggle the town maintained its opposition to the Royalist cause.

THOMAS MALBON'S CIVIL-WAR ACCOUNT

"*A breefe & true Relacon. of all suche passages & things as happened & were donne in and aboute NAMPTWICH in the Countie of CHESTER & in other plac'[es] of the same Countie.   Togerther w*th *some other things in other COUNTIES (not farr distant) acted & donne by some of the Com'anders officers & Soldiers of the said Towne of NAMPTWICHE (after the same was made a GARRISON for KINGE & PARLIAM?,) scythens* [since] *the* v*th of August 1642   Soe trulie as the wryter hereof cold* [could] *come by the knowledge of the same, viz   —*"

Commissioners of Arrey & Com'issioners for the Milicia   "Uppon or about the Eleaventh of August 1642 Sr will'm Brereton, & the Deputie Lieftente for the said Countie of Chester (beinge Com'issioners for the Mylicia) wth some Considerable strength for the setlinge of the Mylicia, as was intended (on the Parham's behalfe) came to Namptwiche   And the Commision rs of Airaye, on the Kings behalfe (hereinge thereof) came the same daye vnto Ravensmore, a myle from the said Towne, (wth purpose to hinder theire p'ceedinge) Having waveied [*i e.* waited] for many Township men both of Namptwiche Hundred, Broxton Hundred & other plac[e]s wth speciall com'andem t to come furnished wth Armes matches powder & Bullets   But to what purpose or intente the Countreymen weire most of them altogether Ignorant   But by mediacon & meanes made vnto both p'ties (by some gents* wch desyred Peace) nothinge was donne att that tyme, But agreed on both sides & soe p mised [promised], That the People & Com'ission rs in bothe p'ties. shold dpte. [departe] home agayne peaceablie, and the Comissione rs of Airaye nor them on theire side, not to come to the Towne that day   Yett neu'thelesse the said Com'issione rs of Arraye wth a greate company (contrary to theire p'mise and agreem t) hearinge that the

---

* According to Burghall's "*Prov dence Improved*," these gentlemen were "*Mr* [Roger] *Wilbraham* of Darfold," and '*Mr Verden* of Chester "

said S^r will'm. Brereton & the deputie Lieftent^s & theire company, weire disperced & gonne awaye, (accordinge as the same was agreed) Came .n a bravado wth greate showtinge & reioycinge into the said Towne, and theire stayed a certyn ty [me] spendinge theire money and drinkinge merrilie w^{thout} offringe any of   .$^{\nearrow}$ [? offence] vnto the Towne & in the Evenynge depted peacablie awaye "

Lord Grandisons   "Afterwards vpon wednesdaye the x\9th of September 1642 beinge
comynge to   . .   [Michaelmas] daye The said Towne of Namptwiche, beinge firme
Namptwiche   for the P [arliament] standinge in opposicon agaynst the Comissioner^{rs}
of Arraye, having   . .[? but] smale p'vision of Armes & Am'unycon and a little ayded by the C   [? common] people neere adioynynge & haveing began to make some [barricades at the] streete ends for theire owne saufeties, was assaulted   [by the royalists] beinge under the Com'and of the Lord Grandison,† . . . . Lord Cholmonceley, Hughe Calveley, Esqre, Heighe Sher [riff]   . of the said countie of Chester and about xiij Troups of Trowpers & Dragoneers amountinge in all to xj hundred horse or more & many other gent, Came vnto the said Towne, to the Aspell Streete End, (where the Chayne was drawen ouer the street ende) & some fewe of the said Towne wth musketts & other weapons weire placed theire sufficient for a tyme to haue opposed them & kepte them furthe   But consideringe that then The Kinge being att Shrowesbury wth great forces And by reason of the feare [i e fair] speeches & p'mises [promises] of the said Lorde not to Wronge the said Towne noe [nor] doe them any harme, The Chayne was withdrawn [&] the said Lorde, Sheryff & whole Army, peaceablie vpon theire said p mises, entered the said Towne   But p'sentlie vpon theire entrance (contrary to theire words and p'misses) they disarmed eu y [every] man and tooke all theire Armes & Armor from them & all that colde bee found in eu'y howse, threatninge that whoesoeu'[er] had any Arms & did not bringe them In, shold bee plundred   And seu'all dayes followinge the [y] yssued furthe (many of them) And took all the Armes from Woodhey, dodington, Haslington, Baddeley and many other places   And plundered many Countrey howses & tooke many horses   And after they had had free quarter in Namptwiche vntill Mondaye then nexte followinge   They depted away wth all they had gotten from thence, and wente to the Kinge and Prince to Shrowesbury   But the Kinge & Prince beinge att that instant att Chester & havinge intelligence of theire cominge to Shrowesbury wente thither to them "

Earle of Derbies   "About the begynynge of December 1642 The *Earle of Darbie*‡ (beinge
cominge into   on the Kings p'tie) ass.sted wth some men and horse, (vth the *Lord*
Cheshire   *Cholmondeley*) entered Cheshire intendinge to have plundered *m^r mayn-
warings*§ of Caryncham & some other of the Deputie Lieftent^s, Commissioner^s for the milicia, & to haue seazed vpon some Parliam^t Carryages wch weire cominge into Cheshire, (but

---

* At the bottom of the first page of the original, the MS is slightly torn, and thus a few words indicated by the dotted lines, cannot be seen, but it is easy to supply these deficiencies   With this exception the MS is in excellent preservation

† Lord Grandison, Lieut -General of the 6th Regt for the King was William Villiers, viscount Grandison in the peerage of Ireland, son and heir of Sir Edward Villiers, President of Munster, and brother to George Villiers, Duke of Buckingham   He died at Oxford on the 29th Sept 1643 from wounds received at the siege of Bristol on the 26th July in the same year   His daughter, the celebrated Barbara Villiers, afterwards Duchess of Cleveland, erected a stately monument to his memory in Christ Church Cathedral, Oxford   (Army Lists, Edwd Peacock, F S A, 1863, p 13)

‡ James Stanley seventh Earl of Derby, K G and K B., Lord-lieutenant and General of Lancashire, who was beheaded at Bolton, 15 Oct 1651

§ Colonel Edward Mainwaring, of Kirmincham Hall, Cheshire.

they miste [missed] of theire purposes), ffor *M*^r *Maynwaringe* & the rest haveing intelligence theirof Raysed the Countrey, wch the Kings ptie p'ceaving fledd   The *Lord of Darbie* by backe wayes into Lancashire, wth his company beinge about twoe hundred   But xxiiij of the said *Lord Cholm*[*onde*]*leys* men & horse, comynge to Northwiche, weire taken theire, theire Armes & horses oeinge taken from them, & theire men sente home on foote

    *Colonell Leigh**** of Adlington (on the Kings pte) wth a considerable force p'senthe afterwards entered Macclesfield in the said countie of Chester   But the said Mr Maynwarynge wth assistance of the Countrey did dryve him thence, & hee, disgysed in a Soldye^{rs} habit, escaped, But his Drummer & more of those of his soldyers weire theire slayne   .   .   afterwards Manchester forces comynge In to Mr. . . . . [? Maynwaringe's] Ayde & hee growinge stronge to the Nu'ber of   .   fyve thousand horse and foote   The Com'issioners of Array hearinge thereof All fledd wth theire goods, some into Chester Citie, some into Shrowesbury, some one waye & some another, And soe alsoe did all Parsons, viccars & others wch took pte wth the Array p tie , not one cold bee mett wth all   The said Mr Maynwaringe did take (wth his company) from Colonell Leighes howse, Armes for one hundred & twentie men   And from Wrynehill Hall, old Armes for as many

Maynwaringe\
his forces comynge to\
Namptwiche

    " Vpon the xth of December 1642, & begynnyinge of the nexte weeke after, a great pte of the said *Mr Maynwarings* force & a brave troupe of Manchester horse & men, came all to Namptwiche, wth Captyns Lieftents, and Com'anders, bringing wth theim Three smale peeces of Ordnance, well mounted, wch weire placed att seu'all streete ends theire   And the Captyns & Souldyers, to the nu'ber of one thowsand trayned eu'y daye, and behaved theim selves very well & honestlie, payinge in all theire quarters what the[y] boughte or agreede for '

    War having been declared between the King and the Parliament, and the Cheshire gentry, with their tenants, being divided in their political opinions, an attempt was made to avert the evils of war in this county by a Convention at Bunbury, where it was agreed that Cheshire should be neutral, and take no part whatever in the threatened struggle   A Civil War Tract (*Cheth Soc Publ* vol ii p 334) alludes to this proposed neutrality, as "*Cheshire's faintheartednesse*"   The Articles of the Agreement were, however, soon broken, and, the "inveteracy of local feeling and bitterness of religious animosity" between opposite parties, were maintained as keenly in this county as in other parts of the kingdom.

    Malbon says —

Peace\
concluded

    "The Com'issioners of Arraye, viz , *Earle Ryvers*,† & his brother, w^r *Thomas Savage* , *Lord viscounte Kilmorey*,‡ *Lord Cholmondeley;* and the rest wch weire fledd to Chester, Reased [raised] all theire force together to Chester wth many Horse & foote from all theire frends & tenants in Shropshire, Cheshire, & Wales, wth many threatnynge speeches to dryve theim awaye from Namptwiche, But the[y] fortifyed theim selves in Chester Citie, and durst not sturr furthe, And att lengthe, they having intelligence that greater Ayde wold come to theim att Namptwiche,

---

  * Colonel Thomas Leigh, of Adlington, Cheshire

  † John Viscou it Savage, of Rock Savage, created Farl Rivers by Charles I

  ‡ Robert Needham, second Viscount Kilmorey, of Shavington, co Salop

and suspectinge that Chester wold be assaulted, They offered p'lye. & mocens (?) [parley and motions] of Peace wch the gent att Namptwiche consented vnto   There were no'iated [nominated] for the Com'ission^rs of Array on theire ptie, The Lord Kilmorey & m^r Bridgeman· and on the other ptie, The for[e]said m^r Maynwaringe and m^r Marbury of Marbury, And the place appoynted was att Bunbury, in the said Countie of Chester, the xxiij^th of December 1642, where the pties nominated did meete the same daye, and made an agreem^t as followeth, viz —

" An AGREEMT made att BUNBURY in the COUNTIE of CHESTER for pacificacon. and settinge the PEACE of the COUNTIE by vs whose names are subscrybed aucthorized theire vnto, by the LORDS and gents COM'ISSIONE^RS of ARRAY & DEPUTIE LIEFTENTS in the said COUNTIE"

Imprimis ytt ys agreed that theire bee an absolute cessacon of Armes from henceforthe w^thin this Countie & noe Armes to bee taken vp to offend one & other, but by Consente bothe of the Kinge and twoe howses of p'liam^t vnless ytt bee to resist force broughte into this Countie

2 —That all (but two hundred of either side) shalbe disbanded tomorrowe beinge Saturdaye, and on Mondaye all on both sides bothe horse and ffoote

3 —That all prsonr^s on bothe sides bee enlarged As for m^r Moreton whoe ys now p'sonr att Manchester (the gent appoynted Deputie Lieftent^s) doe declare that hee was taken w^thout theire privitie or encouragem^t by some Trowper^s of Manchester vpon a pryvatt quarrell for takinge powder & other goods belonginge to one of Manchester yett they will use theire utmost endeavor to p'cure his enlargem^t, & desyer that the lyke endeavers bee vsed by the Lords & other^s Com'issioner^s of Arraye for the enlarginge of m^r Danyell of Daresbury

4 —That the fortificacons att Chester, Namptwiche, Stockporte, Knottesforde, & Northwiche, or any other Towne in Cheshire, (latelie made by either p'tie) bee p'sentlie demollished

5 —That all goods and Armes taken on bothe sides (nowe remaynynge in the Countie in specie) bee furth wth restored, and for all others that are taken furthe of the Countie, ytt ys p'mised on bothe pts that sythens [since] the b'nefitt of the pacificacon redounds to the whole Countie That they will vse theire vtmost endeavor^s for a joynte contrybucon of the Countie towards satisffaction of the owners

6 —That the Lords and gents Com'issioner^s of Array before the viij^th daye of Januarye nexte will p'cure [procure] from his Matie a letter, thereby declaringe, That inregard a peace ys made in the Countie, Hee will sende noe forces into this Countie, And yf any other p'son shall contrary to suche declaracon bringe forces into this Countie (passinge for forces w^thout doinge any hostile acte onelie excepted) The said Lords & gents will Joyne to resiste theim   And yf any forces (w^thout the consent bothe of the Kinge & bothe howses of Parliam^t) shall come into this Countie (the passage forces w^thout doinge any hostile Acte onelie excepted) The said gents (nomynated Deputie Lieftent^s) will resist theim & vse theire vtmost endeaver^s therein

7 —Inregard (that by the blessinge of God) theire ys lyke to bee a peace w^thin the Countie (yf this agreement bee observed) ytt ys agreed that the Com'issioner^s of Array shall not any further putt the Com'ission of Arraye in execucon, nor the gent no'iated Deputie Lieftent^s the ordynance of the Milicia, or execute theire Com'ission

8 —Lastlie all the said pties doe agree and p'myse eyche [each] to other in the worde of a Gent and as they desyer to prosper, That aswell they theim selves as alsoe all theire fiends, tenants, servants and all other (in whome they haue any Interest) shall as muche as in theim lyes, p'forme this agreem^t And ytt ys further desyred that all the said pties Joyne in a peticon vnto his Matie & bothe howses of p'liam^t for puttinge an ende to the great distracons and misery fallen vpon this kingdom, by makinge a speedy

peace   And ytt is agreed that Sr George Bouthe & all others wth in this Countie, whoe haue appeared either as Com ission^{rs} of Array or as Depu:ie Lieftents by reason of the ordinance of Parliam^t shall (with all con-vaynyente speede) subscry be this Agreem^t *

The makers of this Agreem^t for the Com'issioners of Array e	{ My Lord of Kilmorrey
	Orlando Bridgeman Esq
for the Lieftents	{ Mr [Henry] Maynwaringe of Caryncham
	Mr Marbury of Marbury

The next daye afterwards (being Christmas Eve) All the Companyes on bothe sides weire disbanded.   The tyme the forsaid Mr Maynwaringe & the forsaid company contynued in Namptwiche was iust a fortnighte.   But this Peace did not longe contynue, but did breake on the Com'issioners of Arrayes side, in that the fortificacons att Chester weire not throwne downe & the said Com'issioners contyneued still in Chester encreasinge theire forces & renewinge theim daylie "

Will[ia]m Brereton comynge to Namptwiche

"Vppon Saturday the xxviijth of January then nexte following 1642-[3] S^r will'm Brereton Baronett (Colonell and Com'ander in Chiefe of the p'liam^t forces in these ptes) Comynge towards Namptwiche, wth reasonable good strength to releave the said Towne (beinge in greate danger to bee plundred & destroyed by the Kinges Armye and Com'issioners of Arraye) in this Countie (contiary to theire p'mises & agreem^t as aforesaid) Sⁱ Thomas Aston wth about fyve hundred horse of the Kinges forces lyinge in wayte for the said S^r will'm , and meetinge wth him & all his

S_r Thomas Aston† Routed at Namptwiche

carryedges & forces hee had neere the end of the Aspell streete att Namptwiche betwixt & Cheeibrooke (beinge more in nu'ber than the said S^r will'm) aboute foui a Clocke in the afternoone The [y] joyned Battell, wch contynued very sore, & doubtfull on bothe sides, vntill about seyven a Clocke in the Nighte ytt beinge soe darke they cold not see one the other   But S^r will'm havinge a case of Drakes vpon Caniyage readie charged, discharged the same vpon the Kinges ptie , wch did some execucon & soe affiighted them, that they weire all scattered & quyte Rowted , And tooke p'soners Captyn Chom'ley, (a base sonne of the Lord Chom'ley) Captyn Bridgemann, & of officers & Soldiers about one hundred , And three score horse or aboue; wth many Aimes, Cloakbages, and pillage (as was thought) to the value of one thowsand pounds , many wounded , & some men & hoise slayn, the certyn nu'ber (beinge a very darke Nighte) cold neu' [never] bee certynlie knowne   S^r will'm Brereton lost a Lieftent, & one Vernon,‡ and William Brereton, (beinge twoe com'on Soldyers), had many wounded (thoughe neither mortaly nor meamed [maimed])   And soe (God gyvinge him the victory) about viij a Clocke in the Nighte hee entered the Towne, wth great reioycinge of the inhabitaunce thereof, & the saufety of the same whoe gave & ascrybed all praise & Glory vnto God for his greate mercyes towards theim (wth his p soners & pillage).

* This "Agreement' for maintaining a neutrality is also preserved, in the same words, in *Harl MSS* 2135, p 83, and endoised on the back "*worth nothinge*"   The Parliament, being determined to resist the King, issued, early in Jan. 1642-3, definite "*Instructions*' to Sir William Brereton, Bart of Handforth, Cheshire, as one of the Deputy Lieutenants of the County , by which he at once became commander of tne Parliamentary forces in this County   The "*Instructions*," which are too lengthy to be given here, will be found in "*Local Gleanings foi Lanc & Chesh*" 1st Series vol I pp 28 & 31

† Sir Thomas Aston, of Aston, Cheshire, Bart , a brave but unfortunate general, died at Stafford, from wounds received there, on 24th March, 1645

‡ The Parish Register records the burial of these two soldiers, viz —
"1642-3 Jan 30 Joseph Banbery, a Lieutenant "
   „   „   Edward Varnam, a soldier "

Captyns w.th
Companyes cominge
to Namptwiche
"On Sonday the Towne was quyett, And vpon Mondaye the xxx.th of January 1642, The foresaid mr Maynwaringe & other greate forces bravely Armed, came in Ayde of the Towne to Sr will m Brereton, And the nexte weeke followinge come vnto him alsoe to Namptwiche Captyn Duckenfield,* Captyn Hyde,† Captyn Marbury, & many other Captyns, and Com'anders wth a good nu'ber bothe of horse and foote, And lykewyse came to them, all or most of the gent. (well affected to the Parliamt) lyvinge in the Countrey, to the nu'ber of twoe thowsand; wch many tymes yssued furthe & broughte In prvision, & great store of prysoners"

Sir William Brereton described this battle in a letter which was first printed in the Proceedings of the Society of Antiquaries for 1855, from the original,‡ by James Wallis Pycroft, F S A, who, however, mistakes the event to which the letter relates, for the *second* battle of Nantwich fought in January of the following year. The letter, which was written a week after the event described, is as follows —

"Sir,

"Theis lines may convey unto you the relation of our late encounter§ with Sir Tho Aston's forces upon Saturday last [28 Jan 1642-3] about six of the clocke at night, at which time Sir Thomas, who had observed our motions since his cominge out of Readinge, as did appeare by letters found with some of his troopers (oui prisoners), who did also acknowledge that hee did waite and observe untill he might assault us, which it seemes was reserved for my welcome into Cheshire and to Namptwich, whither I sent my seriant maieor [Serjeant-major] Lothian and Capt Bromhall with about fiftie diagooners upon fryday night, who possessed themselves of the towne about seavon of the clocke on Saturday morninge, and were assaulted by 300 horse of Sr Tho Astons about five of the clocke in the eveninge at 3 or 4 passages at one and the same time, where they were bravely resisted and repulsed, and one of their men and horse slaine They did retreate about one mile, and did there make a stand, and layd an ambusment (their horse being lined with their new raysed Shropshire dragooners), whose light matches were our onely guides and directions how to take our aimes at the enemie, of whom we rec'd intelligence by many countrymen, that they did lurke for us in a place of advantage, notwithstandinge which wee were constrayned by force to make way thorow them to the relief of the towne which (as was conceaved) could not make defenc one houre longer (the towne so much asserting newtrality and to maintaine the late accommodation), and our men being deepely engaged, and as wee feared in danger to bee opposed by multitudes of the enemie, whom wee first charged, and that so feirsely and successfully (the Lord assisting, to whom bee the whole glorie ascribed), that their dragooners, which were under *Sir Vincent Corbett*, were presently disordered and many of them ran away without ever givinge fier

The most eminent comanders amongst them were not much more fortunate *Sir Tho Aston*, as it is sayd, was a prisoner, his horse being slayne and him selfe constrayned to fly away many miles on foote, and some say hee hath a bullet in his buttocke, and was not attended with more than eight or ten men, when he came to Whitchurch, *Sir Vincent Corbet* (who, they say, was also a prisoner, but both of them unknown to us in the darke) did make an escape on foote to Ore [Over] which is full five miles, both of them conceaving their arms a burthen, which they threw away After our dragooners had given the first charge, and that wee

* Robert Duckenfield, of Duckenfield, Esq For a biography of this celebrated Lieutenant-colonel, see Earwaker s *East Cheshire*, vol ii, p 13-14

† Edward Hyde, of Hyde, Cheshire, Esq, who died in 1669

‡ The original letter is among Bishop Tanners MSS Bodl Lib Oxford 62 2 f 537

§ This battle, which was the first victory achieved by Sir William Brereton, is mentioned in Josiah Rycroft's *"Survey of Englands Champions,"* (1647), in John Vicars *"England's Worthies,"* (1647), and in *"Cheshires Successe,"* London, 25 March, 1642-3, which was reprinted in 1819 by Dr Ormerod, *Hist Chesh* vol I, p xxxvi (Old Edition)

had seconded them, there being no other horse but myne owne troope (Capt Edward's troope being in the reare guarding our wagons, where they performed good service), and wee being in a lane, compassed with hedges on both sides, and they in the feild within a few yards of us, wee were upon a sudden soe intermingled in such confusednes as, if the Lord had not strucken them with terror and amazement, it had fared much worse with us, our forces being devided, some in the towne before and others guarding our wagons, but their courage departed from them, the Lord delivered them into our hands, to whom I desire the whole honour and glorie may be attributed for whom alone it belongs This successe being farr beyond what could be expected from us (who were at that time much disproportionable in number, and much tired by 2 or 3 longe and foule dangerous marches from Derby to Leeke, and thence to Congleton, and not any one of the country [i e. Cheshire] troopes of horse being joyned with us who came from Derby), so soon as I received the instructions from the Parliament, and hearing at Leeke of their intention to surprize this towne, we were constrayned to hasten thither, and to march alone with the forces I brought from London, our Cheshire troopes not being in readiness to accompany and assist us, whose absence the Lord was pleased to supply by his immediate assistance, for whilst wee were in this confusion intermingled in the darke, they having possessed themselves of our word, which was "Christ,' it was with much difficultie that wee could distinguish their men from ours, but that the Lord was pleased therein to direct wonderfully Wee tooke then prisoners and still possess the *lord Cholmondeley his sonne* (who some say was to bee *Sir Tho Aston's* leivetenent colonell), *Capt Bridgman*, and divers others of their officers and commanders Wee have very neere 100 prisoners and the greatest parte of Sir Tho Aston's owne troope, who are well armed and well furnished and handsome men Almost all our souldiers got good pillage, not only very good and rich garments, but some of them 40li. [£40] in gold, some 50, and others had much more Loste few of my troope and Alderman Edward's troope without prisoners, some of them being possessed of one, some of 2, some of 3 or more prisoners and their horses but many of their armes were thrown away and lost, which the country people found and gathered up the next morning The horse and so many of their armes as could be found I did cause to be seized upon for the publique service but by reason [of] *Capt Goldegayes* company of dragooners leavinge their horses at large, being constrayned suddenly to charge on foote in the lane we are constrayned out of their horses to recrute that troope, many of which horses wee recovered, but divers of them were carried away with the streame of their horses when they fled in much disorder and distraction, some of them calling out, '*Away, away, wee shall bee all slayne!*' many of them beinge slayne, many others miserably slasht and wounded, and some as wee heare dead by the way. Indeed when wee came into towne, wee wanted the leivtenent collonell, Capt Goldegay, and all my servants, and one of the quarter-masters, the most whereof it pleased God to restore unto us the next day There was slaine on our side, upon the ground, Capt Gouldegay *his leivtenant*, and *Corporall Best*, one of my corporalls, and some others wounded, since dead. *Capt Goldegay* and *Capt Lea* are wounded, but not mortally I hope, and so are divers of our souldiers Another of my corporalls, *Appletree*, is sore wounded All my servants and those were scattered the first night, and came not unto mee until the next morning I alone have sustayned the greatest losse all my corporalls are slayne or dangerously wounded, and a[ll] of my best horses which were led are taken and detayned *The towne begins to comply with us, though they were exceeding starke and backward, and wee are fortifying the towne, and preparing to put the instructions in execution* The Commissioners of Aray fortifie at Chester, and draw in the inhabitants of Salop and Welchmen But I do not doubt, by God's assistance, but this countie will approve themselves well affected and it shalbe the duty of my care to improve my utmost endeavour to do you service, the Parliament, and in particular to approve myselfe

Your most faithfull servant,

WILL BRERETON"

[Endorsed] "Mr Brereton Feb 4 1642-3"

When the County gentlemen mentioned on page 145 with their companies rallied round Sir William Brereton, Nantwich became a garrison town for the Parliament. He further increased his army by issuing warrants to summon all between sixteen and sixty years of age to meet at a general muster at Tarporley and Frodsham on the 21st Feb. 1642-3   An interruption occurring at *Tilstone-heath*, near the former town, where opposing forces were entrenched, a skirmish ensued, " but," says Malbon, " in the end, bothe sides retreated, the one ptie to Chester, and the other to Namptwiche, where they contynued that weeke vntill they had fortefyed all the Towne round aboute wth stronge Trenches & mudwalls of Clodds & Earthe "*

On Monday, the 13th March, 1642-3, Sir William Brereton stormed the town of Middlewich, where Sir Thomas Aston again sustained a complete defeat, with great loss of men and arms   Many prisoners were brought to Nantwich, and "vpon Wednesdaye nexte after was a very soleme daye of thankesgyvinge held att Namptwiche, wth preachinge, prayers & Ringinge of Bells "—*Malbon*

Having related particulars of the battles at Salt-heath near Stafford, and Stockten-heath near Warrington, the Malbon MS says—

Prisoners removed
to Manchester
"Vpon Loe [Low] Sondaye att Nighte, about midnighte, was p'sone^rs removed from Namptwiche, & sente to Manchester, (wch Colonell Brereton had longe kepte theire) viz Sr *Edward Mosley*,| *Colonell Ellys*, *Maior Gilmore*, *Captyn Cholmley*, *Captyn Massie*, *Captyn Hurleston*, *Captyn Johnes*, *Captyn Eaton*, *Captyn Horton*, & *Captyn Morrys*, whoe weire garded thither wth twoe Companyes of Dragoners & theire saufelie deliv'ed '

Captyn Massie
plu'dred
"Vpon the xth of Aprill 1643 The Kinges ptie , wch lay in Whitchurch, yssued furthe and plu'dred *Captyn Massie*, of Moshowse, [near Audlem] & tooke awaye from him Three score head of Cattell, & some of his howshold goods & horses from many othe^rs. the newes thereof beinge broughte to Namptwiche, some companyes, beinge speedyhe readie, marched towards Whitchurche, thinkinge to haue mett theim befoie they had gotten into the Towne, but they came halfe an hower to[o] late   Yett notw^thstandinge, the[y] mett wth some of theire company, slewe three of theim, tooke xij Oxen, some Armes, wch they had throwen awaye in theire fleight, & xv p'sone^rs whereof yonge m^r Bulkeley of Buntingsdall was one "

Battell at
Burledam
"The nexte daye afterwards Intelligence was broughte to Namptwiche that Whitchurch forces (beinge very stronge) entended wth theire Carts to fetche all the goods that Captyn Massie‡ had; where vpon the[y] Reased almost all the forces in Namptwiche, bothe horse & foote, to the nu'ber of one thowsand or more, And marched towards Whitchurch.   Att Burledam, they mett the Kinges ptie , But after a shorte skirmishe they fled back towards Whitchurche, yett not

* Mr Partridge says (Hist of Nantwich p 74) the earthworks cost in constructing £335 8s 7d   and that some remains of them existed when he wrote (1774)   I have found no proof of the former statement , and the latter seems improbable when it is remembered that the complete removal of all fortifications, after the War was over, was every where carried out according to the letter of the law so that all might be forgotten as soon as possible by succeeding generations The oldest native townspeople that I have conversed with, have been unable to point out the site of the earthworks

† Sir Edward Moseley, Bart , of Rolleston, co Stafford, and Houghs-end in Lancashire, and manorial lord of Manchester, who was taken prisoner at Middlewich

‡ Captain William Massie of Denfield and Audlem, who died 1668

soe speedylie, but fyve of theim were slayne, & some p'soners of theim taken, wᵗʰout losse or hurte of any, onelie the[y] tooke three of our men p'soners, viz *John Abnett, Thomas Parker, & Captyn Croxtons man* & horse wᶜʰ the[y] carryed wᵗʰ theim to Whitchurche, And the nexte daye after the[y] sente them to Shrowesbury. And the Namptwiche forces retorned home in saufetie, havinge preserved Captyn Massie from any further plu'dringe att that tyme."

Sr Richard Wilbraham decessed

"Vppon Mondaye in Easter weeke the third of Aprill 1643 Sʳ *Richard Wilbraham*, of Woodhey, Knight, and Baronett, a verie worthie gent, and a good Justice of the Peace, & p'vidente for his Country, beinge kepte prsoner by the Kinge, eu' [ever] scythens his Maᵗⁱᵉˢ first comynge to Chester Citie, first in Chester, & afterwards to Shrowesbury, where hee ended his Lyfe And towards the later ende of the same weeke, was broughte to Acton Churche (a myle from Namptwiche) where hee was p'vatlie Buried * (the occasion of his ymprsonmᵗ was neu' [never] certynlie revayled)."

An Alarum on Chester

"The nexte weeke after Easter most of the Captyns, officers, trowprs and Dragoners marched from Namptwiche vp & downe to p'serve the Country from plu'dringe, and on Saturday in the same weeke, The[y] faced the Citie of Chester, came to Boughton & killed one of the Citie garde And gave a stronge Alaram vpon the Citie, they of the Citie tooke one of the Namptwiche soldyers p'soner & noe more donne att that tyme But the daye followinge beinge Sundaye & on Monday nexte after, they all marched backe to Namptwiche agayne"

Battell att Cholmley howse

"Vpon Tuesday mornynge, att Springe of daye, the vj of April 1643, most of Namptwich forces marched to Cholmeley howse (a garrison kepte by the Kinges ptie) beinge enformed that foure hundred of theim theire weire in that garrison And comynge neere to the Howse they found theim ready a waytinge theire comynge, whoe yssued furthe, & theire was for the p'sente a fierce & crewell battell But after a whyle the Namptwiche forces havinge slayne & wounded many of theim, did dryve theim into the howse & planted theire Drakes about the garden and wᵗʰ theim and the muskett shott, discharginge att the howse did muche harme, soe as they hard [heard] a greate crye in the howse But after some shott on bothe sides, & Namptwiche forces, seeinge the advantage that they in the howse had of theim, They wᵗʰdrewe of[f] from the howse & marched backe agayne to Namptwiche, havinge [? leaving] many of theim wounded, theire was Slayne of that side Seriant maior Lestead [?] his seriant and one Wade a Com'on Soldyer wᶜʰ they broughte alyve to Namptwiche but hee died prsentlie afterwards And about three score of the Kinges ptie. horses. But the Bodie of the Lieftenᵗ they cold not fetche awaye, but lefte the same behinde theim ytt was reported that theire weire fyftie & twoe slayne of theim in and aboute the howse "†

---

* The early Registers at Acton have been lost, the earliest vol now existing commences 30th Oct 1653, so that the exact date of his burial cannot be given King Charles first came to Chester on the 23rd Sept 1642 and went thence to Shrewsbury, taking with him "Sir Richard Wilbraham, Sir Thomas Delves, Mr Mainwaring of Peover, and Mr Wilbraham of Deerfold "—(Burghall's Diary, Cole MSS Brit Mus)

† Nantwich Burial Register records —"April 19 1643 John Wade, soldyer
      ,,   ,,   William Douglas, sergant
      ,,   ,,   Robert Hay, Lieutenant '

Malpas Burial Register records —"April 22 1643 2 Soldiers slain att Cholmondeley
    May 11   ,,   A soldier that died att Cholmondeley "

Prysoners removed

"The same Tuesdaye in the Nighte weire sente p^rsone^{rs} to bee kepte att the Hall of Crewe, viz Sr *Edward Mosley*, & *Maior Gilmore*, (wch had byn sent backe from Manchester) m^r *Dudley Norton*, and m^r *Sarrnge* (the Towne minister) And vpon Wednesday weire apprehended & sente p'soners to Dodington Hall, *Edward Olton, Roger Wright, John Wilkes, Will'm Barnes, John Leighe, Edward Hitchenson* & some othe^{rs} for that they weire held to bee malignants & suspected to have betrayed the designe vnto Cholmley the Nighte before   But upon ffrydaye nexte after Edward Olton and John Wilkes weire deliu'ed & sente home, And upon the same daye att Nighte Maior Gilmore, m^r Norton, and m^r Sarrnge weire removed from Crewe Hall & carryed to Stockporte & Sr Edward remayned att Crewe"

During the next six months the royalist forces in Shropshire under Arthur, Lord Capel, harassed the garrison of Nantwich, and obtained at different times great plunder of cattle and provisions from farm-houses and mansions in the neighbourhood   On thrice occasions they advanced close to the lines of the town, but were repulsed   After the first of these attacks, Sir William Brereton retaliated by a successful assault on the royalist garrison at Whitchurch on 30th May, 1643   Foraging parties from Nantwich at various times obtained great booty, but on one occasion, a company under Captain Bulkeley was surprised and defeated by Lord Capel with great loss on the 20th June, 1643   Details of these military exploits are chronicled by Malbon, as follows —

Lord Capell* & others, his firste comynge

"On the xxth of Aprill 1643 Colonell Breretons horse beinge furthe of [the] Towne   The kinges forces came from Whitchurch & Cholmley even wthin sighte of the Towne, And tooke from Derfold, litle Acton, Ravensmore & Sound, & all the Countrey thereabouts, all the Kyne & yonge beasts they cold fynd, to a very greate nu'ber, and from the elder *will'm Jackson*, & many othe^{rs}, all or most of theire howshold goods, takinge them all awaye, & alsoe the[y] tooke, att litle Acton, *Richard Edgley* of the Hall of More, p'son^r   The ffoote Companyes in the Towne, (beinge onelie lefte to tend the Towne) for feare lest the Towne had byn taken, Durst not yssue furthe to Rescowe any thinge from theim   The nu'ber of theim beinge in horse (att least) fyve hundred, beside ffoote Companyes (the nu'ber not knowne certynlie)."

Alarams 2 dayes

"On Tuesdaye the . . . [? 25] daye of Aprill 1643 An Alaram was beaten vp in Towne of Namptwiche & most of the forces yssued furthe, but did neither meete or heere of the Kinges ptie, And vpon Wednesdaye (beinge the exercyse day) Another Alaram was beaten, & Bells Ronge backewards, and almost all the forces in the Towne yssued furthe, & did heere that the Kinges ptie. had taken about xx^{tie} Kyne and yonge beasts from *Thomas Litler*, dwellinge neere Ravensmore, & had sent furthe two of theire Trowpers to waine Carts for Carryage awaye of Haye from Baddeley, But those twoe weire taken wth theire horses & Armes, & alsoe a foote Boye belonginge to m^r *Thomas Walley* of Cholmley, & broughte in p soners, & the rest

* Arthur Lord Capell was the only son of Sir Henry Capell   and was M P for his native County of Hertford in the Long Parliament   He was created Baron Capell of Hasham   6th Aug 1641, and having been taken prisoner, was ultimately beheaded, together with the Duke of Hamilton, and Earl Holland, in the Palace Yard at Westminster on 9th March, 1648-9   His arms were, *Gules, a lion rampant between three crosslets fitchée, Or*   In allusion to which, after his death, this distich became current —

"Our Lion-like Capel undaunted stood
Beset with crosses in a sea of blood "

fledd & one of theim slayne   And the same daye, *St Edward Mosley* was broughte p'son[r] backe agayne to Namptwiche "

Broughte [prisoners]   " On Satuidaye the xxx[th] of Maye 1643, some horse & foote did march
from   furthe of Towne towards witchurche, And neere that Towne they tooke
Waitchurch   *Captyn Morris*, A Leftent & a quaiter m[r] [master] & about iiij Com'on
Soldyeis & broughte theim p'son[rs] to Namptwiche, And alsoe three score Kyne and yonge
Beasts, And the same att Night Colonell Bieieton wth his horse retorned to Namptwiche."

Drayton   " On Thursdaye att Nighte in Maye 1643, some horse & foote aboute
Battell   Midnighte marched furthe of the Towne towards Drayton (where *S[r] Vincett
Corbett* & aboute three hundred Cavaliers horse & foote laye, begynynge
to make some workes (for theire saufetie) aboute the Towne   But a litle after Sonne
Rysinge Namptwiche forces comying thether, on the sudden (before they weire furthe of
theire Bedds), entered the Towne the[y] havinge neithei gaide noi scouts abioad, but
secure (as they thoughte), And killed nyne of them, tooke many p'sone[rs], horse & Armes,
Soe that all or most of Namptwiche foote Soldyers weire horsed home, & many of them
had 2, 3, or 4 musketts & Kaibines a peece, Beside app'ell [apparel] & other goods of
theires   And alsoe thiee Ensignes, foure Drumes & other weppons   But S[r] Vyncett fled
in his shiite & wascot leaving his app'ell behind him, w[ch] *Captyn Whitney* had wth his
money & many letters in his Pockett   *Captyn Kynnaston* & *Captyn Sandford* weire theire
Slayne, beinge Cavaliers   Namptwiche forces did noe wronge nor harme to the Towne,
but onelie thieve downe theire workes, after the Cavaliers weire all fledd & slayne, &
taken p'son[rs], & then retorned back to Namptwiche in saufetie w[th]out losse of any man,
savinge some fewe Com'on soldyers about three or foure w[ch] weire hurte in the streetes
w[th] shotts furthe of wyndowes "

Lord Capell   " On Wednesdaye in the Evenynge the xviij[th] of Maye 1643, The Lorde
comynge agaynst   Capell w[th] a greate Company of Cavaliers bothe of Whitchurch and
Namptwich   Shropshire & other places to the nu'ber of xv hundred oi more (as was
supposed), came agaynst Namptwiche (almost to the Aspell Streete end) & shott at the
towne   & they in the Towne lykewise att them (havinge notice by the Scouts of theire
approche, & beinge well p'vyded to haue bidden them welcome), slewe three of them &
wounded othei some of them, where they contynuynge, indeavoringe to plante foure
peeces of ordnance (w[ch] they broughte with them) about Malpas-field But fyndinge all the
groundes thereabouts to[o] heighe over the Towne, (not fitting theire purpose) And the
Towne Gunner throwinge wyld fier Balls a mongest them (beinge not able to staye)
betwixt on[e] & twoe a Clocke on Thursdaye mornynge, the[y] marched backe to Whitchurche wth gieate disgrace, havinge p formed nothinge nor soe much as hurte one man -
onelie the[y] killed a calfe of *mr Thomas Maynwarings*, w[ch] they lefte behind them, &
brooke some Barnes for Haye, Wherevpon theire was a Ryme made on them, viz

    The Lord Capell wil[t] a thowsand & a halfe
    Came to Bartons Crosse* & theire they kild a Calfe
    And stayinge theire vntill the breake of Daye,
    The[y] tooke theire heeles & fast the[y] fled away

* " *Bartons Cross*," now simply called "*The Cross*," is in Stapeley township, on the east side of Nantwich.

Att that tyme Colonell Brereton & all the horse were att Stafford from whence wth his horse hee retorned to Namptwich on ffryday evenynge. '

    *   +

Thomas Malbon, having related how Warrington was surrendered into the hands of Sir George Booth, the lord of that town, continues his narrative as follows —

Whitchurch taken

"The xxix^th of Maye beinge Mondaye aboute vj or vij a Clocke in the Nyghte, Colonell Brereton, wth the horse & almost all the foote in Namptwiche together wth all the Townesmen (exceptinge some fewe to garde the Towne) marched towards Whitchurch And came thether aboute three a Clocke on Tuesdaye mornynge, whoe sett vpon the Towne & the[y] did Resist them wth all theire power, bothe horse & foote (beinge in the Towne as was supposed) about vj or vij hundred   The Namptwiche foote soldye^rs ffyringe very fearcely vpon theym, and they in the Towne did the lyke, maynteynynge theire workes & Towne very bravely   But ytt pleased God, after twoe howers fighte, very galanthe on bothe sides, that Namptwiche forces (wch weire about Eyght hundred) killed some of the Gunne^rs and othe^rs at theire workes neere the Claye pitts, dryvinge the Townesmen from theire workes, & entered the Towne, wth losse of one man onelie slayne outrighte twoe or three sore wounded wch dyed afterwards And beinge in the Northe pte. of the Towne (many othe^r Streets beinge not entered but lyinge open) Theire horse & many of the townesmen & Soldye^rs fledd   But theire was taken about xxtie p^rson^rs, one very fayre foote Collo^rs, foure good peeces of Ordnance, very many Armes, and much money & brave app'ell of the Lord Capells & other gent Twoe Covered waggons, powder, Bulletts, matches, & goods of the Soldye^rs greate store, many Drumms, one Trumpett & many horses, the Soldyers havinge most of the pillage. Soe that theire weire scarce any Soldye^r, but hee retorned backe either horsed, or well laden wth pillage, or both, onelie takinge them, not doinge the Towne any harme, And about iij a Clocke the same daye in the afternoone, They retorned all back agayne vnto Namptwiche, leavinge much Cheese, goods & Am unycon behind them onelie for want of Cartes and carryage wch vpon ffryday nexte after weire fetched thence, & broughte to Namptwiche, beinge wagons & Cartes Loades of Cheese, Bacon, Malte, Wheate, Corne, Armes, & goods, fourteene loads, wch came all saufe w^thout any opposicon [opposition], takinge noe mans goods but onelie the Cavaliers "

Booties taken from Shocklage & thereabouts

"On Monday the xij^th of June 1643 some companyes of Dragone^rs marched furthe towards the Holte (beinge then the fayre daye theire) And in ffarne [Farn] gave them an Alaram, wch affrighted them sore   But they bended theire course towards Shocklage in wch pte the[y] tooke fourescore and eighteene good Oxen & Cattell   And many horses & att Nighte retorned wth them all saufe to Namptwiche "

Mr Leeches howse & Company of Array taken

"On Saturdaye the vth of June 1643 some Companyes marched furthe to Carden & sett vpon m^r *Leeches* howse (a Com'ission^r of Arraye) whoe did oppose them, But in the end they gott the howse, apprehended him; broughte him wth them p^rson^r, plu'dred his howse, Kild a servant maid wth shootinge att the howse, & broughte wth him, some other^s, and some horses alsoe to Namptwiche "

Ammunycon
broughte to
Namptwiche

"Upon Tuesday the xiij of June Colonell Brereton havinge byn att Liverpoole, for vnloadinge of a Ship, wch was come thether from London wth his greate ordnance & Am'unycon. came wth his troupe of horse to Namptwiche & broughte with him *Doctor Byrom** p'sonei, & ij Loads of his owne Am'unicon in saufetie beinge accompanied wth many brave Captyns & com'anders "

Mr Bostock
did penance
at the Cage

"On Saturday the xvij of June 1643 *John Bostocke* of Tatnull [Tattenhall] Esqr, Learned in the Lawes, Clerke vnto the Councell of wari at Nampt-wiche beinge taken wth the Acte of Adultery wth one Alice Chetwood in the vicarage howse in Namptwiche, vpon the Sabothe daye att tyme of Dyvyne servis (where hee then lyved) was by Judgm^t of the same Councell adiudged to stand in the markett place, vpon the markett daye, (beinge Saturdaye) duringe most pte of that daye wth papeis vpon his Brest (signifyinge his offence) wch was executed accordinglie wth his w——e standinge by him '

The evell merche
to Hanmer

"Upon Tuesday the xx^th of June 1643 Colonell Breretons troupe, *Captyn Bulkeley* & many other troupeis & Dragoneis marched furthe of Namptwiche behynd whitchurche to Hanmiyre [Hanmer] & further, (for what entente was not certynlie Knowne), where they weie sett vpon by the Lord Capell, & Welshe forces, (whoe had laid an ambush for them), who dispersed and scattered all the same Namptwich forces, beinge to[o] stronge foi them   Soe that many of them weie taken p^rsoneis some slayne,† many of them wounded, (althoughe some of the Kinges ptie weire slayne and speciallie some of theire Com'anders of gieate sorte) wch was the worst days worke that ever Namptwiche forces had from the Begynynge   Att wch tyme the[y] had the *Lieftn^t Colonell & Captyn Sankie*, Captyn of Colonell Breretons horse taken p^rsoneis but noe more Com'anders "

Chester

"On Mondaye Eveninge xvij^th of Julye 1643 Colonell Brereton wth almost all the forces in Namptwiche bothe horse and foote (exceptinge Captyn Massye and ye trayned bands ot Namptwiche Hundred) Togeither wth all the forces in the Countie (on the phiam^t ptie) And some furthe of Stafford & Manchester marched towardes Chester Citie att that Nighte intendinge to haue entered theire outworks before they had byn awari and soe donne, yf a messengei wch was sente with letters from old *mr walthall or his wyfe*, had not gyven notice to the Citie, wch was not aboue twoe howers before the forces came thether   But vpon that notice the forces in the Citie weire p^rsentlie Ready & did vehementlie oppose the said Namptwiche forces, havinge made exceedinge stronge works & mounted fourtie peeces of ordnance on the Castle, & other theire workes, that noe good could be donne (althoughe the[y] laye about ytt on the Lande side vntill Thursdaye mornynge, shootinge & dischaiginge theire musketts & some ordnance wch was bioughte thether (on bothe pties) & some slayne on bothe sides And p'ceyvinge the[y] weire not then lykely to doe any good for wynnynge of the Citie, (but by a longe siege) & hearinge that the Lord Capell had drawen gieate companyes furthe

---

* ² Doctor John Byrom of Salford who eventually was one of the promirent chaiadeis in the iejoicings at Manches-ter at the Restoration

† In Philip s *Civil War in Wales*, vol i, p 161, it is related that ' in the breeches of one of the Nantwich piisoners was found the suiplice of Hanmei Church ''   About twenty yeais ago, the body of, perhaps, one of the slain was found outside Hanmer, lying across a ditch, only covered with a few inches of soil as if hastily buried   There were buttons and othei evidences of its being the body of a soldier two hundred years ago —(Infoimation by the Rev M H Lee, Vicar of Hanmer)

of Shrowesbury & Reased the Trayned bands in Shropshire, & beinge advanced towards Chester as far as to Orton Maddocke, Colonell Brereton reased his seige & marched backe to Namptwiche, wth his ordnance Carryage and all in saufety, havinge lost onely twoe com'on Soldyer^s & foure other wounded, but not mortaly. The reporte was afterwards that theire was slayne in the Citie xv whereof on[e] was a woman & the other a Childe "

Lord Capell came agayne agaynst the Towne the 3rd tyme

"Upon Thursday in the afternoone the third of August Lord Capell wth a great force to the nu'ber of three thowsand came to Ravensmore, appearinge att the firste not aboue twoe or three Troupes of horse, Colonell Brereton beinge then at Stafford   The Soldyers & some Townesmen yssued furthe of Namptwiche p'ceyvinge theire nu'ber soe fewe, wth good store of horse wch when the Enemy p'ceaved they broughte vp more of theire horse, (beinge readie in Baddington Lane) & advanced towards Namptwiche forces   So they p^rsenthe fyred on bothe sides   But the Kinges ptie. still increasinge the Towne forces retreated homewards, w^thout much harme onelie *Lieftent Ashley*^r was, by mischance, slayne by one of his fellowes, & *Dicke Massie & one other Com'on Soldyer* weire slayne wth a Cannon Bullett from the Enemy   That nighte the Kinges ptie wth many loades of Carryage & foure greate peeces of ordnance laye quyctelie vpon Ravensmore   And the same Nighte & the daye followinge the Soldyer^s in the Towne fyred & burned all *m^r walthall's* outbuyldings on the Heath-side, fyringe the Hall, wch receyved some harme, but was not burned downe, & alsoe the[y] burned *Thomas Cu'[m]berbach's* howse, & Stable, widowe *Podmores* howse & Stable, *Marchants* Barne, All the coates [cottages] on the Heathe next towards the Towne   *Roger Wrights* Barne, *Thomas Burrowes* Barne, *Saboth Churches* Barne, *John Yardleys* Barne *Massie & Bromhalls* howses at NEWE TOWNE   and they caused *Richard Wicksteeds* Barne & all the Coates & dwellinge howses on Acton pavem^t to bee pulled downe for feare lest the Enemy sholde bee sheltred theire; Upon ffryday mornynge about Sixe a Clocke, they assaulted the Towne on the southe side, betwixte *Marche Lane & Weeuer;* (beinge a very thicke darke mist, fitt for theire purpose), And beinge very neere the works before the[y] weire Seene of any of the Townesmen, ffyred very vehementlie & plaid wth theire Cannons agaynst the Towne very muche, as fast as ever they cold discharge, but (thanks bee to God) did noe harme att all, neither slewe nor wounded any, but onelie one hurte in the side of his Necke, wch was not mortall), And they receyved the lyke from the Towne, bothe wth musketts & ordnance, and soe contynued on bothe sides vntill betwixt ix & x a Clocke in the affore noone   The mist beinge then gonne & the Sonne shynynge fayre, and the Kinges forces p^rceyvinge them selves neere[r] the works, then [than] they ymagined, & p'ceyvinge the great daunger [they] weire In, fledd as fast as they cold, But not soe fast but the ordnance and muskett shott, did overtake them, in suche man'[ner] as about xlte [40] of them weire slayne, & xvj [16]

* Nantwich Register records the burials of these three soldiers —

        " 1643 Aug 5 Edward Ashley Lieutenant "
            ,,   ,,   Richard Massey, trouper "
            ,,   ,,   Allen Swanick, trouper '

sore wounded, (as was credeblie reported), & some of theim of good sorte, whose names cold not bee Knowne, & theire upon they beinge fledd & gonne for the rest of that daye and the Nighte followinge the Towne was in quyett   Althonghe about midnight An idell Alaram (gyven by the watch) by reason of sparks of fyer wᶜʰ they sawe p'ceedinge from seu'all [several] howses & Barnes wᶜʰ weire burned the daye before, thinking they had byn lighte matches of tne Enymyes   Many companyes bothe Horse and foote, (hereing of the beseiginge of the said Towne), came furthe of Lancashire & Staffordshire to theire *Ayde come to* ` Ayde, And vij score Dragoneʳˢ came from the Morelands in Staffordshire, *Namptwiche*   soe farr as Haslington on Saturdaye the vᵗʰ of Auguste in Ayde of the said Towne, where they did quarter them selves that Nighte, beinge wᵗʰin fyve myles of the said Towne & hearinge the Enymye was fledd the[y] retorned back agayne to theire owre homes "

Other reinforcements from Wales, under Sir Thomas Middleton, of Chirk, an able and active parliamentary general, came to Nantwich and strengthened the garrison   In after years, when the Parliament held the reins of government, Sir Thomas Middleton, finding he had helped to establish a more intolerable tyranny than that which he had formerly opposed, changed his opinions, and, in 1659 took up arms in connection with Sir George Booth, in order to restore the ancient constitution *   He is mentioned in "*The Mystery of the Good Old Cause,*" in 1660, as " Sir Thomas Middleton, major-general for Denbigh, and five other counties, who hath manifested his loyalty to his Prince, and is a true patriot of his country "   Though not loyal to King Charles I, his patriotism was none the less, when Malbon wrote —

Thomas Middleton   " Upon Saturdaye mornynge aboute Noone Colonell Brereton came wᵗʰ *cominge to*   some fforces to Namptwiche beinge the xix of August 1643, And about viij *Namptwiche*   a Clocke att Nighte Sʳ *Thomas Middleton* wᵗʰ greate forces, Seyvon [seven] *19 Aug 1643*   greate peeces of ordnance, some cases of Drakes, and aboute fourtie Carryage of Armes and Ammunycon came alsoe to Namptwiche where hee contynued for a certyn space "

Dirtwiches   " On Mondaye the xxviij of August aforsaid *Captyn Croxton*† *& Captyn* *the workes*   *Venables*‡ Companyes (wᵗʰ other wᶜʰ laye in garryson att Cholmley) marched *destroyed*   to bothe Townes of Dirtwiches,§ beinge places wheire Salte was made wᶜʰ the Kinges side had, And there they defaced cutt in peeces & spoyled all theire workes, pumps, and Salte pitts & broughte some of theire Pannes to Namptwᶜʰ, whereby all their Salte makinge was spoyled, wᶜʰ found the Kinges armye att Shrowesbury, Wales, & many of theire quarteʳˢ, Salte   The Lord Caple [Capell] havinge before made p'clamacon that non shold fetche any Salte from Namptwiche "   ⸴   *   ⸴   ⸰   ⸴

The whole Army   " Vppon the xiiij of September 1643 a greate pte of the p'liamᵗ Army *removed to Wem*   Marched furthe of Namptwiche in the afternoone & were quatred in Blakenall, Checkley, Dodington & the Townes thereabouts.   And vpon ffridaye the nexte

* Pennants Tour in Wales, vol i p 364   Edit 1810

† Captain or Colonell Thomas Croxton of Ravenscroft, co Cheshire

‡ Captain Venables, afterwards Governor of Chester   he was sent by Cromwell as General of the Forces, together with Admiral Penn, against Hispaniola and Jamaica —(" *Civil War Tracts,*" p 354   Chet Soc Pub vol ii)

§ *Dirtwich,* or *Foulwich,* in Broxton Hundred

daye after Colonell Brereton, S[r] Thomas Middleton & all the rest of the Army (excepte the trayned band of Namptw[ch] Hundred & some Soldye[rs] w[ch] laye in garrison att Cholmley) marched furthe of Towne, wth all S[r] Thomas Middletons ordnance & drakes vnto whome all the rest (quartred furthe of Towne before) resorted   And the nexte Nighte The[y] quartred att Drayton & in all the Townes & villages thereabouts keepinge theire Randevous theire vntill Tuesdaye nexte followinge   And then sendinge furthe theire warrants they called In all that Countrey thereabouts to a Gen'all Muster & contynued att Drayton vntill ffrydaye the xxij of Septemb[er] nexte followinge   And then all the whole Armye marched thence to Wem and fortifyed that Towne, quartring theire Army in all the Townes & places nexte adioynynge "

*   ʳ   ᴶ   ɪ   *   *   *   *   *

While the parliamentary forces were being concentrated at Wem with a view to an early attack on Shrewsbury, Lord Capell again marched against Nantwich   The train-bands bravely defended the town on Monday, the 16th Oct 1643, and early the following morning Lord Capell retreated on the approach of Colonel Brereton and Sir Thomas Middleton, who entered the town a few hours after, as told by Malbon, as follows —

Lord Capell marchinge to Namptwiche   'On Saturdaye the xxiij[th] of October 1643 Intelligence was sente to Namptwiche that the Lord Capell wth very greate forces to the nu'ber of three thowsand and more, vij score Carryages, three greate peeces of Ordnance & a Morter peece weire agayne comynge agaynst the Towne   The Townesmen especiallie the howsholde[rs] & many othe[rs] besides the Gardes (w[ch] weire doubled) did watche all Nighte.   But hard [heard] noe more of them, but that they weire quartred att Whitchurche, Combermeyre, Marburye, Norbury, Burleydam & the places thereabouts. Vpon Sondaye mornynge theire was an Alaram in Towne, w[ch] did muche affrighte them (but w[thout] cause)   On Sondaye Nighte a greate Garde was sett in Towne but all was quyett, But on Mondaye the xvj[th] of October 1643 about one a Clocke in thafter noone the said Lord was advanced to Acton wth all theire Army, Carryages, before any intelligence came to Towne   Then some Diagone[rs] & twoe foote companyes yssued furthe of Towne towardes them att Acton, & fyred upon them, & did dryve them into Acton Churche, w[ch] some of them tooke for saufeguard, but many of the rest tooke Derfold Howse   But by reason the Enymy had taken those two stronge holds, The townesmen retreated into the Towne fyred att them, as the[y] sawe occasion, over the walles   The Enymy dispersed them selves into the fields, & downe Henhull Lane to Beamebridge, contynuallie shootinge att the Towne wth theire musketts, to smale purpose, but came not neere the walles, w[ch] the Townesmen prceyvinge, some well spirited men of the Towne, vpon theire owne accorde, w[thout] any com'and, leaped over the walles wth theire musketts well charged, & Ran disorderlie towards them, fyringe vpon them, & the Enymy the lyke on them agayne all one afternoone, vntil almost Nighte, that the Enymy bothe horse & foote fled, some of them beinge slayne & aboute sixe or eighte of them taken prsonr[s], & soe for that tyme all [was] quyett on bothe sides   That Nighte all the Townesmen, & Countrey men w[ch] come In to Ayde the Towne, beinge greate Company bothe of men & horse, Did all watch att the Walles, (the Enymy beinge then att Acton & Derfold), They expectinge howerlie to bee assaulted by the Enymy, & that they wold fall vpon the Towne · but vpon Tuesdaye mornynge, when a greate assault was expected to haue byn made by the Enymy, worde was broughte to the Towne that the Enymy, (very manfullie), weire all fledd & gonne awaye about midnight, wch was att the first not credited, but p^rved trewe About vij a Clocke on Tuesdaye mornynge Colonell Brereton, Sr Thomas Middleton, & Colonell Greaves, wth almost all theire Armes marched to Namptwiche, (exceptinge a Considerable nu ber lefte behind theire att Wem, for saufegarde thereof,) to haue releeved and Ayde the Towne (not hearinge of the Enymyes dep'ture) And beinge come thether & the Enymy fled they sente after theim some forces whoe tooke about fourtie of the meane^r sorte of the Enymyes p^rsoner^s the best weire fledd, whiche was all the Enymy then lost, savinge three slayne att Acton, And soe (by Gods mercy) the Towne was then p^rserved w^thout losse of any one, savinge two shott in the Armes, thoughe not muche the worse "

    ✻   ✻   ✻   ✻   ✻   ✻   ✻   ✻   ✻

Another account of this assault is contained in a small quarto tract of 6 pp., entitled "*Shropshires Misery and Mercie manifested in the defeat given to the Lord Capels . . Armie by the Forces of Cheshire and Shropshire** . . . London, Nov 8, 1643,*" as follows —

"That when they [*i e.* the Lord Capell's forces from Shrewsbury &c] all came against *Namptwich* upon Munday *October* 16 [1643] they were so confident of surprizing the same as that the Lord Capel (as it is reported) returned backe all the *Chester* horse which were tendered unto him and coming to his assistance, returning this answer, that he had strength sufficient to take *Namptwich*, to which end he did speedily (& that before notice was given of his aproach) seize upon and possesse himselfe of *Acton* Church and *Dartford* [Dorfold] house, and attempted to force theire passage by the way of Beame-bridge, but by the valour of those few men who were left in the Town they were repulsed from passing the water, not without the losse of divers of theire men Foure whereof were found dead in the ditch those that attempted to undermine the walls in the darknesse of the night were taken prisoners, and this night, and the next morning there were nere forty prisoners taken, besides many horses and Armes, and many of their men run away And upon the newes of our aproach to their reliefe, they sent away their carriages, and marched after them with speed towards *Wem* "

"This was the fifth time they did come before and attempt this poore Town of *Namptwich*, which the Lord hath miraculously preserved and defended, and returned them allwayes backe with shame and dishonour "

Malbon next relates how Lord Capell, being repulsed at Wem, and pursued by Col Brereton, retreated to Shrewsbury Col Brereton, having put the town of Whitchurch "to CCC^li [£300] ransome, beinge a Cavalier place, to save ytt from plu'dring," came to Nantwich, and the next day a few horse soldiers going from Nantwich towards Chester, "came to Andford [Aldford] where they tooke *Captyn Davenport*, wch had broken p^rson [prison] att Namptwiche, *Captyn Lieftent^t Harte,*† *Cornet Leighe, Cornet Maynwaringe, Cornet Healey, Ensigne Thornycrofte,* a quarter maister, a Surgeon, yonge *Mr Tannatt* of Broxton, *Captyn Leigh,* or his Lieftent wounded, but not taken, some soldye^rs slayne & dyvers com'on

---

* A copy of this scarce tract is in the possession of J P Earwaker, F S A, to whom I am indebted for the above extract

† "Henry Hearte, Leinetenant," was buried at Nantwich on 16 March, 1644-5 —(Par Reg)

Pr'soners att Soldye^{rs} taken p^rsoner^s vpon ffrydaye the xxth of October 1643 Vpon
Churton & Saturday the xx1st of October, They were all broughte p^rsoner^s to Nampt-
Andford [A¹dford] wiche, whither the Reste of the Army retorned, non[e] of Namptwiche
forces neither slayne nor wounded, savinge one *Bulkeley* a com'on Soldye^r, wch was taken
plu'dring in Andford [Aldford] p^rsone^r by the Enemy by reason hee did not marche away
wth his followe^{rs} ''

Sr Edwd ''On Mondaye morninge the xxi1j of October some of Sr Thomas
Broughton & his 2 Midletons troupe, wth some othe^r of the Companyes in Namptwiche
Sonnes p^rsone¹s marched furthe of Towne into Wales & broughte in *Sr Edward Broughton*
& twoe of his sonnes p^rsoner^s to Namptwiche from theire owne howse ''

Holte taken ''On Tuesday the vij of November Colonell Brereton & Sr Thomas
firste tyme midleton wth theire Companyes bothe horse & foote marched forthe of
Namptwiche agayn towards Wales The firste Nighte they quartred att
woodhey, Ridley, & thereabouts on Wednesdaye the vnjth of November 1643, they
marched forward & quartred att Barton-on-the-hill Stretton, & the Countrey thereabouts,
where they had Alaram gyven them by the Kinges ptie. at Holte, but they drave them
backe, & slewe some of them wthout any losse. And vpon Thursdaye, Lancashire forces
came & Joyned wth the p'liam^t forces & marched altogether to Holte & ymedyatelie fell
vpon the same. And by one a Clocke in thafter noone (throughe a pollicie) wonn the
Brydge & (by gods assistance) a litle after, the Towne, wthout losse of any man ;
Althoughe the Kinges forces were in horse supposed to bee about one Thowsand, & theire
foote vij hundred, yett notwthstandinge they all fledd And oure foote followinge them in
p'suite, fell upon theire Arere of horse, & tooke *Captyn Preece, Captyn Johnes, & Lieuftent
Salusbury* p^rsoner^s, wch weire sente to Namptwiche, wth many othe^{rs} taken p^rsoner^s, &
Some of them slayne, & the Rest rowted & scatt1ed ''

Hardern [1 e ''On Thursdaye Nighte, after they had taken Holte & left a considerable
Hawarden Castle] ptie theire, They marched to wrixam [Wrexham], where they weire well
¹aken entertayned, & quartred theire that Nighte, And the nexte daye marchinge
furthe^r into Wales tooke Harden Castle, & putt therein a Garrison, And, contynueing in
Wales, the gentry & Com onaltie submitted them selves & Joyned wth them, soe that
the Army was greatly encreased, where for a tyme the[y] remayned ''

The movements of Lord Capell, though often unsuccessful, had been troublesome to
Sir William Brereton, and gave time for the Royalists to strengthen Chester Thither
now the Parliament army had marched, and, occupying the Castles of Beeston, Holte, and
Hawarden, purposed weakening the City, by cutting off all communication and supplies.
But the arrival of troops in the estuary of the Dee towards the end of Novembei, 1643,
sent from Dublin by the Marquis of Ormond, Lord Lieutenant of Ireland, in aid of King
Charles, caused Sir William Brereton hastily to withdraw from Wales and retreat to
Nantwich, and from that time the war assumed a more serious aspect The Irish Army,
as it was called, though both soldiers and officers were native Englishmen, carried terror
with them from the time of their landing and thus reinforced, Lord Byron advanced
from Chester, of which he was Governor, against Nantwich Hawarden Castle, Beeston

Castle, and Crewe Hall, surrendered in succession, and n an engagement near Middlewich the Parliament forces were defeated with great slaughter So rapid was this march that before Christmas Nantwich was environed by the Royalist Army Several determined attacks on the garrison were, however, gallantly resisted by the town soldiers, and after a siege of about seven weeks Lord Byron sustained a complete overthrow at Acton, on 25th Jan 1643-4, from the united forces of Sir William Brereton and Sir Thomas Fairfax, and fled back in haste to Chester

The Malbon MS relates these events with great minuteness of detail, as follows —

Parliam^t forces   "Colonell Brereton & the reste of the P'liam^t forces remaynynge in
retorned furthe   Wales where they p'[ro]spered well (havinge many gent & other^s resortinge
of Wales   vnto theim) But havinge intelligence that greate forces weire come from Ireland & landed in Wales to the nu ber of twoe thowsand & fyve hundred, They all marched backe agayne to Holte, and on ffryday the xxiij^th of November sente theire Ordnance backe to Namptwiche, And vpon Saturday they all marched, some to Namptwiche, other some to Northwiche, & Lancashire men into Lancashire wth all theire Carryage w^thout either fighte or battell wth the Enymy, leavinge Harden Castle vnreleeved, wherein was Mr Ince a faythfull Mynister & firme for the p'liam^t, and about one hundred and twentie Soldyers in greate daunger to haue byn destroyed, & lykewise many other frends, gent, & other^s in Wales, wch had byn aydinge vnto theim, lefte all to the mercy of the bloddy Irish Rebells But the falte was in Lancashire Soldyers wch wold not staye "⁵

Harden Castle   "Vpon or about the third of December 1643 Harden Castle was delivued
delivued to the   vp to the Kinges ptie in Chester upon composi'con, *viz* That the[y] shold
Kinge   depte wth one Colo^r flyinge, & the other Rowled vp, wth halfe of theire Armes & some Truncks & goods, wch was p'formed But some of theim wch came furthe of the Castle, in theire retorne homewards towards Wrixam [Wrexham] weire crewelly vsed by some Welshmen, whoe did beate & wound some of theim, slewe other some, & tooke the Wates[?] & Clothes from other some But the fyfte of December, the foresaid m^r Ince, and some of the Soldyers, came saufe to Namptwiche On Saturdaye mornynge the ixth of December 1643, vj of the Irishe Soldyers did over Runt them from Chester, & come to Namptwiche wth theire Armes, where they weire entertayned "

Beeston Castle   "On Wednesday morninge the xiij^th of December 1643, a litle before
delivued to the   Daye, and after the Moon was sett, *Captyn Sandford* wth viij of his fyerlocks,
Kinge   (beinge in the Kinges ptie) gott into the vpper warde of Beeston Castle, by a byeway, throughe treachery, as was supposed For a litle after hee was entred, *Thomas Steele*, then gou'nor of the said Castle, after a shorte ply [parley] betwixt theim, Receyved Sandford into his Lodginge in the Lower warde, (beinge a very stronge hold), where they Dyned together, & much Beere was sente up into the heigher warde, by the said Steele vnto Sandfords Soldyers, And, after dyn^r, an Agreem^t was made betwixt theim, That Steele shold deliu'^r vpp the Castle wth all am'unycon, goods, p'vision, & what els,

---

* A Tract entitled "*Perfect Diurnall*" No 21, p 164 Dec 18, 1643, quoted in "*Civil War Tracts*" (Chet Soc Pub) p 152, says—" The Manchester men are returned home to divert General Kinges design either against Manchester or into Cheshire "

† That is, six soldiers deserted the Irish Army, and were welcomed at Nantwich

p^rsentlie to the said Captyn Sandford   hee & his Soldye^{rs} beinge about three score to dpte away onelie wth theire Colo^{rs} & Armes, wch was wickedly & treacherouslie p'formed by the said Captyn Steele   And the same daye att Nighte, they all came to Namptwiche, where the said Steele was p^rsentlie ymprissoned, & Kepte closse for feare the soldy^{rs} in the Towne, (wch did Rise in greate multitudes) wolde haue killed him   Theire was in the said Castle muche wealthe, & goods of gent & othe^r neighbour^s, broughte thether for saufety to a greate value, wch the Enymy had, beside halfe a yeres p'vision, att the leaste '

A Skrimage att Burford

"The same daye att Nighte, & almost eu'y Night afterwards & eu'y daye the Kinges ptie gave Alarams vpon the Towne vntill Sondaye nexte afterwards

On Sondaye mornynge, att Sermon tyme, The Kinges ptie was advancing towards the Towne & gaue them an Alaram   The Captyns wente from Churche & drewe all theire Soldye^{rs} together, wth *Seriant maior Lothian*   And some of the horse advanced to Burfoote [Burford] neere Acton, where the Kinges ptie was, & fallinge vpon some of theire horse (before the foote cold bee drawne together) some of the Kinges ptie weire slayne, other some wounded, and some horse & men taken p^rsoner^s (not wthout losse on the other side), And the said Seriant maior Lothian was taken p^rsoner by them before the foote companyes cold come from the Towne vnto them, (althoughe they made a greate speed)   But they weire fledd soe that the foote Soldye^{rs} had noe sight of them   But on the same Sonday att Nighte they gaue the Towne another Alaram, Soe that from the tyme the Castle was lost, vntill that tyme, the Towne was neu' [never] in quyett, neither did they goe to Bed either daye or nighte "

The beginninge of the greate siege agaynst Namptwiche

' The Kinges forces advanced towards the Towne of Namptwiche vnto Stoke, Hurleston, Brynley, Wrenbury and all the Countrey thereabouts, Robbinge, Plu'dring & takinge eu'y mans goods, all the next weeke after vntill ffrydaye the xxijth of December 1643   Vpon wch daye they passed ou' [over] the River of Weever to Aldelem, Hankelow, Buerton, Hatherton Blakenhall, Wibunbury & all the reste of the Townes thereabouts   And vpon Saturday the[y] marched to Barthomley, gyvinge an Alaram vpon the Hall of Crewe, wherein Colonell Brereton had placed a Garrison for the Parliam^t "

Barthomley Churche

"The Kinges ptie comynge to Barthomley Churche, did sett vpon the same, wherein about xx^{tie} Neighbours where gonne for theire saufegarde.

But *maior Connaught*, maior to *Colonell Sneyde*, (whom they in the Churche did take for the *Lord Brereton*),* wth his forces by wyelcome entred the Churche   The people wthin gatt up into the Steeple, But the Enymy burnynge formes, pewes, Rushes, & the lyke, did smother them in the Steeple that they weire Enforced to call for quarter, & yelde them selves, wch was graunted them by the said Connaught, But when hee had them in his power, hee caused them all to be stripped starke Naked, And moste barborouslie & conti'y. [contrary] to the Lawes of Armes, murthered, stabbed and cutt

* " *Lord Brereton* "   This was William, second Lord Brereton, of Brereton Hall, Cheshire, a distinguished Royalist serving in Lord Byron s army   He was taken prisoner with his wife and son, at Biddulph Hall   co Stafford   on 2c Feb 1643-4, and suffered sequestration of his estates, compounding for them at the excessive price of £1738 18s   He was buried at Brereton, 21st April, 1664, and four of his daughters afterwards resided in Hospital Street, Nantwich, and were buried in the south transept of Nantwich Church   (See *postea*)

the Throats of xij of theim,* viz m^r John ffowler (Scholem^r), *Henry ffowler, m^r Thomas Elcocke, James Boughey, Randall Hassall, Richard Steele, & Richard Steele, [bis] Will'm Steele, George Burrowes, Thomas Hollins, James Butler, & Richard Cawell,* & wounded all the reste, leavinge many of theim for Dead   And on Christmas daye, and Ste Stevens Daye, the[y] Contynued plu'dringe & destroyinge all Barthomley, Crewe, Haslington, & the places adiacent takeing all theire goods, victualls, Clothes, and stripped many, bothe men & women almost naked   And vpon Christmas daye 1643, towards Nighte, a nother pte of the Kinges forces, marched to Sandbach, most crewelly plu'dring & spoylinge eu'yone."

<small>Battell in Bouthe Lane</small>

'On St Stephens daye [26 Dec] 1643.   The Namptwiche Army, (savinge those lefte to tend the Towne) beinge att or about Middlewiche & Hulmes Chappell, marched towards Sandbach, & in Bouth Lane, neere Middlewiche, mett the Kinges forces, where theire was a greate Battell, but the Parliam^t side, beinge as ytt seemed not stronge enough, Retyred backe to Middlewich, and the Kinges ptie in p'suite after theim, did dryve theim awaye, where they lefte theire Magazen, & many slayne & wounded on bothe sides, ytt was reported that the pliam^t ptie. slayne & taken p^rsoners weire aboute twoe hundred   But what the Kinges ptie loste was neu[er] knowne. 't

<small>Hall of Crewe yelded to the Enymy</small>

"A Gairison [being] putt into the Hall of Crewe for the p'liam^t ptie, The Kinges forces laid greate Seige agaynst the same howse, And on St Johns Daye [Dec. 27], in Christmas 1643, they in the howse, slewe from the howse about three score of the Kinges ptie, & wounded many, But the Kinges forces encreasinge to a very greate nu'ber, And Namptwiche not able to releave theim, & they in the howse wantinge bothe victualls and Amunycon, vpon Innocents daye [Dec 28] att Nighte, not able to houlde out any longer, & p'ceyvinge noe Aide comynge to theim, (althoughe as valiant Soldyers as any weire) weire enforced to yeld upp the howse & theim selves p^rsoners to the Kinges ptie, havinge quarte^r gyven theim, And beinge in theire custodie (to the nu ber of one hundred or more) weire all putt p^rsoners into the Stable, & afterwards putt into Betley Churche"

<small>Enymy beseiged the Towne Round</small>

' On Saturday Nighte, the xxxth of December, about foure hundred of the Kinges forces came backe ou'[er] the water to Wrenbury, & the places thereabouts & in short tyme beseiged the Towne Round on that side, & another pte. of theim were att Wistaston, Willaston & the rest of the Townes [townships] on another side"

<small>Derfold and Acton Churche.</small>

"Upon Tuesday, the second of January 1643[-4] They entred into Derfold howse, wthout resistance, soe that those in the Towne weire enforced to tende the Wal[l]es bothe daye & Night   But Acton Churche

<hr>

* Although Mr Hinchliffe (Hist of Barthomley, p 41-2) attempts to cast suspicion on the accuracy of this account, it is remarkable that *Lord Byron*, in a letter to the Marquis of Newcastle, dated 26th Dec 1643, avowed and defended the massacre saying, "*The Rebels had possessed themselves of a Church at Bartumley, but wee presently ocat the n forth of it, and put them all to the sword, which I find to be the best way to proceed with their kind of people, for u ercy to them is cruelty*"—(Civil War Tracts, p 154)   To the same effect it is said in "*Certaine Informations*," No 52, p 409, Jan 15, 1644   "*We also hear that those Irish have hewed a godly minster in peices, and so have begun a new Irish massacre in England,*" alluding to this School-master, probably in holy orders, and the son of Richard Fowler, then Rector of Barthomley

† The forces here overpowered and routed by Lord Byron, were "a part of Colonel Ashtons (of Penketh, co Lanc) regement from Lancashire, going to assist Sir William Brereton"—*Perfect Diurnal*, No 25 p 199, (quoted in Civil War Tracts, p 153)

was Kepte wth a reasonable force by *Captyn Sadler*, sente furthe of Towne who did defend ytt very manfullie agaynst many assaults & Cannon shotts made by the Kinges ptie. firom the Churche, the p'ham^t ptie Killed the Canoneire & twoe more of them, And alsoe the widowe Parson dwellinge neere the Churche & fyve of theim in hir howse weire alsoe slayne wth shott from the Churche."

Dodington Hall

"The fourth of January, 1643[-4] the Kinges Army beseiged Dodington Hall, wherein was *Captyn Harwar* for the p'liamt, wth about one hundred men well Armed & p'vision and Magazen sufficiente for a fortnight, yett the same was deliu'ed to the Kinges ptie. wth all the Armes, amunycon, & p'vision in the Howse, w^thout any greate resistance, And the said Captyn, & all his Company depted. [departed] awaye, onelie wth theire app'ell, & went to Wem, not beinge suffred to come to Namptwiche ' *

Comynge of the Enymy

' The Towne beinge Nighte & Daye offred to bee assaulted by the Kinges forces, and contynuall allaroms gyven all that weeke, On Saturday, the vj^th [?] of January 1643[-4], some forces yssued furthe of Towne, & fetched into the Towne, syven [seven] of the Kinges cairryages laden wth goods & p'vision, & most of theim drawen wth good Oxen, wch soe raged theim, That they prsentlie wente & burned *Thomas Evansons* howse & Barne, *Saboth Churches* Lodge, & many stacks of haye, & some other Lodges lykewyse "

Ann Davenporte Slayne

' The Kinges forces, havinge compassed the Towne Round, contynued theire allaroms agaynst the Towne bothe daye & Nighte, and on Wednesdaye Night [10 Jan] they, havinge planted a greate peece of Oidnance neere Derfold Howse, did, about xj a Clock in the Night, shoote & discharge many gleed [*i e,* hot] Redd Bulletts into the Towne, whereof one of theim did light in a hovell of Kidds of m^r *Thomas Wilbrahams*,† att the upper ende of Welshe Rowe towards Derfold, and sett the same on fyer, but throughe gods mercye, & help of many woemen carryinge water & takeinge greate paynes (for the men durst not remove from the Wales [walls]) did quenche the same, litle harme beinge done. But they seeinge the fyer, shott very fast wth theire Canons att the fyer,‡ intendinge to Kill those wch came to quench the same, and did kyll a daughter of one John Davenpoit§ wth a Canon Bullett, wch was the first that was either slayne or wounded in the Towne, from the first beygynnynge of the seige "

---

* This assault and the other victories of Lord Byron above mentioned are also given in a curious and scarce pamphlet entitled "MAGNALIA DEI a Relation of some of the mary Remarkable Passages in Cheshire, Before the Siege of Namptwich, during the Continuance of it, And at the happy raising of it by the victorious Gentlemen *Sir Tho Fairfax* and *Sir William Brereton* London Printed for *Robert Bostock*, dwelling at the Signe of the Kinges Head in Pauls Church-yard 1644"
The Account of the siege of Nantwich contained in the Rev J Partridge's "History of Nantwich," is taken from this pamphlet

† Mr *Thomas Wilbraham* of Townsend, Nantwich, had died in Sussex on 18th Oct 1643 but his son *Roger Wilbraham,* many years after, thus alluded to this circumstance in his "Journal"—"The Christmas after my father s death (A° 1643) the Towne being then a Garrison for the Parliamt was closely besieged by the Irish Army, who made severall shott, which endangered the firing of House at ye Townsend where I then lay senseless of ye Danger we were in, under a sore fever," &c

‡ This cannonade on the 10th January, 1643-4, followed Col Geo Booth s refusal to yield up the town after Lord Byron had sent a peremptory summons to surrender. The Summons was first printed in the tract "*Magnalia Dei* '

§ The Parish Register records the burial of this young woman but gives the name as *Margery*—
"1643-4 Jan 10 Margery Dau. of John Davenport."

Geffrey Minshulls
howse & Barne

"On ffryday mornynge, the xijth of January 1643[-4], many of the Kinges forces beinge in and about *Geffrey Minshulls* howse & Barne, & att *Thomas Duttons* howse, neere vnto the Towne, some fewe yssued furthe of the Towne, & fyred Mr Minshulls Barne, & twoe Coates of Duttons, wch weire burned downe to the grounde, & tooke twoe p^rsone^{rs}, & killed ix or x (as was reported) & broughte in a woman p^rson^r alsoe, wch had xx^{tie} halfe crowne peices in hir pockett, w^{thout} losse of any man, savinge twoe wch were a litle hurte '

"The seige thus contynuynge & the Towne neu' [never] in quyett scythens [since] the losse of Beeston Castle, beinge wholie Surrounded by the Kinges ptie., Soe that the Markett was lost & non durst come to Towne to bringe either any p'vision or fuell, nor fetch any Salte, nor any yssue forth or come In, yett (blessed be god) theire was not for the p^rsent any want of any needfull thinge, althoughe the office^{rs} & Soulde^{rs} in Towne, beside townesfolke, weire many "

Throughout the siege, the garrison of Nantwich was under the command of Colonel George Booth, the grandson and heir apparent of Sir George Booth, Bart, Lord of Dunham Massey and Warrington, who, though nearly eighty years of age, acted as one of the deputy-lieutenants at the commencement of the War. The Colonel, who so gallantly defended the town, fifteen years after came with forces to Nantwich as Sir George Booth, then the prominent supporter of Charles II, (see *posteâ*), and ultimately became the first Lord Delamere

The cannonade of the 10th Jan having failed, Lord Byron* despatched a second summons, dated 16th Jan.; which together with the spirited reply of Colonel Booth, are here given as they were first printed in "*Magnalia Dei*," (1644), as follows —

"*To the Inhabitants and Commanders of the Towne of Namptwich* "

"Whereas I am certainly enformed as well by divers of the Souldiers who are now my prisoners, as by severall other creditable persons, that you are not only in a desperate condition, but that the late Summons I sent to the Towne hath been suppressed and concealed from the Inhabitants thereof, and they most grossely abused, by being told that no mercie was intended to be shewed by this Armie to the Towne, but that both man, woman, and child should bee put to the sword, I have therefore thought fit once more to send unto you, that the minds of the people with you, may be dispossest of that false and wicked slander, which hath been cast upon this Armie And I doe charge you (as you will answer Almightie God for the lives of those persons, who shall perish by your perfidious dealings with them) that you impart and publish the said Summons I sent to the people with you and that you yeeld up the Towne of Namptwich into my hands, for his Majesties use, and submit yourselves to his Majesties mercie, which I am willing to offer unto you Though I am confident, that neither of yourselves, nor by any aid that can come unto you, there is any possibilitie for you to escape the hands of this Armie If you please to send two gentlemen of qualitie to me, the one a Commander, the other a Townes-man, whereby you may receive better satisfaction, I shall give safe conduct and hostage for their returne

I doe expect a present answer from you,

JOHN BYRON "

"Jan 16, 1643"[-4]

* John, first Lord Byron, who, after his defeat at Nantwich in the following week, became the royalist Governor of Chester, had been raised to the Peerage by the title of Baron of Rochdale, on 24th Oct 1643

[*Reply of Colonel George Booth to Lord Byron's Summons.*"]

"We have received your last Summons, and do returne this answer that wee never reported, or caused to be reported, that your Lordship, or the Armie intended any such crueltie, wee thinking it impossible for Gentlemen and Souldiers so much to forget humanitie and if any have informed you otherwise, it is their owne conceit, and no realitie Concerning the publishing of your former Summons, it was publikely read amongst the Souldiers and Townes-Men, as your Trumpetter can witnesse, and since that time multitudes of coppies of it have been dispersed among the Townes-Men and others, and from none hath it been concealed and detained For the deliverie of this towne, Wee may not with our consciences, credits, or reputations, betray that trust reposed in us, for maintaining and defending this towne, as long as any enemy shall appeare to offend it. Though we be termed Traytours and Hypocrites, yet we hope and are confident, God will evidence and make knowne to the world in his due time (though for the present we should suffer) our zeale for his Glorie, our unfaired and unspotted loyaltie towards his Majestie and sinceritie in all our professions

GEORGE BOOTH"

On the 18th Jan a more determined attack on the town was made, but Lord Byron was repulsed with the loss of some of his best generals, as related by Malbon

"On Tuesday, the xvjᵗʰ of January 1643[-4] some of many Companyes in Towne, yssued furthe att the Scownce* on mᵣ Tho Maynwaringes backside towards vid [widow] Bromehalls Barne, where the Kinges forces weire, & att the end thereof, had made some walles & works for theire prservacon, But the Townesmen quyethe entered the same, & drove them awaye, & found some of theire clothes, thenc killed some of them, & broughte in some Armes & Ammunycon, wᵗʰ loss onelie of one *Blackshawe*† (a good Soldyᵉʳ) whoe ventered too fair. Vpon Wednesday, the xvijᵗʰ of January, The Kinges ptie. shott very muche agaynst the Towne, and discharged theire Canons foure score & sixteene tymes, (as was noted by some), but did neither execution nor harme att all. But upon Thursdaye mornynge, directlie att Break of Daye, The Kinges forces did very fiercely assaulte the towne on eu'y side, But the Towne defended them selves, beinge then ready att the Wal[l]es, very valiantlie & resolutelie to Dye, Rather then [than] loose the Towne where theire was for the space of an hower & somethinge more, very good servys performed on bothe sides But then the Kinges forces fledd when ytt was fayre daylighte, noe faster than theire legges could carry them Leavinge behind theim theire Skalinge Ladders, & many wood Kidds, wᶜʰ they had broughte wᵗʰ theim, & some of theire Armes, And about one hundred dead Bodies, wᶜʰ they cold not take wᵗʰ theim, (for hast[e]) & many wounded *Captyn Sandfordt‡* was slayne behind the mounte on *Richard Wicksteeds* backside, and a gent, one of his fyerlocks, & taken there over the Wal[l]es the gent was taken alyve, but dyed the same daye, & some other of theire Com'anders weire alsoe slayne,

* "*Scownce*," or *Sconce* ie fort, or mound

† "1643-4 Jan 19 Hugh Blackshaw soldier,"—(Nantwich Burial Reg) And on the same day, "*Richard Barker, Robert Woodcock, Richard Hough*, and *John Warburton*, soldiers" (*Ibid*)

‡ Captain Thomas Sandford was the second son of Robert Sandford of Sandford co Salop It is said that he and some others killed before Nantwich were removed to Chester and Buried in the Cathedral —(*Cheshire Sheaf*, No 417) It is also stated in Edmund Ludlow's *Memoirs*, Edit 1698, Vol 1 p 77, that Captain Sandford's assault was made "whilst the works were but slenderly defended, the Guard consisting for the most part of Townesmen, who were then gone to dinner But it so happened, that a boy of the age of 15 firing a musquett from the Town, shot him dead in the place, which discouraged his souldiers from any further attempt "—(*Cheshire Sheaf*, No 527)

whose names cold not bee learned * But the Towne Soldye^{rs} had the pillage & Armes of them all. Theire weire slayne of the Townesmen *John Beckett, Robte Goldsmithe,* butcher, & *John Warren,*† wch dyed afterwards, and three com'on Soldyc^{rs} wounded "

The fi1 ste greate
assaulte on
Nampt..che
xv.ij of January
1643[-4]
Captyn Sandford
Slayne

" Theire was found in Captyn Sandfords pocketts, when hee was stripped, (this Sandford was Captyn of fyerlocks, & the same man wch entered firste into Beeston Castle, when Captyn Steele deliu'ed the same), The manner of the designe for the said assaulte sente from *Colonell Richard Gibson* in mann' [manner] following, viz. —"*Maior Harwar* wth the regiment vnder his Com'and, & the fyer locks, wth the Scaling Ladders, They and all the Dragoneers, Armed wth fyer-locks, or Snaphanches, to fall on first soe neere vnto the fall of the Ryvei, on this [Acton] side of the Watei as may bee, on the lefte hande of the Bulworkes, Then to be second[ed] with a hundred musketteers, Then a stronge bodie of pikes, then a reserve of musketteers, & let the Soldie^{rs} carry as many faggotts as they can; This to bee att fyve a Clocke in the mornynge Upon discharge of a peece of Ordnance and to fall on the Wall, att discharge of some peece of ordnance January xvij 1643. Word *God and a good Cause.*"

There was alsoe found in Captyn Sandfords pocketts a letter written in theise words, viz —

" *I o the officers Souldyers & Gentlemen in Namptwiche theise* —
Gent

let these resolve yor Jelousies, concerninge oui Religion I vowe by the faythe of a Christian, I knowe not one Papist in our Army And, as I am a gent, we are not Irishe, but trewe borne Englishe, & Reall p'testants alsoe, Borne & Bredd Praye you mistake us not, but receyve vs into your fayre esteeme And knowe wee intend Royallie [loyalty] towards his Matie & wilbe noe other then faythfull in his servys

Thus gent beleeve from yo^{rs}

THOMAS SANDFORD "

There was alsoe found upon him another letter dated the xvth of January 1643, viz.
" Gent

Your Drum can informe you, Acton Churche, y^s noe more a prson, but now free for honest men to doe theire dovocon therein Therefore bee p^rswaded from your Incredulitie, & Resolve God will not forsake his Anoynted Lett not your zeale in a badd cause Dazell yor Eyes any longer, but wype away your vayne conceipts, that haue too longe led you into Blynde error Louth am I to vndertake the trouble of p'swadinge you into obedyence, because your erronyous opynyons doe vyolenthe oppose reason amonge you But ever (yf you love your Towne) accepte of quarter, & yf you regarde your lyves, worke yor saufetie by yeldinge yor Towne to the Lord Byron for his Maties use yow now see my battery vs fixte, from whence fyer shall Eternallie visitt you, day and Nighte, to the terror of your old and females & confusion‡ of your Thatche howses Beleeve me gent I haue laid by any form^r delays and am nowe resolved to battei burne and storme you Doe not wonder that I wryte unto you (havinge officers in Cheefe aboue mee) tis onelie

---

* Mr Partridge speaks of the "activity of the Towr s Women, headed by a heroine of the name of Brett who defended the woiks with the utmost bravery and did great execution on the 18th Jan when the desperate assault was given by pouring hot brine upon the assailants one of whom gaining the wall, too prematurely cry d out *the town is our own* " As this episode is not mentioned in any contemporary account, the truth of the story probably has no better foundation than the tradition of the town

† None of these names occur in the Burial Register at this time

‡ "*Confusion*" is written "*consumftion*" in the Cole MS. Brit Mus.

to advyse (because I haue some frends amongest you whose saufety I wish,) That you accepte of my Lord
Byrons condicons Hee ys gracyous and will charitablie consider of you

Accepte of these as a somons that you furthewᵗʰ surrender youre Towne and by that testimonie of
your fidelitie & fealtie to his Matⁱᵉ you maye obteyne favour My fyer locks (you know) have done strange
feates bothe by Nighte and by Daye, and howerlie we will not fayle in our pryvatt visitts of you You have
not yett receyved any Allarams wherefore expecte suddenly to here [hear] from

Thomas Sandford, Captyn of ffyerlocks

ffrom my battery and approaches before
your Welshe Roe the xvᵗʰ of January 1643 "

The Assaulte   "The Towne contynuynge still beseiged all round on eu'y side, Althoughe
ytt was supposed, the[y] had slayne & wounded on theire side, & that did
over Runn* them, A thowsand† att the leaste, att that assaulte, Soe that noe Markett
was Kepte, nor any p vision, or fewell broughte to the Towne, & many Cattell Kepte
wᵗʰin the wales, [walls] for feare of plu'dringe, & neither haye nor straye [straw] cold bee
had for them, Inregard of the greate store of horse, for s'vice Kepte in the Towne, Soe
that thinges began to bee scarce bothe for man & horse, yett ytt pleased God, vpon
thawinge of a greate Snowe, (wᶜʰ then was) That the Reever Weever began to Ryse,
And the Kinges ptie being afrayde that the water wold take down a platt they made
for theire passage over the Reever, a little below Beambridge, for theire free passage to
releeve one the other, (for Beamebridge beinge a fayre Stonne Bridge, almost but newely
made, was a greate pte of ytt beaten downe,) On the xxiiij of January 1643[-4], They
conveyed over the Reever all theire Ordnance & Carryages, & most pte of theire horse
& ffoote towards Acton Churche."

Weever   "On Thursday [sic for Wednesday] the xx4ᵗʰ of January 1643[-4], The
[River]   Ryver was Reesed soe heighe that theire platt was carryed downe, & they
by noe meanes cold passe the Reever, the on[e] to the other, wᶜʰ the
Townesmen p'ceyving, tooke advantage of the same, yssuynge furthe vnto ther workes,
rounae about that side of the Reever towards *Beameheathe*, dryvinge all theim theire awaye,
& did level and throwe downe all theire works and broughte in much Haye and fewell
And for feare lest they (vpon fall of the water) should haue retorned agayne, The[y] fyred
a very fayre newe howse of *mr Jeffrey Mynshulls*, the Barne, Stable, & all buyldinges
belonginge to the same, and also another greate Barne of his on the Heath side neere
Milston lane,‡ And lykewyse they, & the Kinges side burned *will'm Brownes* Barne, *James*

---

* *Over-run* i e to desert, or run away

† The Royalist losses on the 18th Jan 1643-4, though perhaps here much exaggerated, were very serious as appears from
particulars in "*Magnalia Dei*," viz —Lord Byron attempted "'o gain the towne by a sudden and violent assault upon
five severall places of the towne at once, and this was done an houre before day, upon notice given to one another by a
shot of one of theire Ordnance, the 18th of Januarie which was a costly assaulte, for they left dead at the *wall lane-end*,
Lieutenant-Colonell Bolton One Captain many Officers and the prime of their soldiers of the Red Regiment many
they cast there into the river, and carried many off dead and wounded At *Wicksteds Sconce* [near the "Nursery on the
north side of Welsh Row] was slaine Captain Sandford and his Lieutenant, and some few soldiers besides left, and many
carried off slain and wounded At *Pillory Street-end* left dead behind, one Captain, two Lieutenants, two Ensignes,
seventeen Souldiers of the Green Regiment, and carried off 60 slain and wounded thence At the back of *Mr Maynwarings*
[? Hospital Street] were left slain two Lieutenants and thirteen Souldiers, and many dead and wounded carried off At
the Sconce near the Lady Nortons [Beam Street-end] was left slain one Captain and 15 Souldiers, besides what was
carried off There are with us of them deadly wounded Officers and Souldiers 18 One of their own party reports they
lost in the assault 300 men but we now understand they lost and had wounded 500 men "

‡ *Mill'store Lane* is still so called

Bullens Barne, *John Wrights* Barne, *Margarett Lathams* Barne, & *Margery Elcocks* Barne; & a Lodge wch was *Doctor Harwars,* And other Coates [cottages] all downe to the grounde; Bee [by] reason they weire places wherein the Kinges ptie had harboured, & mighte a donne agayne, when they had gotten over the Reever, And donne greate harme to the Towne, as they had donne before, (standinge all neere to the Towne) "

The Siege of the 25th of January 1643[-4]   "The same daye, beinge the 24th of January 1643[-4] *Gen'all ffearfax* [Fairfax] *Colonell Brereton,* & many other Colonells & Com'ande^rs wth theire owne & Lancashire forces, to the nu'ber of three thowsand fyve hundred & fyftie horse, & three thowsand foote marched all towards Namptwiche to remove the seige, (unknowne to the Towne), And comynge to Dalameyre forrest, met some of the Kinges forces, wth whome they fought, & killed some of theim, & tooke fortie p'son^rs And restinge theim selves that Nighte att *Tilston,* & on *Tilston Heathe,* (havinge but simple quarter), nexte daye the[y] marched towards Namptwiche; (beinge aoout fyve myles thence), But beinge intercepted att *Barbridge,* wth more of the Kinges ptie they fell vpon theim, killed some & tooke thirtie p^rsoner^s. And vpon Thursdaye, the xxv^th of January 1643[-4], drawinge to *Hurleston,* (twoe myles from the Towne) The[y] weire a wair [aware] of the whole bodie of the Kinges Army att Acton advancinge towards theim   There the Battell began, betwixt theim, very fiercely, (about halfe an hower past three in thafter noone), equall on bothe sides, But before fyve a Clocke, many of the Soldyers of the Trayned bands yssued furthe of Towne, and fallinge vpon the Arreare of the Kinges ptie, They all fledd & weire vtterlie Rowted, (throughe Gods assistance)   Theire weire taken p^rsoner^s, Sr *Michell Erneley,* S^r *ffrances Butler, Colonell Gibson, Colonell Warren, Col fflctewood* and many Captyns, Lieftent^s, Corporalls, office^rs, and Com on Soldye^rs; to the nu'ber of xvj hundred or thereabouts One greate Brasse Ordnance, ffoure other smaler peeces of ordnance, & all theire Carriage, magazen, & p'vision, and alsoe all the money & treasure, wch they had plu'dred & gotten (during all the tyme the seige lay agaynst the Towne, wch was about Seaven weekes), vp and downe all the Countrey & marche in Staffordshire about Betley, & the necrer pte of that Countie adioynynge to Cheshire, wch was broughte into the Towne, (althoughe some of the Soldyer^s gott some of the money vnknowne to the Cheefe Com'anders), But yf Daylighte had not fayled, theire had but fewe of theim escaped   the Nighte beinge very darke, the Kinges ptie. cold not be pursued, (as was intended), But the fighte beinge ended, many of the p'liam^t forces, bett good fyer, & contynued in the *Lady field* att Acton Churche all Nighte   That pte of the Kinges side wch had taken Acton Churche and Derfold Howse, called for Quarter, wch was graunted.   Theire was slayne* of theim about fourty, & on the other side but three; nor but fewe wounded, And thus (throughe Gods mercy & assistaunce,) the Seige was Reased, & the Towne p^rserued from a most bloddy malicious Enymy. All the Com'on sorte of the p^rsoner^s, to the nu'ber of fyfteene hundred & more, weire putt into the Churche at Namptwiche, where they contynued ffryday, Saturday & Sondaye, (maintayned by the Towne), And then many of theim tooke vp Armes for the p'liam^t, And weire listed vnder Seu'all Captyns, and all the wounded weire putt furthe of Towne, wch weire able to goe, and some of

---

* The slain are supposed to have been buried in a field known as *Dead-men's Field,* not far from Acton Church

Drawn by W.Hinchliss F.S.A.

Engraved by J. Syds.

NANTWICH CHURCH, N.W. VIEW.

(Fac-simile of engraving in Lysons' *Cheshire*.)

theim dyed * Theire weire amongest theim about CXX^{tie} [120] weomen taken alsoe, wch weire putt furthe of Towne, onelie some poore weomen in the Towne, tooke the best of theire Clothes from theim, wch they had gotten by plu'der

Noe Servys nor "On Sunday, the x\vij of January 1643[-4] Inregarde the p^rsone^{rs} weire
Sermon in the in the Churche, theire cold bee noe Servys, (havinge but one Churche in
Churche the Towne,) but praye^{rs} & Preachinge weire att *m^r Thomas Wilbrahams Howse*, *m^r Hugh Hassalls the Crowne Gallery*, & the *Ladie Nortons* bothe forenoone & afternoone "†

Pr'soners taken "The names & nu'ber of p^rsone^{rs} of note, taken att Reasing the Seige,
at the Reasing as appered by a Liste, weire *Maior Gen'all Gibson, S^r ffrancis ffletewood, S^r*
of the Seige *Michell Erneley, S^r ffrancis Butler, Sr Rauffe Done, Colonell Warren, Colonell Gibbes* and *maior Hammon* [d], foureteene Captyns, thirtie Lieften^{ts}, sixe & twentie Ensignes, twoe Cornetts, two Quarter maisters, ffourtie seriants, threescore & three Corporalls, twentie gent. of Companyes, ffourtie Drumers, twentie Cariyages, Sixe peeces of Oidnance; a hundred & twentie weomen, And fyfteene hundred Com'on Soldye^{rs} "

The names of "The names of the cheefe Com'anders wch came in Ayde of the Towne
Com'anders w'h to rease the Seige viz *Sr Thomas fferfax, Gen'all, Sir Will'm. ffearefax*, his
reased the Seige Kinsman, *Colonell Brereton; Colonell Maynwaringe, Colonell Duckenfeild; Colonell Bouth, Colonell Brighte, Colonell Allen, Colonell Lambert, Maior Copley, maior Morgan; maior Spencer*, & many othe^{rs} of Note Lancashire Com'ande^{rs} *Colonell Holland*,‡ *Colonell Ashton*,§ *Colonell John Bouthe*,‖ *Sir Thomas Malevery, S^r will'm. Consiable*, & *Colonell Rigbies*¶ Reigm^t conteyninge in nu'ber in all about Seyven Thowsand "

The markett "Upon the nexte Saturdaye after the Seige was reased theire was a
began agayne greate markett in Towne began agayne And plenty of all needfull things att Reasonable Rates, wth greate rejoyceing & praysinge God for the same "

Daye of "On Wednesdaye, the laste of January 1643[-4], A soleme daye of
Thanksgivinge, thankesgyvinge was held at Namptwiche, in the same places where Servys & Sermons weire the Sabothe before '

Nantwiche "And vpon Thursdaye, the firste of ffebruary 1643[-4], The Churche
Churche cleansed was freed from all the p^rsone^{rs} wch had byn theire, from pollucon & beastliness com'itted by them, & all the Mattes & bosses were burned, & all the pewes

---

* Only four soldiers are recorded in the Burial Register, in the three days following the great battle, viz —
"1643-4 Jan 26 John Holland sergant
     „   „   27 William Eckerson [and] Isack Cheetum, Soldiers
     „   „   28 Thomas Brookes Lieutenante

† These houses were —
1 —*Townsend* in Welsh Row
2 —*The Crown Inn*, in High Street the 'gallery" being the whole of the top story, wh ch had a continued range of windows from end to end until alterations were made about Christmas, 1871
3 —*The Hall* at Beam Streed-end on the site of the Crewe Almshouses
   ‡ Colonel Richard Holland, of Heaton, in Prestwich, Governor of Manchester
   § Major-general Ralph Ashton, or Assheton, of Middleton, M P for Lancashire
   ‖ Colonel John Booth, of Woodford, Cheshire, a younger son of Sir George Booth of Dunham, the elder, afterwards Knighted
   ¶ Col Alexander Rigby, M P for Wigan, Lancashire.

& seates made clayne & washed,* And on Sondaye, the fourthe of ffebruary 1643[-4], prayers & preachinge began publiquely agayne in the saide Churche "

Colonell Brereton leaveth for London   " On the Seconde of ffebruary 1643[-4], Colonell Brereton sett forwards towards London to the P'liamt   But retorned not to Namptwiche agayne vntill midsomr nexte afterwards "

The signal overthrow of the Irish Army and Chester forces at Nantwich, according to Clarendon, was very disastrous to the Royal cause   He remarks, "It cannot be denied the reducing of that place at that time would have been of unspeakable importance to the King's affairs, there being between that and Carlisle no cne town of moment (*Manchester* only excepted) against the King   and those two populous counties of Cheshire and Lancashire (if they had been united against the Parliament) would have been a strong bulwark against the Scotts "†   An official account of this important victory by Sir Thos Fairfax was dispatched to the Earl of Essex, who presented it in Parliament on Feb 1st , and on the following day the House of Commons ordered,—"That on the next Lord's Day [Feb 4] following, publique thanks should be rendered unto Almighty God for the forementioned victory of Sir William Brereton against the English-Irish , and that a Copy of the said Order, with the names of the chiefe Commanders and Officers which were taken and slaine of the enemies in that defeat should be read by the Ministers of the several congregations in and about the City of London and Westminster.   And the names of such Ministers who should refuse to publish the said Order should be returned unto the Parliament, which was performed accordingly '‡

Sir Thomas Fairfax's despatch, which was first printed in *"Magnalia Dei,'* together with two other printed lists of the prisoners taken at Acton Church on 25th Jan 1643-4, from a vol of single sheet pamphlets preserved in the British Museum, are here given as follows —

SIR THOS FAIRFAX'S LETTER TO THE EARL OF ESSEX

" May it please your Excellencie,"

" I Desire your pardon, that I haue not given your Excellencie an account before this of the great mercie God hath shewed us in giving us a happy Victory over the Irish Army, to a totall ruine of their foot, and purchase of their chiefe Commanders.

Upon the 21 Jan I marcht from Manchester towards Namptwich to relieve that Towne, with 2 500 foot, and twenty-eight troops of Horse , the Enemies Forces were above 3,000 foot, and 1,800 horse   The first encounter we had were with a Party of theirs upon the Forrest of Delamore, where about thirty were taken Prisoners , About six miles further they maintained a Passage against us with about 200 men, I caused some Foot and Dragoones to bee drawn out to force it, which, by Gods assistance they did in halfe an houres space, and there took a Major and some prisoners , Having advanced some two miles further,

* A charge of 5s was put down in the "Church Book" (now unfortunately lost) "for pitch to purify the place on their departure " *Cheshire Sheaf*, No 673

† Clarendon's *History of the Rebellion*, Vol iv, p 427 Edit 1826

‡ See a Vol of Weekly Pamphlets in Brit Mus entitled —"*C R Mercurius Civicus* London's Intelligencer or Truth related from thence to the whole Kingdome to prevent mis-information " No 4/37 From Thursday, Feb 1 to Thursday, Feb 8, 1643[-4],"

we found a good Body of them planted about Acton Church, a mile from Namptwich, We drew up within Cannon shot, which sometimes played upon us, but without hurt, God be thanked, Wee there understood that the Lord Byron, who had besieged the Towne on both sides of the River, was prevented by the over-flowing of the water, from joyning with that part at Acton Church but heard that he was taking a compasse to get over the River to joyne with it, we resolved to fall upon that party at the Church, before he should get up to it, but staying to bring up our Rere and Carriages, we gave him time to obtain that hee sought for * Then wee resolved to make way with Pioneers through the Hedges, and then to march to the Town to relieve it, and to adde some more Force to ourselves to enable better to fight with them, but being a little advanced on our march, they told mee the Enemy was close upon the Rere, so facing about two Regiments, being *Colonel Hollands,* and *Colonel Boothes,*+ I marcht not farre before wee came to bee engaged with the greatest Party of their Army, Then the other part presently afterwards assaulted oui Front, there *Sir William Brereton* and *Colonel Ashton* did very good service, and so did *Colonell Lambert* and *Major Copley* with the Horse They were once in great danger, but that they being next to the Towne were assisted by forces which came to their succour in due time, Wee in the other Wing, were in as great dis-tresse, but that the horse commanded by *Sir William Fairfax,* did expose themselves to great dangers to encourage the foot, though capable of little service in those narrow Lanes, yet it pleased God, after two houres fight they were forced by both Wings to retreat to the Church, where they were caught as in a Trap A List of what we took, I have here sent you Excellency" &c

Your Excellencies most humble servant

Namptwich 29 Jan 1643[-4]

THO FAIRFAX."

"A List of the Prisoners [Sir Thos Fairfax s List] taken at Acton Church January 25 1643[-4] near Namptwich ' (Printed in ' Magnalia Dei, in 1644)	"A Catalogue of all the Names of the Prisoners taken at the raising of the Siege at Namptwich, by that valiant Commander, Si Thomas Fairfaxe, &c, being a true Copy of the I st presented to his Excellency & by his Excellency presented to both Houses of Parliament the first of February 1643 '[-4] (Single Pamphlets Brit Mus No 669 f 8/46 pag 105 Printed for Edward Husbands, Feb 1, 1643[-4])	"Extraordinary Newes from Colonell John Barher, Governour of Coventry to a merchant of London, shewing how Sir William Brereton hath raised the siege from Namptwich in Cheshire Prison-ers taken' &c [Dated] "Januar 30 1643"[-4] (Single Pamphlets, Brit Mus No 669, page 104 Printed according to Order, London by E G for John Rothwell, 1643-4)
Major General Gibson	Sergeant Maior Generall Gils	Sergeant major-generall Gibson
Colonels Sir Michael Enrley	Sir Michael Earnely	Sir Michael Earnly, Col
,, Sir Richard Fleetwood	Sir Richard Fleetwood	Sir Richard Fleetwood, Col
George Monk‡	Colonell Monck	Colonell Monks
,, Warren	Colonell Warren	Colonell Warren
Lieutenant-colonel, Sir Francis Butler	Sir Francis Boteler	Sir Francis Butler, lieutenant-colonell
,, Gibbs	Lieutenant-colonell Gibbs	Lieutenant-colonell Gibbs
Major Hammond	Maior Hammond	Major Hamond

* Partridge in his History (p 72) and Platt (p 109) both relying on the account of the battle by Lord Clarendon, state that Lord Byron had *not* been able to concentrate his forces at Acton, and in the previous account Malbon says, part of the Royalist forces had effected the passage of the river after the thaw set in, but the rest were prevented by the rapid rise of the flood

† *Col John Booth,* (p 167) uncle to Col George Booth, Governor of Nantwich For interesting particulars relating to both Colonels, see Beamont's "*Annals of the Lords of Warrington,*" pp 80-90

‡ Col George Monk, born in Devonshire, 6 Dec 1608, had served in the army in Spain, and in the Netherlands and had been Governor of Dublin He was still a prisoner at Nantwich on 7th April 1644 (*Ches Sheaf,* Vol II p 39), but was afterwards removed to the *Tower* of London Being liberated, he became servant of the Commonwealth but after Cromwell's death, he exerted himself for Charles II, who created him Duke of Albermarle He died 3rd Jan 1670, and was buried in Westminster Abbey

Captains —Atkins	Captains —Atkins	14 Captains —Atkins	
,, Sydenham	,, Sydenham	,, Liddington	
,, Finch	,, Finch	,, Tinch	
,, Disney	,, Disney	,, Disney	
,, Fisher	,, Fisher	,, Fisher	
, Cooke	,, Cooke	,, Cooke	
,, Ward	,, Ward	,, Ward	
,, Dean	,, Deane	,, Deane	
,, Lucas	,, Incasse	,, Incas	
,, Litcole	,, Lydcot	,, Ledcote	
,, Betts	, Bets	,, Deetes	
,, Spotswood	,, Spotwood	,, Shotterwood	
,, Bambridge	,, Banbridge	,, Bawbridge	
,, Willier	,, Willier	,, Willis	
Lievtenants Long	Lieutenants Long	19 Lieutenants Long	
,, Norton	,, Norton	,, Norton	
,, Roe	,, Roe	,, Rowe	
,, Pawlet	,, Pawlet	,, Pawlett	
,, Goodwin	,, Goodwyn	,, Goodwin	
,, Liverson	,, Liverson	,, Kinerstone	
, Duddleston	,, Duddleston	,, Dulaton	
,, Pate	,, Pate	,, Pate	
,, Morgell	,, Morgall	,, Morgell	
,, Lestrange	,, Strange	,, Strange	
,, Shipworth	,, Skipworth	,, Shipworth	
,, Ankers	,, Ankers	,, Ancars	
,, Billingsley	,, Billingsley	,, Billingley	
,, Castilion	,, Castillian	,, Custelion	
, Milner	,, Milliner	,, Milliner	
,, Bradshaw	,, Bradshaw	,, Bradshaw	
,, Walden	[omitted]	[omitted]	
,, Lyons	,, Lyons	,, Lionnes	
,, Poulden	,, Poulden	,, Goulden	
,, Smith	,, Smith	,, Smith	
Ensignes —Brown	Ensignes —Brown	26 Ensignes —Brown	
,, Brereton	,, Brereton	,, Brewreton	
,, Bach	,, Bach	,, Batch	
,, Fines	,, Fynes	,, Ihnes	
,, Wright	,, Wright	,, Wright	
, Davis	,, Daniell	,, Dampell	
,, Touthwood	,, Touthwood	,, Southwood	
,, Addisse	,, Addis	,, Addise	
,, Smith	[omitted]	,, Smith	
, Mahoone	,, Naham	,, Vahan	
,, Rise	,, Keyes	,, Reise	
,, Dendsworth	,, Doudsworth	,, Doreworth	
,, Musgrave	,, Musgrave	,, Musgrave	
,, Femicock	,, Pemy-cock	,, Pennycocks	
,, Dunsterfield	,, Damsterfield	,, Dunstermile	
,, Elliar	,, Elliar	,, Elliard	
,, Eiclash	,, Iclasse	,, Itlack	
,, Philips	,, Phillips	,, Phillips	
,, Heard	,, Heard	,, Hewde	
,, Thomas	,, Thomas	,, Thomas	
,, Morgan	,, Morgan	,, Morgan	
,, Lewis	,, Lewes	,, Lewes	

Ensignes —Godsclue	Ensignes —Godsclue	Ensignes —Goodfellow
,, Busby	,, Busby	,, Busby
,, Terringham	,, Tiringham	,, Terringham
,, Wither	,, Wither	,, Withers
Cornets Lee	Cornets George Lee of Hylest and one	[omitted]
,, Carpenter	Carpenter	[omitted]
Quarter-Masters Lee .	Quarter Master Lee	[omitted]
,, Petty	,, Petty	[omitted]
Sir Ralph Done also taken	Sir Ralph Done is also taken	[omitted]
Mastr Shurlock* chaplaine to a Regiment	Mr Shimlock, Captaine Lieutenant to a Reigment	[omitted]

Gentlemen of Companies	20	Gentlemen of Companies	20	Gentlemen of Companies	20
Serjeants .	41	Sergeants .	41	Serjeants	41
Drums	40	Drums	40	Drummers	40
Corporals .	63	Corporals	61	Corporals	63
Canoneers	4	Canoneers	4	[omitted]	
Colours	22	[omitted]		[omitted]	
Women (many whereof had long knives)	120	Women (many whereof had long knives)	120	Women with long knives	120
Common Souldiers	1500	Common Souldiers	1700	Common Souldiers	1700
Ordnances (five of brasse)	6	Ordnance	6 peeces	Ordnances	6 Peces
Carriages	20	Carriages	20	Carriages	20
Divers Wagons Rich plunder [omitted] [omitted]		Divers of the Wagons Rich plunder [omitted] [omitted]		[omitted]	
				Priests	40
				Horse .	120
Slain Lieutenant Coll Vane in the fight [25th Jan]		Slain Lieutenant Colonell Van, and many common Souldiers, some affirm 200 on the Right Wing, besides the Left wing		[omitted]	
Lieutenant Colonell Boulton in the assault before the Town [on 18th Jan]		There was slaine at the siege [on 18th Jan] Lieutenant Colonell Boughton, and four Captains, amongst whom Samford [Sandford]		[omitted]	
[omitted]		The Enemy shot 80 or 100 fiery hot Bullets into the Town, but none did execution, but one in a stack of wood "		[omitted]	

This victory was the crisis of the war in Cheshire Henceforward the Parliament maintained the ascendancy. CREWE HALL was re-taken on the 5th Feb , and DODDING-TON HALL two days after CHOLMONDELEY CASTLE surrendered on the 8th July, 1644, and BEESTON CASTLE, after nearly a year's siege, on the 15th Nov 1645, the King having been the sad eye-witness of his ruined hopes at *Rowton Moor* on the 24th Sept. in the same year. In the meantime rigorous measures had been adopted by the Parliament to maintain the war Committees of "*Sequestrators*" were formed for the purpose of fining all who still retained their Royalist opinions, or who refused to subscribe to the "*Covenant*" for Presbyterian uniformity The estates of wealthy '*Delinquents*" were seized by them, and the rents were regularly collected by appointed officials in each district,

---

* Richard Sherlock, afterwards D D , and Rector of Winwick, co Lancashire, from 1660 till his death in 1689 He was born 11th Nov 1612, at Oxton, in Wirrall, Cheshire   (See Anthony a Wood, Vol IV, p 259-261)

who accounted for their monies, &c to the Council of War   Poorer people atoned for their "*delinquency*" by suffering imprisonment and the loss of their household goods, which were valued and sold by auction for the "*publique use.*' In *Harl MS* 2166, are preserved many pages of Sequestrators Accounts, Lists of Delinquents, Inventories, &c. for Nantwich Hundred, from which the following extracts are taken chiefly relating to the town.

"A catalogue of the names of every & severall delinquents in the division & alotment of Marc Folineux, one of the Collectors for Namptⁱᶜʰ hundred as ffolloweth "

LORD CHOLMLEY , sequestrated in the year 1643   The total Half-year's Rents for houses,* gardens, chief rents in Nantwich, Alvaston, Woolstan wood, Leighton, Willaston, Wistaston in 1644, occupying five pages of accounts

	£	s	d
.	37	10	5

(Half-yearly rent)

MR MASTERSON, Total half-year's Rents for 1644, for property in High-town, Welsh Row, Beam Street, Mill Street, &c , and the following lands in Nantwich (which appear to have extended from Pillory Street to Shrewbridge, including what is now the Shrewbridge Hall Estate)

						£	s	d
The Horse Croft	3 Acres, prized to per Annum				.	2	00	00
Shors field	10	,,	,,	,,	,,	6	13	04
Bricke field	12	,,	,,	,,	,,	6	00	00
Greene field	16	,,	,,	.	,,	.	8	00	00
Oxe Pasture	18	,,	,,	,,	,,	.	9	00	00
Longe Meadowe	7	,,	,,	,,	,,	4	11	00
Calues Croft	6	,,	,,	,,	,,	3	00	00
Grastons Croft	1	,,	,,	,,	,,	1	00	00
Milne Meadow	2½	,,	,,	,,	,,	1	12	06
Cros field	10	,,	,,	,,	,,	.	6	13	04
Bathing Meadow	6	,,	,,	,,	,,	3	18	00

£	s	d
19	5	8

(Half-yearly rent)

| 14 | 0 | 0 |

(Rental of walling) for 1644

The late MR ALEXANDER WALTHALL† of Wistaston   His estate in Nantwich consisting chiefly of *Walling-land* and salt-houses   His cottages "were ordered for the maintenance of the soldiers "   The *yearly* sum claimed in 1645 was   .. £23 6 4

JOHN BICKERTON, land and personal property in Nantwich, per ann   £4 0 0

EARL RIVERS, House property in Nantwich   ,,   £2 16 8

MR BAVINE, rents and walling in Nantwich   ,,   £34 10 10

MR FOWLER, walling rents in Nantwich   ,,   .   £4 0 0

SIR THOMAS WILBRAHAM of Woodhey
   Rents in Nantwich in 1644 half-yearly   £59 13 2
   Walling in Nantwich   ,,   ,, ...   £30 13 4
MR RICHARD WIXSTED Junr Houses and land per annum   .   £12 16 8

The late LADY NORTON now *Mr Thos Dodd*
   Rents of Houses &c in 1644 per annum   £25 2 0
   ,,   Lands   ,,   ,,   £42 6 8

---

* Among the houses in Nantwich, are mentioned —

"*Beame Street Hall*," made into a Prison, and occupied by Richard Acton
"*The Porche house*" in Welsh Row, the residence of Roger Wright

† Alexander Walthall, Esq , of Wistaston, was buried at Wistaston, 1st March, 1645-6 —(Wist Reg) An Inventory of his household goods cattle, &c as sold at Nantwich ' for the vse of the Publique" will be found in *Harl MSS* 2166 f 28/33, occupying several pages, and amounting to £48 00s 04d

Amongst the lands occur —

	£	s	d
Bolywall field* valued at per annum	5	0	0
Marchefield banck† ,, ,,	8	0	0
Three parcells of land in the occupation of Mr Thos Dodd, within the walls valued at per annum	8	0	0
The Hall (Beam St End) valued at per annum	10	18	4
Orchard and Yards ,, ,,	0	10	0

	£	s	d
The late Mr HUGH WILBRAHAM, for the year 1644	£7	18	0
Mr WEEVER, for rents for whole year 1644	£3	0	0
Sr JOHN PERSALL ,, ,, ,,	£22	15	10
Mr BROMLEY of Bagington, half-yearly rents, 1644	£17	17	10

Among the *Inventories* preserved, is that of the Town Minister, who, in the words of Jeremy Taylor, a contemporary divine, might have said "I am fallen into the hands of publicans and sequestrators and they have taken all from me. '

"*A TRUE INVENTORY of the goods late Mr SARINGE a delinquent late minister of NAMPTWICH for his delinquency was imprisoned & voted a delinquent by the Sequestrators the wich* [sic] *Goods were seyzed on by the Sequestrators & Collectors & aprised by the aprisors for namptwich hundred*" [Also] "*A true Accompt of the Goods late Mr SARINGE as they were sold for the use of the Publique by the Collector & apprisor for namptwiche hundred in the Publique store howse of the garrison as ffoloweth* "—

	Prized at			Sold for		
	£	s	d	£	s	d
Imprimis One Longe table	00	15	00	00	18	00
Item One Paire of tounges	00	00	04	00	00	04
Item One old Paire of bellowes	00	00	10	00	00	10
Item One litle table	00	03	04	00	03	04
Item One Throne chiere	00	01	00	00	01	00
Item One chamber Pott	00	00	08	00	00	08
Item two Lethren stools	00	02	00	00	02	00
Item one litle lethren chiere	00	02	00	00	02	00
Item one High bedsted with testrum of stofe	00	13	04	00	13	04
Item one litle table	00	04	00	00	04	00
Item one Joint coupbord	00	10	00	00	10	00
Item one Joint Coupbord with a box in it	00	12	00	00	12	00
Item one close Stooll & one old Panne	00	03	04	00	03	04
Item one Bedsted with a testrum of stofe	00	08	00	00	08	00
Item one truckle bedsted	00	03	00	00	03	00
Item one old fflocks bed	00	06	08	00	06	08
Item one litle Plaine Bedsted	00	04	08	00	04	08
Item one o d fringe [frying] Pane	00	00	06	00	00	06
Item one clos [clothes] tubb (i e a wash-tub)	00	05	00	00	05	00
Item one churne	00	01	04	00	01	04
Item one Saltinge Bassin & one Cheese bord	00	01	04	00	01	04
Item one litle Bruinge [brewing] Tressell	00	00	04	00	00	04
" Total aprisement is	£04	18	08			
[Signed] ' Marc Folineux Collector "	" The totall some of the sayell is			£05	01	08

* Most likely a field adjacent to *Bully-wall Well*, in Birchin Lane, Willaston.
† *Marsh-field Bank*, in Woolstanwood

"The *total Recepts* of all the Rents belonging to the severall delinquents before mentioned, which were received in monies & in delinquents goods for the use of the Publique since the 29th August 1644 untill the eleventh of Nouember 1646 by Marc Folireux Collector, Doth mount vnto the some of"   £573 00 04

"The *totall Recepts* of all the foresayd Rents Receued by order of Havage for the vse of the Publique by the sayd Collector since the 29th of August 1644 untill the eleventh of Nouembre 1646 mounts vnto the some of   £306 19 07

The totall some of the Rents arrear & unpayd, (same dates)   [no sum given]

The *totall disboursement* of all these Seuerall Rents & Goods late belonging to delinquents which were disboursed to the treasurer & to diuers other Persons by Severall Oiders for the vse of the Publique, by the foresayd Collector, since the 29 August 1644 untill the eleventh of Nov 1646 mounts &c   £580 02 08

Disbursed of this Accompt more than Receued which is to be charged upon the next Accompts, the some of   £07 02 04

The totall sum remaininge due to mee, settinge all the overplus Recepts of the last Accompts & the sayle of the goods of John Patricke, which is ten shillings ten pence   £05 18 03
besides the Collectors fees since the 11th Nov 1646 till the 1st Feb 1647   [no sum given]

The particulars of payments from the Rents &c of Mark Folineux's district are contained in eight pages of closely written manuscript, and are much too long to be given here· the following selected items will sufficiently illustrate how the public monies were expended.

				£	s	d
1644 Sept 26 Payd to Mr James Croxton treasurer for the vse of the Publique				2	0	0
Nov 2 Payd do do do				11	16	8
Aug 30 Payd to the Collector Marc Folineux				0	2	6

[A long note here states that 2/6 was the usual sum per day for horse and man, for services of the Collector in valuing goods, &c. Similar payments occur repeatedly]

1644 Oct 22 Payd to Collector M F. for one days service in assistinge Tho Wilson Collector in his division, in the saysure [seizure] of the Estate of *Mr Cotton* of Combermere, a delinquent   0   2   6

Nov 14 Comitie to repayre the Sentrye houses which were decayed in the Garrison of Namptwch   2 10   0

1644-5 Jan 17 Payd to Henry Hayes by Order from Sequestrators for monie that hee had layed out for the maintenance of the Almes-men [at Welsh Row Head] wich aie maintened out of Si Tho Wilbr'ms Estate   .   5 10   0

Jan 28 Payd to Will'm Baerns by Order from Sr Will'm Breieton Comander in Chiefe for the quartringe of the sayd Sr Will'm Brerctons men servants   .   0   5   0

Jan 30 Payd to Mr Robt Lunt Comisary for the Garison in Cheese wich was receued for delinquents Rents 1 10   0

	£	s	d

Feb 15 Payd to M F for two dayes service in going in the Countrey by Warrand from the Consell of Warr to Gather Provision to it Cheese & Corne for the Reliefe of the leagres & armes that are before biston [Beeston] Castell & Chester wich provision was delivered to the Comisarie   .   .   .   0 5 0

Mar 10 Payd to eaygth [eight] of Capt Houlse's Soldiers that assisted me in the sejzure of the goods late of Peerce Dod, wich goods were in Mr Mathew Mainwarings house, and the said Mr Mainwaring Refused to deliuer the sd goods for the vse of the Publique, therefore the Sequestrators hired the sayd soldiers to take the sd goods & bring them to the store-howse   ..   0 2 0

1645 April 5 Payd to Willm Becket Comissary the some of eaygth [eight] shillings & two pens, wich was to pay the thrashers that thrashed the corne late John Bickerton, a delinquent 0 8 2

April 12 Payd the Belman of giuinge warninge through the towne concerninge trespeses done by Catell on Mr Mastersons fielde [which had been staked out by soldiers four days previous] 0 0 2

July 24 Payd to Rich Hickock by Order from the Sequestrators for the discharge of tickets for the quartering of soldiers hee being a poore man & not able to forbaire [?]   1 5 0

July 29 Payd to Philip Moulton Carpenter, by Order from Collonall Croxton Gouenor of Namptwch for ourke [work] done by him for the Garrison   .   .   .   0 5 2

Sep 29 Payd John Tenche Showemaker by Order from the Sequestrators, &c for boots & showes &c   .   3 3 6

Oct 2 Payd to Lady Leigh by order from the Consell of Warr & deputie leftenents in pt of 50li [£50] pr annm allowed her by the sayd Consell beinge for Captn Cheswis arrers her husband & [who] was slayn in the Parliaments service   ..   .   2 0 0

1645-6 Jan 2 Payd Mr Bradshaw Receuer of the Kings Rents for the hole yeares *Rent of the fee farme for the Court of Namptwich* payable by the Estate of the Lord Chomlie &c.   9 0 0

Jan 15 Payd Raph Leftwich & Rich Weild aprisors for Namptwich hundred for one dayes seruice in assistinge mee to seize & aprise a Cowe wich was for a Heriott due to the Publique by the death of Mr Tho Walthall tenant to Mr Bromlie of Bagington, a delinquent &c   .   ..   00 4 0

1646 April 28 Payd Mr Bradshaw Receuer of the Kings Rents, for the Rent of *a tenth of the water mils of namptwch* wich mils the Publique doth inioye, for three whole yeares 1643-4-5, beinge 5/- pr annm   .   0 15 0

July 25 Payd to John Pratchett a Poore Almes-man by Order &c for the rent of his Almeshouse,*to be used for a Sentry or gard-house for the vse of the Garison   0 2 0

July 25 Payd Widow Hanwaye & Jean Fowses for winnowinge the corne that was pte of the Goodes late of Mr Alexander Walthall Senr [Wistaston Hall] a delinquent   0 7 1

July 25 Payd to Will'm Fowses & John Vaughann labourers for 12 days service &c. in thrashinge the foresayd Corne &c   .   ..   1 0 0
    [Several payments of 5/- for a man with his team, drawing the goods of Mr A. Walthall from Wistaston to Nantwich]

* This must have been Welsh Row Head Almshouse as John Pratchett's name does not occur in the list of Wright's Inmates preserved in the earliest volume of the Treasurers Accounts

	£	s	d

1646 July 24 Payd to John Bramall & Rich Hussey, watchmen, by Order from Colonel
Croxton, the quantity of soe much barley as mounted to the value of £02 06s 08d,
being in pre of their pay due to them for watching prisoners at the Common Prison at
Namptwch   .   ..   2   6   8

Oct 12 Payd to Rogr Butler by Order &c for Executinge the office of the Clarke of
the Marquett [market] in Namptwch   1 18   0

Oct 14 Payd to Tho Bickerton by Order &c for haye that was taken from him for the
vse of the publique, in the time of distresse, & he being a very poore man & not able to
forbeare it 0 12   0

Nov 21 Payd to Margaret Jonson late seruant to Mr Alexandre Walthall Senr a
a delinquent, there dwellinge with him at his daeth [death] for part of a yeares wages .   0 14   0

June 16 Payd to the Pauer [paver] & to other ourkemen [workmen] & labourers, by
Order from the Sequestrators, for the Repayringe of a Comon-waye in namptwch Comonly
called the moncks-layne wich was spoyled by the trope horses when att sundrey times they
were drawen to Exersise, the way beinge unpasable &c   1 10   0

Nantwich continued to be the head-quarters of Sir William Breieton, the great
Parliamentary General for Cheshire, and the adjacent Counties until the end of the War.
After the surrender of the Halls of Crewe, Doddington, and Cholmondeley, there was no
more fighting in the immediate vicinity of the town.   The inhabitants were, however,
alarmed more than once by news of the near approach of Prince Rupert's Army, from
time to time, troops, arms, ammunition, and prisoners were sent to, or conveyed from the
town, at Church, thanksgiving and humiliation days were kept, as occasion required; the
populace were sometimes the eye-witnesses of military executions, and for several days
they were disturbed by a serious riot amongst the town Soldiery.   Particulars relating
to these local matters are told by Malbon as follows —

"On Monday the xxix of January 1643-4, *Thomas Steele* (late badd
Thomas Steele   governor of Beeston Castle) whoe before had Judgem̄t do dye by a Councell
Executed   of warr, was shott in the Tynkers Crofts att Namptwiche, behind the
Churche Leanynge his Backe to the Crosse wall theire (after a very longe confession and
repentance of his Synnes made) By twoe Com'on Soldyers, the one shott him in the
Belly, & the other in his Throate, whoe was presentlie carryed awaye, beinge laid in a
coffyn standinge on the grounde by him, broughte into the Churche Yarde & buryed
ymedyatlie neeare the Rowe of Gravestones on the Northe side of the heighe Chauncell "*

---

* The Rev Henry Newcome in his *Autobiography* (Chet Soc Pub p 95) speaking at large of Steele's "confession,"
says, "At his death he disclaimed all treachery "   He is said to have been the third son of Thomas Steele of Weston, co
Chester, (Ormerod, New Edit Vol III p 98), and the family name is still found in the neighbourhood of Barthomley
His burial is recorded as follows —"1643[-4] Jan 29 Captaine Steele Shott '—*(Nant Bur Reg)*

Interesting particulars relating to the Steele family are given in Hinchliffe's "*Barthomley*," pp 352-3, Earwaker's
"*Local Gleanings Magazine,* pp 322-336 and in Dr Howard's "*Miscellanea Genealogica*"   The marriage of a *Thomas
Steele,* but whether the unfortunate captain or not is uncertain, occurs in Nantwich Par Reg thus —

"1629 Sep. 5 Thomas Steele and Jane ffurnyvall '

Crewe Hall gyven up

"On Mondaye the fyfte of ffebruary 1643[-4], Namptwiche forces havinge beseiged Ciewe Hall, (kepte by the Kinges ptie.) from Thursdaye befoie, thoughe att a farr distance, Began to assaulte the Howse, wch when Captyn ffisher p'ceyved, whoe kept it for the Kinges vse, desyred a ply. [parley], wch was yelded vnto, And then ytt was agreed, That hee & theim theirein shold all p'senthe depte awaye & yeld up the howse, leaving theire Armes behind theim, wch they did, being in nu'ber (wth those wch weire wounded) one hundred & twentie & many of theim came the same daye to Namptwiche, where they were ent[er]teyned   But the Captyn had carried him selfe soe baschie towards the Neighbourhood thereabout that the Countrey people wold have killed him when hee was come furthe had hee not byn p'served by those to whom hee had yelded vp the howse"

Dodington surrendered

"Upon Wednesdaye the vij^th of ffebruaiy 1643[-4], Dodington Hall, beinge alsoe kepte by the Kinges ptie, was alsoe assaulted by Namptw^ch forces, & upon some Shott wth theire greate ordnance, wch they had broughte wth theim, wch the Captyn in the Howse p'ceyving, & knowinge theire was noe hope of any Ayde, lykewyse desyred a plie [parley], wch was condescended vnto, The Agreem^t was that the howse sholde bee deliu'ed vp, & the Souldye^rs & wounded shoulde depte awaye wth fourtie of theire Armes, whereof the greatest pte of theim wth theire Armes came to Namptwiche, where they were ent[er]tayned The nu'ber in all beinge about .   The[y] left behind theim almost twoe hundred Armes, And good store of victualls, powder, matches & Bulletts

Thankesgyvinge & Humiliacon Dayes

"On Tuesdaye the xiij^th of ffebruary 1643[-4], A soleme daye of thankes-gyvinge was held in Namptwiche & att Acton   And vpon Thursdaye after a daye of humyliacon."

A gibbett erected att Namptwiche

"Upon Shrove Tuesdaye, the fyfth of Marche, 1643[-4], A Gibbett was sett vp in Namptwiche, whereupon was executed the same daye, (beinge adiudged by the Councell of warr) one *Browne*, a Com'on Soldye^r, for wilfullye killinge, one *Alfleete** a Comon Soldye^r in the Streete, when hee was drunke, not knowinge what hee had done, when hee was sober, as hee said & confessed on the Ladder"

An Alaram on Namptwiche

"On the xviij^th of Marche 1643[-4], about one a Clocke after Midnight, *Colonell mariowe*, wth his horse, gave an alaram on the Towne, & drave awaye many Cattell wch was the first allarom gyven to the Towne scythens the seige was reased.'†

A fast att Namptwiche

"On Wednesdaye the xxix^th of Marche 1644 was a soleme fast held att Namptwiche, wth prayer & preachinge most of the daye."

Allaroms

"On Wednesday mornynge in Easter weeke 1644, about three a Clocke in the mornynge, An Alarom was beaten vp in the Towne of Namptwiche vpon a Reporte

---

* The Parish Register records the burial of "*Richard Aght, soldier*," on the 4th March, being the day before this military execution He may have been identical with the unfortunate "*Alfleete*"

† Burghall adds, "This Colonel Marrow, who was a great plunderer, took off all my goods, and drove me from my house [at Bunbury] and having a call to preach a^t Haslington, May 1, 1644, I tarried tnere two years, upon thirty-four pounds a year —(*Providence Improved*)

Colonel Marrow, a distinguished royalist died at Chester on the 19th Aug 1644, from wounds received the day before in a skirmish at Sandiway, co Chester —(Malbon MS)

broughte that the Kinges forces [Prince Rupert being at Shrewsbury] weire seene vpon Ravensmoore. But the scoutes Rydinge furthe sawe non, Soe all was p'sentlie quyett. On the seyventh of Maye 1644, Theire was another Allarom aboute twoe a Clocke in the Mornynge (wthout cause) "

Captyn Stanley att Cholm'ley Castle

"Upon Thursdaye the viijth of Maye 1644, *Captyn Cheswys* with a fewe horse, yssued furthe of Towne And neere Cholm'ley Hall Hee tooke fyve men and horse wth theire Armes, and slewe one, wch fyve hee broughte p'soner^s to Namptwiche, And the same daye att Nighte *Captyn Stanley* wth his horse & most of the horse in Towne wth many foote Companyes marched forth to Cholm'ley (Beinge then Garrisoned by the Kinges ptie) & theire gaue them an Allarom & Som'ond [summoned] the Howse But they wthin wold gyve them noe answere, whereuppon they gave three volyes of shott agaynste the Howse But they wthin did shoote very litle. Soe when the[y] sawe the[y] cold not enter the howse, The[y] broughte allonge wth them a hundred Sheepe, some Lambes, and some goods, wch they found in an out howse theire, for they in the howse had all theire horse in the Hall, And soe retorned in the mornynge all backe & saufe to Namptwiche "

*   *   *   *   *   *   *   *   *   *   *   *

Cholm'ley Howse yelded vp

"On Sondaye [7th July 1644] they [i e Nantwich forces]* marched towards Cholm'ley Howse in the Evenynge wth three or foure peeces of Ordnance, & iiij cases of Drakes where the two voluntier Companyes from Namptwiche, wth theire two Captyns, & other of the office^{rs}, *Captyn George Malbon*,† and *Captyn Thomas Malbon*,† gardinge the greate Brasse peece of ordnance did meete them The Mondaye mornynge towards spiinge of daye the[y] had planted theire ordnance (the greatest of them) wthin Pistoll Shott of the Howse And about three or foure of the Clocke in the mornynge, after they had Som'ond the Howse, The[y] playd vpon ytt wth theire ordnance & shott ytt many tymes throwe, (being a tymber howse) They in the Howse, wth theire Musketts, did shoot very fast att them & about fyve a Clocke in the mornynge the[y] killed one *Rauffe Mylton*, a seriante vnder maior Croxton But the p'liam^t forces playinge on the howse wth theire ordnance & smale shott contynualhe, did beate them furthe of the Howse to theire workes, where they did shoote & maynteyne the servys (beinge but a fewe in nu'ber) very bravelie, & killed *maior Pynkney*, a braue com'ander, and about foure or fyve more‡ of the p'liam^t side. But the same daye, beinge the eighte of Julye 1644, they att the Howse, p'ceyvinge they weire not able to stand out, about on[e] a Clocke in thafter noone, havinge a fierce assaulte made vpon them, called for Quarter, wch was Graunted, and *Captyn Horton* (Captyn of the Howse) lett downe

---

* Under Basil Fielding, Earl of Denbigh, Sir Thos Middleton, Col George Booth, and Col Maynwaring

† Burghall gives these names as *Malton* (*Brit Mus MS* and Poole's printed version of Burghall's *Diary*) but they were in reality, the two sons of *Thomas Malbon*, the author of the Civil War Account, who mentions that they also successfully attacked *Dirtwich*, in this county, on the 12th Sept 1644 *George Malbon* had a Major s Commission from the Council of State in 1650 and *Thomas Malbon* occurs as Captain of a Cheshire troop in the same year

‡ According to the Parish Register, eight soldiers were buried at Nantwich on the 9th July, 1644, amongst them are mentioned *Major Pinkey*, and *Serjeant Milton* and probably the others were slain at Cholmondeley and brought to Nantwich for interment Their names are —"*Richard Boand*, soldier, *Thomas Brassell*, sergant *Robert Hool* soldier *William Davenport*, soldier, *John ffearnough*, soldier, *Raphe Milton*, Sergant, *Raphe Meare*, soldier, *Eswell Pinkey*, Mager "

the drawe Bridge , opened the Gates; and the Lord of Denbigh, Colonell Bouthe, & the reste of theire officers, & some of theire Soldye^{rs} entred the Howse, wheie they tooke Captyn Horton, & the reste in the Howse p^rsoners, beinge in nu'bei about three score and sixe, wth all theire Armes & p'vision, leavinge the goods in the Howse a praye for the Soldye^{rs}, whoe pillaged the same   And then leavinge *Captyn Lownes* wth his Soldyers in the Howse, they all marched wth theire prysoners, Ordnance, & Carryages to Nampt-wiche that Nighte   Non in the howse of the Kinges side was either slayn or hurte. The nexte daye afterwards, beinge Tuesdaye, att Namptwiche was kepte a soleme daye of thankesgyvinge.''

Armes sente to
Namptwiche "On Saturdaye the xxth of July 1644 Colonell Breieton did send fyve hundred and fyftie Armes to Namptwiche. And a litle afterwards retorned thether himselfe.''

Parker
executed "Upon Saturdaye, the xth of August 1644, one *Parker*, a troop[er] vnder Sr *Thomas mydleton*, was adiudged to dye by a Councell of warr in Nampt-wiche, for the wilfull kyllinge m^r *Randull Smythe* & on[e] . .   . *Browne* in haslington , & wounded many othe^{rs}, beinge either madd or drunke And on Tuesdaye nexte followinge he was executed att Namptwiche; and afterwards hanged in cheynes on Haslington Heath, neere vnto the place where hee com'itted the murthers.''

Tarvyn iiade
a Garrison
Markett Towne "On ffryday the xxxth of August 1644, All the forces att Namptwich, excepte maior Croxtons & the Towne companyes, marched furthe to Middlewiche, where the[y] quartred that Nighte, And the nexte daye to Northwiche, & greate Budworthe, & then to *Tarvyn*, wch the[y] fortefied wth stronge workes, made ytt a Markett Towne, & therein putt a Garrison, And anothei garrison att *Huxley Hall*, & another att *Olton Hall* neei litle Budworthe ''

Executions att
Namptwich "On Mondaye the xxiij of September Colonell Breieton, wth many of his company retorned backe [after taking Montgomery] to Namptwiche ''
* * * * * * * "On the xxvj of September 1644 Theire weire foure Soldye^{rs} hanged att Namptwiche, beinge soe adiudged by the Councell of Warr, for Runnynge from theire Cullo^{rs} [colours] to the Enymy, wch weire taken att Mountgom'ry, viz *Will'm Walley, Richaid Hollenworth, Will'm. Strongitharm*, and *Will'm. Poole* ''

Captyi George
Becke't dyed "On Sondaye the xvijth of Novembei 1644 *Captyn Geoige Beckett*, beinge wounded twoe monthes befoie att Shocklage, dyed att Namptwiche   And was seemlye buryed the nexte daye in the Heighe Chauncell, neere the Communyon Table ''*

* This Burial is not recorded in the Registers but there was formerly "*a stone in the middle of the Chancell* '' inscribed "*Captaine George Beckei, son of George B of Soo* [? Sound] *yeoman, bivd Nov* 18, 1644 ' – (*Harl MSS* 2151)

Twoe Irishe hanged

"On ffrydaye, the xvij^th of January 1644[-5] Twoe native Irishe borne, viz *Derby Covan & Mortoughe Colane*, wch weire taken p^rsoner^s att Andforde [Aldford] when Colonell Brookes troupes weire some of theim taken in theire quarter^s by theim of Chester, were tryed by the Councell of Warr, & hanged att Namptwiche accordinge to an ordinance of Parliam^t "

A daye of Thankesgyvinge

"On Thursday the xviij of January 1644[-5], There was held att Namptwiche A Solem daye of thankesgyvinge for deliu'inge the Towne when ytt was beseiged & assaulted, that tyme twelve monthes, & for all other of Gods greate blessings, p^rservacons & favours towards the said Towne.* The same daye att Nighte Reporte came to the Towne that the Kinges ptie, beinge foure hundred horse wth muskettier^s behind theim weire come to Whitchurche. Whereupon the Townesmen & Soldiers weire all com'anded to stande vpon theire Garde, for p^reservacon of the Towne of Namptwiche."

Hawkyns shott att Namptwiche

"On ffrydaye, the xxiiij^th of January 1644[-5], Lieftent Hawkyns, als. *Huggyn*, was adiudged by the Councell of Warr to Dye for that hee was an Irishe man, had taken the Covenante, p'ved for the p'liamt and afterwards went to the Kinges ptie, he was shott at the Chauncell ende in Namptwiche "

Persons in Shrowesbury broughte to Namptwiche

"On Saturday the first of Marche 1644[-5] *Baronett Lea*, Sr *Richard Lowsen*, Sr *John Weild* sen^r & Junr, Doctor *Lewyn*, Doctor *ffowler*, Doctor *Arnewaye*, Herbert *Vaughan*, Edward *Kynnaston*, ffrancis *Sandford*,† ffrancis *Thomas*, & Thomas *Owen* esqrs, Edward *Owen* Lieuten^t Colonell, Captyn *Stanley*, ffrancis *Smythe*, gents, Thomas *Johnes*, Esq, Captyn *Ranesford*, Alderman *Gibbons*, Captyn *Yonge* & Sr Thomas *Whitmore* weire sente to Namptwiche p^rsoner^s from Shrowesbury And vpon the viij^th of Marche 1644[-5] weire sente to Namptwiche after theim, p^rsoner^s, Captyn *Lucas*, Maior *Ranger*, Captyn *Cressye*, Captyn *Harrison*, m^r *Tunner*, Captyn *Betts*, Sr *John Peshall*, Sr *Nicolas Byron*, Captyn Edward *Leighton*, Captyn *Talbott*, Captyn *Pontesbury Owen*, m^r *Spurstowe*, Lieftent Thomas *Owen*, m^r *Robte Sandford*, m^r *Trevyns*, Thomas *Betton*, maior *Littleton*, and m^r Richard *Otley*, All in nu'ber xxxviij."

Prisoners removed

"On Saturdaye the xv^th of Marche 1644[-5], some of theise p^rsoner^s weire removed from Namptwiche to Manchester, And the nexte day after (beinge Sondaye) some of theim more weire removed to Eccleshall Castle "

---

* Partridge says, (Hist Nantwich, 1774, p 74) "In commemoration of the raising of the siege, which [happened on St Paul's Day [25 Jan] 1643-4, upon every anniversary of it, *till of late*, the inhabitants wore sprigs of *Holly* in their hats in token of victory and the day itself upon that account was called *Holly-Holy-Day* "

† *Francis Sandford*, brother to Capt Thomas Sandford who had been slain on the 18th Jan 1644, (p 164), was a prisoner on parole at Nantwich in May, 1645, when Sir William Brereton granted him leave of absence for ten days to visit his native home at Sandford His "*pass*" has recently been printed in the "*Cheshire Sheaf*," No, 719, from the original document still preserved at Sandford, as follows —

' These are to desire and require all those whome it may concerne to suffer the bearer hereof, *Mr ffrauncis Sandford*, to pass thence scu'all Scouts and Courts of Guard from this Garrison of Namptwich to Sandford in Shropshire, and back againe w^thin ten daies after the date hereof

Given under my hand at Namptwich, 12th of May, 1645

WILL BRERETON '

To all officers and souldiers in service for Kinge and Parliamt "

[Countersigned on back]   " John Gobbett
                           Will Alexander "

Irishmen   "On Wednesday, the xj^th^ of June 1645, Many of the p^r^soners sente
hanged   from Tarvyn, about fourteene or fyfteene in nu'ber, weire tryed att Namptwich by the Councell of warr, whereof three of theim weire adiudged to Dye, being
Native Irishe; And the same day in the afternoone they weire all three hanged, (By the
ordinance of p'liam^t^)"

Colonell Brereton   "On ffryday the xiij^th^ of June 1645 Colonell Brereton wente from
going to the   Namptwiche towards London, beinge called vp to the p'liam^t^, & beinge
p'liamt   one of the Knights for Cheshire,* But stayinge a whyle in Stafford towne,
he sente vp *Captyn Stones*, (then Govenor of Stafford) wth but a smale Troope of horse,
whoe in his Journey mett wth some of the Kinges forces & fallinge on theim tooke fyfteen
of theim p^r^sone^rs^ & sixe hundred poundes in money (some reporte viij hundred poundes "

Three executed   On Saturday xxj^st^ of June 1645 Three Native Irishe weire executed att
Namptwiche "

     "You heard before howe Beeston Castle was unwyslye deliu'ed vp to Captyn Sandford
for the Kinges vse by Captyn Steele then Governor thereof for the p'liam^t^, vpon or about
Beeston Castle   the xiij^th^ of December 1643, wch was held by the Kinges ptie vntill
deliu ed   Sonday the xv^th^ of November 1645, And then *Captyn Vallatt*, Governor
thereof, after almost a twelve monthes seige, wth aboute fyftye sixe in his Company,
beinge broughte into greate wante of victuals, havinge not any food in the Castle (but
onelie water), not for to haue maynteyned theim twoe dayes, & seeinge the same blockt
vp, and Chester aloee beinge w^th^out hope to bee releeved, vpon a plye [parley] w^th^
Colonell Brereton, & an agreem^t^ betwixte theim was concluded, That they wth all theire
Armes, Colo^rs^ flyinge, Drumes beatinge, & twoe Carte loades of goods, shold instantlie
depte. awaye, & deliu'[er] vp the Castle to the said Colonell Brereton, wch was the same
daye p formed And when a Considerable force was putt into the Castle by the said
Colonell, The said *vallatt* wth his Soldiers havinge a Convaye w^h^ theim was broughte
vnto Denbighe, whether hee had a desyre to goe But twentie of *vallants* [sic] Soldiers,
when they weire come furthe of the Castle, Laide downe theire Armes, & eu'y of theim
desyred that they might have lycence to goe to theire homes, wch was graunted Theire
was neither meate, Ale, nor Beere, found in the Castle, save onelie a peece of a Turkey
pye, Twoe Bisketts, a lyve Peacock & a peahen "

Beeston Castle   "Chester beinge deliu'ed vp aboute the third of ffebruary 1645[-6],
defaced   presentlie afterwards command was gyven & warrants sente to the seu'all
p'ishes of Bunbury, Tarporley, Wrenbury, & Acton, & some other places
& Townshipps, neerest adioyning ffor the pullinge downe, and vtter defacinge of Beeston
Castle, wch before Whitsunweeke 1646 was p'formed Onelie the Gatehowse in the lower
warde, & pte of some Towers in the heigher warde, weire lefte standinge, wch scythens

---

* This was the Long Parliament that sat from 3rd Nov 1640, to 20th April, 1653 Sir William Brereton, first
Baronet of Handforth co Chester, also sat in two other Parliaments during the reign of Charles I, viz in the
Parliamt 17th March, 1627-8, to 10th March 1628-9 (3 Car I) and that of 13th April 1640 to 6th May 1640 (16 Car I)
He was created a Baronet by Charles I on the 10th March, 1626-7 at the age of 22, his "*Travels into Holland and the
seventeen provinces* in 1634, and "*through Scotland & Ireland*' in 1635, have been published by the Chetham Soc He
received grants of money and lands for his services to the Parliament, including the archiepiscopal palace of Croydon,
where he occasionally resided and where, on the 7th April, 1661, he died For a biographical account of Sir William
Brereton, see Earwaker's "*Last Cheshire*," vol I, pp 255-9

are pulled downe & utterlie defaced   This Castle was buylded, as appeareth by Auncyent Manuscripts in *A° dni* 1220, by Earle Randull, the third Earle of Chester "

                            " Upon Tuesdaye the xiiijth of July 1646 A great Mutynye was made in Namptwiche by some of the Rude & unseemlie sorte of the Towne Souldyers to the nu'ber of iij hundred or thereabouts, wthout either com'and or Ayde of theire Captyns or head officers, beinge all in Aimes & forcinge many honest Townesmen to Joyn wth theim, did by vyolence drawe some of the Comittee of Sequestracons for Namptwiche hundred (beinge in peaceable man r executing theire office for the State) furthe of the office where all theire Books & records weire, & fetched other some of theim (and one of the Collectors) furthe of seuall howses, wheire they weire att Dynner, And putt them all in the Com'on Pryson in Namptwiche amongst Cavaliers, Theeves, & horse stealers (wch weire then theire) havinge byn the Com on prson from the firste makinge the Towne a garrison for thowsands of Lothesome, Lowsy, wounded & maymed Souldyers, wheire many of theim had Dyed, & noe outlett for theim to doe theire needs In but onelie the prson howse, wca was soe filthie & stinkinge that ytt was Gods mercy that they cold endure ytt   Neither wold they allowe them to haue either meate or Drinke, nor quarter in any other howse or place, althoughe ytt was desyred bothe by the heighe Sherryff of the Countie, & many of the Deputie Lieftents & Justices of the Peace beinge then in Towne (sittinge then qter [Quarter] Sessions). But not able to medle wth suche a Rude multitude on the sudden vnlesse they should haue leased the Countrey, or called In the Trayned bands, wch wolde haue bredd a greater mischeefe Neither wolde they willinglie haue allowed theim stooles or quyssions [cushions] to reste on But onelie the flower [floor] or baie bordes for the space of twoe dayes and a halfe & twoe Nights, abusing theim in wordes, callinge theim Rounde headed Rouges [rogues], abusing theire wyves, childien & servants by the names of whores, & all evell wordes the[y] colde devyse, not suffring them to bring theim any sustenaunce, but what was pivatlie convayed vnto them back wayes, throwe holes of the Prysen, neither wolde they suffer them to goe furthe for doinge of theire needs duringe the whole space of ffyftie foure howers (Layinge nothinge to theire charge) but alledged that theire wages was pte. vnpaid Althoughe they knewe that the same Com'ittee never paid them, nor noe other Souldyers any; neither had they any wariant to pay theim any ffor they receyved theire paye alwayes from the Treasurer, By warrant from the Deputie Lieftents But as some of theim said, They wolde Beate Jacke for Gill, yett they wold not dehu[er] theim furthe, vntill Colonell Lothian & some other gents had vndertaken for theire paye The honble lower Howse of Com'ons beinge made acquynted wth that greate abuse vsed vnto the said Com ittee, did appoynte a Com'ittee to examen the buysiness, And sente downe orders to the Deputie Lieftents of the Countie of Chester, Both to examen witnesses and certefie But they did neither by reason they weire eithei in some faulte for not beinge more caiefull to see the Souldyers paid, or els beinge much tro'bled wth the Busines of the Countrey.   But the said Com ittee had never any satisfac'on for the same."

                       " On the xvth day of January 1646[-7] Namptwiche Towne was disgarrisoned, & all the paye from Captyns, officers & Soldyers taken from theim: & they all discharged by the Deputie Lieftents of Cheshire by order from the p'liamt, wch tooke effecte in ffebiuary nexte after "

With this extract from Thomas Malbon's very quaint and interesting MS, the Civil War troubles, of which Nantwich had had a full share, may be said to end Some time after, a complete list of all the "*Delinquents*" in Nantwich Hundred was drawn up, stating how and when certain persons had already been discharged from sequestration, and showing why others were still under arrest This official list consisting of one hundred and two names signed by three sequestrators, appears to have been very carefully made out It is contained in *Harl MSS* 2128, and is here printed in full, as follows —

' *A true & p'ticular note of all the delinquents sequestered wch have any Lands or estate in Namptw^ch hundred either lying in the hundred or furthe of the hundred & also what orders wee haue receyved wth the dates thereof for suspending of theire Sequestrac'ons and whoe standeth still under Sequestrac'on & lykewise whoe are discharged from Sequestrac on & p'doned whose estate Reall or P'sonall are not worthe two hundred pounds wch have taken the Negative oathe & Covenant accordinge to the Resolve of the 8th of December 1646, As followeth und'* "

JOHN EARLE RYVERS,* wee have not as yett, any order concernynge him

RODERT VISCOUNT CHOLM[ONDE]LEY (a) By order from Goldsmyths Hall Dat the 3 of Decemb 1646 his sequestracon ys suspended & his Rente ordered him from the xth of Sept before upon Oxford Articles &c

ROBERT VISCOUNT KILMOREY (b) By order from Goldsmyths Hall of the 22 April 1647, his Sequestrac'on was suspended & upon Oxford articles to receyve his Rents from the xij of August before

SR THOMAS WILBRAHAM [of Woodhey] BARONET (c) was sequestered in 1644, & by order from Goldsmyths Hall dat 20 Junii 1646 his sequestrac'on suspended

SR THOMAS ASTON, BARONETT, An order from the honble Com'ttee of Lords & Com'ons for the deposit-inge of the Rents in the tents [tenants] hands, dat 18 Sept 1646 An other order of 16 of Dec 1646 for taking the Sequestrac'ons of[f] &c (d)

SR THOMAS SMYTH, [of Hatherton] KNIGHT,(e) & THO SMYTH ESQ his sonne & heire sequestered in Chester By order from Goldsmyths Hall of 26 January 1645[-7] theire sequestrac'ons were suspended

SR THOMAS DELVES (f) [of Doddington] *Knight* & *Baronett* By order from Goldsmyths hall dat Oct 20 1646, his sequestrac'on was suspended

SR HUGH CALVELEY,(g) Knight, wee have receyved noe order concernynge him

ALEXANDER WALTHALL,(h) [of Wistaston] senr Ar [Esq] dead & the lands descended to his sonne, were - by convayaunce & adidged [? adjudged] good by Mr Bradshaw under his hand dat 12 Marie 1646, & confirmed by Sr Willm Brereton, Mr Henry Brooke & Mr John Leighe under theire hands.

JAMES POOLE [? of Poole Hall, Wirrall] Ar^r [Esq], a papist
THOMAS POOLE, gen [t], a papist

---

* The amounts of fines here given in the notes are taken from "*A Catalogue of the Lords, Knights and Gentlemen, that Compounded for their Estates* Printed for Thomas Dring 1655 London and Chester Re-printed by Roger Adams 1733" Earl Rivers, who was a County Magistrate, was driven from the Bench by order of Parliament on 1st Oct 1646, and fined £1 110 He died 10th Oct 1654, at Frodsham Castle

(a) Fined £7,742

(b) Fined £2,306 with £120 per ann settled on the Ministry

(c) Fined £2,500 (f) Fined £1,484 10s (g) Fined £1,455

(d) Sir Thos Aston had died on 24th March, 1645 6

(e) Fined £2,150, with £110 per ann settled

(h) Fined £164 He died in Feb 1645-6

DOROTHY POOLE, vid [widow], a papist

JOHN MYNSHULL(*i*) [of Vale Royal] Esqr , By order from Goldsmyths Hall of the 21 Nov 1646, his sequestrac'on was suspended

THOMAS MYNSHULL [? of Erdswick] Esqr , hee remayneth still under sequestrac'on   but the trustees have the lands ordered theire by an order from the honble Com'ittee of Lords and Com'ons, dat xiiij July 1647

WILL[IA]M HASSALL [of Hassall] Esq deceased   But his mother & his wyfe have all his lands by Convey-aunce for theire lyves made long scythens [since]

RICHARD GRYFFYN(*j*) [of Bartherton] Esq   hath Compounded, but his order ys not come downe as yett, But onelie an order from Goldsmyths Hall dat 9 Feb 1647 not to lett his lands   But the 4th of March 1647[-8] wee did receyve another from Goldsmyths Hall for suspendinge of his ffathers sequestrac'on

HUGH WILBRAHAM(*k*) [of Draketon] Esqr   An order from Goldsmiths Hall dat x Nov 1646 for depositing his Rents in the tents [tenants] hands from the first of Oct last upon Oxford articles &c   And another order dat 25 ffeb 1646[-7] for suspending his sequestrac'on

RICHARD GREENE(*l*) [? of St. Martins in the Fields] Esq , noe order concernynge him

JONATHAN WOODNOTH(*m*) [of Shavington] Esq , noe order concernynge him

PEERS DOD, gent ,(*n*) noe order concernynge him

RICHARD WICKSTEED(*o*) [of Nantwich] Junr , his sequestrac'on suspended by order from Goldsmyths Hall, dat 15 Aug 1646

JOHN WILSON(*p*) [of Chester] noe orders concernynge him

Parson [THOMAS] FOWLER,(*q*) of Whitchurch, [Salop]   noe order &c

Parson [FRANCIS] ROWLEY of Coppenhall , noe order &c

THOMAS POOLE a papist , noe order &c

THOMAS WICKSTEAD,(*r*) [of Hampton, Cheshire, yeoman], a papist , noe order &c

GEORGE BICKERTON(*s*) [of Horse Hall, Cheshire], noe order &c

GEORGE PARSON, a papist , nothinge in oure hundred

THOMAS BREYNE [? of Acton parish], a papist noe order &c

WILLIAM HINTON (*t*) [of Burton, Cheshire, gent], noe order &c

ROBERT GRYFFYTH, discharged beinge under the value of CCli [£200]

HENRY GRYFFYTH, under the value of CCli [£200]

MR [WILLIAM] BROMLEY of Baginton(*u*) [Warwickshire] sequestered att Coventree   An order from Goldsmyths Hall dat 25 Jan 1646[-7] for suspending of his Sequestrac'on

MR [THOMAS] BROMLEY(*v*) of Hampton post, [Cheshire], sequestered in Broxton Hundred & suspended by order from Goldsmyths Hall dat 20 Aug 1646

MR [RALPH] SNEYDE(*w*) of Keele [Staff Esq], noe order concernynge him

---

(*i*) Fined £740

(*j*) Fined £50

(*k*) Fined £362

(*l*) Fined £463 10s

(*m*) Fined £400

(*n*) His household goods sold at Nantwich for £24 10s 2d   Inventory in Harl MSS 2166

(*o*) Fined £210

(*p*) Fined £142 10s

(*q*) Fined £130

(*r*) Fined £56

(*s*) Fined £55 10s

(*t*) Fined £90

(*u*) Fined £424

(*v*) Fined £320

(*w*) Fined £1000, with £100 per ann settled on the Ministry

MR LAWTON[x] of Lawton, sequestrac'on suspended by order from Goldsmyths Hall, Dat Sept 1646

MR RANDULL ECERTON,[y] of Betley, [Staff] noe order &c

WILLIAM LORD BRERETON[z] [of Brereton] Rents deposited in his tents [tenants] hands by order from
    G H dat, 19 June 1647

ROBERT EICCCKE[a] [of Acton, nr Nantwich] By order from G H dat 16 Maii 1646, his sequestrac'on
    suspended

THOMAS HALM[AR]AF , paup[er], under the value &c.

JOHN PAGE , noe order concernynge him   (being a paupr) but discharged beinge under the value of CCli

RANDULL GRYFFYTH , noe order concernynge him

CAPT RICHARD WALTHALL[b] [of Wistaston] noe order &c

JOHN POWNALL noe order &c

MR [JOHN] SARINGE[c] mynister, [of Nantwich] noe order &c

JOHN BARNETT , noe order &c

HENRY VERNON[d] [of Haslington] Esq was sequestered (to our remembrance) about March 1644 &
    suspended at G H by order of the 9th of December 1645

WILLIAM ALLEN[e] [of Baddiley, Cheshire] gent , was sequestered in Ao   & by order fiom G H date
    2 Junii 1646 sequestracon suspended

MRS COTTON vid [widow of Thomas Cotton Esq of Combermere, being Elizabeth dau of Sir George
    Calveley, Kt] discharged by order fiom the Com'ittee of Lords & Com'ons dated 26 June 1646, &
    Restituc'on to bee made her

THOMAS MAISTERSON[f] [of Nantwich] Esq , was sequestered in 1644, hath made his composic'on &
    sente up his money & 4 March last hee did shew vs an order for suspending his sequestrac'on

RAUFFE CARDIFF noe order &c

WILLIAM IRISH , noe order &c

ROBERT CROSBIE , discharged, being under the value of CCli

JOHN FYTHIAN, paupr under the value of CCli

EDWARD HASSALL ,[g] fledd & gonne , & whether lyvinge or dead wee knowe not, but hathe very litle to
    mayntayne all his children

RAUFE HORTON[h] [of Coole Pilate] gent   His sequestrac'on suspended by order from G H dat xxvj
    Julii 1646

ROBERT HORTON[i] [of Coole Pilate] gent fledd & gonne beinge urged to take the Negative othe but
    hathe nothinge that wee knowe of

WILLIAM LEVERSAGE [of Wybunbury Parish] Esq   his sequestrac'on suspended by order from G H dat
    14 Aug 1646

CAPTYN JOHNES[j] noe order &c

THOMAS WEEVER p'[ar]doned beinge vnder the value of CCli

CHARLES WALLEY[k] [of Chester] gent , his sequestrac'on suspended by order from Goldsmyths Hall dat
    24 Julii 1646

(x) Fined £630
(y) Fined £1,511
(z) Fined £1 738 18s
(a) Fined £18
(b) Grandson of Alexander Walthall, senr before
mentioned   Perhaps he was not fined, as the family
goods had been sold, and his father s purse drained

(c) Mr Saring's goods sold, see p 173
(d) Fined £500
(e) Fined £90
(f) Fined [?] £630

(g) According to Harl MSS 2166, his household goods sold at Nantwich for £28 14s 5d   On another page a note
states that the goods were delivered to Thos Steele of Leighton " to and for the keeping of Edward Hassalls three litle
children," on account of the death of their mother at the same time as the goods were seized

(h) Fined £128   (i) Fined £10   (j) ? whether the same as "John Jones of Namptwich, gent , who was
fined "£25"   (k) Fined £268 10s

WILLIAM BV[R]OM , under the value p'dce [aforesaid]

THOMAS CALCOTT(*l*) gent , his sequestrac'on suspended by order of the Com'ittee of Lords & Com'ons, dat 14 July 1647

JOHN PATRICKE, under the value p'dce

MR ROBERT WEEVER dead & his wyfe hath all his lands in Joynture by good convayaunce

EDWARD DODD(*m*) [of Edge] Esq sequestered in Broxton hundred & a moietie of the Lady Nortons lands compounded for by his sonne and another part for his daughter

THOMAS WARBURTON, dead & his wyfe pardoned beinge under the value &c

GEORGE COTTON(*n*) of [Combermere] Esq sequestered in Ao 1644 suspended by order from G H dat. 6 March 1645[-6]

JOHN BICKERION, p[ar]doned, under the value &c

HALTON WEAVER, p[ar]doned &c

THOMAS HOLLAND, pauper, p[ar]doned &c

JOHN SHERSHAWE, paupr, pardoned &c

BOBERT LATHOME , noe order &c

MR KELSALL, viccar of Audley , noe order , nor any lands in our hundred

MR. JOHN KELSALL(*o*) mynister, noe order nor any lands in our hundred

MR [RANDLE] SILLITOE(*p*) mynister [of Church Lawton], noe order nor any lands in our hundred

THOMAS ROWLEY, nothing in our hundred

WILLIAM KELSALL, voted the 8th March 1644[-5] noe lands in our hundred

CHRISTOPHER HOLFORD, about the same tyme, vnder the value pdce

MR [LAWRENCE] NEWTON mynister [of Church Minshull] about the same tyme, under value

RANDULL MYNSHULL, about the same tyme, under value pdce

THOMAS WALLES, about the same tyme noe order &c

THOMAS HILDITCH, about the same tyme noe order &c

THOMAS SIDWAY, 27 March 1645 , & taken of[f] by order from G H dated 27 March 1646

RANDULL CHURCH [? of Nantwich] gent 12 Junii 1645 nothing in our hundred.

JOHN MALKYN, 19 July 1645, noe order , but a poore man & lyveth by Alsellinge [Ale-selling]

RANDLE HALLM[AR]KT 7 Oct 1645 a poore alseller p'doned being under &c

RICHARD DUNNINGE , the same day , noe order but lyveth by Aleselling

THOMAS DAVIS , 4 Nov 1645 noe order &c

MR RICHARD WILSON,(*g*) mynister　　　　　　27 Jan 1645[-6] noe order &c

MR JOHN BRESSIE ,(*r*) 19 Maii 1646 , dead & his meanes in our hundred belongeth to his mother

JANE WAGGE vid [widow] 5 of Sept 1646, p'doned being under value

RICHARD HEATH sequestered in Broxton Hundred, noe order &c

CHARLES WICKSTEED 20th Aug 1647 hath nothinge

RICHARD WILKES *Juni* , 7th October 1647 noe order

JOHN NORRIS(*s*) sen'' of Bolton was sequestered att Manchester, the 27 March 1645 , whoe had some monie oweinge him in Namptwiche wch ys receyved & accompted for

(*l*) ? whether the same as John Caldecott, of Bickley Gent (Cheshire) who was fined £9

(*m*) Fined £93 6s 8d

(*n*) Fined £666 13s d4

(*o*) ? whether the same as John Kelsall of Trafford, gent , who was fined £236

(*p*) Fined £8 10s

(*q*) ? whether Richard Wilson of Chester, gent , who was fined £22

(*r*) Bressie or Brassey of Willaston

(*s*) Fined £50

MR THOMAS CHOLM'[ONDELEY](t) beinge sequestered in   . [Broxton] hundred haveing some small Rents in oure hundred did bring vs an order from Goldsmyths Hall dated quinto Nov 1646, for depositing the Rents in ye tents [tenants] hands & from the xth of Sept last havinge the benefitt of Oxford Articles & his Order for suspendinge of his Sequestrac'on ys dat 7 Decem 1646

SR JOHN PE[R]SHALL [of Checkley] *Bart* was discharged from his Sequestrac'on by the Com'ittee of the Lords & Com'ons by Order dat 3 March 1646[-7] His grandfather(u) being Sequestered by the Com'ittee of Stafford

MR THO DOD [of Nantwich] order from G H dat x Oct 1645, for allowinge him halfe of the Lady Nortons lands

MR BOVELL order from G H dat 2 Junii 1646 for suspending of his Sequestrac'on

MR STANLEY BURROWES(v) [of Bickley] his order from G H dated 18 Sept 1646 do

MR JOHN KING(w) [of Cholmondeley] gent Order from G H dated 7 Dec 1646, for the suspendinge of his Sequestrac'on "

[Signed by three Sequestrators] "THOMAS HARWAR
"ROBERT WILKES
"THOMAS MALBONE "

Resuming the local events in the Malbon MS —

A greate ffyer in Namptwiche

"The xxij of Marche 1646[-7] beinge Mondaye, a litle after Nyne a Clock in the Nighte, theire happened a greate and terrible fyer in Nampt- wiche, throwe the Negligence of the Ostler in Swan Stable, wth a Candle, wch in three howers did consume & burne a greate p[ar]te of the same Stable, The Blacke Lyon Stable, & pte of the Lambe Stable, beinge all neire togeither, wth muche of the Haye, Strawe, & materialls therein, togeither wth pte of the Swan Howse, and pte of *Will'm Pratchetts* Kitchen, & pte of some other buyldinges, Beside many thatched howses neerest adioyninge weire vncovered, as vidowe *Arcalls* Kitchen, *Henrye Hoyase* [?] howse, beinge newly thatched, and pte. of *mr Walthalls* horse Mylne, To the greate losse and damage of the Owners But ytt pleased God, there was but smale wynde, & good helpe by reason of many Soldiers quartred in the Towne that Nighte, wch tooke greate paynes, or else the fyer begynnynge in the very harte of the towne, & water scarce, the whole Towne had byn in greate danger of burnynge "

Another ffyer att Namptwiche

"The xiij of August 1647, Another greate ffyer, beinge in the Welsh Roe in Namptwiche, on the outside of the dwellinge howse of widowe *Bebbington*, beinge a thatched howse, betwixte xj & xij of the Clocke in the daye, wch hapened by Shootinge att a Crowe on the said howse, wth a Birdinge peece, Kyndinge* in the Thatche, burned exceedinglie, & fyred *Michell Davenports* howse, beinge nexte adioynynge, wch howses, by reason of a greate helpe weire quicklie uncovered, & bothe had harme by the fyer, but Davenports howse had the greater harme, and also Davenports

(t) Fined £2 10s,

(u) The grandfather probably being Sir William Pershall, *Recusant*, [i e papist] who was fined £604 15s

(v) Fined £298 3s

(w) Fined £50

* "*Kinding*," i e lighting, or igniting, a word still commonly used

fyred *John Prees* howse, beinge nexte adioyninge, wch spoyled a greate pte. of one Baye,* and Began to enter on *Reginald Kynseyes* howse, But ytt pleased God, that the same hap'ninge in the Daye and the Towne reased, & greate helpe came, or els the whole streete, especiallie that side, had byn burned. And about a moneth before All the roofe of a Wichehouse of *m^r wilbrams* & *Dorothy Brown* was burned as they weire walinge & makeinge Salte, wch yf ytt had happ'ned in the Nighte might haue] endangered a great pte. of the Towne "

Plague att Wistaston   " The Plague began in Wistaston, beinge a litle p'ishe of one Towne-ship, not twoe myles from Namptwiche, a litle after midsom^r 1647 & conty'ued about Nyne weekes, in wch space theire dyed xxvj p'sons.† The same began in the howse of widowe *Scott*, a Bleacher of Clothes "‡

Malbon, describing the overthrow of the Scotch Army at Preston on the 17th Aug. 1648, by General Cromwell, says —

" Theire weire broughte p^rsoner^s to Namptwiche, p'sons of accompt, viz. *Earle Traquerne* [Traquaire], *Lord Cornegy*, *Lord Lunton*, *Lord Ramsay*, *Si James Lasly* [Leslie], *Sr Nicholas marsmath*, four maiors, twelve Captyns, eleaven Lieftent^s, three Ensigns, three Cornetts, one quarter^mr, fyve ministers, fyfteene gent. of quallitie, & aboute one thowsand Com'on Soldier^s They were almost all of them a fortnighte in Towne, The greate men & better sorte of them weire well quartered in Innes, & other sufficient howses, & the Com'on Soldye^rs weire kepte in the Churche '

Prisoners Removed   " On Tuesday the fyfte of September 1648 the Noblemen weire removed to Warwick Castle, But the weeke before all the Com'on sorte in the Churche, weire sent abroad to seu'all Townshipps in the Countrey, wch vsed to sett furthe the Trayned bannds,§ eu'y towneshipp had double the p^rsoner^s to quarter to the nu'ber of the trayned bands The Mynisters, Captyns, and other officers quartered in the Towne for a long tyme afterwards."

" Kinge Charles Behedded neere the Banquettinge House att Whitehall, London, on Tuesday the xxx^th of January 1648 " [-9].

After the great tragedy was enacted which astounded the whole nation, and which is thus simply mentioned, without note or comment in the Malbon MS, Parliament nomi-nated an executive of extreme members, thirty-eight in number, to administer the affairs of the government, and everyone was required " to be true and faithful to the *Commonwealth* as then established without a King or House of Lords." Great political changes brought about the " Reign of Terror," when the country was divided into militaiy governments,

* " *Bay* " an architectural term applied to houses, it appears to have meant the sections into which they were divided by the principal beams supporting the gables The expression is used in the memorandum relating to the Great Fire by the Parish Clerk (see p 104) Farmers still speak of a *hay-bay*, or *corn-bay*, meaning that *part* of the out-build-ings, where hay or corn is stored

† No burials are recorded at Wistaston in this year, the parish register there having been very irregularly kept from 1646 to 1652

‡ *Bleaching* and *Dyeing* was a trade carried on at Wistaston until not many years ago The *Dye-house* beside the stream in the valley near the Hall, was occupied for several generations by the family of *Boote*

§ In the 17th century the only standing army recognized by law was the rustic soldiery raised in every town and village, known as the *Trainbands*, or the *Militia*, which met for drill once a month, was officered by a local gentleman, and was called up once a year for drill and inspection at some pre-arranged meeting place for the surrounding district each with a major-general at its head, who exercised arbitrary power, arrested suspected royalists, and condemned many to death for treason against the Commonwealth, and among the rest a townsman named *John Sare*, as will be noticed presently

Burghall, in his "*Providence Improved*,' (Cole MS. Brit Mus) relates concerning the spring of 1651, "there was great drought in March, April, May and June; but upon seeking God by prayer and fasting we had supply of raine in due time"*

Among the Wilb MSS preserved at Delamere is the following Order relating to the paving of Marsh Lane in 1651 —

"*The g nrll* [general] *Sessions of y*ᵉ *Peace for y*ᵉ *Keepers of y*ᵉ *Liberty of England by aut*[*h*]*ority of Parliament held at Nantwich y*ᵉ 15*ᵗʰ day of July* 1651, *Before* Tho Mainwaring, Hen Birkenhead, Tho. Cronson, Hen Bradshaw & Gilbert Gerrard, *Esqrs*, *Justices of y*ᵉ *Peace, within y*ᵉ *County &c.*

"Upon yᵉ Humble Petition of Divers Gentl and other yᵉ Inhabitants of Nantwich and other adjacent townes, That whereas yᵉ Lane lyeing betweene Nantwich and Ravensmoore called yᵉ *Marsh-Lane*, beinge a very great Roade from Shrewsbury, Welshpoole, Whitchurch, and from divers parts of Wales to Nantwich and other pts of this Countrey, wᶜʰ said lane all yᵉ winter season is altogether unpassable, so yᵗ yᵉ Countrey people thereabout are either prvented from comeing to their usuall Market or necessitated to go a farr greater way about oner yᵉ sᵈ Moore and through many difficulties alsoe And seeing this Benche is informed that yᵉ said Lane can noe other way be made passable but by *rayseing a cawsye, and making a pauemt* throughout yᵉ same, yᵉ charge whereof will amount to a farre greater sume than possibly can be dispended by the Inhabitants of those Townes wherein yᵉ said Lane lyes, without yᵉ totall ruine of theire Estates, being a very few & alsoe poore Inhabitants, and being a worke of such extreame necessity It is therefore thought fit & ordered by this Court that foure payments of a Mize shall be levyed upon Nantwᶜʰ and yᵉ Fees thereof Three payments of Mize upon yᵉ Towncships of Baddeley, little Acton, Edlaston, Sound, Brumhall, Wrenbury ffryth, Smeton-wood, Dodcot cu' Wilkesly, Norbury, Marbury cu' Coyesly, & Wirswall, (all wᶜʰ said Townes being likely to have a more frequent & beneficiall use of yᵉ said Lane when repayred) & upon yᵉ residue of yᵉ sᵈ Hundred of Nantwᶜʰ two payments of a Mize for & towards yᵉ makeing of yᵉ sᵈ *Cawsye & Pavements* And for yᵗ end, yᵉ head Constables of yᵉ sᵈ Hundred are hereby required forthwith to issue forth their warrants to all yᵉ petty Constables within their severall Divisions thereby strictly com'anding euery of them im'ediately to collect & gather by distresse or otherwise yᵉ sᵈ seuerall payments imposed on yᵉ sᵈ Towneships as aforsaid And yᵉ money soe by them gathered to pay unto yᵉ said head Constables, soe as they may not fayle to pay over yᵉ same unto Rogᴿ Wilbraham of Nantwᶜʰ Esqr, Gabriel Wettenhall, John Delves, Robt Wilkes, & Tho Noden, Gents, all of Nantwᶜʰ aforesᵈ at or before the 23rd August next ensueing, which said Gentlemen are by this Court nominated and appointed Overseers of yᵉ said worke, and hereby desired to act and direct therein for yᵉ setting forward of yᵉ said worke as to them shall seeme fit And alsoe to receive yᵉ money collected, and to pay all such workemen as are imployed therein, as occasion shall require And after yᵉ said Lane is soe sufficiently repayred then it is from time to time soe sufficiently to be keepte in good repaire by yᵉ Townes only which heretofore haue accustomably repaired yᵉ same"

"Humph. Million *Dep Cler Pace*"

---

* A reference to one of the fast days about this time, when "divers ministers prayed and preached," and amongst the rest "Mr Burghall,' then Vicar of Acton, will be found in the "*Life of Lieutenant Illidge*," of Nantwich, a book said to have been written by the Rev Matthew Henry in 1710 (Edit 1836, p 10)

Malbon records that Charles II, then the uncrowned King, with his army passed through Nantwich on his way to Worcester, as follows —

"The Scotts forces wth theire Kinge weire in Namptwiche on Monday the xviijth of August 1651, but did not much harme; onelie tooke Aimes & Cheese; and the nexte daye afterwards march ed awaye   And after they had Garrisoned Worcester, the Parliam^t forces, com'anded by Lord Gen'all Cromwell stormed the same & quyte Rowted the Enymy, the third daye of September 1651   And Cheshire forces came home agayne on Tuesday ixth of September 1651 "*

A letter had been sent to the Magistrates, Constables and inhabitants of Nantwich requiring in his Majesty's name the payment of £3000 before five o'clock the following morning, for furnishing shoes and other necessaries for the Army —*(Calendar of State Papers)*   Roger Wilbraham, of Townsend, in his Family Journal, noticing the arrival of "*the forelorn of the Scotch Army,*" says, they "*were incensed to find so few in Towne,*' and then modestly adds, "*It is known who was chiefly instrumental to save ye Towne from plunder* "

The *Earl of Derby* having been taken prisoner at "*Sandford Bridge in Shropshire,*"† was taken to Chester, "where,' says Malbon, "by a Councell of Warr hee & Sr Tymothye *ffetherston, & Captyn Benbowe,* weie all tried & had Judgmt to dye on Wednesday the first of October 1651, viz   the said Earle to bee beheaded att Bolton in Lancashire that day ffortnight, afterwards Captyn Benbowe to bee shott att Shrowsbury the same daye; & Sr Tymothye to bee beheaded att Chester that daye three weekes, wch was all p'formed accordinglie "

"The nexte weeke afterwards *John Saer, John Benbowe,* & some othe^{rs} weire alsoe tryed by a Councell of Warr att Chester & weire adiudged to dye   *John Saer* was hanged vpon the Comon Gallowes att Chester on Tuesdaye the ffourth of November , where some more weire hanged for seu'all offences the same daye beinge condemned att the assizes att Chester held on the weeke before "

The trial of John Sare, (*Saer* or *Sayer*, as his name is variously spelled), is alluded to in *Mercurius Politicus* (No 71 p 1137 dated Oct 9th-16th, 1651) in a note of "*news from Chester,* ' as follows —

"The Court Martiall sate here again on Wednesday last and have sentenced *long John Sayers of Namptwich,* one of the biggest Fellows in the Nation to be executed at Boughton "

A broadside giving his "last dying speech " on the scaffold, in which he avowed his loyalty to the King, has recently been printed in Earwaker's "*Local Gleanings,*" (1st Series, vol ii, p. 79-81), commencing as follows —

---

* The Parish Register records the burial of a soldier—

"1651 Aug 22 Richard Royston a soldier in the Scotch Army '

† *James, Earl Derby,* together with the *Earl of Lauderdale* and *Sinclair* were taken prisoners by Capt Oliver Edge, a Lancashire man   The story is told in the *Memoirs of Capt Hodson, of Coley,* who was present on the occasion, and who fixes the place on "*the road abo it half a mile south of Nantwich*   This would be in *Cheshire* and though there is a place called *Sandford Bridge* in Cheshire, about 4 miles south of Nantwich, I am inclined to think Malbon would not be likely to have made a geographical error in the name of the county, and that Capt Hodson, who probably was not so well acquainted with the neighbourhood was wrong in fixing the situation of Sandford Bridge so near to Nantwich

"The chief heads of *Mr John Saers** speech, and other passages at the time of his execution at West-Chester, he being the portliest man the three Kingdomes afforded, whose Coffin was two yards and a halfe in lengthe, yet too short to containe his Corps, he suffered the 20th day of October 1651 "+

Roger Wilbraham *(MS Journal)* notices an almost total eclipse of the sun

"The most memorable eclipse of the Sunne that hath been knowne wth us was 29 Mar 1652, which lasted 2 hrs 45 min, betwixt 8 &° 11 of ye clocke in the morning It proved to be a clear calm day, so that in a Basin of water set for ye purpose I sensibly perceived how the darknesse increased & how it wrought off "‡

"On Sondaye the \\th of June 1652, The p'ishoners of Lawton beinge in the Churche in thafter noone, he[a]reing Gods worde, A greate storme comynge wth wynde thunder & Lightninge The thunder bolte & Lightninge or what els, pleased God, entred in att one of the Steeple wyndoes, brooke the Greate Bell wheele did much harme in the Steeple breakinge the Roofes & floores & came downe amongest the People & killed eleaven dead, viz · a sonne of John Pursels, Will'm Beeche of Audley p'ishe [a webster], Will'm. Meaiham [collier] of the same p'ishe, Thomas Poole, of Road, [Rode] Blacksmith; John Hughton, servant to widowe Hancocke of Road, Will'm Brereton, s'vant to John Stonyer, Peter Capper, s'vant to Richard Merry, John Parker [a beggar lad], ffrancis Lowe, Carpenter, John Hall [blacksmith], John Pursell, Carpenter § Besides to the nu'ber of xij more or thereabouts stricken, & sore astonyshed, not killed, But not any of them had any wounds nor harme to bee seene, onelie some of them weire blacke in some pte. of theire Bodies "—*(Malbon)*

"The \\th of Aprill 1653, beinge wednesdaye, the *Lord Gen'all Cromwell, maior Gen'all Harrison,*‖ & others of the officers of the Army, havinge a greate Company of ffyer-Locks neer them, Came into the Parliament howse, the Parliamt sitting, And then & there told them of the[i]1 evell carryage in the publique buysiness, & greate wast & expence of Treasure And tooke the Speaker furthe of the Cheere & putt him furthe of the howse tooke the Mace & suche Wrytinges as weire then in the howse & then all the rest of the Howse arrose & wente theire wayes & the Lord Gen'all locked the doore, putt the keye in his Pockett, And after wente to Whitehall and discharged the Councell of State "

---

* The following mentions of the *Sare* family, inn-keepers in Nantwich, occur in the Parish Register —

"1605 April 16 John Sare, Inkeper " [Buried]
1605 Oct 20 John son of John Sare, of the blak Leopard " [Bapt]
1638 July 8 Eliz dau of John Sare, of the Black Lyon " [Buried]
1638 Dec 4 Jane, wief of John Sare, of the Crowne " [Buried]
1641 Sep 5 Rich son of Little John Saer " [Bapt]
1643 Oct 15 Rich son of John Saer of the black lyon ' [Buried]

† There is a discrepancy in the date of Sare's execution from Malbon's account, which may possibly be wrong

‡ The Parish Register of Brignal, in Yorkshire, records —" 1652 Mar 29, The *darke Mondaye*, the sunn being eclipsed 10 in 12—that is ten parts in twelve darkened, so that the day seemed as twilight —(Burn s Parish Registers, p 192-3)

§ This last name is wrong It should have been " Antony a Yorkshire lad, a collier,' as appears in a list of killed, and description of the catastrophe by Randall S llito, the Rector of the Church, with which, with this exception, Malbon's list of names fully agrees (See Earwaker s *Local Gleanings Magazine*, p 15-18)

‖ In Platt s *History of Nantwich*, p 81, and in Ormerod s *Cheshire*, New Edit vol iii p 437, Major-General Thomas Harrison, the regicide, and " one of the five who appointed the time and place for the King's execution, ' is stated to have been born at Nantwich This, however, is not correct, the name of Harrison is very rarely met with in the Parish Registers, and, after a careful search I failed to find his name in those records He is said to have been the son of a butcher in or near Newcastle-under-Lyme —*(Peacock's Army Lists, p 33-4)*

It has been stated that during the Commonwealth more than ninety-six and a half millions were raised by Parliament from such sources as the sale of Crown lands in England and Ireland, Sequestrations of, and Compositions for Estates, Postage, Wine Licences, Duties, Excises, &c * Hence in the Calendar of State Papers, under date 2nd Nov 1652 occurs the name of *James Smith*, of Nantwich, farmer of the Excise for the City and County of Chester of all exciseable Commodities, salt, soap, hats, and tobacco pipes excepted, who renewed his lease, which expired on the 25th December, for nine months longer for £1000, being an advance of £108 6s 8d per quarter

By Act of Parliament passed on 24th Aug 1653, all marriages after the 29th of that month were to be performed before a magistrate, the banns having first been published on three several Lord's days in Church after the morning service, or (at the option of the parties) in the market place on three several market days, between the hours of eleven and two   Certificates of the ' publications ' having been produced and examined before a local magistrate, the man to be married, taking the woman by the hand, pronounced these words —†

"I, A B , do here, in the presence of God, the searcher of all hearts, take thee, C D. *for my wedded wife, and do also in the presence of God, and before these witnesses, promise* *to be unto thee a loving and faithful husband "*

Then the woman, in like manner, promised to be *"a loving, faithful, and obedient wife,"* after which, the magistrate declared them man and wife, "no ring, no blessing, no religious ceremony being considered necessary.'   The first of these *Civil Marriages* at Nantwich took place on 16th Jan. 1653-4, and the last on 16th Nov 1656, the total number registered being seventy-one   In no case does the name of a magistrate occur as in some parish registers, but according to a Memorandum on the first page of the then new Register Book, the appointed Registrar for the parish was *Mr Edward Hayes.* The following extracts show how these marriages were recorded, the most important entry being the marriage of *Roger Wilbraham, of Townesend, Esqre*

1653-4 "William Jackson & Sarah Bebington after publication three several markett days in Namptwich Markett, were married the 16th January '

1654 ' Capt Robt Wright & Mrs Anne Wilkes, after publication three several markett days in Namptwich Markett were married the 26th June "

1656 " Roger Wilbraham Esq & Mrs Alice Wilbraham after pub three severall Saboth days at Church, were marrid the 17th April "

1656 " Willm Clowes & Mary Comberbach, a.ter publication three several markett days in Namptwich Markett, were married the 16th November

"1655 A litle before Bartholomewe Daye 1655 was the greatest ffloodes by reason of a boundance of Rayne, as noe man lyvinge had seen the lyke   Weever did tutche the bottom of Namptwch Bridge, drowned all *Mislesiche* & the lower ende of welsh Roe, and the Reever Ranne throwe *mr Hassalls* gates a full Mylne water & drowned the streete vnto the Poste att *Kendalls* doore, & did very muche harme in drowninge many wiche howses & especially in many water works betwixte the Mylnes & Bryne pitt   But in Northwiche where Weever & Done did meete ytt did farr more harme "—*(Malbon MS)*

* See Fellowes' " *Historical Sketches,*" Appendix p lxxv, where the total amounts under different heads are given

† See an interesting article on " Marriages during the Commonwealth Period, ' in Mr Earwaker s *Local Gleanings Magazine,* pp 190 & 309

The above account is followed by a notice of repairs at the Brine Pit at Nantwich during the summer months of 1656, at a cost of £300 This memorandum, which is given in the chapter on the Salt-trade, is the last paragraph in the Malbon MS

Roger Wilbraham *(MS Four)* records two remarkable deaths the one of local interest, and the other of national importance, as follows —

"My uncle Mr Raphe Wilbraham, my Fathers youngest Brother dyed at Peele House in Tarvin Parish (which belonged then to my Father-in-law) upon the eve of St. Bartholom[ew] *ano* 1657 A right charitable good Man Who (as is said ot Cornelius) gave much Almes, and by his last Will & Testament Bequeathed his whole substance (which was considerable) to the poor,* Whereof I procured a share for this Towne of N The residue was put into ye hands of ye Ch[urch]wardens of neighbour-ing Parishes to remain in Stock for their Poor "

"O [liver] C [romwell] $\left\{ \begin{array}{l} \text{Terror Ang Sco et Hib} \\ \text{obiit et abiit suo loco} \end{array} \right\}$ 3 Sept 1658 "

In 1659 the restoration of the monarchy was generally desired, for the country was wearied with the war, and the Commonwealth had become a tyranny. It was arranged that the Royalists in each County on a certain day should rise and assert the claims of Charles, but when the time came, Sir George Booth, in Cheshire, and Sir Thos Middleton, in North Wales, were the only generals who attempted to carry out this design Sir George Booth seized the City of Chester, but failed to take the Castle, which was defended by Colonel Croxton, and on the 19th Aug 1659, about nineteen days after the "Rising' first commenced, Sir George was defeated and his army scattered at Winnington Bridge, near Northwich, by General Lambert The country people called it not the "*Cheshire Rising*," but the '*Cheshire Race*"† Both armies passed through Nantwich, and both Generals were entertained at Townsend House, by Roger Wilbraham, who writes con-cerning these visits, as follows —

"1659 Aug 11th Sir Geo Booth (afterwards Lord Delamere) being then in arms to restore Kg. Charl 2nd, tooke up his Quarters at my H[owse] for one night The Monday following [Aug 15] Maj Genl Lambert, who was sent with forces to suppress the rising in Cheshire and Lancashire took up his Quarters at my house, wch was filled with officers, & were the more straitened my w[ife] lying in at that time of her 3rd child After three nights stay to refresh his men, he marched towards Northwich, and met Sir G Booth's forces upon the skirt of the forest of Delamere, which were easily dispersed, wanting arms, ammunition, and experienced officers to lead them, 19 Aug 1659

G. F. Wilbraham Esq. has another interesting family paper relating to Genl Lambert's visit to Townsend,—

"Monday the 15th of Aug 1659

'General Lambert with his Armie consisting of 5,000 men horse and foot, came to Nantwch & staid therin till Thursday ye 18 of August The *Generall, Adjutant General Nelthrop, Colonell Swallow*, one *Lister* brother in law to the Generall, and one *Friar*, Chaplain to ye Generall & theire servants & horses quartered at my house At meals there was for ye most part as many as ye table would hold, viz *Col Briscoe, Col Ashley, Major Creed*, & others of ye principall officers, all upon free Quarter, for which ye Genl gave to my servants 24s. They went hence ye same day of ye same month in wch ye Scotch Army came hither 8 years before "

* See Church Monuments, and List of Charities.　　† See Philip Henry's "*Diaries*," p 69

The great army of the Commonwealth was soon after disbanded. "The Winter after," says the same writer, "afforded little else but distractions, and these counties were full of discontented soldiers. The year following [1660] was Englands Jubilee, when K. Charles 2nd was restored an° Reg. xii; after so many years exile, after the martyrdom of his Father by those bloody Regicides who killed & tooke possession of the Kingdom, until he came at last whose right it was. His Majesties return & Restoration, for the more solemnity was contrived to his Birthday, 29 May, *an*. 1660. The solemnity was made what it was when King David was brought from Mahanaim to Jerusalem."—*(Wilb. MS. Journal.")*

THE CROWN INN.

Annals since the Restoration.

ERHAPS few towns in England had greater cause to be thankful for the Restoration of the Monarchy than Nantwich; and here, in commemoration of King Charles' Coronation-day, (St. George's Day, the 23rd April, 1661), that day of universal rejoicing, a curiously constructed Dial was placed on the west front of the Parish Church. The Dial, which had already disappeared in 1818,* was thus described by Partridge in 1774;†—"Its form is orbicular, and within the orb at the top is a sun rayonant, from which depends a label with this inscription—

SOLEM QUIS DICERE FALSUM AUDEAT,‡

and in the border round the top, another, to wit,—

DoMIno pro paCe popVLo sVo parta."§

The latter inscription was a chronogram; the Roman capitals (MDCLVVI) being intended for the year of the coronation of King Charles, to which event this quaint conceit referred.

An interesting record occurs in the Calendar of State Papers, dated June (?) 1660, stating that *James Hickes*, who had been Clerk in the Post Office at Nantwich since 1637, (and who had, no doubt, seen great changes under the Commonwealth, when the practice of farming the Post Office revenues was adopted), was still retained "for continuance of employment in the said office, and of his accustomed salaries;" the "road now [1660] bringing in £4000 a year."

Still earlier mentions of the Post Office occur in the Parish Registers:

"1621. Mar. 13. Thomas Cheshire, a letter bearer." [Buried].
"1622. Ap. 12. Mr. Roger Mainwaring Post Maister." [Buried].
"1635. Feb. 19. Elizabeth, wife of Mathew Alvaston, foote-post." [buried].

---

* Platt's History of Nantwich, p. 64.　　　† Partridge's History of Nantwich, p. 41.

‡ *Translated :* Who dares to say the sun is wrong ?

§ *Translated :* To the Lord for peace obtained for his people.

In 1663 the Town Bridge was first built of stone, mainly through the exertions of Roger Wilbraham, Esq , who writes —

"Our Town Bridge wᶜʰ was of timber, being in decay, I obtained of the Justices of the Peace at the Quarter Sessions held here in July 1663, that we might have a substantial Stone Bridge It being referred to me by the Bench to contract with some sufficient workman, I agreed with *Tim Adams,* Mason, to build the bridge, as it now is, for which he had £90 of the County, & the Materials of the Old Bridge

My little boy, a Twin of 2 years old, was the first corpse that was carried over the new Bridge the begins of July 1664 "*

At the last Herald's Visitation of the County Palatine of Chester by William Dugdale, Esq , Norroy King of Arms, dated 3rd Sept 1663, and 6th July, 1664, the following persons, belonging to Nantwich, occur in the list of "*disclaimers of Gentility*" for Nantwich Hundred, numbering in all sixty-six These were branded "*no gentlemen,*" and had no right to bear arms because they failed to appear before the Herald to prove their claim, and pay the required fees. Their names were —†

GEORGE HENSHAW,	ROGER COMBERBACH,	THOMAS BROMHALL,
THOMAS LANGLEY,	JOHN WICKSTED,	THOMAS WRIGHT,
RANDLE CHURCH,	THOMAS BULLEN,	JOHN ACTON.

JOHN DELVES, natural son of Sir Thomas Delves, Bart

WILLIAM MEAKIN, save his right as Attorney-at-law to use the title of Esquire

Of those who, attending to the summons of William Dugdale Esq , appeared before him and had their claims to gentility allowed, occur the names of ROGER WILBRAHAM, ESQ , and THOMAS MAISTERSON, ESQ , of this town

At this time, owing to the general want of small change, tradesmen and shopkeepers here, as elsewhere, issued unauthorized copper tokens of the value of the penny and half-penny, which were payable at their respective places of business, until they were declared illegal by Act of Parliament passed on the 16th Aug 1672, when Charles II half-pence and farthings were made current The following list of eight Nantwich Tokens has recently been printed,‡ to which I have been able to add three others

1 *Obverse* RICHARD BICKERION IN NAMPTWICH [In four lines].

    Reverse HIS HALF. PENY. R B 1666 [In four lines]

Richard Bickerton was a brewer by trade, and died in 1669

2 *Obv* THOMAS BROMHALL IN NAMPTWICH. [In four lines]

    Rev HIS HALFE PENY 1665 T E B [In four lines]

Thomas Bromhall, mercer, according to a Rate Book for 1691, appears to have lived at the corner of High Town, where Hospital Street and Pillory Street diverge, at that time called "*Pye Corner,*" and now occupied by Mr P H Chesters Thomas Bromhall was buried on 31st Jan 1700-1 —*(Par Reg)*

3 *Obv.* *William Crossley his halfe Penny* [In four lines]

    Rev IN NAMPTWICH 1666, [device] A Ship

* The burial Register records —" 1664 July 2 Roger, son of Roger Wilbraham, Esq "

† The list is preserved in *Harl MSS* 2142 f 168, (Brit Mus), and in *Ashmolean MSS* 857 f 250-1 (Bodl Lib)

‡ Mr Earwaker s '*Local Gleanings Magazine,*" p. 287

4   *Obv.*   DANIEL IACKSON [device] The Mercers' Arms. (octagonal)
      Rev   IN NAMPTWICH [in the centre] HIS I^D 1669

5   *Obv*   THOMAS IACKSON [device in centre] The Ironmongers' Arms
      Rev.   IN. NAMPTWICH 1666 [in the centre] HIS. HALF PENY

6.   *Obv.*   ELIZABETH PRICE. IN [device in centre] The Arms of the Price family,
             VIZ   *a chevron embattled between three spear-heads*
      Rev   NAMPTWICH 1666. [in centre] HER. HALF PENY

The *Prices* had been resident tradesmen in the town for at least a century previous to 1666 A Mrs Elizabeth Price, probably the same as mentioned above, and the last of the family, was buried at Nantwich on the 27th Feb 1691-2 —*(Par Reg)*

7   *Obv*   IOHN TFNCH 1666 [in the centre] I M T
      Rev   IN NAMPTWICH [in the centre] HIS HALF PENY

John Tench was a tanner The middle initial letter stands for the christian name of his wife, Mary He married "*Mrs Mary Demock, after publication three severall markett days in Namptwich Markett,*" on the 6th March 1653-4, and was buried at Nantwich on the 14th Nov 1675—*(Par Reg)* The Tench family were respectable residents here as early as 1545 (see p 98), and occur in the Registers as "dyers," "tanners," "mercers," "gentlemen," &c The last mentions of the family are as follows —

                " John Tench Attorney buried in the Church 5 Feb 1756 "
                " Miss Mary Tench [buried] 2 Dec 1780 "
                " Thomas Tench [buried] 5 May, 1783 "

8   *Obv.*   IAMES WILSON 1666 [in the centre] HIS HALF PENY
      Rev   IN NAMPTWICH [in the centre] I A. W.

James Wilson, silk-stocking weaver, was buried on the 19th Dec 1699 —*(Par Reg)* The initial A stands for his wife's christian name

Besides the above Nantwich tokens, I have two others in my possession which have not hitherto been described

9   *Obv*   *William Cappur his halfe Penny* [In four lines].
      Rev   IN NAMPTWICH 1666 [device in centre] A Ship

Possibly William Cappur kept the "Ship" Inn The family continued to reside in the town until about thirty or forty years ago The following extracts from the Parish Register will be of interest

        " 1726 Aug 4 Jacob, son of Raph Cappur Inholder " [Bapt]
        " 1753 Sep 16 James son of Ralph Cappur, Cheesefactor ' [Bapt]
        " 1780 Aug 17 George Cappur, Cheesefactor, & Lydia Maddocks [married] by Lycence "
        " 1785 Nov 27 George, son of George Cappur, Cheesefactor, & Lydia his wife " [Bapt]
        " 1790 Oct 19 Ralph, son of George Cappur, Cheesefactor, & Lydia his wife, born '

10 *Obv*   GEORGE B . . [in the centre] The Mercers' Arms
      Rev   IN NAMPTWICHE   [in the centre] G B. I. E

The edge of this token, being worn away, the *surname* and *date* cannot be deciphered

11   *Obv*   IOHN TENCH IN [in the centre] a Shield with half figure of a female.
      Rev   NAMPTWICH 1665 [in the centre] I. M T.

This coin which is apparently a farthing token, is in the possession of Mr Bowers, of Broad Lane, Nantwich, and is in an excellent state of preservation

Lord Ossory, travelling from Oxford to Dublin, passed through Nantwich with his retinue, on the 10th Feb. 1667, and here an incident occurred which provoked some merriment in the town "At Nantwich they met the noble Captain Baker, with the badge of his office at his breast he caused much amusement because he had bought a new cap of beaten black satin, to ride *bareheaded* before my lord 10 miles of the way "[*]

"Our Great Bell in Nantwich, being above 2000ʰ [*i e* about a ton] in weight, chaunced to be cracked, and was cast anew at Wellington, in Shropshire, by one Clitheroe. *Robert Parker*, Mercer & *Jo[hn] Dean*, Barber, Churchwardens anᵒ 1669, wᶜʰ cost the parish near £30."[†]

In 1670 Roger Wilbraham, of Townsend House, Esq , was made Sheriff of the County; and, concerning the Spring Assizes held at Chester, 11th April, 1670, before Sir Job Charlton, Chief Justice, he writes as follows —

"It came to my thoughts sitting in yᵉ chair, that two worthy gentⁿ and of good repute in their time had been arraigned at yᵉ same Barr near upon C [100] years before upon an Appeal brought by the widow of R Cr [Roger Crockett] for yᵉ supposed murdr of her Husband, who chanced to be slain in a fray at N [ant wich];   yᵉ Jury at Chester, finding yᵉ Prosecution was evidently malicious [were moved] to acquit yᵉ sᵈ Gentlemen [Richard Wilbraham and Richard Hassall] whose innocence, wᶜʰ in a while after, was remarkably cleered by yᵉ confession of that same dangerous witness which his guilty conscience extorted from him, where himself for Theft came to be arraigned at Chester, and was found guilty of yᵉ Felony for which he was arraigned and expecting to have suffered for his offence, being (as he sᵈ) pricked in conscience, he confessed to an eminent Divine Mr Goodm[an of Chester] that he was suborned by his Mistr[ess] & induced by her large promises to endanger the lives of yᵉ sᵈ R W & R H , by a false oath, to gratify his sᵈ Mistr[ess] whose importunity had wrought to prsist in what he had sworne falsely & against his knowledge befoie yᵉ Coroner, which shewes the temper of yᵉ wretched woman whose malice would have made those innocent Gentlemen a sacrifice or otherwise she meant to serve her Avarice of them whom she falsely accused, & upon that score the rather chose to prosecute them by *Appeal* than by *Indictment* But missing of her aime, & fearing they might prosecute her, she left yᵉ Country and was never heard of after And yᵉ said R W lived prosperous many years after to see their end that had conspired his And that a descendant of the same family after C [100] years should come to possess yᵉ Chair so near unto yᵉ Barr where his Ancestor had his Tryal, this coming seasonably to mind, it did very much raise & affect his Thoughts, who had yᵉ whole story by Tradition, having likewise seen an Authentic Registr of those proceedings   Hœc olim meminisse &c "

"Mr. Randle Shenton s house, kill & Barnes were burnt at noon-day [15 July, 1672] near Nantwych, through the carelesness of servants drying Hemp upon yᵉ Kyll Hee was then at Coventry & saith about 1 a clock yᵗ moining hee arose affrighted with a light shining in at window, wᶜʰ was a star extra-ordinary, supposing yᵉ Town had been on fire, & that meeting one of his neighb. in his way homewards, one of his first qu was, is my house safe fiom fire His loss is generally computed to neer 400 ˡᵇ [£] in building, goods, malt, chees, tow, &c "—("*Diaries of Philip Henry M A* " p 254).

[*] Calendar of State Papers 1666-7, vol CXCI

[†] Roger Wilbraham's MS Journal

[‡] Cf pages 99-101

In 1676 the Widows' Almshouses in Welsh Row were founded by Roger Wilbraham; and mainly by his recommendation, in the following year, a House of Correction and Workhouse at Beam Street-end were established *

On the night of the 2nd Jan 1679, Townsend House was entered by burglars In a long Memorandum, Roger Wilbraham, says, they took "ye plate we had in use, 7 Buttery linen, a coat of my sons, some of ye servants clothes &c. By what they eat & drank we guessed they could not be fewer than 5 or 6 in company That which made them ye bolder & us insensible of ye disturbance was that it chanced to be a rugged [boisterous] night but not dark. I made all ye inquiry I could Sent ye marks of ye plate I lost to all ye market Townes within 20 miles round us, but could make no discovery."

The years 1680 and 1681 were years of great mortality, the Registers recording 110 and 104 burials respectively "The small pox being rife in the Town in 1681, I thought it not safe," says Roger Wilbraham, "to adventure Stephen my young^r son to goe any longer to ye Towne Schoole '

"The Duke of Monmouth came to this Towne 9th Sep. 1682,† honourably attended. dined with his train of attendants at y^e *Crowne*, and went hence after dinner to Peele, thence to the Horse race of his own appointing at Wallasey; which as appeared after was not well resented at Court, having notice of his popular reception in these parts '

Roger Wilbraham, who here alludes to the "Protestant Duke," as he was called, says later on concerning the rebellion of 1685, "Amongst others in this county that were suspected of disloyalty the Ld Brandon eldest son of ye Earl of Macclesfield & Hen[ry] Ld Delamere [eldest son of Sir George Booth, afterwards first Lord Delamere], were impeached of H T [High Treason] The former was found guilty by a Middlesex Jury, but after some time had his pardon The latter had his trial at Westm^r Hall, & was happily acquitted by his Peers, the K [ing] & Q [ueen] being present which was January [14th] 1685[-6] Both kissed King Jas. hand at Chester in Aug 1687 "

The Wilbraham MS Journal contains the following memorandum —

"1683 It happened that the Beame over the Pulpit in our Ch[urch], (of which we had no suspition) fell point blank into ye pulpit, which had it happened but half an hour sooner, would have been a startling sight to us that met that morninge to joine in Prayer. To see a Beame of that length carried in our sight from one side to the other side of ye Church—For so it was, that the end of the Beam wch rested upon the south wall was wholly perished, ye end over ye pulpit was sound, & fast mortised into ye wall plate, & so drew the beam to ye opposite side, wch we conceived might hang for a space perpendicular over the pulpitt, till the weight of the beam wrested the tenon out of ye mortis in ye wall plate & then dropt end-wise, shivered the cover of the pulpit to pieces, struck through ye bottom of ye pulpitt a foot into ye ground And stood not upright, but something inclining, as if God had purposely sent this dumb messenger to preach Repentance to a stupid Auditory It chanced that Sr Tho Wilb[raham of Woodhey] came that afternoon to Towne I had the favor of his company, to

---

* Cf the "*Towne Concernes*," and for the subsequent history of these institutions, under date 1767, &c

† The celebrated Philip Henry made the following entry in his Diary — 1682 Sep 9 D of Monm past through Nantw[ich] tow[ards] Chest'—some applauding others vilifying—*studia in contraria vulgus*."—(*Diaries of Philip Henry*, M A , p 317)

see this Dumbe show And took the boldness to tell him, that unless he pleased to befriende us with a Tree out of *Woodhay Bache*, for Love or Money, we should be at a losse who very freely gave us a Tree yᵗ made the beam which carries his cognizance [coat of arms] as 'twas meet it should

This further advantage we had by this accident, that it gave us occasion to suspect the other Beams, & upon search we found most of them deficient, & took that opportunity to strengthen them where need was "

This accident, the exact date of which is not given,* appears to have led to extensive repairs to the roofs of the Church, spreading over several years, the cost of which was defrayed by Church rates, and private liberality   In the absence of " *Churchwardens' Accounts,* ' the following entries taken from Roger Wilbraham's Pocket Almanacks for 1689, 1698, and 1700, will be of interest

1689 "One of yᵉ middle Beames wᶜʰ was given by my Ancestor (as I suppose by yᵉ Coat thereon, when yᵉ Roofe [i e the Clerestory] of our Church in Nantwch was raised) being now much decaied & ready to fall, was taken down To supply which I procured another out of Woodhay Bache (whereon is my Coat of Armes, as I now quarter it), wᶜʰ cost me 2 Ginneys, which I paid to the then Ch Wardens *Wm Hale & Tho Twisse*, Ano dni 1689, Septr 25 "

"The next beam was given by yᵉ Lord Cholmondeley "

1698 "Oct 6 To *Mr Wright* & *Mr Audley* Ch Wardens, A Lay of yᵉ whole Old Rent for repairing yᵉ Roofe of yᵉ South Ile [i e Transept] of yᵉ Church, £3 9s 4d "

Above the tower arch in the South Transept is still to be seen a board, inscribed " *John Clowes Workeman* 1698 ," and another, fixed to one of the cross beams, says,— " *This Roofe was Repared and three new Beames put up when Benjamin Wright & Geo Avdley were Wardens* 1698 " In the North Transept also, is a board inscribed "*This Roofe was repared and three new Beames put up when John Comberbach and John Church were wardins John Clowes workeman* 1699 "

Roger Wilbraham in one of his pocket books, made the following entry —

"1700 March 13 Pd to John Church & his ptner [John Church & John Denton, Churchwardens] a Lay of yᵉ whole Old Rent for glazing & pointing yᵉ Church & Steeple £3 9s 4d "

In 1687 the notorious sycophant Bishop of Chester, Dr T Cartwright, made a short stay at Nantwich on his journey to London, where he arrived on the 7th April   He says in his Diary —‡

"March 28 We went from the Colonel's [i e Colonel Whitley of Chester] to Nantwich, where we dined at the post house [the " Crown "] with *Mr Stringer* [the minister], *Mr Mainwaring, Mr Wilbraham*, the churchwardens [*Thomas Stringer* and *Richard Peeter*] and two officers, and from thence we went that night to Stone " &c

* The Rev Philip Henry in his Diary for 1684 under date Jan 1st, says, " I heard that a *month since* one of yᵉ mayn Beames of yᵉ Roof of Nantwych church falling, beat yᵉ Pulpit & desk all to peices, not past half an hour after the Minr Mr Stringer & yᵉ congregation were gone out from morning prayr on a Tuesday — ' *Diaries and Letters of Philip Henry, M A* " p 322

† Exactly one hundred years after the roof of the Clerestory was again in a dangerous state of decay (See under date 1789)

‡ Dr Cartwright s Diary, p 40 (Cam Soc Pub 1843)

In 1689 the Parish Register records the burials of ten soldiers, who perhaps died of some infectious disease, during the months of June, July and August * JAMES, aided by Louis XIV, had landed in Ireland on 12th March, and probably these ten soldiers had belonged to the *Duc de Schomberg's* army which landed near Donaghadee on 12th August, to oppose the deposed King's invasion On Friday night, 6th June, 1690, King William III, being on his journey to Ireland before the Battle of the Boyne, slept at Combermere Abbey, and set out next day [probably passing through Nantwich] for Hoylake, where he embarked for Ireland †

"1690 Oct. 7th About 7 of ye clock in ye morning there happened the most sensible [*i e* perceptible] earthquake that I have known wch overthrew the topp of my Hall Chymney, and endamaged others in the Town There was about 6 weekes before a much gentler Earth Quake God grant us to make use of these shakings to sitt loaser to ye world "

Roger Wilbraham, who wrote the above memorandum, also gives six long paragraphs (here abbreviated) as instances of God's Judgments during sixteen years on persons *"who being over wicked came to an untimely end "*

"*Robert Salmon*, a day labourer, having got drunk at an alehouse near the Bridge fell into the river at the Bridge & was drowned " [Buried 9 Oct 1677]

"*Megg Blagg*, being drunk, was burnt to death, in her own Kitchen " [Buried 5 March, 1677-8]

"*Robert Brooke*,‡ carpenter, drunkard and profane Swearer, who was struck dead in a wood after felling a Birch tree on Whitsun eve " [Buried 1 June 1680]

"*Widow Maddu*, a Dyer, going home late at night full of drink, thinking to have gone over ye *wooden Bridge* [the Little Bridge across the channel] at ye lower end of Welsh Row, she missed the Bridge, & falling into ye Channell, was carried by the stream [there had been much rain previously] into ye River and was *doubly drowned* " [Buried 15 Jan 1682-3]

"*T Wood*, a webster, who lived with his daughtr that sold Ale at a Howse near ye River side in Mill St, went in open day to ye *flood gates*, we call them wch receives ye wast waters above ye mills there he putt off his cloathes & left them upon the Bank & jumpt into ye water where it was deepest & drownded himself ' [Buried 16 May 1688]

"*Widow Savage*, a Taylor, being drunk and going from the Almshouses at Welsh Row Head, by the fields behind Townsend, towards her own home was drowned "in a lake near my Orchard wall at ye gate entring into ye *Lyon Lane*, wch was not above ankle deep " [Buried 15 April 1689]

"*Cicely Eaton*, hearing of a Christening at *Beam Bridge*, thither she went & having got more drink to her share than she could carry home, sett her down upon ye Battlements of the Bridge & fell backwards into ye River " [Buried 5 Oct 1694]

---

* The Burial Register gives their names as follows —

"1689 June 12 William Wilmott, a souldier	June 28 James Phillips, a souldier
,, 16 Robert Lightborne, a souldier	July 6 ————, a souldier
,, 18 William Wright, a souldier	,, 23 Robert Cole, a souldier
,, 18 James Powell, a souldier	, 25 ————, a souldier
,, 28 John Briscoe, a souldier	Aug 26 ————, a souldier '

† Memoirs and Correspondence of Field Marshall Viscount Combermere, pub 1866

‡ "1680 May 30 One Brookes of Nantwych aged about 55, a sawyr, a loose p'son, went with others on this day being Sabb day in the afternoon to Chorley hay to steal a pole for a *May-pole*, having agreed with a fiddler to attend ye setting of it up next day, After hee had given a few strokes with an Axe, towards ye falling of it, it pleas d God, hee was struck down himsf & dy'd immediately without speaking one word in ye very same place "—(*"Diaries of Philip Henry M A ,"* p 288)

Another list of untimely deaths is here appended, taken from the Burial Register —

" 1634   Sep 27   John Chell drowned in a well
1634-5   March 5   John sonne ot Richd Podmore, being choaked with bread & butter "
1640   May 15   Zacharie Gill found drowned in Weeuer "
1646   June 1   William Allat drowned at Shrobridge
1648-9   Feb 7   Randle Twis, faling of [f] a car' Broke his neck
1649   May 2   Richard Hall cutt his own throte
1649   Oct 31   John, son of John Wright, glover, was drowned
1651   Nov 27   Edward Rogers, drowned in the Towne well
1655   March 26 William Maddock, Milner, drowned
1658   Jan 22   Raphe Pratchett hanged himself
1660   April 30 Anne Simcock killed with a cart
1663   March 30 John Wilbraham slayne
1663   March 31 John Myddleton poysoned himself
1664   May 7   Abraham, son of Richard Gill drowned in a well
1665   Dec 19   Thomas Weaver, buryed at Afton, who dyed suddenly
1667   Oct 7   Elizabeth, wife of ffrancis ffleete slayne by her husband
1668-9   Jan 20   Roger Bartley died suddenly
1670   May 28   James son of Thomas Burroughs, drowned
1673   Oct 29   Katherine Minshull who was drowned in the Weever
1677   June 13   John, son of Richard Barker, mercer, was drowned
1678   July 22   Mary Wife of Thos Briscoe, poysoned herself
1678   Sept 10   William, son of John Bromley, junr , was drowned in a swine-tubb
1679   May 30   Tnos son of John Hall, with a cart [killed]
1680   Dec 2   Ca herine Bankes dyed suddenly
1680   Dec 3   Jane Crockett scalded in a turnell of worte
1682-3   Feb 3   Thomas Price hanged himself
1684   Dec 9   Thomas Whittingham dyed suddenly
1685   April 5   Thomas Simcock dyed suddenly
1685   July 22   Joan, sonne of John Evans, scalded in a salt-pan
1685   Nov 29   Peter Houlse, Drowned
1686   July 28   John Moyle Drowned
1688   June 7   John Emmery Drowned
1691   May 22,   Margaret dau of Thomas Sefton, drowned
1693-4   Feb 27   John Leake killed with a fall off a ladder
1700-1   Jan 8   Thomas Beech labourer killed with a wagon
1701   July 4   Margaret Gardner, scalded with brine
1701   July 17   Jonathan Richards, a boy, drowned
1702   March 29 John son of Stephen Morriss kill'd by his brother, about 10 years of age, with a gun
1703-4   Feb 4   Henry Rutter, Attorney, killed by a fall ot a horse *
1703-4   Feb 11   Richard, son of Thomas Wilkes yeoman, killed with drinking brandy *
1703-4   Feb 21   Thomas ffurnivall, mercer, buried at Sandbach, died suddenly *
1704   June 11   Ambrose Pickerin, Barber, Drowned
1707   July 7   Thomas Wickstead, Gent , killed by a fall of a horse
1707-8   March 2   Sarah dau of Roger Leather, Glovr, Drowned
1708   Nov 8   Martin Cain a soldier stab d & killed by his Serjeant
1708-9   Jan 4   William Hayles, shoemaker, dyed suddenly

* These three sudden deaths are mentioned in the Life of Lieut Richard Illidge, of Nantwich and Cheerbrook, and are entered in the Burial Register *seriatim*

The Annals of the Town during the latter half of the seventeenth century are here supplemented by a very interesting memorial, entitled "*The Towne Concernes*," written in the year 1682, by Roger Wilbraham, Esq, of Townsend House, who was then in the sixtieth year of his age. It is preserved amongst the Wilbraham MS collections at Delamere, and is contained in the fly sheets of a pocket Almanac, dated 1673, on the inside cover of which is written, in the same small, neat hand-writing, "This was my son Toms Almanack, who to my gr [eat] grieve died 8° September 1675, *ætat* 18, His d [ear] Mother died that day 12 mon after, 8 Septr. 1676, *ætat* 47 ' In this account Roger Wilbraham reviews, with characteristic naivete of style, several important changes and events that had taken place in the town during his life-time, events and changes with which he had been directly concerned. The use of certain colloquial expressions that are familiar sayings at the present day, is worthy of the reader's notice, and, although some of the events have already been mentioned in chronological sequence in the previous pages, it has been thought best, notwithstanding the repetition, to give these reminiscences exactly as they were written, two hundred years ago, without alteration or abridgment

"*THE TOWNE CONCERNES*"

' The Towne hath 2 especiall Priveledges wch have bin upheld by such necessary Bylaws as have bin made by Juries from time to time in ye Court Leet held for ye Barons of Wich Malbank, *als* Nantwich

The one of these Priveledges is y^e *Salt-spring* which is of great Antiquity, as appeares by Domesday Book The other priveledge is ye Benefit that is & may be made by the improvem^t of a large plott of Land, adioning to ye Towne which wee call y^e *Beam Heath* ye property whereof together wth ye possession hath bin in ye Inhabitants of Nantwch for above 400 yeares, by conveyance from *Bressey* in ye time of K Hen 3 ᵈ Which said priveledges while they held y^m [them] to their Customes were very beneficiall & helpfull to ye Towne But Matters of p'fitt [profit] being subject to Usurpation, neithr of these Priveledges yeeld that profit to ye Towne that they did heretofore & chiefly through ye remisnes & neglect of Officers intrusted to manage these Concernes

The ancient Way of makeing Salt wth us, was in Lead Pans, whereof every Wich H [ouse] had six of equal gage & in those they boyled their Salt with Wood cloven & fitted for ye purpose, every Wich H. in its turn, or *kale*, (as wee phrase it,) by direction of y^e *Rulers of Walling*, who are sworne to deale iustly & uprightly between ye Owner & Occupier, & to see, that none take benefit of ye occupation, but the Inhabitants, & that no Occupier exceed his stinted time & Gage This was ye Way & usage of making salt in this Towne till the vi^th yeare of King Charles I [1632]. And then it was that some fancifull persons, thought it would be more for their profit to boyle their Salt in *Iron Pannes* (of equall Gage with the six Leads) with *Pitte-coale,* pretending y^t Wood grew scaice, & y^t therefore it concerned them (while ye Law allowed them to make ye best of their owne) to make their com'odity at as light chaige, as they could which was their Plea at ye Councell Bord, & they carried it for ye Projectors, against all ye reasons & allegations of

---

* See under Alvaston Township where full translations of this and other ancient deeds relating to the Heath are given

yᵉ much greater & more substantiall pt. of Inhabitants, who opposed this projeᵭ foreseeing the detriment & disadvantage that would inevitably ensue thereupon both to yᵉ Towne & Countrey.*

For since then we find by sad experience that yᵉ salt yᵗ is made with coale is nothing so good, yᵉ Trade much slacker, yᵉ Woods wᶜʰ were preserved to serve the Salt-works are now cut downe & destroyed to make worse Iron then wee had then from beyond the seas, & the Coale Mines, which sholde serve yᵉ Countrey, are much exhausted by what is spent here, & elsewhere for making of salt. All which inconveniences my Father and others concerned, endeavoured to have prevented, but were over-ruled has hath bin declared.

And the Natives will reape but little p'fit from yᵉ *Heath* If Strangers after they have dwelt a yeare in yᵉ Towne are permitted to put their cattle to the Heath, who (as it is said) pay not one penny to yᵉ reliefe of yᵉ poore A great Abuse this is & a Reproach to yᵉ Towne "

" A Memoriall of yᵉ Concernes of yᵉ Towne since Xmas anᵒ 1649"

"After my elder Brothers decease, who died 19 Decem. 1649, I was invited by some, yᵗ thought their yeeres & experience in the Towne Affaires would have swayed me as they listed, to appear & interest myself as occasion might be in their publique Meetings Which I did, & found that their Meetings most what consisted of Strangers, who fled hither for shelter when yᵉ Town was a Garrison, & having bin Under Marshalls, Com'issaries, Quarter-Masters &c , in the late Warr, had a Mind to be Quarter Masters still. & controllers of other Mens Purses For it was then in yᵉ power of half a dozen of yᵐ [them] who had no concerne in Towne save a rented H.[ouse], (for which it may be yᵉ Landlord paid the Taxes,) with yᵉ assistance of as many poor Trades-Men in Towne who paid not a pen'y to Church or Poor, to give away as pleased themselves, (while others negleᵭed to move) to yᵉ Church Officers & Constables when they demanded it, a whole old Rent, or more, when the halfe perhaps, or 2 parts at most would have sufficed

Whereupon the more consciencious officers, to whom such a Lay was granted, trobled themselves no furthʳ but to colleᵭ their Due of those yᵗ were best able & willing to pay, & yᵉ residue of yᵉ Lay granted them, they never concerned themselves to colleᵭ. And when such a Lay was granted to other officers, (to whom all was Fish yᵗ came to yʳ Nett,) they having a Grant of more than their due Disbursements, made no Bones to pocket up yᵉ over-plus. When this was perceived, & that yᵉ remisnes of yᵉ Gentlemen, & more Substantiall Inhabitants was that which imboldened Strangers & Mechanicks to rule all at their pleasure, I did associate myself wᵗʰ some of yᵉ best rank, whom I took to be most true

---

* The great change here alluded to, appears to have been forced on the town, in spite of ancient customs, by the establishing of rival works higher up the Weaver, as related by William Webb (King's *Vale Royal*) about 1621 He says "*Austerson* hath had goodly woods that hath been the chief store-house and nursery of that fewel they call *Wich-wood*, [oak and hazel] which being of twenty years growth, or thereabouts, is most fit for that service, and hath been usually fallen by yearly falls, as they call them, and sold to the town of Nantwich, for the boiling of their salt Sir Robert Needham hath, in this age of ours found out by the side of Weaver, at Baddington, a seth or pit of that brine whereof they make great plenty of very good white salt, as also, upon the bank on the other side, in the lordship of *Hatherton*, in the lands of Sir Thomas Smith In both which they have taken a more profitable way of boiling their salt in *pans of iron*, to which the *pit-coals*, which are their ordinary fewel of that country, and whereof there is great abundance not far off, in the confines between the two counties of Chester and Stafford, is found a cheaper and more compendious way than that of boiling in pans of lead with fewel only of wood, used in all the Wiches "

hearted, (having experienced some y^t spoke fair to be otherwise) we resolved to put our Oare into ye Boat with them y^t then ruled all, & to have a little more Inspection into Officers Accounts, & to proportion our Lay to their Disbursm^{ts}, not to their Demands, when we found them unreasonable And those that are sensible what sumes have bin spared since this course was taken, have reason to take their diligence in good part, who have attended all publique Meetings, to save their owne, & their Purses

When the prophanation of ye Sabbath was more penal[*] then now it is, It is well known, that care was taken to Choose Church Officers yeerly as made it their Business to suppresse all disorders that trenched upon ye Sabbath, & through Gods Blessing upon their eart [heart] things were reduced to that passe, y^t I think there was scarce a Markt Town within many Miles, where there was better Order, & more due observacon of ye Sabbath And I myselfe have imputed our deliverance from ye plague wch did often threaten us from o^r Neighbour Townes to Gods gracious acceptance of our zeale to his service and publique worshipp.

My endeavours have not bin wanting to have suppressed ye supernumerary Ale-Houses in this Towne And when consideration was had of this matter by encouragement of ye Justices of Assize an^o 1655, one halfe of them were thought sufficient, and ye groundes wee went upon were to continue those, & those onely,—

1. That kepte good Order.

2 Those that had fitt Houses & accomodations for Travellers & quartering of soldiers.

3 Those were thought fittest to be continued who had no Trades nor other way of Livelihood, & holding this course without respect of persons, or ill will to any, the number came to be lessened by one halfe But importunity prevailed with ye Justices of P, to re-admit most of those that were thus laid aside as unfitt Whereof complaint being made to ye Judges of Assize, they ordered ye Justices of P. to see to the effectual suppressing of unnecessary Ale-houses Whereupon ye same thing was re-attempted in this T[own]. And yett all this availed not, nor I believe ever will, to suppresse them

Ano 1651 The fortnights Collection in ye Church was found insufficient to relieve the poor, by reason that many and some of ye better Quality in Towne, did frequently absent themselves those Sabbaths y^t ye fortnights Collection was Whereupon I prevailed that there might be an an'uall Assessm^t made throughout the Parish, & that to be confirmed by ye Justices of P the one moiety to be collected by ye O^{r}seeis of ye Pool [i e. Church-wardens] presently after their entrance upon their office, & the other moiety at Michaelmas after, that so they might have wherewth to relieve ye poor monthly Which Assessm^t did almost double ye Fortnightly Collection, & not above halfe a dozen were Assessed more then [than] what they voluntarily pd. before This course began 1651 & continues to this day with little regret.

Ano 1655. Upon occasion of Majo^r Generall Fleetwood (who was the then Protector Cr[omwell's] son in Law) his passing through this Towne out of Ireland, he was importuned by a Factious party in Town, who knew his Temp[er], to interpose his Authority, y^t one *Haydock* who was their Chaplaine, might be admitted as an assistant to *Mr. Jackson*,

---

[*] In 1580, by Statute of Parliament, a fine of £20 per month was inflicted for not attending Church, and on the 8th March, 1604, licence was granted to John Talbot to be absent from Church, on paying £20 per month (See *Calendar of State Papers*, under those dates)

o^r Minist^r, to preach one p^t of ye Lord's Day, or else a Lecture once a Week   Which was propounded by the Majo^r Genl to my selfe & some few of ye Towne, who came to wait upon him at his Quarters, knowing nothing of the Matter, with ample promises of civilities to Mee & large Priveledges which he woulde procure for ye Towne, if I wolde effect his desire in this   Which I excused as well as I knew how upon such a Surprise   And when they thought to bring in ye same Haydock by strong hand, I improved my interest ye most I could to discountenance him   Who finding ye Towne generally bent to mischieve rather then [than] to hear him, he desisted and quickly after quitted ye place, & as a congregational Pastor, is by degrees become a Romish Priest, as I am informed

The Inhabitants of Nantw^{ch} by an ancient Charter exemplified under ye Seale of ye County Palatine, which is in my Custody   have bin exempted time out of mind from being impan'elled upon Juries with Foreigners at Assizes & Sessions held for this County which priveledge was ill resented by ye Justices of Peace   Whereupon on behalfe of ye Towne, I made applications to *Judge Bradsh[aw]* late Chief Justice of Chester, & obtained his allowance of ye said Charter in open Court *Ano* 1654   And since then I obtained ye like allowance of Sr *Job Charlton* Ch Justice of Chester, *an*^{o} 15° Car [1664-5] And since then prevailed with Sr *Geo Jeffreys* our present Chief Justice 32° Car 2 [1680] to do the same   Whereby o^r priveledge is established, notwithstanding ye endeavours of those y^t grudged us this Priveledge, to have suppressed it *

Ano 1659   There was a project y^t had many Abettors of in'ovating & utter overthrowing o^r Customes of Walling, & of introduceing 2 great Panes [Pans] into every Wich-House, that sholde have made a doble proportion of salt   for ye sole Benefit of ye occupiers, without any increase of rent, or colour of advantage to ye Lords & Owners of Walling, with design also of thrusting out ye poorer sort of occupiers, who were not of ability to be at ye charge of altering their Works, & furnishing their Wich-H[ouse] with so costly Pans   This was strongly attempted by Divers of ye abler Occupiers of Walling, who minded their private advantage, more then [than] ye publick good   which upon y^t account I opposed, & having 2 of ye Rulers on o^r part, wth much adoe, & much ill will, we p^{r}vented for that time   But through con ivance of ye Rulers from time to time, who are alwaies Occupiers of Walling ye Pannes are more and more inlarged to ye prejudice & detriment of all that are Owners & not Occupiers of Walling   which it is found by experience doth not advance the Trade, & it is feared will in time (by Gods just judgm^t) come to be nothing worth, which hath bin ye Rise & inriching of most families in Town †   R W [? Robert Wilkes] One that was a chief promoter of ye great Pans   soon after designed to have invaded another of the greatest priveledges belonging to ye Town by attempting to sink a Marle-pitt upon y^e *Beam-Heath*, near to a Field of his, out of which he designed to marle the said Field, without consent (indeed in defiance) of ye Towne which indangered a Mutiny   whereupon the Town met & resolved to oppose him, to prevent others from attempting ye like, whereupon he desisted   And this project had no better successe than y^t of ye great Panes, and himselfe got neither credit, noi profit by either

---

* See also page 79   † Half a century elapsed after 1659 before the ancient Salt Customs were finally abolished, perhaps Roger Wilbraham saw those changes looming in the future when he penned these words

Some years after this, yᵉ last Lᵈ Cholm[ondeley] or his Agents for him, under pretence that Strangers of late years had abused us by counterfeiting oᵣ Heath Mark and that my Lᵈ hearing of it had in Kindnesse sent us his own peculiar Mark, which we might see was not so easy to counterfeit as ours, and that it should bee at our Service, if wee pleased to use it insteade of oᵣ owne, which Mark was tendered us in yᵉ Church at a publique Meeting appointed by his Steward Mr. Ad——, who, to induce us to accept his Lorsᵖˢ profer, told us, that He being Lᵈ of yᵉ Towne, his Mark must needs be most proper for us, and more safe, being not so easily counterfeited To which after some silence, answear was made That we could not com'and another Mark with that freedom yᵗ wee might doe our owne That our Mark was so well knowne that if a Horse or other Beast shold stray off yᵉ Heath, yᵉ Owner might more boldly challenge his Goods having yᵗ Mark then [than] be put to contend with his Lordsᴾ We owned his Lordsʰᴾ to be Ld of yᵉ greatest pt of yᵉ Towne, but to have nothing to do with the *Heath*, which is not within yᵉ Barony So that upon all accounts we hold it best, for us to stick to our old Mark, & that if it had bin counterfeited, it behoved us to look yᵉ better to it for time to come Whereupon this matter fell, & since then we have heard no more of it

Ano 1663. Finding the Poor to increase by the dayly recourse of Strangers who stole in upon us, I procured a Survay to be taken, and presented a List of them (being then in number 782) to the Justices of P at yᵉ Quarter Sessions held in this Towne 7 July 1663 At which Sessions, a Lay Mize was charged upon yᵉ County, for yᵉ case of Market Townes, & other places that were found to be overcharged with poor And of that there was 50ˡⁱ [£50] alotted to this Towne by my procuremᵗ, & since then thrice 50ˡⁱ at so many payments, whereof I had the disposeall, by order of yᵉ Justices, for putting forth Orphans & other poor Children Apprentice, & other charitable uses; which hath exceedingly eased the Towne, as may appear by the Securities which I have in my hands, to Witnesse for mee what my care hath bin to put that Money to the furthest, to ease the Towne of those yonglings that eate up yᵉ Breade that sholde have sustained yᵉ Aged Poor

I likewise procured for the Towne a considerable Sume [sum] parcell of my Uncle Mr Raphe Wilbrahams estate, who left his whole estate reall & personal to yᵉ Poor indefinitely & without discriminacon * at yᵉ disposeall of his executors, of whom I obtained £400 for yᵉ Poor of Nantwᶜʰ, yᵉ designe whereof was to set yᵉ poor on work. But having no *House of Correction* or *Work House*† at that time, nor of many yeers after in this Towne, the Interest of yᵉ Money as it came to my hands hath bin faithfully distributed to yᵉ Sick, aged, & most indigent poor from time to time as appeares by yᵉ Notes in My Custody, which will sufficiently evidence that I have bin a Friend to yᵉ Towne & no bad Steward for yᵉ Poor

I also obtained other 50ˡⁱ out of my said Uncles estate in recompence of yᵉ Annuity of ˣˡⁱ [£10] which for several yeeres was pᵈ to *Mr Edw Hayes* out of yᵉ profits of yᵉ 400£ alotted to this Towne Which 50£ being left to my dispose, I designe for yᵉ Town-Schoole [Grammar School] for yᵉ teaching of so many children (whose parents are not of ability to keep them to Schoole) as the interest of yᵉ 50£ will amount unto

* See page 193   † By Act of Parliament 43 Eliz 1601, town authorities were required to afford relief to the impotent see to the apprenticing of poor children and provide work for the able-bodied by means of a convenient stock of flax, hemp, wool, thread, &c   No Work-house for that purpose was provided at Nantwich until 1677   Roger Wilbraham drew up another Poor List in Jan 1683, when the number was reduced to 281

Our Towne Bridge over the River as appears by Sundry Orders of yᵉ Justices at Chester hath bin repaired & maintained at yᵉ Town charge, & upon that consideracon we were alwaies exempted from contributing to yᵉ chaige of repairing yᵉ County Bridges untill yᵉ year 1652, that the then Justices of P repined at our not contributing to other Bridges And thereupon against our Will oidered ours to be a County Bridge,* & us to contribute with the County to all the County Bridges   After his Maⁱᵗᵉˢ Restauracon, when yᵉ known Lawes came to be in force again, Some of us began to think yᵉ Countrey might haply put it upon us to maintain oᵣ owne Bridge at our charge, after 12 yeeres contribucon to yᵉ County Bridges   Whereupon to put yᵉ mattʳ out of doubt, we caused our Bridge to be presented at the Quarter Sessions in Town anᵒ 1663, to be in decay. Whereby yᵉ County might be put to prove [proof], Whether it did belong to us, or them to repaire And for lack of defense on their part, it was established a County Bridge And wee had Ninety Pounds by Ordei of yᵉ Justices to make it a substantiall Bridge of Stone & xx Marks [£13 6s 8d] afterwards to pave yᵉ sᵈ Bridge, and so many yards at either end thereof   The overseers were of my nomination to yᵉ Justices, & yᵉ Work was compleated the year aftei by *Tim Adams*, Mason, who had yᵉ Materials of yᵉ Old Bridge by Bargaine, & yᵉ sᵈ 90£ allotted us as aforesᵈ †

The Plague being so hot in London & other places, anᵒ 1665, that never was the like It concerned us (yᵉ Towne being a Throughfare) to use all possible diligence to prevent the Infection that might come by Passengers & God knowes wee were in dayly Feare, & under dreadful expectation of yᵉ arrow that walkes in darkness being shot amongst us   But through mercy (For not unto us, but to his Name yᵗ kept us, be yᵉ praise,) we escaped it   I cannot say that I was more Active then [than] others   But am sensible that I was as much concerned, & as great a sharer in yᵉ Deliverance as any Person in Towne, & have the more reason to remember it with Thankfulnesse

From that time that yᵉ Towne was in such p'ill [peril] to yᵉ yeer 1675, (which was much imbittered to mee by yᵉ Losse of my 2 eldest sons, who were both hopefull & deservedly dear to me, & were snatched from mee within yᵉ compasse of 4 Months,) I had fewe opportunities of doing yᵉ Towne any considerable service   This year 1675 being a yeaie of scaicity, I was so much the more concerned for yᵉ Poore   But of that I shall say no more, Being in matters of this nature, the Left hand is not to know wᵗ yᵉ Right hand doth

Ano 1676 Soone after yᵉ death of my D [ear] W [ife] who left this Life & Mee disconsolate that day Twelve months that my Eldest son died, It was much upon my Spirit to do something extraordinary for yᵉ Poor   And yᵉ Legacy wᶜʰ my W [ife] left in newe Halfe crowne pieces and new shillings to be distributed to poor Widowes in our owne Street, was that (perhaps) which gave mee the first hint to make some more lasting provision for poor and aged Widowes; & straight it came into my thoughts that I had 3 Well built houses under a Roofe at yᵉ lower end of yᵉ same street, wᶜʰ wᵗʰ little adoe would soon be converted to an *Almes House* for six poor Widdowes, each House having

---

* This Order was made at the General Sessions at Middlewich on 27th April, 1652, before Henry Brooke, Tho. Stanley, Tho Mainwaring, Esqrs , and other Justices of the Peace   The order, which is signed by Humphrey Milton, Deputy Clerk of the Peace states that the " Wiche Bridge lyinge ouer yᵉ Weauer is yᵉ greatest & most frequented Road within this County "—(Wilb MS Coll)

† Cf page 196

convenient Apartments for 2 persons, who by co-habiting together might mutually succour & solace each other & thereupon instantly I went & warned yᵉ Tenants of those Houses to provide themselves Dwellings elsewhere betwixt & Christmas, not discovering anything of my purpose Which accordingly they did, & as my strength would permit, made it my Business to repaire & furnish yᵉ sᵈ Houses for yᵉ purpose & indowed yᵉ same with Lands of inheritance to yᵉ value of Forty Marks [£26 13s 4d.] yeerly, for yᵉ Perpetuall maintenance & sustentation of six poor aged Widdowes, to be chosen out of this Towne by me & my heires & having pitched upon six whom I thought fittest to prefer to this my Charity, I provided them Gownes, wherein they went orderly to Church yᵉ day after their admittance being oʳ Lady Day 1677, which yᵗ yeer fell out to be yᵉ Sabbath Day, & had yᵉ Almes Women to Din'er that day, that I might have opportunity to Blesse God with them, & to begg his Blessing upon that which he put into my Heart to do for yᵉ Poor, sith it hath pleased him to favour mee so far as to let me see it effected to my Hearts content

Many of the poore amongst us through a habit of idleness growing insolent for lack of a House of Correction at hand, & others as clamorous for maintenance, who had no list to work, & yet made it their Plea to yᵉ Justice, that they coulde not have worke to earn a livelihood, Wee made urgent application to yᵉ Justices of P at yᵉ Quarter Sessions held in this Towne July 1677, & obtained an order for a House of Correction & Work H [ouse] forthwith to be sett up in this Town,* (wᶜʰ was a thing yᵗ had bin long wished) and a Lay was granted for raising so much money through yᵉ County as sufficed to p'chase a fair Brick House, outhouses, &c, at yᵉ further end of yᵉ Beam Street, which by yᵉ care of yᵉ Treasurers *Mr Thos Wicksted & Mr Rich. Seyvill* is now put into good repaire † And thereupon to set yᵉ poor of yᵉ Towne on work, I delivered 200ʰ [£200] of the 400ʰ [£400] which by my procuremᵗ was allotted to this Towne out of my uncle *Mr Raphe Wilbraham* his estate, For wᶜʰ 200£ I have a Receit under the hands & seales of yᵉ Treasurers before named, & their Assumpsit to imploy yᵉ same for setting yᵉ Poor of yᵉ Towne on Work which if duely inspected will be sundry waies helpfull and beneficiall to yᵉ Towne, care being Taken, to secure it, yᵗ yᵉ Money be not lost

After yᵉ death of *Mr Jackson* our Minister, who died yᵉ begin'ing of winter anᵒ 1677, when *Mr. Crewe* assumed a right of presentation to yᵉ Curateship of Nantwich & would impose upon us against our consent, I laboured what in mee lay by Letters & other applications to yᵉ Bishop, being at that time unable to travell or stir much in yᵉ Busines, to have prevented *Mr Crewes* imposing upon us, & would have given out of my owne Purse as much as the Profits of yᵉ Easter Roll (under wᶜʰ Mr Cr [ewe] claims a right of Advowson) cost his Grandff[ather] *Sʳ Rand[ulph] Crew*, which as I have heard was 100 Marks [£66 13s 4d] & if it would be accepted I would give 100ʰ [£100] gladly, that yᵉ Towne might have the nomination of their owne Minister, to which oure Counsell tells us we have a good right by prescription, if yᵉ Bishop would have heard what we had to say for ourselves, But the Bishop being at London, this Busines was transacted there

---

* This was not a Workhouse in the modern sense of the term but a place where work was provided for the able-bodied poor, who lived at their own homes and received relief there The House of Correction was a prison for idle vagabonds, or paupers, who, being able, refused to work (See Annals, 1767)

† The MS Journal states that "£20 salary was granted us for yᵉ Master, & I [Rog Wilb] had the favor of nominating the first Mr to the Bench, wᶜʰ was Cap M '

to oᵣ disadvantage & disappointment, by yᵉ restless endeavours of *Mr. Str.* [*inger*]* in compliance with *Mr Crew*, & under his Title (such as it is) to thruste himselfe upon us, which he did to yᵉ dissatisfaction of yᵉ whole Body of yᵉ Towne & parish I wish it may turne to his & our good in Conclusion · which is more than at present I have in prospect, considering his temper, and that he hath so much disobliged yᵉ whole Towne, that it will be hard for him to recover yᵉ Love he hath lost amongst us.

Three things more I have endeavoured of very great concernemᵗ to yᵉ Towne, which, I would gladly have accomplished

One is, The inclosing of a considerable part of yᵉ *Beam Heath*, which may well be spared for a settled maintenance for yᵉ Minister, & schoole [Free Grammar School] & something in certainty for yᵉ Poore yeerly, to ease yᶜ Towne This hath bin obstructed by yᵉ *Lords of Alvaston*, who have a peculiar interest in the Com'on, which renders them little, & no possibility of improveing their interest, & yet will not assent to yᵉ inclosing of any part of yᵉ sᵈ com'ons having as much or more allowed them then [than] they do or can make of their priveledge.

Another Mischiefe to yᵉ Towne is yᵉ Liberty that Owners of Cottages in Town take to admitt Strangers & Inmates into such Cottages, without regard of secureing the Towne. [*i e* from becoming chargeable as paupers to the town] I myselfe have undertaken to be responsible for my Tenants, if any of them sholde become burdensome. others promise faire, but performe nothing Notwithstanding we have a good order made by Sʳ *Thos. Milward* late Justice of Chester to redresse this, which Order was procured by my father & other Gentlemen of yᵉ Towne in his time [viz.· in 1632, see page 130] Which Order might easily be revived, but yᵗ selfe prevailes too much with yᵉ generallity of Men

A third Mischiefe is —That wee cannot agree of yᵉ old Rents in Towne, there beinge severall Books of yᵉ old Rents made at severall times, which amout to yᵉ same sume in yᵉ whole, but differ in particulars, & every man being willing to pay by that Book yᵗ eases him most, oᵣ Assessments when they come to be collected fall short of the Sume intended Which yᵉ Officers of late yeeres perceiving, when they come to be re-imbursed require a greater Lay than needs, to yᵉ end it may satisfy them & so both Poor & Rich that are willing to pay their Laies, pay constantly above their share, & others wᵗ [what] they list. I myselfe have oft times, when this abuse hath bin complained of at our Meetings, undertaken to pay by any one Book, so that might be establisht But when that comes to be done, one or other is absent of those who have no leasure to meet, when it is not for their profit

For ten yeeres from yᵉ time that I had a concerne in Towne, & took upon me to interest myselfe in their concernes, I ever found the people tractable & governable, beyond what might be expected from a people that had yᵉ Raines in their owne hands, till those unhappy differences before spoken of which happened aᵒ 1659, were sett on foot, & from that time those that could not have their Will then, declined our Meetings in yᵉ Church & gave leaue to those that wolde to take yᵗ troble of manageing yᵉ Towne concernes, whilst they themselves minded their owne ; yet did not this discourage mee to appeare at all Meetings, Where I ever spake my Mind freely, which if it tended to ease the

---

* The Wilb MS Journal, alluding to the death of Mr Jackson, who had been Minister of Nantwich for thirty years says, "In compliance with Mr Crewe's pretensions, another lesse deserving was thrust upon us, that was born among us G *Str*"[*inger*].

Towne it was well accepted, if it were matter of charge, it was taken in good part, being it was knowne to all I was to bear a considerable share my selfe. And if those whom I have faithfully served for so many yeeres, will not Witness this for mee, I have this Witness in my selfe, that I have done it, and not served my selfe of Them

Remember mee, O my God, for Good

I have not left this in Writing to tell the World what I have done, But to minde [remind] my sonne of what Strephon told his companions on his death Bed.

"The pleasures wch from virtuous Deeds we have
Procure ye Sweetest slumbers in the Grave"

Whither I am hastening, and having lived to see many changes, am the more concerned (for ye short time I have to live) to prepare and wait for my appointed change"

"Sic ŏ sic juvat vivere, sic perire"

[Dated] "Feb 2nd 1682"

After the death of Roger Wilbraham, Esq, at Townsend, on the 5th March, 1707-8, his son, Randle Wilbraham, Esq of Rode, removed to Nantwich, and became the head of the house and historian of the family He mentions two great changes, one of local interest, and the other of a general character, that are noteworthy. The Ancient Customs of Walling, which had become too antiquated for the times, passed away, (see Account of the Salt Trade *posted*,) and the simple manners of country gentlemen were relinquished for a more fashionable life. Randle Wilbraham, speaking of the death of his father-in-law in the family Journal, says —

"ffeb 3 1709[-10] Dyed s^r Richd Brooke of Norton, Bart, an honest ffriendly Gentleman, whose hospitality justly gained him the prayers of the Poor & Applause of the Rich *att a tyme when that good and Ancient way of House keeping was decry'd to bring in new & more pernicious ffashions* Tom Hide, son of Edward Hide, of Norbury Esq, Kinsman & companion to Sr Richard, was so affected with the loss of soe kind a ffrend, that himself survived but a few hours"

In the seventeenth century few gentlemen made journeys to London, or any other expensive journey, but upon important business, and their wives never, by which providence they enjoyed and improved their estates in the country, and kept good hospitality in their house, brought up their children well and were beloved by their neighbours * But in the reign of Queen Anne, as travelling became easier, and literature was more disseminated, country gentlemen paid less attention to local matters, and, adopting the new manners of Society, frequently left their country residences to enjoy the luxuries and gaieties of Town life

Randle Wilbraham *(MS Journal)* writes as follows —

"May 1709 Thos Wettenhall Esq, my kinsman & neighbour dyd [died] of a Feavour † A sober gentleman, a good Majestrate and very useful in his place I promised myself great satisfaction in his conversation by my removall from Rode to Namptwich, but instead thereof I succeeded in his troublesome office" [viz as Magistrate]   "att ye desire of H Earle of Cholmondeley"

* See Lord Clarendon's Life, quoted in Disraeli's "*Curiosities of Literature*," p 253. (Edit 1867)
† Thos Wettenhall Esq was buried, without memorial, at Nantwich on the 19th May, 1709 *(Par Reg)*

"April 7 1711 Severall younge men & women took a Boat from y[e] Mill at N   and rowed up the river   but soe carelessly & unskilfully (the water being high) that the stream drew y[e] Boat under the Bridge att y[e] Flood-gates   & the apprehension of so imminent danger made them leap out of the boat, whereby three persons perished * the rest were saved "

Feb 16 1711 [12] Mem[d]   Five daughters of William late L[d] Brereton living in this Towne at Mr Goldsmith's house in Hospitall Street   The youngest Frances dyed there   And Mr Peak late Vicar of Bowden came to mee from the other ladies her sisters to desire shee might bee interred in my Buriall [place] to w[ch] I consented & appointed the place, viz   att the head of S[r] David Cradock's monum[t] '

Some explanation is necessary to give interest to this last memorandum

"Mr Goldsmith's house," has been already alluded to in these pages as the probable site of St Nicholas Hospital (p 52-3)   It is mentioned in the will (dated 25th March, 1684) of John Goldsmith, Gent, as follows —"As I am unable to assure to my said wife [Anne] the use of my dwelling-house in Nantwich, as I had before promised, owing to its being settled on my son John, I further leave her, should my son refuse to let her inhabit the said house with him, the sum of £40, but if my son John sh[d] kindly permit my said wife, Anne Goldsmith, and Elizabeth Weston, my grand-daughter, to dyett with him without requiring from them more than £16 per annum during my said wife's widowhood, then the £40 not to be payable to her "†   According to a Nantwich Rate Book for 1691, John Goldsmith is assessed for the house, and Madam Anne Goldsmith, his step-mother, for her personal estate, proving that at that time she did "dyett with him."   By her own will in 1701, she leaves £20 for her step-son "to defend his right to his house, wherein he now lives,' in case my grandson, "does not give my said [step-]son Gouldsmyth a discharge or release from any claim he may hereafter lay ' to it   John Goldsmith also mentions (Will, 1684) his "niece M[rs] Anne Brereton," who was one of the ' five daughters of William late [2nd] Lord Brereton "

The Goldsmiths became connected with the noble family of Brereton, of Brereton, in this county, by second marriages, and thus the relationship between the two families was only distant.

Anne Goldsmith, the second wife of John Goldsmith, Gent,‡ was the daughter of Sir Thomas Smith, of Hough, who had been Mayor of Chester in 1622, and Sheriff of the county in 1623   Her sister Mary Smith married George Cotton, son of Thomas Cotton of Combermere, and was re-married to Sir Robert Holt, of Aston, near Birmingham, whose first wife was Jane, the sister of William, second Lord Brereton §   Although it may appear strange that John Goldsmith should have described M[rs] Anne Brereton as his "niece," it is very remarkable that an acquaintance was long continued between these two families

---

* The Parish Register records the burial of two persons, the third no doubt being buried elsewhere —
               "1711 April 9th   John Judson and his daughter Sarah drowned '

† Additions and Corrections for "A Royal Descent and other Pedigrees and Memorials,' by Miss Thomasine E Sharpe, p 33, (Privately printed, only 40 copies   1881)
   The Parish Register records the burial of the testator as follows —
                    ' 1684 April 24   John Gouldsmyth, Gent "

‡ This marriage is recorded in the Parish Register thus —
               "1666 May 24   John Goldsmith, Gent, and M[rs] Anne Smith "

§ Cf Brereton and Smith Pedigrees in Dr Ormerod's Cheshire, (New Edit) vol iii pp 89 and 503 and the Goldsmith pedigree in the Chapter on Family History postea

William, second Lord Brereton, who was a heavy sufferer during the Civil War, (pp 159, *n*, and 185), at his death, left four sons and six daughters   All the daughters, except one, Margaret, died unmarried, and of these, four were interred in the Wilbraham burial place, which occupied an area of 16 sq ft in the South Transept of Nantwich Church, the fifth being *the Honble. Elizabeth Brereton,* who was buried at Brereton on the 6th April, 1723.   The Parish Register thus records the burials of these aged maiden ladies —

> "1711-2 Feb 16 Honble Mrs Frances Brereton, Spinster "
> "1716   Dec 1 Honble Mrs Mary Brereton, Spinster "
> "1718-9 Jan 4 Honble Mrs Anne Brereton, Spinster "
> "1720   May 14 Honble Mrs Jane Brereton, Spinster "

The *Rev. John Peake,* late Vicar of Bowden (1689-90) had been deprived of his living as a Non-Juror, for refusing to take the oath of allegiance to King William III

Resuming the extracts from *Randle Wilbraham's* Journal —

"Sept 17th 1713 The five Bells belonging to the Church of N were taken down, in order to cast into six by *Abram Rudhall* "[*]

' Oct 6th 1713 About 6 at night a foine [fine, *i e* great] fire broke out on ye Top of a Rick of Oates adjoining to a Barne of *Mr John Comberbach* in Pillory St, wch in short time consumed ye sd Barne & most of ye Corne therein (as the providence of God ordered) it was a calm night and tho' a Thatcht house stood within 5 foot of it, yet it was preserved, and no further harme ensued "

"The summer of 1714 was a great Drought which did much accelerate corne Harvest that there was Barley cut before Midsummer, & I bought in the markett at N new barley for use July 17 of the same year "

On Monday Ap 5, 1714, Began the first Assizes in the year of my Shevalry [Shrievalty] wher[e] *Sr Joseph Jekyll Kt* sate sole Justice, & there being not much business the Judge went out of Chester on Fryday, & gave mee a Dismission leaving my Deputy *Mr Kent* to attend the Recorder of Chester[†] who hee had constituted his to call the Court that Day & the next "

"K[in]g George proclaimed in Nantwich on Wednesday ye 4 Aug 1714 "

"Sep 20 1714 The later Assizes in the year of my Sheriffry commenct att which both Justices were present I was much out of Order all the Time but was much comforted to think it was the last The Judges went out on Fryday ye 24th & I returned home leaving my undersheriff with some men to attend the Judges Deputy "

It was the usual custom then, and for more than a century after, for the High Sheriff of the County to make a grand state entry into Chester to meet the Judges, and thus, Randle Wilbraham Esq, arrayed in a costly dress and fashionable wig, and bearing in his hand a "white wand " (the badge of his office) rode from Nantwich to Chester in the state carriage drawn by richly caparisoned horses led by a liveried postillion, with a long procession of gentry, tenantry, javelin men, a running footman, servants &c, amid the clanging of bells in all the parish Churches along the road and at Chester   Of course, all this entailed considerable personal expense, which was further increased by

---

[*] The *Rudhalls* of Gloucester were noted bell founders there for about a century, and were succeeded in or about 1774 by the name of *Mears*

[†] The Recorder of Chester at this time was also a native of Nantwich,—Mr Roger Comberbach, whose son, Roger Comberbach LL B was Prothonotary of the Palatinate of Chester

costly entertainments, gifts, &c * at Chester, in maintaining the dignity of the high office. This seems to be the explanation of the words of Randle Wilbraham, that, after the second Assizes he *"was much comforted"* From the following list of expenses in his own handwriting, still preserved at Delamere, it is clear that the office carried with it no light pecuniary burden, especially when it is remembered that the sums here given would be perhaps equal to three times the amounts at the present time

"ACCᵀ of the CHARGES of my SHERIFFRY Begun Dec 22 1713 & ending Dec 10 1714 "

	£	s	d	£	s	d
To the Trumpeters who came to offer their service	00	02	00			
To Postage of the Dedimus from London	00	03	06			
To Namptwich Ringers	00	06	00			
Expenses att Chester when I gaue security in yᵉ Excheqr	01	02	08			
To the Ringers att S. Mary s in Chester	00	05	00			
To the Prisoner att the Castle	00	02	06			
To the Bailiff Itnerant att yᵉ Exchequer	00	05	00			
To the Guard at the Castle	00	02	06			
To the Trumpeters when wee agreed [i e engaged them for the procession]	00	02	00			
Expence att my going to Chestr a second time	00	12	00			
To cos Raphe Wilbraham for getting my name rectified	03	04	06			
The Drapers Bill for Cloth Lining & trimming for 40 Liveries	91	08	02			
Mr Seavill Drapr his particular Bill	22	10	00			
To Philip Dean for 17 new Javelins & cleaning 5 old	01	17	00			
ffor Dying old fringe for the Staves	00	03	00			
ffor Lace for my Mens Hatts & other particulars frō Chester	06	08	04			
Expense att my going to Chest to prepare for yᵉ Assizes	00	10	00			
pᵈ to Tom farington Taylor his bill for work	13	10	00			
To Mr Bowler, his Bill for Stockings	03	17	00			
To Gervase Walker his Bill for hatts	08	05	06			
To Robert Brown his Bill for gloves	01	07	06			
To the Herald att armes for my Banners	03	00	00			
To the Bayliffe for my White Ward	00	02	06			

	1st Assizes Ap 5, 1/14			Latter Assizes Sep 20		
	£	s	d	£	s	d
To the Drummers at Namptwich	00	02	06	00	02	06
To the Towne fiddlers	00	02	06	00	02	06
To John Fleet, my Porter, to keep out th Rabble yᵉ morning I went	00	01	00	00	01	00
To the Drummers belonging to Chester Castle	00	05	00	00	05	00
To the City Musick	00	05	00	00	05	00
To the Vergers att the Choir	00	10	00	00	10	00
For a Mourning Sword [on account of the death of Queen Anne]	00	08	00			
to Sr Tho Brookes Servants where I lay at yᵉ Time of yᵉ Assizes	00	07	06	00	10	00
to yᵉ Postillion	00	10	00	00	05	00
To yᵉ Trumpeters their Wages, a guinea a peace	02	03	00	02	03	00
To my owne Musick	01	00	00			
To a Musician who plaid on the Bass viall				00	10	00
To Ringers at the severall Churches on yᵉ Rode & att Chester	02	15	00	01	13	00
To the Prisoners att the Castle	00	10	00			
To the poor of St Michaels Parish	01	10	00			
To the poor att my coming out				01	00	00
To Mr Bennett Wyne Marcht his Bill	16	05	00	11	11	00
To Mr Henry Leghs men who brought Venison	00	10	00			

* About 1745 an Association of County Gentlemen was formed for the purpose of reducing the customary expenses which heretofore fell to the lot of each High Sheriff   (See No 653 "*Cheshire Sheaf*)

	£ s d	£ s d
Expence att the Glashouse	00 11 06	
To Mr Hughes his Generall Bill for my entertainment & Horses	48 12 06	53 00 00
To Mr Hughes his Servants, att the Inne	01 10 00	01 10 00
To Mr Williams my Chaplain ye first Assizes 2 Jacobus'	02 11 06	——
To Mr Gibbons [Rector of Nantwich] my Chaplaine the latter Assizes	——	02 11 00
To my Footman [? the running footman] Philipp Nettles	00 05 00	00 05 00
To Joseph Davie for his pains & attendance	01 01 06	01 00 00
To Hamnett Oxon for Carriage of my Clothes to & frō Chester ..	00 11 00	——
For Carriage of two Boxes from London	00 11 06	——
For a Sword for my Groom	00 05 00	——
To Mr Bennetts Wine Cooper	00 05 00	——
To Faringtons Men [tailors in Nantwich] for Beverage [i e Beer-money]	00 02 06	——
To the Cook att Chester	01 00 00	——
To Tilcock the Sadler his Bill	01 07 10	——
To Hayles [of Nantwich] the Shoemaker	01 10 00	——
pd to my son Randle for things bought for me at London	32 01 03	——
More to him for cloths &c for my son Roger	18 02 09	——
Expence att proclaiming King George att Chester	01 10 00	——
for a New Gray Cloth Coat	03 00 00	——
Occasionall expences not before specify'd	——	01 02 00

	£ s d
[Total]	£384 08 06
This Doubly charged	4 10 00

	£ s d	£ s d
Recd back for the profitts of the County Court	55 00 00	£379 18 06
The Sheriffs Fee allowed on passing his Account	20 00 00	
A present of Wine from Clutton Wright esq	01 00 00	
A buck from H Legh of High Legh, Esq att the first Assizes	02 00 00	
A present of Wine from Mr Bromhall	00 18 00	
A present of Wine and Sturgeon from the undersheriff	03 00 00	
	£81 18 00	

Sep 28 1716 Mr Grantham, to whom I did lett the profitts of the County Court complaining much that his Bargaine was hard, I returned to him 5li wch must be added to my charge	05 00 00
So that ye Whole Charge amounts to	£303 00 06

Amongst "the names of Roman Catholics, Non-jurors, and others who refus'd to take Oaths to his late Majesty King George I," in 1715,* two persons are mentioned in this locality, namely — "*Laurence Hill,* of Nantwich, Yeoman," whose property was valued at £4 2s od , and "*Anne Chesceyss*" [or *Cheswiss,* as now pronounced] "of Spurstow, spinster."

The Wilb MS Journal next records as follows —

"April 9, 1716 By reason of the great number of Scots & others taken att Preston (upon an Insurrection made on behalf of Jas son of Jas II agst Geo Dk of Hanover, then reigning Kg of Gt Brit) & detained in prison in ye Shire Hall att Chester The Assizes usually held there was by adjournment att Nantwich before *Sr Joseph Jekyll & Edwd Jeffries Esqrs alias Winnington* The said Judges taking up their lodgings at my howse '

"Septr 24th 1716 Assizes held as before and the Judges lay at my howse"

* This list was first printed in 1745, and reprinted for John Russell Smith in 1862

The County Assizes had been held at Nantwich on a former occasion, 112 years before, owing to the plague at Chester in 160₁, and the unhealthy state of the Castle was the cause of the removal of both Assizes to Nantwich in 1716   According to the Cowper MS the winter of 1715 was "very severe, and the snow lay a yard deep in the roads   Many of the prisoners (among whom was Lord Charles Murray the son of the Duke of Athol & several gentlemen besides a great number of privates) died in the Castle by the severity of the Season   many were carried off by a malignant fever, and most of the survivors were transported to the plantations in America "*

"March 25 1718 I [Randle Wilbraham] got the Town Charter signed by SPENCER COWPER ESQ , who succeeded Jekyll at Chester Assizes "

"Decr 4th 1723 was first held a Faire† in this Towne prsuant to a Patent newly granted to H[ugh] Earl of Cholmondeley "

' The next day [5 Dec 1723] there happened a fire in a house‡ late Madews next door to the Ship ale-house , wh[ich] threatened much damage to the Towne , but by God's blessing our endeavours, the same was extinguisht without further harme than ye burning down most part of ye house where it began, & some small detriment to ye next   *Laus Deo* "

"On Munday Jan 18, 1724[-5] Dyed the Rt Honble Hugh Earle of Cholmondeley & was succeeded in his Honrs by his Brother George , tho[ugh] a good part of the estate was before settled upon George his sd Brothers son on his marriage with Mary sole Daughter of the Honrble Robert Walpole Esqr "

"1727 *Mem'd* that about the later end of June after a long fit of Wett weather succeeded by a sudden Heat & Drought, a Distemper more epidemicall than has been known in ye memory of Man Began to show its Malignity on the sea coasts of Lancashire, & in short time spread itself into this & the neighbouring Countys & almost all over England   It sometimes seiz'd with violent symptoms of a putrid Feavour , other while with intermissions which grew shorter till the Feavour was continuall, & tho[ugh] it might bee computed that not aboue one in Ten dyed, yet those who escaped, did it with great Difficulty after 5 or six weekes illness and at last generally ended in a Quotidian, Tertian, or Quartan Ague, with much dissipation of spirits, & prostration of strength   what was peculiar & observable in this disease was, that it was most frequent among servants, Labourrs *&* people of meane condition, *&* rag'd more in Proportion in Country Villages§ than in Populous Citys *&* Market Towns , *&* therein was usually observed to affect the outskirts worse than ye more inward parts   In the cure the following Method was found most successfull   If it seiz'd violently at the first, then bleeding was found usefull   If it did intrmit at first, Bleeding was omitted, *&* vesicatorys [blisters] were rais'd in proper places, to draw off ye humour from ye neiues , which were much affected where there was Intermissions the Bark [Peruvian] had not its usual effect, *&* then recourse was had to salt of wormwood *&* juice of Lemons, mixt with snake root *&* other warm *&* nervous medicines, administered with ye Bark

As to my owne family, My sons Roger & Tom, being gone to Offerton were seiz'd with it there   But by Gods blessing & the care of Dr Jackson of Manchester, after six weeks they return'd without any remaining ill symptoms   At home the Cook & Foot-boy, were by seuerall Relapses ill & weak aboue two months but hitherto *though scarce any house in the neighbourhood has escaped* yet it has made noe further progress among my Domesticks   *Laus Deo Amen* "

* Quoted by Dr Ormerod *Hist Chesh* vol I p 248 (New Edit)

† This fair commonly called *Dirty Fair*, is still held

‡ Though not mentioned in the Memorandum, there appears to have been loss of life at this fire according to the following line in the Burial Register —" 1723 Dec 7 Philipp Cooper Burnt to Death

§ Thus in the adjoining parish of Wybunbury, which about this time had an average death rate of about 50 annually, the Register records 121, 136 and 102 burials for the years 1728, 1729, and 1730 respectively

"Dec 4 1728 Having in the year before Giuen a short Account of a Distemper then reigning in this Country, I was in hopes I might haue dismist that subject, but find occasion to repeat the like remark in this present year 1728 About Midsum'er, the same Feavour re-kindled with the same malignity or greater than before Many dyed of it, & those who escap'd Death fell into Agues Quartan, Tertian, Quotidians & some of Anomalous kind About ye middle of October ye Feavour grew less frequent, but ye Ague more Epidemical This Town & the neighbourhood thereof felt it more seuerly, than the year before & p'ticularly my ffamily My Wife, my Gr-son Dick, my daughter Mary, ye Cook, Chambermaid, my Wiues [Wife's] Maid, my Groom, Tho Huxley,* & my son Harry were attack'd by it Where the Quinquina [Bark] was taken in great Quantitys, & for a long space of Time, it seldom return'd but where it was taken in such Quantity only as heretofore had been thought sufficient, it return'd with much seuerity, & ye Patients were forc't to repeat it to 4, 5 or 6 ounces What the Spring may produce God only knows But if the distemper continues wch depriues poor People of getting their bread by their labour, & that the Crops of corne proue noe better than they haue done for the last two yeares the Case will be deplorate"

The above account is the last of the local events contained in the Wilbraham MS Journal, and it will now be seen how much of interest relating to Nantwich would haue been lost to posterity, but for the memoranda left on record by the four successive Mr. Wilbrahams of this town, during a period extending over more than a century and a half. Although there is no special reference in the Parish Register to these years of great Mortality, the number of burials during those years furnish ample proof of an unusually large death-rate. In 1727 are registered 154 burials, of which 91 occur during the six months from August to January. In 1728 there were no less than 209 burials, chiefly of young people, "paupers," and "widows," 51 being recorded in the month of January 1728-9. In the following year the number of burials is 117, and in 1730, 110, and it was not until 1731 that the death-rate of the parish decreased to a normal average of 66.

On the 31st May, 1727, Chancellor Gastrell granted a Faculty to William Maisterson and six other gentlemen of the town to build a South Gallery in Nantwich Church, which, in after years, became the place where the principal families of the town sat at Church, untill its removal in 1855. It contained six front pews (two under each arch), and twelve back pews in two rows, separated from the front pews by an aisle. Some idea of the cost of this Gallery may be arrived at from the following receipt, and particulars on a plan of the gallery, preserved at Delamere. (Wilb. MS. Coll)

1729-30 "Jan 3 "Recd From Randle Wilbraham Esq Twenty four pounds and ten shillings for three seats in the New South Gallery in the Parish Church of Namptwich that is to say, £14 10s 0d for the third front seat from the East End £6 0s 0d for the seat next behind it, No 10 and for the next behind that, No 15, £4 Being reasonable Rates proportioned to the whole charge expended in erecting the sd Gallery, and assessed and agreed unto by us Commoners appointed to build the sd Gallery .

£	s	d
24	10	0

Wm Maisterson, John Bromhall, Ran Wilbraham, John Wixsted, Thos Williams, Geo. Audley, Matt Gleave "

* Randle Wilbraham records his death as follows —"Aprill the 30th 1729 Dyed my faithfull & Diligent servt Thomas Huxley of an Acute Feavour who is the first servt who dyed out of my Howse, tho' I haue been an Housekeepr 40 years, & haue seldom had less numbr than eight at a time & sometimes more " His burial is entered at Wybunbury as follows —"1729 May 2 Mr Thomas Huxley Steward to Randle Wilbraham of Nantwich Esq
" On the 21st June 1730 Randle Brereton, a servant to Randle Wilbraham Esq " was buried at Nantwich *(Par Reg)*

The Plan gives the following information respecting the *front pews*.—

			Ft In	£ s d.	
Jno Bromhall Esq	⎱	under eastern	6 10	£14 5 0	⎫
Wm Maisterson Esq	⎰	Arch	8 0½ ·	£14 5 0	
Ran Wilbraham Esq ·	⎱	under the	8 3	£14 10 0	£ s d.
Mr Thos Williams ·	⎰	middle arch	8 3½	£14 5 0	Total 80 0 0
Mr Geo Audley ·	⎱	under the	8 6	£11 10 0	
Mr Jno Wixsted	⎰	west Arch	8 4½	£11 5 0	⎭

In August 1729 *Horse-races* were first inaugurated at Nantwich   They continued to be held annually for two or three days at the end of June, or beginning of July, on Beam Heath, for about a century   They were mainly upheld and patronized by County Gentlemen, who kept valuable studs of highly bred horses, and who, on the race days, resorted to the Cock-pit at the *Griffin Inn** in the morning, saw the horses run on the Course in the afternoon; and went at night to the Play at the *Crown Assembly Room*, or at the *Old Barn*† at Hospital Street-end, until the *Play-House* was built‡ in Dog Lane, early in the present century by Charles Mare, Esq , of the Manor House, in Beam Street   In 1820 Mytton's§ " Mandeville " won the gold cup at Nantwich, and in 1822 the "sixty-five guineas," on the same course, but the old turf-loving sport of the gentry was then fast declining.   A few years after Mr Mytton's career as a sportsman had ended, and meanwhile, in 1824, Mr Benjamin White, shoe manufacturer, and Mr Davies, salt manufacturer, rented the Race-course, and ploughed it up, and although races were run afterwards on the '*Ley Ground*,' and, for a few years on the '*Ox Pastures*,' having lost their former popularity they were soon altogether discontinued   In like manner after the death of Charles Mare, Esq ,‖ the patron of the Theatre, the Messrs Stanton, with their talented " Company of Comedians," which had so long visited Nantwich and other towns in Cheshire and the adjacent counties, now failed to 'draw a house ,' and so the Theatre was closed, and, in 1840, partly pulled down   The gallery of the Play-house was converted into the present Odd Fellows' Lodge Room, and a row of cottages was built on the site of the pit, stage, and green-room   The following mentions in the Parish Register of a resident jockey, dancing-masters, and 'men of the sock and buskin,' associated as they were with the gaieties and amusements of the town in former days, will be of interest.

" 1738 Dec 15 Thos s of Henry Johnson, Dancing Master " [Bapt Reg]
" 1743 Aug 25 Wm s of John Wheeler, Comedian   [Bur Reg]
" 1745 Sep 12 Catherine wife of Jonn Doncaster, Jockey " [Bur Reg]
" 1750 Aug 22 Ann, dau of Wm Quelch, a player " [Bur Reg]
" 1750 1 Feb 17 John Doncaster, Jockey " [Bur Reg]
" 1761 July 23 Eliz d of James Bath, a Player " [Bapt Reg]

* The "*Griffin Inn*," one of the oldest houses in High Town, is now occupied by Mr E H. Rhodes

† This picturesque "*Old Barn*" of wood and thatch, which was a very commodious building, was pulled down in or about April, 1883

‡ About the same time an adjacent Inn changed its name from the "*Elephant and Castle*" to that of the *Shakespeare Tavern*

§ This was the celebrated Jack Mytton, of Halston, Esq , whose son of the same name was for many years a land agent for Lord Kilmorey, and died a few years ago at his residence near Nantwich

‖ Charles Mare, (the son of Matthew Mare, Esq of the Broomlands, in Hatherton, a retired potter who died in 1814,) was a ship-builder in Liverpool, and failed in the large sum of £500,000   He died at Nantwich on the 8th March, 1838, aged 51, and was buried at Wybunbury

"1767 Jan 27 Robert Endas s of Saml Stanton, Player " [Bapt Reg]
"1782 Sep 25 Mary dau of George Fairburn, comedian, & Margaret his wife Recd " [Bapt Reg]
"1797 Aug 22 Samuell Stanton, Gent Buried "* [Bur Reg]
"1809 Mar 22 George Stanton, Comedian [Bur Reg]
"1812 July 12 Emilia dr of Charles Stanton, comedian, & Sarah " [Bapt Reg]

Two gravestones on the north side of the Churchyard were placed to the memory of two of Mr Stanton's company of theatricals, and inscribed as follows —

"James Smith, Comedian who died Aug 8, 1828 Aged 50 "
"Henry Wood,† Comedian, who died Jan 26, 1836 Aged 55 "

On the 19th April, 1731, the Rev Thos. Brooke, Rector, preached a special sermon in the Parish Church, on the occasion of a *Spring Flower Show* held in the town

In the same year, (Oct 15th) a Vestry Meeting decided

"That there shall be an altar-piece made and erected with Ten Commandments Lords Prayer and Creed wrote upon the same, suitable ffor the Chancell And the Churchwardens shall collect and pay att the parish Charge what cannot be gathered by subscriptions for the same "‡

This order was duly carried out by filling up with stone more than half of the East Window, as shown in the East view of Nantwich Church in Lysons' "Cheshire " Forty years after, Mr Partridge wrote— "The Altar-piece is a work of handsome modern architecture executed by that ingenious architect *Mr William Yoxall* of this town, lately deceased "§—(*Hist Nant* p 25) It was removed when Lord Crewe restored the Chancel, but an external disfigurement to the Church, viz the Rectory House, described by that writer as "a genteel brick fabrick built by Dr Brooke, Dean of Chester, and Rector of Nantwich, towards which in consideration of his great merit and affectionate regard borne him, his parishioners largely contributed, "—(*ibid* p 42) and designed most likely by the same architect, continues to the present time.

Important alterations, too, were made in the Churchyard between 1735 and 1739, according to the Minutes of the Vestry Book, as follows.—

"1735-6 Feb 4 Agreed "there shod be a handsome flag'd rode from the dean's [Dr Brooke] garden to the Chancell Door "

"1736. Aug 1 Agreed "there shall be a flagg road made between ye Light [lich]-gates [Iron gates opposite Pepper Street] on ye North side ye Church to ye West Door, two yards Broad, to be done with white flags from Kelsall Hill "

"1737 July 31 "to get sand to level and regulate the churchyard, & repair pavements "

"1738 Sept 28 to make a pavement from the Turnstile leading to the Market House [in High Town] to

---

* See Church Monuments in the North transept of the Church

† Henry Wood died in Church Lane in great poverty and left two daughters one of whom survived till 1876 gaining a livelihood in Nantwich as a teacher of music and dancing

‡ This extract, and others given on subsequent pages, are taken from the "*Town Vestry Book*, ' a paper book, in parchment backs, containing the minutes of parish Meetings, &c from the 15th Oct 1731 to the 15th June 1777 This volume, which is minus pages 1 and 2, is now preserved at the Rectory House It is stated on p 51, that there were three earlier volumes of the *Church Vestry Book*, commencing in the years 1619, 1706 and 1717 respectively, all of which are now unfortunately lost Roger Wilbraham, Esq,, states that he had caused a note of all deeds relating to the Town in his possession to be entered into the Church Book, so that should any, or all, of these earlier volumes be still in existence it would be a graceful act on the part of the owner to restore them to the Town, and the safe custody of the Rector of the Parish

§ I have an excellent engraving of Crewe Hall drawn by this Architect in 1742 His burial is recorded thus —
"1770 June 6 Mr William Yoxall (Par Reg)

the West Door of the Church , also, the churchyard to be raised and levelled where necessary "
" 1739 July 8 To erect Piers and Iron Gates at the end of the *Church Lane* entering the church-yard "

On Saturday, the 14th May, 1737, "about six in the evening the Sessions and Market House at Namptwich fell down, by which nine persons were killed The building had been erected but sixteen years and six months before At a Quarter Sessions it gave evident signs that it would soon tumble.' —(*Gent Mag* 1737, p. 314)

Towards the erection of this Market Hall, with a Sessions Room above, in 1720, George Frederick, Prince of Wales, Earl of Chester, &c., (afterwards King George II.) gave £600, and a full figure of the Prince, carved in gritstone, ornamented the South side of the building. When the disaster occurred the statue was broken across the middle, but the upper part of the effigy may still be seen in the garden of Burland Hall, in Acton parish, standing on a rockery overshadowed by yews, where it is locally known as the "King of Burland " The throng of the market would, doubtless, be over before the accident happened, or there must surely have been greater loss of life, but Partridge says, "many were terribly bruised and hurt." The Register records the following burials; others, being probably country people, would be interred in their own parish graveyards, as, for example, *James Burscoe*, of Stapeley, in Wybunbury churchyard

> " 1737 May 15th Mary Ickin, a Pauper, kill d by the Market house falling in this Town, the 14th, buried
> the 15th "
> „ „ 16th ·Patient, Daughter of Jane Smith, kill d at the same time and place "
> „ „ , Catherine, Wife of Thos ffletcher, Taylor, kill'd at the same time and place, And Sarah
> Hewitt Wid '
> „ „ „ James Burscoe, of Stapeley, yeoman, kill d by the fall of the Market House in Namptwich
> where many more lost their lives —(Wybunbury Burial Reg)

This public Hall was rebuilt but in no better manner than its predecessor, for, in or about the year 1759, "while the Justices were holding their Sessions, a sudden crash so greatly alarmed the court that in the hurry and confusion of getting down, many people, expecting the whole fabric to fall every moment, were much hurt.' —(Partridge's *Hist. Nant* p 82-3) In consequence of these accidents and alarms, the Quarter Sessions were removed from Nantwich to Knutsford, in the year 1760, and the upper room was taken down, the lower part of the building being retained as the market place for those who attended with baskets of butter, eggs, poultry, and provisions This Market Hall, which met with the requirements of the town until 1868, was a low building in the High Town, opposite Castle Street Its roof was supported by brickwork on semicircular arches that rested on nine granite columns; the only ornament being a plume of feathers (the badge of the Prince of Wales) on the cornice above the central pillar on the south side.

"On June the 8th 1737, between 5 & 6 o'clock in the afternoon, a dreadful fire broke out in the salt-house going over ye bridge, which was burnt down to the ground with 5 more houses the fire was so fierce, and the wind so high, that the wind blew up ye sparks on the other side the street, but by the great number of hands, and by the having water so near at hand, and in such great plenty by constantly pouring the water on the houses they prevented its spreading, tho' the damage done is very considerable "*

---

* From Steel s Collections for Cheshire, c 1750-60 —*(Gough Coll Bodl Lib)*

A meeting, called by the Churchwardens and Constables, was held in the Parish Church on the 17th July, 1737, when it was agreed by the gentlemen and freeholders of the town, "that the Churchwardens & Constables should erect an Engine House at the end of Mr Cappur's [the Lamb Inn] Stable, *viz* the end next the Church Yard, and to purchase an Engine and other implements proper for extinguishing of fire" A rate was levied for the purpose on 28th August; but it was not until 1740 that an Engine was purchased, and not until the 9th Nov 1746, that "it was agreed to buy 2 doz. Leather buckets for extinguishing fires at 5s. 6d a piece, plain without painting."—(Town Vestry Book)

This Engine-house, which stood opposite the Rectory, was taken down in 1853, when Lord Crewe built another in Pillory Street, nearly opposite the "Gaol-house" on land given by the Marquis of Cholmondeley, and that, too, was taken down when the present Engine-house in Market Street was built in 1869.

On page 202 mention is made of a person being drowned in the *Town Well* in 1651, and for many years after that date the inhabitants obtained their supply from *open draw-wells* in various streets of the town. In the "*Town Book*" it is recorded that—

"At a Vestry held at the "George," the 3rd Feb 1737-8, It was agreed that the *Draw well in Hospital Street* should have a pump fixed in it, and the pump in the *Beam Street* should be repaired, and likewise the pump in the *Pillory Street* be repaired at the Town Charge by the present Constables, Thomas Massie & Joseph Onions"

"At a Vestry in the Parish Church held 11th [?] March 1752, It was agreed that *the Well in the Welsh Row, which has some time since had a pump put into it*, shall be repaired now and henceforward at the charge of the Town, and the expense of putting the said pump down shall be likewise paid by the Constables of the said Town"

Alterations in the Churchyard of a very permanent character were made by order of the Vestry in 1738 and 1739, as appears by the following minutes —

"At a Vestry held at the Crown and Sceptre, [now called The Crown Hotel] on the 28th Sept 1738 it was agreed that Jos Jackson, and Richd Cartwright Church-wardens make a pavement from the Turnstile leading to the Market House to the West Door of the Church, like that from the Iron Gates leading into Pepper Street to the West Door Also, the Churchyard to be raised and levelled where necessary"

"At a Vestry on the 8th June 1739, Richd Cartwright and Samuel Higgenson, Churchwardens," were ordered to "erect Piers and Iron Gates at the end of the Church Lane, entering the Church Yard"—*(Town Vestry Book)*

To remedy evils in the management of public business by the Town Officers, *new Rules and Orders* were drawn up and signed by the following leading Gentlemen on the 25th Nov 1734, but it was not until the 4th Jan 1738-9, after much opposition, that the Rules in an amended form, (here given) were finally agreed to. The list of names is as follows —

ROGER WILBRAHAM ESQ	GEO. AUDLEY.	RICHARD CHURCH
WM MAISTERSON ESQ J P	THO. WICKSTED	HENRY HAYES.
EDWARD WETTENHALL ESQ.	THO MARSHALL	STEPHEN HASSALL
JOHN WICKSTED	THO WILLIAMS	THOMAS SWETINAM
JOHN MASEREY	A WOODWORTH	JOHN MASTERSON.
CLUTTON WRIGHT.	THOMAS READE.	JOHN JOHNSON.

TOWN RULES AND ORDERS   1738

" *Officers in General*

"I   That no Person shall upon pretence of serving any Office within the Town & parish aforesaid retain or deduct his proportion of any public tax, it being a Duty which the Law binds upon him when thereunto nominated and elected "

" II   That no Levy for the said Town or parish shall be granted at any meeting Unless three at least of the Freeholders in the said Town or parish shall be present thereat Nor any bargain made for any publick work above the Rate of twenty shillings unless notice be given in the Church, and such a Meeting be held as aforesaid "

" III   That all officers receiving any Books for the collecting any tax shall at the Expiration of their Office deliver up their Books, and charge themselves with the whole Assessment and return A Schedule of the names of all such persons as refuse or neglect to pay, and the reason why such could not be collected that further proceedings may be had thereon as the case requires "

" IV   That no Beverage shall be given by any Officer of this Town or parish, or allowed upon his Account in any publick work whatsoever "

Church wardens

" That no further sum than two pounds ten shillings be charged or allowed for their expences at the Visitations that they allow no more than 8s per Diem to the Ringers, nor expend any greater sum than 2s of the Parish money for the refreshment of any Strange Minister "

Constables

I   " That they expend none of the Town's money on Days, or pretended Days of publick Rejoyceing, but on Days hereafter named , and then only 10s each day , To witt

The 20th Day of January, being the Prince of Wales' Birthday ,

The 29th Day of May, the Restoration ,

The 11th Day of June, his Majesty's [Geo II] Accession ,

The 30th Day October his Majesty's Birth-day

The 5th Day of November, the Deliverance from the Papist Plott "

II   " That they give none of the Town's Money to those that come with permitt passes, or those Men that carry the Hallbeards [Halberds] at Fairs "

III   " That they pay to each Constable on the other Libertys in Town 2s for Serveing the Office and such sums as they shall pay down and expend in Repairs of their Stocks, and other Necessary Disburstments [*sic*] and expence, in the Execution of their Office, and shall be allowed the same in their Accompts "

Overseers of the Poor

" That the Overseers appear the first Monday in every Month by ten a clock at the Poor-House, and there give in their Accompts and take Directions how to proceed in their Distributions "

Eight years after, on the 29th Jan 1746, it was decided that the following gentlemen " compose the Monthly Vestry for the Managem^t of the Publick Business of the s^d Township of Nantwich , to meet at the schoolhouse [in the Church-yard] at Eleven o'clock in the forenoon upon the first Monday in every Month, to enquire into the Proceedings of the respective officers of the s^d Township, & the Publick Business thereof, And to give such Orders and Directions relating thereto as shall be found necessary for the benefit and Advantage of the Inhabitants "

ROGER WILBRAHAM ESQ	MR THOMAS PRATCHITT	MR THOS. MASSIE
THOMAS MAISTERSON ESQ	MR. ANDRW WOODWORTH	MR. JOSEPH SKERRETT
EDWARD WETENHALL ESQ	MR. RICHARD YOXALL	MR ROBERT TAYLOR
MR. WM WATKISS	MR THOS YOXALL	MR. HENRY HAYES
MR. [GEO] AUDLEY the elder	MR JOHN OULTON	MR TOMKINSON
MR. JONATHAN HALL	MR THOMAS WALLEY	MR AUDLEY the younger
MR. THOMAS WICKSTED	MR RICHD CHURCH	MR GEO GIBBONS
MR. RICHARD LEVERSAGE	MR WM COOKE	MR. JOSEPH ONIONS

This Committee of local legislators was annually re-elected   On the 28th May, 1746, they exempted *John Dawson* from holding any Town Office, on the condition of his "paying to the Overseers of the Poor the sum of 8 guineas to be imployed in putting out 2 or more boys to be apprentices, ' and on 27th Nov 1748 *Mr. Plant Maddocks*, a lawyer, claimed similar exemption on the payment of 10 guineas to be imployed for the use of the Town "

Serious robberies in the town probably, made it necessary for the Vestry to pass the following *"Order relating to Thieves"* on March 26th, 1744

"That every Inhabitant of the said Town receiving stolen goods knowingly or who shall at any time hereafter take in any Inmate and Harbour or wilfully permitt or suffer any Thief, Robber, Pickpocket, Rogue, Vagrant Vagabond or Sturdy Beggar to lodge in his, her or their dwelling-house, cottage, barn, stable or other out-building within the said Town contrary to the Laws in being, or any of them, then every Inhabitant so offending shall for every such offence or misdemeanour be prosecuted at the Publick charge of the said Parish   And that the Constables shall carry on such Prosecution &c with the utmost Rigour and be allowed in their accounts all reasonable charges and expences thereof '

At the same meeting the following resolution was entered —

' It appearing that the present *Beadle* of the Town, *John Shufflebotham*, hath not only been remiss and negligent in the execution of his Office, but hath absolutely refused to execute the same when thereunto required, It was therefore agreed and ordered that he be, and accordingly he is, discharged from the said office, And that *Henry Buckley* shall succeed him and enter upon the said office immediately and that the *Constables* of the said Town shall pay him the usual salary as hath been heretofore allowed for executing the same "—*(Town Vestry Book)*

Another extract is here given from the same book relating to the *Town Constables*

"At a Vestry held at the Poor House [in Queen Street] on the 10 Feb 1747-8, it is agreed, That for the future the 13s 4d a piece usually paid to the Constables of the Barons Fee, & the 2s a piece usually paid to the sub-Constables of particular districts within the township of Nantwich, for the serving their offices, shall not be paid or allowed (it being deemed their Duty to serve their offices *gratis*)

And that there shall be nothing allowed for *Bonefires* for the future upon any Account

And it is likewise agreed that the sd Constables from henceforth shall not have any Lay [Rate] Granted them, but shall be reimbursed their reasonable charges by the Overseers of the Poor for the time being at their Quarterly payments "

Two centenarians, who were brothers, died in this town in February 1748, as noticed in Steel's MS Collections for Cheshire, c. 1750-60.*

"In February 1747-8 died at Nantwich two brothers of the name of Stockton, the one in the 102nd and the other (who left a buxome young widow) in the 101st year of his age."

* This MS is preserved amongst the Gough MSS in the Bodleian Library.

One of them was buried at Acton, and the other at Wybunbury the burial at the latter place, however, is not recorded but both are mentioned, with slight differences as to age, in the Acton Register, which, within nine months after, has another remarkable entry, here given —

> "1747 [-8] Edward Stockton of Hurleston (was aged) 105 buried 16th Feb
>   His brother buried at Wybunbury the same week, aged 103 '
> " Mr Davis, Denbigh, a passenger from London died in the Stage Waggon by Darfold Gates   Buried Nov 6th 1748 "

About the middle of the eighteenth century this country was visited by a *Cattle Plague*, which called forth the attention of Parliament   By the Act, 20 Geo II. *c* 5 [1746-7] entitled, " An Act to enable his Majesty to make rules, orders and regulations more effectually to prevent the spreading of the distemper which now rages among the horned cattle in this kingdom", it is provided that the regulations therein contained be read in all Churches after prayers on the first Sunday after their receipt, and every month while in force.   The plague was of long continuance and widespread   It was enacted that after May 1750, no beasts should be sold unless with an attested copy of a certificate from a Justice of Peace, proving that such beasts had already been in possession of the owner for at least fifty days; failing to comply with that restriction, the seller was subjected to a penalty of £10   All Cattle Fairs were prohibited being held at Chester, by order dated 18th June 1750, until further notice   The distemper was particularly fatal in Barthomley, Wybunbury, and other parishes in this neighbourhood in the months of January, March, and April, 1749, and in the Spring months of 1751 and 1752.*

Under date the 9th Dec. 1753, the *Town Book* says it was agreed " That the Room on the north side of the Chancell shall be forthwith fitted up in a proper manner as a Vestry Room for the use of the Parish "   It was customary then for Parish business to be conducted in the Church after the Sunday morning service , or more frequently at one of the principal ale-houses in the town.   Partridge has the following remark on Vestry meetings, which may here be quoted   " After a long time lying neglected, it [the Vestry] was put into decent repair, [probably in 1753 as above stated] the mutability of time, however, has occasioned it to be again neglected and disused , at present [in 1774] the parochial business commonly transacted at Vestry Meetings·is done at the north end of the broad ile "† [i e in the Lady Chapel]

A Church Rate was granted by the Vestry on 27th March, 1757, of a " whole old Rent," to defray the Churchwardens' (John Walker and Richard Taylor) " Charges and and Disbursements hitherto expended, & also towards enabling them *to rebuild the Battlements & repair the Breaches lately made in the North side of the Church* "—(Town Book) This damage was the result of a violent storm, which did still greater injury to Acton Church, as recorded in the Register there —

> " *Memorandum*   On Tuesday March 15th 1757
> Abt noon, the upper Part of the Steeple, was by the excessive violence of the Wind or Tempest, suddenly blown down, & falling upon ye roof of ye Church broke it entirely, and destroyed most of the Pews and a Gallery erected therein at the West End

---

* See Hinchliffe s " *History of Barthomley*," p 351

† Partridge's *History of Nantwich*, p 25   The Vestry has again been used for Town's Meetings during the present century , but all parish business has for some years been conducted at the Church House opposite the Rectory

> The estimate of damage given in
> To obtain a Brief was 1,760 & upwards
> but exceeded by £   600 at least
>
> 1,760 pounds
> Height of New Tower from Church Flagg Floor to the highest part of Battlement, 28 yards 3¾ inches "

Parish Books frequently give curious information concerning the management of the pauper class and the law of settlement in the eighteenth century   Overseers were diligently to enquire what persons in the parish had not gained a legal settlement, and who were liable by law to be removed to their own parishes, and to remove them   All Overseers being remiss in their official duties, might be prosecuted at the public charge   The Town Book records —

> "At a Vestry held in the Parish Church of Nantwich upon Sunday the 2nd Oct. 1757 it is unanimously agreed, That the present Overseers of the Poor of the Township of Nantwich, *William Sprout* and *John Eaton*, shall forthwith make a full enquiry into the measures taken by *John ffenna* & several other Inhabitants of the township of Wardle in procuring a marriage to be solemnized between Thomas Cleas, a poor Almesman, in the township of Nantwich, & Ann Bickerton, otherwise Gilbert, a pauper, belonging to the sd township of Wardle   And which said Marriage has been represented to have been unduly accomplished by the sd John ffenna &c in order to gain the sd Ann a Settlemt in the sd township of Nantwich & to charge the Inhabitants of the sd township of Nantwich with her maintenance   And it is further agreed & ordered, That the sd William Sprout & John Eaton as Overseers, shall apply for an Information against the persons who shall appear to have been concerned in procuring such undue marriage & take such other methods & proceedings as they shall be advised in order to punish the offenders & to obtain a suitable satisfaction "

On the 23rd March, 1759, a cheesefactor named John Stevenson, of Bickerton, co. Chester, was committed to Chester Castle for shooting Mr. Francis Elcock, Attorney-at-law, of Nantwich   The affair was as follows —Stevenson, being apprehensive of an arrest from some of his creditors, shut himself up at home, and to deter anyone from attempting to seize him, kept fire-arms by him   Nevertheless, a person, who had but one arm, got admittance by stratagem, and served him with a writ, but as soon as Stevenson knew the business, he took up a pistol, and presenting it, the bailiff ran out of the room.   Mr. Elcock then went to the house, and threatened to burst open the door   Stevenson thereupon fired through the door, and wounded Mr Elcock so terribly that he died the next day *   This led to a very remarkable trial, lasting several hours, on Friday, the 27th April, 1759, at Chester Assizes   The Jury found the fact as laid in the indictment, but brought in their verdict *special* in regard to the legality of the arrest, the Sheriff having, according to custom, signed his warrant for the apprehension of Stevenson, leaving a blank therein for the names of the special bailiffs, which were afterwards (but *before the arrest*) inserted by Mr   .   Elcock, a relative of the deceased, one of whom arrested the said Stevenson   This special point of law was argued before the Honble Justice Noel, and Taylor White, Esq, Justices of Chester, who took time to deliver their opinion   Justice Noel then, in a learned and pathetic speech, supported by adjudged cases, declared

---

* Acton Parish Register thus records his burial —
   ' 1759 March 24 Francis Elcock, killed by Stevenson a Bankrupt Cheese Factor [in] Cholmondeley "

his opinion, that the prisoner's crime, found by the special verdict, could amount at most to Manslaughter only, whereupon the prisoner was burnt in the hand, and discharged from the indictment for murder *

1760   The Court of Quarter Sessions, which had from time immemorial been held about Midsummer, was removed to Knutsford, as before mentioned

' On Thursday 18 Septr 1760, a foot-match between a gentleman of Cheshire and a gentleman of Staffordshire, 200 yards for 200 guineas, was decided on Beam Heath, when Cheshire proved victorious."†

"1764 Oct 18 Benjamin Bourne, exciseman, [buried] who first cut his throat and afterwards fell into a pitt and was drowned   The Coroner's Inquest brought in their verdict Lunacy "—*(Parish Register)*

"1765 Sep 30th At Namptwich, Mr Samuel Jackson, had this year, a crop of oats, of about 8 statute acres, which were 6 feet high and upwards   It is supposed, that almost every grain produced 11 or 12 stems, and that most of the stems produced about 280 grains, the razoms or ears being covered 18 inches long, and though it is common for one chaff to contain two grains, it is very remarkable that, in this crop, one chaff frequently contained three, the least of which had a good kernel in it.   Upon threshing and winnowing a thrave or 24 sheaves, the produce was 7 measures [each of 45 or 50℔s] of fine marketable corn, and ½ a measure of light corn, 36 quarts to the measure   The above were Dutch Oats, and had been sown but once in this kingdom "‡

In the same year, 22nd Oct , a Faculty was granted by Bishop Peploe to William Watkis, gent , of Welsh Row, Nantwich, to build a second North Gallery, eastward, in Nantwich Church.§

1765   No Burials are recorded for the month of March, a wide space being left in the Register to indicate that fact   The following year, however, was one of great mortality in the spring and summer months   The total number of burials in 1765 was 71 , in 1766, the numbers were as follows —

Jan — 9	April—20	July— 40	Oct — 7	
Feb — 7	May— 37	Aug —13	Nov —5	203 Total
March—12	June—31	Sep— 19	Dec —3	

In 1767 the *House of Correction and Workhouse*, at Beam Street end, were converted into seven Almshouses by John Crewe, of Crewe, Esq   The first Workhouse or *Poor-House*, under the Act 9 Geo. I c 7 [1723], which enabled Overseers to purchase or hire a house or houses to *lodge* the poor, had been provided prior to 1748, by appropriating several houses in Queen Street for that purpose.   Heretofore the poor had received town relief at their own homes, but, now, the pauper class must inhabit the building set apart for them   This Poor-house fulfilled the wants of the town until 1780, when a new *Poor-House* or *Workhouse* was built on the Barony.   (See next page.)

* This remarkable trial was privately printed with the following title —" *The Trial at large of John Stevenson*, [&c] *at Chester Assizes, on Friday 27th April 1759* [&c]   *Taken by Mr Ralph Carter, of Nantwich*   Printed for John Wilkie, at the Bible, St Paul's Churchyard, price One Shilling "

† Newspaper Scrap Book in possession of J P Earwaker, Esq

‡ *Annual Register* for 1765 p 129 and *London Chron* 1765, p 256

§ "*Chesh Sheaf*, " Vol II, No 1351

The earliest mentions of the parish poor-house in the Registers are —

"1748 Oct 21 Wm Hindley, Governor of the Poor-House " [Buried]
"1755 Jan 25 Sarah dau of John Kenyon Governor of the Poor House ' Buried.
"1757, June 7 Eliz Wareham, widow & pauper out of the Workhouse [Buried"

The London "*Chronicle*" for 6th Oct 1767 relates the following outrage by a lunatic at Nantwich

"1767 Sep 23 Saturday se'nnight a person of this town, being disordered in his senses, became so outrageous, that two neighbours were called in to give their assistance, who pursued him upstairs Before they could catch him, he rushed into a chamber, and shut the door Then they broke the door when unhappily for one of them, his throat was cut by the madman, who, unknown to anyone had a razor in his hand, concealed in a handkerchief He was at last secured The wounded man languished till Monday, when he died "

Another minute in the Town Book, in the handwriting of the Rector, the Rev. John Smith, mentions projected alterations in the Church, that were most likely carried out

"At a Vestry held this Day, 7th Jan 1770, in the Parish Church of Nantwich, it is agreed that the Church Wardens shall (as soon as may be) lay before the Gentlemen of this Town estimates for erecting a New Door at the West End of the Church, & it is likewise agreed that the Rector of Nantwich, for the time being shall have the use of the new erected Pew, in place where the Old Clock stood in lieu of a Pew in the South Gallery now belonging to the Rectory, which Pew is to be disposed of for the Benefit of the Parishioners of the said Parish

[Signed] JOHN SMITH, Rector	WILLIAM WALKIS	G AUDLEY
PLANT MADDOCKS	WILLM HENNETT	WM GREENWOLLERS
	GEO GARNETT	

Tennis-ball playing in the Churchyard had resulted in so much damage to the Church windows, that coercive measures were taken by the Vestry in 1776 and 1777, not only to put a stop to "Ball-playing" but 'to prevent Gaming of all sorts in the Churchyard, whereby much Profaneness and many Indecencies & evil consequences have arisen " Parish prosecutions of offenders, however, failed to prevent this desecration, and in the memory of people still living, the churchyard continued to be the public playground of the town   More effectual means were adopted about fifty years ago, when Mr Foster, an ironmaster in South Staffordshire, and a native of this town, (see under ALVASTON, *posted*) enclosed the north side of the Churchyard with iron railings

1779 April 6 The Rev John Wesley preached in Barker Street Chapel, which had been hired for worship, by the first band of his followers in this town, two years before. He preached there a second time on the 17th May, 1781 —(Wesley s "*Journal* ')

The Chester and Nantwich Canal, which had been in course of construction from May 4th, 1771, was finished at a cost of £80,000, and opened in August 1779, but, unfortunately, was not brought into the town

In 1779 and 1780 a new Work-House was erected on the Barony, on land given by the Marquis of Cholmondeley. Beside the sum of £450 from the funds of certain Charities, which was invested for its erection the following local gentlemen and tradesmen were shareholders.

SIR ROBERT SALUSBURY COTTON, Bart of Combermere

GEORGE WILBRAHAM, Esq of Delamere

JAMES TOMKINSON Junr

WILLIAM YOXALL [Attorney]

GEORGE GARNETT [Cheesefactor]

RICHARD WICKSTED [Surgeon]

GEORGE CAPPUR [Cheesefactor]

JAMES CALDWALL [Linendraper]

WILLIAM PHILLIPS [of the King's Arms Inn, High Street]

GEORGE PAYNE [Gent. of Hospital Street]

WILLIAM FOSTER [Mercer ?]

JOHN EDDOWES [Grocer]

JOSEPH JACKSON [Maltster]

CHARLES GIBBONS [Attorney]

THOMAS MASSIE 2 shares [Chandler]

WILLIAM SPROUT Junr [Linen Draper]

JOSEPH SKERRETT [Upholsterer & Auctioneer]

THOMAS JACKSON

WILLIAM WATKISS [Attorney]

HENRY TOMKINSON [Attorney]

ROBERT TAYLOR [Tanner]

CHARLES BATE [Attorney]

BENJAMIN HEWITT 4 shares [Shoe manufacturer, afterwards a Banker]

ROBERT TAYLOR [Junr Tanner]

SAMUEL HODGSON 2 shares [Wine Merchant]

JOHN TOMLINSON

[Rev] JOHN KENT [Grammar Schoolmaster]

PETER BAYLEY [Attorney]

RICHARD LEVERSAGE 2 shares [Ironmonger]

JAMES FOSTER [Stay maker]

SAMUEL BARROW [Esq J P]*

The New Work-house was opened in June, 1780, the Governor being Mr Charles Shrimpton,† and the first burial of an inmate, recorded in the Parish Register in red ink, is as follows —

"1781 Sept 25 William Pemberton, The first Interd from the new Poor-house '

John Howard, the Philanthropist, in his 'Accounts of Lazarattos" &c (pub 1789, p 209) gives an interesting report of the Debtor's Prison, Town Gaol, and Workhouse, on his visit to Nantwich, Aug 1st, 1788

"Nantwich Prison for Debtors	No alteration 1788 Aug 1 No prisoners
Nantwich Town Gaol	No alteration The two damp dungeons still used
	No allowance 1788 Aug 1 Prisoners 2 "

"The Work-house at Nantwich was erected in 1779, on the common, and about 11½ acres of land enclosed, for which 2 6 a year is paid to the lord of the manor The house is visited weekly by the gentlemen of the town in rotation It was clean, and great attention seems to be paid to the inhabitants The rooms are too low, and the upper parts of the windows too far from the ceilings Five shillings a month is allowed for tobacco and snuff, yet the use of tea, though purchased with their own money, is ordered to be punished by confinement in the dungeon Aug 1 1788 there were eleven men, sixteen women, ten boys, seven girls " [Total, 44 persons]

Another story was added, and other alterations and additions were carried out by the first Board of Guardians, under the Poor Law Act that constituted it Nantwich Union Workhouse 1835, and exactly one hundred years after its first erection, the very handsome "Childrens' Home" was built by Mr Madeley, of Nantwich, from designs by J. A Davenport, Esq., Surveyor and Sanitary Inspector, of Nantwich. On the 3rd April, 1881, according to the Census returns for that day, the population of the Workhouse was—142 males, and 80 females, total 222

* This list is taken from an Overseers' Book now in the possession of Mr Johnson Oat Market, Nantwich to which I have added the trades and professions from Directories, printed in Chester Guide of 1782 and 1789

† His Burial Register is as follows —
"1806 April 4 Charles Shrimpton aged 81 Governor of the Poor-house '

In 1780 George Wilbraham, Esq , of Townsend, built in the Welsh Row, and almost exactly opposite his residence (which he shortly after quitted) four parallel rows of wooden shops or stalls named the *York Buildings* * for the convenience of holding a Cloth Fair For many years previous travelling cloth-merchants, linen-drapers, &c had visited the town at the Great Fair, and at Christmas Rag Fair, their wares having heretofore been exposed on stalls in the streets   Mention is made of one of these merchants in the Baptism Register, thus —

"1765 Feb 28 Thos son of Thos Stubbs Rag Fair merchant "

The rents collected from the merchants for stallage on the 4th Sept 1783, being the day of the third annual Cloth Fair, amounted to £34 15s 9d , according to the accounts of Mr Audley, agent for George Wilbraham, Esq , in a Memorandum Book now in the possession of W Holland Blades, Esq , of Stapeley, from which the following extracts, giving some particulars of the cost of erecting York Buildings, and incidental entries of the prices of articles of food, wages, &c , now exactly a hundred years ago are taken

			£	s	d
1783 Ap	1	pd for a Quire of paper	0	0	9
,,	5	pd Ch Wild for hanging Miss Reeves pew	0	17	0
,,	5	pd for a Hind Qr of Veal 22 lbs at 3d	0	5	6
,,	5	pd ,, Breast of Veal	0	1	1
,,	5	pd ,, Small Round of Beef at 4½d Beef Stakes 1d	0	5	3
,,	5	Allowed in Mr Penlingtons Bill for Polleys Hat from London	1	6	0
,,	5	pd Mr Wilbrahams Bill in full to Mr Dutton for Locks, Hinges, Nails, &c [for York Buildings]	15	1	0
,,	9	To inform Mr Wilbraham respecting an encroachment of York Buildings Wall			
,,	9	To speak to Mr Wilbraham about Buildg a proper place for carrying on the Cotton Weaving Business			
,,	12	Recd from Mr Ratclife 2 yrs and a half Rent for a Pew due 25th March last	2	5	0
,,	12	Recd from Ch Walker for 2 sittings	0	3	0
,,	12	Pd Ch Walker for his Cart 17 days and a half	0	17	6
,,	12	pd for a Loyn of Veal, my own calf, 9 lb	0	2	3
,,	12	pd for a Beef Stake	0	0	3
,,	12	pd for a Qr of Lamb for John 7 lb	0	3	0
,,	19	pd Johnson Lime man, for a load of Lime had in Feb last weight 22 cwt 1 qr at 1s 4d per cwt	1	9	8
,,	26	pd Perrin for a Loyn of Veal at 2d	0	1	4
,,	26	Mr Fox a Bill for Mr Wilbraham for Lead Gutters at York Buildings	5	10	10
,,	26	pd Wm Parsons for 5 days	0	5	0
,,	26	pd Sandbach Carrier for putting up paper &c abt the Fair in York Buildings	[sum not given]		
May	17	pd Ch Thos 5 days for Mr Wilbraham	0	5	10
,,	17	pd Thos Minshull Bricklayer, 5 days, 15s 10d Grains 2d	0	16	0
,,	17	pd Strettles 1 Day Gardiner	0	1	4
,,	17	pd Chimney Sweeper for sweeping house and Parlour Chimney	0	0	9
,,	17	pd Ch Thos for 8 young Ducks & old one	0	2	6
,,	17	pd John Weever for a Suit of Cloathes	0	9	0
,,	24	pd Coman for Advertizmts for York Buildings	0	5	0
,,	24	pd for flour for Batch at 12½lbs, for 1s	0	3	0
,,	24	pd for a couple of green geese	0	2	0
June	14	pd Qr of Lamb 8½ lbs at 4d	0	2	8
,,	14	pd Beef 8 lb at 4d	0	2	8

* On the site of York Buildings has since been erected the Primitive Methodist Chapel, in Welsh Row

	£	s	d
June 21 pd Almswimmin £5 5s od, Maiden do £1 10s od	6	15	0
,, 21 pd Mr Pass for a pr of Apple pots for Mr Wilbraham	0	11	9
,, 21 pd for my own Calves head, Feet, liver &c	0	2	0
,, 21, pd for Qr of Calf for Mr Wilbraham 36 lbs at 3½d	0	10	6
,, 21 pd Mulliner for a load of Malt	2	2	0
,, 28 pd peas ½ a peck 6d potatoes 3 lbs at 1½d	0	0	10½
,, 28 pd Magee his Ballance for Slates at York Buildings	6	0	0
July 12 pd Lightfoot for a Stone Cistern 7s od , a Harthstone 1s .	0	8	0
,, 26 pd Leg of Mutton from Shenton 7 lbs	0	2	4
,, 26 Oak troughs Iron work to Do for two Center Roofs for York Buildings	12	9	0
,, 26 2 pair Gates of Dressing Posts	3	13	4
,, 26 Joiner for making 10 doz of Tressels	1	0	0
Aug 9 pd Beef 11 lbs 3s od Veal 25 lbs, at 3½d , 6s 9d	0	9	9
, 9 pd Jno Blakeman Sawyer for Sawing 1 day and ¾ at 1s 4d	0	2	4

1781   July 8 Dr. William Wrench, Surgeon, of Nantwich,[*] restored a boy who had been drowned in the Canal   For his successful treatment he was presented with a silver medal by the Royal Humane Society, which had been established only a few years before   The medal is now in the possession of W Holland Blades, Esq , and represents—

Reverse—*A wreath*, within, this inscription   " Dr Wm Wrench restored G Farrington July 8, 1781 ' round the edge, "*Hoc pretium sine servato tulit*" (*i e* He has obtained this reward for saving the life of a citizen)

Obverse—The motto, "*Lateat scintillula forsan*" (*i e* perhaps, a little spark may yet be hid), the figure of a naked boy blowing the spark of a torch into a flame   "*Soc · Lond in resucitat inter moriuorum instit* MDCCLXXIV " (*i e* Society established in London for the recovery of those in a state of suspended animation   1774)

1786   The following remarkable instances of mortality in one family within a week, occurred at Nantwich —"On the 23 Aug died Mrs [Hannah] Maddocks [*née* Hassall] relict of the late Mr Plant Maddocks   On the following day died Mr John Hassall [Joiner] brother to the above lady   And on the 27th (only three days after) died Mrs. [Elizabeth] Hassall, relict of the said Mr. John Hassall '   The Parish Register corroborates the above Newspaper extract, their burials following *seriatim*, on Aug 29th, 30th, and Sept 2nd

1788   On Friday night, the 30th May[?], "One of the most dreadful thunderstorms ever remembered in England was felt at Chester, Frodsham, Nantwich Stockport, and other parts of the County   This storm was, however, but of short duration, and went off with a plentiful shower of hailstones, as large as small gooseberries " &c   (Newspaper extract)

---

* Dr William Wrench who resided in a curious old house that stood on the site of the present District Bank was the son of Richard Wrench, Surgeon, of Nantwich, who was descended from an old family of that name in Davenham Parish Cheshire
    RICHARD WRENCH died at the age of 85, and was buried at Nantwich on the 27th Nov, 1806   He had married Elizabeth, widow of Mr Richard Rockett, of Hough, *née* Birch and grand-daughter of Stephen Wilbraham of Nantwich, on 28th Sept 1750   She died at the age of 78, and was buried at Nantwich on 2nd Aug 1800   Their issue was *William*, *John*, (who was an apothecary in Wybunbury parish, and married Margaret Oulton on 18th Oct 1781) and two daughters, *Mary* and *Ann*
    DR WILLIAM WRENCH was baptized on the 14th July 1751 and was buried at Nantwich on the 13th July 1821   He was twice married first to Ann, daughter of William Penlington Esq , of Mill St Nantwich, on 8th Feb 1776, by whom he had two daughters *Anne* and *Mary* , and secondly to Mary Harris of Hospital St , Nantwich on 20th Nov 1785 by whom also he had two daughters, *Margaret*, and *Catherine*   Catherine Wrench was married on the 26th July 1821 to Thos Young of St Pancras, Lieut in the 33rd Regiment of Second Foot , whose daughter Anne Wrench Young, the wife of W Holland Blades Esq , died on the 22nd March, 1879

Among the *Additional Charters* in the British Museum is preserved a *Church Brief*, which describes the deplorable and ruinous state of Nantwich Church in 1789, as follows

"A very ancient structure become so ruinous that the Inhab^ts cannot with safety assemble therein to attend divine service, the whole Roofs of the Nave of the Church are in such a state of decay that they are prevented from falling only by transverse Beams of timber laid across the centre Isle over the Roof and principal Beams of the Roof, stayed to the transverse Beams by Bars of Iron to prevent the Roof from falling   That great part of the Walls and Battlements are fallen down and the other part in a state of great decay   The buttresses which support the side Walls, are from length of time much decayed, and have in part fallen down, and some other parts are very near in the same state, by which decay very considerable settlements appear in the quadrancal or supporting Arches of the side Isles   Part of the floors and covered ways and staircases of the Steeple is decayed and must inevitably be repaired at a great expence   The Stone Work of the Windows is so much decayed that some parts have fallen down, and others must be taken down and made new "

With the above report, an estimate for the necessary repairs by *Messrs James Cheney* and *Thomas Cartwright*, (two local builders), amounting to £1,283 12s 0d was presented by the inhabitants of the *" Parish and Chapelry of Nantwich"* at the General Quarter Sessions, where application was made for licence by King's Letters Patent for a *Brief* granting a collection throughout England, the town of Berwick-upon-Tweed, and the counties of Flint, Denbigh, and Radnor, according to Act of Parliament 4 Queen Anne, for the purpose of restoring the Church, the inhabitants, as was stated, being unable to raise the required sum   The Brief is dated at Westminster the 30th July 29 Geo III [1789], and the following persons were appointed receivers of the Charity or Collection.

THE RIGHT HON EARL OF CHOLMONDELEY	SAMUEL BARROW, ESQRE
THE HON WILBRAHAM TOLLEMACHE	PETER WALTHALL, ESQRE
SIR ROBERT SALUSBURY COTTON, Bart.	JAMES TOMKINSON, ESQRE.
SIR JOHN CHETWODE, Bart.	THOMAS WETTENHALL, ESQRE.
JOHN CREWE, ESQRE	WILLIAM STEVENSON, GENT.
GEORGE WILBRAHAM, ESQRE	WILLIAM HILDITCH, GENT

And the Ministers and Churchwardens of the Parish.

The Roof was completed in the following month according to the following entry in Burial Register

"1789 Aug, 26 *Thos Gyles, grocer*   N B *The first corpse y^t was bro't for Interment under ye new Roof of ye Church* "

W Cowdroy's "Chester Guide" for 1789, has the following interesting paragraph relating to Nantwich, on page 82.

"It is a pity, but that the same gentlemen and principal tradesmen who exerted themselves in erecting the work-house before mentioned for the relief and comfort of the poor, and who have this year also set on foot a liberal subscription for a new roof, on the nave or body of their antient and venerable Church, . . would once more immortalize themselves, for the credit of the town, and the health of the inhabitants, by removing the *slaughter-houses* and *shambles* from their present situation, being now a *real nuisance* in the centre of the town   If the slaughter-houses were situated below the bridge, and the spot of ground, called *Snow-hill*, was allotted and formed into a square, sufficient to contain the Shambles, fish-market and green market, there would be more convenience, as well as decency   These reforms would greatly contribute to the purity of the air, and healthfulness of the people, for bad air is next to bad water, a frequent cause of sickness, particularly of the putrid kind "

Following this suggestion, a Company was formed called the "*Union Society*," and new shambles were built, as told in Adam's "*Weekly Courant*" for Tuesday, 17th Jan 1792

"The new shambles, upon a quadrangular plan, surrounded with covered passages for purchasers, erected near the Corn Market in Nantwich, was opened on Saturday last [Jan 14th] and very justly met with the commendation of the magistrates and the inhabitants of that town This very laudable undertaking has been carried out at the expense of the Union Society in Nantwich, and there is no doubt but the tenants of those sale shops will meet with every encouragement from the inhabitants and neighbouring gentry, as this improvement will cause the long-accustomed nuisances of having butchers' standings and benches in the open streets to be removed"

"At Nantwich market on Saturday [Jan 14] the average price of wheat was 5s 0½d, barley 3s 10½d, and oats 2s 8¾d per bushel Winchester measure"

The "*Union Inn*," built by the same "Society," in the summer of the same year, was advertised as "A Large, new, handsome, Sashed House, three stories high, cellared under, with gateway, &c, very advantageously situated in the centre of the High Town, and near the new erected Shambles, to be Let, very suitable for a public house,"—(Chest. Chronicle for 7 Sept 1792) It was first tenanted by *Mr John Lightfoot*, and soon became a busy Coaching House, but neither the enterprise of the Union Society nor the newspaper article could persuade the butchers to use the new Shambles. They even continued to stand in the streets for some time after the opening of the *New Market Hall* in 1868, and as foot-pavements were then unknown in the town, people had to jostle their way through the crowd, on market and fair days, with great inconvenience, and often not without danger from cattle, and other varieties of street locomotion The butchers, however, were at last shamed out of their opposition and prejudice, and the "*long-accustomed nuisance*" ceased about seventy-seven years after the erection of the *Shambles*, which were, consequently, used for another purpose, and acquired another name About 1782 George Wilbraham, Esq left the town, and subsequently disposed of most of his Nantwich property, and so the Cloth fair was removed to the "*Shambles*" in the Union Inn yard Many years after, an upper row of shops with a gallery was added for their accommodation, and ever since they have borne the name of "*Yorkshire Buildings*" The annual cloth fair at Christmas time, which usually lasted about six weeks until the "*New Market*,"* continued to be a busy scene until about the year 1840, when these travelling tradesmen ceased to visit this and other towns in the county, a change that was gradually brought about by a variety of circumstances. Resident tradesmen, some of whom came originally as travelling tradesmen, and had settled here, began to regard the cloth fair at the busiest time of the year, with jealousy and envy. Country servants and the poorer inhabitants of the town, who had been the chief purchasers at the cloth fair, began to improve the style of their dress, and smock frocks, linsey petticoats, and cheap shoddy were in less demand, and as they received advanced wages payable at different times, and not all at Christmas as heretofore, farm servants were better enabled to do business with the tradesmen of the town

It is not my intention to attempt an exhaustive account of the changes and improvements that have taken place in this country town during the present century. To do so

* *i e* On the Saturday after Candlemas Day, (Feb 2)

would extend these annals to a wearisome length   Still it will be necessary to allude to some of the principal changes, and chronicle a few events of local interest, taken from the Parish Registers, old newspapers, Directories, and Guide Books, and from what the poet Wordsworth has called "*oral records*"

The transmission of goods along the main road between Chester and London, was formerly effected by *Wakeman's Waggon,* with wheels nearly a yard broad, and drawn by a team of nine horses   a fact very suggestive of the then bad state of the turnpike roads. *Mail-Coaches,* and vehicles that were dignified by the name of "*Machines,*" also regularly passed through the town   Two Chester Guide Books, dated 1782 and 1789, give the following information —

   1782   "The London Post comes in [to Chester] by the *Nantwich* Road, early on Tuesday, Friday, and Sunday mornings   goes out on Monday, Wednesday, and Saturday, at half past eleven in the morning"

   1782   "The London Post comes in [to Chester] by the *Nantwich* Road, early on Monday, Thursday, and Saturday mornings , goes out on Monday, Wednesday, and Saturday, at ten at night '

   1782   "The *Machines* go [from Chester to London] by the *Nantwich* Road, in Summer time, on Monday, Wednesday, and Friday nights, and perform in two days   *Fare,* £1 11s 6d   In Winter time on Monday and Thursday nights, and perform in two days and a half   *Fare,* £1 11s 6d "

   1789   "The New and Elegant [Coach] Royal Chester, in 36 hours, by way of *Nantwich,* Lichfield and Northampton, to London , every Sunday, Tuesday and Thursday mornings at seven   *Fare,* inside, £2 2s 0d , outside, £1 1s 0d "

   1789   "The London Waggons go out from Mr Wakeman's, the Wool-hall, Northgate Street, [Chester] every Wednesday and Friday mornings, at four o'clock, and Saturday evening at six   return Wednesday, Friday, and Saturday, at noon   Perform in six days "

Some years after two coaches commenced running from Nantwich to Manchester on alternate days, the fare being eight shillings , the shoemakers, who could not afford to pay for this luxury, either sent their parcels of shoes by the Carrier's cart, or carried them on their backs as they travelled on foot to attend Shudehill market.

In 1792, at the corner of Church Lane lived John Groucott, a *spinning-wheel maker ,* employed by people in the town and neighbourhood who, for many years after that date, continued to wear home-spun apparel.   Farmers came to market on their working horses with long fetlocks, their wives being commonly seated behind them on pillions , from which they alighted by means of the horse-block, then a necessary appendage to an inn *

Most of the cottages,—timbered houses with thatched roofs,—were inconveniently low , and were entered, generally, by descending one or two steps, to the ground floor, which was often laid below the level of the street.   According to a Survey of the town in 1792, stables, barns, and maltkilns, stood in close juxta-position with dwelling houses, in the lines of the streets that branched from the centre of the town   A few shops in High Town were then mere open stalls, with hanging shutters , the rest had windows with small panes of glass, the dark and crowded interiors being very different from the orderly arrangement and ample dimensions of shops at the present time   There were then no decorated shop fronts, but over the door of a draper's establishment, for example,

---

   * A *horse-block* is represented in the illustration of the Wilbraham Almshouses, in Welsh Row

would hang a linsey petticoat, or a smock frock, which, stretched on a pole passing through each sleeve, resembled very much a boat s square sail.

Of the principal houses in High Town, the one already mentioned as the " Griffin Inn," (p 218) affords an interesting specimen   The old builders seem to have designed business houses much on the same plan as cottages, making the gable end to face the street, and carrying a great extent of premises behind,—room after room, with several staircases, thus rendering the inner rooms of these long, narrow houses somewhat dark and dismal

At the "Crown" and "Lamb" Inns were kept post-boys and post-horses; but beside these necessary inns, were many ale-houses. Old people say, that from the west end of Beam Street, in a short distance, could once be counted no less than sixteen ale-houses ! But if those days were merrier than now, they were certainly not more peaceable.

Sports and pastimes were of a noisy and rough character. Partridge alludes to a spirit of rivalry and strife, and perhaps animosity between the young people of the town who lived on opposite sides of the river   (*Hist Nant* p. 10)   Many people now living remember the practice of bull-baiting at the Union, the Market Hall, opposite the Wilbra-ham's Arms, at Cartlake, or on the Barony   After the Griffin Inn was closed, the *Cock-pit*, for the convenience of the "royal sport," was removed to the Pigeons in Welsh Row, and was resorted to at Easter and Whitsuntide, the cock-breeders and trainers living in a dingy court, then called Bowker's Yard in Wall Lane   *Billy Boff* of Beam Street kept a badger and a bear, and frequented all the wakes and fairs in the neighbour-hood, as also did *Thomas Hayes*, of Hospital Street, who, though a weaver by trade, was more celebrated as a *bag-race runner*

Nantwich has long been famous as a sporting-town, and the probability is that if the following contest, (the account of which is taken from an old newspaper) had been generally known beforehand, the event would have been quite sufficient to have brought labour almost to a standstill, as, indeed, a coursing day, a pigeon race, or a trotting match has done in times more recent

1800   "On the 6th March a singular and well contested race was run over Beam Heath near Nantwich, between Mr Barrowcliff, who rode his Welsh horse, "Punch," twice round the race-course, two miles, and Mr Yardley, who ran on foot, with his hands tied on his back once round the course   The race was won by Mr Barrowcliff beating Mr Yardley not more than four yards, and was performed in 5 min and 56 seconds   Mr Barrowcliff is six feet two inches high and his horse is 17 years of age, and only 13 hands one inch in height "

1801   Two notorious burglars, named *Clare* and *Gee*, who lived at Ravensmoor, near Nantwich, and who had committed several depredations in the town and neighbourhood, were apprehended and taken to the Gaol-House in Pillory Street, and afterwards to Chester, where they were convicted at the Spring Assizes   *Gee* (Clare's nephew) being transported for life, and *Clare*, condemned to be hanged with two other robbers, Thomson and Morgan, on Gallows-hill beside the river Dee, at Boughton.   Just as the cart, which brought the three malefactors to execution, was being turned opposite the gallows, Clare gave a sudden spring, and by jumping and rolling reached the precipitous bank of the Dee, threw himself into the river, and sinking through the weight of his irons, was drowned   Jack Ketch was determined to fulfil his official duty, and the other criminals were kept in awful suspense until the body of the drowned man was recovered. After the triple execution, as the bodies were conveyed to Chester Gaol for interment, attended by a noisy crowd, the cart was upset by its drunken driver opposite St Michael's Church This execution and its disgraceful scenes, being the last at Boughton, took place on 9th May, 1801 *

"1802 March 16th & 17th A main of cocks of 13 main and 12 bye-battles was fought at Nantwich, between Sir Robert Leighton and Sir Thomas Mostyn, Barts , which was won by the former, one ahead in the main , the byes were equal "†

In 1803 part of Beam Heath was enclosed pursuant to Act of Parliament (43 Geo. III cap 123), and in opposition to a few persons who, at that time received the only benefit of Common right, and who excited the poor of the town to rebel Fences were wilfully destroyed by them , and at last a body of soldiers was sent from Chester , and some of the rioters were captured, tried at Chester, and imprisoned

Owing to the threatened and expected invasion of England by Buonaparte in 1803, great preparations were made for war; and here as elsewhere, every man between the ages of fifteen and sixty, was compelled to learn the use of arms At Nantwich, Sunday was the day appointed for military drill, the exercise ground being a field near the Common, afterwards called *Volunteers' Field;* a name still existing in *Volunteers' Row* Here

"Striplings, all in bright attire
And graced with shining weapons, weekly marched
From this [green] valley, to a central spot
Where, in assemblage with the flower and choice
Of the surrounding district, they might learn
The rudiments of war "

The names of the officers of the Nantwich Volunteers, which was the largest company in the county at this time, Chester excepted, were as follows ‡

Colonel—John Crewe, Esq of Crewe   1st Dec 1803

Major—Robert Salusbury Cotton Bart   5 Sep 1803.

Captains—James Bayley, William Sprout, Thomas Garnet, Peter Bayley, William Harwood Folliott, James Tomkinson 5 Sep 1803

Lieutenants—Benjamin Rodenhurst, Richard Leversage, John Pratchett, John Jasper Garnett, Peter Sprout, William Kent 5 Sep. 1803

Ensign—John Needham Cliff, William Sutton, William Martin, William Lowe, Robert Holland. 5 Sep. 1803

Adjutant—Peter Wetenhall 18 Oct. 1803.

Quarter-Master—John Pratchett

Surgeon—William Kent

Infantry. Six companies , 420 men

Nantwich Volunteers were accustomed to "Camp out" at Newport, Salop The Chester Chronicle of 22nd June, 1804 says:—

"Tuesday June 19th the Nantwich Loyal Volunteers marched into that town, on their return from Newport, where they have been on permanent service for 21 days "

* Hemingway's *Hist Chester*, vol II, p 297 , and *Cheshire Sheaf*, vol I, p 198
† Chesh Sheaf, No 1485 Cock-fighting was practised in Nantwich after the year 1825
‡ Local Gleanings, 4to series, vol II, p 222

During the Napoleonic wars, Ballotting Serjeants were busy at the "Crown Inn," where, sometimes, large sums (seventy or eighty guineas) were paid as redemption money for respectable men who were "drawn" to go for soldiers Recruiting Serjeants also paraded the town on market-days, at fairs, races, &c , to the strains of drum and fife, enticing youths to enlist into His Majesty's Militia Force, their head-quarters being the "Star" Inn, (*now* "Royal Oak") in Beam Street, one room of which was long known as the *Soldiers' Parlour*, where many a country yokel was "trepanned," and afterwards suffered "the smart," that is, he was cajoled into accepting the enlisting shilling, after which his freedom could only be purchased within four days, on payment of a guinea The rendezvous of ballotted men this district was Chester, whence they were sent to Plymouth where the Militia recruits were under training. and thence to the Seat of War.

An amusing incident in connection with a soldier s wedding at Nantwich is thus told in the Chester "Chronicle," dated Friday, Dec 7th, 1804

"Monday last [Dec 3] at Nantwich, Mr Scholfield, sergeant of the Army of Reserve, to Miss Betty Hallwood [? Hollowood] of Beam Bridge This marriage being against the consent of the lady's friends, the brother of the bride actually stript to fight the parson in the church for marrying them, who was obliged to procure constables to keep the peace during the nuptial ceremony, after which the bride was borne off in triumph by the bridegroom under one arm, and a corporal of the same regiment under the other, to the no small gratification of a large concourse of spectators"

In 1803 the present balustraded stone Bridge (now called the Welsh Bridge on the Government Survey Map) of one arch, was built by Mr William Lightfoot, mason, of Snow-hill, in this town The former stone bridge had existed 140 years (See pp 196 and 208).

1804 Nantwich Races were held this year on Wednesday and the two following days, the 11th, 12th and 13th of July.

1805 The following advertisement appeared in the Chester "Chronicle" of Friday, March 22nd, 1805

"The old customary *Salt-Ley* will be opened on Tuesday the 23rd of April next. Terms &c

The ley of a horse for the first four weeks at 10s 6d per week   £2 2s 0d

Ditto for the second four weeks from 21st of May at 8/- per week   £1 12s 0d

Horses may continue for a month longer after the first ley, at eight shillings per week (with due notice)

Half-price to be paid when the leys are engaged, and the remainder before turning in

The established credit of the Salt-ley makes it unnecessary to say more, than that the greatest care will be taken, and strict attention observed

☞Apply to Edward Bellis, Salt-Ley, Nantwich, Cheshire

Nantwich, 3d Month, 18th, 1805 "

The "*Salt-Ley*," or "*Heating-horse Meadow*" is the field between Wall Lane and the River Such were the properties of the grass, that it was commonly said horses were either killed or cured by eating it The field was at last overstocked in the dry summer of 1826, and some of the horses, to use a homely phrase, were "*clemmed,*" and so, like the Quaker's dog, the field got a bad name, and has never since regained its former notoriety. Possibly the dry season may have killed some of the indigenous grasses in this once far-famed field

1808 On Saturday, the 12th November, the firm of *Broughton, Sprout and Garnett* opened a new Bank, in High Town, in premises next to the Griffin Inn Tokens issued there were thus inscribed —

> *Obv* The Arms of the Town, surrounded by " NANTWICH TOKEN VALUE ONE SHILLING."
> *rev.* In the centre, "AT THE OLD BANK," surrounded by " ONE POUND NOTE FOR
> 20 TOKENS."—(Platt's *Nantwich*, p 77)

Though called the *Old* Bank, it was not the *first* Bank in the town Some years before, Benjamin Hewitt, a wealthy Shoe-merchant, had started one in Hospital Street at the house now occupied by S H. Munro, Esq. M D Mr Hewitt died aged sixty-four, on 8th Oct 1808 and his bank, which was afterwards managed by his son, failed in Feb. 1816 The proprietors of the Bank in High Street were Charles Delves Broughton Esq , of Almington Hall, co. Staffordshire, William Sprout Esq ,* of Nantwich, John Garnett Esq , of Nantwich, who took another partner, William Sutton Esq , a proprietor of salt-works at Lawton, who died at Shardlow, near Derby, aged eighty-five, in Feb 1814 This bank failed, when there was a general commercial depression, on 13th Feb 1826

On Sunday, 13th Nov 1808, the Wesleyan Chapel, which had been built at a cost of £3,300, was first opened, the services at 10 a m and 6 p m being conducted by the Rev. John Gaulter, preacher, a native of Cheshire, who became president of the Wesleyan Conference in 1817

On Wednesday, the 25th Oct. 1809 was celebrated with demonstrations of loyalty the jubilee of His Majesty King George III. In the evening of the same day a new Organ, built by Mr Grey, of London at a cost of £1000, (Platt's *Hist Nantwich*, p 31) and placed in a gallery under the tower of the Church, was first publicly played, and a selection of Sacred music performed, the soloists being "Miss Travis, Mr Miller, Mr Jones and Mr. Keefe" The Sermon was preached by the Rev James Cotton, cousin to Lord Combermere —(*Nantwich Parish Magazine*, Aug 1875).

1810. James Boston, of this town, commenced running a Coach between Nantwich and Chester, once a week, leaving the " Three Pigeons" at Nantwich for the first time on 17th April, 1810, at 8 a m ; and returning from " The Blossoms," Chester, on the following day at 3 p.m. (Chester "*Herald*')

1811. A lawsuit relating to the Mills at Nantwich and Bartherton between Sir Thomas Broughton, of Doddington, Bart , and Messrs Michael Bott & Co , after pending several years, and occupying two days in Court in 1810, was finally decided at Chester Assizes in Sept 1811 in favor of Messrs Bott & Co (Chester "Chronicle" 13 Sep. 1811)

When corn and provisions were at famine prices, a public meeting to consider the propriety of petitioning Parliament against the proposed alteration in the laws relating to the importation of Corn, was held on 31st May, 1813, Michael Bott, Esq being Chairman. The following resolutions, advocating Free Trade principles, were adopted —

> " 1 —That a Bill, now before Parliament, is highly prejudicial to the interests of the Manufacturers of this Empire, & what is of the most vital importance, they cannot rival other markets, if the prices of the necessaries of life are are not brought nearer to those of other countries

---

* A portrait in oil of Wm Sprout may be seen at the Savings' Bank, in Welsh Row

2 —That we think there is no necessity for any duty on importation to increase or regulate the price of corn, & therefore for the welfare of the Community at large, petitions ought to be presented to both Houses of Parliament praying that no duty be imposed on Corn & Grain, to be imported into this Country, but that as well the importation as the exportation of Corn, be free from any duty whatever "

Samuel Platt, servant, killed by the wheel of a Wagon being drawn over his head in Nantwich   Buried 7 May 1813— *(Par. Reg)*

Thomas Gayter wheelwright, found suffocated and drowred in the water of a lime-pit, in Nantwich   Buried 6 June 1813 —*(Par Reg)*

On 17th May, 1814, SIR STAPLETON COTTON, the renowned hero of the Peninsular War, was raised to the Peerage, by the title of BARON COMBERMERE   The return of his lordship to Combermere Abbey was marked by great rejoicings in the neighbourhood   At Wrenbury, on the 29th May, four sheep were roasted on the village green, and three barrels of stout Cheshire ale provided for the feast, at which about two hundred sat down.   His lordship was chaired and carried by four tenants, colours flying, and the band playing God save the King, amid loud huzzas   After the dance, in which his lordship led off with Miss Harding, the whole village in the evening, was illuminated, and thus ended that day of village festivities   On Wednesday, 20th July, Nantwich had its demonstration in honour of Lord Combermere, when a grand dinner was given at the Assembly Room, furnished by William Holyoak,[*] of the Crown Inn   His Lordship, in the full dress of a Lieutenant General, decorated with military orders, was received by the gentlemen of the town at Newtown, and conducted to an "Antique triumphal Car, adorned with ribbands and drawn by men   The procession, consisting of trumpeters, constables, and gentlemen on horseback, the Lodge of Freemasons (of which his Lordship had held the highest office), and members of different Clubs, passed through the principal streets, which everywhere displayed flags and festoons of evergreens.   At the Market-Hall, in the centre of the town, the Freemasons having arranged themselves in a circle, Brother Fawcett (one of Mr. Stanton's Company of Comedians) presented an address to his Lordship, who descended from the car, to express his appreciation of this honour   From thence, the procession moved under a triumphal arch of laurel, surmounted with a crown and G R, to the entertainment provided at the Crown Inn   At night the whole town was illuminated; the west window of the Church was lit up with a transparency by Mr. Robertson, of Faith, Hope, and Charity, the houses of Messrs Hewitt, (Banker), Berks, (Tanner), Broughton & Co s Bank, Bott & Co.'s Factory, Edleston, and Elwood's Office, (Attorneys), Walton, (Auctioneer), Tomlinson, Washington Cliffe, Wrench, (Surgeon), Gardner, (Surgeon), Johnson, (Chemist), Owens, (The Lamb), Leversage, (Ironmonger), Cappur, (Cheesefactor), and Sprout, (Banker), were ornamented with various designs in variegated lamps, very fully described in the Chester "*Chronicle,*' 22nd July, which devotes an unusually large space to an account of this Thanksgiving-day at Nantwich, that was only surpassed by the remarkable reception accorded to Lords Combermere and Hill, on the 15th of August in the same year, at the ancient city of Chester.

* William Holyoak afterwards became Governor of Nantwich Workhouse, and died in that office   A gravestone to his memory in the Churchyard on the south side of the Church, is inscribed —" Sacred | to the Memory | of | William Holyoak | who departed this Life | July 12, 1828, Aged 76 Years | Also | Elizabeth Wife of | William Holyoak | who died November 15th 1830 | Aged 80 Years | "

He was the uncle of George Jacob Holyoak, the free-thinker, a native of Birmingham, who for some years conducted a paper called " The Reasoner," and is now (1883) living in London

The year 1814 is generally memorable for the long continued "great frost" and heavy fall of snow, which broke up in the month of February, followed by a remarkably hot summer, the hottest days being from the 21st to the 28th of July, both inclusive

"Edward Lowe, son of Willm & Eliz Lowe was killed by the overturning of a Coach, and buried 10 Aug 1816 Aged 13"—*(Par Reg)*

On 27th Dec 1820, the Duke of Wellington, being the guest of his friend and companion in arms Lord Combermere, passed through Nantwich, *en route* to Chester, where honour was done to the hero of Waterloo (Hemingway s *Hist. Chester*, vol II p 268-9)

In 1821 an Act of Parliament was obtained entitling householders in Nantwich to participate in the profits of Beam Heath

The coronation-day of George IV, 19th July, 1821, was celebrated in this town with lively demonstrations of loyalty, as the yeomanry and volunteers, headed by bands of music, paraded the streets   (Macclesfield and Cheshire Advertiser, 28 July, 1821).

Joseph Sherratt, who was drowned in the Weaver on the 23rd December, 1821, at Shrewbridge, in attempting to guide the Salop Coach of Messrs Farrar and Cooke, through a deep flood, was buried on 10th Feb. 1822, *(Par Reg)* his body having been in the river nearly seven weeks

In 1824 was established the Nantwich Auxiliary of the Bible Society   It originated with several benevolent ladies who, for five years previous, had associated themselves for the purpose of disseminating copies of the Scriptures and Psalter. (First printed Report of the Society, dated 1825)   The Twenty-ninth Report (dated 1853) records that to William Smith, Esq , of Stapeley, "more than to any one individual, are to be ascribed the formation and continued prosperity of this Auxiliary, and several of its Branch Associations "   The first list of officers was as follows —

President.

Right Hon Earl of Rocksavage [afterwards (1828) Marquis of Cholmondeley]

Vice-Presidents.

Rev R Hill, of Hough.	George Wilbraham Esq , of Delamere.
Rev. W. Garnett, of Tilston.	E Davenport Esq., of Calveley
Sir John Chetwode, Bart., of Oakley.	James Caldwell, Esq , of Lindley Wood
John Harding, Esq , of Wrenbury	Michael Bott, Esq , of Nantwich
Charles Clarke, Esq , of Cholmondeley	

To which in 1826 were added the names of John Dudley, Esq., of Wharton Lodge; Rev. Thomas Brooke, Rector of Wistaston, and in 1829, the names of George Tollett, Esq , of Betley, Rev. James Campbell, of Tilston, John Jervis Tollemache, Esq , of Tilston Lodge [now Lord Tollemache].

The first Committee was —

Mr John Downes	Mr George Jackson	Mr Benjamin White
Mr Robert Parker.	Mr Thomas Nixson	Mr Richard Stretch
Mr William Pearce	Mr John Barker	Mr Robert Adams.
Mr Ralph Cappur	Mr Thomas Bostock.	Mr. Thomas Wilson
Mr John Withenshaw	Mr. Edward Jones.	Mr. Joseph Nixon.

Mr William Jervis	Mr John Eardley	Mr Richard Vernon
Mr Robert Harrison	Mr John Barker	Mr William Wordley
Mr. George Moores	Mr James Plevin	Mr Thomas Deriemer.

Treasurer—John Jasper Garnett Esq

Secretaries

| Rev G Vawdrey, Vicar of Wrenbury | William Smith, Esq ,* of Stapeley |
| Rev B Senior | Croudstan Tunstall, of Alvaston |

The first balance sheet, dated 1st Sept 1825, showed an income from subscriptions, donations, &c of £264 10s 6d , and an expenditure of £248 19s 3d   The first meeting was held at the Old Brewery, now Harlock s Clothing Factory, on the site of the Townsend House   Succeeding annual meetings were held at the Theatre until 1829, at the Wesleyan Chapel until 1839, at the National School until 1859, and since then at the Town Hall. Some idea of the work of the Society in its early years may be gathered from the fact that for the first fifteen years of its existence the average amount of subscriptions in Nantwich *alone*, was £110 per ann   The sixth Report (1830) states that in Nantwich a hundred and ninety families had been found destitute of a copy of the Scriptures, and in that year the Society had purchased Bibles and Testaments to the amount of £241 †

1826 John Edgeley), who was accidentally suffocated and smothered in a ditch of water by a horse, which he was r ding, falling upon him therein, was buried 6 July 1826 Aged 47 —*(Par Reg)*

   William Taylor, who was accidentally drowned in the Chester and Ellesmere Canal in the township of Hurleston, was buried at N 31 Aug 1826, aged 66 —*(Par Reg)*

   John Burgess was found suffocated and drowned lying in a ditch of water by the side of the road in Hurleston on the 23rd day of December   Burd 26 Dec 1826 Aged 49 —*(Par Reg)*

1827 John Billington was accidentally scalded to death on 11th Sept and Buried 14th Sept 1827 Aged 5 —*(Par Reg)*

1828 Mary Vernon, not being of sound mind, memory & understanding, but lunatic & distracted, drowned herself in the river Weaver at Nantwich   Buried 10 July 1828 Age 22 —*(Par Reg)*

   Mary, wife of John Turner, being of unsound mind &c did drown herself in a pit of water on Beam Heath, in this parish   Buried 11 Aug 1828 Aged 55 —*(Par Reg)*

   Mary, wife of John Bebbington, accidentally burnt to death   Buried 27 Aug 1828 Aged 53 —*(Par Reg)*

On 17th Dec 1828, a number of Nantwich shoemakers and others of the town and neighbourhood were implicated in a great poaching affray on the Darnhall estate, causing much excitement in the town   One of the number, Burrows, peached , and the ringleaders were apprehended and imprisoned in the " Round House " on Snow Hill   They were tried at Chester, six or seven were sentenced to fourteen years' transportation, and the rest to short terms of imprisonment   Through a technical flaw in the indictment, the same not specifying whether the offence was committed after twelve at noon, or twelve at night,—a discovery made by the astute lawyer, T. W. Jones, Esq , of Hough,—they were liberated after some months' imprisonment on board the "Justicia " convict hulk at Woolwich   At the time of their apprehension, public feeling was so strong in their favour, that serious riots took place every time they were brought before the local magistrates ; and eventually a detachment of soldiers was sent from Chester. While the prisoners were

* William Smith, Esq , was Secretary for ten years, and Treasurer for eighteen years, until his death in 1853 when he was succeeded by Thomas Cawley, Esq , who continues to act as Treasurer for the Society

† Samuel Harlock, Esq has in his possession an almost complete set of the printed Reports of this Society, which has now existed above half a century , from which the above information is obtained

being conveyed away, chained together in carts and waggons, a scuffle took place in Marsh Lane. Major Tomkinson of Dorfold read the Riot Act, and the rioters, after a few blows from the butt end of the guns, were soon dispersed, some of them being afterwards imprisoned for aiding and abetting the escape of the poachers Mr. George Williamson, one of the released convicts, afterwards became a useful and respected townsman " His death, (on 25th Aug 1868) seems to have been felt as a public loss, and his remains were attended to the grave by a great number of sorrowing friends, including the children and teachers of the Nantwich Primitive Methodist Sunday School, who wished to sing a hymn at the grave but were not allowed to do so by the Rector,"* a circumstance that produced great animosity between Churchmen and Dissenters, and eventually, in 1875, resulted in the formation of a Nonconformist Cemetery.

1829. Shrewbridge Hall built by Mr. Michael Bott.

As several inaccuracies occur in a note on Shrewbridge Hall by Mr Helsby, (Ormerod's *Cheshire*, new edit vol III p 440), it will not be uninteresting here to give the true history of the estate from private papers and legal documents

The present estate was formed by Mr. Isaac Horton, Currier, of Hospital Street, Nantwich, who, between the years 1780 and 1790, purchased lands amounting altogether to nearly eighty acres, from the Maistersons, Peter Walthall Esq, Messrs Briscoe, and Perrin. About that time and for some years after, Shrewbridge farm was rented by Mr. Michael Bott, of the firm of Buch, Bower, and Bott, for supplying the apprentices engaged at the Cotton Factory with bread, butter, cheese, milk, vegetables, &c. Mr Horton died intestate in April, 1803, leaving an only daughter, Mary Horton, sole heiress, to whom administration of her father's property was granted by the Chancellor of Chester on 20th Sept 1803 Mary Horton was married at Liverpool* on 14th Oct 1805 to Mr Michael Bott, having two days previous (12th Oct) made a marriage settlement of the estate in favour of the issue of that marriage Mrs Bott died in 1822, and was buried at Wybunbury on the 23rd April of that year, and, in consequence of the children of this marriage dying in infancy, another agreement was made shortly before her death, dated 4th April, 1822, by which the ultimate limitations of settlement were to Mr Michael Bott his heirs and assigns for ever, in fee simple. The final agreement was made in the Lord the King's Court of Chester, in the Common Hall of Pleas, on 10th April, 1822, before the Hon Chas Warren, Justice of Chester, and the Hon. Samuel Marshall, serjeant-at-law, when Mr. and Mrs Bott levied a fine to one Peter Taylor of the estate at Shrewbridge, by the description of "1 Messuage, 1 Barn, 3 Stables, 2 Shippons, 2 gardens, 1 orchard, 20 acres of land, 30 acres of meadow, 50 acres of pasture, common of pasture for all cattle and common of turbary with the appurtenances in Nantwich "

Mr. Bott married secondly Miss Williamson of Chester, in 1828, by whom he had four sons, John, Thomas, Charles, and Philip, who all survived their father. In 1829 Mr Bott pulled down the old farm-house, and on its site built a handsome mansion of white stone, (for many years locally known as Bott's Hall), surrounded it with ornamental pleasure grounds at a cost of about £10,000, and further increased the estate by various

* Johnson's '*Nantwich and Crewe Monthly Illustrated Journal* " a Local Magazine commenced in June, 1868, and finished December, 1868

† "Chester Chronicle" for 18th Oct 1805 The marriage is also entered at Nantwich on 14th Oct 1805

purchases to 108 acres   There he resided, giving the strictest attention to the management of his estate, until his death, which took place on the 29th Dec 1846. He was
buried at Wybunbury, on 7th Jan following, and by his will dated 24th Dec 1844, proved
at Chester 8th April, 1847, and sworn under £14,000, his property was to remain in the
hands of trustees until his youngest son attained the age of twenty-one years, when it was
to be sold and divided amongst his sons, legacies also being left to certain relations and
other legatees

After the death of Mr Bott, the estate was claimed by Mr Richard Horton, shoe
manufacturer, of Nantwich, as heir-at-law of his great-great-uncle Mr Isaac Horton, the
father of the first Mrs Bott   An ejectment suit was tried at Chester Assizes on 5th Aug.
1857, in the Exchequer of Pleas before Lord Chief Justice Cockburn, but at once quashed
when the defendants, Messrs Philip and Charles Bott, produced the legal settlements, which
had been persistently withheld from the plaintiff, who, therefore, was led to expend several
hundred pounds in order to satisfy himself and his relations of this barring claim

The Hall and estate were purchased in 1878 by J M Bennett, Esq, of Manchester,
for £15,000, who endeavoured, but failed, to sell it to a Company, for converting the
Hall into a Sanitorium with Brine Baths, which scheme finally collapsed in Sept 1880

Great distress was felt amongst the labouring classes in the winter of 1830,* and in
the early part of February, a committee headed by the Rector (Rev H R Gretton) collected in the town for the relief of the poor subscriptions amounting to above £120.

In the same month George Edwards, who was one of an organized gang of horse-
stealers that had frequently visited this neighbourhood, was committed to Chester Castle,
by the magistrates, no less than five charges for this offence having been preferred
against him

On Tuesday, 9th Feb 1830, Mrs. Elizabeth Woolsey drowned herself in a watercourse
which runs into the Weaver. The verdict before Faithful Thomas Esq, Coroner, on the
next day was lunacy (Chester *Chronicle*)

Another Inquest was held on 16th Feb. 1830, on Mr John Cooke, aged 88, who the
day before, had been drowned in the Weaver   The deceased was nearly blind, and it
was supposed he had left home early, according to his usual custom, and missing his way,
walked into the river at a dangerous and unprotected place near the Bridge

On Saturday, 28th Aug 1830, Elizabeth, wife of Thomas Shaw, mercer, of High-town,
died under very painful circumstances. On the Thursday previous she had boiled a leg
of mutton in a saucepan, that had a few days before been used to boil arsenic for the
purpose of destroying rats   Having prepared dinner, Mrs Shaw sent some of the broth
to a young man who was sick, and partook of some herself   The Rev John Hughes,
Wesleyan Minister, was invited to dinner, and he and Mr. Shaw were in the act of
eating some of the broth, when Mrs Shaw was taken suddenly ill, and as the use previously
made of the saucepan recurred to her mind, she desired them to eat no more   The
young man minister, and husband narrowly escaped being poisoned, but medical assistance having failed, the wife died —(Chester *Chronicle*, 3 Sept)   She was buried in the
churchyard on the north side of the Chancel, where a flat stone exists to her memory.

* There had been several years of trade depression, in which Bank failures were common, throughout the country,
these bad years were followed by strikes in the Cotton districts in 1830

Tuesday, 26th Oct 1830   Demonstration with procession, and grand Dinner to Lord Combermere at the Crown Assembly Room, Nantwich, previous to his departure for parliamentary duties in London —*(Ibid)*

Wednesday, 8th Dec 1830   The Nantwich branch Bank of the Manchester and Liverpool District Banking Company, opened in Barker Street, under the direction of Messrs Robert Harrison, William Smith, of Stapeley, and Croudson Tunstall, of Alvaston. —*(Ibid)*

1831. In this year the Liverpool and Birmingham Junction Canal which crosses the western extremity of Nantwich township, was in process of construction.

George Foxley, an idiot of the extraordinary age of 105 years, was Buried at Nantwich on 12 Sep 1831 —*(Par Reg)*

1832. This year is remarkable for the erection of Gas Works by a company of local gentlemen, and for the outbreak of Cholera, which was confined almost entirely to Wych-house Bank and the two Wood Streets   (Dr Williamson's Report in *Board of Health Report*, 1850, p 11)

The Parish Register records —

" Samuel Latham, the younger, of Wych-House Bank, The first Corpse dead of Cholera   Buried 11 Sept 1832   Aged 23

In the same month there were eight Cholera interments, five from Wood Street, one from Wych-House Bank, one from Welsh Row, and one from Newtown —*(Par Reg)*

Frances daughter of George and Sarah Bowker, who was accidentally killed, by the wheel of a Chaise, in the gateway of the Crown Inn, was Buried 9 Sep 1832 Aged 6 —*(Par Reg)*

1834. The Gas Works became the property of ten shareholders, and has continued to belong to a private Company to the present time

In September of this year was formed the first Temperance Society in this town.

The Register records as follows —

" William Orme did strangle himself Age 86 Buried 3 Jan 1834

John son of Joseph Latham, accidentally killed by the falling of a wall at the Old Brewery   Age 10   Buried 7th March 1834

Hannah, Widow of Saml Kirk, cut her own throat on 5 Aug 1834

Jane, wife of Thos Serjeant, Butcher, drowned herself in a water-tub, Buried 9 Nov 1834

Richard Steele, butcher, who was accidentally killed, by a blow on the hinder part of his head from the sail of a windmill [near Mount Pleasant, in Windmill Lane, now called *Crewe Road*]   Buried 18 Jan 1835   Aged 72

Samuel, son of John Green, who was drowned whilst Bathing in the Weaver, Buried 10 June, 1835   Aged 10

Elizabeth, Wife of William Burgess died by the visitation of God, Buried 11 Dec 1835 Aged 50 "

William Farnworth, aged 67, died in an apoplectic fit 18 Nov 1835 —(Chester *Chronicle*, 27 Nov)

The Workhouse on the Barony was enlarged in the year 1835, and surrounding parishes and townships formed into the Nantwich " *Union*," the management of paupers and vagrants being taken away from "Overseers" and given to the first elected "*Board of Guardians*," pursuant to the " Poor Law Amendment Act" of 1834 (4 & 5 Will. IV. c 76)

The ancient custom of ringing the Pan-cake, or Guttit Bell on Shrove Tuesday ceased in or about the year 1836

James Bromhall, joiner, who was accidentally crushed to death, was buried 1 April 1836, Aged 66 —*(Par Reg)*

Joseph Tinsley, who was accidentally killed by being thrown off a pony and being dragged in the stirrup leather, was buried 20 Oct 1836   Aged 14 —*(Par Reg)*

In 1837 the National Schools were built on land given by the Marquis of Cholmondeley.

On 10th Aug 1837, the High Sheriff, Charles Peter Shakerley Esq of Somerford Hall, declared at Chester, Sir Philip de Malpas Grey Egerton, Bart , and George Wilbraham Esq , duly elected Members of Parliament for the Southern Division of the County, for the first Parliament of Queen Victoria. The returns of the Poll were as follows —

EGERTON *(Conservative)*	3136
WILBRAHAM *(Liberal)*	3032
EDWIN CORBETT, of Darnhall *(Conservative)*	2646

The Register of electors numbered 7084. Plumpers for Wilbraham 2551, for Egerton 176, for Corbett 29. The polling days were the 7th and 8th Aug , and at Nantwich the numbers were, according to the printed Poll Book, as follows —

WILBRAHAM	849
EGERTON	511
CORBETT	421

Unpopular among the lower orders since the events of 1825, and terrified when a wag brandished a pheasant on a pole before his eyes, Mr Corbett, the Darnhall squire, hastily left the polling-booth at the Market Hall, and reaching the river, made his escape from the noisy crowd, by jumping in and wading through it   In the Welsh Row, a country voter was killed, by falling headlong from the top of a coach as it was being carelessly driven past the Black Lion Inn

1838 John Cawley, aged 30, being lunatic drowned himself in the Weaver   Buried 4 June 1838 —*(Par Reg)*
       William Lockett, aged 69, being lunatic, hung himself in his workshop   Buried 28 Oct 1838 —*(Par Reg)*
1839 Thomas Davies, aged 17, who was feloniously killed by Joseph Skerratt, was buried 24 Jan 1839 —*(Par Reg)*

1840. Typhus fever of a very malignant kind considerably increased the mortality of the town , in the Union Workhouse there were no less than fifty-six cases at one time.—(Dr Williamson's Report in *Board of Health Report,* 1850, p. 11)

In this year the Primitive Methodist Chapel, Welsh Row , and the Wesleyan Day and Sunday Schools were built; and the Potato disease made its first appearance *

1841   At the general election for members of Parliament in this year, GEORGE WILBRAHAM, ESQ., who advocated the fixed corn duty, was thrown out, and from that time retired from Parliamentary duties   The successful candidates were —

SIR PHILIP DE MALPAS GREY EGERTON, BART *(Cons)*	3110
JOHN TOLLEMACHE, ESQ *(Cons)*	3034

George Wilbraham Esq. polled 2365 votes, the Register numbering 6972   There was no contested election in this Division of the county from Aug 1841 until April, 1880.

* The late Richard C Edleston, Esq , Attorney, of Nantwich, who died in 1871, devoted his attention for several years to the study of this disease, with great success   and ' in Cheshire " says Mr Salisbury *(Border Counties Worthies)* "his name will be remembered with respect, for the efforts he made during the potato famine to prevent the spread of that terrible infliction "   His invention for the better culture of the potato may be briefly stated as follows — Whole potatoes, carefully selected, were planted at unusually wide distances apart   After the tops appeared, they were earthed up in mounds with a spade, and when grown about a foot high, the stems were carefully divided and soil added to the top of the mound   Hence the stems instead of growing erect, inclined downwards on the sides of the mound   By this means it was found that the disease (which usually came in August) was prevented passing down the stem to the tuberous roots   This new method of culture was not generally adopted on account of the extra cost of labour   but the few farmers who tried the experiment were satisfied with the results   for not only was the disease prevented but the crop was greatly increased   Mr Edleston also professed to have discovered a prevention for the pleura and, some say, for the foot and mouth distemper in horned cattle   but these secrets, unfortunately, were never divulged   He was the son of Richard Edleston Esq   Attorney, of this town   and was baptized at Nantwich on the 20th Sept 1816   He was a well-known supporter of field sports, and an authority on all matters connected with coursing possessing, himself, some of the best greyhounds in the country

William Robinson, Master of the Free Grammar School, hanged himself in the Schoolroom, and was buried on the north side of the Churchyard, 1 July, 1841   Aged 32 —*(Par Reg)*

Thomas Kettle, timber drawer, committed suicide, and was buried 16 July 1841   Aged 36 —*(Par Reg)*

1843   On Whit-Sunday a fire occurred in Hospital Street, which totally consumed a row of thatched cottages opposite the Wesleyan Chapel, and damaged the Wesleyan Schools.

1846.   The Savings' Bank built in Welsh Row, and the Mechanics' Institute established in High Town, which latter had a short-lived existence.   Typhus fever again visited the town, and prevailed for nine months   (Dr Williamson's Report)   This year was a general failure in the potato crop throughout the county

1848.   Salt-baths, which had been commenced but a short period before on the Snow-Hill, were removed, and the old *"Round House"* (prison) in close proximity was taken down, and a Police Office erected on its site   The last criminal detained in the "Round House" (which notwithstanding its name, was a rectangular building), was *Mary Gallop*, for poisoning her father at Crewe.   She was hanged at Chester in 1844   In the new Prison on the site, the first and only murderer confined prior to her trial at Chester, was Sarah Featherstone, for the murder of her child.   She was condemned to be executed, but respite was granted, and she was imprisoned for life.

The Cholera.

In June, 1849, the plague of Asiatic Cholera visited the town, and in the short space of fourteen weeks nearly 1000 cases were reported out of a population of about 6000, resulting in about 180 deaths.   All the inhabitants were more or less affected by the peculiar atmospheric cause of cholera, but the epidemic appeared in its severest forms near the river, in the localities of the Wood Streets, Gas Alley, Wych-House Bank, Mill Street, and also in Hospital Street, and chiefly among the lower classes, although it was remarkable that the Irish population, who were generally attacked by typhus in 1846, escaped, comparatively speaking, from this horrible disease   Many people fled from the plague-stricken town, and trade came almost to a standstill.   No markets were held; and no fair in September, even country milk-sellers refused to come to the town, and grass grew in the streets   Funerals took place daily, and at all hours; and, as it was deemed necessary to bury the dead as soon as possible, alarming reports were circulated that some had been buried alive.   Thirty-seven deaths occurred in the week ending the 10th July. On the 14th inst a house to house visitation was commenced and continued until the contagion died out, by a committee consisting of the Rector, Dr Williamson, Mr Thomas Johnson and others, who with praiseworthy zeal, were untiring and heroic in their attentions to the distressed and afflicted poor   When the epidemic was at its height, sufficient grave-room for the dead could not be found in the ancient Churchyard   In this exigency, a parcel of land on the Barony called *Finger-post-field*, belonging to the Workhouse, was purchased for £400 raised by public subscription, and on the 20th July, 1849, licence was granted by the Bishop for the burial of the dead, Episcopal Consecration being deferred until the 19th July in the following year.

Two consecutive entries in the Parish Register, will be of interest, the former giving the name of the last person buried in the Churchyard, and the latter according the first interment (a Cholera victim) in the new Burial Ground, which has ever since been the Parish Cemetery. The names are —

' Joseph Clarke, of Mill Street, aged 41 years buried 20 July 1849 by W A Stevenson (Curate) '

' James Chesters, of Snow Hill, aged 60 years, buried 21 July 1849, by A F Chater (Rector) "

To the names of those ascertained to have died of Cholera Morbus the Rector has added in the margin of the Register a capital C, the earliest victims being as follows —

"William son of Jno & Ellen Edwards of Wood St aged 5¾ yrs   Buried 23 June 1849
Thomas son of Jno & Ellen Edwards, of Wood St aged 3 yrs 8 mos   ,,   ,,   ,   ,,
James Ankers, of Wych House Bank, aged 50 years   ,,   27   ,,   ,,
Sarah, dau of Saml & Sarah Bullock of Welsh Row, aged 11 months   ,,   28   ,,   ,,
Elizabeth, wife of John Trickett, of Wood Street, aged 27 yrs   ,,   ,,   ,,   ,,
Jane, dau of Thos & Eliz Singleton of Mill Stone Lane, aged 11 yrs   ,,   2 July   ,,
James, son of Will & Abigail Gilbert of   do   do   aged 7 yrs   ,,   ,,   ,,   ,,

The following numbers taken from the Register show the mortality in this town from the 1st June to 31st Dec 1849

From 1 June to 23 June	7	
,, 24 June to 30 June	18	Buried in the Churchyard
,, 1 July to 20 July	81	
,, 21 July to 31 July	47	
,, 1 Aug to 31 Aug	33	
,, 1 Sep to 30 Sep	24	Buried in the Cemetery
,, 1 Oct to 31 Oct	16	
, 1 Nov to 30 Nov	11	
,, 1 Dec to 31 Dec	12	
Total	249	

As the plague abated, many suggestions were made by the local medical faculty for purifying the air and disinfecting the houses It was thought at one time, that the firing of cannon in the streets would sufficiently disturb the atmosphere, but it was finally decided that a cup of vitriol should be distributed to every house, and at a given signal, namely, the ringing of the Church Bell, every householder was ordered to fumigate the house with closed doors, and this plan seemed to have the desired effect. In August, when the half-deserted town presented a most melancholy appearance, and the greatest distress prevailed amongst the poor, the noblemen and gentry of the neighbourhood raised a fund and placed it at the disposal of the Rector, who distributed therewith a liberal supply of nutritious food, and rendered assistance to the various benefit clubs, most of which were at that time in a state of insolvency

The terrible calamity above described, of which, strange to say, no memorial stone exists in the Cemetery, may be regarded as the greatest crisis in the history of the town in modern times, for since the cholera visitation a spirit of improvement and progress have been infused into the inhabitants which cannot be traced in times prior to that event. The immediate outcome was the improvement of the sanitary condition of the town, and provision for a better water supply from Baddiley Mere, by a newly constituted Local

Board of Health. During the intervening thirty years great liberality and local efforts have been manifested in the restoration of the ancient Parish Church, and beautifying of the Churchyard, the erection of a commodious, though not handsome, Town Hall, and Market Hall, and the removal of old property in the centre of the town The opening of Railway communication with the manufacturing districts giving rise to increased trade, the introduction of machinery into the shoe and tailoring industries, the laying down of footpaths in the streets, the erection of several important public buildings, and better built houses, all these things have tended to raise the town to greater importance at the present time than in past ages Of these and minor events still fresh in the memory of the present generation, a brief notice will next be given, thus bringing to a close this already long chapter of Annals

1850 On 29th Sept the following nine gentlemen were elected as members of the first Local Board of Health in this town, namely —

REV A F CHAIER, Rector	MR EDWARD HARRISON
MR JOHN BARKER, Currier	MR JOHN SMITH, Draper
MR JAMES HOWARD, Gentleman	MR WILLIAM JOHNSON, Tailor
MR WILLIAM BOTT	MR WILLIAM FOWLES, Auctioneer (Clerk
MR GEORGE LATHAM, Architect	pro tem)

The first meeting was held at the Rectory, on 4th Dec. 1850, when the Rector was unanimously voted chairman MR JAMES BROADHURST being appointed Clerk, at £20 per ann., and MR THOMAS JOHNSON to the combined offices of Inspector of Nuisances and Rate Collector at £25 per ann Subsequent meetings were held at the Registry Office, Hospital Street

1851. Road made across the Barony

1852. The Unitarian Chapel renovated at a cost of £300

1853 The old Engine House, in the corner of the Churchyard opposite the Rectory taken down, and a new one built by Lord Crewe in Pillory Street, on land given by the Marquis of Cholmondeley (Cf p 221)

1854-5 The town drained by General Lee Esq C E

1855. St Anne's Catholic Chapel built, and the Restoration of the Parish Church commenced by G G. Scott, Esq , the Churchyard being finally closed by Order in Council, although no interments had taken place since 1849

1856 The last salt-work of three pans finally closed

1858 Shoemakers' Strike against the introduction of machine-made tops Wesleyan Chapel enlarged and improved at a cost of £400 The Ebenezer Chapel built at a cost of £1100, on the site of the old " Tabernacle."

On 1st Sept the Crewe and Shrewsbury Railway was opened for traffic, and on the 13th of the same month the newly built Town Hall and Corn Exchange, which cost over £2,500, was opened the day being kept as a festival. The streets were decorated with mottoes and evergreens, and a high class concert was given, at which, amongst other artistes, Miss Clara Novello sang

1859. A Poultry and Dog Show was held this year, and has since been annually held on or about New Market, in the month of February In May Mr Leonard Gilbert,* a native of this town, introduced the first Sewing Machines into his Shoe-factory.

Oct 16th, Mr Deriemer, a respectable inhabitant, died in the Parish Church during divine service

1860. The old Grammar School demolished, and the New Grammar School built

1862 Nantwich Cotton Mill closed during the Cotton Famine, but re-opened about two years after (in the spring of 1864) by a Cotton Spinning Co

1863 March 10th. Demonstration celebrating the marriage of H R H Albert Prince of Wales The very dry summer of this year was followed by a winter remarkably mild Green peas were gathered out of gardens at the end of November; and roses were in bud and bloom on Christmas day

On the 6th Oct 1863, a shock of earthquake was felt in this neighbourhood and in many other parts of England The Rev W F Shaw, curate of Acton, near Nantwich, described it as follows —

" Between half-past three and four o'clock [a m.] we were aroused by the smart shock of an earthquake It shook the windows and bedsteads violently, and lasted, I should suppose, for nearly a a minute The sensation produced, I can compare to nothing better than a huge giant taking the opposite posts of the bed and shaking them violently "†

On Monday, the 19th Oct 1863, the Railway between Nantwich and Market Drayton was opened, and in the same year was commenced a Festival of the united Choirs of Nantwich, Malpas and Middlewich Parishes, which continues to be held annually.

1864 The Manchester and Liverpool District Bank was in course of erection, the architect being Alfred Waterhouse, Esq, of Manchester, the contractor Mr Richard Beckett, of Hartford, and the sub-contractor, Mr Thomas Bowker, of Nantwich. It was opened on the 2nd June, 1866.

1865-6 The ancient Frog Channel, from Welsh Row Head to the second Wood Street, converted into a culvert

The pestilence amongst cattle, known as the *Rinderpest*, broke out in the summer of 1865, and continued its ravages in this neighbourhood until the following summer. The plague swept across the county (beginning, it is believed, in Dodcot-cum-Wilkesley,) with terrible severity

1866 A day of Humiliation was held at Nantwich, on Wednesday, 28th Feb The Rector preached from *Hab* iii 17 18, and a collection was made for the farmers who had lost cattle by the Plague. In this year, the Churchyard was improved by the planting of trees and ornamental shrubs, mainly through the liberality of James Broadhurst, Esq., and F W Hobson, Esq.

---

* This gentleman, to whose enterprise and ability the prosperity of the shoe-trade in this town is mainly due, was elected Mayor of the City of Chester in the year 1878

† *Nantwich Guardian* for 10th Oct 1863, which also contains the following description of the same occurrence from the pen of the late Charles Dickens " I was awakened by a violent swaying of my bed from side to side, accompanied by a singular heaving motion It was exactly as if some great beast had been crouching asleep under the bedstead, and were now shaking itself and trying to rise "

The *Cheshire Sheaf* records similar shocks of earthquakes felt in this county on the following dates, *viz* 14th Sept. 1777, 10th Nov 1795, (vol 1 pp 289, 324), 1st June 1801, 11th Jan 1878 (vol II p 1, 233)

1867 A public park formed on the Barony, and planted with shrubs at considerable expense. The scheme, which was unpopular at the time, has since proved a complete failure *

1868. The present Market Hall erected, and a new thoroughfare constructed called Market Street The Hall, which was built on land given by John Tollemache, Esq, M P, at a cost of about £2000, was opened without any demonstration whatever on the 30th July, the Old Market Hall in High Town being shortly afterwards taken down

On the following day (Friday, 31st July), a few minutes before two in the afternoon, a serious fire broke out on Snow Hill Some sparks from James O'Neil's smithy having ignited the thatched roof of a neighbouring stable, (the wind blowing freely at the time), the burning thatch was carried across the street, and in about half an hour, the fire spread from Snow Hill along the Swine Market as far as Mr Carrington's shop at the corner of High Street. Owing to scarcity of water after a long dry season, and an inadequate supply from Baddiley Mere, great alarm was felt at the rapid progress of the fire. After some delay the town water was obtained and the fire engine vigorously worked Six houses, four stables, and a blacksmith's shop were totally destroyed, and five houses were unroofed or otherwise injured This disaster led to the immediate formation of the Nantwich Volunteer Fire Brigade

The Town Hall, the greater part of which had been taken down on account of the insecure foundations, and re-built at a cost exceeding £1050, was re-opened on 11th Aug. in the same year.†

1870 Almshouses at Welsh Row Head re-built by John Tollemache, Esq, M P

1871 Church Infant School built in Market Street

1872 By Act of Parliament, the ancient privilege of Jurors claimed by the inhabitants of the town, became null and void

Messrs Harding and Co's Clothing Factory on the Barony commenced working in June.

In December the block of old houses and shops, situated in High Town, were taken down, thus greatly improving the centre of the town

1873 The Baptist Chapel in Market Street built The opening services were conducted by the Revs J. Clifford, M A, and Dr Jabez Burns, two celebrated London preachers who took great interest in the re-establishing of the Baptist cause in this town

1874. The Cotton-mill again became a Corn-mill as in ancient times

A new band of teetotal advocates, called the Independent Order of Good Templars, purchased the old Baptist Chapel in Barker Street, for a Good Templars' Hall

A second Church Day School built in second Wood Street.

1875 Early in this year an attempt was made to form a Public Cemetery under the management of a Burial Board The vote of the Vestry on 3rd Feb decided in favour

---

* The so called "Park," having long been in a sadly neglected state, and is now (1883) likely to be transferred to the Local Board of the town, and another scheme is under consideration for carrying out the original intention of providing a park and recreation ground, which promises to be a success

† It is proposed to further improve the Town Hall, which has this year (1883) been transferred by the Trustees to the Local Board

of the proposed scheme by a majority of 18 out of 80 present; but a poll of the town being demanded, an adverse vote was given on the 8th Feb , by a majority of 82 out of 918 votes; whereupon the leading Nonconformists, who had already formed themselves into a Company, and purchased land in Willaston, carried out their own project, and in November was opened the *Nantwich General Cemetery*.

Another project, which was being discussed at the same time, met with a similar fate. It was proposed by certain gentlemen, strangers to the town, to make Nantwich a Brine pumping station, and convey the brine by pipes to Ellesmere Port, there to be manufactured into salt, but the scheme, being unpopular in the town, and meeting with great opposition from the neighbouring gentry, was abandoned in May of this year

- On Wednesday, 28th July, the Rev C. H Spurgeon, of London, preached two sermons in the Market Hall to the largest audiences, perhaps, ever assembled for religious purposes in this town

In August, died Mr Thomas Hassall, Almsman (Beam Street Almshouses) a native of this town, having completed the hundredth year of his age

In the same year the Independent and Unitarian Chapels were renovated, and an Organ added to each, the Co-operative Society was formed in June; and the Liberal Club opened in a house in Pepper Street in November.

1876   Combermere Abbey narrowly escaped destruction by fire in February.

On 30th March, Mr Jackson, of Mill Street, formerly manager of the Cotton Mill for many years, was buried in a vault in the Independent Chapel yard

The Wesleyan Chapel enlarged, at a cost exceeding £2000, and the Midland Bank erected on the site of former banking premises.   -

1877   On 6th Sept the Friendly Societies of the town held a Demonstration to celebrate the centenary of the "Friendly Knot" Society.

Oct 14th A severe storm of wind damaged some of the pinnacles of the Church, roofs and chimneys of houses, &c , and uprooted many fine trees at Dorfold, Shrewbridge and in the neighbourhood.

1878   Feb 28th to March 2nd was held a Grand Bazaar in the Town Hall, in aid of the Restoration of the Porch and West Front of the Church, realizing more than £1000.

In July and August the Church Bells were quartered and re-fixed

In the latter month, F. E. Massey, Esq , of Alvaston Grove, served an injunction against the Local Board for polluting the River Weaver.

On the 12th Sept. was an imposing Masonic Demonstration

1879.   Great distress amongst the poor was felt during the severe frost of January and February   The hard winter was followed by a cold spring and wet summer   There was a heavy fall of snow on May-day   Plum trees were not in blossom until after the 12th May, and farmers could not turn out their cattle according to custom on that day, owing to the scarcity of grass.

April 5th. William Sherratt, of Willaston Terrace, murdered his wife by strangulation He was condemned, with recommendation to mercy at Chester Assizes, his sentence being eventually commuted to imprisonment for life.

A Cocoa House in Pillory Street ("*The Three Cups*") opened on 26th December.

1880. On 27th Jan Miss Janet Ramsay, of Dysart Buildings, was buried in a vault in the Independent Chapel yard.

April 8th Polling day at the General Election; being the first contested Election since 1841 in this Division of the County. The town was in a disturbed state

Early in March the impending lawsuit relating to the pollution of the river Weaver in the case of Massey *v.* Nantwich Local Board, was settled by an arrangement between the plaintiff and defendants

The Children's Home built in connection with the Union Workhouse

1881 The first interment in the Parish Cemetery under the recent Burials Act took place on Friday, 4th Jan , when the Rev. F. Moon, Independent Minister, conducted the ceremony at the funeral of Emma, wife of Mr J F. Crompton, and daughter of Mr. Charles Laxton, of this town

At the by-Election, after the death of Sir Philip de Malpas Grey Egerton, Bart , M P , Henry J Tollemache, Esq. was returned in the Conservative interest, the polling-day being 22nd April.

Michael McKale, of Spring Gardens, climbing a tall elm tree at Hospital Street end, in search of young rooks, between one and two o clock on Sunday morning, 22nd May, fell, as was supposed, eighty or ninety feet, and was found at six o'clock insensible He died two days after.

Brine discovered at a depth of thirty feet at Parkfield, Nantwich, on 16th Sept.

Dec 1 The Peoples' Hall opened , and in the same month the Conservative Club House, a very handsome building, was inaugurated by a Bazaar, which was opened on 16th Dec. by the Right Hon Lord Combermere

1882 The forty-sixth Annual Cheshire Agricultural Show held on the 31st August in Dorfold Park

Mr. Charles Laxton, who had been Special High Constable for Nantwich Hundred from Feb 1841 until 1857 , and Superintendent of the Police for Nantwich Division (under the Constabulary Act) from 1857 to 29th Sept. 1874, when he retired through failing health , died on the 29th Sept. 1882 He had been one of the principal founders of the Nantwich Volunteer Fire Brigade in 1868, and held the post of Captain until 1879 A Fireman s funeral was accorded to him, which was witnessed by a large concourse of people

A monthly Cheese Fair commenced on the 9th Nov.

Mrs. Cooper, of Hospital Street, accidentally killed in the hunting field on the 29th December

1883. On May-day the newly erected Brine and Medicinal Baths, on Snow Hill, were publicly inaugurated in the presence of about two hundred and fifty spectators, by Henry J. Tollemache, Esq M P , of Dorfold Hall. It is not a little singular that nearly two hundred years ago Nantwich followed Droitwich in abolishing the ancient salt customs; and in this present year of grace, by establishing saline Baths, Nantwich has again followed in the wake of Droitwich, where similar baths were opened on the 1st Jan. 1876 It may also be pointed out that if the opening ceremony had been arranged to have taken place but two days later, it would then have corresponded exactly, in time and place, with the annual Ascension-day Festival of olden times

TRADES OF THE TOWN.

The Salt Manufacture.

EVERYONE admits that the rise of Nantwich was due to the presence of its BRINE SPRING; which, according to Mr. Partridge, has long been called the "*Old Biot.*" Nowhere, however, in any ancient deed or record that has come under my notice, has this local name occurred; nor can it be stated with any degree of certainty how long the Brine Pit has been in existence. Although most Cheshire writers contend that the Romans were acquainted with the Salt-springs in this county; stronger evidence is yet required before it can be positively asserted that Nantwich, and the other Wiches, really existed at so distant a period of history. If the convergence of roads (see p. 8) implies the existence of a small Roman station, (which, it must be remembered, is not mentioned in the Roman "*Itineras,*") it still remains to be shown to what century we are to look for the founding of the Salt-towns of Cheshire; for the Roman occupation of Britain embraces a period of 450 years; a period equal to the interim that has elapsed since the commencement of the Wars of the Roses. About 650 years after the Romans left Britain, occurs the *first* mention of the Brine Pit at Nantwich. In late Saxon times the salt-spring and salt-houses here belonged to the Earls of Chester, and certain thanes (the King claiming rights of royalty); and in Norman times to the Baronial family of Malbank;* but after the death of William, third Baron of Wich-Malbank, the wich-houses, brine-pit, right of toll, &c., descended with the divisions and sub-divisions of the Barony to various manorial lords, and eventually to principal families in the town and county. Some of the wiche-houses, or "*bullaries,*" as they are often called in old deeds, were granted to Religious Houses. Besides the grants of salt-houses by the Barons of Wich-Malbank to the Abbeys of St.

---

* See Account of the Salt Laws &c., in Domesday Survey, on pp. 10-12.

Werburgh and Combermere early in the twelfth century, the religious houses in the town, the Hospital of St John,* and St Mary's Nunnery at Chester, the Monasteries of Wenlock and Lilleshall in Salop, and the Priory of St Thomas at Stafford, all derived emoluments from the Salt-houses in Nantwich in pre-Reformation times. From the Register of Bishop Norbury, it appears that in 1326 the people of "Wychmanbury" (probably a miss-spelling of Wych Malbank) were liable to furnish salt for the Bishop's table; and being at that time very remiss, were to be threatened with excommunication.†

In feudal times tenant farmers were required to render a service called "*salicher*," or carrying of salt from the nearest Wich. Few particulars relating to the manufacture of salt in Nantwich are known, from the year 1245, when King Henry III ordered a temporary stoppage of the works, until the Tudor period of history, when the revenues appear to have increased to many times the value recorded in Domesday Book. At the Dissolution of the Monasteries some of the wiche-houses in this town reverted to the Crown, and were afterwards sold to local families. Two such sales, *temp* Eliz., showing the value of salt-houses three hundred years ago, are here given from the *Cal. State Papers* (Domestic Series, vol ccxxxiii) —

"1590 July 12 Purchase by Roger Wilbraham, of Dorfold, Esq., of *three wiche-houses and a half*, in Namptwich, of the yearly value of £4 13s 4d at the price of £136 6s 8d

1590 Oct 10 Purchase by Richard Sawyer of *one wich-house* in Namptwich of the yearly value of 33s 4d, for which he payeth £66 13s 4d"

The Messrs Lysons (quoting *Rymeri Fœdera* vol. x p 761) say, the art of making salt was imperfectly understood in the fifteenth century, and King Henry VI invited *John de Sheidam*, of Zealand, with sixty persons in his company, to come to England "to instruct his subjects in the improved method of making salt." A hundred years later, so inadequate was the supply of salt, and so imperfect the method of obtaining it from brine, that between the years 1563 and 1580 many salt-works were established at Blyth, Hull, Boston, Lynn, St Bees, and other coast towns, by Dutchmen, who obtained patents from Queen Elizabeth granting the exclusive privilege of manufacture by a new method, called "*making salt upon salt*," (Cal of State Papers), a method, explained by Mr. T. Lowndes, in his "*Brine-salt Improved*" (Edit 1746, p 14) as follows —"The Dutch in purifying their Salt, always blend with the French Bay Salt, a great quantity of Spanish and other Mediterranean salts, this process is frequently called *making salt upon salt*"

A century later still, the salt of the Wiches was of very inferior character. Lord Macaulay, describing the mineral wealth of this country in 1685, says,‡ "The salt which was obtained by a rude process from brine-pits was held in no high estimation. The pans in which the manufacture was carried on exhaled a sulphurous stench, and when the evaporation was complete the substance which was left was scarcely fit to be used with food. Physicians attributed the scorbutic and pulmonary complaints which were common

* In the "*Palatine Note Book*," vol 1 p 273, mention is made of a Latin Charter on vellum still extant "being a Grant of some Saltworks called '*Saynt Mary Wychehous* near the '*Nunne Wychehous*, the Wode-strete, the land of John Lenell & the *Salt Works* of Randulph Scholehall, Chaplain of the Blessed Mary in the College of St John, Chester' to Richard Keffes Chaplain Given at Wich Malbank by Willm Sawrdyn & Cecilia his wife on the Monday before the feast of St Martin [11 Nov] 6 Hen V ' [1419] Seal attached

† From the Lichfield Registers, vol 1322-1358, obligingly communicated by J P Earwaker, F S A

‡ History of England, vol I p 155 (Longman's Edit 1871) quoting various Nos of Philosophical Transactions 1669-1684

among the English to this unwholesome condiment   It was therefore seldom used by the
upper and middle classes, and theie was a regular and considerable importation from
France "

Half a century later still and seventy years after the discovery of Rock Salt at
Marbury, near Northwich, the Government returns of imported salt. for seven yeais ending
Lady Day 1743, (the greater part of which was the celebrated Bay-salt of France, obtained
by natural evaporation in the neighbourhood of Rochelle), averaged no less than 106,000
Bushells each 84 ℔s., or nearly 4,000 tons per annum *

It will not be necessary to trace the history of the manufacture any further, as
Nantwich has had no share in the gieat development of the salt-trade of Cheshire in
modern times.   As will presently be seen, the greatest obstacles to improvement were the
restrictions of custom limiting the production to certain fixed quantities that might be
considered large in ancient times, but which, judged by modern standard, appear insig-
nificantly small

Leland, who visited Cheshire a few years before the suppression of the Monasteries,
thus describes the salt-towns in his "*Itinerary*," (Edit 1769, vol v fol 82)—

"NORTHWICH is a prati Market Towne but fowle [*i e* dirty] and by the Salters† Houses be great
stakkes of smaul clovyn woode, to seethe the salt water that thei make white salt of The salt water
Pitte is hard by the Brinke of Dane river, the wich, within a good But shott, runnith into Wyver

Ther be ii [two] Salt Springges at MIDDLEWICH, that stondith, as I remember, upon Dane river,
and *one* at NANTWICH, the wich yeldith more salt Water than the other iii [three]   Wherefore ther be
at Nantwich a iii hunderith salters † [*i e* three hundred persons engaged in making salt].

The Pittes be so set abowte with Canales [wooden pipes, or channels] that the salte Water is facily
derivid [easily distributed] to every Mannes Howse

And at the Nantwiche very many Canales go over Wyver River, for the Commoditie [convenience]
of deriving the water to the Salters Troughes [technically called *ships*, (see *posted*)]

They seethe the Salt in Furnesses of Lede [lead], and lade out the Salt, some in cases of wicker,
thorough the wich, the water voydith, and the salt remaynith

A mile from Cumbremeie Abbay, in time of mind, sank a Pease of a Hille having Trees on hit,
and after in that Pitte sprang salte water, and the Abbate ther began to make salt but the Menne of
the Wichis componid with the Abbay that ther should be no salt made   The Pitte yet hath salt water,
but much Filth is faullen into hit '

The next account of the salt-manufacture, written about the year 1580, (but not published until 1656) is that by WILLIAM SMITH, a native of Old Haugh, in the parish of
Warmincham, who was educated at Oxford, and became Rouge Dragon Pursuviant in
the College of Arms   The learned CAMDEN, who is said to have been a compiler rather
than an original observer, appears to have been indebted to William Smith for the
description of Nantwich salt-works, which he printed about the year 1590, in his "*Britannia*,"
and hence it is doubtful whether Camden ever visited Nantwich, although it is very likely

* Mr Lowndes' "*Brine-Salt Improved*,' p 36

† It is clear that *salters* means *wallers*, who were chiefly women, the termination *er* being the Old English feminine
Some, mistaking salters for *salt-works*, have assumed that Nantwich salt-trade was in its greatest activity in Henry VIII
reign, and that since that time the trade has gradually declined in importance Platt (*Hist Nantwich*, p 78) absurdly
states that there were 220 works in Nantwich in Elizabeth s reign, all of which were destroyed by the fire of 1583,
except *one*

that he was personally acquainted with the Cheshire antiquary and official of Herald's College   Both accounts, which greatly resemble each other, are here given as follows —

SMITH'S ACCOUNT   c 1580

(Printed in King's *Vale Royal* 1656)

" Nantwich is accounted the greatest town in Cheshire, next to Chester, and standeth upon the river Weever * * * Here at this town is great store of white salt made   it hath one salt-spring (which they call a brine-pit) standing hard upon the river Weever, from whence they carry the brine to the wich-houses, saving such houses as stand on the further side of the river   Within the said houses are great barrels set deep into the earth, which are all filled with salt-water, and then when the bell ringeth, they begin to make fire under the leads every house hath six leads, wherein they seethe the said salt-water, and as it seethes, the wallers (which are commonly women) do, with a wooden rake, gather the salt from the bottom, which they put into a long basket of wicker, which they call a salt-barrow, and so the water voideth, and the salt remaineth "

CAMDEN'S ACCOUNT   c 1590

(Gough's Edit 1806, of Camden's *"Britannia,"* vol iii, p 43)

"Wever runs by Nantwich not far from Middlewich to Norwich [Northwich]   These are famous salt-wiches or pits, where the brine, or salt-water, is drawn out of pits, and not poured upon burning wood as the antient Gauls and Germans used to do, but boiled over the fire to extract the salt   I have no doubts but the Romans were acquainted with these pits and that they laid a salt-duty thereon   For from Middlewich to Nor[th]wich runs a noble road, raised with gravel to such a height as easily to be known for a Roman work gravel being very scarce all over these parts, and therefore now carried from this road to private houses

Nantwich is accounted the largest and best built town in the county   It has one brine-pit about 14 feet from the river, out of which the brine is conveyed in wooden troughs into houses, where are several casks fixed in the ground which they fill with this salt water, and on ringing of a bell, the fire is lighted under leaden kettles of which there are six in each house, and the water boiled, and women called Wallers, with little wooden rakes draw up the salt from the bottom, and put it into baskets out of which the water drains, and the salt settles "

No doubt during the vicissitudes of five centuries the penal laws, privileges, and customs recorded in Domesday Book had passed away, but that the same feudal servility existed in the sixteenth century, will be seen in the following code of regulations, dated 1563, which are said to have then been observed "during the tyme whereof the memorie of man is not to the contrary "   These *"Customes '* prove that the Rulers of Walling (always four in number) as curators of the Brine-pit, inspectors of the wich-houses, and watchful guardians of the Lords of Walling land, had almost unlimited authority over the work-people, and kept up a spy-system, that not only for long years prevented any innovation, but was productive of frequent discontent as evidenced in the few extracts already given from the Court Leet Rolls (see pp 72-77)   Only a small proportion of the pans were worked at a time, each wich-house having to wait its turn for its proper supply of brine, hence there would be no liberty of action amongst the wallers and briners, and there could be no incentive to industry, for, if any one attempted to produce more salt than custom allowed, he was in danger of having his wich-house forcibly pulled down and his lead pans destroyed by the Rulers, and by them he would be charged at the next

Court Leet with obtaining by fraud the Lord's Brine.

These "*Customes*," which are preserved amongst the Wilbraham MSS, afford interesting information relating to the Manufacture of salt three hundred years ago, that will be quite new to the present generation

ANCIENT SALT LAWS AND CUSTOMS

"The CUSTOMES OF WALLINGE and makeing of Salt in Wich Malbanke, in the Counne of Chester, which haue bin had and used during the tyme whereof the memorie of man is not to the contrary, with the number of the wich-houses or salt houses in the sayd Wiche, presented at the Court houlden at the Wiche aforesaide the xiith day of October in the fifte yeare of the Raigne of oure Soueraigne Ladie Elizabeth [1563] by the grace of god Queene of England, ffrance, and Ireland, defender of the faith, &c , before SR HUGH CHOLMLEY, KNIGHT, Stewarde of the Wiche aforesaid, by the oathes of *Roger Maisterson, Roger Walthall, Roger Wettenhall* the elder, *John Lugh, Humfrey Mainwaring, Oliver Mainwaring, John Maisterson, John Rutter, Jeffray Minshall, Thomas Mainwaring, Reginold Wright, Roger Crockett, Roger Harwar,* and *Richard Church*

1 —First the said Jurie upon their oathes say that there is and of right ought to be *two hundred and sixteene wiche-houses** in the said Wiche, and noe more, euerie of them being a house of sixe leades

2 —*Itm* they say that euerie of the said wich houses haue and of right ought to haue yearely for eurie of the said wich houses twelue daies walling, that is to say, sixe daies of the newe yeare, and sixe daies of the Barons weekes,† and to be free at the brine-pitt or sethe for bryne to serue [serve] the occupation and walling of twelue daies

3 —*Itm* they saie that by the said Custome noe p'son [person] nor p'sons shall or may wall or make anie salt, or haue the occupacon of anie of the saide walling, vnles hee or they shall presentlie haue dwelled and inhabited the saide Towne by the space of one whole yeere then last past, and that noe forreiner dwelling out of the libertyes and boundes of this Towne shall haue anie occupacon of walling wthin the Towne

4 —*Itm* that none of the said inhabitants shall wall or haue the occupac'on of anie more walling in the said Towne other then [than] as insueth that is to saie, noe manner of married man aboue three dozen of leads, that is to saie, the walling belonging to sixe wich-houses noe widdowe woman or single p'son being a batchler wch is not and hath not been married as aforesaid, or anie other p'son or p'sons haueing anie handcrafte or occupation within the said Towne aboue the number of eighteene leades walling

___

* This expression is not synonymous with *salt-works*, as has often been erroneously stated An explanation will be will be found on another page in this chapter

† The occupation of a wich-house was reckoned from year to year, not however for twelve months, but for a period fixed by the Manorial Court, and entered on parchment deeds from time to time An original deed of this kind dated 24th March, 1579-80, witnessed by Sir Hugh Cholmley, knight Steward of Nantwich, and twenty-six of the inhabitants, and having the Town Seal appended is now in the possession of G F Wilbraham, Esq This deed states that from the 17th June, 1573, to the 29th June, 1576, was a "*full terme of foure yeares for the occupation and makyage of salt,*" the several years being dated as follows —

	The Baron's Weeks began	The New Year began	Names of the Rulers
1st year	17th June, 1573	11th October, 1573	Reynold Wright / Richard Robinson / Richard Maddocke / John Moyle
2nd year	14th April 1574	8th September, 1574	do
3rd year	9th February, 1574-5	24th June, 1575	Thomas Wright / John Tenche / Richard Wycksted / Richard Crewe
4th year	10th October, 1575 / 29th June, 1576	25th January, 1575 6	Humphrey Ithell / Hugh Mynshull / Robert Goldsmith / Robert Lytlor

5 —*Itm* that noe psons dwelling in one house in the said Towne shall by anie manner of waies or meanes wall or haue the occupa'con of anie more walling at the most then [than] three dozen leads walling as be foresaide except all occupyers being tabled * with others being occupyers and that noe childe dwellinge with his or her father, the father liueing, being vnder the age of twentie yeares shall haue or be suffred to haue or occupie anie of the said walling

6 —*Itm* the said Jurie doth saie and prsent that once euerie yeere, that is to saie, at the Great Court yearely holden after the ffeast of St Michell th' archangell, the Jurie at the same Court sworne uppon their oathes shall nominate and appoynt fower of the honest and skillfullest occupiers of the said walling to be RULERS, and ouer-seers of the said walling for that yeere, wch said Rulers being sworne before the STEWARD shall haue, and at all tymes haue had full power and authoritie to rule and order the saide walling as beforesaide, and as hereafter is and shall be declared, viz. that euerie the said occupiers walling for a single house, (that is to witt, for eighteene leades or lesse), shall wall but single, therefore walling the first weeke shall stand and not wall ye later [latter] for that eighteene leads

7 —*Itm* anie pson walling† for a double house, that is to saie, for xvj leads or aboue unto three dozen, shall wall double according to the number of his leades aboue viij leads, that is, xvj leads to wall once double, xxiij leads twice double, xxvij leads thrice double, xxx leads fower times double, xxxiij fiue times double, and three dozen leads sixe times double

8 —*Itm* they saie that the sayd Rulers soe sworne haue, and haue had as beforesaide authoritie from time to time, at euerie Kinding‡ to enter into euerie of the sayd wich-houses, and to search and foresee that none of the sayd inhabitants walling as beforesaide shall occupie or wall but orderlye as before sayde, and if anie of the said inhabitants shall attempt to doe ye contrary, then the said Rulers haue and shall haue full authoritie & power to stopp and sett euerie of them by breaking down the wiche houses, dores, or walls, or by strikeing or knocking or puttinge downe of the same leads or otherwise at the discretion of ye said Rulers for reformation of the said disorder or misdemeanorr of walling, and if anie of the said wallers or occupiers of walling in the saide Towne resist or lett [hinder] the said Rulers to rule as in this rolle is Contayned, to forfeitt to the Barons of ye saide Towne for euerie such offence or disorder the summe of xls [40/-] bating one halfpennie, and further that the said Rulers shall and may lawfully call and take the whole officers and inhabitants of the sayd Towne or as manie of them as be neere and will come to aid and assist them to enter into the wich-house as aforesaid and stopp and lett [hinder] the sayd disorder or misrule in walling or if they or anie of them soe called and reasonablie required therevnto, refuse to aid and assist the said Rulers as beforesaid, to forfeitt likewise the summe of   vjs viijd [6/8]

9 —*Itm* the sayd Jurie say and prsent that the custome aforesaide is, and the tyme whereof the memorie of man is not to the contrarie, hath bin that all and euerie pson and psons whatsoeu'[er] that they themselues, or anie his or their antecessor or antecessors, p'decessor, or p'decessors, whose right interest or estate he or they then haue, wch haue had, or hereafter shall fortune to haue, the possession or occupacon of anie of the said wiche-houses or walling by the space of three yeares then last past, if he or they will find sufficient suertyes to the said Rulers of the two honest psons wthin the sayd Towne by obliga'con in the summe of xlli [£40] to saue and keepe them, the sayd Rulers, harmeles against euerie other pson or psons. then claymeing the said walling, that then uppon such suertyes soe found, the sayd Rulers shall prmitt and suffer ye sayd ptie [party] soe fynding suertyes, to haue and occupie the saide wallinge soe claimed untill the said matter betwixt the said pties [parties] shall be ordered by due course of the lawe or order taken in some of the King or Queenes Maties Court or Courtes, or otherwise agreed upon the said pties § and if the

---

* "*Tabled*" i e living at the same *table*, and so synonymous with *lodger*, who boarded in the same house

† "*Walling*" signifies *boiling*   ‡ "*Kinding*" i e kindling, or lighting of the fire

§ The meaning appears to be —that in cases of dispute in the ownership or occupation of wiche-houses, any person who had been in possession for three years immediately preceding, was to be allowed to occupy until the case was decided in a Court of Law, on the condition of his entering into a bond of £40 to the Rulers of Walling Otherwise, he was liable to immediate ejectment by the Rulers

said ptie haueing yᵉ possession by the space of three yeaɾes, as before saide, refuse to fynde suertyes as beforesaid, then if the other ptie will ard doe fynde like suertyes as beforesaid, that then the saide Rulers shall likewise pɾmitt & suffer the saide ptie soe fyndɪng suertyes to occupye and enioy the said wallɪng as before sayde and if neither of the saide pties haue been ɪn possession or occupacon of yᵉ said wallɪng soe then ɪn varɪance by the space of three yeares then last past, and both or either of them will fynde suertyes as before, or if neither of them will fynde such suertyes, that then and ɪn all such cases the saide Rulers shall stopp and lett [hɪnder] euʹɪe [every] of the sayd pties soe pretendɪng tɪtle untill they shall haue trɪed their rɪghte as beforesayd, and if the one of them will fynde suertyes as beforesaid, and the other refuse soe to doe, that then the said Rulers shall p'mɪtt & suffer the said ptie soe fyndɪng suertyes, as before sayd, to haue the occupacʹcn of the said wallɪng then ɪn varɪance, untill the sayd matter be determɪned as beforesaide.

10 —*Itm* the sayd Jurɪe pɾɪsent that the saide custome ɪs that euerɪe pson & psons whatsoeveɪ wᶜʰ haue oɪ of rɪght ought to haue anɪe rent or renᵗs whatsoeuʹ[er] goɪng out of euerɪe the saide wɪche-houses or wallɪng, and that if the wallɪng belongɪng to the said wɪche-house or wɪche-houses be walled ɪn anɪe other place ɪn the saide Towne, that then he or they that ought to have any such rent or rents, shall and may fɪom tɪme to tɪme, enter ɪnto anɪe of the saide wɪche-houses, where the said wallɪng shall fortune [happen] soe to be walled, and there to dɪstraɪne for the said rent or rents, soe beɪng due for the wallɪng there walled, as beforesaid, as well as if the said dɪstresse had fortuned to bee founde uppon the saide landes, out of which the said rent ɪs or shalbe goɪng

11 —*Itm* the said Jurɪe pɾɪsent that the custom ɪs and allwaɪes hath bɪn, that ɪt shalbe lawfull foɪ euerɪe pson and psons beɪnge occupɪers from tɪme to tɪme, to make new and amende the *theets* [channels] wherein the bryne runneth ɪn all such places betweene yᵉ bryne-pɪtt and the wɪch-house, as hath bɪn used and accustomed of aunɪent tɪme and that euerɪe pson and psons and their brɪneɪs [drawers of brɪne] shall and may lawfulhe at all tɪmes haue fɪee ɪngate and outgate & passage to and fro the said theetes, uppon whose grounde soeuer they lye, to follow their brɪne, and to amende and repaɪre their said theetes accordɪnghe wᵗʰout anɪe contradɪction of the said owners of such ground where anɪe such theetes do lɪe ''

THE RULERS' OATH

"You shall well and truely execute & serve yᵉ Office yᵗ shall appertaɪne to yᵉ Rulers of Wallɪng for this yeer next comɪng you shall endeavoɾ yoɾselues to yᵉ uttermost of yoɾ Wɪtts, cunnɪng, & knowledge, to sett [let] forth yᵉ occupation of wallɪng to yᵉ most profit, behoof & advantage of yᵉ Occupɪers of yᵉ same, & for yᵉ com'onwealth of yᵉ Towne And that noe pson or psons shall wall for hɪmself aboue 3 dozen leads to yoɾ knowledge nor anɪe Man for them beɪng suspected wɪthout swearɪng And yᵗ Crafts-men [tradesmen], Wɪddowes, & Yong Men shall not Wall aboue 18 leads to yoɾ knowledge, & accordɪng to yᵉ former Customes heretofoɪe made And yᵗ you nor any of you shall wall yᶜ oftener for yoɾ owne profit or advantage to yᵉ hurt of yoɾ neighbours, but fervently and ɪustly shall use the said office foɪ yᵉ best com'on-wealth of yᵉ said Occupɪers And also you shall delay no tɪme ɪn settɪng [letting] forth yᵉ occupation whereby yoɾselues may haue advantage & yoɾ neighbors dɪsadvantage, but at all tɪmes see yᵗ the same occupation may proceed truely & ɪustly, accordɪng to yᵉ aunɪent Customes of Wallɪng wɪthɪn yᵉ said Towne, and for yᵉ most com'onwealth of yᵉ Lords and occupɪers wɪthout any manner of delay or detractɪng of Tɪme dureɪng yᵉ said Office And if there be any suspected psons that say they wall foɪ themselves, and you thɪnk they wall for other Men, you shall sweare them or ɪnforme the Stewarde to take theɪɪ oathes upon a book, that the profit, behoof, use and advantage shall come clearly wɪthout fraud, covɪn, [ɪ e to quɪet by flattery] or any other manner of deceɪt whatsoever to themselves

These poɪnts and all other that appertaɪne to yoɾ Office, you shall, will and truely keepe to yᵉ uttermost of yoɾ power & skɪll, So help you God &c ''

Other Regulations, orders, &c have already been given in the "Injunctions" of 1535, and in the Court Leet Rolls (see *Manorial History*) The first great change in the manufacture took place in 1632, when small *iron-pans* were substituted for lead-pans, of the same size and guage,* each being about a square yard in area, and the use of *coal* instead of wood (see pp 203 and 206)

On 26th Aug 1617, the salt-works were visited by Royalty, as told by Webb, (see *Annals*, p 121). From that description it may be inferred that little alteration had taken place in the *Brine-Pit*, which appears to have then flowed as a natural spring, out of which the *briners*, or drawers of brine, (*men*), lifted the salt-water with buckets A considerable sum of money was expended in improving the Pit in 1656, according to the *Malbon MS*, which says —

"On or aboute the xviith daye of June 1656 greate works att the Brine pitt veire began & con-tynued vntill the 9th of September nexte followinge, wth outany intrmission, Savinge the fayre weeke, wch cost about CCCli [£300]"

"*Thomas Malbon Jun*, *Thomas Sparrowe*, & *John Watson* beinge the Rulers *Wilham Thrushe* another Ruler (but then dead)"

Whatever those improvements were, the pit does not seem to have been deepened to any great extent, for in 1669 Dr William Jackson described it as follows —

"In Nantwich the pit is full seven yards [deep] from the footing about the pit, which is guessed to be the natural height of the ground, though the bank [Snow Hill] be six foot higher accidentally raised by rubbish of long making salt, or *walling* as they call it In two places within our township the springs break up so in the meadows as to fret away not only the grass, but part of the earth, which lies like a breach at least half a foot or more lower than the turf of the meadow and has a salt liquor oozing as it were out of the mud, but very gently" (Phil Trans vol iv p 1060, dated 15 Nov 1669)

These natural salt-springs are still to be seen in precisely the same condition, the one near Beam Bridge, the other near Shrewbridge Snow Hill, and Water-load, on the east side of the Weaver, and the Wood Streets and Wych-House Bank on the opposite side of the river, were the localities of Wich-Houses in former times. Several accounts of the manufacture of salt in the latter half of the seventeenth century are preserved The remarks of Roger Wilbraham (see "*Towne Concernes*") on the Walling Customs in 1659, which he lived to see abolished, must now be read *cum grano salis* Dr Jackson gave details in 1670 in *Philos. Trans* Nos 53-4, and John Ray, the naturalist, in 1691, left an account, which has recently (1874) been reprinted by the English Dialect Society. But the most interesting account of all, which is given below, is from a MS at Macclesfield, by Thomas Branckner, M A, Grammar School Master there, who, in 1675, was sent by the Trustees of the School to Nantwich to enquire concerning the wiche-houses belonging to that school situated in Wood Street, Nantwich † In his report to the Trustees he gave the following description of the salt-works in this town.‡

---

* Lead-pans, found at Northwich many years ago, are preserved in the Museum at Warrington, the dimensions being 3½ ft × 2½ ft × 6 inches, and weighing 2 cwt 1 qr 18 lbs A modern salt-pan of ordinary size has an area of 1500 square feet *Iron-pans* had been used at South Shields in salt-making as early as 1489 See Surtees' *Durham* vol ii p 95, and Sir Will Brereton's *Travels*, Chet Soc Pub vol i pp 86-9

† The present Wood Street school occupies part of the site of the Walling Land once belonging to the Macclesfield Grammar School

‡ For this account I am indebted to the kindness of J. P Earwaker, Esq, F.S.A.

" Considerations about ye SALT WORKS at NAMPTWICHE belonging
to ye SCHOLE of MACCLESFELD.   1675 "

" June 10th, 1675   I went with Mr. Normandsel to Namptwich about the wallings of
salt that belong to Macclesfeld Schole out of the Brine-pit in that Town   And the Information which there I had about that business as far as I could learn was this —

In Namptwich there is only one large Brine-pit out of which salt is made by many
persons each according to their respective concern.

The brine they say was once in one man's possession, but in process of time and
compact it is now the partial right of a great many, and now some have one dozen,
others two, others 3, and one I hear hath 17 dozen, that is, walls 17 times while he
that hath but 1 dozen walls once.

A Walling is boyling of salt for 26 hours, which in that place is called one days
walling, 2 hours being allowed supernumerary to 24 for cleansing ye work, as they call it.

Four of these days walling is called a *kinding* or kindling, that is 104 hours, and so
long the fire continues when once it is kindled in any wiche house (or house allotted for
boiling of salt)

By reason of the several interests in ye same brine there are above 20 wiche houses,
and all ye owners have a part of ye common brine, yea there are some that have right to
ye brine whose houses are now fallen down, and they boil their salt in houses elswhere
borrowed or hired

There be troughs to convey each mans brine from ye common pit whither he pleases
for his use & every man knows his own troughs

Macclesfeld Schole hath 3 dozen days walling but, but [i e only] one house, which
was once thought sufficiently employed by 1 dozen wallings, the other two houses are
down   yet will it quit nobodys cost to erect new ones, because by ye decay of the salt trade
such houses must needs ly [lie] still frequently so long, as soon to fall to decay again

All owners of Brine contribute to maintaining the common pit, for cleansing it, and
reparing ye walls and timber, &c

And because all ye owners had their title from one, they are now a society or
corporation, and have lawes to preserve ye community & each man s proportional propriety

Hence it follows, that no man must wall beyond his proportion that, within ye same
compass, as he that is greatest hath walled his, he also that is meanest may wall his also *

And to this end there be at every Michaelmas Court Leet, 4 Rulers chosen who are
sworn to their office for one year   These Rulers are—

    1.—To estimate the price and vent [sale] of Salt, and

    2 —To allot the time of every man's walling according to proportion, and to see that
    none of ye houses be left so unemployed that they decay for want of use

    3.—To be present (one or more of them) at ye beginning and end of every fire that
    is kindled in any wiche house, to see and be able to make oath of it that their
    kindings began and ended according to right

---

* John Ray says (c 1691) —" The lords of the pit appoint how much shall be boiled as they see occasion, *that the
trade be not clogged*

"When there is occasion for salt to be made the Rulers cause a cryer to make proclamation, that so all parties
concerned may put to their fires at the same time, and so when they shall cease at a determinate hour, at which they
must give over, else they cause their salt to be marred by casting dirt into it or the like "

4 —To keep an exact account of every days walling in each house throughout their year, and also to record in what house and for how many dayes any man borrowed or hired his walling   And to register yᵉ names of yᵉ chiefe workman in each kindling and under whom he wrought

5 —To make taxes that concern ye charge of ye wich-houses and brine-pit

Other officers they have but yᵉ particulars I have not met withall.   These Rulers order that account which they call their *Making Meet*, that is, according to rise or fall of salt, so they may all of them wall sooner or later their whole course   Of this, the Rulers, as was said, are judges, and they order that in such or such a time all the proprietors shall have all their wallings according to *kale* (or call)

And because in this *making meet* perhaps the time may be (by reason of ill trade) so so long as that those that have but small interest would not have sufficient employment for their houses, therefore the Rulers have power to debar any man from walling all his whole number in his own wiche-house, that soe he may sell it, or set [*i e* let] it to be done in some other house, that all ye houses may be preserved

As for instance, the Schole of Macclesfield hath right to 36 days walling in one making meet   Yet if ye Rulers see cause they will order that we shall not wall our whole 36 in our house, but only 24, 28, or 32 as the trade is, and the rest of ye wallings we must be obliged to take in some other house for ye common good   For the brine is ye same whither so ever it be carryed, the charge of *Pumping** (which each proprietor bears for himselfe) is ye same   and the charge of setting up ovens and pans &c is ye same in all, for it must be renewed every kindling

This *Making meet* was, when trade was quick, every halfe year, and the former halfe year, or *first making meet*, they call the *new year*, the later halfe year, or making meet, they called the *Barons weeks* (of Malbank, I suppose, whose ye brine once entirely was). But now by reason of the many other pits of brine in Cheshire, these times of *Making meet* are not within 12 or 18 or 21 months, and it is reasonably feared that they will shortly be extended to 24 months.

The whole number of wallings in ye Rulers books is accounted by 6, or half-dozens, and belonging to ye whole pit there be in one making meet 216 halfe dozens, of which Macclesfeld schole hath 6   And yet by some accidents or other, they may not all be walled out in any *one making meet*

Each wiche house hath 2 *ovens*, a *ship*, a *chamber*, or *store*, and 2 *iron pans*   All ye pans in ye town are to be of one assize, for dimension and depth

The *Pans* are to boil ye brine in   The *Ovens* are furnace holes, or fire places to make fire under the pans and are furnished with *bearers* and *crosse bars* all of iron to make ye coal fire on, so as it may have vent for ye ashes to fall through, as is easy to conceive

The fire that is made in ye ovens is carryed back into another room through two stone pipes, at ye end of which rises ye chimney that vents ye smoak of both, and this back room is called ye *chamber* or *store*, because there they set ye wet salt to dry in their *barrows*

---

* This is the earliest mention of brine being raised out of the Pit by *Pumping*

Barrows are made of rods or splints, in shape like a very long eggshell open at one end, they contain 2 measures, [i e 2 bushels, or 112 ℔s] The 2 pans in each wiche-house make of these *barrows* 7 each 5 hours

The *ship* is a long and deep trough that runs along ye side of ye wich-house within; to hold brine brought thither by ye troughs without, and they are made so large as to hold brine for 4 days walling, or one kindling

Out of these *ships* at each 5 hours end, they fill their pans, and as soon as ever ye water is in ye pans they prepare their white of eggs and blood &c to cleanse ye brine, for it brings off a dirty scum, all to one corner of ye pan This they take off and put it into a trough hard by for that purpose, till they can have time to carry it out, and this is ye chiefe part of their muck or manure as they call it, which as it is blended with all sorts of sweepings and cleansings of the wiche-house, else is sold for 10ᵈ 11ᵈ 12ᵈ and sometimes more by the cart load

The *Barrows* of dry salt are sold now for 15ᵈ or 16ᵈ the barrow "

[END OF MR BRANCKNER'S ACCOUNT]

In addition to the above details, other particulars of the process of manufacture, by Dr William Jackson, about the year 1670, are given in ' *Philosophical Transactions*" Nos 53 and 54, as follows —

"The pit at Nantwich is seven yards deep, but the general depth is not above four It yields one pound [℔] of salt for 6 ℔s of brine The pans in which the salt is boiled are set on iron bars, and closed up on all sides with clay and bricks After filling them, they put into the brine, a mixture of brine and cows' or sheeps' blood, two quarts into a pan of 360 quarts This occasions a scum, which they take off, and continue the fire as quick as possible till half the brine be wasted They then replenish it, adding a mixture of whites of eggs and brine When the scum of this is removed, and part of the brine wasted, they throw in a quarter of a pint of strong ale, slackening their fire and lading in what is called *leach brine*, which is such as runs from the salt when it is taken up before it hardens After all this is in, they boil it gently till a thin crust rises, which is the first appearance of the salt. This sinking, the brine gathers into corns at the bottom of the pans, and they take it out with their *loots* or *wooden rakes*, long square boards with handles, and put into *barrows*, or pyramidal wicker baskets, which, after the leach brine is drained out, they remove into their hot-house to dry "

On the 24th Feb 1691, an assessment of 6½d in the £ upon all estates, both real and personal, within the township of Nantwich, was made pursuant to Act of Parliament for the collecting of the sum of £48 12s 4d., being the quarterly payment of the Royal Aid, towards carrying on a vigorous war against France. There were at that time, according to Ray, about *fifty* wiche-houses, which, together with the other houses in the town, were assessed in their due proportions. But besides these, is particularized the assessment of the *Walling*, calculated on the customary 216 vessels of brine supplied to the wiche-houses, namely, 18 dozens (18 × 12 = 216) at 6½d per doz., amounting to £2 18s. 6d , "Maxfield [Macclesfield] walling excepted "*

* From the Rate Book, *penes*, G F Wilbraham, Esq

Shortly after, the ancient customs of walling, which had become too antiquated, were discontinued and the Lords of Walling overthrown, brine was no longer supplied to the wiche-houses in fixed quantities at stated intervals, but the pit and works were simply let to tenants at certain rentals without restrictions as to working *

How this came about, is told by Randle Wilbraham in the Wilb MS collections, as follows —

ANCIENT CUSTOMS ABOLISHED

'The beginning of June 1696, SAMUEL ACTON of Namptwich, Tobacconist, began to sink a Brine Pitt, in the Woodroom belonging to a wich-house, wch hee had purchased of one Braine, wch did much alarme the Ancient Proprietors or Lords of Walling, and the Rulers threatening to disturb this Innovator, Hee apply'd to the H[igh] C[our]t of Chancery & from thence obtained an injunction to Quiet the possession of his new Brine pitt, wch being finisht & Brine found therein, hee began to make Salt Nov 13th 1696

The Proprietors† on the other hand, prayd upon their Answer that the Injunction might bee dissolved, upon severall allegations, and upon a hearing the Lord Keeper Somers ordered that these four severall issues should bee Tryde att common Law in *Cur Ban Reg* [the Court of King's Bench], viz. —

I — *Whether there bee such a plott of Lande called Walling Land*

II — *Whether Mr Actons Brine pitt bee within the compasse of the Walling land*

III — *Whether there bee any Ancient Customes to restraine the use of the brine springs flowing in the said Walling Land*

IV — *Whether Mr Acton by drawing Brine out of his new Pit, did diminish the Brine of the old Pit, & to what degree"*

Upon the Tryall most of the issues were found for the Proprietors, except the second, wch being the ground of their complaint, the injunction was not like to bee dissolved, without that was prov'd and therefore, presuming that they had hard measure from the Jury, and their cause not sett in a true light they mov'd for a new Tryall, and a view [re inspection of the land], & obtained an Order for itt, and therein prevailled in every One of the issues, upon full proof and evidence

But the record being returned into the Ct of Chancery, the Proprietors found a new Lord Keepr upon that Bench The seale being taken from the Ld Somers,‡ and given to Sir Nathan Wright serjeant att Law, who having been of Mr Actons councell in his cause, was forward to take umbrage att any thing, that might assist & favour his Client, who having got some Affidavits drawne, that the Jurye were treated with Wine, and that the Gentlemen who came down upon the view were influenc by our Councell, wch attended them upon their sd view, (The fact in truth was only this, One of the Jurye drinking noe malt liquor,

---

* Droitwich, in Worcestershire, had a few years before taken the initiative by overthrowing similar trade customs there as recorded in the Holt and Gregson MSS (vol xix, p 140, Liverpool Free Pub Lib) as follows —

"In Jas I time every person employed in making salt, sometime before the Day fixed for beginning to make it (for then also it was made only one half of the year) gave notice to sworne officers of the number of Phats [pans] he occupied For each Phat, these officers delivered to him 18 vessels of brine six from the bottom of the Pit, where the brine was stiongest, six from the middle & six from the top where weakest 216 vessels made the whole half-years *Walling*, an Anglo-Saxon word for boiling

In Chas II reign, the thanks of the Corporation were given to Winter Norris for extending the sale of Salt & in the same reign one, Gardener, was encouraged to sell Wich salt in Berkeley in Gloucestershire, none having been sent before so great a distance

In the first year of William & Mary [1688] an Act was passed for better regulating the Salt at Droitwich, and under this Act the Governors & proprietors of salt-works, prevented every one from sinking new Pits until Robert Stigner Esq sunk two pits upon his freehold abt the year 1690 The Corporation sued him, & he defended himself at the expense of £6000, which after various tryals was finally determined in his favour in the year 1695 In consequence of this determination many persons sunk pits upon their own land, the main spring was destroyed, the trade greatly extended and Salt reduced from 2s to 4d per Bushell '

† The defendants in this law-suit were — HUGH LORD CHOLMONDELEY, RICHARD WALTHALL ESQ, RICHARD WRIGHT ESQ THOMAS BULLEN SABOTH CHURCH, HUGH DELVES, THOMAS STRINGER, GEORGE CUDWORTH, the plaintiff being Samuel Acton

‡ Lord Somers, Chancellor of England, having been dismissed from office in 1700

Mr Bromhall sent him from his owne house, a Pint of Sherry, and Mr Hawkins one of the Councell for the Proprietors did goe along with the Jury on the viewe, but never said or did anything to influence them) The Lord Keeper ordered a new Tryall & would not allow the proprietors to have the costs recover'd in the last, wch amounted to about £180 *

By this tyme with such various successes both p'tys [parties] were growne weary (& their purses being out of breath) were inclined to parley   What Mr Actons expenses were is best knowne to himself, but the Proprietors besides ye losse of their Walling, wch was imploy'd towards the maintenance of the suit, had by severall assessments of 40s and 50s per dozen upon their Walling, rais'd considerable summs, and those who wanted ready money to pay downe their Quotas, took un severall large summs upon interest, and being jointly bound drew upon themselves a debt in the whole amounting to £800   wch made it high time to put an end to so unprofitable a contest   whereupon Mr Masterson for Mr Acton, and I [Randle Wilbraham] for the proprietors, mett att Weston, and att last agreed that Mr Acton should have a lease of the Towne Walling for the terme of 11 years, att the Rent of £100 per ann , wch Rent by consent of the Proprietors was to be imployed towards the payment of the debt beforemention'd, and that after the expiration of the said Terme of 11 yrs Mr Acton should demolish his new pitt, and make no further use of it   This Terme did commence att Lady Day 1702

Prsuant to the Agreem^t last mentioned, Mr Acton had the Towne Walling, tho hee made but little use of it, but within two or three yeares of the expiration of his Terme , Finding I suppose sweetness thereby, hee agreed with Mr Hugh Delves for an orchard, and some few Cottages, & Gardens in Middle-stich [between Wood Street and the River] out of the compasse of Walling Land, and there sank a Brine Pitt, and erected a Wich-House, without any obstruction

Upon the expiration of Mr Actons Terme in the Towne works, The Wichouses for the most part, being either demolisht,† or much out of repaire, and the proprietors utterly unprovided of Panns, Irons, and barrows, for the making of Salt , they agreed with Mr Acton for a further Terme of Two years, att the rent of £108 per ann , wch is to commence this prsent Lady Day 1713

To satisfie my posterity how this branche of the Revenue of our family came to be lopt, I have thought fitt to insert this short memoriall   R W " [Randle Wilbraham]

In spite of the enterprise of Mr. Acton, the salt-trade at Nantwich did not increase, owing to circumstances that led to the centralization of the trade in Mid-Cheshire.   In 1670 the first bed of Rock Salt had been discovered, when searching for coal, at Marbury, near Northwich, though some years elapsed before mining operations were commenced   About the year 1700 brine-springs were discovered at Winsford ‡   In 1721 (7 Geo. I) an Act of Parliament was obtained by which the Weaver was made navigable from the Mersey to Winsford Bridge, thereby facilitating the transit of coal from Lancashire and manufactured salt to Liverpool as an article of *export*.   Deeper pits were sunk at Winsford and Northwich, and a stronger brine obtained at depths varying from thirty-five to seventy yards, *"some brine being drawn from Rock Salt Pits, that had"* (probably through bad mining) *"fallen in"*§   Speaking of the flooded pits, the same writer says, " this Brine varies much in strength, some is so weak as not to be used without a solution of rock

---

* In one of Roger Wilbraham s Pocket Almanacs is the following entry —

"1698   Oct 19. To Mr Delves one of ye Rulers of Walling to carry on ye suit against Acton, £5 0s 0d "

† The Will of Richard Horton, landlord of the Lamb Inn, Nantwich, dated 1 Feb 1714, and proved at Chester 10 Oct 1715, mentions three several properties and vacant lands, on Snow Hill, which had formerly been the site of wiche-houses

‡ See ' Salt-trade," by Wilckins, *Holt and Gregson MSS* , vol xix, p 242   Liverpool Free Public Library

§ *Ibid*, p 235

salt; whilst other Brine is nearly saturated." From that time, probably, commenced the subsidence of land in the neighbourhood of Northwich, which has, in later years, by continuing the practice of flooding old mines, assumed so serious an aspect.

To resuscitate the fast declining salt-trade an attempt was made to connect this town with Liverpool and the export trade by lengthening the navigation of the Weaver from Winsford Bridge to Nantwich. For this purpose an Act of Parliament was obtained in 7 Geo. II [1733-4] by WILLIAM MAISTERSON, ESQ., and THOMAS WILLIAMS, GENT., both of Nantwich; which, unfortunately, was never carried out, "owing," says Partridge, "to the jealousies and disputes betwixt the inhabitants and the persons employed to solicit the Act, who were deemed to have acted too partially in favor of themselves, and precluding

THE OLD "LAMB" HOTEL.

in a great measure the advantages the other subscribers to the expense in obtaining the Act ought to have enjoyed."—(*Hist. Nant.* p. 59). No less than 222 names of townspeople and local gentry occur,* as "Commissioners for determining controversies," in the Bill, which states that Nantwich was the largest town in the County. From that time, however, Nantwich became of secondary importance as a salt-town; the trade was confined to local districts, salt still being carried in packs on horse-back into Salop, the neighbouring counties, and North Wales.

---

* Of these names the following may be mentioned:—The Rt. Hon. Lord Kilmorey; Hon. James Cholmondeley; Sir Robt. Salusbury Cotton, Bart.; Sir Philip Chetwode, Bart.; Rev. Thos. Brooke, LL.D.; John Crewe, Esq.; The Earl of Dysart; Rev. Joseph Harwar, Vicar of Acton; Roger Wilbraham, of Nantwich; Roger Wilbraham, of Dorfold; Roger Wilbraham, of Hough; Randle Wilbraham, of Rode; Peter Walthall; Gabriel Wettenhall; Nathaniel Wettenhall; Edward Wettenhall; Clutton Wright; Thomas Wicksted; John Wicksted; Samuel Watkiss; Ashton Williams; George Salmon, of Hough; John Starkey, of Wrenbury; John Pratchett, of Worleston; Francis Elcock; John Bromhall; Edward Windsor; Esquires, &c., &c.

Probably about this time the picturesque custom of *"Blessing the Brine,"** on Ascension day, when the inhabitants assembled in gala dress round the *"Old Biot,"* which was dressed with flowers and rustic finery, to pass the day in dancing, feasting, and merriment, died out.—(*Partridge*, p. 59-60).

Whilst the Parish Registers seldom mention the *"wailers"* and *"briners"* of olden days, perhaps, because they were of the lowest class of the inhabitants, the names of principal salt-makers, Rulers, Officers, and Excise-men frequently occur in those records. Of the last named, implying the existence of the salt-duty, the following are early mentions in Burial Register

> "1698 May 11 Baddington, son of William Petty of Dirtwich, Excise Officer
> ,   23 Shusanna, dau of Arthur Keay, Salt Officer
> 1702 Dec 20 Backwell, son of Richd Wilson, supervisor of ye Salt Duty,
> 1705 July 7 Zachariah Turnpenny, salt-officer, buried at Acton
> 1712 Nov 11 John Goodwin, Gent , supervisor of the Salt Duty
> 1726, July 22 Jorathan Brown, Gent , Collector of the Salt Duty "

John, first Lord Crewe, was mainly instrumental in bringing about the repeal of the Salt duty "which bore very heavily upon Cheese makers, and forced them to an habitual and most demoralizing evasion of the law   Salt-smuggling was a trade countenanced and supported by almost every farmer in the county "†   During the French war the duty rose to 15s. per bushell or £30 a ton, and it was not until 1822 that it was reduced to 2s per bushell; the duty being finally repealed in 1825.   In 1774 there were only "two salt-works of five large pans of wrought iron" belonging to Richard Hassall, one situated in Water-Lode and the other on Wych House Bank, these produced about five hundred tons of salt per annum, the duty (5s. per bushel of 56 ℔s) then amounting to £5000   The Chester Canal, which was finished in 1779 but was not brought into the town, failed to revive the long lost trade, and according to a printed Survey of the town dated 1792, the salt-house on Wych House Bank is described as *"in decay and un-used "* After the death of Richard Hassall,‡ the son of the Salt-proprietor above mentioned, in 1820, Mr Davis succeeded to the last salt-work, which was situated between Water-Lode and the Bridge In the hope of obtaining a stronger brine, he first made three new borings on the Wych House Bank, and afterwards deepened the old pit,§ and superseded the old horse "gin" with a steam pump, having mortgaged the works in the sum of £4000 to George Walker, Esq , of Chester, who bequeathed them to his only daughter, the wife of the Rev Dr. Burton, sometime incumbent of All Saints', Manchester.   In 1837 J H. Bradley, Esq , (now of Droitwich) leased the work for twenty-one years, and sub-let it first to Mr. Ellicker, and afterwards to Mr. Beckett, who in 1845 withdrew in favour of Mr Thomas Wright Townley, the last salt-manufacturer of Nantwich, the works being finally closed in the year 1856

In these last days, Lord Crewe received, by ancient right, 10s. per ann as toll for

---

* The late Lieut -Col Egerton Leigh M P , in his *"Cheshire Ballads,"* gives a song entitled *"Blessing the Brine "*

† Hinchliffe s *'Barthomley,"* p 305   The duty was felt a great hardship, because, in 1818, when manufactured salt might be exported duty free, the home consumer was taxed in the excessive duty of £30 per ton

‡ In the Churchyard are two flat stones thus inscribed —
    [1] " Richard Hassall, Salt-Proprietor, who departed this life life Sept 7, 1812, aged 83 years "
    [2] " Richard Hassall, who departed this life 15 March, 1820, aged 65 years "

§ The present depth of the Brine Pit is, according to recent soundings, 57 ft —(Information by W Cooper, Esq)

brine, manufactured in the three pan-houses, (one of which is still standing) which produced about twenty tons of salt per week. A ton of coals was required to make a ton of salt, which was sold at 18s to 20s. per ton.

It is an interesting fact that an upper room in the salt-works was let by Mr Townley to the *Rev. H. Alcocke*, Catholic Priest of Crewe, who held meetings there until ST ANNE'S CHAPEL was built, and thus gathered together the Roman Catholic Church of modern times.

A project for making Nantwich a brine pumping station was mooted and abandoned in 1875. After having been closed for about a quarter of a century, the ancient BRINE-PIT was purchased by William Cooper, Esq, of White-Hall, Welsh Row, who in 1882 had it cleaned out at considerable expense, for the purpose of supplying the newly erected MEDICINAL BATHS with brine.

Corn Mill and Cotton Factory.

The earliest mention of Nantwich Mill occurs in one of the undated Sneyd Charters preserved at Keele, Staffordshire, which is believed to date back as far as 1228 (See p 6).

In ancient times a corn-mill was an important accessory to a manor, and often embraced the monopoly of a wide circuit of country, within which no one could grind corn without paying *molage* or toll to the dominant miller. Mr Beamont says, the millers "took toll in kind, and, consequently, making no bad debts, were a sure source of profit to their owners, who were able, therefore, both to afford higher rents, and, as few other tenants could, to pay them in money."[*] Manorial rights over the mill at Nantwich, as in the case of the Brine-pit, were exercised by the different lords of the town, thus, for example, according to an *Inq p m* 16 Ric II [1392-3] RICHARD DE LEFTWICH held *inter alia*, the eighteenth part of the profits of the water corn-mill here. From the "Rental" given on page 62, it appears that early in the sixteenth century, the LOVELL and AUDLEY shares of the Mill had been purchased respectively by WILLIAM CHURCH, of this town, and SIR RANULPH EGERTON, KT, who died 4th March, 1528, and was buried in his newly founded Chantry Chapel in Bunbury Church, his will (dated 26th March, 1525) providing for two Chantry priests "*to be maintained out of his Mills in Nantwich* and wyche-house and other lands." &c.

In the following century the *Egerton* family appear to have become sole proprietors of the Mill. The *Inq p m* of RALPH EGERTON, ESQ, 18 Jac I [1621], found him "*possessed of lands in Wich Malbank and water of Weever in Namptwiche,*" his heir being SIR RICHARD EGERTON, KT, of whom Webb says, in his description of the town (c 1621), that the "*fair and profitable mills for the service and use of the town are his inheritance.*" Sir Richard died 15th Feb. 1627-8, and was succeeded by his son and heir, RICHARD EGERTON, who dissipated his estates, worth £5000 per annum, in gaming, and thus the Corn Mill came by purchase into the possession of ROBERT CHOLMONDELEY, *Baron* of Wich Malbank, about the year 1650, and continued in the same family for nearly two hundred years, until it was sold by GEORGE second MARQUIS OF CHOLMONDELEY, about the year 1840, to MESSRS. BOWER & Co.

---

[*] Cheshire and Lancashire *Domesday Book*, 1863, p xxxi

THE COTTON-MILL.

About the year 1789 the Corn-mill was changed into a Factory for Cotton-spinning; the original firm being MESSRS. BIRCH, RANDLES, and BOWER, MR MICHAEL BOTT, of Burton-on-Trent, becoming a partner in 1790 The cotton manufacture had been intro- duced into the town about 1785, in a building on the Weaver on the site of gardens now opposite Bowers Row, and adjacent to the Waterworks This Cotton Factory and Waterworks, in 1792, belonged to MESSRS EDLESTON & Co., though it was commonly called *Fogg's* Mill, (from Ralph Fogg, Cotton-Master) and was destroyed by fire in 1799 The other Mill in 1797 was considerably enlarged, and steam machinery was added, mainly through the enterprise of Mr Bott, and from that time it was spoken of as *Bott's* Mill.* This Cotton Mill, which was a source of great gain to the company was worked chiefly by children apprentices of both sexes, procured from workhouses and foundling hospitals in various parts of the country,† and even from Ireland A rigorous system of labour was enforced by overlookers, the factory being worked night and day by two sets of hands. Sir Robert Peel's Act for ameliorating the condition of children apprentices in Cotton Factories came into operation in June, 1802; and as a result the Mill apprentices, though still hard worked, were well-fed, well-clothed, and lived in a large, airy house that stood on the site of the present "Ebenezer ' Chapel, under the superintendence of an elderly matron They had recreation in an adjoining yard, and their religious instruction consisted in their attendance every Sunday at the Parish Church At the sale of machinery in 1874, the following curious notice relating to runaway apprentices was found amongst some old papers

"Whereas several of the apprentices belonging to the cotton works in Nantwich have absented themselves without the approbation of their master, this is to give notice, that whoever will restore to the proprietors of the said cotton works, any of the said runaway apprentices, shall be allowed one guinea as a reward, and sixpence per mile as expenses for every mile exceeding eight, necessarily travelled with them for that purpose or half a guinea for such advice by post letter, or otherwise, as will lead to their apprehension ; and whoever harbours or employs any of them after this said notice, will be proceeded against with the utmost rigour

The usual dress of the above Apprentices for Boys on *Sundays* an olive drab woollen cloth coat and waistcoat, turned up with green, and green side seams or welts, and leather breeches

Working Dress Jacket and waistcoat of the same cloth and facings, linen trousers, a felt hat, or leather cap, and the buttons on both dresses are stamped Bott & Co Nantwich

Girls' Sunday Dress An olive or drab calico gown with apron of the same, a dark coloured woollen petticoat

Girls' Working Dress Bedgown and petticoat of the same, or in lieu of the bedgown, a linen brat apron with sleeves "

---

* The Parish Register records —
    "1786 Sep 22 William, son of William Peers, Cotton Manufacturer ' [Baptised]
    "1790 Dec 12 Ralph son of Ralph Fogg, Cotton Master " [Buried]
    "1791 Dec 28 Richard Galley of N cotton Manufacturer married Elizabeth Davies of Nantwich "
    "1792 July 12 Joseph Davies, Cotton spinner, & Ann Clutton of N married "
    "1793 Feb 19 James Sproson an Apprentice to Bott & Co ' [Buried]
    "1794 June 1 John Hayes, apprentice to Mr Bott, and killed by a wheel at ye Cotton Mill " [Buried]

† Mrs Sarah Steele, widow, who died on 16th Nov 1878, at the advanced age of 98, informed me that she was brought from Cirencester co Gloucester, in the year 1788 being at that time only 8 years old, to be apprenticed at *Bott's* Mill She well remembered the destruction of the smaller Mill, and used to say that she was the first to raise the alarm of fire Interesting letters relating to cotton-mill apprentices will be found in Gent Mag for 1804, p 491-4 711, &c

In 1825 Mr Bott withdrew and retired to his newly built mansion at Shrewbridge, the firm then being *Messrs. Bower and Wright* Mr. Bower died in 1834, and was succeeded by his son THOMAS BOWER, ESQ , two new partners, named LOWE, joined, and purchased the mill from the Marquis of Cholmondeley, raised it to its present height, and added new machinery For two years after 1846 the mill was idle, it was then sold to *Mr. Whitelegge*, who, during the cotton famine (1861-5), sold it to *Messrs Terrington, Gill & Co* , from whom it was purchased by *Mr. William Hodgson* in Nov. 1873 In the spring of 1874 the female operatives struck for a shilling per week advance in their wages, (their earnings then being 9s. per week) which was refused, the mill being finally closed in the beginning of June, 1874 Fortunately many of the women found employment in the new Clothing Factory on the Barony, but some families were obliged to leave the town. After having been used as a Cotton Spinning Factory for about eighty-five years, it was again purchased for a *Corn Mill*, by Mr John Whittingham, of Bartherton Mill Part of the premises is utilized as a Foundry for making Agricultural Implements, and the upper story of the wings as a Clothing Factory

𝔚𝔢𝔞𝔟𝔦𝔫𝔤 𝔞𝔫𝔡 𝔖𝔱𝔬𝔠𝔨𝔦𝔫𝔤-𝔗𝔯𝔞𝔡𝔢𝔰.

Mr Partridge says (*Hist Nant* p 58) "the *Bone-lace and Knit-stocking* trades, which were heretofore considerable in this town are now [1774] quite declined.' *Bone-lace Weaving*, so called because *bone* pins were used instead of metal pins, which were too expensive, and *Frame-work Knitting*, carried on by means of the old Stocking-frame invented by William Lee, of Woodborough, Notts, in 1589, were trades once widely spread over the country. During the Protectorate the stocking-frame knitters obtained a charter, by which they exercised a monopoly in many towns, until 1753, when legal proceedings were taken, which eventually set aside the charter, and the trade became centralized in the counties of Nottingham and Leicester.

Frequent mentions of persons engaged in these occupations are to be found in the Parish Registers, from which the following extracts are selected —

```
' 1630    Aug  22  Thomas son of Thomas Smith, bone-lace weaver [Baptised]
  1651-2  Feb  22  John, son of Thomas Dutton, Silke weaver [Baptised]
  1671-2  Jan  28  Randle, son of Thomas Massey silk weaver [Baptised]
    „         March 5  Randle, son of Richard Marshall, silk-stocking weaver [Baptised]
  1683-4  Feb   8  John Millington, Silk weaver [Buried]
  1699    Dec  19  James Wilson, silk stocking weaver [Buried]
  1707    July 13  William son of William Dale, frame-work Knitter [Buried]
  1707-8  Feb  15  Jonathan, son of Thomas Noden, Frame-work Knitter, [Buried]
  1715 6  Feb  15  James ffletcher, Frame-work Knitter [Buried]
  1742    Oct  19  Thomas Marshall Stocking-Knitter [Buried]
  1792    Feb  20  Thomas Sant, frame-work Knitter & Mary Owen of Acton [Married] "
```

This Thomas Sant was the last person who worked a stocking loom in this town in and after the year 1825

𝔖𝔥𝔬𝔢𝔪𝔞𝔨𝔦𝔫𝔤.

For three hundred years at least, tanning and shoemaking have been important trades in Nantwich. The names of *Tench, Oulton, Wright, Combeibach, Wettenhall,* &c , occur in sixteenth and seventeenth centuries as tanners, whilst shoemakers, cordwainers, and cobblers are mentioned in the Registers more frequently than any other class of men   Comparatively little change took place in the art of shoemaking until about twenty-five years ago   In former times the master-shoemakers were many and poor   They worked in their cottage homes with two or three apprentices, (the master's wife or daughters working, too, as hand-binders,) and attended the shoe-market at Shudehill, Manchester, every Friday , performing the journey, sometimes by the Carrier s cart. but oftener on foot   The following prices of a pair of men's shoes at the dates here given, are taken from the Account Books of the Wright's Trustees , it would be curious to know what the earnings of the poor shoemakers were in those days.

A pair of men's shoes in 1656 * cost 3s , in 1738, 4s , in 1768, 4s. 6d , in 1769, "leather being dearer," 5s , in 1800, 6s , in 1825, 7s 6d , in 1838, 9s 6d   In 1825 an industrious workman could make *one pair* of men's shoes in one day for which he received 1s 10d., few earned more than 9s per week, though working from twelve to sixteen hours per day   Hand-binders (women) earned on an average 3s 6d to 4s 6d per week. Boys were apprenticed for seven years, and received 6d. per week for the first year, 9d. per week for the second year; and so advancing 3d. per week each year   It may not be generally known that *"rights'* and *"lefts'* in shoes were, at the beginning of this century, things unknown in the trade.   The principal manufacturers in this town in 1825 were Messrs John Davenport, William Davenport, and Thomas Barker, who being capitalists, opened small factories, (*"Colleges"* they were called), and employed more labour   No change of any importance occurred until the introduction of *"machine bound boot-tops,"* by Mr Bostock, of Stafford, in July, 1858   In the following year Mr Leonard Gilbert, a native manufacturer, in spite of the bitterest opposition and ill-treatment from his fellow townsmen, introduced sewing machines, and built the first Shoe-factory   In course of time the other masters, one by one, purchased machines, and the men, after suffering privation and want, the trade society's funds being exhausted, began to succumb to the inevitable   Scarcely, however, had these troubles subsided, when another innovation aroused old prejudices   *"Rivetting"* or *"tinkering-shops,'* as they were derisively called, were established with a view of superseding *"stitch-work, '* and again, great opposition was raised on the ground that it was impossible to manufacture boots *ad infinitum,* and suppose that feet, somehow or other, would be found for them,—the demand always keeping pace with the supply   But the fears of the old shoemakers were gradually dispelled during the decade of commercial prosperity from 1865 to 1875, when high-storied factories were erected, finding more employment for work-people of both sexes at increased wages The trade, however, was seriously affected by two strikes, the first commencing on 10th May, 1872, and lasting thirteen weeks, until the 21st August, and the second beginning

---

* The wages paid by King James I to his shoemaker are recorded in *Cal State Papers,* vol 119, dated 28 Jan 1621-2 , thus —" Grant to John Smith of the office of Shoemaker to the King with the fee of 12d per day for life "

on 8th May, 1873, and terminating on the 14th July, a period of nine weeks. In consequence of these strikes, a considerable amount of the shoe-trade was alienated from the town, and has not at present been recovered; many of the manufacturers have thereby suffered great loss; and, but for the establishing of Clothing factories, the position of the workpeople must have been deplorable in the extreme.

Gloving and other decayed trades.

Gloves were made at Nantwich more than three hundred years ago, as proved by the Parish Register.

> "1574-5. March 19. Ellen, dau. of William Shenton, *glover.*" [Baptized].
> "1575-6. Jan.   2. Eliz. dau. of Henry Clarke, *glover.*" [Baptized].
> "1580-1. March 24. Margaret, dau. of George Debrah, *glover.*" [Baptized].

In former times gloves were expensive articles, the importation of foreign made goods being prohibited until the year 1825. The trade was carried on at Nantwich on a small scale until April, 1863; the last manufacturer being Mr. William Davies, of Pepper Street, whose female apprentices are still remembered for their neat attire and extreme cleanliness.

The Parish Registers afford abundant evidence of other occupations in the eighteenth century that have since passed away; such as *Peruke-makers; Tobacco manufacturers; Flax-dressers; Dyers; Stay-makers; Straw-plaiters; Thread-makers*, &c. Tobacco and Thread were manufactured in Barker Street, in buildings still standing. A *Dye-house* occurs in a Rate Book in 1691 in *Middlesiche;* the *straw-plaiters* lived, until about fifty years age, in Wood Street, Wall Lane, and Vauxhall.

Clothing Factories.

On the site of Townsend House, in Welsh Row, commodious premises were built by MESSRS. GEORGE HARLOCK & CO. for the manufacture of moleskin, corduroy, &c. goods, about thirty years ago; and within the last ten years a new trade, namely,—the cutting out and making up of cloth for ordinary wearing apparel, has been introduced; and now gives employment to several hundreds of the population. The first factory, on the Barony, built by MESSRS. HARDING & CO. of Manchester, was opened in June, 1872, and has since been several times enlarged. Others have embarked in the same business; and the trade promises to supersede the manufacture of shoes.

The Chapel of Saint Mary,

NOW CALLED

Nantwich Parish Church.

ANTWICH CHURCH is sometimes, though rarely, mentioned in ancient records as an *ecclesia*. It is more frequently styled a "*capella;*" because from a remote period Nantwich, ecclesiastically considered, has been a *chapelry* within the ancient parish of Acton. That Nantwich, like the important towns of Macclesfield and Congleton, did not possess an independent Church of its own, and was not a separate ecclesiastical parish,* was clearly shown by Dr. Ormerod, who refuted the arguments put forth by Mr. Partridge in favour of the opinion that Nantwich never was a chapelry within Acton parish; it will therefore be necessary only to notice—

(1)—That no church or chapel existed at Nantwich when the Domesday Survey was taken *c.* 1087; the parish churches then being at Acton, Wybunbury, and Barthomley.

(2)—Nantwich is not mentioned as a separate parish in either of the great Ecclesiastical Valuations prior to the Reformation, *viz.*: in Pope Nicholas IV Taxation *c.* 1291; nor in *Valor Ecclesiasticus*, 26 Hen. VIII [1535].

(3)—After the Dissolution of the Monasteries, Nantwich is described as being in the parish of Acton.†

(4)—That Sir Peter Leycester, in his Catalogue of Cheshire Churches in 1669, mentions Nantwich as a parochial Chapel within Aghton [Acton] Parish.

(5)—And that as late as 1789, according to a Church Brief now in the British Museum, the town is described as the "*Parish and Chapelry of Nantwich.*"‡

* The term *Parish* is synonymous with "*vill*" or "*township;*" and is not necessarily an ecclesiastical division. For much interesting information on this subject, see Toulmin Smith's "*The Parish*," pp. 1-43. (London, 1857, second edit.)

† See the Survey of the Monastery of St. Werburgh in Dr. Ormerod's *Cheshire*, vol. I, p. 274.(New Edit.)

‡ To these evidences may be added the authoritative statement of Bishop Gastrell, who says "Nantwich Church has been lately styled a *Parochial Chapel* in the Bishop's Instrument for the confirmation of seats, anno 1671." (*Not. Cest.* p. 225. Chet. Soc. Pub.)

As has already been stated, about the year 1130, by the charter of Hugh Malbank, the parish Church of Acton and the Chapel of Wich Malbank were granted to the then newly erected Abbey of Combermere by which grant the Abbey was enriched and the parish starved Most likely for more than a hundred years after the appropriation of Nantwich to Combermere, the officiating priests here would be monks of that Abbey. But the legislature in course of time, perceiving how Churches throughout the country were impoverished by the exactions of Monasteries, first enacted that churches should be served by secular priests, and not by monks of their own order, and afterwards, when it was found that the religious houses abused this law, it was further enacted by the Councils of Bishops at Oxford in 1220 and at Worcester in 1240 that Curates serving in this way should be endowed as perpetual Vicars, and this endowment was often made out of small tithes * It was not until the year 1285 that the Bishop of Lichfield compelled the Abbot of Combermere to find a perpetual Vicar for Acton Church, and endow the Vicarage with small tithes and certain other profits of the cure (alterage and oblations) to sustain a *Chaplain* and *Clerk* in the *Chapel of Wich Malbank* The deed relating to the Ordination of the Vicarage is preserved at Lichfield, of which the following translation is taken from Acton Parish Register, the record having been entered therein about a hundred years ago by the then curate, William Morgan, B A †

ENDOWMENT DEED OF ACTON VICARAGE

"In the Name of God Amen We Roger‡ by divine permission Bishop of Litchfield & Cov[entry] lately exercising our Visitation in the Arch-deaconry of Chester have found that the Vicarage of Acton is not endowed in any certain Portions, and that the care of the whole Parish did not belong to the said Vicar which usage has occasioned the no small danger of Souls For which reason, We by these Presents, do ordain that the Vicar for the time being shall have the *entire Cure of the said Parish*, that he may be able to answer meetly to us, and to our Successors for the same

And the said Vicar shall receive in the said Church of Acton & in the Villages to the same anciently belonging all oblations & obventions to the Altar in any manner belonging, so as that the *Abbot & Convent of Combermere* shall only receive Tythes of Corn & half the Tythe of Hay in the aforesaid Villages

But the Vicar shall receive in the Chapel of Wrenbury all oblations and Obventions to the Altar of the said Chapel, in any manner belonging

Also the Vicar shall receive in the *Chapel of Wich Malbank* all oblations accruing or arising upon the days Nativity, [Dec 25] Easter Sunday, the Assumption of the blessed Virgin Mary, [Aug 15] and All Saints', [Nov 1], and all oblations for purification of Women after child-birth *But the Vicar shall support a Chaplain to officiate in the said Chapel with a sufficient Clerk at his own expenses* And we will that the said *Chaplain* swear as is fitting on the holy Evangelists that he will be diligent & faithful &

* See Blackstone's "*Commentaries,*" and "*Defence of Pluralities,*" by Wharton, (Edit 1703) for information on this subject

† The Rev William Morgan, Curate at Acton, was afterwards Rector of Wistaston, from 1789 to 1823

‡ "ROGER D MOLEND, *alias* LONGSPEC, Bishop of Litchfield, was a nephew to King Hen III, by one of King John's natural children, and on the resignation of Roger d Weseham, he was raised to the See by the interest of his uncle Richard Earl of Cornwall, the King's Brother He lived beyond the Seas in great splendour and luxury, and in order to keep in favour with the Religious Houses of his Diocese he commuted for his non residence and neglect of all Pastoral care by appropriating many Churches to them, without reason or conscience But on the advancement of John Peckham, a Black Friar, to the See of Canterbury he was compelled Aº 1283 to reside on his Bishopric, and was severely reprimanded by that Virtuous and Upright Prelate for the great neglect of his Charge On this he visited every part of his Diocese and corrected many of the errors and irregularities which had crept in during his long absence, and died Aº 1295 a very old man "—*(Acton Parish Register)*

will in no wise commit any deceit or fraud in the Portions belonging to the said Abbot and Convent. And the same *Priest shall by no right claim the Tythes or obventions* * but if it shall happen that any shall be made by the faithful in Christ to him he may receive them so long as the Tithe or Obvention shall in no manner be assessed

Dated at La Lee the Ides of March [March 15] *Ann Dom* 1285 In the Ninth Year of our Consecration."

Acton continues to be a vicarage, and a list of the vicars for now nearly six hundred years will be found in Dr. Ormerod's *Cheshire*, Vol III.† The patronage of the living and the great tithes of the parish were retained by the Abbey until its dissolution, when they were sold by the King to Richard Wilbraham, of Woodhey, in or before 1544 (*Harl. MSS* 1967 f 5), and so descended to the Tollemache family, the Right Hon Lord Tollemache of Helmingham now being *ipso facto* lay-rector of the Parish Whilst the institutions of clergymen to Acton have been regularly recorded in the Episcopal Registers of Lichfield and Chester, during that long period, the *Chaplains* of Nantwich, being merely priests appointed and removed by the Vicar, find no place in those records, and hence no complete list of them can be given prior to the Reformation Two names of Chaplains in early times are here given, one occurring in 1285, or the very year when the above interesting endowment deed was executed, and the other a quarter of a century before that date Amongst the Wettenhall Charters in *Harl MSS* f 113, is the following deed —*(translated)*

"I Richard chaplain and rector of Baddilegh Church anno 1259, concede and quitclaim to *Henry de Sondbach, chaplain of the Chirch of Wich Malbank* all that land &c which I have held for a term of 35 years &c

These being witnesses Dno [Sir] John chaplain of the Hospital of St Nicholas, William Daulin, Laurence the clerk, John de Wrenbury, Nicholas Calveley, Thomas son of Matthew and many others 44 Hen III " [1259-60]

Another deed enrolled in the *Calendar of Fines* dated 13 Edw I [1285] states that William Dymmock and Margaret his wife acknowledge certain tenements described as—

"One burgage and one acre of land in Nantwich, being those which *Richard Froward, chaplain*, formerly held and lying in Hospital Street to be the right of William Wodenot of Swanle[y], to hold by him and his heirs, of *God and the Blessed Mary of the said town* for perpetual alms at the yearly rent of 1d for tapers for the *Blessed Mary in Nantwich* '   .

The following deeds prove that gifts were made for the better sustentation of the services in Nantwich Church in early times

(Translation)—"I Randle Wode of Wich Malbank and Margery my wife daughter and executrix of the will of Thomas Bickley *alias* Wright as executor of the will of the late David Bickley, have given conceded and relinquished to *Ranulph Crue* and *Richard Pikton wardens* [p'positis] *of the Chirch of the Blessed Mary in Wich* aforesaid, all that third part of a burgage and one wich-house of six leads with appurtenances in the said Wich called I amburcots to have and to hold &c

Dated 10 Dec 14 Edw II " [1320] — (*Harl MSS* 2074 f 166 a)

---

* The reason of this was because Nantwich was merely a *parochial Chapel*, which Sir Peter Leycester defines as " having all the rights and ceremonies [baptisms, burials &c] as the mother church or parish church hath, *except the tithes* so that indeed they are as lesser parishes, created within the greater for the benefit of the neighbourhood "—(Preface to Antiquities of Bucklow Hundred

† The name of a Puritan Vicar, not given in the New Edition of Dr Ormerod's History, incidentally occurs in Nantwich Parish Register— ' 1643-4 Feb 4 Rachel dau of Edward Boulde minister ' [Baptised]
" 1645 June 1 Mary dau of Maister Bould vicker of Acton [Baptised]

In the Cheshire Recognizance Rolls mention is made of Beatrix Huedoghter[*] leaving to Roger Rondulph, chaplain [most likely of Nantwich] who was living in 1338, "an acre of land in Wyghtreton [Wistaston] *for the support of a chaplain to celebrate divine service in the Chapel of St. Mary, Nantwich,* for 12 years at 6s yearly"

About thirty years after the date of the Endowment Deed, (i e about 1315) the Vicar of Acton (probably "*Thomas de Prestecote*") found it necessary to compromise the oblations at Wich Malbank, according to the following extract of an Inquisition taken at Minshull before Thomas le Yong, Eschaetor, 28 Edw III [1355]

    Translation—"Also they [the jurors] say that the Vicar of Acton for certain masses of the same Abbot [Richard de Rodierd ?] hath given the same Abbot thirty acres of land in Acton, that is to say in exchange and for *the four days oblations in Wich Malbank* for the term of his life, forty years having since elapsed, and the aforesaid land with all its issues is worth 15s 4d yearly" (*Harl MSS* 506 f 13)

Whether succeeding Vicars received the "*oblations*" or not, record does not say, but the probability is, that these offerings ultimately found their way into the treasury of the Abbey. In *Harl. MSS* 1967 are many pages of particulars relating to Abbey lands in Nantwich dating as far back as 17 Edw I [1289], which prove how for two hundred and fifty years the Abbey was constantly acquiring property in the town, and sometimes defending their claims in legal courts

Probably in the latter half of the fourteenth century, the Chapel of St Mary, to which the foregoing account relates, was rebuilt, forming the present Parish Church Several theories have been advanced to account for so large and beautiful a Church in so small a town The Rev. J Partridge, in his admiration of the building, not only denied that it was a Chapel within Acton Parish, but magnified it into a Collegiate Church with a Dean and six priests or prebends! (*Hist Nant* p 45) The fact that Lichfield diocese (which prior to 1541 included the county of Chester) had ruri-decanal divisions, amongst which was the Rural Deanery of Nantwich, cannot prove Nantwich Church to have been of Collegiate foundation. It has recently been suggested that the Church may have been the munificent gift of Robert Burnell, Bishop of Bath and Wells, who died 1292 [†] This theory, put forward on the assumption that Combermere Abbey was too poor, and the inhabitants of the town too few, to have built this Cathedral-like Church, implies that that rich prelate was the patron of the living as well as founder of the Church, and if this be accepted as correct, it must then follow that the Church of Nantwich was dedicated to St Nicholas and the list of chaplains given on pages 49-51, would then be the Rectors of the parish in pre-Reformation times These fancies, however, receive no support from documentary evidence, but are directly contradicted by the clear statements of the deed on page 273-4, dated 1285 and the few records relating to the Church and its priests, when the great crisis in Ecclesiastical affairs—the Reformation—came, unmistakeably proving the Church in this town to have been a dependency of Combermere,—an *Abbey Church*[‡]—and to have continued to be such until the dissolution of that Monastery When it is remembered that the work of rebuilding Churches in mediæval times was usually spread over a number of years, the older structure being gradually removed as funds were forthcoming for the new, that the Architecture of the Church proves the *Nave* to have been of earlier

[*] The patronymic "*daughter*" (long since disused) is similar to the common patronymic "*son*" which has survived to these times
[†] *Cf* Manorial History, p 41
[‡] Astbury Church, in this county, is another remarkably fine specimen of an Abbey Church

date than the *Transepts;* which, again, are earlier than the *Choir* and *Chancel;* (a period
of, perhaps, fifty or sixty years having elapsed from the commencement to the completion),
that it was erected when Gothic Architecture was at its zenith, on abbatial estates, out
of the plenitude of the riches of the Abbey, and by the benefactions of Religious Gilds
in the town, and wealthy people in the neighbourhood, as evinced by memorials of ancient
families in heraldic glass that once adorned the windows of the church, it is no wonder
that the present building far exceeded the mother-church at Acton in size and beauty.
The following extract of a deed preserved in the Dodsworth MSS (vol xxxi f 134 Bodl
Lib), although undated, clearly refers to the time when the work was still in operation,
since the persons named therein, viz *William Wodenote,* living in 1399, *Sir Nicholas
Audley,* who died in 1391, and *Henry Mareshall,* who occurs several times on the Recognizance Rolls between the years 1380 and and 1404, were contemporaries of *Sir David
Cradock, Kt* (the *traditionary* founder of the Church) and *Richard Wyche,* who contributed
to the fabric and had his arms in one of the windows (*Cf* Annals, p 84). The extract
is as follows *(translated)*—

"William Wodenote* gave to the *fabric of the Chapel of the Blessed Mary of Wich Malbank* land
lying between the land of Sir Nicholas de Audley and the land of Henry Mareshall near the graveyard"

Mention has just been made of *Religious Gilds* or, *Fraternities* as they were sometimes
called, which were to be found in small country towns as well as in corporate or Cathedral
cities   The following interesting deed exhibits a glimpse of social and religious life in the
town, when, long before the introduction of Poor Laws, the inhabitants enrolled themselves
in societies for purposes of brotherly aid, the distribution of local charity, the sustentation
and reparation of the Church, and various other good objects.   By this deed two persons
were admitted by the Stewards (officials under the President or Dean of Gild) into full
benefit of the Gild, which not only provided for the members in the circumstances
of life, but cared for them even after death   The original deed, formerly in the
possession of "Mr. Wilbraham of Nantwich," is not now known to be in existence, but
a copy in Latin is preserved in *Harl MSS* 2074 f 166 a which has a rough drawing of
a seal depending therefrom, representing a naked child with outstretched arms, holding
what appears to be a flower or branch in each hand   The following is a translation —

"To the beloved holy and devoted children in Christ *William Houe* any *Sibyl* his wife, with all
others whatsoever

We, *William Ruddock* and *William Lynche* stewards [*seneschalli*] of the *Gilds* or *Fraternities* of
Wich Malbank lawfully deputed send greeting, that by the prayers of the Saints ye may obtain celestial
joys   Forasmuch as out of God's gifts to you, you have contributed to the sustentation of the aforesaid
Gilas and to the six priests in the Church of the Blessed Mary of Wich Malbank aforesaid, for the daily
celebration for the brethren sisters and benefactors alive and dead, We freely admit you to the partici-
pation of all masses which shall be celebrated in the said church and to all other and singular
"*cantilenas*" [masses chanted] works and prayers which by our brethren are performed   We promise
according to the tenor of these presents in life as also in death, and furthermore we concede that after
your deaths, prayers for your souls shall be offered by the said priests and brethren of the said Gilds

* The *Wodenote* arms in glass adorned one of the East windows of the North Transept   It may be added that
particulars relating to the building of Churches during the Middle Ages have very rarely been handed down to these
times   and hence it is impossible to assign exact dates for the erection of mediæval Churches   The ancient records now
extant, relate almost entirely to lands, and seldom to other matters of local importance

with the prayers for those lately deceased, masses, exequies, and prayers being performed as by the brethren is accustomed to be done   In testimony whereof to their children living and dead we append to these presents our seal of office

    Dated on the 8th day of January in the year of our Lord 1461 "

    Though the information concerning the number of Gilds and their patron Saints is very meagre, it is worthy of note that in 1461 there were no less than six Chantry priests supported by these societies, and probably as many altars in the Church where prayers were daily said   One, called the Gild of the Holy Cross, is referred to in an inscription amongst the ancient heraldic glass, and very probably at Nantwich, on the Invention of the Holy Cross [May 3], the annual Gild Festival was held, with processions and amusements, just as in the neighbouring villages *Wakes* were held every year on the Saints days of their churches, because there were no Religious Gilds there to conduct the ceremonies.* Some rules regulating the town Gilds are given in the "*Injunctions*' &c dated 1538 (pp 30, 32).   The Gild Hall, situated in the churchyard, was, after the Reformation, converted into a Grammar School

    Mention has already been made of the Deanery of Nantwich and Chaplains of St. Mary's in the will of Randle Wettenhall, dated 1437 (see p 93)   Another reference, a few years earlier, occurs in the probate of a will preserved amongst the extracts of Wettenhall deeds in *Harl. MSS* 1967 f 118, as follows —*(translated)*

    "The will of Robert le Mercer of Wich Malbank was proved, &c before us in our *Christian Deanery of Wich Malbank*, in the Church of the Blessed Mary of the said town, on the 24th July, 10 Hen V [1422] and administration granted to John de Wetenhall Esq " &c

    Beyond the grant of a wiche-house and walling-land to *Nicolas Harwar*, Chaplain, and his successors, in 1515, there is nothing of importance to relate concerning the Church until the Reformation   RANDLE STEVENSON, *curate* of Nantwich, is mentioned in the will of *Laurence Maynwaring* of Nantwich, in the year when the Papal Supremacy was abolished in England.   This very interesting Will, which has already been printed in Cheth. Soc Publ, vol xxviii, p 188-9, is as follows —

Testamentum Laurentii Maynwaryng

    "In ye nayme off God ame ye xxth off July in ye yer' of or Lord God MCCCCC and xxxiiij [1534] I Laurens Maynwayryng hole and p'fyte [perfect] off mynd mayke my testame't I com'end and betake my sole to God allmythty and my body to be buret in ye Nontwyche churche   I giffe to ye sayd churche vjs viijd [6 8] p'vidyt [provided] yt no mor' be askyt by reson off any custom for my bureall   Also I will yt ye abbey [abbot] off Co'burner' have his due porcion for my mortuarye†   Also I giffe to Sr Thomas Ankers‡ xs [10s] desyring hy' to say a trentall§ off masses in ye Nontwyche church for

---

* See articles on "The History of Gilds," by C Walford in "*The Antiquarian Magazine and Bibliographer*" 1882   On page 186 is the following description of the anniversary feast of the Gild of the Holy Cross at Abingdon   "The fraternity hold their feast yearly on the 3rd May, and then they used to have 12 priests to sing a *Dirige*, for which they gave them 4d a piece they had also 12 minstrels, who had 2s 3d besides their diet and horse-meat   At one of these feasts (A D 1445) they had 6 calves, valued at 2s 2d apiece 16 lambs 12d apiece 80 capons 3d apiece 80 geese 2d apiece 800 eggs, which cost 5d the 100, and many marrow bones creame and floure besides what theyre servants and others brought in and pageants and plays ard May-games to captivate the senses of the zealous beholders

    † Mortuary," see explanation in a foot-no e on page 93

    ‡ "*Sn*," here used as a title of courtesy similar to the modern word *Rev*, and in the sixteenth century was generally applied to one who had taken a degree   *Thomas Ankers*, a priest, occurs in the Clergy List, c 1533-4, (*Piccope MSS* Chet Lib) as a private chaplain to Mr Mainwaring of Baddiley

    § "*Trentall*," i e thirty masses

m) sole my wife child and all crysten soles   Also I giffe to ye sayd Sʳ Thomas vᵈ [5d] desyring hy' to say dirige and masse off ye V wonds* for a frend ji ye *curet* will schew hy' off and vij d [7d] to pore fokes for ye sayme p̃son latly dep'tyd [departed]   Also I will yᵗ Anker [*sic*] fad' [father of] my p̃ntes [apprentice] schall have xiij ꝑ p'yydit yt my sayd p̃rente' will p'forme his prenteschypseᵈ as long as [he] was absent and make gud suche cappes as he sold wen he went   And wher[as] John Mynton dyd desyre me to giffe hy' a cappe and I dyd p'myse hy y'for [therefore] I bequeth hy' a cappe off ye best yᵗ I have   I giffe to Robt mv prent' a serke and his workyng scher[es]   I giffe to *Ranald Stèson* a cappe ye [best] off ye ij prestes capp'[s]   I giffe to my cosyn Olev' Maynwayring a daggar and a pollax and to Hu'fray Maynwayring a thycke cote and a pollax   I giffe to Schenton wyffe a buschell off whete and to hui son my prent' a Kendall jacket ij serke howse [stockings] schone [shoes] and a cappe   I giffe Jonc my bastard doghtur vjˢ vijᵈ [6s 8d]   To John Fleecher a gowne and a salet and to John Ankers a jacket and a payre off hoose   Also I giffe and beqweth to my ij doghtors for yayr [their] chylds parts yᵗ is to Magery seve' pounds sterlyng and ye beste sylver pese and all biokyn mone[y] in my cofer   to Margaret vijᶫ and ye beste panne   to Anne vijᶫ and my beste gowne   Also when my detts beqwethis and fun'all expensis be payd then I giffe, &c ye resydue off all my guds and tacks and gronde to Ellen my wyffe   Also I orden and make my trysty cosyn Hu'fray Maynwayring and Ellen my wyffe my executors and my trusty cosyn Olev' cv'sear off this testament   Wyttenes John Maynwayring gentillma' John Prachett and *Ranalld Stènson curatt*   Giffen ye day and ye'r beforesayd "

[No date of probate]

A complete list of the Clergy in the various Deaneries of Cheshire, dated *circa* 1533-4 is preserved amongst the Piccope MSS (Chetham Lib)   The names of the clergy connected with Nantwich Church at that time were as follows —

Dns [Sir] REGINALD STEVENSON [the *Curate*, paid out of the income of the Church
                                                              ("*ex fructibz ecclie*")]

Dns [Sir] RALPH MYNSHULL   ⎫
Dns. [Sii] CHRISTOPHER WENINGION   ⎪
Dns [Sir] JOHN OLIVER   ⎬ "*Conduct p' Wilhelm flecher et alios iconimos*"
Dns [Sir] WILLIAM ROLINSON   ⎭

Four of these names occui again as priests serving at Nantwich Church in Bishop Biids Visitation, dated 16th May, 1548, namely,   *Reginald Stevenson, Christopher Wenington Ralph Mynshull,* and *John Olyver,"* and in the place of William Rolinson, two other priests are given, viz   "*Dns* [Sir] *Thomas Nu'ter,"* and   *Dns* [Sir] *John Brasnell,* '+ who were most likely identical with "*Thomas Porter"* and "*John Brasentt"* as they are called in the Chantiy Roll, also dated 1548   It appears, too, fiom the Chantiy Roll that *Dns* [Sir] JOHN CROXTON succeeded Reginald Stevenson as incumbent of Nantwich in 1548, and that John Olyver iesigned his post in or about the same year   The last named priest however continued to receive an annual pension until the year 1568 according to the followirg receipt, and similai ones still extant §

* "*Mass of the fiue wounds,*" that is, the Mass at the high or principal altar in the Chancel of the Church, which had five crosses carved on the top slab symbolical of the five wounds

† The testator was evidently a tradesman in Nantwich, and may have belonged to the Manwarings of Baddiley though his name does not occur in the Cheshire Visitation of 1580   or in any of the Cheshire pedigrees that I have seen

‡ *John Brasnell,* (*Brasmell,* or *Brasernt,* as his name is variously spel ed) paid his Composition for First Fruits to the Crown, as incumbent of the Lady Chapel, on the 10th July 38 Hen VIII [1546]   (*Record Soc Publ vol viii, p* 396)

§ Mr Earwaker's transcripts of "*Miscellaneous Receifts,* West Hall (Cheshire) Papers, vol iv   Dated c 1560-8

"Paid to Sir John olyver his holle yeres pencon going owte of the late Monestor' of comberm' ended at the feast of seint Michell th'arcangell last past   C^s " [100s]

In 1536 the *Valor Ecclesiasticus* was completed, giving effect to the Stat 26 Hen. VIII [1535] that transferred the first fruits and tenths to the Crown, which heretofore had been forwarded to Rome   The Commissioners for the Rural Deanery of Nantwich, SIR THOMAS FOULESHURST, KNIGHT, WILLIAM VENABLES, ESQ, RICHARD SNEDE and RICHARD HASSALL, in their Survey of Combermere Abbey, returned as follows relating to Nantwich

Income of the Abbey in Temporals

Rents and Profits in Wich Malbank   , xiiij^{li} xiiij^s v^d [£14 14s 5d]
Great tithes of Acton, Cholmeston, Wich Malbank, Badyngton, &
Leghton, total   xxij^{li} vj^s viij^d [£22 6s 8d]
Easter Roll of Wich Malbank   viij^{li} vj^s viij^d [£8 6s 8d]

Payments

To Robert Bagenhall bailiff [of the Court for the Abbot's Fee] in
Wich Malbank, per ann   xxxiij^s iv^d [£1 13s 4d]

In *Harl MSS* 1967, p 147 is the following rental of the Abbey lands in Nantwich, dated 31 Hen. VIII [1539], being the last year's revenues to Combermere

	£	s	d
"Farm of the Easter Roll* of Wich Malbank	8	6	8
Farm of tithes of grain from the Mill of Wyche	0	5	0
Farm of oblations, and obventions [?] called the *rood box*	0	3	4
Rectory and glebe of chancell	4	0	0
The accounts of Thomas Wright Bailiff, for assessed rents	0	10	10
Farm of the land of 5 salt-houses of six leads in Beam Street in the tenure of Gilbert Walthall			
One salt house of Roger Harwar of 12 leads			
One salt-house at the end of the bridge demised by the relict of Laurence Rope	15	3	4
One salt-house of 12 leads demised by Henry Sparke in Baywardshale [in Nantwich]			
One 6 leads demised by George Maisterson			
One salt-house in the tenure of Isabella Walker in Beamestreete			
Farm of a mill in Wich Malbank demised by Oliver Mainewaring	0	3	4
Total	£28	12	6

* *The Easter Roll* was at this time leased to William Maisterson of Wich Malbank, by John, last Abbot of Combermere, by an Indenture dated 25th April 1538 for the term of 60 years   By this deed William Maisterson claimed—
  "all the Tythes called the Ester Rolle or the Ester Booke and all oblacons, Weddyngs & Buryings * * * of the p'isshe of Wyche Malbanke '
The subsequent history of the Easter Roll is given on another page

Nantwich Church, which had been so intimately connected with Combermere for more than four hundred years, was now no longer a dependency of the Abbey; for on the 27th July, 1539, JOHN MASSY,* the last abbot surrendered his Monastery to the King. In anticipation of this change, Sir Thomas Fouleshurst, Knight, steward of Nantwich, in his "*Injunctions*" dated May 7th, 1538, provided and ordained that the whole town should be assessed and the inhabitants be required to pay towards the support and maintenance of the Church. (*Cf.* p. 30).

---

* *John Massy* or *Massie* was first sub-prior of the Monastery of Combermere, and afterwards (in or before 1535) became the Abbot. He retired upon a pension of £50 per annum, which was regularly paid to him until 1563. (West Hall papers, vol. iv.) He died in 1564-5, and was buried in Chester Cathedral,—(Special Commissions 16 Eliz. [1574], Record Office) "in the north ile," in accordance with his Will, which was proved 4 Feb. 1564-5; and which is printed in Vol. LI *Cheth. Soc. Publ.* pp. 56-7.

Chantries and Altars.

The history of the chantries here is very scant, no early deeds, throwing light on the foundations and dedications, having occurred   Concerning ST GEORGE'S CHAPEL, the only record is a line in *Hail MSS* 2074 f 166 a, which states that it was "neere the [stone] pulpit as it now stands,' and here, says Mr Partridge, (*Hist Nant* p 33) " Margaret Leech, widow, by her last will bearing date 1545 appointed her body to be buried " The last chantry priest of St George's Chapel was Peter Blage, [or Blagg] who, after the suppression of Chantries, retired on a pension of £4 which was paid to him as late as 1562 (West Hall Papers, vol iv)   No mention is made of this chantry by *name* in any of the surveys at the Reformation, though it may be included in the Chantry Roll given below, but that an altar actually existed in the North Transept is clear from the remains of an aumbry, piscina, and

> "a little Gothic niche
> Of ancient workmanship, that once had held
> The sculptured image of some patron saint "

The LADY CHAPEL, being an early extension of the North Transept, is stated in the same MS. and on the same page, to have been "*endowed*.'   Hence it is mentioned in the Ecclesiastical Survey 26 Hen VIII [1535], by which it appears that it was originally founded by the ancient family of *Praers*, but, who the said *Roger Praers*, the founder of the "obit" was, is difficult to say.   In the new edition of Ormerod's History of Cheshire, Vol III, pp 299, 301, 482, he is said to be ' *Roger Praers, chaplain* '* who granted Wybunbury to his son "*Richard ye clerk*" in the time of King John (!), a statement which cannot be accepted, since the Lady Chapel could not possibly have existed much before the time of Richard II

The survey before mentioned records as follows concerning the Lady Chapel
"CHANTRY IN THE CHAPEL OF WICH MALBANK " [1535]
WILLIAM WRIGHT, chaplain of the same

	£	s	d
Clear value in tithes to the same chaplain for celebrating masses for the soul of *Roger* Praers deceased and his predecessors, founders of the same chantry	7	6	8
Also, paid for the obit of the said Roger to the chaplain, priests and all poor persons according to the same chantry foundation†		26	8
And clear remainder	6	0	0
Also, the Tithes		12	0

In a survey of the Rural Deanery of Wich Malbank 33 Hen. VIII [1542] this chapel occurs again, as follows :—

"Chantry in the chapel of Wich Malbank"—£0 12s 0d , subsidia £0 10s 9¾d ,

and lastly in the Chantry Roll of 1548 [1 & 2 Edw. VI], when the name of another chaplain is given, *William Wright* being probably dead or removed

---

* Mr Helsby produces no proof for this assertion   It seems more reasonable to suppose that "*Roger son of William of Blackhurst*," one of the Masters of St Nicholas Hospital from 1365—1374, was the *Roger Praers* who left an *obit* to Nantwich , being probably the son of *William Praers* of Blackhurst in the neighbouring parish of Baddiley, who occurs in the Plea Rolls 32-36 Edw III (1358—1362)

† *Praers' Obit* continued to be paid to the poor for many years after this date by the *Wilbraham* family, and this charity under the name of *Prior's Obit*, is still dispensed by the churchwardens (See *List of Charities*)

[Description] " The Chauntery Within the sayd Church of Namtwyche "
[Incumbent] " JOHN BRASENTT* of the age ot lx yeres Incumbent there "

" The yerely Valewe vij¹ vjˢ viijᵈ	[£7 6ˢ 8ᵈ]
" In almes to poore ffolks xxvjˢ viijᵈ	[26ˢ 8ᵈ]
" The clere Remayn vjˡⁱ	[£6 oˢ oᵈ]
" Plate and Jewells † x oū7 [10 o7 weight]	
" Goods and Ornaments, None	
" Leade & Bells, None	

Of the *Chantry* in the South Transept nothing is known   It is not mentioned by name in any of the surveys   nor has the name of the Saint to whom it was dedicated been handed down   Mr Partridge calls it the " *Kingesley aisle,*" and among the ancient heraldic glass remaining in one of its windows in 1572, were the figures of a male and female kneeling with hands folded in prayer.   The man had a chaplet of roses round his head, dressed in plate armour, and sword by his side, on his breast was a tabard of arms, and on the lady's kirtle the arms of Bromley   Between the two figures were the Arms of Kingsley impaing Bromley ‡ and the following imperfect inscription —

"   𝕶𝖎𝖓𝖌𝖊𝖘𝖑𝖊𝖞 𝖊𝖙 𝕸𝖆𝖗𝖌𝖆𝖗𝖊𝖙 𝕭𝖗𝖔𝖒𝖑𝖊𝖞 𝖚𝖗𝖔𝖗 𝖊𝖏𝖚𝖘."

" The rest of the Glasse broken where the superscription was '—(*Harl MSS* 2151 f 80)

From this it seems highly probable that John Kingesley was the founder of this Chapel, and that it may have been consecrated by the Bishop of Lichfield and Coventry in 1405, according to the following record, which, however, does not mention the dedicatory saint.

" Licentia celebrandi Divina in Capella de Namptwych, an 1405 "§

The Rev T W Norwood, Vicar of Wrenbury, has recently pointed out the square head-dress or ornament in the east and west windows of this Chapel, which illustrates a fashion peculiar only to the early years of Henry IV reign, and thus fixes the date of the erection of this Chantry Chapel about the year 1405

Towards the end of the reign of Henry VIII, the King decided on appropriating the revenues belonging to Collegiate Churches, Chantries, Fraternities and Stipendiaries, and, as a preliminary measure to their sale, he appointed a Commission in 1545-6, to re-value that kind of property   The suppression of the Chantries &c was, however, finally carried out by Edw VI in 1548, in which year the following return was made, giving the names and incomes of the last Catholic clergy at Nantwich

THE CHANTRY ROLL FOR NANTWICH, 1548 ‖ [1 & 2 Edw. VI].

" *Namtwyche* "

" Md   The said towne of Nantwiche is a graet town and hath Ml viijᶜ [1800] hoslyng people within the same and is very necery [necessary] to haue a gramer scolle [grammar school] within the same And also a Vicar and Assistant to serue [serve] the Cure accordingly "

* Or *John Braswell, cf* p 278
† " *Jewells,*" i e anything reputed precious, and made of valuable materials or richly adorned   Hence the Cross of wood plated with *silver,* that then stood on the *rood screen,* is called a Jewell in the Inventory of Church goods
‡ *Cf* Chapter of Annals, p 92
§ Hulm MS from the Lichfield Registers, quoted by Bishop Gastrel in his " *Notitia Cestriensis,*" Cheth Soc Pub   Translated, this line would read —Licence to celebrate Divine services in the Chapel of Namptwich in the year 1405
‖ The names of the Commissioners who made this return were " Hughe Cholmelev, Willm Brereton, Knyghts, John Ascote, James Starkey, George Browne, Thomas Carne Esquyers, John Cheching, Thoms ffletewoode & Willm Laton Gents, Comyssyonᵉˢ " (From the Original in the Record Office)

[1]   *The fflower Servyces in the same Churche*
          JOHN CROXTON of thag' [the age] of l [50] yeres
          XPŌFER [CHRISTOPHER] WYNNINGTON* of xl [40] yeres
          RAUF MYNCON [MYNSHULL] of xxx [30] yeres
          THOMS PORTER,* hauing eu'y [every] of them iiijli xiijs iiijd [£4 13s 4d]
      "The Yerely Valewe xxjli xxd [£21 0s 20d *sic*, but should be 8d]
      "Repuses yerely xxvijs iiijd ob [27s 4½d]
      "The clere Remaine xixli xiijs iiijd ob [£19 13s 3½d]
      "Plate, Jewels Goods, ornamts, leade & Bells   none
      "Stokk of redy money xxli [£20]
      [To which is added] "This is discharged for that noe such sume p'med [promised] to be paid or
      deliuered According to the will of Randall Carbor vintenei of london nor Any such Chauntery hadu
      begynnyng or contynuaunce '

Lands graunted for Terme of yeres yett to Come {
  The yerely Valewe vjl xiijs iiijd [£6 13s 4d]
  Reprises yerely lxxs xd ob [70s 10½d]
  The Clere Remain lxijs xd ob [62s 5½d]
}

Lands graunted by   Gyllette belonging {
  The yerely Valewe xv js [17s]
to ye sayd s'vice for terme of yeies
  Reprises yerely vnjs [8s]
  The Clere Reman ixs [9s]
}

Then follows the "*Chauntery* [Lady Chapel] *within the sayd Churche*," which has
already been given on page 282, followed by "*the ffree Chauntries of St Lawrence and St
James*," (page 54) and "*the ffree Chauntry of St Nicholas*," (page 51) both of which are
described as "*w'hin ye sayd Towne*," but not within the said Church, and, therefore,
independent religious edifices

    In the same year, 1548, when the pecuniary difficulties of the Government led it to
gather up what was left of Church property after the spoliations of former years Commissions were issued ordering "true and perfect inventories to be taken of all goods,
plate jewels, and ornaments" still to be found in any churches, chapels, &c Accordingly
LAURENCE SMITH, KT, RONDELL MAYNWARYNG, KT, and RICHARD HASSALL, J P, as
Commissioners for Nantwich Hundred returned as follows for Nantwich Church

    Namptwiche has iiij chalices, whereof iij are gilt,† and the fourthe ungilt, on[e] cross of wood
plated wth silv'[er],‡ and a rynge of five bells,§ and on[e] litle anton' bell "||

    It is further stated that whereas at Audlem, Mynshull and Wybunbury the church-
plate, vestments, &c, had been sold and "bestowed upon the church reparacon," at
Nantwich and at other Churches in the Deanery the plate, ornaments, &c, were "not
alienated or put awaye" With this record, the history of the Church in Roman Catholic
times may be said to end, for within the next twenty years, the Rood-screen with its
cross, (and most likely the sanctus bell, the plate, vestments, altars in the chantry chapels,
&c) had disappeared, as proved by the following extract from the original will of Thomas
Maynwaring,¶ of Nantwich, now preserved at Chester

---

* These two priests were living in 1556 on a pension of £4 each per arnum —*(Pension Roll)*
† Most of tne country churches had chalices of the meaner metals, pewter, &c
‡ From this return it would appear that only at Nantwich and Malpas, amongst the Cheshire cnurches, did the Cross
on the *rood-s'reen* exist in 1548, and at the latter place it is described as "*a pi[e]ce of a broken crosse sylv[re]d*
§ At Mynshull the church bell had been taken possession of by Rondnll Mynshull of Holgreve, and "broken and
bestowed to his own private use,' before the taxing of the inventory there
|| The "*little anton* (? altar] *bell*" was probably a *sanctus bell*   ¶ Thomas Maynwaring died in January, 1572-3
the record of his burial being the first now to be found in the Parish Registers

"The xxvj day of March 1568 I Thomas Maynwaring of the wiche malbanke sonne of Humffrey maynwaring [&c] give my boddie to be buryed in the Church of the Namptwiche nere vnto the place where the *stenes dyd stoud whiche dyd goe into the Roodlofte*, yf I fortune [happen] to decease or Die in or neare the said towne of Namptwiche, or else to be buryed in some other Christen Churche and I gyve towards the reparacon of the sayd Churche of Namptwiche the somme of iijs iiijd . [3s 4d]

Heraldic Glass and Ancient Monuments.

As has already been stated, much heraldic stained glass adorned the Church prior to the Reformation   Memorial windows commemorated aristocratic families who had been benefactors to the building   and associated with their arms, no doubt, was the common phrase,— "*Orate pro anima,* ' words which afterwards became so offensive that edicts in the reigns of Edw VI and Elizabeth ordered their destruction   And hence in 1572, when the first Randle Holme visited the Church, only *one* inscription of this kind then remained in glass, and *one* in brass   Much of the ancient glass armoury, however, existed for a century later at the least, according to Church notes taken by Elias Ashmole in 1663   These notes, which are now preserved at the Bodleian Library, (*Ashmo MSS* vol 854, f 305—318), serve to corroborate similar notes by successive Randle Holmes' in *Harl MSS.* 2151 f 80 &c. at the British Museum   It is necessary to point out that in the latter MSS the ancient glass is not *always* distinguishable from the later glass armoury; but Elias Ashmole was more careful in noting which was the old, and in what part of the Church it was to be found, for example, drawings are given of "*Armes in the windowes of the South Cross,*" [i e South Transept] viz   *Kingslegh, Delves* and *Fulleshurst* which are said to have been "*set vp long since,*" and *Mainwaring* and *Wilbraham* which are described as "*lately set vp,*" and again "*in the windowes of the body of the Church*" [i e the Nave] three coats of arms in the south windows are specified as being "*very old,*" viz —those of *Oulton, Poole* and *Rope,* of which the last named escutcheon still exists in the middle window of the south aisle; while three other coats are mentioned as being "*in a south window* [of the nave] *of late tyme set vp*"   By collating the two MSS some idea of the internal appearance of the Church and of the armorial devices of the chief local families in the fifteenth century may be obtained.   The list, which is necessarily imperfect, is as follows, the * prefixed to the name indicating that the arms were remaining in 1663.—

I IN THE CHANCEL
(1) *In the East window.*
*AUDLEY   Gules, a fret Or.
*FULLESHURST   Gules, fretty Or, a chief Ermine
(2) *In the South window*
*WICH MALBANK   (the Arms of the town) Quarterly Or and Gules, a bendlet Sable.
*VERNON. Argent, on a fesse Azure three garbs Or.
*STAFFORD (or *Bagot*) Argent, on a chevron Gules a crescent Or, between 3 martlets (?) Or.
*FULLESHURST   Gules fretty Or, a chief Ermine
*MAISTERSON   Ermine, a chevron Azure between three garbs Or.
*PRAERS   Gules, a scythe Argent
*CHOLMONDELEY   Gules, in chief two esquiers helmets garnished Or, in base a garb Or.

SHIELDS OF ARMS.

(3) *Situation not specified in Harl MSS   Date* 1572

RAVENSCROFT impaling BROMLEY   Argent, a chevron Sable between three ravens heads
proper *(Ravenscroft)*   Argent on a chevron Gules five bezants Or *(Bromley)*.

WETTENHALL (ancient) Vert a bend Or [Dr Ormerod says Ermine].

II   IN THE SOUTH TRANSEPT.

(1) *In the East windows*

*KINGESLEGH   Vert, a cross engrailed Ermine *

*FULLESHURST   Gules, fretty Or, a chief Ermine

*DELVES: Argent, a chevron Gules fretty Or between 3 turves Sable.

(2) *In the West windows*

*DOMVILLE   Azure, a lion rampant Argent collared Or

*WETTENHALL   Vert, a cross engrailed Ermine *

Below this coat was remaining in 1572 the following inscription —

" **Orate p. tratribus et sororibɬ. sce. Crucis q' fecerunt ista'. fenestra'.** "

(Translation)—Pray for the Brethren and Sisters of the Holy Cross who made this window

(3) *In the South window*

*AUDLEY   Quarterly, 1 and 4 a fret Azure *(Audley)*, 2 and 3 Ermine a chevron Gules
(?   . . .)†

*BULKELEGH *alias* WRIGHT impaling BUTLER   Sable on a chevron Argent a fleur-de-lis
Or between three bulls' head cabossed Argent. *(Buckley or Wright)*   The Butler
quarterings are added

(4) *Situation not given in Harl MSS   Date* 1572

VERNON   Argent, on a fesse Azure three garbs Or

ST PIERRE   Argent, a bend Sable, debruised in chief by a label of 3 points Gules

CRADOCK   Argent on a chevron Azure three garbs Or.

STAFFORD.   Argent on a chevron Gules a crescent Or, between 3 martlets Sable

MAISTERSON   Ermine a chevron Azure between three garbs Or.

III.   IN THE NORTH TRANSEPT

(1) *In an East window*

*WODENOTE: Argent, a cross voided Sable

IV   IN THE NAVE

(1) *In the South windows*

*ROPE   Gules an orle of pheons Argent, a lion rampant Or ‡ ⎫
*POOLE   Azure, an orle of fleur-de-lis Argent, a lion Rampant Or. ⎬ Said in Ashmo MS.
*OULTON   Quarterly Vert and Gules, over all a lion rampant Argent. ⎭ to be "*very old*"

(2) *In West end window*

WICH MALBANK   (Arms of the town)

MAISTERSON   Ermine, a chevron Azure between three garbs Or

---

* The *Kingeslegh* or *Kingsley* glass is described under *Kingsley Chapel*   No satisfactory explanation has hitherto been given of the coincidence in both device and tinctures of the arms of Kingsley and Wettenhall

† Partridge speaks of Lord Audley s arms as existing "in fine condition" in 1774, in this window, and regrets that no precaution was taken to preserve it   *(Hist Nant* p 32)

‡ Still existing in the middle window of the South aisle of the Nave

(3) *In the North windows.*

Four coats are given by Elias Ashmole, but it is uncertain whether they are ancient or modern

(5) *In the Clerestory windows, South side*

*AUDLEY   Quarterly, 1 and 4 a fret Azure (*Audley*), 2 and 3 Ermine a chevron Gules

(6(*In the Clerestory windows, North side*

*WICH MALBANK   (The Arms of the town)

V In other places in the Church windows, the exact situation not stated in *Harl. MSS* (Date 1572)

COMBERMERE. Quarterly Or and Gules, a bendlet Sable, and over all a crosier per bend sinister, Or *

WICH   Argent, on a chevron Gules an annulet Or (or 5 Besants Or, according to *Hail. MSS* 2119 f 119), between three Quatre-foils

WOLFALL or MERTON   Argent, three greyhounds heads

MAINWARING *impaling* BROOKE   Argent two barrs Sable, an annulet Sable for difference (*Mainwaring*), Or a cross engrailed party per pale Gules and Sable (*Brooke*) †

Of this heraldic glass only one coat now remains *in situ*, namely, that of the ancient family of Rope   Some fragments of old stained glass, which Mr Norwood thinks is illustrative of the legend of St George, were removed from the North Transept (St George's Chapel) to the Choir some years ago, and now fills up the tracery of one of the south windows there

Before leaving this subject it may be well to allude to Mr Partridge's imperfect description of another shield dated 1338 (!), which, he says, was in one of the south windows of the nave at the time he wrote, "being the earliest date extant in the church" (*Hist Nant* p 36) From a rough drawing of it by the last Randle Holme in *Harl MSS*. 2151, it appears to have represented an alliance between two very ancient and notable families, namely, *Erdeswick* (a shield with a bend, no colors given) impaling *Stafford* (Argent, on a chevron Gules five bezants Or) with an inscribed scroll as follows —"*Thomas Erdeswik Margaret Staford* 1338 "   Below, however, it is added—"this character doth not bespeak this coat to be so auntient as 1338 " a remark which must be received as proof that it was not ancient glass at all, especially when it is known that no mention is made of this glass in the Church notes by the earlier Randle Holmes', nor by Elias Ashmole

Besides the above memorials of glass armoury, the first Randle Holme (in 1572) mentions the following armorial bearings *on wood*, "these coates are on the roofs [Transepts and Nave] of the said Church:—*Wilbraham*, [of Woodhey] *Bulkley, Mainwarnge, Delues, Masterson, Egerton, Bassett*, and [? Audley]. *(Harl MSS)*

The last Randle Holme gives a drawing of another shield *in stone*, and adds,—" on the outside the Chancell on the north side is cut in stone about a yard from the ground this coate, ' i e on a shield an engrailed cross (*Wettenhall*)   This carving which is not

---

* Dr Ormerod gives the Arms of Combermere Abbey slightly different, viz —" Quarterly Or and Gules, a bendlet Sable, debruised by a crosier *in pale* Or, the head turned sinister ways "

† This was Roger Mainwaring, Eschaetor of Cheshire 10 Hen VIII, the second son of Randle Mainwaring of Car n-cham   He married Mary (or Margaret) dau of Thomas Brooke of Leighton, and died 5 Oct 2 Hen VIII [1510]

now to be seen, may have indicated the place where Randle Wettenhall, according to his will dated 20th Oct 1437, was buried   (See chapter on *Annals*, p 93)

Although the Church was rich in heraldic glass in pre-Reformation times, it had very few ancient monuments, two only being noticed by Randle Holme in 1572, one in marble and the other in brass

The former is described as "The tombe of Sr George [should be *David*] Cradock* cut in Allablaster with his coate on his brest" In *Harl MSS* 2151 p 80, a rough drawing of the tomb is given, and an engraving of the same will be found in *Gent. Mag* for 1805, Vol. II, p 706   A broken part of the effigy of the Knight in the lower room (Crypt) of the vestry, is all that now remains of the monument   It originally stood in the South Transept, and was an altar-tomb of red stone, the sides being ornamented with shields included in quatre-foils   On the top was the recumbent figure of the Knight in alabaster, habited in plate armour, with conical helmet and gorget of mail, his hands clasped on his breast and a sword at his side   The legs were not crossed, the feet rested on a lion, and the head reposed on the crest, which was the head of a lamb   A notice of this monument occurs in Samuel Derrick's Letters (Vol I p 9), which alludes to two remarkable traditions of the town concerning it   He says—

"Here we were shown the Monument of the Founder [of the Church] Sir Roger de Caradoc, an ancient British Knight who was said to have been descended from the renowned *Caractacus* (!)   It is of white marble and much defaced by *Cromwell's* (!) soldiers from whose violence nothing neat, elegant or venerable was sacred "

The arms on the tomb were *"three garbs on a chevron,"* which correspond with the heraldic glass on page 285, where the colours are given †

The other ancient monument, placed at the *"North end of the Church"* was a brass representing a knight in armour, his feet resting on a greyhound, and on either side of his head shields charged with a griffin segreant   Round the sides of the brass, commencing at the feet of the warrior was this inscription —

"𝕳𝔦𝔠 𝔍𝔞𝔠𝔢𝔱 𝔍𝔬𝔥𝔦𝔰. 𝔊𝔯𝔦𝔣𝔣𝔦𝔫 𝔪𝔦𝔩𝔦𝔱𝔦𝔰 𝔮𝔲𝔦 𝔬𝔟𝔲𝔱 𝔡𝔦𝔢 𝔩𝔲𝔫𝔢
𝔭𝔵. 𝔭𝔬𝔰𝔱 𝔣𝔱𝔲. 𝔰𝔯𝔦. 𝔪𝔦𝔠𝔥𝔦𝔰. 𝔞𝔯𝔠𝔥𝔦. 𝔞𝔫𝔫𝔬. 𝔡𝔫𝔦. 𝔐.𝔠𝔠𝔠.
𝔏𝔵𝔵𝔵𝔵 𝔠𝔲𝔦𝔤. 𝔞𝔦𝔞. 𝔭'𝔭𝔦𝔱𝔦𝔞𝔱𝔲𝔯 𝔡𝔢𝔲𝔰. 𝔞𝔪𝔢𝔫."

(*Translation*)—Here lies Sir John Griffin knight‡ who died on Monday next after the feast of St Michael the Archangel [29 Sept] in the year of our Lord 1390, On whose soul may God be merciful   Amen

---

* Here is another variation of the name   Dr Ormerod also, by a clerical error, printed the name *Sir John* Cradock, the real personage being *Sir David* Cradock, which last name s given by Randle Wilbraham in his MS Journal, by Pennant in his tour from Chester to London, p 32 (Edit 1782), and by Partridge, (*Hist Nant* p 32)   No mention of "*Sir George*" or "*Sir John*" occurs in the Cheshire records, but *Sir David Cradock* and his son *Sir Richard Cradock* no doubt were really living Knights   (See Annals, p 83)

† It is interesting to note that the Cradock family have in modern times been long connected with Audley and Betley, having had possessions in some of the townships on the Wybunbury side of Nantwich and in the neighbourhood of Stafford   but whether the Staffordshire branches of the family and the Cradocks of Nantwich are descended from a common ancestor, I have not been able to ascertain   A '*Thomas Cradock, Gent ,*' who lived and died at Nantwich, was "*buried at Audley* 27 *April* 1762   —(Nantwich Par Reg)   He was the brother of John Cradock of Betley, Esq , who died leaving two daughters   and was the last male descendant of the Betley branch of that family —(Information by T F Twemlow Esq of Betley Court)

‡ Sir John Griffin held the manor of Barthelton near Nantwich, which continued to be held by his posterity, until it was sold by Richard Griffin in 1666 to the Delves family of Doddington

The Church since the Reformation.

FTER the great changes in Ecclesiastical affairs that had taken place during the reigns of Henry VIII and Edward VI, Nantwich was classed amongst the "*discharged livings;*" that is, such as were exempted from the payment of *first-fruits* and *tenths* to the Exchequer, on account of the smallness of their incomes. Such livings were often called "*scandalous livings*" during the sixteenth and seventeenth centuries, because they had been deprived of their glebe lands, tithes, &c.; the revenues therefrom being either retained by the Crown, or diverted to individuals who could show a claim by purchase. Thus the Tithe-hay of Nantwich, and the Tithes of corn, grain, and pulse in Woolston-wood, Willaston, and Alvaston, belonged to the Mainwaring family of Nant-wich; until Thomas Mainwaring, the elder, Gent., and William Mainwaring, Gent., sold the same, in 1635, to Raphe Judson; who, by his will, proved on the 17th Aug. 1648, devised the same to his wife, Rebecca Judson; from whom they were purchased by Roger Wilbraham Esq. of Townsend on the 16th April, 1657.[*] These, together with his tithes in Leighton, he values in his Rent Roll, dated 1659,[†] as follows:—

	£	s.	d.
"Tythes of Leighton, and Tythes of my owne lands in Namptwich, in possession ...	20	0	0
"The Tythe-Hay of Namptwch wch was Judsons	6	13	4

The same Roger Wilbraham also purchased on the 31st Dec. 1678, from Robert Hyde, Gent., "*certain tythes of Namptwich which had formerly belonged to the Abbot of Combermere;*"[‡] which, together with the "*Tithe-hay of Namptwich,*" were assessed for the relief of the Poor in 1834, at £4; being at that time in the possession of his descendant, George Wilbraham, Esq., of Delamere.[‡]

Other Tithes in Alvaston and Nantwich-Willaston were purchased, in 1719, for the sum of £200, raised by subscription, and given to the Rector of Nantwich and his successors.[§]

By deed dated 1st May 15 Car. I [1639] the living of Nantwich had been augmented by "*tithes formerly of the dissolved free Chapel of St. Lawrence,*" which for nearly a hundred years previous had been in the possession of the Wright family of this town. By that deed Margaret Woodnoth (*née* Wright) and Elizabeth Davenport (*née* Wright), widows, of Nantwich, conveyed—

---

* From authorized copies of the original Indentures preserved at Nantwich Rectory.

† Minshull Accounts, in the possession of G. F. Wilbraham, Esq.

‡ "Valuation of Buildings, Lands, Tithes, and other rateable property in the Township of Nantwich &c. 1834. Printed by E. Carven, Bookseller, High-Street, Nantwich, 1835."

§ Bishop Gastrell's "*Notitia Cestriensis,*" Chet. Soc. Pub. vol. viii, which states that Mr. Crewe, of Crewe Hall; Mr. John Bromhall; and Mr. Randle Wilbraham of Townsend; each subscribed £50.

"their tithes of hay, hemp, flax, pigs, onions, and garlick in Wich Malbank, Willaston, and Leighton, and in Milne Street, High Towne and the Welsh Row in the town and parish of Wich Malbank" *in trust* "to raise £26 to provide and buy two silver Flaggons and a silver Patten, and deliver the same to the Churchwardens of the Parish Church of Wich Malbank, to be by them and their successors for ever used in the Celebration of the Sacrament," and afterwards "*to the use of the preaching Minister in and for the said Town of Wich Malbank*"*

In 1839, when the Tithe Commutation Act came into operation, Mr. France, of Bostock, co Chester, raised a most unexpected claim to the small tithes of Leighton township, which were relinquished by the Rev H Gretton, Rector of Nantwich, in the year 1840, when Leighton was separated from Nantwich parish.

Another source of Church revenue which fell into lay hands was the *Easter Roll*, or *Easter Dues*, being a *personal tithe* of twopence from every householder in Nantwich, for each member of his family, due annually at Easter The history of the Easter Roll from the dissolution of Combermere Abbey to the present time is of a very interesting character, since it became, in a very strange manner, associated with the advowson of the Church, as will next be shown.

The Easter Roll, which according to *Valor Ecclesiasticus* (1535) was let to farm for £8 6s. 8d, was by an Indenture dated 25th April 30 Hen. VIII [1538] leased for a term of sixty years by John, Abbot of Combermere, to WILLIAM MAISTERSON, of Nantwich, at an annual rent of £8, payable to the Abbot at the feast of the Nativity of St. John Baptist [June 24] The deed states the rights and privileges to be—

"Pryve [personal] Tythes called the Ester Rolle or the Ester Booke and all oblacons Weddyngs & Buryings cumynge or happenynge or that hereafter shall cume or happen durynge the t'me [term] of Yeres underwryten of the pisshe [parish] of Wyche Malbanke aforeseid beinge due to the seid Abbott & Convent at the clause [close] of Ester or w'tn any tyme of the yere when the seid Tythes oblac' Weddyngs or Buryings shall happen" &c †

This lease in all probability became null and void about fourteen months after, when the same Abbot surrendered his Monastery with its revenues into the King's hands The Crown appears to have retained the Easter Roll of Nantwich until 1592, and out of its profits to have paid the annual stipend of £4 13s 4d. to the Town Curate. By Letters Patent‡ dated at Westminster 27th June 34 Eliz [1592], Queen Elizabeth granted a lease of the Easter Roll of Wich Malbank to ROGER WALTHALL, HUGH HASSALL, and ROGER WILBRAHAM, for their lives and the life of the longest liver of them, "*for the use and benefit of the said parish of Wich Malbank,*" subject to the annual rent of £3 6s 8d payable to the Crown, and after the decease of any of them, a payment to the Crown of 30s in the name of a heriot "And the aforesaid Roger Walthall, Hugh Hassall, and Roger Wilbraham, and their assigns shall pay £4 13s 4d yearly due to the *Curate of Wich Malbank*, and so yearly from time to time for his *stipend* '

---

* From a printed copy of the Deed, now at Nantwich Rectory, printed in 1784, by order of the Rev John Smith Rector, from the original Indenture then in the Diocesan Registry at Chester, which has since that time been lost
The "*two silver Flaggons,*" which were purchased twenty years after (1659), form part of the present Communion Plate of the Church, there is also a "*silver Patten,*"—a thin, beaten plate (without date or inscription), which may also have been bought by the Trustees, as directed above

† Authorized copy of the original deed at Nantwich Rectory

‡ I have a full copy of this Latin deed, taken from one preserved amongst the Wilb MSS, which is too long to be given in its entirety The principal facts, however, are given in this paragraph

In the next lease of the Easter Roll, a clause was inserted, which attempted (illegally) to pass the *advowson*, or *right of presentation* as accessory, incident, and appendant to the right of collecting Easter Dues. The deed is here given in full * *(Translated)*—

" By Letters patent bearing date the 30th July in the fourth year of our reign [1628] as well under the Great Seal of England as of the Seal of the County Palatine of Lancaster, I King Charles do grant and concede to Ralph Wyse and Henry Harryman [? Harrison†] both of London, Gents, and their heirs and assigns for ever all that *Easter Roll* or *Easter Book* of Wich Malbank in the county of Chester, and all and singular the smaller tithes coming growing or renewing of and in the parish of Wich Malbank with all and singular its rights members and appurtenances then or late in the tenure of Roger Walthall, Hugh Hassall and Roger Wilbraham or their assigns said to be of the yearly value of 66s 8d and formerly parcel of the possession of the late Monastery of Combermere in the said county of Chester, and all and singular *the Advowson donation free disposition and right of patronage of all and singular the Rectory Church Vicarage Chapelry and of all other ecclesiastical benefits of these presents thus granted* &c to hold the said Ralph Wyse and Henry Harryman their heirs and assigns in fee farm for ever   To be held of our heirs and successors of our Manor of East Greenwich‡ in the co of Kent in fealty and in free and common socage and not *in capite* nor by Knight's service paying yearly to us and our successors 66s 8d &c in two equal portions on the feasts of the Annunciation and St Michael the Archangel "

The Easter Roll was next passed to Sir Ranulph Crewe,§ of Crewe, Kt , by Indenture dated 3rd March, 1631, for the sum of £66 13s 4d , subject to the annual Crown Rent of £3 6s 8d as before, and remained in that family until the year 1820, when by an Indenture dated 24th Feb 1 Geo IV [1820]

"between the Rt Hon John Lord Crewe Baron Crewe of Crewe, *Patron of the Parish Church* of Nantwich and Richard Henry Gretton, Clerk, *Rector of the Parish and Parish Church of Nantwich*, Witnesseth that the said John Lord Crewe for divers good causes &c and for augmenting the living of the said R H Gretton and his successors *Rectors* for the time being of the Parish of Nantwich aforesaid, and in consideration of 5s &c hath granted bargained sold and assigned to the said R. H. G and his successors Rectors of the Parish &c all and every the offerings, oblations obventions commonly called the *Easter Dues* or *Easter Roll* of the Parish of Nantwich aforesaid and of right due and payable to the said John Lord Crewe at the feast of Easter yearly, from the several inhabitants for the time being of the Parish of Nantwich &c subject nevertheless to the Annual Rent of £3 6s 8d payable to the Crown in respect of the same, &c by the said R H G and his successors, Rectors for the time of the Parish of Nantwich "||

For many years after the dissolution of Combermere Abbey, the Curate of Nantwich received a fixed stipend of £4 13s. 4d. per annum , which was further supplemented by other sums collected in the town (see p 30), and hence as the parishioners were compelled to sustain their minister, they claimed the right of choosing and appointing him. In Puritan times the incumbents were styled *Ministers*, and, the living being a *donative*, that is, given to clergymen by the parishioners without presentation to, or institution by, the

* From an authorized copy of the original Latin deed now at Nantwich Rectory
† The name *Harrison* is here introduced from another copy of the same deed *penes me*
‡ " *Manor of East Greenwich* " a legal phrase signifying the possession of the Crown
§ Papers at Nantwich Rectory, and *cf* page 209
|| Original deed by the first Lord Crewe now preserved at the Rectory, Nantwich   The Easter Dues ceased to be collected about the year 1868 The present Rector, however, still pays the same Crown Rent annually

Bishop, no list of their names is to be found at the Diocesan Registry of Chester, until after the passing of the Act of Uniformity, (19th May, 1662), which rendered Episcopal ordination imperative. Fortunately, however, the names of the Nantwich Ministers for a period of seventy years (1560—1630) have been preserved in an original document, which is here printed for the first time.

"*My Co.[usin] To [m] Maynwaryng touchine o[u]r Curate and his Wages*"[*]

"I doe remember & wyll testefye that theis mynysters wch have beene off the Namptwiche Churche have beene placed & displaced bye the gentellmen & others off the towne w^thout the Consent or approbation eyther of the Lorde Bishopp or anye other parson [person] whatsoever

"First, *(Sr) Richard Hargreve* was displaced & after him, the gentellmen toocke on *(Sr) Wylliõ[m] Warde*, & vppon some dislicke hee was displaced, then the[y] toocke one *(Sr) John* . I remember not his Sirname, but the[y] called him *(Sr) John off Warryngton* vppon dislicke off him the gentellmen putt him foorthe & toocke in *(Sr) Wilhã Warde* agayne whoe reemayned to his dying daye

After him the gentellmen chose *Mr Hollford* w^thout the consent of anye Ordynarye, & hee reemay[n]ed to his deathe vppon the place beē g [being] then voyde Byshopp lloyde sent heeyther one *Mr Holland* & woulde have placed him heere, but the gentellmen wth the rest off the towne, would not suffer him to bee here, in that they [i e the] Byshoppe hathe noe titell or ryghtte to place anye Mynister amongst vs, but did expulse him from us & chose *Mr Bradwell* w^thowt his the Bishopp Consent or approbation for our Curatteshipp is but stipendarye allowed from the Kinge butt fourteene nobles [£4 13s 4d] p Ann, wch ryghtte & titell wee have bve lease from the latte Quaene Elizabethe, and paye iij^li vj^s viij^d [£3 6s 8d] p an, beesydes the reeperac'on [repairings] & xxx^s [30s] att the deecease off eu ye [every] one of the leasees, as the lease wyll testifye & for the other I am able & wyll wittenesse that itt is true"

"*Mr Clayton* was never lawfullye Elected to the Curatteshippe off Namptwiche, neyther did, or doe the moste (as wyl be proven) houlde him for our mynyster or Curatte"

"THO MAYNWARYNG"

The Curate's Wages.†

"The Town hath a lease of ye Curats place (w^ch *Mr Saving* now hath) for 3 liues paying yearely 5 markes [£3 6s 8d] & to repaire ye chauncel & by ye same lease we are to pay to y^e *Minister* of ye Towne 14 nobles [£4 13s 4d] wch the towne makes up £10 p ann of their owne accord & giues him moreover the weddings, burialls, christnings and churchings wch come to about 40s p ann Now to pay this £10 the Towne ha^the ye Proctors book‡ wch comes to about £15 p ann And this is thus raysed —

ffirst £5 8s 0d forth of ye whole walling, vizt out of euery 6 leads sixpence, their being 216 six leads walling

Then for euery man servant in ye Towne 6^d and for euery woman servant 4^d Then for euery Cow whereof the milk comes into ye Towne 1^d And a hal[f]penny for euerie Calfe calued w^thin the parish, except *woolston-wood* wch answears but ye 3^d pt [third part] of Tythes wch are p^d by Leighton, vizt smoke,§ cowes, and calues, & ye white tithes || Willaston and Aluaston pay all tythes belonging to a vicar ¶

---

* This interesting document, *penes me*, formerly belonged to the MS collections of the late T W Jones, Esq, Solicitor, of Nantwich
† This Terrier is preserved amongst the Wilb MSS at Delamere
‡ On the 19th May, 1703, was buried "Robert Oldfeild, *Proctor*," *(Par Reg)* whose duty it was to collect these fruits of the benefice
§ *Tithe of Smoke*, sometimes called *smoke-penny* or *smoke-silver* was money paid to the minister instead of *Tithe wood*
|| *White-tithes* i e the tithe of hay
¶ Probably the vicar of Acton In 1705, the Tithes of Willaston were held by Mr Simon Degge, of Nantwich, ' from whom' (says Rev Sam Edgeley, Vicar of Acton,) "I cannot learn" Gastrell's *Notitia Cestriensis*, Chet Soc. Pub p 200

My Lady Norton payes yearely 2s for tythe Geese, but they are worth 10s p ann

George Whittakers payes 20s. for Onions & Garlick, worth p ann 30s   Also 5s for euery chamber vnder the schoole [*i e* the Grammar School in the Church Yard] & 16s for *Ric Barkers* house, all wch are of th' inheritance belonging to ye Towne

"Also, 10s is paid for a Mortuary for euery one dying worth £40 in goods, & 6s 8d if worth £30, and 3s 4d if worth £6 6s 8d   & for euery man or woman buried in ye church 3s 4d , and for euery child is 8d , and for euery one buried in ye chancel 6s 8d "

"Theis directions I [Thomas Wilbraham*] had fro[m] my Cos Tho. Mainwaring 15 Dec 1629 "

On the death of Mr. Richard Jackson, the last of the Nantwich *Ministers* or *Curates*, in 1677, John Crewe, of Crewe, Esq., (grandson of Sir Ranulph Crewe, Kt., the purchaser of the Easter Roll in 1631) "assumed the *right of presentation* to ye Curateship of Nantwich," and was supported by the "restless endeavours" of Gabriel Stringer, a native of the town, who sought and obtained the preferment †   The original presentation of Mr. Stringer is not now preserved at the Diocesan Registry   but it was in existence when Bishop Gastrell wrote, stating that he was admitted as perpetual Curate of the Church of Nantwich on the presentation of John Crewe, of Crewe, Anno. 1677 ‡

On the next vacancy of the benefice in 1690, *Anne Crewe Offley*, eldest daughter and co-heiress of John Crewe, Esq , exercised the right of patronage   and, in presenting *Peter Lancaster* to the Bishop, besought his Lordship "to admit and institute him *Rector* of the said Church with its rights and all belonging thereto, and declare and set forth the same publicly by his [the Bishop's] authority "§   All succeeding clergymen have been similarly presented, and have received institution as Rectors of Nantwich, but it is very noteworthy that the title, Rector, does not occur in the Parish Register until the year 1714, or thirty-seven years after the death of Richard Jackson, Minister of Nantwich

Whilst ancient Rectories, with their glebe lands, soon recovered from the effects of the Reformation, and have in recent times greatly increased in value, Stipendiary Curacies, like Nantwich, which could only be augmented by gifts and endowments, increased but slowly in value; and as late as 1786, (Bacon's "*Liber Regis*") the annual income was only £27 3s 4d !   It would seem that the restitution of tithes and gifts to the incumbent have *ipso facto* made the living *rectorial,* and the district in which the tithes were collected an *ecclesiastical parish* separate and distinct from Acton, of which it was originally a part   These changes, however, were brought about in a very gradual manner, and not by any legal act or process.   No suspicion appears to have been cast upon the right of the Crewe family to the advowson of Nantwich from the year 1677 until 1840, when the legality of the claim was questioned by the Rev. Robert Mayor, Vicar of Acton   Legal opinion was obtained showing that Lord Crewe's title was then wholly unimpeachable, according to Stat. 3 & 4 Will IV [1833] c. 27, which enacted —

---

* Thos Wilbraham records in the Wilb MS Journal —

          " My Cosen Thos Mainwaring, my Lady Norton s son, dyed 10 Aug 1638 '

He was buried on the following day—

          " 1638 Aug 11th Thos Mainwaring, Gent , in the Beame Street "—*(Par Reg)*

† See Roger Wilbraham's " *Towns Concernes* " page 209—210

‡ Gastrell's *Notitia Cestriensis*, p 225   Chet Soc Pub

§ From the original presentation, dated 11th Aug 1690, signed and sealed , and now preserved at Chester Diocesan Registry

"That after the 31st Dec 1833 no *quaie impedit* or other suit shall be maintainable to enforce a right to present to any benefice after the period during which three clerks in succession shall have held it having been appointed adversely to the right of the party so claiming if such three incumbencies amount altogether to 60 years " (Sect 30)

Sect. 33 "limits the right to maintain such suit absolutely to 100 years "

Sect 34 "extinguishes the right of the party out of possession after the determination of the period of limitations "

The Clergy List.

I CURATES OR MINISTERS

For reasons already given, the list of incumbents of Nantwich Church commences about the time of the Reformation, the first name being—

[*Sir*] REGINALD STEVENSON. *Temp.* Hen VIII

He occurs as Curate between the years 1533 and 1548   (*cf.* pp. 277-8).

[*Sir*] JOHN CROXTON, 1548

The Chantry Certificate of 1548 recommended the appointment of a Vicar with an assistant to supply the spiritual wants of the town   Accordingly the King's Commissioners, on the 13th July, 1548, appointed the oldest of the four priests, *John Croxton*, to be the *Stipendiary Curate* of Nantwich, the other priests retiring on pensions of £4 per ann   The deed of appointment states —

"That the *Chapel of the Nauntwich in the parish of Acton* shall continue,* and that JOHN CROXTON one of the four Stipendiary priests in the same *Chapel* shall serve the Cure there, and shall have yearly £4 13s 4d "†

John Croxton resigned his Curateship, (? date), but was living in the parish of Audley (Staffordshire) on a pension of £5 per ann , about the year 1570 ‡

[*Sir*] RICHARD HARGREVE   *Temp.* Queens Mary and Elizabeth.

The date of his appointment has not occurred   but he was Curate here in 1560, and in 1562, having received in both those years his annual stipend of £4 13s 4d. from Richard Legh, of West Hall, Esq , the receiver of Crown revenues in Cheshire, according to the following entry in the West Hall Papers, vol. iv.—

"Paid to Ric' hargreve assistent in the Church of Namptwiche his hole yeres penc'on ended at ye feast of seint Michell th'arcangell last past   iiijli xiijs iiijd "

Having been displaced, he was succeeded by—

* "*Continue* " that is, shall not be demolished as the *Hospitals of St Nicholas*, and *St Lawrence*, with their Chapels, Altars, &c , and as *Combermere Abbey*, and many other religious edifices were about that time
† The original document, which mentions other similar appointments in Cheshire, has been recently printed in Mr Earwaker s "*Local Gleanings Magazine*" pp 307 309   The name Croxton is, however given *Crapon*, no doubt a misreading of the original that might easily have been made , as those who are acquainted with the kind of handwriting in use 300 years ago, will readily allow
‡ Special Commissions, 16 Eliz [1574] No 3258 Diocese of Chester, 38th Report of Deputy Keeper of the Public Records

[S*ir*] WILLIAM WARD.

Who must have been appointed early in Queen Elizabeth's reign, and being displaced was succeeded by—

[S*ir*] JOHN*   "*of Warrington*"

This Curate was displaced in or before 1572, and was succeeded by William Ward.

[S*ir*] WILLIAM WARD   1572—1583

Re-appointed 1572, and continued to be minister here until his death; his burial, however, not being recorded in the Register   He commenced keeping the Parish Register 1st Jan. 1572 (see chapter on the Registers), and during his incumbency, the high-pitched roofs of the Transepts appear to have been removed, and the flat panelled oak ceiling substituted, according to the following inscription in Roman capitals still discernible on a beam in the North Transept —

> "ANNO DOMINI 1577   THOMAS CLEASE MADE AND FENISHED
>
> THIS WORKE IN THE 19 YERE OF ELIZABETH QVEENE THE
>
> 4 DAYE OF NOVEMBER. THOS WRIGHT RYCHARD WYNTED YE CHVRCH WARDENS '

He was succeeded by—

[M*r*] WILLIAM HOLFORD, *Minister*   1583—1604

The Parish Register records, "*Dec 12th 1583 William Holford Minister entereth*"   In the reign of Elizabeth, Puritanism spread rapidly in the south of Cheshire   From 1571 to 1604, ministers were only compelled to subscribe to those of the thirty-nine Articles which concerned the faith and sacraments, and not to points of discipline and Church government, but the Canons of 1604 required the subscription of the clergy to the Articles touching rites and ceremonies, and in the following year, three hundred of the Puritan clergy were driven from their livings for their refusal to conform; and amongst the rest, *Mr John Paget*, a very learned man, "*preacher of God's Word*" at Nantwich, under the Minister Mr. Holford, of whom more presently   Shortly before *Mr Paget* came to Nantwich, religious feeling had run so high as to necessitate legal proceedings by which, on 21st July, 1595, a Commission was appointed to inquire touching certain "lybelles and Rymes" dispersed in the town of Nantwich to the scandal of the preachers of God's word

"ELIZABEIH &c   To our trusty and welbeloved *Sr hugh Cholmondeley Knighte, Thomas Wilbraham* [of Woodhey], *Henry Delues* [of Doddington], *Thomas Smith* [of Hatherton], *Willm hu'sage* [Liversage of Wheelock], and *hugh Beeston* [of Beeston], the elder, Esquires, or to any two of them   Greetinge

Whereas We are credibly enformed That certeyne lewde and seditious p'sons haue of late dispersed certeyne infamous and slaunderous lybelles and Rymes in the towne of Namptwiche tendinge to the slander and discreditt as well of the preachers & ministers of gods Worde as of others of good creditt and reputation By oc'con [occasion] Whereof much inconvenience and breach of our peace is like to ensue if it be not p'vented   Wee mynding the speedie reformation thereof for the quiet and peaceable gou[ern]ment of our Subjects and the due punyshment of such offenders doe by theise pr[e]sents authorize and requier yow or any two or more of yow at such daies and tymes as shall be agreed vppon by yow &c to assemble yourselves at the said towne of Namptwiche and to cause to come before yow &c all such p'sons as yow shall thinke meete   and to exam' theym by such Wayes and meanes as yow shall thinke convenyent eyther by othe or otherwise &c   And such as yow shall fynde to be any Waye guiltie or vehemently suspected thereof to take theym bounde for their appearaunce in our Exchequer

* His surname has not occurred   No information relating to this incumbent or his predecessors is to be found in the Parish Registers, owing to the hiatus between 1545 and 1572

at Chester at such tyme as yow shall lymytte and appoynt   And of your facts doings & prceedings therein to certifie us into the saide Exchequer at or before the first daie of September next cominge together with such exa'i'acons [examinations] as you shall take in this behalfe

Wytnes or seale at Chester the xvj daie of July 37th of or Raigne "* [1595]

Very interesting particulars relating to Mr John Paget have recently been printed,† from which the following brief biography is compiled, a few extracts from the Parish Register, and an old pedigree book, furnishing additional information concerning that eminent Puritan divine

Mr John Paget

He is believed, though it is not certain, to have been descended from the *Pagets* of Rothley, co Leicester   He was educated at the University of Cambridge, "where he was esteemed for the most part to surpasse his contemporaries." "After some few yeares spent in places of lesse note," says R. Paget in an Address prefixed to a vol of Sermons by John Paget, entitled '*Meditations of Death*' published after his death at *Dort* in Holland, in 1639, "he was called to the ministry of the Church of Christ, at Namptwich, about the yeare 1598   The extraordinary diligence and paines he tooke there, both in publick and private, with persons of all sorts, and the blessed successe, hath bene already witnessed by the lively Epistles of Christ ministered by him.   But when the times would not beare his continuance in that place, where his labours were so profitable, and where he was then so beloved, he followed the hand of God's providence guiding him into the Nether-lands, in the yeare 1605 "   He is described as possessing "rare skill in the languages that conduce unto the understanding of the originall text of the Scriptures, for he could to good purpose and with much ease make use of the Chaldean, Syriack, Rabbinicall, Thalmudicall, Arabick, and Persian versions and commentaries "   Whilst at Nantwich he published a book, now of great rarity, entitled "*A Primer of Christian Religion, or a forme of Catechising, drawne from the beholding of Gods works*, &c   By I P London 1601 "   Small 8vo 183 leaves   This book is dedicated "*To my beloved friendes in the Namptwich*," and is signed "*John Paget* "

At Nantwich, too, he married   Dr Ormerod places him in the Maisterson pedigree as the husband of *Bridget* daughter of Richard Maisterson, of Nantwich, and the Parish Register records —

"1601-2 Feb 8 Mr John Pagett, preacher, and Bridget Thrushe"‡ [Married]

This apparent error is made plain in old MS pedigree book of Cheshire families preserved at Dorfold Hall, in which on page 123 is the following —"*Brigetta qua nupsit I Thrush deinde Joh Pigett concionator verbi Dei in Amsterdam in Hollandie* "§

Driven away from Nantwich in 1605 for his Nonconformity, he fled to Holland, where he first preached and taught in the Army, until he was admitted minister of the English Church at Amsterdam‖ on 29th April, 1607, where he was pastor for about thirty years

---

* *Cheshire Recognizance Rolls*, Pub Record Office

† J P Earwaker's *East Cheshire*, Vol I p 390, and *Local Gleanings*, 4to series, Vol I, pp 33, 40

‡ *Bridget Thrush* remained in a state of widowhood only a few weeks, her former husband having been buried at Nantwich in the November previous   "1601 Nov 10 *George Thrushe, Gent dyed of a consumption* ' Buried]

§ *(Translated)*—Bridget [Maisterson] who married first Thrush, afterwards John Pagett preacher of God's Word at Amsterdam in Holland

‖ Sir William Brereton, Bart, in his "*Travels in Holland* ' in 1634 records on "*June 12th we dined with Mr Pageatt* " (p 57) and that the Church   *allowed unto Mr Pageatt* 1100 *gilders* [£110] *per annum* ' (p 67)

"untill age and the infirmities thereof growing upon him the Magistrates of that City vouchsafed him the honour of an Emeritus" He died in 1637-8, and in the Vol of Sermons before mentioned, his widow *"Briget Paget* speaks of these Meditations of my deare Husband of blessed memory" &c He was the author of *"An Arrow against the Separation of the Brownists,"* Printed at Amsterdam 1618, a controversial pamphlet, dated 1635, and a posthumous book entitled "A Defence of Church Government" &c. 1641

By a singular coincidence *Mr Thomas Paget,* younger brother of *Mr John Paget* married a Nantwich lady, as recorded in the registers

"1613 April 6 Mr Thos pagett, preacher, & Margery Gouldsmith '

He was minister of Blackley Chapel, in Manchester parish, at the time of his marriage; where he remained till he was deprived of his living by Bishop Bridgman in 1631 He fled to Holland to escape imprisonment or fine, and there in 1639 succeeded his brother at the Church in Amsterdam. Returning to England in 1646, he was Rector of St. Chad's, Shrewsbury, for ten years, and from 1657 till his death in 1660, Rector of Stockport. One of his sons, Nathan Paget, a physician, was the intimate friend of the poet Milton, and a relative of the poet's third wife, Elizabeth Minshull. (See Minshull pedigree)

Of the incumbent, *Mr William Holford,* very little is known Both he and his wife died when the Plague was rife in the town (See p 114)

He appears to have died intestate, but an inventory of his goods was filed and administration granted to his relatives, in 1608.*

MR JOHN BRADWALL   1605—1623

After the death of Mr Holford, the right of the *"Gentlemen"* to appoint the next minister was questioned by Bishop Lloyd, who gave institution to a certain *Mr. Holland.* In opposition to the Bishop, however, the parishioners expelled Holland,† and chose *Mr. Bradwall,* who came to Nantwich, seven months after the death of the previous minister ‡ His name occurs in the Registers as follows —

'1605 May 31 John Bradwall, minister, entereth here "--*(Par Reg)*
'1605 Dec 14 Samuell son of John Bradwall minester ' —[Baptized]
'1608 Aug 31 John sonne of Mr John Bradwall minester "—[Buried]
"1608 Sep 12 Ann dau of Mr John Bradwall minester "—[Buried]
"1612 June 16 Annes Conesrak Mr Bradwall's mother or minester '—[Buried]
"1623 4 March 7 Mr John Bradwall, preacher & minester of the word of God —[Buried]

To his memory a monumental tablet was erected *"by the Communion table,"* but it does not appear to have been in existence in 1663 when Elias Ashmole visited the Church. The inscription from *Harl. MSS* 2151, is as follows —

"Here lyeth the body of the holy and religious pastor   . . mr John Bradwall, who did zealously & laboriously discharge the office of the ministry   for the space of two and 30 yeares, 18 yeares of wch was dilligently bestowed on this towne of namptwch being much admired both in life and doctrine He came to this towne 18 May 1605 and deceased 5 March 1623-4 "

* Wilis at Chester 1545—1620 (Record Soc Pub)

† Failing at Nantwich, *Mr Hugh Holland* was presented by the Bishop, on 5th July, 1606, to the Rectory of Wistaston, which living he only occupied about a year

‡ Several events in connection with the Church, during the incumbency of Mr Bradwall, will be found noticed in the *Annals,* pp 115—120

Mr. Bradwall's widow seems to have survived until 1645, her burial register being as follows —

> "1645 May 6 Mrs Ellen Bradwell widowe "

Among the names of minor clergymen between the years 1636 and 1642 occurs *Joseph Bradwall*, who was most likely a son of Mr John Bradwall

> "1636 Aug 25 Joseph Bradwall, clerk, and Margaret Wicksteed [married] at Acton '
> "1639 Jan 19 Mary dau of Joseph Bradwall minester " [Baptized]
> "1642 Aug 29 Mary dau of Mr Joseph Bradwall minester " [Buried]

He must have died before 1648, as another assistant minister here married his widow in that year, as recorded in the Parish Register —

> 1648 July 17 John Roberts, minister and Margaret Bradwall, widow ' [*Marr Reg*]

[*Mr*] MATTHEW CLAYTON   1624

The appointment of *Matthew Clayton* as Curate of Nantwich, after the death of *Mr John Bradwall*, was again the cause of disagreement and ill-feeling in the town, some holding that *Mr Clayton* was not "lawfully elected'   A memorandum in the Registers states —

> "That in March 1624, after the death of John Bradwall late mynister here, was placed by the Churchwardens to bee mynister one Matthew Clayton a good gospeller "*

The last word is almost illegible, and other remarks which followed, have been erased, perhaps because they were offensive to their registrar or some of his successors   The names of the Churchwardens for the years 1624 and 1625 are not given in the Register   A Matthew Clayton, (most likely the same clergyman) was curate of Witton, near Northwich, from Nov 1616, to the year 1619,† and the same name occurs again as second minister at Middlewich in 1646 ‡   Matthew Clayton was one of the fourteen ministers who asked the Rev John Ley, of Astbury, to write his "*Sunday a Sabbath*, 1641 "

The following extracts from the Registers are of interest.

> "1626 April 27 Mathew Cleaton, mynister, and Eleanor Mynshull   [Married]
> "1626 July 13 Elizabeth, dau of Mathew Clayton, clerk " [Bapt]
> "1626 March 6 Katherine Jerram, wyfe to Steephen Jerram, *preacher of gods Word in this towne* " [Buried]

No other mention of *Matthew Clayton* has occurred   His successors at Nantwich, according to the following memoranda in the Burial Register, appear to have been—

PETER FROGG, c 1627

[*Mr*] PETER LEIGHE, *appointed* 13th July, 1627, *resigned* 1632

[*Mr*] THOMAS BOYSE, 1632—1633

[*Mr*] JOHN SARING, M A , 1633

Memd 1627 July That in this month *Peter Frogg* being *minister* in this towne, fallinge into extreame sicknesse departed away home voluntarilie, and afterwards was placed att Mynshull and there

---

* The term "*Gospeller*' was originally a derisive epithet applied to those who read the Scriptures to the unlearned poor   Gilbert Burnett, D D (Author of History of Reformation), in "*a Sermon preached on the Fast-Day* 22 Dec 1680, at St Margaret s, Westminster, before *the Honble House of Commons*   says, 'There were two things that were visible in the practice of those who first embraced the Reformation among us , the one was the great pleasure they took in reading the Scriptures, from whence they were in derision called "*Gospellers* "   When Bibles were first set up in Churches and went at such rates that ordinary people could not buy them   what a running was there to Churches, and what crowds gathered all day long about *such as could read*, to hear this blessed Word "

† Dr Ormerod's *Cheshire*, New Edit , vol iii, p 156

‡ History of Nonconformity in Cheshire, pp 164 and 477

dyed   And aboute the 13th daye of this month *Peter Leighe* was by the Churchwardens,* with the consent of the gent & others, placed mynister here during pleasure "

" *Mem^d* [1632 March] That att Michaelmas last past [29 Sep 1631] *Mr John Saringe* was hyred & entered to bee the aforenoone Preacher of gods worde att Namptwiche, as assistante to Mr PEELER LEIGHE "

[Signed] William Mainwaring, Gent ⎞
                      ⎬ Churchwardens
Thomas Walthall Gent ⎠

Mem^d That att Michaelmas this p^rsent year 1632 MR THOMAS BOYSE came to bee readinge minister at Namptwiche, and att Christmas *Mr Mainwaring*† schoolem^r went awaye to Wibunbury and *Mr Robert Symons* came to bee schoolemar in his place whome *Mr Boyse* doth assiste "

Of PETER FROGG, there is nothing further to relate

PETER LEIGH is believed, though it is not certain, to have left Nantwich in 1632 for Chester, where, during the Commonwealth period he appears to have been minister at St Oswald's, and afterwards at St John's.   Being ejected in 1662, he became Nonconformist minister at Knutsford ‡

The burial of MR BOYSE is recorded at Nantwich within nine months of his appointment as minister here

" 1633 June 8 Mr Thomas Boyse Minister at Nantwich buryed "

JOHN SARING, having been incumbent for ten years (1633—1643), suffered imprisonment and the loss of his goods during the Civil War troubles.   He was still a prisoner at Nantwich on the 8th Dec. 1646 (p 185), and, on gaining his liberty, "was forced to quit the country,' although he "was a very worthy man "§   His name will be found mentioned on several pages in this work

RICHARD JACKSON   1647-8 —Oct. 1677.

No account of the appointment of Richard Jackson is given in the Parish Register, but from the fact that the living of Nantwich was augmented by Parliament *c* 1648, by the Commissioners sitting at Goldsmith's Hall, London, for compositions with the Delinquents, (Sir Thomas Smith [of Hatherton] and Sir Thomas Delves [of Doddington] Knights), by which £50 per ann   went to Wybunbury and the rest [sum not stated] to Namptwich,"‖ it may be presumed that *Richard Jackson* was a Presbyterian parson appointed by the Parliament, against whose decision the parishioners, (who had successfully withstood Bishop Lloyd's attempt to force a clergyman on the town in 1605), would now, of course, be powerless   His name occurs in the list of signatures to the Cheshire " *Attestation*,' drawn up by the celebrated MR LEY, of Astbury, and subscribed at Northwich on 6th July, 1648, but in 1662, he must have conformed, for he continued to be

---

* The Churchwardens were *Thomas Malbon*, gent   and *Richard Huwar*, Apothecary   See also pages 126—134 for other mentions of the Church, Ministers, officers, repairs, &c

† *Mr Edward Mainwaring* succeeded *Thomas Tidman* as Schoolmaster at Wybunbury   and after the death of *Samuel Cole*, vicar of Wybunbury in July 1659   he appears to have been vicar until 1693, when on the 7th Dec he was buried as " minister of Gods Word and Vicar of Wybunbury "—*(Wybunbury Par Reg)*

‡ History of Nonconformity in Cheshire, pp 13 and 442   See also *Cheshire Sheaf*, vol ii, pp 101, 110, 121 and 162

§ Walker's *Sufferings of the Clergy*

‖ See Earwaker's   *Local Gleanings*," quarto series, Vol II, pp 170-1

Minister here until his death in 1677. Richard Jackson,* who was about twenty-eight years of age when appointed to the Curacy of Nantwich, married, and had issue a daughter, and two sons, (George) both of whom died in infancy

' 1651 April 26 Richard Jackson Minister and Margaret Broomhall " [Married]

" 1651-2 March 7 Anne dau of Richard Jackson, Minister [Bapt]

" 1656-7 March 10 George son of Rich Jackson, Minister " [Buried]

" 1663 Dec 20 George son of Ric Jackson Minister " [Buried]

" 1677 Oct 15 Mi Richard Jackson, Minister [Buried]

He died intestate, but an Inventory of his goods was taken on the 14th May, 1677; and administration granted to his widow, Margaret Jackson, on the 15th Dec 1677 A monument was erected to his memory within the Communion, and inscribed as follows —†

' Richard Jackson, minister of Nantwich 29 years, was interred on the 15'h Oct in the 57th year of his age *Anno* 1677 "

GABRIEL STRINGER   19 March, 1678—1690

Gabriel Stringer, Curate or Minister, was the first clergyman at Nantwich to receive institution from the Bishop, on the presentation of John Crewe, of Crewe, Esq ‡

He was the son of Gabriel Stringer, of the Red Lion [*now* Wilbraham's Arms] Inn, and had been Curate of Little Budworth in this county, from June, 1674. His marriage is recorded, but there is no mention of issue either in the Registers or in his Will

" 1679 80 Feb 24 Gabriell Stringer & Margaret Wicksted oy lic[ence] frm Chancellor Dated 19 ffeb "—[Par Reg Matrim]

Dr. Thos Cartwright, Bishop of Chester, in his " Diary " (Camden Soc. Publ) enters as follows —

" 4 Dec 1686 I wrote to Major-General Worden of making Mr Stringer of Nantwich my surrogate "

" 15 Dec 1686 Mr Gabriel Stringer, minister of Nantwich, sent me a cheese weighing 80 ℔s "

The will of Gabriel Stringer is of an interesting character. An abstract from the probate copy at Chester is here given

" In the name of God Amen 21 ffeb 1689 I Gabriel Stringer Minister of the parish of Namptwich, co Chester, [&c] doe make & ordeine this my Last will & Testament in manner following declaring that I dye in the Com'union of the Church of England & in vtter detestation of either Popery or Phinatisism [fanaticism] &c   and whereas I am possessed of three severall Cottages situate in the Beame Street in Namptwich the demise of the Right Honble Hugh Lord viscount Cholmondeley for Three Lives [&c] I give devise bequeath & Assigne the same to be habited Rent free by sixe poor widows if the same may be found and for Lack of such to the Antientest of the maides to make up that number the same to be Elected & Chosen from time to time of such as are or can be found in the Welsh Rowe in Namptwch by my Honrd & well beloved freinds Thomas Cholmondeley of vale Royall Esq   Charles Mainwaring of eightfeild [Ightfield] in co Salop Esq   Peter Wilbraham of Derfold Esq Roger Wilbraham of Namptwich Esq and their heirs or by my Exors [&c] *Item* my will is that the

* Richard Jackson, minister of Nantwich, is mentioned in Zach Crofton s " *Bethshemesh*," 4to London, 1653, p 228 A Richard Jackson, but whether the same individual or not, is uncertain, occurs as a member of Gonvil and Caius Coll Camb in 1641 2 (See Vol of *Protestations*)

† J W Platt's *History of Nantwich*, p 63

‡ See Roger Wilbraham's " *Towns Concernes*," p 210

s^d widows or other psons. so cohabiting in the s^d Houses shall have yearly pd. [paid] them by my s^d Executors the yearly sume of fforty shillings by Quarterly payments & Likewise at every Christmas each of them a Purple Russett Gowne [&c.]   *Item.* I give & Bequeath to my Deare mother Isabell Stringer my new wich-House in Namptw^ch which I lately built Together with three dossen Leades walling of their M^aties Inheritance which I have now in Lease for a considerable terme of yeares with the Rents & p'fitts thereof for the terme of her naturall Life shee paying the old Rent Reserved [&c.] and Likewise giveing & disposeing yearly during the time of Lent upon Wednesday & friday half a Crowne a day in Bread to the poore of ye s^d Towne of N. & after her death the aforesaid Gentlemen to dispose of the wich-house & walling for the putting poor children of the s^d Towne of N. (them of the Welsh Rowe having the preference) Apprentice or for the encouraging the Benefit of divine service to be Read in the week days by the minister of the s^d Towne of N. [&c.] or for the Instructing or Cattechising of such poor Children by ye s^d Minister vpon Wednesdays ffridays or Holydays.   *Item.* I give [&c.] to the Minister of the Towne of N. for the time being the sume of 20 sh. yearly for the preaching of two Sermons one on St. Paules day [Jan. 25] with Relation to Loyalty* & the other on the day of my funerall yearly encouraging Charity.   *Item.* I give [&c.] to my Brother Stephen Stringer & his wife each of them a Guinney to buy them Rings [&c.] to my sister Alice Wilkes 40 sh. [&c.] to my sister in law Sarah Stringer one broad peice of Gold.   *Item* to my Hon^red freinds Thomas Cholmondeley Charles Mainwaring Peter Wilbraham & Roger Wilbraham each of them a Guinney to buy them a Ring.   *Item* the Residue of my estate to my brothers John & Thomas Stringer [&c.] equally to be devided between them *&* whom I make executors [*&c.*] requesting them [*&c.*] to keep the Cottages Hansomly Repaired by nogging† with Brick [*&c.*]   In witness &c.

Gabriel Stringer."

The date of probate is 13th Aug. 1705; Gabriel Stringer having been buried at Nantwich on 1st July, 1690.—*(Par. Reg.)*

II. RECTORS.

PETER LANCASTER, M.A. 1690—1695.

Presented 11th Aug. 1690 by Anne Crewe Offley, on the death of Gabriel Stringer.

"1690. Aug. 20. Mr. Peter Lancaster, Minister, entered."—*(Par. Reg.)*

According to Anthony á Wood,‡ Peter Lancaster was the son of a clergyman in the bishopric of Durham.   He entered St. John's College, Cambridge; but left to enter Baliol College, Oxford, where he took his degree of B.A. 15th May, 1684, and M.A. 7th July, 1686.   He was twice married, his second wife being the daughter of John Lowndes, of Nantwich, glover.

"1692. Dec. 2. Prudence wife of Peter Lancaster clerke."—*(Burial Reg.)*
"1695. Oct. 21. Peter Lancaster cler. & Mary Loundes by Publicacon."—*(Marr. Reg.)*

He resigned the living of Nantwich on the 11th Oct. 1695, and became Rector of Tarporley in this county, being presented thereto by Sir John Crewe, Kt., of Utkinton, 12th Oct. 1695, which living he held till his death in 1709.   He was collated to the thirteenth Prebendary of the third Stall of Chester Cathedral, 2nd May, 1694, in which church he was buried without memorial, 17th May, 1709.   Having died intestate, administration of his goods was granted to his father-in-law, John Lowndes, on 15th June, 1709.

---

* St. Paul's Day, 1643-4, was the date of *Parliamentarian* victory at Nantwich.   (See Account of Civil War, p. 166).

† "*Nogging;*" a local word, meaning to fill up the interstices between the frame-work of a timber building."

‡ *Fasti Oxonienses,* 2nd part, p. 399.

He was the author of a *"Tract on the rights of the Clergy to exemption from road rates;"* and a translation from Greek into English of *"A Discourse of Envy and Hatred* in the first vol. of Plutarch's Morals. Lond. 1684."*

JOHN BRADSHAW, M.A. 1695—1711.

Presented on 15th Nov. 1695, by Anne Crewe Offley, on the resignation of Peter Lancaster.

> 1695. Nov. 29. Mr. John Bradshaw Minister entreth here."—*(Par. Reg.)*

He was educated at Emanuel College, Cambridge; and took his B.A. in 1686, and M.A. in 1700.

John Bradshaw, and Peter Lancaster (as Rector of Tarporley) both signed the "Loyal address of the Clergy of the Diocese of Chester to Queen Anne in 1704," congratulating the Queen on the successes of the English arms at Blenheim and Gibraltar.†

An order having been made on 22nd Feb. 1704, by the Governors of Queen Anne's Bounty, for ascertaining the value of Church livings throughout the country, John Bradshaw, on 10th Oct. 1705, certified Nantwich to be £10 per ann., excepting contributions. The Tithe Hay of one small lordship belonging to the *Rectory* was valued at forty shillings, and a *Library* was then founding, and being settled by the clergy of the Deanery. The following extracts from the Registers give information relating to his family.

> "1698-9. ffeb. 12, Jinny Dau. of John Bradshaw, minister." [Bapt.] (Buried March 2, 1699-1700).
> "1700. June 5. John son of John Bradshaw minister." [Bapt.]
> "1702-3. Jan. 14. Jinny dau. of John Bradshaw clerke." [Bapt.]
> "1704. July 24. Harcourt son of Mr. John Bradshaw Minister." [Bapt.] (Buried 1 Nov. 1704).
> "1711. July 21. Martha wife of Mr. John Bradshaw Minister." [Buried.]
> "1711-12. Jan. 5. Mr. John Bradshaw Minister." [Buried.]

GEORGE GIBBONS, M.A. 1711-2—1719.

Presented on 7th Feb. 1711-2, by John Crewe, of Crewe, Esq., on the death of John Bradshaw.

> "Mr. Geo. Gibbons was inducted March 6th 1711-2." *(Par. Reg.)*

He was educated at St. John's College, Cambridge; and took his B.A. in 1698, and M.A. in 1709. He married *Mary Hussey,* of Nantwich, at Peover, on 5th Feb. 1713-4—*(Nantwich Reg.)*; and in all the baptismal entries of his children, he is styled *Rector,* being the earliest mentions of that title in the Parish Registers.

> "1714. Nov. 19. George son of George Gibbons, *Rector* and Mary his wife." [Bapt.] (Buried 10 Aug. 1715.)
> "1715-6. Jan. 13. Mary dau. of &c. [similar to above] born 7th inst. and baptized 13th.
> "1716-7. Jan. 22. Samuell son of &c. born 14th baptized 22nd. (Died 31 March; buried 2 April, 1717.)
> "1717-8. ffeb. 27. Lucy dau of &c. „ 12th „ 27th. (Died 12 March; buried 14 March 1717-8.)
> "1718-9. ffeb. 5. Peter son of &c. „ 21st Jan. baptized 5th Feb.
> "1719-20. ffeb. 16. George son of &c. „ 12th baptized 16th.
> "1719-20. Mr. Geo. Gibbons, Rector, Dyed ye 25th & was buried ye 29th Feb.

THOMAS BROOKE, LL.D. 1720—1757

Presented on 27th June, 1720, by John Crewe, of Crewe, Esq., on the death of George Gibbons.

> 1720. July 8. "Mr. Thomas Brooke, Rector, entereth here."—*(Par. Reg.)*

Thomas Brooke was a son of Benedict Brooke, of Buglawton and Handforth, co. Cheshire, and was educated at Queen's College, Cambridge, where he took his B.A. in 1713, and M.A. 1717. He became LL.D. in 1732.

---

* *Fasti Oxonienses,* 2nd part, p. 399.　　　　　† Local Gleanings, Quarto Series, Vol. II, p. 83.

In addition to his Nantwich preferment he was installed *Dean of Chester* 18th July, 1732, and held the Rectory of Winslow, co Bucks, and that of Doddleston, co Cheshire, from 15th June, 1739

The building of a new Rectory house at Nantwich, to the expense of which, Partridge says, "the parishioners largely contributed," the erection of the South Gallery in the Church in 1727, and improvements in the Churchyard between 1735 and 1739, (see Annals p 217—221), are indications of great activity in the parish during the incumbency of this Rector

In 1722 Bishop Gastrell valued the living as follows —*

	£	s	d
Reserved out of the Easter Roll, belonging to Mr Crewe	4	13	4
Dwelling house and garden	3	0	0
House given by Mr Sparke [given in 1515]	0	10	0
Left by Mrs Arne Smith [given probably in 1681]	1	0	0
Compensation for t the hay in Alvaston [given 1719]	2	0	0
Tithe pigs, geese, hemp, and flax [given in 1639] †	1	0	0
Left by Roger Wilbraham [of Townsend] for reading prayers on Litany days (*Wednesday*) [given in 1700] ‡	5	0	0
Surplice Fees	10	0	0
Twelve lead wallings not to be certainly valued	—	—	—
Yearly contributions [not given	—	—	—
Total income of the Benefice	£27	3	4

Mr Partridge says, Dr Brooke "was an excellent preacher and a most amiable man," and gives an Elegy, probably original, on the Rector's death, (*Hist Nant* p 26-27) the following lines being an extract

> "Methinks I see him venerably great
> With form majestic fill the preacher's seat
> His voice, how charming! still, methinks, I hear,
> Ever distinct harmonious strong and clear
> His manly looks our free applause bespeaks
> Ere from his lips the flow of rhetoric breaks
> With wrapt attention his whole audience hang
> While heavenly truths seemed mended from his tongue"

A singular anecdote is told by Hemingway (*Hist of Chester*, Vol I, p 320), that the Dean "was so athletic a man as to be able to raise the great bell of Chester Cathedral without assistance, in which he was very fond of exercising himself"

Four published sermons are evidence of his learning and ability §

1 —" *The Perfection of God displayed in his Works, and the Obligation that ariseth to Us from a Consideration of them* "

"A Sermon, Preach'd in the Parish-Church of Nantwich   At the Florists Meeting there April 19 1731 By Tho Brooke, A M Rector of Nantwich London Printed for the Author, by T Wood

* Bishop Gastrell's "*Notitia Cestriensis*" (Cheth Soc Pub Vol VIII 1845)

† Margaret Woodnoth's and Elizabeth Davenport's gift in 1639

‡ "An Annuity of £5 p an out of land in Coppenhal to ye Minister of Nantwich for yᵉ reading the prayers appointed by yᵉ Church upon Litany Dates & Holy Dates by *Roger Wilbraham* [of Townsend Nantwich] anno 1700 ' (Extract from a Pocket Almanac, dated 1673, in possession of G F Wilbraham, Esq) This sum of £5 is still annually paid to the Rector

§ Copies of these Sermons are in the possession of John Downes, Esq, of Nantwich

in Little Britain MDCCXXXI   Price 1sh   Psal cxlv 10"
Dedicated "To the Gentlemen, Gardiners, and Others, Who attended the Florists Meeting"

2 —"*St Paul's Argument to Felix consider'd*"
"A Sermon Preach'd in the Cathedral Church of Chester, Sept 17th 1732   Being the Time of the
Assize there   By Tho Brooke LL D   Dean of Chester   London   Printed for the Author, by T
Wood, in Little Britain MDCCXXXIII   Acts xxiv 25"

3 —"*The Duty and Reward of Charity*"
' A Sermon Preached before the Rt Honble the Lord Mayor, [Westley] the Court of Aldermen, the
Sheriffs, and the Governours of the several Hospitals of the City of London, at the Parish Church of
St Bridget, on Tuesday in Easter-Week 1744 By Thomas Brooke LL D Dean of Chester   London
Printed for the Author, by Henry Woodfall, jun in Little Britain 1744   Psalm xli verse 1"

4 —"*The Pleasure and Advantage of Unity*"
"A Sermon Preached in the Cathedral Church of Chester, at the Assizes, Sept 2 1746, Before the
Honble Mr Sergeant Skinner, Chief Justice and the Honble John Talbot, Esquire, the other Judge of
the County Palatine of Chester   By Thomas Brooke LL D Dean of Chester   Printed London by
H Woodfall jun &c   Published at the Request of the High-Sheriff and the Gentlemen of the Grand
Jury, [whose names are thus given]

RALPH LEYCESTER, ESQ, *High-Sheriff*

THE RT HONBLE THOMAS, LORD VISCOUNT KILMOREY

SIR PETER DAVENPORT, KNT

LYNCH SALUSBURY COTTON, ESQ	CHARLES GORDON, ESQ	JAMES CROXTON, ESQ
THOMAS BRERETON, ESQ	JOHN BASKERVILE, ESQ	GEORGE LEGH, ESQ, of Outrington
PETER BROOKE, ESQ	THOMAS SWETTENHAM, ESQ	GEORGE GERRARD ESQ
PETER SHACKERLEY ESQ	THOMAS HUNT, ESQ	ROBERT CLOWES, ESQ
GEORGE LEGH, ESQ, of Tatton	GEORGE HYDE, ESQ	JOHN PINLOT, ESQ
FRANCIS JODRELL, ESQ	EDWARD WRIGHT, ESQ	JOHN DAVENPORT, ESQ
Psalm cxxxiii Verse 1		

His family register at Nantwich is as follows —

' 1721 April 15 Thomas son of Thomas Brooke Rector [Bapt]
1723 Octob 29 Ann dau of &c [Bapt]
1724-5 March 22 Mary dau of &c [Bapt]   (Buried at N 4 Dec 1725)
1726-7 ffeb 19 Samuell son of &c [Bapt]
1728 Sep 27 Robert Salusbury, son &c [Bapt]
1730-1 March 22 William son &c [Bapt]
1733 June 8 Benedict son &c [Bapt]
1736 May 30 Rhoea dau &c [Bapt]

Two other children, whose baptisms are not recorded here, were buried at Nantwich,
viz. —*Elizabeth*, on 8th March, 1721, and *Mary*, 31st Oct 1723.

Doctor Brooke s burial is thus recorded —

1757 Dec 20 *Thomas Brooke* LL D Dean of Chester, and Rector of this Parish buried in the Chancel "

The Registers also record the burial of his mother, *Mary Brooke*, on 8th Sep. 1747,
and of his widow, *Esther Brooke*, on 2nd April 1771   The family did not continue to

reside at Nantwich, and on the death of Robert Salusbury Brooke, Esq, of Chelford, in 1814, the family in the male line became extinct *

The names of three Curates in succession, (the Revs *Thomas Wettenhall, John Twemlow*, and *Thomas Adderley*) occur in the Registers, their presence being necessary when Dr. Brooke was non resident

JONES READE, D D   1758, Feb 19 —1769

Presented on 10th Jan 1758, by John Crewe, Esq, after the death of Dr Brooke. No record of Dr Reade's induction, nor, indeed, of any of his successors is preserved in the Parish Register, but the *"Act Book"* at Chester states that he received Institution on the 19th Feb 1758.

Dr. Reade graduated at Jesus College, Oxford; B.A. 16th Oct 1739, M.A. 19th June 1742, B D 26th May, 1749, and D D. 18th July, 1755

Nothing has occurred worthy of remark concerning this Rector, who held the living of Nantwich little more than eleven years

JOHN SMITH, B A   1769—1792

Presented by John Crewe, Esq, on the resignation of Jones Reade. Instituted 26th May, 1769

I cannot state, with certainty, at which University he was educated, several persons named John Smith occurring in the old Clergy Lists, contemporary at Oxford and Cambridge †   He was twice married

"1770 Dec 28 Jane the wife of John Smith Rector, buried at Wistaston"

"1779 May 21 Rev John Smith Clerk of this Parish & Mary Mears of Nantwich spinster" [Married]

He published a small book of Metrical Psalms and Hymns for occasional use in Public Worship, printed by E Snelson, of Nantwich. Enlarged editions were printed here in 1808, 1813 and in 1816, by A Fox, Nantwich. He also printed four Sermons

1 —"*A Vindication of the Freedom of Pastoral Advice*" &c.

"A Sermon preached in the Parish Church of Nantwich, on Sunday Sep 10, 1775, by John Smith A B Rector of the said Parish, from Gal IV 16   Nantwich Printed and sold by R Taylor and E Snelson, for the Author &c   Price Sixpence"

2 —"*The Nature of Christian Charity, or Love stated   its excellency proved   and the practice of it enforced*"

"A Sermon preached in the Parish Church of Nantwich, on Friday, Nov 24, 1780, before the Trustees of the Alms-houses founded by the late Sr E Wright, Lord Mayor of London, and the Governors of the Work-house, lately erected, within the said Parish   By John Smith A B Rector of Nantwich, 1 Cor xiii 13   Nantwich Printed by Edmund Snelson" &c

3 & 4 —"*Polygamy indefensible*"

"Two Sermons Preached in the Parish Church of Nantwich   By John Smith A B Rector &c   On Sunday the 10th of December 1780   Occasioned by a late Publication, entitled "*Thelyphthora*," to

* Mr Earwaker's *East Cheshire*, Vol II, p 367
William Brocke, Esq, of Hartford co Chester, died in or about 1798, his will being dated 10 Dec 1798
    Ann Brooke was married to Peter Walthall of Wistaston 1 March, 1764,—*(Nantwich Par Reg)* and died 26 Nov 1802, aged 79, being buried at Wistaston on the 2nd Dec 1802 —*(Wistaston Reg)*

† A portrait of the Rev John Smith, Rector of Nantwich, was engraved for the "*New Spiritual Magazine*" for 12th June, 1784, published by Alex Hogg 16 Paternoster Row   The Magazine contains no biographical notice of this Rector.

which is prefixed "A Letter to the Rev Mr Madan" Gen 11 24 Printed London, Alex Hogg, Paternoster Row, 1780 "

His burial is thus recorded in the Parish Register —*

"1792 Oct 20 Rev John Smith Rector of Nantwich, Aged 57 '

ANTHONY CLARKSON, M A 1793—1819

Presented by John Crewe, Esq , on the death of John Smith Instituted 2 Jan 1793.

He graduated at St Peter's College, Cambridge, B A 1770, M A 1776 Previous to his appointment to Nantwich, he had been at St Peter's Church, Derby, and had married a native of this town, Mary, daughter of William Watkiss, Esq , of Welsh Row, on 3rd Nov. 1778 —*(Par Reg)*

The return of small livings made by the Governors of Queen Anne's Bounty, Feb 13th, 1809, states the living of Nantwich "to be *not augmented* or *charged*, and of the yearly value of £106 3s 9d , arising from tithes, composition for tithes, surplice fees, stipend, rents, and official house ' †

The Rev. A Clarkson was buried at Nantwich on 10th March, 1819, aged 70 years, and his widow, who resided in Hospital Street, was buried on 1st Sept 1834, aged 86 — *(Par Reg)*

The following is an exact copy of a Request for Sequestration of Tithes preserved in the Diocesan Registry

"*To the R^t Rev Father in God William* [Cleaver] *by Divine permission Lord Bishop of Chester.*"

"The Petition of *Samuel Barrow* of Nantwich Esq , *Richard Smith* (nephew of the undermentioned John Smith) and *John Knight* of Whitchurch, in Salop, Gent , Whereas your Lordship having sequestered the Fruits Tythes and other profits of the Rectory of Nantwich, co Cest , to *Charles Hall James Read* (since deceased) & *Samuel Jackson* the then Wardens And we being desirous that a Sequestration of the same may now be granted to Us, that all possible care may be taken of the profits of the said Rectory for the use of the Revd John Smith the Rector thereof after paying the stipend assigned by your Lordship to the officiating Curate thereof & all other burdens incumbent on the said Rectory, do therefore pray that your Lordship would be pleased to grant Us a Sequestration of the said Rectory for the purposes aforesaid "

Dated April 28, 1792

SAMUEL BARROW
RICHARD SMITH
JOHN KNIGHT

[To which is added in the Bishop's handwriting]
"Granted May 16, 1792, WILLIAM CHESTER "

The first *Curate* licensed under this sequestration was *James Turner*, who was appointed Sep^t 23rd, 1792 It has not been thought necessary to give a complete list of licensed Curates , but the following names will be of interest

William Leversage, of Nantwich, M A , Brasenose College, Oxford. Appointed 1795. Buried at Nantwich 11th March, 1803

---

* The Parish Register from January to December, 1789, is signed "J Wilson, Offg Minister " who was afterwards incumbent of Donnington, co Lincoln, and married one of the daughters of the Rev John Smith She died at Donnington, 28th April 1809

† Dr Ormerod's *Cheshire*, Old Edit , Vol III, p 234

John Latham, B A , Queen's College, Oxon , from 25th Sept. 1796 , Stipend £40 per ann   Afterwards Rector of Baddiley

Thomas Brooke, B A , Christ College, Cambridge, appointed 1814 , afterwards Rector of Wistaston, from 25th May, 1825, until his death on 25th Feb 1873.

Rev. Will Godwin, A.M., 1817 , Stipend £75 per ann &c.

RICHARD HENRY GRETTON, M A   1819—1846.

Presented by John Lord Crewe, of Crewe, on the death of Anthony Clarkson. Instituted 28th April, 1819   He was educated at Clare Hall, Cambridge, taking his degree of B A in 1808 and M.A in 1812

During his incumbency dissent increased much in the town   The system of Church Rates was strongly opposed in noisy Vestry meetings; and the Rector was subject to so much annoyance that on 3rd Dec. 1844, he resigned this living, and accepted the Head Mastership of the Radcliffe Grammar School, at Stamford, co Lincoln , his brother, Rev Fred. Edw. Gretton, B D , being Rector of St Mary's in that town at the time   Finding, however, his duties there uncongenial, and the living of Nantwich still vacant, he sought re-institution , and on 15th March, 1845, he was presented by the Hon. Dame Emma Cunliffe Offley, the only daughter of John first Lord Crewe, and sister to John second Lord Crewe, who had died on 4th Dec. 1835   The Rev Robert Mayor Vicar of Acton, who had a few years before disputed the right of the Crewe family to the advowson of Nantwich, was now required by a Commission " from the Lord Bishop of Chester, dated 1st April, 1845, "*to qualify the Rev Henry Gretton Clerk to the Rectory and Parish Church of Nantwich,*" (*Act Book* Dioc. Registry) and accordingly Mr. Gretton was re-instituted on 10th April, 1845, and continued to be Rector here until his death, which took place on 1st Feb. 1846.

He was J P for this district.   His only published sermon was one preached in the Church on Monday, 7th Sept 1835, on the occasion of the first Anniversary of the Nantwich Temperance Society, 1 Cor. ix 25.   He married Frances, dau. of John Bennion, Esq , of Chorlton, on 22nd April, 1822, *(Par Reg)* but had no issue.   This Rector, his wife, and her four sisters, (maiden ladies* long resident in Nantwich), were interred in a vault in Malpas churchyard, in this county, where two flat stones, within high iron railings, are thus inscribed —

" Richard Henry Gretton, M A Rector of Nantwich, died Feb 1, 1846   Aged 60 years
" His wife daughter of John Bennion Esq of Chorlton, died Jan 5, 1848   Aged 70
Esther Bennion of Nantwich and formerly of Chorlton, died Jan 18, 1848   Aged 72
" Ellen Bennion, sister of the above, died Jan 20, 1848   Aged 69 years
" Mary Bennion, sister, died Oct 7, 1850   Aged 86
" Elizabeth Bennion, sister, died Feb 9, 1855   Aged 85

ANDREW FULLER CHATER, M.A.   1846—1872

Presented on 30th March, 1846, by the Hon. Dame Emma Cunliffe Offley, on the death of Richard Henry Gretton.   Instituted 6th April, 1846.

He was the son of the Rev. James Chater, who for twenty-two years "laboured zealously" (as stated in Mr J A Hine's *History of Christian Missions* from the Reformation to 1842) as a Baptist Missionary at Serampoor, Rangoon, and in Ceylon, and died

---

* They were great benefactresses to the Church and poor   The income of Nantwich benefice was increased to £285 per ann by the bequest of the last surviving sister

on his voyage home in 1828   James Chater helped largely in the translation of the Holy Scriptures into the Indian languages, and in 1815 published a Grammar of the Cingalese language, which was printed at the Government Press, Colombo, and dedicated to the Governor of Ceylon, Lieut. Gen. Sir Robert Brownrigg   Andrew Fuller Chater, so named after the distinguished divine Andrew Fuller, (who for many years was secretary to the Baptist Missionary Society), was born at Colombo, Sept 29th, 1814   He was educated first at Mr Harley's school in Chester, then at Lyde House School, Bath, under the Rev. Thos Hale, D D, Principal, for more than four years as a boarder, and was there awarded by the Examiners, the chief distinction, viz the Marquis of Salisbury's Gold Medal, and afterwards at Frome Sellwood Grammar School, under the Rev William Williams, Head Master.   In 1834 he entered King William's College, Isle of Man, as Assistant Classical Master, under the worthy Principal of the College, the Rev Edward Wilson, Fellow of St John's, Cambridge, and afterwards Prebendary of Lincoln Cathedral. He took his degree of B A. at Trinity College, Dublin, in 1842, as a Classical Moderator, and obtained the Silver Medal   After travelling on the Continent with his pupils, the sons of the late Solicitor General for Ireland, Mr Green, he was ordained Deacon by the Bishop of Cork in 1844 for the Curacy of Drumcondra, close to Dublin, and Priest in the following year by Archbishop Whateley, when he became a Curate of St Thomas', Dublin, under the Rector Archdeacon Magee, at which time the Rev Wm Connor Magee, the present Bishop of Peterborough, was chief Curate of St Thomas'   Andrew F Chater left this Curacy in 1846 for the Rectory of Nantwich, with the highest testimonials from the Archbishop, Archdeacon, and others   Being on a visit to his brother, the Rev D S. Chater,* Curate of Nantwich, at the time of Mr Gretton's death, the Rev A. F Chater, by request, preached the funeral sermon of the deceased Rector, and produced such a favourable impression in the town, that several persons at once interested themselves in obtaining him preferment, particularly Miss Diana Mainwaring,† sister to the late Sir Harry Mainwaring, of Peover, Bart., a lady who was the last descendant of the ancient family of *Wettenhall*, resident in this town, and who had great influence with the then patroness of Nantwich living

The Rev A F Chater, who became a Canon of Chester Cathedral, and Rural Dean of Nantwich, died at Bournemouth, co Hants, on 24th Jan 1872, and was interred in the Parish Cemetery at Nantwich   Over his grave has been erected a handsome stone tomb, representing an ancient sarcophagus, at a cost of £32 18s, raised by voluntary contributions at Church on Sunday morning, 4th Feb 1872, after the funeral sermon, preached from Heb xiii 7, by the Rev John Ellerton, M.A, Vicar of Crewe Green

The tomb is inscribed—

"𝔥ere rests in 𝔭eace 𝔗he 𝔅ody of 𝔄ndrew 𝔉uller 𝔠hater 𝔐.𝔄.
𝔯ector of this 𝔭arish: 𝔄fter he had served his generation, by
𝔗he 𝔚ill of 𝔊od he fell asleep 𝔍anuary 24 𝔄.𝔇. 1872, aged 57 years."

---

* The Rev Daniel Sutcliffe Chater was Curate of Nantwich from 1845 to 1847 and Head Master of Acton Grammar School near this town from 1848 to 1861 in which latter year he became Vicar of Blackawton co Devon   I am indebted to this clergyman for the above particulars relating to the parentage and education of his much esteemed brother

† Miss Diana Mainwaring died in Hospital Street on 5th Oct 1861, and was buried in the Parish Cemetery

When the Lord Bishop of Chester held his third Triennial visitation of the Diocese, in Chester Cathedral, Nov 1874, he remarked as follows concerning the late Canon Chater.

"Andrew Fuller Chater was singularly diligent and pains-taking in the discharge of all his Pastoral Obligations, through the twenty-six years of his being Rector of Nantwich During a visitation of Cholera under which that town suffered very severely, he truly *put his life in his hand*, and had his immediate and ample reward in the general and permanent improvement of its sanitary condition, which was then effected. Among other works which have followed him, he left his mark upon the Parish deep and strong, in the well and wisely managed Restoration of its remarkably fine Church ' — (*Nantwich Parish Magazine*, Dec. 1874).

Exception, however, must be taken to the last words of these, otherwise, just remarks of Bishop Jacobson The wanton way in which the monuments and flat tombstones in the Church were treated is evidence that *all* the "Restoration" work was *not* "well and wisely managed;" and it is now surprising that the whole parish did not rise and protest against this act of dishonour to the dead   With the exception of five tablets now in the Transepts, all the mural monuments &c were destroyed, and not even a written record of them preserved ! *

This "Restoration" commenced in 1855, extended over several years under the superintendence of the late Sir Gilbert Scott, Architect, and consisted chiefly of the removal of the pews and galleries of seventeenth and eighteenth century date, the lowering of the floor to the original level of the bases of the doors and pillars of the Nave, the fitting of the Nave and Transepts with carved oak seats, the raising of the roofs of the Transepts, the opening out of the flat plaster ceiling in the Nave, thus disclosing a good timber roof, and the scraping off accumulated layers of plaster and whitewash from the walls

The total cost of the "Restoration ' associated with the name of Canon Chater was £6,109 1s 2d, of which £4372 5s 9d was raised by subscriptions from the nobility and gentry in various parts of the country and by the Parishioners   Among the principal contributors to this fund may be mentioned — †

	£	s	d
The late Miss Bonnion of Nantwich	500	0	0
The Right Hon Hungerford Lord Crewe who restored the Chancel and filled the East			
Window with stained glass, at his sole cost, and in addition gave	200	0	0
The Most Hon the Marquis of Westminster	100	0	0
The Most Hon the Marquis of Cholmondeley	100	0	0
The Right Hon the Earl of Cottenham	25	0	0
The Right Hon the Viscount Dungannon	25	0	0
The Lord Bishop of London	10	0	0
The Lord Bishop of Chester	50	0	0
The Right Hon Lord de Tabley	5	0	0
George Fortescue Wilbraham Esq , who, in addition to the gift of the memorial stained			
glass in the South Window, gave	50	0	0
John Tollemache, Esq , M P (*now* the Right Hon Lord Tollemache)	50	0	0

* I am informed that when the plaster was being removed from the walls, and these memorials were carelessly thrown among the dust and *débris* that the Rector and others become alive to the destruction and attempted to save them , but no mention of the monuments, &c , having been made in the specifications, the contractor claimed them as materials !

† From the " List of Subscribers,' printed by E H Griffiths, Nantwich, 1862, copies of which are still to be had

NANTWICH CHURCH.

Wilbraham Spencer Tollemache, Esq , Dorfold Hall	25	0	0
Edward Delves Broughton, Esq	101	0	0
Rev A F Chater, Rector of Nantwich	205	0	0
John Downes, Esq , Nantwich	25	0	0
William O Foster, Esq , Stourton Castle	100	0	0
T P Lowe, Esq , Nantwich	50	0	0
J H Kent, Esq , Nantwich	50	0	0
William Church Norcup, Esq , Betton Hall	50	0	0
Randle Wilbraham, Esq , Rode Hall	20	0	0

The Church was re-opened on the completion of the Chancel by special services on the 8th and 9th Oct 1861,' the preachers being the Lord Bishop (Graham) of Chester, the Revs C J Vaughan, D D , Vicar of Doncaster, E Clayton, Rector of Astbury, and W H Egerton, Rector of Whitchurch, Salop.

FOSTER GREY BLACKBURNE, M A. 1872. (The present Rector)

Presented 15th Feb 1872, by Hungerford Lord Crewe on the death of A F Chater Instituted and inducted Rector by the Lord Bishop of Chester, on 12th March, 1872, in Nantwich Church

The Rev F G Blackburne is the son of the Rev Thomas Blackburne late Vicar of Eccles near Manchester and brother to the Rev Henry Ireland Blackburne, Rector of Warmingham, and belongs to the family of Blackburne of Hale co Lancashire   He graduated at Brasenose College, Oxon , B A 1861, and M A 1864, and was formerly Curate at Bebington, co Chester, 1864-7 , and of St Oswald's Chester, 1867-72, and Deacon of Chester Cathedral 1868-72   In recognition of his services there, he was appointed Honorary Minor Canon of Chester Cathedral, 25th June 1872, by the Dean and Chapter

The work of Church Restoration has been resumed by the present Rector. The West Window, by Gilbert Scott, Esq , not being approved of, the same architect designed another which was completed in 1875 at a cost of £300, and was filled with memorial stained glass by Clayton and Bell, at a further cost of £800   In 1876 the North Window was repaired at a cost of £100, and filled with stained glass by C E Kempe, at a further cost of £300   In 1877 the memorial (Martin) glass was added by Clayton and Bell.

From April to September in 1878 the South Porch underwent thorough repair, under the direction of Thos. Bower, Esq , architect, a native resident, and pupil of Sir Gilbert Scott, who had died on the 25th March in that year   The whitewash was removed from the interior walls, a groined roof added, and new floors laid down. The walls, windows, niches, gurgoyles, parapet and pinnacles, and the curious lean-to appendage of the exterior, (anciently used as a Priest's Chamber) were all repaired

In the following year the buttresses of the West front, the West windows of the North and South Aisles, a buttress on the east side of the South Transept, and the pinnacles of the Nave, were renewed in accordance with the old design

The entire cost of the work done in 1878-9 amounted to £1959 5s 3d , so that, within twenty-five years probably no less a sum than £10,000 had been expended in beautifying and repairing the fabric of this Church.

Monumental Inscriptions

NOW DESTROYED.

ESIDES the ancient monuments and inscriptions mentioned on pages 282, 284, 287; there were many others, together with shields of arms, hatchments, tables of Charities, &c., once in the Church, which have at various times been removed. Copies of them, and in some instances rough drawings, have been preserved in the Church notes in *Harl. MSS.* 2151; and in *Ashmo. MSS.* 854. Of these inscriptions, the principal ones were printed in 1819 by Dr. Ormerod;[*] who added to the list some of the later memorials then existing in the Church; but as no complete account of the monuments was taken before their ruthless destruction in 1855, it is impossible to say, exactly, how many of them remained in the Church at that time. A chronological arrangement of the old monuments, classified according to the families they memorialized, is here given from the above sources.

Maisterson Monuments.

On the south side of the Chancel, between the Altar-rail and the south door, was an altar tomb of alabaster, with an incised marble top representing the figures of JOHN MAISTERSON, and his wife, MARGARET, the daughter of William Bromley, of Dorfold, Esq., each with their hands joined in prayer. The drawing of the tomb in *Harl. MSS.* indicates (between their heads) a shield of arms—*Maisterson* impaling *Bromley;* and round the edge of the tomb the following inscription:—

"Here lyeth the body of John Maisterson, gent., together with Margaret his wife; which John and Margaret had issue Margaret, who marr. to Rondulph Stanley of Alderley: which John died x Dec. M.DLXXXVI." [1586].

Nearly in the middle of the incised slab, the two figures are cut across by two parallel lines, between which is the following verse in black letter—[†]

"Within this fadinge tombe sepulted lyes
John Maisterson and Margaret his wyfe,
Whose soules do rest above the vaulted skies
In paradice with God, the lord of lyfe.
Which John wrought meanes to build this Namptwiche towne
When fire had frett her face, and burnt her downe."[‡]

Above this tomb, "in a frame near the atchievements of the family" was suspended the following quaint metrical inscription, which, together with the tomb, was destroyed in 1855.

"An Epitaph vppo' ye Death of John Maisterson, Gen 1586.

Nowe Malbank mourne, lament your losse, lay mirthe asyde, be sade,—
Lett fall your straeninge siluer tears for him that made you glade
Your Joy and Jewell wears to duste, his bones are clad in clay,
Your Piller and your Proppe is gone gone is your gemne and stay
The turrett trewe and steedfast towre is battred to the grounde,
The captane cheefe of all the charge, dead in the campe is founde
Traile downe youre Ensignes and retire, the steede hath loste his breathe
Lett trumpet r sound, strike one tne drum, the dumpe of dreedfull deathe
Fowle of youre scattringe shott at ones, dragg on your pearring picke,
Close up youre gates, shutt up youre doores, you neuer saw the like
Pull downe youre hangings and begene to attire youre walls with blake
Send forthe youre greefed sighes, youre happe is gone to wreack
This dismall day canicular, one this tenthe day of December
Your towne was burnde, your frend did die that was youre cheefest member
Youre extreame losse he did repaire, he wypte youre tears away,
But now youre glorie and youre gain, shall be no more youre stay
John Maisterson hathe chaunged his life, to Malbanke heanie greefe,
Good channge to him, hard channge to them that felt his sweete releife
Unto the poore he franckly gaue, the needie shall him wante,
To those that lacke, his happie hand was neuer proued scante
When this poore Towne to ashes fell, deuourde with firie flame,
Bv pittie moued, he founde the way, howe to repare the same
Whoe by the grace of our good Queene, and nobles of this land,
This poor Towne was builte up againe, in state as it dothe starde
The timber had els growing in woods, which nowe sweete dwelings are,
Soe had the seats and plotts of ground, remain'd to this day bare
Had he not bin, this Towne had bin noe Towne as nowe it is,
That which he had, he did procure, the trauaille all was his
His deeds weell doone noe faute can foyle nor deathe the same expell
Nor ruste nor tonge can tuch his life, nor furies slaignt can quell
Nor thoghe that deathe dothe put downe life, & nature yealds her dewe,
Yete this Towne shall from age to age his Pearles fame renew
The liuing and the unborne tow, and all that snall sucseede,
The roofes and walls shall blase his fame, for this his worthy deede
His endless labour in this case deserues an endless crowne
With goulden garlands of great thankes, and wraythes of high renoune
The Soun shall witness of his woorks, suruayde with his bemes so brighte
Soe shall the moone and statly stars, that vewe the same by nighte
And all good hearts shall yeald him prayse and moniment his name,
And so long as the world endures shall spread abroad his fame "

On the North side of the Chancel were two painted tablets, with the following inscriptions in Roman capitals, and shields of arms

"HERE BENEATH LYETH YE BODY OF THOMAS
MASTERSONE OF WICH MALBANK, ESQ WHO FIRST
MARRIED FRANCES, COHEYRE TO SIR JOHN DONE
OF UTKINTON, KT, BY WHOM HE HAD ISSUE 2
SONES & 2 DAUGHTERS, WCH ALL DYED YONGE
AFTER HE MARRIED MARY DAUGHTER TO THO
MAINWARING OF MARTIN, ESQ AND HAD ISSUE
MARY, RICH & KATHERINE YT ALL DYED YONGE,
THOMAS, ROBT JOHN, ELIZABETH, MARY, KATH-
RINE, FRANCES, BRIDGET, MARGRETI & HELLENA,
ALL NOW LIVINGE, YE SAID THO DYED ON THE
16TH DAY OF FEBRUARY AN° D NI 1651 "*

ARMS Two shields, (1) *Maisterson* impaling *Done,* and (2) *Maisterson* impaling
Mainwaring

MAISTERSON has six quarterings in each.
1 *Maisterson,* 2. *Mainwaring* (a crescent
sable for difference), 3 *Blundeville,* earl of
Chester, 4 *Lupus,* 5 *Praers,* 6 Azure, three
bugles Argent, strung Gules

The impalement of DONE has six quarterings. 1 *Done,* 2 *Kingsley,* 3. the forest of
Delamere s badge, 4. *Legh* of East Hall
5. *Alpraham,* 6 *Weever*

The impalement of MAINWARING has ten
quarterings 1 *Mainwaring,* 2 *Blundeville,*‡
3 *Lupus,* 4 *Praers,* 5 *Glegge,* 6 *Sutton,* 7
Azure, a lion rampant Argent [*Crewe*],‡ 8
Merton , 9 . , 10 as 1 ‖

"HERE BENEATH LYETH YE BODY
OF THOMAS MAISTERSON OF
WICH MALBANKE, ESQ, WHO MARRIED MARY,
DAUGHTER TO THOMAS PALMER OF MARSTON, IN
YE COUNTY OF STAFFORD, GENT, BY WHOM
HEE HAD ISSUE TWO SONNES AND ONE DAU-
GHTER, THO RICH AND MARY, ALL
NOW LIVEING THE SAID THO DI-
FD ON THE 7TH DAY OF APRILL
A° D NI 1669 '†

ARMS *Maisterson* impaling *Palmer,* Argent,
on two barrs Sable, three trefoils slipped
Argent, 2 and 1, in chief a greyhound
courant Sable, for difference a mullet
Sable

CREST on a wreath a greyhound seiant
Sable, on the shoulder a trefoil as in the
arms

Near the above were two shields of arms, with the initials and dates, R M 1617,
and E M 1626; the memorials of RICHARD MAISTERSON, and his wife, ELIZABETH
MAISTERSON the daughter of Sir Thomas Grosvenor, of Eaton, Kt *(Harl MSS)*§ These
were not mentioned by Dr Ormerod

On the stone Pulpit, a brass with inscription, and the arms of Leech and Dawson,
quarterly, viz —1 and 4, Ermine, on a chief indented Gules an annulet between two
ducal coronets Or, *(Leech),* 2 and 3, Azure, on a bend engrailed Argent three daws
Sable, *(Dawson)* ¶ The brass remained affixed to the pulpit in 1795,*⁎ and its exact

* " 1651 Feb 18 Thomas Maisterson Esq —*(Bur Reg)*
† " 1669 April 9 Thomas Maisterson Esq "—*(Bur Reg)*
‡ *Cf* page 53
', The arms of this monument will be found fully described in *Gent Mag* 1805, part 2, p 706, from Church notes
taken in 1795
⎧ ' My Cosen Rich Maisterson died 21 Oct 1617 —*(Thos Wilbraham s MS Journal)*
§⎨ " 1617 Oct 23 Richd Maisterson Esqr '—*(Bur Reg)*
⎩ " 1626 Mar 1 Elizabeth Maisterson widowe "—*(Bur Reg)*
¶ Cheshire Visitation 1580 Harl Soc Publ p 137   *⁎ Gent Mag for 1805 p 706

position is indicated in an engraving of the pulpit given as frontispiece to Platt's History of Nantwich, 1818; at which time, however, another brass had been substituted, inscribed thus —"This burying place, which was formerly the Leighs', [*sic* for Leech's] belongs to Sir John Chetwode, of Oakley, Bart, being three yds. and a half broad as it is now Meered out."[*]

The original brass was inscribed as follows —[†]

"𝕳𝖊𝖗𝖊 𝖑𝖞𝖊𝖙𝖍 𝖇𝖚𝖗𝖞𝖊𝖉 𝖙𝖍𝖊 𝖇𝖔𝖉𝖞 | 𝖔𝖋 𝕵𝖔𝖍𝖓 𝕷𝖊𝖈𝖍 𝖑𝖆𝖙𝖊 𝖔𝖋 𝖙𝖍𝖎𝖘 𝖙𝖔𝖜𝖓𝖊 𝖔𝖋 𝕹𝖆𝖒𝖕𝖙𝖜𝖎𝖈𝖍, 𝖌𝖊𝖓. 𝖜𝖍𝖔 𝖉𝖊𝖕'𝖙𝖊𝖉 | 𝖙𝖍𝖎𝖘 𝖑𝖎𝖋𝖊 𝖙𝖍𝖊 𝖑𝖆𝖘𝖙 𝖉𝖆𝖞 𝖔𝖋 | 𝕸𝖆𝖗𝖈𝖍 𝖎𝖓 𝖙𝖍𝖊 𝖞𝖊𝖆𝖗𝖊 𝖔𝖋 𝖞𝖊 | 𝖎𝖓𝖈𝖆𝖗𝖓'. 𝖔𝖋 𝖔𝖚𝖗 𝖉𝖔𝖒. 𝕷.𝖃. | 𝖔𝖓𝖊 𝖙𝖍𝖔𝖚𝖘𝖆𝖓𝖉 𝕮𝕮𝕮𝕮𝕮𝕏𝕮𝖁𝕳𝕳𝕳." [1598][‡]

Crewe Monument.

At the east end of the South Aisle of the Nave, was a carved marble monument fixed to the wall, which was taken down in 1729, when the South Gallery was erected A rough sketch in *Harl. MSS.* 2151 represents a figure kneeling under an arch, with two shields, (1) *Crewe,* (2) *Crewe* impaling *Mainwaring,* and this inscription.—

Johannes Crewe	
ex antiquâ familiâ de Crewe	
oriundus, vir pius,	*(Translation)*
susceptam ex Alicia	John Crewe descended from the ancient family
Maynwaring uxore reliquit	of Crewe, a pious man, left issue, by Alice Main-
sobolem Ranulphum,	waring his wife, Ranulphe, Thomas, Lucretia,
Thomam, Lucretiam, Prudentiam	and Prudence He lived 74 years, and died in
Vixit annos 74, obiit	the year of our Lord 1598 [‖]
anno Domini 1598	

Clutton Monuments

On the north-west tower-pier were three tablets. The *first,* a shield of arms with initials and date, the *second,* a Latin inscription, imperfectly or wrongly transcribed in *Harl. MSS.,* the *third,* an inscription, part of which was legible in 1819.

[1] "The Arms of R C 1610"[§]

[2] "Tho Clutton ⁑ sepultus est, 19 Sep ano 1628 "[¶]

[3] "Here underneath lyeth burd the bo[dy] of ELIZ eldest dau unto Rich[ard] Clutton of this town, gent, deceased, & late wife of I HO MALBON of Bradley, gent, who dep'ted this life 21 day of March haueing had issue by the same Tho 2 sonnes & 7 dau 1622 "[*]

---

[*] Platt's History of Nantwich, p 32

[†] *Harl* and *Ashmo MSS*

[‡] His burial is entered thus —"1598 April 1 John Leeache gent "—*(Nant Reg)*

[‖] The Register of John Crewe s burial has been given on page 36

[§] Argent, a chevron Ermines, cotised Sable, between three annulets Gules —(Chesh Visit 1580 Harl Soc Pub, page 67)

"Richard Clutton my cosen died 15 day of Nov 1610 "—*(Wilb MS Journal)*
"1610 Nov 16 Richard Clutton Gent a Laweyer "—*(Bur Reg)*

[¶] "My cosn Tho Clutton dyed 17 Sep 1628 "—*(Wilb. MS. Journal).*
"1628 Sep 19 Thos Clutton, gent "—*(Bur Reg)*

[*] "Cozen Eliz Malbon died 21 March 1622 '—*(Wilb MS Journal)*
"1622 March 23 Elizabeth wife of Thos Malbon, Gent '—*(Bur. Reg)*

Minshull Monuments.

These were situated at the East end of the North Aisle of the Nave; "On a little mon* on the piller on the back of the pulpit." (Not mentioned by Dr. Ormerod)

" In sacra sacræ virginis memoria' Margarettæ Minshull expirantis 22 Aug 1616	*(Translation)*—Sacred to the memory of the holy virgin Margaret Minshull who died 22 Aug 1616
Virgo spousa fulgetra tibi nupta vocarer	A virgin spouse by lightning slain
Mortua sum, moriens, virginitate fruor	I gave my troth to thee in vain
Nupta tamen christo, sum virgo, spousa marita	'Twas mine to die a wife and maid,
Virgo mihi, tibi sum, spousa, marita deo "	And thus within this tomb be laid
	Yet I in Christ have placed my choice
	And will in him my Lord rejoice
	A maiden to myself and thee
	My only spouse the Lord shall be *

Rough sketches of the next two mural tablets are given in *Harl MSS* The pedigree monument had carved pillars, heraldic shields, cherubim with expanded wings, &c, but both were almost wholly concealed by the North Gallery from 1765 to 1855, in which latter year they were destroyed

[1]

" To the memory of RICHARD MINSHALL,† son and heire of Mr Thomas Minshall, of this Towne of Nantwiche He married *Elizabeth*, daughter of Richard Wilbraham of Lincolnes-inn, Esq son and heyre of Mr Richard Wilbraham of this towne He lived wonderfully beloved, being a most sweet, affable, pleasant and generous na`ure, upright in his dealings, charitable to the poore, and a great lover and maker of peace

He died very piously upon the 17th day of February 1637, being the 56th year of his age, leaving behind him no child, but his good name, which his most dear, and sorrowful wife here registers in his deserving character

I wish so longe a peace unto thine urne
As till it harbour such another guest.
If so, untill the world to ashes turne
Thy ashes will unrak'd be like to rest "

ARMS *Minshull* impaling *Wilbraham*

Both Richard Minshull and his wife were buried in the Wilbraham burial place in

[2]

GEOFFREY MINSHULL, ESQ ,§ in due respect to his ancestors hath erected this monum*

NICHOLAS MINSHULL, a second brother of the house of Minshull, marr with *Alice*, dau of *Yewen Clutton*, by whom he had issue, YEWEN, who marr. with *Jane*, daug of *James Calveley* of Peckforten, by whom he had issue EDWARD, who marr *Margaret*, dau of *Hugh Mainwaring* of Namptwiche, who died on 2 Dec. 1557, and left behind him GEFFREY, who marr with *Ellen*, daug of *Wm Bromley* of Dorfold, who died upon St Stephen's day [26 Dec] 1603,‡ being aged 64, and left behind him EDWARD, JOHN, RICHARD, RANDLE, MARGARET and ELIZABETH

EDWARD marr with *Margaret*, daug of *Thos Mainwaring*, of Namptwiche, who died upon Tuesday morning, 17th January 1627,|| being aged 68, and had issue GEFFREY,§ EDWARD, MARGARET, and ELLEN Margaret died a mayd upon Thursday morning, 22nd Aug 1616 being aged 20

GEFFREY marr with Mary dau of Sir Edwd

---

* For this translation I am indebted to the kinduess of Wm Beamont, Esq , of Orford Hall
" 1616 Aug 23 Margaret daughter of Edward Mynshull Gent "—*(Bur Reg)*
† " 1637 Feb 20 Mr Richard Mynshull "—*(Bur Reg)*
‡ " 1603 Dec 28 Geffrey Minshull, mercer "—*(Bur Reg)*
|| " 1627 Jan 21 Edward Minshull, Gentleman "—*(Bur. Reg)*
§ " 1668 Dec 1 Geffrey Minshull of Stoake, Esq "—*(Bur. Reg)*

the South Transept, where were two flat gravestones, with a brass plate engraved with their arms and names. (*Ashmo MSS* Vol. 854, p. 310).

RICARDUS MINSHVLL OBIIT 17 FEB. A.D. 1637.

ELIZABETH MINSHVLL UXOR RICHARDI. A D. 1658

Fitton of Gawsworth, bart., and had issue now living Edward, Richard, Thomas, Anne, Jane, Margaret, Mary and Ellen"

"Within this glasse a patterne you may see
Of human change, and tyme's mortalitie
In vaine it were t'expresse this place hath tride
Their birth, their breeding, how they liv'd and died

To the memory of GEFFREY MINSHULL of Stoke (Acton parish) Esq. who set up the above Pedigree Monument, a tablet was afterwards placed in the same North Aisle, and in the same words as the concluding sentence of the above inscription, only that it was written in Latin, and of course gave the date of his death, viz. "27 Nov. 1668 Æt 76."

Mainwaring Monuments.

On the east wall of the South Transept, were four mural tablets (with armorial shields) inscribed as follows —

[1]

"A breviat upon the life and death of RANDULPH MAINWARING, gent, who departed this life the 18th day of February, anno 1610, and was buried on the 19th day of the same month, ætat sui 77"*

[2]

"Here lyeth interred the bodies of WILLIAM MAINWARING† of Wich Malbank, gent, who died on the 22nd April, anno 1637, and also Martha his wife, daughter to Thomas Mainwaring of the same place, gent She died on 7th Septr 1658, leaving issue only one daughter, Anne, wife to *John Brock*, gent both now liveing"

[3]

"Here lyeth the bodyes of MATHEW MAINWARING‖ of Wich Malbank gent, who married *Margrett*, daughter to Thomas Minshull of the same place, gent, and had issue 14 children He died [? was buried] on the 19th day of Jan 1651, and she died [? was buried] on the 21st of Oct 1652"

[4]

"Anna uxor Johannis Brock | generosi, filia atq. hæres | Gulielmi Mainwaring de Wico Malbano | generosi, hic jacet sepulta obiit quarto die | Decembris a° Dom 1666"

(Translated)—Here lies entombed, ANN wife of John Brock, gentleman, daughter and heiress of William Mainwaring of Wich Malbank, gentleman, she died on the 4th Dec in the year of our Lord 1666 ‡

---

* "1610 Feb 19 Rondulph Mainwaring Gent Dyed at age of 77 "—*(Bur Reg)*
† "1637 April 24 Mr William Mairwaringe "—*(Bur Reg)*
 "1658 Sep 9 Mrs Martha Mainwaringe "—*(Bur Reg)*
‡ "1666 Dec 6 Ann wife of John Brock, Gent "—*(Bur Reg)*
‖ "1651 Jan 19 Matthew Mainwaringe gent "—*(Bur Reg)*
 "1652 Oct 21 Mrs Margaret Mainwaringe wid '—*(Bur Reg)*
Of the first three tablets to the Mainwaring family, none were in existence in 1803, according to Mr Bowman's letter to Mr Joseph Hunter, mentioned on page 310 *note* But the fourth is mentioned by Dr Ormerod as being still in the Church in 1819, and it may probably have remained until 1855

Besides the above monuments, were several hatchments, (not mentioned by Dr. Ormerod), with initial letters and dates, as follows —

"Tho manwaring 1638" ["Thomas Manwaring Gent in the Beame Street, 11 Aug 1638"— (*Bur Reg*)]

"I M   1597"   ["Judith wiffe of Rodger Manwaring, gent 2 July 1597."—(*Bur Reg*)]

"R M   1622"   ["Mr Roger Manwaring Post Maister 12 April 1622"—(*Bur Reg*)]

"B M   1637"   ["Mris Bridget Manwaring wief of Mr Arthur Manwaring 21 Feb 1637." (*Bur Reg*)]

"T M   1645"   ["Thos Mainwaring, Gent, 15 Feb 1645"—(*Bur Reg*)]

"I M   1638"   .   ["John Manwayring gent, Hospell St 3 Jan 1638"—(*Bur Reg*)]

"H M   1621"   ["Mr Hugh Manwaring of the Crowne Gent Ap 4, 1621"—(*Bur Reg*)]

"G M   1641"   ["Geo[rge] son of Thomas Mainwaringe Gent 5 Feb 1641"—(*Bur. Reg*)]

Church Monuments, in the Lady Chapel.

[1]. In 1663 Elias Ashmole wrote—"In the East corner of the North Cross" [*i e* Lady Chapel] "hangs a large Tablet, whereon is painted the Pictures of an old man & an old woman to the Brest, with these Armes (*Church* impaling *Mainwaring*) ouer their heads; & under the pictures this Epitaph" A rough drawing of these portraits is given in *Harl MSS* 2151, and Dr Ormerod described them as "an aged male and female figure holding up their hands in prayer, both having large ruffs, the man has a venerable beard and red cap edged with lace, the female a close cap and high-crowned hat."

> "Here under lyes the body
> of Thomas Church, gent
> Aged 71, who married Anne
> daughter of Thomas Mainwaring,
> gent and dye' the 6 of July
> anno 1634"

ARMS Argent, a fesse engrailed Sable, between three greyhounds heads erased, Sable, collared Or, *(Church)*, impaling *Mainwaring*, a mascle for difference

The Burial Register records as follows —"1635 July 8th Mr. Thos Church" This discrepancy, and the probable error in the age here given, will be noticed in the account of the Church family. The painting hung in the Lady Chapel until the "Restoration" of the Church in 1858. What became of it, is not now known.

[2]. Next was a tablet with the Arms of *Church* impaling *Wilbraham* with this inscription —

"Ricardus Church, filius et hæres Ranulphi Church, gen qui duxit Elizabetham filiam Thomæ Wilbram gen Vixit annos 43 Obiit 21 Oct 1637 obiit autem illa 19 Jan 1638, et reliquerunt sex filios viventes, et quatuor filias defunctas"

(Translated)—RICHARD CHURCH, son and heir of Ranulph Church, gentleman, who married Elizabeth daughter of Thomas Wilbraham, gentleman He lived 43 years He died on the 21 Oct 1637 * She also died on the 19th Jan 1638, and left six sons now living and four daughters deceased

---

* Thomas Wilbraham s MS Journal states as follows —

"My Cos Rich Church of hospell street died 21 Oct 1637"

And the Burial Register —

"1637 Oct 23 Mr Richard Church of the Townsend" [*i e* Hospital street-end]

[3] A gravestone under the "steeple" *(Harl. MSS.)* inscribed "Tho Church 1652."*

[4]. Above the crown of the arch that divides the North Transept from the Lady Chapel, is a wood tablet inscribed with capital letters (written from left to right) as follows:

"RICHARD CHURCHE MERCER GAVE THIS BEAME"

Probably this was Richard Church, the builder of Church's Mansion, who contributed to the flat, panelled, oak ceiling of the North Transept, which was erected in 1577, according to another inscription on wood, still existing in the same roof (See page 294).

Wright Monuments,

consisting of two flat gravestones in the North Transept, and a tablet with a coat of arms of ten quarterings, given in the *Harl* and *Ashmo MSS*

[1] "Richard son of Robert Wright gentleman, was buried on 31st day of March anno dni 1652"

[2] "Elizabeth dau & coheire to Tho Maisterson Esqi late wife to Capt Robert Wright of Wich Malbank died on the 26th day of March 1653'†

On the South-east tower pier was a Monument having this inscription *(Ashmo MSS.* Vol 854, p. 309).

"In memory of HUGH DAVEN | PORT second son of Sr John Daven | port of Davenport Knight & ELIZABETH his wife one | of the two co-heirs of Rich | ard Wright of Namptwich gen | & of RALPH WOODNOTH‡ second son | of John Woodnoth of Sha | vington Esq & MARGARET | his wife the other coheire | of the said Richard & also of RALPH WOODNOTH | the only child of the | said Ralph & Margaret | all wᶜʰ persons lye interred | underneath & neere this | Monument 8 Nov 1654"

"At the top of the Monument are these Coates"

(1) *Davenport* impaling *Wright*

(2) *Woodnoth* impaling *Wright*

Special interest attaches to this monument, which is not mentioned by Dr Ormerod as existing in 1819, though it was certainly there in 1795 (see *Gent Mag* 1805 part 2, p 706-7), from the fact that the two ladies mentioned thereon conveyed, in 1639, certain tithes to the preaching Minister of Nantwich, (see page 288). The date on the monument indicates the time when it was set up. Thomas Wilbraham, Esq, in his MS. Journal, says, "*My Cosⁿ Hugh Davenport dyed 17 Ap 1630*," and from family papers now in the possession of G F Wilbraham, Esq, it appears that Hugh Davenport, by permission, was interred in the Wilbraham Burial place in the South Transept; and beside him his widow, *Elizabeth Davenport,* was buried in 1653 by the permission of Roger Wilbraham, Esq Another entry in Wilb MS Journal, records the death of Ralph Woodnoth junior, thus —

"*My young cos Raphe Woodnoth died 13 Aug. 1638,*"

* "1652 April 11 Thomas son of Mr Saboth Churche "—*(Bur Reg)*

† Their burials occur in the Registers, as follows —
" Richard sonne of Captᵘ Robert Wright 31 March 1652 " [Buried]
" Elizabeth wife of Captayne Robert Wright 28 March 1653 " [Buried]

‡ A pedigree of the Woodnoth family of Shavington, from the time of William the Conqueror until King James I, will be found in Dr Ormerod s *Cheshire,* vol iii p 506 (New Edit) It is stated in Lyson s *Cheshire,* p 831, that the family became extinct in 1637 This is inaccurate for Jonathan Woodnoth, who was an attorney-at-law and agent to Sir Ranulphe Crewe, conveyed the Shavington estate to Thomas Turner, of Barthomley, yeoman, in Oct 1661 The last known member of the family was another Jonathan Woodnoth (grandson of the said Jonathan) who became chargeable to Shavington in the year 1707, a payment having been made to him by the Overseers of the township of £1 7s for clothing

His father, *Ralph Woodnoth*, having pre-deceased him in 1635, and his mother, *Margaret Woodnoth*, surviving him until 1649; to whose memory a "Marble gravestone was placed at the entrance into the Chancell," inscribed —

"MARGARETA UXOR | RADOLPHI WODNOTII | SEPULTA 8° die Junii | 1649."—*(Ashmo MSS)*

Consistent with these remarks the Burial Register records as follows

' 1630 Ap   16   Hughe Davenport Esquier, buryed '
' 1635 Dec 20   Mr Raphe Woodnothe of the Bell "
" 1638 Aug 17   Raphe Woodnoth, gent, of the Bell "
" 1649 June 8   Mris Margaret Woodnoth widowe '
" 1653 Oct 30   Mris Elizabeth Davenport widdowe '

Dr. Ormerod mentions "a memorial [in the Lady Chapel] of THOMAS WICKSTED Esq (died Jan 11th 1769, aged 60) and of GRISSEL his wife, only daughter of Charles Fletcher of Wigland Esq. died Aug 18, 1784, aged 82)."[*]

Other memorials mentioned in *Harl. MSS* 2151 are as follows —

(1)   John Bradwall minister of Nantwich (See page 296)

(2)   "On graue stones in the higher end of the Chancell,"

"Here lyeth the body of Richard Walthall gen who died the 13 day of Jan 1623 "[†]
"The same on a brasse on' [over] the com'[munion] table," together with two shields, rough drawings of which are given

(3)   "On a table[t] by the stone pulpit," the arms of "Woode of Dorington 1635."[‡]

(4)   "On a Tablet fixt on the Rood Loft," *Ashmo. MSS* 834, p 308).

"Here lyeth Interred the body of ANNE late wife to Jo[hn] DELUES, gent., by whom she had issue 3 sons & 3 dau wch Anne was ye dau of Hugh Mainwaring the sore of John, who im'ediately desc[ended] fro[m] Hugh the seventh sone of Randle Manwaring of Carincham Esq She finshed her mor'all course Feb 23 Ano redempcionis nre 1636 ætat sui 41 "[||]

(5)   "On a stone in the middle of the Chancell ."

"Under this stone lyeth Interred | the body of Captaine George | Beckit son of Geo B of Soo | [? Sound] yeoman burd nouemb 18 | 1644 '

(6)   On a gravestone "in the steeple part "

"Here lyeth ye bo[dy] of Leut Rich Radmore who was slaine at Ravensmore ye 9th of May 1645 "[§]

(7)   "Here interd lyeth the body of mris Kate Golborne | wife of mr Rich Golborne of Chester she died sept | 18 [? 8] 1645 '[¶]

(8)   ' Frances interd to Peter Leigh of High Legh | in the county of Chester esq wife to Will | Edwards Alderman of Chester buried | 28 April 1645 "[.*]

(9)   ' Under this stone lyeth the body of John | Clife gen who was once a cittizen | of London, & was interred the 29 | of March ano 1645 "[††]

---

* '1769 Jan 11 Thomas Wicksted "—*(Bur Reg)*
"1784 Aug 21 Grissell widow of Thos Wicksted, Esq of *Town Well* "—*(Bur Reg)*
† "1623 Jan 15 Richd Walthall Esqre ' —*(Bur Reg)*
‡ "1635 Sep 18 Margaret wife of Mr John Woode of Dorrington '—*(Bur Reg)*
|| "1636 Feb 27 Anne wife of John Delues, Gent "—*(Bur Reg)*
§ No record in the Parish Registers   N B —A place about a mile from Burland Hall, in Acton parish, is still known as " *Radmore Green* "
¶ "1645 Sep 9 Catherine wife of Mr Richard Golborne "—*(Bur Reg.)*
.* "1645 April 28 ffrancis wife of Captaine Will Edwardes Alderman of Chester '—*(Bur Reg)*
†† "1645 March 29 Mr John Cliffe "—*(Bur Reg)*

(10) "Under this stone lyeth the bo[dy] of Jo[hn] Bromhall of Soond who was interred the 7 of April, ano dni 1645 "*

(11) On a gravestone in the South Aisle of the Nave, an inscription to
"Radulphus Burroughes de wico Malbo gen qui obiit 3 die Oct ano dni 1651 " and to his wife "Margareta filia Hugo Allen, de eadem villam, mercator" &c she died 21 Nov 1650 †

(12) "Under a blew marble lyeth the bodyes of mr dod Baron of Escheqr, his wife, and the lady margret Norton, which lady was buried 29 March 1644 "‡

(13) The Arms of *John Griffin* impaling (?), with initials and date "I G 1623"

Thomas Wilbraham records "*Mr John Griffin of Bartherton died* 21 Sep. 1623," and his burial entry at Nantwich is dated 24 Sep. 1623 §

Near the hatchments of John Griffin on a tablet was —
' Here lyeth the body of *Martha Griffin* one of the dau of John Griffin of Bartherton Esq, who died the 25 day of Feb 1665 aged 55 yeares "
She was buried at Nantwich two days after her death —*(Par Reg.)*

(14) On a pillar near the pulpit a tablet, with Coat of Arms and Crest
"Neere this place lyeth | Robt Parker gen He married | Margaret dau of Edw Massy of Namptwich gen He had issue | 3 sones & 5 dau wch Robt died 21 Nov [?] 1664 ' ||

Dr. Ormerod mentions "a coffin shaped slab with a cross thereon ornamented with oak leaves springing from the shaft, the head formed by four oak leaves conjoined within a circle, probably relating to some members of the Order of St. John of Jerusalem, who had lands here." It was situated in the South Aisle of the Nave, near the South door: and is now to be seen under a young birch tree in the churchyard. Some flat stones were removed into the churchyard at the time of the "*Restoration*" of the Church, under the superintendence of the Rector, but most of them, together with many others in the churchyard, are now under the greensward.

Monumental Inscriptions.

(NOW IN THE CHURCH).

At the present time there are several mural monuments in brass and marble, and a few flat tombstones in the aisles of the North and South Transepts, which now are partly, and soon will be altogether, illegible. Of these, only six date back to the seventeenth and eighteenth centuries.

* "1645 April 7 John Bromhall of Renbury parrish ' —*(Bur Reg)*
† "1650 Nov 22 Margret wife of Raphe Burrowghes, gent "—*(Bur Reg)*
  "1651 Oct 3 Raphe Burrowes gent "—*(Bur Reg)*
‡ "1644 Mar 29 Margaret Lady Norton "—*(Bur Reg)*
  "1648 Sep 31 Margaret wife of Edward Dodd Esq ' —*(Bur, Reg)*
  "1648 Nov 30 Edward Dodd Esq "—*(Bur Reg)*

§ The manor of Bartherton, with its mill, &c, which had long been in the possession of the Griffin family, passed after the death of Richard Griffin, who was also buried at Nantwich on 21 Dec 1655, to the family of Delves, from whom it has descended to the Broughtons of Doddington

|| "1664 Oct 13 Robert Parker "—*(Bur Reg)*

Wilbraham Monuments

A tablet of black marble on the south wall of the Kingsley Chapel, which was originally affixed to the south east tower pier, on the 12th July, 1636, *(Wilb MS Journal),* and which has the Arms and Crest of the Wilbrahams, is inscribed as follows —

MARMORI HUIC VICINI

UNA OBDORMISCUNT SENEX PROAVUS, PUERQ' PRONEPOS,

[UTERQUE RICHARDUS WILBRAHAM]

ILLE

EX PATRE FUIT RADULPHO, FILIO
RANULPHI, FILII SECUNDI THOMÆ
WILB'HAM DE WOODHEY, AR PROGNATO.
VIR, PRÆTER PIETATEM, QUI CLARUIT,
SAPIENTIÆ MENSURA, JUDICII PONDERE,
ET ANNORUM NUMERO OLIM INSIGNIS,
QUI EX UXORE SUA ELIZABETHA
FILIA THOMÆ MAISTERSON GENEROSI,
QUATUOR HABUIT LIBEROS, (VIDELICET,)
RICHARDUM WILBRAHAM ARMIGERUM
ROGERUM WILBRAHAM EQUITEM AURATU'
THOMAM WILBRAHAM GENEROSUM ET
RADULPHUM WILBRAHAM DE DERFOLD, AR'
OBIIT 2° DIE FEB A° SUI JESU 1612
ÆTATIS SUI 88°

ISTE

PRIMOGENITUS FUIT FILIUS THOMÆ
WILBRAHAM AR' (FILII ET HÆREDIS
RICHARDI WILBRAHAM AR' FILII
RICHARDI SENIORIS PRIUS MEMORATI)
EX RACHAELE CONJUGE EJUSDEM
THOMÆ, FILIA ET HÆREDE JOSUÆ
CLIVE DE HUXLEY AR' SUSCEPTUS,
PUER OPTIMÆ SPEI, CANDIDISSIMÆ
INDOLIS, INGENIIQ' PRÆCOCISSIMI
QUI DUM PROAVI PREGRESSI VESTIGIA
VIRTUTEM ANHELANS, SEQUERETUR,
ANIMAM IN CURSU HOC EFFLANS, IDEM,
CŒLUM, IDEM ET SEPULCHRUM INVENIT
OBIIT 23° DIE JULII A° SALUTIS 1633
ÆTATIS 12°

TEMPORE NON UNO VIXERUNT, HIS TAMEN UNA,
LUX DATUR, ATQ' HIC VELATI NOCTE QUIESCUNT
DAT MORS QUÆ VITA NEGAVIT"

[*Translated*]   Near this Marble

sleeping together, lie an aged great-grand-father, and a boy his great grand-child,
(Both named RICHARD WILBRAHAM)

This

was descended from his father Ralph son of Ralph, second son of Thomas Wilbraham of Woodhey Esq   He was a man who, besides excelling in piety, was remarkable for his great wisdom, sound judgment, and length of years   Who, by his wife, Elizabeth, daughter of Thomas Maisterson, gent, had four sons, namely —

Richard Wilbraham, Esquire
Roger Wilbraham, Knight
Thomas Wilbraham Gent, and
Ralph Wilbraham of Derfold, Esquire

He died on the second day of Feb in the year of his Saviour 1612, in the 88th year of his age

That

in descent was the son of Thomas Wilbraham Esq (son and heir of Richard Wilbraham Esq, the son of Richard, the elder, before mentioned) born of Rachel, wife of the same Thomas, daughter and heiress of Joshua Clive, of Huxley, esquire   He was a boy of the greatest promise, the kindest disposition, and most precocious mind, who, longing for the virtue that might enable him to follow in the footsteps of his great-grand-father before him, found, while thus breathing out his soul, the same heaven, and the same tomb

He died on the 23rd day of July in the year of Grace 1633 at 12 years of age

They lived not at one Time, yet to them one day is given
But here they rest together veiled in Night   Death gives what Life denies

On the other side of the great window in the same Chapel, is another marble tablet to the memory of ROGER WILBRAHAM, of Townsend, Esq., the historical collector for Nantwich, another great-grandson of the first *Richard Wilbraham*, of this town When Dr. Ormerod visited the Church this monument stood near the one just given, on the East wall of the South Transept, and "at the side was a small kneeling figure, habited in a furred gown, ruff, and square cap, intended, most probably, for the person commemorated in the inscription"

ARMS: 1 and 4 Argent, three bends wavy Azure, *(Wilbraham)* 2 Argent, on a fesse Sable between three wolves heads erased Sable, three mullets Or, *(Clive)*. 3 Ermine, on a bend Gules, coticed Gules, three crescents Or, *(Huxley)*.

CREST On a wreath a wolf's head erased.

H S E

Rogerus Wilbraham de Wico Malbano armr

vir ex indole minime famæ appetens,

morum vero gravitate, scientiæ copia,

vitæ integritate,

non incelebris,

qui religionis et literarum studiis

penes totus incubuit,

Nec amicis interim, nec patriæ defuit

Uxorem habuit

Aliciam Darfoldensem,

cognatam sibi, et cognomine,

amore et virtute multo intimius conjunctam

undecim liberorum pater, quatuor tandem reliquit

superstites,

duos filios totidemque filias

Ranulphus natu maximus

hoc posuit Monumentum

optimo parenti filius pientissimus

Obiit anno { æræ Christianæ MDCCVII
{ ætatis suæ LXXXV

[*Translated*] —Here lieth Roger Wilbraham, of Wico Malbank, Esq , a man who, though fame was not his aim, yet could not but be known for his sound morals, great wisdom, and uprightness of life , and though much given to the study of religion and letters, yet failed not in his duty to his friends or his country He had to wife, Alice of Darfold, who, though she was allied to him in kindred and in name, was still more so by her love, her affection, and her virtue He was the father of eleven children , four of whom, namely, two sons and as many daughters survived him, and are still living , of whom, Randle, his eldest son, in duty to the best of parents, has set up this monument

He died in the year { of the Christian era 1707,
{ and of his age 85

In the aisle of this Transept, is a flat stone,* (partly under the Organ screen,) which has an oval brass, with Wilbraham Arms engraved thereon, and the following inscription in Roman capitals —

* Beside this stone is another inscribed "*Elizabeth Wilbraham, Relict of Ralph Wilbraham of Dorfold, Esq* ' She was the dau of John Bromhall, of Nantwich and the Hough, her husband died in 1731, and she was buried at Nantwich on 12th Oct 1748 (*Par Reg*)

"RADULPHUS WILBRAHAM   LINCOLNIENSIS HOSPITII OBIIT A° DNIJ 1657"

[*Translated*]—Ralph Wilbraham, of Lincoln's Inn, died in the year of our Lord 1657

Ralph Wilbraham, who was born in London on the 13th Nov 1601, was admitted of Lincoln's Inn on the 16th July, 1619, and, dying unmarried at Peel House, in Tarvin Parish, on the eve of St Bartholomew, 1657, left all his estate to the poor in general. (See page 193, and List of Charities)

"1657 Aug 27 Mr Raphe Wilbraham"--(*Nantwich Bur Reg*)

There still exists a brass in the South Transept, on which a very curious composition in Latin, eulogising him for his charitable disposition, has been engraved as follows —

"Ne lateat Posteros quantum funus sit, cui affectus noster justa solvere conatur, quale nomen quod devoto Pietatis Officio æternitati consecramus, sic Famæ Posthumæ tradere placet

Radulphus Wilbrahamus, tam moribus quam natalibus vere Palatinus, Patriam habuit eximiam Nobilitatis altricem Cestriam, magnâ utrinque inclaruit ex inde parentelâ, quam tamen minor ipse natu majorem meritis reddidit illustrem a propriâ virtute splendorem acquirens ac si nullam a prosapiâ vendicasset Inter avitas imagines Honoris non Imago, sed angustus Prototypon præluxit, antiquos retro Patres nobilitans serus nepos, fœnus que sanguini rependit generis sui instaurator, a quo multum decoris si recepit, plus retulit

Apud Wici Marbani candidissimas salinas* educatus, qua fuit in agendo prudentia, qua in dicendo per urbanâ festivitate, patrio quasi sapore mores et loquelam fæliciter condivit, cujus salibus* nil candidius, nil innocentius

Quoties gustui et palato erudiræ Quiritum coronæ adblandiri libuit, Deus bone! quam Sirenibus attentas inhiantium aures, quibus amœnitatum oblecta mentis delinivit deliciæ selectiorum ingeniorum, Gratias crederes Musis sociatas unius ore locutas, nescio quo procante illapsu ultra Philtrum aut Mercurialem caduceum captans et incantans auditores!

Diceres alterum Ulissem Homericum, a peregrinatione reversum, æquæ homines ac libros edoctum, nisi quod Penelope destitueretur Rigidus enim Cultor cælibatus maluit progeniem adoptare quam gignere, en itaque viduas, orphanos, detorsos, tamæ perituros, tanquam tot Lazaros in sinu *Wilbrahami* recumbentes

Quid memorem multiformem linguarum varietatem mutuo quidem sed æmulo quasi fœdere sic conjunctam, ut qui loquentem audiret, peregrinam a vernacula discernere non posset

(*Translation*)—"Let it not be a secret to our posterity how sad is his death, to whom our affection will pay his due What a name is his, we consecrate to eternity in our dutiful love, and so hand down his memory to posthumous fame

Ralph Wilbraham, a Prince in all truth by manners as well as birth, had the renowned county of Chester for a foster-mother, on all sides his great parentage is illustrious, which he, though younger in years, made older by his merits, acquiring an illustrious splendour by his own virtues, even if he claimed none from his descent Amongst the forms of his ancestors, the form of honour shone not forth, but its more august Prototype he the offspring, ennobling his ancestors, and he, the founder of his race, paying interest to his blood, to which, if he received much glory from it, he gave still more

Educated near the salt-springs of Wich Malbank with what prudence did he act, with what pleasant courtesy did he speak! He preserved, as it were, with a seasoning inherited from his birthplace his morals and conversation, than whose wit nothing was more brilliant, nothing more harmless

How often it pleased his taste to find delight, in the Civic crown! Bounteous God! what an eloquent companion, what a pleasant guest! with what enchantment, he held the ears of his gaping listeners, with what delights did he entrance choicer spirits, you would think that the Graces, united to the Muses, were speaking in the mouth of one capturing and carrying along his hearers with a kind of gentle motion, beyond any Philtre or Mercurial wand!

You would say he was a second Ulysses returned from his wanderings, learned in men and books (except that he had no Penelope) for, a strict admirer of celibacy, he preferred to adopt children rather than beget them widows and orphans, bowed down and perishing from want, lying like so many Lazaruses in *Wilbraham's* bosom

How can I speak of his varied knowledge of languages united in him, with so mutual yet rival a bond, that he who heard him speak, could not discern if he were speaking his mother tongue or a foreign language

* There is a play on the Latin words here, which it is almost impossible to render into English *salinas*—salt springs *salibus*—the salt of wit

Quid verba narrem cum facta videam quid Artes recenseam, quibus adeo excelluit sui similes, liberales quas tamen Pietati vectigales fecit Non loquitur magna, sed facit, quid Hominum et Angelorum linguæ sine Caritate, illa primas habeat, illa procluceat tanquam inter stellas Luna minores Eleemosyna, viaticum in terris, thesauris in Cœlis

Radulphus eleemosynarius suâ munificentiâ inauravit sæculum hoc ferreum Exteras invisit regiones ut exulantem reduceret Charitatem, absoluta Peregrinatione jam reversurus in superum Patriam integras facultates omnes opes divitiasq' Pauperibus, quasi Mercatoribus, (ut fit) tradidit cum fœnore recipiendas in cœlo gnarus quod patrimonium Deo creditum nec Resp eripit, nec Fiscus invadit, nec calumnia forensis evertit

Egenos adeo ex asse hæredes constituit ut nec legaverit sibi vel tumulum vel Epitaphium, utrumque tamen cognato Genevæ defuncto cum extruxit, sibi ibidem erexit aliud dedignatus quam illud perenne pietatis et ingenii monumentum antea plus quam semi sepultus cum charissimo consodale repetitus exequias, alterumq' funus noluit

Frustra Marmore Tegitur qui cunctorum pectoribus tumulatur

Ex quo Christo se dicavit non fratrum aut affinium memor, neminem in carne novit immo carnem suam non agnovit, cutem qui nunquam curavit, de Corpore, prorsus incuriosis, totus de Animâ sollicitus integrum se cum suis Holocaustum Deo in flammâ charitatis obtulit, consummatæ Perfectionis apicem quis dubitat illum attigisse? qui omnia profudit pauperibus, qui sic secutus est Christum, procul dubio assecutus est

Alii aurum inaurantes divitis propinquos locupletavit insta fluminum aquas suas in mare mittunt Illæ terras sitientes rigavit, nec oleum suum in plena sed in vacua vasa in fudit

> Quas tulit acceptas Christi *Wilbramanius* amori
> In Christi moriens membra refudit opes
> Scilicet hæredem cum se sentiret Olympi,
> Hæredem contra scripsit Eipse Deum "

Why should I speak of words, when I can behold his deeds? How can I recount his talents in which he so excelled! What revenues he gave away in his generosity! He spoke not of great things, but did them What are the tongues of Men or Angels without Charity! Charity should have the first place, it should shine forth like a Moon of Mercy amongst the lesser stars a provision on earth, a treasure in Heaven

Ralph the charitable has gilded this iron age with his munificence He visited foreign lands to bring back the wanderer Charity, himself now about to return from his Wanderings to his home on high. He lent his substance, wealth, and all his means to the Poor, as if they were Merchants (as is the custom) to be received back by him in heaven with interest knowing that his patrimony was only lent him by God, his Money-bags corrupted him not, the scandal of the market turned him not aside

He left his heirs so penniless, that he did not even bequeath means to build a tomb or write an Epitaph for himself, yet he erected a tomb and inscribed an Epitaph for a kinsman who died at Geneva for he thought him not unworthy of an everlasting monument for his piety and talents, having before that attended the last rites of his dearest friend, half buried, as it were, himself, he would not have another funeral ceremony even for himself.

In vain can he be read of in Marble who is buried in the breasts of all

He so dedicated himself to Christ, that he, mindful not even of his brethren or relations offered no one as a sacrifice to God in the flame of charity Who can doubt that he reached the highest point of Charity, who poured out all his riches to the poor? Who so followed Christ, though he followed him with trembling at a distance

Others gild gold, make their rich neighbours richer, like rivers that pour their waters into the sea He watered the thirsty land, nor did he pour his oil into full but into empty vessels

> This good man *Wilbraham* great wealth possessed
> And dying gave all back to Jesus breast
> For, sooth, he thought himself of Heaven the heir,
> And as an heir did God receive him there

It is, perhaps, not generally known, that the above Wilbraham monuments were *all* that ever existed in this Church to the memory of that worthy family. To these have recently been added memorial stained glass, at a cost of £500, executed by Wailes, of London, in the large window of the South Transept, and a brass engraved as follows —

> "TO THE GLORY OF GOD
> AND IN MEMORY OF HIS KINDRED WHOSE
> BODIES ARE BURIED IN A VAULT BENEATH
> ✠ THIS WINDOW IS DEDICATED BY
> GEORGE FORTESQVE WILBRAHAM, A D 1858

✠ ROGER WILBRAHAM of NANTWICH ob^t 1754. ✠ MARY DAUGHTER
OF THOMAS HUNT, WIFE OF ROGER WILBRAHAM OBIIT 1760.
✠ MARY WILBRAHAM ob^t 1741 ✠ THOMAS WILBRAHAM ob^t 1802
✠ GEORGE WILBRAHAM of DELAMERE LODGE, ob^t 1813. ✠ MARIA
DAU. OF WILLIAM HARVEY, WIFE OF GEORGE WILBRAHAM ob^t 1822
✠ MARIA WILBRAHAM ob^t 1794 ✠ ROGER WILBRAHAM ob^t 1784 ✠
LOUISA WILBRAHAM ob^t 1797 "

On the west wall of the South Transept, the arms of *Walley* impaling *Wright*, (recently re-painted) and a brass thus inscribed —

"HIC JACET

VIR PIUS, SUBDITUS FIDELIS, MEDICUS PERITUS, PAUPERIBUS CONSANGUINEIS
CONJUGIS SUÆ CHARÆ RELATIVIS, ET
ALIIS AMICUS VERUS PEPETUUS, ET GENEROSUS
GULIELMUS WALLEY

OBIIT XXXI DIE JANUARY ANNO $\left\{ \begin{array}{l} \text{SALUTIS MDCLXXX.} \\ \text{ÆTATIS SUÆ LXVII} \end{array} \right.$

ELIZABETHAM UXOREM SUAM PER DILECTAM, BENIGNAM,
ILLAM MATRONAM AC PERDECORAM FILIAM ROGERI
WRIGHT GENEROSI HEU, IDEM CLAUSIT SEPULCHRUM.

OBIIT XXIV DIE FEBR ANNO $\left\{ \begin{array}{l} \text{SALUTIS MDCLXXX} \\ \text{ÆTATIS SUÆ LXXII.} \end{array} \right.$

CREDE CHRISTIANE ET NON MORIERIS
NAM FIDE CHRISTI MORIENTES RESURGENT."

[*Translated*]—Here lies William Walley, a pious man, a loyal subject, a skilful physician, a true, constant, and to the poor, to his own kindred, and the relatives of his dear wife, and to others a genuine friend. He died on the 31st day of January in the year of Grace 1680, and of his age 67 Also, his beloved wife, Elizabeth, a kind matron, and very comely lady, the daughter and heiress of Roger Wright, gent. She is buried in the same tomb. She died on the 24th day of February in the year of Grace 1680, and of her age 72.*

Believe O Christian! and you will not die, for by faith in Christ, the dying shall rise again

Between the two west windows of the South Transept, a mural tablet, thus.—

"M S

THOMÆ WETTENHALL

de Wico Malbano in com Cest arm

et CATHARINÆ uxoris ejus

ex qua

unicum filium Thomam

et quatuor filias

Catharinam, Amiciam, Margaretam

---

* The Register records —" 1680 Feb 4 William Walley Doctor of Phisick " [Buried]
" 1680 Feb 27 Mrs Elizabeth Walley *vid* " [Buried]

et Susannam, superstites
suscepit
Qui quidem THOMAS obiit
xviii° Octob aº MDCLXXVII
CATHARINA vero
xiv° Maii anno MDCLXXXIII."

[*Translated*]—Sacred to the memory of THOMAS WETTENHALL of Wich Malbank, in the county of Chester, Esq, and CATHARINE his wife, by whom he had an only son Thomas, and four daughters, Catharine, Amicia, Margaret, and Susannah, now living Which same THOMAS died on 18th Oct in the year 1677, also CATHARINE on 14th May in the year 1683 *

With the above, ends the list of monuments relating to the old families of Nantwich, preserved to these times Of the monuments belonging to the present century, three mural tablets are on the East side of the South Transept

A black marble to the memory of—
"RALPH FOX
of Nantwich died
Feb 9, 1820 Aged 77
MARGARET FOX
of Nantwich died
Jan 6, 1822 Aged 73"
A white marble with an urn —
"Sacred to the memory of
MARY
second Daughter of the late Mr JAMES MEEK, formerly of this place, who died on the 18 Jan 1816
ÆT 22 years"
"This lovely bud so young and fair
Call'd hence by early doom,
Just came to show how sweet a flower,
In Paradise would bloom"
"Blessed are the Dead that Die in the Lord"

An alabaster monument, somewhat tumid and vulgar for the time it was written —
"Sacred to the memory of
WILLIAM,
the only child of WILLIAM and MARY SPROUT, of this Town,
who died on the 15 April 1807
in the eleventh year of his age.

THE DAWN OF HIS INTELLECT PROMISED A DAY OF BRIGHTNESS | HE WAS ENDEARED TO ALL BY SWEETNESS OF DISPOSITION, | AND EMINENTLY, TO HIS PARENTS BY FILIAL | AFFECTION AND OBEDIENCE | THEIR CONSOLATION FLOWS FROM THE WORDS OF THE SAVIOUR | —"OF SUCH IS THE KINGDOM OF HEAVEN" |

There are flat gravestones in the aisle of the South Transept, (but partly hidden by modern seats), to *Sprout*, a banker, *Plevin*, a saddler; *Richard Leversage*, Ironmonger, who died 1st March, 1839, aged 71, *Rodenhurst*, formerly a freeholder in Coole Pilate, and resident in Dysart Buildings, Nantwich, and [*Ann*] "*Relict of William Hewitt* ob Sep 1 1780" These names will soon be obliterated.

In the North Transept are two memorial stained glass windows, on the east wall (1)—An Angel window, representing Gabriel, Michael the Archangel, and Raphael, and below a brass plate, with arms, and engraved thus —

* "1677 Oct 23 Thos Wettenhall Esq "—*(Bur Reg)*
"1683 May 17 Mrs Catharine Wetenhall widow"—*(Bur Reg)*
In *Harl MSS* 2151 is given a coat of arms, (*Wettenhall* impaling *Clutton*) with initials and date,—I W 1623 Probably intended for the grandmother of this Thomas Wettenhall, whose burial is recorded thus —
"1623 Nov 9 Jane, wiefe of Mr William Wettenhall —*(Par Reg)*

"In Dei gloriam et in piam memoriam Locum tenentis Prefecti Caroli Cuyler Baronetti, filii Ducis Cornetii Cuylei Baronetti cui | natus ante diem quartum Kal Febr Anno Salutis 1794, obdormivit in CHRISTO et in spe beatæ resurrectionis ante diem decimum Kal | Sepr Anno Salutis 1862 ætatis suæ 69 hanc fenestram ejus Vidua Catharina Francesca Cuyler mœrens ponendam curavit " |

To the Glory of God and in pious remembrance of Deputy Lieutenant Charles Cuyler Bart son of General Cornet Cuyler Bart , who was born on 29th Jan in the year of Grace 1794   He fell asleep in Christ and in hope of a blessed resurrection on 23rd Aug in the year of Grace 1862 and of his age 69 His sorrowing widow Catherine Frances Cuyler has caused this window to be placed *

(2)—A window representing the Transfiguration   below a brass engraved thus —

"In memory of William Lowe Esqre long resident in Nantwich as a Solicitor, who died 21st Dec 1812, and of Elizabeth his Wife, | who died in July 1822, and who, with several of their children and grandchildren are interred in the Chancel of the Church, this | Window was erected to the Glory of God, by their sole survivor in the Parish T P Lowe, Esqre , Solicitor on the 21st Decr 1864 "†

On the wall dividing St. George's Chapel from the Lady Chapel, is a marble tablet with carved work representing the Muse of Comedy, masks, clowns, &c , thus inscribed —

"Underneath this marble are interred the remains of
SAMUEL STANTON,
who many years presided over a company of Comedians
in this neighbourhood, with credit and respect , and
was deservedly esteemed in private life as an honest man
He died suddenly Aug 20, 1797 aged 60 years
His wife ELIZABETH STANTON
also died suddenly (in London) Oct 2, 1790   Aged 57 years,
and was buried at Barnes in Surrey
Her truly benevolent disposition
excited the Love of her Acquaintance and the Poor
Their seventh son, ROBERT, died April 2, 1795, aged 22 years,
and was buried at Walsall
Their surviving children have raised this tribute of affection
to their memory "

Between the two windows of St George's Chapel, is a brass inscribed in capital letters —

"TO THE GLORY OF GOD AND IN MEMORY OF
EDWIN JACKSON KENT A NATIVE OF NANTWICH
WHO DIED MARCH 24TH 1878   AGED 65 YEARS
THIS TABLET TOGETHER WITH . ALTAR STEPS FRONTAL . &C
IS OFFERED BY HIS WIDOW AND CHILDREN "

Above is a tablet of white marble within a black border, surmounted by an urn ; with the following inscription —

* Sir Charles Cuyler lived for some years at Poole Hall near Nantwich   He was buried in the Parish Cemetery at Nantwich, and his daughter, who was accidentally burnt to death about the same time, was buried there also

† The late Rev Thomas Brooke B A Rector of Wistaston, from 1825 to 1872, and Justice of Peace, married the sister of Thomas Philip Lowe, Esq , of Nantwich whose son, Charles Stuart Brooke, Esq now occupies the same residence and offices of the late William Lowe Solicitor, Esq

"Sacred to the memory of
Ensign CHARLES HALL of the 38th Regiment of Foot,
(Only Son of the late Dr CHARLES HALL of this town)
Whose amiable Disposition endear'd Him
to his numerous Friends
He died of a Fever, brought on by excessive
Fatigue, soon after his Return from Spain
at Plymouth,
on the twenty-first Day of January 1809,
Aged 28
His sorrowing Sisters SUSANNAH & ANN
have caus'd this Tablet to be erected
in Token of their affectionate Regard "

In the aisle of this Chapel, are several flat gravestones to the memory of the Hall family of Nantwich The inscriptions are partly hidden by modern seats, and are now nearly illegible. Two of them relate to the sisters, *Susannah* and *Ann,* and Charles Hall, M D , their father, as follows —

(1)—"John Hall Surgeon died January 30th 1767 aged 43 "*

(2)—"John [?] Hall Surgeon died July 3, 1785 [?] aged — Also Elizabeth Hall spinster, Daughter of the above John & Mary Hall died Oct 12, 1801 Aged 48 "

(3)—"Charles Hall M D Mortalis esse decessit "†

(4)—"*Susanna* eldest dau of late Charles Hall [died] Aug 8, 1823

(5)—"To the memory of *Anne,* Wife of W M Brady, M D & last surviving Daughter of the late C Hall M D Died April 25th 1835 aged 47 years "

Also another stone in the same aisle —
[Richard] "Wicksted M D who departed this life March 26, 1810 aged 70 years "

In the Lady Chapel is a mural tablet—
"To the memory of | SAMUEL HODGSON Esquire | who died on the 16th of September 1807 | at the Age of 72 Years | This Monument is erected | by his surviving Relatives | as a tribute of respect to his Virtues | and a token of their affection " |

A lancet window in the North Aisle of the Nave, is filled with memorial stained glass representing four examples of Patriarchal faith, and inscribed —
IN MEMORY OF EDWARD HALL MARTIN | OF HENHULL
BORN OCT 3 1799 DIED JAN 25 1866 " | †

A brass under the West Window of the Nave, is inscribed —
"THIS WEST WINDOW WAS COMPLETED NOV 1875
TO THE GLORY OF GOD AND IN MEMORY OF
ANDREW FULLER CHATER M A
RECTOR OF NANTWICH FROM A D 1846 TO A D 1872
IN WHOSE TIME THIS CHURCH WAS RESTORED AND MADE FREE '

* Buried 2 Feb 1767 —*(Par Reg)*   † Buried 26 Nov 1805 Aged 75 —*(Par Reg)*

‡ The subjects Abel, Enoch and Noah were added to the first memorial (Job) in memory of Mr and Mrs Martin by the members of their family and Lord Crewe, in March, 1877 The artists being Messrs Clayton and Bell of London —*(Parish Magazine)* The late E H Martin, Esq was articled with Messrs Tomlinson & Welsby, Solicitors of Nantwich, and ultimately succeeded to their practice He was buried in Acton churchyard, between the sundial cross and the east boundary wall

𝔇𝔢𝔰𝔠𝔯𝔦𝔭𝔱𝔦𝔬𝔫 𝔬𝔣 𝔱𝔥𝔢 ℭ𝔥𝔲𝔯𝔠𝔥.

HE CHURCH is dedicated to St. Mary. At the present time, however, it is erroneously called the Church of SS. Mary and Nicholas. The late Sir Gilbert Scott, in his Report on the Restoration of Nantwich Church (1854), adopted this double dedication, possibly on the authority of Bacon's edition of "*Liber Regis;*"[*] or on that of the old antiquary, Browne Willis,[†] who wrote in the early part of the eighteenth century, and who appears to have confounded the two separate religious foundations of St. Mary's Chapel (or Church) and St. Nicholas' Chapel. As there is great danger of this error being perpetuated,[‡] it should be clearly understood that not a single instance is to be found of this double dedication in pre-Reformation times; and to adopt it now is both incorrect and absurd; as those Chapels have been shown, in the foregoing pages, to have been two distinct religious edifices in different parts of the town. There seems to be in the Church itself sufficient proof in stone, of the original and single dedication. In the Chancel groining, and over that part of the Church between the altar-steps and the east window, are four carved bosses, (see illustration) representing:— (1)—*The Eternal Father;* (2)—*The Coronation of the Virgin;* (3)—*The Virgin and an Angel,* (Regina Angelorum); (4)—*The Assumption of the Virgin.* If these have any meaning at all, it seems reasonable to suppose that, according to the common practice of ancient times, Nantwich Chapel, (or Church) would be dedicated to God the Father, under the patronage or invocation of the Blessed Virgin, the chief of Saints and Queen of Angels, whose name was thus associated with the High or Principal Altar.

The Church is built on high ground near the centre of the town; in a graveyard, which was formerly larger than it is now,[§] and which has recently been planted with ornamental trees and shrubs.[‖] Partridge made the following remarkable statements in 1774:

> "Entering the Church from the churchyard, we now *descend,* though it is certain our ancestors *ascended* some steps into it; and in digging graves, pavements and gravestones have been discovered at the depth of two yards or more. Though the churchyard is a very large one, and seemingly sufficient

---

[*] "*Liber Regis*" contains the following return; the part in italics being J. Bacon's additions to the original:—
"NAMPTWICH *(St. Mary & St. Nicholas)* olim cap. ella⌐ to Acton. *John Crewe esq. Patr. now* ⌐1786⌐ *held by institution as a Rectory £27 3s. 4d. certified value.*"

[†] Partridge's *History of Nantwich,* p. 34.

[‡] A few years ago, a banner with the emblems of both saints worked in coloured silks was presented to the Church; and, when the Porch was "restored," although the proposal of filling the empty niches over the doorway with new statues of the Virgin Mary and St. Nicholas was, happily, not carried out; one of the corbels was, unfortunately, newly carved from a fancied resemblance in the original to three children borne up by the wings and hands of St. Nicholas.

[§] In digging the foundations for the present District Bank, coffins and remains were unearthed.

[‖] *Cf.* p. 298. The inscriptions on the principal gravestones in the churchyard are given in various parts of this work.

for the interment of all the dead, yet that illaudable custom prevails here, of burying within the Church, but these graves are not very eligible ones, for scarce are they got a foot below the surface, but the coffins are immerst in water "*—(*History of Nantwich*, p 42)

When the above was penned the bases of the pillars of the nave were completely hidden, the floor having been raised in 1615, (see page 120) At the Restoration of the Church in 1855, the floor of the nave was lowered two feet, to its original level, which is approached from the South porch by *descending* four steps. The same writer, who may have been inaccurate in the first sentence above quoted, also says, (*ibid*, p. 40) the Church "*stands upon springs*," and in this, he is literally correct, the Church being built on a bed of sand that is saturated with water The late Mr Sprout for many years strongly advocated the draining of the Church, but it is believed, that if his suggestion had been carried out, the fabric would have given way At the present time a fixed quantity of water is drawn away by pumping every week, in order to keep the Church as dry as possible without causing damage to the building

The general appearance of this handsome structure is exhibited in the three plates, namely —

1 —The *fac-simile* of the north west view given in Lyson's "Cheshire,' showing the Perpendicular window anterior to the "Restoration" of the Church

2 —A north-east view, giving a good idea of the Chancel, with its curious low-pitched roof, ' magnificent pinnacles in two ranges to the buttresses, a richly pierced parapet, and windows of great beauty The east window, with its beautiful crocketted canopy, taken in combination with the exquisite buttresses and groups of pinnacles which flank the east end of the Chancel, form a design extremely beautiful and unique."†

3 —A south-west view, which, like the north-east view, is reproduced on a reduced scale from the excellent drawings of Messrs Bowman and Crowther, in the "Churches of the Middle Ages " and which is introduced as giving an idea of the appearance of the Church in the early part of the fifteenth century, before the roof of the nave was altered

Of the external sculpture, the grotesque gurgoyles of the choir and north aisle of the nave, the ornaments on the south transept, and the evangelistic symbols on the porch, are worthy of notice, but owing to the friability of the sandstone of which the Church is built, these are either much worn away, or have of late years been renewed For the want of pointing, some parts of the exterior, particularly the south side of the Church, and the tower, are peeling off in flakes, and thus going to decay

Cruciform in design, the Church is justly admired for its symmetrical proportions; having a *Nave* with side aisles of four bays, a *Choir* and *Chancel* of three bays, and two *Transepts* of three smaller bays Between the transepts is a square area *(Interstitium)* over which is a rather low octagon tower, with a picturesque stair turret on the north side

---

* The last interment in the Church, I believe, was Mary Howard, the wife of James Howard, Esq , of Brookfield, Nantwich, and daughter of John Hill of Walgherton She died on the 1st Aug 1847 and in 1865 her grave in the North Transept was opened, and found to be full of water, her remains were removed to Wybunbury churchyard and re-interred beside her husband, who had died on the 18th March, 1865 The removal of the Organ from the Lady Chapel to the South Transept, in 1875, was partly owing to the injury it was sustaining from the damp

† Gilbert G Scott's Report on Nantwich Church in 1854

The internal dimensions are as follows —

		Ft	in		Ft	in	
The Nave		70	0	in length,	57	0	in breadth
The Chancel	. .	52	0	,,	24	6	,,
The South Transept		37	6	,,	27	6	,,
The North Transept		39	9	,,	27	6	,,
The Interstitium		34	0	,,	34	0	,,

The total length from E to W is about 156 ft
The total length of the Cross, from N to S , is 111 ft.
The height of the Tower to the parapet is 94 ft.
And to the top of the stair-turret 101 ft.

On referring to the ground plan of the Church, two irregularities in the building will be seen, namely —the west window is placed out of the centre of the west front, and the axis of the choir and chancel is not in the same line with that of the nave, being inclined towards the south about nine inches, a peculiarity found in many Cathedrals and old Churches *

Built in the fourteenth century, Nantwich Church belongs to the Decorated style of architecture, but the gradual change from the Decorated to the Perpendicular style is exhibited in the Chancel, and in the Chapel of the South Transept. The late Sir Gilbert Scott, in 1854, discovered on and near the site of the west door some remains, of thirteenth century date, of a former Church, and he was of opinion that the builders of the present Church allowed that portion to remain as the oldest feature of the then newly constructed building   This fact explains why at the "restoration" of the Church, the west door was re-constructed in imitation of the Early English style of architecture †

The *Nave*, the oldest part of the Church, is lofty and has four acute arches, elegantly pointed, thrice recessed with wave mouldings, on clustered piers, that have under-cut abaci and bell-shaped bases. A series of pointed arches are formed in the *side aisles* by curved ribs of stone from the pillars of the nave to the flying buttresses The *Clerestory*, probably of late fifteenth century date, has a modern roof and on each side eight segmental-arched windows The line of the original high pitched roof of the Nave is still discernible over the west window, and the superiority of the original design is shown in the S W view of the Church   Of the fittings of the nave, oak carved seats brass eagle lectern,† font in Caen stone, and oak pulpit, all are modern except the last named   The oak pulpit is inscribed —

- MAYE 9 1601 DAYE -
- THOMAS FINCHE JOYNER MADE THIS -

Above it, formerly, was a sound board, and below, the minister's seat, where prayers were read, and still lower, the clerk's seat and churching pew, where most marriages

---

* Well known examples occur at St Peters at Rome Ratisbon, Norwich, Peterborough, Lincoln and York Cathedrals, at St Mary s, Oxford, &c

† The Rev T W Norwood says that "*wimples*" and "*wave-mouldings*" characterize the whole structure and serve to fix the date of the Church, which is middle and latish Decorated work, with nothing earlier   Certain details, (e g "pointed bowtells" in the Lady Chapel, "under-cut abaci" in the Nave piers, "stiff leaved foliage" on the West Tower arch, and "concave base mouldings" in the same arch) which at first sight seem earlier, being associated with later forms, can only be regarded as survivals of earlier forms, rather than indications of earlier work

‡ The Lectern was the gift, by will, of the late Mrs Mary Evans (nee Cappur) of Hospital Street, widow It was placed in the Church on Christmas Eve, 1873

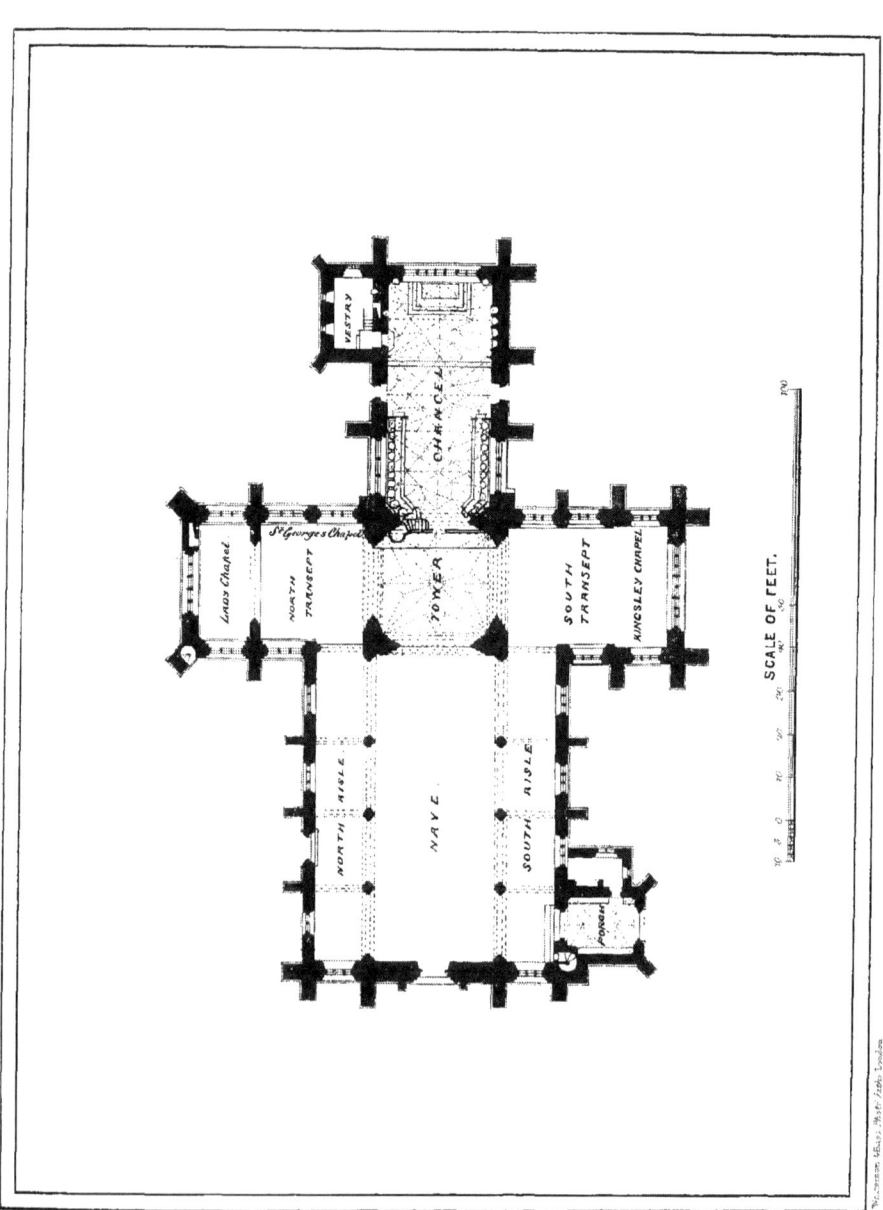

VESTRY

CHANCEL

TOWER

St George's Chapel

NORTH TRANSEPT

LADY Chapel

SOUTH TRANSEPT

KINGSLEY CHAPEL

NORTH AISLE

NAVE

SOUTH AISLE

PORCH

SCALE OF FEET.

10 5 0 10 20 30 40 50 60 70 80 90 100

were solemnized Humorously spoken of as the *"three-decker,"* and after having been affixed to the second pillar on the north side of the nave for two hundred and twenty-two years, (see page 130), it was destroyed at the ' restoration" of the Church, except the top story, which was placed in its present position beside the north-west tower pier An oak chest with initial and date, (W 1676) upon which the weekly dole bread (ninety loaves) is placed, was given by a parishioner, Thomas Cawley, Esq , about forty years ago On the east wall of the nave is some seventeenth century decorative painting, representing a Cross in a circle, with I.H S , and on either side tables of the Law Below is the verse "He that hath my commandments and keepeth them, he it is that loveth Me, and he that loveth Me, shall be loved of my Father" Round the arch are these words, which are, however, incorrectly quoted from John I 17, "The law came by Moses but Grace and Truth by Jesus Christ "* The restored north door of the nave is not now used A modern oak screen separates the south aisle from the transept. The restored west window, the second of its kind, dated 1875, has seven lights with geometrical tracery ; and is filled with memorial stained glass, the general subject of which is "Christ in His Temple " The *South Porch*, originally of late Decorated work, has a *Parvise,* or upper room, in which is a library† of 190 vols , founded about 1704, (see page 301), and an *East Room*, containing an open-fire place. The porch was restored in 1878, when stone groining was added in place of the former flat ceiling, and stained glass, by C E Kemp, of London , two lights being given anonymously, a third by Randle Wilbraham, Esq , of Rode Hall , and a fourth by the late Miss Bennett, of Willaston Hall ‡

The *Transepts*, the *Lady Chapel*, and the *Interstitium* are of late Decorated work, the difference in style between these parts and the *Nave* is well exhibited on the opposite sides of the bases of the west tower-piers From 1859 to 1875 the Lady Chapel was used as the Organ chamber, and since then as a Choir Vestry. The north window, after having long been in a sad state of decay, was renewed, and the ' *Jesse*" glass added anonymously, with these words in black letter —

"Ad laudem Dei Patris Filii et Sancti Spiritus
‚ hæc fenestra dedicata est M.DCCC.LXXVI."§

Both Transepts are fitted with seats like those of the nave. The *Interstitium* has wood vaulting of recent date, and is fitted with choir-seats and two prayer desks Attached to the north-east tower-pier is the stone pulpit (see page 280) which is of Transition to Perpendicular in style

The *Kingsley Chapel*, of early Perpendicular work, has remains of a piscina, and fragments of ancient glass in the east window. The restored south window of eight lights illustrates, in stained glass, by Wailes, the early life of our Lord as foretold by the prophets, each of whom are represented bearing scrolls with the following texts —

* The practice of inscribing Scripture passages on the inside walls of Churches is said to have commenced after a conversation on the subject between Queen Elizabeth and Dean Nowell at St Paul s, on 1st Nov 1561 (Hone s *Every Day Book*," vol ii p 684-5) Sentences of holy Scripture were painted on the walls of Nantwich Church in 1615 and 1633 (See pp 120 and 130)

† Inside the Church may be seen a shoulder-headed doorway, now filled up, that formerly led from the library to the South Gallery
The porch has a stone bench on either side, where in former times the destitute poor were relieved

‡ Miss Bennett died on the 6th Aug 1880, and was buried at Wybunbury

§ *Translated* —' This window is dedicated to the praise of God the Father, the Son, and the Holy Ghost 1876

Isaiah vii 14	The Annunciation	*Jer* xxiii 6	The Presentation
Amos ix. 11	The Salutation	*Zech* iii 8.	The Epiphany.
Micah v 2	The Birth	*Mal* iii 1	Jesus in the Temple.
Dan vii 13	The Angel host.	*Ezek* xxxiv. 23	The Baptism

In the tracery twelve angels in white robes bear scrolls with the following texts — *Isa.* ix. 6, *Rev.* v 12, *Psalm* lxxii. 10, 11; and *Isa* xi 2

It may here be mentioned that none of the original mullions of the windows of this Church now exist, and the windows behind the organ, which were originally of Decorated work, have at some period, long ago, been made to harmonize with the Perpendicular windows of this Chapel

The *Choir* and *Chancel* are very handsome, and of late Decorated work, with pear tracery, *c* 1380 It has already been conjectured (see page 276) that William Wodenote's grant of land may have had some connection with the erection of the Chancel of the Church, for as the Rev. T W Norwood has recently pointed out, the same "*string-course*" and "*pear tracery*" are exhibited in the Chancel of Bunbury Church which was built by Sir Hugh de Calveley in 1386.* Along the central stone beam of the richly groined roof are eleven bosses, (carved in stone), representing the following subjects in order from east to west, that is, commencing with number xi in the accompanying plate.

XI	The Eternal Father	V	The Nativity
X	The Coronation of the Virgin	IV	The Flagellation.
IX	The Virgin and an Angel	III.	The Crucifixion.
VIII	The Assumption of the Virgin	II	The Resurrection
VII.	The Annunciation	I	The Appearing to Mary (*Noli me*
VI	The Immaculate Conception (?)		*tangere*,—"Touch me not ")

In the *Choir* are twenty canopied stalls† of ancient workmanship, having seats with *misereres*, ornamented with carvings of animals, foliage, human figures (a pair of wrestlers; St. George and the Dragon, monks and nuns, &c), and subjects grotesque and satirical. One specimen may be selected for description.

On the left hand	*In the centre*	*On the right hand*
Reynard as a monk returning from hunting, with right arm outstretched carrying a goose by the neck, a hare hanging from a stick across his left shoulder	Three trees, with birds, at the foot of which a fox is laid on his back, shamming dead, that he may catch prey for his cubs, which are seen in holes at the roots of the trees	Reynard as a monk going out a hunting In his right hand is a bow, and in his left a bottle(?), arrows are seen protruding from under his left arm

Another miserere has the monogram ☩ ℳ.𝔖. and the word **merci.**

---

* Bunbury Church is situated about nine miles from Nantwich On the 24th June 10 Ric II [1386] a warrant was issued "to John Doune forester, and Roger de Moldeworth, '*equitator*' of the forest of Delamere for delivery to Hugh de Calveley of 20 mastich trees for making scafoldes to be used for the repairs of the church of Bunbury which the said Hugh proposed to make "—*(Chesh Recog Rolls)* In the same year Sir Hugh de Calveley had licence to found a college or chauntry for one master and six chaplains to celebrate mass for the King, for himself and his ancestors The Chancels of Nantwich and Bunbury have some architectural details in common and in the latter still exists an altar tomb with the figure of Sir Hugh, the founder

† A Bishop's head, with a mitre, is represented amongst the carvings on the sides of the stalls

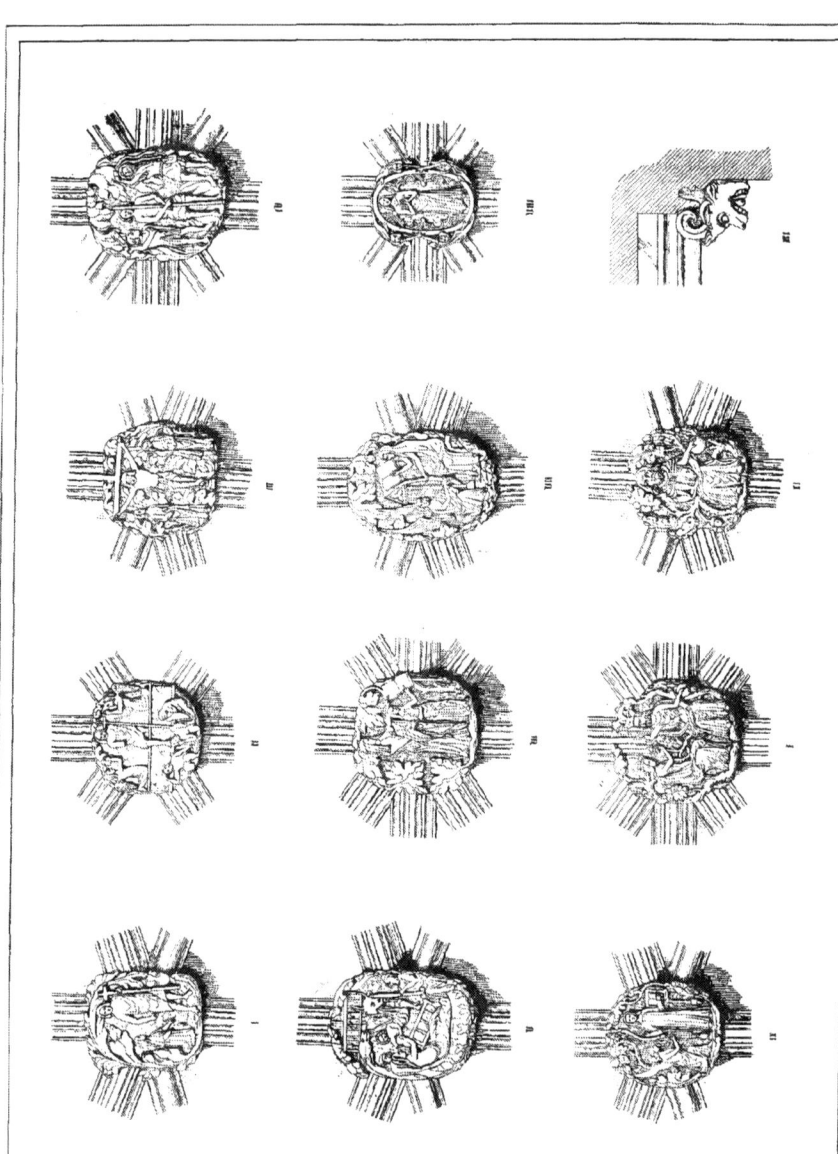

The *East window* of seven lights, consists of a repetition of small windows of flowing tracery, so combined as to give the whole work the appearance of the Perpendicular style It is filled with stained glass by Clayton and Bell, the subjects, designed in tabernacle work, being —The Agony, Judgment Hall, Scourging, Crucifixion, Taking down from the Cross, Entombment, and Resurrection   Above are represented the prophets, *Moses* and *Elias* occupying central positions, and below, the Evangelists and great Apostles *   A somewhat singular feature of the Chancel is, that it has a *north* as well as south door The Communion table (Altar) rests on a massive carved oak frame, thus inscribed —

"GIVEN BY THOMAS CLOWES CLARKE OF THIS PARISH 1638 "†

On the wall above, in letters of gold, is, "And I, if I be lifted up from the earth will draw all men unto me "   Handsomely carved piscina and three sedilia‡ with canopies are situated in the usual place, and on the opposite side is a "restored" Saint s niche

On the north side of the Chancel, and *within* the altar-rails, is a low door leading to the *Sacristy* or *Vestry*,§ which is entered by descending two steps to a floor paved with glazed tiles of patterns *"in cavetto"* from remains found in 1855-8   This room with its open fire-place and chimney, no doubt was, formerly, a priest's chamber   Descending two steps more, the *Crypt*, which is partly underground, and lighted by three narrow windows, is entered   It has a piscina and aumbry, indicating an altar, and contains the mutilated figure of the Cradock monument. (*Cf* p 287)

The Vestry also has an upper chamber lighted by three exterior windows, and a fourth looking into the Chancel, which, from the presence of iron hinges, appears to have been in former times, a door

The octagon *Tower*, on a square base and in the same style of architecture as the Transepts, is the only unrestored part of this noble edifice.   It contains six bells, bearing these inscriptions —

[1] PROSPERITY TO THIS TOWN & PARISH   A R 1713   (Smallest bell)
[2] PEACE & GOOD NEIGHBOURHOOD   A R 1713
[3] ABR RUDHALL CAST US ALL   1713 ‖
[4] GOD SAVE THE CHURCH & QUEEN ANN   A R 1713
[5] PROSPERITY TO ALL OUR BENEFACTORS   A.R 1713
       (This bell strikes the hour of the day)
[6] THO. TALBOT. HUMPHREY HALES. CHURCHWARDENS. 1713   (Tenor Bell)

Mentions of the bells occur on previous pages.   Prior to 1713 there had only been five bells   The tenor bell is 3 ft 8½ in in diameter, and weighs about 15 cwt., the note being F.   The smallest bell weighs 6¼ cwt , and the total weight of all the bells is about

* The East window, and the whole of the Chancel were restored by the munificence of Hungerford Lord Crewe

† *Cf* pp 115—117

‡ Anciently these were seats for the officiating priest, deacon, and sub-deacon

§ Precisely the same arrangement is found at Bunbury, the door entering the vestry on the north side of the Chancel, being within the altar rails

‖ Abraham Rudhall, of Gloucester, bell-founder   The family of Rudhalls carried on the business as early as 1684, and are said to have made the enormous number of 3,594 bells prior to 1774 (*Cf* page 213)

From an entry in the Burial Register, it would appear that a person was killed either at the time, or very soon after, the present bells were hung

"1713-4 Jan 22 Mark, son of Mark Topham, kill d by the 4th Bell clapper " three tons   In 1878 the bells were quartered, new wheels and ropes were added, and the framework thoroughly repaired at a cost of £113 8s. 0d, by Messrs Warner and Sons, of London

The custom of ringing the "*Guttit*" or "*Pan-cake bell*" on Shrove Tuesday, at 11 a m ceased about forty years ago, and the *Curfew bell*, rather more than twenty-five years ago

THE CHURCH PLATE.

The present Communion Plate is the same as that described in an Inventory now preserved at the Rectory, dated 20th June, 1763,* namely —

[1] CHALICE, (London Hall Mark 1604) with a loose lid on which is engraved the date—1605

[2] CHALICE, (London Hall Mark, 1633) without a lid   It is inscribed, and dated, the figures being in the centres of four roses, as follows —
    "(1) *Ex dono* (6) *Aliciæ* (3) *Wilbraham* (3) *de Dorfould*"†

[3] Two large FLAGONS (London Hall Mark 1659) each inscribed—
    "The guift of Eliz Dauenport and Margt Woodnoth, widdowes,
    To ye Church of Namptwich, 1659"‡
And above the arms and crests of the Davenport and Woodnoth families

[4] SILVER PATEN, no date, but supposed to have been given by the same ladies

[5] Two SILVER ALMS DISHES (London Hall Mark, 1732-3), no date, but inscribed —
    "*The Gift of Mrs* ELIZ. WILBRAHAM, *Relict of* STEPHEN WILBRAHAM ESQ'R"§
To the above have recently been added —

[6] A BRASS ALMS DISH; given in 1872, superseding the former PEWTER DISH ‖

[7] An old APOSTLE SPOON, not of English workmanship, added in 1873

[8] A SILVER STRAINER (London Hall Mark 1822) given in 1879

---

* See Article in *Cheshire Sheaf*, vol ii p 243, by the Rev. F G Blackburne, Rector of Nantwich

† Alice Wilbraham, the donor was the wife of Ralph Wilbraham, who built the present Dorfold Hall, and daughter of Thomas Mainwaring Gent of Nantwich   She was married at Nantwich on the 7th Feb 1580-1, and died here in 1635   Thomas Wilbraham *(MS Journal)* says —"My Ant Alce Wilbraham died 21 Martii 1635 "

Her burial is thus entered at Nantwich—
    "1635 Mris Ales Wilbraham, widdowe, died at Namptwich, buried att Acton March the 23 "—*(Par Reg)*

‡ *Cf* pages 288-9

§ Randle Wilbraham, Esq, of Nantwich *(MS Journ)* says —"12 June 1708 My only Brother, Stephen Wilb[raham] married Elizabeth the dau of Thos Hoole of Bostock, & widow of Crispin Birch "   She survived her second husband 21 years and was buried at Nantwich on the 26th Jan 1753 —*(Par Reg)*

‖ This large Pewter Dish which is preserved in the "aumbry" in the Lady Chapel, bears the following inscription
    " A citizen of London gave this bason and two bread
    plates to the Church of Nantwich April 4 Ano Dom 1640 "
Query, whether it was the gift of John Clife, gentleman, who is mentioned on page 318

The Parish Registers.

N the abolition of the Pope's Supremacy in England, Thomas Lord Cromwell was placed at the head of Ecclesiastical affairs under the title of the King's Vicar-General; and to his wisdom was due the introduction of Parochial Registers. Injunctions were set forth for their commencement in Sept. 1538 (30 Hen. VIII); and though, in many parishes and chapelries, those injunctions met with only a tardy compliance, at Nantwich, Registers were commenced in the following year, as proved by the heading of the first page; as follows:—

"The pairyshe of Wychemalbanck."

"Anno Domine M.DXXXIX,º the xvjº daye of Novembre in the xxxjº yeare of the Raigne of our most gracyous and dread sowergne Henrye the eighte by the grace of god Kinge of England and of ffraunce and Lord of Ireland defender of the faythe &c. and on earth Supreame head under god of the churche of England."

"This booke contenteth a Register for the Wychemalbaucke aforesayd wherein is wrytten the day monethe yeare of every Christeninge Weddinge and Buryinge."

This volume, written on paper, and originally bound in calf backs, is now, unfortunately, but a fragment; consisting of only nine leaves of Baptismal entries from the 17th Nov. 1539, to the 5th June, 1545. Then comes a space, from which many leaves have been torn out. That records were kept after the latter date, is proved by the following extract from the "Minshull Accounts and Memoranda," now in the possession of G. F. Wilbraham, Esq.

"The Juste agge [age] of me Thomas mynshull written wth my owne hande owt of the cheresoninge bowke safelie kept in the chorche beinge there sett Downe that I was bowrne iu to the woorlde the sixt Day of meay beinge the year of 1552."

The missing pages probably brought the record down to 1558; after which, according to the title page of the next volume, no registrations were made for fourteen years. In consequence of the general laxity in keeping registers throughout the conntry, the Registration Act was amended in the 1st, 7th, and 39th years of Queen Elizabeth's reign; and, accordingly, this old neglected volume was again called into requisition; and from Jan. 1572-3, entries of Baptisms, Marriages, and Burials were re-commenced by William Ward, the then incumbent, and the series have since come down in successive volumes to the present time with almost unbroken continuity. These volumes may be divided into *Old* and *Modern* Registers. The former, from which the extracts given below are taken, are comprised in eight volumes, extending, as a complete series, over a period of two hundred and forty years (from Jan. 1573 to Jan. 1813); the latter, in which a formal arrangement under different heads became imperative by Act of Parliament, are contained in fourteen volumes. All these volumes are in an excellent state of preservation, and every care is now taken of them by the present Rector, who keeps them locked up in an iron safe in the Rectory House   When it is remembered that Parish Clerks, Churchwardens, and Clergymen have at different times been the custodians and registrars, it is remarkable that the Registers have been handed down having scarcely suffered either damage or loss. They appear, on the whole, to have been well kept, as very few alterations, interpolations, erasures, or gaps occur

The utility of the Parish Register as a book of record was recognized by the churchwardens of the sixteenth and seventeenth centuries, as evidenced by many interesting memoranda which have already been given in the chapter of Annals   Entries relating to the principal local families will be found in their pedigrees, or in other parts of this work. The extracts given below are selected as illustrative of the "Annals of the poor," as alluding to notable persons, who, though not belonging to the old families of the town, have found a place in these records, or as being otherwise curious and interesting

VOLUME I 1539—1545

This volume commences with the baptisms of four illegitimate children, and throughout its pages the names of both father and mother, whether legal or reputed, are duly recorded   The registrar, who signs his name in Nov 1542, as "*Thomas Bulleyne me possidet*," has also given at the end of each year, (March 24th,—old style) the total number of Baptisms, divided thus —

Year	Legitimate	Illegitimate	Total
1540	62	15	77
1541	52	8	60
1542	69	15	84
1543	69	13	82
1544	56	9	65

From these figures it will be seen that in 1540 the base-born children reached nearly 20 per cent, and for the five years, they amount to more than 16 per cent of the total number of recorded baptisms   With one exception they appear to have belonged to the lower orders of the town   These facts afford evidence of the poverty and degradation of the labouring classes, who, at that time, seldom entered the bonds of matrimony   (See Froude's History, vol 1 p 4 and 5)

"*Christnings*"

1539 Nov 17   Joane ffounderdam alijs greene D of Nicholas ff & Esabell Davyeson illigittimat *
1539 40 Feb 7   Eliz the D of John Manwaringe gent and Jane w[ife]
1540 April 18   John the S of John Rutter and Alice his weife
1540 May 23   Margaret the D of Rich Rutter & Elizabeth his w
1541 April 14   Robt sonne of Roger Crokett & Alice w a twinne}
                Roger sonne of Roger Crokett & Alice w a twinne}
1541 July 10   Thomas S of Richard Hassall Esquire and Justice of peace & Margret his wief
1542 May 1   Roger S of Roger Crokett & Alice in pöch Wybunbury natus
1544 Oct 17   Roger S of William Bromley gent & Ellen
1544-5 March 4   Edward S of Raphe Brooke, gent & Margaret

* This is the first recorded baptism in the Registers

VOLUME II   Jan 1572-3,—Sept. 1653

The title page of this volume has an illuminated border   A vine, bearing leaves and clusters of grapes, branches out from a central point at the bottom of the page, and entwines itself round two columns   On the pedestal of each column stands a female figure, *Faith* and *Hope*   In the middle of the top of the page, is a shield of the Royal Arms, (France and England quarterly) surmounted, crest-like, with a dove, representing *Love*, and thus completing the trio of Graces, and under the shield is the motto, *"Dieu et mon droit"*   Within this border is written, very neatly, the following —

"Anno Reg Regin
Elizabeth 13
A REGESTER OF THE
PARISHE OF WICHE
MALBANKE.

Beginninge the first Day of Januarie in the
yeare of our Lord God on[e] thousand fiue
hundred seventy & tow, at which
time ther was no Regester of the
said Wichmalbanke to be
founde
for the space of fourtine yeares befor, till one
William Warde was admitted Curatie
there, who in the day & yeare
aforesayd began the first
of this Regester
as followeth

✠

Anno D'ini   1572. '*

In 1603 (1 Jac. I) it was ordered by a Canon of the Church that all Registers should be written over again on *parchment*, and accordingly Hugh Price, haberdasher, of this town, was employed to transcribe the entries from the 7th Jan 1572-3, to the year 1603, contained in the old paper volume   The almost total absence of alterations and errors, and the characteristic neatness of the writing (the years being in red ink, which is still bright and fresh) are evidence of the ability and accuracy of the copyist, whilst the much admired title page remains a proof of his artistic skill in embellishment when art and learning were only possessed by few

From 1603 to the end of the volume, the register appears to have been kept by the Senior Churchwarden during his year of office

Marriages

1572-3 Jan   29   James Bullenn and Ellen Edwards †
1574   June 18   Richard Brooke of Chester married Alice Colly of Aulm [Audlem]
1575   Aug 20   Richd. Crompton of the parish of Coona in ye county of Sallop to Joan Masterson

---

* This is subscribed "p *Hugh Price*," who is mentioned in the same volume as follows —
   1590-1   Feb 8   Hugh Price & Alice Coultonn [Married]
   1591-2   Jan 16   Mary d of Hugh Price, Haberdasher [Baptised]
   1614-5   Jan   1   Hugh Price the Author of this Booke [Buried]
† This is the first recorded marriage

1581	Oct 28	Thomas Baker, musysyon, & Joan Boult
1607	Dec 12	Jasper Wicksted, & Margaret Maddocks at St Werburg, Chester
1607-8	Feb 9	John Gibbons, & Mary Smethwicke, by dispensation
1609	Dec 18	Edmund Sparrow marryed his mayd
1621	May 10	Robert Lawton and Margaret Church dau of Thomas Churche of Bunbury, by a licence
1621	Sep 8	Edmund Warrington, & Susan Meakin, both of Bartomley parrishe by certificatt
1634	May 6	ffoulk Griffin and Ann Maddock mari at Acton
1639	April 18.	William Dod gent & Ann Lotham married at Awgdlem [Audlem]

Baptisms

1573	Nov 24	Edmund s of Rondull Wright *
1576	April 10	Jasper the son of Jasper Rutter, gent
1576	April 21	Margaret the dau of John Hudson of London
1576	May 8	Ellen, d of Rondulph Manwaringe of Sarsenshead †
1576	Oct 8	Thomas son of William Bromley, gent
1578	Aug 21	Richard son of Richard Griffen, gent
1580-1	Jan 28	Thomas, s of William Snelson of London
1582	Aug 22	Thomas, s of Robert Briskooe, *fletcher* ‡
1582	Oct 5	Jane d of Thomas Clowes of the Lampern Bridge §
1592-3	Feb 28	Margery d. of Thomas Willett of Towne well [Welsh Row]
1602	July 10	Roger, s of Roger Lecher, drumer [drummer]
1605	Nov 8	Richd s of John Brayne, gent of Acton p'ishe
1606	Sep 7	Kathren daughtr of Laurance Hopkin, *perigrine* [gipsy]
1606	Oct 26	William s of John Leigh de Swanne [i e of the Swan Inn]
1607	Oct 7	Thomas & Anne, twinnes, of William Ince, *cherurgion* [surgeon]
1610-11	Jan 20	Mark, s of Willm Parttidge, *chapman* [hawker]
1613-4	Feb 13	Lawrence, s of Richard Woodward of Shrowbridge
1629	April 19	Richard, sonne of John Creswall, *booke bynder*
1629	April 27	Catharine, daughter of Lawrence Eyton, of Leighton, Esq
1630-1	March 7	Marie the daughter of a poore Irishe woman
1647 8	Jan 16	John son of Mr William Dodd of Allim [Audlem] pish [of Highfields]
1648	Oct 29	Mary d of Raphe Walley *potte-karier* [see Salt petre man, under Burials 1629]
1649	Dec 23	Mary dau of Richard Wilkes of Cheere-Brooke

Burials.

1572-3	Jan 7	Thomas Mainwayringe, gent ‖
1573-4	March 23	Silber Wathew, gentlewoman ¶
1576-7	Jan 19	Thomas Towyearould *.

* In the margin, by a later hand, are the initials E W , no doubt added to point out the baptism of one whose memory is still green, viz Sir Edmund Wright, Kt , founder of an Almshouse in this town The Almsmen's Feast is still held on the 24th of November annually

† That is, Saracen's Head, an Inn in Beam Street A Saracen's head was the badge of Lord Audley

‡ "*Fletcher*, i e arrow-maker Implying the use of the long bow, and the practice of archery

§ Probably the "*Little Bridge*," that crossed the *Channel* in Welsh Row, not far from the Welsh Bridge *Lampern*, or *Lompon* is synonymous with channel or open drain

‖ This is the first recorded burial An extract from his Will has been given on page 284

¶ "*Wathew,*" this is probably one of the many ways of spelling *Walthall*, a very respectable family that afterwards settled at Wistaston

*. "*Towyearould,*" or Twoyearold, a family name found all through the Registers, and only lately died out in the town

1577	July	9	Sibbell Griffen, gentlewoman
1577	Nov	21	William Rutter of Wigen in lancashire
⋖1578	Dec	6	Thomas Vaughan of church stretton, gent
1581	April	7	Ellen Bromley, late wife of Wm Bromley, gent
1582	March	29	Rondell Rutter, *minister*
1582	Oct		Roger Wathew gent dyed the 4th daye & was buryed the 7th
1583	June	20	Richard Maisterson *carryer*
1585	April	2	Isabell Cotton, gentlewoman
1585	Dec	26	James Bulleine, Cutler, off the age of 74 yeares, he had five wyves and twentie foure children *
1588	Aug	15	John Manwaringe of the Hawkes Head, gent.
1589-90	March	14	Owinn Mowdy born in cambridge
1591-2	Feb	10	Thomas Baker, *harper* †
1593	Sep	28	Maximilian Savage, gent
1596-7	Jan	26	Rondull Seaboll, *piper* [i e bag-piper] †
1597	Aug	29	Richd Meakin, of the pumpe
1597	Sep	3	Richd Ciewe clayman
1602	March	28	Rauffe Wilbram of the Anngell, Smith
1603	Nov	5	Arthur Minshull with the long berde [beard]
1606	Nov	16	Peter Knowsley, sometyme of the Ambutts
1607	May	24	Richard Hewsonn, *pursmaker*, of Aspell [Hospital] Street
1607	Sep	18	Margaret wyfe of John Steete Recusant [i e Roman Catholic] buryed at Wistanson.
1611	Aug	25	Ann Hassall, widdow, genner [gentlewoman] a mirror of vertue
1611	Aug	31	Anne, wyffe of Edward Diggens, *scrivenner* ‡
1613	March	29	Rodger Brouck, whiseler, smith §
1614	Dec	11	John Corbet, an ancient poore man
1617	May	26	Richard Lewis, *Minister at Acton*
1618-9	March	19	Hennie Talley whose dwelling was in Saint Allowes, was buried
1621	June	13	Richard Wilkes of the beame streete, an ancient townsman
1621	Aug	21	Richard Bookeley, of the pepper Streete, an ancient townsman
1621-2	March	3	Thomas son of John Rudierd, stationer
1629	Nov	26	John Couper, *a salt-peeter man* ‖
1631-2	Jan	28	Mary daughter of Houlsie, Poyntmaker [pin-maker]
1632	Aug	13	Mrs Ales Birkenhead ¶

* At Willaston, in the year 1876, died Mr Jonathan Kitchen, for many years a butcher in Nantwich, who even out-Harried Harry VIII, having survived his sixth wife!

† The services of these players would be in requisition at marriages, and other festivities, wakes &c

‡ "*Scrivenner*" i e one who drew up and engrossed writings

§ "*Whiseler*' This appears to have been his nickname Many like instances occur, and some amusing stories are still told in the town of people in the past generation who were better known by their nickname than their proper surname

‖ The office of *saltpetre man* was a very obnoxious one All animal fluids were, by proclamation 3 Car I 1627, ordered to be preserved by families and an officer was authorized to collect the same from house to house once in 24 hours in summer, and once in 48 hours in winter, for the purpose of supplying nitre for the gunpowder manufacturers (See an Article on this subject in Chambers' *Book of Days*, vol 1 p 666) This town official is traceable at a later date, under the name of "*potte-harier*' (See *Baptisms*, 1648)

¶ "*Mrs*" for *Mistress*, a title of courtesy of frequent use in parish Registers, &c, is sometimes used to describe a *maiden*, as well as a *married*, lady Her name occurs in the *Index to Chester Wills* (Record Soc Publ Vol iv p 23) as follows — "Alice Birkenhead, of Wych Malbank, *spinster*, 1632 '

In the *Cheshire Funeral Certificates* (Record Soc Pub Vol vi p 171 is mentioned another Mrs Alice Birkenhead, buried in the same year, on 13th November, at Backford, co Chester, who was the wife of Henry Birkenhead, of Backford, Esq.

1635-6 Jan 20 Syon Venables, Rectoi of Thurstington
1636-7 March 8 Gilbert Woollam one of the Almsmen [at Welsh Row Head]
1637 Oct 10 Yewyn son of Thomas Mynshull of Mynshull, buried
1638 June 21 Thomas Mynshull the Almsman being the first [i.e of Sir Edmund Wright's Almsmen]
1638 Aug 5 William Smallwood miller of the Wych Mill
1638 Sept 18 Mr Ridgwaye brother to the Earl of Londonderry, died
1638 Aug 31 Peter son of William Iobley, Salt-peeter man
1638 Oct 12 Edwd Richardson, barbar, buried in the night
1640 June 24 Richard Venables Esquire
1641 July 2 Lady Leigh buried at Wibunburie *
1641-2 Jan 28 Ann, dau of William Clarke, faulkner [falconer]
1645 July 31 Nickolas son of Chidley Coote, Lieutenant Collonl †
1646 June 8 Mary, wife of Maior Philipp Mainwaring Buryed at Goostree ‡
1647 April 12 Matthew Mainwaring, gent , & Constable of Dublin castle
1647 Dec 30 Edward Moore tapster at the Lamb
1648 Aprill 25 Sir Thomas Delves [Kt and Bart of Doddington] buried at Widdenbury §
1650-1 Feb 26 Jane, dau of Mr Willm Dodd of Highfields [Audlem]

VOLUME III.   1653—1678

This parchment volume was commenced pursuant to an Act passed by the "Barebones Parliament," dated 24th Aug 1653, which required that a "Parish Register" (i e. Registrar) be chosen by every Parish, to be approved of, and sworn by, a Justice of the Peace for the Registering of births, burials, and marriages.

On the first page a memorandum of the appointment dated 3 Oct 1653, is entered as follows —

> "Forasmuch as it appeareth unto mee by severall Certificates under the hands of several persons inhabitants within the Parish of Namptwici that MR EDWARD HAYES is a fit person to be parish Register within the said Parish These are therefore to certifie all whom it doth or may conceane that I have confirmed him the said Mr Hayes to be Parish Register in the Parish aforesaid And have also given him his oath to execute the said office faithfully according to the late act of Parliament in that case made and provided Witness my hand and the day and yeare first above written "
>
> [No signature]

At the same time it was enacted that marriages should be celebrated by a local Magistrate, and not by a clergyman.‖

At Nantwich the names of the Magistrates, before whom the marriage contracts were ratified, are not recorded, but in the adjoining parish of Wybunbury, the entries of marriages are much fuller,—e g.

---

* Wybunbury Register records her burial thus —" 1641 Julie 2 buried Ladie Dame Elizabeth Lee "

† "Chidley Coote," the same family name occurs again in these Registers under Baptisms 1691 and 1693

‡ The total number of soldiers entered in the Burial Register from 29th March, 1642, to the 17th March, 1645-6, amounts to 188 Of these, 91 were buried in 1643 38 in 1644, and 48 in 1645   The greatest number of military burials occur in the following months —19 in Jan 1643-4, 27 in Feb 1643-4, 11 in July 1644, 21 in Oct 1645

§ His burial is entered at Wybunbury on the 24th April

‖ Cf page 192   The fees were not to exceed the following sums —

Publication and Certificate	12d	Entry of Birth of Child .	4d
Entry of every Marriage	12d	Entry of every Death	4d
Certificate from the J P (if desired)	12d		

Poor people living upon alms were excused all Registration Fees

"1655 Nov 13 Were married as this is to Certifie all whom it doth or may concerne Thomas Cornes of Namptwich parish and Anne Yonge of hatherton in wibunbury pish before Thomas Mainwaring Esq one of the Justices of the Peace for this Countie in witness of Mr Smith of Audelem and Mr Charles Standish and diuers others "

"1655-6 Feb 25 This is to certifie all whom it doth or may concerne that Robert Timis of hatherton in the pish of wibunbury and Allis Rowley of Keele were married before Tho Bratt Esq one of the Justices of the peace for the county of Stafford In witness of John Blackburn, John Timis and diuers others "

"1655-6 March 3 This is to certifie, [&c] Richard Pemberton of hatherton [&c] and Elizabeth Yeavenson of Longehill in the pish of Audelem weare marryed before Thomas Mainwaring Esq [&c] in witness of Mr Samuel Cole cler [vicar of Wybanbury] Humphrey Hayles and diuers others "

Out of seventy-one civil marriages recorded at Nantwich, only seven are stated to have been published in the Church   From the year 1656 the registrars here adopted the simplest form of recording marriages, (merely giving the names of the parties), whereas in the neighbouring parish of Wistaston, after King Charles Restoration, the mode of entry, for several years, was as follows —

" William Colbach and Ann Soot both of Namptwich their banes [banns] of Matrimony being published three several times *accordinge to the Lawes Ecclesiastical of this Realme* in Namptwiche Church, were marryed the twenty-seventh of Jannarye," [1678-9 at Wistaston Church] —*Wistaston Reg*

Marriages

1660   Dec   6   Robert Burroughes gent * and Anne Hopkin
1667   June 13   Hugh Whitney of Poole, gent , and Mrs Eliz Wright †
1674   Sep. 27   Mr John Wettenhall and Mrs Ann Jackson ‡

Baptisms

1661-2   Jan 26   Eliz d of John Middleton, *slater*
1663   July 14   John, s of Richd Pemberton of Broad Lane
1663   Aug 9   Thos s of Thos Price, *Paver*
1671-2   March 18 ffrancis d of Rich Griffin Esq
1672-3   March 3   Ann d of Rich Griffin Esq
1673   Sep   1   Ermine, dau of Hughe Delues §

Burials

1654   May 1   Katherine wife of Richd Griffin, Gent
1655   Oct 22   Ellen Shephilbotham ‖

* He was the eldest son of *Thomas Burroughes*, Attorney, of Nantwich, (the son of *Ralph Burroughes*, of Alpraham) by his wife, Anne, daughter of Randle Palyn, of Bickerton   The family of Thos Burroughes, who was buried at Nantwich on 16th Feb 1646, was as follows —
  1 *Robert Burroughes*, who married, first, Jane, dau to John Benyon, of Ashe, co Salop, and, secondly, Anne, dau to Thos Hopkins, of Tilstode, co Salop, who was buried at Nantwich 31st Jan 1670   He was Churchwarden in 1651, and was buried at Nantwich 13th Dec 1677   He entered his name and pedigree at the Visitation of 1663
  2 *Ralph Burroughes*, who married Margaret dau of Hugh Allen (See p 319)
  3 *Thomas Burroughes* who was Churchwarden of Nantwich in 1663
  4 *Anne Burroughes*, wife of Gabriel Wettenhall (See Wettenhall Pedigree)
  5 *Elizabeth Burroughes* wife of John Abnet of Nantwich
The name Burroughes is of frequent occurrence in Acton Parish Registers

† This Hugh Whitney is not mentioned in the account of the family in Green's " *Whitney's Emblems*," Introd page xl—xlii   ‡ See *Wettenhall Pedigree*

§ *Ermine Delves* was the eldest and last surviving daughter of *Hugh Delves*, of Nantwich, Gent , who died at Doddington and was buried at Wybunbury on 14th June 1712, (*Wybunbury* and *Nantwich Registers*) and grand daughter of *John Delves*, (natural son of Sir Thomas Delves, of Doddington, Bart) and Anne, his wife, whom he married on the 2nd July, 1623 (*Cf* pp 196, 318)   By her will, dated 1st Feb 1728, Ermine Delves spinster, left a Charity for the erection and sustentation of Almshouses for four poor men, natives of Nantwich, and of 50 years of age, at the least, and their wives, and belonging to the Church of England (See *Charities*)

‖ Shephilbotham, is now spelled Shufflebotham.

1655   Dec 21 Richd Griffin, Gent (*Cf* page 319 *note*)
1662   May 10 John Browne a soldiei in Col fflowers Regt   •
1664   Feb 27 Mrs Martha Griffin
1665   July   5 Edmund Griffin, Gent
1668   Feb 16 Sir Joseph Throckmorten
1673   April 4 Mrs Anne Jones, Widow *
1673-4 Jan 20 George Croxton Esq buried at Middlewich †

VOLUME IV.   1679—1740

This parchment volume was commenced when the Act (30 Car II cap. 3), intituled
"*An Act for burying in Woollen*" came into operation, which had for its object the
lessening of the importation of linen from beyond the seas, and the encouragement of
the woollen and paper manufactures in this kingdom   The law, which was rigorously
carried out, required an affidavit to be brought within eight days of the burial, under a
penalty of £5, that the deceased was not shrouded in linen, exception only being made
for persons dying of the plague   So particular were persons to be, that neither thread nor
cotton, but only *worsted*, might be used for sewing the shroud   This Act was not finally
repealed until 1813   No violation of the law is recorded here, and, what is still more
remarkable, for *ninety years*, during which Parish Clerks were the Registrars, no allusion
whatever is made to this curious Burial-law   In 1769, and three succeeding years, the
Rev John Smith, Rector, entered the burials in the following manner, and signed his
name at the bottom of each page

Burials in Woollen Shrouds

1769	No Certificate Notice given	Thomas son of John & Jane Amson	Aug 28
,,	Notice given Sep 9 No affidavit	Mary White	Sep 1
,,	Notice given Sep 9 No affidavit	John Nixon	Sep 7
,,	No notice in this case necessary	Margarei d of Chas Wild	Sep 7
,,	Notice given Dec 23 No certificate	Mr Richard Cooper Surgeon	Dec 17
1770	No notice in this case necessary	Mr Chas Salmon, burd at Middlewich	July 16
,,	An Affidavit made by Elizabeth Cliffe widow and Ann Thomason Spinster before the Rev Mr Kent	Jane wife of John Smith Rector buried at Wistaston	Dec 28
1771	Notice given Ap 10 No affidavit	Esther Brooke widow of the late Dr Brooke Dean of Chester & Rector of Nantwich	Ap 2

The total number of such entries, from 20th July, 1769, to 2nd Oct 1772, amount to
255   After the latter date, the name of the deceased person is simply given, by the
Parish Clerks who again became the registrars for a few years

* This lady gave to Wrenbury Church as follows —

"Mrs Hannah Jones of Namptwich gave the sum of Fifty Pounds to be disposed of as followeth, viz, £10 towards
buying a Silver Flaggon foi the Use of ye Sacrament in ye Parish Church of Wrenbury   *Item* £10 to buy a Velvet Pulpet
Cloath and Cushion for Adorning the Pulpett   *Item* £10 to the Schoolmaster of Wrenbury, the Interest to be paid to
him Annually upon St Thomas' Day by the Churchwardens for the teaching two Poor Boys to Read, out of Broomhall
and Sound   *Item* £20, the Interest thereof to be paid annually upon St Thomas' Day by yo Churchwardens to ye Poor
of the Townships of Broomhall and Sound"

† Very probably George Croxton, of Ravenscroft, Esq, one of the last of an ancient family that became extinct by
the death of Thomas Croxton in 1696 —(Lysons' *Cheshire*, p 380)

From the year 1678 to 1688 there were two hundred marriages solemnized in Nantwich Church, of which one hundred and thirty-nine were by licence, and sixty-one by publication of banns

Marriages.

1679 April 29 Joseph Poynton of Manchester & Margaret Wright of Namptwich by license from Mr Adams Suragate of Manchester dated the 25th of Aprill

1679 Oct 6 Anesiphorus Hickson & Jane ffisher, widow, by licence from the Chancellor [John Wainewright LL D] dated the 5th Oct

1680 Aug 24 Edwd Dodd and Jane Hanson by licence from Mr [Laurence] Fogg [afterwards Dean of Chester] dated the 17th Aug

1681 May 22 John Goodale* and Hannah Kirkham by licence *extra p'vintiam*

1688 July 12 Thomas Brooke Esq [of Norton] and Mrs Grace Wilbraham by licence from Mr Stringer [of Nantwich] dated July 7th

1688 Sep 6 Samuell Barrow Gent, & Mary Astle, by Licence from Mr Stringer dated Sep 6th

1689-90 Jan 13 Solomon ffoley, clerk, & Margaret Wettenhall by Licence from Mr Stringer dated Jan 13

1702 Sep 30 Samuel Walker, cler, & Elizabeth Loundes, by Publicacon

1707 Nov 5 Robert Withenshaw, tanner, & Anne Churche, by licence from Mr Bradshaw dated Nov 5

1711 April 27 Henry Bennett of the City of Chester, gent, & Elizabeth Comberbach by Licence from Mr Olliver [Vicar of Audlem] dated Ap 24

1719 June 11 Creswell Taylner Esqre & Martha Willdigg by Licence from Mr Gibbons [of Nantwich] dated June 11th

1720-1 Feb 14 William Wright Esq † & Mrs ffrancis Alice Wilbraham by Licence from Mr Brooke [of Nantwich] dated ffeb 13

1722 May 26 William Calkin of Waverton, Cleric, & Jane Sherwin, spinster, by Licence from Mr Brooke dated May 25

1723 Aug 11 John Sanders Esqr & Mary Bayley by Licence from the Chancellor of Chester dated Aug 9 ‡

1723-4 Jan 15 Peter Weever of St Sepulcher's Parish, London, & Catharine Pratchett of Nant parish, by Licence from Doctor's Commons Dat Jan 7 G Paul, Registrar

1724 Ap 23 William Furnivall Gent & Margery Jackson by Licence from Mr Brooke [of Nantwich] dat Ap 21

1724 Ap 23 Peter Furrivall Gent & Marget Jackson by Licence &c dat Ap 23

1729 May 27 Samuel Stretch & Elizabeth Wilkenson, by Licence from Mr Brooke dat May 27

1729 July 26 William Noble & Margaret Jones, by Publicacon, a soldier in the Princes Regiment

1730 Nov 26 John Cotes of Woodcote in the county of Salop Esq & Dame Rhoda Delves of Doddington in the County of Chester widow, by Licence from Mr Harwar [of Acton] Dat Nov 25 §

1733 May 3 Thomas Lowe Gent & Elizabeth ffurnivall, spinster by Licence from Mr Hanson Dat Ap 27

---

* Another John Goodale, (? whether a son of this marriage) is mentioned in a monument now in the Baptist Chapel Nantwich

† William Wright, Esq , o: Mottram, in this County

‡ A child of this marriage was born and died at Nantwich , see 1735 *postéa*, see also Burials 1735 6

§ *Dame Rhoda Delves*, was the fourth wife of Sir Thomas Delves The Rev Thos Cotes, M A , Vicar of Acton from 1787 to 1798, belonged to this Shropshire family

1734-5 Jan 29 Richard Walmsley Esq & Margaret Williams by Licence from the Revd Doctor Brooke Dated 28 Jan

1738 Aug 10 Thomas Hall Esq * & Elizabeth Bayley Spinster by Licence from the Revd Doctr. Brooke Dated the 9th

1739 June 1 Edward ffletcher Gent & Margery Wetwood, by Lic [&c] Dated May 29

1740 May 15 Joseph Skerratt & Sarah Shenton, by Lic [&c same day]

＊

Baptisms

1691 Dec 23 John sonne of Capt Chidley Coote, second son to my Lord Caloony in the Kingdome of Ireland

1693 Aug 6 Mary dau to Capt Chidley Coote, &c

1697 May 8 Catharine dau of Robt Peplow, Minister of Moreton-sea, Salop

1699 Aug 2 Richard Chance, a Bastard child lost at the Heath side

1703 May 22 Thomas son of William Simpson, Packsaddle-maker

1703 Aug 26 George, son of Thomas Polley Gent [Thos another son, bapt 11 March 1707-8]

1703 Oct 26 Elizabeth, dau of Capt Washington Shirley second son to Robert Lord fferrers, Baron of Charteley

1705 Dec 1 Joseph, son of Thomas Newans, Pipe-maker

1709 March 26 Willm s of Charles Boote, Perriwigg-maker

1710 Nov 20 Thomas son of Thomas Hewitt of London, Attorney

1712-3 Jan 10 Hannah wife of Samuell Dutton, aged about 34 years †

1713 Dec 18 Robert son of John Booth Esq ‡ [Buried 26 May, 1716]

1714 May 5 John, son of Robert Withenshaw, Tanner

1714 July 6 Thomas son of Balzar Oulfon, Gent

1714 Nov 28 Morrice son of Daniell ffrith, Gent

1715-6 Jan 11 Thomas son of Robert Withenshaw [Robert W died in or before 1721]

1716 July 12 John, son of John Edwards, *Surveyor of the Windows* §

1718 Dec 11 James son of James Bealey [Bayley] junr Gent

1719-20 Feb 23 Elton son of Thomas Wood ||

1720 Nov 13 Samuell son of Thomas Sanders ¶

1722 Oct 8 Thomas Mainwaring*٭ son of Peter Wilding, Supervisor of the Ale Duty

1725 Aug 8 Mary, dau of Wm Lister, Excise Officer

1727-8 ffeb 11 Maurice son of Radcliffe Searle, clerke

1729 March 25 George son of Radcliffe Searle Rector of Thernsway,٭٭٭ in Lincolnshire [Buried 26 Jan 1730-1]

1730-1 Feb 7 Radcliffe son of Radcliffe Searle Rector of Thornsway, Lincolnsh

1732 June 15 William son of Radcliffe Searle Rector of Thoreseway &c [Buried 22nd June]

---

* This was Thomas Hall, Esq of the Hermitage, near Holmes Chapel, who obtained *jure uxoris* the manor of Cotton, near Middlewich The issue of this marriage was *Thomas Bayley Hall* Esq who after residing on the paternal estate at Hermitage for 60 years, died at the age of 83 in Sep 1828 (See mentions of this family in "*A Sketch of the History of Holmes Chapel,* ' by T W Barlow, Manchester, 1853)

† This is the first recorded instance of an adult baptism

‡ ? Whether John Booth Esq belonged to the family of that name settled at Twemlow, near Middlewich, which became extinct in the male line by the death of Thomas Booth Esq in 1786 (Lysons *Cheshire,* p 770)

§ The window-tax was imposed by Act of Parliament in 1695 This barbarous tax on the light and air of heaven was not repealed until 1851, (¹) the assessors being commonly called *Window-peepers*

|| To which is added ' Had his head shot off by a cannon ball in Flanders where he was a soldier '

● To which is added by a later hand "Who died Vicar of Knutsford "

٭٭ This is the first instance of a double Christian name, two other sons were named respectively, Arthur Mainwaring Wilding, and Peter Mainwaring Wilding ٭٭٭ Thoresway is a village 5 miles S E of Caistor, in Lincolnshire

1734-5 March 13 Hannah Tuesday, a Foundling

1735-6 ffeb 16 John son of John Sanders Esq of Koneley in co Warwick

1736 Sep 7 Charles son of Thomas Prince, *the town's hunts-man*

1737 May 16 Ann d of Richd Bell, *jarsey-weaver*

1739 Aug 11 Thos son of Thos Hewitt of ye Kingdom of Ireland

1739-40 March 16 Thomas son of John ffardoe *Chester carrier*

1740 May 24 Thos son of Acton Cartwright, a thatcher [To which is added "drowned in the further pool at Dorfold"]

Burials

1680 Sep 13 John Smith, a stranger dyed at the Red Lyon [now Wilbrahams Arms]

1684 May 12 Richard Griffin Esq

1684 July 23 Elizabeth wife of Charles Wright of Leighton, gent

1689 Sep 4 Mris Margaret Griffin, widow

1690-1 Jan 27 John Gibbons *Barber-Chyrurgion*

1691-2 Jan 16 Christopher sonne of Condrade Killingbough

1691-2 ffeb 18 Polycarpus Cæsar

1693-4 ffeb 2 Charles Cardiffe, Gent

1695-6 ffeb 13 ffrances wife cf John Ioundes buried at Chester

1696 Sep 14 John Brock, Gent

1698 July 5 Shusannah dau of Robert Peploe Clerk of Moreton-sea in Salop

1699 Oct 17 Alexander Humpston, *Boddys-maker* [Stay-maker]

1700 Oct 29 Margaret wife of John Lovatt, Gent, Quartr Master

1702-3 Jan 1 Catherine Oakes of Chester, Spinster

1703 May 5 Henry Bird, of Burton upon Trent, Gent

1704-5 Jan 12 Ellinor wife of Mr John Steele of Leighton buried at Wybunbury

1705 Dec 11 Thos Eavons, *pedlar*, burd at Wibunbury

1705-6 Jan 2 William Harrison senr, *Dawber* *

1706 Dec 13 John s of John Younge, *Heel-maker*

1706-7 ffeb 12 Doctr Robert Moyle, Cleric

1707-8 ffeb 27 Richard Novell of the City of Chester, *Limner*

1709-10 March 5 Eleanor dau of Mr Thomas Harvey Minister of Hargrave

1710 Dec 28 Gertrude wife of Arthur Glegg, Gent

1711-2 Jan 3 Henry Cobb attorney } both buried at Wybunbury in one Grave
Marg wife of Henry Cobb }

1716 Nov 15 George son of John Loundes, Clerk

1716 Dec 2 Mris Anne Wetenhall† widow, buried at Wistaston

1717 June 29 Thomas Talbot, *clockmaker* ‡

1719-20 March 23 Elizabeth dau of Nathaniel Payne, Gent

1720 Sep 6 Thomas Polley Gent

1726 Dec 18 Richd Moreton & Willm Moreton his son, both in a coffin

1727 Aug 15 Edmund Griffin Esqre

1727 Nov 29 John Warden, of the parish of Calder in North Brittain

---

* "*Dawber*," ie plasterer Cottages were formerly built of "Raddle" (interwoven sticks) and 'Daub' (clay) Though the occupation of "*dauber*" has passed away, a few specimens of such house-building still exist

† Her husband, the Rev John Wetenhall, Rector of Wistaston, was buried there, 16th May, 1704

‡ In Musée de l Hôtel de Cluny (Paris) there is a curious old clock, without date, but having on it the name of "*John Naylor, Nantwich, Cheshire*"

1727-8 March 17 Mrs Ann ffurnivall, spinster, Buried att Sandbach

1728-9 Feb   2 Richard Ravenscrofte, of Willaston, *dumbe*

1728-9 March 13 Sarah Leversage widow
                   Stephen Leversage her son } Buried at Sandbach

1728-9 March 21 A strange man found drown'd in Weever

1729   March 28 Ralph Horton Esq * Buried at Aulem [Audlem]

1729   Aug   29 John Massey *Chanlor*† [Chandler] Buried at Wrenbury

1729-30 Jan   29 John Parker, *Broker of Cloathes*

1730-1 Jan   24 Ann dau of the Revd John Loundes, decd Curate at Coppenhall

1732   July   2 Richard s of Richard Blagg, *Breeches-maker*

1732   Oct   16 Hannah Watkis buried at Sandbach   [In Sandbach Register called "Mrs Hannah
                      Watkiss, *widow* "]

1732   Dec   6 Slater Chaworth Gent Dyed the 1st

1732-3 Feb   25 Edward Parrot, steward to Sir Jno Chetwood

1735-6 March 22 John Sanders Esqre of Honeley, in co Warwick, Dyed at Nantwich the 17th
                      Buried at Honeley

1736   July   13 Richard Robinson, *Mugman* ‡

1736-7 Feb   10 John, s of John Walley, *fishmonger*

1737   May   6 Samuel Watkiss, Gent , buried at Wrenbury

1737   Aug   15 John Brayne, Gent , buried at Acton §

1737   Oct   3 William Jackson, Glover, kill'd by an ox at Crewe Hall

1737   Oct   25 Thomas Lovekin, Victualer, burd at Wybunbury

1737   Oct   30 Mary dau of George Moores, *Whiting-Master*

1738   May   24 Wm s of Wm Meers, *Cordwainer*

1738   June 12 Jane, dau of John Sanders Esq deceased at Madeley

1738-9 Jan   16 John Pratchett Gent, burd at Acton ||

1738-9 Feb   5 Eliz wife of William Hunt, *flax-dresser*

1739   April   6 Joseph Child, *net-maker*

1739-40 Jan   5 The Rev John Twemlow, Curate here

1740   June 30 Dorothy wife of ye Revd Samuel Lowe of Bunbury

1740   Sep   12 The Revd Daniel Barnet, Buried at Wrenbury

---

* Ralph Horton Esq was probably the last descendant of a family that had resided and owned lands in Coole-Pilate, near Nantwich, from the time of King Henry IV   (Lysons *Cheshire*, p 473)

† This John Massey is mentioned on a board now in the vestry of Wrenbury Church, thus — 'Mr John Massey, late of Nantwich, chandler, out of true respect to his Native Parish gave in his life-time a handsome silver chalice for the use of the Communion Service in the Parish Church of Wrenbury "

        John Withenshaw
        John Sproston } Churchwardens 1730

He fulfilled the office of Churchwarden at Nantwich in 1716 and 1717   His descendants for four generations, (Edward, Thomas, Richard, and Samuel successively) were Chandlers and Soap-boilers, at the corner of Mill Street and Barker Street   Mr Samuel Massie succeeded to his father's business in 1839, but, owing to the falling off in the candle trade by the introduction of composite candles, followed by oil-lamps and gas, he gave up the chandlery business about 1846 and commenced selling flour, bread-stuffs, and groceries, a trade that offered great profits at the time of the potato famine

‡ "*Mugman* " i e a dealer in earthenware   Formerly, on the north side of the Churchyard, was held the *Mug-market.*

§ The *Brayne* family resided in Acton parish for several centuries   Brayre-Hall, now a farm-house, is in Aston-in-Mondrem   The last of the name was another John Brayne, Esq , who died in the early part of this century (Lysons' *Cheshire* p 362, 472, &c)

|| The Pratchetts were connected with Worleston as well as Nantwich and are frequently mentioned in both Nantwich and Acton Registers   The last representative of this old family was a maiden lady, who died at Nantwich a few years ago, but the name is still preserved in *Pratchett's Row*, Nantwich

VOLUME V

This volume contains Marriages from 1741 to 1754, and Baptisms and Burials from 1741 to 1785 Towards the end of the volume will be found the following *memoranda* concerning the final change in the office of Registrar, from lay to clerical hands, and so for the last hundred years the Registers have been kept by the Rector of the Parish, or his Curate.

> "5 Nov 1762 Then pursuant to Doctor Reades [the Rector's] Request Richard Yoxall Parish Clerk Delivered to the Reverend Mr George Astley Curate of this Parish this Register Together with Three other Register Books belonging to the sd Parish The oldest of which begins in the year 1572 *

Mr Yoxall died the next year Different handwritings indicate different registrars, and for the next few years the entries are very meagre, consisting simply of names, omitting *trades, professions,* &c , almost the only additional information being the word "*pauper*," in the case of poor people, who probably paid no registration fee The registrar in 1764 is more particular in his entries, but in April, 1765, neither baptisms nor burials are recorded; and a wide space is left to indicate the omission From July, 1769, to Oct 1772, the registers were well kept, as has been already mentioned, by the Rector himself (Rev. John Smith) who signed his name at the bottom of every page But after the latter date, he appears to have relegated registration, perhaps, to his Curate. Other irregularities occurred as stated in the following *Memoranda* in the Rector's own hand —

> "*Mem* An Account of Funerals from this time [31 March 1782] to the 27th Dec 1782 is contained in a book which was in the possession of Thos Child late Parish Clerk† at the time of his decease, & which his widow has repeatedly refused either to deliver up or suffer the account to be transcribed
>
> Witness our hands this 26 day of April 1784
>
> John Smith Rector
> Thos Birchall ⎫ Churchwardens
> Wm Philipps ⎭
>
> "*Mem* The said Book has since been delivered up by the late Parish Clerks widow, from which the following entries of Funerals from March 31 1782 are made & continued to the end of the said year "

During the incumbency of John Smith, an occasional note at Easter states that an "*account of Funerals was returned to Court*"

Marriages

1744	July 30	John Tollett Gentleman, & Maria Redsdale, by licence &c
1747	Aug 17	Plant Maddocks and Hannah Hassall, by licence &c
1750	Sep 28	Richard Wrench & Elizabeth Rockett, widow, by licence &c
1751	May 18	William Sprout & Mary Fitton, widow, by licence &c
1751	Dec 5	Samuel Palin & Ceiceley Delves, widow, by licence &c
1722	June 28	Charles Wrench & Martha Griffies, by licence &c

Baptisms

1741	June 26	Eliz dau of Crewe Chetwood, Esqre ‡
1742	Sep 11	Richd son of Leonard Morrey, Gent §

---

* The earliest paper volume appears to have been lost at that time , but it had been found before 1831, when returns were made for the "Parish Register Abstract " (Add MSS 9335, Brit Mus)

† Thomas Child Parish Clerk [buried] 21 Dec 1782 —*(Par Reg)*

‡ Anna, another dau bapt 26 Jan 1742-3

§ Joseph, another son, bapt in 1748

1743	April 14	Catharine dau of James Williams, Gent
1745	May 1	Joseph, son of Joseph Skcrrett, *Upholster* *
1746-7	Jan 11	Catharine Maria† dau of James Tomkinson, Attorney
1747-8	Feb 11	John son of John Broadbent Gent
1748	July 5	Mary‡ dau of William Watkiss, Gent
1754	July 12	Plant son of Plant Maddocks, born 12th
1759	June 24	James son of James Bayley Junr Esquire
1763	Jan 24	George son of William Bailey, Gent
1765	May 22	Sarah dau of William Brooke, *Woman's Taylor*
1765	Aug 19	Stephen, son of Joseph Hassall of Brassie Hall [Willaston]
1767	Apr 23	James Wilkenson of Willaston in Nantwich Parish, adult of the age of 63
1769	Sept 1	Received into the Congregation John Underwood the son of James Bagley, Malster, who was privately baptized July 2, 1769 §
1769	Sept 20	Received into the Congregation Margaret daughter of the Rev John Smith, Rector of Nantwich & Jane his wife, who was born at Mucclestone Wood in the co of Stafford July 13, 1769 & privately baptized July 17, 1769 §
1769	Oct 4	Zillah dau of James Stockton
1769	Oct 15	Joan the child of Joseph Salmon, Gent , of Weaver Bank
1769	Nov 18	Thomas son of Thomas Bayley, Gent
1771	Aug 10	Richard Wickstead son of Rev James Thomas Vicar of Bolton-le-Sands, Lancashire
1778	Sep 1	Peter‖ son of Mr Peter Bailey, attorney at Law, & Sarah his wife
1780	May 1	James son of Mr Peter Bayley, Attorney at Law, Born Nov 1, 1779
1781	Sep 11	Matthew son of Peter Bayley Attorney at Law, & Sarah his wife, Born May 16th & Recd
1779	January	Harry son of Thos & Eliz Woodward Innkeeper recd 15th January, but born ye Day before ye Beginning of the preceding Nantwich Races
1780	June 7	A illegitimate child Baptized at Beam Bridge, John
1780	July 9	Peter s of James Boyer, *Clerk of Salt works*, recd
1783	May 21	William Plant, son of John Pratchett Gent, & Ann his wife born 2 March last

Burials

1741	July 21	Roger son of Francis Williams Gent buryed at Acton
1741-2	ffeb 1	William Cobb, gent buryed at Wybunbury
1742	July 31	Willm Maisterson Esqr *Buryed in the Chancel by leave from Mrs Crewe* ¶
1742	Oct 24	Phœbe Lewis, a *traveller*
1742	Dec 30	John Johnson, *Jersey comber*

* This son lived to be 87, and was buried in the Churchyard in 1832 (see page 53 *note*)

† The earliest *double* baptismal name of a female

‡ She became, in 1778, the wife of Rev A Clarkson, Rector of Nantwich, Other children baptized were *Ann*, 2 Oct 1749, *Hannah* 27 Nov 1750, *Catharine* 28 Oct 1756, *William* 20 March 1759, *Charlotte* 24 June 1763

§ This kind of entry commenced when John Smith became Rector of the Parish and kept the Registers

‖ Peter Bayley was afterwards educated at Rugby, and Merton Coll Oxford, and entered himself at the Temple, with the view of studying for the bar He gave more attention, however, to literature than to the law, and wrote "Sketches from St George s-in the-Fields," "Idwal," "A Queen's Appeal" a poem in the Spenserian stanza, and other poems He died in 1823 —(Salisbury s "*Border Counties' Worthies*") Mr J E Bowman, of Nantwich, in a letter addressed to Joseph Hunter, the antiquary, dated 10th June, 1803 speaks of Peter Bayley as a rising artist, as well as a poet —(*Hunterian Corresp* vol ii f 289, Add MSS 24865, Brit Mus)

¶ This is the first *recorded* instance of an interment within the Church When such burials were of frequent occurrence the registrars thought it unnecessary to state the fact, but when the practice of burying within the Church became less common, and confined chiefly to the privileged classes, entries like this begin to appear

1742-3 ffeb 27 Catharine dau of Jas Bayley, *Oxford carrier*.

1743 June 1 Wm son of Wm Joynson, *Threadmaker*

1746 April 13 Richd Walthall, *Gaoler of Chester*

1746 Nov 13 Willm Barrett, a Blindman

1746 Oct 16 Enoch son of Thos Cope, Gent [Mary, a dau bapt on Nov 30 in the same year]

1747 July 6 Moulton Griffin Esqre

1750 Aug 30 William Jackson, *Peruke-maker*

1750 Nov 8 Wm Hodgson Gent buryed at Chester

1751 March 27 Thomas Tagg, Gent burd at Acton *

1753 Dec 15 George Beckett, coachman to Mr Wilbraham

1755 March 21 Edwd Evans shoomaker, *buried by the Club*

1755 March 26 Thos Leversage, mercer, *buryed in the Church*

1755 April 20. Ann, wife of Thos Rowe, *Brass founder*

1756 Nov 23 Eliz Daughr of John Lewin *Plushweaver*

1757 Feb 16 George Bryan, Officer of Excise dyed 11th being a Publick ffast, buried at Acton

1757 March 18 Ashton Williams Gent *Buried in Church*

1757 March 23 Eliza, d of Ann Simson a Comberland vagrant

1757 June 21 ———— a pauper & soldier, buried by the Overseers

1757 July 8 Thos Bird, peruke maker, buried in the Church by Mr Jos Lea of London

1758 Oct 19 William Butler, Gent buried at Audlem

1761 Feb 27 Sarah dau of Chas Davenport, *Turnpike Keeper* †

1762 Oct 4 John Pratchett Gentleman Buried at Acton

1764 Jan 8 James Topham, *apparitor* [Beadle]

1764 May 23 Mrs Brain Buried at Acton

1764 May 28 Mrs —— Watkiss Buried att Wrenbury

1767 June 28 Mrs Gilbert [buried] at Uttoxiter

1767 June 29 Robert Eachus [buried] at Middlewich

1767 Aug 10 Mrs Bayley wife of Mr Matthew Bayley [Buried] at Wrenbury

1768 July 22 Henry Johnson Gent [buried] at Bunbury ‡

1770 Feb 14 Mrs Barrow, widow, buried at Wrenbury

1770 July 16 Mr Charles Salmon, buried at Middlewich

1771 May 31 Edmund Griffin, of Burland Esq §

1773 Feb 28 William Watkis, Gentleman

1774 Nov 20 Mr Martin from London

1775 Dec 18 Mr George Audley Coroner and Attorney at Law

1777 March 14 *Miss* [first instance of this title] Margaret Yoxall

1777 Aug 30 Thos s of Thos Robinson, killed in fighting ||

* Thomas Tagg, Gen , owned lands in Worleston   See Ormerod's *Cheshire*, vol iii, p 357, New Edition, and *Cheshire Sheaf*, vol ii, p 363

† Toll-gates and toll-houses in this neighbourhood, were removed about the year 1875

‡ Henry Johnson is said to have been an Apothecary in Nantwich   To the memory of his wife, Jane, whom he had married at Bunbury in 1735, and who was buried there on the 9th April, 1741, he erected in the Chancel of Bunbury Church an altar tomb (with a long inscription and epitaph in verse which is still preserved) and pedestal on which stood the figure of his lady in stone of "shapeless sculpture"   The statue was afterwards taken down, and buried in the churchyard, where it remained until it was again brought to light by the sexton, John Smith, on the 4th May, 1882, when digging a grave   It has since been placed in the Church again , and an account of the discovery and an engraving of the figure appeared in the Palatine Note Book for July, 1882

§ Edmund Griffin was the last of the ancient family of Griffin, of Nantwich and Bartherton   (Lysons' *Cheshire*," p 383)

|| The scene of this fight was Snow Hill, the combatants being Charles Tomlinson and Thomas Robinson   Tomlinson was tried and imprisoned at Chester and when liberated was branded on the hand

1777   Oct   7   Thomas Pratchett Gent
1777   Dec   8   Sarah Salmon aged 95 *
1778   March 2   Luke Hines, Hackney coachman
1779   March 9   Ann Bloor, aged 94
1779   Sep   26   Ann Daughr of John Dawson *Printer*
1780   May   21   Joseph Meakin broke his leg the 16th
1780   April 23   Sarah Williamson midwife much lamented
1780   July 13   Mr George Payne [buried] at Wistaston
1781   March 3   David Thomas kill'd by the Machine [? A Coach]

VOLUME VI

Lord Hardwick's "*Act for the better Preventing of Clandestine Marriages*," (26 Geo II 1753) required that the Register of Marriages should be contained in a separate book, according to a printed form   The first entry is as follows   the italics representing the words filled in by the Registrar in *writing*

"*John Pemberton* of [*this*] Parish *Cordwainer*
and *Margaret Stringer* of [*this*] Parish *Spinster*
were married in this [*Church*] by [*Banns*] this *fifteenth*
Day of *April* in the year *one thousand seven hundred and fifty-four*
          By me   *T Adderley* [*Curate*]
This Marriage was solemnized between us { the mark **X** of *John Pemberton*
                                          { the mark **X** of *Margaret Stringer*
          Presence of { *Richd Yoxall*
                       { *Jno Harding.*'

Succeeding volumes have a similar, though improved, formal arrangement down to the present time

Marriages.   1754—1776

1755   Jan   19   James Hammond Merchant of Worcester & Amabilia Walthall
1755   Feb   9   George Payne, Mercer, & Amy Stone both of Nantwich
1758   July 16   William Pratchett Distiller & Martha Gleave
1759   Nov   11   Daniel Comberbach of Sandbach, Victualler, & Sarah Lea of Nantwich †
1763   April 29   William Knowles Esq of Great Budworth & Mary Kent, Spinster, of Nantwich
1764   May   13   Samuel Barrow of Wrenbury Esq, & Anne Bayley, Spinster of N
1764   July   2   Mark Topham of N *Threadman* & Clerk of the Senr Society & Mary Smith of N
1765   Oct   24   George Potter of Leigh, Lanc Gent, & Mary Kent, spinster of N
1771   Jan   1   Richard Crawford Massey of Great Budworth & Sarah Audley, dau of George
                  Audley Esq
1773   Aug   19   William Pratchett of Acton, Gent, & Elizabeth Pratchett, spinster of N
1775   Nov   11   Ralph Audley Gent & Joan dau of William Penlington Esq of Nantwich
                  Signed Ralph Audley

Joan Audley late Joan Penlington being married in August last to the said Ralph Audley in North Briton commonly called Scotland   [? at Gretna Green]

1776   Feb 8   William Wrench Surgeon & Ann Penlington Spinster aged 18 yrs & upwards, by &
                with the consent of Willm Penlington her natural & lawful Father.

* She was the daughter of John Gibbons, and baptized 13 Jan 1683-4, according to a marginal note in the Register.
† Omitted in Dr Marshall's "Genealogical Account of Comberbach Family," p 11 & 12

VOLUME VII *Marriages.* 1775—1812

1780	Aug	17	George Cappur Cheesefactor and Lydia Maddocks
1781	June	14	Plant Maddocks Gent and Catherine Cappur by Licence
1781	Oct	18	John Wrench of Wybunbury Parish Apothecary, and Margaret Oulton
1782	March	21	Thomas Nixon Attorney at Law and Sarah Maddocks
1782	May	21	John Pratchett of Acton, Gent and Ann Maddocks spinster
1789	Feb	10	William Lowe Gent and Elizabeth Stone of N spinster
1792	May	28	Thomas Garnett, Gent and Mary Horwood of N spinster
1795	Feb	24	William Sprout Linnen Draper and Mary Marsh of N
1797	May	21	Charles Gibbons Esq of Whitchurch and Joan Kent
1800	April	1	John Thompson schoolmaster and Elizabeth Mounfield of N
1800	Aug	20	Prussia Salmon Gent and Mary Walker of N
1803	Aprill	11	Prussia Salmon Gent and Elizabeth Cowap widow of N
1806	Feb	9	Sampson Cartwright Confectioner and Emma Perry, of N
1807	June	1	John Richardson* Esq of Bunbury and Mary Craven †
1808	Jan	3	John Bolland Surgeon, and Elizabeth Davies of N
1811	Apr	25	Edward Kent Esq and Penelope Jackson
1812	Feb	6	Charles Delves Broughton Esq and Mary Ann Atkinson of Manchester
1812	May	21	Peter Sprout Gent and Ann Maule of N

VOLUME VIII

As early as William and Mary's reign, a tax was imposed on the registrations of Baptisms, Marriages, and Burials   After having been several times amended, it was enacted in 23 Geo. III that after the 1st Oct 1783 a stamp duty of 3d (under a penalty of £5) was required for every entry in the Parish Register   Allusion is made to this law in the second extract.

Baptisms.   28 March 1785—31 Dec 1812

1785	June	16	Recd William 2nd son of Thomas Wettenhall Esq and Catharine his wife Born March 28, 1785, and baptizd the 30th of ye same month
1785	Oct	5	George, son of James Moore, soldier, and Sarah his wife [to which is added] " Duty excused "
1787	July	31	Diana Dr [daughter] of Thomas Wetenhall Esq and Catherine his wife was born the 14th of March, baptizd the 16th and recd into the Church of Acton 31 July
1789	Feb	27	William, son of Wm Tomlinson Gent and Eliz his wife, born 19 Oct 1788

* This *John Richardson, Esq*, afterwards purchased for a residence the large old house within walled grounds at Hospital Street end   and there his son, John Richardson, Esq , died on the 23rd July, 1880, at the age of 58 years   In the latter half of the seventeenth century, the house appears to have been the town residence of the Minshulls of Stoke Hall, in Acton parish   After the death of Sir Edward Minshull, Kt , in Jan 1672, his widow, the Dowager Lady Mary Minshull, enjoyed the Nantwich house as portion of her jointure   There she resided in 1674, at which time it was known as "*The New Bell,*" (Notes and Queries, 1st series   vol vi, p 109), a name suggestive of having originally been built as an Inn   She still occupied the same house in 1691   according to a Rate Book of that date   and most likely continued to reside there until her death in 1693   A century after the house belonged to George Garnett, Esq , from whom it descended to his son, the Rev W Garnett, Rector of Tilston, in this county and, after his death in 1829, to the Rev W B Garnett, (now W B Garnett-Botfield, Rector of Shifnall) who sold the house to the above-mentioned John Richardson Esq , whose son of the same name, lately deceased, has left it to George Garnett, Esq , of London

† *Mary Craven* was the daughter and co-heiress of Richard Craven, Esq , of Stoke Hall   The lordship of Stoke, in Acton parish, was held by the Minshull family (see p 314 and Minshull Pedigree) from the year 1610 until it was sold by Edward Minshull, Esq , in 1719, to Thomas Williams, Cheesefactor, of Nantwich whose son, in 1753, conveyed it to Roger Wilbraham, Esq   In 1781 it was purchased of the Wilbrahams by Richard Craven, Esq , who died at Stoke Hall on the 19th July, 1804, and left his lands to his three daughters —*Elizabeth Craven*, the wife of John Jasper Garnett Esq of Nantwich, *Mary Craven* the wife of John Richardson Esq of Bunbury , and *Anne Craven*, spinster

1789	Oct	20	Thomas son of Richd Edleston Gent and Elizabeth his wife
1789	Oct	31	Margaret Alsager, Daur of James Sheridan of ye Midddle Temple, London, Esqr and Catharine his wife *
1789	Dec	14	George son of Wm Lowe Gent and Eliz his wife, born 17 Nov 1789
1791	April	21	Charles son of Thos, Nixon, Atturney and Sarah his wife, priv[ately] bapt 22 March
1792	Sep	18	Arabella Maria dau of Peter Bayley Esq and Sarah his wife, bapt 2 Aug 1790
1793	Dec	10	Thomas son of Thomas Hall, Liquor Merchant, and Fanny
1796	May	11	William son of William Sprout Linen Draper and Mary
1800	Aug	15	Matthew son of James Bayley Esq and Penelope
1801	Jan	13	George, son of Wm Harwood Folliott Esq and Catharine
1802	Jan	27	Weston son of James Bayley Esq and Penelope
1803	June	12	John son of John Withenshaw Currier and Mary
1805	March	19	Henry son of King Nixon, Tanner, and Mary
1807	Oct	9	John son of John Downes, Merchant, and Eliz
1809	Sep	16	Charles William son of Samuel Bradbury, *Organist*
1812	Aug	2	John Nelson son of John Squarebridge Methodist preacher and Catharine his wife
1812	Sep	9	Thomas son of John Downes, Shoe-merchant and Eliz
1812	Dec	28	Joseph Gardner son of John Bolland surgeon and Eliz

Burials

1785	June	16	John, son of Richard Edleston, Attorney
1789	Feb	24	John Lamb, sergeant of ye Militia, fifty years in his Majesty's service, and died in ye 83rd year of his Age in a moment's sickness
1789	Sep	1	John Cliffe (commonly called Major Cliffe) Pauper
1789	Oct	12	George Clowes, Apparitor
1789	Dec	9	Thomas Massey, accidentally drowned
1790	Ap	10	Thomas Wright, almsman, pauper, drowned by accident
1792	No burials are recorded in March, only 3 in April, 1 in May, and 3 in June
1794	May	2	Mrs Eaton widow of the Revd Mr Eaton
1795	July	12	Deborah Holding, aged 95
1797	Feb	10	Thomas Robinson, Gaol-keeper
1798	July	13	Edmund Snelson, stationer [and printer]
1798	Nov	29	Thomas Becket, aged 91
1799	Jan	20	Peter Minshull, aged 92
1799	Feb	1	Sarah Hope, widow, aged 80
1799	Feb	10	Mris Francis Maisterson, aged 96 †
1799	Feb	15	Mrs Ann Taylor, aged 80
1800	Feb	17	Thomas Keay, Tobacconist Manufacturer
1800	Nov	23	Catharine dau of Luke Punshon, Engineer
1803	March	3	Thomas Nixon, Attorney at Law
1803	May	31	John Clowes, Clockmaker, and of his Majesty's Navy
1804	June	8	George Cooper, aged 90
1804	June	17	Lydia Hall, aged 90

* James Sheridan, of Nantwich, married Catharine, fourth daughter of James Williams, of Nantwich, and Anne Wilbraham, his wife (See *Alsager Pedigree* in Ormerod's *Cheshire*, vol iii, p 323, New Edit)

† The death of this aged lady is mentioned in *Gent Mag* 1800, part ii, page 698

1804   Aug.   28.   Mary widow of Revd. Mr. Kendall.
1804   Dec.   19.   Elizabeth wife of Ralph Ratcliffe, Gent, aged 71.
1805   May   24.   Job Mee, chimney-sweeper.
1806   May   20.   Andrew Rogers, Pedlar, aged 94.
1807   Oct.   1.   Thomas Percival, labourer (commonly called Passover).
1809   Ap.   14   Sion son of Sion Cooper.
1809   May   "Not one buried."
1810   Jan.   29   Anthony Spencer, aged 98
1811   July   21.   Isaac Smith Methodist preacher.
1811   Dec.   24.   John Martin, solicitor, from Newcastle.
1812   Sep.   13   Ann widow of William Shenton, Joiner, aged 85.
1812   Sep.   22.   Mary, widow, of Jonathan Dutton, Joiner, aged 83.
1812   Dec.   31.   Mary, widow of William Plant, aged 82.

This, the last entry in the old registers, is signed "*Anthony Clarkson Rector.*" The next and succeeding register books down to the present time, contain printed forms. From these volumes a few extracts have been given in the chapter on Annals.

SWEET-BRIAR HALL.

Charities.

O Tables of the Charities are now to be found in the Church. Formerly, tablets giving the names of benefactors to the poor were affixed to the walls of the Church; but, many years ago, their names and gifts were obliterated with paint, and afterwards, the boards were removed as useless. The list of Charities here given, which I have endeavoured to make as complete as possible from various available sources of information, includes several names and benefactions that have never before appeared in print. To give a full account of even the principal Charities would extend these pages to a needless length; but those who are interested in the subject will find many particulars relating to legacies bequeathed to the poor of Nantwich, and for parochial purposes, (some of which have been lost, and others misapplied), in the thirty-first Report of the Charity Commissioners, 1837, pp. 644—664.

The earliest known list of Charities, dated 1665, which appears to have been taken from a similar one then in the Church, is preserved in *Harl. MSS.* 2176, f. 60; as follows:

" A Cataloughe of what Charitabel giftes haue beene given vnto the towne
and Church of namptwiche."

Mᴬᴿ HENRY SPARKE gaue six leade wallinge of Inheritance for euer towards the maine-taynace of gods divine seruice.

[PRAER'S OBIT, of very ancient date] giuen from yᵉ house of woodhay 26s. 8d. to bee yearely delte to the poore upon euery St. Thomas day [Dec. 21] for euer.

Mʀ ALDERMAN WALTHALL of London gaue 100ˡⁱ. [£100] to bee lent out from fiue yeares to fiue yeares for euer to foure tradesmen by 25ˡⁱ. [£25] a peice paying euery of them yearly for the same 20s. to bee distributed yearely to the poore at yᵉ discretion of the Maior or Bayliffe or Communaltie there.

S#R ROGER WILBRAHAM [of Dorfold] KNIGHT, borne in this Towne, founded an Almes-house there for six poore almes men, whereof 4 are to be Chosen in this Towne, and 2 forth of Acton Parish, and gaue euery one of them yearely foure markes [£2 13s 4d] and euery other yeare a gowne

> Also, hee gaue 4#h [£4] to bee yearely distributed vnto the poore on goode friday for euer

MR OLIVER WILKES, of London, gaue 10#h [£10] to bee lent out freely euery yeare to 5 poore men by 40s a peice att the discretion of the Churchwardens

MRS MARGARETT SLADE borne in this Towne gaue lands in Haughton for the yearely distributinge of 3#h [£3] euery good friday and 3#h [£3] euery St Thomas day to six score poore householders for euer att the discretion of the Church wardens

MA#R ANTHONY CLOWES, Haberdasher of London, also borne in this Towne gaue the bookes of Acts and Monuments* and soe much sand and quarrell as raised and laid the body of this Church att his owne cost and charges

S#R EDWARD [sic for Edmund] WRIGHT, KNIGHT, *Lord Motor of London*, borne in this Towne gaue first in his life-tyme 12#d weekly in bread to 12 poore people during the space of nere 20 yeares, and after this, alsoe before his death erected a verie fayre and spacious Hospitall for vi poore men, and to maintaine this famous foundatyon hath for euer setled 32#h [£32] and to bee distributed in such relacyon there vnto As By deed and Record more pticularly aperes directed

S#R THOMAS CRW [Crewe] KNIGHT, borne in this Towne gaue certain fee farme rents in Bugglawton amounting to 22#h [£22] per an um to bee distributed yearely to the poore of the Hospell street for euer

MR RICHARD MINSHALL of this Towne gaue y#e inheritance of 2 sixe leade wallinge, the profitts of the one six leade to the then preacher & his successors, y#e profitt of y#e other six leade to be bestowed in bread for the releif of poore householders yearely for euer.

MR SAMUELL GOULDSMITH, citizen and mercer of London, borne in this Towne, gaue 50#h [£50] to remaine in stocke y#e increase to be bestowed in bread & to be dealt to the poore upon euery Lords day for euer

MR RICHARD VENNER, citizen of London, borne in this Towne gaue 30 shillings yearely to be giuen to the poore euery Lords day in bread accordingly

RICHARD HARWAR of this Towne, apothecary, gaue y#e inheritance of a house in peper Street in which Thomas Clowes y#e p'rish Clerke sometime dwelt, y#c rent and profitt thereof to bee distributed to y#e poore yearely and for euer

MRS MARGARET WOODNOTH, MRS. ELIZABETH DAUENPORT, daughters and coheires of Richard Wright of this Towne, Gent, gaue two faire siluer flaggons for y#e use of y#e communion & alsoe y#e tithes of hay within Aluaston and certain small tythes in certain streets of this Towne & other adiacente townships for y#e better maintenance of y#e preacher of this Towne & his Successors for euer

---

* Fox's "Book of Martyrs, the Acts and Monuments of the Church"

RANDLE LIGHTFOOTE of weston in y⁰ parish of wibunbury, yeoman, Gaue to this Towne 44 Pounds, yᵉ increase to be bestowed in bread and to be dealte to yᵉ poore euery Lords daye for euer.

MRS MARGERY MAISTERSON daughter of John Maisterson of this Towne, Gent , Gaue 20 Pounds to yᵉ behoofe of yᵉ grammar school and for yᵉ aduancement of good literature therein 1662

THOMAS CLOWES late Clerke of this parish.Church Gaue yᵉ Communion Tabel

JOHN MINSHALL late rector of Sidmouth in yᵉ county of Daven-shire son of John Minshall of this Towne, Gent , by his last Will and testament Gaue 40ʰ [£40] to remaine in Stocke and yᵉ yearely increase to bee distributed to yᵉ poore of this Towne for euer

ELIZABETH, daughter of JOHN BLAGE of this Towne, and late wife of JOHN DAVIES, locksmith, in yᵉ life-time of her said husband and with his consent Gaue yᵉ sum of 10 Poundes to be put forth for the benefitt & behoofe of yᵉ natife Poor of yᵉ mill Street in this Towne

MARGERY TOMSON, Widdow, sister of yᵉ said *Elizabeth*, by her last will and Testamente Gaue 5ʰ [£5] to bee impersed [employed] for yᵉ same benefitt of yᵉ poore of the same mill street 1665."

In a book containing copies of Deeds, &c , relating to Nantwich, now in the possession of G F Wilbraham, Esq , of Delamere, is the following Memorandum by Randle Wilbraham, of Townsend House, relating to the *Consolidation* of certain Charities in 1704, and an Account of the Charities vested in the Churchwardens, for the year ending 26th March, 1713, as follows —

I   "*CHARITIES· ANNO DNI* 1704"

"The Gentlemen and other inhabitants of the Towne of Namptwich considering that diverse summs of money, wᶜʰ had from time to time by well disposed persons been given and bequeathed to the Poor of the sᵈ Towne were in Danger to bee lost, thought fit to collect the said severall summs into One,—& to dispose the same for the purchase of lands , wᶜʰ might bee a more permanent profitt , & bee managed with less trouble & hazard   An opportunity then offering of Lands to be sold neare the Towne, being the inheritance of *Matthew Wright, Gent*, with whom a bargaine was made , the severall summs under-written were called in & apply'd to that purpose —

" The deeds are now in   custody "

The Gifts of—		MR DELVES	05£
ELIZABETH BLAGG, widow	10£	MRS HEACOCK	20£
ROGER COMBERBACH	40£	THO SUCKLEY	04£
WILLIAM WALLEY, Apothecary	40£	OLIVER WILKES	02£
WIDOW TOMSON	05£	MRS SEGRAVE	10£
ALDERMAN WALLTHALL	63£	MR RICHARD WICKSTEAD	20£
MRS KNIGHTLY	10£	MRS MARGERY MAISTERSON	20£
SIR THOS WILBRAHAM	25£	MRS ANNE SMITH	70£
MR JOHN MINSHULL	40£	WILLM PHYTHVAN	20£
MRIS ANNE MINSHULL	05£	THOS BRISCOE	05£
RANDLE LIGHTFOOT	44£	ROGER WILBRAHAM ESQ.	45£
TOTAL		£503	

Lost —Of money given by ALDERMAN WALTHALL   37£
      „   „   ,   „ MR SAM GOLDSMITH   50£
      „   „   ,   „ OLIVER WILKES   08£
                                 95£

The above sum of £500 was expended on Dec 17th, 1706, in the purchase of the following lands from *Matthew Wright*, of London, son and heir of *James Wright*, of Nantwich; viz :—

	A	R	P
A pasture in Nantwich called *New-Town field*	6	1	16
A close in Acton called *The Bell-field*			
Land adjoining, next to Acton Pavement called *Chapel Croft* }	7	1	8
Land in Henhull called the *Wall Croft*	2	2	23
Total	16	1	7

As stated below, these lands produced, in 1713, an annual rent of £20 18s od The Churchwardens, who have had the management of this fund to the present time, incurred the popular odium in the early part of this century by not applying the increased rents to charitable purposes, but merely expending a certain sum as the interest, and carrying a large surplus to the use of the parish in aid of the church levies In 1828 the Liverpool and Birmingham Junction Canal was cut, passing through *Bell Field* and *Chapel Croft*, and 2a 1r 12p was bought by the Company at £200 per acre, a further sum of £50 being paid for under-cutting the soil for the purpose of raising the embankment These, and other sums of recent date, have been invested in the Funds, and according to the Government returns, the Consolidated Charities, in 1862-3, produced as follows —

Income	£	s	d	Disbursements	£	s	d
From Land	46	0	0	Paid for weekly dole of bread, 90 loaves	47	18	7
„ £501 18s 7d Consols and other				„ to Rector, for the poor	2	0	0
securities	14	19	10	„ to Parish Clerk	2	0	0
				„ to Bellman	0	8	0
				„ to Grammar School for educating			
				boys	6	13	3
	£60	19	10		£58	19	10

II "*CHARITIES RECEIPTS AND PAYMENTS OF THE CHURCH WARDENS OF NAMPTWICH March 26th, 1713*"

"*Rents to be received by the C W. of the parish of Namptwich yearly*

	£	s	d
For Mr Venners Gift	1	10	0
„ Mrs Slades Gift	10	0	0
„ Widow Kemps House	2	10	0
„ Newtown field	8	0	0
„ Croft by the Almshouse } [Consolidated Fund]	4	0	0
„ Lands held by Davenport }	8	18	0
„ T Proudmans House	1	0	0
„ A Legacy of Mrs Masterson	1	0	0
	36	18	0

"To be paid by the Churchwardens yearly"

			£	s	d
To the Minister and Poor	⎫		2	10	0
To the Parish Clarke	⎪	[Richard Harwar's Gift] ⎰	1	4	0
To the Schoolmaster [Grammar]	⎬		3	14	0
To the Bellman	⎭	⎱	0	4	0
To Poor householders on St Thomas Day & good Friday Mrs Slades gift			10	0	0
To the Poor of Mill Street .			0	18	0
To the Poor of Pillone Street			1	0	0
To the Poor of Welsh Row			1	0	0
For a School House for ye Charity [Blue-cap] Boys			1	0	0
	Total		. £21	10	0

"The ballance of these sums, viz £15 8s od (Lays and Taxes being deducted) is to be distributed to the poor in bread by the C W in the Church"

"There is likewise a Legacy of 4£ per ann granted out of Walling to the poor, wch has not been paid since the walling became invaluable ' [i e about 1696]

"Also there belongs to the poore the sum of £: 6s 8d payable by ye heirs of Sr Thos Wilbraham [of Woodhey], whose ancestor purchased Partridge's Land out of wch the said Rent of £1 6s 8d issued, being given for an obiit by PRAERS "

"There belongs likewise to the Churchwardens to receive yearly—

	£	s	s
"The Rent of *Goughs House* in Barker Street	1	10	0
Also a Legacy given by Mr Plover to buy Sacrament wine	2	0	0
A Rent from Mr Hussey [Parish Clerk] for the under-Rooms of the school-house " [in Church yard]	0	15	0
"To the use of the Church ..	£4	5	0"

BENEFACTORS TO THE CHURCH AND POOR

Date	Donor and Purpose	Amount.
		£ s d
Ancient	ROGER PRAERS' *Obit*, to the poor, annually [a]	1 6 8
1515.	HENRY SPARKE, rent of a salt-house to the Minister, annual value in 1722	0 10 0
1590	ROGER MAINWARING, of N to 12 eldest poor folk in N. 4s each, every Good Friday [b]	2 8 0
1612	REV HUGH ASSWILL of St. Tewe, Cornwall, to the poor. (*see Annals*)	1 10 0
1613	SIR ROGER WILBRAHAM, of Dorfold, Kt , Almshouses for 6 poor men	— — —
	Do Do. Dole annually on Good Friday	4 0 0
Unknown	LADY WILBRAHAM,[c] in augmentation of Almshouse endowment, per ann. . ..	12 0 0

a Still in the hands of the Churchwardens

b See Roger Mainwaring's Will, proved 1 May, 1590 *Che' Soc Pub* Vol liv, p 152.

c 'The Lady Grace Wilbraham, the wife of Sr Richard Wilbraham, Bar of Woodhey, 14 March 1661-2 "—(*Acton Burial Register*)

Date	Donor and purpose.	Amount.		
		£	s	d
1630.	M*ris* Margaret Slade,*d* widow, of Poole, to 60 poor householders, pr ann	12	0	0
1633	Sir Thos. Crewe, of Steane, Kt., to poor in Hospital St , per ann *e*	22	0	0
1634	Ann Wright, spinster of N. by Will dated 25 Sep. 1634, to the poor	10	0	0
1637.	Richard Minshull,*f* of N , rent of a salt-house to the Minister	—	—	—
	Do. rent of a salt-house to the poor	—	—	—
1638	Thomas Clowes, Parish Clerk, gave the Communion Table	—	—	—
1638.	Sir Edmund Wright, Kt of London, Alderman, built an Almshouse for 6 poor men , Endowment per ann *g*	32	0	0
1639.	M*ris* Margaret Woodnoth, widow, of N gave part of the Communion Plate, and certain Tithes to the Minister *h* M*ris* Elizabeth Davenport, widow,	—	—	—
1657.	Raphe Wilbraham,*i* Esq , to the poor	400	0	0
	Do to the Grammar School	50	0	0
1662	M*ris* Margaret Maisterson, spinster, to the Grammar School	20	0	0
Anie 1665.	Alderman Walthall, of London, to be lent to four tradesmen for 5 years, at £1 int per ann , which interest to be given to the poor	100	0	0
	Oliver Wilkes, of London, to be lent to five poor men	10	0	0
	Anthony Clowes, of London, raised the floor of the Church, and gave Fox's "*Book of Martyrs*"	—	—	—
	Samuel Goldsmith, of London, bread to the poor every Lord's Day	50	0	0
	Richard Venner, of London, bread to the poor every Lord's Day	1	10	0
	Richard Harwar, apothecary, of N , the rent of a house in Pepper Street, to the poor	—	—	—
	Randle Lightfoot, of Weston, bread to the poor every Lord's day	44	0	0
	Rev. John Minshull, of Sidmouth, to the poor, interest of	40	0	0
	Elizabeth Davies, of N to the poor of Mill Street	10	0	0
	Margaret Thomson, of N , widow, to the poor of Mill Street	5	0	0
1676	Roger Wilbraham, of Townsend, Esq , Almshouses,*j* for six widows, the endowment, £24 per ann , afterwards augmented by *Randle Wilbraham Esq* , of Nantwich in 1721, and by *Peter Sprout*, Gentleman, of Nantwich in 1834	—	—	—
1681.	M*ris* Anne Smith, to the poor	70	0	0

d Deed dated 25th Feb 5 Chas I, [1629-30] She was the daughter of Lawrence Wright, Gent of Nantwich and married John Slade, of Poole, who left a Charity to Wybunbury, and was buried at Nantwich, 25th May, 1625 —*(Reg)* "Mistress Margaret Slade, buried at Nantwich] 6 Sept 1630 —*(Ibid)*

e From land in Buglawton   *f* See Minshull Pedigree

g Deed dated 20 Aug 14 Chas I [1638]

h See pp 288, 334

i Raphe Wilbraham left all his estate to the poor at the disposal of his executors who, in addition to £450 for Nantwich, gave to the poor of *Baddiley* £10 *Audlem* £63 6s 8d *Wrenbury* £50 *Wybunbury* £50, and *Acton* about £185 To his memory a brass and grave-stone still exist (See page 322)

j These houses were built by Thos Wilbraham Esq , in 1637 and were endowed by his son, Roger Wilbraham as an Almshouse, under circumstances related in "*Town Concerns*" (Annals) and in the Chapter on Biography The deed was dated 15th Jan 1676 7 and the income issued out of lands in Betchton, near Sandbach

| Date | Donor and purpose | Amount. |
| | | £ s d |

1683 WILLIAM PHYTHIAN,[h] of N   to Grammar School, to educate a child
      out of Beam Street 20 0 0

1689 WILLIAM HODGKIN,[l] Gent of N , 20 *de* 3*ro* 24*per* of land in Alvas-
      ton to be applied in apprenticing children .... — — —

1700 ROGER WILBRAHAM, of Townsend, Esq Annuity to the Minister[m] ... 5 0 0

1701 RICHARD PEEVER,[n] Apothecary of N., to buy Sacrament Wine, per ann ... 2 0 0

1703-4 MRIS MARTHA CHORLTON,[o] widow, of Southwark, to the poor (com-
        monly called " *the Widows Mite* 200 0 0

Ante 1704 {

  ROGER COMBERBACH,[p] by will, proved 8 Oct 1678 to poor in Hospital
    and Barker Streets 40 0 0

  WILLIAM WALLEY, M D, of N ,[q] bread to the poor 40 0 0

  MRIS ELIZABETH KNIGHTLY, to 10 poor widows in Hospital St 10 0 0

  SIR THOMAS WILBRAHAM, of Woodhey, Bart · 25 0 0

  MRIS ANNE MINSHULL[s] 5 0 0

  MR [Hugh] DELVES,[t] to the poor 5 0 0

  MRIS [Margaret] HEACOCK, widow,[u] to the poor 20 0 0

  THOMAS SUCKLEY 4 0 0

  MRIS SEAGRAVE[v] 10 0 0

  RICHARD WICKSTEAD,[w] to the poor 20 0 0

  THOMAS BRISCOE, to the Grammar School 5 0 0

1705 ROGER WILBRAHAM of Townsend, Esq , by Deed dated 20 Nov 1705,
      an Almshouse for 2 old Maids. The endowment £3, each, per ann
      afterwards augmented by *Randle Wilbraham*, of Nantwich, Esq , in
      1721, and by *Peter Sprout*, Gentleman, of Nantwich, in 1834 ..... — — —

k "William ffithian [buried] Dec 16, 1683 —*(Par Reg)*

l "William Hodgkins Gent , 'buried] Jan 1, 1689-90 "—*(Par Reg)* Owing to the altered state of the shoe-trade, the number of applications became insufficient to absorb the income of this Charity Accordingly since 1873, by the approval of the Charity Commissioners £60 has been applied per annum to provide six exhibitions (free scholars) to the New Grammar School at Nantwch

m See page 302 *note*

n "Nov 19, 1701 Richard Peever, Apothecary "—*(Bur Reg)* The field charged with this £2 is still called "*Peever Meadow*"

o Mrs Martha Chorlton, (one of the daughters of Sir Edmund Wright) was waited upon by Thomas Maisterson of Nantwich then Treasurer of the Wright's Trustees, on 30th Jan 1702-3, "att her house in the Parke, in Southwarke, upon an intimation given to the Trustees, of a Charitable designe in her towards the poor of Namptwch "—*(Treasurer's Book of Wright's Trustees)* "1717 *Mem* That Tho Maisterson esq in his life time did declare publickly at a meeting of the Trustees in the Church that Mrs Chorlton was herself an Anabaptist, & did strickly appoint that none should be excluded her charity on account of Dissent fro ye Church of Engl —*(Ibid)*

p Roger Comberbach gave to Wybunbury £10 and to Audlem £10 He was buried at N 29 Sep 1678 —*(Par Reg)*

q "William Walley, Doctor of Phisick [buried] ffeb 4, 1680-1 "—*(Par Reg)* See Monuments, page 324

r " Sir Thomas Wilbraham de Woodhey Barronett 19 Aug 1692 "—*(Acton Bur Reg)*

s Probably " Anne wife of Edwd Minshull Esq of Stoake [who was buried] 2 Aug 1694 "—*(Par Reg)*

t Probably Hugh Delves (son of Hugh Delves, Gent of Nantwich) who was buried 22 March 1680-1 "—*(Par Reg)*

u " Mrs Margaret Heacock widow [buried] 25 Dec 1691 '—*(Par Reg)*

v " Mrs Elizabeth Seagrave, widow, [buried] 22 Oct 1690 "—*(Par Reg)*

w " Richard Wickstead Gent, [buried] 21 April 1681 '—*(Par Reg)*

Date	Donor and purpose	Amount.
		£ s d
1711	SIR JOHN CREWE, of Utkinton, Kt , to the poor in Hospital St , land in Wardle, then producing per ann *x*	10 0 0
1711	MRIS ANNE CREWE OFFLEY,*y* of Crewe Hall	5 0 0
c. 1721	RANDLE WILBRAHAM, of Nantwich, Esq	163 0 0
c 1721	CATHERINE MAINWARING	27 0 0
c 1721	JANE EDGELEY*z*	10 0 0
c 1721	STEPHEN WILBRAHAM, of Nantwich, Esq	500 0 0

To the Charity (Blue-cap) School

		£ s d
Ante 1713	THOMAS PROUDMAN, of N ,*zi* bread to poor in Welsh Row, per ann.	1 0 0
	MARY MAISTERSON,*a* bread to poor in Pillory St interest of	20 0 0
	. . GOUGH, producing per annum in 1713	1 10 0
1722	ERMINE DELVES,*b* spinster, of N property in Love lane	— — —
1738	MATTHEW MEAKIN,*c* of N. gent. £200	

To erect Alms-houses in Love lane

		£ s d
1725	BRIDGET WOOD,*d* of N , widow, to poor of Beam Street and Wall Lane, the interest of	350 0 0
1734	JOHN BROMHALL,*e* of N & of Hough, Esq , to Charity (Blue-cap) School	50 0 0
1735	ZACHARIAH TURNPENNY,*f* of N , gent to Charity (Blue-cap) School	10 0 0
1736.	THOMAS WETTENHALL, of N , to educate four poor boys at the Grammar School, per ann.	2 0 0
1741	JANE LOWE,*g* spinster, of N , to buy a Crimson Velvet pulpit cloth and cushion for the Parish Church *(Will)*	20 0 0
1767	JOHN CREWE, of Crewe, Esq , Almshouse in Beam Street for seven families, decayed tradesmen having the preference	— — —
1768	ANN RATHBONE,*h* widow, to poor widows in Beam St , on Christmas Day	1 0 0
1775	JOHN EYTON, to the poor in bread, the interest of	20 0 0
Ante 1779	MARY [or *Hannah*] HICKSON,*i* of Clotton, to the poor in Barker Street, on St Thomas Day, interest of	10 0 0

x This Charity and that of Sir Thos Crewe, Kt dated 1633, were annually distributed amongst the poor in Hospital Street, (the native Street of *Sir Thomas*, and his brother, Sir Ranulph Crewe, Kt , the grandfather of *Sir John Crewe*) until the year 1733 Thirty-four years after, (*i e* in 1767) John, first Lord Crewe, diverted the donor's original intentions by erecting and endowing therewith an ALMSHOUSE, for married men with families, decayed tradesmen having the preference in *Beam Street*

y Eldest daughter of John Crewe, of Crewe, Esq and wife of John Offley, of Madeley, Esq She died 15th May, 1711, and was buried at Barthomley

z The wife of Samuel Edgeley, Vicar of Acton She was buried at Acton on 3rd Jan 1728-9 *(Acton & Nant Bur Reg)*

zi In Dec 1872 twenty shilling loaves were given to poor people in Welsh Row —*(Parish Magazine)*

a " Mris Mary Maisterson vid 9 May 1684 "—*(Nantwich Burial Register)*

b " Ermine Delves, Spinster, buried at Wybunbury 18 April 1729 "—*(Nantwich Burial Register)*

c Matthew Meakin, Attorney, 9 Jan 1740 "—*(Nantwich Burial Register)*

d " Bridget Wood, buried at Acton, 5 Oct 1725 "—*(Nantwich Burial Register)*

e " John Bromhall Esq 3 April 1735 '—*(Nantwich Burial Register)*

f " Zachariah Turnpenny Buried at Acton 13 March 1738-9 "—*(Nantwich Burial Register)*

g Jane Lowe was the younger daughter of Samuel Lowe of Newton Hall, Esq , near Middlewich After her father s death in 1703, she resided in Nantwich until her death, which took place in 1741 She was buried at Middlewich, 10 Sep 1741 (Information by A E Lawson Lowe, Esq , of Shirenewton Hall, near Chepstow) A pedigree of this family, which was in no way connected with the Lowes, Solicitors, of Nantwich, will be found in Dr Ormerod s *Cheshire*, New Edit Vol III p 182

h *Ann Rathbone*, late wife of Rev Isaac Rathbone, Grammar Schoolmaster

i In Dec 1872, poor people in Barker Street received 5s 11d each —*(Parish Magazine)*

Date	Donor and Purpose.	Amount.
		£ s d
1793	ELIZABETH WALKER, spinster, of N , to six maids, each £5 per ann (called "*The Maids' Mite*") total sum	959 0 0
1827	THOMAS BECKET, of N , the rent of a pew in Church, to be distributed in bread to widows in Welsh Row, and the two Wood Streets, in 1836 produced per ann.	2 5 0
1829	WILLIAM SPROUT, of N. Esq., in augmentation of several Charities, gifts to Rector, Organist, &c , total sum about	6000 0 0
1834	PETER SPROUT, of N Gentleman, in augmentation of several Charities, gifts to Rector, Clerk, &c , total about	2200 0 0
1846	MARY SWAN, (by will 1837) to poor in Hospital Street; total	1000 0 0
1851	GEORGE FOLLIOTT,*j* Esq , of Vicars Cross, Chester, distributed in coal to poor people in winter time , total amount	180 0 0
1856	MARY BENNION ⎫ ELIZABETH BENNION,*h* ⎬ of Nantwich, spinsters, in augmentation of the endowment of Wilbraham Almshouses at Welsh Row Head	738 13 7
1864	MARY JANE HALL, of Wistaston, in augmentation of Miss Walker's Charity .	200 0 0
1866	MRS ANN PEMBERTON, in augmentation of Miss Walkers Charity .	50 0 0
1873	MR HYDE, to the poor, (applied to the building of Wood St School)	100 0 0

These Charitable Trusts have been vested either in the Churchwardens as representatives of the Parish, or in a kind of corporate body known as the Wright's Trustees

Of those *now* in the hands of the Churchwardens, are—

1. Praer's Obit
2. Slade's.
3. Harwar s.
4. Peover's.
5. Consolidated Charities (1704.)
6. Proudman's.
10. Folliott's
7. Meakin and Delves.
8 Hickson's.
9 Swan's.

The Charities *now* under the management of the Wright's Trustees, are—

1 Sir Edmund Wright's, Almshouse
2 Hodgkin's, Apprenticing Charity
3 Mrs Chorlton's, Widows' Mite.
4. Meakin and Delves', Almshouse.
5 Bridget Wood's Charity
6 Elizabeth Walker's Maids' Mite
7 William Sprout's
8 Peter Sprout's.
9. Miss Hall and Mrs. Pemberton's.
10 Mary and Elizabeth Bennion's.

I have a list of the Churchwardens for Nantwich from 1568 to 1789 (a few names only wanting) which, however, is too long for insertion, but, a complete list of the Wright s Trustees, which will be of interest as giving the names of leading townsmen, contemporary at intervals during the past 245 years, is here appended.

j In Dec 1872, fifty-three poor people each received 2 cwt of Coal —*(Parish Magazine)*

h This lady largely augmented the income of Nantwich living To the above long list of names may be added Mr Thomas Cawley who gave the present gas-standards in the Church Mrs Evans Mrs Kent and others whose names have already been mentioned in the foregoing pages as benefactors to the Church

NAMES OF THE WRIGHT'S TRUSTEES *

The original Trustees appointed by Sir Edmund Wright by deed dated 20th Aug. 1638, were as follows —

Thomas Maisterson, Esq

Thomas Wilbraham, Esq

Alexander Walthall, the younger, Esq

Thomas Bavand, Esq

Roger Wright, the elder, of the High Town, Gent.

Richard Wright, son and heir apparent of Roger Wright, Gent

Lawrence Wright, the elder, Gent

Randle Church, the elder, Gent

Jeffrey Massey, Gent

Ralph Woodnoth, Gent †

Richard Wright, of the Stone, Gent

William Grafton Gent

John Saring, Clerk [Minister of Nantwich Church]

The first Indenture for perpetuating the Trust is dated 7th April, 1666, when *Richard Wright* and *Jeffrey Massey*, being the only surviving trustees,‡ elected the following gentlemen.—

Thomas Maisterson, Esq

Richard Walthall, Esq

Thomas Wettenhall, Esq

Randle Church, Gent.

Richard Wright, Gent son and heir apparent of the said Richd Wright Sabboth Church, Gent

William Walley Gent

Richard Wright, Gent son and heir apparent of Matthew Wright, Gent

Thomas Wright, Gent

Robert Parker, Gent

Richard Jackson, Clerk [Minister of Nantwich Church]

By Indenture dated 1st Nov 1681, *Richard Wright*, then Clerk, Batchelor of Divinity; *Richard Wright*, Gent, and *Robert Parker*, Gent, being the only surviving Trustees, elected the following —

Edward Minshull, Esq.

Richard Walthall, Esq.

Thomas Maisterson, Esq.

Thomas Wickstead, Gent.

John Brock, Gent

John Goldsmith, Gent.

Roger Wright, Gent

James Wright, Gent

Richard Wright, Gent.

Roger Stone, Gent, Apothecary

By Indenture dated 5 Oct 1702, *Thomas Maisterson, Richard Wright*, B D, *Roger Stone, Roger Wright*, the only surviving Trustees, elected the following —

Randle Wilbraham, Esq

Richard Walthall, Esq

Thomas Wettenhall, Esq

Clutton Wright, Esq

William Jackson, Doctor in Physic, Gent

Thomas Wickstead, Gent

Sabboth Church, Gent

Hugh Delves, Gent

John Comberbach, Gent

---

* In the weekly issues of the Whitchurch Herald from 25 Nov 1871, to 27 Jan 1872, Mr Thos Dunning, of Nantwich, printed a series of abstracts of Indentures Leases, Deeds, &c, relating to the Charities in the hands of the Wright's Trustees, from papers which had long been in the possession of the Pratchett family of this town Although these articles excited little or no interest in the town when they appeared they will be of the greatest service to anyone who will undertake to write a full account of Nantwich Charities   From these articles, and from deeds preserved in the Deed chest of the Trustees this list of names is obtained

† Ralph Woodnoth, probably never executed this deed, being buried on the 17th Aug 1638

‡ These gentlemen were the only acting Trustees for several years prior to 1666, and it is remarkable how soon they assumed an independent position contrary to the express wish of the Founder

By Indenture dated 26 Aug 1717, *Randle Wilbraham, Clutton Wright, Richard Walthall, Roger Wright,* and *John Comberbach,* being the only five surviving Trustees, elected the following —

William Maisterson, Esq   John Bromhall, Gent
Ralph Horton, Esq.   Matthew Meakin, Gent.
Jonathan Goldsmith, Esq   Richard Stone, Gent
Roger Wilbraham (son and heir apparent   George Gibbons, Clerk [Rector]
    of Randle Wilbraham,) Gent

By Indenture dated 24th Nov. 1732, *Roger Wilbraham, William Maisterson, Clutton Wright, John Bromhall,* and *Matthew Meakin,* being the only five surviving Trustees, elected the following —

Thomas Brooke, Clerk, **LL.D.** [Rector].   Thomas Williams, Gent.
Peter Walthall, Esq.   Thomas Wickstead, Gent.
Edward Wettenhall, Esq   George Audley, Gent
Matthew Wright, (son and heir apparent   Richard Maisterson, Gent
    of Clutton Wright,) Gent.

By Indenture dated 24th Nov 1745, *Roger Wilbraham, Edward Wettenhall, Thomas Brooke, Thomas Wickstead, Thomas Williams, Richard Maisterson,* and *George Audley,* being the only seven surviving Trustees, elected the following —

Thomas Maisterson, Esq   Thomas Pratchett, Gent.   Alexander Elcocke, Gent
John Hall, Surgeon, Gent   Ashton Williams, Gent.   Thomas Yoxall, Gent.

By Indenture dated 5th Dec 1761, *Thomas Maisterson, John Hall, Alexander Elcock, Thomas Wickstead, Thomas Yoxall,* and *Thomas Pratchett,* being the only six surviving Trustees, elected the following —

George Wilbraham, Esq *   Plant Maddocks, Gent.   John Oulton, the elder, Gent.
John Hall, Surgeon Gent.   Thomas Williams, Gent.   William Hewitt, Gent
                               George Payne, Gent.

By Indenture dated 24th Nov 1779, *George Wilbraham, Alexander Elcock, Thos. Yoxall, George Payne, William Hewitt,* being the only five surviving Trustees, elected the following —

Samuel Barrow, Esq   William Philips, silk-mercer.
James Tomkinson, the younger, Esq.   Joseph Skerrett, upholsterer
George Garnett, Gent, cheesefactor   Richard Liversage, Ironmonger.
Richard Wicksted, Surgeon, Gent.   William Kent, Apothecary.
Thomas Yoxall, the younger, Gent   George Dutton, Ironmonger
William Wrench, Surgeon, Gent   Benjamin Hewitt, Merchant

By Indenture dated 26th Dec 1817, *James Tomkinson, William Wrench,* and *Joseph Skerrett,* being the only three surviving Trustees, the two former of which declined to act, elected the following —

---

* Never executed this Deed of Trust

William Sprout	John Jasper Garnett	Edward Kent
Benjamin Rodenhurst	John Downes, Junr.	William Acton
Richard Liversage	Samuel Walton.	Thomas Downing.
William Kent	John Pratchett	John Richardson

By Indenture dated —— 1829, *Joseph Skerrett, William Sprout, Richard Liversage, William Kent, John Downes, William Acton,* and *John Richardson,* being the only seven Trustees surviving, elected the following —

William Welsby, Attorney	George Cappur, Cheesefactor
William Massey, Silversmith	John Eyton, Banker.
Thomas Deriemer, Grocer.	Henry Tomlinson.

By Indenture dated 31st Oct. 1839, *William Massey, Thomas Deriemer, George Cappur,* and *John Eyton,* being four surviving Trustees, the rest being deceased, except John Richardson and Henry Tomlinson, who had resigned, elected the following —

William Ellison, Wine Merchant.	William Salmon, of Mount Pleasant, Esq
Joseph Henry Kent, Surgeon	Thomas Bower, Cotton-spinner
William Hall, Wine Merchant	Thomas Williamson, Surgeon
James Latham, Maltster.	Edward Hounsum Griffiths, Bookseller and
Richard Martin, Grocer	Stationer

The last Trust Deed was executed on 22nd June, 1866, when *William Hall,* (who resigned at the same time) *Joseph Henry Kent, Richard Martin* of Acton, *Thomas Bower,* the elder, (late of Nantwich, then of Hankelow), Gent , *Thomas Williamson,* and *Edward Hounsum Griffiths,* being the only surviving Trustees, elected the following —

> THOMAS CAWLEY, of Nantwich, Ironmonger.
> JOHN SUTTON NIXON, of Nantwich, Currier and Leather Merchant
> EDWARD SWINFEN BELLYSE, of Springfield, Nantwich M.D.
> HOLLAND BLADES, of Stapeley, Chemist
> WILLIAM WALLEY DOWNES, of Nantwich, Esq , Banker
> FREDERICK WADE HOBSON, Gent , Manager of the District Bank
> THOMAS BOWER, the younger, Architect, of Nantwich
> JOHN MARTIN of Nantwich, Chemist

WRIGHT'S ALMSHOUSE

Edmund Wright, Esquire, one of the Aldermen of London, (afterwards, in 1641, Lord Mayor,) "out of his pious intention and charitable disposition towards the poor inhabitants of Wich Malbank," conveyed by deed dated 20th Aug 1638 (14 Car I.) to thirteen Trustees, his newly-erected Almshouse at Hospital Street end, and "all that parcell of land lying and being on the back side of the same Almshouse and containing 1 ro 2 per or thereabouts , and "a Yearly Rent Charge of £32 per ann. issuing from a farm called *Ryefields* in the parish of Hillingdon, co Middlesex," the whole "to be held in trust to the uses, intents, and purposes expressed and declared" by the Founder as follows —*

---

* The original "Deed Gift," which is too lengthy for insertion here, is still preserved in the Deed chest of the Trustees , together with a copy of the same

1 —The Almshouse to be "for the use and benefit of six poor men"* of the age of fifty years at least, natives of the town, and belonging to the Church of England †

2 —The Trustees to pay each almsman 20s quarterly, and provide on Christmas Day each pensioner with a new shirt, a pair of stockings, and a pair of shoes, at a total cost of 40s

3 —The Trustees to meet at the Almshouse every year on the 24th November, at 8 a m , and view the Almsmen , then repair unto the Church of Wich Malbank, together with as many of the said Almsmen as should be able to go there to hear divine Service and a Sermon , after which, the said Trustees should have a Dinner of the value of 20s , and be attended by the said Almsmen, and after dinner, they should read unto the Almsmen then present certain " *Orders*," (see below), and punish by suspension of the allowance or expulsion from the Almshouse any who should offend against those Orders

The 24th November, which was the anniversary of the Founder's baptism, (see p. 338), henceforward became a red-letter day in the town, known as the " *Almsmen s Feast.* ' In 1658 the " Dinner for ye Feoffees and Almsmen wth them " cost £1 , and in 1664 Mr. Gabriel Stringer of the "Red Lion," provided the dinner for nineteen shillings ! This feast, which in 1799 was held at the " *Bowling Green*," has for many years been held at the " *Crown*" and the " *Lamb*" Inns in alternate years A quart of ale has been allowed to each Almsman at the dinner since 1712 , besides other quantities of "strong drink" paid for by generous gentlemen, who were often witnesses of the third " Order" being violated before the conclusion of the old men's feast-day

According to a Memorandum in the Treasurer's Book, dated 24th Nov 1793, owing to "the high price of provisions and other causes," the Trustees appropriated 22s out of other Charities towards the Dinner, in 1797, the sum of £3 3s , and in 1825 the following sums —

```
0 10  6 from Sir Edmund Wright s Charity (then in debt)
0 10  6  ,,   Mrs  Chorlton's (the Widows' Mite)
3 11  6  ,,   Hodgkin s Apprenticing Charity
0 10  6  ,,   Miss Walker's (the Maids' Mite )
2  1  5  ,    Meakin and Delves'.
0 10  6  ,,   Bridget Woods'
───────
£7 14 11
```

It is perhaps to this period of the history of the great Feast Day that the custom began of inviting tradesmen of the town to dine with the Trustees , and, for the better maintenance of this Charity dinner, one of the Trustees, Wm Sprout, Esq , left the sum of £5 per ann   At a meeting of the Trustees held at the Savings' Bank on 16th Nov. 1877, it was agreed that the *Trustees*' Annual Dinner be discontinued , the Almsmen having their feast as heretofore

The foundation Deed further directs —

* Between the years 1800 and 1840, some of the houses were kept vacant for long periods in consequence of great expense in repairs

† On the death of John Cooper Almsman, in 1835, Peter Bolis, the only candidate for the vacancy, was not admitted because he was not a Churchman   He was a candidate at five different times, and was at last elected, 8th Dec 1836, having before that time conformed

4,—The Trustees to give "the Ministers that should preach the Sermon" (on the 24th Nov) "10s for his pains,' and to reserve £4 yearly for gowns for the Almsmen to be given them every second year *

5 —That Roger Wright be appointed Treasurer for life, and keep accounts in a book which should be prepared and kept for that purpose, and after his death the Trustees to elect a Treasurer

6 —After the displacing or death of an Almsman, notice to be given on the next Lord's Day, in the Church, by the "minister" of the vacancy, and of the election of another Almsman "upon the Thursday se ennight after such notice"

7 —Candidates for these "places" must be single men, and must produce certificates that they were "born in the town, above the age of 50, poor and unable to get their living by labour, of good honest behaviour and conversation, and a professor of the Religion and Doctrine of the Church of England"

8 —If several competitors for one vacancy, they must draw lots, in the presence of five Trustees, the successful one being he who drew the lot upon which was written "Praise God for thy Founder"

9 —A candidate of the name of *Wright* to be admitted without casting of lots, in preference to anyone else

Out of 197 poor men who have been recipients of this Charity since the erection of the Almshouse, fifteen have had the name of *Wright*. The last, Robert Wright, aged 64, was admitted 31st Aug. 1837, and died the following year. John Wright, aged 73, was a candidate in Nov 1844, but was not elected. It is not stated why.

The Deed concludes with a long proviso for the appointment of new Trustees, of which the following extract gives all that is necessary to be known

"The said Edmund Wright did further declare that within six months after the death of eight of the said Trustees before named or thereafter to be named, the five surviving Trustees should nominate and elect eight other able and sufficient men in the place or rooms of the said deceased Trustees wherein such who were or should be of the kindred or Name of the said Edmund Wright should be preferred and chosen before strangers" &c.

EMANUEL

"*Orders sett downe and decreed by the Right Worshipfull Sir Edmund Wright Knight borne in this Towne, sometime Lord Maior of the Cittie of London, and Sole Founder of this Almes-house which are to bee observed and kept by all and every person and persons that shall be Elected, Admitted and Received to take the benefit of his Bounty and Charity in this House.*† †

I It is Ordered and Decreed that all and every person and Persons that shall be elected, &c. shall Professe and bee of the present Faith now maintayned in the Church of England and shall duely frequent the House of God and his Holy Ordinances soe long as God shall bee pleased to give him or them Health and Ability of Body ‡

II It is Decreed that all and every such Almsman or Almsmen shall every morning and evening daily humble him and themselves in prayers & Devotions before Almighty God, and shall amongst other petitions pray for the flourishing estate of this Commonwealth, blesse God for their Founder and pray for his Posterity

---

* Gowns and Hats have been delivered to the Almsmen once in *three* years since the year 1771 An Almsman in his dress is given in the illustration of the Gateway to the Almshouses It represents William Bramhall, who was admitted on 22nd May, 1856, and died on 23rd April, 1883, aged 85 years having been an Almsman close upon 27 years

† These orders are taken from "*A true Copy of the Original* renew'd 1823" Printed by A Fox, Nantwich

‡ "1702 paid for repairinge the Almsmens Seats in Church £00 03s 00d '—*(Treasurer's Book)*
"1728 Nov 18 Paid Jo Illidge for mending a Desk in the Almsho & repairinge Almsman Seat in Church, £00 02s 06d "—*(Ibid)*
"1782 Feb 11 It was ordered that Richard Wicksted, Almsman, should be suspended for the space of 3 months, and his allowance stopped for absence from Church and other misdemeanours "—*(Ibid)*

III It is Decreed that all and every Almes man and Almes-men forbear swearing, Drunkenness, and all such scandalous Vices, and shall carry and demean him and themselves Christianly, truely, & peaceably, and shall not willingly doe or suffer to bee done any wrong or prejudice to this Almeshouse or to any the appurtenances thereof *

IV It is decreed that all and every Almesman, &c shall Reside and Inhabit in such rooms and parts thereof as shall be Allotted unto him or them &c And shall not suffer any other person or persons to Lodge therein Except such as the Feoffees and Trustees of this house, &c shall think fitt to allowe to attend those Almesmen that shall be Sick, Blind, Lame or impotent †

V It is Decreed that upon the death or Expulsion of any of the said Almesmen, The new Gowne Cognizance &c which shall be delivered to any Almesman or Almesmen within two years next before his or their Death or Expulsion, shall be delivered to the Treasurer of the said Almeshouse for the time being, and shall bee by him delivered to such as shall bee next Elected and Received into the Roomes or places that shall soe happen to become Void

VI It is Decreed and Ordered That the poor men borne and to bee borne in the Towne of Wichmalbank is to bee Understood of such men onely, who being soe borne, are also knowne to the Feoffees and Govenours of this House to have Resided and Dwelled three Years at the Least Last past in the said Towne before hee or they can bee capable of the benefit of this Foundation ‡

VII It is Decreed that all and every Almesman of this house, if hee or they shall bee able shall walke Orderly in their Gowns and other garments allowed them by their Founder to the Parish Church of Wichmalbank before the dead Bodies of all such Persons especially as shall bee of consanguinity or Allyance to the said Founder And also before such other persons of Quality as the Feoffees & Trustees of this House or any three of them shall think fitt to Appoint

VIII It is Decreed that none of the Almesmen of this House shall Begg any Almes of any Person or persons whatsoever But shall either Labour in some honest Imployment as hee or they shall bee able or else Content themselves with the Allowance given by the said Founder, And other such free helpes as it shall please God to vouchsafe unto him or them by good Benefactors, All which shall bee putt into a Box and Distributed amongst them by the hands of the Treasurer of this House as hee in his Discretion shall think fitt

IX It is Decreed that none, &c shall either marry and take to Wife or Harbour and keep any Woman as an Harlot or give any Entertaynement unto any Vagrant person or persons into his or their House or Houses that may any way bee offensive or Chargeable to the said Towne

X It is Lastly Determined and Decreed, That if any of the Almesmen of this House shall breake any of the Orders and Decrees aforesaid, That then such Offender or Offenders shall be immediately Punished by Fyne Suspension or Expulsion off & from his or their Place or Places by the Feoffees and Trustees &c And upon Suspension or Expulsion another fitt Person or Persons to bee Elected and Placed in his or their Roomes or Places within one and twenty Days then next Following

Finally, the Founder earnestly entreats all the Feoffees and Governours of this House As they tender their Truth and Trust to God and him That they will have all due and strict regard in their Elections to the Directions of his Deed and these Orders well weighing and considering every Qualification therein mentioned giveing Capacity to Election And rendering the most equal Construction and just Prelation of each said Qualification to the uttermost and best of their Judgments and Consciences That soe God may bee glorified The Feoffees and Trustees duties discharged and the truly Poor Comforted "

* 1828 Nov 24 Peter Moss was fined one quarter's salary for getting drunk and also abusing in gross language M-John Berks, residing at Church's Mansion Other instances of fines and suspensions for drunkenness occur

† 1735 Nov 26, Samuel Lea had 10s of his quarterly pension stopped "for Lying out of his Almshouse
"1745 June 24 Willm Topps pay stop'd Because he would not Inhabit"

‡ In 1835 Joseph Sant was admitted, but received no pension from Wright's Charity for three years, not having resided in Nantwich the prescribed time

Extracts from the Treasurers' (Wright's Trustees) Accounts.

"*Mem.* In the yeare of our lord God 1655 Richard Wright, of Wich Malbank, son of Roger Wright one of the Trustees put in a ffaire Byble fixed unto a Moovinge Deske in the house of Henry Wright one of the Almesmen to be preserved and kept by the present & future Almesmen for the use of the Hospitall June 1665 "

"In Witness [where]of
Will Grafton "

			£	s	d
1656 July 24	2 horse load of lyme	2s 8d			
	2 horse load of sand	0s 4d			
	100 of cou'nge Tyle & carr	1s 8d	00	04	06
,, ,,	pd John Hill and his labourer for 3 dayes at the Almeshouses & the walls there		00	05	06
,, ,,	pd for makinge the Morter & Berridge [and allowance for beer] and a labourer to help at the walls with stones		00	01	02
,, ,,	To three men two dayes for clensing the ditch, before the Almshouse, & removinge earth before ye walles		00	05	00
,, Agt Christide next	Paid now for xij yards and a halfe of Lynan cloth to make the 6 Almsmen Shirts, xvjs vjd, and for making the 6 Shirts 2s 0d		00	18	06
,, ,,	Paid to Mr Jackson for his Anivisary Sermon		00	10	00
,, Dec 23	Paid Thomas Proudman for six pair of Shooes for the Almesmen		00	18	00
,, ,,	Paid Thomas Langley for six pair of white Kersey stockinge for the Almesmen at 19d the pr		00	09	06
,, ,,	Paid for a Diner for the ffeoffees and Almesmen 24th Nov 1656		01	00	00
1657 Nov 24	Paid Robert Bins cloathier for 27 yards & halfe to make Gownes for *five* Almesmen att 2s 10d the yard, abating 5d at all and six yards Minikin att 20d ye yard, all†		04	07	06
,, Dec 10	Paid Edward ffrith for makinge of five new Gownes for 5 of the Almesmen & hee found thrid, & Canvas for the Capes		00	08	00
1661 March 25	Paid John Wright, Reginolde Blagg, Richard Jeffes, Richard Cheswis, Richard Symons, & William Cartwright the six Almesmen all nowe liveinge in the Almeshouse to eu'ye of them their severall Quarters pay before hand untill the 24th of June next 20s a pece		06	00	00
	"Mem The six almesmen aboued freely gave eu ye of them 2s a peece unto Margerye Salmon beinge Neice to the founder to relieve her necessitie at present, xijs "				
1661 June 24	The usual quarterly payment to the six Almesmen, "whereof 5s " was stopped from William Cartwright "for being severall tymes Drunck, and 2/6 was given to Joseph Robinson towards Cartwrights debt, and the other 2/6 given to Cartwright himself "				
,, Sep 30	'Wm Cartwright the sixt Almesman whoe for his Grosse Misdemeanrs stands for prsent expelled or suspended And the old Gowne & this Michas Quarters pay to be disposed of at the discretion of the Treasurer & ffeoffees "				
,, Sep 30	'Whereof giuen freely in Charity to the suspended Almesman Cartwright		00	02	00
,, ,,	Also given Margerye Salmon Neice to the founder beinge nowe a widowe, aged, & in great pouertie towards her livelihood forth of the said vacant Quartridge		00	05	00
,, Nov	Paid Sam Salmon & Jo Poole for making 6 Capps		00	03	00

* There had been a death this year,—Laurence Oulton, and the election of another Almsman was suspended a quarter for necessary repairs Total income for 1657—£32, total Disbursements—£30 16s 8d

† In 1738 one hundred years after the founding of the Hospital, the cost of clothing was as follows —

	£	s	d		
6 pairs of shoes	1	4	0		
6 shirts, thread and making	1	0	9		
6 pairs stockings	0	9	0	Total . .	£9 8 2
6 gowns and hats	6	2	5		
Making gowns and hats	0	12	0		

In 1838, two hundred years after, the cost of clothing for five men, one house being then vacant, was as follows —

	£	s	d		
To Robert Massey for 5 pair shoes	2	7	6		
,, Henry Tomlinson for 5 Cloaks & Hats	10	10	0	Total	£14 19 3
,, Thos Shaw, for Shirts, Cravats and Hose	2	1	9		

			£	s	d
1661 X.mas	To Margery Salmon, out of ye vacant Quartridge		00	05	00
,, ,,	To Wm Cartwright ye prsent suspended Almesman		00	00	06
1662 March 25	To Margery Salmon out of ye vacant Quartridge		00	03	06
	To Wm Cartwright ye suspended Almesman in his great want & pouertie		00	01	00
	[Cartwright was admitted again, received his gown and a quarter's pay June 1662, but was finally expelled about June, 1663]				
,, Dec 24	To Margery Salmon, aged & poor as aforesd		00	02	00
1663 March 25	To Margery Salmon aged and poor as aforesd		00	01	00
,, Septr 29	To Margery Salmon, &c		00	02	00
1664 June 24	To Marg Salmon, &c		00	02	00

It is very remarkable that Sir Edmund Wright's niece should have been in destitute circumstances scarcely twenty-five years after the founding of the Almshouse Messrs Lysons state that "the six almesmen contributed 2s each to relieve her necessities in 1661, and agreed to give her a further allowance of 5s a quarter"—(*Cheshire*, p 711). The latter statement, it will be seen, is incorrect. Margery Salmon received at various times (all enumerated above) between the years 1661 and 1664, certain sums out of the funds of this Charity, allowed by the Treasurer, Richard Wright, (who at that time was almost sole Trustee, and was a distant relation of the aged widow), during the suspension of the incorrigible Cartwright.

1668 March 20	For a load of lyme to make up the gate & sett the worke over the door		00	01	04
,, ,, ,,	To Mr Banks in pte of ye Summe agreed on for setting up the Armes &c over the door		01	00	00
,, ,, ,,	To John Johnson, Mason, in pte for his stone-worke ouer the door & for the gate		01	00	00
,, ,, ,,	More to the sd Jo Johnson & his man in full to him for their worke		00	14	06
,, ,, ,,	For some lead & pins for ye saide worke		00	01	01
,, ,, ,,	More to Mr Banks in full for his stone worke 10s , and for *painting & guilding* the same 13s 4d		01	03	04

One of the first acts of the Trustees elected in 1666 was to erect the present Stone Gateway (see illustration) and Coat of Arms with the inscription carved in. stone as follows —

Arms Sable, a chevron between three bulls' heads cabossed, Argent *
Crest A bull's head on a wreath.

"SR EDMVND WRIGHT KT. BORNE
IN THIS TOWNE SOLE FOVNDER OF
THIS ALMESHOVSE A'NO DOM. 1638 "

To pay for these additions, one almshouse was kept vacant from Christmas, 1666, to March, 1670, and for half a year, three houses were kept empty The gateway and front wall, which were originally built nearer to the houses than at present, were taken down and re-built in their present position in the year 1837.

---

* These Arms belonged to the ancient family of *Bulkeley* (*Cf* p 285) From the fact that the *Wrights*, of Nantwich, (who are said in the old pedigrees to have descended from the family of *Bichley* or *Bulkeley*,) do not appear in any of the Cheshire Visitations, it is believed they had no right to use these Arms In a note in Dr Ormerod's *Cheshire*, vol iii p 695, it is assumed on the evidence of this stone carving, that Sir Edmund Wright improperly used the Bulkeley Coat It may be, however, that the Trustees of 1666, and not Sir Edmund, are responsible for the presence of these Arms on the Almshouse

GATEWAY TO WRIGHT'S ALMSHOUSES.

	£	s	d
1668 Sep 29 For 800 setts for a hedge att turther end of the garden 4/o, and for 600 more 3/-	00	07	00
" " For 2 days work to set them & to make the mudd wall fit for them	00	03	04
" " For sixe burne ¸bundles¸ of Thornes 1js , & for a cay for 2 men to berre the Thornes in the gutter by the Almshons \\jd	00	03	09
1669 Sep 29 To John Dutton for laying the Gate in o¸le & for po¸nting all the stone worke of the portall	00	04	00

1674 Lady Dav "William Fleete d¸ing vpo 3 dayes before the quarter end, whereby he was prevented of his Quarter s pay, Save only giuen To his poore diseased aged wife and two diseased children towards his buriall &c £00 06s 08d "

This is one of the instances of *married* pensioners   His poor widow was one of the first inhabitants of Roger Wilbraham's Almshouses   Her burial is thus recorded —

"1679 July 24 Jane Fleete, wid Almeswoman "—*(Par Reg)*

The following Mem is entered under date 2nd Jan 1717—18 —

"It was agreed by a good majority of the Trustees then present yt hereafter no married person shall from henceforth be admitted an Almsman in Sr Edmd Wright's Hospitall, the same being contrary to ye declar'd Will & direction of ye founder notwithstanding that such direction may have sometimes been dispensed with by some former Trustees "

"John Bromhall, Treasurer "

"At a Vestry Meeting Aug. 8, 1800, it was judged highly necessary that a proper woman should be appointed to the care of the Almsmen on account of their Inability and frequent Indispositions, when the daughter of Thos Wicksted was elected, and that the vacant house should be repaired for her to inhabit for her care & attention to them, and that one of the women who receives the Widows' Mite should live with her " Her successors were Mary Wright and Elizabeth Wright, the latter of whom died about 1840.

	£	s	d
1678 Nov Given to a poor kinswoman of the founders	00	02	00
1682 March 25 Paid for binding & clasping the Bible	00	04	00
1685 June 25 "*Mem* Roger Stone, of Wich Malbank one of the Trustees putt into the Almshouse a Booke of Comon Prayer to be perserued & kept by the present & future Almsmen for the vse of the Hospitall "			
1703 April 2 For a bottle of Sack at ye election of New Trustees (omitted in last yeares disbursements)	00	02	06
1712 Nov 24 Paid for Ale which the Almesmen had	00	01	00
1728 Nov 16 Paid Mr Jonathan Taylor Binding a B ble, which is at the Almshouses	00	03	00
1731 Sep 29 Pd for a Coffen for Richd Lynn (deceased almesman)	00	08	00
" Gave Ale to ffunerall	00	01	00
1733 May 12 Paid Mr John Tench for hire for a horse to Hough to get Mr Bromhall to execute the new Trust Deed	00	01	00
1750 Jan 29 Receivd of Mark Topham for goods sold that were John Dean s an Almsman deceased	00	08	02
" " " Paid for Coffen for John Dean	00	08	00
" " " 30 Pd for Ale for the funerall	00	03	00
1758 Ap 5 Pd Jno Hassall (being the Deputy Overseer) for attendance on Bowers (Almsman) when Ill 3 weeks 6s , Bowers Coffin & Church Fees 9s 2d , Ale for 3 men to carrie him to Church 4s , Saml Bowerey who was chose in his room 10d	01	00	00
" (Which was Bowers quarters' pension due at Midsummer, had he lived till then)			
1768 Sep 29 Pd J Davenport for 6 pair of Shoes, Leather being now much dearer	01	07	00
1769 Xmas Pd 6 pr Shooes	01	10	00
1772 *Michaelmas* William Bowerey, one of the Almsmen (by Old Age) was so reduced that he could not assist himself, so he was removed Oct 16th into the poor house, and John Vaughan was elected in Bowereys Room "			

		£	s	d
1783 June 24 Fined 5 Almsmen for suffering the wall to be injured & refusing to tell by whom it was done		00	12	06
,, Sep, 29 Stopt with Richd Wicksted (Almsman) the Repairs of his Windows which he neglgently broke		00	01	02
1795 Nov 24 "At Anniversary Meeting in the Vestry it was resolved, that in consideration of the very high price of Grain & all other Provisions, a sixpenny loaf of house-hold bread shall be distributed every week to each of Sir Ed Wright's Almsmen, till further orders "				
The distribution commenced on Sat Dec 5th " Rich Wicksted, (Treasurer)				
1795 Dec 21 Paid Clerk Burchall for proclaiming Wright's Election & other Meetings of the Trustees		00	01	04
1827 " Mem Nov 24 Messrs Broughton & Garnett Bankers having become bankrupt on 13th Nov 1826, and being indebted to the Charities in a Balance of Cash in their hands with interest thereon £136 7s 4d , and in Nantwich Notes in the Treasurer s hands £13, making together the sum of £149 7s 4d The Treasurer in the succeeding accounts has only credited the Charities proportionably with the Dividends he has received on that account ' ' Wm Acton, Treasurer '				

The Income and Expenses for the year 1877 were as follows —

			£	s	d
Income	One year's Rent Charge due Sep 1877	.	£32	0	0
Expenditure	One year s Pension to 6 Almsmen, at 20s each per quarter	..	24	0	0
	Rector for Sermon		0	10	0
	For Anniversary Dinner		1	0	0
	Hats and Cloaks (once in three years)	.	11	5	6
	Six pairs of Boots @ 13s 6d each	.	4	1	0
	Clothing (Shirts and Stockings)	..	2	3	0
	Water Rate 6s per ann , Repairs various sums .	.	.	..	
	Balance against this Charity 24th Dec 1877 ..	.	£37	9	10

Owing to the insufficiency of income, the endowment being exactly the same now as it was 245 years ago, some of the pensioners in the early part of this century quitted the Almshouse for the Workhouse , while others died in great poverty and neglect Mr. William Sprout's gift in 1829, however, increased each Almsman's pay £10 per annum and the pensioners since that time have been better sustained than at any former period of the history of this Hospital.

Sir Roger Wilbraham's ALMSHOUSE at Welsh Row Head, was originally a low brick building of one story, the only ornament, in the centre, being a stone tablet of the Arms of Wilbraham, of Dorfold, and the date 1613. It stood close to the road, and had a garden behind divided into six plots When Partridge wrote the six almsmen were supplied with a warm gown faced with blue, and a cap, once every two years, a pair of shoes every year, and forty shillings per annum Of late years a sum of money has been allowed, which the almspeople expend themselves in clothing.

The Almshouse was re-built in 1870, by John (*now* Lord) Tollemache on the site of the former garden plots, in two groups of three houses each. These comfortable dwellings of two stories, with their gardens in front, are an ornament to the west end of the town. The inmates are old married men, and on their deaths their widows are allowed to remain during their widowhood, if they conduct themselves properly

The WIDOWS' HOSPITAL and OLD MAIDS' ALMSHOUSE in Welsh Row, the foundation of Roger Wilbraham, Esq , of Townsend, are sustained by his descendant, G F. Wilbraham, Esq.

The ALMSHOUSE at Beam Street-end is sustained by Hungerford Lord Crewe, of Crewe Hall.

The Grammar School.

LTHOUGH the exact date of the foundation of Nantwich Grammar School has not occurred, it is certain that the school was established more than three hundred years ago.* The Chantry Roll of 1548 (page 282) alludes to the necessity there was for such a school; and in many places the revenues of the suppressed Chantries and Free Chapels were, by Act of Parliament I Edw. VI. c. 14, applied to the establishing of Grammar Schools. This, however, was not the case at Nantwich. Some years must have elapsed before one was commenced; or Gerard, the herbalist, who was born at Nantwich in 1545, would probably not have been sent to school *"to Wisterson, two miles from the Nantwitch."*† Webb, in his "Itinerary of Nantwich Hundred" c. 1621, (King's Vale Royal) says:—

> "The school was founded by Mr. John Thrush and Mr. Thomas Thrush, of London, woolpackers, and is well and sufficiently upheld and maintained to the furtherance of teaching the children of the poor and others; and an ancient and grave schoolmaster of very near fifty years continuance, Mr. RANDAL KENT, yet teacher there with a learned assistant, a master of arts of Queen's college in Oxford, whose name is *Mr. Shenton,* of laudable pains and industry."

The exceptionally long period of half a century that Mr. Kent had been master, carries the history of the school as far back as 1572 (14 Eliz.); in which year the name of a scholar, Humphrey Mainwaringe, also occurs, (page 101). A note in *Harl. MSS.* 2074, f. 166, states, that the School-house was formerly the *"Gild-Hall:"* and that *"the woolpackers armes, & the names of the said psons.* [John and Thomas Thrush] *in the school chamber is all that proues the place to be of their foundation."* The founders above named, who were natives of the town, are said to have purchased the Gild-hall, in the Churchyard, for the purpose of a school, from Queen Elizabeth.‡

What the original endowments were, or how the school was supported in the early years of its existence, is not known. The names of benefactors in later times will be found in the list of Charities. To the Wilbraham family of this town, for a great number of years, belonged the right of nominating the Masters, a list of whose names, though, perhaps, incomplete, is here printed for the first time.

---

* It is very singular that no mention is made of the Grammar School at Nantwich in Carlisle's "*Endowed Grammar Schools,*" published in 1818.

† John Gerard's "*Herbal,*" Edit. 1599, p. 1091.

‡ Lysons' *Cheshire,* p. 712; and Dr. Ormerod's *Cheshire,* vol. iii, p. 436, New Edit.

MASTERS OF THE OLD GRAMMAR SCHOOL.

MR RANDLE KENT,* from *c* 1572 to 1623   This master, who was most likely the first, enlarged the school by adding a handsome wing or porch on the south side   It had two inscriptions †   One giving the date of creation and the builder's name —

> "RICHARD DALE, FREE MASON,‡ WAS
> THE MASTER CARPENTER IN MAKINGE
> THIS BUYLDINGE. ANNO DOMINI 1611"

The other, being the Schoolmaster's epigraph, as follows —

> "*Ranulphus Kent, hujus scholæ gymnasiarchus, singulari suo in bonas literas amore, et summâ in natale solum pietate, hanc ipsam musarum sedem novo hoc adjecto ex suis ipsius impensis auxit et donavit.*"§

Although the Kent family is frequently mentioned in the Parish Registers, the baptism of Randle Kent is not recorded , perhaps, owing to the hiatus in the Register after 1545; but he may have been a younger son of the family mentioned just before that date

> "1542 Allice, D of Roadull Kent & Jane   March xviii —*(Bapt Reg)*
> "1544 John, S of Randull Kent & Joane   Feb xxvj "—*(Bapt Reg)*

It is noticeable that no less than four persons of the name of *Kent* have been masters of this School   In the *Itinerary*, already quoted, Mr Webb relates that King James I visited the school on the 26th Aug 1617, and stayed "while an oration was pronounced by one of the scholars "

The death of the aged master, and that of an usher in the school, are thus noticed in the Wilbraham MS Journal⸱

> "Oula Mr Kent the schoolmaister dyed 18 Jan 1623-4 "
> "Toby Tench the usher died 18 Oct 1624 "
> "1623-4 Jan 20 Mr Randle Kent, an ancient schoolemaister '—*(Bur Reg)*
> "1624 Oct 19 Tobias Tench "—*(Bur Reg)*

MR WILLIAM SHENTON, M A   It is presumed from the following entry in the Register, that Mr Shenton, who was first an assistant in the school, succeeded Mr Kent, as head-master , but no mention of his resignation or death has occurred.

> "1630 Nov 7 John son of Mr Willm Shenton, Schoolemaister '—*(Bapt Reg)*

MR . . MAINWARING.   After having been master for a short time, he resigned at Christmas, 1632 (p 298), and succeeded Thomas Tudman, as schoolmaster at Wybunbury ‖——*(Wybunbury Par. Reg.)*

---

* The Head-masters of the School, like the Ministers of the Church during the seventeenth century have the designation 'Mr', which was similar to the modern title of "Revd , and, possibly, indicated the possession of a university degree

† Both inscriptions were legible in 1842, when Mr C J Richardson published the plate of the Porch, in his "*Second Series of Studies from Old English Mansions,*' which has been re-produced on a reduced scale for this work

‡ In the illustration will be noticed a masonic emblem (intersecting triangles) as an ornament

§ *(Translated)*—Randle Kent, high master of this School, out of his great love of sound learning, and his extreme affection for his native place, at his own expense both enlarged this Temple of the Muses and gave it this addition

‖ The singular coincidence in name of Schoolmaster and Vicar at Wybunbury has led to an inaccuracy in a foot-note on page 298, which it will be necessary here to correct   *Edward Mainwaring*, Vicar of Wybunbury from 1659 to 1693, was the second son of Henry Mainwaring, of Carincham, Esq , who marred Frances, daughter of Sir Edward Fitton, of Gawsworth, Bart , in the year 1626   Mr Mainwaring, who left Nantwich for Wybunbury in 1632 could not, therefore, have been identical with Edward Mainwaring, who at that time was most likely an infant

MR ROBERT SIMONDS. There is a reference to Mr Simonds, or "Symonds," as his name is spelled in the Baptism Register in 1633, in the Registers of St John's College (Cambridge) 1636-7, where it is stated that "Thos Kirketon, a native of Hinckley co. Leicester, was two years at school at Nantwich under Mr Simonds, and was admitted sizar in St John's under Mr Lacy, on 25 Jan 1636-7.' Robert Simonds was one of the witnesses of Cecily Maisterson's will dated 19 Jan 1634-5, and now preserved at Chester

MR JOHN DOLMAN. His signature occurs as Schoolmaster in a petition dated 1642,* and in the "Remonstrance" (p 138) in the same year

MR WILLIAM SWALDEN This name is given on the authority of the following line in the Register of Baptisms

' 1661-2 Jan 5 John son of Mr Willm Swalden, Schoolmaister "

MR THOMAS KENT I have not met with the date of his appointment, but the Register records his burial, as follows —

"1686 Nov 4 Mr Thomas Kent, Schoolmaster, burd at Warmingham "†

MR . . MILLINGE, apparently the next master, resigned in June, 1692 His name is not mentioned in the parish Registers

MR JOHN BOYDELL The following entries are taken from a pocket Almanac, in the handwriting of Roger Wilbraham, Esq, of Nantwich, now preserved at Delamere.

"1692 June 30 To Mr Millinge at his leaving ye schoole 5s

  ,,   Dec 17 To ye School Mr at breaking upp for Christm a quarters pay 10s

  ,,   ,,   To 5 Boyes that Acted   2s 6d

  1693 Sep 15 To Mr Boydell or Schoolemr a qt [quart] of Sack to welcome him to N, 2s 6d "

Regular quarterly payments of 10s are made to Mr Boydell, and to his usher, Mr. Pratchett, 2s 6d. per quarter Both are also mentioned in the Registers

"1692-3 Jan 22 Thomas sonne of John Boydell Schoolmaster '—(Bap Reg)
"1696 July 26 Martha dau of John Boydell clerke ' [i e in holy orders] —(Bap Reg)
"1699 April 23 Sarah dau of Thomas Pratchett Schoolemaster "—(Bap Reg)
"1704 Oct 8 Mary dau of Thomas Pratchett Schoolemaster "—(Bap Reg)

The date of Mr Boydell's death or resignation has not occurred

During the seventeenth century the exact dates of the appointments of Masters to the Nantwich Grammar School, or "The High School" as it was then called, to distinguish it from the endowed Charity School in the town, are preserved in the Diocesan Act Books at Chester

MR SAMUEL TOWNSEND Nominated by Randle Wilbraham, of Nantwich, Esq, 15th Feb 1716 He appears to have resigned in 1721, and was buried at Nantwich on 6th June, 1729 —(Par Reg.)

* See Account of the Wilbraham family postea

† His burial is also recorded at Warmingham, and probably he was a native of that parish There is a Silver Paten in Warmingham Church with the following inscription —"The Gift of Samuel Kent of Sandbach, Mercer, for the use of the Communion Service in the Parish Church of Warmingham 1740 " (Reverse side)—" He was born at the House called the Lane End, in Elton, in this Parish, July 12, 1679 ' (Obligingly communicated by the Rev Canon H I Blackburne, Rector of Warmingham)

REV JOHN KENT, Clerk (in holy orders) Nominated by George Wilbraham of Hefinston Grange, Esq, 26th June, 1721. The exact date of his resignation or death has not occurred, but the next nomination in the Bishop's Registry is that of Mr Adderley It is worthy of note that a line in the Parish Register mentions another clergyman schoolmaster, as follows —

"1730 April 27 John, son of the Revd William Duncalfe, *Schoolmaster* ' [Baptized]

REV. THOMAS ADDERLEY Nominated by Roger Wilbraham, of Nantwich, Esq, 20th Dec. 1732, his testimonial to the Bishop for licence being signed by Roger Wilbraham, Tho Brooke, (Rector), Will Maisterson, Clutton Wright, Edwd Wettenhall, and Thos Williams After the death of the "Rev John Twemlow, Curate,' who was buried at Nantwich 5th Jan 1739-40 *(Par Reg)* Mr Adderley became Curate under Dr Brooke, the Rector, and Dean of Chester, and, as the whole ministrations of the parish would devolve on the Curate during the non-residence of the Dean, most likely Mr Adderley found it necessary to resign his school. The Register records —

"1750 Dec 2 Eliza wf of the Rev Thos Adderley, Buried in the Chancel"
"1762 May 20 The Revd Mr Thomas Adderley, Curate ' [Buried]

REV ISAAC RATHBONE, *clerk* (in holy orders). Nominated by Roger Wilbraham, Esq, 15th March, 1744 He had previously been elected Master of the Free Grammar School at Acton on 3rd Jan 1725-6, (Acton *Par Reg*), and resigned that post to accept the mastership at Nantwich He was also incumbent of the Chapel of Wettenhall, in Over, until his death The Register records —

"1742-3 Jan 19 Isaac Rathbone, clerk, & Ann Morris, widow, [married] by Licence" &c
"1767 Aprill 17 The Revd Mr Rathbone [buried] at Acton "

His widow left a Charity to Nantwich (See page 361)

REV JOHN KENT He is described as "of Nantwich," and was nominated by George Wilbraham, Esq, on 29th May, 1771, the school having probably been vacant since the death of Mr. Rathbone This John Kent on the 9th May, 1767, also succeeded Mr Rathbone as Chaplain of Wettenhall *(Diocesan Act Book)* He is mentioned by Mr Partridge *(History of Nantwich*, p 57) as a worthy successor to the first Grammar School-master of that name

REV MATTHEW BLOOR, M A Nominated by George Wilbraham, Esq, on the resignation of John Kent, licence from the Bishop dated 15th Jan 1792, his testimonial being signed by the Rev William Morgan, Rector of Wistaston Rev Joseph Partridge, Curate of Baddiley and Chaplain of Woodhey, and Rev John Kent, Curate of Wettenhall This is the last appointment preserved at Chester Diocesan Registry

REV JOHN LATHAM. Nominated by George Wilbraham, Esq The exact date of his appointment has not occurred, but he was licensed Curate of Nantwich at an annual stipend of £40, on 25th Sept 1796 He was educated at Queen's College, Oxon, and is first mentioned in the Register as follows —

"1798 April 12 John Latham, Clerk of Nantwich and Elizabeth Snelson [Married]

His eldest son Edmund was baptized at Nantwich 2nd April, 1799, *(Par Reg.),* and to the memory of another son, James, who died in the twenty-first year of his age, on 1st June, 1824, is a gravestone in the churchyard near the South door of the Chancel;

beside which, another flat stone records that the Revd. John Latham died Oct. 26th, 1836, in the 64th year of his age. Having resigned the mastership of the school, the Rev. John Latham became curate of Baddiley, near Nantwich, which is said to be the smallest parish in the county. At that time the parson, clerk, and sexton of the parish, all resided in Nantwich, according to the following rhyme, then current in the town.

> "I, John Jackson went to ring,
> I, John Moore went to sing,
> I, John Latham went to pray,
> And all the congregation stayed away."

OLD GRAMMAR SCHOOL.

After the resignation of Mr. Latham, the Grammar School was vacant for several years, owing to the very small emoluments, which, added to the fact that there was no residence provided for the master, deterred clergymen without preferment from accepting the school. Thus for the first time in the history of the school, the next master, Mr. Robinson, was a layman.

WILLIAM ROBINSON. Appointed by George Wilbraham, Esq., on 29th Nov. 1831. The Charity Commissioners, who visited Nantwich in 1836, reported concerning the endowment and condition of the school, as follows:—

£4 os od per ann from Mr Wilbraham, who for this sum appointed *four* free boys from the town
£6 12s od per ann (variable) from the Churchwardens, on account of certain bequests to the school
(see page 361), for which *four* more free boys were appointed from the town viz, two by the
Churchwardens, and two by Mr Chas Mare of the Manor House in Beam Street

In addition to the eight foundationers, Mr. Robinson had nine boarders, and fifty
day-boys Mention is also made of £2 per ann formerly paid to the Master, having
been lost "for a long time." (Thirty-first Report Charity Commissioners, 1837, page 644)

Mr. Robinson was educated at St Bees, and was married at Nantwich to Ann, dau
of William Stoneley, on the 8th March, 1832 —*(Par. Reg)* He committed suicide by
hanging himself on the 28th June, 1841, at the early age of thirty-two years; and was
buried on the 1st July, in the churchyard, on the north side of the Chancel, where a flat
stone covers his grave, and that of an infant daughter

REV THOMAS PRESCOTT, B A   Appointed by George Wilbraham, Esq , after the
death of William Robinson, in 1841   He was the son of the Rev Peter Prescott, for
some time Superintendent Wesleyan Minister in this town   Having resigned, his successor was

REV THOMAS TALBOT DAY, the last master of the old Grammar School   After a
short time he left the town, and the school was finally closed in or about the year 1858
When alterations were made in the churchyard, in connection with the restoration of the
Parish Church, the ancient timbered school was pulled down, a new one having been
built at Welsh Row Head in 1860   Throughout the present century, if not earlier, this
school was rivalled by the neighbouring Grammar School at Acton, which has produced
some who have distinguished themselves in after life, no list of boys educated at the
High School at Nantwich is known to exist.

The Charity, or Blue-cap School.

Parochial endowed Charity Schools which were designed for the children of the poor,
originated at the close of the seventeenth century, in efforts to counteract the proselytism
of James the second's papists.[*]

The general mode of founding these schools was as follows [†]—The Clergyman of the
Parish expressed in a few lines the necessity and usefulness of the design on a roll of
parchment, to which benefactors subscribed their names and the sums of money given,
these subscribers forming the first governing body of the school. Among the general
Orders, it was imperative that the Master should be a member of the Church of England.
He was required to teach and explain the Church Catechism twice a week, and to take
particular care of the manners and behaviour of the children, to bring them to Church
twice every Lord's Day and on Holy Days, and to the Clergyman to be catechised in

---

[*] Fosbroke s "*Ariconensia,*' 2nd Edit 1818 p 107

[†] "An Account of the Methods whereby Charity Schools have been Erected and Managed" (15 pages) was published
in connection with "a Sermon (30 pages) preached by Richard Willis D D Dean of Lincoln in the Parish Church of St
Andrews, Holborn, 8 June 1704 Being Thursday in Whitson-Week, At the first Meeting of the Gentlemen concern'd in
Promoting the Charity Schools in and about the Cities of London and Westminster ' Printed by J Downing, for M
Wotton, at the Three Daggers near the Inner-Temple Gate in Fleet Street 1704 '

Church when any number were sufficiently prepared   When the boys could read competently well, the Master was to teach them to write a fair legible hand, with the grounds of Arithmetic, to fit them for services or Apprentices.   School hours were from 7 to 11 a m , and 1 to 5 p.m., in summer; and from 8 to 11 a m , and 1 to 4 p m , in winter.

The first mention of the Charity School at Nantwich is in a quarto pamphlet entitled "*An Account of the Charity Schools in Great Britain and Ireland, &c*, London, 1712," which gives the following information relating to the school here.

' Forty boys taught, who wear blue caps that their behaviour may be the better observed abroad. The Master's salary is £10 a year paid by two ladies The Minister hath set up another for 30 girls, the charge of whose education is defrayed out of the offertory *

One of the ladies here mentioned was, most likely, Mrs Anne Crewe Offley, the patroness of Nantwich living, who dying 15th May, 1711, left by Will, £5 per annum to the school (see page 361) No further information has occurred relating to the Girls' Charity School, but many years afterwards the Register records the following burial

" 1784 Oct 13 Charlotte Blagg, School Mistress '

No school was ever built at Nantwich, but the upper story of a house† in Pepper Street was rented for the purpose from the Churchwardens (as Trustees of Harwar's Charity) at £1 per annum, which is stated to have been received in the Accounts for 1713 (page 358).

Bishop Gastrell in his *Notitia Cestriensis* in 1721, speaking of Nantwich Charity School, says, nothing was then "*settled*," *i e* the monies subscribed were not permanently invested. Donations amounting to £700, of which £663 were the gifts of Randle and Stephen Wilbraham, Esqrs , remained in the Wilbraham family, who from time to time appointed the master and elected the free boys   From 1796 to 1850 the sum of £5 was annually applied to this school out of Hodgkin's Charity. Two other sums were given by John Bromhall, Esq , and Zachary Turnpenny, in augmentation of the Master's salary, and to buy books   From the Treasurers' Books of the Wright's Trustees, in whom those sums were vested, the following names (except the first) of Schoolmasters occur, which list is here printed for the first time

LIST OF MASTERS OF THE CHARITY SCHOOL

THOMAS LOWE.‡ From *c* 1711—1742 His burial is thus recorded.—

" 1742 Sep 16 Thos Lowe, maister of the Charity School "—*(Par Reg)*

THOMAS DAVIES. 1742—1766 He received the first payment from Bromhall's Charity, according to the Treasurer's Book, as follows —

			£	s	d
1746 Dec. 25	Paid Mr Davis being one half of the money as agreed on by the Trustees at the last Annual Meeting		3	7	9
1747 May 1	Paid Mr Taylor [stationer] for six Spelling Books 3s , and two Bibles in three vols 6s 6d , for the use of the Blew-cap School		0	9	6
1747 Dec 9	Paid Mr Davis		1	10	0

* Re-printed in Local Gleanings, 4to Series, Vol I, p 224

† The house was pulled down at Christmas 1879 and on its site Mr Jackson, Draper, has erected a commodious residence

‡ There is an entry in the Bapt Reg as follows —" 1714 May 12 Sarah dau of Thomas Lee schoole-master " Query whether "*Lee*" is intended to be "*Lowe*"

His burial is thus registered —

> "1766 Jan 19 Thomas Davies, Schoolmaster "—*(Par Reg)*

JOSEPH HILDITCH. 1766—1772   He appears to have been the recipient of these Charities as Schoolmaster until his death in 1772

> ' 1772 Oct 23 Joseph Hilditch Schoolmaster "—*(Bur Reg)*

REV. JOSEPH PARTRIDGE. 1772—1796.   He was born in 1724, and was the son of Joseph Partridge of the Red Lion *(now* Wilbraham's Arms) Inn, Nantwich, who is described in the Parish Register as the *"London Waggoner."*

> '1722 Oct 13 Joseph Partridge and Sarah Tew,* by licence from Doctor's Commons, Thomas Gyles, junr,
> Surrogate, Dated Oct 4th "—*(Mar Reg)*
> "1724 May 1 Joseph son of Joseph Partridge, Waggoner '—*(Bapt Reg)*
> 1756 Aug 15 Joseph Partridge, London Waggoner "—*(Bur Reg)*
> '1772 Jan 9 Sarah Partridge, widow "—*(Bur Reg)*

On the first anniversary of his father's death, Joseph Partridge, who had already married, had his only child baptized at Nantwich Church   The entry in the Register is interesting as revealing the fact that he had succeeded to his father's business, as "Waggoner," *i e* proprietor of the Road Waggon for the carriage of goods to and from London

> "1757 Aug 15 Jane daur of Joseph Partridge, Waggoner '—*(Bapt Reg)*

When forty-two years of age, however, Joseph Partridge had succeeded in qualifying himself for the Church of England without going to the university, and on the 26th Aug. 1766 he obtained licence from the Bishop to be Master of the Free Grammar School at Acton, on the nomination of several of the Trustees of the School *(Diocesan Act Book);* and, about the same time, he became Curate at Baddiley and Chaplain of Woodhey Two years after, he and his wife are noticed in a pasquinade, entitled *"Nantwich Notables* 1768,' printed in the "Cheshire Sheaf," No 985, as follows —

> "Ye Cassocked Waggoner, drole Tale   Mr P.   t   ge"
> "Modern extravagance   Mrs P   t   ge"

He relinquished Acton School for the Mastership of Nantwich Charity School in Aug. 1772, which, together with his Curacy and Chaplaincy, he retained until his death   His burial, and that of his widow, are recorded thus —

> "1796 Oct 29 Revd Joseph Partridge "—*(Bur Reg)*
> "1806 Jan 5 Mary, widow of the Revd Joseph Partridge "—*(Bur Reg)*

A gravestone in the churchyard has this inscription —

"In Memory of
THE REVD JOSEPH PARTRIDGE,
who departed this life on the 25th of
October, 1796, aged 72 years.

All that was Good in me to God I owe,
My Sins and Follies from Myself did flow,
And I with full Conviction must disown
From future Woe, where find the safe Retreat !
The Good how little, and the Guilt how great !

* " *John Tew Waggoner*, " probably the father of Sarah Tew, was buried at Nantwich on 14 May, 1722 *(Bur Reg)*

Faith and Repentance shew'd the way to Bliss,
Those Means apply'd, my End I shall not miss
Humbly thro' CHRIST'S atonement then I trust
At the last Day to rise among the Just "

" Also, Mary wife of the above reverd
Joseph Partridge, who departed
this life on the 1st of January 1806,
Aged 79 Years '

Joseph Partridge published the following works —

1 —A folio pamphlet of 46 pages entitled " *The Anti-Atheist* A Didactic Poem in Two Parts By Joseph Partridge of Namptwich, Cheshire Manchester Printed by Joseph Harrop, at the Printing Press, opposite the Exchange, MDCCLXVI " [1766]

2 —" An Historical Account of the Town and Parish of Nantwich, with a particular relation of the remarkable Siege it sustained in the Grand Rebellion of 1643 Shrewsbury printed by W Williams 1774 "

In the above work the author thus notices the School he taught. " Forty poor boys are cloathed and instructed in English and the older part in writing, supported chiefly by the charitable appointments of the family of Wilbraham of Town's-End, which cloathes the boys Mr. Crewe of Crewe hath generously augmented the salary They are denominated Blue-Caps, from a cap of woollen cloth of that colour which they wear "—(*History of Nantwich*, page 57)

3 —"The Renovation of the Heart, the only True and Acceptable Fast A Sermon preached in the Parish Church of Baddiley in Cheshire, on Friday the 27th of February 1778, being the day appointed to be observed as a general fast "

"Published at the request of several of the parishioners by the Revd Joseph Partridge, Curate of Baddiley, Nantwich Printed for the Author by R Taylor and E Snelson, Nantwich Price Sixpence "

JOHN THOMSON, or *Toby Thomson*, as he was generally called, was master for no less a period than fifty-five years (!) that is, from Jan 1797, until Dec 1851; and amusing stories are still told by old inhabitants of the system of school management and discipline adopted by that old-fashioned and eccentric pedagogue

The income of the School in 1836 was as follows —*

	£	s	d
From GEORGE WILBRAHAM, ESQ			
On the 30th Jan in each year, for each of the 40 free boys, a stout drab jacket, a blue cloth cap, a band, a pair of shoes, a pair of stockings, amounting altogether, including the making to	23	3	11
For Master's Salary, per annum	11	0	0
From LORD CREWE, per annum	5	0	0
,, HODGKIN's Apprenticing Charity, per annum	5	0	0
,, BROMHALL's and TURNPENNY's Charities per annum	3	3	0

The forty free boys were wholly selected by Mr. Wilbraham's agent at Nantwich, out of the parish, and were not admitted before the age of eight. They were required to pay for stationery, and sixpence in winter for fire-money. In July, 1836, there were, besides, thirty boys received upon the master's own terms *

* Charity Commissioner's Report for 1837, p 645

Mr. Thomson, who was married in 1800, (see page 351), died in Beam Street, at the advanced age of eighty-seven years, and was buried in the parish Cemetery on the 15th March, 1852.

MR. . . . . . BINNS was the last master of the Charity School; and held that position only about six months. From June, 1853, to November, 1860, the balance in the hands of the Wright's Trustees from Bromhall's Charity due to the School, amounted to £14 6s. 1d.; which sum was paid to E. D. Broughton, Esq., as receiver for the Nant-wich Grammar School Trust; and the Governing Body of that School incorporated this Charity in the Endowment at the same time.

The New Grammar School.

The present Grammar School and Master's residence at the end of Welsh Row, were erected by GEORGE FORTESCUE WILBRAHAM, ESQ., of Delamere, who endowed the same by investing the sum of £500, according to the scheme, dated 22nd March, 1860, directed by the High Court of Chancery, for consolidating the Grammar and Blue-Cap Schools Charities. At the same time the RT. HON. HUNGERFORD LORD CREWE transferred to the official Trustees, in respect of the Blue-Cap School, the sum of £200. For these sums, G. F. Wilbraham, Esq. nominates four free boys, and Lord Crewe two free boys, in the parish of Nantwich. The school is controlled by nine Trustees; the original names being Lord Crewe, G. F. Wilbraham, Esq., the Rector, two Churchwardens, Wilbraham S. Tollemache, Esq., Messrs Edward H. Martin, Thomas Williamson (Surgeon), and E. H. Griffiths. Meetings are held twice in the year; viz.: Monday fortnight after Midsummer day, and on Christmas Day. The Masters of the New School have been as follows:—*

1.—MR. WILLIAM BROOKS, appointed 25th April, 1860; resigned 19th April, 1862.

2.—MR. H. C. BARBER, appointed 30th June, 1862; resigned Aug. 1866.

3.—REV. J. V. CRISPIN, appointed 13th Oct. 1866; resigned Christmas 1871.

4.—MR. *(afterwards Rev.)* ROBERT BOURNE B.A. (London) appointed April, 1872; resigned Dec. 1875.

5.—REV. JERMYN S. HIRST, B.A., appointed Jan. 10th, 1876. Present Master.

---

* This list of names was kindly supplied by T. W. Hensley, Esq., Solicitor, one of the Trustees of the School.

Nonconformity in Nantwich.

NE of the results of the Reformation under Henry VIII was the rise in the latter part of the sixteenth century of religious sects who claimed the right of private judgment in the interpretation of Scripture as opposed to enforced subscription to formulas of creed; and a free and extemporaneous form of prayer as opposed to a fixed Liturgy. When James I became King of England there were two established religions in the kingdom; Episcopacy in England, and Presbyterianism in Scotland. In course of time the latter religion gained many adherents in England, and other societies sprang up, *Independent* in their government, one of which was distinguished by the practice of *adult* baptism, known as *Baptists,* and nicknamed by their opponents, *Ana-baptists,* or the *re-. baptizers.* Puritanism, too, had spread rapidly in Cheshire during the reigns of Elizabeth and James, and though Mr. John Paget was silenced at Nantwich, in 1605, (page 295), nonconformist ministers had their "solemn assemblies," and their "glorious monthly exercises at Northwich, Namptwich, Knutsford, Macclesfield, &c. in and after 1627."[*] The Long Parliament abolished Episcopacy in 1646; and during the Protectorate, Richard Jackson was the Presbyterian clergyman of the parish until the passing of the Act of Uniformity in 1662; when, not having the conscientious scruples of some, he conformed, and so retained his living.

Ejected ministers, numbering throughout the country, it is said, two thousand, afterwards became the heads of *new* Nonconformist churches, which at first met in secret, and multiplied in spite of persecution. The Rev. Philip Henry, in his Diary under date 16th Feb. 1672, says:—[†]

"Came forth the K.[ing's] Declaration for Indulgence: the Church of Engl. establisht; pœnal lawes suspended agt. all non-conf. & Recusants [*i.e.* Roman Catholics]; separate places promis'd to bee licens'd; Papists to meet in private houses only."

[*] Paget's "*Defence of Church Government,*" London, 4to., 1641.

[†] "*Diaries and Letters of Philip Henry, M.A. of Broad Oak, Flintshire.* Edit. by Rev. M. H. Lee. Vicar of Hanmer, 1882." p. 249.

NANTWICH.

Under this Indulgence, which only remained in force about one year, licence was granted to ROBERT FOGG to be a Presbyterian teacher in the house* of *John King* in Nantwich, and two other houses† were licensed as meeting houses, namely —the house of *John Malden*, and *Robert Fogg*, both in Nantwich (*Cal. State Papers*, Dom Series, 1672, No. 185).

Interesting particulars are known of *Robert Fogg* Born about the year 1596, he had been appointed Rector of Eccleston, Lancashire, in 1627, of Hoole, Lancashire, in 1641, and of Bangor Is-y-coed in 1646, from which last living he was ejected in 1662; and, in his old age, came to Nantwich. He "went constantly to Church at Acton or Nantwich, and preached after sermon on the Lord's day, and also on week days, and in the latter part of his time he lived alone, (his second wife proving a Papist, and her sons having entered the King's army), and kept his coffin by him" He was buried at Acton on the 21st April, 1676 ‡

On the "30th Nov 1682, orders were published in the Churches of Cheshire to present all that come not to Church and to the Sacrament if above sixteen." (Philip Henry's "*Diaries*," p 319), and for a few years the Dissenters here, as elsewhere, were silenced, but when the Toleration Act of 1689 was passed, there were two distinct congregations of Protestant Dissenters in this town, namely, the *Presbyterians*, and the *Baptists*.

PRESBYTERIAN MEETING HOUSE AND MINISTERS.

The first Meeting-House of the Presbyterian society in Nantwich was situated in Pepper Street, on the site of cottages now belonging to Mr Thomas Johnson, of Acton. One of the deeds of that property, dated 16th Feb 1749, describes it as a "*Warehouse or Ancient and decayed piece of Building formerly used as a Meeting-House*" In a Rate Book dated 1691, it is entered as a "*Kiln,*" being, probably, a malt-kiln; and here the celebrated nonconformist divine, Matthew Henry, the son of Philip Henry who also occasionally visited Nantwich, commenced and finished his remarkable preaching career At the age of twenty-three, Matthew Henry, who had then just completed his education at Grays Inn, came from London to Broad Oak in June, 1686, and spent some days at Nantwich with his friend George Illidge, "and preached every night to a considerable company."§

The first pastor who settled at Nantwich was—

REV WILLIAM TURTON, M.A. 1688.

Mrs Savage, of Wrenbury Wood, the sister of Matthew Henry, in her Diary, says —

"In the year 1688 we had old Mr Turton for a while at Nantwich"

* This house was "*Sweet-briar Hall*," (see illus ration) The earliest deed relating to this property, dated 1701, mentions John King as owner and occupier for many years prior to that date and the Rev Samuel Lawrence as tenant of that part of the house to the right of the oriel window Both occupied these premises in 1691, according to a Rate Book of that date

† These houses I have not been able to identify

‡ See "*Palatine Note Book*," vol ii, p 216 "*Nonconformity in Cheshire*," and "*Philip Henry's Diaries*," which contain many references to him

§ Tong's *Life of Matthew Henry*, Edit 1716, p 52 This biography contains several allusions to George Illidge and other zealous Presbyterian dissenters at Nantwich The Illidge family belonged to Wybunbury parish and many entries of their names occur in the Registers there, and some few in Nantwich Registers George Illidge who is stated to have frequented the ministry of Philip Henry, was the son of Lieut Richard Illidge, of Nantwich and Cheerbrook, whose life, written by the Rev Matthew Henry was published in 1710 and re-printed in 1836

He had been ejected from Rowley, in Staffordshire, in 1662, and removed from Nantwich to Birmingham, where he died in 1716   He was succeeded by—

REV SAMUEL LAWRENCE   Sep 1688.—April, 1712

Samuel Lawrence was the son of William Lawrence, a dyer, of Wem, where he was baptized 5th Nov 1661   Philip Henry characterized his father as "an intelligent, holy, useful man"[*]   His uncle, the Rev. Edward Lawrence, M A, of Magd Coll Cambridge, ejected (1662) from Baschurch, co. Salop, settled as minister in London, and was there known to Matthew Henry   When a child, Samuel Lawrence had a remarkable gift for learning   He was taught Latin at the Free School, Wem, under Mr. Roderick; was next sent to Newport School under Mr Edwards, and afterwards had as tutors the following ministers in succession   Philip Henry at Broad Oak, Mr. Tallents at Shrewsbury, and Mr Malden at Alkinton, near Whitchurch, where he improved much in Greek and Hebrew   He completed his education at the Dissenting Academy of Mr Charles Moreton, whose school was broken up under the tyranny that followed the Act of 1662, its master being obliged for safety and liberty, to sail for New England   Samuel Lawrence, after having been three years an usher under Mr. Singleton, Grammar Schoolmaster of Clerkenwell Close, became domestic chaplain to Lady Irby, widow of Sir Anthony Irby, of Dean's Yard, Westminster   When the liberty for Dissenters commenced in 1687, he began to preach in a meeting-house ' lying very near to my Lady's '   "In the year 1688 he came down into the country to see his relations, and a society of Dissenters in and about Nantwich being then in quest of a minister, after several motions made to them had miscarried, desired Mr Lawrence to come and spend a Lord's Day with them, which he did to their great and universal satisfaction, so that they unanimously chose him to be their minister, and after some time taken to consider of it and consult his friends, he accepted it, but went first to London to take leave of his friends there.   The Lady Irby was extremely loth to part with her chaplain, and was very angry with *Mr Baxter* and *Philip Henry* for persuading him to go to Nantwich, but thither he came in September of that year."   Ordained at Warrington in the beginning of November, he zealously laboured here for twenty-four years, and was never 'taken off from his work till the last Sabbath of his life"   Though of a weakly constitution, he preached every Saturday about noon to the country people that attended the market, and frequently on week-days in the country about   He regularly attended the meetings of the Cheshire Ministers twice a year, and in his nonconformity he was "considerate and conscientious"   "His whole conversation in the world was blameless, and without rebuke, and, like Demetrius, he had a good Report of all men, he was of a peaceable spirit, bearing and forgiving, a very good scholar and very communicative of his knowledge.   The year before he died he "read University learning, both philology and philosophy," *gratis*, "to two or three hopeful young men who came and tabled [lodged] near him in the Town for the benefit of his conversation "

Samuel Lawrence died of a fever on Thursday, 24th April, 1712, in the fifty-first year of his age; and was buried in the Chancel of Nantwich Church, being followed to the grave by a great many true mourners, amongst whom was his "intimate bosom friend"

* Funeral Sermon of William Lawrence, by Philip Henry, on 26th Feb 1694-5

Matthew Henry, who on that day preached a funeral sermon in the Pepper Street Meeting-House, which was published and from which the above particulars are obtained.* Matthew Henry often preached to the congregation at Nantwich, on his visits to Mr Lawrence, and to his eldest sister, Mrs Savage, of Wrenbury Wood. On 21st Oct. 1707, an Ordination Fast was held at Nantwich, the evening was spent in examining the Candidates at *Mr Lawrence's* house, *Mr. Lawrence* began, *Mr Irlam* prayed, *Dr. Holland* preached from Acts xxvi, 17, 18, *Mr. Henry* took their Confessions and Vows, and left this memorial of the meeting —

> "We were in all about twenty Ministers, the Candidates discovered much seriousness, we were much refresh'd and there were none to make us afraid"

Samuel Lawrence was twice married   "He left behind him a sorrowful widow,† three sons by his first wife, and two daughters by his second, and a dear and tender mother in the 80th year of her age." Some of his correspondence has recently been published by J E Bailey, F.S.A., in the Palatine Note Book, vol ii, p 98-9

Several mentions of these early Presbyterian dissenters occur in the Parish Registers, as follows —

> " 1686 July 27 George Illidge & Ellen Seavill [married]
> 1687 July 14 Elizabeth dau of George Illidge, shoomaker Baptized by Mr Henryes
> 1689 May 19 Mary d of George Illidge, shoomaker, Baptized by Mr Lawrence
> 1691 June 21 Martha d of George Illidge, shoomaker, Baptized by Mr Lawrence
> 1698 Oct 16 Thomas s of Thomas Hassall, Baptized by Mr Lawrence
> 1700 June 9 Robt s of Thomas Hassall, shoomaker, Baptized by Mr Lawrence
> 1705 Aug 5 Richd s of John Gill, Currier, Baptized by Mr Lawrence
> 1707 May 18 John s of Thomas Bikerton Glover Baptized by Mr Lawrence
> 1700 March 25 Wm s of Samuel Lawrence, Presbiterian Minister, bur at Acton
> 1700 April 26 Sarah wife of Saml Lawrence, Presbiterian Minister, bur at Acton
> 1712 April 28 Saml Lawrence, Presbiterian Minister " [Buried]

REV JOSEPH MOTTERSHEAD. 1712—1718.

He was ordained at Knutsford on 5th Aug 1712, and came from Kingsley to Nantwich. During the short term of his ministry, *Matthew Henry* preached his last sermon in the Pepper Street Meeting-House, on 21st June, 1714, from Jer. xxxi, 18. Sir Thomas Delves, Bart, had invited the celebrated divine and his old friend George Illidge to spend the evening at Doddington Hall, but, being indisposed, Matthew Henry dined at Mr Mottershead's house, and, after a restless night, died there of an apoplectic fit the following morning at eight o'clock   Three days after, in the same Meeting-House, was preached *"A | Sermon | upon the | Mournful Occasion | of the | Funeral | of the Reverend and Excellent | MR MATTHEW HENRY | Minister of the Gospel | Preach'd at | Nantwich, June 25, 1714   The Day | on which the Sacred Corps was carried | thence to be interr'd at Chester, | By John Reynolds, Minister [of Shrewsbury] in Salop" | London   Printed 1714   8vo. pp 40*

The Parish Registrar noted the event in the Burial Register as follows —

> "1714 June 25 Mr Matthew Henryes buried at Chester "

---

* "A Sermon Preach'd at the Funeral of Mr Samuel Lawrence, Minister of the Gospel at Nantwich, in Cheshire Who died there, April 24 1712, in the 51st year of his Age and was buried April 28   To which is added a short Account of his Life   By Matthew Henry, Minister of the Gospel ' Printed "*London* .   1712 " 8vo pp 48

† The widow of Samuel Lawrence, died suddenly at Newcastle-under-Lyme, and was buried at Nantwich, 10th Nov 1718 —*(Par Reg)*

Little is known of Mr. Mottershead, his congregation is said to have numbered three hundred, of whom ten were gentlemen (*Wilson MSS.* Dr Williams' Library, London). He was married, and had a son buried and another baptized, at Nantwich, as recorded in the Registers

> "1714 May 22, Joseph son of Joseph Mottershead, Presbiterian Minister " [Buried]
> "1716 Sep 13 Joseph son of Joseph Mottershead, Presbiterian Minister " [Baptized]

He removed to Manchester in 1718, where he lived many years in much reputation, and was succeeded at Nantwich by

REV WILLIAM VAWDREY 1719—1728.

Mr. Vawdrey, who was ordained in 1718, came from Allostock to Nantwich in 1719. The population returns of Bishop Gastrell* in 1721, state that at Nantwich there were 157 Presbyterian families Shortly afterwards the Society left the old Meeting-House, and built the present Chapel in Hospital Street, as related in the diary of Mrs. Savage, as follows —†

> "1725 March 28 This week ground is bought for the building of a new Chapel at Nantwich, &c
> 1725 Tuesday, May 4 Our friend Mr Braddock came hither from Namptwich, and brought us good tidings Chapel work begun, and great encouragement from some of our friends, especially at Manchester [most likely Mr Mottershead's congregation], where they have collected £40 for us
> 1725 June, Wednesday This week our friend *Mr* [George] *Illidge* called on us, who had been at London, Bristol, and other places negotiating for us 50£ collected
> 1726 Wednesday, 18th May, a day much to be remembered We went to Namptwich and most of our family to the dedication of our NEW CHAPEL there I should have remarked how our good minister [Mr Vawdrey] took leave of the old chapel with that text *"If thy presence go not with us carry us not up hence"* Mr Owen preached first, then Mr [John] Gardner [of Chester] Mr Lawrence [of Newcastle] prayed A very full congregation Mr Vawdrey's good humble remark affected me, 'I must endeavour to preach better, you to hear better, and both to live better, and then our light will shine indeed' I would own the goodness of God that we may set up our Ebenezer—hitherto kept, helped, taught *very few alive now that were members of this society when we began in the old chapel* One generation passes away and another comes but the word of the Lord endureth for ever
> 1729 January 3 The most considerable event of the past year has been the removal of our dear minister Mr Vawdrey from Namptwich to Bristol, borne away from us by a violent importunity "

Mr. Vawdrey, who resigned at Midsummer, 1728, was succeeded by

REV. THOMAS HAYNES. 1729—1745

The Diary of Mrs. Savage mentions this minister.

> "1729 Thursday, August 7 This day Mr Haines our new minister and cousin Eddowes's daughter, came to see us, &c
> 1731 Tuesday, March 1st This week our minister Mr Haines and cousin Betsey Eddowes‡ were married at Namptwich, &c

---

* *Notitia Cestriensis*, Chet Soc Publ, p 222

† The extracts here given are taken from the fuller extracts of the Diary as printed in "*Nonconformity in Cheshire*," 1864, p 130—132

‡ *Betsy*, or *Elizabeth Eddowes*, was the eldest daughter of John Eddowes, Ironmonger, of Nantwich who was cousin, by marriage, to Mrs Savage The marriage is recorded at Nantwich on the 2nd March, 1731-2 By his second wife, John Eddowes had four sons, one of whom, *John* Eddowes, born c 1722, will be be noticed presently in connection with Joseph Priestley

1732 Wednesday   19th At Namptwich, a double lecture, *Mr* [Thomas] *Colthurst* [of Knutsford] preached first, from *Gen* III 15, ' *The seed of the woman shall bruise the serpent's head* ' Blessed be God for Jesus Christ, that blessed promised seed   He came in the fulness of time, and has wrought our eternal salvation for all his elect   Afterwards *Mr Dobson* of Salop, whose subject I thought well followed, 1 Pet v 12 ' *The true grace of God wherein ye stand* '

                .   Tuesday morning, in bed, I said over to myself the Assembly's Catechism—an excellent form of sound words which I was taught in my childhood, and trust I shall hold fast, and am glad to find that notwithstanding sad decays those good old things I do not forget "   &c

This last significant remark seems to have a tacit allusion to changes of religious thought and differences of opinions amongst the members of the Nantwich society

Mr. Haynes, who took no prominent position amongst the dissenting ministers of his day, removed from Nantwich to Sheffield in 1745,[*] and was succeeded by *Mr Meanley*

At a meeting of the Cheshire Ministers held at Knutsford on 3rd Sept 1745, according to the Minute book, " *Mr. Meanley*, at the request of his people at Nantwich, consented to ordination next meeting" which was fixed to be the " first Tuesday in May next." [1746]   Before that date, however, the union of Presbyterian ministers was broken up by divisions arising out of the Arian controversy   Some, called *Subscribers*, required subscription to the Doctrine of the Trinity and the Divinity of Christ, others, though differing much in their views and opinions, maintained the fundamental principle of the old Dissent, viz   non-subscription to creeds—and were known as *non-subscribers*.   Of the latter was Mr Meanley.   The society, though afterwards adopting Socinian views, retained the Chapel as the representatives of the old Presbyterians, but here, as elsewhere, it has since been called the *Unitarian Chapel*

UNITARIAN MINISTERS.

Rev Richard Meanley   1745—1758
He removed to Platt, near Manchester, and died there in 1790

He was succeeded by

Rev Joseph Priestley.   Sept. 1758—Sept. 1761.

This minister, afterwards the celebrated Dr. Priestley, came from Needham Market, in Suffolk, to Nantwich, at the age of twenty-five, having been introduced to the congregation here by a former minister, Mr Haynes, of Sheffield.   An interesting account of his settlement and life in this town is related in his autobiography,[†] as follows —

"Mr Haynes, perceiving I had no chance at Sheffield, told me that he could recommend me to a congregation at Nantwich, in Cheshire, where he himself had been settled, and as it was a great distance from Needham, he would endeavour to procure me an invitation to preach there for a year certain   This he did, and I gladly accepting of it, removed from Needham, going thence to London by sea, to save expense   This was in 1758, after having been at Needham just three years

At Nantwich I found a good-natured friendly people, with whom I lived three years very happily, and in this situation I heard nothing of those controversies which had been the topics of almost every conversation in Suffolk, and the consequence was that I gave little attention to them myself   Indeed

[*] On the oak wainscotting in one of the pew aisles on the east side of the Chapel, is a brass inscribed as follows —
" In Memory of | John, son of the Revd | Thomas and Elizth Haynes | who Died Janry 6th 1758 | Aged 17 " |
[†] Memoirs of the Rev Dr Joseph Priestley to the year 1795   Written by himself "   Birmingham, 1810, p 31-36

it was hardly in my power to do it, on account of my engagement with a *school*,* which I was soon able to establish, and to which I gave almost all my attention, and in this employment, contrary to my expectations, I found the greatest satisfaction, notwithstanding the confinement and labour attending it   My school generally consisted of about thirty boys, and I had a separate room for about half a dozen young ladies   Thus I was employed from seven in the morning until four in the afternoon, without any interval, except one hour for dinner, and I never gave a holiday on any consideration, the red letter days, as they are called, excepted   Immediately after this employment in my own school rooms I went to teach in the family of *Mr Tomkinson*,† an eminent attorney, and a man of large fortune, whose recommendation was of the greatest service to me, and here I continued until seven in the evening   I had therefore but little leisure for reading or for improving myself in any way, except what necessarily arose from my employment   Being engaged in the business of a school-master, I made it my study to regulate it in the best manner, and I think I may say with truth, that in no school was more business done. or with more satisfaction, either to the master or the scholars, than in this of mine

Many of my scholars are probably living,‡ and I am confident that they will say that this is no vain boast

At Needham I was barely able, with the greatest economy, to keep out of debt (though this I always made a point of doing at all events), but at Nantwich my school soon enabled me to purchase a few books, and some philosophical instruments, as a *small air-pump, an electrical machine*, &c   These I taught my scholars in the highest class to keep in order, and make use of, and by entertaining their parents and friends with experiments, in which the scholars were generally the operators, and sometimes the lecturers too, I considerably extended the reputation of my school, though I had no other object originally than gratifying my own taste   I had no leisure, however, to make any original experiments until many years after this time

As there were few children in the congregation (which did not consist of more than *sixty persons*, and a great proportion of them travelling Scotchmen) there was no scope for exertion with respect to my duty as a minister   I therefore contented myself with giving the people what assistance I could at their own houses, where there were young persons, and I added very few sermons to those which I had composed at Needham, where I never failed to make at least one every week

Being boarded with *Mr Eddowes*,§ a very sociable and sensible man, and at the same time the person of the greatest property in the congregation, and who was fond of music, I was induced to learn to play a little on the English flute, as the easiest instrument, and though I was never a proficient in it, my playing contributed more or less to my amusement many years of my life   At Nantwich I had hardly any literary acquaintance besides *Mr Brereton*,‖ a clergyman in the neighbourhood, who had a taste for

* The *School-house*, which was pulled down about forty years ago, fronted Hospital Street   It was a black and white building, and had an upper room that extended over the gate-way that led to the Chapel yard

† This was *James Tomkinson, Esq*, who married Katherine Wettenhall, and was the first of the family to settle at Nantwich, and the purchaser of Dorfold estate

‡ The last surviving scholar of the philosopher schoolmaster was Mr Thomas Hassall, of Nantwich, who died in 1829, aged 82 years   and was interred in the grave-yard connected with this Chapel, without any memorial stone   With the science lectures delivered at Nantwich more than 120 years ago, Mr Priestley commenced that extraordinary series of experiments and discoveries which afterwards entitled him to the honourable distinction of being the Father of pneumatic chemistry

§ This was Mr *John Eddowes* who died 18th March, 1789 aged 67, and was buried in this Chapel   To his memory is a flat stone on the floor, the inscription of which is perfectly legible   The late Joseph Hunter compiled a pedigree of the Eddowes family of Whitchurch and Nantwich, which is preserved amongst the Add MSS Brit Mus 24,444 f 106

‖ "The Rev Joseph Brereton, LL B, Vicar of Acton, who was born at Helmingham, in Suffolk, the seat of the Rt Hon Lionel, Earl of Dysart, in whose family his father, Mr Thomas Brereton, was domestic steward   At the early age of fourteen he was entered a commoner of Queen's College, Cambridge, and from his low stature at that time he got the appellation of the "Little Man of Queens' by which name he was generally known whilst he continued at the University   Soon after taking his LL B degree, and before he had attained to Priest's Orders, he was presented by Earl Dysart to Acton vicarage   He was a man of strong passions, but endowed with great natural talents which were rendered more conspicuous by his diligent acquirements of knowledge in every branch of useful refined Science   He died 6th March, 1787, and was buried at Lower Peover, in this county, aged 67 '—(*Acton Parish Register*)

astronomy, philosophy, and literature in general   I often slept at his house, in a room to which he gave my name   But his conduct afterwards was unworthy of his profession   Of dissenting ministers, I saw most of Mr Keay, of Whitchurch, and Dr Harwood, who lived and had a school at Congleton, preaching alternately at Leek and Wheelock   Being both of us schoolmasters, and having in some respects the same pursuit, we made exchanges for the sake of spending a Sunday evening together every six weeks in the summer time   He was a good classical scholar, and a very entertaining companion

In my congregation there was (out of the house in which I was boarded) hardly more than one family in which I could spend a leisure hour with much satisfaction, and that was *Mr James Caldwell's,*[*] a Scotchman   Indeed, several of the travelling Scotchmen who frequented the place, but made no long stay at any time, were men of very good sense , and what I thought extraordinary, not one of them was at all Calvinistical

My engagements in teaching allowed me but little time for composing anything while I was at Nantwich   There, however, I re-composed my *"Observations on the Character and Reasoning of the Apostle Paul"*   For the use of my school, I then wrote an *English Grammar* [printed 1761], on a new plan, leaving out all such technical terms as were borrowed from other languages, and had no corresponding modifications in ours, as the future tense, &c

My removal to Warrington was in September 1761, after a residence of just three years at Nantwich   In this new situation I continued six years , and in the second year I married a daughter of Mr Isaac Wilkenson, an ironmaster, near Wrexham, with whose family I had become acquainted, in consequence of having the youngest son, William, at my school at Nantwich   It was while at Warrington, that I published my *'Chart of Biography,'* though I had begun to construct it at Nantwich "

To the above account it may be added that Mr. Priestley, while at Needham, had published a work entitled *"The Scripture Doctrine of Remission, &c.* 1755 ," which shows that he had then embraced Unitarian doctrines   It is unnecessary here to trace the biography of this eminent man any further.

A photograph of the earliest oil portrait of Joseph Priestley supposed to have been painted during his short stay in this town, was presented to the Trustees of the Chapel, by the Rev. Jas Yates, M.A., F.R S , and still hangs in the Vestry.   It represents him having a full-bottomed wig, the costume of the Divinity students when they left the Academy at Daventry to settle in the ministry   Later portraits of Priestley have a wig with curls   The photograph was delivered to the subscribers to the Priestley statue at Oxford in 1861

Joseph Priestley[†] was succeeded at Nantwich by

REV JOHN HOUGHTON   1761—1771

John Houghton, who had been trained in Dr Doddridge's Academy at Northampton from 1747 to 1751, completed his education at Glasgow, and was first appointed to *Hyde*

---

[*] *Mr James Caldwell,* who lived at Hospital Street-end, died 15th July, 1791 and was buried in Nantwich Church-yard   A tombstone with inscriptions, which formerly covered the family vault was removed a few feet in Aug 1879, when the new footpath was made along the north side of the Churchyard   *Cf* page 53 *note*

[†] A Portrait and Memoir of Dr Priestley is given in *"The Monthly Repository of Theology and General Literature,"* Vol X 1815

Dr Priestley had a stammering utterance   He says (*Autobiography,* p 43) "for the first two years I was at Nantwich, this impediment had increased so much that I once informed the people that I must give up the business of preaching, and confine myself to my school   However by making a practice of reading very loud and very slow every day I at length succeeded in getting in some measure the better of this defect, but I am still obliged occasionally to have recourse to the same expedient "

in 1758, where he remained until he succeeded Priestley as minister and schoolmaster at Nantwich   He published "*A New Introduction to English Grammar, in the easiest Method possible for the use of Schools, London*   ;' and edited a book entitled "*Sacrificium Missaticum Mysterium Iniquitatis*, or a Treatise concerning the sacrifice of the Mass (never before printed) by the Reverend and Learned *Mr. Henry Pendlebury*, M A , of Christ's College, Cambridge,' &c *London* . . . MDCCLXVIII " [1768].   The latter work was published by subscription, and in the printed list of subscribers occur no less than seventy-three local names.

Mr Houghton removed in 1771 to Elland, co. Yorkshire, in 1782 to Wem; and in 1788 to Norwich, where he died.

REV. RICHARD HODGSON. 1771—1799

Mr Hodgson, who succeeded J Houghton, came from Monton to Nantwich in 1771. He ministered to the congregation and conducted the school for nearly thirty years. and in 1799 or 1800, removed to Doncaster.

The next two names are given on the authority of the History of Nonconformity in Cheshire (1864, p 133), but it is doubtful whether either of them were settled or appointed ministers

REV. ROGER MADDOX, 1800, for a short time.

REV.   . . . PARTRIDGE. 1800 –1801.

REV WILLIAM JOHNS 1801—1803. Removed to Manchester

REV DAVID WILLIAM JOHNS (or Jones ?) 1804—1815. Removed to Whitchurch

REV FRANCIS KNOWLES 1816—1823.

He was a native of Sheffield, and, though not educated for the ministry, he published several pamphlets on religious subjects, entitled "*Observations*," &c.,   His most important work was "*The Balance of Scriptural Evidence*," &c , in three vols , in which Unitarian and Trinitarian arguments are contrasted in parallel pages   Mr. Knowles collected the materials for this work while at Nantwich, although the book was not published until 1835. He removed to Park Lane Unitarian Chapel, near Wigan, and there died.

REV. JAMES HAWKES. 1823—1846.

From 1800 to 1813 Mr Hawkes had been minister at Duckenfield, where he originated a Sunday School   His next appointment was to Lincoln, and from thence he came to Nantwich in 1823, and conducted the school with great ability, first in the old school-house, until it was taken down, and afterwards in the present school-room over the vestry in the Chapel   Mr. Hawkes died at Nantwich, and was buried in the Chapel, being the first pastor who had died here since Samuel Lawrence, 134 years before.   A mural tablet on the south wall is inscribed as follows.—

"In memory of Ann wife of the Rev James Hawkes who died June 13th, 1826, aged 53 years Also Rev James Hawkes Minister of this Chapel for 23 years died May 19, 1846, aged 75 years "

REV. FRANCIS HORNBLOWER 1849—1853

After the death of Mr Hawkes, the cause having for many years been in a low and declining state, and the chapel suffered to fall into a ruinous condition, no minister was appointed for three years   In 1849 efforts were put forth to renovate the chapel.   It was found necessary to make a new roof, and the south wall was partially taken down and rebuilt, the pulpit being removed from the opposite side of the chapel to its present position, and the oak pews being re-modelled   These repairs and improvements were effected at a cost of over £300, and the chapel was re-opened on 10th Dec 1849, the preachers being the Rev. R Brook Aspland, of Duckinfield, and the Rev Franklin Howorth, of Bury   In the same year Mr. Hornblower had been appointed pastor and under his ministry Unitarianism in Nantwich revived   It may be mentioned that the celebrated actor Macready attended the ministry of Mr Hornblower on his occasional visits to his aunt, Mrs Forshaw, who then resided in Hospital Street

Mr Hornblower married a daughter of William Roscoe, Esq, of Allerton Hall, banker, M P for Liverpool in 1806, and a well-known author   She was a talented woman, and published a volume of poems in 1843, and one of the Hymns in the Martineau collection is by her pen *   Mr Hornblower died at Nantwich in 1853, and was buried at Liverpool. Since his death the congregation has again decreased, and his successors, who have been for the most part young students, have remained only for short periods   Their names are as follows —†

REV THOMAS BOWRING   1853—1857   Resigned
REV. ROBERT WILKINSON   1859—1861   Resigned
REV THOMAS WILLICOTT   Feb 9, 1862—Feb 28, 1864.   Resigned.
REV. E W HOPKINSON   July 10, 1864—March 22, 1868   Resigned
REV. JAMES MACDONALD   Feb 7, 1869—Dec 28, 1873   Resigned
REV T B BROADRICK   Dec 20, 1874—March 11, 1877   Resigned
REV JOHN HARDING MATTHEWS   Feb 3, 1878   Present Minister.

The Chapel, which still retains its original oak pews and pulpit, is 37 ft by 28 ft, and 18 ft 6 in high   It is lighted by four circular-headed windows, decorated with architraves and moulded cills, and is capable of seating about 230 persons   An organ was purchased in Aug 1875, and the Rev S A Steinthal, of Manchester, preached on the occasion of its opening   Besides the memorials of the dead already mentioned, is a mural tablet on the south wall of the chapel inscribed to

"Mary Street Baron, wife of Peter Baron formerly of Walshaw house Lancashire, whose remains were deposited beneath this Pew on the 2nd of November 1821 at the age of 45 Years   Also the said Peter Baron died Dec 13th 1831 aged 56 years"

A small graveyard behind the chapel, which was closed for interments about thirty years ago, and is now in a very neglected state, has in it three gravestones,

(1) "Ann, wife of Thos Cooke, died 12 Sept 1834," (2) "Joseph Hassal died 24 May 1833, aged 77," also "Sarah, his wife, died 30 May 1843, aged 78, also a daughter, Emma Vaughan Hassal, died 11 March 1829, aged 20," (3) "John Bolland, Surgeon, died 28 April 1850, aged 67 years," who belonged to a family of that name at Bolesworth

It is a singular fact, as will presently be seen, that the three old Dissenting Chapels in this town,—the Presbyterian, the Baptist, and the Friends' Meeting-house,—were all built in or about the same year

* This Hymn commences—   "My father! when around me spread,
                                              I see the shadows of the tomb ' &c

† The names of the Ministers of this Chapel since Mr Willicott, have been supplied by Philip Barker, Esq, The Grove, Nantwich, to whom I am also indebted for other particulars relating to this Chapel

THE BAPTIST CHAPEL, MINISTERS, &c

The earliest mention of a society of Baptists in Nantwich occurs in a book having the curious, if not absurd, title,—"*A History of the Baptists among the Welsh from the time of the Apostles to the present year By* [Rev.] *Joshua Thomas* [of Leominster] 1778 pp 504 " The author states (pp 158—160) that during the years of persecution (1678—1688) the Baptists at Nantwich, for security, held their meetings in the salt-*mines* [an error, no doubt, for salt-*houses*] the pastor being the RƐV S [amuel] ACTON, who maintained the doctrine of a general redemption, and was a gifted and acceptable preacher   He also remarks that several members of this society, who had removed to Newbridge, near Wrexham, travelled a distance of twenty-two miles to partake of the Lord's Supper with the brethren and sisters at Nantwich.*

In Grey's "*Examination of Neals*," (vol iv p 410) is printed the following Address to King William III, in 1688.

' From the ANABAPTISTS at NAMPTWICH '

"Though we want Words to express our Gratitude for so great a Blessing as the free Exercise of our Religion which is now by your Majesty granted unto us, and all others in so full a Manner as could be expected from none but such a Prince, as Heaven designed for the highest Pattern of Royal Goodness and true Policy, yet the Sense of it has made so lasting an Impression upon us, that (we trust) that it shall not be possible for any of your Subjects to serve your Majesty with more ready Obedience and stedfast Loyalty, than we shall do in our Station to the utmost of our Capacity

Dread Sovereign, that Almighty God who hath established you upon the Throne to correct the Mistakes of past Ages, and make the present happy in the enjoyment of an entire Liberty of Conscience, will crown your Majesty and your Royal Posterity with all temporal and eternal Blessings, making your reign over us glorious and happy to the utmost Wish of your most loyal and obliged Subjects and the Terror of your Enemies, we shall ever pray " [First printed in "Gazette, No 2244 "]

One of the congregation about this time was Mrs. Milton (widow of the immortal poet) who came to reside at Nantwich in the year of the Revolution (1688)   It is worthy of note that Milton in his Latin treatise on "*Christian Doctrine,* ' translated and published some years ago, expounds the views of Baptists very strongly as to the immersion of believers only, as against the sprinkling of infants, and on that account it may be, his widow associated herself with the Baptists here, in preference to other Protestant Dissenters in the town

MR SAMUEL ACTON,† who has already occurred in these pages as a tobacconist, salt-proprietor, and the first known Baptist minister, must have been a wealthy man   In 1691 he resided in one of the principal houses in the town,‡ now (1883) called "The Elms,"

---

* Information of Simon Jones, Esq of Wrexham, who has a copy of the book

† Samuel Acton does not appear to have been a native of Nantwich   Query, whether he belonged to the Actons of Little Budworth and Bunbury parishes

‡ Rate Book, dated 1691, *penes* G F Wilbraham, Esq

in Mill Street Bishop Gastrell says there were in 1721, 109 Anabaptist families in Nantwich,* but whether they then worshipped in Mr Acton's salt-houses, or had a meeting-house elsewhere, is not known

The first Baptist Chapel, a low brick building, that has been much altered of late years, was built in Barker Street in 1725 The late T W. Jones, solicitor, of Nantwich, who defended a trustee of the Chapel in a law-suit at Chester, says, "The earliest document connected with this Chapel which has fallen under my notice bears date 1726, followed by subsequent Deeds renewing the Chapel Trusts from time to time" In the then new Chapel, or its grave-yard, Mrs Milton is believed to have been buried, (neither line, nor stone, however, remains to prove the fact) a few days prior to the 10th Oct 1727, on which day her will "was proved at Chester, in common form of Law, by John Allcock, one of the Executors, power reserved to *Samuel Acton*, the other Executor."

No later mention of Mr. Samuel Acton has occurred, but he cannot possibly have lived long after, and may, too, have been buried in the Chapel which had been erected under his superintendence, of this, however, there is no positive proof, the Parish Register being silent on the matter, and the old records of the Chapel having been lost for many years † Of his published Sermons, the earliest is entitled —

" Dying Infants Sav'd by Grace, Proved, And the Blessed Man with his Blessedness Described In a Sermon preached near Namptwich, in Cheshire, at the Burial of a deceased Infant July 25, 1695 By S[amuel] A[cton] Matt xviii, 3 1 Cor xiii, 7 Lond Printed for the Author &c 1699 4to pp 32 "‡

The Rev. W Tong (Life of Matthew Henry, 1716, p. 387) speaking of the funeral of Matthew Henry on the 25th June, 1714, says, "the Day before *Mr. Acton*, Minister to the Baptist Congregation, had taken very particular and Respectful Notice of the great Loss the Church of God had sustained "

In 1714 Mr. Acton published the following Sermons —" *The Folly of Wise Scepticks*," Jeremiah viii, 8, " *Gospel Compulsion*,' Luke xiv, 23, " *Salvation by Grace*," Ephesians iv, 5. In 1717, a " *Discourse on the Sacrament*," and in 1718 a small book entitled " *Uncompromised Truth*, or an Attempt at Unity among Christians, together with an Appeal to my Brethren of the Baptized Churches of Great Britain and Ireland." In this book

*Bishop Gastrell's " *Notitia Cestriensis* " The Bishop also mentions another meeting-house for Anabaptists with about 40 members in Wybunbury parish, where there were at that time 24 Dissenting families, of whom fourteen were Anabaptists The field in which this meeting house stood, in *Blakelow*, is still called *Chapel-Field*, and Mr Thomas Pedley, of Willaston, aged 75, remembers conversing with old people in his youth, who said that stones from the grave-yard of the old meeting-house were used up in building cottages in the neighbourhood Wybunbury Parish Register contains the following interesting entries —

" 1723 June 1 Elizabeth Dunbibb, a stranger, interred at Blakelow Meeting-house within the Township of Wibunbury "
" 1726 Aug 21 Joseph Allen, of Weston, a young youth of about 18 years of Age [Baptized] having not Recd Infant Baptism because Born of Anabaptistical Parents "
" 1732 May 1 Elizabeth Smith, of Hough, Spinster, born of Anabaptistical parents, publicly Baptized in the Parish Church of Wybunbury '
" 1743 Jan 1 John Sparepoint, of Stapeley, born of Anabaptistical parents Baptized publickly "
" 1762 May 1 Mary Birchall about 30 yrs of Age, Born of Anabaptistical parents, Bapt into the Church "

† The only mention of Samuel Acton, in any Parish Register, that I have seen, is an entry at Wybunbury, recording his marriage, late in life, as follows —

" 1725 June 22 Samuel Acton of Nantwich Parish, Gentleman, and Lydia Maddocks of the City of London, widow, p' lic dat 21 June "

He is stated, in the late Rev R B Aspland's MS collections (vol iii, p 148), now in the possession of his son in London, to have died in the year 1728

‡ Roger Wilbraham, of Townsend House, makes an entry in one of his pocket Almanacs, that he had written a paper in " Nov 1692 " entitled " An Answer to S A [Samuel Acton] his cavils to Mr Lawr [Rev Samuel Lawrence] Argum [ent] for Infant Baptism "

the writer remarks that he had been for *forty years* lamenting the disadvantages arising from contentions, and for upwards of *thirty years* had been endeavouring through the exercise of friendliness and goodwill to promote charity," &c. For three years the REV. ISAAC KIMBER ministered to the congregation, at the invitation of Mr. Acton, the latter probably having arrived at an advanced age. Mr. Kimber, who was born in 1692, and is known as a biographical writer, and author of a History of England, 4 vols. 8vo., is said to have preached a funeral sermon on the death of Mrs. Milton, on 10th March, 1726,

entitled " *The Vanity and Uncertainty of Human Life*," &c. The date here given, which is clearly an error, may be accounted for by the fact that Mr. Kimber's sermons were published posthumously by his son, Edward Kimber, in 1756; but much suspicion has been cast on the truthfulness of the statement altogether, as "not one word occurs that has relation to the deceased" in the printed sermon.* Mr. Kimber's abode at Nantwich was rendered uneasy by the unkind behaviour of some of the principal persons of the congregation because he would not subscribe to certain Articles. Even his intimacy with the minister of the parish, and also with Mr. Vawdrey (Presbyterian minister) was objected to, though both were very pious and learned characters. He was obliged on these accounts to leave Nantwich in 1727. He took leave of his flock in a pathetic sermon, and most of the congregation wept.†

GROTESQUE CARVING.
(See page 332 note.)

The next settled minister was the REV. JOHN ASHWORTH, who removed to London in 1740, and was succeeded by the REV. JOHN GREEN, who was minister here in 1743.‡

A marble mural tablet, formerly in the Barker Street Chapel, and now built into the wall of the school-room in the new Chapel, Market Street, commemorates a lady of the congregation about that time, as follows:—

" Near this place lies the Body
of LYDIA wife of JOHN GOODALE Gentleman.
A Woman
Endow'd with the most amiable Qualities
of Fine Natural Understanding,
Which She had greatly improv'd by Reading & Meditation.
To her Husband, Relations, & Neighbours
Tender, Generous & Humane.
To relieve the Needy & Succour the Distrest
Forward, Earnest & Impatient.
And in her Duty to her Creator
Regular, Devout, & Fervent.
She died Universally lamented,
December ye 17th 1746.
Aged 40."

* See Hunter's *Critical and Historical Tracts,* No. iii, p. 72. London: Jno. Russel Smith, 1850; and articles in the *Athenæum* for Sept. and Oct. 1849, &c.

† The late Rev. R. B. Aspland's MS. collections, vol. ii. p. 353.

‡ MSS. in Dr. Williams' Library, Red Cross Street, London; quoted in "*Nonconformity in Cheshire,*" p. 135.

A line in the Parish Register mentions this Chapel as follows —

"1759 March 6 Ann Tomkin, widow, Buried at the Anabaptist Meeting House '

The Rev R B Aspland says, the Chapel came into the hands of some Calvinistic Baptists, through the influence of a Mr Price, but the congregation declining, it was at last closed about the year 1772. One of the trustees, Mr Roger Maddock, in 1777, let the Chapel to the first Wesleyan Methodist Society, which continued to worship there for thirty years. The Rev. John Wesley, on two occasions, preached there, and there, too, in 1785, an eccentric townsman, *Joseph Whittingham Salmon*, Gent, who held Swedenborgian doctrines, preached his own wife's funeral sermon, from Rev. vii, 13—17, which was printed at Leeds in the same year.[*] Soon after the year 1808 an attempt was made to re-establish the Baptist Society, and one of the new Trustees, a native shoemaker, MR JOHN COOPER, became the first minister. A house was purchased for a minister's residence, and the sanction of the Bishop obtained, certifying it as a place of worship, according to the following petition late in the possession of Geo. Wild, Esq, J P, of Stockport

"*To the Right Reverend Father in God B Edw. Sparke by divine permission Lord Bishop of Chester*"

" We whose names are hereunto subscribed being his Majesty's protestant Subjects dissenting from the Church of England have agreed to set apart for the public worship of Almighty God a dwelling house now in the holding and occupation of Saml Penkethman situate in Hospital Street in the Parish and Town of Nantwich, the County and Diocese of Chester, and desire that the same may be registered according to the Act of Parliament made in the first year of the reign of their late Majesties King William and Queen Mary entitled ' An Act for exempting their Majesties protestant subjects dissenting from the Church of England from the penalties of Certain Laws,' as witness our hands this 25 March 1812

Saml Penkethman	Thos Cooper	William Fairbrother
John Cooper [Minister]	Wm Cooper	Thomas Hassall
Samuel Lovatt	Ralph Tilsley	Thomas Louvatt
John Davies	John Tilsley	Matthew Pickering "

The above document is endorsed as follows "The 28th day of March 1812. Registered in the Public Episcopal Registry at Chester, according to the Act within mentioned. Wm Ward, Depy Regr " " Extracted by Edwd Jones, Procter."

Mr. Cooper, who was still minister in 1820, removed to Coseley, in Staffordshire, and afterwards to Wisbeach, and then to Sutton, in Lincolnshire, where he died. Before leaving Nantwich, he installed as his successor, his journeyman shoemaker, *Mr Thomas Foster*, whose name occurs in the Parish Register, as follows.—

"1831 Jan 13 Thos Foster, Genl Baptist Minister, and Mary Hughes " [Married]

---

[*] JOSEPH WHITTINGHAM SALMON printed a second edition of this Sermon in 1787. He was the author of "*Moral Reflections in Verse Begun in Hawkeston Park, May 20 and 21, 1794*" &c. Printed by E Snelson of Nantwich 1796, which was reprinted in an abridged form, the third Edition, entitled, "*The Beauties of Hawkestone Park*" &c, being printed at London in 1817. Another poem by the same writer, entitled "*The Beauties of Boothes, the seat of Willoughby Legh, Esq*' papeared in 1820

He was the son of Charles Salmon of Nantwich, Gent, who married Martha Whittingham 1 Jan 1747 *(Acton Par Reg)* J W Salmon was twice married first to his cousin Mary, dau of Charles Salmon of Willaston, whom he married on 19 Jan 1769 *(Nant Par Reg)* by whom he had issue a son, the Revd William Salmon, B A, (bapt 27 June 1775) who was Vicar of St Peter's Church Stockport, 1811—1816, and afterwards curate at Nantwich, and whose daughter *Annette*, though born at Stockport on 12 Feb 1811 was baptized at Nantwich on 22 Dec 1817 and on 28 Nov 1833, became the wife of Thos Bower, Cotton-manufacturer, of Nantwich *(Ibid)*

There are many entries relating to the Salmon family in Nantwich and Wybunbury Registers

The next minister, also a townsman, was *Mr. Thomas Hammersley* These three ministers adopted Unitarian views, and the congregation decreased until it became extinguished Mr Hammersley took possession of the house in Hospital Street, and the Chapel, and eventually an action was brought against him by the other trustees, which was tried at Chester before Justice Williams at the Autumn Assizes in 1840, but decided in his favour For several years the Chapel stood a mournful monument of the zeal of a by-gone age, until it was obtained by a new society of *General Baptists,* that had been gathered together by Messrs Kirkham, Johnson, Pedley and others This society finally removed to new premises in Market Street on the 14th Nov. 1873, and sold the old Chapel in the following year to the Independent Order of Good Templars. The pastors of the new society have been as follows —*

REV J. B. LOCKWOOD,† Jan. 1864 to Dec 1865. Resigned

REV E EVANS, April, 1866 to Sep 1869 Resigned

REV EDW KNIGHT EVERETT, Nov. 1869 to Dec. 1871 Resigned

REV ROBT PEEL COOK, May, 1872 to Sep. 1881. Resigned.

REV PRICE WILLIAMS, Aug. 1882. Present Minister.

THE FRIENDS' MEETING HOUSE

A Society of Friends, originally called *Seekers*, and afterwards *Quakers*, in derision from the quaking they exhibited in their enthusiasm, appears to have existed in this neighbourhood in the Commonwealth period Edward Burghall, vicar of Acton, in his "*Providence Improved*," says :—

"1660 March 16 *Two Quakers* came to disturb me in the public congregation I so ordered my studies, that the sermon was pat against them, they had liberty to speak, and were answered, at last one of them denied the Scriptures to be the word of God, on which they were, with shame, turned out by the congregation "

"1660 June 9th *Two Quakers* came into my church with a lanthorn and candle, while I was preaching, their design was (as they confessed) to have lighted a sheet of paper, which they had, as a sign of God's anger burning against us "

In explanation of the vicar's remarks, it may be suggested that open disputings during public worship at that time were neither uncommon nor regarded as a mark of indecorum, and very likely the two quaker declaimers here mentioned on two different occasions, were merely disturbers, or fanatics, for whose actions and opinions the society founded by George Fox was in no way responsible ‡ The names of several quakers in this neighbourhood, who, about the year 1670, had been convicted as recusants for not attending divine service at their parish churches, and had had their estates seized, occur in a roll preserved in the Bodleian Library, Oxford, as follows —"*Thomas Brassey,* of Willaston, *Joseph Powell,*

* This list of ministers was obligingly communicated by Mr Richard Forey

† Mr Lockwood came from Tarporley, and had formerly officiated for seven years at Hebdon Bridge, Yorkshire He preached his first sermon at Nantwich on 1 Jan 1864

‡ The Rev Philip Henry, of Worthenbury, in 1659 was also annoyed by such like individuals, whom he also calls " *Quakers* set on by others who wished ill to his ministry " Of those who were Quakers by honest conviction, Philip Henry mentions *Mary Moody* who left his congregation and turned Quaker, because she refused to partake of the Lord's Supper " (Philip Henry's *Diaries and Letters* 1682, pp 66, 285)

of Acton, *John Sharples.* of Hatherton, *Daniel Moore*, of Hankelow, and *Thomas Coines,* of Barthomley "~

The Quakers suffered severe persecution in Charles II reign; and in 1685, it is said, no less than 1,460 were imprisoned in Englana and Wales; and great numbers sailed to America, and settled in the newly founded Quaker colony of Pennsylvania, amongst whom were many from Cheshire, who probably built the city of Chester in that State. The first mention of this Sect in the Parish Registers is as follows —

> " 1715 Dec 30 Shussannah Duce, Aged about 42 yeares, *Quaker* " [Baptized]

In 1721 there were thirteen Quaker families in Nantwich —*(Notitia Cestriensis)*

The Nantwich Friends' Meeting-house, and Burial Grouna, is situated in Pillory Street   The land, about eight hundred and twenty-one square yards, was conveyed in 1724 to Benjamin Claridge, of Winsford, and another, together with some buildings thereon, in trust for the use of the people called Quakers, ¯as the site of a building for religious worship, and as a place for the burial of their dead   In the following year a Meeting-House was erected, the cost of which, as also the purchase money for the land, were raised among Friends of Cheshire Quarterly Meeting   The Meeting-house underwent a thorough repair about the year 1850, at a cost of £206   A stable formerly belonging to this property, was taken down a few years ago to provide a better entrance to this secluded and well-kept ground †

Of the Quaker families resident in this town about a hundred years ago, may be mentioned, *Adkins, Bellis, Claridge, Fallows, Morrey, Mulliners, Stretch,* and *Tunstall.* When the burial-grounds in the town were closed by order of the Board of Health in 1850, special exception was made in the case of the Friends', owing to the smallness of the Society, and during the last thirty years only about half a dozen interments have taken place ‡

INDEPENDENT OR CONGREGATIONAL CHAPEL

The evangelical movement, which was commenced within the Established Church by the Rev. John Wesley, and among Nonconformists by the Rev George Whitfield, reached Nantwich before the end of last century, and led to the formation of the Wesleyan and Independent societies   It is stated that when Whitfield visited the town in 1753, he was assaulted by a mob and taken over the flood-gates at the Mill, to Marsh Lane, where the rabble obtained a bull, intending to drive it among the congregation, but being thwarted in their designs by the animal falling into a pit, they left him to deliver his discourse § More than twenty-five years elapsed before a society of Independents was formed by Captain Jonathan Scott, who has been called the Cheshire Whitfield. He was the second son of Capt Richard Scott, and was born at Shrewsbury in 1735   Entering the army in his seventeenth year, he rose to the rank of Captain in the 7th Dragoons, and was present

---

* The List for Lancashire and Cheshire is printed in Mr Earwaker's *Local Gleanings Magazine,* 4to series, Vol I, P 233-4

† These particulars are taken from a pamphlet entitled ' Some Account of the Trust Property, Belonging to the Society of Friends within the limits of Cheshire Monthly Meeting, Prepared by Direction of that Meeting   Third Month 1855

‡ For this information I am indebted to Samuel Harlock, Esq , Brookfield, Nantwich.

§ Whitfield s Life, p 131 , and Letter 997

at the battle of Minden, 1st. Aug. 1759. He commenced preaching to the soldiers of his regiment; and being induced to sell his commission in 1769, he devoted his after years wholly to missionary work, settling first at Wollerton, and visiting Newport, Whitchurch, Newcastle, Nantwich, and other Cheshire towns In 1773 he had a thousand hearers at Stoke-on-Trent, and in the following year he was ordained at Lancaster to the office of "presbyter or teacher at large" In 1780 Capt Scott and the Rev William Armitage of Chester, came to Nantwich and opened a preaching room,—a coachmaker's shop, in Barker Street, (on the site of a row of houses called *Oak Buildings*) the leading members of the small society then being Mr Henry Kitchen and Mr John Smith. Another supporter of the cause was Samuel Barrow, Esq, J P, who lived at a large house, since converted into cottage tenements, on the south side of Hospital Street, and who, in 1796, offered £50 per ann for the support of a settled ministry, an old female servant of his, likewise, leaving a legacy of £20 towards the erection of a "chapel or meeting-house if ever there should be one '

The Chapel was built in 1801, in Church Lane, and met the requirements of the society until 1842, when the present Chapel in Monks' Lane, was built at a cost of £2,200, the old Chapel being retained as a Sunday School, and for week-day services Of the principal supporters in past years, may be mentioned the families of Cummings, Groucott, Hilditch, Jackson, Nixon, Thomson, and Williams In Jan. 1880 the congregation sustained a severe loss in the death of Miss Janet Ramsay, of Dysart Buildings, Nantwich, who for sixty years had been a most liberal supporter,—not only of the Congregational Church, but of other good objects outside her own denomination Besides contributing very largely towards the erection of Monks' Lane Chapel, she bore the sole expense of enclosing the garden (given by her brother, Gilbert,) and Chapel with a substantial wall in 1861, in 1871 she invested £700 in Manchester Corporation Bonds, the interest to be a perpetual annuity in augmentation of the pastor's stipend, and in 1875 she presented the congregation with a very fine-toned Organ at a cost of nearly £400

Memorials of the dead on mural tablets in the Church Lane Chapel still remain to—

(1) "*Rev Robert Smith*, forty years a Minister of the Gospel of Jesus Christ and late Pastor at Church Lane Chapel Nantwich, died 20 March 1822, aged 73"

(2) "*Elizabeth Smith*, died 1 Sep, 1814, aged 63"

(3) "*Sarah*, dau of *Rev Peter Henshall* of Nantwich, died 19 June 1823, aged 2 yrs 4 mths The following curious epitaph is added —

> Dear Sarah s left this vale of woe and sin below,
> Triumphant borne away on bright seraphic wings,
> Her infant soul is fled to Regions high and fair,
> Where now for ever Jesu s love she sings,
> Now in full glory she beholds the Saviour's face,
> Which infant thousand thousands more Behold,
> And with the numerous, glorious Blood-bought Race,
> She sweetly sings his praise to harps of Gold '

(4) "*Henry Kitchen*, aged 68, died 29 Jan 1821, He was more than Forty Years a stedfast Member of that Church, which he in his youth through Divine Providence was the humble means of first establishing, and for several Years, with the assistance of a Friend and Companion he supported the Ministry of the Independent Church"

(5) "*Henry Kitchen* [son of the above] died 20 Sep 1869, aged 77 years He was upwards of 50 Years connected with this Sabbath School as a Scholar, Teacher & Superintendent.'

(6) "*John Ramsay*, Tea-dealer of Nantwich, born in 1795 at Laggansarroch, parish of Colmonell, Ayrshire, died 23 Jany 1834, aged 39 years"

(7) "*Andrew Ramsay*, Draper of Nantwich [brother to the above] died 27 April 1835, aged 56 years, also, *William Ramsay*, Tea-dealer of Nantwich [another brother] died 24 Aug 1835, aged 35 years"

(8) "*Robert John*, infant son of Peter and Janet Cumming, died 25 April 1852"

(9) "*Ann Groucott*, died suddenly 30 April 1876, aged 25 years"

(10) "*Edgar Whitfield*, son of Rev E J Sadler & Ann his wife, died 28 July 1854, aged 4 months 2 Sam vii, 23"

In the grave-yard of Monks' Lane Chapel are memorials to—

(1) Joseph Jackson, d ed 25 March, 1876   Aged 76
Ann, [his wife] died 14 Jany 1853   Aged 51
Samuel [the r son] died 22 July 1819   Aged 8

(2) Ann Steele, died 20 June, 1855   Aged 63

(3) Henry Bilditch, died 21 May, 1854   Aged 36   [Tablet in the Chapel]

(4) Samuel Kitchen, died 24 April, 1859   Aged 67
Hannah [his wife] died 29 Dec 1870   Aged 84

(5) Peter Cumming, died 11 June, 1869   Aged 69

(6) Gilbert Ramsay, died 15 June, 1857   Aged 77
Janet Ramsay [sister to the above] died 22 Jan 1880   Aged 82 } [Tablet in the Chapel]

List of the Ministers.

It is a remarkable fact that all the ministers of this Chapel have, in their turns, resigned the pastorate   Their names are here given, and the year in which they commenced their ministrations, as follows —

The Revs Mr. Gardner, 1796, William Jones, 1799, John Tisier, 1800, John James,* 1804, Robert Smith,† 1807, Peter Henshall, 1819, Mr. Senior, 1825, Mr. Bury, 1834, Mr. McLean, 1835, J Simson, 1840, E. J Sadler, 1852, E L Adams, 1856, R. S Lewis, 1866, H S Payne, 1873, and the Rev F Moon (the present pastor) 1879

This society was most prosperous under the ministry of Mr. Simson, who rendered assistance to the Rector and the town during the visitation of Cholera in 1849, but since his resignation in 1851 the congregation has very greatly diminished

WESLEYAN CHAPEL

It has been previously stated, that a Methodist society existed in Nantwich as early as 1777, in which year, and for thirty years after, the members worshipped in the old Baptist Chapel in Barker Street   There, on two occasions, the Rev John Wesley preached, namely, on the 6th April, 1779, and again on 17th May, 1781. (Wesley's *Journal*)   At that time Nantwich was included in the Chester circuit, which then extended sixty miles to the south as far as Bridgenorth.   Parson Greenwood, who was appointed

---

* Mr James was frequently assisted by Capt J Scott who had married, as his second wife, the widow of Samuel Barrow, Esq, in 1802 and who came to reside at Nantwich   The Captain died on the 28th May, 1807, and his widow on the 10th Sep 1810, both being interred at Queen Street Chapel Chester

† Robert Smith resigned Jan 10th, 1818, and died at Nantwich   (See Monument above)

a second time to Chester in 1789, visiting Nantwich, made the following remark in his sermon " My present congregation is just the same number as I have been absent from the circuit, namely, 23 "* In 1803 Congleton and Nantwich were made into a separate circuit, Messrs Shelmerdine and Pinder being then ministers The Nantwich Society, in 1806, increased from one hundred and twenty-seven to two hundred, and in the following year property was purchased in Hospital Street for £700, and a commodious Chapel of the same dimensions and on the model of Congleton Chapel, together with two preachers' houses, were built at a cost of £3,300.† In Oct. 1808, Nantwich was made the head of a circuit that extended as far as Bickerton, Winsford Alsager, and Buerton, and on 13th November of the same year the new Chapel was opened by the Rev J Gaulter ‡ The leading Wesleyan families at that time were *Allwood, Bebbington, Kennerley, Mellor, Penkethman, Vernon, White, Wood,* and *Withinshaw.*

In 1835, when the Warrenite agitation broke out, the following members of society, viz *James Blagg, Anthony Gilbert, Richard Horton,* and *Thomas Stanyer,* were publicly expelled by the Rev John Smithson after service one Sunday evening, as were others on the following day These became the nucleus of another society§ that worshipped first in a school-room in Pall Mall, and afterwards purchased the old Castle-house, and fitted it up as a Chapel, calling it " *The Tabernacle,* " which has since been pulled down, and on its site was built in 1857 the present *Ebenezer Chapel* in Castle Street

The Hospital Street (Wesleyan) Chapel, which is the largest in the town, and capable of accommodating more than a thousand people, was improved in 1858 at a cost of £400; and a new organ by Sweetland, of Bath, was purchased for £300, in the following year. In 1876 the Chapel was enlarged by the addition of a new front, re-pewed, and beautified, at a further cost of about £2,300.

For forty years (1808—1848) Nantwich continued to be the head Circuit-town, but after that time, owing to the rapid rise of the town of Crewe, the Circuit for twenty years was called the Nantwich and Crewe Circuit, the latter town having a resident minister from the year 1860. The following list of ministers appointed by the Annual Conference since the formation of Nantwich Circuit was drawn up by the Rev Jabez Ingham in 1869, in which year Crewe was formed into a separate Circuit

LIST OF WESLEYAN MINISTERS
Nantwich Circuit

Stephen Wilson,	1808 to 1809,	William Jones,	1808 to 1809
John Denton,	1810 ,	William Brocklehurst	1810
Daniel Campbell,	1811 to 1812,	John Squarebridge,‖	1811 to 1812

* No account of the origin of Methodism in Nantwich has occurred, but, when the Rev John Wesley was travelling to the north of England in March, 1753, it is said, that "at Nantwich he was saluted with curses and hard names, and soon afterwards the mob pulled down the *chapel* "—(Whitfield's Works vol iii, p 35)

† The above particulars are from a Memoir of Mr John Withinshaw, of Nantwich, by the Rev J B Holroyd in the Methodist Magazine for 1842, pp 399—401, from the Rev John Beaumont s "*Experience, Travels, Sermons, Treatise on Melancholy and other writings,*" 1808, pp 372, 391, 395-6, and from '*A Memoir of the late Benjamin White, of Nantwich,* by the Rev A Watmough, Wesleyan Minister" Printed by T Johnson, Nantwich, 1850

‡ The Rev John Gaulter was of Cheshire birth, and became President of the Wesleyan Conference in 1817

§ The new society of seceders from the "old Body" was called the '*Wesleyan Methodist Association*" It continued to bear that name until its amalgamation with the Wesleyan Reformers in 1857, and since that time the society has belonged to the *United Methodist Free Churches*

‖ John Squarebridge was Supernumerary in 1813 See also Register extracts, p 352

Joseph Brookhouse,	1813 to 1814,	James Allen,	1813 to 1814
John Simpson, Senr	1815 to 1816,	Thomas Harris,	1815 to 1816.
John Draper,	1817 to 1819,	John Hague	1817 to 1818
Moses Dunn,	1820 to 1821,	James Mortimer,	1819 to 1820
James Bogie,	1822 to 1823,	Thomas Eastwood,[a] .	1821 to 1822
Richard Smetham,	1824 to 1826,	Robert Watkin,	1823 to 1824
		James Smetham,	1825 to 1826
Thomas Gee,[b]	1827 to 1828,	Robert Bentham,	1827 to 1828.
John Hughes,	1829 to 1830,	Charles Janion,	1829 to 1830
Thomas Hill, ...	1831 to 1833,	Hugh Carter,	1831 to 1833.
Thomas Preston,	1834 ,	John Smithson, . .	1834 to 1835.
Richard Tabraham,[c]	1835 to 1836,	Richard Smetham,	1836.
Richard Smetham,	1837 ,	Wright Shovelton,	1837 to 1839
Peter Prescott,	1838 to 1840,	Thomas Stokoe	1840[d] to 1842
James B Holroyd,	1841 to 1843;	John Cannel, Abraham Stead,	} 1843 to 1845
Adam Fletcher,	1844 to 1846,	Joseph Lowthian, John Clulow,	} 1846.
Abraham Watmough,	1847 to 1848,	William Henley,	1847[e] to 1848

Nantwich and Crewe Circuit

Abraham Watmough,[f]	1849 ,	William Henley,	1849
James Godden,	1850 to 1852,	William Swallow	1850 to 1852.
John Boyd,	1853 to 1854,	Robert Lewis,	1853 to 1854
William Davies,[g]	1855 to 1857,	Henry Needle,[g]	1855 to 1857
John G Wilson	1858 to 1860,	Henry Oldfield, .	1858[h] to 1860 [i]
James Mowat,	1861 ,	Thomas Brackenbury,.	1861 to 1863
Samuel Allen,	1862		
Robert H. Hare,	1863 to 1865,	Charles G. Turton,	1864 to 1866
Jabez Ingham,	1866 to 1868,	Charles Crawshaw,	1867 to 1868.[j]

Nantwich Circuit

John B Dyson,[k]	1869 to 1870;	Charles Crawshaw, .	1869.
Joseph Midgley,	1871 to 1873,	George Scott,	1870 to 1872.

a A Pamphlet entitled '*Animadversions on a Sermon by Francis Knowles preached at the Socinian Chapel, Nantwich, March 2, 1823, and also upon some other of his Publications*," by Thomas Eastwood, was printed at Nantwich by E Jones in 1823   *b* A flat Gravestone in the Churchyard on the south side of the Chancel, records— 'Underneath | lie the remains | of the | Rev Thomas Gee | who for 32 years | was a laborious | and useful Preacher | in the Wesleyan Methodist | Connection | He died in this Town | May 24th 1836   Aged 64 years | Blessed are the dead, ' &c   His daughter was married to the late George Latham, Architect, of Nantwich

c In Mr Ingham's list *Thomas Thompson* is given in error for *Richard Tabraham* who died in 1878, having been a Wesleyan Minister from the year 1813

d George Poole was a Supernumerary minister from 1840 to 1846   *e* William P Peck was third Minister in 1847

f A Watmough was the author of "A History of Methodism in the City of Lincoln, ' in 1829

g The wives of these ministers died within three days of each other and were buried in the same grave in the Parish Cemetery   A tombstone states—" Mary, wife of Revd Hen Needle, died 14 Nov 1857 Aged 34 Years "
" Sarah, wife of Revd Willm Davies, died 17 Nov 1857, Aged 64 Years "

h Henry B Britten was supernumerary minister from 1859 to 1866

i The Ministers residing at Crewe before the separation of Crewe from Nantwich were as follows —*James Jackson Wray* 1860—1862, *Wesley Brunyate* 1863—1865, *Joseph Workman* 1865—1867 *James Kent* 1865—1868, and *Austin Davey* 1868

j William Wears was Supernumerary minister in 1868

k J B Dyson was the author of a History of Methodism in Leek (1853, 12mo pp 92), of Methodism in Congleton, (1856 12mo pp 186) and of Methodism in the Isle of Wight (1865 12mo pp 344)

John Hooton, ...	... 1874 to 1876;	James Cooke,	... 1873 to 1875.
		Mark Shaw,...	... 1876.
Mark Shaw, ...	... 1877 to 1878;	Buckley Yates,	... 1877 to 1879.
George Cartwright,	... 1879 to 1881;	Samuel Green,	... 1880 to 1882.
John Bramley,...	... 1882 ;	Samuel Wilson,	... 1883.⎫ Present
(Present Superintendent Minister.)		Henry Wadsworth (Audlem) 1883.⎭ Ministers.

PRIMITIVE METHODIST CHAPEL.

It remains to speak of another Methodist Society that originated in Staffordshire with Messrs. Hugh Bourne and William Clowes, in the early years of this century, and became established as a Connexion in 1819. The first missionaries that came to Nantwich, William Clowes and John Wedgewood, preached on the Barony in 1817; but several years elapsed before the society obtained a footing in the town. Foremost amongst the leading members of the infant society were Mr. Thomas Bateman, of Chorley, and Mr. Taylor, who, on the 1st Aug. 1826, purchased on their own responsibility, (for the society was then as poor as it was small) a building in Marsh Lane for £100, and fitted it with seats, gallery, and pulpit, and there this new sect of nonconformists, known then by the name of *Ranters*, worshipped until the year 1840; when, mainly, through the exertions and perseverance of Mr. Bateman, (Mr. Taylor having died in 1837) the present Chapel was built in Welsh Row, and opened on the 21st October in that year. At first Nantwich was included in the Burland Circuit of Primitive Methodism; but since 1844 a minister has resided in the town, and the Chapel has been the head of the Circuit. In Nantwich, the late Mr. Thomas Wood was an active supporter of this denomination for upwards of half a century; and principally through the influence and liberality of his brother, Mr. John Wood, a second Chapel, called the Wood Memorial Chapel, was built in 1881 on the Barony.*

* For the above particulars I am indebted to the kindness of Mr. Thomas Bateman, of Chorley, who, a few years ago, fulfilled the office of President of the Primitive Methodist Conference; and who, though now 84 years of age, is still an energetic worker in the cause with which he has long been intimately associated. His name will long be remembered for the integrity and ability he has shown in the discharge of several important official positions of trust; and for the valuable services he has willingly rendered through a long series of years to the furtherance of good objects beyond his own denomination, in his native parish of Wrenbury, in Nantwich, and in other places in the neighbourhood.

MISERERE CARVING.
(Described on page 332.)

Alvaston Township.

LVASTON township, which is situated to the north-east of Nantwich, is not mentioned in the Domesday Survey of 1086, being at that time included under *Acton*, of which parish it then, like Nantwich, formed a part. In early deeds it is variously spelled *Alvaston, Alvandeston*, and *Alwaldeston*: the last apparently being the original Saxon name, signifying the *All-wood-town*. Alvaston, and its adjacent township of *Woolstan-Wood*, which is also, for a similar reason, omitted in Domesday Book, most likely formed part of the Acton Forest,* which is stated in that record to have been nine miles long and one and a half broad. The "*Wood*" is first mentioned in Hugh Malbank's Charter to Combermere Abbey, *c.* 1130, by the appellation of the "*Creche*," a name perhaps of Norman origin, which, though in use in 1557, (see "*Articles*," p. 407) has since been lost. Besides the "wood" there has been from the earliest times in Alvaston, a "waste," called "*Beam Heath*," a name still in common use and co-eval, perhaps, with the first settlement of English people in this neighbourhood. *Beám* is Saxon for *tree*; and as applied to the heath, it refers to the extent of the waste, which, in former times, would be defined by the line of the forest or by certain boundary trees, commonly called in Anglo Saxon charters the "*mearcbeám*."† In Saxon times the inhabitants of Nantwich had the right of pasturing their cattle on the "Waste," and gathering firewood in the forest of Alvaston. These privileges of common right were admitted as "belonging to the town" of Nantwich in the Charter of 1130 above-mentioned; but subsequently the Lords of Alvaston somehow (probably by first enclosing and improving small portions, and then exercising what was afterwards called "*the lord's right of approvement*") obtained parts of these lands and settled there. To prevent further encroachments and appropriations of the common lands, an Agreement was made between the townspeople of Nantwich and the lords of Alvaston; by which the former renounced all claim to a certain part of

---

* In the adjacent township of Willaston, or Wistaston, was formerly a place called "*Wylde-cattes-heth*," a name suggestive of one kind of forest occupant.

† See Kemble's *Saxons in England*, vol. i, p. 53. Perhaps the word *Creche*, or *Creach*, which is found elsewhere as *Crouch*, meaning cross oak, may have been given because of the number of crossed or marked boundary trees.

the township within limits particularly defined, then held by the lords of Alvaston, whilst the latter agreed that the rest of Alvaston should remain as common land for the benefit of the community in Nantwich, reserving to themselves, however, the sole right of pasturing their cattle for forty days in the year Although the original deed is not known to exist, an *Inspeximus* and *Exemplification* of it, and three other charters relating to the common land in Alvaston, were enrolled by Richard Maisterson, and Richard Wilbraham, Gents., of Nantwich, in *Recognizance Rolls (Cheshire)* 30 & 31 Eliz. [1593], three of which deeds are now in the Record Office. Copies of all four deeds in Latin are still preserved amongst the *Wilbraham MSS* at Delamere, and are here given, *(translated)* as follows —*

"*AN INDENTURE written and made between RICHARD DE ALWALDESTON and others and all the men of the whole commonalty of the vill* [town] *of WICH MALBANK*"

"This is the Agreement made between *Richard de Alwaldeston clerk, William fitz* [son of] *William*, of the same place, *Thomas fitz Cradoc* of Weston, *Richard fitz Roger, Godith* his wife, *William* son of *Thomas Totigrewe* [or Totigreux] and *Agnes* his wife of the one part and all the men of the whole commonalty of Wich Malbanc of the other part Beginning on the tenth day of April in the year of Grace M CC LXXXV [1285] and so to endure for ever, namely, that the aforesaid Richard, William, Thomas, Richard, Godith, William and Agnes have granted and by this present writing have confirmed for them and their heirs and assigns to the aforesaid men of Wich and their heirs *that they may for ever have free common of pasture for all manner of their moveable animals everywhere sustained in the wood and in all the waste of the said vill of Alwaldeston at all times of the year except only forty days, that is to say between the Feast of St Michael* [29 Sept] *and the Feast of St Martin* [11 Nov] But so that neither the aforesaid Richard, William, Thomas, Richard, Godith, William, and Agnes, nor their heirs or assigns shall at any time enclose or approve any part of the said wood and waste neither shall they or their heirs or assigns require claim or in any mode whatever be able to require or claim anything therein, but that the same shall for ever lie and continue in common And for this concession and agreement and confirmation of this present writing all the aforesaid men of the said Wich have granted for themselves and their heirs to the Richard William Thomas Richard Godith William and Agnes that they their heirs and assigns may in any way whatsoever approve as may seem best to them without challenge or contradiction of the said men of Wich or their heirs a certain place of the said Waste lying within the underwritten boundaries that is to say, under "*Schaslar*" in the field which is called the "*Brockefield*" near the "*Sonsteresty*"† following the knoll on the other part from "*Crooked brock*" [crooked brook] as far as to the "*Sichet*" [runlet,] which lies opposite "*Marle*," and so by that sichet ascending as far as to the "*great oak*" that overhangs the same sichet and from thence directly as far as to the "*Red Clough*"‡ so as the divisions and metes have been there laid down and so following from thence the Red Clough from that part as far as to "*Roberdesheye*" [Robert's-hay] But so that neither the said men of Wich nor their heirs or assigns shall at any time claim or be able to claim any thing within the said place while it shall be enclosed and because the parties aforesaid are willing that the aforesaid agreement should remain firm and established unshaken between them for ever they have granted that it should be affirmed in the Chester Roll which is called the *Domesday* § and for

---

* For these translations I am indebted to the kindness of Wm Beamont, Esq , of Orford Hall

† Query, whether the name, the "*Rising Sun*, in this township is a corruption of this local name

‡ "*Red Hall*" is the name of an old farm house in Wistaston, close to the boundary of Alvaston

§ This deed, however, is not mentioned amongst the deeds of the *Cheshire Domesday* given in Dr Ormerod's "*Miscellanea Palatina*'

greater security to the two parts of this chirograph have put their seals These being witnesses, the lord [*domino*] *Reginald de Gray*, Justiciary of Chester, the lord *Richard de Massey*, the lord *Ralph de Vernon*, the lord *Richard de Sondbache*, *Thomas de Crewe*, *Thomas de Prayers*, *William Wodenoth*, *Thomas de Alstanston*, *William* the clerk, and many others "

The next three deeds relate to a tract of ten acres of land in Alvaston which was granted by a charter without date, and consequently before the year 1300, by the lords of Alvaston to *Robert de Bressey*, who quit-claimed the same in favour of the townspeople of Nantwich in 1307.   These charters are as follows. *(translated)*—

I

" To all the faithful in Christ to whom this present writing shall come *Richard de Bromhall* clerk, *William fitz* [son of] *William de Alvaldeston*, *Richard* called the chariotecr [" bigator "] of Alwaldeston, *Goduce* his wife, *William* also called *Totigrewe* [or Totigreux] and *Agnes* his wife, the signior lord of Alwaldeston, send eternal greeting in the Lord Know ye that by our common assent we have given and granted and by this present Charter have confirmed to ROBERT DE BRESCY one place of our land in Alwaldeston in our wood which is called CRECHE between the King's highway which leads from *Marchefford* near Wich Malbank To have and to hold of us and our heirs to the before named Robert and his heirs and assigns (men of religion and the chief lords of the fee excepted) freely quietly and entirely as we have measured it as an inheritance for ever with haybote* in our wood of Creche and with all other commons and easements or liberties to our vill of Alwaldeston belonging rendering for the same to us and our heirs from him and his heirs and assigns three shillings in silver at two times in the year, namely, on the feast of St John the Baptist [24 June] eighteenpence, and on the Feast of St Martin [11 Nov] eighteen pence for all services customs and demands to the beforenamed place of land belonging And because we mean this our gift grant and confirmation of our Charter to be kept firm and stable for ever we have strengthened it by the impressions of our seals These being witnesses *Thomas the lord of Alstanton*, *Richard de Henhull*, *Randle Cotere* *Philip de Stapeley*, *William Chanu*, [? Cheney] *Hugh de Blakenhall* and many others '

II *A Charter of Robert de Bressy to all the men of the Commonalty of Wich Malbank*

" Know all men both present and to come That I ROBERT DE BRESSY have given granted and by this my present charter have confirmed to *Richard de ffouleshurst*, *William of the Fountain*, [" de fonte "] *William de ffouleshurst*, *Hugh* of the same place, *Richard Cradock* of Wich [Malbank], *William Colfox*, of the same place *William Wildebor*, *Richard Adcock*, *William Machin*, *Roger Russel*, *Randle Russel*, *William* of the Fountain, *junior*, and all other men of the whole community of Wich Malbank, All that place of land with all the fruits growing upon the same and with all other easements and appurtenances & c in the vill of Alwaldeston and containing in itself ten acres of land and which we have recovered by an azzize of *novel dissesin*† in the county of Chester against *William fitz Richard de Alwaldeston*, *William fitz William*, *Thomas Cradock* and other persons natives of the same vill, for a certain sum of money to me in hand paid To have and to hold of the chief lord of that fee for me and my heirs for ever, freely quietly hentably entirely lawfully fully and peaceably as I the aforesaid *Robert de Bressy* the aforesaid place of land by its metes and bounds as it is enclosed by a ditch, have more fully or freely held it or in any manner could have held it with all its commons and easements to the said place of land in any manner belonging Doing for the same to the chief lord the services due and of right accustomed for all

---

* *Haybote* i e an allowance of timber out the lord's wood towards the making and keeping up of fences

† The term "*dissesin*' signified an unlawful dispossessing a man of his land From this it is clear there had been litigation between the townspeople of Wich Malbank and the lords of Alvaston

secular services things and demands whatsoever And that this my gift and confirmation of this present Charter may remain firm established and unshaken for ever I have strengthened it by the impression of my seal These being witnesses [Domino] the lord RALPH DE VERNON, the lord URIAN DE ST PIERRE, KNIGHTS, *William de Wistaston, Richard de Rope, Geffrey Griffin, Patric Crewe, Randle Coterel, Richard de Henhull*, and others

Dated at Alwaldeston on Wednesday in the morrow of Saint James the Apostle [25 July] in the year of our Lord M CCC VII " [1307]

III   *Charter conveying the same land to the Commonalty of Nantwich*

" To all the faithful in Christ to whom this present writing shall come ROBERT DE BRESSY sends eternal greeting in the Lord Know ye that we have remised released and for me and my heirs have for ever quit claimed to *Richard de ffouleshurst, William of the Fountain, William de ffouldshurst, Hugh of the same place, Nicholas Cradock* of Wich, *William Colfox, William Wildebor, Richard Adcock, William Machin, Roger Russel, Randle Russel, William of the Fountain, junior* and all other the men of the whole community of the vill [town] of Wich Malbanc all that place of land with appurtenances which I have in Alvaldeston and which to the aforesaid men of Wich Malbanc by my certain Charter I have enfeoffed as in such Charter is more fully and plainly contained together with all my right and claim which I have or might have or might in any manner have or claim in the aforesaid place of land, so that neither I the said ROBERT DE BRESSY nor my heirs or any other in my name or in my right any right or claim in the aforesaid place of land with its appurtenances shall at any time hereafter claim or demand or be able to claim or demand In testimony whereof to this present writing I have set my seal, These being witnesses the lord RALPH DE VERNON &c Dated at Alvaldeston on Thursday next after the Feast of St James the Apostle [25 July] in the year of our Lord M CCC VII ' [1307]

The common land, thus secured by the above interesting deeds nearly six hundred years ago, has ever since been jealously guarded by the community Until the end of last century these ascertained rights were protected by the regulative powers of the old Court Leet which annually elected two officers, called *Heath-Keepers*, who watched the interests of the townspeople, saw the common domain was equitably enjoyed, and carried out the custom of " stint of common," by which only a limited number of animals of the commoners could be turned out on the waste It may be inferred from one of the " *Injunctions* " of 1538 (page 31) that a considerable portion of the *Creche* forest was at that time not cleared for pasture or cultivation as herds of swine, that were reared and kept by the householders in ancient times for their supply of salt-pork, (then the chief article of flesh-food), were confided daily to the charge of a professional swine-herd, who drove the animals into Alvaston wood for the harvest of acorns and beech-mast No other mention of this town-officer has occurred, and it is noticeable in the following " *Articles* " dated 1557, preserved amongst the *Wilb MSS*, and in the extracts already given from Court Rolls still later, *(temp Eliz.)* that the animals mentioned are beasts, cows and horses

'*ARTICLES concerning the usage & occupacon of the COMMONS and WASTE belonging to the towne of NAMPTWICHE commonly called BEAME HEATH and CREACHE agreed and determined by the inhabitants of the said Towne the xij [12] day of March in the third and fourth years of the Raigne of our soueraigne Lord and Ladie King Philip & Queene Mary Anno Dni 1557* "

"*ffirst* it is by the Consents aforesayd ordered and agreed that all the sayd Wastes and Commons shall be inclosed with hedges railes and gates as here before hath bin used and the same for to be kept severall from all forreiners who haue noe right nor good interest to any Com'on of pasture within or uppon the sayd wastes & Com'ons, and alsoe that none of the sayd Inhabitants shall putt anie of their beaste or cattell into the sayd wastes and Com'ons from ye feast of the Annunciacon of our Ladie [25 March] unto the xth [10th] daie of May and that euery one wch shall put at the first marking wth the burne anie beaste or horse to pasture in or upon the p'misses shall pay for eu'ry [every] beaste ijd [2d], and for euery horse iiijd [4d] for to be imployed & bestowed upon the sayd hedges railes or gates and other defences of the p'misses, and att all tymes after when any beaste shall be marked jd [1d] for a beaste , and ijd [2d] for a horse

2 Alsoe it is ordered and agreed that noe one shall at anie time haue in or vppon the p'misses aboue the number of iiij [4] beastes in lay, or to the lay of iiij beastes, and that all and euerie pson [person] & psons haueing aboue ij beastes in or uppon the p'misses shall paie yeareley to the hands of such honest and well disposed psons as shall be nominated and appoynted by the most substantiall men the wch now be and hereafter shall be elect for the ordering of the same, for euene horse viijd, and for euerie beaste iiijd, all which sumes of money soe payd shall be distributed & giuen by the sayd psons unto such the poore and needie neighbours of the sayd inhabitants as shall not haue, nor are able to haue anie beaste going wthin the premisses, and as by the discretion of the sayd psons as shall be thought most needfull

3 Alsoe it is condiscended and agreed that the sayd honest & well-disposed psons shall cause a booke to be made as well of their severall receiptes as of their p'ticular payments, and that they or two of them at the least shall yearly wthin iiij daies after the ffeast of St Michell [29 Sept] make declaracon & Accounte before the gentlemen and other substantiall honest men of the sayd Towne wch shall be thought meetest for the hearing of the same , and if it shalbe thought necessary after such declaracon and accounte made yearely for to nominate and appoynt other like men for to execute ye p'misses as is before sayd, that then all such money as shall remaine not distributed the same money to be deliuered unto the same men then appointed as is aforesaide

4 Alsoe it is further condiscended ordered and agreed that this aiticle and all things herein contained shall be observed and kept without minishing or alteration unlesse it may be conuerted to greater or more benefits for the use aforesayd, and ye same to be done by the whole consent ot all those who now be and hereafter shall be authorized by the whole inhabitants of the sayd Towne or by the greater number of them

5 Alsoe it is agreed and determined that there shall yearely fower [4] substantiall honest men of the sayd inhabitance be elect and appoynted who shall haue the charge as well with the marking and takeing in of all beaste and cattell wch shall be putt to pasture vppon the sayd wastes and Com'ons , as with the making of hedges, railes, gates and other defences necessary for the same, and if the foresayd fower [4] men at euery time hereafter shall by their discretion and good policie invent or fynd anie thinge concerneing the vsage and occupation of the p'misses wch now is or hereafter may be beneficiall and necessary for the Com'onwealth of the sayd inhabitants and now omitted in this booke, that then the sayd fower men and all others wch hereafter shall be elect & appoynted to the sayd charge shall from tyme to tyme open & declare the same unto the aforesayd gentlemen and other substantiall honest persons who by the advice of the fower men shall take order, and direction therein as shall appertaine

6 Alsoe it is ordered and agreed that a *Pinfolde* shall be made and sett upon the sayd Wastes or Com'ons in such place as by the sayd gentlemen and psons aforesayd shall be thought meete & convenient, and that the sayd fower men who shall haue the ouer-sight & charge of the sayd wastes and Com'ons shall yearhe att such tyme & tymes as to them shall seeme most convenient to driue or cause to be driuen all the sayd Wastes and Com'ons all & such beastes and Cattell as shall be found trespassing in or upon the p'misses, the same for to impound and there to remaine untill such tyme as the owners if they be of the sayd inhabitants haue payd for the impounding of euery beaste iiijd, or as the impounders & the owners can agree, and that euery forriner and stranger haueing anie beastes or cattell impounded for trespassing

through escape or negligence, the same for to paye for euery beaste viij^d or at the discretion of the impounders Provided allwaies that if any beastes or cattell of forriners or strangers or others who shall claime or pretend anie interest right or title for to have Com'on of Pasture within any part or parcell of the p'misses be found trespassing & impounded as aforesayd, that all and euery such beaste & cattell soe impounded shall remaine in the sayd pounde untill the owners thereof shall obtaine the Kinge and queenes maties writt of Replevie or otherwise by due Course of the Lawe borrow the same, & in case the impounders or anie of them shall att anie time hereafter be impleaded, sued, or otherwise molested for or concerning the executing of ye sayde charge & office that then all and euery of the sayd inhabitance haueing beaste or cattell pasturing in or upon the sayd Wastes and Com'ons that they euery of them shall be for the lawfull assisting & aiding of the sayd officers indifferentlie be taxed & cessed by the gent'emen and the others honest substantiall psons of ye said Towne what they euery of them shall giue and pay as well towardes the charges & expense of the sayd officers as in all other causes & pursuits for the quiett useing & occupying of ye p'misses

7 Alsoe it is ordered condiscended and agreed that the *tenants of the towneshipp of Alvaston* may & shall peaceably occupy & enioy their com'on of pasture in & uppon all the aforesayd Wastes & Com'ons wth as manie & like number of beastes and Cattell as was determyned lymitted & agreed betwixt the inhabitants of ye sayd towne of Namptwiche and the tenants of the said towneshipp of Alvaston at such times as the sayd Wastes and Com'ons was last inclosed from all forreiners & strangers, that is to witt ye sayd tenants and their assignes to haue soe manie beastes & other cattell as to the lay of twentie-fower beastes dothe amount at all seasons of the yeare from the Annunciation of our Ladie [25 March] untill ye 10th daie of May onely excepted

8 Alsoe it is ordered by the consente aforesayd that none of the inhabitants aforesayd not haueing cattell of his or their owne or otherwise, as kine borrowed or hired to giue them milke, shall haue or occupy any pte [part] or pcell [parcel] of the same Com'ons or Waste with anie Cattell colourably to free anie strangers or other psons there uppon, paynes [fines] of such sumes of money as the aforesayd fower men shall thinke meete for euerie such trespasse being first duely proved

9 Alsoe it is ordered by the consent aforesayd that if anie article, clause or sentence expressed or mentioned within this booke shall chance hereafter to be preiudiciall, hurtfull or against the com'onwealth of the sayde towne of Namptwich or to the inhabiters of the same, that the gentlemen and others of the most substantiall and honest psons then inhabiting in the sayd towne may at anie time or times be at libertie with the consents & agreements of the sayd inhabitants or ye greater number of them for to augment, minish, alter, or to make frustrate and voide any such article, clause or sentence, and the same to converte to better purpose if occasion shall serve accordinge to the purport true meaning and intent before specified

In witnesse whereof wee the sayd inhabitants haue putt to oure owne seale and sett to oure owne hands the daye and yeare aboue written "

From the above "Articles" it will be seen that one of the duties of the Heath-Keepers was the marking of cattle on the Ley ground Roger Wilbraham *("Towne Concernes* p 207") relates how Lord Cholmondeley, in or about the year 1660, attempted to infringe this custom by adopting his own mark, an innovation that was resented by the townspeople, fearing lest his lordship, who was Lord of the Barony, might eventually claim to be Lord of the Commons also In the early years of the present century, when the authority of the Court Leet was fast declining, the collective ownership of *Beam Heath* was more firmly established by two Acts of Parliament, which gave power to inclose and improve by cultivation two hundred acres, and eighty-nine acres, respectively

By the first Act (43 Geo. III, 1803) the Common Land, estimated at about four hundred acres, was vested in twenty-one Trustees, viz —

JAMES BAYLEY	ISAAC CHURCH	JOHN PRATCHITT
THOMAS BEBBINGTON, Junr.	WILLIAM GARNETT, clerk	JOSEPH SKERRETT
EDWARD BELLYSE	RICHARD HASSALL, Junr	WILLIAM SPROUT
GEORGE CAPPUR	BENJAMIN HEWITT	THOMAS STEELE
WASHINGTON CLIFF	RICHARD LEVERSAGE	THOMAS TAYLOR
JAMES COOPER	JOHN MINSHULL	DANIEL TOMLINSON
THOMAS CLOWES	RICHARD PARRATT	JAMES WRIGHT

This Act directed that the largest portion of the Common should remain as pasture; twenty-four cow-gates being reserved for Alvaston; two hundred acres to be tilled; thirty acres kept as potato ground, and other portions set apart for obtaining gravel, sand, &c, to repair roads in Nantwich and for obtaining clay for bricks for Nantwich. The profits, after paying all expenses, to be divided annually (in January) among inhabitant householders entitled by the Act to receive the same The Rector of Nantwich to receive tithe, and the Heath to be exempted from all poor and parish rates

An Amended and Enlarged Act was obtained on 30th May, 1823, (4 Geo. IV) the number of Trustees being increased to thirty-two, viz. —

JAMES BAYLEY	WILLIAM GARNETT, clerk	JOHN PRATCHITT
JOHN BAKER	JOHN JASPER GARNETT	BENJAMIN RODENHURST
THOS BEBBINGTON, Junr.	EDWARD KENT	JOSEPH SKERRETT
WILLIAM BETTELEY	JOHN LATHAM, clerk.	WILLIAM SPROUT
GEORGE CAPPUR	JOHN LATHAM	THOMAS STEELE
WASHINGTON CLIFFE	RICHARD LEVERSAGE	CROWDSON TUNSTALL
JAMES COOPER	JOHN MINSHULL	WILLIAM TOMLINSON, Senr
THOMAS COPESTICK	WILLIAM MASSEY	HENRY TOMLINSON
JOHN DOWNES	CHARLES MARE	DANIEL TOMLINSON
THOMAS DERIEMER	JAMES PARRATT	JOHN WITHENSHAW
JOHN EARDLEY	JAMES PLEVIN	

The chief provisions of the Act are as follows —

1 —Vacancies in the number of Trustees to be supplied at the next General Vestry, new Trustees being nominated and elected by a majority of the inhabitants then present

2 —Two Heath-Keepers to be appointed, and paid a salary

3 —Eighty-nine acres of Common land to be enclosed and improved

4 —Persons entitled to benefit are defined to be,—All inhabitant householders for the space of seven years, or if born, or having served seven years apprenticeship in Nantwich, and the widows of any such persons dying after having been so resident

5.—A schedule of Leys to be made out annually in January, and no person to turn into the Ley more than 2 horses, or 3 two-year-old Colts, or 4 one-year-old Colts, or 3 Cows, or 4 Heifers; or 5 Stirks, or 20 Sheep

6 —Persons having left the town, and returning again, must be resident householders in Nantwich for two successive years before they shall be entitled to Leys upon the said Heath.

7 —The Trustees may lease the enclosed lands for agricultural purposes for terms not exceeding fourteen years

8 —The prescribed times for opening and closing the Leys to be —

For horned cattle, horses, colts   from 12 or 20 May to 12 or 20 Nov.

For sheep   from 12 or 20 May to 4 December

9 —Allotments for procuring gravel, sand, &c , to repair roads in Nantwich.

10.—Allotments for making bricks, or tiles, to be sold to the inhabitants.

11 —Allotments for Potato-ground, at a rent not exceeding 3d. per rood of 8 square yards

12 —When the surplus of Income amounts to £500, the same to be distributed in equal shares amongst the inhabitant householders of Nantwich entitled to the benefit of Leys

13 —The accounts to be audited annually in June

14 —The enclosed lands to be exempt from all Statute Duty and Composition, and all other poor and other Rates

15 —The Rector of Nantwich to receive tythes of these lands

In conclusion, it is worthy of remark that, after the vicissitudes of centuries, the inhabitants of Nantwich are still, as in Saxon times, the free allodial proprietors of their common land, which has of late years so increased in value as to have produced in 1879 an annuity of twenty-two shillings to each householder, the recipients numbering about twelve hundred and fifty

The Common Land above treated of embraces about two thirds of the township The remaining third seems to have been the part of Alvaston that fell to PHILIPPA BASSET on the first division of Nantwich Barony, (see page 23), and that subsequently passed to the ALVASTONS of Alvaston From the family, who thus acquired the local name these lands descended to the PRAERS of Baddiley. By *Inq* 23 Ric II [1399] "Letice, widow of William de Praers, held in fee the fourth part of the manor of Alvaston, of Sir John Lovell, *in socage*, val per ann 20 shillings " The manor next passed by marriage to the BROMLEYS of Baddington, and the PIGOTS of Butley, and was held by them in 1427-8 (*Inq p m* 6 Hen. VI) After that date the descent of these lands cannot be traced. In 1666 the landed proprietors were "*Mr Richard Wright*, of Namptwich, *Sir Thos Wilbraham*, of Woodhey, *Randle Minshull*, a minister of Exeter, and *Mr Randle Dod*, of Edge, who sold the manor of Alvaston being a 4th part to *John Greenough* Mr of Arts" (*Harl MSS* 2010 f 21). The principal estate, consisting of an old mansion and demesne, called WINDY ARBOUR, formerly the property of Richard Vernon, gent, was sold in 1788 by Charles Clowes, Esq , to Messrs James, William and Thomas Foster,* of Nantwich, and is still the property of their descendant, W O Foster, Esq , of Aspley Park, near Droitwich Another estate, with a modern Hall called ALVASTON GROVE, was formerly the residence and property of Mr Croudson Tunstall, a quaker gentleman; and now belongs to Francis Elcocke Massey, Esq , who is the representative of the Elcocke family of Poole, near Nantwich

---

* The Foster family left Nantwich and became iron-masters in South Staffordshire They gave the iron railings when the Churchyard at Nantwich was first enclosed The family vault in the Churchyard has a flat stone (within iron railings) inscribed as follows —

"In Memory of *James Foster* of Windy Arbour, who died Feb 2 1805 aged 73 years,
Also of *William Foster*, who died June 12, 1812, aged 78 years
Likewise of *Henry Foster*, who died March 9, 1817, aged 42 years
And of *Thomas Foster* , who died Aug 17, 1817, aged 79 years "

For many years an annual horse-race was run on a course in Alvaston, until the year 1824, when the land was enclosed and cultivated In 1689 William Hodgkin, by will, bequeathed his lands in Alvaston, consisting of 20a 3r. 24p for the purpose of founding an Apprenticing Charity for Nantwich One of the fields, known as the *Brick Barn Field*, contains a spring that was once locally famous for its curative properties in cases of bad eyes A few years ago an exchange of land was made between the Beam Heath Trustees and Baron von Schroeder, of the Rookery Hall, who has since constructed a private carriage road across the Ley ground

𝔚oolstanwood Township.

WOOLSTANWOOD, which is not noticed in Domesday Survey of 1086, may have been included, as its name implies, in the Acton forest at that time It first occurs in the *Inq* 16 Edw. I. (see page 23) as having been divided between PHILIPPA BASSET and ELEANOR MALBANK, co-heirs of the last Norman Baron of Wich Malbank The *first share* appears to have passed, like Alvaston, to the families of PRAERS and BROMLEY, and is supposed to have been purchased by the CHOLMONDELEY family in the sixteenth century, and sold by the Marquis of Cholmondeley towards the end of the eighteenth century to Mrs. Anne Elcocke, of Poole, from whom it has descended to Francis Elcocke Massey, Esq, of Alvaston Grove The other share is said to have been held by the BULKELEGH family for a period of seventy years (1360—1430), but it cannot be traced further with any degree of accuracy In Henry VIII reign "the capital messuage and mill" of Woolstanwood belonged to the GRIFFINS of Bartherton, from whom the "*house & milnes*" were purchased by SIR HENRY DELVES, of Doddington, prior to 1666, at which date "the King was Lord of the Wastes of Wooleston Wood, but the tenants appeared at the Nantwich Hundred Court," (*Harl MSS* 2010, f 21) The estate just mentioned was sold by the REV. SIR THOMAS BROUGHTON, BARI, early in the present century to THOMAS WICKSTED, Esq, of Nantwich

At the present time the principal landed proprietors of Woolstanwood are, F E Massey, Esq ; Geoffrey J. Shakerley, Esq, of Pimley Manor, co. Salop; and the trustees of Mrs. Lloyd [*]

Woolstanwood, or *Ouston-wood* as it was formerly sometimes spelled, contains about five hundred and ninety acres of land, and has an agricultural population In this outlying part of Nantwich Parish, a small society of Wesleyan Methodists regularly met for worship at Marshfield Bank Farm, from the year 1830 until 1870, when a Chapel was built in connection with Crewe Wesleyan Circuit

---

[*] See Dr Ormerod s *Cheshire*, Vol III, p 456, New Edit

Willaston Township.

(PART OF.)

ILLASTON, a township on the east side of Nantwich, is now ecclesiastically divided (though when that division was made I am unable to state) into two parts, namely :— *Wybunbury-Willaston*, and *Nantwich-Willaston;* the former containing five hundred and sixty-three acres of land in Wybunbury parish; and the latter 406*a*. 3*r*. 38*p*. in Nantwich parish.

Willaston is referred to in the Domesday Survey of 1086, as follows :—*

> " Isdem Willelmus tenet Wilavestune. Ulviet liber homo tenuit. Ibi i virgata geldabilis.
> Terra est dimidia carucata. Ibi est i bordarius. Valebat V solidos. Modo ii solidos."

(Translated)—" The same William holds Wilavestune. Ulviet, a free man, held it. There is one virgate rateable to the gelt. The land is half a carucate. There is one bordar. It was worth five shillings; now two shillings."

Some little explanation will render this brief record more intelligible to the general reader. In the time of King Edward the Confessor, ULVIET, a Saxon freeholder, was lord of the manor of Willaston; the estate then being worth five shillings. In 1086, it was under the lordship of William Malbank, first Baron of Wich Malbank, at which time it had decreased in value to two shillings. The extent of the manor is described as "*half a carucate*," or about ten acres of land; and of this, a "*virgate of land*," that is, the arable land, amounting perhaps to half of the manor, was rated in the King's taxes. The tenant farmer who ploughed with his yoke of oxen and lived in his timber cottage on the estate, is called a "*bordar*," because he rendered as rent and service to the Baron of Wich Malbank for his holding certain quantities of poultry, eggs, and other articles of food for the lord's table.

After the death of William, third Baron of Wich Malbank, Willaston fell to the share of his daughter *Philippa Basset* (page 23). From the time of Henry III to Henry VIII, during a period of three hundred years, the manor belonged to the family of CHANU or CHENEY,† a name still applied to the brook that passes through the township. In or about 1530 the manor, described as a " Capital Messuage [Hall], 11 messuages, 300 acres of land, 50 acres of meadow, 500 acres of pasture, 60 acres of wood, and 100 acres of moss and heath in Willaston, Wistaston, Otedische, Walgherton, Acton and Hurdeleston," was sold by JOHN CHANUE, *of Chanuex hall‡ in Wyxsterton* [or Willaston] *gent."* to RICHARD SNEYD, whose direct descendants have owned these lands, but have resided at Keele, in

---

* The Domesday Book of Lancashire and Cheshire ; translated by William Beamont, Esq., p. 35.

† The descent of this manor is very fully traced by Mr. Helsby in the New Edition of Ormerod's *Cheshire*, Vol. III, page 487—491.

‡ In a field, called the *Moat-field*, belonging to Cheerbrook Farm, and nearly opposite the Willaston Board Schools, is still to be seen the outline of the *Moat*, which, most likely surrounded the old Hall of Willaston.
In the will of Roger Mainwaring of Nantwich, Gent., proved 1st May, 1590, mention is made of a house "*in Beamestreete* [Nantwich] *called* CHEYNYE HALLE *wherein Mr. Edwards the surgeon dwelte.*"—(Chet. Soc. Publ. liv, p. 155-6). This may have been the town residence of the Cheney family. Nearly two hundred years after, in Rate Books dated 1779, 1781, and in the Wright's Treasurer's Book under date 1788, mention is made of another *China* or *Cheney Hall*, and a Barn, belonging to it, situated in Barker Street or Love Lane. It was pulled down in 1788; two Almshouses being erected on the site of the Barn.

Staffordshire. John Bayley, Esq. purchased part of the estate, and in 1731 built the present Willaston Hall. In 1860 Ralph Sneyd, Esq disposed of the remaining lands in Willaston, the purchasers being Messrs. L. Salisbury (about a hundred and fifty acres), Edward Birchall, John Cliffe, Owen Lunt, Philip Barker, and Thomas Pedley, and about sixty acres by the representatives of James Bayley, Esq , J P , who now resides at the Hall

Of *Nantwich-Willaston* there is little to record Two *Inquisitions*, now in the Record Office, relate to claims of Right of Road through this part of the township One of these, dated 1525, has already been given on page 97, the other, dated the 26th July, 14 Eliz. [1572] mentions a road

> "From a certain pasture in Wigstarson [Willaston] held by *Lawrence Wright* to the town of Nantwich namely, from the said pasture through a certain close of Land in Wigstarson aforesaid called *Sandyhole*, and thence to a certain lane called *Birchin Lane*, and thence to the said town of Nantwich, and so back again The jurors named in the Inquisition said that the said Lawrence and every tenant of the said pasture ought to have such road from and to the same as is before described "

A field belonging to Red Hall Farm is still called the *Sandyhole,* and perhaps the roads mentioned in the Inquisitions correspond with the two field-roads leading from Nantwich to Wistaston Church,—the one from Sandy Lane, and the other from Birchin Lane

An estate, or hamlet, called *Bressey* or *Brassey Green*, was the residence for several generations of a family of that name, which in ancient times was connected with the adjoining parish and township of Wistaston ROBERT DE BRACY did homage and service to William, Baron of Wich Malbank, for his lands in Wistanston * Another ROBERT DE BRESCI, *of Wildcatsheath,* his wife, *Alice*, his son, *John;* his brothers, *Thomas, Hamon,* and *Nicholas,* are all mentioned in a charter, which is witnessed by Randle de Olton, then Sheriff of Cheshire, Richard de ffouleshurst, William Hamelin, Richard de Rope, and Thomas Chanu, and dated 16 Edw III [1342] † In a Rental of Willaston, dated 22 Hen VI [1443-4]‡ is mentioned *"Jo braysey pro 1 acr 6s 8d '*

The following entries from Nantwich and Wistaston Parish Registers, relating to the Brasseys of Willaston, in later times, will be of interest

> " 1578 Thomas Brassie thelder was buried the 10th December "—*(Wistaston Reg)*
> " 1583 June 3 Elizabeth d of John Brassye of Willasonn "—*(Nantwich Bapt Reg)*
> " 1591 John Brassye was buried the 21st June "—*(Wistaston Reg)*
> " 1614 John Brassye of Willaston was buried 20 April ' —*(Wistaston and Nantwich Reg)*
> ' 1615 John the son of Danyell Brassey bapt 1 Oct , buried 12 Oct "—*(Wistaston Reg)*
> " 1617 Oct 15 Anne Brassey, widowe de Willaston "—*(Nantwich Bur Reg)*
> " 1620 The fourteen daye of December was buryed Thomas brassey a gret buriall —*(Wistaston Reg)*
> " 1631 Margaret Brassy, widdowe was buryed 29 May "—*(Wistaston Reg)*
> " 1639 May 23 Raphe sonne of Thomas Brassie gent of Willaston '—*(Nartwich Bapt Reg)*
> " 1669 Sep 30 Married Thomas Raumore pish Clarke [of Wybunbury] and Mary Bressie daughter of Mr Ralphe Bressie of Willaston per licence ' —*(Wybunbury Par Reg)*
> " 1701 Mary Brassye of Willaston Buryed 28 April ' —*(Wistaston Reg)*

* Dr Ormerod s *Cheshire,* Vol III, p 330, New Edit quoting Dr Williamson's " *Villare Cestriense* "
† *Harl MSS* (British Museum) 2077, f 110
‡ *Iord,* f 100 *h*

This is the last mention of the name of Brassey of Willaston in any of the local registers that I have seen; and possibly she may have been directly related to *Thomas Brassey* of Willaston, whose name is given in the list of Quakers, *c.* 1670 (page 397).

A modern farm-house now occupies the site of *Brassey Hall*, and retains the old name. Two adjacent fields are still called the "*Hall-field*," and "*The Park.*"

One of the principal residences in Nantwich-Willaston, called "*Mount Pleasant*," was built shortly before 1828 by the late William Salmon, Esq.; and is now occupied by his nephew, Henry Daniel Hill, Esq. On this rising ground formerly stood a windmill, that was blown down some years ago. *Windmill Lane* (now *Crewe Road*) and *Birchin Lane* locate the scene of Sir William Brereton's victory on the 28th Jan. 1642-3. (See page 145). For a few years after 1825 Nantwich races were run on the "*Ox Pastures;*" and in this part of Nantwich parish land was purchased in 1875 for a Nonconformist Cemetery.*

* Owen Murphy, of Love Lane, aged 45 years, was the first to be buried in this Cemetery, in Nov. 1875. In less than four years, that is down to 18th Sep. 1879, there had been no less than 249 interments.

OLD HOUSES IN HIGH STREET.

Family History.

GLANCE over the foregoing pages will at once show that the history of a town is the history of the people that have lived in it. On nearly every page mention has been made of former inhabitants of Nantwich, and many particulars concerning them will be readily found by consulting the index at the end of this volume. It now remains to give further details in tabular or narrative pedigrees of some of the principal families, and short biographies of a few native celebrities. In ancient times the most important families were the *Malbanks*, the *Maistersons*, the *Fouleshursts*, the *Wyches*, the *Cradocks*, the *Griffins*, and the *Wettenhalls;* and notable individuals such as *Wildebore*, *Russsell*, and *Kingsley*. Since the beginning of the sixteenth century there have been generations of *Maisterson, Wettenhall, Griffin, Crowe, Leech, Hassall, Tench, Crockett, Rutter, Sparke, Bebbington, Cheney, Wilbraham, Wickstead, Wright, Mainwaring, Church, Comberbach, Goldsmith, Minshull, Walthall, Clutton, Burroughes, Malbon, Delves, Pratchett,* &c.

Of these, the *Maistersons* were the longest resident in the town; and in the subjoined pedigree they are traced through fifteen generations, embracing a period of no less than five hundred years, in direct succession from *Robert Maisterson*, of Wich Malbank, who was living in 1297, to *Thomas Maisterson*, of Shrewbridge, (Nantwich) who was living in and after 1780. Though never manorial lords of Nantwich, they formed alliances with some of the best families in the county; and the natural inference is that they must have held estates elsewhere; for, in former times, even more so than now, the possession of land constituted the gentleman. Amongst the Cheshire Inquisitions preserved to modern times, only *two* relate to this family; so that it is now impossible to say what possessions they had in ancient times, or to test the accuracy of the earlier descents of the family, which are based on the memorials of *Laurence Maisterson* in 1611, referred to on page 89. Besides the exploits of the renowned hero, *Thomas Maisterson, Esq.,** already given; particulars relating to others of the family who distinguished themselves in various wars prior to the seventeenth century, are embodied in the pedigree.

---

* Mr. Helsby (Ormerod's *Cheshire*, vol. iii, p. 439, New Edit.) has added the following interesting information relating to Thomas Maisterson, Esq., from Lichfield Registers, viz.:—that he "*had license for an oratory in his house in Nantewyche* 12 *Dec.* 1398."

The following abstract of the earlier Inquisition just mentioned, will be of interest as affording an instance of *might* over-ruling *right*, which was not of uncommon occurrence in feudal times

"*Inquisition p m* of WILLIAM MAISTERSON who died on the 18th July 10 Hen VII [1495] without any heir because he was a bastard and had no issue of his body lawfully begotten. He died seised of 2 salthouses of 6 leads in Nantwich lately held by Richard Bekyngham and John Haryson ; another of 12 leads held by William Ypurs Chaplain , another of 6 leads held by Robert Bromley , a messuage held by John Leek , 2 messuages with gardens adjoining held by Thomas Basfford , 9 shill annual rent issuing out of a messuage lately held by Adam Wetenhall , 18 shill like annual rent issuing out of a messuage lately held by Thomas Starkey 4 messuages and gardens adjoining late in the separate holdings of Richard Hill, William Mynshull Edward Thatcher and John Harison

Richard Wyche, Chaplain, and Robert Littlelovere being seised in fee *(inter alia)* of these messuages, salt-houses, gardens, hereditaments and premises in Nantwich aforesaid, did by their deed, grant them to *John Maysterston*, senior, and the heirs of his body on the body of Catharine his wife, the daughter of John Dutton of Halton, lawfully begotten, with remainder to the right heirs of the said John After the death of the said John, who died without leaving any heir of his body, the said premises descended to *John Marchomley* as his next of kin and heir , viz the son of *Margery* his sister , by virtue whereof he was seised of the said premises in fee, & continued so seised until he was *forcibly disseised* thereof by WILLIAM MAISTERSON a bastard, supported by Sr William Stanley Kt and was kept out of the possession thereof all his life, but after his death John Marchomley his son, to whom the right of the said premises descended, entered upon the said premises, and was seised thereof, but a parcel of the said premises so restored to him, the said WILLIAM Maisterson re-entered and died seised thereof"

The other Inquisition *post mortem*, dated more than a hundred years after the preceding one, relates to the possessions of THOMAS MAISTERSON, son and heir apparent of RICHARD MAISTERSON of Nantwich, Esq , whom he pre-deceased Two Inquisitions were taken after his death , one on the 14th June 4 Jac I [1607], and the other, which was taken at Chester Castle, and was a very long one,—the original being contained on seven skins,—on the 8th Jan 15 Jac I [1617-8]. After quoting a lengthy Indenture by which property was acquired by his father's marriage with Elizabeth Grosvenor, and mentioning lands "formerly the lands of Lord Lovell, and a capital messuage in which *Richard Maisterson* inhabits held of the King as Earl of Chester, with a mill, dovecotes, 70 acres of land, 20 acres of meadow, 70 acres of pasture lying in Wich Malbank and called *Presthume*, held of the King as formerly belonging to the dissolved priory of Trentham, co Stafford, in socage " the Inquisition goes on to say that *Thomas Maisterson Gent* of Nantwich

"Died seised of 47 messuages, 8 salt-houses, 1 Mill, 1 dovehouse, 56 gardens, 200 acres of land 80 of Meadow, and 40 of pasture, and £7 18s 8d rent in Nantwich , the reversion in fee of a Croft called *Lodge Croft* there, after the death of Lawrence Maisterson, Gent &c

Also lands in Oldcastle, Stockton, Willaston, Wigstaston, Worleston and Chester The said Thomas Maisterson married Catharine Dorrington, and died on the 19 April 1 Jac I [1604] leaving *Thomas Maisterson*, son and heir, who was born after the death of his father, namely on 8 Dec 1604 "

JOHN MAISTERSON, great-uncle of the above, who died in 1586, was famous for his noble exertions in connection with the rebuilding of Nantwich after the great fire of 1583 (see Monument) The Maistersons of Nantwich and Woodford, in this county, were fined for their loyalty to King Charles I, and Henry Maisterson, D D, a native of this town, was deprived of his church preferment, and ejected from Cambridge University, together with the master, Dr Beal, and other fellows, in 1643 * Though the exact date of his birth or baptism has not occurred, his parentage, as proved by several wills still preserved at Chester, is shown in the subjoined pedigree His father, *John Maisterson*, had been dead more than ten years when HENRY MAISTERSON† was admitted fellow of St John's College Cambridge by royal mandate 6th Sept 1634 In the following February his mother, Cecill Maisterson, died Her will, which though very interesting, is too long for insertion here, expresses that her youngest son should be educated at Cambridge, as her eldest son had been The will says —

"*Itm* my will is that my [eldest] sonne *Henry* (if he please) shall have the best bedd, wᵗʰ the furniture which was my mothers, he giveing to his [youngest] Brother John the bedd he hath att Cambridge when hee shall come thither, my trust & hope being that by his Brothers good endeavours, and his unkle williams helpeing hand, hee may be, in due time fitted for the university and mainteyned there '

These intentions were dutifully carried out when, in 1647, Henry Maisterson obtained for his brother John, his admission into St John's College, having himself been *Concionator* [preacher] at Michaelmas, 1643, and admitted Senior on 15th Jan 1645-6

The following notice of him occurs in a very scarce pamphlet entitled "*An Accusation of Dr Arrowsmith, Mr* [Master, after Dr Beal] *of St John's college in Cambridge By Petition of Robert Waidson Esquire and Doctor of Physick of the University of Cambridge Printed ᴀᴅᴄᴊʟ* [sic] 4to On page 30 is this instance of mis-government — ‡

"Dr Masterson admitted to be a senior, after he had been sequestered in Cheshire , And by his temporall means is outed by the statute, and for not keeping of his exercises in the Colledge before he commence Doctor, and after he was made senior here, was sequestered by M Fortune, for what I know, without it is for giving ten pounds in money unto the King, and the Colledge plate which was none of his own, which truly I think he ought to restore to the Colledge, and doe desire it This Doctor Masterson got his sequestration deferred at London, under a pretence that he hath been a madman these many years, and that you may see the madness of this man, he got his brother *Sir Masterson* [John Maisterson, B A] a deboched [debauched] fellow, and a prisoner for the Kings service taken in waire, to be made Fellow [John Maisterson, admitted Fellow 7 Ap 1647], whilst *Captain* [John] *Smelt* for the Parliament mist a Fellowship [He is however entered in the Coll Reg as admitted Fellow, 7 Ap 1647, and Senior 21 Ap 1657]

This Doctor since [no date given] had the degree of Doctor conferred upon him by the University, and he is one of our Seniors, so that by Statute he is to be supposed *one of the wisest of us* I am sure he is wise enough to save his money Now if he shall be judged to be *non suæ memoriae compos, fatuus, vel idiota*, I do humbly desire the Parliament, that I may have the tuition of him It is *quid pro quo*, for I have been under his tuition ever since he was senior Now if he be wise enough, I shall then humbly desire the composition for his Sequestration, as a thing the State has been cheated on, if I had

---

* *History of St John's College, Cambridge*, edited by J E Mayor, M A , 1869, p 224, &c

† Another *Henry Maisterson*, of Nantwich, gent , in his will, which was proved at Chester on 19th March, 1605, bequeaths a garden on the *Castle Hill* " in Nantwich, a pasture in Stapeley called *ssrobstall* " "two pastures in Worleston called the *Barrefields* ' (now called Berry Meadow) 'and one p[ar]cell of ground in *Anesey* ' (Annisey field being still one of the fields of Mile House Farm in Worleston) These lands descended to *John Maisterson*, the father of Henry Maisterson, D D

‡ From a copy of the pamphlet *tenes* J F Bailey, Esq , F S A , who kindly sent me the above extract

not discovered it   And let Dr Masterson, with all the distinctions he hath, take off this Dilemma , if he doe, I will give him leave to pay my Garragaskins [breeches], as hee uses the phrase "

Henry Maisterson* was Zachary Cawdrey's (afterwards Rector of Barthomley, 1648—1684) tutor, at that time [1641 and *posted*] one of the Fellows at St John's, Cambridge The quarrels among the old and new Fellows at Cambridge are alluded to in Newcome's Autobiography, (Chet. Soc Pub) Newcome, who went up to College for the second time, in May, 1645, was received ' to be sizar to Mr Maisterson,' [*i e* John Maisterson] "who was after senior Fellow , and though, good man, he was distempered & jealous, and very suspicious of everyone, and oft of his sizar, yet it pleased God to give me favour in his eyes, and I lived very comfortably in his service and respective [sic] to me "   " I was also afterwards Mr Maisterson s proper sizar, which was a fine place, of little service & good help, as is known to be in that College "—(*Autobiography* pp 8 & 295)

John Maisterson, who is mentioned in the previous extract, was entered in St John s College Register as " John Maisterson, son of John Maisterson, gent , of Namptwich, Cheshire , born at Namptwich, school Repton (Mr Whitehead) 2 years, admitted pensioner 22 March 1641-2, surety Mr [Henry] Maisterson aet past 17 ' He is also alluded to by Mr Newcome (*Autobiography* p 151) many years afterwards, as follows —

" 12 July 1665 My old friend *Mr. John Maisterson*, came to me [at Manchester] this night, and was with me all night   We discoursed of old matters when in the university together , and great things we have both seen since that time "

Of the later descendants, I have not discovered the parentage of *Thomas Maisterson*, of Shrewbridge, nor *Martha Maisterson* , nor of "*Richard Maisterson*, of Nantwich, Gent ," who is mentioned in the following pedigree, but whose will, proved at Chester on 30th June, 1747, mentions his two sons, "*Captain Maisterson*," and *John Maisterson* (who was married and had two sons, *Wooley*, and *Richard*, and a daughter, *Elizabeth*), and a daughter who was then married to a Mr Edwards, and had one son, *Winwood*, and three daughters, *Margaret*, *Ann*, and *Ursula*.

The Maisterson Mansion, the residence of the heads of the family in the seventeenth and eighteenth centuries , and the names of fields situated on the south side of the town, once their possessions, have already been noticed on pages 125 and 172

* Anthony a Wood, *Fasti* ii 179, says that Henry Maisterson, D D was after 1653 "*beneficed at Namptwich*, and died in 1671 " The former statement must be incorrect, as the incumbent at Nantwich from 1648 to 1677 was Richard Jackson   The latter statement is correct , he was buried at Nantwich on 12th Aug 167: —(*Par Reg)*

Maisterson Pedigree.

Authorities: Harl. MSS. 2119, p. 42; Visitations 1580—1663; Dorfold Pedigrees; Wilbraham MS.; Wills at Chester; Parish Registers.

ARMS. Ermine, a chevron azure between three garbs Or.

CREST. On a wreath a tiger passant Argent.

Swayn filius Magistri

Rogerus Filius Magistri

Siwardus vocatus Magisterson

ROBERT MAISTERSON, of Wich Malbank, 26 Edw I [1297-8] Then surviving and holding land in Wich Malbank (*Dorfold Ped.*) = Cecilia...... .... died 1312

ROBERT MAISTERSON, son and heir = Agnes, dau. of William Wilbraham 26 Edw. I. [1297-8] (*Dorfold Ped.*) 5 Edw. II. [1311-12]

THOMAS MAISTERSON of Wich Malbank, Esq., son & heir = Katherine dau. of Sir [Hugh] de Dutton, co. Halton, co. Cest., by his wife Joan, dau. of Sir Robt. de Holland. (see Beamont's *Hist. of Halton, p. 43.*) Escheator of Cheshire 1300-1 & 1395-6: Attorney-general of Cheshire 29 Oct. 1301. (*Chesh. Rolls.*) Distinguished in French wars from *knight* of Ed. III. to Hen. V. Died at a "great age, early in Hen. VI." probably c. 1427.

Nicholas Maisterson Esq. second son 1331.

Margery dau. and heir of Thomas Dawkinson.

Ralph Maisterson 1349. ob. ante 1396.

Richard or Robert] Maisterson Esq., who died possessed of one half of a salt pit of 6 leads in Nantwich, with successive remainder to his brothers *Ralph* & *William*, who being dead before 1396, the property was granted by the King to the Prior & Convent of Rowton. (*Chesh. Recog. Rolls.*)

Wm Maisterson 25 Edw.III [1351] ob. ante 1396.

Thomas son of William 3 Hen. IV. [1401-2]

RICHARD MAISTERSON, Esq., 19 Ric. II. [1395. & 25 Hen. VI. Seneschall to Thos. Holland, duke of Exeter, for his manors of Sponley & Adderley in co. Salop. = Joanna dan. of Ralph Egerton of Wrinehill, co. Staffs.

Thomas Maisterson Esq. Seneschall together with his brother 8 Hen. V. [1420.] (*Dorf Ped.*)

John Maisterson 1374. Grants lands, the inheritance of his mother, to his son *John*, and his right heirs. Sep. 1396, (*Chesh. Recog. Rolls*)

Nicholas Maisterson, dead in 1449.

Alice Maisterson.

Nicholas Maisterson

Margaret Maisterson (*Dorf. Ped.*) Heiress to estates in Nantwich after the death of her brother *John* Maisterson. = Robert Marchomley son and heir of *William* Marchomley of Marchomley.

John Marchomley son & heir cisseised of Nantwich estates by William Maisterson.

John Maisterson said to have been buried in Acton churchyard in 1412.

THOMAS MAISTERSON, Esq., son and heir, 13 & 39 Hen. VI. [1434 & 1460] & 7 Edw. IV. [1467] = Cecilia dau. Wm. Leycester, of Tabley, 14 Hen. VI [1435].

NICHOLAS MAISTERSON son and heir, 7 Edw. IV. [1467.] He is the first of the family mentioned in Cæsh. Visit. 1580. = Ellena dau. of Mathew Fostock, of Elton, Gent., 2 Edw. IV. [1462] (*Dorf. Ped.*)

John Maisterson, son & heir = Katherine dau. 7 Hen. IV. [1405] & 33 Hen. VI. [1454] Died without legitimate issue (*Dorf Ped.*) of John Dutton, of Halton.

John Maisterson (*Dorf. Ped.,* to which is added "*quæri*," or more probably *William Maisterson. Inq. p. m.* 11 Hen. VII. [1495.]

A   B   C

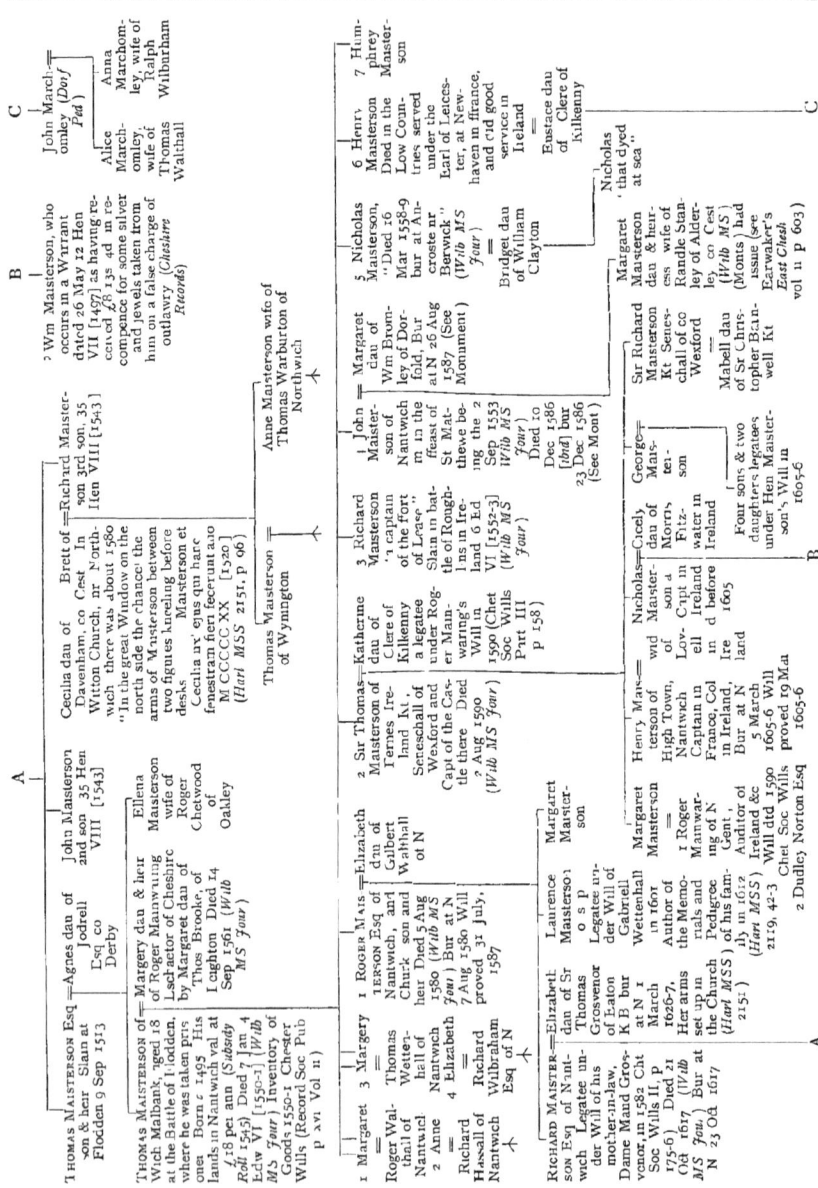

A

B

C

Thomas Maisterson son, & heir apparent Bap 14 July 1581 D in his father's lifetime 19 Apl 1604 Bur at N same day Inq p m taken on 14 June 1607 and on 8 Jan 1617 18

John Maisterson Executor of his uncle Henry M Will 1605-6 Dead before 31 May 1624, on which day an inventory of his goods was taken

Richard Maistr son

William Maisterson of Nantwich Churchwarden at N 1632 Will proved 18 Feb 1647-8 o. s. p

= Cecill dau of Manwaring of N d in Feb 1634-5 (Wrb MS) Will proved 14 Feb 1634-5

Henry Maisterson D D eldest son Tutor in St John's Coll Camb ejected 1643 Bur at N 12 Aug 1671

Richard Maisterson of Hunterson Gent Bur at Wybunbury 14 July 1662

John Maisterson, youngest son, b c 1621, of St John's Coll Camb Living in 1665

1 Margery 2 Elizabeth 3 Anne M Bap at N 16 Sep 1621

1 Lawrence Maisterson who for the service he did in Spaine, positinugall, fraunce, the netherlands, & Ireland, had from Q Eliz a reward of 4s p day till he should be better advanced with a charge of a company of horse & foot Bur at N 30 Sep 1610

= Anne dau of John Woodnoth of Shenton [Shavington] co Cest Bur at N 2 May 1645

2 Roger Maisterson married & lived in Ireland "This man slew Theobald Toole in single figat before the army, one of the valiantest heines that ener was in Ireland"

3 Anthony Maisterson unmarried 1612
4 Anne Maisterson ob a mayde

Catherine dau and heir to Anthony During ton, of Cotton, co Saff Gent

Mary Maisterson married 1 Lawrence Pope of Stapeley, Esq (2) John Smith of Morville, co Salop Esq

Margaret Maisterson married 1 Edward Butler of Bewsey, Esq o s p 2 Sir John Gibson Kt D L of Welburne co York Had Issue Edw Gibson, age 16 in 1612

Frances Maisterson m Robt Cooke of Molesley, Gent, co York

Bridget Maisterson who mar (1) John Thrusfie and (2) on 8 Feb 1601-2 (N Per Reg) John Paggett, Preachr of God's word at N and after wards to the company of Merchants at Amsterdam [Dod Pd & Harl MSS 2119 p 43]

Margaret dau & heiress of Henry Wright of N Mar at N 9 Mar 1618 9

Mary Maisterson Bur at N 30 Sep 1604

= Captain Thomas Maisterson slain at the Isle of Ree

Elizabeth Maisterson co-heir d 26 Mar bnr 28 Mar 1653 (See Mont)

= Capt Robert Wright of N Gent Mar 23 Oct 1650

Jane Maisterson co-heir, wife of Car of Hoole(?) co Cest

(First Wife)
Frances, 3rd dau and finally co-heiress of Sir John Done of Utkinton, Kt, co Cest Bap at Tarporley 31 Mar 1603, and bur there 23 Apl 1629, having died within two days of her father (Chesh Funeral Certif p 70) Burghall, noticing her death, says she was "a pattern of piety".

= Thomas Maisterson of Nantwich, Esq Posthumous and only son born 3 Dec 1604 Bap not recorded because of the hiatus in Registers Had livery of his father s lands 20 Car 1 [1631] June 20 Suffered sequestration in Civil War D 16 Feb, bnr 18 Feb 1651-2, at N (see Mont)

(Second Wife)
Mary dau of Thomas Manwaring of Melton, co Cest Bap 18 May 1666 Bur at N 9 May 1684

Richard ob infan Bur 31 March 1652

Richard M bur 3 Sep 1650

John M bap 4 March 1648-9 Bur 5 Sep 1663

Robert M living 1651

1 Elizabeth M wife of Thos son of Willm Wilbraham of Kees Heath nr N Living 1663 (Visit)

2 Mary M wife of N Welch of N o s p 1663

3 Catherine
4 Frances
5 Bridgett living 1663

Margaret bur 15 Oct 1662 (Reg)

Helena bapt 4 Sep 1651 living 1663

1 Richard, living 1635, then about 8 yrs old
2 Thomas
1 Grace
2 Elizabeth All died young

Thomas Maisterson, Esq. Born in 1636 or 1637 (Visitation) Died 7 Apl 1666 but 9 Apl (Reg) Monument)

= Mary dau of Thos Palmer of Marston co Staff Gent man at N 23 Dec 1660 Bur at N 27 July 1715 (Reg)

Richard Maisterson Bapt 13 Dec 1664

B

Mary Maisterson Bapt 5 March 1666

Thomas Maisterson Esq Bapt 18 Sept 1662 Bur 13 Sep 1712

= Catherine dau of Bapt 20 Jan 1743-4

A

Richard Maisterson of N Will dated 15 Oct 1746 Proved 30 June 1747 = pre-deceased her husband

Captain Masterson | John Masterson = Elizabeth M | Richd Masterson | a daughter = Edwards

Wooley Masterson

2 Wm Maisterson Esq 2nd son & heir Bap 3 April 1692 Churchwarden 1733 Bur in Chancel of N Church, by leave from Mrs Crewe, 31 July, 1742 = Martha dau of — Bur in Chancel of N Church 18 Dec 1751

Margaret Henrietta | Ann | Mary Swain | Ursula

1 Thomas eldest son, bap 6 Aug 1689 Bur 24 Sep 1700 (Par Reg)

3 Roger Maister-son, Bap 12 May 1693

4 Robert Master-son, Bap 20 June 1698 Bur 1 Nov 1700

5 Richard Maisterson Bap 9 Oct 1701 Bur 12 Oct 1701

6 John Maisterson Bapt 13 Dec 1704 Ch'warden at N 1734 & 1742 for Alvaston

1 Catherine M Bap 16 Mar 1690 = Baltasar Hortls-ton, mar at Acton 25 Sep 1713 (Acton Reg)

2 Mary M Bap 14 Dec 1694 = Ralph Brom-ley, mar 9 March 1740 (N Par Reg)

3 Ursula Maisterson Bap 21 Dec 1695 Bur 1 Nov 1700

4 Anne Maisterson Bap 18 Apl 1697 Bur 23 Oct 1698

5 Eliz Maisterson Bap 2 Dec 1699 Bur 7 Oct 1703

6 Frances Maisterson Bap 3 Jan 1702-3 Bur at N 10 Feb 1799 A spinster aged 96 yrs Her death is noticed in Gent Mag 1800, pt ii, p 698, & in Lysons Cheshire, p 710 Will proved 7 March 1799

7 Ann Dorothea Masterson Bap 10 Oct 1708

8 Eleanor Masterson Bap 4 June 1711 Bur as a spinster in the Chancel of Nant Church, 13 Nov 1754

1 Catherine Masterson Bap 11 April 1723 (Reg)

2 Mary Maister-son, Bap 25 April 1725 (Reg) Living 1789 at Holden in Yorksh Spinster

3 Anne Maister-son Bap 1 Dec 1726 Bur 16 March 1732-3 (Reg)

4 Hester Maister-son Bap 13 May 1732 (Reg)

1 Richard Maisterson Bap 20 Oct 1730 Supposed to have had cestendants living in London in 1817 (Ormerod's Cheshire, vol iii, p 439, New Edit)

Ann Maisterson Buried in Chancel at Nantwich, 9 July 1754

Thomas Masterson Bap at N 30 Oct 1756 ? Whether the same as Thomas Masterson mentioned in a deed dated 24 June 1786 belonging to Flr House property, now own-ed by John Withinshaw, Esq (Cf p 241)

Harry Masterson Bur 7 Jan 1739-40

Winwood Edwards

5 Richard Maisterson Bap 9 Oct 1701 Bur 12 Oct 1701

Martha Masterson = John Hoare Esq of Con-way nr N 11 April 1746

Thomas Masterson Esq of Shrewsbridge, Nant Nephew of Frances Mais-terson Churchwarden in 1748 Died intestate Bur at N 9 Mar 1768 (Par Reg) = Mary dau of — She administered to the goods of her late husband 14 Mar 1768

William Masterson Bap at N 28 April 1789 Living 1789

Mary Katherine Frances All living in 1789

Edmund Masterson Bap 16 July 1760 Buried in Charcel at Nantwich, 24 March 1761

THE WILBRAHAM FAMILY

The WILBRAHAMS resided in Nantwich, at Townsend House in the Welsh Row, for two hundred years, that is, from 1580 to 1780   The family, which is one of the most ancient in the county, can be traced back to the early part of the thirteenth century, the earliest known ancestor being RICHARD DE WILBURHAM, who was Sheriff of Cheshire in 53 Hen III [1269], and died about 2 Edw. I [1274]   This Richard, who is stated to have been twice married, *first*, to Margery, eldest daughter and co-heir of Warin Vernon Baron of Shipbroke, by Ada, daughter of William third Baron of Wich Malbank, and *secondly*, to Letitia, eldest daughter of William de Venables, lord of Warmincham and Radnor, co Cest , is supposed to have derived his name from the manor of *Wilbraham* in Cambridge, where the family was located as early as the reign of Henry II. (Ormerod's *Cheshire*, old Edit vol iii, p 126)   Following in succession were WILLIAM WILBRAHAM living in 1312, WILLIAM WILBRAHAM, who died in 36 Edw III [1363], RALPH WILBRAHAM, who died in 11 Rich II [1388], and THOMAS WILBRAHAM, who died at the early age of thirty-eight, in 11 Hen IV [1410]   The next successor, THOMAS WILBRAHAM, settled at Woodhey, and became lord of that manor in right of his wife, Margaret, heiress of John Golborne.   He had five sons, three of whom became ancestors of different branches of the family   *Thomas*, the eldest, succeeded to the Woodhey estates, which were held by his descendants in the male line, until the death of Sir Thomas Wilbraham, of Woodhey, Bart , who died on 5th Aug 1692 , *Richard*, the progenitor of the Wilbrahams of Brindley and Rease Heath, in Acton parish, who became extinct in the eighteenth century, and *Randle Wilbraham*, the ancestor of the Nantwich Wilbrahams, now represented in direct descent by George Fortescue Wilbraham, Esq , of Delamere House, as shown in the accompanying pedigree   Of RANDLE WILBRAHAM and his successor RALPH WILBRAHAM little is known   A curious mistake, however, occurs in Ormerod's *Cheshire*, (New Edit. vol. iii, p. 379), where Randle Wilbraham is stated to have been the *great-grandfather* of *Richard Wilbraham*, and to have died in 1548   It will be noticed in the pedigree that the date of the marriage covenants of Thomas Wilbraham of Woodhey, father of the said Randle Wilbraham, is fixed at 1401-2, and allowing a wide margin for the consummation of the marriage after that date, in case the contract was made during the childhood of Margaret Golborne, the heiress of Woodhey, as was not uncommon, *Randle Wilbraham*, the second son of that marriage, must have been born before 1420, and if so, in 1548 he would have reached the patriarchal age of one hundred and twenty-eight years !   The express statement of Richard Wilbraham in his Family Journal, is the best refutation of the error   He writes as follows —

"yt Randull Wylbrahm my *grannffather* Dyed the second daye of march in the xiij yere of the reigne of Kyng Henry the sevonth A⁶ Dni 1498 "

RICHARD WILBRAHAM, who came to reside at his newly-built Townsend House on 6th Aug 1580, commenced the remarkable family memorial, to which the successive heads of the family have contributed to the present time   Having lived to see his four sons rise to positions of wealth and honour, he died at Nantwich at the advanced age of eighty-seven, and was succeeded by his grandson, Thomas Wilbraham.   The following is an abstract of his Inquisition *post mortem*

"*Inq p m* taken at Wich Malbank 23 Oct. 11th Jac 1 [1614] before Sir Rich Wilbraham, Kt, and Henry Mainwaring Esq Eschaetors, Ralph Wilbraham, and George Cotton, Esqrs, Commissioners, after the death of Richard Wilbraham, Gent, on the oaths of Robert Whitney, John Haughton of Haughton, Thomas Brooke of Leighton, William Allen of Brindley, John Aston of Aston, Ralph Hayle(?) and Randle Smith of Brindley, Richard Wilbraham and William Pratchett of Worleston, William Salmon of Wild Heath, George Cudworth of Newhall, Robert Massey of Coole Lane Laurence Wode of Wysterson, Thomas Smyth of Checkley, and Peter Walton of Sound, gentlemen, Jurors, who say that Richard Wilbraham on the day of his death was seised in his demesne as of fee, of and in a capital messuage in Wich Malbank, with garden and lands (pasture and meadow) adjoining, also a messuage, garden, orchard and lands formerly belonging to Sir William Davenport Kt, value 3s 4d, four pastures called the *frog-greaves*, in Wich Malbank and Acton, value 13s 4d, also the manor of Bechton with water-mill, 8 cottages, 20 gardens, 20 orchards, 40 acres of land, 100 acres meadow, 40 acres pasture, &c Also the messuage and farm called the *hall of ffulshurst* in Sound, also 30 acres land, 10 acres meadow, 20 acres pasture &c in Buerton, a messuage with garden orchard and lands in Newton near Tattenhall, a messuage with lands in Faddiley and Brindley, a messuage with lands in Somerford Radnor two messuages &c in Walgherton and Hatherton, a messuage and lands in Bloore (Staff), Two pastures, one called the *pease fflatt* in Acton, the other the *Brown-Hull* in Wich Malbank, one croft called the "*Cawsey Croft*" in Henhull, five pastures and one meadow called *Shuttshawes* and *Wichfeild* in Wich Malbank, 19 messuages with gardens &c in Wich M, four salt-houses each 12 leads, and 8 salt-houses each 6 leads in Wich M, Rents in Hankelow, Brindley and Faddiley a parcel of land called the *Horse-croft* in Wich M formerly in the tenure of Rich Maisterson, Gent an annual free rent of 2s from the west side of a pasture called the *Green-feild* in Wich M, rents in Great Wood Street, also tithes of corn and wood in Leighton, Messuages in Wich Malbank in the occupation of Thomas Malbon, William Webb, Gents, William   , Dorothy Brooke, widow and John Sparrow, val 10s, also other lands in Wich M in common and free burgage value 40s They say Rich Wilbraham died on 2 Feb 161(-2, and that Thomas Wilbraham Esq is next heir, being the son of Richard Wilbraham of London Esq deceased, son and heir of the said Rich Wilbraham, and that he is aged 22 years and upwards"

THOMAS WILBRAHAM, the grandson of Richard Wilbraham, was born and brought up near London, and was a well educated and accomplished gentleman He was admitted of the Society of Lincoln's Inn, and of Brazenose Coll Oxon in 1613, and at a time when very few travelled abroad, he spent two years on a tour in France, Spain, Germany, and the Low Countries. "for the better experience and knowledge of the Languadges," as stated in his *Licence to Travel*, dated Whitehall, 17th June, 1614 He made a second journey to France in 1618 Of these travels he has left the following brief account in the family Journal —

"*Memorandum* yt the 20th of July 1614 I went from London for France in company with Sr Tho Edmonds the French Ambassadour & Sr Tho Darnall my familiar friend And tooke shipping at Douer in one of the Kinges Ships called the Answeare the 25 July 1614 at 3 of the clock in the afternoon, & by God's good protection of vs we landed prosperously at Boulongne in France the next morning by 9 of the clocke the 29th of the same month we came to Amiens where the day following we saw the Duke of Longueville make his solemne entrie, & the 11 of August we came to Paris, &c

Md that the 18 of Oct 1613 The Kinge of Spaine was married to the K of France his eldest sister at Burgos in Spaine And the same day the K of ffrance was married to the K of Spaine his sister at Bordeaux in France The D of Lerma was Deputie for the K of France, and the D of

Guise for the K of Spaine   And the 9th of Novemb following the 2 sister-in-laws exchanged their native countreys meeting vpon the river Behobie·′ wᶜʰ deuides France & Spaine, *where I then was,* and came wᵗʰ th' Infanta of Spaine to Bordeaux, where vpõ the 23 November the marriage was solempnly consummated in St Andrew's Church betwixt the K of France & her, and vpo the 29th day the King and Queene made an entree into Bordeaux and were received wᵗʰ great state & Pompe

The 3rd of December 1615 I imbarqued in a shippe at Bordeaux to go to Rouen in Normandy, but by a contrary wind we were driven to Rochel the 8th day, & during oʳ stay there the Prince of Condé was received by 4,000 musketiers into the Towne, & 300 of his followers wᵗʰ him, who with the Rochellers entered into a league & combination agˢᵗ the K but were not able to crosse his designes the 23 day of the same month we went for Rouen & arrived there the r Jan aftʳ   Before oʳ departure frõ Rochel the Duke of Neuers came fro the french K thether to treat wᵗʰ the Prince of Condé for peace

Memorandum yᵗ the 1 May 1616 I tooke my iourney from Paris to Nancy the Court of the Duke of Lorraine, from thence into the higher Germany, & soe to Heidelberg in company of my Lord Gray from thence I went through the low Countreyes & tooke shipping at Dunkerke & landed in England at Margat 29 July 1616   God's holy name be ener thanked & praysed "

Of the second tour he records —

" *Md* That vpon Monday 10 August 1618 at 7 of the clocke in the evening I took shipping at Douer in company of Sr Tho Darnell and Sr Peter Wentworth and made my second iourney into France where we landed at Diepe the next day at 3 o'clock after noone

I returned forth of France accompanied wᵗʰ Sr John Maynard & we landed at Douer 29 Octob 1618   Thanks be to God who still protected me in all my iourneys both by sea and Land in Spaine, France, Germany & diuers other contreys and forraine places "

In the year 1617, the intervening year between the first and second continental tour, he had the great honour of entertaining King James I, as already mentioned, *(see Annals)* at the family seat, *Townsend House,* in Welsh Row, where, after his marriage, he continued to reside until the outbreak of the Civil War   Though a Royalist in principle, he took no active part in the war, being at that time fifty-three years of age, and in ill health, yet, says Roger Wilbraham, his son, he "had a taste of the troubles being made a Prisoner in his own Howse, for refusing to lend Monies to carry on the Warr against his Sovereign K. Char., whose sworne servant he was.   Being set at liberty he retired into Sussex where he spent some time with his kind Friend Sr Tho. Pelham Bart, in his House at Halland, where he dyed of a Fevr 18 Oct 1643 "

In *Harl MSS* 2135, p 17, is preserved the following letter in the handwriting of Thomas Wilbraham, dated 9th Oct 1642; which will be of interest   It does not appear to whom the letter was addressed

" Good Cousin,

Many troubles fall upo or contrey, and vpo or friends but especially vpon this vnfortunate Town [Nantwich] for the folly of some few wch are fled, for besides ye losse and terror it hath already sustained by theis late devour-ing Troopes, The King hath imposed a Fine upo it of two thonsand pound, without making any distinction between the innocent and ye guilty   It is thought also that now at th' Assyzes or Towne wilbe indicted, and seuerly proceeded against   In all wch p'plexityes how I must behaue myself, I must entreat yor advice, being absent at ye Bathe† all the while theis actions of Rebellion were in agitation, whereof I haue ye testimony of diuers of best credit in or Towne, wch I haue here inclosed, sent yow for my instification (if there be cause) and can haue more hands enowe [enough]

---

* Query whether the River Bidassoa   † *i e* the town of Bath

to it if it were requisite also hercinclosed is a note of some pticlers which I heare wilbe charged vpo the Towne
I am not well able to travel my self in regard of my old paine wch I cannot yet be cured of   I haue sent my man of
purpose to yow wth theis things yt in case I be namcd yow will make my excuse, and mooue yt those yt were innocent & ignorant of theis proceedings no way allowing or approoving them may not be involued wtn ye delinquents
nor beare any pt of their clame or burden   It may be for my names sake* I may find some aduersaries otherwise I
think I should find none, for in regard I am sworne his Matie servant I was very cautious   It was tould me yt
this last week Mr Sheriff in ye hearing of my Ld Chomley and others did averre yt I sent & armed men to rescue
Steele our constable when he was vnder arrest, wch is most false   I myself was then at Bathe [Bath] and left but
onely on[e] man at Nantwich wch was this messengr & he will depose yt at that tyme he was forth of ye Towne
What I write to yow I will make good by the testimony of all my neighbours I haue appointed my man to stay till
Tuesday to bring me word how things are carried wch ye Lord graunt may be for the good of vs and our friends,
wch I am much afraid of, for I received a letter vpon Saturday fro Sr Ric Wilb intimating yt something wilbe
done at this Assyzes agst or Towne or our friends or both   I pray [as] there snalbe occacion, doe what good yow can
for them [and also] for those yt cannot be there to make their owne defence

I shall entreat yow to draw me a Petition to his Matie for my owne iustification wch I will eyther deliuer myselfe
or procure some to do it for me   I thinke it were not amisse if I made mention of my readiness at all tymes to do his
Matie ye best seruice yt lay in my power   That in the yeare 1639 when he went in pson to make warre against ye
Scots whom he then took to be his enemyes, without eyther letter or summons fro his Matie I furnished myself
with a cuirasiers Armes and three horses at my owne charge & went to nis Matie to York, where I tendred my
seruice to him for wch he gaue me his hand to kisse, and gaue com'and to my Ld chamberlain yt I should be sworne
of his Privy chamber   I wayted vpo his Matie all yt iourney in wch imploymt I spent betwixt 3 and 4 hundred
pounds His Maties father was pleased to make vse of my house to lye at, and at my owne charge I entertained &
lodged the Earle of Strafford & his company when he came last forth of Ireland vpo his Maties seruice   That I was
farre fro home when theis fortifications & tumults were in Nantwich &c

And therefore being his Maties sworne servant and loyall subiect to desire I may be seuered fro ye delinquents,
and not pay or contribute any thing for their salt &c   Yow may put in or take out what yow please But certainly
before I will pay any money for other mens errors, I will preferre some Petition or other as yow shall advise me   It
yow please to doe this any tyme this week I hope will serue turne I am almost a sleep as yow may see by my
scribling and therefore fro this sheet I will goe to another and bid yow and all my Cousins godnight who am

9 Oct 1642   Yor assured lov Cousin

                                                                THO WILBRAHAM "

' I had forgott to tell yow yt I heare Mr Sheriff hath foisted in my name
among ye rest into his Catalogue   I [beg] yow keep theis inclosed papers "

George F. Wilbraham, Esq has in his possession the original " Certificate from the
Maior of Bristol [John Lock] dated 14 Sep. 1642, to permit Thos. Wilbraham to travel
safely from Bristol into Cheshire on his return from Bath," and the following "*Petition*"
from the town of Nantwich exonerating him from certain charges, which is signed by
influential townsmen irrespective of their avowed opinions

"Wee the Inhabitants of Nantwich whose names are subscribed being desired to testifie ye truth
on ye behalf of Mr Tho Wilbraham of oure Towne doe averre that ye sd Mr Wilbraham had no hand
at all in advising or making any bulwarke or fortifications in ye sd Towne, or in making any opposition,
but when ye sd devises were made, he was at Bathe in summersetshire for ye use of those hot springs
for the recouery of his health, in wch journey he was absent for ye space of about six weeks, and returned but ye day before my Lord Grandison brought his troops into oure Towne, for ye opposing of whose
entry Mr Wilbraham imployed no help, but came purposely thither to perswade those yt were most
refractory, and we doe confesse and beleeve yt by his prswasions the Towne was better satisfyed that no
hurt was intended against it "

[Signed] Tho Maynwaryng   John Dolman, scoolemaister   John Saring, Minister
         Mathew Mainwaring   William Lee Bayliffe & Dom   Rich Wright
         Edw Hayes   Ran Churche   Henry Wicksted

* Alluding to the Wilbrahams of Woodhey and Dorfold, who were not loyal   After Sir Richard Wilbraham's death
his son, Sir Thomas Wilbraham of Woodhey, Bart , being a Royalist, suffered sequestration, compounding for his estates
in £2,500

Thomas Wilbraham was succeeded by his son and heir THOMAS WILBRAHAM, who, at the time of his father's death, was in France. Little more than seven years after, "he dyed of Bleeding at his House in Nantwich 19 Dec 1649," and his estates, which, by reason of the late war, "stood deeply charged with Debts & Portions,' descended to his brother, Roger Wilbraham

ROGER WILBRAHAM, like his great-grandfather, Richard Wilbraham, lived to a great age at Townsend House, where he was born on 3rd Nov 1623. He was educated first at Repton School, Derbyshire, and for three years, commencing June, 1640, at Catharine's Hall, Cambridge, under Mr S Lynford, B D   He was admitted of Lincoln's Inn in Easter Term 1642, and was called to the Bar in Easter Term 1649, but his elder brother dying in the same year, Roger Wilbraham relinquished his law practice for the life of a country gentleman, and came to reside at Townsend House   He married Alice, daughter of Roger Wilbraham, of Dorfold, Esq, by whom he had eleven children.   In the family Journal is a pathetic account of his domestic afflictions and bereavements, ending with the death of his wife, whom he survived thirty-one years

He writes as follows —

"This dark year 1675 was ushered in by the death of Mr Upshan,* the Vicar of Acton, who was a burning and shining light, but his lamp went out within less than a year and a half after his coming into this neighbourhood to the grief of his parishioners & all good men that knew his worth

It pleased God within a few weeks after to take from me my second son Rich W in the 16th year of his age, who died with us upon Whitsun-eve 1675, of a stoppage in his breast, occasioned by over-heating himselfe at schole   He was a spiritfull well-humored Boy & had a secret way of attaching love wch endeared him to his mother & me, & to his Brother, who was but newly come from Oxford, who came seasonably to divertise me after his brothers death

I had not thoroughly mastered my grief, when it pleased God, a fresh tyde of grief broke in upon us both, who had set our hearts too much upon our eldest son, who was now arrived to the years of manhood, & yet as obsequious as he had ever been from a child   It was the last week in August that I took him with me to Chester, it being the Assize week, where a drowsiness took him in the Shire Hall, which much indisposed him, & made me hasten home the next day, taking Beeston Castle in our way, wch I had promised to shew him   Coming home he grew more indisposed, & to prevent a fever he was let blood, & in hope to procure him a gentle sweat he had a dose of Gasgon powder, wch affected what was designed, but went not off as we hoped it might, but made him more restless, till God took him to rest, wch was upon Wedny evening 8 Septr 1675, while we were at prayers with him, after he had with the greatest violence that nature could exert, raised up his whole Body in bed, as if he would take Heaven by violence, and so departed away at 19   Anno Dom 1675

The effects of these repeated griefs might have been prejudicial to my health, the former affected my eyes with a violent rhume, wch put me to paine, & endangered my sight   The latter so sow'red my blood that it found vent at my mouth, that 3 weeks that my son Tom dyed   But after 2 or 3 daies, by the help of timely meanes, by Bleeding, stopped, & I recovered to survive a greater loss the year following than either, or both the former

The year following, I went with my wife for a diversion to the Bath [Somersetshire], the week

---

* The Rev Wm Upshan, who had been Rector of Lawton, co Cest from c 1662—1674, died in April, 1675   A grave-stone on the north side of the chancel floor in Acton Church states that he was "interred on the 19th April 1675," (so also *Acton Parish Register*) ' in the thirty-second yeare of his age "   His death is noticed by the Rev Hy Newcome, (*Autobiography*, p 212, Ci et Soc Pub) who endeavoured to get the living of Acton for his son, but Mr Samuel Edgeley, chaplain to Sir Thos Wilbraham, of Woodhey, obtained the preferment

before Whitsuntide, wch had she used for a refreshment might have advantaged her but the over frequent
use of the waters in conformity to her sister the Lady B [ellot]* insensibly rob'd her of her spirits & brought
her so weak that had not Mr Ford an able Apoth in whose house we lodged, upheld her with proper
cordials, in likelihood she had died there, but God would that she sh^d dye in her owne Bed, & brought
her home to sett her concernes in order, having the pre-apprehension of her change that she was not minded
I should know

At Barthol-tide (wch is our Fare) to be out of the bustle we went to Moreton Her sister the Lady
Bellott brought her home stayed with us 3 daies The day after being 8th Septr 1676, I went abroad upon
business, whereof my wife took advantage to spend the whole day in her closet, being the day 12 months
that her dear Tom died At my return in the eveng she came out of her closet to welcome me home,
supp'd with me & discoursed with me of the Business I went about We went to bed at our usual time
About midnight she awakened & having a slight cold, coughed twice or thrice, which awakened me I
asked her how she did She said, Well, but for her cough which said, she fetched 4 or 5 faint sighs &
turned her over I asked her again how she did, but she gave me no answer & though I conjured her of
all loves to speak if she was able, she gave me not a word In this consternation I rose hastily out of Bed,
called the servants, and sent for a neighbour, that was oft with her But whatever could be done, could not
bring back the spirit wch she had breathed into the hands of God All that Grief will allow me to say of
her is, that she was knowne to be an humble, pious, virtuous, discreet woman, an ornament to her sex, &
a crown to her husband, but woe is me (may I say) the crowne is fallen from my head †

It was a just Quarter of a year before I returned to my widow-bed, & that while I had no rest in my
spirit, sleep became a straunger to me, and while I lay musing I thought of erecting a monument that
might transmit the memory of my D [ear] wife to posterity, it came into my thoughts, that I had in our own
Street, three well built houses, under a roof, with convenient apartments, that might easily be converted into
an Almshouse, for half a dozen poor aged widows, and thought better to devote something of this nature to
the Honor of God and to her memory that had been mindfull to lay something by, to be distributed to poor
widows in her own street I gave notice forthwith to the Tenants of these houses to remove at Christmas
coming and till then I c^d proceed no further in this affair

From All-Hallow to Christmas my Fa[ther]-in-law declined very fast, being arrived to the 88th year of
his age, (wch was the yeai in wch his grandfather, [Richard Wilbraham, of Townsend,] my great grandfather
died) I had not seen him of 2 mo[nths], being confined to my chamber Upon New Year's day, I had
the convenience of his coach to bring me to Dorfold to take my last leave of him, who died in his sons
arms, the morning after, in a good old age, full of daies, wealth and honor ‡

After the Holy daies were over, and my dr [dear] Father-in-law laid to rest I made all possible haste
to fitt the houses wch were now in my possession for the reception of six aged widows, that I had there in my
thoughts I endowed the same by deed executed with Livery, with lands [in Betchton] to the value of
xxiiij^li [£24] per ann, for a constant and perpetual maintenance for so many poor aged widows for ages

* Anne, daughter of Roger Wilbraham, of Dorfold, Esq, and widow of Sir John Bellot of Moreton, Bart, who had
died on 14th July 1674

† Amongst Roger Wilbraham s papers occur the following lines on the motto " In portu quies" belonging to his
paternal coat of arms, written, as he says, "in my chamber after God had bereaved me of my Dear wife "

" All thy waves & thy Billowes are gone over Me "—Ps 42 7

In Portu Quies, was my Mott'
When seas were calm, wch now are not,
If God give grace to persevere,
Though seas do rage I will not fear
Grant me O my God to have vitam in patientia, mortem in valo

Rogr Wilbraham 1676

‡ Acton Burial Register records his burial as follows —

"1676-[7] Jan 8 Roger Wilbraham de Dearefould Ar [miger (Esq)]

to come. Which done the six widows took their lodging in the said almshouse; two in each house (for society) upon the eve of the Blessed Virgin M[ary] 1676. The day following being Sunday the said widows went orderly in their gowns to Church; took their places in a seat wch I had provided for them in the face of the Pulpit; dined with me that day; and joined with me and my family to beg a blessing upon this charitable mite which God enabled me and inclined my heart to cast into the Corban, and lent me life to see it accomplished."

WIDOWS' ALMSHOUSE.

After the death of his wife, Roger Wilbraham devoted much time to reflection and study; and although he did not publish any work, he left behind him MSS. (forty in number) on subjects chiefly theological and historical. He was very methodical in his manner of life, as proved by the numerous memoranda crowded into the fly-leaves of his small pocket almanacs, giving the minutest particulars relating to his crops; how he disposed of his wheat, barley, oats, &c.; his household expenses; the cost of his son Stephen's education at Cambridge; regular gifts at Christmas, the Fair, &c.; to the members of his family, his domestics, the Parson, Schoolmaster, the poor; &c.

A few extracts, illustrating, as they do, the home-life of a country gentleman two hundred years ago, are here given as follows:—

Commonplace Accounts of Roger Wilbraham.

1672. Nov. 19. Winnow'd upp ye Oates fro. Leighton of stricken Meas. 16.
    ,,   Delivered for ye Stable before my groom is going to Oxf.* 3 measures.
    Dec. 20. All ye Tythe Barley from Leighton was but 34 measures & 2 of w[i]ght Corne.
    ,,   Given to Neighbours at Xmas† .. .. 14 measures.
    ,,   To be Malted .. .. 20 measures.
1672-3. Jan. 28. Pd. for a bushel of otes in ye Market .. .. 5s. 4d.

* The groom probably was sent to Oxford to bring young Thomas Wilbraham home from the University for the Christmas holidays.

† Poor people and servants seldom tasted wheaten bread.

1672-3 Feb 20, Win'owed up of Otes, 3 daies thrashing   30 measures

     [Entries occur about every fortnight of Oats "Delivered to ye Stable" 2 or 3 measures at a time, for his Bay Horse, and other horses]

1675 Nov 25 Winnow'd up of Barley I had out of the say f [uld]* in Henhull Carried to the Granary 48 measures

     Dec 21 Sent to Darfold to be malted 21 measures

       Barley given to poor Neighbours at Xtm 12 measures

1675-6 Marc 15 Delivered out for Buttery & for Diet Drink 4 measures

     ,,   22 Delivered for small Beer 1 measure   [Many such entries]

1676 August I had to my pt [part] of ye wheat which T Stringer sowed in Parkers furthr Field 41 Thraves & ⅜

     Oct 12 Thrashed 26 Thravest & ½, which yeelded 37 measures ‡

1677-8 Jan 2 Win'owed upp, 37 measures of Otes§ which I had for Tythe out of one of ye presthuries, sow'd by T Stringer

     Jan 3 Carried into ye Granary out of ye lower Cheese Chamber 60 measures of Malt which I had of Mr Winser for rent of Sharps Crofts at xijˢ ye Bushell

     Feb, 19 Bought of wid[ow] Becket 5 pecks of Darby Malt for Ale for myself   [Several similar entries]

1678 Dec Given of ye wheat to p [oor] neighbours 5 measures, & 7 measures of Barley for their Xmas Batch

1688-9, Jan By an order from Mr Gonge (my son Ste[phen's] Tutor) I transmitted to his correspondent Mr T Clarke a Tradesman in London to c eer my sons expenses 40 li [£40] For which I had a Bill from Mr Salmon, Cheese Factor, in Nantwich, who ordered me to pay ye like sume to Rich Shore of Baddiley For which I have Shores acquitance, pd X date 12 Jan 1688-9

     Feb 22 Tench his Note for Sugr & Spices since ye week before Christmas last   £1 13s 6d pd by Marg Fisher

     Mar 2 Pd to Mr Banks, by my servant W Grocutt, who gave me a Bill for £21 10s which Bill was transmitted to Lynsey ye Coachmaker, at London, for Coach & harnesse for 2 Horses, having Mr Minshulls Letter for £20 more, wch ye sd Mr Lynsey had of mee in November last for ye sd Coach & harnesse, in all £41 10s

1689 April 15 Pd to my daughter Ally her allowance for Lady-day qr £10

     ,,   To Marg Fisher, housekeeper, a yeeres wages due at Lady day last, 40s

     ,,   To Alms-women by W Greene, for Last Quarter, £4 10s 0d

     April 20 Pd ye Glover at Whitch[urch] for 2 pair of Sham[?]Gloves by him yt brings Bread to or Market   2s

     May 4 I gave to my Grandc[hild] & Godson R W [Richard Wilbraham]|| 10 Guinees, wch I put into his Fathers hands upon condition to give ye child when he comes to be a man ye silver kan which was my wifes bequest unto my son Ran[dle] W [ilbraham]

     May 13 To or Clerk my Eastr dues for my selfe & my servants   2s 2d

     ,,   More for my son & his servants   1s 0d

     May 23 To Mr Stringer our Minister, & W Hale, Ch Warden, for relief of ye distressed protestants driven out of Ireland   £5 0s 0d

     ,,   To Mr Stringer my contribucon for half a year from Xmas last   £1 0s 0d

     ,,   Pd to Will Hayles, his note for shooes, deducting what he owed me for Tythe   £1 9s 6d

     June 24 Pd the Collectors for my degree of Esqr   £5 0s 0d

     ,,   More for me & my daugh A W for or polls   2s 0d

     Aug 10 I had Mr Salmon his Bill to his Correspondent for £30 to be paid to Mr T Clarke at ye Ship & Star in Cheap-side, for ye use of Mr Lea my son Stephens Tutor which Bill I sent by ye next poste after to Mr Clarke Pd Mr Salmon ye money by my servt W Greenold   £30 0s 0d

     Sep 12 I parted with my old servt peg Fisher who has served me now 13 yeers since her Mistrs Death I gave her over & besides her wages, 3 years ago, £10, & at parting 20s

     Sep 28 To Rogr W[illia]ms for 11 daies ditching ye ground I hold in my owne hands, having my man Hilditch to help him those daies   7s 4d

     Oct 16 I paid to Deborah Dawson for Bread for ye poor 4s weekly for 9 weekes, ye last distribucon was upon Wednesday Oct 16 ..   ..   £1 16s 0d

---

     * Most likely *Causway Field* or Meadow, mentioned on page 7

     † A "*Thrave*" was generally 12, but sometimes 24, sheaves of Corn —*(Cheshire Glossary)*

     ‡ The "*Measure*," or bushel of wheat, in Cheshire, also varied in different localities, ranging from 70lbs to 80lbs Four measures made a load

     § A *Measure of Oats* varied from 45lbs to 50lbs

     || Richard, the eldest son of Randle Wilbraham, died of a fever on 6th Feb 1706, in the 18th year of his age. *(Wilbraham MS Journal)*

1689 Dec 21 I sent my son at Bettley a Quartr of ye Beef & a side of a Doe , & a haunch of ye same to my neighbour
    – Mr Wrt [Wright]

Dec 27 To Miss Bellot* for her new-year's gift a Ginney

Dec 28 To our Minister, Mr Stringer   20s
        To ye stranger that has assisted him this last Quarter   20s

1691 2 Mar 9 An ague seized in ye mth of March, wch preyed much upon my spirits and left me weak, & confined to
    my chair 6 weeks after

Mar 13 To Mr Lancaster our Minister a Ginney

Mar 24 To Dorothy this Quarter s wages   12s 6d

Mar 28 Recd of Mr Roger Wilbraham for Bread delivered to ye Towne by his order 4s weekly for 27 weeks, ye
    last distribucon was ye Wednesday next after Laay Day, 1692   £5 8s od

1692 April 21 For 3 Holl[an]d Shirts for my selfe   £1 2s 6d

April 28 To ye Collectors of ye Roll Money, ye first quarterly paymént for my degree of Gentleman   20s od
   ,,   More upon ye account of finding a light horse   20s od
   ,,   Head money [Easter Dues] for myselfe, my daughter, & 3 servants   5s od

May 5 Pd my daughter for 4 quilted night caps bought of Bet Meakin   5s 6d

June 30 To or Minister, Mr Lancaster   20s od

1692 Aug 5 Sr Thos Wilbranam, of Woodhey, Bart ,† died at Weston in Staffordsh whereupon his corpse was
    brought to Acton Church that day fortnight, and laid in the vault made by his Lady mother, daughter and
    co-heir of Sir Roger Wilbraham, Kt

Aug 24 Given in Farings —
    To my son Rand , to my D[aughter] Brook, & to my daughter Ally to each of them a French Pistol † to
    my s[on] Steph a Pistol & 10s in silver   £3 3s 9d
    To ye children at Wincham in Toyes   2s 6d
    To my servants viz —To W Gr 2s 6d   To Lawr 2s , To Pen W 1s 6d , To ye two new Maies 3s ,
    To Randles man 1s   10s od

Sep 14 I did sett unto Ellis Key, Carpentr ye house at ye back of ye Widdowes Hospital wherein Laz Ward
    now dwelleth for one whole yeere from Michaelmas next for 24s to be paid quarterly Recd in earnest, 1s

Sep 10 To Ad Meanly for boring at Betchton to search for Brine,§ 40s of which 8s was to ye Smith To Jos
    Davy to assist 10s , to Joseph Dyer 10s   Toto £3

Sep 17 Recd of Mr Tho Broom of Betchton in lieu of a Heriot‖ at the death of his father, T Broom £3 os od

Oct 14 To Mr Humphrey Milton,¶ who held ye Courts for me at Clive & Betchton, 10s for ye charges of
    dineing ye Juries I am accountable to Ran Jackson & Jos Davy

Oct 14 Pd my son Rand[le] for 5 pound of Tabacco, whereof I gave him 1 pound   10s

Oct 26 To Raphe Bursco for making me a Freel Coat , Silk wastcote & Breeches for my son Stepher   17s od
   ,,   Pd for a Green Cheese sent to my D Wilbr at Rode   6s od
   ,,   To Churchwardens for distribution among ye poor   £6 10s od

Nov 29 I gave to or Minister Mr L[ancaster], 20 hlf-crowns ye day his wife dyed, supposing his circumstances
    might require it

Dec 3 To my son Ste[phen] at his going to Rode to Christen his Brothers third Son   20s od

[Customary Christmas gifts to his family, grandchildren, servants, the poor, the Parson, Grammar Schoolmaster and
boys, and Almswomen]

1692-3 Jan 11 To Jo Hall Senr for a side of Bacon & a role of Brawn   18s 9d

Feb 20 My son Rand his 2nd son T W died of weakness occasioned by breeding his teeth, aged 2 yeeres &
    upward, & was interred at Astbury in ye burial belonging to ye Hall of Rode He was dear to me upon
    sondry accts & to his Godmother A W

   * Probably Mary, the eldest daughter of Sir John Bellot, of Moreton, Bart , by his wife Ann, daughter of Roger
Wilbraham, of Dorfold, Esq (Ormerod's *Cheshire*, New Edit vol iii, p 44)

   † He was the last male descendant of the eldest branch of the Woodhey Wilbrahams

   ‡ The *French Pistol* varied in value from 17s to 18s It would then be worth 17s 11d

   § Another entry proves that brine was not only discovered, but worked, at Betchton

   ‖ *Heriot*, a customary payment due to the Lord of a Manor on the death of a tenant, generally paid in kind, but
here in money

   ¶ See *posteá*

1692-3 Feb 21 To my son Steph when he went to ye Funer[al] of his little nephew T W   20s 0d

Mar 17 To my son Rand his Disbursemts & expenses at Chester in my concerne wth J Cartwright in ye Consistory Court & for a 4dt [quart] of Brandy [9s]   £4 9s 0d

Apl 27 For a wrought cup & cover wch I sent for to Chester for my son St[ephen's] godson   £3 4s 6d

Apl 29 Pd for wine wch was had of Rich Horton [Lamb Inn Nantwich] at ye funeral of my little Gr ch T W in Feb last   £2 11s 0d

1693 May 5 For scouring ye *Shutshaw Ditch*, along ye Marsh Lane 45 roods, @ 2d ye rood, 7s 6d , whereof ye Tenant W Fleet paid ye one half & I, 3s 9d

May 26 Pd to Garnet of Haughton for a House Dog   8s 0d

,, To my Daught for 2 pair of sheets wch she bought for ye house £1 0s 6d , muslin for cravats, 11s   £1 11s 6d

June 9 Pd to M Stones wife 20s in pt for Cambd[en's] Britan[nia] now in ye presse & am to pay her 20s more when I receive ye Book   [A subsequent entry says, I received ye Book 11 April 1695 & sent her 20s , Toto   40s]

June 21 Wages for Midsummer Quarter to my servants, viz To Wm Gr[ocu]t £1 Jane Key 12s 6d , (I gave her 5s) Cook Maid, 12s

Aug 4 Paid to Haymakers for the *Frog Greaves* viz Sarah Judson 5 days, 2s 6d , Margaret Hitchenson 4 days 2s Hannah Wright 3 days, 1s 6d , Widow Harop 2 days & half 1s 3d , Hugh Manning 1 & half 10d 8s 1d

Aug 14 Given for ye Redemption of Christian Captives*   £1 10s

Aug 15 To Ruscoe for mending ye Jack   1s 8d

Aug 24 I had three score Ginnies of Jo Br[omhall] mercer, at 21s 8d apiece, for which I sent him ye value in silver by Wm Grt [Grocott]   £65 0s 0d

Sep 19 To Lawr Steel of Leighton for 2 Loads of Turves   5s 0d

Sep 20 To Mr Delves & Mr Peever towards ye last Cheese yt was sent to ye Judges .   15s

Oct 12 To my son Rand for his attendance at ye Assizes at Chester, over & above his Disbursemts in ye Concerne for a Pew in Lawton Church, 2 French Pistols [each 17s 6d] & 10s   £2 5s 0d

Nov 2 I recd of J Bromhall mercer one of ye present Ch Wardens a Hundred Broad pieces of gold wch I took at 24s a piece, wch amounts to £120 in silver, wch sume he found in ye Wardens Box & belongs to ye Poore of this Towne of Nantwch

1694 Ap 9 To J Bromhall, his Bill for my Godson Dick Wilbr his first Coat, Breeches & Wastecote   £2 9s 3d
To ye Taylor for making ym   4s 5d

May 26 Pd to my Collier Wm Heath for 6 dozn of coals @ 11s 6d ye doz , being 12 Cart loades   £3 9s 0d
July 3   Do '   do   do   £3 9s 0d
1 Cart load of slack   5s 9d

June 14 Received of T Wickstd for ye 1st & 2nd kinding in both my wich houses ye sum of xiiij h   £14 0s 0d
1694-5 Feb 14 Recd then of Mr Acton by deputation of J Bromhall for 3 kindings of 4 daies   £6 0s 0d

March 5 To Rich Wilbram Bart & Ric Minshull Ch Wardens their lay for my House & Lands ⅓ ye old Rent   35s 6d

1695 May 4 Pd to Tho Willms Constable of Henhul by order of ye Justices of P to remove Mar Eaton & her family out of Henhull   £16 4s 9d

May 13 Pd to Edmd ye Thatcher for 11 days work & ½ at ye *red lyon* stables & at Jamesons House   23s
To my man Law H to pay Judson for drawing 50 Thraves of winter straw to thatch ye stables belonging to ye Red Lyon Inn   12s 6d

May 18 For a bushell of Oats bought in ye Market   6s 5d
,, 3 Measures of Mill-corn   6s 3d

May 18 To my son Steven, 10£, wch is to serve him for Cloathes & expences till Allhallowtide next   £10 0s 0d

June 20 To my daughter Ally at her going to Rode to have her picture taken a Ginney   £1 1s 0d

July 8 To ye Brief [Collection] for ye fi e in York   5s 0d

July 15 Recd by my son Rand for a Heriot on ye death of Wm Shaw of Betchton   £4 0s 0d

Sep 20 To Mr Broadbent for a pair of worsted stockings   3s 6d

* The allusion here is to the nefarious slave-traffic of the Turkish pirates of Tunis and Algiers (the Sallee rivers of history and fiction,) that infested European seas in the 17th century, and even until quite recent times, robbing ships of their merchandise and taking sailors and passengers captive Collections in Churches, for the purpose of raising a fund for purchasing the freedom of ' Christian Captives " taken by ' Infidel Turks " were common in every parish in England

1695 Sep 25 Recd then of Mr Cartwright of ye Hall of Lee (by ye hand of Mr Edgeley, Vicar of Acton) 14 Ginneys
              @ 30s a piece in full ye costs taxed upon him by order made in ye Kings Bench after a tryall in ye hall of
              pleas at Chester, for a Pew in Lawton Church   £21 0s 0d
     Dec 20 Recd of my new Tenant Unwin for a capon 15d , for a hen   9d
        ,,   Recd of Mr Wilbraham a Salt toll o. 8d yearly for ye years 1693-4-5
1697-8 Mar 5 To Wm Hales for 2 pr of Shooes for my son Steven   9s od
1698 May 9 Pd to Hilditch, sho-maker, & his ptner ye last yeeres Tax for my son Steven as Gentleman Bachelor   6s
              And now that he is not of my family, nor resident, ye sd Collectors p'mised me to leave him out of ye roll
              for ye yeere to come
     Oct 15 Two measures of Rye for ye House   11s od
1698-9 Feb 2 For 37 Measures of Malt @ 4s 5d a measure   £8 3s 6d
     Jan 8 A Measure of Corne 5s 4d , 3 Meas Oates 3s 4d   a Bushel Oates   9s
1699 Aug 28 A Bushel of Wheat   £1 3s 8d
1699—1700 Jan 13 To Sam Burgess of New Castle 8 doz of Candles @ 4s 6d   36 od
1700 June 10 Pd ye Collectors of ye Tax for Windowes for ye yeere last past*   10s od
     June 21 Bought in ye market of Jo Heyward of Hunsterson a red cow & calf   £4 10s od
     July 29 Recd of Mr Horton of ye Lamb by Order of Mr Throp, being ye rent for ye Salt work in Betchton for
              3 months, viz April, May, June   £20 0s od
     Aug 10 Sent my son Steven at London a Bill for £11 1s 6 , a ginney of it was for Sr Paul Ricalts history of ye
              Turks, wch he sent me , & for his maintenance 10£   £11 1s 6d
     Dec 4 To T Bowers, Gardener, for Trees to replant my Orchard & Wall Fruit, 78 trees in number £2 14s od
1700-1 Jan 2 To Ja Clowes for bleeding my daug Ally & for other attendance   1s od
     Feb 3 Pd to Mr Andrew Taylor, Goldsmith, for a small patin & chalice of Silver for Hargreave Chapel
              £2 18s 6d
     March 13 Pd Jo[hn] Church & his p'tner [John Denton] a Lay of ye whole Rent for glazing & pointing ye
              Church & Steeple   £3 9s 4d
1701 Sep 1 Given to ye Brief for repairing ye Minster at Chester, A Ginnie
1701-2 Feb 27 A kind friend & neer Relation of mine, who knew me to be a smoakr of Tobacco, presented me with a
              Tobacco stopper of Ivory wch ye carver has beautified with sundry Figures, &c
1702 May 24 Bought at Whitchurch Fare 5 Cowes to feed, cost £16
     June 11 Bought at Holt Fare, 5 Cowes to feed, cost £13 6s 4d

For many years Roger Wilbraham was an active and never-failing guardian of the
rights and interests of the town, as evidenced in the memorials of his public life contained
in his "Towne Concernes" (pp. 203—211). On one occasion a public honor was accorded him, which he relates, with no small pride, in the family Journal, as follows —

"My youngest Daughter Grace W was married to Tho Brooke, eldest son of Sr Rich Brooke
[of Norton], 12 July 1688, Sr Thos Bellot Bart, gave the Bride in or Chancel at Nantwch, where
the marr was solemnized Sir Ric Br[ooke] & his Lady, my son Rand[le] & his wife, sistr to the
Bridegroom & other Relations on both sides being present

The better sort of ye Town did me ye honor without my seeking (hearing that my son & his wife
came along with Sr Richard Brooke & his train) to meet them on Horseback some miles out of the
Town all in a manner that had, or could procure horses Those of the meaner sort, especially in our
own streete, expressed their gratulations in that way, that it might be noticed I had their Love, in
returne of the good offices which I have done for ye place of my Birth & abode for many yeares &
wherein it is known I have a Concerne "

Roger Wilbraham stands pre-eminent as an antiquary, having been an assiduous
collector and transcriber of ancient deeds, as well as the local chronicler of his own times;
and but for his industry, much that is contained in these pages would never have been

* See page 344 note

known to the present generation   At the Restoration of the Monarchy (1660) he was
nominated as one of the intended new order of Knighthood, styled "Knights of the Royal
Oak," (the institution of which was, however, never carried into effect) his estate being
valued at that time at £1,000 per ann   In 1669-70 he fulfilled the office of High Sheriff
of the County, and was the first native townsman to hold that high position   To his
memory a marble monument still exists in the Church (see p 321), and in wealth, in
manners, in character, and in religion he resembled in a striking degree his contemporary,
the Worcestershire Knight and Squire, Sir Roger de Coverley.

RANDLE WILBRAHAM, the son and successor of Roger Wilbraham, was forty-four years
of age at his father's death   He had been educated at Cambridge, having been admitted
as a gentleman commoner of Catherine's Hall in July, 1680.   After his marriage in 1687
he resided at Rode, in Astbury parish, from whence he removed to Townsend House,
about the year 1710, Rode Hall, henceforth, becoming the seat of his second son, Randle
Wilbraham, the eminent lawyer and M P, who became the ancestor of the Wilbrahams
of Rode, and of Bootle Wilbraham, of Lathom House, co Lancashire, now Lord
Skelmersdale.

Randle Wilbraham, who thus became head of the family, was the last to leave any
records relating to Nantwich in the MS. Journal   Following the example of his father,
he took an active interest in local affairs, and appears to have been one of the foremost
County gentlemen of his time.   He was a Wright's Trustee for thirty years, he originated
a Consolidated Charity Scheme, to prevent the loss of bequests to the poor, and by his
and his brother Stephen's benefactions, the Blue-cap Charity School was mainly endowed.
He was succeeded by his eldest son in 1732

ROGER WILBRAHAM, Esq, who had been educated at Brazenose College, Oxon., came
to reside at Townsend in Oct 1738, from Chester, after his second marriage   He died
in 1754, leaving three sons, the eldest, *George*, being then under age.

GEORGE WILBRAHAM, Esq, who was educated at Trinity College, Cambridge, passed
some years of his early life in France, Italy, Turkey, Greece, and the Levant   He was
the last of this worthy family to reside at Townsend House, which, having fallen much
into decay, he quitted about the year 1780.   In 1784, and subsequently, he purchased
lands bordering on Delamere Forest, and built, after a plan by Wyatt, the house which
has ever since been the family seat   He is chiefly remembered as one of the first to
introduce an improved system of agriculture into Cheshire

GEORGE WILBRAHAM, Esq, the next successor, who, from 1831 to 1841, in four
Parliaments, represented first the whole County, and afterwards the Southern Division,
was always the popular candidate at the elections in this town, and although the family
have now been removed from Nantwich for upwards of a century, the present representative, GEORGE FORTESCUE WILBRAHAM, Esq, who is the direct descendant of Sir
Richard Wilbraham of six hundred and fifty years ago, has, in respect of the place of his
ancestors, recently rebuilt and re-endowed the Nantwich Grammar School, and erected a
memorial stained glass window, near the ancient family vault, in the Parish Church

The following family portraits in oil are preserved at Delamere House.

1.—In the Dining Room, Roger Wilbraham Esq. of Dorfold, by *Vandyke.*

2.—In the Hall, Randle Wilbraham Esq. of Nantwich, dated 1711, by *Otley.*

3.—   „   Stephen Wilbraham Esq.   „   „   „ by *Otley.*

4.—In the Study, Roger Wilbraham Esq.   „   „ 1741, by *Fellowes.*

5.—In the Dining Room, George Wilbraham Esq. of Nantwich, by *Battoni.*

6.—   „   „   George Wilbraham Esq. of Delamere, M.P., by *Sir M. A. Shee.*

7.—   „   „   George Fortescue Wilbraham Esq. of Delamere, by *S. E. Williams.*

The later history of Townsend Mansion, of which no drawing is known to exist, will be found on page 123. Before giving the pedigree of this worthy family, it will be necessary to point out that the Wilbraham Coat of Arms, although blazoned correctly in Dr. Ormerod's *History of Cheshire*, is, by mistake, incorrectly drawn in the new edition of that work.

𝔚ilbraham 𝔓edigree.

Authorities: The Wilbraham MS. Journal; Dorfold MS. Pedigrees; Visitation 1664; Parish Registers, &c.

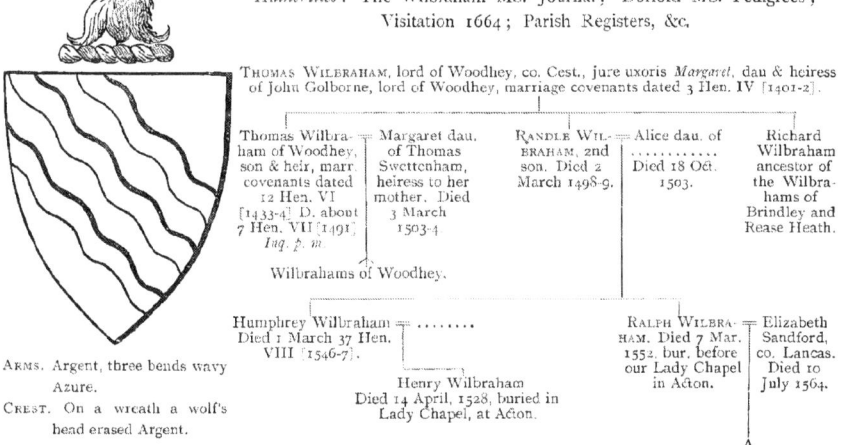

THOMAS WILBRAHAM, lord of Woodhey, co. Cest., jure uxoris *Margaret*, dau & heiress of John Golborne, lord of Woodhey, marriage covenants dated 3 Hen. IV [1401-2].

| Thomas Wilbra-ham of Woodhey, son & heir, marr. covenants dated 12 Hen. VI [1433-4] D. about 7 Hen. VII [1491] *Inq. p. m.* | Margaret dau. of Thomas Swettenham, heiress to her mother. Died 3 March 1503-4 | RANDLE WIL-BRAHAM, 2nd son. Died 2 March 1498-9. | Alice dau. of .... Died 18 Oct. 1503. | Richard Wilbraham ancestor of the Wilbra-hams of Brindley and Rease Heath. |

Wilbrahams of Woodhey.

Humphrey Wilbraham ⊤ ....
Died 1 March 37 Hen. VIII [1546-7].

Henry Wilbraham
Died 14 April, 1528, buried in
Lady Chapel, at Acton.

RALPH WILBRA- ⊤ Elizabeth
HAM. Died 7 Mar.   Sandford,
1552, bur. before   co. Lancas.
our Lady Chapel   Died 10
in Acton.   July 1564.

A

ARMS. Argent, three bends wavy
Azure.

CREST. On a wreath a wolf's
head erased Argent.

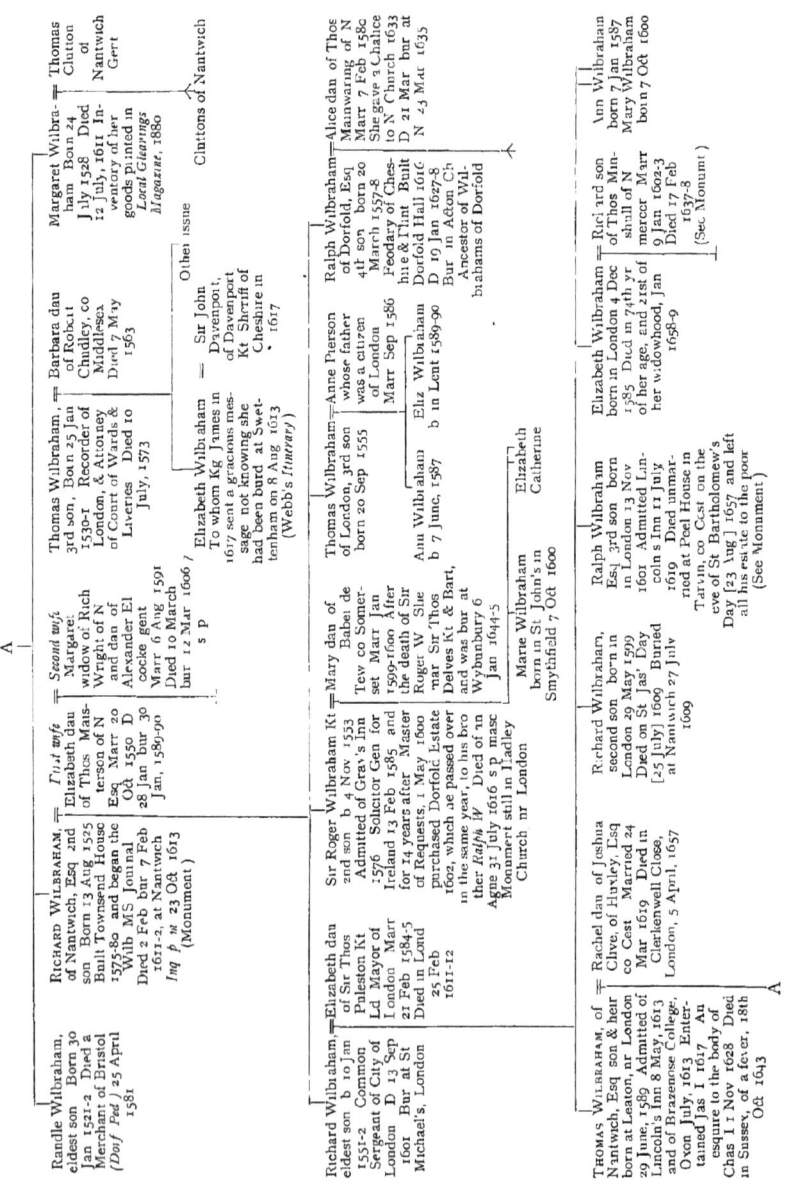

A

Rachel Wilbraham born 7 Mar bap 18 March 1626 Elizabeth Wilbraham, born 17 Dec bap 23 Dec 1631 Died 17 July bur 18 July, 1637

Richard Wilbraham 6th son born 19 Sep bap 25 Sep 1633 Apprenticed to a mercer in Paternoster Row, and died within a quarter of a year after he was bound 22 Nov 1650

Geo Wilbraham 5th son born 27 April, bap 4 May 1628 Died of a consumption, 17 May bur 19 May 1637

Raphe Wilbraham 4th son Merchant of London Born 28 Sep bap 2 Oct 1625 D it Wimbledon Aug 1665, "when so many thousands died weekly of the plague"

Ann Wilbraham b 28 Nov bap 7 Dec 1665 Died 9 Sep bur 10 Sep 1666 Grace Wilbraham B 28 Dec bap 8 Jan 1667 Marr Thos, son of Sir Rich Brooke, Bart 12 July 1688

Rachel Wilbraham, b 20 Sep bap 24 Sep 1664 Died 19 Sep bur 20 Sep. 1666

Elizabeth Wilbraham Born & bap 13 Aug 1659 bur 3 Feb 1659-60

Roger & Alice twins b 28 June 1662 Roger died 1 July, 1664 Alice marr to Raphe Wilbraham, of Dorfold, at Wrenbury Church, 26 May, 1709 She died 9 Jan 1713-14

Elizabeth W m to Win Falconer Esq of Chester, 7 Jan 1730 (N Par Reg) Mary Wilbraham, mar to Thos Cheatham Esq of Glossop, 13 Mar 1738-39 (N Par Reg)

Frances W m to Win Wright Esq of Stockport & Mottram, 14 Feb 1720 (N Par Reg)

5 Hy Wilbraham M A of Brazenose Coll Oxon Rector of Shelford, Oxon where he died unmarried

4 Thomas Wilbraham, LL D F R S Fellow of All Souls Oxon Fellow of Coll of Physicians o s p

Diana dau of John Plumtree of Nottingham, mar 1752 died at Westminster 2 Nov 1757

Richard Wilbraham, eldest son b 18 May, bap 22 May 1621 D "of a burning fever" 23 July, bur at N (See Monument)

Thos Wilbraham 2nd son born 17 Nov bap 1 Dec 1622 D unmarried of a bleeding at N 19 Dec. Bur 24 Dec. 1649

Roger Wilbraham 3rd son of N Esq & heir to his brother Thos Wilb Born 3 Nov bap 6 Nov 1623 Sheriff of Chesh 1669 Died 15 Mar bur 19 Mar 1707-8 (See Monument)

Alice dau of Roger Wilbraham, of Dorfold Esq and Mary Ravenscroft of Bretton, his wife Marr at Acton 17 April 1656 Died 8 Sep bur 14 Sep 1676

Stephen Wilbraham of N Esq Born 4 July, bap 13 July, 1669 Marr 12 June 1708 Bur at N 26 Feb 1732-3

Elizabeth dau of Thos Hoole of Bostock, and widow of Crispin Birch Bur at N 26 Jan 1733

3 Randle Wilbraham, of Rode, Hall I I I D &c Educated at Brazenose Coll An eminent law yer M P for several years Ancestor of the Wilbrahams of Rode, co Cest & of Bootle Wilbraham, now Lord Skelmersdale, of Lathom House, co Lancash.

Dorothea only dau of Andrew Kendrick Esq Marr at Tarporley 24 Aug 1722

Richard Wilbraham, 2nd son b & bap 27 Aug 1660 Died 27 May 1675

Randlf Wilbraham of N and Rode, Esq born 24 Aug bap 5 Sep 1663 Sheriff of Cheshire 1714 Died 19 Sep bur 23 Sep 1732

Mary dau of Sir Richard Brooke, Bart of Norton Marr 25 Oct 1687 at Aston Chapel, near Norton Bur at N 15 Jan 1738-9, aged 75 years

(2nd wife) Mary Verr, dan of Thos Hunt Esq of Mollington, Barrister-at-law Marr in 1738 Bur at N 13 Sep 1760

A

Thos Wilbraham eldest son born at Dorfold Hall, 23 May, 1657 D 8 Sep bur 11 Sep 1675

2 Roger Wilbraham of Nantwich Esq Born c 1694 Educated at Brazenose Coll Oxon Dep Lieut of Cheshire 17 Sep 1725 Bur at N 25 Sep 1754, aged 60 years

(1st wife) Eliz dau of Thos Brooke, of Norton M at Trinity Ch Chester 31 Dec 1731 Died in childbed to Oct 1737 Bur at N 14 Oct 1737

1 Richard Wilbraham, eldest son b 13 Jan 1688-9 Died of a fever 6 Feb 1706-7 Bur at Astbury, where a Mont still exists to his memory

Grace, born 26 April, 1735 Died 10 May, 1735

Thomas Wilbraham, born 10 Aug 1731 Died Sep 1738

Mary Wilbraham, born 22 April, 1736 Bur 22 May 1741

A

Thomas Wilbraham Born Jan 1751 Died unmarried Buried at Nantwich 13 Dec 1802 (See Brass in Church)

William Wilbraham Capt in the Navy
=
Julia, dau of Lewis Montober, Esq

Roger Wilbraham of London, Esq F R S & S A Fellow of Trinity Coll Camb Bap at N 11 Jan 1743-4 See notice of him in Chester Archæolog Journal, Part V, 1856-7, and Gent Mag June, 1829 M P for Helston and Bodmin Author of "A Cheshire Glossary" Died unmarried in the 87th year of his age, 3 Jan 1829 Buried at Twickenham, where is a Monument to his memory

Emma Wilbraham Living unmarried in 1845.

Louisa Wilbraham Born 1 July, 1786 Bur at Nantwich, 21 Oct 1797

Maria Wilbraham Born 26 July 1775 Bur at Nantwich, 14 May, 1794

GEORGE WILBRAHAM, of Nantwich and Delamere House Esq son and heir Born 4 April 1741 Sheriff of Cheshire 1791 Died at Delamere 3 Dec 1813, aged 72 Buried at Nantwich 16 Dec 1813
=
Maria dau of Wm Harvey of Chigwell, co Essex Esq Marr 13 Oct 1774 Died at Chigwell aged 66 Buried at Nantwich 23 Sep 1822

GEORGE WILBRAHAM of Delamere House, Esq son & heir Born 8 March 1779 M P for Cheshire 1831, for South Cheshire 1834, 1835 & 1837 Sheriff of Cheshire in 1844 Died at Delamere 24 Jan 1852 Aged 73 years Buried at Weaverham
=
Lady Ann Fortescue, dau of Earl Fortescue of Castle Hill, Devonshire Marr 3 Sep 1814 Died at Delamere 28 Feb 1864 Buried at Weaverham

Roger Wilbraham eldest son born 25 Jan 1777 Died 2 Feb 1784 Bur at N aged 7 yrs

Hugh Wilbraham Purchased lands in co. Mayo, Ireland

Henry Wilbraham of Lincoln s Inn Born 25 July 1823 Died 13 Feb 1883 Bur at Weaverham

Thomas Edward Wilbraham A Capt in the Army

Roger William Wilbraham of Tunbridge Wells, Esq Born 29 July, 1817

GEORGE FORTESCUE WILBRAHAM, of Delamere, Esq., J P Born 4 Aug 1815 Barrister-at-law Sheriff of Cheshire 1858 Still living (1883) unmarried
=
Louisa, dau of Robt Gosling Esq, co Surrey Marr Sep 1850

1 Arthur George Wilbraham Born 17 Feb 1856

2 Hugh Edward Wilbraham Born 22 June 1857

3 Herbert Vere Wilbraham Born 19 Dec 1858

4 Henry Dudley Wilbraham Born 27 May 1862

5 Fredk William Wilbraham Born 18 Nov 1864

5 William Robert Wilbraham Born 14 May 1871

Alice Mary Wilbraham

Beatrice Augusta Wilbraham

Ada Louisa Wilbraham

THE CHURCH FAMILY.

The family of CHURCH, whose original name appears to have been *Churchehouse*, has been seated for many generations in Cheshire They had estates at Middlewich, Occleston, Alvaston, Wistaston, Church Coppenhall, and Nantwich In 29 Hen. VI. [1451] *Richard del Churchehouse* occurs in connection with lands in Wyghtreton [Wistaston], according to a lease dated 30th July, 1451 * In 14 Edw. IV. [1474-5] by a deed in Mr. Norcup's possession, John Marchomley, son of Robert Marchomley, and John Marchomley, son and heir apparent, (see *Maisterson Pedigree*, page 420), John Bromley, Richard Cholmondeley of Cholmondeley, and William Cholmondeley, granted to *John Churchehouse* and his brother *Nicolas Churchehouse* of Grayste [Gresty] all that land with its buildings, gardens, orchards, &c situate in "Hospitull Strete" bounded by the land of William Hassall, John Bromley, Edward Wetenhall, and Nicolas Maisterson On that land was erected in 1577 the present "*Church's Mansion*," which belongs to A W. Radford-Norcup, Esq , of Betton, Salop, the present representative of the eldest branch of the Church family of this town In 13 Hen VII [1497-8] "*Nicolas Churche, chaplain*," who may have been identical with *Nicolas Churchehouse*, just mentioned, granted by deed to Ralph Malbon certain lands in Haslyngton, and Balterley † The first mention of the family in the Parish Registers is in 35 Hen VIII. [1543], when "*William Kyrke* alias *Churche*" was the head of the family. His grandson of the same name migrated into Shropshire, where he acquired partly by marriage and partly by purchase very large estates at Betton, Tunstall, Tyrley, and Amington, which on the death of the last male heir in 1780, were divided among the several co-heiresses At the dissolution of the Monastic Orders, Sir Rowland Hill, the opulent Lord Mayor of London, purchased vast estates in the neighbourhood of Drayton, and the Betton estate was granted to him by King Henry VIII, by deed bearing date 25th Sep 32 Hen VIII [1540] Sir Rowland conveyed it to his nephew, Rowland Barker, through whose sister, Isabell, one moiety came by marriage into the Church family ‡

RICHARD CHURCH, the eldest son of William Kyrke or Churche, built the Hospital Street "Mansion," which is represented in the accompanying plate, and resided there § His Inquisition *post mortem* now in the Record Office is much defaced and time-worn, but the following brief abstract, though imperfect, proves that he died possessed of considerable landed property

"*Inq p m* taken at Nantwich 17 April 35 Eliz [1593] before Thomas Cholmondeley, Junr , Kt , Escheator, and Ralph Wilbraham, and these Commissrs Hugh Cholmondeley, Richard Wilbraham, Jasper Rutter, and Richard Clutton, gents , on the oaths of   Whitney,   Richd Wilbraham, Willm ffuleshurst, John Cheswis, &c [names illegible] who say that Richard Church, of Nantwich, Gent , died seised of one messuage and one wiche-house of six leads in Wich Malbank , one messuage and 1 acre of land in Worleston , 1 Messuage, 20 acres of land, 10 acres of meadow and 20 acres of pasture in Coole-lane , also 2 messuages   20 acres of pasture in Newhall ,   also 2 messuages in Stafford , 22sh rent in Alderly, Salop , rent from Thos Smyth in Nantwich 8d [?], another rent of 16s 4d for mill-field and corn-mill , also rent of 8s 4d in occupation of Humphrey Brooke , 6s 4d rent from Richard Weever, gent , for property in Acton , another rent of 5s for one messuage

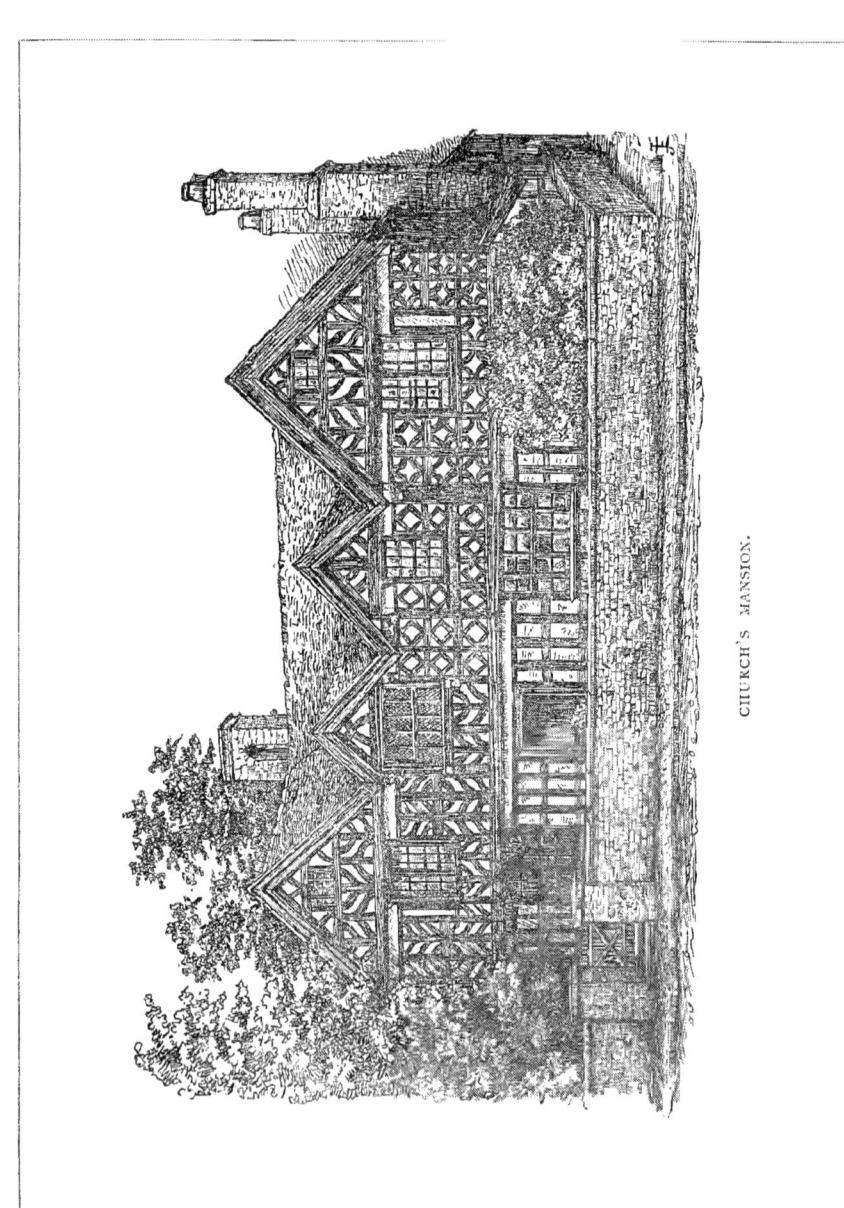

CHURCH'S MANSION.

in Nantwich called *Preyers Hall*, formerly in the possession of John Seckerston, another rent of 5s for property in N formerly the possession of Margaret Maynwaring de Marton, widow, annual rent of 3s 6d in Poole in the occupation of Willm Malbon, annual rent of 3s in Little Acton formerly the property of Thos Chetwode, gent, another rent of 16s from Oliver Cartwright formerly the property of Robt Goodier, gent, another rent of 12d from John Crewe, another rent of 6d for messuage of Ralph Twoyeareold, all which [with other small rents] the said Richard Church by his Will [dated 21 June, 1592] left to his son William Church   Besides these Richard Church died seised of a messuage in Hospital Street, of 3 mess, 20 acres of land, 10 acres of meadow, 20 acres of pasture in Church Coppenhall, 20 acres of land and pasture in Monks Coppenhall, 1 messuage, 20 acres of land, 6 acres of meadow, and 10 acres of pasture in Worleston,   120 acres of pasture and grazing in Oulston and Newton near Middlewich, 10 acres of pasture in Warmincham, certain rents in Monks Coppenhall and Woolstan Wood [all specified], also his house in Hospital Street, with appurtenances, garden, pasture, Dovecotes, stables and buildings 10 (?) cottages and 5 gardens in Wich Malbank, &c

That the said Richard Church died on the 27 Aug 34 Eliz [1592] and that William Church, his son, is his next heir and of the age of 33 and upwards "

Of the Will of Richard Church, now preserved at Chester, and alluded to in the above *Inquisition*, the following are the principal items —

Abstract of Richard Church's Will

"In the name of God Amen, the 21 June 1592

"ffirst I give &c to Margery Church my wife £100 also *wyndmill-field*, also *Malpas-field*, also occupation of salt for 40 years, if she live soe long, and at her death to my son Randle Church, also the barnes and buyldings in *Byrchin Lane*, and certayne gardens lyinge on the North syde of the Churche "

"I give to my son William Church my whole terme & interest in the *Barne Field* adioyning to the Heath, one silver-salt dooble guilt, one drynkinge boole double guilt, one silver pott   I give to my sonne Randull three cottages and gardens in Ospell Street, Also these legacies to Thos Church 20£, to John Church 40s, to Mary Wettenhall 20£ to Humphrey Renolde 20s, to Robert Wright 20s, to William Wright 20s, also Renold [Wright] 20s, to my god-daughter Elizabeth Church 20s, to Mr Sherston, [? Shenton] 20s   The property in the co of Chester and elsewhere to my son William Church, also his howse in Hightowne, also *Birchin Lane* Croft in Wigterson [Willaston] also *Rease Meadow* in Worleston, Wiche-house in Wich Malbank in the occupation of Elen Masterson widow, Lands in *Cowe* [Coole] *Lane,* Cottage and lands in Newhall, Cottage and Land in Stafford, Betton coppice in Adderley, certain rents in Hatherton, Wich Malbank, Acton &c, and at his death to descend to my sonne Rondull, &c   I give to Rondull Church the house or messuage wherein I now dwell in the Ospell Street with gardens meadowe dovehouse stable & buyldings thereunto belonging, with other cottages, also lands in Church Coppenhall, Monks Coppenhall, Warmingham, Middlewich, Occleston, five wiche-houses in Middlewich," &c

[Provision for his wife, who was made his sole executrix, his two sons being overseers of his Will]

An Inventory of his goods, appraised by William Churche, Randle Churche, Thomas Churche and Nicolas Gouldsmythe, dated 12th Oct 1592, accompanies the Will, and amounts to £216 13s. 4d.

The eldest son of Richard Church settled at Betton, in Salop, where the family continued for several generations, as already stated, whilst RANDLE CHURCH, the second son resided at the "*Mansion*" left him by his father, and died there at an advanced age (probably not less than eighty-six years), having survived his eldest son, RICHARD, and his grandson of the same name   A "memorandum" accompanying the will of the said Richard Church, now preserved at Chester, is worthy of being quoted here.

"Whereas I Randull Church of Na'ptwich was named by my sonne Richard Church to be his executor together with my sonne Randull Church of Bullingbroke in the county of Lyncolne I being very aged & also very sickly do renounce to be executor and hereunto I have set my hand in the p'[re]sence of the praysors of the testators goods & chattels the viij day of Jan 1637[-8]

By me Ran Church the elder"

[Witnesses] "Roger Wright, Randall Hampton, Richard Wright, James Bullen '

After the death of this Randle Church, in 1648, the *Mansion* in Hospital Street seems to have become the propeity of the eldest branch of the family at Betton, and, as will presently be seen, was tenanted by the first and second SABOTH CHURCH of Nantwich, in succession, who belonged to the younger branch of the Church family (see Pedigree) I have not been able to trace the descendants of Randle Church beyond his grandchildren, one of whom, however, deserves special notice   This was THOMAS CHURCH, the fourth son of Richard Church, who was born about 1618, and afterwards became a tutor in Brazenose College, Oxon   He matriculated there at the age of sixteen, in 1634, and was Fellow in 1642   Being asked, on 14th July, 1648, whether he would submit to the visitors, he said "I am not satisfied how I can submitt to this Visitation, without incurring manifest perjury '   Accordingly he was removed from his Fellowship 17th Oct 1648, by order of the Committee of Lords and Commons —(Walker's "*Sufferings*," &c vol. ii p 102).   He was, however, restored to his Fellowship in 1660; and obtained the degree of B D   He bequeathed £300 for the purchasing of lands, that out of the revenues thereof two poor scholars of his kindred born in Nantwich, or in default of such any born in Cheshire, should receive £7 apiece, &c.   He also ' gave £25 to the Chapel of the College, with which was bought a silver dish to put the offering money therein at times of Communion "   He died 19th Feb 1676-7, and was buried in the Cloisters belonging to Brazenose College *

Another Thomas Church, D D. was educated at Brazenose, Oxon, but whether belonging to the same family I am unable to say.   He was born in 1707, was instituted to the Rectory of Battersea, Prebendary of St Paul's 3rd Jan 1743-4, B A 22nd April, 1726, M A 10th July, 1731   Wrote against the Methodists as a vindication of the miraculous powers of the first three centuries, in answer to Middleton 8vo 1749   For this work Oxford gave him the degree of D D 23rd Feb 1749-50.   He also wrote an Analysis of the works of Bolingbroke, 8vo, 1755.   He died on 23rd Dec 1756 †

EDWARD CHURCH, second son of William Church, *temp.* Henry VIII, became the founder of the younger branch of the family that has continued without interruption to the present time   His death must have occurred in or before 1560, according to the following extract in *Harl MSS* 1967, f 116 *d*

"2 Julii 2 Eliz [1560] Rich Walthall son and heir of Roger Walthall of Wich Malbank, gent, and Margt his wyfe, demised to Thomas Church sone of *Edward Church, late of Wich Malbank dece[ase]d*, and John Church another sone of ye sd Edwd Church the Capitall Messuage in Wistanston in occupation of John Alexander [of Wistaston] hend p 4 annrm "

THOMAS CHURCH, who succeeded his father, lived in Puritan times, and gave his second son the curious Christian name of *Sabbath* (or *Saboth* as it is usually spelled in the

---

* Anthony á Wood's "*Hist of the Coll & Halls in Univ Oxon* ' 4to 1786 p 361 & 374

† See Alex Chalmers, F S A Biog Dict Vol iv, p 313 (Edition 1813)

Parish Registers and in old Deeds), a name that has been perpetuated, as will presently be seen, through seven generations   The principal clauses of his Will, dated 6th May, 1635, (11 Car I) are as follows —

> "I Thomas Church of Wich Malbank, gent &c ffirst I deuise & bequeath unto Ann Church my wife all that my Messuage or Burgage lyinge and beinge in Wich Malbank, as also one Messuage Burgage & Cottage with the Stable and Garden thereto belonging lvinge and beinge in *Castle Lane* in Wich Malbank, and one great pasture &c adioyning Ridley field for the term of her natural life," &c [also lands in Edlaston] on "condition that she p'mitt & suffer Edward Church my eldest sonne to haue & enioy the moytie and one haulfe of my said pasture called by the name of " *Wichfeild* or *Shuttshaw* and adioyninge to *Ridley ffeild* " [Permission given to his wife to sell. if she think proper, his wiche-houses, bryne, &c]   " Also I giue to my said sonne Edward my drawing Table in the Great Chamber next to the *Cage*, one guilded Silver salt, & my Signett goulde ringe &c   I do giue and bequeath vnto Sabath Church my second sonne one silver cupp p'cell guilt called a Beaker   Also, I giue vnto Thomas Church my sonne Sabaths sonne and my godsonne one wyne cupp p'cell guilt   Also, I giue &c vnto my third sonne John Church 20li and one silver Beaker   Also I giue &c to Thomas Church my sonne Edwards sonne & my godsonne my guilt Boolle or Cupp   Moreover I giue vnto my two daughters 20 shillings a peece   Also I giue to all and euery of my grand-children 5 sh a peece   I make my said wife Ann Church my true and sole executrix'   [Inventory dated 18 July, 1635, accompanying the will, amounts to £311 11s 10d]

The date of the will, and the entry on the 8th July, 1635, of his burial in the Parish Register, prove that the monumental Tablet formerly in the Church was incorrect as to the year of his death (see p 316)   In like manner the age of Thomas Church, which is there given as seventy-one, is apparently an error, for, according to the deed just quoted, his father was already dead in 1560, that is, seventy-five years before.

Of the seven successive Saboth Church's, a few particulars not given in the pedigree, may here be added

The *first* SABOTH CHURCH purchased on 20th March, 1662-3, from Sir Edward Minshull of Stoke, Kt., for £180, two fields in Broad Lane, Nantwich called *Peartree field* and *Peartree Meadow*.   These lands descended to the *next* SABOTH CHURCH, who sold them for £320, on 16th Feb 1696-7, to his nephew, John Bromhall, Esq *   According to a Rate Book,† dated 1691, these lands, and the house *("Church's Mansion")* where Saboth Church then lived   were assessed as follows —

	s	d
"Mr Churches ho[use] & orchard [Hospital Street end]	2	8½ "
" More his land at Broad Lane	4	10½ "
" More his field and Barne	7	3¾ "

This Saboth Church was named to be taken into custody with thirteen other Cheshire gentlemen, who, being loyal to the Stuart dynasty, were disaffected to William III, in 1696 ‡   The tradition of the family is that he was detained a prisoner three days.

---

* Family deeds, now in possession of Mrs Church

† Peres G F Wilbraham, Esq , Delamere

‡ The original Warrant, signed by Thomas Lee and Roger Mainwaring, by order of the Lord-Lieut of the County, empowering Roger Mainwaring and Cornett John Johnson, and the town Constables, to take the several persons named therein into custody, and to search their several houses for arms and horses, was dated 10th March, 1695-6   It will be found printed *in extenso* in J H Hanshall's *History of Cheshire*, 1823, pp 499—500 *note*

The *third* Saboth Church married into a respectable family named Wolfe, of Shaving-ton, the marriage settlement dated 10th Feb 1723-4, mentions the following property, which remained in the family until within a few years ago.

" All that one Meadow in N with the Barn standing thereupon, lying next to a pasture commonly called *Ridley Field* One Messuage and one Shop with their Appurtenances situate in High Town adjoining to the *Pudding Lane* [Castle Street], and one Messuage, Stable and Garden, situate in *Pudding Lane* &c in the possession of John Church* and Elizabeth Bagnall widow as undertenants of the same Four cottages in Pepper Street† &c One barn upon the Snow Hill, halfe a barn lying in the Water Load, and six dozen Leads of Walling " &c

The above was the marriage portion of Anne Wolfe,‡ who died in Jan 1736-7, and was buried at Wybunbury, on 1st Feb following, leaving issue *Elizabeth, Hannah, Martha, Sabbath,* and *Thomas* Saboth Church married secondly Rebecca Wolfe, of Shavington, on 29th Oct 1737, and had issue *Martha,* and *Charles*. He appears to have lived in Shavington, Willaston, and Nantwich, at different periods of his life. The *fourth* Saboth Church resided on his property at Newtown, in Nantwich, where until recently the family have been located The *fifth* Saboth Church, whose eldest son was born before his father's marriage, willed his estate to his second son, Thomas, whose son and grandson wasted the patrimony, and brought the family to poverty. The *sixth* Saboth Church was a farmer in Acton parish, and the *seventh* is still living, a septuagenarian, and childless, at Acton.

In *Harl MSS* 2119, f 183, is a rough drawing of the Arms of the Church family similar to the blazon given on page 316 A Crest is also added, which may be described as follows —

CREST.—On a wreath, a greyhound's head erased Sable, spotted and collared Or

* John Church occurs as occupier of this property in a Rate Book of 1691 The house, shop, &c , were sold by Mr Church to the present occupier, Mr William Lovatt, a few years since The illustration on page 415 shows part of the front in High Town, and that on page 110, a side view of the same house in Pudding Lane or Castle Street

† The site of the cottages in Pepper Street was recently purchased from one of the Church family by Mr Joseph Jackson, of Nantwich

‡ It may here be noted that the tradition of *General Wolfe*, of Quebec fame in 1759, having spent his boyhood at the Yew-Tree House, in Acton parish, (as related in *Historical Facts connected with Nantwich,*" &c Printed at Chester, 1851, p 52) cannot be substantiated General Wolfe, who was born at Westerham, in Kent, in 1726, was in no way connected with the neighbourhood of Nantwich , and the local tradition has no better foundation than the fact that a respectable family of that name has been long resident in the vicinity of the town, and the desire of some to connect the brave hero with their own county

Church of Nantwich, and Betton co. Salop.

Authorities Harl MSS 2119 and 1535, Nantwich Parish Registers, Wills at Chester, Wilb MS Journal, Visitation 1613, Family Deeds, &c
The descent of the Shopshire family being continued by the present representative of the family, Alexander W Radford-Norcup, of Betton Hall, Esq

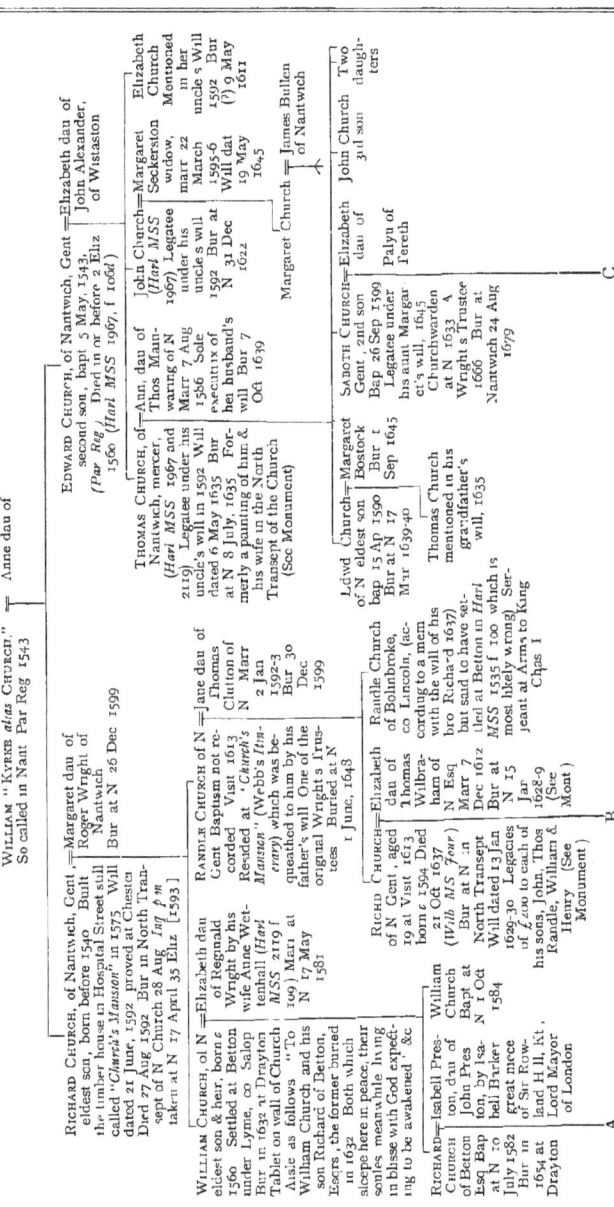

WILLIAM "KYRKE alias CHURCH." So called in Nant Par Reg 1543 = Anne dau of

EDWARD CHURCH, of Nantwich, Gent = Elizabeth dau of second son, bapt 5 May, 1543, John Alexander, (*Par Reg*), Died in or before 2 Eliz of Wistaston 1560 (*Harl MSS* 1967, f 106d)

Elizabeth Church Mentioned in her uncle s Will 1592 Bur (?) 9 May 1611

John Church = Margaret (*Harl MSS* Seckerston 1967) Legatee widow, under his marr 22 uncle s will March 1592 Bur at 1595-6 N 31 Dec Will dat 1622 19 May 1645

Thomas Church, of = Ann, dau of Nantwich, mercer, Thos Mann-(*Harl MSS* 1967 and waring of N 2119) Legatee under his Marr 7 Aug uncle's will in 1592 Will 1586 Sole dated 6 May 1635 Bur executrix of at N 8 July, 1635 For- her husband's merly a painting of him & will Bur 7 his wife in the North Oct 1639 Transept of the Church (See Monument)

Margaret Church = James Bullen of Nantwich

John Church Two 3rd son daugh-ters

RICHARD CHURCH, of Nantwich, Gent, = Margaret dau of eldest son, born before 1540 Built Roger Wright of 1560 the timber house in Hospital Street still Nantwich called "*Church's Mansion*" in 1575 Will Bur at N 26 Dec 1599 dated 21 June, 1592 proved at Chester Died 27 Aug 1592 Bur in North Tran-sept of N Church 28 Aug *Inq p m* taken at N 17 April 35 Eliz [1593]

RANDLE CHURCH of N = Jane dau of Gent Baptism not re- Thomas corded Visit 1613 Clutton of Resided at "*Church's* N Marr Mansion*" (Webb's *Itin-* 2 Jan erary*) which was be- 1592-3 queathed to him by his Bur 30 father's will One of the Dec original Wright's Trus- 1599 tees Buried at N 1 June, 1648

Lloyd Church = Margaret of N eldest son Bostock bap 15 Ap 1590 Bur 1 Bur at N 17 Sep 1645 Mar 1639-40 Legatee under his aunt Margar et's will, 1645 Thomas Church mentioned in his gra^ndfather's will, 1635

Saboth Church = Elizabeth Gent, 2nd son dau of Bap 26 Sep 1599 Palyn of Churchwarden Fereth at N 1633 A Wright s Trustee 1666 Bur at Nantwich 24 Aug 1679

WILLIAM CHURCH, of N = Elizabeth dau eldest son & heir, born c of Reginald 1560 Settled at Betton Wright by his under Lyme, co Salop wife Anne Wet-Bur in 1634 at Drayton tenhall (*Harl* Tablet on wall of Church MSS 2119 f at N (?) Mari at Antie as follows "To N 17 May Wilham Church and his 1581 son Richard of Betton, Esqrs., the former buried in 1632 Both which sleepe here in peace, their soules meanwhile living in blisse with God expecti-ng to be awakened". &c

RICHARD CHURCH = Elizabeth of N Gent, aged dau of 19 at Visit 1613 Thomas born c 1594 Died Wilbra-21 Oct 1637 ham of Bur at N in N Esq North Transept Marr 7 Will dated 13 Jan Dec 1612 1629-30 Legacies Bur at of £400 to each of N 15 his sons, John, Thos Jan Randle, William & 1628-9 Henry (See (See Monument) Mont)

Randle Church of Bolinbroke, co Lincoln, (ac-cording to a mem with the will of his bro Richard 1637) but said to have set-tled at Betton in *Harl MSS* 1535 f 100 which is most likely wrong) Ser-jeant at Arms to King Chas I

RICHARD = Isabell Pres-CHURCH ton, dau of of Betton John Pres Esq Bap ton, by Isa-at N 10 bell Barker July 1582 great niece Bur in of Sir Row-1654 at land H II, Kt Drayton Lord Mayor of London

William Church Bapt at N 1 Oct 1584

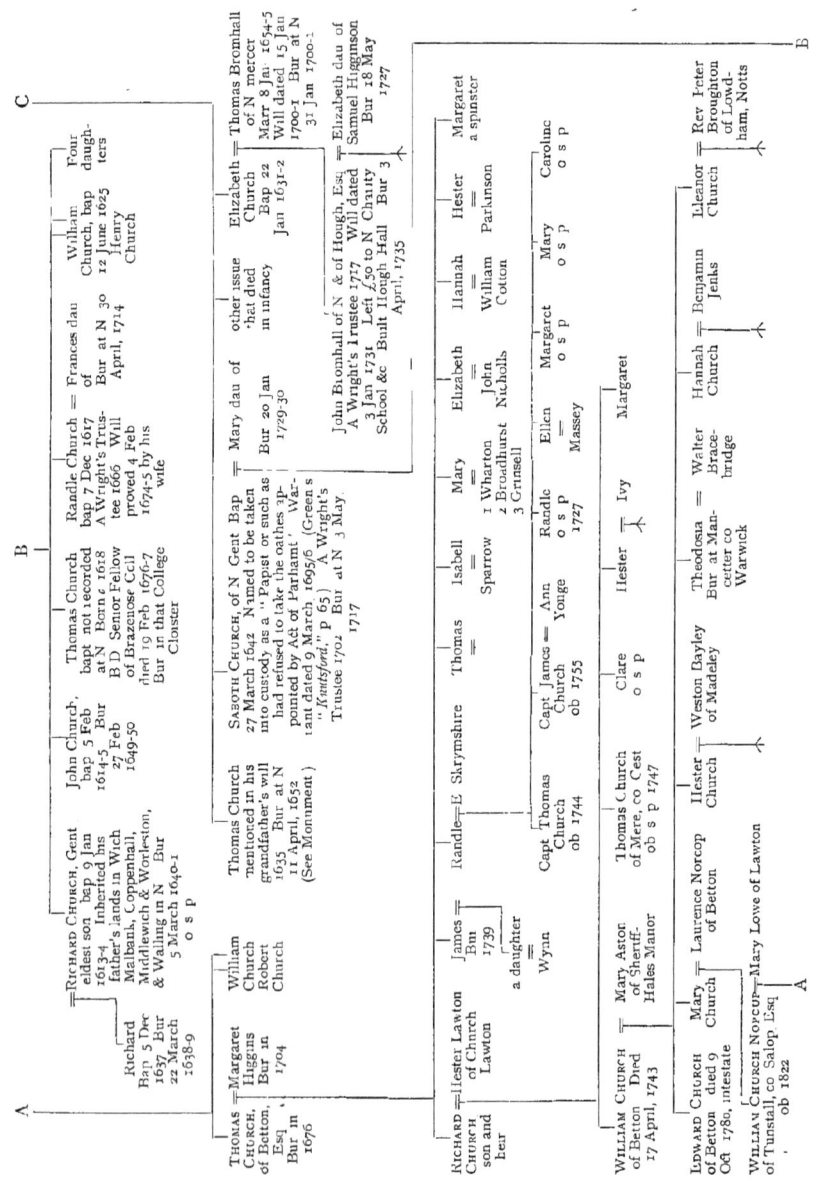

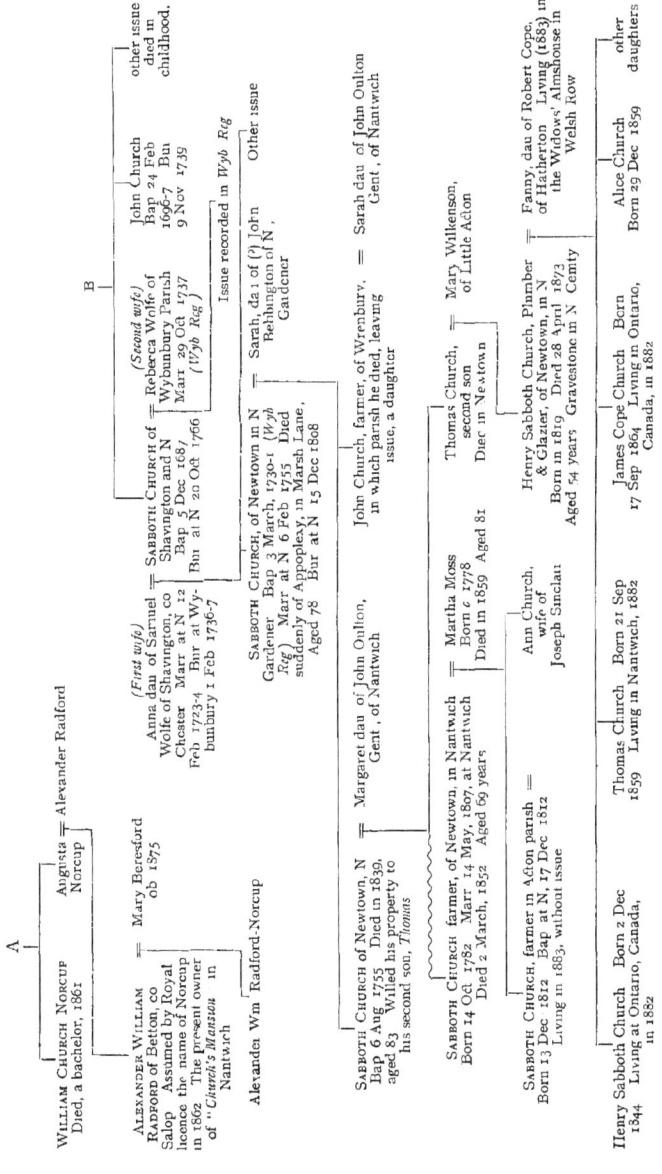

A

WILLIAM CHURCH NORCUP
Died, a bachelor, 1861

Augusta = Alexander Radford
Norcup

ALEXANDER WILLIAM = Mary Beresford
RADFORD of Betton, co   ob 1875
Salop Assumed by Royal
licence the name of Norcup
in 1862 The present owner
of "Church's Mansion" in
Nantwich

Alexander Wm Radford-Norcup

B

(First wife)
Anna dau of Samuel = SABBOTH CHURCH of = (Second wife)
Wolfe of Shavington, co   Shavington and N   Rebecca Wolfe of
Chester Marr at N 12   Bap 5 Dec 168/   Wybunbury Parish
Feb 1723-4 Bur at Wy-   Bur at N 20 Oct 1766   Marr 29 Oct 1737
bunbury 1 Feb 1736-7   (Wyb Reg)

John Church
Bap 24 Feb
1696-7 Bur
9 Nov 1739

other issue
died in
childhood.

Issue recorded in Wyb Reg

SABBOTH CHURCH, of Newtown in N = Sarah, dau of (?) John   Other issue
Gardener Bap 3 March, 1730-1 (Wyb   Rehbington of N,
Reg) Marr at N 6 Feb 1755 Died   Gardener
suddenly of Apoplexy, in Marsh Lane,
Aged 78 Bur at N 15 Dec 1808

John Church, farmer, of Wrenbury, = Sarah dau of John Oulton
in which parish he died, leaving   Gent, of Nantwich
issue, a daughter

SABBOTH CHURCH of Newtown, N = Margaret dau of John Oulton,
Bap 6 Aug 1755 Died in 1839,   Gent, of Nantwich
aged 83 Willed his property to
his second son, Thomas

SABBOTH CHURCH farmer, of Newtown, in Nantwich = Martha Moss   Thomas Church, = Mary Wilkenson,
Born 14 Oct 1782 Marr 14 May, 1807, at Nantwich   Born c 1778   second son   of Little Acton
Died 2 March, 1852 Aged 69 years   Died in 1859 Aged 81   Died in Newtown

SABBOTH CHURCH, farmer in Acton parish = Ann Church,   Henry Sabboth Church, Plumber = Fanny, dau of Robert Cope,
Born 13 Dec 1812 Bap at N, 17 Dec 1812   wife of   & Glazier, of Newtown, in N   of Hatherton Living (1883) in
Living in 1883, without issue   Joseph Sinclair   Born in 1819 Died 28 April 1873   the Widows' Almshouse in
Aged 54 years Gravestone in N Cemty   Welsh Row

Henry Sabboth Church Born 2 Dec   Thomas Church Born 21 Sep   James Cope Church Born   Alice Church   other
1844 Living at Ontario, Canada,   1859 Living in Nantwich, 1882   17 Sep 1864 Living in Ontario,   Born 29 Dec 1859   daughters
in 1882   Canada, in 1882

THE MAINWARING FAMILY

The MAINWARINGS were connected with Nantwich for about three hundred years. Three separate branches, that settled here late in the fifteenth century, are traceable to a common ancestor, the eldest branch descending from illegitimate issue of *Sir John Main-waring*, of Over-Peover, eldest son of RANDLE MAINWARING, ESQ of the same place, who died at an advanced age in 1456, and the two younger branches from *Hugh*, and *William*, respectively fourth and fifth sons of Randle Mainwaring, of Carincham, who was the third son of the said RANDLE MAINWARING, ESQ, of Over-Peover

First—*The eldest Mainwaring line*   Slight variations occur in the earlier descents in different old MS pedigrees,* which cannot now be rectified, as no Inquisitions or deeds relating to this branch of the family are known to exist   A few particulars from the Registers, and Wills at Chester, &c, however, prove the correctness of the later descents in the subjoined pedigree

Thus, JOHN MAINWARING, gent, who resided in the Beast Market, in Beam Street, mentions in his Will, dated 24th April, 1581, his eldest son, *Roger*, his wife, *Cicilie*, his daughter-in-law, *Margery* (wife of the said Roger Mainwaring)   and his grandchildren, *Richard*, and *Margaret*   He gives unto his "loving sister *Ales Crockett* one Crowne of gould of the value of vˢ for a token," and to his son-in-law, *Thomas Minshull*, "a bible."

ROGER MAINWARING, who succeeded his father, John Mainwaring, resided at Beam Street-end (*cf* page 124), and acquired a very considerable property in town and elsewhere, which is minutely described in his Will and Inquisition *post mortem*, both of which are extant. A few extracts from his Will which is printed in full in vol liv Chet Soc Publ, and occupies nearly fourteen pages will not be uninteresting

"I bequethe unto my lovinge wief MARGRET M my chief mansion house at the townsende of Namptwiche wᵗʰ all the buildings and gardens thereunto app'teyninge, three fields called *Tynkers Crofts* lyinge together adioyninge on the southeste and southeside of the same house , ' &c   "all my lands in *Woolston woode* called *Marchforde* grounde conteyninge five fieldes and two meadowes wᵗʰ a new barne ," &c   "two howses and gardens wᵗʰ a litle pece of waste sometime called the *Mixon* in the *church lane* in Namptewiche ," &c   "lands and gardens called *Masons yardes* in N " &c

"I give &c unto THOMAS M my youngest sonne my beste silver pott being all guilte and also my beste sworde," &c   "five pounds yearlie ,"   and £100 when he shall come of age &c   "I give, &c unto RICHARD M my eldest sonne all suche howses, lands &c as are before given unto my wief after her deathe or decease" &c   "two messuages in Beamestrete in N one called the *Saracens hea*," &c   "one other howse in the same strete wherein my mother [Cicely] dwelleth, nexte the *horsemylle* of Henry Manwaringe of Carincham esquier " &c

"several wiche-houses and walling , and land that had been leased by the late Abbot of Combermere for 80 years to his *grandfather* OLIVER M , and his *father* JOHN M , both deceased"   "one burgage in Berwick upon Tweed lyinge neare nnto the northweste gate of pallace wᵗʰin the said towne of Berwick, wᶜʰ said howse was purchased and morgaged for debte dulye owinge unto me by Roberte Arderne gent customer of the same towne and the same is fforfeited unto me divers yeares sithence [since] the seekinge for the possession whereof hathe beene omytted and delaied by reason of *my service and goinge unto Ireland ,"* &c   "my greate cheyne of goulde with all my goulde buttons" &c.

apparel, swords, daggers, armour, "*bookes imprinted or written*," deed chests, and "one other cheste of imbowed worke of walnutte tree beinge a Frenche cheste gotten at Newhaven warres" &c

* This will be seen by collating the pedigree printed in the "*Visitation of Cheshire* 1580," (Harl Soc Publ) taken from *Harl MSS* 1424, f 106 with other pedigrees in *Harl MSS* 1535 f 340, in the Add MSS (British Museum) 24 444, p 77, and in other volumes of MS pedigrees of Cheshire families in private libraries, notably at Dorfold Hall, near Nantwich and Condover Hall, Salop, &c

"Unto my younger sonne JOHN M two howses lyinge togeather in the Beamestrete the one *Cheynye Halle*" &c   "and the other in the tenure of *my aunte Alice Crokett* wydowe" &c

"I give &c unto MARY M my eldest daughter" £200 &c   "unto my other daughter MARGARET" [subsequently sole heiress to his estate] £200 &c

"I give &c unto my nephewe ALEXANDER MAINWARING £16 13s 4d , and to *John Mainwaring* his basterd brother 6s 8d " &c   "Unto my sister ANNE SWINGLEHURST 20 nobles [£6 13s 4d] &c   "Unto my brother [in-law] *Thomas Minshull* one angell of golde [10s] for a token, and to my neese *Margarett* his daughter 40s , unto my cosen *Robert Croket* the elder tailor 10s " &c   "Unto *Thoms Maisterson esquire* my faithfull ffather in lawe and good frend on[e] portegewe of goulde " [£3 10s] &c   "and to my mother in lawe *Katheryne* his wyfe twoe angells of goulde to be made in a ringe wth my name in it to be sente unto her into Irelande " &c   "and lastlie to be geven and distributed amongst the poore people my neighbours in the towne of Namptwiche the daye of my buriall" [sum left blank] &c   Total legacies £600
also a charity left to the poor of Nantwich (see page 358)

"And my desier is that my bodie may be buried at the upper ende of the highe chauncell on the north este side of the same above the door called the *revestry* door wthin the churche of Namptwich " &c   "and at both endes of the grave may be raised the marbell pillars and the greate tombstone of marble that came out of Ireland as the mason shall best devise the same " &c   "I will that there be a table of brasse to be made at London whereon shalbe written the date and yeare of our Lorde of my deccase out of this lieff and also what yssue or children I then hadd wth all their severall names and the same table of brasse to be set in a faire stone in the church wall even righte over the verie middest of my said tombe stone " &c *

The above Will, which is dated 18th April, 1589, was proved on the 1st May, 1590, the testator, Roger Mainwaring, having died on the 1st March, leaving Richard Mainwaring his son and heir, aged thirteen years five months eleven days, as stated in his Inquisition *post mortem* taken on the 2nd Sept in the same year   Roger Mainwaring was "Auditor in Ireland." It is very remarkable that several of the Maisterson family of this town held important positions in Ireland, and were the contemporaries of Sir Roger Wilbraham, also a native of Nantwich, who was then Solicitor General for Ireland

The coat of Arms assigned to Roger Mainwaring (*Harl MSS* 1424) was blazoned as follows —

     ARMS —*Argent, two bars Gules within a bordure† goboné Or and Sable*
     CREST —*An ass's head proper, erased, maned, and haltered Or*

After the death of Roger Mainwaring, his widow, Margaret, was re-married at Nantwich, to Sir Dudley Norton, whose Funeral Certificate is as follows.—

NORTON FUNERAL CERTIFICATE ‡

"ARMS —*Argent on a chevron azure between three crescents of the second a crescent of the first for difference* [Norton], *impaling Ermine a chevron Azure between three garbs Or* " [Maisterson]

---

* These directions for erecting a tomb and monument to his memory were never carried out , nor is his burial recorded in the Parish Register

† The "*bordure goboné*" was probably used to prove the family had become legally legitimate   (See Boutell's *English Heraldry*, p 197)

‡ This Funeral Certificate, which supplies a missing generation of the Norton family in the pedigree given on page 124 *note*, has already been printed in Dr Howard's "*Miscellanea Genealogica et Heraldica*" vol 1 p 139, from a Book of Funeral Certificates, Ayscough MSS

" The Honᴮᴸᴱ Sᴿ Dudly Norton Knᴛ principall Secretary to the State and one of the privie Councel departed this mortal Life the 27th of July 1634   He had to wife Margrᵗ Dᵣ of Sᵢ Thomas Masterson of Fearnes in the County of Waxford Kᵗ by whome he had Issue *Dudly Norton* his only Sonn who hath to Wife Katherin Dᵣ of Captⁿ Hercie Wolferston of Statfould Esqr in Staffordshire by whome he hath Issue *Henry Norton*   She was relict of John Bromfeild of Bullthornes in Staffordshire

Margaret wife of Sᵢ Dudly Norton before mar[ried] to Rogeᵢ Manneringe sometime Remembrancer of the Exchequer of Ireland

Sᵣ Dudly Norton was buried in the Choue of Christ Church Dublin yᵉ 30th of July "

Mainwaring Pedigree.

(ELDER LINE)

Authorities   Harl MSS 1424, &c , Wills, Parish Registers, &c

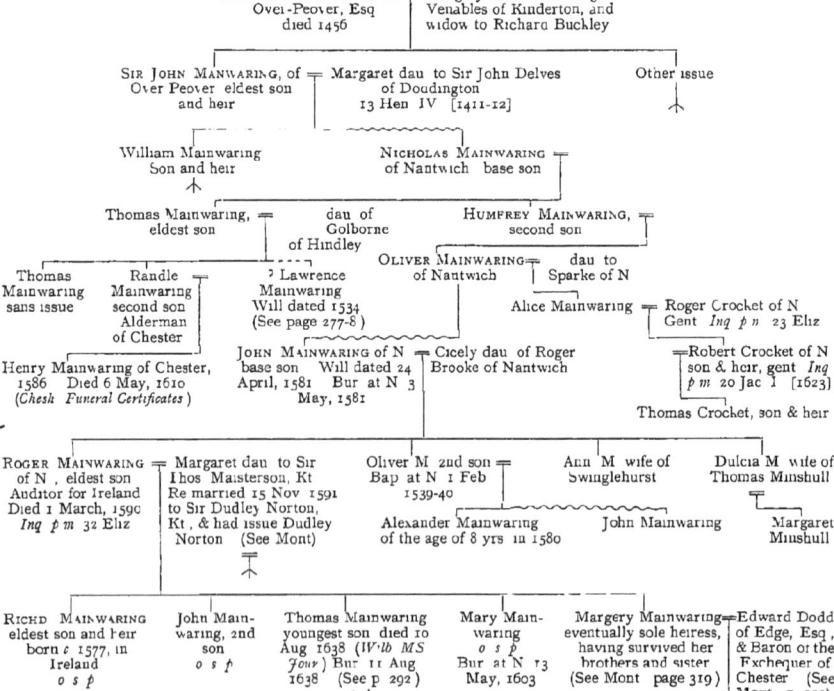

Of the *second Mainwaring line*, the descendants of HUGH MAINWARING, of Nantwich, fourth son of Randle Mainwaring, of Carincham, no reliable information has occurred beyond what is contained in the Will of his grandson, ROGER, and in the Inquisition *post mortem* of his (probably) great-grandson, HUGH   Abstracts of these are as follows —

1.—WILL OF ROGER MAINWARING, dated 1 Oct 1510 *

" My body to be buried in Nantwich Church , I bequeath to my brother *William Mainwaring* my best Gowne my best Dublet my best Hose and my best Shirte , to my brother *Hugh* my second Gowne furred with fox , to my brother *Robert* four yards of tane to make him a gowne   I bequeath to Robert Mainwaring John Bret Thomas Symcock Thomas Wright Richard Ince William Maisterson Nicholas Savage and Rondell Anteley each of them one mark of money [13s 4d] a jacket a pair of hose a cow and a calf   "I will that if *Margaret* my wife depart that Thomas Masterson haue my tacke of Swanley the wch is 15th yere behind   The residue of my Landes and goods I give and bequeath to Margaret my wife the time of her life and then I will that they be devided between my *two children,* and the cheefe place at the *Beyme Streete end* I will that   Glegg haue it beside his pte and if ought come to the one of my children I will it remayn to the other and for default of issue betwixt them both it to remaine to the heirs males of my brothers *Oliver*, *Robert* and *Hugh* as it appears by a tail deed   I ordene and make my executors Margaret my wife, and Richard Brooke her brother, and the overseers that this be performed the honble father in God William Bishop of Lincoln in whom I putt all my trust and under him John Egerton John Mainwaring Ralf Delves William Hondford and Richard Cholmondeley Esquires, these being witnesses Sr Nicholas Mainwaring my curate, William Mainwaring gent , and Rondell Anteley with others

Given the day and year aforesaid "

2 —INQUISITION *post mortem* OF HUGH MAINWARING   19 Jac I †

"Inquisition taken at Wich Malbank on 28 Sept 1621, before Hugh Mainwaring Esq Escheator, and Peter Daniell Esq feodary, &c finds that Hugh Mainwaring, of Wich Malbank, gentleman, died seised of a burgage house and garden, held of the Barons of Wich Malbank in socage, value per ann 2s , three acres of land and three acres of pasture commonly called the *Brown Hills* in Wich Malbank, value per ann 5s   The said Hugh died on 2nd April last past‡ [1621] leaving *George Mainwaring* his son and heir, aged 13 years, on the 19th June last past ' [1621]

Of the *youngest branch* of the MAINWARINGS of Nantwich some interesting information is here given from Inquisitions *post mortem* and Wills, &c

I HUMPHREY MAINWARING, who died at a very advanced age in 1583, had six sons, *Oliver, Thomas, John, Laurence, Randle* and *Roger*, all of whom, except the first named, attained to manhood, married, and left issue   He had also seven daughters, one of whom, *Alice*, became the mother of the celebrated Lord Chief Justice, Sir Ranulphe Crewe.

1 THOMAS MAINWARING died in his father's lifetime, and by his Will (an extract of which has already been given on page 284), he bequeathed to his father his "golde ringe desyringe and prayinge hym to stand good grandfather and father" to his wife and children   He left legacies to his daughters, namely to *Alice* £40, to *Ann* 40 marks [£26 13s 4d], to *Margaret* his bastard daughter £10, to his wife, *Margaret*, two crofts in Henhull, one

* Taken from a copy of the Will preserved in *Harl MSS* 1967, f 131
† Public Record Office
‡ Thomas Wilbraham, Esq of Nantwich, in his MS Journal, enters as follow —
          " Hugh Manwaring of the Crowne died 2 Apr 1621 "

wiche-house of six leads, and his tithes of corn and hay in Nantwich, Alvaston, Willaston, and Woolstanwood, as long as she remained his widow, his other lands being left to his sons, *Thomas, Matthew, John* and *Richard*. He appointed as his executors his father, his wife, his brother *John*, and his brothers-in-law *John Leech* and *John Crewe*.

His Inquisition *post mortem*, taken on 29th Sept 21 Eliz [1579] finds that "he died seised of 2 messuages, 30 acres of land, 10 acres of meadow, 12 acres of pasture, and 2 of wood in Monkes Copenhall, 3 acres of land and 2 of meadow in Nantwich all held of the Queen by the 100th part of a Knight's fee, value per ann. £3 8s 0d, also a salt-pit and a moiety of a salt-pit in Nantwich in a place called *Burwaites Hold* [which he granted to ffeoffees, namely, John Leech of Nantwich and Laurence Wright of Huxley] to the use of Margaret his wife for life, 2 burgages and 3 gardens in Nantwich, a moiety of certain tithes of corn, grain, and herbage, annually growing &c in Willaston and Alvaston, and a moiety of all and singular the tithes of hay &c in Nantwich, and a 6th part of such tithes of corn and grain in Woolstanwood The said Thos. M. died seized of the above premises and tithes, but long before the said Thomas had any interest in the said tithes, Queen Elizabeth by her Letters Patent dated 23 June in the fifth of her reign [1563] granted the said tithes to Randle Maynwaring his executors and assigns from the feast of the Annunciation then last past [25 March, 1563] for term of 21 years [*cf* page 288]

The said Thos M died on the 5th Jan 15 Eliz. [1572-3] leaving Thomas Mainwaring his son and heir aged 20 years 2 months '

2 JOHN MAINWARING, third son of Humphrey Mainwaring, by his Will dated 6 Dec 1596, left his interest in the tithes of corn of the parish Church of Dawlish, in Devon, to executors for the use of his wife *Margerie*, and his daughters, *Cicelie, Elizabeth, Margerie, Margaret,* and *Dorothy,* and his son *Laurence Mainwaring* To his son, *Humphrey,* his signet ring and best wine bowl, to his son *Roger,* his wine bowl "wch my uncle Olyver gave me," to his mother-in-law *Clutton,* a gilt spoon, to his brother-in-law, Richard Clutton, his "brooch, ' to his brother Rondull Mainwaring, "two paire of spectacles," to his "cosen" Thos Mainwaring, his ' dyall," to William Ince, his "shorte sworde wth the dagger belonging to the same, ' to Dorothy, "vi silver spoones of the appostles, and to Laurence my sonne the other half dosen of silver spoones of the appostles" His Inventory amounted to £127 14s 4d

3 RANDLE MAINWARING, fifth son of Humphrey Mainwaring, by his Will dated 31st Jan 1610, left 40s towards mending the leads over his pew in the Church of Nantwich To his wife, Ann, to his eldest son *John,* to his son *Rondull,* and daughter *Ellen Minshull,* (children by a former marriage) and to his sons *William, Thomas,* and *Roger,* by his second wife, he left various legacies, and his household goods, the Inventory of which, taken on 23rd Feb 1610, amounted to £419 9s 9d

His Inquisition *post mortem*, taken on 23rd Sep. 9 Jac. I [1612] finds that he died on 18th Feb last past [1611-12], leaving *John Mainwaring* his son and heir, aged forty years and upwards at the time of the taking of the Inquisition. He left a wiche-house between Wood Street on the east side and little Wood Street on the west side, together with the *lignarus* [wood-room] and profits thereto belonging to trustees, to the use of his sons, *Thomas* and *John,* with remainder to *William* and *Roger* in succession

His widow, Ann Mainwaring, left a Will, (which is in the handwriting of "*Thomas Malbone*" of Nantwich, who, together with *Hugh Price*, witnessed the same), dated 12th Aug 1615, in which she desires 'to bee buryed in the p'ishe Church of Wich Malbank neere unto my late husband," and bequeaths legacies to her sons, *William*, *Thomas*, and *Roger*, who were all under the age of eighteen years, to her "sister Margery, wife of Thomas Ley clarke pson. of Muckleston," to her brother-in-law Roger Mainwaring, to Margaret Mainwaring "my brother Roger Mainwaringes daughter a Crowne in goulde and my Saddle wth ytt furnyture." The Inventory of her goods, taken on 1st Dec 1615, amounts to £437 6s 8d

(*a*) JOHN MAINWARING, the eldest son of the above Randle Mainwaring, made a very curious Will, (dated 13th Sept 1638) in which, after a long profession of his faith, he says, "I give vnto Mr Saiing or to some of the godlie men in his absence to speake some fewe words to the people that shall gather att my fun'all* that they be admonished of ther mortalitie and be taught how they must dispose them selues in this life &c. x^s ' [10s.] . . . . . . "I doe give vnto my cussen John Manwaringe my vncle Roger's sonne a booke called m^r Perkins vppon the creede in lewe of my love towards him," . . . "vnto my Uncle Weston a booke called the deceitfulness of mans heart in lewe ' of my love towards him,' . . . "vnto my cussin Ric Bagnall towe bookes, the one called m^r Perkinst vpon Mathewe & the other called Barkers sermons in lewe my love towards him," . . "vnto John Pratchett blacksmith a booke called the casts of conscience in lewe of my love towards him " He makes his wife, *Jane*, his sole executrix, and gives to his nieces *Arne* and *Martha Manwaring* x^s [10s] "a peece to buy ether of them a ringe in lewe of my good will towards them " Inventory, dated 12th Jan 1638-9, amounts to £257 3s 10d

(*b*) WILLIAM MAINWARING, another son of the above *Randle* Mainwaring, died more than a year before his half-brother John Mainwaring. By his Will, dated 22nd April, 1637, he left several houses in Nantwich, lands called *Daubies Crofts* in Tarporley, lands called *sitchfields*, messuages, tithes in Willaston, Alvaston, Woolstanwood, and wichehouses in Nantwich the lease of *Walfield* and *Birchin-lane* ground &c. to his wife Martha, his sole executrix, until his daughters, *Ann* and *Martha*, attain the age of twenty years. Inventory of goods dated 15th May, 1637, amounts to £295 2s 10d.

His Inquisition *post mortem*, taken on 19th Sep. 13 Car I [1637] states that he died on 22nd April last past [1637] leaving *Ann Mainwaring*, aged seven years ten months two days, and *Martha Mainwaring*, aged five years three months eight days, his daughters and heiresses.

II. THOMAS MAINWARING, who died in the life-time of his father, Humphrey Mainwaring, married Margaret, daughter to Randall Crewe, of Nantwich, by whom he had four sons, *Thomas*, *Matthew*, *John* and *Richard*, and three daughters, *Alice*, *Anne*, and *Margeret*.

1 THOMAS MAINWARING, the eldest son, married Margaret, daughter to Richard Lee, of Lea, in Wybunbury parish, and had issue six sons, *Thomas*, *George*, *Richard*, *Matthew*,

---

* See page 36, where this curious burial custom, known as *lating*, is mentioned

† The book here mentioned was probably "*Exposit on of Christ's Sermon on the Mount*," by William Perkins, folio, 1608

Arthur, and *John*   He died in Feb 1645-6, shortly after Inquisitions *post mortem* ceased to be taken.   His Will is not now preserved at Chester, but his death is mentioned in a letter written by his nephew, Roger Wilbraham, Esq., of Dorfold Hall, to John Crewe, Esq., of Utkinton, on receiving intelligence of the death of Sir Ranulph Crewe, Kt., of Crewe Hall, who was cousin to the said Thomas Mainwaring.   The letter, which contains interesting particulars relating to the state of the county just after the surrender of the City of Chester into the hands of Parliamentary forces, is here printed in full from the original now in the possession of J P Earwaker, Esq., as follows —

[Endorsed] "*ffor y*ᵉ *wor*ˡˡ [worshipful] *John Crew esqr at Westminster these*"
"Sr

I mourne wᵗʰ yoʷ for yoʳ loss in yᵉ deathe of yᵉ good ould man, but reioyce wᵗʰ yoʷ both in yᵉ goodnes of him who pᵣserued him vnto yoʷ so longe, and in his mercies who hath giuen yoʷ (I hope) a heart to submit vnto his good will and pleasure   the truth is he was yᵉ *glorie* of his p[ro]fession, yᵉ *grace* of his Countrey, and a *propp of comfort* to his frends, amoungst whom ther is few more weakned then my selfe ther beinge not many more interested in his affections   but this learnes vs how rightly to *value creature* comforts, to be thankfull for them whilst we enioy them, but not to sit [set] oʳ Rests vpon them   Sʳ yoʳ two ould cosins on whom yoʷ were so tender are now p[ar]ted, Thomas [Mainwaring] being 87 had he liued vntill August, dyed yᵉ 13ᵗʰ of this pʳsent, and knew of yᵉ deathe of sʳ Randull, but spake much of him   Mathew [Mainwaring] yet liues to mourne both, for whom poore ould man he sheeds more teares then yoʷ woulde thinke possible to come from such drie eyes

we are now (thanks he to god) in possession of Chester, and vthington,* I hope, will shortly possess many goods yᵗ [that] were carried thither   yoʳ *writinge* sʳ R B [?] p[ro]tests vnto me he hath faithfully deliu'ed vnto M Wright, & so hath others, some of yoʳ goods and p[ro]mised more   my la[dy] Gamull† acknowledgeth a guilt boale giuen her by Marrow,‡ for wᶜʰ she wilbe accountable   we are yet in an vnsetled condicon there, though yᵉ p[ar]liamᵗ hath giuen vs a good entrance by giuing vs a Gou'nour we may well confide in   oʳ greatest business wilbe to giue *satisfaction* to yᵉ souldiers for yᵉ mounthes [month's] *pay we* p[ro]mised them to p[re]vent yᵉ Citie [of Chester] from plunder   this not wᵗʰstandinge oʳ engagemᵗ to them, to make good at a mounthes end, and their p[ro]mises to vs to be gone, yet yᵉ Reformathoes§ and yᵉ Lankeshire horse do still irfest yᵉ Countrey and wholy destroy it where they come & will not I feare be gotten out wᵗʰout they be enforced   Hawarden Castle hath articled [i e agreed] to be deliu'ed wᵗʰin xxtie daies yf not releiued   in yᵉ interim a cessacon of armes   yf yᵉ Hoult do so and both adioyned to Chester it would be a great strengthninge to these pts [parts]   I wish Chester may be pʳserued both in its im'unities and priuellages, though it hath hithervnto bin yᵉ ruine of vs all   yoʷ hear oʳ two great lords Chom' [Cholmondeley] & Killm' [Kilmorey] wᵗʰ many of their adherents now cominge vp to compound though they go a *strange way to it* (by Oxford) amoungst these yoʷ will find *Honest H*[ugh] wilbraham whose carriage [i e gentility], I hope (yᵉ Iurie excepted) will pleade his innocense and render him in a better capacitie [i e he will be better able to plead his innocence] then many of yᵉ rest   sʳ Tho[mas] Wilb[raham]‖ is more indisposed in bodie then in mind to come up, his ladie *worse*, hauinge bin hardly able to sett her foote to yᵉ ground this 3 weekes   this I hope by yoʳ good names, [?] my co[usin] J B   [?] & sʳ W B[rereton's]

* The *Crewe* family, and the Wilbrahams of Dorfold favored the cause of the Parliament during the Civil War

† *Lady Gamull*, the wife of Sir Francis Gamull, at whose house in Lower Bridge Street, at Chester, his majesty King Charles I lodged on Wednesday Sep 24th 1645

‡ *Colonel Marrow*, a distingu shed Royalist, whom Burghall, in his *Providence Improved*, calls "a great plunderer "

§ *Reformado i e* an officer, who having lost his men, is continued on whole or half pay   (Bailey's *Dictionary*)

‖ Sir Thomas Wilbraham, of Woodhey, who died in 1660

certificate wilbe no pruudice vnto them, they resoluinge to come so soon as they are able   I pray com'end me to *both* y^r *sistr*, yor selfe, y^e rest of o^r frends as yo^w se[e] them   excuse this hastie scrible, beinge more *af aid to loose* y^e bearer, then eu' [ever] yo^w shall haue cause [to lose] ye true affection of s_r

yor most faithfull frend

and readie kinsman to serue yo^w

Rog^r wilbraham "

" Dat Feb y^e 17th 1645 "

SEAL.

2   MATTHEW MAINWARING, brother to the above Thomas Mainwaring, married Margaret, daughter to Thomas Minshull of Nantwich, by whom he had issue fourteen children   (See Monument)   His name has been handed down as the author of the now very scarce Romance of Vienna,* (4to 1621), a curious specimen of euphuistic writing, which is interspersed with much original poetry, and, what is still more remarkable, contains, in the pages prefacing the story, commendatory verses of considerable merit by his relatives, Thomas Mainwaring, John Mainwaring, Ralph Mainwaring, Richard Minshull, and Thomas Crockett †   The Romance is entitled —

"The Honor of true love and Knighthood, wherein is storied ye valorous atchieuements, famous triumphs, constant love, & finall happines, of the well-deseruing, truly noble and most vaitant Kt Sr Paris of Vienna, and ye most admired amiable Princess, the faire Vienna "   " London Printed for Richard Hawkins, and are to be sould at his shop neere Serjeants Inne in Chancery lane "

Here follows the author's shield of Arms, alluded to in a couplet describing the title, thus —

"If that the bars were red, and scutch'on white,

The coate would shew who did this story write "

Another edition, which, like the earlier one, contains title-page, four preliminary leaves, and 180 pp , was printed at London for

" George Percivall and are to be sould at his shop at ye Signe of ye Bible in fleetstreete neere the Cunditt "

Matthew Mainwaring, like his brother Thomas, lived to see the outbreak and close of the great Civil War *temp* Charles I, and, as may be inferred from the notice of him on page 175, was himself a Royalist in principle   He died in January, 1651-2, having nearly completed the ninetieth year of his age   Another *Matthew Mainwaring,* but whether his son, or nephew, is doubtful, is mentioned as follows in the Burial Register —

" 1647 April 12 Matthew Mainwaring gent , & Constable of Dublin Castle "

There are many entries in the Registers in the latter half of the seventeenth century of the Mainwarings of this town , but further information is required before they can be connected with those in the accompanying pedigree   The last male descendant of the family appears to have been " *John Mainwaring Esq. of Nantwich,*" who was buried at Acton on 20th April, 1766   *(Acton Par Reg)*

---

* Two copies of this work are preserved in the Bodleian Library, Oxford, and another copy was in the library of the late James Crossley, Esq , F S A , of Manchester which was purchased many years ago for £8 10s   Besides these, no other copies are known to exist   It has been proposed to re-print the work for the Chetham Society
† The verses by these local rhymers have recently appeared in an interesting article on Mainwaring s " *Vienna,*" in the *Palatine Note Book*, vol iii, pp 156—159

Mainwaring Pedigree.

(YOUNGER LINE.)

Authorities: Harl. MSS. 1535, f. 347-8; Visitation of Cheshire 1580; Wilbraham MS. Journal; Wills; Parish Registers, &c.

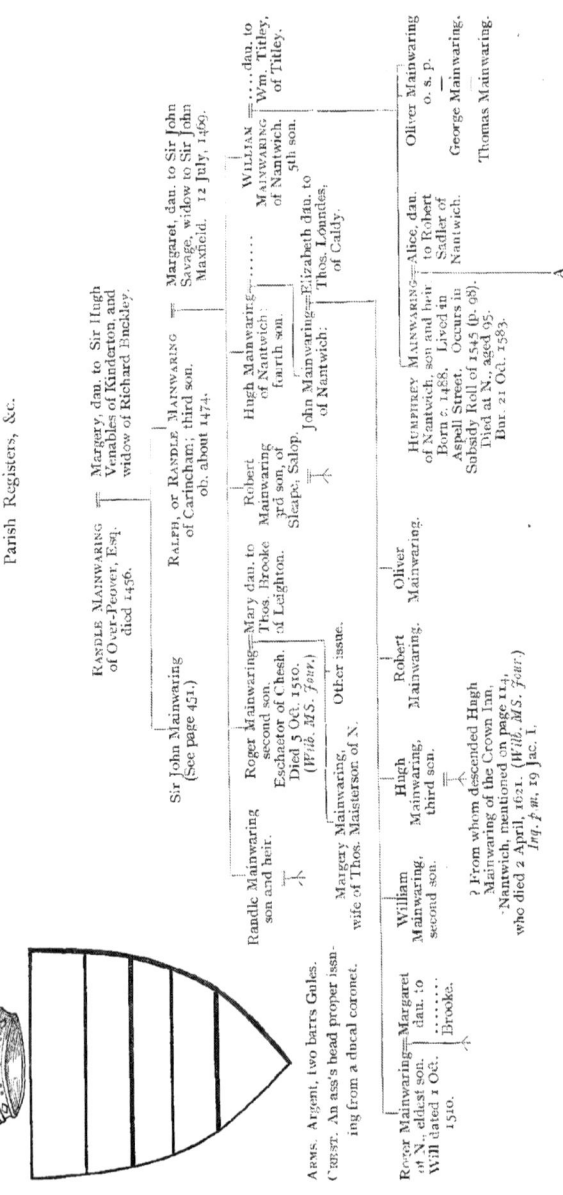

ARMS. Argent, two barrs Gules. CREST. An ass's head proper issuing from a ducal coronet.

RANDLE MAINWARING of Over-Peover, Esq. died 1456. = Margery, dau. to Sir Hugh Venables of Kinderton, and widow of Richard Bnckley.

RALPH, or RANDLE MAINWARING of Carincham; third son. ob. about 1474. = Margaret, dau. to Sir John Savage, widow to Sir John Maxfield. 12 July, 1469.

Sir John Mainwaring (See page 451.)

Roger Mainwaring second son. Escheator of Chesh. Died 5 Oct. 1510. (*Wilb. MS. Jour.*) = Mary dau. to Thos. Brooke of Leighton.

Robert Mainwaring 3rd son, of Sleape, Salop.

Hugh Mainwaring of Nantwich; fourth son.

WILLIAM MAINWARING of Nantwich. 5th son. = ...dau. to Wm. Titley, of Titley.

John Mainwaring of Nantwich. = Elizabeth dau. to Thos. Lowndes, of Cathy.

Randle Mainwaring son and heir.

Margery Mainwaring, wife of Thos. Maisterson of N. — Other issue.

Roger Mainwaring of N., eldest son. Will dated 1 Oct. 1510. = Margaret dau. to .... Brooke.

William Mainwaring, second son.

Hugh Mainwaring, third son.

? From whom descended Hugh Mainwaring of the Crown Inn, Nantwich, mentioned on page 14, who died 2 April, 1621. (*Wilb. MS. Jour.*) *Inq. p. m.* 19 Jac. I.

Robert Mainwaring.

Oliver Mainwaring.

HUMPHREY MAINWARING, son and heir of Nantwich. Born c. 1488. Lived in Aspell Street. Occurs in Subsidy Roll of 1545 (p. 98). Died at N., aged 95. Bur. 21 Oct. 1583. = Alice, dau. to Robert Sadler of Nantwich.

Oliver Mainwaring o. s. p.

George Mainwaring.

Thomas Mainwaring.

A

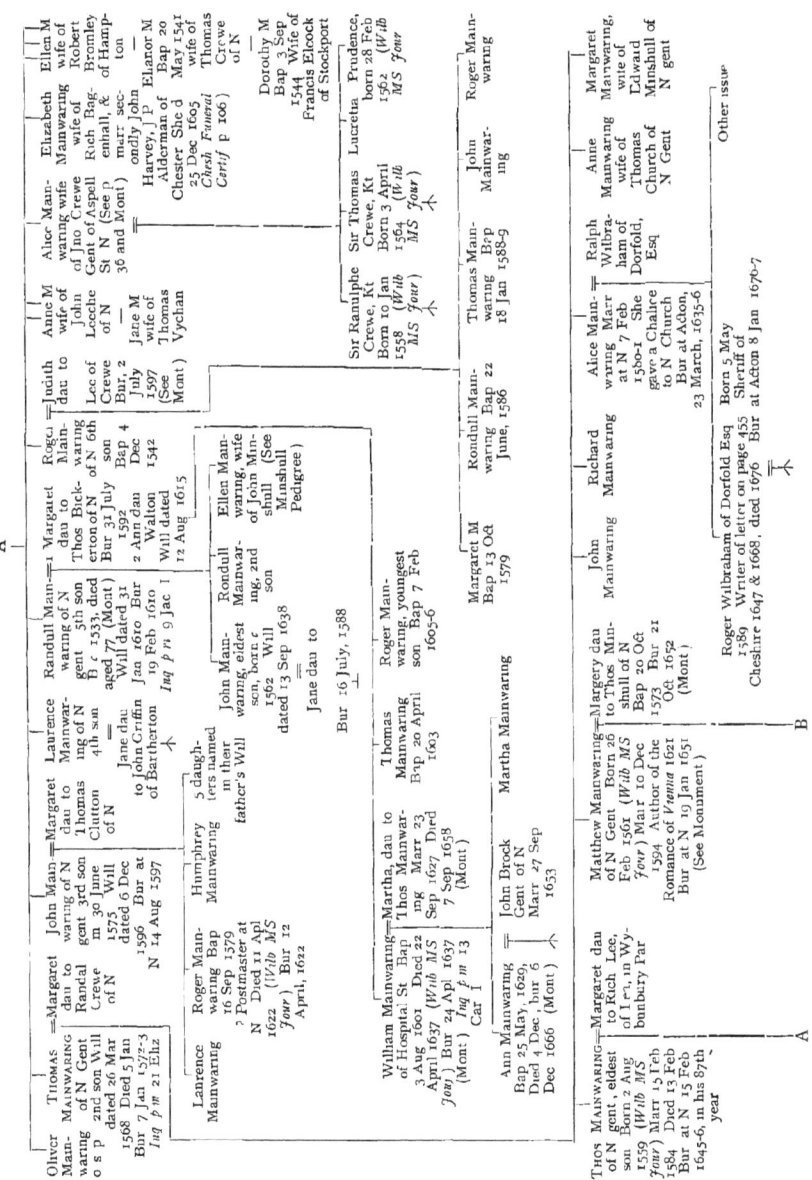

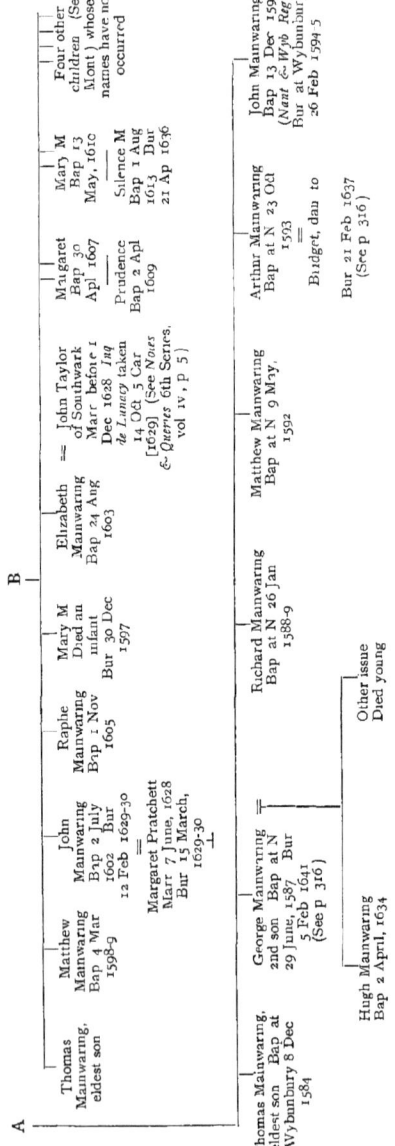

A

Thomas Mainwaring, eldest son

Matthew Mainwaring Bap 4 Mar 1598-9

John Mainwaring Bap 2 July 1602 Bur 12 Feb 1629-30
=
Margaret Pratchett Marr 7 June, 1628 Bur 15 March, 1629-30

Raple Mainwaring Bap 1 Nov 1605

Mary M Died an infant Bur 30 Dec 1597

B

Elizabeth Mainwaring Bap 24 Aug 1603
=
John Taylor of Southwark Marr before 1 Dec 1628 Inq de Lunacy taken 14 Oct 5 Car [1629] (See Notes & Queries 6th Series, vol iv, p 5)

Margaret Bap 30 Apl 1607
Prudence Bap 2 Apl 1609

Mary M Bap 13 May, 1610
Silence M Bap 1 Aug 1613 Bur 21 Ap 1616

Four other children (See Mont) whose names have not occurred

Thomas Mainwaring, eldest son Bap at Wybunbury 8 Dec 1584

George Mainwaring 2nd son Bap at N 29 June, 1587 Bur 5 Feb 1641 (See p 316)

Hugh Mainwaring Bap 2 April, 1634

Other issue Died young

Richard Mainwaring Bap at N 26 Jan 1588-9

Matthew Mainwaring Bap at N 9 May, 1592

Arthur Mainwaring Bap at N 23 Oct 1593
=
Bridget, dau to Bur 21 Feb 1637 (See p 316)

John Mainwaring Bap 13 Dec 1594 (Nant & Wyb Reg) Bur at Wybunbury 26 Feb 1594-5

WETTENHALL AND TOMKINSON FAMILIES.

Like the Maistersons, the WETTENHALLs of Nantwich and its neighbourhood, were a very ancient family   The earliest Wettenhall resident in the town occurs as far back as the fourteenth century, and doubtless the family descended from ancestors that settled in the township of *Wettenhall*, in this county, from which they took their name   In the new edition of Dr Ormerod's "*Cheshire*," (vol III. p 479—480) will be found a revised pedigree of the ancient line, which the editor acknowledges to have been difficult satisfactorily to trace out, owing to the absence of Inquisitions *post mortem* * deeds, &c and the mention of so many bearing the same name, *John* On the second line of descent, (*ibid*, p 480-1) the accompanying pedigree, containing additional information from local registers, and the will of Gabriel Wettenhall, &c , is based, but it is remarkable that few memorials of this once important family have been handed down to these times

In *Harl MSS* 1991, p. 152, is preserved a copy of the will of Gabriel Wettenhall, of which the following is an abstract

Will of Gabriell Wettenhall.

"In the name of God Amen. The 11th Sept 1601 I, Gabriell Wettenhall of the towne of Namptwich, gent , being sick in bodie [&c.] doe make my last will and testament in manner and forme following —

ffirst I give and bequeath my soule to Almighty god [&c] and my body to the earth there to be buried att the discrecion of my exors   *Item.* I give [&c] unto *William W.* my son and heire apparent all and singular my Messuage, wiche-houses, lands, tenements [&c] situate in Wichmalbank, Hurdleston, Henhull, Yardley in p'ish of Torpley [Tarporley] and Coole , the joynture of *Anne* my wife made unto her before our intermarriage for term of her natural life always excepted and foreprised, to have and to hold [&c] to the heires males of the bodie of the s^d William W. lawfully begotten [&c] And for default of such Issue male to my dearly beloved *uncle John Wettenhall* and his heires , and for default of such heires to my dearly beloved *uncle William Wettenhall* and his heires , and for default [&c] to the right heires of the said William Wettenhall my son, according to the last will and test. of *Thomas Wettenhall* father to mee the s^d Gabriell

Item   I give &c unto *William* my son   [the leases of several lands, *Thackers Croft* in Nantwich, lands in Alvaston]   "the moytye of one salt-house

---

* The only Inquisitions now extant relating to this family are those of I —JOHN WETTENHALL [? of Nantwich] who '' died on Sunday next after the feast of St James the Apostle [25 July] last past [1498] leaving *Roger Wettenhall* his son and heir aged one year on Sunday next after the feast of St Michael the Archangel last past [29 Sept 1498]   He died seised of a messuage in Nantwich lately held by Edward Mynshull , 12 messuages there , a salt-house of 6 leads there in the holding of John Broke   The said John W by a writing dated 20 Jan 6 Hen VII [1490-1] granted an annuity of 20s issuing out of all his lands and tenements in N to *Robert Sadler* for term of his life   By another writing dated 26 Nov 9 Hen VII [1493] he granted another annuity of 8s issuing thereout to *John Broke* and Jane his wife and their assigns for 41 years   By another writing dated 2 June 5 Hen VII [1490] *Adam Wettenhall*, the father of the said John, and the said John demised to *Robert Sadler* of N and his assigns two pastures there called *Iynkers Crofts* for the term of his life at the yearly rent of 18s ' —(*Inq p m 14* Hen VII   Pub Record Office)
II —ROGER WETTENHALL gent , [? of Nantwich] who died 1 April 1622, leaving *John W* his grandson his heir, aged 15 years 3 weeks   He died seised of 11 messuages, 17 gardens, 12 acres of land, a salt-house, and 40s rent in Nantwich — (*Inq p m 19* Jac I)

"the waynscott, joyned worke paynted or stayned, clothes and glasse, all cupboards, desks, tables, formes, bedstidds, stooles, [&c] wth in my Mansion house in N. wherein I now dwell," [&c] "my Signet of gold & certain rings of gold, one silver salt wth a couer, and a picture of a man broken of[f] engraven wth goldsmiths worke all gilt,* one silver Bowle wth a couer thereunto p'cell gilt, one silver Cupp p'cell gilt wth T.W. graven in the middest of the same, eight silver Spoones, sixe whereof haue three lres [letters] punched upon the end of euery Spoone, the other two haue R D upon the end of either of them, together with the keyes of my cupboard, deske & presse [chest] in the chamber where I lye, and the keyes and chest where my evidence lye" "my best pott, best pan, best payre of candlesticks, best possenct, best sadle of Mastyne [?], alsoe my Armoui and furniture for war"

"my bookes, evidence, writings, muniments, my malte kilne, stable, and furniture, &c   *Item* I give [&c] to *Anne Wettenhall*, my wife, one little drinking cupp for wyne of silver all gilt, with three Apostle spoones, &c [other articles of furniture]   "and the rest of my goods and chattels,"   "two parts to my sd. son *William*, & the third parte to my sd wife *Anne*

Item I give [&c] to be distributed among the poore wth in the Towne of Namptwiche the summe of fyve pounds

Item. I give to the overseers [Richard Maisterson, Richard Walthall, and my loving brother-in-law Thos Mynshull of Erdeswick, Esq, Randle Stanley of Adderley, Esq, and John Griffyn of Barderton, Esq] of this my last will, xx^s each, &c

Item. I give &c   [legacies of 10s each to] *Richard Whicksteed* th' edler, cozen *Lawrence Maisterson, Margery Wettenhall* my uncle William Wettenhalls daughter, [also legacies of 5s each to] *William Whicksteed, Alexander Whicksteed,* and *Mr. Randle Kent,* Schoolem^r " &c, &c.

Gabriell Wettenhall "

Thomas Wettenhall, of Nantwich, who resided at White Hall in Welsh Row, and was the sixth in descent from the above-named Gabriel Wettenhall, succeeded in the year 1797 to the estates, and took the name and arms of the Mainwarings of Peover, in this county, and thus became the ancestor of the present line of Baronets of Peover

By the marriage of *Katherine Wettenhall*, in 1738, this family became allied with that of the Tomkinsons, who came originally from Staffordshire.

James Tomkinson, Esq, the first of the family to settle in Nantwich, was an eminent attorney and solicitor By his extensive practice, and parsimonious habits, he amassed a large fortune, and in 1754 purchased the Dorfold estate, and went to reside at the Hall At his office in the Welsh Row, Lloyd Kenyon,† (afterwards first Lord Kenyon, Chief Justice of the Court of Kings Bench), was articled in 1746, completing his term of clerkship there in the year 1753 ' While Mr Kenyon was a clerk," says a well known

---

* The silver salt-cellar was usually placed in the middle of the table on great occasions, and divided persons of quality who sat at one end of the table from inferior persons who sat at the opposite end

† Lloyd Kenyon, the second son of Lloyd Kenyon, Esq, of Gredington, co Flint, by his wife Jane the daughter of Robert Eddowes, Esq of Eagle Hall, co Cheshire was born on 5th Oct 1732 In 1780 he was appointed Chief Justice of Chester in 1782 Attorney-General, in 1784 Master of the Rolls, and in 1788 Chief Justice of the Kings Bench, being raised to the peerage by the title of Baron Kenyon Gredington

writer,* " it was the custom for attorneys who had to attend the Assizes to ride to the assize town on horseback The city of Chester, where the courts always sat, was twenty or more miles from Nantwich ; and once, as Mr. Tomkinson and his clerk were riding side by side, Mr Kenyon asked his master to tell him what was the most important thing in law " "Oh, yes," replied his master, " I will tell you what of all things in law is the most important to be attended to , but it must be on the condition that you pay for the dinner we are to have on our way at Bar Hill to-day " Supposing that this mean condition would be acceded to, Mr Tomkinson told his clerk, that of all things in law to be most attended to, evidence was the chief They arrived at Bar Hill, and after dinner, when the landlord's bill came in, Mr Tomkinson tossed it over to Mr Kenyon, saying that it was his concern , but he affected surprise, and handed it back again , upon which Mr Tomkinson reminded him of the condition he had made on the way. The clerk said that if there was any such condition his master must give evidence, which, as the party in a cause could not give evidence, was a complete *estoppel;* and thus the master was caught by his own device." The same writer says, " Kenyon who had been an invaluable servant, remained with his master seven years , at the end of which time he expected to be taken into partnership, but happily for Kenyon s future, no partnership was offered ; the reason being that of Mr Tomkinson, though he was very rich, it might be said that *crescit amor nummi quantum ipsa pecunia crescit.*"†

Of the descendants of James Tomkinson, Esq , particulars are given in the subjoined pedigree.

* " *Notes on some English Judges and other men of Law,* ' by W Beamont, Esq

† Other stories illustrative of the hoarding propensities of this grasping lawyer, are still told by old inhabitants of the town

Wettenhall and Tomkinson Pedigree.

Authorities: Harl. MSS. 1424, f. 149; 2119, f. 65 and 109; Wills; Parish Registers; College of Arms; Ormerod's *Cheshire;* &c.

ARMS. Vert, a cross engrailed Ermine.

CREST. An antelope's head Argent, attired Gules, issuing from a ducal coronet of the second.

THOMAS WETENHALE, descendant of the younger line of Wettenhall of Wettenhall.

THOMAS WETENHALE of Nantwich. = Elizabeth dau. of .... Palein of Wohdhey. (N.B.—*Elizabeth* is here given as the Christian name, on the authority of Hunter's Pedigree Add. MSS. 24,444, p. 167, British Museum.)

WILLIAM WETTENHALL of Nantwich. Occurs in an Inquisition of Right of Way dated 6 Sep. 2 Edw. VI. [1549] = Elizabeth dau of John Leche of Nantwich. (*second wife.*)

Joanna dau of Thos. Wettenhall of Cholmondeston (*first wife.*)

Margaret at N. 5 Nov. 1593.

1 Roger Wettenhall of Coppenhall, who married Isabella, dau. to Thos. Maisterson, & had issue. *Inq. p.m.* 13 May 1573-
2 John Wettenhall.

3 William
4 Hugh
5 Richard
6 Gabriel
7 Robert
8 Henry
Elizabeth

Roger Wettenhall of Cheer Brook, Willaston. = ... dan. of Damory.

Thos. WETTENHALL of Nantwich, 1566. Bur. at N. 3 Feb. 1578-9. = Margery dan. of Thos. Maisterson of N.

(*Second wife*) = Anne, dau. of Thos. Gamull of Buerton. Marr. at N. 13 Jan 1593-4. Bur. at N. 28 Aug. 1617.

(*First wife*) Catherine the dau. of Wm Bromley of Harford [Dorfuld] Bur. 5 Sep. 1592.

GABRIEL WETTENHALL of Nantwich. Gent. Will dated 11 Sep. 1601 (see *Harl. MSS.* 1991, f. 152.) Bur. at N. 22 Sep. 1601.

William Wettenhall legatee, together with his brothers Gabriel & John, under the will of Roger Manwaring of N., dated 18 April 1589. = Isabella, dau. of ..... Skrinshaw.

John Wettenhall, of Hennys, (?) co. Richmondsh. = Dorothy, dau. of Wm. Deyville, of Chickwould.

Margaret Wettenhall. Bap. 13 April 1589.

WILLIAM WETTENHALL, Bap. 4 May, 1584. Bur. 14 Feb. 1670-1. = Jane dau. of Richard Chiton, of Nantwich. Married 20 Sep. 1601. Bur. 9 Nov. 1623. Arms formerly in South Transept of N. Church.

A

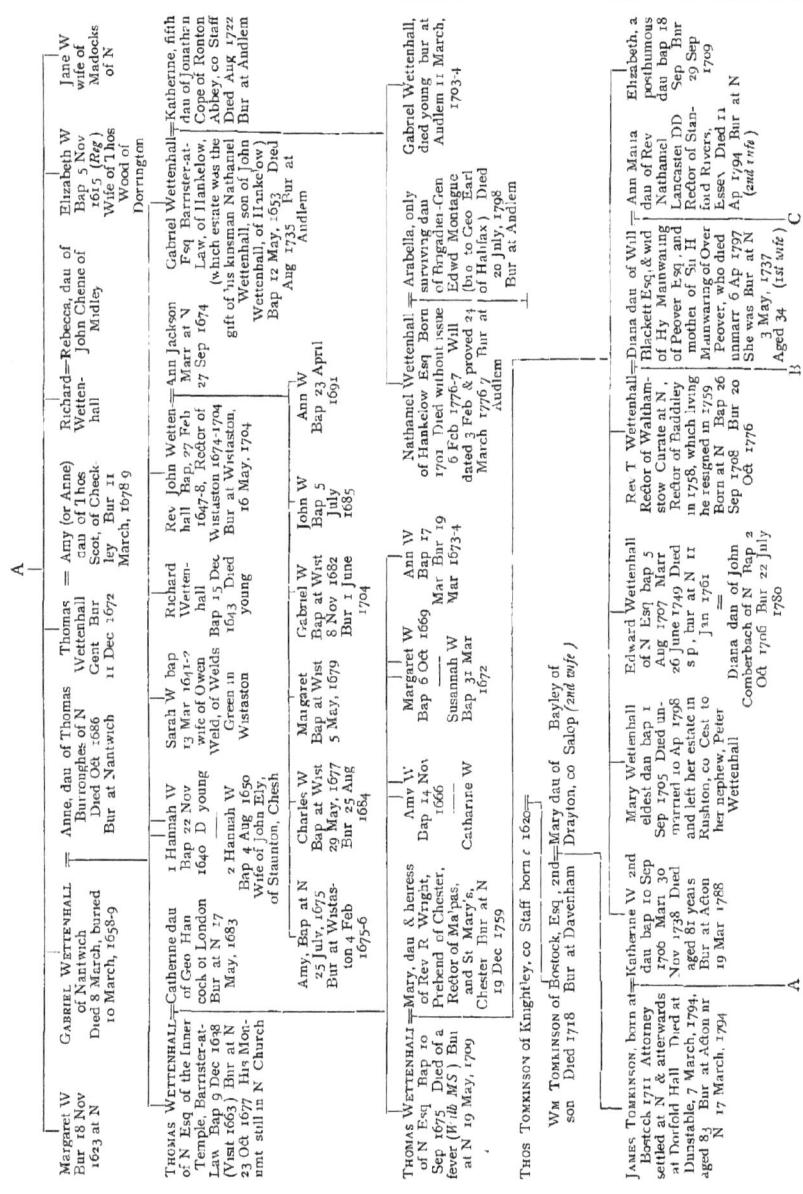

C

Richard W of London Stockbroker in 1810

Charlotte, dau of Wm Watkis Esq of N Bur at Afton 16 April, 1789
Elizabeth Bap at N 8 April, 1789

Rev Lancaster Wettenhall, twin brother of Peter W Rector of Lawton Marr at N 23 May, 1786

Mary Ann Bap at N 23 April, 1795

Peter Wettenhall of Ravenscroft Hall born in 1749 — Frances, dau of Thos Ravenscroft Hall born in 1755, living 1817. Other issue

Robert Wettenhall died in Australia, 1877

Edward Wettenhall of City of London Born in 1749

Mary Wettenhall Bap 21 Dec 1735. Other issue that died young

(See Ormerod's Cheshire, New Edit vol iii, p 481-906)

Diana Mainwaring, Born 14th, Bap 16 March, 1787, at N Died in Hospital St, N, a spinster, on 5 Nov 1861 Bur in the Parish Cemetery at N, where is a stone to her memory

Catharine Maria Bap at N 23 July, 1783 Bur at Afton 13 Nov 1791

Edward Bap at N 23 Nov 1792

William Born 28 March, 1785 Bap at N 30 March, 1785

Elizabeth

Margaret twins, died young

Catharine Maria Bap 11 Jan 1746-7 Marr in 1771 to Rev George Cotton LL.D, Dean of Chester

3 Edward Tomkinson of Bostock and afterwards of Harkelow, by devise of Nathaniel Wettenhall Born at N 21 Sep, bap 23 Sep 1743 Assumed name of Wettenhall 1798 — Sarah, dau of Jas Marsden Born Aug 1753 Died 16 Feb 1776 Bur at Davenham

William Wettenhall of Hankelow Born at Manchester, 1772

Anna Maria died unmarr 1826

Arabella Gen Rich Egerton of Laton Banks

Susan, dau of Thomas Tarlton of Bolesworth Cheshire Died 1879

Frances Beatrix Bap 17 Nov 1774 Died unmarried 16 Sep 1834

4 Wm Tomkinson Esq of Willington Hall, Lat-perley, Lent Col Officer in 16th Dragoons in 1809 Served with distinction in Peninsular War 1809—1814 and at Waterloo received 2 Medals & 4 clasps Severely wounded in the passage of the Domro 1809 Born 18 Jan 1790 Died 1872

B

A

2 Henry Tomkinson of Dorfold, Esq, bap 29 Aug 1741 Died aged 80 Buried in Afton Church in 1822 — Anne, dau and heiress of John Darlington of Aston, Esq Died 26 Aug 1826, aged 76 Bur in Afton Church

Thomas Wettenhall Bap at N 21 Dec 1736 Marr 21 June 1781. Heir to his uterine half-brother Sir H Mainwaring of Over Peover in 1797 Assumed the Name and Arms of Mainwaring Died 4 July, bur 8 July, 1798, at Peover — Catharine, youngest dau of Wm Watkis Esq of N Survived her husband Lived in Welsh Row Died at Parkgate 28 June, 1804

Sir Hen Mainwaring Bart, of Over Peover Born 25 April 1782 Bap at Nantwich 23 Sept 1782 Created Bart 25 May, 1804 Sheriff of Chesh 1806 Died 11 Jan 1860

(From whom the present line of Baronets of Peover)

1 Rev James Tomkinson Born 26 Dec 1739 bap at N 18 Jan 1739-40 Rector of Davenham Died in 1819 — Mary, dau of John Wood of Bath Esq Bur at Afton 31 May, 1791

James Tomkinson, born at Afton 2 1785 An Officer in 17th Light Dragoons o s p 1860

3 Rev Hy Tomkinson of Reasse Heath a student of Middle Temple in 1809 Succeeded his brother as Vicar of Afton, which he held 18 yrs Died, aged 52, on 9 June, 1838 Bur in Afton Church (Monument in Afton Church) — Harriet Sophia dau of Shakespear Phillips Esq Died at Lower Seymour St London, aged 79, 31 Dec 1881 Bur in Afton Church

1 Edwd Tomkinson Bap 8 Mar 1773 Died unmarried in 1819, aged 46 Bur in Afton Church

2 Rev Jas Tomkinson of Dorfold Hall, LL.B Vicar of Afton from 14 Feb 1820 to 22 July 1820 Died 5 Oct 1841, aged 60 Bur in Afton Church — Julia, dau of John Nesham Esq of Houghton-le Spring Died 4 April, 1861 Bur in Afton Church, aged 82 years

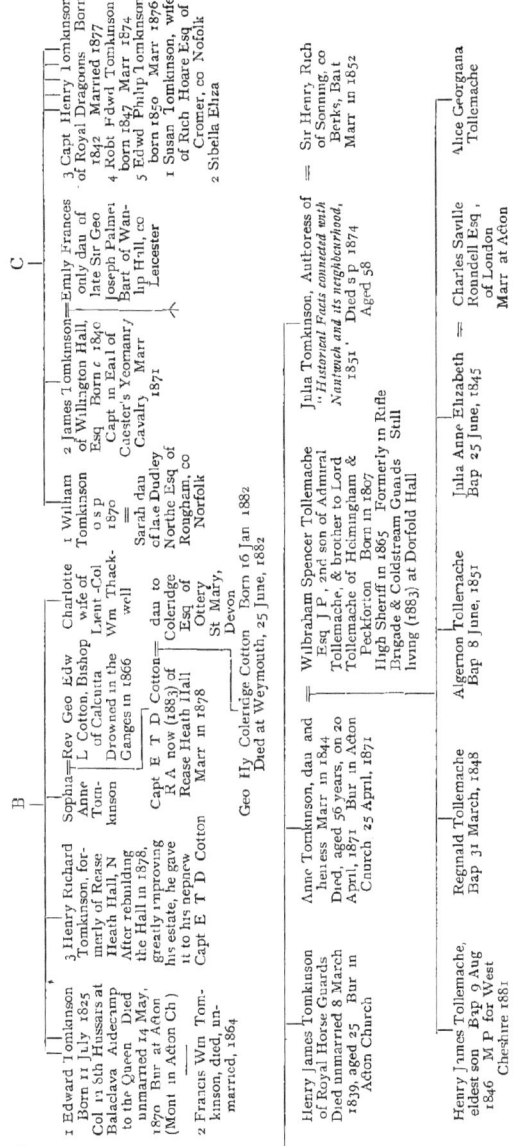

A

1 Edward Tomkinson Born 11 July 1825 Col in 8th Hussars at Balaclava Aidecamp to the Queen Died unmarried 14 May, 1870 Bur at Acton (Mont in Acton Ch)

2 Francis Wm Tomkinson, died, unmarried, 1864

B

Sophia Anne Tomkinson = Rev Geo Edw L Cotton, Bishop of Calcutta Drowned in the Ganges in 1866

3 Henry Richard Tomkinson, formerly of Rease Heath Hall, N After rebuilding the Hall in 1878, greatly improving his estate, he gave it to his nephew Capt E T D Cotton

Capt E T D Cotton, R A now (1883) of Rease Heath Hall Marr in 1878

Charlotte wife of Lieut-Col Wm Thackwell

= dau to — Coleridge Esq, of Ottery St Mary, Devon

Geo Hy Coleridge Cotton Born 16 Jan 1882 Died at Weymouth, 25 June, 1882

1 William Tomkinson o s p 1870

= Sarah dau of late Dudley Northe Esq, of Rougham, co Norfolk

2 James Tomkinson of Willington Hall, Esq, Born c 1840 Capt in Earl of Chester's Yeomanry Cavalry, Marr 1871

= Emily Frances only dau of late Sir Geo Joseph Palmer, Bart of Wanlip Hall, co Leicester

3 Capt Henry Tomkinson of Royal Dragoons Born 1842 Married 1877

4 Robt Edwd Tomkinson, born 1847 Marr 1874

5 Edwd Philip Tomkinson born 1850 Marr 1876

1 Susan Tomkinson, wife of Rich Hoare Esq of Cromer, co Norfolk

2 Sibella Eliza

C

Henry James Tomkinson of Royal Horse Guards Died unmarried 8 March 1839, aged 25 Bur in Acton Church

Anne Tomkinson, dau and heiress Marr in 1844 Died, aged 56 years, on 20 April, 1871 Bur in Acton Church 25 April, 1871

= Wilbraham Spencer Tollemache Esq J P, 2nd son of Admiral Tollemache, & brother to Lord Tollemache of Helmingham & Peckforton Born in 1817 High Sheriff in 1865 Formerly in Rifle Brigade & Coldstream Guards Still living (1883) at Dorfold Hall

Julia Tomkinson, Authoress of "Historical Facts connected with Nantwich and its neighbourhood," 1851 Died s p 1874 Aged 58

= Sir Henry, Rich of Sonning, co Berks, Bart Marr in 1852

Henry James Tollemache, eldest son Bap 9 Aug 1846 M P for West Cheshire 1881

Reginald Tollemache Bap 31 March, 1848

Algernon Tollemache Bap 8 June, 1851

Julia Anne Elizabeth Bap 25 June, 1845

= Charles Saville Roundell Esq, of London Marr at Acton

Alice Georgiana Tollemache

THE MINSHULL FAMILY.

Various branches of this Cheshire family have lived at Erdswick, Hampton, Chester, Nantwich, Stoke, and Wistaston, all claiming descent from the parent stock that settled at Minshull in Norman times   Although the race is not yet extinct, they no longer possess lands in this county.   Two lines of descent come within the scope of this history, namely, the *Minshulls* of Nantwich and afterwards of Stoke Hall, and the *Minshulls* of Wistaston and Nantwich, one of whom, ELIZABETH MINSHULL became the third wife of the poet MILTON.

An abstract of the Inquisition *post mortem* of GEIFREY MINSHULL, gent , of Nantwich, who died on 26th Dec   1603, has already been given on page 6   In the same year had died his brother THOMAS MINSHULL, whose Inquisition *post mortem*, dated 4th Dec Jac I [1605], finds that

> " THOMAS MINSHULL gent died on the 13th Jan 45 Eliz. [1602-3] leaving *Richard Minshull* his son and heir aged 21 on the 26th Dec last past.   He died seized of a messuage and shop in Nantwich in a street called the *Hightown*, three other messuages and three gardens in *Pepper Street,* an annual rent of 4s out of the lands of Arthur Minshull deceased in Pepper Street , and lands in Burland and Faddiley, late the inheritance of Edward Ithell " &c

JOHN MINSHULL, Esq , second son of Geffrey Minshull, resided on the Heath-side, Nantwich, and died there as recorded in the Parish Register   In his Inquisition *post mortem*, dated 11th Sep 14 Car. I. [1638], it is stated that

> " he died seized of a messuage in Nantwich, and two pastures thereto belonging called *Beame-Bridge Field,* and *Duneley Hill ,** also of cottages, a salt-pit of 12 leads, and lands in Alvaston, Willaston, and Wareton *alias* Wavreton near Bostocke , and enffeoffed Philip Mainwaring Esq , Thomas Wilbraham Esq , and Hugh Allen, merchant, thereof in trust for the settlor for life, with remainder as to part, to *Thomas Minshull* his second son for life
>
> He died on 27 Feb 10 Car I [1634-5] leaving *Geffrey Minshull* his son and heir, aged 30 years and more "†

EDWARD MINSHULL, the purchaser of Stoke Manor, married Margaret, daughter to Thomas Mainwaring of Nantwich, and sister to Matthew Mainwaring, author of the romance of *" Vienna '*   His son and heir, GEFFREY MINSHULL, of Gray's Inn, Gent , in the year 1617, brought himself into debt and to the *King's Bench Prison*, where he solaced his days of captivity by writing a series of Essays, which he sent to his uncle Matthew Mainwaring. who generously assisted him in his misfortunes   In the following year these experiences of prison life were printed under the title of—

> " Essayes and Characters of a Prison and Prisoners   Written by G M of Grayes-Inne, Gent
> Printed at London for Mathew Walbancke, and are to be solde at his Shops at the New and Old Gate of Grayes-Inne 1618 "

The title-page has a wood-cut representing a ferocious looking gaoler standing beside a prison door, with staff in hand, and keys chained to his waist, and this rhyme —

---

* *Dunelay Hill*, or *Dunnilow-field* (*cf* page 7) and *Beame-Bridge field* are adjoining fields at the northern extremity of the township

† The son and heir of John Minshull was baptized in 1588 (*Par Reg*) and consequently at the time of his father's death must have been *considerably* more than 30 years of age

"Those that keepe mèe, I keepe, if can, will still,
Hee's a true Jaylor strips the Diuell in ill"

It is dedicated to "*his most loving and ever respective kind uncle Mr Matthew Mainwaring, of Namptwich, in Chesshire,*" concerning whom the author says "Why should I feare, since you have alwayes been my anchor, when I have been ship-wiackt, and many times saued my poore barque when it was ready to split?" There have been three editions of this book, the first in 1618, another in 1638, and the third, of which only one hundred and fifty copies were printed in 1821, and all are now extremely scarce. A few extracts, illustrative of Geffrey Minshull's punning style of writing, will not be uninteresting

The following lines appear on the fly-leaf —

"A Prison is a House of Care,
A Place where none can thrive,
A Touchstone true to try a Friend,
A Grave for one alive
Sometimes a place of Right,
Sometimes a place of Wrong,
Sometimes a place of Rogues and Thieves
And Honest men among"*

The Character of a Prison.

"A prison is a graue to bury men aliue, and a place wherein a man for halfe a yeares experience may learne more law, than hee can at Westminster for an hundred pound" * * * "It is a little commonwealth although little wealth be common there, it is a desart, where desert lyes hoodwinckt, it is a famous citie wherein are all trades, for here lies the Alchymist that can rather make *ex auro non aurum*, than *ex non auro aurum*"† * * * * * * * * * * * * *

The Character of a Prisoner.

"A prisoner is an impatient patient, lingering vnder the rough hands of a cruell phisitian, his creditor hauing cast his water knowes his disease, and hath power to cure him, but takes more pleasure to kill him"

Of Creditors.

"A Creditor hath two paire of hands, one of flesh and blood, and that nature gave him, another of iron, and that the law gave him, but the one is more predominant then [than] the other, for mercy guids the one, and mammon the other" * * * * * * * * * * * *

The Character of Companions in Prison

"Three kinds of persons thou shalt be sure to find in prison, *a Parasite*, who will no longer faune than thou wilt feed him, *A John Indifferent*, when present, will be with thee, when absent, against thee, hee is *hic et vbique* *A True-hearted Titus*, come stormes, come calmes, come tempests, come sunshine, come what can come, hee will be thine and sticke to thee" * * * * * * * *

The Character of Visitants

"Visitants are men, for the most part, composed all of protesting promises, and little or no performance they are like your almanacks, which, when they prognosticate faire weather, it is a million to a mite if it proue not contrary they are like the German clocks, which seldome goe right, their tongues run faster then

* These lines were copied and printed on a board which hung at the west end of the Hall in the Old Tolbooth, Edinburgh (*Vide* R Chambers's Traditions of Edinbcro', p 79)

† It is very remarkable that Hogarth, in 1735, in his "Rake's Progress" (Plate vii *In the Fleet*) represents an Alchemist in the Debtors Prison "placidly pursuing the quest which has beggared him"

[than] the clocke on Shroue-Tuesday , &c   They are like the ringes and chaines bought at St Martines, that weare fair for a little time, but shortly after will proue alchimy, or rather pure copper   They are like the apples which grow on the bankes of Gomorrah, they have crimson and beautiful rindes, but when they come to gather them, they crumble all to dust " *   *   *   *   *   *   *   *   *   *

Of Jaylors

"Cruelty becomes them worst of all men , a prisoner is a poore weather beaten bird, who hauing lost the shoare, is driven by tempest to hang upon the sailes and tacklings of a prison   the jaylor is the saylor, and if hee beate that bird off to sinke her in the seas, when by climbing vp to the maine top, or perhaps by lifting vp his hand, hee may take it and lend it heat from his warm bosome, it is an argument that his heart is made of the same rocks that lie in wait to destroy ships in the ocean "   *   *   *   *   *

A Locker up at Night.

"The belman of the city and he haue almost offices alike, yet herein they differ, that the belman hath his dog following him, but this night walker grows into the habit of a dog by his currishness "   *   *   *

'Some are of opinion that English prisons lock vp none but Englishmen, but I say they are all Hungarians "

Geffrey Minshull advises those who are compelled to borrow to pay as soon as they can , remembering the blood-thirsty creditor, the " Jew of Malta " (Shakespeare's *Shylock*). There are many classical allusions and quotations, proving the author to have been a scholar

In *Harl MSS* 2119, f 155, is preserved a copy of the grant of a Crest to SIR RICHARD MINSHULL, of Bourton, co Bucks, Kt , (see accompanying pedigree) dated 4th July, 1642, which traces his descent for eighteen generations back to RICHARD DE MINSHULL *temp* William the Conquerol , and mentions the first grant of Arms and Crest to Michael Minshull *temp* Richard I, as follows —

"And Whereas the said Michaell did take the cross (*suscipere crucem*) and went with the Kinge of England Richard the first into the holy land and served him in that warres against the Sultan Saladine who was there vanquished and for the proice [prowess] of the said Michaell he had given him the Crescent and Starre for Armes they being the device of that Kinge he used for that voyage, and the sd family hath sithence born for their Crest two Lions Pawes holdinge a Crescent "

Whether the above account of the origin of the coat-armour of the Minshulls is mere tradition or not, I cannot pretend to say , but these Arms were allowed to Edward Minshull, of Nantwich, and to Geffrey Minshull, of Stoke, in the Visitations of Cheshire in 1613 and 1664 respectively, according to the records at the College of Arms, London

Minshull of Nantwich and Stoke.

Authorities: Harl. MSS. vols. 774; 1080; 1424; 2119; 2112; &c. Visitations 1613 and 1664; Privately printed pedigrees by John Bellamy Minshull, Esq., of London; Parish Registers; Church Monuments; &c.

ARMS. Azure, an estoile of six points Argent, issuing from and partly included within the horns of a crescent of the second.

CREST. On a wreath two lion's gambs Gules, supporting a crescent Argent.

Edward Minshull, of Nantwich, son of Hewen Minshull, of Clutton, co. Cest.; and grandson of Nicolas Minshull of the family of Minshull of Minshull. Died 2 Dec. 1557. = Margaret, dau. to Hugh Mainwaring, of Nantwich, gent. Buried at N. 14 Jan. 1572-3.

1 Edward Minshull, eldest son. Built old Hall at Kinderton near Middlewich. Died 8 Dec. 1620. Bur. at M. = (1st wife) Prudence .... Left issue. = (2nd wife) Ellinor Swettenham. Marr. 18 May, 1589. Left issue.

2 Geffrey Minshull, of N. mercer; born c. 1539. Subscribed £25 for defence of England against the Spanish Armada. Died 26 Dec. 1603. Aged 64. Inventory at Chester 1603. Inq. p.m. 2 Jac. I.

3 William Minshull. Living in 1620. (Visit. of Devon.) = Ellen, dau. to Wm. Bromley, & sister to Sir Thos Bromley Kt. Ld. Chanc. of England & Sir Geo. Bromley Kt. Justice of Chester. Bur. at N. 3 July, 1598.

4 Yewen Minshull. Bap. 3 June 1541.

(1st wife) Dulcia dau. to John Mainwaring of the Beast Mkt N. Marr 31 Dec. 1574. Bur with infant child 26 June, 1576. = Thos. Minshull, of N. mercer, of Twerling Gate, N. Born 6 May, 1552. Bur. at N. 14 Jan. 1602-3. Will dat. 1602. Inq. p.m. 2 Jac. I. = (2nd wife) Elizabeth dau. to Richard Wright of N. Marr. 16 Aug. 1581.

1 Emma, wife of John Warburton.
2 Margaret M Bap. 26 Sep. 1544. Wife of John Lytler, Alderman of Chester; Mayor 1605. He died 2 Ap. 1619. (See Chesh Funeral Certif.)

Richard Minshull of N. mercer; bap. 2 Jan. 1602-3. Died 17 Feb. Bur. 20 Feb. 1637-8. Will proved 1638. Left his lands to his half-sister. (Mont.) = Elizabeth, dau. to Richard Wilbraham. Born 1585. Bur. at N. 13 Jan. 1658-9. (See page 437.)

Matthew Mainwaring of N. gent. = Margaret Minshull. Bap. 20 Oct. 1573. Died 21 Dec. 1652. Marr. 10 Dec. 1594. Died 19 Jan. 1651. Had issue 14 children. (See Monument.)

A — 1 Edward Minshull of N. Born c. 1559; marr. 8 Feb. 1589-90; purchased from Sir Thos. Aston, and his son John, the Manor of Stoke, by Indenture dated 10 Sep. 1611. (See Cheshire Sheaf, No. 982.) Died 17 Jan. Bur. 21 Jan. 1627-8. Aged 68. Will proved at Chester 1628. = Margaret, dau. to Thomas Mainwaring of N. gent.

B — 2 John Minshull "of the Heath Side," N. Esq. Bur. at N. 27 Feb. 1634-5. Inq. p.m. 14 Car. I. = Ellen to Randle Mainwaring.

3 Randle Minshull M.A. Author of Antiquities of Cheshire; a MS. dated 1591. From his great learning called "Scholar Minshull." Bur. at N. 17 May, 1639. = Eleanor dau to Richard Griffin, Esq. of Bartherton. Bur. at N. 22 March 1614-5.

C — (1st husband) Thomas Ekcocke of N. gent. Had issue (Harl. MSS. 2161.) = Elizabeth Minshull, 2nd dan. Her sister, Margaret, died unmarried. = (2nd husband) Edward Hayes of N. gent, aged 21 at the Visit of 1613 (Harl. MSS. 1535 p. 245.) Cf. pp. 131 and 340.

Edward Hayes. Bap. 23 Oct. 1625.

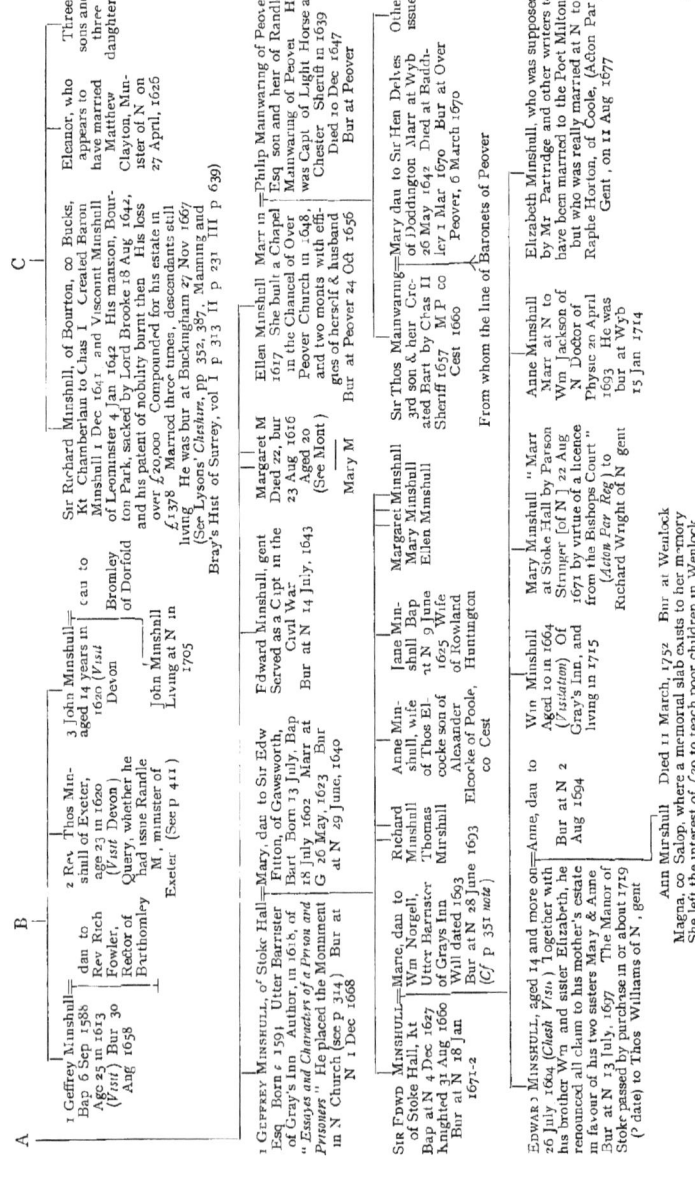

A

B

C

1 Geffrey Minshull═dan to Rev Rich Fowler, Rector of Barthomley
Bap 6 Sep 1586
Age 25 in 1613
(*Visit*) Bur 30
Aug 1658

2 Rev Thos Minsull of Exeter, age 23 in 1620 (*Visit* Devon) Query, whether he had issue Randle M, minister of Exeter (See p 411)

3 John Minshull aged 14 years in 1620 (*Visit* Devon)═dau to Bromley of Dorfold
John Minshull Living at N in 1705

Three sons and three daughters

Eleanor, who appears to have married Matthew Clayton, Minister of N on 27 April, 1625

Sir Richard Minshull, of Bourton, co Bucks, Kt Chamberlain to Chas I Created Baron Minshull 1 Dec 1641 and Viscount Minshull of Leominster 4 Jan 1642 His mansion, Bourton Park, sacked by Lord Brooke 18 Aug, 1644, and his patent of nobility burnt then His loss over £20,000 Compounded for his estate in £1378 Married three times, descendants still living He was bur at Buckingham 27 Nov 1667 (See Lysons' *Cheshire*, pp 352, 387, Manning and Bray's *Hist of Surrey*, vol I p 313 II p 231 III p 639)

1 Geffrey Minshull, of Stoke Hall,═Mary, dau to Sir Edw Fitton, of Gawsworth, Bart Born 13 July, Bap 18 July 1602 Marr at G 26 May, 1623 Bur at N 29 June, 1640
Esq Born c 1591, Utter Barrister of Gray's Inn Author, in 1618, of "*Essays and Characters of a Prison and Prisoners*" He placed the Monument in N Church (see p 314) Bur at N 1 Dec 1668

Edward Minshull, gent Served as a Capt in the Civil War Bur at N 14 July, 1643

Margaret M Died 22, bur 23 Aug 1616 Aged 20 (See Mont)
Mary M

Ellen Minshull Marr in 1617 She built a Chapel in the Chancel of Over Peover Church in 1648, and two months with effigies of herself & husband Bur at Peover 24 Oct 1656

Philip Mainwaring of Peover Esq son and heir of Randle Mainwaring of Peover He was Capt of Light Horse at Chester Sheriff in 1639 Died 10 Dec 1647 Bur at Peover

Sir Edwd Minshull, kt═Marie, dau to Wm Norgell, Utter Barrister of Grays Inn Will dated 1693 Bur at N 28 June 1693 (*Cf* p 351 *note*)
of Stoke Hall, Bap at N 4 Dec 1627 Knighted 31 Aug, 1660 Bur at N 18 Jan 1671-2

Richard Minshull Thomas Minshull

Anne Minshull, wife of Thos Elcocke son of Alexander Elcorke of Poole, co Cest

Jane Minshull Bap at N 9 June 1625 Wife of Rowland of Huntington

Margaret Minshull Mary Minshull Ellen Minshull

Sir Thos Mainwaring═Mary dau to Sir Hen Delves of Doddington Marr at Wyb ley 1 Mar 1670 Bur at Over Peover, 6 March 1670
3rd son & heir Created Bart by Chas II Sheriff 1657 M P co Cest 1660

Other issue

From whom the line of Baronets of Peover

Anne Minshull Marr at N to Wm Jackson of N Doctor of Physic 20 April 1693 He was bur at Wyb 15 Jan 1714

Edward Minshull, aged 14 and more on═Anne, dau to ... Bur at N 2 Aug 1594
26 July 1664 (*Chesh Visit*) together with his brother Wm and sister Elizabeth, he renounced all claim to his mother's estate in favour of his two sisters Mary & Anne Bur at N 13 July, 1677 The Manor of Stoke passed by purchase in or about 1719 (? date) to Thos Williams of N, gent

Win Minshull Aged 10 in 1664 (*Visitation*), Of Gray's Inn, and living in 1715

Mary Minshull "Marr at Stoke Hall by Parson Stringer [of N] 22 Aug 1671 by virtue of a licence from the Bishops Court" (*Aston Par Reg*) to Richard Wright of N gent

Elizabeth Minshull, who was supposed by Mr Partridge and other writers to have been married to the Poet Milton, but who was really married at N to Raphe Horton, of Coole, (Aston Par) Gent, on 11 Aug 1677

Ann Mirshull Died 11 March, 1752 Bur at Wenlock Magna, co Salop, where a memorial slab exists to her memory She left the interest of £20 to teach poor children in Wenlock

Another branch of the Minshull family, which is traced in the subjoined pedigree through several generations down to the present time, is introduced mainly to show the descent of *Elizabeth Minshull*, the third wife of the great poet Milton

MRS ELIZABETH MILTON

During the last thirty years much has been written concerning this lady, who at the age of thirty-six, was left a widow, and afterwards resided at Nantwich for nearly half a century.

Toland (*Life of Milton*, 1698, p. 39,) spoke of her as "Elizabeth, the daughter of Mr Minshall, of Cheshire, recommended to him [Milton] by his friend Dr Paget" Later biographers and historians, by mistake, (as modern discovery has satisfactorily shown) have claimed for her the honor of high birth, and cast dishonour on her character. Thus, Partridge, in 1774, stated that she "was a daughter of   Minshull Esq of Stoke, three miles from Nantwich'* Pennant, in 1782,† and Dr. Ormerod, in 1819,‡ relying upon the supposed accuracy of Partridge, connected her with the same family, the Cheshire historian giving her father's name as Sir Edward Minshull, Kt, of Stoke Hall, and, as recently as 1851, an authoress§ states that "Milton was received at Stoke Hall as the husband of Elizabeth Minshull'

On referring to the previous pedigree it will be seen that Elizabeth, the daughter of Sir Edward Minshull, was a single lady until nearly three years after the death of John Milton, and that on the 11th Aug 1677 she became the wife Raphe Horton, Gent., of Coole Pilate, near Nantwich *(Par Reg)* The same lady is mentioned by name as "*Mrs. Elizabeth Horton*" in her mother's, the Dowager Lady Mary Minshull's, Will in 1693 When it is remembered that the great poet was married to Elizabeth Minshull at Aldermany Church, London, on the 24th Feb 1662, he being at that time totally blind, it is most likely that Milton did not travel far from the metropolis after that event, and absolutely certain that he never visited either Stoke Hall or Nantwich

The true parentage of the poet's third wife was first pointed out by the late John Fitchett Marsh, Esq., of Warrington, in a volume of "*Milton Papers,*' printed for the Chetham Society in 1851, who showed by legal documents in his possession that her father was Randle Minshull, a yeoman farmer of Wistaston, near Nantwich. This discovery led to a diligent search in the local Registers, and amongst the Wills at Chester, and after a long discussion in the "*Athenæum*," and in "*Notes and Queries*," during the years 1853—5, it became an established fact that Mrs Elizabeth Milton was born in Wistaston parish, and not at Stoke Hall, in Acton parish ‖

Probably she was born at Weld's Green, where for four generations her forefathers had resided She was baptized at Wistaston Church on 30th Dec 1638; and at the age of about twenty-four years was married to John Milton, having been introduced to him

* Partridge's *History of Nantwich*, p 87 So also Platt in his *History of Nantwich* 1818, p 87, who gives the father's name as "T Minshall Esq of Stoke '

† Pennant's "*Tour from Chester to London*," 1st Edit p 35

‡ Dr Ormerod's *History of Cheshire* Vol III Old Edit p 191, New Edit p 361

§ Miss Julia Tomkinson's "*Historical Facts connected with Nantwich*," p 50

‖ The late Messrs T W Jones and Thomas Turner, Solicitors, of Nantwich, Thomas Hughes, F S A , of Chester, and the late Rev Joseph Hunter (see his "*Sheaf of Gleanings*,) were all deeply interested in the subject and took part in the discussion

by his intimate friend, and her relative, Dr Nathan Paget * After the death of the poet on the 8th Nov 1674, she remained for a few years in London, apparently living in the house of her deceased husband in Artillery Walk, Bunhill, where she was frequently visited by Dr Paget, who, dying in Jan. 1678-9, left her, by Will dated 7th Jan and proved the 15th Jan in the same year, a legacy of £20 On the 4th June, 1680, her brother, *Richard Minshull*, of Wistaston, frame-work knitter, invested a part of the sum of £600, (the two-thirds of her husband's effects to which she was entitled as widow and administratrix, the poet having only made a nuncupative will) in purchasing the lease of a farm at Brindley,† in Acton parish, from Sir Thomas Wilbraham, Bart , for three lives, viz —Mrs. Milton, Mary Minshull the wife of the said Richard Minshull, and that of his son Richard Minshull, and for the benefit of whichever of the three should live longest Two months after this investment had been secured, her brother Richard died, and was buried at Wistaston on 6th July, 1680 These bereavements following one another in so short a time, most likely led Mrs. Milton to leave London about the year 1681, and in 1688 she is found living in Hospital Street, Nantwich, with Mrs Mary Noden,‡ widow of Ralph Noden, and formerly widow of Richard Minshull, the brother of Mrs. Milton She then appears to have occupied a small house in Pillory Street, near (? whether the old "black-and-white ' cottage *adjoining*) the one in which Mrs Lea, saddler, now resides, for the remaining years of her life § Though the exact date of her death is not known, it must have taken place on, or within a day or two after, the 22nd Aug 1727 Her Will,‖ dated on that day, and still preserved at Chester, was a very simple one, for the aged widow had only her household goods to leave, and these were to be equally divided amongst her "nephews and nieces [not mentioned by name] in Namptwich," her executors being her "loving friends *Samuel Acton* and *John Allecock*¶ [or *Allcock*] both of Namptwich " Accompanying the Will is a "A True and perfect Inventory of the Goods & Chattels of late Mrs. Elizabeth Milton, appraised by us whose names are undernam'd [*John Wright* and *John Allcock*] this twenty sixth of August 1727," comprising, in seven common law folios, one hundred and eight different items, and amounting in the aggregate to £38 8s 4d. This Inventory** was exhibited by the only acting executor, *John Allecock*, at Chester on the 10th Oct 1727, when Mrs Milton's Will was proved

Amongst the "items" may be mentioned—

* Dr Nathan Paget was cousin to Randle Minshull, the father of Elizabeth Minshull (See Goldsmith Pedigree)

† On the 22nd Oct 1720 Mrs Elizabeth Milton signed an agreement with *John Darlington*, yeoman, letting to him her farm and premises at Brindley, at a rent of £30 per annum , and on the 16th June 1725 there is a further transaction between him and the same tenant

‡ Mary Noden, widow, was buried at Wistaston on 18th Jan 1712-3 —*(Nant Par Reg)*

§ The late T W Jones Esq traced out Mrs Milton's abode in Nantwich from old Rate Books , and he makes this statement in a letter *penes me*

‖ Mrs Milton s Will will be found printed in ' *Milton Papers*," p 33-4 —(Cheth Soc Pub 1851)

¶ This *John Allecock*, of Nantwich, figures in the *Elcocke* pedigree (Dr Ormerod s *Cheshire* , vol iii p 353, New Edit) as the son of *Francis Elcocke* of Whitepoole ! With the editor of that work, however, must rest the *onus probandi* how the Allecocks, who scarce ranked amongst the tradesmen of Nantwich belonged to a neighbouring family of landed gentry

** An exact copy of the Inventory of Mrs Milton's goods was printed in full by T W Barlow in his "*Cheshire and Lancashire Historical Collector*," vol ii p 98—100, on 1st Aug 1854 It may also be found in the *Transactions of the Historic Society of Lancashire and Cheshire*, for Feb 1855

	Valued at
" Mr Milton's Pictures* & Coat of Arms	£10 10 0
2 Teaspoons and 1 silver spoon, with a seal and stopper, and bitts of silver	£0 12 6
1 Pencil Case	£0 3 0
2 Cane Chairs & 2 velvet cushins	£0 17 0
A Large Bible	£0 8 0
2 Books of Paradise	£0 10 0
Some old Books & few old pictures	£0 12 0
A Totershell knife & fork,† wth other odd ones	£0 1 0
Tobacco Box	£0 0 6
Blk & White Gown & Pettycoat	£0 5 0
A Fine Cloak and Hood	£0 17 6
A Norwich Gown and Petticoat	£1 5 0
A Calimancoe Gown	£0 14 0
A Quilted Petticoat	£0 8 0
An old Norwich Gown & Coat	£0 10 0
2 Silk Handkerchiefs	£0 5 0
3 pr of Old gloves	£0 1 0
The best suit of twad cloaths‡	£0 3 0
The Worser do ‡	£0 1 6
2 pair Ruffles‡	£0 2 0
3 Old check aprons	£0 1 0
2 Silk Aprons	£0 2 0
A pair shoes & 2 pair Cloggs	£0 2 6
1 Mask and Fan	£0 2 0

* These portraits are believed to have been, the one when he was a school-boy and the other when about twenty (See *Notes and Queries*, 2nd series, No 116, 20 March 1858) Partridge (*History of Nantwich* page 88) states that one of the pictures was purchased by one of the Wilbrahams of Nantwich then a student of Brazenose College Oxon , and by him was presented to the University But it is a remarkable fact that neither of the picture galleries at Oxford has a portrait of Milton See also Marsh s Tracts on Portraits of Milton, 1860, Milton Ramblings 1861, by M Leigh Sotheby , and " The Antiquarian Magazine and Bibliographer for July 1882, for information on this subject

† The late T W Jones (*Notes and Queries*, 1st series, vol xi , p 109--110, dated 10 Feb 1855) says, "After the most diligent enquiries in this town and neighbourhood I have not been successful in discovering any of the articles of the Inventory except one of the knives and forks ' This was given to him by one of the *Hassalls* of Nantwich in 1852 In 1857 it was exhibited before the Archæological Society by the late Joseph Hunter, Mr Jones having sent an affidavit declared on oath before Thomas Brooke, Rector of Wistaston and J P , on 29th Sep 1854, by *Thomas Hassall*, the elder, of Beam Street in Nantwich, joiner, aged 75 years, and *Thomas Hassall*, the younger, attorney's clerk, his son, aged 41 years, to the effect, that the knife and fork were the property of *Anne Hassall*, daughter of the elder Thomas, who died in 1832, aged thirty, and on her death came into the possession of her father They further affirm that the said *Anne Hassall* lived many years in the service of *Miss Elizabeth Webb*, a wealthy maiden lady who resided in Castle Street in Nantwich and as they believe, died there in the month of March, 1828, at the age of 83 years and upwards and that the said Elizabeth Webb, some years before her death, gave to the said Anne Hassall, as she frequently told them the said knife and fork as great curiosities and informed the said Anne Hassall that they had belonged to Mrs Elizabeth Milton who lived in the town of Nantwich, and was the widow of the Poet And the said Elizabeth Webb, who told the said Anne Hassall (as she informed them) that her grandfather owned the said knife and fork, and was on very intimate terms with the said Elizabeth Milton and her family The younger *Thomas* declares that when a boy he used to visit his sister at the house of Mrs Webb, and often read to her, and had heard her say, that she had given the said knife and fork to his sister, as valuable relics And he, the younger *Thomas Hassall*, further declares that the Rev John Latham, late of Nantwich clerk deceased, was particularly intimate with the said Elizabeth Webb, and managed her affairs, and that he had often heard him speak of the said knife and fork having belonged to the said Mrs Milton

The above declaration is authenticated by the signatures of the two Hassalls Mrs Elizabeth Webb is distinctly remembered by many persons now living at Nantwich, and there is independent evidence of the residence with her of Anne Hassall, as her servant, and a person who was much esteemed by Mrs Webb, and intended to have been benefitted by a Will, which by some accident was never executed (See *Archæological Journal*, 1857, vol, xiv , page 89—90)

‡ These are believed by Dr David Masson (*Life of Milton* 1880, vol i , page 748) to have been ' Milton's old suits of gray in Bunhill fifty-three years before The same writer, who submitted the Inventory to practised feminine judgment expresses his opinion that Mrs Milton s house at Nantwich consisted of "a single chamber, with a small attached scullery " The ' black-and-white house alluded to above as the probable residence of the widow, answers the description, only that it possesses, in addition, an upper chamber

	Valued at		
2 pr of Spectacles	£o	1	6
'Coles [coals]	£o	o	6
A pair Bedsteads and hangings .	£o	18	o
A feather Bed and Bolster, weight 94℔ at 6d	£2	7	o
2 Quilts and pair of Blanketts, old patched ones .	£o	10	o
1 Chest of Drawers and frame	£o	13	o
In Money	£o	17	o

[Pewter dishes, pails, brass fender, fire irons, old tin candlesticks, old looking glass, cooking utensils, &c]

Though the burial of Mrs Milton is not recorded in the Parish Registers, it is commonly believed that she was interred either in the old Baptist Chapel, or its grave-yard, in Barker Street   Allusion has been made to a funeral sermon supposed to have been preached in that Chapel on the occasion of her death, see page 395   Respecting the imputations first cast upon her conduct by Richardson, who derived his information from one of Milton's unkind daughters,—imputations that have been repeated by Dr Johnson, Pennant, and others,—sufficient evidence has been brought forward proving them to be entirely groundless   Between the years 1785 and 1791 Mr Warton ascertained from depositions preserved in the Prerogative Office, that Milton's widow was neither the *"termagant'* nor *"cheat'* some biographers had made her; but, on the contrary, that she had kindly treated her blind husband, and acted honestly by his children, who had been very undutiful to their father   Aubrey, the contemporary of Milton, who occasionally visited Mrs Milton, after the poet's death, speaks of her as having *"a peacefull and agreeable humour,"* and Christopher Milton, the poet's brother, declared upon oath, that Milton *"complained but without passion, that his children had been unkind to him; but that his wife had been very kind and careful of him."**

The late Thomas Turner, in a letter dated July, 1854,† addressed to J F Marsh, of Warrington, states on the authority of a highly respectable lady upwards of eighty-four years of age, then living in Nantwich, "that persons in Nantwich, known to possess but narrow incomes were said to have *Mrs. Milton's Feast, just enough and no more."*   This local proverb has been obsolete for many years.

It is very singular that another family named Milton, in no way connected with the Poet Milton, resided in Nantwich and at Stapeley; and still more remarkable that they should have been proprietors of a dwelling house abutting on the graveyard of the Baptist Chapel from 1650 to 1710   Soon after the latter year, it was transferred by sale, and in 1720 got into the possession of Mr. Samuel Acton ‡

These Miltons were as follows —

I.—HUMPHREY MILTON, Gent, who, together with the Earl of Ardglass, in Ireland, and Richard Green, Esq, conjointly held part of the manor of Stapeley, near Nantwich, in 1662, was descended from a family in the vicinity of Middlewich   For many years he presided over the Manor Court of Betchton for Roger Wilbraham, Esq, of Townsend, who makes an entry in one of his pocket books of the death of Mrs. Alice Milton and

---

* See *Milton Papers*, Chetham Society Pub page 10—13
† I have a draft copy of the letter in Mr Turner's handwriting
‡ Turner correspondence with Mr Marsh

her daughter Matilda within a month of each other in 1695. His first wife, *Elizabeth*, was buried at Nantwich on 10th Nov 1654. apparently without issue   On 22nd Feb. 1656, he married, secondly, Alice Palmer, of Nantwich, by whom he had two sons and three daughters, viz. —

1. *Humphrey;* of whom more presently.

2 *Thomas Milton,* baptized 20th April, 1662; and buried at Nantwich 8th Dec 1693. He was married, and had issue Ralph Milton, who was buried at Cheadle 6th Aug. 1692.

1 *Matilda Milton* baptized 17th Feb. 1660, died a spinster in Welsh Row, buried 24th Dec 1695

2 *Alice Milton,* baptized 26th Dec 1663, and married on 15th Aug 1693, to Joseph Hodgson

3. *Katherine Milton,* baptized 23rd Sep 1666, buried at Nantwich 1st Feb 1667

Humphrey Milton was buried at Nantwich on 26th Oct. 1672, and his widow survived until the 20th Nov 1695, being buried at Nantwich three days after   He was succeeded by his eldest son,—

II.—Humphrey Milton of Stapeley, Gent, who had been baptized at Nantwich on 1st Dec 1659 He appears to have lived on his property at Stapeley, which his father had increased in 1670 by the purchase of Mr. Green's part of Stapeley manor   He fulfilled the office of churchwarden of Wybunbury in 1696-7, and was buried at Nantwich on 28th Sept 1701, leaving a widow, *Ursula*, who was buried at Wistaston on 3rd Feb. 1708, and one son, *Humphrey*

III —*Humphrey Milton,* baptized 6th Nov 1684, was the last of the family He occurs as an attorney   By his wife *Ellen*, who was buried at Nantwich 26th Nov 1736, he had two children, *Eleanor*, and *Humphrey*, both of whom died in childhood, and were buried at Nantwich, the father being buried there on 13th March, 1724-5

From the above it will be seen that there were *three* Mrs. Miltons* contemporary in Nantwich in the year 1695, namely, *Alice Milton, Ursula Milton,* and *Elizabeth Milton,* the Poet's widow

THE GOLDSMITH FAMILY

Closely allied to the Minshulls of Wistaston, were the *Goldsmiths* of Nantwich, a local family of note, concerning which many interesting particulars in the following pedigree are given

---

* Under date 8th Dec 1768, is recorded the burial of another Mrs Milton, whom I have not been able to identify — *(Nantwich Parish Register)*

Minshull Pedigree.

(SECOND LINE)

Authorities Harl MSS 2039, f. 163, Visitation of Lancashire 1664, Privately printed pedigrees by John Bellamy Minshull, Esq., of London, "*Milton Papers*" (Chetham Soc Publ), Wills at Chester, Parish Registers of Wistaston and Nantwich

JOHN MINSHULL, fourth and youngest son of John Mirshull of Minshull Built a residence upon a moiety of the estate (*Weld's Green Farm*) obtained *jure uxoris* = younger dau and coheiress to Robert Couper a freeholder in Wisterson [Wistaston] near Nantwich

RONDULL MINSHULL, of Weld's Green Will dated 21 Dec 1590 proved 23 May, 1595 Printed in *Cheshire Sheaf*, No 1102 Bur at Wistaston 21 Feb = Margery, dau to Roger Rawlinson of Crewe Bur at W 11 Feb 1591-2

Joan Minshull, marr Meakin She living in 1606

A daughter who married Rondull Meakin

| (*First wife*) Alice, dau to Bur at W 2 March, 1590-1 | = | THOMAS MINSHULL, of Weld's Green Bur at W 23 Sep 1606 Will dated 15 Sep 1606, proved 23 Oct 1606 Printed in *Cheshire Sheaf*, No 1117 | = | Dorothy, widow of Randle Goldsmith. marr 17 July, 1592 (*Nantwich Reg*) She survived her second husband (*Second wife*) | 6 William Minshull Bap 1590 Living 1606 | 5 Robert Minshull Bap 31 Aug 1586 Bur 15 Dec 1589 |

Ellen dau to Nicolas Goldsmith of N, mercer Bap at N 8 March 1582-3, marr at W 13 Aug 1599 Bur there 4 Jan 1623-4 (?) = 2 Rondull Minshull Bap 25 Sep 1577 Bur 8 Feb 1591-2

3 Thomas Minshull Bap 7 May, 1585 Bur 27 Jan 1601-5 4 John Minshull Bap 18 Aug 1588 died before 1590

THOMAS MINSHULL, 2nd son Bap 18 May, 1613, settled in Manchester as an Apothecary Aged 51 in 1664 (Dugdale's *Visit of Law*) He rebuilt Chorlton Hall, Manchester = Ann, dau to Jas Lightbourne of Manchester

1 RICHARD MINSHULL, of Weld's Green, eldest son Bap 9 Jan 1574-5. He wrote letter dated 3 May 1656 to his son Richard, concerning his pedigree in answer to enquiries of Randle Holmes Letter in *Harl MSS* 2039 f 163, and printed in *Milton Papers*" p 44-5 Bur at W 25 June, 1658, aged 86 = RANDLE MINSHULL Bap 13 May, 1605 Bur at Wistaston 22 July, 1660 but only recorded at N

Anne Boote Marr at Acton 8 Feb 1633-4 Bur at Wist 16 Dec 1675

RICHARD MINSHULL Bap 14 Ap 1616 Alderman of Chester 1647 Mayor 1657 wrote letter, dated "Wystaston 20 May, 1656," to Mr Alderman Holmes of Chester, preserved in *Harl MSS* 2039 f 164

Anne Minshull Bap 22 May 1643

Thomas Minshull Bap 12 June 1645 Peter Minshull Bap at N 10 Feb 1650 Bur at W 4 Aug 1657

Mabell Minshull Bap 13 Jan 1601-2 Marr by licence to John Boote, I Nov 1625 Bur as wrd at W 26 Jan 1668-9

Ellen Minshull Bap 24 May, 1635 = John Milton, the Poet, of London Marr at St Aldurmanbury, London, 24 Feb 1662-3 Died 8 Nov 1674

ELIZABETH MINSHULL Bap at W 30 Dec 1638 3rd wife of the Poet Milton Died at N Aug 1727, in her 89th year Will dated 22 Aug 1727, proved 10 Oct 1727, with Inventory

Richard Minshull Bap 7 April, 1641 Frame work-knitter Witnessed a bond to his sister Eliz Milton 4 June, 1680 Bur at W 6 July, 1680 = Mary Henshaw Marr at N 17 Sep 1670 Survived her husband, & marr secondly Ralph Noden, & survived him She was bur at W 18 Jan 1712-3

John Minshull Bap 1648 Died intestate 1720 (*Milton Papers*)

George Minshull Bap 7 May, 1680 Apothecary in N Bur at W 11 Aug 1728

Daughters, nieces of Mrs Milton, living 1727

Randle Minshull Bap 5 March, 1671-2

John Minshull Bap 23 Feb 1674-5

Richard Minshull Bap 19 Dec 1676 Bur 3 June, 1681

Ellen Minshull Bap 24 May, 1635

A

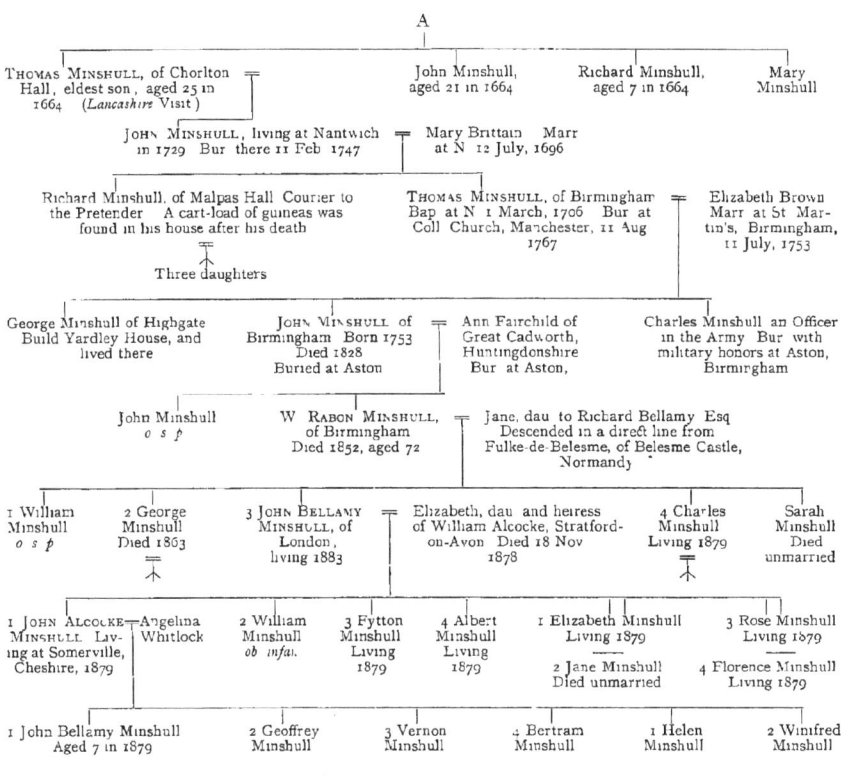

A

Thomas Minshull, of Chorlton Hall, eldest son, aged 25 in 1664 (*Lancashire* Visit)	John Minshull, aged 21 in 1664	Richard Minshull, aged 7 in 1664	Mary Minshull

John Minshull, living at Nantwich in 1729 Bur there 11 Feb 1747 == Mary Brittain Marr at N 12 July, 1696

Richard Minshull, of Malpas Hall Courier to the Pretender A cart-load of guineas was found in his house after his death

Three daughters

Thomas Minshull, of Birmingham Bap at N 1 March, 1706 Bur at Coll Church, Manchester, 11 Aug 1767 == Elizabeth Brown Marr at St Martin's, Birmingham, 11 July, 1753

George Minshull of Highgate Build Yardley House, and lived there

John Minshull of Birmingham Born 1753 Died 1828 Buried at Aston == Ann Fairchild of Great Cadworth, Huntingdonshire Bur at Aston,

Charles Minshull an Officer in the Army Bur with military honors at Aston, Birmingham

John Minshull o s p

W Rabon Minshull, of Birmingham Died 1852, aged 72 == Jane, dau to Richard Bellamy Esq Descended in a direct line from Fulke-de-Belesme, of Belesme Castle, Normandy

| 1 William Minshull o s p | 2 George Minshull Died 1863 | 3 John Bellamy Minshull, of London, living 1883 | Elizabeth, dau and heiress of William Alcocke, Stratford-on-Avon Died 18 Nov 1878 | 4 Charles Minshull Living 1879 | Sarah Minshull Died unmarried |

| 1 John Alcocke Minshull Living at Somerville, Cheshire, 1879 | Angelina Whitlock | 2 William Minshull ob infai. | 3 Fytton Minshull Living 1879 | 4 Albert Minshull Living 1879 | 1 Elizabeth Minshull Living 1879 | 3 Rose Minshull Living 1879 |
| | | | | | 2 Jane Minshull Died unmarried | 4 Florence Minshull Living 1879 |

| 1 John Bellamy Minshull Aged 7 in 1879 | 2 Geoffrey Minshull | 3 Vernon Minshull | 4 Bertram Minshull | 1 Helen Minshull | 2 Winifred Minshull |

Goldsmith Pedigree.

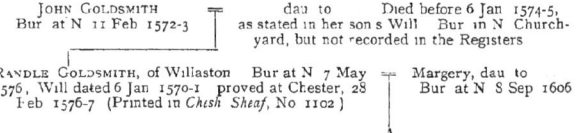

Authorities Privately printed pedigrees by Miss T E Sharpe, of Kensington, in her "*Royal Descent,*" "*The Genealogist,*" vol ii, pp 309 315, Parish Registers, The "*Cheshire Sheaf,*" &c

John Goldsmith Bur at N 11 Feb 1572-3 == dau to Died before 6 Jan 1574-5, as stated in her son s Will Bur in N Churchyard, but not recorded in the Registers

Randle Goldsmith, of Wollaston Bur at N 7 May 1576, Will dated 6 Jan 1570-1 proved at Chester, 28 Feb 1576-7 (Printed in *Chsh Sheaf*, No 1102) == Margery, dau to Bur at N 8 Sep 1606

A

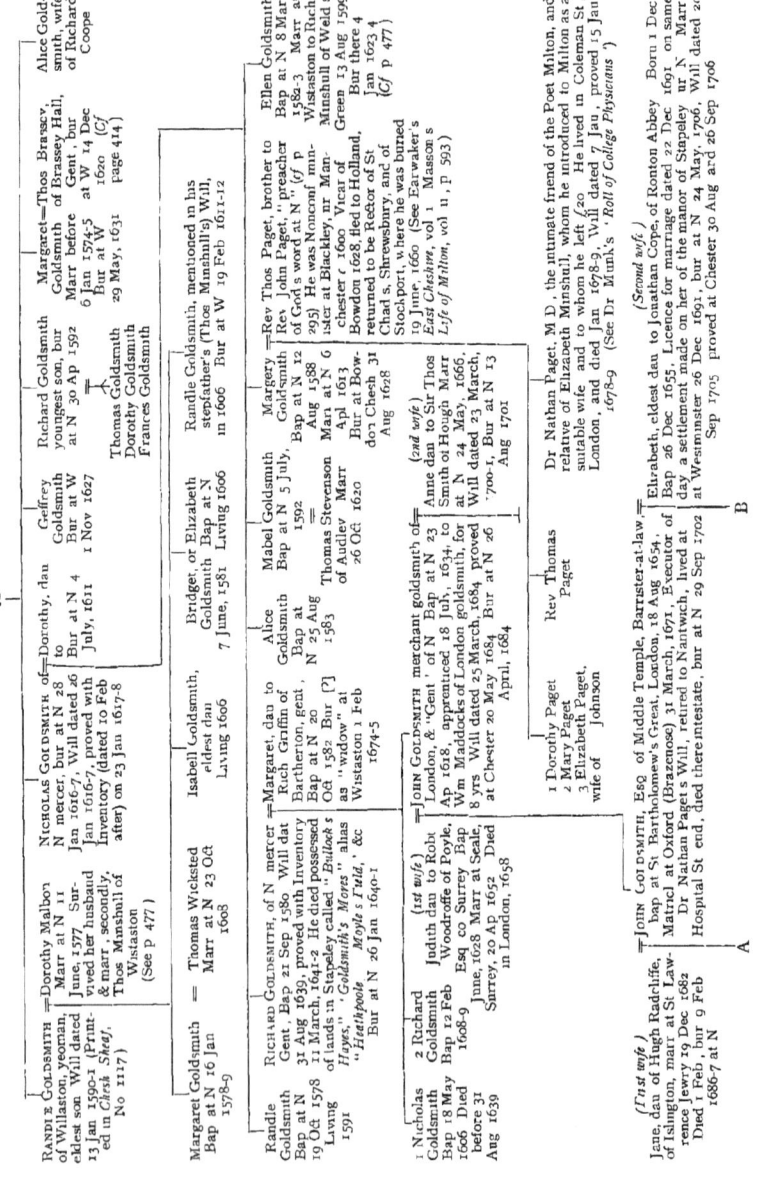

A

Alice Goldsmith, wife of Richard Coope

Margaret—Thos Brassey, Goldsmith of Brassey Hall, Marr before Gent, bur 6 Jan 1574-5 at W 14 Dec Bur at W 1620 (Cf 29 May, 1631 page 414)

Richard Goldsmith youngest son, bur at N 30 Ap 1592

Thomas Goldsmith
Dorothy Goldsmith
Frances Goldsmith

Randle Goldsmith, mentioned in his stepfather's (Thos Minshull's) Will, in 1666 Bur at W 19 Feb 1611-12

Ellen Goldsmith Bap at N 8 Mar 1582-3 Marr at Wistaston to Rich Minshull of Weld s Green 13 Aug 1599 Bur there 4 Jan 1623 4 (Cf p 477)

Rev Thos Paget, brother to Rev John Paget, "preacher of God's word at N " (cf p 295) He was Noncomf mnnister at Blackley, nr Manchester r 1600 Vicar of Bowdon 1628, fled to Holland, returned to be Rector of St Chad s, Shrewsbury, and of Stockport, where he was buried 19 June, 1660 (See Earwaker's East Cheshire, vol 1 Masson s Life of Milton, vol 11, p 593)

Margery Goldsmith Bap at N 12 Aug 1588 Marr at N 6 Apl 1613 Bur at Bowdon Cheeh 31 Aug 1628

Geffrey Goldsmith Bur at N 1 Nov 1627

Bridget, or Elizabeth Goldsmith Bap at N 7 June, 1581 Living 1606

Mabel Goldsmith Bap at N 5 July, 1592 = Thomas Stevenson of Audley Marr 26 Oct 1620

Anne dau to Sir Thos Smith of Hough Marr at N 24 May, 1666. Will dated 23 March, 1700-1, Bur at N 13 Aug 1701 (2nd wife)

Rev Thomas Paget

Dr Nathan Paget, M D, the intimate friend of the Poet Milton, and relative of Elizabeth Minshull, whom he introduced to Milton as a suitable wife and to whom he left £20 He lived in Coleman St, London, and died Jan 1678-9, Will dated 7 Jan, proved 15 Jan 1678-9 (See Dr Munk's 'Roll of College Physicians')

Elizabeth, eldest dau to Jonathan Cope, of Ronton Abbey Born 1 Dec Bap 26 Dec 1655. Licence for marriage dated 22 Dec 1691, on same day a settlement made on her of the manor of Stapeley ur N Marr at Westminster 26 Dec 1691, bur at N 24 May, 1706, Will dated 20 Sep 1705 proved at Chester 30 Aug a^d 26 Sep 1706 (Second wife)

B

RANDLE GOLDSMITH =Dorothy Malbon of Willaston, yeoman. Marr at N 11 eldest son. Will dated June, 1577 Sur-13 Jan 1590-1 (Print-vived her husband ed in Chris Shef, & marr, secondly, No 1117) Thos Minshull of Wistaston (See p 477)

NICHOLAS GOLDSMITH of =Dorothy, dau N mercer, bur at N 28 to Bur at N 4 Jan 1616-7, Will dated 26 July, 1611 Jan 1616-7, proved with Inventory (dated 10 Feb after) on 23 Jan 1617-8

Margaret Goldsmith = Thomas Wicksted Bap at N 16 Jan Marr at N 23 Oct 1578-9 1603

Isabell Goldsmith eldest dau Living 1606

Randle Goldsmith Bap at N 19 Oct 1578 Living 1591

RICHARD GOLDSMITH, of N mercer Gent. Bap 21 Sep 1580 Will dat 31 Aug 1639, proved with Inventory 11 March, 1641-2 He died possessed of lands in Stapeley called "Bullock s Hyes," "Goldsmith's Mores," alias "Heathpoole Moyle's Fuld," &c Bur at N 26 Jan 1640-1 =Margaret, dau to Rich Griffin of Bartherton, gent. Bap at N 20 Oct 1582 Bur [?] as "widow" at Wistaston 1 Feb 1674-5

Alice Goldsmith Bap at N 25 Aug 1583

1 Nicholas Goldsmith Bap at N 18 May 1606 Died before 31 Aug 1639

2 Richard Goldsmith Bap 12 Feb 1608-9

Judith dau to Robt Woodroffe of Poyle, Esq co Surrey Bap June, 1628 Marr at Seale, Surrey, 20 Ap 1652 Died in London, 1658 (1st wife)

JOHN GOLDSMITH merchant goldsmith of London, & "Gent" of N Bap at N 23 Ap 1618, apprenticed 18 July, 1634, to Wm Maddocks of London goldsmith, for 8 yrs Will dated 25 March, 1684, proved at Chester 20 May 1684 Bur at N 26 April, 1684

1 Dorothy Paget
2 Mary Paget
3 Elizabeth Paget, wife of Johnson

JANE, dau of Hugh Radcliffe, of Islington, marr at St Lawrence Jewry 19 Dec 1682 Died 1 Feb, bur 9 Feb 1686-7 at N (First wife)

JOHN GOLDSMITH, Esq of Middle Temple, Barrister-at-law bap at St Bartholomew's Great, London, 18 Aug 1654. Matricul at Oxford (Brazenose) 31 March, 1671, Executor of Dr Nathan Paget's Will, retired to Nantwich, lived at Hospital St end, died there intestate, bur at N 29 Sep 1702

A

A

Judith Goldsmith Bap at N 4 Oct 1683 Bur 28 Mar 1684

Jane Goldsmith Bap at N 10 Mar 1684-5, Marr her cousin Geo Dodd of the same place Marr in 1708 Bur at Audlem 4 Jan 1734 (*Nant Reg*)

= George Dodd, Esq, of Highfields nr Audlem, one of 17 children of

Anna Goldsmith Bap 23 Nov 1692 Bur 28 Jan 1692-3 at N

Dr Jonathan Goldsmith Bap at N 8 May, 1694 Educ at Brazenose Coll Oxon B A 13 Oct 1715, M A , 13 June 1718, Bach & Doc of Medic 11 June, 1724, F R C P 25 June 1726 Gulstonian lecturer 1728 Censor of College 1729, elected to Roy Soc 15 Jan 1729-30 & Fello v Jan 29 He resided in Norfolk St Strand & died there 17 April, 1732, aged 38 Bur at St Clement Danes 24 April, 1732

= Elizabeth, dau to Wm Farrington, of Worden Hall, co Linc & widow of Rich Atherton, of Bewsey, Lanc Marr at Weld Chapel Southgate Micdlesey, 20 Aug 1729 bur at Leigh to April, 1742, aged 40

Judith Goldsmith, eventually heiress of her brother Bap at N 21 Jan 1695-6 Died 23 Feb 1760 Bui at Beckbury

= Walter Stubbs, of Beckbury Hall, co Salop Marr at Kemberton Salop, 11 Aug 1712 Died 13 Oct 1754 Bur at Beckbury

B

A daughter

Jane Dodd, heiress = William Baker, Esq of Locrminster. Born 1711 Died a relative of the Wettenhalls of Hankelow, an architect Born 1705, marr at at Highfields 17 Bridgenorth 1736, died 29 Nov 1771 March, 1783 Aged 56 Bui at Audlem Table to Aged 72 his memory in the Church there

From whom the Bakers of Highfields, now extinct in the male line since the death of William Baker, Esq, J P, who died in 1863, and William Baker, Esq J P, his son, who died in 1876, to whose memories a stained-glass window, over the Highfields Pew in Audlem Church, was unveiled Christmas Day 1879

Walter Stubbs, who married and left issue from whom many descendants are now (1883) living The lands in Stapeley, which had been in the Goldsmith family for over 100 years, described in 1747 as the "Manor of Stapeley, consisting of 6 messuages, 10 cottages, 300 acres of land, 50 acres of meadow, 100 acres or pasture, and 50 acres of heath" were sold by Messrs John Dutton and Orlando Stubbs, trustees under the Will of Mrs Walter Stubbs to Mr William Salmon, of Nantwich, in 1765-7, the purchase money being £2 580 In 1810 the manor was the joint property of Charles and Prussia Salmon Esqrs The Hall, which was moated round, was then in ruins and infested with rats, so that James Bayley Esq, to whom these lands descended, took it down and re-built the present Stapeley Hall farm-house, now (1883) the property of his grandson, James Bayley Esq J P, of Willaston Hall

JOHN GERARD.

Of the few native worthies John Gerard, the Herbalist, stands pre-eminent. His great work, a folio volume of 1392 pp., founded on translations of Dodonæus and other foreign authors, and illustrated with more than eighteen hundred woodcuts, chiefly from the Dutch Herbal of Tabernæmontanus, is thus entitled:—

"The Herball, or Generall Historie of Plantes, Gathered by John Gerarde of London, Master in Chirurgie. Imprinted at London by John Norton 1597."

This work, which contained many errors and plagiarisms, was re-issued with corrections in 1633 by Thomas Johnson, and became a standard work for English students. The inscription round the portrait, which is here reproduced from the engraving in the first edition of that work, slightly reduced, states the author to have been fifty-three years of age in 1598. Hence he would be born in 1545; but, in consequence of the lapse of the

Registers at Nantwich, no record of his baptism is preserved, and the only mention of
the family* name occurs amongst the Baptisms, thus —

"1578 Aug 23 Alice, daughter of William Gerard"

Incidental allusions to his birth-place, school-days, travels, and to his final residence
in London as a surgeon and superintendent of the gardens of Lord Burleigh, occur in the
"*Herbal*"   For example, speaking of "*Cuckowe Flowers*," he says —

"In Northfolke, they are called Caunterbune bels, at the Namptwich, in Cheshire, *where I had
my beginning*, Ladie smockes, which hath giuen me cause to christen it after my countrie fashion "—
(Page 203)

"I haue found it [*i e* the *Raspis*, a species of Bramble] among the bushes of a cawsey neere
vnto a village called Wisterson, *where I went to schoole*, two miles from the Nantwitch in Cheshire "—
(Page 1091)

"I haue not seene any one tree thereof [*i e* the Laurel] growing in Denmarke, Swenia, Poland,
Iuonia, or Russia, or in any of those colde countries where *I haue trauelled* "—(Page 1223)

The Herbal was dedicated to the Right Hon. Sir William Cecill, Kt, Baron of
Burghley K G, Lord High Treasurer of England, &c ,† and in the "epistle dedicatorie"
Gerard writes —"under your Lordship I haue serued and that way imployed my principall
studie, and allmost all my time now by the space of *twenty yeeres*"   Hence Gerard was
already settled in London in 1577 as superintendent of the gardens of Lord Burleigh in
the Strand, and at Theobalds in Herts, concerning which he says, "a man doth behold
a flourishing show of summer beauties in the middest of winters force, and a goodly spring
of flowers, when abroad a leafe is not to be seene .   I haue added from forren places
all the variety of herbs and flowers that I might any way obtaine, I haue labored with
the soile to make it fit for the plantes, and with the plantes to make them to delight in
the soile, so that they might liue and prosper vnder our climate, as in their natiue and
proper countrie "

From several allusions to Cheshire and Nantwich in the Herbal, it may be presumed
that Gerard, in his manhood, visited the place of his birth   He says —

"*Phalaris pratensis* is called in Cheshire, about Namptwich, Quakers and Shakers."—(Page 81)

"*Buckwheate* prospereth verie well in anie ground be it neuer so drie or barren, where it is commonly sowen to serue as it were insteede of a dunging   It quickly commeth up and is very soone ripe,
it is very common in and aboute the Namptwiche in Cheshire, where they sowe it as well for foode for
their cattell, pullen, and such like, as to the vse aforesaide "—(Page 83)‡

' *Turneps* flower and seede the second yeere after they are sowen   for those which flower the same
yeere that they are sowen are a degenerate kinde, called in Cheshire about the Namptwitch, *Madneeps*,
of their cuill qualitie in causing frensie and giddinesse of the braine for a season "—(Page 178)

"I haue found *Horse Radish* wilde in sundrie places as at Namptwich in Cheshire, in a place
called the *Milne-eye*." [*i e* Mill Field]—(Page 187)

"*Bistorta* is called in English Snakeweed, in Cheshire *Pashions* and *Snakeweed*, and there used
for an excellent pot herbe "—(Page 323)

* An earlier mention of the *Gerard* family in this locality occurs in the *Inq p m* 1 Hen VII [1485-6] of SIR JOHN
BROMLEY, KT of Baddington, who "died on Sunday in the vigil of Pentecost last past leaving Margaret, the wife of
Peter Gerard, his next of kin and heiress" * * * * ' and also leaving———[obliterated] *Gerard* another of his next of kin
and heirs aged 4 years " &c , &c
   † Lord Burleigh, who expended £10 weekly to keep the poor employed in his gardens, died on 8 Sep 1598
   ‡ The last grower of Buck-wheat in this neighbourhood was Mr Goodall, a farmer, of Cheerbrook, who died about
20 years ago   (Information of Mr S Fitton, of Cheerbrook, Willaston)

" *Wall-flowers* flowei for the most part all the yeere long, but especially in wintei, whereupon the people in Cheshire do call them Winter Gillo flowers "—(Page 371)

' *Small Navelwort (Umbilicus Veneris minor)* groweth vpon the Alpes neere Piedmont, I founde the same growing upon Bieston castell in Cheshire "—(Page 424)

" I haue founde *Haies-eaies (Bupleui um)* growing naturally among the bushes vpon Biestone castell in Cheshire [and] the *Stone Crukforle* "—(Pages 485, 839)

" The people in Cheshire, especially about Namptwich where the best Cheese is made, do vse *Ladies Bedstraw* (Gallium) in their Rennett, esteeming greatly of that Cheese aboue other made without it "—(Page 968)

" *Whortlebernies* grow vpon the hils in Cheshire called Broxen hils, neere vnto Beeston castle, 7 miles from the Nantwich The people in Cheshire do eate the black Whortles in cieame and milk, as in these south parts we eate strawberries '—(Page 1230)

' The *Wilde Ashe* or *Quicken tree*, groweth vpon high mountaines, and in thicke high woods in most places of Englandc, especially about the Namptwich in Cheshire "—(Page 1290)

In 1596 Geiard lived in Holborn, then the most aristocratic part of London, where he had an extensive garden, and in that year he issued his "*Catalogus arborum, fiuticum, ac plantarum, tam indigenarum, quam exoticarum, in horto Johannis Gerardi ciuis & chirurgi, Londonensis, nascentium,*' of 24 pp printed in Fetter Lane, being the first complete garden catalogue ever published. A second edition, enumeiating 1,071 plants, dedicated to Sii Walter Raleigh, Knight, appeared in 1599 These Catalogues were re-printed for private circulation by Benjamin Daydon Jackson, F L S, in 1876, with a biographical notice of Gerard, from which the following particulars are obtained

John Gerard, who is supposed to have been descended from a youngei branch of the Gerards of Ince, in Lancashire, was elected a member of the Court of Assistants of the Barber-Suigeons 19th June, 1595, and was subsequently appointed Junior Warden, and on 15th Jan 1598, to be one of the examiners of candidates for admission to the freedom of the Barber-Surgeons Company, and finally in Aug 1608 he was elected Master of that Company He died in Feb 1611-2 and was buried in St. Andrew's Chuich, Holborn, on the 18th of that month, but there is nothing to indicate the exact spot It is said he was married, and his wife, whose name has not transpired, is also stated to have assisted him in his profession To the above notice it may be added that Queen Anne (consort of James I) granted on 14th Aug 1604, to John Gerard, Surgeon and Herbalist to the King, a lease of a garden plot adjoining Somerset House, on condition of his supplying her with herbs, flowers, and fiuit. Gerard gianted the said plot to Robert Earl of Salisbury, who surrendered it to the Queen on 27th June, 1611 *(Cal of State Papers.)*

THE MALBON FAMILY

The MALBONS are said to have descended from "a younger branch of the baronial family of Malbank, as appears by a deed of Joan, one of the co-heiresses of William de Malbank, the last Baron of that family, by which she grants lands in Bradeley, (which continued to be the residence of his posterity for several centuries) to her relation, WILLIAM MALBAN "* For so ancient a family, it is remarkable how seldom they are

* Lysons' *Cheshire*, p 838, quoting *Harl MSS* 2022, f 16 The co-heiress *Joan* married Reginald Valletort (see *Malbank Pedigree*, p 24) to whose heirs *George Malbon*, in 1592, paid a chief rent for his Bradeley demesne (See *Inq p m*)

mentioned in the County Records   There are references to THOMAS MALBON, and his wife, ELLEN, in the *Plea Rolls* 11 Hen IV [1409—10], about which time his Inquisition *post mortem* was taken, to WILLIAM MALBON,* on a Recognizance Roll, dated 6th Sep. 1474, to WILLIAM MALBON, and his daughter *Agnes*, THOMAS MALBON, and his son *John*, and RALPH MALBON, all of whom occur on a *Plea Roll*, dated 13 Hen VII. [1497-8] (See page 440)

Under the township of Haslington, in which Bradeley is situated, in the *Subsidy Roll* of 1545 (page 98) RALPH MALBON is mentioned as assessed at 14s for goods valued at £8   Possibly he was the father, or near relative, of GEORGE MALBON, of Haslington, whose Inquisition *post mortem*, now in the Record Office, is as follows   *(translated)*—

Inq p m taken at Wich Malbank, on the 9 May 35 Eliz [1593] before Sir Hugh Cholmondeley, the younger, Kt, Eschaetor, and Thomas Wilbraham, Esq, Richard Wilbraham, Ralph Hassall, and Ralph Wilbraham, Gents, feodaries, &c after the death of *George Malbon* of Haslington, in the county of Chester, by the oath of Thomas Mynshull, Richard Brereton, Thomas Chetwoode, Esqrs, Robert Whitney, Thomas Brooke, Richard Horton, John Chefors, John Witter, Richard Wilbraham, Roger Wettenhall, Robert Alger Randle [?] Poole, William Salmon, Robert Rawley, and William Salmon, Gents, who say that GEORGE MALBON died seised in his demesne as of fee of and in 1 messuage 10 acres of land 8 acres of pasture 4 acres of meadow and one water-mill with water-course belonging to the same mill in Haslington, which he held of the heirs of Reginald de Valletort in socage by the service of 3s 6d per ann, and rendering 12d per ann to Thomas Vernon of Haslington, Esq on the feasts of St Martin [11 Nov] and St John the Baptist [24 June] by equal portions being of the total value of 20s per ann   Also the said George Malbon died seised &c of 1 toft and 4 acres of arable land which he held of the Queen as Countess of Chester by Knight service *in capite* of the value of 3s per ann That the said George died on the 11th Nov before the taking of this Inquisition, and that *Thomas Malbon* is his son and heir of the age of 16 years on the 14th March last past [1592-3]   The said George Malbon had to wife Matilda, the daughter of William Leversage, who is now living at Haslington

THOMAS MALBON, who was under age at the time of his father's death, was born, as may be inferred from the above Inquisition, on 14th March, 1577-8   He obtained livery of his father's lands at Bradeley by Writ dated 20th Aug 1599,† and, in 1616, according to a tablet with armorial carvings that once adorned old Bradeley Hall,‡ re-built the home of his ancestors   For many years, however, he was connected with Nantwich, where, on 14th Feb 1597-8, he married for his first wife, Elizabeth, eldest daughter to Richard Clutton, Lawyer of Nantwich, and himself followed the profession of the law   In 1623 he occurs as Sir Ranulphe Crewe's *Steward* for his Manor Court of the Countess of Warwick's Fee, as appears by the following copy of a Presentment from the Court Rolls in his own handwriting §

Countess of Warwick's Fee

"View of Frankpledge with Court Baron of Sir Ranulphe Crewe, Knight Serjeant-at-law of the King, and lord of the said Fee, held at Wich Malbank in the county of Chester on the 21 Oct. 21 James I, 1623, before *Thomas Malbon*, Gent, Steward of the said Court

---

* He may have been identical with *William Malbon*, aged 52, who was present as a Juror at Wistaston Church on Saturday next before the feast of St Thos the Apostle [21 Dec] 5 Edw IV [1466] when the *prob ætat* (proof of age) of John Bruen was taken

† Cheshire Recognizance Rolls   ‡ Bradeley Hall has been a farm-house since about the year 1720

§ The heading and the names of Jurymen in the original, *tenes me*, is written in Latin.

Names of the Jury for the lord and King.

THOMAS SHENTON, of Stoke	THOMAS MAYKYN, of Cholmeston
RALPH STOCKTON, of the same	THOMAS HODCSON, of the same
THOMAS HIGHFIELD, JUNR, of the same	JOHN DAYE, of the same
WILLIAM SAVAGE, of Wich Malbank	EDWARD ASTON, of Aston
EDWARD MASSIE, of the same	HENRY PENDLETON, of the same
THOMAS CARTWRIGHT, of Stoke	WILLIAM ASTON, of the same
HUGH FILCOCKE, of Cholmeston	JOHN WATSON, of the same

The said Jurye upon their Othes doe p'sent [present] —

That the \th daye of Julye in the 21 James I [1623] One Baye trottinge Mare wth a peece cutt furthe of the vtter pte [outer part] of the Eare from the Mare, wth a Saddle and Brydle was taken vp att Cholmeston aforesaid, as a *wayfe*, and steyed [seized] by the Baylyff for the vse of the Lorde   And afterwards was p'ved [proved] to have byn the goods of one Thomas Mynshull wch was apprehended for stealinge a Nagge from one Rondull Betteley of Cholmeston aforesaid & was executed* for the same att Chester att the assize holden theire the xxixth daye of Septr in the said year 21 James I "

[Subscribed in the same handwriting]

"A true Copy of the examination by me the said

THOMAS MALBON Steward of the said Court, 1624 "

Thomas Malbon fulfilled the office of Churchwarden at Nantwich in 1626 and 1627 (page 126), and during those years kept the Parish Registers   In 1642 he signed the "*Remonstrance*" (page 139), in 1644 he was one of the Committee of Sequestrators; and in 1651 he wrote the account of the Civil War in Cheshire and the adjacent counties, from which extracts have been given relating to Nantwich and its immediate neighbourhood on pages 140—182

His first wife, *Elizabeth*, died on 21st March, 1622-3, and was buried at Nantwich, (see Monuments, page 313) leaving as issue two sons, *George* and *Thomas*, and seven daughters, *Margery*, baptized 7th Nov 1601,† *Dorothy*, baptized 19th Feb 1605-6, four daughters whose baptisms are not recorded at Nantwich, and *Katherine*, baptized 28th Oct 1621.

By his second wife, *Sarah*, who only survived her husband about five months, and was buried in Barthomley on the 22nd Nov 1658, he had no issue.

Thomas Malbon was buried in Barthomley Church on the 23 June, 1658, and on the south wall a brass was placed to his memory, inscribed as follows —‡

"UNDERNEATH LYETH BURYED THE BODIE OF THOMAS MALBON OF BRADELEY, GENT., ONE OF YE ATTORNEYS BEFORE THE JUDGES OF CHESTER, WHO DEPARTED THIS LYFE THE 21ST DAY OF JUNE 1658."

The Rev Edward Hinchliffe (*Hist of Barthomley*, page 35) says, the "achievements" of the Malbon family "were hanging upon the walls over their graves when I was young, dusky and ragged mementos of the departed, but, unfortunately, they were taken down without authority, and, as I am told, their sound and well-seasoned oak backs were applied

---

* This execution is not mentioned in the '*List of Public Executions in Chester from the 16th Century*,' contained in Hemingway's *History of Chester* 1831 vol II p 296

† The Baptism of *Margery Malbon* was originally entered (by mistake as it would seem) at Nantwich under date 18th March, 1603-4, but this error is corrected in her father s own handwriting to 7th Nov 1601 (See *Bap Reg* at Nantwich)

‡ Hinchliffe s *Barthomley*, p 35

to the repairs of the pigstye doors of the glebe farm " It may also be added that the stones, which formerly covered the Malbon vault, have of late years been removed into the churchyard, and now form part of the pavement along the north side of the Church They have lozenge shaped brasses, with Arms engraved, *(Or, two bendlets componé Argent and Gules)** and inscribed as follows —

"Sarah the wife of Thomas Malbon of Namptwitch, Gent, died 20 Nov 1658 '

"Thomas Malbon, of Bradley, Gent, died ye 21st day of June 1658 '

"Catharine, first wife of George Malbon of Bradley Gent 1644 "

"Elizabeth, second wife of George Malbon of Bradley Gent, died 27 Sep 1654 "

"George, son and heir of George Malbon of Bradley Gent, died 27 Oct 1708 '

1 GEORGE MALBON, of Bradeley, gent, eldest son of Thomas Malbon, was born *c* 1598. He was married at Nantwich to Catharine Wood on 24th Sep 1639, who was buried at Barthomley in 1644, leaving a son, *George Malbon*, afterwards of Bradeley, who died on 27th Oct. 1708 His second wife, *Elizabeth*, died on 27th Sep 1654, and was buried at Barthomley †

2. THOMAS MALBON, second son of Thomas Malbon was baptized at Nantwich on 11th July, 1613, and buried there on 4th Aug 1688 Both brothers became officers in the Parliamentary Army, and distinguished themselves at the taking of Cholmondeley Castle (page 178) By his wife, *Elizabeth*, he had a son, *Thomas*, baptized at Nantwich 13th Dec 1655, and buried there on 30th July, 1697, from whom probably descended *Thomas Malbon*, of Bridgemere, gent, who was Churchwarden at Wybunbury in 1692, and had three sons baptized there namely —*Thomas*, baptized 1st Dec 1687, *George*, baptized 21st May, 1689, *William*, baptized 10th March, 1691-2

It will not be necessary to trace the family further,† but it may be remarked, that although the Bradeley Hall estate has been alienated from the family since the year 1720, the local newspapers of this present year (1883) recorded the death of a Mr George Malbon, at Bradeley Green, aged forty-nine years, on 27th March, 1883

THE WRIGHT FAMILY

From the middle of the sixteenth century to the early part of the eighteenth century the WRIGHTS ranked amongst the principal families of the town. Prior to the year 1540 nothing certain is known of the family, and there is little to relate concerning them beyond what is contained in two Inquisitions *post mortem*, and a few Wills, abstracts of which are here given in proof of the descents in the subjoined pedigree. It has, however, been assumed that RONDULL WRIGHT, the brother of *Edmund Wright*, and father of *Sir Edmund Wright*, was the son of EDMUND WRIGHT, whose name is also given in some old MS pedigrees as *Edward Wright*. Although the probability of this descent may be admitted from the Christian name of *Edmund* only occurring in that branch of the family,

* If, as has been supposed, the Malbons descended from the ancient family of Malbank, it is very remarkable that they never entered their names at any of the Heralds Visitations and thus proved their right to bear arms, No claim to such distinction appears to have been made until 1663-4, when it was disallowed by Sir William Dugdale (See Dr. Ormerod's *Cheshire,* vol iii p 318, New Edit)

† For further information, see Lysons' *Cheshire,* pp 399 and 838, Hinchliffe's *Barthomley,* p 74, Earwaker's *Local Gleanings relating to Lancashire and Cheshire,* vol ii p 283

positive proof is wanting owing to the hiatus in the Parish Register between the years 1545 and 1572

EDMUND WRIGHT, (afterwards *Sir Edmund Wright*) the son of Rondull Wright, was born at Nantwich, and baptized there on 24th Nov 1573 (see pp. 338 366)   He was a successful adventurer in trade in the metropolis, where he rose to be an Alderman, and eventually, in 1640-1, when the Long Parliament had assembled, to be the Lord Mayor. Sir Edmund Wright Alderman of London, is mentioned in the return by the several wards of the City of London specifying the names of such persons as are conceived able to lend his Majesty, Charles I, money upon security, towards the raising of the sum of £200,000 according to Order in Privy Council at Whitehall on 19th May, 1640 *

In 1640 (Nov or Dec) Sir William Acton, Knight and Bart, was discharged from his office of Lord Mayor of London by the House of Commons and *Sir Edmund Wright, Grocer*, substituted †   The date of his death has not occurred   His gifts to his native town have already been noticed, and need not be repeated, but a clause in the Almshouse Deed may here be alluded to   The Founder directed that a candidate of the name of *Wright* offering himself for an Almsman's "place" should be preferred to anyone else, doubtless thinking he was thus providing a home for his poorer kinsfolk   At that time the *Wrights* were as numerous in Nantwich as the Leighs, Davenports and Massies are said, in the old proverb, to have been in Cheshire   No name occurs so often in the Parish Registers in the seventeenth century, they lived in every street in the town, and belonged to every grade of society from Esquires and Gentlemen, to respectable tradesmen, work-people and cottagers   For example, (and this is by no means a solitary instance,) in the Baptism Registers in the course of *five* weeks, *five* different families are mentioned; thus —

> " 1653 Aprill 3 Richard sonne of Richard Wright in the wale lane "
> ,,   ,, 10 Thomas sonne of Jonn Wright glouer
> ,,   ,, 24 Edward sonne of Arthur Wright "
> ,   May 1 Dorothy dau of John Wright Junr "
> ,,   ,, 15 Henry sonne of Robert Wright in the welsh roe "

Notwithstanding the multitude of Wrights in the town, it is a remarkable fact, that after the death of *John Wright, Almsman*, about Christmas 1666, no person of the name of Wright had benefit of that Charity for nearly forty years, the next being *Henry Wright*, butcher, "being of kindred to ye founder," who was elected on 28th June, 1705.

Inquisition post mortem of Richard Wright, 31 Eliz. [1589].

"*Inq p m* taken at Wich Malbank on 13 Sep 31 Eliz [1589] before Hugh Beeston, Senr, Esq   and Thomas Burroughes Gent deputy Eschaetors, John Ward, of Frodsham, and Richard Clutton, Gents, Commissioners, after the death of *Richard Wright, Gent*, by the oathes of Ralph Leftwich, Thomas Mynshull, Esqrs, George Bostock, John Hankye, Roger Hockenhull, John Cheswis, Thomas Brooke, Richard Horton, Roger Wettenhall, Richard Wilbraham, William Pratchett, John Cawton, Hugh Wareton, William Salmon of Coole-lane, and William Salmon of Wildheath [Willaston] Gentlemen, who say that Richard Wright, father of the said Richard Wright had by deed dated 1 Oct 2 Eliz [1559] (quoted in this Inquisition) granted a Messuage or Burgage called " *The Bell*," and one salt-house of six leads in Wich Malbank,

---

* Calendar of State Papers, Car 1 Domestic Series
† Orridge's " *Citizens of London and their Rulers* "

two acres of land and two acres of pasture in Henhull called the *Wallcrofte*, to Margaret daughter of Alexander Elcocke formerly of Stockport in consideration of her marriage with the said Richard Wright Senr and to their legitimate heirs &c failing these to his right heirs   The said Richard Wright died seised of the above property and of one vine garden, 2 meadows, 1 pasture called *Peretree field* in Wich Malbank another pasture called ' *Chapel-croft*," and half of another pasture called the " *Chapel-field*" adjacent, lying in Acton, 20 acres of land, 12 acres of meadow, 20 acres of pasture, and 40 acres of wood in Wych Malbank, Henhull, and Monks Coppenhall   also, *the tythes of the formerly dissolved free chapel of St Lawrence*, also 4 pastures in Wich Malbank, 1 meadow and pasture and wood, called *Coppenhall-hey*, in Coppenhall, 1 pasture or croft called peretree-field in Monks Coppenhall, 1 pasture or Croft called *Roughfield* in Henhull, *Shutshawe* pasture in Wych Malbank, 13 messuages or tenements in Welsh Row, "*le hospell*" St, "*le pillorie*" St, and High Town in Wych Malbank   The aforesaid Richard Wright died 20 Aug 30 Eliz [1588] and Margaret Wright, aged 12 yrs 6 mo and 5 days, and Elizabeth Wright, aged 1 yr and 10 months, when this Inquisition was taken, are his heirs ' &c

These daughters, many years afterwards, in 1639, conveyed their interest in the tithes above mentioned to the preaching minister of Nantwich Church   Richard Wright, senr, father of the above Richard Wright, had died in 1585, and his Will, now at Chester, is as follows —

Will of Richard Wright   Proved 1585

"In the name of God, Amen 2 May 20 Eliz [1578] I Richard Wright of Wich Malbank, the elder, &c I give &c vnto Margaret my wyffe 40s yearly yssuing out of a field called *wychefield* in Stapeley for 4 yeares, and afterwards to my sonne Henrie Wright for the terme of 4 yeares & the remainder of the terme to James Wright another of my sonnes   *Item* I give &c to Richard Wright my sonne and heire apparent one neste of silver bowles being three and my best silver salte &c my wife to have the use of all the plate during her natural life   *Item* I give &c to the said Richard that dozen of silver spoones wch I bought of mr ffulleshurste and four bedds and my beste gold ringe &c   *Item* I give to Cicilie Wright my daughter three score poundes of money   *Item* I give &c to my younger sonnes Jerome Wright, Henrie Wright ffrancis Wright, James and Roger Wright, to euery of them £33 6s 8d   Also I give &c to my bastard daughter, (yf she will be ordered by my seide wife) tenne poundes &c , to my old loving fiends Mr William Massie of Denfield one double ducett, and the rest of my goodes to my wyffe [whom] I make sole executrix &c And I make &c my brother in law Thomas Elcocke parson of Bartomley, my brother Thomas Wright, and my cosin Lawrence Wright overseers &c   R W "

The following Inventory of goods at the "*Bell Inn*," dated 9th Nov. 1585, accompanies this Will

		li	s	d
Itm,	xviij bedds wth the furnyture	xxxvij	xj	iiij
Itm	in lynynge [linen]	vj	—	—
Itm	in wyne	xxxv	—	—
Itm	in brasse potts & pannes and such lyke	iiij	viij	—
Itm	in Iron vi grates wyth hondyarns [hand irons] wythe fyre skyurners [screens] tongs and such lyke	—	xxxij	—
Itm	in pewter lxxxviij peces	—	xxxiij	ij
Itm	xiiij candell stycks	—	xx	—
Itm	in qnysshens [cushions] x	—	v	—
Itm	a carpet & cubbord cloth	—	vj	—
Itm	in tables formes & Chayres	—	xl	—
Itm	in trene ware	—	xx	—
Itm	viij chests	—	xx	—
Itm	in plate praysed to	xlv	—	—
Itm	in Cattell	xxv	—	—

The other Inquisition *post mortem* is that of LAWRENCE WRIGHT, of Nantwich, which, however, was not taken until twenty-one years after his death

"*Inq p m* taken at Wich Malbank on 9 July 21 James I [1625] before Hugh Mainwaring Esq Eschaetor, and Peter Daniell Esq Feodary &c after the death of Laurence Wright Gent deceased, by the oaths of Robert Auger, Robert Poole, of Auger [Alsager], William Boulton of Hankilowe, John Cartwright of Aston, William Wast of Hunstaston, Thomas Scott and Thomas Smith of Checkley, Thomas Shenton of Stoke, ffrancis Betteley of Burland, Olliver Pollett, John Moulton of fadeley, John Gallamore, William Gallamore senior, and William Gallamore Junr of Betchton, Hugh Wheelock of Betchton, Randle Grafton of Worleston, and Nicholas Hussie of Baguley, Gents jurors, who say that *Laurence Wright* on the day before his death died seized in his demesne as of fee of and in 15 acres of land, 15 acres pasture, 6 acres meadow, and 15 acres of heath in Henhull, 5 acres land, 3 acres pasture, 2 acres meadow, and six salt leads in Namptwich, 6 burgages or cottages, two salt houses and 12 acres of land in Namptwich, a messuage called Chadknik in Romiley in the county of Chester formerly purchased from Queen Elizabeth, also certain tithes of corn, wool, and lambs in Baddington Woolston Wood and Namptwich, formerly belonging to Queen Elizabeth, &c The Jurors say that Laurence Wright died 5 Aug 1603, and that *Laurence Wright*, his son and heir is at the time of taking this Inquisition 48 years of age and more, and that the said Laurence Wright, son and heir, Margaret his wife, and Robert his son occupied all and singular the premises, lands, &c The said Robert Wright died 14 Jan 1616, and the said Margaret died 18 Feb 1617"

Will of Laurence Wright Proved 1603

"In the name of God Amen, the 6 June 1 James I [1603] I LAURENCE WRIGHT of Wich Malbank, gent &c

Item I bequeath to my sing'ler good *Mr Henrie Birkenhead Esqr* my golde Ringe with the deathes head

It I bequeath to *William Newton Esq* sonne in lawe my rapier and dager and tenne shillings in gold, and to my daughter Margery his wyffe tenne shillings in gold

It I bequeath to my daughter *Elizabeth Weyver* 10s in gold

It I bequeath to my son in law *John ffyges gent* and to *Cecell* his wife together 10s in gold

It I bequeath to my son in law *John Slade* and *Margaret Slade* his wife together 10s

It I bequeath to *Robert Wright* one of my younger sonnes and to his heirs for euer all those messuages and lands in Wich Malbank wch I lately purchased of Peter Dutton gent, Elizabeth his wyfe, and Richard Massie Gent, and also a messuage in beame streete &c in the holding of Thomas Minshull, also a messuage in High Towne wch I lately purchased of Raphe Wright &c also a wiche house of sixe leads lying in Mistlesiche in Wich Malbank

It I give &c to Margaret my wife a pasture called the broad-lane field for her life, remainder thereof to my sayd sonne Robert his heirs &c Also to Robert my sonne my land in Woolston wood wch I holde of William Hassall gent and my best cloake

It I give &c to *Thomas Wright* my youngest sonne a messuage in Welsh Row &c a messuage in Barkers street &c also my interest in demeanes meadow other[wise] demeanes bache in Wibunburie wch I holde of the dymise of Thomas Smyth Esq, also a wiche-house of sixe leades in Wich Malbank two messuages in beame street and nyne gardens in Monks lane &c

It . my wyfe Margarett to have certain lands for seven yeares if she soe longe live towards payment to my sonne *Laurence* duringe three years after my decease tenne poundes, also paying my sonne Robert at the ende of his apprenticeshipp fortie poundes, and to my son Thomas &c fifteene poundes

It I give to my daughter *Dorothie* 300li and to my daughter *Ann* 200li [After disposing of his furniture, plate, jewellery, &c, the Will says,] I give &c vnto my sonne Thomas my bookes of Lawe and Latin books, and the reste of my bookes to be divided among the rest of my sonnes" &c

The Inventory accompanying this Will, dated 10th August 1603, amounts to cccccccxli xiijs iiijd [£621 13s 4d]

Will of Roger Wright, mercer   Proved 1604

"In the name of God Amen, the 27 June 1604 I ROGER WRIGHT of Wich Malbank mercer, &c
My bodie to be buried in the p'ishe church yarde of wiche Malbank

It I give &c unto my deare and lovinge mother *Margaret Wilbraham* in Remembrance of the love
and dewtie I beare her in gold vjs viijd

It I give unto my well beloved brother [in-law] *Lawrence Wright* in gold vjs viijd

It I give unto my welbeloved brother *Henrie Wright* in gold xs

It I give to my sister in law *Anne Wright* his wife in gold xs

It I give to my loving brother *ffrancis Wright* one debt of viijli and in money xxs

It I give unto my welbeloved brother *James Wright* &c xli

It I give unto *Roger Wright* sonne of the said James iijli vjs viijd

It I give &c unto my sister *Elizabeth Minshall* &c in golde xs

It I give unto my welbeloved sister *Cycill Haughton* in golde xs

It I give unto *Anne Haughton* my god daughter &c xls

It I give unto my welbeloved father in law *Mathew Wright* to make him a ringe in golde xxs also
my ryding gray cloak &c

It I give to my poore nurse Anne Younge &c xxs also to Henry Young her husband my old apparell

It I geve to my wyves [wife's] grandmother Elizabeth Wright widow iijli vjs viijd to my wyves uncle
William Wood in money xls   All the reste of my goods &c I give unto *Marie Wright* my wife and make
her my sole executrix   *p me* Roger Wright "

[*Codocil*] "I give unto *Roger Wright* my godsonne sonne of Roger Wright of the High Towne in
gold xs " &c

The Inventory of stock in his shop, household goods, &c which is more than two
yards in length, is dated 14th Nov 1604

Will of Henry Wright, Innholder.   Proved 1607

"In the name of God Amen The 9 Aug 1607 I HENRY WRIGHT, of Wich Malbank Innhoulder
&c I give &c to my onelye daughter *Margarett Wright* 100li   I give &c to my brother *ffrancis* 40s in
golde and to every one of his children vs   I give &c to my brother *James* my bandore [a musical instru-
ment] his owne picture and mine my book of the abridgment of statutes my silver sorde and daggar and
40s &c   I give &c to my brother *Jerom Wright* 40s &c.   I give to my loving sister *Elizabeth Minshull*
40s   I give to my loving sister in law Margaret Georges 40s   I give to my brother in law *mr John
Woodnoth* a debt of £3   I give to my father in law *mr John Woodnoth* 40s in gould   I give to my cousin
Richard Mynshull my Vyoll de Gamboe [bass-viol, which in the Inventory is valued with other musical
instruments at £2], to Thomas Tench 10s , I give &c to my cossen *Roger Wright* of ye High Towne 10s ,
to Richard Hurwar 10s ; also to mr John ffrancis of Chester 10s and my great velvett saddle   I give to
Randull Sparrowe my man my lease I have in the *beare howse* vnder such conditions as I now have it
Also Mr Wilbraham's garden behind the Church and £10 in money , and the rest of my goods to my
loving wyffe *Anne Wright* sole executrix "

The Inventory taken 15th Oct 1607, amounts to £268 18s 6d

Will of Anne Wright, spinster.   Proved 12th May, 1635

"In the name of God Amen   The 25th Sept 1634 I ANNE WRIGHT one of the daughters of
Lawrence Wright, of Wich Malbank, gent , &c

It I give to my cosen *Henry Wright* son to Lawrence Wright my brother woods and lands in Minshull

Vernon called the Milne Hey Gibbons field the great Brooke flatt the little Brooke flatt in trust to pay the rents &c by £6 yearly to *Roger Wright* my brother and *Alts* his wife

It I give to the said Henry Wright my yellow bed and the furniture carpitts needlework and tente work qushions two stools for *Elizabeth Weever* my sister

It I give to *Thomas Wright* my brother p[ar]son of Wilmslow my great silver gilte bowle with a cover whereon my fathers armes are engraven and to his wife my best purse imbroadered with pearle and gould

It I give to *Laurence Wright* my brother my best bedd curtain vallences and other furniture and £10 &c

It I give to *Laurence* son of my brother Laurence another silver gilt boole with a cover

It I give to *Thomas, Edward, Elizabeth, Dorothye,* and *Margaret* [children] of my said brother laurence £10 a peece

It I give to *Elizabeth Wiever* my sister sixe qushions of neildwork which the s^d Elizabeth did work with platt stich Speeds Chronicle, Josephus, and £10

It I give to my sister *ffiges* [and her children, *William, Thomas, Sarah, Francis,* and *Jane,* legacies of £5 and £10] &c

It I give to *Richard Clutton* gent sonne of my sister *Dorothy Clutton* deceased my great Joyned presse, a feather bed &c And all the rest of my goods in my trunk marked E C to *Richard Clutton, Laurence Clutton, Margaret Wright,* and *Elizabeth Clutton,* children of my said sister Dorothy Clutton at such time as Richard Clutton shall come to 21 years and in the meantime to be kept for their use by Richard Clutton Esq their uncle

It I give to Roger Wilbraham Esq my best gould ring with a dyamond

It I give to my kinsman Roger Wright of the High Towne £10 wch he oweth me To Thomas Wilbraham of the Townsend Esq my best seeinge glasse

It I give to Margarett Warde Anne Newton Margery Kelfall daughters of my sister *Newton* deceased £10 a peece

It I give to the Poor of the Pr'she of Bunburie 5£ &c and £10 to be distributed to the poore of Namptwich

It I give to cousin *Mathew Wright* son of my kinsman *James Wright* deceased £10, to *Margaret* wife of the said Mathew Wright my best gowne and petticoat of moe heare my cloak sangard hood pillin and all other my riding furniture &c '

Other sums are left by the testatrix to persons named in this interesting Will, and the Inventory of her goods, taken on 1st Dec. 1634 amounts to the very large sum of £1,196 5s 4d

Will of Matthew Wright, gent Proved 28th May 1663.

"In the name of God Amen I Matthew Wright of Wich Malbank, Gent &c *ffirst* I doe hereby give devise [&c] vnto my Executors all that one p[ar]cell of wood or woodland called *Coppenhall Hey* & the meadows thereunto belonging [&c] for the terme of 4 yeeres after my decease and after to my son and heir apparent *Richard Wright* and the heirs of his body [R W to pay to the said executor £360] Also I give [&c] to my sonne Richard one brewing panne in the brewhowse all Iron gratts belonging to my messuage called *the Bell* one Jack in the Kitchen all the shelves in the howse one great bedstead in the p'lor chamber, & my signet Ring I give unto my sonne James * * * * [Legacies of 20s to buy a ring to each of the following friends namely, to Leftwich Oldfeild, Esq, to "my brother in law William Bentley doctor of Phisick," to Thomas Ursgate Gent, to William Meakin, gent] * * * * "And whereas my cozen *Elizabeth Davenport* deceased in her life time by her Conveyance did grant unto my sonne *James Wright* certaine lands lynge in or neere Wich Malbanke of the yearly value of £23 18s 4d and soe received by mee since I came in possession thereof the which I charge my said Executors to bee Accountable for to my said sonne James hee allowing £10 by the yeare vpon such Account for his table [board] app[ar]ell and Schooleing which I have found for him   And lastly I doe hereby ordayne and make *Ann Wright, Elizabeth Wright,* and *Margaret Wright* my loving and dutiful children executrices of this my last will and testament [&c] In witness &c on 1 Aprill 1663

MATT WRIGHT[1]

After a careful search in the Parish Registers, I have failed to find the baptisms of RICHARD WRIGHT, B D , and of CLUTTON WRIGHT, Esq , consequently their parentage must remain doubtful until positive proof is forthcoming   The latter gentleman may have been the son of Margaret Wright (*née* Clutton) who is named in the Will of her aunt Anne Wright, spinster, on page 491

The Lysons (*History of Cheshire,* page 369) say that the Wrights of Nantwich became extinct with the death of EDWARD WRIGHT, Esq in 1745, who died unmarried and in-testate in that year   This statement is proved to be correct by the administration of his effects still preserved at the Probate office, Chester, dated 22nd Oct 1745 , which states that " Ann Wright, of Nantwich, spinster, William Bailey, of Congleton, Gent , Thomas Tagg, of Nantwich, gent , Charles Montague Lyon, of Winsford, salt-officer, and Richard Church, of Nantwich, gent , entered into a bond of £500 on the 16th Sept 1745   Ann Wright as administratrix of all the goods &c of Edward Wright to the use and behoof of Sophia, wife of Thomas Tagg, Charlotte, wife of Charles Montague Lyon, Margaret, wife of William Bailey also natural and lawful sisters of the decedent and of all others."

This last generation of the Wrights is clearly shown in the subjoined pedigree

Wright Pedigree.

Authorities   Harl MSS 2119, f 77 , Inquisitions post mortem , Wills at Chester , Parish Registers , &c

ROGER WRIGHT, === Margaret, dau to Rich Leech of N
of Nantwich   (*Harl MSS* 2119)   Margery Bradfield
Subsidy Roll 1545   of N *Harl MSS* 1424, f 25 , and *Visit Chesh* 1580, preserved at Condover Hall

A

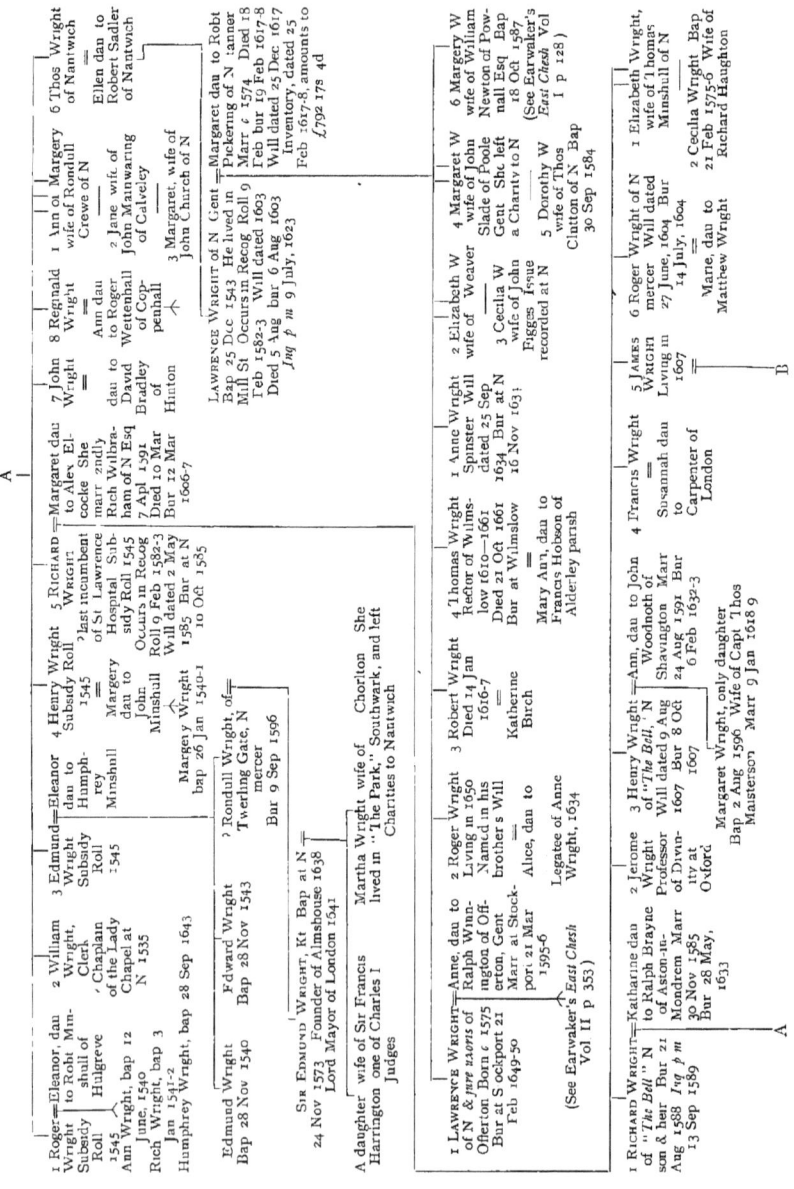

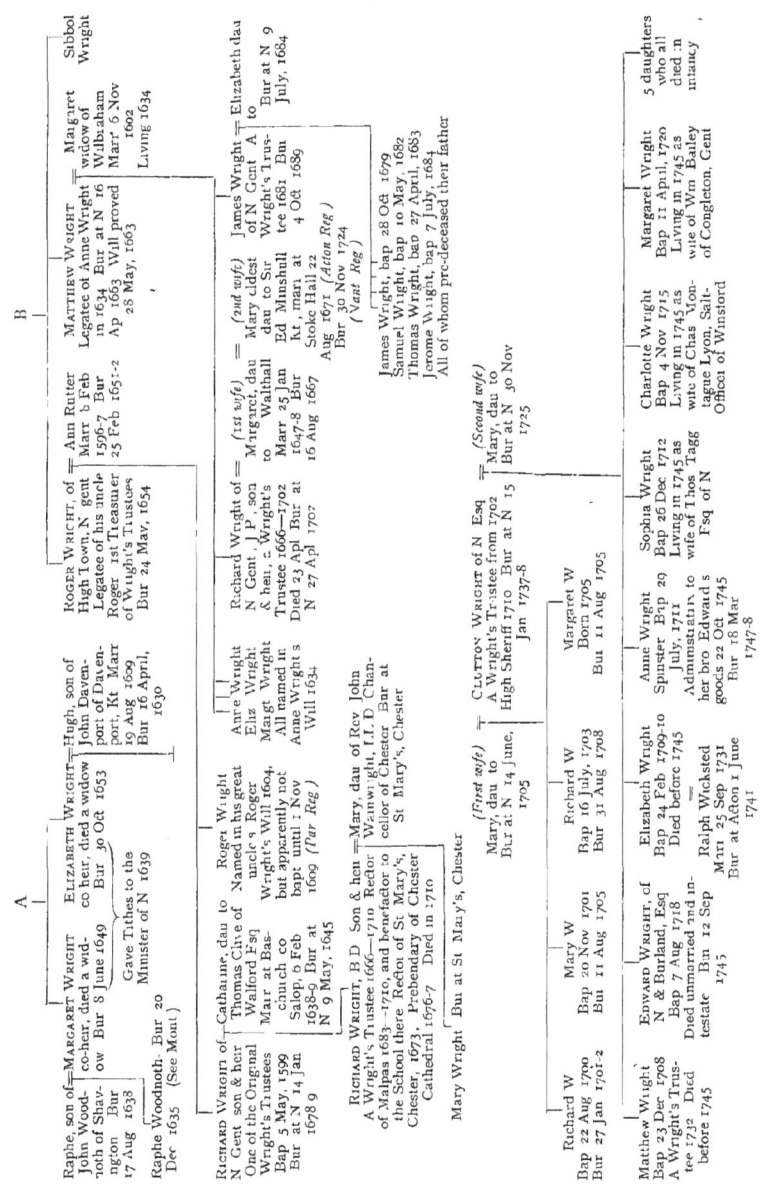

A

Raphe, son of ⸺ MARGARET WRIGHT ⸺ ELIZABETH WRIGHT ⸺ Hugh, son of
John Wood-   co heir, died a wid-   co heir, died a widow   John Daven-
noth of Shav- ow Bur 8 June 1649   Bur 30 Oct 1653   port of Daven-
ington Bur   port, Kt Marr
17 Aug 1638   Gave Tithes to the   19 Aug 1609
        Minister of N 1639   Bur 16 April,
Raphe Woodnoth: Bur 20   1630
Dec 1635 (See Mont)

RICHARD WRIGHT of ⸺ Catharine, dau to   Roger Wright   Anre Wright   Margt Wright
N Gent son & heir   Thomas Clive of   Named in his great   Eliz Wright   All named in
One of the Original   Walford Esq   uncle s Roger   All named in   Anne Wright s
Wright's Trustees   Marr at Bas-   Wright's Will 1604,   Anne Wright s   Will 1634
Bap 5 May, 1599   church co   but apparently not   Will 1634
Bur at N 14 Jan   Salop, 6 Feb   bapt until 1 Nov
1678 9   1638-9 Bur at   1609 (Tur Reg)
      N 9 May, 1645

RICHARD WRIGHT, B D Son & heir ⸺ Mary, dau of Rev John
A Wright's Trustee 1666—1710 Rector   Wainwright, L.L.D Chan-
of Malpas 1683—1710, and benefactor to   cellor of Chester Bur at
the School there Rector of St Mary's,   St Mary's, Chester
Chester, 1673, Prebendary of Chester
Cathedral 1696-7 Died in 1710

Mary Wright Bur at St Mary's, Chester

        (First wife) ⸺
        Mary, dau to
        Bur at N 14 June,
        1705

Richard W   Mary W   Richard W   Elizabeth Wright
Bap 22 Aug 1700   Bap 20 Nov 1701   Bap 16 July, 1703   Bap 24 Feb 1709-10
Bur 27 Jan 1701-2   Bur 11 Aug 1705   Bur 31 Aug 1708   Died before 1745
          Ralph Wicksted
          Marr 25 Sep 1731
          Bur at Afton 1 June
          1741

Matthew Wright   Edward Wright, of
Bap 23 Dec 1708   N & Burland, Esq
A Wright's Trus-   Bap 7 Aug 1718
tee 1732 Died   Died unmarried and in-
before 1745   testate Bur 12 Sep
      1745

B

MATTHEW WRIGHT ⸺ Ann Rutter   ROGER WRIGHT, of ⸺ Margaret Wright   widow of
Legatee of Anne Wright   Marr b Feb   High Town, N gent   Wilbraham
in 1634 Bur at N 16   1596-7 Bur   Legatee of his uncle   Marr 6 Nov
Ap 1663 Will proved   25 Feb 1651-2   Roger 1st Treasurer   1602
28 May, 1663   of Wright's Trustees   Living 1634
        Bur 24 May, 1654

James Wright ⸺ Elizabeth dau
of N Gent A   to
Wright's Trus-   Bur at N 9
tee 1681 Bur   July, 1664
4 Oct 1689

Richard Wright of ⸺   (1st wife)   =   (2nd wife)
N Gent, J P, son   Margaret, dau   Mary eldest
& heir, a Wright's   to Walthall   dau to Sir
Trustee 1666—1702   Marr 25 Jan   Ed Minshull
Died 23 Apl Bur at   1647-8 Bur   Kt, marr at
N 27 Apl 1702   16 Aug 1667   Stoke Hall 22
          Aug 1671 (Afton Reg)
          Bur 30 Nov 1724
          (Nant Reg)

James Wright, bap 28 Oct 1679
Samuel Wright, bap 10 May, 1682
Thomas Wright, bap 27 April, 1683
Jerome Wright, bap 7 July, 1684
All of whom pre-deceased their father

CLUTTON WRIGHT of N Esq ⸺ Mary, dau to
A Wright's Trustee from 1702   Bur at N 30 Nov
High Sheriff 1710 Bur at N 15   1725
Jan 1737-8

    (Second wife)
    Mary, dau to
    Bur at N 30 Nov
    1725

Margaret W   Anne Wright   Sophia Wright   Charlotte Wright   Margaret Wright   5 daughters
Born 1705   Spinster Bap 20   Bap 26 Dec 1712   Bap 4 Nov 1715   Bap 11 April, 1720   who all
Bur 11 Aug 1705   July, 1711   Living in 1745 as   Living in 1745 as   Living in 1745   died in
    Administration to   wife of Thos Tagg   wife of Chas Mon-   wife of Wm Bailey   infancy
    her bro Edward s   Esq of N   tague Lyon, Salt-   of Congleton, Gent
    goods 22 Oct 1745   Officer of Winsford
    Bur 18 Mar
    1747-8

Sibbol
Wright

THE COMBERBACH FAMILY.

The COMBERBACHS of Nantwich were tanners in Barker Street for four generations, from ROGER COMBERBACH, who carried on that trade in the latter part of the sixteenth century, and died in the year 1603, to his great-grandson, JOHN COMBERBACH, who says—

" May ye 1 day 1691 I began the Trade of Tan[n]ing "

And again—

' I follow'd the Tanning trade Eighteen years and some odd months "

ROGER COMBERBACH, by his Will, dated 14th March, 1602 (proved 1603) bequeaths his goods, &c to be divided between his wife Margaret, and his children, *Thomas, Roger, John,* and *Margaret* Mention is made of his mother-in-law Salmon, his brother Richard, to whom he gave his "cloake," his 'men servants" who were "to continue to tanne out the lethr in the pike after as my executors shall thinke fittest "

He was buried at Nantwich on 18th March, 1602–3, and his wife, Margaret Salmon, whom he had married on 12th June, 1592, was also buried here on 6th Feb. 1638 His second son, ROGER COMBERBACH, who has already been mentioned amongst the "disclaimers of gentility" (page 196), fulfilled the office of Churchwarden in 1636, and was buried on 29th Sept 1678, his personal estate being appraised at £6182 8s 4d By his Will, proved 8th Oct 1678, he left a Charity to the poor of Hospital Street and Barker Street.

JOHN COMBERBACH, third son of the first-named Roger, was succeeded by his son, JAMES COMBERBACH, tanner, of Nantwich, who was buried on 20th Oct. 1696, and left three sons, namely —

1 *Roger Comberbach,* who became in 1688 clerk of the Courts of Pentice, Crownmote and Portmote for Chester, in 1700 Recorder for that City, and subsequently a Welsh Judge His grandson of the same name, assumed the name of *Swettenham* on inheriting the ancient possessions of that family at Somerford Booths, in this county

2 *John Comberbach,* who has already been mentioned as a tanner at Nantwich in and after the year 1691, and who is also described in the parish Registers as a maltster His descendants continued at Nantwich until the beginning of the present century, one of the last of the family being *John Comberbach,* who was buried at Nantwich on 4th Nov 1800, at the age of eighty-one

3 *James Comberbach,* who settled at Chester, and fulfilled the office of Mayor of that City in 1727

For further particulars relating to this family the reader is referred to an interesting volume entitled "*Collections for a Genealogical Account of the Family of Comberbach,*' (Lond 1866) by George W. Marshall, LL B., who has treated the subject in a very able and exhaustive manner.

The present Rector of Nantwich has a very curious engraving of the South West Prospect of Nantwich Church, undated, and subscribed "*John Comberbach* Delin," and "*W Pritchard* Sculpo " Its chief curiosity is, however, its inaccuracy of detail and faults of perspective, so that, although the print may be scarce, it is of no intrinsic value

THE WICKSTED FAMILY

The following pedigree, which is re-printed from Dr. Ormerod's work with such additions as the Parish Register affords, supplies all that has occurred relating to this once important family

Wicksted Pedigree.

Authorities: Dr. Ormerod's Pedigree in *History of Cheshire*, Vol. III p. 233 (Old Edit.) p. 442 (New Edit.) which is based on Visit. 1613, and records of the College of Arms. Parish Registers; &c.

ARMS. Argent, a bend Azure, charged with three garbs Or, between three crows Sable, beaked and legged Gules.

CREST. On a wreath two serpents proper, issuing from and twining round a garb Or.

JOHN WICKSTED, a younger son of ....Wicksted of Wicksted. *temp.* Hen. 8. = Anne, dau. to ....Henry Bradford.

HENRY WICKSTED, son and heir. of Welsh Row. Bur. at N. 10 March, 1610-11. Will proved at Chester 1611. = Mary, dau. to Henry Hassall of Hankelow.

Thomas = Agnes (? Anne) Wicksted. dau. to ......

Margaret W. Bap. at N. 18 July 1541.

Anne W. Bap. 19 Dec. 1542.

Elizabeth Wicksted.

John W. Bap. at N. 2 Nov. 1544. = William Kent.

Margaret Wicksted.

Cicely = John (? Roger) Wicksted. Rutter.

Elizabeth Rutter. Bap. at N. 24 June, 1542.

Ann Rutter. Bap. at N. 15 March, 1543-4.

RICHARD WICKSTED, of N. gent. Born 1513. Bap. not recorded at N. Purchased the Weaver meadows & other property at N. of Thos. Bromley; which were, *inter alia*, settled by his son & heir *Richard Wicksted*, as a jointure upon. *Lucretia Yonge*, on her marr. with *Rich. Wicksted*, grand-son of the purchaser, by Indenture dated 29 Nov. 12 Car. I. 1636). Inur. at N. 25 July, 1623. Administration of his effects granted to Rich. W. his son at Chester 22 Oct. 1623. Inventory still at Chester. = Margaret, dau. to Roger Walthall. Bur. at N. 30 Mar. 1629. Will dated 13 Mar. 1626, proved at Chester by her sole executor Ralph Wicksted 12 April, 1629.

Anne Wicksted Bap. 24 Oct. 1544.

Henry Wicksted, Marr. Anne dau. to Lewis ap Reece.

Henry Wicksted = Ellen dau. 2nd son Marr. 23 May, 1574. to John Rutter.

Eleanor.

Elizabeth.

? Hugh Wicksted who marr. Anne Cluton. She was bur. at N. 30 Oct. 1605.

Thomas Wicksted of Shrewsbury. Died 1623. = Eleanor dau. to Rowland Langley of Salop. Living 1626.

John Wicksted 2nd son; mercer of N. Marr. 15 June 1608. Living 1626. = Margaret, dau. to Wm. Browne.

Margaret W. Bap. 25 March, 1618.

Ralph Wicksted of N. Church-warden 1635. Died 1638. Inventory of his goods at Chester.

Robert Wicksted, administered to his bro. Ralph's goods 9 Oct. 1638. = Margaret dau. to Rev. Thos. Elcock.

Elizabeth, wife of Ralph Huxley 1613. Living 1626.

Ann wife of Wm. Judson 1613. Living 1626.

RICHARD WICKSTED of N. gent, eldest son & heir; settled his lands 1636, preparatory to the marr. of his son Rich. W. Bur. at N. 21 April, 1681.

(*1st wife*) Mary, dau. to William Browne of N. Marr. 17 Dec. 1669. Bur. 25 Oct. 1611.

(*2nd wife*) Ann dau. to Thos. Bromley. Marr. at N 27 May 1614. Bur. at N. 16 Jan. 1633-4. Arms with initials AW formerly on one of Tower Piers of N. Ch. (*Harl. MSS.* 2151.)

(*3rd wife*) Jane dau. to ...... Marr. before 1636. Bur. at N. 2 Jan. 1644-5.

Richard ob. infan. Bur. 27 Oct. 1610.

Margaret, aged 2 Visit. 1613. ? whether marr. to Joseph Bradwell, clerk. 25 Aug. 1636. (see p 297).

A

A

RICHARD WICKSTED, gent. of N, son and heir Born = Lucretia, dau. to John Yonge of Pembly, co Salop, gent Settlement before marriage
after Herald's Visit 1613 Bap not recorded at N dated 29 Nov 1636, described as the "relict of Richard Wicksted late of Wiche
Party to a deed "7 Oct 1642, containing a further Malbank, gent deceased" in an assignment of part of her jovnure to her son Thos
settlement of lands upon his wife Lucretia Bur at Wicksted, dated 1 Sept 1673 Party to the settlement after the marriage of her son
N as "Richard Wicksted, the younger gent Thos Wicksted, with Susannah Haycock, dated 2 Apul. 1675
20 Feb 1651-2 Buried at N 11 Dec 1690

Ellen Wicksted
Bap 10 Aug 1627
Bur 15 April 1629

(1st wife)=John Wicksted=(2nd wife) THOMAS WICKSTED, of N gent = Susanna dau to Richard Wicksted, of Mickley, co Cest Elenor =Edward Manley,
Mary gent Living in Anna Smith named in the settlement 1642 Haycock gent Described in the Settlement 2 April Wicksted gent Marr at
Bur at 1642, but dead marr 1 Jan Party to the Assignment 1673 Marr in 1675 1675, as "the younger brother of Thomas only dau the Hall of Sme-
N 8 before 3 April, 1667-8 Bur settled his lands after his mar- Bur at N 24 Wicksted" Died in Aug 1678, very sudden- wick by licence,
April, 1675 at N 22 riage, by Indenture dated 2 April Feb 1685-6 ly at shrewsbury, under circumstances related 26 May, 1676
1666 Dec 1674 1675 Bur at N 26 Nov 1701 by Roger Wilbraham Esq of Townsend (who 1 Lucretia Manley
was paying him a visit at the time) in Will MS Jour 2 Prudence Manley
John Wicksted Bap 29 Sep 1668 Thos Wicksted Richard Wicksted Bur 16 Mar 1678-9
Attorney Marr at Wistaston 16 Bap 13 Sep Bap 29 June, 3 Edward Manley
July, 1696 1670 1673 Bap 23 Nov 1680

Mary Jebb of Nantwich

THOMAS WICKSTED, of N gent Bap 11 = Katherine, dau to Samuel Watkiss, of Aston, co Salop, Margaret Wicksted Susannah Wicksted
April, 1683 Killed by a fall of his horse gent Marr at Wem, 27 May 1795 Bap 17 April 1677 Bap 7 Dec 1678
Bur at N 7 July 1707 Marriage articles dated the day before Bur 18 April 1677 Bur 21 Dec 1678

THOMAS WICKSTED of N Gent, Attorney = Grissel, dau to Charles Fletcher, of Whitchurch, Salop, Esq
Posthumous son Bap at N 4 March, Bur at N 21 Aug 1784 (See Monument, page 318)
1707-8 Bur at N 11 Jan 1769 (N B — Upon the death of her brother, John Fletcher, of Lichfield, Esq,
(See Monument) without male issue the manor of Wigland and other property in co
Cest was vested by settlement in her son Thomas Wicksted)

THOMAS WICKSTED of N =Anne, eldest Charles Wicksted (1st wife) = Richard = (2nd wife) Grissel Bap 28 Elizabeth Bap 18 Frances WICKSTED
Esq Bap 3 April, 1732 dau to John Bap 9 Feb 1737 Anne, dau Wicksted Margaret dau May, 1734 Bur Dec 1735 Marr Bap 5 July, 1739
o s p 27 Jan 1814 Bur Bennion, of Bur 18 Apl 1716 to Samuel Bap 6 to Joseph 29 Sep 1734 to Simon Horner, Marr at N 4 July,
at Malpas Will dated 16 Chorlton, s p Gerrard of Feb Richardson of of Hull, 12 Feb 1771
July, 1803 co Cest Moreton Say 1743-4 Beeston Mary Bap 17 1772 Had issue a =
Samuel Wicksted co Salop Bur at N 1 Feb 1736 Bur son an dau, both William Jolliffe
Died an infant Feb 1731 17 Nov 1752 died s p Merchant of Hull
Bur 18 Feb 1744-5 s p co York

Mary Anne Wicksted Mary Wicksted
Living unmarried
1815

Martha Wicksted, wife of James Swan of Wavertree
co Lanc Marr "t Childwall" had issue James Wicksted
Swan Esq, B A, of Trinity College, Cambridge

A

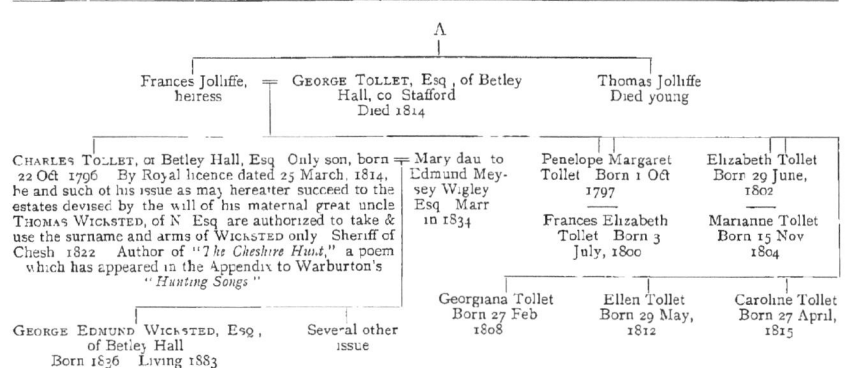

Accounts of other local families not less interesting or important than some that have been treated of in this already long chapter, such, for example as the CLUTTONS, the DELVES, the PRATCHETTS, might have been included had time and space permitted   A notice of the *Cluttons* of this town has appeared in an article contributed to Mr Earwaker's "*Local Gleanings Magazine*," (pp. 260-6, and 297-304), where I have endeavoured to show how different in appearance the interiors of respectable houses in country towns like Nantwich must have been two or three hundred years ago   Concerning the Inventory of Margery Clutton's goods, which is there printed in full, as appraised by Hugh Mainwaring, Matthew Mainwaring, Roger Wright and John Maisterson, Gents, on 25th July, 1611, I have said that the heavy, scant, plain furniture, consisting only of long tables, stools, and forms (only eight chairs are mentioned in that lady's house, which contained fourteen rooms) chests, cupboards, and bedsteads, the valuable plate for special, and the abundant service of pewter for common use, chests containing beef and bacon, which had been either salted in brine or dried in the smoke of the capacious kitchen-chimney, other chests with stores of home-spun linen, &c, the former suggesting the slaughter of stall-fed oxen in summer time for the supply of meat from Michaelmas to Whitsuntide, when markets were irregularly attended owing to the bad state of the roads, and the latter suggesting the spinning of flax and carding of wool by the family and servants during long winter nights, one solitary "*seeinge glasse*," (what would our ancestors have said to the staring mirrors of drawing-rooms of the present day?) no clock, no fender, no pictures, few books, &c., and the absence of many common conveniences and elegancies of these days;—all these are evidence of the simplicity and frugality of our ancestors in their domestic arrangements, while they afford a striking contrast to the luxury and ostentation of modern tastes and fashions.

Doubtless many persons, who have received but a passing notice in this history, will be rescued from obscurity by some future genealogist who may be engaged in tracing out their posterity. Thus, for example, it is an interesting fact that about the year 1650 a family in humble life, named *Sharples,* emigrated from Nantwich, or its immediate neighbourhood, to America; where their descendants have continued, and are now represented by merchant princes of that name in Philadelphia; relatives of the late Colonel J. Lemuel Chester, D.C.L., LL.D., who some years ago personally searched the registers at Wybunbury for the purpose of tracing out the ancestry of that family.

It has been pointed out in the foregoing pages that Nantwich has had two important crises in its history,—the Great Fire of 1583, and the scourge of Cholera in 1849. It is also noteworthy that during the period that intervened between the calamity of three hundred years ago, and the outbreak of the Civil War, the town produced its greatest men;—men of learning, wealth, and position. May the spirit of improvement and activity which has manifested itself since the latter event, in like manner, prevent this ancient town from becoming a decayed town; and, as education advances, may men of intelligence and enterprise again be produced that shall be the boast of future days; and may the bells long continue to ring out, and ring out truly, to the inhabitants around, " PROSPERITY TO THIS TOWN AND PARISH, PEACE AND GOOD NEIGHBOURHOOD."

ADDITIONS

AND CORRECTIONS.

ILLIAM MALBANK is said (on page 16) to have been the founder of ST. NICHOLAS HOSPITAL; and in further proof of that statement it may be added that an Inquisition *post mortem*, dated 6 Hen. IV. [1404-5] recites that "William Maubank [Malbank] formerly Lord and Baron of Nantwich died seized of the site of *St. Nicholas Hospital in Nantwich*, a Hall, and 2 salt-pits with all the lands and perquisites belonging to the said Hospital. These were granted by him to God and to St. Nicholas of the said Hospital in pure and perpetual alms to support a certain priest celebrating Divine service in the said Hospital for ever."[*]

Dr. Ormerod, in his additions to the *History of Cheshire* (Old Edition) mentions a "singularly curious oak chest," said to have once belonged to St. Nicholas Hospital in Nantwich, which he purchased from a tenant at Erdswick Hall in this county. He says the chest had belonged to the Astons of Hulgreve Hall, who participated in the divisions of the religious spoil at the Reformation. In his description of the chest, the Cheshire historian was of opinion that the carved work in the centre of the front represented the coronation of Henry VI, and so approximately fixed the date of its construction. But the celebrated architect A. Pugin, who gives three excellent engravings of the chest, suggests that the centre-piece is a representation of the Holy Trinity and the Virgin.[†]

WILLIAM HILL, the last Master and Priest of the Hospital, paid his Composition for first-fruits to the Crown, on becoming Incumbent of the said Hospital, on 28th March 32 Hen. VIII. [1541].—(*Record Society Publ.* vol. viii. p. 394.)

On page 52, line 22, *dele* the words " (see map.)" The reason for this will be found in the Preface.

---

[*] Public Record Office; and transcripts of Cheshire Inquisitions *penes* J. P. Earwaker, Esq., F.S.A.
[†] See Pugin's "*Examples of Gothic Architecture*," 1822, vol. ii. pp. 22—28. Plate xliv.

Page 54—RICHARD WRIGHT, the last Incumbent of St. Lawrence Hospital, paid his Composition for first-fruits to the Crown on 19th Oct 37 Hen. VIII. [1545.] (*Ibid* p. 395)

On page 56, line 2, for "aftewards" *read* afterwards
On page 56, line 21, for ' SIR JAME" *read* SIR JAMES.
On page 56, lines 27 and 31, for "siezed ' *read* seized.
On page 68, line 18, for "chimnies" *read* chimneys
On page 97, line 5, for "grandfather" *read* grandson.

On the gravestone alluded to on page 97 are the words "*See the adjoining stone;*" referring probably to the gravestone of *Maria Sparke* All that is decipherable of the now imperfect inscription is—*

"MARIA SPARKE. Conditur hoc Maria . 1595 "

Page 98 —The following abstract of the Inquisition *post mortem* of Roger Sparke, probably identical with Roger Sparke named in the Subsidy Roll of 1545, may here be added

Inquisition p m dated 27 May 11 Eliz [1569]

"ROGER SPARKE Gent died [date not given] leaving *Robert Sparke* his son and heir, aged 18 yrs 6 mo 3 wks and 4 days He died seised of 5 messuages, 2 salt-houses, 100 acres of land, 40 of pasture, 10 of meadow, 10 of wood, 100 of bruery [heath] and 10 of moor, and 3s rent in Nantwich Wolstanwood and Burland, and 20 acres of land in Henhull which descended to *Philip* Sparke his younger son in taile *Blanche* the wife of the said Roger Sparke survived him, and had a third part of all the said lands and tenements for her dower during her life "

Page 99, three lines from the bottom The Inquisition *post mortem* of Roger Crockett Gent of Nantwich, who died on 19th Dec 1572, was taken at Nantwich on 28th Aug 23 Eliz [1581], when *Robert Crockett* his son and next heir was found to be of the age of 20 years 3 months and upwards

On the 20th Aug 20 Jac I. [1623] Robert Crockett, late of Nantwich, Gent, was found to have died on 13th March 9 Jac I [1612-3] leaving *Thomas Crockett* his son and heir, aged 30. *(Inq p m)*

Isabell, the wife of Robert Crockett, is named in the Will of John Davenport, of Wistaston, Gent, dated 8 Jan. 1595-6 *(Chesh Wills* Cheth Soc. Pub. vol li p 182)

Page 105, nineteen lines from the bottom *John Wydenbury* [or Wybunbury] who is mentioned as the landlord of the *Swan* Inn in 1583, is named in his father's Inquisition *post mortem,* an abstract of which is as follows —

Inquisition p m dated 13 Dec 24 Hen VII [1508]

" ROBERT WIBBUNBURY died on Thursday next before the feast of St Michael the Archangel [29 Sep] last past [1508] leaving *John Wibbunbury* his son and heir, who was the age of one year and upwards on the day of the taking of this Inquisition He died seised [*inter alia*] of lands in Briddesmere, Checkley, Wystaston an annual Rent of 12s issuing out of a messuage in Nantwich held by Ralph Toore [? Goore] and 11 gardens and 3 acres of land, and 3 acres of meadow there , &c Also lands in Newhall, a messuage in Nantwich aforesaid called the "*Swanne,*" &c He granted the same to Ralph Delves, Esq, [of Doddington] John Wynyngton of the Hermytage [in Wybunbury] Thomas Maynwaryng and others and their

* I am indebted to J Brooking Rome Esq F S A President of the Devonshire Association, for an exact copy of the Sparke memorials, which was received too late for insertion on page 97

heirs to the use of Catharine Maynwaryng the daughter of Randle Maynwaryng of Kermyncham Esq, who was then the wife of the said Robert, for her life, who survived him and was living at the time of the taking of this Inquisition '

The Certificate given on page 114 is signed by the following Town Officers and Jurymen, namely—

RICHARD CLUTTON, Sen^{lus} [i e. Seneschal or Steward of the Cholmondeley Court].

John Church ⎱ Bailiffs	Rychard Maystersone	Edward Massye
Rauffe Elcock ⎰	William Hassall	tho tench
William Huxley ⎱ Constables	Hughe Manwaring	Richard Wilbraham
Raphe Massie ⎰	Rand Minshall	tobyas Tench 1605

It has been stated (pp 114, 215) that the Assizes were held at Nantwich on two occasions, namely, in 1605 and 1716 By the following extract of a deed it appears that the Chester Courts were also held at Nantwich in 1648.

"Fine levied in the King's Court of Chester at Wich Malbanc co Chester, 3 April 24 Charles [1648] before John Bradshaw Esq Justice of the said lord the King at Chester, and Peter Warburton, Esq, the other Justice of the said lord the King there " &c *

Page 138 —ANDREW BOWRY is mentioned in the local Registers thus —
"1637 April 11 Married Andrew Bowrye minister of Gods word and Anne Slade "—(Wybunbury Reg)
"1646 May 3 Thos son of Andrew Bowrie Minister "—(Nantwich Bapt Reg)

Page 176 —Capt Thomas Steele is said to have been a cheese-factor (Newcome's Autobiography, p. 95). In the Register of Baptisms is the following entry —
"1632-3 Feb 24 Sarah, dau of Thomas Steele factor "

Page 177 —Doddington Hall. Wybunbury Register records—
' 1643-4 March 24 Thomas Banforth a souldier slaine at dodington was buried "

Page 186 —Dele note (o) JOHN KELSALL was the son of William Kelsall, vicar of Audley (See Hinchliffe's Barthomley, p. 169). His name occurs in the Wybunbury Register as follows —
"1667-8 March 3 Baptized John sonne of Mr John Kelsall Cler' at Barthomley "

Page 187.—THOMAS HARWAR appears to have belonged to a family resident at Bridgemere in Wybunbury Parish The Registers there contain many entries of their names, among the rest are —
"1650 May 30 Buried Thomas Harwar senior gent "
1658 May 12 Buried Capt Thomas Harwar of Bridgemere "
"1662-3 Jan 10 Buried Thomas Harwar of Bridgemere, gent from Nantwich "

Page 201 —In the Churchwardens' Accounts at Wybunbury, under date 1688, occurs the following entry of parish money paid to —
"Edward Carter, Morice Carter & Robert Merrill being protestants disbanded from
Ireland & having the Countrey disease   .   .   .   .   £00 01s   06d "

Page 231 —Slaughter-houses In the early years of this century the inhabitants were accustomed to see offensive refuse and carrion in undisturbed heaps in the principal streets

* Kindly communicated by J P Earwaker, Esq F S A

of the town, the town officers being very remiss in their duty of attending to the proper cleansing of the streets (*Cf* page 68.) Old people now living remember an open shop that stood in the centre of the town, on the site of handsome premises now occupied by Mr. S Harlock, where Mr. E Barrowcliffe, butcher, *killed* and *dressed* his meat, before exposing it for sale

Page 239—In 1819 Dr Ormerod stated (*IIist Chesh*) that there were *three* fairs held in this town, namely, on March 26th, September 4th, and December 4th, to which he might have added another fair held on the first Saturday after Candlemas Day [Feb 2], then, and *now*, called *New Market* In the same year another fair was commenced on the second Tuesday in June, and called the *New Fair*. (Advertisement in the Macclesfield "*Courier*," 5th June, 1819) This fair is still held on the same day, and is commonly known as the *June Fair*

In the last line on page 243, for "the Marquis of Cholmondeley ' *read* John (now Lord) Tollemache

On page 247, line 25, the Unitarian Chapel was renovated in 1849, *not* 1852.

Page 248, line 20 It is an interesting fact that the Nantwich Association of Parochial Choirs is the oldest in the Chester Diocese (*Nantwich Parish Magazine*, Sep 1883)

Page 250 line 14 Thomas Hassall is stated to have completed his hundredth year at the time of his death in 1875, on the affirmation of his son, Charles Hassall, of Nantwich, now living This, however, is incorrect The same Thomas Hassall, joiner, is mentioned in a foot-note of page 474 as being seventy-five years of age in 1851, consequently, in 1875 he would be ninety-six years old This is further corroborated by the entry in the Parish Magazine of his burial, thus —

' 1875 Aug 11 Thomas Hassall, Beam Street, *aged* 96 years

Another inmate of the same Almshouses, *John Horton*, was buried on the 6th Dec. 1879, at the advanced age of ninety-five *(Ibid)*

Page 251—In the present year (1883) the brine at the Old Pit, near the Town Hall. was analysed by Dr. Frankland, D C L , F R S , whose report of the proportionate chemical ingredients is as follows

	Grains of Saline matter per Imperial Gallon
Chloride of Sodium	14697 01
Chloride of Potassium	135 28
Bromide of Potassium	1 67
Carbonate of Lime	15 49
Carbonate of Soda	6 95
Sulphate of Lime	455 99
Chloride of Magnesium	157 90
Sulphate of Soda	353 09
Alumina and Peroxide of Iron	2 53
Silica	47
Nitrate of Soda	47

In the summer of 1883 Alderman J. M. Bennett, Esq., of Manchester, commenced boring operations in the field called *Bathing Meadow*, belonging to Shrewbridge Hall Estate, and discovered brine at a depth of about 140 feet.

Page 252, twelve lines from the bottom; for "Itineras" *read* Itinera.

Page 253.—Several salt-pits (wich-houses) in Nantwich belonging to Lilleshall Abbey were leased to Roger Mainwaring on 20th Dec. 16 Hen. VII. [1500]; and to John Leech, on 13th July 17 Hen. VIII. [1525]. (*Record Soc. Publ.* vol. vii. p. 169).

Page 271, line 20; for "age" *read* ago. *Apropos* of glove making, although the manufacture ceased over twenty years ago, the *Nantwich glove*, as a superior article in the trade, is still sold.

Page 301-3.—To the notice of Dr. Brooke, it may be added that an oil portrait of him in wig and gown, is now in the possession of E. Delves Broughton, Esq., of Wistaston Hall, near Nantwich.

Page 305.—The death of the Rev. A. Clarkson was announced as follows in the Macclesfield "*Courier:*"—

"On March 3. [1819] at Nantwich in the 71st year of his age Anthony Clarkson A.M. *Chaplain to the Duke of Leeds*, and Rector of Nantwich, and of *Langwith co. Derby.*" (Communicated by J. P. Earwaker, Esq.)

Page 399-400. To the account of the Independent Chapel it may be added that—
Mrs. Scott, the widow of Capt. Scott, invested the sum of £1000 in trustees for the benefit of the Minister for the time being of the Independent Chapel in Church Lane, Nantwich.

Also, that the late Miss Janet Ramsay, in memory of her brother Gilbert, founded a scholarship, known as the "*Gilbert Ramsay Scholarship*," of the annual value of £30, open to all students entering the Lancashire Independent College, Whalley Range, Manchester, for the full curriculum.

Page 400, line 14, for "1819" *read* 1849.

Page 400, line 17, for "Kitchen" *read* Hilditch.

Page 445, line 16, for "have" *read* has.

Page 463, line 8, for "Wohdhey" *read* Woodhey.

Page 472, line 20, insert *of* after the word "wife."

THE EDDOWES FAMILY.

To the passing notice of the EDDOWES family in the chapter on Nonconformity, is here appended the pedigree alluded to on page 389 *note*, containing the names of several persons mentioned in that chapter, and in the later descents, showing the connection of the family with the BOWMANS of Macclesfield and Nantwich, three of whom, natives of this town, have, during the present century, risen to eminence, and as such deserve special mention before concluding this volume

The EDDOWES family appears to have been originally of Welsh extraction   An ancient pedigree, still extant, traces the family back to Howel Dhu, Prince of Wales, and Tudor Trevor, Earl of Hereford * A "JOHN EDOW, of Hanmer, living *temp* Eliz and James I ," and another "JOHN EDDOWES of the Middle Temple 1673," who entered his pedigree at the Heralds' College, are mentioned in the Salisbury MS , in the possession of Sir Watkin Wynn, and possibly they were related to the undermentioned *Ranulph* and *Roger Eddowes* of Whitchurch, Salop

RANULPH EDDOWES (or *Eddowe*, as his name is also spelled) of Tybroughton, near Whitchurch Gent , in the year 1606 sold to his brother, *Roger Eddowes*, for the sum of 200 marks, a messuage in Whitchurch, with four closures of land, &c , which he had purchased from William Chydlowe, Gent   These lands, described as "neere the Hall of Hinton," had been in the possession of the Chydlowe family as early as 8 Henry V [1420].†

ROGER EDDOWES, of Whitchurch, Mercer, by his will dated 17th March, 1646, bequeathed the property purchased from his brother, to his son *Joshua Eddowes* and his heirs, on condition of his paying to his three brothers, *William, Randulph*, and *Ralph*, £100, and the like sum to the children of his brother *Thomas*, deceased, all by instalments within a certain period after his decease   He was also possessed of some freehold property in Whitchurch, which descended in a direct line to *John Eddowes*, of Nantwich, who, dying without issue 1789, left it to *Ralph*, only son of his cousin, *John Eddowes*, of Chester

Roger Eddowes was buried at Whitchurch on the 18th Nov 1648

ROGER EDDOWES, of Whitchurch, grocer and ironmonger, the son of Ralph Eddowes, and grandson of the above Roger Eddowes, was born about 1648 or 9   By a letter to his brother *Joshua*, dated 5th March, 1693, it appears that his property was very respectable, though, from the circumstance of his having portioned off his whole family of six children during his lifetime, and the general terms of his Will, which is dated 19th April, 1716, it is difficult to ascertain what he died possessed of   He does not seem to have retained much for his own expenditure, since his wants were few   "That he was a sincerely pious and virtuous character,' writes the father of Sir W Bowman in 1808, "cannot be doubted after perusal of a few invaluable letters written to his brother Joshua when in London, and now in my possession   They prove him to have been a man of considerable literary qualifications for that period   The principles of virtue which he so carefully instilled into his children, are yet the most valuable inheritance of their descendants, who are thus worthy of a name, *honourable* for being *his* "

He settled Broughall upon his eldest son, *John Eddowes*, on his marriage in 1703

* Sir William Bowman Bart , has an " Ancient Pedigree of the Eddowes s, copied from a MS folio volume, *penes* Athelustan Corbet, Esq , of Ynysymaengwyn, near Aberdovey "
† Deeds *penes* Sir W Bowman, Bart

JOHN EDDOWES, of High Town, Nantwich, ironmonger and grocer, where he was settled early in 1704, was born at Whitchurch in 1678   He had £150 on his first marriage, together with the Freehold and Copyhold property in Whitchurch heretofore in the possession of his grandfather which was settled upon his issue.   The Rev Matthew Henry was consulted about this marriage, as appears from the following extract from his Diary —

"30 Jan 1702-3   In the evening with cousin Eddowes, finishing the treaty between him and cousin Crue, and with ye Recorder about drawing ye Articles "

The marriage settlement, by which Susannah, eldest daughter of William Crue, of Chester, ironmonger, had £150 to her marriage portion, was executed the following day, and was witnessed by the Rev Matthew Henry, "who spent some time at Cousin Crue's in prayer, committing the work to the Lord "

In 1722 John Eddowes purchased an estate at Stapeley, containing about thirty acres, which descended to the issue of his second marriage   The following disinterested act of friendship bears a most honourable testimony to his character.   When his uncle, Joshua Eddowes, named his intention of leaving him the bulk of his property, he replied, that as it had pleased God to bless him with a competency, he would relinquish his claim in favour of others equally related, and who stood in greater need, whereupon he furnished him with their names and circumstances, agreeably with which his uncle made his Will, and appointed him his executor, with a legacy of £100.   The trust, which was extensive and very complex, devolved to the widow and children of John Eddowes, who were not exonerated from it for forty years after his death   He and his descendants occupied the house in High Street (see illustration on page 110) for upwards of a century

JOHN EDDOWES, of High Town, Nantwich, tobacconist and grocer, to which business he succeeded on the death of his mother, *Anne Eddowes*, was born in 1722   At his house, in and after the year 1758, the Rev. Joseph Priestley boarded. (See page 389).   On the death of his brother *George*, John Eddowes enfranchised the land at Broughall from the Duke of Bridgewater, 5th July, 1765, for £30 13s 9d   To his nephew, *Ralph*, he gave his estate at Stapeley, the property in Whitchurch, which had continued for five generations in the family, and the reversion of Broughall   He died unmarried, on the 18th March, 1789, and was buried in the Unitarian Chapel, where a flat stone still remains to his memory

After the death of John Eddowes, the business in high Town, Nantwich, succeeded to his distant relative, EDDOWES BOWMAN, whose connection with the Eddowes family is shown in the subjoined pedigree, which contains other details relating to both families

Eddowes and Bowman Pedigree.

Authorities A Pedigree on parchment compiled by John Eddowes Bowman, of Nantwich, attested by Joshua Eddowes, of Shrewsbury, Printer, his grandfather, on 18th Feb 1808, collated with a MS pedigree by the late Joseph Hunter, F S A, now preserved in *Ada MSS* Brit Mus 24,444 f 106, the later generations by information of Sir William Bowman, Bart., of Joldwynds, Dorking, Surrey

RANULPHE EDDOWE, of Tybroughton, nr Whitchurch, Salop, Gent In 1606 he sold to his brother *Roger E*, for the sum of 200 marks, a messuage in Whitchurch with four closures of land, &c	ROGER EDDOWE, of Whitchurch, Salop, mercer Will dated 17 March 1646 Bur at Whitchurch 18 Nov 1648 ═	Elizabeth, dau to Bur at Whitchurch 12 Jan 1645-6
	A	

A

| John Eddow | Thomas Eddow Died before 1646 | Joshua Eddow, Heir to his father's estate | William Eddow | Randulph Eddo | Ralph Eddowes, of Whitchurch, Died 31 Jan 1704 | Sarah, dau to John Hotchkiss Bur 24 May 1698 | Margery Eddow |

Elizabeth, dau of Rowland Nevitt of Oswestry. V D M. One of the ejected ministers

Joshua Eddowes of London Gent Acquired a handsome property there Died, unmarried, 27 July, 1732 By his Will dated 23 Oct 1731, he left to relatives and legatees the total sum of £4,790

Sarah Eddowes, wife of Robt. Wilson of Wrenbury Wood Married at Wrenbury, 8 Nov 1683

Savage Eddowes of Wrenbury Wood

Sarah, eldest dau to Rev Philip Henry, of Worthenbury & Broad Oak, Flintshire, and sister to Rev Matthew Henry Authoress of Diary quoted on pp 387 8 Left Wrenbury c 1732 Died in 1752, aged nearly 88 years

Elizabeth Eddowes

John Savage of Wrenbury Wood Bap 27 Dec 1651 Marr 28 Mar 1687 Died c 1729

Roger Eddowes of Whitchurch, grocer and ironmonger Eldest son born c 1648-9 Marr in Feb 1676-7 Will dated 19 April, 1716

Margaret Eddowes

Sherratt

Hannah Eddowes

Bradbourn

Margt Sherratt

Philip Savage Bur at W 2 March 1720-1

Other issue Died young

John Wickstead   Ann Wickstead

Sarah Wickstead   All named in Joshua Eddowes Will

Susanna dau to

(1st wife) Susannah, eldest dau to Wm Crue of Chester ironmonger Marr 10 Ap 1703 Died suddenly 26 Sep 1719 Bur in N CH

John Eddowes of N ironmonger & grocer, eldest son Born at Whitchurch 1678 He settled at N in 1704 Died in 1738 Bur in N Church

(2nd wife) Anne, dau to ... Head of Maccles-field

Samuel Eddowes of Whitchurch

Sarah Eddowes, only daughter

Ralph Eddowes of Whitchurch, grocer

(1st wife) Wickstead of Whitchurch

(2nd wife) Eleanor dau to Wm Car-ter of Shrewsbury

Joshua Eddowes of Wrexham, grocer Will dat 12 Ap 1733

Elizabeth dau to Broadfoot She had £500 for her marr portion

Joshua Eddowes of Shrewsbury, Printer, youngest son, b 15 Apl 1724 Editor of 'Salopian Journal' Died 25 Sep 1811 Bur in Meet ing-House Yard, at Shrewsbury

Lydia dau to William Philips of Horsemans Green, nr Hanmer, co Flint Born 1 Feb 1728 Marr 13 Sep 1753, died 20 Mar 1803 Bur in Meeting-House Yard

Daughter, wife of Hugh Johnson of Knutsford

Other issue who married and left issue (See Hunter's Pedigree)

Thos Eddowes of London, mercer Died at Axe Inn Aldermanbury 1751

Roger Eddowes o s p

Elizabeth Eddowes eldest dau Marr at N 2 Mar 1731, to Rev Thos Haynes of N and afterwards of Sheffield, V D M (See page 387)

Mary Eddowes

Sarah (or Susannah) Marr to Jas Green Marr to of N Clock-maker o s p

George Eddowes of N Settled at Sheffield as a Tobacconist Twice married Died 16 July, 1761

John Eddowes, of N Tobacco-nist and grocer Born in 1722 Died unmarried 18 Mar 1780 Bur in Unitarian Chapel, N (see p 389)

Wm Eddowes, of Sheffield, M P, Died unmarr aged 29

Roger Eddowes of Maccles-field

Samuel Eddowes, of Stone, Staffs, Yeoman

John Eddowes, of Maccles-field, Tobacconist

Susannah Eddowes, only dau Born 1727 Died 1762

Henry Bowman, of Macclesfield, grocer Born 26 Oct 1725 Died 16 July 1773

Samuel Eddowes, of Macclesfield, grocer Died 16 July 1773

B

A

B

WILLIAM EDDOWES, of Shrewsbury, Printer, only son born 2 Oct 1754, died 4 Feb 1835 == (1st wife) Elizabeth, dau to Joshua Ridgway of Bronnington, Flint

== (2nd wife)

Lydia E
Elinor E

EDDOWES BOWMAN, of N Born at Macclesfield 12 Nov 1758 Settled at N 1775 Succeeded the late *John Eddowes* in the business of Tobacconist & Grocer in 1789, retired therefrom in 1812 afterwards a Banker Died at Shrewsbury 30 Sep 1844, aged 85 yrs == **CATHARINE EDDOWES** Born 5 Oct 1759 Marr at Shrewsbury 25 Nov 1784 Died at Shrewsbury 28 March 1851, aged 91 years

John Eddowes Rector of St Jude's, Bradford, Yorks

Sarah E, wife of Hy Bowman Esq, Architect   other issue

Mary Eddowes, Born 2 Feb 1794, Wife of W Nealor, Died without issue

John Bowman
Mary Bowman
ob infan

Sarah Bowman
Born 20 May 1757
Died, unma red, aged 17

JOHN EDDOWES BOWMAN of N and afterwards of Welshpool, Wrexham, and Manchester, Banker, Esq, eldest son, born at N 30 Oct 1785 Marr his cousin-german An eminent naturalist & geologist F L S, F G S, &c Died 4 Dec 1841 Buried at Manchester == **ELIZABETH EDDOWES** Born 23 May, 1788 Marr 6 July, 1809 Died in 1859, Buried at Manchester

Wm Eddowes Born 27 July, 1789

Lydia E Died, aged 10 years

SIR WILLIAM BOWMAN BART LL D, F R S, F L S, F G S, &c Born at N 20 July, 1816, Created Baronet 1883 Surgeon to King's Coll Hospital, and the Royal London Ophthalmic Hospital Now (1883) living near Dorking, Surrey == **HARRIET**, 5th dau to Thos Paget, Esq, Surgeon, of Leicester

JOHN EDDOWES BOWMAN, Esq Born at Welshpool 7 July, 1819 Professor of Practical Chemistry at King's College, London Died at Kensington 10 Feb 1856 == Ellen, 4th dau to Thos Paget, Esq, Surgeon, of Leicester Bn 8 Jan 1814 Marr 5 Jan 1844 Died 9 May, 1866

Henry Bowman
Born 9 Nov 1788
Died 20 July
1873, aged 34

Catharine Bowman
Born 19 June, 1792
Died, unmarried 25
Jan 1872, aged 79

Eliza Bowman
Born 19 Apl 1812
Marr 11 Aug 1836,
to Geo Smith Kenrick Esq She died
without issue 16 Nov
1838 Bur at Varteg,
South Wales

HENRY BOWMAN Esq Born at N Feb 1814 Settled at Manchester as an Architect Died 14 May, 1883 Buried at Dorking, Surrey No issue == Sarah dau to John Eddowes

Eliza Bowman
Eldest daughter

Fanny Poole
Bowman Born
22 July, died
27 Oct 1848

Mary Bowman
Marr 24 May 1877
to Alfred Bray Kempe
Esq, F R S, 3rd son
of Rev J E Kempe,
West., & Prebendary of St Paul's

Agnes Bow
man Marr
14 Nov
1876

John Wm Bow-
man
Born 28 Sep 1877

== John Conyers
Merriman,
Esq, Surgeon,
Kensington

Ruth Agnes
Margaret Harriet

JOHN FREDERICK BOW
MAN, Esq Born 1 Nov
1850 Educ at Eton A
Solicitor in London == Cecilia Charrington
second dau to Edw
Charrington, Esq
of Bury's Court,
nr Reigate

EDDOWES BOWMAN,
M A, eldest son
Born 12 Nov 1810
Died unmarried 10
July, 1869, Buried
at Manchester

WM PAGET BOWMAN
Esq Born 25 Sept
1845 M A of Univ
Coll Oxford, Barrister-at-Law Registrar
to the Corporation of
the Sons of the Clergy
Marr 9 Aug 1870
Living in 1883 == Emily Frances, 4th
dau to Hon Capt
Wm Swabey, R H A
D L, and J P, for
Bucks, sometime of
the Exec Council of
Prince Edwd Island
A Waterloo Officer,
& of the Swabeys of
Langley Marish, Bucks

REV ARTHUR GERALD BOWMAN
M A Born 14 Feb 1854 Vicar
of St Andrew's Westminster == Edith, 3rd dau of late Wm
Paget, Esq, of St Anne's
Manor, Sutton Bonnington,
Notts Marr 30 July, 1879

Dorothea Percy
Bowman

Humphrey Ernest
Bowman B 26 July, 1879

HARRY ERNEST BOWMAN,
M R C S, Eng Born 29
April, 1855 Now (1883)
an Artist

Paget Melvyn Bowman, born 1873
Muriel Paget Bowman, born 1875
Guy Eddowes Bowman, born 1878

Angela Bowman
Born 4 Oct 1852
Died 8 Oct 1852

JOHN HERBERT BOWMAN, Esq Born 27 Sept 1846 Under Secretary in Bank of England == Catharine, dau to John S Lister, Esq Marr in 1872 Died 26 April, 1874

GEORGE CYRIL BOWMAN
Born 2 Jan 1849 == Frederica Caroline, dau to John J Merriman, Esq, Surgeon, Kensington Marr 17 April, 1873

Edith Bowman == George W Molineux, Esq of Eastbourne Marr 29 Sep 1883

Herbert Lister Bowman
Born 15 March, 1874

Paget John Merriman Bowman
Born 29 Aug 1874

Ethel Mary
Bowman

THE BOWMAN FAMILY.

The ancestors of the BOWMANS mentioned in the above pedigree belonged to East Cheshire and Derbyshire, and trace their descent from John Bowman, who died Oct 31st, 1661   The first to settle at Nantwich was EDDOWES BOWMAN, who succeeded *John Eddowes* in the business of tobacconist and grocer in High Town, in the year 1789, from which he retired in 1812, and became a partner with Mr Hewitt in a Banking speculation, that proved unsuccessful, and collapsed in Feb 1816 (see page 237)   In 1814 he purchased from the Leversage family of this town the house in Hospital Street, known as *Sweet-briar Hall* (see illustration page 353)   In 1817 Messrs Joseph Skerrett and Benjamin Rodenhurst, Assignees of the estate and effects of Messrs Hewitt, Bowman, and Bowman, (Bankers) bankrupts, together with Miss Catharine Bowman, and Mr Eddowes Bowman, sold the property to Miss Mary Bennion, whose sister, Miss Elizabeth Bennion, bequeathed the same to Miss E H McClure, afterwards the wife of the late Edward Butterworth, Esq.

The Bank failure above mentioned caused the Bowman family to leave Nantwich in 1816, and to seek their fortunes elsewhere   Eddowes Bowman died at the age of eighty-five years on the 30th Sept 1844, having lived to see his son, *John Eddowes Bowman*, and some of his grandchildren rise to distinction

Of JOHN EDDOWES BOWMAN, who pre-deceased his father in 1841, mention has already been made in foot-notes on pages 310 and 348   He was personally acquainted with Bewick, the celebrated engraver, and was a life-long friend of the antiquary, Joseph Hunter, F S A , with whom he corresponded much   Some of his letters are preserved in the British Museum amongst the Hunterian correspondence   As a young man while at Nantwich, he appears to have been eager, though under difficulties, in the pursuit of knowledge   Thus in a letter to his friend, dated "Nantwich 7 Nov. 1803," lamenting the disadvantages for study under which he was then placed, he writes —

"Indeed I never knew such a town as ours is , there is scarcely a person that takes any delight in any species of literature , excepting a very few, who from fortune or other obstacles, are excluded from me , so I am quite solitary, and never hear any literary news, and very seldom can see a Magazine "

In another letter, dated 31st July, 1803, he mentions the visit to the town of the brothers LYSONS, for the purpose of collecting information, and obtaining sketches, for their then forthcoming History of Cheshire , and says, that one of them preached in the Church.

In 1816 John Eddowes Bowman left Nantwich for Welshpool , and about ten years after moved to Wrexham   In both these towns he found leisure to pursue with ardour those botanical and geological studies which occupied all the moments he could spare from his business as a Banker, and the passion for which induced him, in 1830, to retire to Gresford, and subsequently, in 1837, to Manchester, where he sought a larger circle of men of congenial tastes   There he died in 1841 of a fever contracted while geologizing in the mountains of North Wales   "The late Mr Bowman," says Sir Charles Lyell, (*Student's Elements of Geology*, Edit 1871, p 382), "was the first who gave a satisfactory explanation of the manner in which distinct coal-seams, after maintaining their independence for miles, may at length unite, and then persist throughout another wide area with a thickness equal to that which the separate seams had previously maintained "   The Rev W S Symonds (*Record of the Rocks*, 1872, p 154), and other writers on Geology, associate him with Professor Sedgwick, Lyell, and other authorities on that science

The following notice of his death appeared in the Manchester Guardian for Dec 11th, 1841.

"The death of this very intelligent and excellent gentleman, which was announced in our last number, will be a great loss to science He was indefatigable in the pursuit of knowledge, and his time and talents were most willingly devoted to its advancement In his botanical and geological investigations he displayed a perseverance, activity, and acuteness, seldom surpassed; and he had no greater pleasure than in the discovery and communication of any new fact illustrative of the wisdom, power, or benevolence of the Deity Soon after the commencement of his residence in Manchester, he became intimately acquainted with the different cultivators of kindred studies; and, by the activity of his mind, and his zeal for the promotion of knowledge, no less than by the accuracy and solidity of his own acquirements, proved one of the most valuable and efficient members of the principal scientific institutions of this town and neighbourhood His exemption from the absorbing avocations of business enabled him to concentrate his whole attention on objects of science, and to afford a kind and degree of assistance in promoting them, which few others had it in their power to give, and the loss of which it will not be easy to replace To those who had the happiness of enjoying his private friendship he was endeared by the amiable cheerfulness and simplicity of his manners; by his unaffected readiness to communicate information, and by his generous ardour on behalf of every object and institution connected with the diffusion of knowledge, and with the extension of the means of human virtue and happiness Those who knew him most intimately can best appreciate the genuine piety and benevolence of heart which formed the animating principle of his character, and pervaded every relation of his domestic life By his associates in the Literary and Philosophical, the Natural History, and Geological Societies of Manchester, his memory will be warmly cherished; and his death will be deeply regretted by the most distinguished members of the British Association, especially when they assemble in this town next year His communications to the Transactions of the Linnæan, Geological and other societies, will form lasting evidence of his acquirements, and valuable memorials to his relatives and friends"

By his wife, Elizabeth Eddowes, who was his cousin-german, he had four sons and one daughter.

EDDOWES BOWMAN, M.A., eldest son of John Eddowes Bowman, was for some time a Professor of Classics in the Manchester New College He died at Manchester, unmarried, on the 10th July, 1869

HENRY BOWMAN, second son of J E Bowman, who was born at Nantwich in 1814, lived for many years in Manchester as an eminent Architect In connection with his partner, J S Crowther, Esq, he published a very handsome work in two volumes, entitled "The Churches of the Middle Ages." Among the plates contained in that work is a series, fourteen in number, illustrative of the Church of his native town, from which three have been re-produced for this history On his retirement, he left Manchester to reside at Brockham Green, near Reigate, and died there on the 14th May, 1883

JOHN EDDOWES BOWMAN, youngest brother of the above Henry Bowman, was born at Welshpool in 1819, and in after life became Professor of Practical Chemistry at King's College, London, and was the author of a "Practical Chemistry,' and a "Medical Chemistry." He died at Kensington in 1854

Another brother of this very remarkable family, is SIR WILLIAM BOWMAN, BART, of London, now living, of whom the following notice has recently appeared in "Men of Mark," 4th Series, page 29 —

"William Bowman, LL D , F R S , was born at Nantwich, Cheshire, on July 20th 1816, being the third son of John Eddowes Bowman, F L S , F G S , a Banker in North Wales, and an ardent Naturalist After being at Hazelwood School under the father of Sir Rowland Hill, of Post-office renown, he resided five years in the Birmingham General Hospital, and entered King's College, London in 1837   In 1840, '41, and '42, he presented papers of value to the Royal Society on *Muscle* and "*The Structure of the Kidney,*" and for the last was accorded the Royal Medal in Physiology   At 24 he was elected a Fellow of the Society , two years after to the Council , and he has since been a Vice-President   He contributed the article "*Surgery*" to the " Encyclopædia Metropolitana ," others to the "Cyclopædia of Anatomy and Physiology ," and published with Dr Todd the "*Physiological Anatomy and Physiology of Man*" a work of wide repute In 1846, being Demonstrator of Anatomy and Assistant-Surgeon at King's College Hospital, he joined the Moorfields Ophthalmic Hospital, and delivered a course of Lectures "*On the parts concerned in the Operations on the Eye, and on the Structure of the Retina*'   Though thus led towards a special branch of practice, he continued to be Surgeon to King's College Hospital till 1862 , and he read the "*Address in Surgery*" before the British Medical Association at Chester in 1866   From 1848, he was joint-Professor of Physiology and of General and Morbid Anatomy in King's College, but withdrew from professorial work in 1855, under the exigencies of a large private practice   His services to King's College Hospital from its foundation, and to the College for 22 years were warmly acknowledged , he was named an Hon Fellow , and is now on the Council   Recently he has become consulting Surgeon to Moorfields Hospital and a Vice-President   Mr Bowman has been many years Vice-Chairman of the Clerical, Medical and General Life Assurance Society   He has taken an active part in improving the class of Nurses for the Sick, as a Member of the Council of St John's House from 1848, and of the Nightingale Fund Council from 1856   His later professional writings have been on practical subjects connected with ophthalmology   He has received many marks of recognition from British and Foreign Scientific bodies "

To the above account it may be added that this eminent gentleman, who has done incalculable service to humanity at large, has, in this month of December, 1883, had conferred on him by her Majesty the Queen the honor of a Baronetcy

FINIS.

GENERAL INDEX.

The NAMES OF PERSONS mentioned in the foregoing pages appear in this Index; except those occurring in the tabular Pedigrees.

NAMES OF PLACES,—*Fields*, *Streets*, particular *Houses*,—are printed in *Italics*   Those far distant from Nantwich are not included in this Index

Names mentioned more than once on a page are only indexed once

The modern way of spelling surnames and place-names has been adhered to in the Index, *e g* Maynwaryng, Mynshvll, &c. appear as Mainwaring, Minshull, &c

ABERCONWAY, 42
Abbot of Chester, 19, 21, 42
—— of Combermere, 86
Abbot's Fee, 20
Abnett, John, 148
ACTON, 10, 155, 156
—— Battle at 158 166
—— Church, 22, 148, 155-6, 160, 165, 166, 169, 224-5
—— Churchyard 89
—— Grammar School, 376, 378
—— Pavement, 153
—— Registers, 148*n*
—— Vicar of, 87
Acton John, 196
—— Samuel, 125, 263, 264, 393-4, 433, 473 475
—— Sir William, 487
—— Thomas, 45
—— William, 365
Adams, Mr 343
—— Rev E L, 400
—— Robert 239
—— Tim, 196
Adcock, Richard, 406, 407
Adderley, Rev Thos , 304, 376
Addisse, Ensign, 170
Address to William III., 393
Adult Baptism, 344*n*
Æthelbald of Mercia, 8
Affray 100
Aghit, Richard 177*n*
Agincourt, Battle of, 89
Agricultural Show 251
Ague, epidemic, 111, 135
Alan, Master 30
Albert Edward, H R H , Prince of Wales, 23
Alcocke Rev H , 267
—— Roger, 85
—— William, 138
Aldersey, Thomas, 107, 108
Aldford, 156 157
Aldithley, see Audley
Ale-houses, 205, 224
Ale-tasters, 68
Alexander, John, 98, 443

Alfleet, a soldier, 177
Alger, Robert, 484
Allat William, 202
Allecocke John, 394, 473
Allen Colonel, 167
—— Hugh, 134, 319, 341*n* , 467
—— John 89
—— Joseph, 394*n*
—— Rev James, 402
—— Rev Samuel, 402
—— William, 139, 185, 425
Allerton Roger de, 49
Almshouses 119, 199, 249, 359, 360, 365
Almshouse Meadow 52
Almshouse, Sir Edmund Wright's, 135, 363—372
Almsmen's Feast 338*n* , 366
—— Seats in Church, 367*n*
Almsmen named Wright, 367, 487
Alsager, Margaret, 352
—— (or Auger) Robert, 489
—— Thomas, 133
Alstonton Thomas 406
Altar piece, in the Chancel, 219
Alva, Robert, 61, 91
—— William, 91
Alvaston Grove, 411
Alvaston, Lords of, 210
ALVASTON TOWNSHIP, 404
Alvaston, John, 76, 77
—— Matthew, 195
—— Richard, 90, 406
—— Rondull, 100—1
—— William, 406
Alwaldeston, Richard, de, 405
—— William, 405
Amboldeside, 82
Amson, Jane, 342
—— John 342
Anabaptists explained, 383
Ancient Monuments, 287
—— Privilege, 249
Ancors, John, 98
Anderton, William 139
Ankers, Anne, 102
—— James, 246
—— John 102

Ankers, Lieutenant, 170
—— Thomas, a Priest, 277
Anntscy Field, 418*n*
Anteley, Roger, 452
—— Rondell, 452
Appletree, Corporal, 146
Apprenticing Charity 360
Arcold, Richard, 128
Arderne, Henry de 61
—— Bartholomew, 45
Ardglass, Earl of, 475
Arian Controversy 388
Armada, The, 111
Armitage, Rev William, 399
ARMS OF THE TOWN 17
Arneway, Doctor, 180
Arrowsmith Doctor, 418
Ascension Day, 10
Ascote, John, 282*n*
Ashley, Colonel, 153, 193
Ashton, Colonel 160*n* , 167, 169
Ashworth, Rev John, 395
Aspell Street, 144 150
Aspland, Rev R Brook, 392
Assembly's Catechism, 388
Assessment of the Town, 210
Assizes at Nantwich, 114, 215-6, 502
Aswall, Rev Hugh, 358
Astle, Mary, 343
Astles, Robert, 78
Astley, Rev George, 307
Aston, Edward, 485
—— Hugh, 97
—— John, 425
—— Richard, 102
—— Sir Thomas, 144, 146, 183
—— William, 485
Atha, John ap, 90
Athol Duke of, 216
Atkins, Captain, 170
Atkinson, Mary Ann, 351
AUDLEM, 159
—— Church, 480
Audley Cross, 95
Audley, Adam de, 22
—— George, 200, 217*n* , 218, 221, 223, 227, 349 350

Audley Henry, 55
—— James Lord, 56, 81
—— Joan, 56
—— John Lord 95
—— Lord, 27, 66
—— Lord, Badge of, 338 n
—— Margaret, 56, 57
—— Mr , the younger, 223
—— Ralph, 350
—— Sarah, 350
—— Sir James, 56
—— Sir Nicholas 56, 57, 276
—— Walter de 89
Austerson Wichwood Forest of, 204 n

B ACH Ensign 170
—— Bach, William, de la, 49
—— Babbington Randle, 134
Baddiley Mere, 149, 246, 249
Baddington Hall, 89
Baddington Lane, 118 153
Baerns, William, 174
Bagenhall Robert, 279
Bagley James, 348
—— John Underwood, 348
Bagnall, Elizabeth, 445
—— Richard, 76, 454
—— Thomas, 75, 76
Bagot, Sir William 84
Bailiff, or Bedell, 69
Bailiff's Accounts, 61
—— Proclamation, 67
Bailey, George, 348
—— William, 348, 492
—— Peter, 348
—— Sarah 348
BAKER FAMILY, 480
—— Baker, Memorial glass, 480
—— Captain, 198
—— Hugh, 90
—— Joan, 118
—— Mary, 90
—— Thomas 338—9
Bambridge Captain, 170
Banaster Richard, 17
Banbery, Lieut Joseph, 144 n
Bancroft Richard 116
Banforth Thomas 502
Bank, Midland, 250
—— The District, 125, 243, 246
—— The Old, 237, 372
Bankes, Catharine, 202
Baptismal names double, 344 n
Baptist Chapel, 249, 393—397, 475
—— —— in Wybunbury, 394 n
—— Petition 396
Barber H C , 382
Barbour, William, 83
Barbridge, 166
Barebones Parliament, 340
Barker, John, 138, 202, 239, 240, 247
—— Philip, 392 n , 414
—— Richard, 163 n , 202, 292
—— Rowland, 440
—— Thomas, 270
Barker Street, 7, 63, 413 n
Barlow, T Worthington, 344 n
Barn, Hospital Street end, 218
Barn-Field, 442
Barnes, William, 133, 149
Barnett, Rev Daniel, 346
Barnett, John 185
Baron, Mary Street, 392
—— Peter, 392
Barons' Fee, 223
Barons-Meadow, 92
Barons' Weeks, 256 n , 261

Barony the 7 22—24, 65, 226
Barr, John 93
Barrett, William, 349
Barrow, Samuel, 22b 231 305 343,
    350 364, 399
—— Mrs , 349
Barrows of Salt, 261
Bartholomew Fair, 429, 432
BARTHOMLEY 15 224
—— —— Church, 485
—— —— Massacre, 159
Bartley Roger 202
Barton, Henry, 57
—— Isabella, 102
—— Thomas, 102
Barton-on-the-Hill, 157
Bartons Cross, 34, 150
Baskervyle, John, 303
Basset, Alice 40
—— Joan, 40
—— Philippa, 40, 411, 412, 413
—— Thomas Lord, 25
Bassford, John, 78
—— Thomas 417
Bate, Charles, 228
Bateman, Thomas, 403
Bateson, John, 86
Bath James, 218
—— Elizabeth, 218
—— William, Earl of, 57
Bathing Meadow, 172 504
Battle, The Great, 144
Bavand, Thomas, 363
Bavine, Mr , 172
Baxter, Rev Richard, 365
—— Thomas 91
Bay, explained, 188 n
Bayordshood, or *Bayvardshals*, 6, 279, 453
Bayley, Ann, 350
—— Arabella M , 352
—— Catharine, 349
—— Elizabeth, 344
—— James, 53 , 235, 344, 346-9, 352,
    414 450
—— John, 414
—— Mary, 343
—— Matthew, 348-9, 352
—— Penelope, 352
—— Peter, 228, 235, 352
—— Sarah, 352
—— Thomas 348
—— Weston 350
Bazaars, 250, 251
Beadle, 223
Beal, Doctor 418
Beam Bridge, 155, 165, 201
Beam Bridge-Field, 467
Beam Heath, 204, 206, 207, 210, 218,
    235, 239 404, 409, 410
—— Articles 407-9
—— Charters 405 7
—— Trustees, 410, 412
Beam Street 6
—— Hall 172 n , 173
Bear Inn, The, 105
Beast Market, 6, 105 449
Beauchamp, John de, 83
Beaumaris Castle 83
Beaumont, Rev John, 401 n
Bebbington, John, 240
—— Ralph, 98
—— Richard 98
—— Sarah, 192
Becket, George, 349
—— Captain George, 179, 318
—— John, 133, 164

Becket, Mr 68, 266
—— Richard 248
—— Thomas, 352, 362
—— William 175
Beech, Thomas, 202
Beeston Castle, 157-8 171, 175 6, 181,
    483
Beeston, Hugh, 487
—— William de, 87
Beete Bridge, 31
Bekingham, Richard, 417
Bell Ann, 315
—— Richard 345
Bell-Field, 357
Bell Foundry at Wellington, 198
Bell Inn, The, 105
—— Inventory of, 488
Bell, The New, 351 n
Bellmen, 39 175
Bells, The Church, 198 333
Bellis, Edward, 236
Bellot, Lady Ann, 429
—— Sir John 429 n
—— Sir Thomas 434
Bellyse, Doctor, Edward S 365
Benbow, Captain, 190
Bennett, Henry, 343
—— John M 242, 504
—— Miss, 331
Bennion Elizabeth, 306, 362
—— Ellen 306
—— Esther, 306
—— Frances, 306
—— Jane, 341 n
—— John, 306, 341 n
—— Mary, 306, 362
—— The Misses, 125
Bentham Rev Robert 402
Bentley William 491
Berkbet John, 130
Berks, John, 125, 368 n
Berry Meadow, 418 n
Best, Corporal, 146
Betchton, Manor Court of, 475
Betley Church, 160
Betteley, Francis, 489
—— Rondull, 485
Betton, Thomas, 180
Betts, Captain, 170, 180
Beveresford, Hugh de, 6
Bewick, the engraver, 509
Bible Society, 239
Bickel, Roger, 74
Bickerton Ann 225
—— George, 184
—— Henry, 98
—— John, 51, 172, 175 186, 386
—— Margaret, 102
—— Richard, 196
—— Roger, 52, 76
—— Thomas, 98, 133, 176, 366
Bickley Hall, 64
Bickley, David 274
—— Thomas 274
Bidulph Hall, 159 n
Bigod, Roger le, 42
Billingsley, Lieutenant, 170
Billington, John, 240
Binns, Mr , 382
Birch, Crispin, 334 n
—— Elizabeth, 230 n
—— Mr , 268
Birchall, Edward, 414
—— Mary, 394 n
—— Thomas, 347
Birchin Lane, 414 5, 442

Bird, Henry, 345
—— Thomas, 349
Birkenhead, Alice 339
—— Henry, 189, 189
—— Ralph, 95
Bishop of Chester 14, 18
—— of Coventry and Lichfield, 50
—— Gastrell's Valuation 96
Blackburn, John, 341
Blackburne, Rev Foster G , 309
—— Rev H Ireland, 309
—— Rev Thomas, 309
Blackheath, Battle of 58, 95
Blackhurst William, 49
—— Roger, 49
Black Lion Inn, 244
Blackshaw Hugh, 163
—— John, 98
—— Margaret, 101
Black Prince, Edward the, 26, 49, 89
Blades, W Holland, 229, 230, 365
Blagg, Ann, 105 n
—— Charlotte 379
—— Elizabeth 356
—— James, 401
—— John, 356
—— Megg 201
—— Richard, 346
—— Peter, 281
Blake, John, 83
Blakelow Chapel, 394 n
Blakenhall 154 159
Blakenhall, Hugh, 406
Blessing the Brine, 9, 266
Blome s Itinerary, 4
Bloor, Ann, 350
—— Rev Matthew, 376
Bloreheath, Battle of, 57, 95
Blount, Alexander le, 49
Blymston, John 102
Blythe, John, 120
—— Thomas 50
Boand, Richard 178 n
Board of Guardians, 228
Boff, Billy, 234
Bogie, Rev James, 402
Bolis, Peter, 78, 366 n
Bolland John, 351-2, 392
—— Joseph Gardner, 352
Bolton, Lieut Colonel, 165 n , 171
Bolywall-Field, and Well, 173
Bone-lace Weaving, 269
Bonfires, 223
Bookeley, Richard, 339
—— Robert, 120
—— William 120
Boote, Charles, 344
—— William, 344
Booth Hall, 31, 63, 72
Booth Lane, Battle of, 160
Booth, Col George, 154, 161 n , 162-3,
        167, 178 n , 179
—— Col John, 167, 169 n
—— John Esq , 344
—— Robert, 344
—— Sir George, 144, 151, 162, 193
—— Thomas, 344 n
Bordar explained, 413
Bostock, George, 487
—— John, 152
—— Ralph, 134
—— Thomas 239
Bos on, James, 237
Bosworth Field, 45, 46
Bothe, Richard, 91
Bott, Charles, 241-2

Bott, John, 241
—— Michael, 127 n , 237, 239, 241, 268
—— Philip, 241-2
—— Thomas, 241
—— William 247
Boughey, James, 160
Bould, Rev Edward, 274 n
Boult, John 338
Boulton, William, 489
Bourchier, Lord F tzwarine, 57, 66
Bourne Benjamin, 226
—— Hugh, 403
—— Rev Robert, 382
Bovell, Mr , 187
Bower, Thomas, 53 268-9, 309 365, 396 n
Bowker, Thomas, 65, 248
Bowker's Yard, 234
Bowling Green, 71, 366
BOWMAN FAMILY, 505
Bowman, Catharine, 508
—— Eddowes, 508, 510
—— Edith, 508
—— Eliza, 508
—— George Cyril, 508
—— Henry, 507, 508, 510
—— Herbert Lister, 508
—— John, 508
—— John Eddowes, 508—510
—— John Herbert, 508
—— Sir William, Bart , 508, 510, 511
—— William Paget, 508
Bowring Rev Thomas 392
Bowry, Andrew, 138, 502
Boyd, Rev John, 402
Boydell, John, 375
Boyer, James, 348
—— Peter, 348
Boyne, Battle of, 64
Boyse Thomas, 297-8
Brackenbury Rev Thomas, 402
Bracy, Robert de, 414
Bradbury, Charles, 352
—— Samuel, 352
Braddock, Mr , 387
Bradeley 483 6
Bradeley Hall, 484
Bradley, J H , 266
Bradshaw Henry, 183
—— John 79 301 502
—— Lieutenant, 170
—— Mr , 175, 183
Bradwall, Ellen, 297
—— John 115-7, 291, 296
—— Joseph, 297
—— Margaret, 297
—— Samuel 296
Brady, W M , M D , 127 n , 327
Bramhall, William, 367 n
Bramley Rev John, 403
Brammall, Henry, 120
—— John, 176
Branckner, Thomas, M A , 259
Brandon, Lord, 199
Brasnell John, 278, 282
Brassell, Thomas, 178 n
BRASSEY, see also BRESCI, BRESSIE,
                            BRESSEY
Brassey Green, 414
Brassey Hall, 348, 415
Brassey, Ann, 414
—— Daniel, 414
—— John 414,
—— Mary 414
—— Margaret, 414
—— Raphe, 414
—— Thomas, 107-8, 397, 414-5

Bratt, Thomas, 341
Brayns Hall, 346 n
Brayne, Edward, 133-4
—— Mrs 349
—— Henry, 85
—— John, 99, 338, 346
—— Richard, 338
—— Thomas 47 184
Breame, Edward, 120
Brereton, Anne, 212
—— Catharine, 29
—— Ensign, 170
—— Honble Anne, 213
—— —— Elizabeth, 213
—— —— Frances, 213
—— —— Jane, 213
—— —— Mary, 213
—— —— Margaret, 213
—— Jane, 213
—— John, 21
—— Lord William, 8, 159, 185, 212
—— Randle, 217 n
—— Rev Joseph, 389 n
—— Richard, 29
—— Sir William, 29, 36, 134 n , 140,
        141, 144-5, 149, 151-7, 160 n ,
        166-169, 174, 181 n , 183, 415, 455
—— Thomas, 303, 339 n
—— William, 5 282 n
Bresci, Alice, 414
—— Hamon, 414
—— John, 42, 414
—— Nicholas, 414
—— Robert 414
—— Thomas, 414
Brescy, Robert de, 5
—— Roger, 42-3
—— William, de, 6, 47
Bressey, Robert, 406-7
—— Thomas, 101
Bressie, John, 44, 186
Brerewood, Robert, 106
Brett, John, 75, 100-1, 452
—— Robert 43
—— William, 90
Brich Barn Field, 412
Bridge, The Little, 201
Bridge The Town 7 32, 86, 87, 125,
        128, 134, 196, 208, 236
Bridgeman, Bishop, 296
—— Captain, 144, 146
—— Orlando, 143-4
—— Sir John, 134-5
Bridgewater, Duke of, 506
Briefs, 106-8, 434
Bright Colonel, 167
Brindley, in Acton, 159, 473
Brindley, Thomas,
Brine Analysis of, 503
—— Baths, 251
—— discovered, 251, 264 504
—— Pit, 11, 73, 121, 193, 259, 503
—— Scheme, 250
—— Spring, 203
Briscoe, Colonel, 193
—— Henry, 133
—— Robert, 338
—— Thomas, 202, 338 356, 360
Britten, Rev H B , 402 n
Broadbent, James, 247-8
—— John, 348
Broadrick Rev T B , 392
Brock, John 315, 315, 363
Brockleburst, Rev William, 401
Brom, Richard, 83
Brome, Hugh, 1.8

Bromfield John 451
Bromhale, Geoffrey, 60
Bromhall, Captain, 145
—— John, 52, 94, 217-8, 265n, 288n, 319, 361, 364, 371, 433
—— Mr, 264
—— Richard, 406
—— Robert, 128 133
—— Roger 98
—— Thomas 95, 107, 196 338
Bromley, Ellen, 114, 314, 339
—— Emlyn, 52
—— John, 20, 34, 89, 95, 202, 440
—— Margaret 92
—— Richard, 87, 88
—— Robert, 117
—— Sir George 35
—— Sir John, 62, 482n
—— Thomas 6, 51-2, 184
—— Walter de, 5
—— William 34, 43, 83, 89 95 98, 103, 105, 175, 184 202, 310, 314, 336, 338 9
Brooke, Ann 303
—— Benedict, 301, 303-4
—— Charles Stuart, 326 n
—— Dorothy, 425
—— Edward, 336
—— Elizabeth, 303
—— Esther, 303, 342
—— George, 123
—— Henry, 114, 183, 208 n
—— Humphrey, 440
—— John 46 460 n
—— Mary, 303
—— Margaret 98
—— Oliver 102
—— Peter, 303
—— Raphe, 336
—— Rev Thomas LL D, 219 239, 265 n, 301-3, 306, 326 n, 342, 364, 376 504
—— Rev Thomas (Wistaston) 474
—— Rhoda 303
—— Richard, 337 452
—— Robert, 201
—— Robert Salusbury, 303
—— Roger, 96, 98, 102, 339
—— Samuel, 303
—— Sarah 348
—— Sir, Richard, 211, 434
—— Thomas, 286 n, 343, 425, 434, 485, 487
—— William 303, 348, 382
Brookfield, 329n
Brookhouse, Rev Joseph, 402
Broomlands, The, 218n
Brothersome, John, 60
Broughall, 505
Broughton, Charles Delves, 237, 351
—— Edward Delves, 65, 382, 504
—— Rev Sir Thomas, 412
—— Richard, 114
—— Sir Edward, 157
—— Sir Thomas, 45, 237
Brown, a soldier gibbetted, 177
—— Ensign, 170
—— George, 282 n
—— John 102 133, 342
—— Jonathan, 266
—— William, 165
Brown hills Pasture, 92, 425, 452
Browne, Maria, 127
—— Mary, 130
—— Nicholas, 104
—— Sir Anthony, 48
Browning John 40

Browning William, 40 44 45
Bruen, John, 484 n
Brunley, Thomas, 47
Brunyate, Rev Wesley, 402 n
Brus, Richard de, 42
—— Robert de, 42
Bruyn, John, 91
—— Randle, 50
Bryan George 349
—— Henry 44
Bryne, John, 99
Buckingham, Duke of, 121
Buckley, Henry, 223
—— Margaret, 102
Buck-wheat, growth of, 482
Budworth, 179
Buerton, 159
Buerton, John de, 85
Bugiawton 37 n 57 n
BULKELEY or BULKELEGH Family, 412
Bulkeley a soldier, 157
—— Captain, 149, 152
—— Mr 147
—— Roger, 42
—— Thomas 44 48
—— William, 91
Bullaries, 252
Bullen, (or Bulleyne) James 103 128 133, 166, 337, 339, 443
—— John, 115, 117
—— Thomas, 39, 196, 263 n, 336
Bullock, Samuel, 246
Bunbury Church, 89, 177 n, 267, 332 n
—— Convention 142-3
Buren Roger 90
Burford near Acton 159
Burgess, John, 240
Burghall, Edward, 139, 177 n, 189, 397
Burghesse, Bartholomew, 43
Burghley, William, 107
Burglary at Townsend, 199
Burgundy, Margaret, Duchess of, 45
Burial Custom, 39, 454
Burials' Act 251
Burials in Woollen, 342
Burke, Robert, 118
Burland Hall 220
Burleigh, Lord, 482
Burleydam, 147, 155
Burnell, Edward, 42
—— Robert, (Bishop) 40, 41, 81, 275
—— Sir Philip, 42
Burnett, Gilbert, D D, 297n
Burns, Dr Jabez, 249
BURROUGHES FAMILY, 341 n
Burroughes, James, 202
—— Ralph, 341 n
—— Robert, 341
—— Thomas, 72, 128, 130, 133, 139, 153 202, 341 n, 487
Burrowes, George, 160
—— Stanley, 187
Burscoe, James, 220
Burton, Rev Dr, 266
Bury Rev Mr, 400
Busby, Ensign, 171
Butchers Stalls, 232
Butler James 160
—— Roger 176
—— Sir Francis, 166-7, 169
—— William, 349
Butterworth, Edward, 509
Button, James, 47
Butts, The, 74
Byron, Lord John, 157, 161-2, 169
—— Sir Nicholas 180

Byrom Doctor 152
—— William, 186

CÆSAR Polycarpus 345
Cage, The, 72 129, 152, 444
Cain, Martin, 202
Calcott, Thomas, 186
Caldwell, Ann, 53 n
—— Elizabeth, 53 n
—— James, 53, 228, 239, 390
—— Margaret, 53 n
Calkin, William 343
Cally, Richard, 102
Caloony, Lord, 344
Calveley, Hugh, 141
—— James, 314
—— Sir George, 185
—— Sir Hugh, 88, 183, 332
Camden s Britannia, 255, 433
Campbell Rev James 239
—— Rev Daniel 401
Canal, The, 227, 243 266, 357
Cannel, Rev John, 402
Capell, Arthur Lord, 149, 150 152
—— Sir Henry, 149 n
Cappur, Catharine, 351
—— George, 125, 197, 221, 228, 351, 365
—— Jacob, 197
—— Ralph, 125, 197, 239
—— William, 21, 138, 197
Carbor Randle 283
Carden Hall 151
Cardiffe, Charles, 345
—— Ralph, 155
Carne, Thomas 282 n
Carpenter Cornet 171
Carriers, 233
—— John, 91
Carrington, Anthony, 249
Cart Lake, 7
Carter, Edward, 502
—— Maurice, 502
—— Ralph, 226 n
—— Rev Hugh 402
Cartwright, Acton, 315
—— Bishop, 200 299
—— John 128, 138, 433-4, 489
—— Oliver, 442
—— Richard 221
—— Rev George, 403
—— Sampson, 351
—— Thomas, 39, 102, 231, 345 485
Castell, John, 85
Castilion, Lieutenant, 170
Castle Hill, 418 n
Castle House, 6, 16, 22, 401
Castle Lane, 76, 444, 474 n
Catchpole, 82
Catholic Chapel, St Anne s, 247
Cattle-fairs prohibited 224
Cattle Plague, 224
Causeway Field, 7, 431 n
Cavales, Richard, 138
Cawdrey, Rev Zachary, 419
Cawell, Richard 160
Cawley, John, 244
—— Thomas 240n, 331, 362n, 305
Cawsey Croft 425
Cawsey near Wistaston, 482
Cawton, John, 487
Census returns, 3, 228
Centenarians, 112, 115, 223
Chadderton, Bishop, 106
Chance, Richard, 344
Channel-lockers, 68
Chantries, 281-2

Chantry Roll, 30, 51, 54
Chano or Cheyne, family, 40
—— John, 97, 413
—— Thomas, 90 1 414
—— William 406
Chapel Croft or *Field*, 54 488
Charities List of, 358—362
Charity School 378—382
Charles II at Nantwich, 190
Charlton, Sir Job, 79 198
Chastel, William de, 83
Chastelyord, 6
Chater, Rev Andrew F , 247, 306, 327
—— Rev Daniel S , 307 n
—— Rev James, 306
Chaworth Slater, 346
Cnecking, John, 282 n
Cheerbrook, 144
Cheese Fair, 251
—— Making, 483
Crefors, John, 404
Chell, John, 202
Cheney Brock, 413
Cheney Hall, 413 n
Cheney, James, 231
—— Robert 102
Cheshire, after the War, 455
—— Rising 154
Cheshire's Faintheartedness, 142
—— Success, 145 n
Cheshire, Thomas, 195
Chester Burnt, 22
Chester, Colonel J I , 499
Chester, Earls of, 13 25, 56, 182
Chesters, James, 246
Cheswiss, Anne, 215
—— Captain, 175, 178
—— John, 45, 440, 487
—— Thomas, 97
Chetwood, Alice 152
—— Anna, 347 n
—— Crewe, 347
—— Elizabeth, 347
—— Philip, 21 265 n
—— Richard, 102, 139
—— Sir John, 231, 239, 313, 346
—— Thomas, 96, 442, 484
Child Joseph, 346
—— Thomas, 39, 347
Children s Home, 228, 251
Chobbam, John, 91
Choir Festival, 248, 503
Cholera, The, 213, 245 6
Cholmondeley Castle, 65, 148, 171, 178, 486
Cholmondeley, Captain, 144, 147
—— George, Earl of, 64—65
—— Hon James, 265 n
—— Hugh, Lord, 64, 91, 200, 216, 263 n , 282 n , 299, 440
—— John de, 6
—— Lord 146, 172, 409, 412
—— Marquis of 65, 141-2, 221, 227 239, 267, 412, 455
—— Reginald, 139
—— Richard, 44, 85, 87, 90 440, 452
—— Robert, Viscount, 37 63 4, 90, 118, 129, 183, 267
—— Roger, 43, 87
—— Sir Hugh, 7, 34, 35, 48, 51, 60 1 63 81, 107, 256, 484
—— Sir Robert, 57, 61, 64
—— Thomas, 135, 187, 299, 300, 440
—— William, 440
—— William Henry, 65
Chorlton, Martha 360
Christening custom, *passim*, 201

Church, Advowson of, 209, 292
—— Banner, 328
—— Bells, 119, 213, 250
—— Building of, 275
—— Burying in 329
—— Chancel 332, 333 n
—— Clock, 207
—— Crypt, 333
—— Damage to, 199, 224
—— Dedication, 275, 328
—— Description of, 328—334
—— Dial, 195
—— Dimensions of 330
—— First Rector of, 292
—— Floor, 120
—— Inventory, 283
—— Library, 301, 333
—— Memorial Windows, 323 325-7
—— Monuments, 310—327
—— Old Engraving of, 495
—— Organ 237
—— Pews, 126, 130, 131 3
—— Plate, 334
—— Porch, 331
—— Rates, 306
—— Remains, 330
—— Restoration, 119, 126, 130, 200, 294, 308-9
—— Situation of, 329
—— South Gallery, 302
—— Tithes, 305
—— Tower 434
—— Vestry, 333
—— Wall painting, 331
Churchyard, 105 219, 221, 227, 247-8, 302, 328, 411 n
Churchhouse John 440
—— Richard, 440
Church Lane, 6, 220 449
Church Lane Chapel 399
CHURCH FAMILY, 440—448
Church Mansion, 124 440
Church Pedigree, 446—448
Church, Anne, 343, 444
—— Edward, 126-7, 132, 443 4
—— Elizabeth, 442
—— John, 200, 442-3, 445, 502
—— Margaret, 124, 338, 442
—— Nicolas, 440
—— Randle, 130 139, 186, 196, 363, 427, 442-3
—— Richard, 70, 103, 112, 124, 127, 133 221, 223, 256, 316-7, 440, 442-3
—— Saboth, 124 132-3 139, 153, 161, 263 n , 317 n , 363 443-5
—— Thomas 71-2 76 103 133, 316 7 338, 442-3
—— William, 34, 76, 267, 440, 442-3
Cnurton, 157
Chidlow, William, 505
Civil Marriages, 340
Clare, Agnes, 102
—— Gilbert 102
Clare and Gee burglars 234
Claridge, Benjamin, 398
Clarke, Ann, 340
—— Charles, 239
—— Herry, 271
—— Joseph, 246
—— Thomas, 101
—— William, 340
Clarkson Rev Anthony, 305, 348 n , 504
Clayton, Matthew, 291, 297
—— Rev E , 309
—— Thomas, 127
Cleaquin, Bertram, 89

Clease, Thomas, 124, 225, 294
Cleaver, Bishop, 305
Clergy List, 293—309
Clerk of Market, 176
Clerks List of Parish 39
Clerkship, Dispute 115
Cliffe, Elizabeth, 342
—— John, 235 318, 334 n , 352, 414
Clifford, Rev John, 249
—— Sir Robert, 46
Clinton, Roger de, 18
Clipesby, Juliana, 38
Clive, Joshua, 320
—— Rachel, 320
Cloaners Fields 7
Cloth Fair, 229
Clothing Factories, 240, 249, 271
Clowes, Alexander, 39
—— Anthony 355 359
—— Charles, 411
—— George 352
—— Jane, 338
—— John 200, 352
—— Nicholas, 39
—— Robert, 303
—— Thomas, 39, 115-7, 333, 338, 355-6, 359
—— William 39 192, 403
Clubs 250-1
Clulow, Rev John, 402
Clutton, Alice, 314
—— Ann 268 n
—— Dorothy 491
—— Elizabeth, 491
—— Laurence 491
—— Margery, 498
—— Richard 76 127 132 4 313 440 484 487, 491, 502
—— Thomas 79 99—100, 103, 313
Coaches 233 237
Coal in Salt making, 204
Cobb, Henry, 345
—— Margaret 345
—— William, 348
Cock Inn, 6, 105
Cockburn, Lord Chief Justice, 242
Cockpit, 218, 234-5
Cocoa House 250
Coden, Elizabeth, 114
Coke Sir Edward, 35, 115, 117
—— William, 87
Colbach, William, 341
Colclough, Richard, 72
Cole, Rev Samuel, 298 n , 341
Colecrome 75
Colfox Nicholas 44 47, 83
—— William, 84, 406-7
Colleges, 270
Colly Alice 337
Colthurst, Rev Thomas, 388
Comet, 122
COMBERBACH FAMILY, 495
Comberbach, Daniel, 350
—— Elizabeth, 343
—— James, 495
—— John 200 213 363, 495
—— Margaret, 132, 495
—— Mary, 192
—— Richard, 495
—— Roger, 134, 196, 213 n , 356, 360, 495
—— Thomas, 132, 153, 495
Combermere Abbey, 17-8, 155, 201, 250, 254, 273, 279
—— Arms of, 286 n
—— Abbot of, 449
Combermere, Baron, 237 9, 251

Common, The 72-3 203-4, 407
Commonplace Accounts, 430—433
Connaught, Major, 159
Constable Sir Wilham, 167
Constables, 68, 223
Constabulary 123
Co-operative Society, 250
Cook, Rev R P, 397
Cooke, Ann, 392
—— Captain 170
—— John 242
—— Rev James, 403
—— Richard 6
—— Thomas, 392
—— William, 223
Coole Lane, 442
Cooper, George, 352
—— John, 339, 366 *n*, 396
—— Mrs, 251
—— Philip 216*n*
—— Sion, 353
—— Thomas 396
—— William, 267 396
Coote, Capt Chidley, 340, 344
—— John, 344
—— Mary, 344
—— Nicholas, 340
Cope, Enoch 349
—— Mary, 349
—— Thomas, 349
Copley Major 167 169
Coppenhall Hey, 488, 491
Corbett Athelstan, 505 *n*
—— Edwin 244
—— John, 339
—— Robert, 46, 99
—— Sir Vincent, 145, 150
—— Thomas,
Corn, importation of, 113
—— Market 6
—— Mill 104 249, 267
Cornes, Thomas 341, 398
Cornegy, Lord, 188
Cornish Rising, 57, 95
Corse present explained, 93 *n*
Cosin, Dr, 130
Coterel Randle 407
—— Richard, 406
Cotes, John, 343
—— Rev Thomas, 343 *n*
Cottages described, 233
Cotton Factory 267
—— Famine, 248
Cotton, Elizabeth, 185
—— George, 186 212 425
—— Isabell, 339
—— Lynch Salusbury, 303
—— Rev James, 237
—— Richard, 112
—— Sir Robert Salusbury, 228, 231, 235, 265*n*
—— Sir Stapleton, 236
—— Thomas, 185 212
Coxhull Forest of, 20
Coulton, Alice 337 *n*
Countess of Warwick s Fee, 25, 484
Court Hall, 32, 63
—— Leet, 66 7, 175, 203
—— Quarter Sessions, 220 226
—— Rolls 70 77, 484-5
Cowap, Elizabeth, 351
Cowper John, 71, 76
—— Spencer, 79, 216
Cradock, John, 31, 287 *n*
—— Nicholas, 83, 407
—— Pelerine, 83

Cradock, Richard, 83, 406
—— Roger, 6 83 501
—— Sir David 5, 83 4, 212, 276, 287
—— Thomas 42 287 *n* 405-6
Cranage Thomas, 97
Cranmere, John, 86
Craven, Anne, 351 *n*
—— Elizabeth, 351 *n*
—— Mary 351
—— Richard, 351 *n*
Crawshaw Rev Charles 402
Crewe, The 6, 82, 404 406
Creed Major, 193
Cressey, Captain, 180
Creswall, John, 338
—— Richard, 338
Crispin, Rev J V, 382
Critchley Marion, 52
Crewe Hall 38, 149 158—160, 171, 177
Crewe, Cicely 102
—— Edmund, 100
—— Hungerford, Lord, 309, 333 *n*, 372, 382
—— John, 36, 38, 52, 71, 103-4 138 9, 209, 226, 231, 235, 265*n*, 288*n*, 292, 313 361, 442, 453 455
—— John, Lord, 219, 221, 266, 290 306
—— Margaret, 102
—— Patric, 407
—— Randall, 454
—— Richard, 74, 89, 102, 256 *n*, 339
—— Sir Clippesby, 37
—— Sir John, 300 361
—— Sir Ranulphe, 35-8, 52, 116 7, 120 126, 209, 274, 290 317 *n*, 361*n*, 452, 455, 484
—— Sir Thomas, 37, 355 359, 361
—— Thomas, 406
—— William 120
Crewe Road, 415
Crockett, Alice, 34, 449
—— Bridget, 101
—— Isabell, 501
—— Jane, 202
—— Raphe 76, 114
—— Richard, 114
—— Robert, 97, 103, 105 450 501
—— Roger, 34, 90-100, 131, 198, 236, 336
—— Thomas, 456, 501
Crofte, James, 107
Crompton J F 251
Cromwell, Oliver, 191, 193
—— Thomas, Lord, 335
Crosby, Robert, 185
Crossley, William 196
Crouth John, 85
Crown Inn, The, 100, 105, 167 *n*, 218, 221
Crowther, J S, 510
Croxton, Colonel or Captain, 148, 154, 175-6, 178-9, 193
—— George, 342
—— James, 138, 174 303
—— John, 278 283 293
—— Randle, 129, 138
—— Thomas, 189 342 *n*
Crue, David, 87-8
—— William, 87
Cucking stool, 7, 66, 72
Cuckoo flowers, 482
Cudworth, George 263 *n*, 425
Cumming Janet, 400
—— Peter, 400
Curate s Wages 291
Curfew Bell, 334
Curious Chest 500
Cutler, Agnes, 90

Cutler, John 90
Cuyler, Catharine Frances, 326
—— Sir Charles, 326

D\, William 92
 Day, John, 485
 —— Rev Thomas T, 378
Dakin, Ralph 94
Dale, Richard, 374
—— William, 269
Dandrehen, Marshall, 89
Daniel Jane 101
—— Robert, 85
—— Peter, 126, 143, 452, 489
Darlington, John, 473
Darnhail, poaching affray, 240
Daukinson Thomas, 60, 87
Daulin, William, 274
Davenports of Bramhall, 60
Davenport Ann 161
—— Captain 156
—— Charles, 349
—— Edward, 230
—— Elizabeth, 54 *n*, 288 334, 355, 359, 491
—— Hugh, 317
—— John Aldersey, 228
—— John, 60, 270 303 501
—— Michael, 187
—— Nicholas, 90
—— Sarah, 349
—— Sir John, 121, 317
—— Sir Peter, 303
—— Sir William, 61, 425
—— William, 66, 178 *n*, 270
Davey Rev Austin 402*n*
Davies, Elizabeth, 351, 359
—— Ensign, 170
—— John, 138, 268 *n*, 356, 396
—— Lawrence, 138
—— Sarah, 402 *n*
—— Thomas, 186, 244, 379, 380
—— William, 271, 402
Davison Isabell 336
Dawson Ann 350
—— John 223 350
—— Robert 88
—— Thomas, 94
Deadmen s Field, 166 *n*
Dean, Captain, 170
—— John, 198
Deanery, Survey of, 54
Dearth, 111-2, 242
Debrah, George, 271
Debtors' Prison, 228
Declaration for Indulgence, 383
Degge Simon, 291 *n*
Deincourt, Alice, 44
—— Sir John, 44
Delamere, Forest of, 166
Delamere, Lord, 162, 199
Delinquents, List of, 171-3, 183
Delves, Anne, 318
—— Ciceley, 347
—— Dame Rhoda, 343
—— Ermine, 341 361
—— Henry, 112, 132 3
—— Hugh, 263-4, 341 *n*, 356, 360, 363
—— John 87, 130, 132, 139, 189, 196, 341 *n*
—— Ralph, 95, 452, 501
—— Sir Henry, 98, 139, 412
—— Sir John, 88
—— Sir Thomas, 135, 139—140, 148 *n*, 183, 298, 340, 341 *n*, 386
Demock, Mary, 197

Deuton, John, 200 401
Derby, The Earl of 34, 76, 141 *n* , 142
   190
Derfold (see Dorfold)
Derimer, Thomas, 240, 248, 365
Despencer, Hugh, 55
—— Thomas, 55
Deudsworth, Ensign 170
Dickens, Charles, 248 *n*
Diggens, Anne, 339
—— Edward 120, 339
Dilkes, Roger, 95
Dirtwich, 154
Disney, Captain, 170
Disseisin, explained, 406
Distress, times of, 242 250
Dobson, Rev Mr , 388
Dodd, Edward, 124, 186, 319, 343
—— James, 95
—— Jane, 340
—— John, 338
—— Peerce, 175, 184
—— Randle 411
—— Thomas, 102 121 172-3, 187
—— William, 45 118, 338, 340
Doddington 88 149, 154, 161, 171, 177
Dog Lane 218
Dog and Poultry Show, 247
Dolman, John, 138, 375, 427
Doncaster, Catharine, 218
—— John, 218
Done, Sir John 121, 312
—— Sir Ralph, 167, 171
Dorford Hall, 61 122 124, 149, 155,
   160-1 166, 224
—— Pool, 345
Dorrington, Catharine,
Douglas, Serjeant 148 *n*
Doune, John, 332 *n*
Downes Edmund 120
—— Elizabeth, 352
—— John 239 352, 365
—— Thomas 352
—— William Walley, 365
Downing, Thomas, 365
Drake, Nicholas 98
—— William, 95
Draper, Rev John, 402
Drayton 150, 155
Drinking and Gaming, 31
Droitwich Salt Customs, 263 *n*
Drought, 134 189, 213
Duce, Susannah 398
Duckenfield Colonel, 145 *n* , 167
Duckworth Rondull, 105 *n*
Dudley, John, 239
—— William, 120
Duddleston, Lieut , 170
Dunbibb Elizabeth, 394 *n*
Dunn, Rev Moses, 402
Dunnillow Field, 7 467
Dunning, Richard, 186
—— Thomas, 363 *n*
Dursterheld Ensign, 170
Dutton, Adam 90
—— Elizabeth, 489
—— George 364
—— Hannah, 344
—— Hugh, 91
—— John, 120, 417
—— Jonathan 353
—— Katharine, 89
—— Mary, 353
—— Peter, 91 489
—— Samuel 344
—— Thomas, 162, 269

Dyehouse, at Wistaston, 188 *n*
Dymmock, William, 274
Dysart, Earl of, 265 *n* , 389 *n*
Dyson, Rev John B , 402

EACHUS, Richard, 138
   Eachus Robert, 349
   Eagle Hall in Wienbury parish,
   461 *n*
Eardey, John 85, 225 240
Early Deeds, 4-6
Earnley, Col Sir Michael, 166—169
Earthquake, Shocks of, 119 134, 201, 248
Easdall, William, D D , 130-1
Easter Dues 431-2
—— Roll 37 116 *n* 209 279 289
Eastwood, Rev Thomas, 402
Eaton, Captain, 147
—— Cicely, 201
—— Rev Mr , 352
Eavons, Thomas 345
Ebenezer Chapel, 247, 401
Eccleshall Castle, 180
Eclipse of the Sun 191
EDDOWES FAMILY, 505
Eddowes and Bowman Pedigree
Eddowes, Anne, 506
—— Elizabeth, 387
—— George, 506
—— Jane, 451
—— John, 228, 387 *n* , 389 *n* , 505
—— Joshua 505
—— Ralph, 505
—— Ranulph, 505
—— Robert 461
—— Roger, 505
—— Thomas, 505
—— William, 505
Edlaston, 92, 118
Edleston, John, 352
—— Messrs & Co , 109, 268
—— Richard 67, 244 *n* , 352
—— Thomas 352
Edge, Capt Oliver, 190 *n*
Edgeley, Arthur, 138
—— Jane 361
—— John, 240
—— Rev Samuel, 291 *n* , 361 *n* , 428 *n* ,
   434
—— Richard 101-2, 149
—— William, 134
Edward II at Nantwich, 82
Edwards, Ann, 419
—— Captain, 146
—— Ellen, 337
—— George, 242
—— John, 246, 344
—— Margaret, 419
—— Mr , 385 413 *n*
—— Ursula, 419
—— William, 318
—— Winwood 419
Edwin, Earl of Mercia, 10, 13
Eggesley Thomas, 90
Egerton, Hugh, 95
—— John 452
—— Ralph 47 62 94
—— Randle 50, 185
—— Richard, 50
—— Sir Philip, 244, 251
—— Sir Ralph, 29, 51, 99, 267
—— Sir Richard, 5, 125, 267
—— William, 96, 309
Eiclash, Ensign, 170
Elcocke Alexander, 138 364, 488
—— Anne, 412

Elcocke, Francis, 225, 265 *n* , 473 *n*
—— Margery 166, 488
—— Raphe, 502
—— Robert, 185
—— Thomas, 160, 488
Elephant and Castle Inn, 218 *n*
Ellerton, Rev John 307
Elliar, Ensign, 170
Ellicker, Mr , 266
Ellis, Colonel, 147
Ellison, William, 365
Emmery, John, 202
Endowment Deed, 273
Epidemic Fever 216 7
Epitaphs, curious, 311, 314 5 320, 321 4,
   399
Escheator's Hall, 63
Eske, Richard, 93
Essays & Characters of a Prison, 467-8
Essex Earl of, 168
Evans, Edward 349
—— John 202
—— Mary, 330 *n*
—— Rev E 397
Evanson, Thomas, 161
Everett, Rev E K 397
Everard, Sir Edmund, 43, 49
Evetts Croft, 118
Excise Officers 192, 266
Executions at Nantwich, 176, 179, 180-1
Eyre John, 85
Eyton Catharine 338
—— John, 123, 361, 365
—— Lawrence, 338

FARDOE, John 345
   Fardoe, Thomas, 345
   Fairs, 42, 66, 81 129, 216, 229,
   503
Fairbrother, William 396
Fairburn, George, 219
—— Mary, 219
—— Margaret 219
Fairfax, General Sir Thomas, 158,
   166—169
—— Sir William, 167 169
Fallows, George, 112
Farrington, George, 230
—— Robert, 138
Fast Days, 128, 136, 177, 248, 381
Fawcett Mr , 238
Fazacreley Roger, 95
Fearnough, John 178 *n*
Featherstone, Sarah, 245
—— Sir Timothy 190
Fenna, John 225
Ferrars, Robert Lord, 344
Field-Names, 7, 172
Fielding, Basil, Earl of Denbigh, 178-9
Figgs, Cecilia, 489
—— John 489
—— Thomas, 491
—— William, 491
Flcocke Hugh, 485
Finch, Captain 170
Fines, Ensign, 170
Fingerpost-Field, 245
Fire Brigade, 249
Fire Engine House, 221, 247
Fire-lookers 68
Fires, 94 104 9, 128, 187, 198, 213, 216,
   220 245, 249, 268
Fisher, Captain 170, 177
—— Jane, 343
—— Richard, 120
—— William, 44

Fithian, John, 185
Fitton Frances, 347 n
—— John, 45
—— Laurence, 91
—— Mary, 347
—— Samuel, 482 n
—— Sir Edward, 315, 374 n
FITZWARINE FAMILY, 50
Fleet Francis, 202
Fleetwood, Colonel, 166—169
—— Major General, 205
—— Thomas, 282 n
Fleshmonger Lane, 6, 44
Fletcher, Adam, Rev , 402
—— Catharine 220
—— Charles, 318
—— Edward, 344
—— George, 134
—— James 269
—— John, 278
—— Laurence, 138
—— Richard, 47
—— Robert, 48 58
—— Thomas, 220
—— William, 98
Floods, 103, 134, 192
Flood Gates, 201
Flower Show, 219, 302
Flowerscroft, 6
Flowers, Colonel, 342
Flux, The, 112
Fogg, Lawrence, 343
—— Ralph 268
—— Robert, 384
Foley, Solomon 343
Fohneux Marc 138 172, 174
Folliott Catharine, 352
—— George, 352 362
—— William H 235 352
Foot-race, 226
Foot-way along Churchyard, 390 n
Forest, Robert 101
Forcy Richard, 397 n
Forshaw Mrs 392
Fortifications, 146, 147, 427
Foster, Henry, 411 n
—— James, 228, 411
—— John, 91
—— Thomas, 396, 411
—— William, 228, 411
—— W O , 411
FOULESHURST, or FFULESHURST, Hall,
    57 n , 425
—— Anna 28
—— Edward, 58 n
—— Eleanor, 44
—— Gregory, 34
—— Hugh, 49
—— Joan, 27
—— Matthew 82
—— Richard, 5, 6, 43, 406 7, 414
—— Robert, 28, 34-5, 66-94
—— Sir Robert, 27-8, 59, 83, 89, 95
—— Sir Thomas, 27-29, 34, 279, 280
—— Thomas 35 44, 47, 87
—— William, 43, 47, 61, 92, 343, 406, 440
Foulke, Ellen, 114
Founderdam, Nicholas, 336
Fountain, William, 406-7
Fournns, Gilbert, 134
Fowler Doctor, 180
—— John, 54 160
—— Henry, 160
—— Rev Richard, 160 n
—— Thomas, 172, 184
Fowles, William, 247

Fox, Acton, 304
—— John, 88
—— Margaret, 325
—— Ralph, 325
Foxley, George, 243
—— William, 101
Frame-work knitting, 473
Frankland, Doctor, 503
Frankpledge view of 66 7
Freemasons' Lodge, 238
Free-warren, 42
Friendly Societies, 250
Friends' Meeting-House, 397
Friston, Thomas, 50
Frith, Daniel, 344
—— Morrice, 344
—— Edward 133
Frog Channel 5, 248
—— *Greaves*, 5, 52, 425, 433
—— Mill, 5
—— Row, 4, 5
Frogg, Peter, 297
Frosts, 115, 128, 239
Froward, Richard, 274
Fullshurst Lane, 93
Furnival, Ann, 346
—— Elizabeth, 343
—— Hugh, 118
—— Peter, 343
—— Thomas, 202
Fusey, Juliana, 38

GAGE, Sir John, 48
    Gallamore, John, 489
—— William, 489
Galley, Richard, 268 n
Gallop, Mary, 245
Gallows, 66
Gamull, Edward, 108
—— Lady F , 455
Gaol House, 69, 221, 228, 234
Gardner, Margaret, 202
—— Jane, 102
—— Rev John, 387
—— Rev Mr , 400
Garnett, George, 227-8, 351 n , 364
—— John, 237
—— John Jasper, 235 240, 351 n , 365
—— Thomas, 235, 351
—— William, 72, 239, 351 n
Gas Works, 243
Gastrell Chancellor, 217
Gaulter Rev J , 237, 401
Gayter Thomas, 238
Gee, Edmund 99
—— Rev Thomas, 402
George, Earl of Shrewsbury, 97
General Baptists, 397
Gerard, Alice, 102 482
—— George, 403
—— Gilbert, 189
—— John, 7 113 373, 481 3
—— Margaret, 482 n
—— Peter, 482 n
—— William, 482
Gerards, Lord, 121
Gibbet erected, 177
Gibbons Alderman, 180
—— Charles, 228, 351
—— Rev George, 215, 223, 301, 364
—— John, 101-2, 338, 345, 350 n
—— Thomas, 34
—— William, 111
Gibson, Colonel, 164, 166—169
Gilbert, Anthony, 401
—— Leonard, 65 248 270

Gilbert, William 246
Gild Hall, 30, 276-7, 373
—— Priests, 30, 32
Gill, Abraham, 202
—— John, 386
—— Richard, 21 202, 386
—— Zachary, 202
Gilmore, Major, 147, 149
Gleave Martha 350
—— Matthew, 217-8
Glegg, Arthur, 345
—— Gertrude, 345
—— Thomas, 98
—— William, 139
Glendower, Owen, 87
Gloving, 271 504
Godden Rev James 402
Goddier, Richard, 103
—— Robert, 98, 102, 105, 442
Godsclue, Ensign, 171
Godwin, Rev William, 306
Godwinsley Croft, 92
Godwinsley, Richard, 5
Golborne, John, 114, 424
—— Kate, 318
—— Margaret, 424
—— Thomas, 114
—— Richard, 90, 318
Goldgay, Captain, 146
GOLDSMITH FAMILY, 476—480
Goldsmith Pedigree, 478—480
Goldsmith, Anne, 212
—— John 120 212, 363
—— Jonathan, 364
—— Margery, 296
—— Nicholas, 6 76 98, 442
—— Randle, 101-2
—— Richard, 120, 127
—— Robert, 164, 256 n
—— Samuel, 355, 357, 359
Gonnins Benjamin, 81
Goodale, John, 343, 395
—— Lydia, 395
Goodman, Rev Christopher 106, 108,
    198
Goodwin, John, 266
—— Lieutenant, 170
Good Templars' Hall 249, 397
Goore, William, 138
Gordon, Charles, 303
Gorste, John, 102
Gospeller, explained, 297 n
Government of the Town, 204
Grafton, Randle, 138, 489
—— William 363, 369
Graham Bishop, 309
Grammar School (new), 382
—— (old), 30, 104, 119, 207,
    248, 277, 373-8
Grandison, Lord 141 n , 427
—— Ottone de, 42
Graston, William, 130
Gravestones, 319, 328 n
Gray, Reginald, 22, 406
—— Robert, 98
Greaves Colonel, 156
Green, Mr , Solicitor General, 307
—— Rev John 395
—— Rev Samuel, 403
—— Richard, 184, 475
—— William, 78 101
Green Field, 425
Greenold, Alice, 102
Greenough, John, 411
Greenwollers William, 227
Greenwood Parson, 400

Gresty Francis, 120
—— Ralph, 97
Gretton Rev R H , 289, 306
—— Rev F E , 306
Grey Mr of London, 235
Griffin Inn, 218, 234
GRIFFIN or GRYFFYN FAMILY, 412
Griffin Ann 341
—— Edmund, 342, 345, 349
—— Ffoulk, 338
—— Frances, 341
—— Geoffrev, 407
—— George, 64
—— John, 101
—— Katharine 341
—— Margaret 315
—— Martha, 319, 342 347
—— Moulton, 349
—— Richard 102, 105 184 338, 341-2, 345
—— Sibbell 339
—— Sir John 89, 287
Griffith Henry, 184
—— Randle, 185
—— Robert, 184
Griffiths E Hounsum, 365, 382
Grosvenor, Elizabeth, 417
—— Gilbert le, 85
—— Sir Richard 126
—— Sir Robert, 85
—— Sir Thomas, 312
Groucott, Ann, 400
—— John, 233
Guttit Bell, 334
Gwyn William, 50
Gyles, Thomas, 231

HAGUE, Rev John, 402
     Hailstorm, 129
     Hale Dr Thomas, 307
Hale, William 200
Hales William, 434
Hall of Shaw, 35,
Hall, Ann, 327
—— Charles, 305 327
—— Elizabeth 327
—— Fanny 352
—— Joan 102
—— John 202, 327, 364
—— Jonathan 223
—— Lydia 352
—— Mary, 327
—— May Jane 362
—— Richard, 202
—— Susannah 327
—— Thomas 202 344, 352
—— Thomas Bayley, 344n
—— William 365
Halmarke, Thomas, 102, 185
—— Randle 186
Hame a Saxon Thane 85
Hamelin, William 414
Hamilton, Duke of 149n
Hammersley, Thomas, 397
Hammond, James, 350
—— Major 167 169
Hampton, Randle, 130, 139 443
Hancockson, John 90
Hangford Sir Richard, 94
Hankelow, 159
Hankelowe, Richard 45
Hankie, John, 487
Hanley Sir William, 62
Hanlow Sir John, 42 49
Hanmer, Battle at 152
Hanson, John, 343

Hanywell, Warin de, 4
Harding Charles 78
—— John, 39 239, 271, 350
Hardwick, Lord, 350
Hare, Margaret, 101
—— Rev Robert H 402
Harefinch Joseph 20
Hargreave Chapel, 434
Hargreave, Richard 291, 293
Harlock, George 123 271
—— Samuel 65 210n 398n
Harris Mary 230 t
—— Rev Thomas, 402
Harrison Captain 180
—— Edward, 247
—— George, 102
—— John, 417
—— Margaret 90
—— Robert, 240 243
—— Thomas, 191
—— William, 90, 290, 345
Hart s-horn Inn, 105
Harvey Eleanor 345
—— Rev Thomas 345
—— William, 324
Harwar Captain 161 502
—— Doctor, 166
—— Joan, 98
—— Major 164
—— Nicholas, 96 277
—— Rev Joseph, 265n 343, 348
—— Richard 120, 126, 298n , 355, 359 490
—— Robert, 96
—— Roger, 256 279
—— Thomas 187
Harwarden Castle 157 8
Harwood Mary 351
—— Rev Doctor 390
Haslington, 154 177n 179
Hassall family, a remarkable circumstance in 230
—— Ann 339, 471n
—— Charles 503
—— Edward, 185
—— Emma V 392
—— Hannah 347
—— Hugh, 127, 132, 289 290
—— John 97
—— Joseph 392
—— Ralph, 95, 484
—— Richard, 97—101 103 160, 198 266, 279, 283 336
—— Sarah, 392
—— Stephen 221, 348
—— Thomas 250, 386 389n , 396, 474n , 503
—— William 184 440 489 502
Hatherton, 159
Hatton, Lady Elizabeth, 35, 115n
—— Sir Christopher, 35 107, 115-7
—— Sir William 35, 91
Haughton, Ann, 490
—— Cecilia, 490
—— John 425
Haward, H 107
Hawkes, Ann, 391
—— Rev James, 391
Hawkins, Lieutenant, 180
Hay, Lieutenant Robert 148n
Haybote, explained, 406
Haydock Mr (Chaplain) 205
Hayes, Edward, 72 127, 131, 133, 139, 192, 207, 340, 427
—— Henry, 174, 221, 223
—— John, 268n

Hayes, Thomas, 234
Hayles, Humphrey, 341
—— William, 202
Haynes, Elizabeth, 386n
—— John, 388n
—— Rev Thomas 387-8
Heacock Margaret, 356, 360
Healey, Cornet, 156
Heard, Ensign, 170
Hearte, Lieutenant 156
Heath-keepers, 68, 407 9
Heath-side, 153 467
Heath Richard, 186
Helde, William de, 5
Hellath-wen, 8
Helsby, Sir George, 97
Hengster, Nicholas, 47
Henhull Lane, 155
Henhull, Richard, 83, 406-7
—— Roger, 22
Henley, Rev William, 402
Hennedt, William, 227
Henry Duke of Lancaster, 89 119n
Henry Rev Matthew, 189n , 384-6, 394
—— Rev Philip, 384-5, 397n
Henshall, Rev Peter 399, 400
Henshaw George, 196
Hensley, Thomas W , 382n
Heraldic Glass 284-7
Herbal, Gerard's 113 481-2
Heriot, explained, 432n
Hermitage, in Wybunbury, 501
Heth, Thomas, 85
Heuster, Nicholas, 62
—— Richard, 72
Hewitt, Benjamin , 228, 237, 364
—— John, 101
—— Sarah, 220
—— Thomas, 344 5
—— William, 325, 364
Hewson, Richard, 339
Heywode, Thomas, 50
Hickes, James, 195
Hickson, Anesiphorus, 343
—— Hannah, 361
Hide, Edward, 211
—— Tom, 211
Hilditch, John, 60
—— Joseph, 360
—— Thomas, 186
—— William, 231
Highfield, Thomas, 485
High prices 372
High Sheriff's expenses, 213 5
High Street or High Town, 6
Hignett, Mr , 65
Hill, Henry D , 415
—— Joan, 34
—— John, 34, 101, 329n
—— Lawrence, 215
—— Rev Thomas, 402
—— Richard, 239, 417
—— Roland, 48
—— Sir Rowland 440
—— William, 51, 500
Hillary, Sir Roger, 56-7
Hinchliffe, Rev Edward, 36, 485
Hindley, William, 227
Hines, Luke, 350
Hinton, Robert, 139
—— William, 184
Hirst, Rev J S , 382
Hitchenson, Edward, 149
Hobson, Frederick Wade, 248, 365
—— Samuel, 125
Hockenhull, John, 46

Hockenhull, Roger, 102, 487
Hodgkin, William, 360
Hodgson, Gabriel, 21
—— Joseph, 476
—— Rev Richard, 391
—— Samuel, 125, 226, 327
—— Thomas, 485
—— William, 349, 412
Hogarth's "Rake's Progress" 468n
Holding, Deborah, 352
Holebeck, or Houleck, 82
Holford, Ann, 120
—— Christopher, 186
—— John 85
—— Mary 63
—— William, 291, 294
Holmes Chapel 160
Holroyd Rev J B, 401-2
Holt, 151, 157
Holt Sir Robert, 212
Holy Cross Gild, 285
Holyoak, George Jacob, 238n
—— William, 238
Holland, Colonel, 167, 169
—— Earl, 149n
—— Hugh, 291, 296
—— Maud 43
—— Rev Doctor, 386
—— Robert, 43, 235
—— Thomas, 186
Hollenworth, Richard, 179
Hollins John, 118
—— Thomas, 160
Hollowood, Betty, 236
Holly Holy-Day, 180n
Honford, Sir John 91
—— William, 452
Hoole Robert, 178n
—— Thomas 334n
Hooton, Rev John 403
Hope, Sarah, 352
Hopkin Ann, 341
—— Katherine, 338
—— Laurence 338
—— Thomas 341n
Hopkinson Rev E W, 392
Hopwood William, 69
Horace, Earl of Orford, 65
Horbott, Richard, 102
Hornblower, Rev Francis, 391
Horobyn, Katherine, 102
—— Richard 101
—— Roger, 132
Horse Croft, 425
Horse Races, 218
Horse Stealing, 485
Horton, Captain, 147, 178-9
—— Isaac, 241
—— John, 503
—— Mary, 241
—— Randle, 71, 77
—— Ralph, or Raphe, 185, 346, 364, 472
—— Richard, 96, 242 264n, 401, 433 4, 484, 487
—— Robert, 185
Hospital Croft, 52
Hospital House, remains of, 53
Hospital, or Hospell Street, 5, 105, 159n
Houe Sibyl, 276
—— William, 276
Hough, Richard, 163n
Houghton, Rev John, 390
Houlford, Ann, 114
—— William, 114
Houlse, Peter, 202
Houlsie, Mary, 339

House in the 17th century, 498-9
House of Correction, 124, 199, 207, 209 226
Howard, James, 247, 329n,
—— John, 228
—— Mary, 329n
Howorth, Rev Franklin, 392
Hudson, John, 338
—— Margaret, 338
Hudd, John, 91
Huedoghter, Beatrix, 275
Hughes, Mary, 396
—— Rev John, 242 402
—— Thomas, 472n
Hull, Thomas 46
Hulse Captain 175
—— Joan, 102
—— Raphe 102
—— Richard, 102
Humpston Alexander, 345
Hundred Court 66
Hunsdon, H , 107
Hunt, Elizabeth, 346
—— Hugh 60
—— Mary, 324
—— Thomas, 120, 303, 324
—— William, 346
Hunter, John, 100, 102
—— Joseph 389n , 472n
Huntingdon, Earl of, 89
Hurleston, 159 166
Hurleston, Captain, 147
—— Thomas 102
Hussey, or Hussie, John, 39
—— Mary, 301n
—— Nicholas, 489
—— Richard, 176
—— Samuel 39
Huxley Hall 179
Huxley, Alice 102
—— Ciceley 101
—— George, 120
—— Thomas, 217
—— William, 502
Hyde Edward, 145n
—— George, 303
—— Mr , 362
—— Robert, 288
Hyne, Thomas, 50

ICKIN, Mary, 220
—— Illidge Elizabeth, 386
—— George, 384-6
Illidge, Lieut Richard, 189n , 202n , 384n
—— Martha, 386
—— Mary, 386
Ince, Ellen, 102
—— Raphe, 102
—— Rev Mr 158
—— Richard 31, 452
—— Robert 120
—— William 76, 338, 453
Incent', Doctor, 54
Inclosure Act, 111
Independent Chapel 250, 398, 504
Ingham Rev Jabez, 401-2
Ingrossers of Corn 122
Injunction against the Town, 250
Injunctions and Ordinances, 29
Inns described, 234
Inscriptions on houses, 109, 124
Irby, Lady, 385
—— Sir Anthony, 385
Irlam, Rev Mr , 386
Iron, importation of, 204

Iron Salt-pans, 259
Irish Army defeated, 168
Irish, William 185
Ithell, Edward, 467
—— Humphrey, 256n
—— John 97
Itinerary, Webb's, 8, 121, 123

JACKSON Ann, 341 400
Jackson, B Daydon, 483
—— Daniel 197
Jackson, Doctor, of Manchester, 216
—— George, 239
—— Joan 101
—— Joseph, 221, 228, 379n , 400, 445n
—— Margaret 343
—— Penelope 351
—— Raphe 119
—— Rev John 400
—— Rev Richard 206, 209 292, 298, 363 383
—— Reynold, 101
—— Samuel, 226, 305
—— Thomas, 128, 197, 228
—— William, 52, 101-2 138 149 192 259 262, 346 349, 363
Jacobson Bishop, 308
James I at Nantwich 121
Jamion, Rev Charles, 402
Jeffries, Edward, 215
—— Sir George, 79
—— Sir Joseph, 213 215
Jennings, John 133
Jervis, William, 240
Jodrell, Francis, 303
Jones, Anne 342
—— Captain, 147 157, 185
—— Edward, 239, 396, 402n
—— Margaret, 343
—— Rev William, 400-1
—— Thomas 180
—— T Wyndham, 125, 240, 394 472-4
John of Gaunt, 89
—— of Peckham, 41
Johns, Rev David W 391
—— Rev William 391
Johnson, Cornet John, 444n
—— Hannah, 342n
—— Henry, 218 319
—— Jane, 349n
—— John, 221, 348
—— Margaret, 176
—— Robert, 138
—— Thomas 218, 245 247, 384, 481
—— William, 247
Johnston, Gilbert, 138
Joynson William, 349
Jubilee England's, 194
Judson, John, 130 212n
—— Raphe, 288
—— Sarah, 212n
—— William, 128
Justice of Eyre 86

KEAY Arthur 266
—— Keay, Thomas, 352
—— Rev Mr , 390
Keble Thomas 28
Keefe, Mr , 237
Keffes, Richard, 253n
Kelfall Margery 491
Kelsall, John, 85, 186, 502
—— William 101 186
Kempe C E , 309
Kendall Mary, 353
—— Rev Mr 353

Kent, Alice, 374
—— Edward, 351, 365
—— Edward Jackson 326
—— Rev James, 402n
—— Joan, 351, 374
—— Rev John, 228, 342, 374, 376
—— Joseph Henry, 365
—— Mary, 350
—— Randle, 119 126, 373-4, 461
—— Samuel, 375n
—— Thomas, 375
—— William, 98 235, 364-5
Kenyon, John 227
—— Lord, 461
—— Sarah, 227
Kerdiff Richard, 97
Kettle Thomas, 245
Key John, 101
Killingbough Christopher 345
—— Condrade, 345
Kilmorev, Lord, 142, 183, 218n, 265n, 303, 455
Kimber, Rev Isaac, 395
Kinding, 187n, 257, 260
King of Burland, 220
King, General, 158n
—— John, 187 364
King's Arms Inn, 228
Kingsley Chapel, 91—2, 282 331
Kingsley Field, 92
Kirgsley or Kyngslegh, Adam, 27 43
—— John, 47, 86—8, 91—2
Kinsey, Reginald, 188
Kinshaw, Richard, 75—6
Kirkbride T W 123
Kirkham, Hannah, 343
—— James, 7
Kitchen Hannah, 400
—— Henry, 399—400
—— Jonathan 339n
—— Samuel, 400
Knight, John, 305
Knightley Elizabeth 356, 360
Knolles Francis, 107
—— William, 350
Knowsley Rev Francis, 391, 402n
—— William, 350
Knowsley Peter, 339
Korkett, Richard, 138
Kynnaston Captain, 150
—— Edward, 180

LACY Henry de 42, 56
—— Lacy, Joan, 56
—— Lady Chapel, 224, 281
Lady Field, 166
Lamb Inn, 96, 433
Lamb, John, 352
Lambert, Colonel, 167, 169, 193
Lamburcots, 271
Lancaster, Rev Peter, 292, 300
—— Prudence, 300
Langley, Thomas, 196
Lating, an old custom, 39
Latham, Edmund, 376
—— George, 247, 402n
—— James, 125 365, 376
—— John, 124
—— Margaret, 166
—— Ralph, 132
—— Rev John, 306, 376-7, 474n
—— Samuel, 243
Lathome, Robert, 186
Laton, William, 282n
Lawrence, Rev Edward, 385
—— Rev Samuel, 384-6
—— Sarah, 386

Lawrence, William, 385
Lawton Church, 191, 433-4
Lawton, Robert 338
Lawton of Lawton, 185
Laxton, Charles, 8, 251
Lea, Baronet, 180
—— Captain, 146
—— Joseph 349
—— Samuel, 368n
—— Sarah, 350
—— Sir Richard 37
—— William, 128-9
Leather Roger 202
Leave-lookers, 68, 73
Lee, General, 247
—— George, 119
—— Quartermaster, 171
—— Richard, 454
—— Thomas, 46 444n
—— William, 427
Leech, John, 48n, 62, 79, 98-9, 103, 313, 453, 504
—— Margaret, 98, 281
Leek, John, 202, 417
—— William, 47
LEFTWICH FAMILY, 60
Leftwich Ralph, 60, 138 175, 487
—— Richard, 66, 267
—— Robert, 60
Leicester, or Leicester, Maud, 102
—— Ralph, 303
—— Richard 139
Leigh, or Legh, Captain, 156
—— Colonel, 142
—— Cornet 156 171
—— Edward, 100
—— Frances, 318
—— George, 303
—— John, 46, 83 149, 183, 256, 338
—— Lady, 175 340
—— of High Leigh, 215
—— Peter, 83 297-8, 318
—— Ralph 44
—— Richard, 46, 293
—— Roger, 72
—— Sir Urian, 114
—— Thomas, 48
—— William, 338
Leighton Township, 1
Leighton, Captain Edward, 180
—— Sir Robert, 235
Leland's Itinerary, 254
Lenox, Duke of, 121
Leper House, 121
Leslie, Sir James, 188
Lestead, Serjeant-Major, 148
Lestrange, Lieutenant, 170
Letfote, Richard, 86
Leversage Richard 223, 235, 228, 325, 364-5
—— Sarah, 346
—— Stephen, 346
—— Thomas, 349
—— William 139, 185, 484 305
Lewin, Elizabeth, 349
—— John, 349
Lewis Ensign, 170
—— Phoebe, 348
—— Rev Robert, 402
—— Rev R S 400
—— Richard, 339
—— Thomas, 45
Lewkenor Sir Richard, 79, 114
Lewyn, Doctor, 180
Ley Ground, 218
Lev, Rev John, 297-8

Ley, Rev Thomas, 454
—— Rev Sir James, 37
Liber Regis 328
Licence to Travel, 425, 427
Lichfield, Bishop of, 273
Lich-gates, 219
Lightfoot, John, 232
—— Randle, 356 359
—— William, 236
Lincoln, Battle at, 22
Lincoln E, 107
Lion Lane, 201
Lister, Mary, 344
—— William, 344
Litcole, Captain, 170
Litler Richard 120
—— Thomas, 149
Little Acton 149
Littlebury, John, 60
Littlelover, Robert, 417
Littleton, Major, 180
Liverson, Lieutenant, 170
Lloyd, Bishop, 296, 298
—— Sir Marmaduke, 79, 117, 134-5
Loblev, Peter, 340
—— William, 340
Local Acts of Parliament, 265 409 410
—— Board of Health, 65, 69, 81, 247
—— Proverb, 475
Lockett, William, 244
Lockwood, Rev J B, 397
Lodge Croft 417
London Ministers, Order to, 168
Londonderry, Earl of, 340
Long Lieutenant 170
Lotham, Ann, 338
Lothburne, 6, 105
Lothian, Colonel, 182
—— Serjeant-major, 145, 159
Loundes or Lowndes, Ann, 346
—— Elizabeth, 343
—— Frances, 345
—— George 345
—— Joan, 125
—— John, 300
—— Mary, 300
—— Rev John, 345-6
—— Richard, 125
—— Thomas, 253
Lovatt, or Louvatt John, 101, 345
—— Margaret, 345
—— Samuel, 396
—— Thomas 105, 396
—— William, 111, 445n
Lovekin, Thomas 346
Love Lane, 6 105, 413n
Love Lane Almshouses, 413n
Lovell, Francis Lord, 45, 50 54
—— Johanna, 45n
—— Lord, 6, 417
—— Sir John 42, 44
—— Sir William, 40, 44-5
Lowe, Edward, 239
—— Elizabeth 326
—— Ellen 114
—— George, 352
—— Hugh, 101
—— John, Vicar of Acton, 192
—— Jane, 361
—— Roger, 102
—— Samuel, 346 361n
—— Thomas, 343, 379
—— Thomas Philip, 326n
—— William, 235, 239, 326, 351-2
Lowsen Sir Richard, 180
Lowthian, Rev Joseph, 402

Lucas Captain 170, 180
—— Thomas, 51
Lunt Owen, 414
—— Robert, 174
Lunton Lord, 188
Lupus, Hugh, Earl of Chester, 13 14 85
"*Lybells and Rhymes*, 294
Lyell, Sir Charles 509
Lynch William 276
Lynford, Rev S , 428
Lyon, Charles Montague, 492
Lyons, Lieutenant, 170
Lysons, the at Nantwich, 509
Lytler, Randull, 101
—— Robert, 256*n*

MACAULAY Lord, 253
Macdonald, Rev James 392
Macclesfield, Earl of 199
Macclesfield Grammar School, 259 260
Macclesfield, Ralph de, 90
Machin, William, 406-7
Macready, the Actor, 392
Madan, Rev Mr , 305
Maddock, or Maddocks Ann, 338, 351
—— Eldred, 134 138
—— John, 52, 133
—— Lydia, 351, 394*n*
—— Margaret, 338
—— Plant, 223, 227, 347 8, 364
—— Richard, 256*n*
—— Roger, 396
—— Sarah 351
—— William, 202
Maddu, Widow, 201
Madeley Roger 138
—— William, 228
Madox, Rev Roger, 391
Madye, Hugn, 47
Magee, Bishop, 307
Magnalia Dei 161*n*.
Mahoone, Fnsign, 170
MAINWARING OR MAYNWARING FAMILY
    449—459
—— Arms of, 450
—— Monuments, 315
Mainwaring Pedigree, (elder line)
    124*n* , 451
Mainwaring Pedigree, (younger
    line) 457—459
Mainwaring, Alexander, 450
—— Alice, 36 452, 454
—— Amicia 56
—— Ann, 316, 318 454
—— Arthur, 133, 316, 455
—— Bertred, 56
—— Bridget, 316
—— Catnarine, 361, 502
—— Charles, 299, 300
—— Cicely, 28 101 449, 453
—— Colonel, 141-2, 167, 178*n*
—— Cornet, 156
—— Diana, 307
—— Dorothy, 453
—— Edward, 141-2, 298 374*n*
—— Elizabeth, 453
—— Ellen, 338
—— George 133, 139 316, 452, 454
—— Henry, 34, 114, 143-4, 374*n* , 425
—— Hugh, 71, 314 316, 318, 449, 452,
    489, 498, 502
—— Humphrey, 34, 36, 98, 101, 103,
    256, 278, 452-3
—— Jane, 114, 134, 454
—— John, 76, 91, 95, 103, 105, 127,
    138-9, 316, 336 339 449—456

Mainwaring, Lawrence 277, 452-3
—— Major Philip 340
—— Margaret or Margery, 5, 314, 442,
    449, 452-4, 467
—— Martha, 315, 454
—— Matthew, 126 7, 132, 175 315, 340,
    427, 453-6, 467 8, 498
—— Mary, 312, 450
—— Oliver 34 98, 256, 278-9 449 452
—— Philip 467
—— Prudence, 114
—— Ralph 56 94 456
—— Randle or Rondull 61, 66, 72, 90,
    94, 105, 283, 286-7, 449 454, 502
—— Ranulph, 28, 91
—— Richard 449—454
—— Robert, 452
—— Roger, 48*n* , 95, 103, 112 114, 124,
    195, 286*n* , 316, 35S, 413*n* , 444*n* ,
    449—454, 504
—— Rondulph, 315, 31S, 338
—— Sir Harry 307
—— Sir John, 449
—— Sir Nicholas, 452
—— Sir Philip 136
—— Sir Randle, 37, 98
—— Thomas, 103, 115, 117 127, 130,
    139 150 163 165*n* , 189, 208*n* ,
    256 283-4 288 291-2, 312 314
    316 334*n*., 338, 341, 427, 452 6,
    467 501
—— William, 114, 127, 130, 288, 298,
    315, 449 452-4
Mainwarings of Karincham, 61
—— of Peover, 140
—— various spellings, 130*n*
Maismath, Sir Nicholas, 188
MAISTERSON OR MAYSTERSON FAMILY,
    416—423
—— Arms of, 312, 420
—— Monuments 310—312
Maisterson Pedigree, 420—423
Maisterson, Captain, 419
—— Catharine, 417
—— Cecil, 418
—— Cecily, 133, 375
—— Elizabeth, 312, 419
—— Ellen, 442
—— Frances 352
—— George, 279
—— Henry, 76, 133, 418-9
—— John, 91, 94, 107, 221, 256, 310,
    417-9, 498
—— Katharine, 98, 450
—— Lawrence, 89, 416, 417, 461
—— Margaret, 124, 310, 356, 359, 451
—— Martha, 419
—— Mary, 361
—— Nicholas, 90 101, 440
—— Richard, 47, 76 89 91 94, 98, 103
    114, 312, 339, 364, 405, 417, 419,
    425, 461, 502
—— Robert, 5, 43 89, 416
—— Roger, 34, 79, 99, 103, 256
—— Sir Thomas, 415
—— Thomas, 21, 44-5, 83, 86-90, 94, 96,
    98, 124 5, 127, 132, 139, 185, 196,
    223, 312, 363-4, 416-419, 450, 452
—— William, 217 221, 265, 279*n* , 289,
    348, 364, 376, 417, 452
—— Wooley, 419
Makin Thomas, 485
Making Meet, 261
Malbank Pedigree, 24
Malbank, Arms of, 17
—— Ada, 424

Malbank Adelia 17 19 24
—— Andelicia 22, 24
—— Auda, 4, 5 22 24 59
—— Eleanor, 22, 24 55, 412
—— Hugh 17, 18, 24 273
—— Petronilla, 18, 19 24
—— Philippa, 6, 22, 24 25
—— William, 11, 14-17, 19, 21 24 413
    424 483 500
MALBON FAMILY, 483—486
Malbon, Arms of 48C
—— Dorothy, 485
—— Elizabeth, 485-6
—— Ellen, 484
—— George, 178, 484 6
—— John 484
—— Katharine 485-6
—— Margery 485
—— Matilda 484
—— Ralph, 97, 440, 484
—— Sarah, 485-6
—— Thomas, 38, 87-8 126-7, 139 178
    187 259, 298*n* , 313 425, 454, 484-6
—— William, 442, 484, 486
Malden John, 384
—— Rev Mr , 385
Malevery, Sir Thomas, 167
Malkin, John 186
Malpas, Church, 64
Malpas Field, 150, 442
Malpas, Hugh, 87 8
Malt Trade, 33
Manley, Richard, 43
Manners of the people, 94*n*
—— of the gentry, 211
Manor House, 218
Marbury, 99, 155
Marchesford, 406, 449
Marchomley, John, 417, 440
—— Margery 417
—— Robert de, 49 440
Mare, Charles, 218 378
—— Matthew 218*n*
Mareshall, Henry, 276
Markets 31, 65-6 162, 167, 232, 248
Market Hall, 220, 232, 249
Market Street, 221 249
Marriages Commonwealth, 192
Marrow, Colonel, 177, 455
Marsh, John Fitchett, 472, 475
—— Mary 351
Marshall, G W , 495
—— Richard, 269
—— Honble Samuel, 241
—— Thomas, 221 269
Marsh-field Bank, 173 351, 412
Marsh Lane 77 153 189
Martin, Edward Hall, 327, 382
—— John, 353, 365
—— Richard, 365
—— Robert, 131
—— William, 235
Martinmas Day, 10
Maserey, John, 221
Masinbaring Matthew 130
Masons Yard, 64, 449
MASSEY, MASCY, or MASSIE FAMILY
—— Edward, 93*n* , 119 132-3 319 485,
    502
—— Francis Elcocke, 250 411-2
—— Jeffrey, 138, 363
—— John 280, 346
—— Raphe 502
—— Richard, 5, 87-8, 153, 350, 406, 489
—— Robert, 425
—— Samuel, 346*n*

Massey, Thomas, 134, 221, 223, 228, 269, 352
—— William 147, 152, 365, 488
Matthew, Toby, 116, 136
Matthews, Rev J H , 392
Maule, Ann, 351
Mautravers family 40
Maynwaryng see Mainwaring
Mayor, Rev Robert, 292, 306
May Pole custom, 201*n*
Maysterson, see Maisterson
McClure Elizabeth H , 509
McHale, Michael, 251
McLean, Rev Mr 400
Meakin, Joseph, 350
—— Matthew, 361, 364
—— Richard, 339
—— Roger, 76
—— Susan, 338
—— William, 196, 401
Meanley, Rev Richard, 388
Mears Mary 304
—— William, 346
Mechanics Institute 245
Medicinal Baths, 267
—— Spring, 412
Mee, Joseph 353
Meek, James, 325
—— Mary, 325
Mere, Ellen, 92
—— Raphe 178*n*
Merrill, Robert, 502
Merton, Randal, 25, 90
Meverell, John, 47
Middle-stych, or Misslesiche, 4 72,192, 489
Middleton Elizabeth, 341
—— John 202 341
—— Sir Thomas, 154—157, 178*n* , 193
Middlewich 147, 160, 179, 254
Midgley, Rev Joseph, 402
Mildmay Walter 107
Military Force, 88*n*
Mill, Rental of, 175
—— Lawsuit, 237
—— Field 7
—— Street, 6, 356
—— Weir 212
Millinge Rev Mr , 375
Millington, John, 269
Milstone Lane, 165
Milne-eye, 482
—— Meadow, 172
Milner, Lieutenant, 170
Milton, Alice, 475
—— Christopher, 475
—— Eleanor , 476
—— Elizabeth, 474-6
—— Ellen, 476
—— Humphrey, 189, 208*n* , 432, 475-6
—— John, the Poet, 393, 467, 472
—— Katherine, 476
—— Matilda, 476
—— Raphe 178
—— Thomas, 476
—— Ursula, 476
Milward, Sir Thomas, 210
Minshull Pedigrees, 470-1 , 477-8
MINSHULL or MYNSHULL FAMILY, 467-9
Minshull, Arms of, 469 470
—— Monuments 314
—— Anne, 356, 360
—— Arthur, 339, 467
—— Edward 6, 98, 139, 314, 363, 467, 469
—— Elizabeth, 296, 314, 393, 467, 472-3, 490

Minshull, Ellen, 453
—— Geoffrey, 6, 71, 76, 103, 112 130, 132-3 139, 162, 165, 256, 314-5, 467, 469
—— Hugh, 250*n*
—— John 46 76 95 99 101-2 127, 184, 314, 356, 359, 467
—— Katherine, 202
—— Lady Mary, 351*n* , 472
—— Margaret, 314, 315, 450
—— Mary, 473
—— Michael, 469
—— Nicholas 314
—— Peter 352
—— Ralph, 98 127, 278, 283
—— Randle, 186, 283*n* , 314, 411, 472-3
—— Richard, 88, 127, 130, 133 314, 355, 359, 433, 456, 467, 469, 473, 490
—— Sir Edward, 351*n* , 444, 472
—— Sir Richard, 469
—— Thomas, 7 71, 99, 106, 108, 113, 184, 314-5. 335, 340, 456, 461, 484—489
—— Yewen 514, 540
Mize explained 99, 114, 119*n*
Moat-Field 413*n*
Moldeworth, Roger, 332*n*
Molend, Roger de, 273*n*
Molyneux, Thomas, 85
Monk, Colonel George, 169
Monks' Lane, 6, 21, 176, 399, 489
—— *Orchard*, 6
Monmouth, Duke of, 199
Montalt, Roger de, 55
Moon Rev F , 251, 400
Moore, Daniel, 398
—— Edward, 340
—— George 240 346 351
—— John, 351
—— Mary 346
—— William, 120, 134
Mordant John, 28
More Hall, 149
More, Randolph, 97
Moreton Rev Charles, 385
—— Richard 47 345
Morgan, Ensign, 170
—— Major, 167
—— Rev William, 273*n* , 376
Morgell, Lieutenant, 170
Morrey, Henry, 120
—— Joseph, 347*n*
—— Leonard, 347
—— Richard 347
Morriss, Captain, 147, 150
—— Stephen 202
Mortality, years of, 111-114, 134*n* , 199, 217, 226
Mortimer, Rev James, 402
Moss House, 147
Moss, Peter, 368*n*
Moseley, Sir Edward, 147 149, 150
Mostyn, Sir Thomas, 235
Mottershead Rev Joseph, 386-7
—— Robert, 138
Moulton John 489
—— Philip, 175
—— Thomas, 48
—— William, 138
Mounfield Elizabeth 351
Mount Pleasant, 415
Mowat, Rev James, 402
Mowdy, Owen 339
Moyle, John, 202 256*n*
—— Rev Doctor R , 345
Mug-Market, 346*n*

Multon Hugh, 45
—— Thomas 90-1
Munro Seymour Hugh, 237
Murphy, Owen, 415*n*
Murray, Lord Charles, 216
Muryell John, 44
Musée de Cluny, 345*n*
Musgrave, Ensign, 170
Mutiny, 182
Myles, Thomas, 130, 138
Mynshull see Minshull
Mynton, John, 278
Mytton, Jack, 218

NANTWICH a Chapelry, 272
Nantwich, Barony of, 17
—— Battle at, 14, 22, 85, 158
Nantwich Church, abuses in, 30
—— Brief, 231
—— a prison, 166
—— Derivation of, 8
—— Description of, 2, 10 11, 123, 125
—— Disgarrisoned, 182
Nantwich-Willaston, 413-4
National School, 240
Naylor, Henry. 51
—— John 345*n*
Needham, Sir Robert, 204*n*
Needle, Mary, 402*n*
—— Rev Henry, 402
Neile, Dr , Archbishop of York, 130
Nelthrop General 193
Neville, Richard, Earl of Salisbury, 57, 95
Newans, Joseph, 344
—— Thomas, 314
Newbold, brook, 118
—— *manor of* 82
Newcastle, Marquis of, 160*n*
Newcome Rev Henry, 418*n*
Newenham, John, 49
Newhall Castle of, 56
Newport, Sir Richard, 52
Newton, Alexander, 52
—— Anne, 491
—— Henry 489
—— Lawrence 186
—— Margery, 489
New Town 153, 243
New Town-Field, 357
"New Year," explained, 256*n* , 261
Nicknames, 339*n*
Nixon, Charles, 352
—— Henry, 352
—— John 342
—— Joseph, 239
—— King, 352
—— Mary, 352
—— Sarah 352
—— Thomas, 239, 351-2
—— Thomas Sutton, 365
Noble, William, 3 , 3
Noden Mary, 473
—— Ralph, 473
—— Thomas 133, 189, 269
Noel, Hon Justice, 225
Nonconformist Cemetery, 249, 425
Nonconformity 383—403
Nonjurors Privilege, 79
Norbury, 155
Norbury, Bishop 253
Norcup, Alexander, 440
Norley, John, 86
Normandsel, Mr , 260
Norton, Arms of, 450
—— Funeral Certificate, 450

Norton, Henry 451
—— Lady Margaret, 124, 139, 165*n*, 172, 292, 319
—— Lieutenant 170
—— Sir Dudley, 123—127 149 450
Northwich, 179, 254
Norris, John 186
Norwood, Rev T W , 332
Novell Richard 345
Novello, Miss Clara, 247
Nowell Alexander, 105

OAKES, Catharine, 345
—— *Oat Market*, 6 105*n*
—— Oats, a remarkable crop of, 226
Odd Fellows' Lodge 218
Offley, Anne Crewe 292, 300, 361 379
—— Dame Emma, 306
—— John, 129, 361*n*
Old Biot 252
Old Brewery, 240
Oldfield Henry 119 402
—— Leftwich 491
—— Robert, 291*n*
Oliver, Rev John, 278, 343
Oton, Edward, 149
—— Ralph, 96
—— Randle, 414
O Neil, James 249
Onions, Joseph, 221, 223
Oratory 86, 416*n*
Organere, John, 91
Oimeshened, John 49
Ormond Marquis of, 157
Orreby, Philip de 55
Ortor Richard, 51
Ossory, Lord, 196
Ostler, George, 120
Oseworth Roger, 228
Ottley Richard, 180
Oulton, Balzar 344
—— Thomas, 344
Oulton Hall, 179
Oulton, John, 83-4 138, 223 364
—— Margaret, 351
—— Thomas, 39, 45
Outrage by a lunatic, 227
Overseers, 225
Owen, Capt Pontesbury 180
—— Lieut Thomas, 180
—— Rev Mr , 387
—— Thomas, 180
Ox Pastures, 218, 415

PACK-HORSES 265
—— Paget, Doctor Nathan, 296, 472-3 479
Paget, Lord, 48
—— Rev John, 185, 294-5 383
—— Rev Thomas 296, 479
—— Sir William, 48
Palin Samuel, 347
—— Thomas, 75, 101
Pall-Mall, 401
Palmer Alice, 476
—— Thomas, 312
Pancake bell 334
Paradise, William, 93
Paris Matthew, 80
Parish Cemetery, 245
Park The, 249
Parker John 98, 101, 346
—— Oliver, 102
—— Richard, 43
—— Robert 132, 138 198, 239, 319
—— Roger, 102

Parker, Thomas, 148, 363
Parliament The Short, 136
Parliamentary Election, 244, 251
—— Forces retreat of 158
—— Roll, The lost, 120
Parrot, Edward, 346
Parson, George, 184
Partridge, Jane, 380
—— Mark, 338
—— Mary 380-1
—— Rev Joseph, 370, 380-1, 391
—— Sarah, 380
—— William 338
Paruise, The, 331
Parys, Robert, 86
Pate, Lieutenant 170
Patricke, John 174, 186
—— Richard, 138
Paul, G , of London 343
Pawlet Lieutenant 170
Payne, Elizabeth, 345
—— George, 228 350 361
—— Nathaniel, 345
—— Rev Henry S , 400
Peake, Rev John, 212-3
Pearce, William, 239
Pearson, John 39, 115-7
Peartree-Field 6 414 486
Pease-flat Field, 425
Pech, Rev W P , 402
Pedley, Thomas 394*n* , 414
Pedro King of Castile, 89
Peers, William, 268*n*
Peever Richard, 200, 360
Pelfe, 66
Pemberton Ann, 362
—— John, 350
—— Richard 341
—— William, 228
Pembroke Earl of, 121
Pemicock, Ensign, 170
Pen Admiral, 154*n*
Penance at the Cage, 152
Pendlebury Rev Henry 391
Pendleton Henry, 485
Penkamane, Thomas 138
Penkethman Samuel 396
Penlington, Ann, 230*n* , 350
—— George 125
—— Joan, 350
—— William, 125, 230*n* , 350
Pennant Thomas 9
People's Hall 251
Peploe, Bishop 226
—— Catharine 314
—— Rev Robert 344-5
—— Susannah, 345
Pepper Street 7, 52
Percival, Thomas 353
Percy Rebellion 87
Perkins Rev William, 454
Perkyn Ralph, 5
Perry, Emma 351
Pershall, Sir John, 173, 180, 187
—— Sir William 187*n*
Petition to King Charles, 137
Peters Lane 6
Petty, Quartermaster, 171
—— William 266
Philips, Ensign, 170
—— William, 228, 347 364
Phythian, William, 356, 360
Piccage, 66
Pick, James, 138
Pickering Ambrose, 202
—— Matthew, 396

Pickerin, Robert, 98, 102
Pikton Richard, 274
Pillory Street, 7 31, 63 66, 165*n*
Pimlot John, 303
Pinder Rev Mr , 401
Pinfold 32 408
Pinkey, Major 178
Plague, at London, 208
—— at Nantwich, 113, 129
—— at Wistaston, 188
Plant, Mary 353
—— William 353
Platt, Alice, 102
—— Samuel, 238
Play-House, 218
Plessetts, Hugh de, 40
—— John de, 40-1
—— Philip de, 40
Plevin, James 240, 325
Plymton Church 96
Podmore, John, 153
—— Richard, 202
Pole, John de la 45
—— Sir Richard, 95
Pollett Oliver, 489
Polley, George, 344
—— Thomas 344-5
Poole Ann 114
—— Dorothy, 184
—— George, Rev , 402
—— James 183
—— Richard, 86
—— Robert, 489
—— Thomas, 183-4
—— William, 179
Poor-House, 226
Poor Law Act, 204
Poor Rate, 205, 207
Population, 3 4
Porch, Memorial Glass 331
Porche House, 92, 93*n* , 172*n*
Porter, Thomas, 278, 283
Post-Office, 195
Potato disease 244
Pott, William 138
Potter, George, 350
Potts Nehemiah 138
—— Thomas 138
Poulden, Lieutenant, 170
Powell, Joseph, 397
Pownall John, 185
Poynton John, 343
Praers Hall, 442
Praers Elizabeth, 26
—— Letice, 411
—— Margaret, 23, 26
—— Obit, 354, 358
—— Richard, 26
—— Robert, 4 22
—— Roger, 47, 48*n* , 94 281
—— Sir Randle 25
—— Thomas, 26, 85 406
—— William, 47 83 86, 89, 281*n* , 411
Pratchett Catharine, 343
—— Elizabeth, 350
—— John, 21, 175, 235 265*n* , 278, 346, 348—351, 364-5, 454
—— Raphe, 202
—— Richard 133
—— Thomas, 223, 375
—— William, 43 52 118, 187, 350, 425 487
—— William Plant 348
Pratchett s Row, 364*n*
Presbyterian Chapel, 384—388
Preece, or Prees, Captain, 157

Frees, John, 188
Prescott, Rev Peter, 376, 402
—— Rev Thomas, 378
Pressing for the Army, 236
Prestecote, Thomas, 275
Presthume Field 417, 431
Prestland John, 102
Preston, Rev Thomas, 402
Pretender s Rebellion, 215
Price, Elizabeth, 197
—— Hugh, 104 337, 454
—— John, 138
—— Mary, 337n
—— Thomas 202, 341
Prices of food, wages &c 122, 229
Priestley Rev Joseph, 387n 390
Priests' Chamber, 309
Primitive Chapel, 229n , 244, 403
Prince, Charles 345
—— John 68, 78
—— Thomas, 345
Principal Houses 123—125
Priory of St Thomas at Stafford, 96
Prisoners, 147, 149, 169-172, 176, 180, 182 188
Proclamation of Fair, 70, 129
Proctors Book, 291
Proudman, Thomas, 361
" Providence Improved," 139, 397
Prynne, Mr , 135
Pudding Lane 445
Pugin, the architect, 500
Pulpit, in Church, 130-1, 330
Pull, Jonn, 91
—— William de 42
Punshon, Catharine, 352
—— Luke, 352
Pye Corner , 196

QUAIN, Mr , 123
    Quakers, 397-8
    Quakers and Shakers, 482
    Quarter Sessions, 100 182 220
Queen Elizabeth, 113
—— Margaret 95
Queen Street, 226
Quelch, Ann, 218
—— William, 218

RABY, Lord, 136
    Race-course, 218, 234 236 412
    Radcot Bridge, Battle at, 85
Radtord-Norcup, A W , 124
—— Thomas 414
Radmore, Lieut Richard, 318
Rag Fair, 229
Railway, 247-8
Raleigh Sir Walter, 483
Ramsay, Andrew, 400
—— Gilbert, 400, 504
—— Janet, 251, 399, 400, 504
—— John, 400
—— Lord, 188
—— Scholarship, 504
Ranesford, Captain 180
Ranger Major 180
Ranulph, Earl of Chester 18 19
Ratcliffe Elizabeth, 353
—— Ralph, 353
Rathbone, Ann, 361, 376
—— Rev Isaac, 376
Ratonrows, 6
Ravenscroft, Richard, 346
Ravensmore, 140, 149, 153, 178
Rawley Robert, 484
Ray, John, 259

Reade, James, 305
—— Rev Jones, 304, 347
—— Nicholas, 102
—— Thomas, 221
Rease Meadow, 442
Rectory House 219, 302
Red Hall, 405n , 414
Red Lion Inn, 433
Red Lion Lane, 93
Registers, The, 113 335—353
Registry Office 247
Regrators of Corn 122
Reign of Terror, 188
Rejoicings at Nantwich and Wrenbury, 238
Remonstrance, 137
Reynolds, Humphrey, 442
—— John, 138, 386
Rhodes Edwin H 218n
Rhyme, a curious, 377
Richard I Crusade, 469
—— II at Nantwich, 86-7
Richards, Jonathan, 202
Richardson, Edward, 340
—— John, 351 365
—— Thomas, 52
Ridgway Mr , 340
Ridle,-Field, 5 32, 92, 100, 128, 444-5
Ridle, Hall, 47n , 157
Rigby, Col Alexander 166
Right of Way, 118, 414
Rinderpest, 248
Rioting, 241
Rise, Ensign 170
Rising The Cheshire 193
Rising Sun, 405n
Rivell, Nicholas, 49
Rivers, Earl John, 40, 142, 172, 183
Rivers Pollution, lawsuit, 251
Road Waggons 233
Robinson, Richard 76, 98, 102-3, 256n , 346
—— Thomas, 76 349 352
—— William, 245, 377-8
Rock Salt discovered, 254, 264
Rock Savage Earl of 65
Rockett, Elizabeth 230n , 347
—— Richard, 133, 230n
Rode Hall, 434
Rodenhurst, Benjamin, 235, 365
Roderick Rev Mr , 385
Rodes, Richard, 102
Roe, Charles, 4
—— Lieutenant 170
Rogers, Andrew, 353
—— Edward, 202
Robinson, William, 278
Roman way, 7
" Romance of Vienna," 456
Rondulph, Roger, 275
Rookery Hall, 412
Rope John 44 47, 94
—— Lawrence, 95, 279
—— Richard, 85, 87-8, 97, 407, 414
Roscoe, William, 392
Rough Field, 488
Round House Prison, 240, 245
Rowe, Ann, 349
—— Thomas 349
Rowley Alice 341
—— Rev Francis, 184
—— Thomas, 186
Rowton Moor, 171
Royal Humane Society, 230
—— Protection 81
Royston, Richard, 190n

Ruddock, William 276
Rudhall, Abraham 213, 333n
Ruderd John, 339
—— Thomas, 339
Rulers of Walling, 68, 258
Runaway Apprentices, 268
Rural Deanery, 275
Russel, Randle, 406-7
—— Roger, 406-7
Rutter, Henry 202
—— Jasper, 72 75-6 103 114 338 440
—— John, 114, 256, 336
—— Richard, 336
—— Rondull, 339
—— Urselo, 114
—— William, 339
Ryder, Margaret, 102

SABBATH observation of 205
    Sadler, Captain, 161
    —— Rev E J , 400
Sadler Robert, 46n
Salicher, 253
Salghall, Roger, 87
Salisbury, Earl of, 89, 483
—— Lazarus 414
Salmon Annette 396n
—— Charles, 342, 349, 396n , 480
—— Geo. ge, 265n
—— Joan, 348
—— Joseph, 348
—— Joseph, Whittingham 396
—— Margaret, 98, 369—370, 495
—— Mary, 396n
—— Prussia 351, 480
—— Robert, 201
—— Sarah, 350
—— William, 118, 365, 415, 425, 480, 484, 487
—— Rev William, 396n
Salt Baths, 245
—— Duty, 266
—— Heath, Battle at 147
—— Lake, or Meadow 7
—— Laws and Customs, 11, 32, 72-4, 77, 203, 206, 256, 263-4
—— Ley, 236
—— Houses, Pits, or Wiche-houses, 81, 247 260-2
—— Smuggling, 266
—— Springs, sanctity of, 9, 12
—— Subsidences, 265
—— Trade suspended, 162
" *Salt upon Salt*," 253
Saltersiche, 57n
Saltpetre man, 339n
Saltworks at Baddington, 204n
Salusbury, Lieutenant, 157
Samford, Thomas de, 4
Sandbach, 160
Sandbach, Henry de, 214
—— Richard, 406
—— Thomas de 85
Sanders, John, 343, 345-6
—— Samuel, 344
—— Thomas 344
Sandford Bridge 190n
SANDFORD FAMILY 40
Sandford, Francis, 180
—— Richard de, 6
—— Robert, 163n , 180
—— Capt Thomas, 150, 158-9, 163-5
Sandiway muster at, 87
Sands, William 109
Sandyhole 414
Sankie, Captain, 152

Sant, Joseph, 368n
—— Thomas, 269
Saracen's Head 338 449
Sarazin, Ralph, 49
Sare, Humphrey, 120
—— John, 133, 189—191
Saring, John, 131, 134, 139, 149, 173, 185, 291, 297-8, 363, 427
SAVAGE FAMILY of Clifton, 59
Savage, Alice, 59
—— John 60
—— Maximilian, 339
—— Mrs, 386
—————— Diary of, 384, 387-8
—r— Nicholas 452
—— Robert, 74 76
—— Sir John, 59, 66, 118
—— Sir Thomas, 59n
—— Thomas 142
—— William, 485
Savings Bank, 245
Savonry, John 68n
Sawrdyn William, 253n
Sawyer, Richard, 253
Scarcity, years of, 111, 122, 208
Scavenging, 77
Schoolhall, Randulph 253n
Scholfield, Serjeant, 236
Schroeder, Baron von, 412
Science Lectures 389n
" *Scold like a wych waller*," 7
Scot, John, Earl of Chester, 80
Scott, Captain, 398, 400n, 504
—— Rev George, 402
—— John, 118
—— Sir Gilbert, 247 309
—— Thomas 489
Scrope Sir Richard 85
Seaboll, Rondull, 339
Searle, George, 344
—— Maurice, 344
—— Rev Radcliffe, 344
—— William, 344
Seavill, Ellen, 386
—— Richard, 209
Seckerston John, 76 98 103, 105 447
—— Randulphe 138
Sefton, Thomas, 202
Segrave, Elizabeth, 356, 360
—— Thomas, 21
Senior, Rev B, 240, 400
Sentry Houses, 174-5
Sequestrators, 171
Sergeant Thomas, 170
Shagh, Thomas 90-1
Shakerley, Charles Peter, 244
—— Geoffrey J, 412
—— Peter, 303
Shakespeare Tavern, 105n, 218n
Sharples, John, 398, 499
Shaw, Elizabeth, 242
—— Isabell 90
—— Rev Mark, 403
—— Rev W F, 248
—— Richard, 118
—— Thomas, 242
—— William, 118
Shelmerdine, Rev Mr, 401
Shenton, Ann, 353
—— John 138
—— Mr, 126
—— Randle, 198
—— Sarah, 344
—— Thomas 39, 101-2, 485, 489
   William, 271, 353, 373-4
Sheridan, Catharine, 352

Sheridan, James, 352
Sherlock Rev Richard, 171
Sherman, Thomas, 88, 90
Sherratt, Joseph 239
—— William 250
Shershaw John 186
Sherwin, Jane, 343
Shiedam, John de, 253
Ship Inn, 105
Ship-money tax, 135
Shipworth Lieutenant, 170
Shirley, Elizabeth, 344
—— Capt Washington, 344
Shocklach 151
Shoemakers strike, 247
Shoemaking, 270
Shops in High Town, 233
Shovelton, Rev Wright, 402
Shrewbridge, 82, 172, 241
Shrewbridge Lane, 76 118
Shrewsbury, 88, 155-6
Shrimpton, Charles, 228
Shufflebotham Ellen, 341
—— John, 223
Shurington, Elizabeth, 98
Shutshaw, 425, 433, 444, 488
Shyre, Johan, 101
Siche-Field, 454
Siddals, William, 78
Sidway, Thomas 186
Sillito, Randle, 186 191n
Simcock, Ann, 202
—— Thomas 202, 452
Simnell, Lambert, 45, 95
Simonds, Robert, 375
Simpson, Ann, 349
—— Rev Joseph, 402
—— Thomas 344
—— William, 344
Singleton, Rev Mr, 385
—— Thomas, 246
Skelmersdale, Lord, 435
Skerrett, Joseph, 53, 223, 228, 244, 344, 348, 364
Skrymsher, Charles Boothby, 95n
Slace, Anne, 502
—— John, 128, 138, 359n, 489
—— Margaret 128, 355 359, 489
Slaughter-houses, 231, 502
Small-pox, 170
Smallwood, William, 340
Smelt, Captain, 418
Smetham, Rev James, 402
—— Rev Richard 402
Smethwick, Mary, 338
Smith, Anne, 356, 359
—— Christopher 20
—— Cicely, 114
—— Elizabeth, 394n, 399
—— Ensign, 170
—— Francis, 180
—— Isaac, 353
—— James, 192, 219
—— Jane, 220, 342
—— John, 90 247 270n 399, 345
—— Rev John 227, 304, 342, 347
—— Laurence, 283
—— Lieutenant, 170
—— Margaret, 102, 348
—— Mary, 212, 350
—— Patient 220
—— Randle, 425
—— Rev Robert 399 400
—— Richard, 71, 101, 305
—— Sir Lawrence, 99, 100
—— Sir Thomas, 37, 122 183, 212, 298

Smith, Thomas, 97, 118, 269, 425, 440, 489
—— William, 240, 243, 254
Smithfield, proposed, 65
Smithson Rev John, 401 2
Smythe, Randle, 179
—— Thomas, 440
Snelson, Edmund, 304, 352
—— Elizabeth 376
—— Thomas, 338
—— William, 338
Sneyd, Colonel, 159
—— John, 91, 413
—— Ralph, 184, 414
—— Richard, 279
Snow, a great fall of, 134, 165, 239
Snow Hill 6, 105 231
Soldiers buried at Nantwich, 201n 340n
Soldiers Parlour, 236
Soldiers Wedding, a, 236
Somers, Lord Keeper, 263
Sonde, John 89
Sonkey, Robert, 93
Sontley, Randle, 34
Soot, Ann, 341
Sound, 149
Sparbacon Lane, 5
Sparepoint, John, 394n
Sparke, Blanch, 501
—— Henry 96 279 354 358
—— Margaret, 98
—— Maria, 501
—— Nicholas, 97
—— Philip, 501
—— Robert, 72, 75
—— Roger, 96 98, 501
—— William, 501
Sparrow Alice 102
—— Edmund, 101 338
—— John, 102, 425
—— Randle, 490
—— Thomas, 130, 132, 259
Spencer Anthony, 353
—— Major, 167
—— Richard, 47, 91
Spring Gardens 251
Sports and Pastimes, 234
Sproson, James, 268n
Sproston, John, 346n
Spotswood Captain, 170
Sprout, Mary, 352
—— Peter, 235 351, 359—360, 362
—— William, 225, 228, 235, 237, 325, 347 351 352 362 365-6, 372
Spurgeon, Rev C H, 250
Spurstow, Richard, 44
Squarebridge, Rev John, 352 401
Sirobistall pastures, 418n
Stafford, William, 61
Stage Waggon, 224
Stallage 66
Standish Charles 341
Stanley, Captain 178, 180
—— Catharine, 59
—— Lord, 59
—— Randle or Rondulph, 310, 461
—— Sir William, 46 8, 66, 417
—— Thomas, 95, 208n
Stanton Charles, 219
—— Elizabeth, 326
—— Emilia, 219
—— Robert 219, 326
—— Samuel, 219
—— Sarah, 219
Stanyer, Thomas, 401
Stanyhurst, John, 90

Stapeley Hall, 480
Stapeley, Peter de, 6 82
—— Philip 406
—— Roger de, 85
Star Inn, 236
Starkey, Edward 101
—— George, 139
—— James 282n
—— John, 90, 265n
—— Thomas, 59 417
Stead Rev Abraham 402
Steele Ann 400
—— Elinor, 345
—— John, 345
—— Richard, 160
—— Sarah, 268n, 502
—— Capt Thomas, 138, 158 9, 176, 502
—— William 160
Steenkirk Battle of. 64
Steven, Ann 120
—— Lawrence, 119
Stevenson John. 225
—— Randle, 277-8
—— Sir Reginald, 293
—— William 231
Steinthal, Rev S A 392
Stocking-frame knitting, 269
Stockport, 149
Stocks, 32 69, 222
Stockten-heath, Battle, 147
Stockton Edward, 224
—— James 348
—— John, 128
—— Ralph 485
—— Zillah. 348
Stoke, Battle of, 45
Stoke Hall 472
Stoke Manor, 91. 467
Stoke Robert de, 92
Stokoe, Rev Thomas, 402
Stone Amy, 350
—— Elizabeth 351
—— Richard 364
—— Roger 363
Stoneley, Ann 378
—— Wilham 378
Stones, Captain, 181
Storms, 128, 129, 224, 230, 250
Strafford The Earl of 136
Strays, 66
Street pavement, 74
Street, John, 339
—— Margaret 339
Stretch, Richard, 239
—— Samuel 343
Stringer Rev Gabriel 200, 210, 292, 299
—— Isabell, 300
—— Margaret, 350
—— Sarah, 300
—— Stephen, 300
—— Thomas, 200 263n
Strong, Rondull, 78
Strongitharm, William, 179
Stubbs, Thomas, 229
St Anne's Chapel, 86, 267
—— Clock 118
—— *Croft* 7, 52, 357
—— Parish, 86
St George's Chapel, 281, 286
St John of Jerusalem Order of, 319
St Lawrence Hospital, 53, 488, 501
St Nicholas Hospital, 41, 48, 212, 274, 500
St Pierre, David 85 87
—— John 61

St Pierre, Urian de, 61n, 81n, 407
St Werburgh Abbey, 17-18
Subsidy Roll, 98, 127
Suckley, Thomas, 356, 360
Suit of Arms 82
Supervisors, 75
Sutton, Ann, 114
—— John 78
—— William 235, 237
Swalden William 375
Swallow, Colonel, 193
—— Rev William 402
Swan Mary, 362
Swan Inn, 6, 105, 501
Swanick, Allen 153n
Swanwyk David 45
Sweating Sickness 99
Sweet-briar Hall 105n 384n, 509
Swettenham Family 495
—— Lawrence, 81
—— Petronilla, 91
—— Thomas 91 221 303
Swineherd 31, 407
Swine Market 6
Swinglehurst Ann, 450
Sydenham, Captain 170
Symonds, Rev W S, 509

TABERNACLE Chapel, The, 401
Tables of Charities, 354
Tabraham, Rev Richard, 402
Tagg Thomas 349 492
Taintree Yard 63
Talbot, Captain, 180
—— John, 205n
—— Thomas 345
Tallents Rev Mr, 385
Talley, Henry, 339
Tanatt Mr, of Broxton, 156
Tarun 179
Taxation of Pope Nicholas, 20
Taylor, Ann, 352
—— Creswell, 343
—— Edmund, 98
—— Jeremy 173
—— Peter, 241
—— Richard, 96, 48n
—— Robert 223 228
—— Thomas, 47 78, 90
—— William 240
Temperance Society 306
Tench, Edward, 98
—— Eleanor, 115n
—— John, 21, 103, 133, 138, 175, 197, 256n, 502
—— Thomas, 197, 490
—— Tobias, 374 502
—— William, 71-2, 76, 98, 103
Tenchersfield 6
Tennis-ball playing, 227
Terringham Ensign, 171
Terrington, Gill & Co, 269
Tew John 380
—— Sarah, 380
Thackers Croft 460
Thanksgiving Days, 147, 167, 177, 179, 180
Thatcher, Edward 417
Theatre, The, 218, 240
Theue, 66
Thomas, David, 350
—— Ensign 170
—— Faithfull, 243
—— Francis 180
—— Rev James, 348
—— Rev Joshua, 393

Thomas, Richard W, 348
Thomason, Ann 342
Thompson, John, 138, 351, 381-2
Thornicliffe, John, 91
Thornicroft, Ensign, 156
Thrave, meaning of, 431n
Three Pigeons The, 237
Throckmorten, Sir John, 79
—— Sir Joseph 342
Thrush, Bridget, 295
—— George, 29,n
—— John, 30, 52 119, 125 373
—— Thomas, 30, 125, 373
—— William, 259
Thunderstorm, 129, 230
Tilsley, John, 396
—— Ralph, 396
Tilstone Heath, 147 166
Timmis, John, 341
—— Robert 21, 341
Tinkers Crofts, 6, 92, 176, 449, 460n
Tisser, Rev John, 400
Tithes, 273-5, 279, 288, 291-2, 301, 453, 489
Titley Thomas, 99
Tochet, James, Lord Audley, 57
—— Sir John, 56-7
Tokens, 196 7, 237
Toleration Act, 384
Tollett, George, 239
—— John, 347
Tolls, 69, 349n
Tollemache, Henry J, 251
—— Hon Wilbraham, 231
—— Lionel, 21
—— Lord 21 65, 239, 274, 372, 503
—— Wilbraham S, 65, 124, 382
Tomkin, Ann, 396
TOMKINSON FAMILY, 461-2
Tomkinson Pedigree, 464-5
Tomkinson, Catharine Maria, 348
—— Charles, 349n
—— Henry, 228
—— James 228, 231, 235, 348 364, 389 461
—— Major, 241
Tomlinson, Henry, 123, 365
—— John, 228
—— William, 351
Tomson, Margery, 356, 359
Topham, James 69, 349
—— Mark, 333n, 350
Topps, William, 368n
Totigrenx, Agnes, 405-6
—— Thomas, 405-6
Touthwood, Ensign, 170
Town Bridge, see Bridge
—— Charter, 79 99, 206, 216
—— Hall, 240, 247, 249
—— Holidays, 222
—— Illumination of, 238
—— Officers, 68, 221
—— Orders, 29, 222-3
—— Riots, 182, 235
—— Wells, 221
Townley, Thomas W, 39, 266
Townsend House, 103, 123, 167n,, 240, 424, 426
Townsend Henry, 35, 79, 114
—— Samuel, 375
Trainbands 188n
Traquaire, Earl, 188
Travelling Scotchmen, 389, 390
Travis, Miss, 237
Trial, a remarkable, 225

Trickett, Henry, 138
—— John, 246
Trevyns, Mr , 180
True John, 98
Tudman, Thomas, 298*n* , 374
Tuesday, Hannah, 345
Tumbrel, 7, 66
Tunstall, Crowdson 240, 243, 411
Turkish Pirates, 433*n*
Turner, Ellen, 102
—— John, 240
—— Margaret 101
—— Rev James 305
—— Thomas, 317*n* , 472*n* , 475
—— William 120
Turnpenny, Zachariah, 266, 361
Turton, Rev Charles G , 402
—— Rev William, 384
Twemlow, John, 98, 304, 346, 376
Twiss, Randle, 202
—— Thomas 200
Twoyearold, Thomas, 338, 442
Typhus Fever, 244-5

ULVIET, a Saxon, 413
Uniformity, Act of, 383
Union Inn, 232
Union Society, 232
—— Workhouse, 244, 288
Unitarian Chapel, 247, 250, 388-392
United Methodist Free Churches, 401*a*
Untimely deaths 201-2
Upshan, Rev William, 428
Urscrate, or Ursgate, Thomas, 138, 491

VALE ROYAL 41 121
Vallet, Captain, 181
Valletort, Joan, 483*n*
Valletort, Reginald, 40, 483*n* , 484
Valor Ecclesiasticus 20 51 54
Vane, Lieutenant-Colonel, 171
Varnam, Edward, 144
Vaughan, Herbert, 180
—— Rev Doctor 309
—— Roger, 21
—— Thomas, 339
Vawdrey, Rev G , 240
—— Rev William, 387, 395
Venables Captain, 154
—— Hugh, 5, 83
—— Letitia, 424
—— Richard 133-4
—— Sion 340
—— Thomas, 102, 129
—— William, 279, 424
Venator, Gilbert, 14
Venner, Richard 355 359
Verney, Richard, 97
Vernon, Auda, 60
—— Henry 185
—— James, 59, 85 111
—— Margery, 424
—— Mary, 240
—— Maud, 60
—— Ralph, 5, 59, 83, 86, 406
—— Richard, 14, 47, 59, 87, 240, 340, 411
—— Roesia, 60
—— Sir Ralph de, 89, 407
—— Sir Richard 28 59 85
—— Thomas 85 112 484
—— Warin de, 4 5, 24 55 59, 60, 424
Vestry Books, 219*n*
—— Meetings, 223-4, 306
Visitations, 196, 308
Volunteers' Field, and *Row*, 235

WADE, John, 148*n*
Wadsworth, Rev Henry, 403
Wagge Jane, 186
Wardson Doctor 418
Waif, 66 485
Wainewright, Dr John, 343
Wakeman s Waggon, 233
Walden, Lieutenant, 170
Walkeley lands 118
Walker, Elizabeth, 362
—— George, 266
—— Isabella 279
—— John, 60, 105
—— Mary, 351
—— Samuel, 343
Wall Croft or *Field*, 7, 357, 488
Wall Lane, 7, 8, 165*n*
Wallers and *Walling*, 254*n* , 257, 260
Walley, Charles, 185
—— Elizabeth, 324
—— John, 108*n* , 346
—— Mary, 338
—— Raphe, 338
—— Thomas, 149 223
—— William, 179, 324, 356, 360, 363
Wallis, Thomas, 186
Walmsley Richard, 344
Walshmon Llewellyn 92
Walsingham Francis 107
Walthall, Alderman, 354, 356-7, 359
—— Alexander, 130, 132, 139, 152, 172, 175-6, 183, 363
—— Amabilia 350
—— Captain Richard, 185
—— Gilbert, 96, 98, 279
—— John, 34
—— Peter, 231, 241, 265*n* , 304*n* , 364
—— Richard, 263*n* , 318, 349, 363, 443, 461
—— Roger, 79, 99, 103, 256, 289, 290, 443
—— Thomas, 120, 126, 139, 175, 298
Walton, Peter, 425
—— Samuel, 365
Warbeck, Perkin, 47, 95
Warburton John, 163*n*
—— Peter, 502
—— Richard, 90
—— Thomas, 186
Ward, Captain, 170
—— John, 487
—— Margaret 491
—— William, 291, 294, 335, 337, 396
Warden, John, 345
Wardour Castle, 43
Wareham, Elizabeth, 227
Wareton, Hugh, 487
Warmundestron, 10, 12
Warrant, John, 114
WARREN FAMILY, 40
Warren, Colonel, 166-7, 169
—— Hon Justice 241
—— John 164
—— Lawrence, 91
Warrenite agitation, 401
Warrington, Edmund 338
Warwick, Earl of, 25, 45, 50
Wast, William, 489
Waterhouse, Alfred, 248
Water-lode, 6, 104
Water-Mill, 60*n*
Water-works, 109
Watfield Pavement, 7
Wathew, Roger, 339
—— Silber, 338
Watkin, Rev Robert, 402

Watkiss, Ann, 348*n*
—— Catharine, 348*n*
—— Charlotte, 348*n*
—— Hannah 346, 348*n*
—— Mary, 348
—— Samuel, 265*n* , 346
—— William, 223, 226-8, 305, 348*n* , 349
Watmough, Rev A , 402
Watson, John, 134 259, 485
Wears, Rev William, 402*n*
Weaver or *Weever River*, 103, 118, 153, 165 264-5
Weaver or Weever, Elizabeth, 489, 491
—— Hatton, 186
—— Peter, 343
—— Richard, 440
—— Robert, 186
—— Thomas 91, 185, 202
Webb, Elizabeth 474*n*
—— William, 425
Webbs' Itinerary, 123, 125
Wedgewood, John, 403
Weild, Richard, 175
—— Sir John, 180
Weld's Green 472
Wellington, The Duke of, 239
Wells Cathedral, 42
Welsby William 365
Welsh Bridge, and *Row*, 5, 87
Welsh Row Channel, 128
Werden, Mr , 140*n*
Weir, 155-6
Wenlock Abbey 21
Wentworth, Sir Thomas, 136
Wesley, Rev John, 227, 396, 398, 400, 401*n*
Wesleyan Chapel, 237, 240, 247, 250, 396 400
—— Methodist Association, 401*n*.
—— Schools,, 244
West Door of the Church, 227
Weston, Elizabeth 212
—— John, 98
Westminster Abbey 17
Wetwood Margery, 344
Wettenhall Chapel, 376
WETTENHALL FAMILY, 460-1
Wettenhall, Arms of, 94, 463
Wettenhall Pedigree, 463-5
Wettenhall, or Wetenhale, Adam, 417, 460*n*
—— Amicia, 325
—— Anne, 345, 460-1
—— Catharine 324-5 351, 389*n* , 461
—— Diana 351
—— Edward, 221 223, 265*n* 364 376, 440
—— Elisot, 44
—— Ellen 60
—— Gabriel, 76, 128*n* , 138, 189, 265*n* , •341*n* , 460-1
—— Henry, 61, 90, 92-3
—— Hugh, 44, 90-1, 97
—— John 5, 47, 60, 90-4, 277, 341 460
—— Margaret, 60, 325, 343, 461
—— Mary, 442
—— Nathaniel, 265*n*
—— Peter 235
—— Ralph 90
—— Randle, 44, 90, 93
—— Rev John, 345
—— Rev, Thomas, 304
—— Roger 100-1 256, 460*n* , 484, 487
—— Sir John, 60
—— Susannah, 325
—— Thomas, 46 7, 90-93, 100-103, 211, 231, 324 351, 361 363 460-1

Wettenhall, William, 5 43, 91 98, 127, 134, 351 460-1
Wheeler John 218
—— William 138 218
Wheelock, Eleanor, 59
—— Hugh 489
—— Joan, 28
—— John, 118
—— Richard, 28, 59, 90
Whembrugge Thomas 91
Whitchurch (Salop) 147-151 155 6 505
White, Benjamin, 218 239 401*n*
—— Mary, 342
—— Taylor 225
White Hall 128, 461
Whitelegge, Mr, 269
Whitelocke, Sir James, 79
White Swan, badge, 95
Whitfield, Rev George, 398
Whitley, Colonel, 200
Whitmore Sir Thomas 180
Whitney or Whytney, Captain 150
—— Geffrey 109
—— Hugh 341
—— Robert 425 484
—— William 45
Whittakers George, 138, 292
—— Thomas 138
Whittingham, John, 269
—— Martha 396*n*
—— Thomas, 202
Whitworth, William, 120
Whorall, Margaret, 102
Wiche Bridge, see Bridge
Wiche-field 425, 444, 488
Wichewood-forest 34 204*n*
Wickham, Henry, D D, 130
WICKSTEAD WICKSTEED, WICKSTED
or WIXSTED FAMILY, 495
Wicksted, Arms of, 496
Wicksted Pedigree, 496-8
Wicksted, Alexander, 461
—— Charles, 186
—— Grissel, 318
—— Henry 74 76, 98 134, 427
—— Jasper 338
—— John 100—101, 133, 196,, 217*n*, 218, 221, 265*n*
—— Margaret 299
—— Marian, 102
—— Richard, 72, 76, 103, 127, 130, 132, 139, 153, 163 172, 184, 228, 256*n*, 294, 327, 356, 360, 364, 461
—— Robert, 139
—— Thomas, 21 184, 202, 209, 221, 223 265*n* 318 363-4 412 433
—— William 72 75-6, 461
Wickstead s Sconce, 165*n*
WILBRAHAM FAMILY, 424—429
Wilbraham, of Rease Heath, 424
—— of Woodhey, 424
—— Almshouses 208 355 372 429, 430
—— Arms of 436
—— Manorial Court, 434
—— Memorial Glass 323 331-2
—— Monuments, 320—324
—— Motto, 429*n*
—— Portraits, 436
Wilbraham Pedigree, 436—439
Wilbraham Alice, 192 321 334 343, 428
—— Anne 352*n*
—— Bootle, 435
—— Elizabeth 122*n*, 314, 316, 321, 334
—— George, 123, 228-9 231-2, 239 244 256, 288, 324, 364 375, 435

Wilbraham George Fortescue, 99, 323, 372, 382, 435
—— Grace 343 434
—— Homfrey, 39
—— Hugh, 139, 173, 184, 455
—— John, 202
—— Lady Grace, 358
—— Louisa 324
—— Mary, 324
—— Margaret, 490
—— Maud 60
—— Peter 299 300
—— Ralph, 98, 207, 320—322, 334*n*, 424 5 440, 484
—— Randle, 211, 217-8 264 265*n*, 288*n* 331 334, 356, 359 360 1, 363, 365, 375, 424 431*n* 434-5
—— Raphe, 51 193, 209 339 359
—— Richard, 34 99—104 112 138 198, 274 314 320 405, 424, 428, 431*n*, 440 484 487, 502
—— Roger 21 52 101 139 140, 148*n*, 189, 192 196 200, 211, 221, 223 253, 265*n*, 288—290, 299 300 320, 324 351*n*. 356 359, 360, 364, 376, 394*n*, 428-9, 435, 475, 491
—— Sir Richard 35 37 60, 139, 140, 148, 358*n*, 425, 433
—— Sir Roger, 54, 126, 320, 354, 358, 450
—— Sir Thomas 21 172, 183 199 356 360 411 424 428*n*, 432, 455, 473
—— Stephen 230*n*, 334 361 433
—— Thomas, 52, 91, 94, 97, 112, 121, 127, 130 132, 135-6, 139, 161 320 324, 359*n*, 363, 424—428, 467 484 491
—— William 95, 424
Wild, Charles, 342
—— Margaret, 342
Wildbor John 6 61
—— Nicholas 83
—— Ralph 92
—— Richard, 6, 94
—— William, 406-7
Wildcatsheath, 404 414, 425
Wilding, Peter, 344
Wilkes, Alice, 300
—— Anne, 192
—— John, 149
—— Lawrence 128, 139
—— Oliver 355-7, 359
—— Richard, 127, 134, 186, 202, 338-9
—— Robert 74-5 131-2, 187, 189
—— Thomas 76 202
Wilkenson, Elizabeth, 343
—— Isaac, 390
—— James, 348
—— Rev Robert 392
Wilson, James, 197, 269
—— John, 184
—— Rev J 305*n* 402
—— Rev Samuel 403
—— Rev Stephen, 401
—— Richard 186
—— Robert, 266
—— Thomas, 100, 138, 174, 239
—— William, 131
Willaston, 160, 413-5
Willaston Hall 413*n* 414
Willaston Schools 413*n*
Willdig, Martha 343
Willesone, Nicholas 85
William Bishop of Lincoln, 452
William III at Combermere, 201
Williams, Ashton, 265*n*, 349, 364

Williams Catharine, 348, 352*n*
—— Francis, 348
—— Gilbert 98
—— James, 348, 352*n*
—— Justice, 397
—— Margaret, 344
—— Rev Price, 397
—— Rev William 307
—— Roger, 348
—— Thomas 217*n* 218 221 265, 351*n*, 364 376
Williamson, George, 241
—— Sarah, 241, 350
—— Thomas, 243 245 365, 382
Willett, Margery, 338
—— Thomas, 338
Willev, Thomas, 95 6
Willicott, Rev Thomas, 392
Wilher Captain. 170
Willis, Rev Richard, 378*n*
Windmill-field 442
Windmill Lane 415
Window-tax, 344*n* 434
Windsor, Edward 265*n*
Windy Harbour 7 411
Winnington Bridge 193
Winnington Christopher 278, 283
—— John, 501
—— Robert de, 60
Winsey John, 128 132
Wistaston, 160
Wistaston Church, 484*n*
—— *Hall,* 504
Wistaston, William 82, 407
Withinshaw John 125 239 344 346*n*., 352, 401*n*
—— Marv, 352
—— Robert, 343-4
—— Thomas, 344
Wither, Ensign 171
Witter, John, 484
Wode, Laurence 425
—— Randle, 274
Wodehouse, John, 50 83
Wodewer, Roger, 85
Wolfe Anne 445
—— General, tradition of, 445*n*
—— Rebecca, 445
Wolferston Captain II, 451
Wood, Bridget, 361
—— Catharine 486
—— Elton, 344
—— Henry, 219
—— John 318, 403
—— Thomas 344 403
—— William 490
Wood Memorial Chapel, 403
Wood Street, 6 100, 243
Wood Street School 249
Woodcock, Robert, 163*n*
Woodhey, 157
Woodhey Bache, 200
Woodken, Richard 138
Woodnoth, John 40 317, 490
—— Jonathan 184 317*n*
—— Margaret, 54*n* 288, 334, 355, 359
—— Raphe, 130, 317, 363
—— William, 274, 276, 332, 406
Woodward, Elizabeth 348
—— Harry, 348
—— Lawrence, 338
—— Richard 338
—— Thomas 348
Woodworth Andrew, 221, 223
Woollam Gilbert, 74, 340
Woolley Lawrence, 111

Woolsey, Elizabeth, 242
Woolstanwood, 412
Wolton Sir Thomas, 46
Worden, Major General, 299
Wordley, William, 240
Workhouse, 199, 207, 209, 226—228
Workman, Rev. Joseph, 402*n.*
Wortleberries, 483
Wotton, John, 40
Wray, Rev. J. Jackson, 402*n.*
Wrenbury, 159, 160
Wrench, Catharine, 230*n.*
—— Charles, 347
—— John, 230*n.*, 351
—— Margaret, 230*n.*
—— Mary Ann, 230*n.*
—— Richard, 230*n.*, 347
—— William, 230, 350, 364
WRIGHT FAMILY, 486—492
Wright, Arms of, 370
—— Monuments, 317
𝕎𝕣𝕚𝕘𝕙𝕥 𝕡𝕖𝕕𝕚𝕘𝕣𝕖𝕖, 492-4
Wright, Alice, 93*n.*, 491
—— Allen, 76, 104
—— Ann, 359, 489—492
—— Anthony, 118, 120
—— Arthur, 487
—— Benjamin, 200
—— Cecilia, 488
—— Charles, 345
—— Charlotte, 492
—— Clutton, 215, 221, 265*n.*, 363, 376, 492
—— Dorothy, 489, 491
—— Edward, 303, 491, 492
—— Elizabeth, 317, 324, 341, 345, 488, 490—492
—— Ensign, 170
—— Francis, 488, 490

Wright, Henry, 98, 102-3, 138, 369, 487-8, 490
—— Humphrey, 98
—— James, 357, 363, 488, 490-1
—— Jerom, 488, 490
—— John, 60, 98, 102, 132, 166, 202, 473, 487
—— Katherine, 127
—— Lawrence, 72, 103, 133, 359*n.*, 363, 414, 453, 488—491
—— Margaret, 93*n.*, 101, 317, 343, 488-9, 492
—— Maria, 490
—— Matthew, 76, 356-7, 364, 490-1
—— Raphe, 489
—— Reginold, 103, 256
—— Richard, 54, 98, 101, 103, 105, 132, 138, 263*n.*, 317, 363, 369—370, 411, 427, 443, 487-8, 491-2, 501
—— Robert, 21, 124, 192, 317, 442, 487, 489
—— Roger, 21, 34, 93*n.*, 98, 114, 118, 127, 133, 138-9, 149, 153, 363, 369, 443, 488, 490-1, 498
—— Rondull, 338, 486
—— Sir Edmund, 52, 54, 98, 338, 355, 359, 486-7
—— Sir Nathan, 263
—— Sophia, 492
—— Thomas, 103, 105, 130, 138, 196, 256*n.*, 279, 294, 352, 363, 452, 488-9, 491
—— William, 281, 343, 442
Wright's Trustees, Accounts of, 369-372
—— Names of, 363—365
Writ of *quo warranto*, 66, 96
Wrottesley, Sir Hugh, 121
Wyatt, the Architect, 435
Wybunbury, 15, 159, 216*n.*, 224

Wybunbury, John, 105, 501
—— Richard de, 88
—— Robert, 501
Wybunbury-Willaston, 413
Wyche-Field, 6, 92
𝕎𝕪𝕔𝕙𝕖 𝕡𝕖𝕕𝕚𝕘𝕣𝕖𝕖, 84
Wyche, John, 84
—— Sir Hugh, 84, 95
—— Sir Maurice, 84
—— Thomas, 84
—— Richard, 84, 87, 276, 417
—— William, 84
Wychehouse-Bank, 6, 243, 266
Wynn, Sir W. Watkin, 505
Wyse, Ralph, 290

YARDLEY, John, 153
—— Yardley, Thomas, 74
—— Yates, Rev. Buckley, 403
Yates, Rev. James, 390
Yonge, Captain, 180
—— Thomas le, 53, 275
Yorkshire Buildings, 229, 232
Young, Ann, 341
—— Ann Wrench, 230*n.*
—— Henry, 490
—— John, 345
—— Thomas, 230*n.*
—— William, 120
Yoxall, Margaret, 349
—— Richard, 39, 223, 347, 350
—— Thomas, 223, 364
—— William, 219, 228
Ypurs, William, 417

ZOUCH, William Lord, 44

NANTWICH
PRINTED BY T JOHNSON, AT HIS OFFICE
IN THE OAT MARKET
1883

Lightning Source UK Ltd.
Milton Keynes UK
UKHW020022070223
416579UK00002B/570

9 781015 671928